Ex Libris

DR. JESS

EUROPEAN EMPLOYMENT LAW

EUROPEAN EMPLOYMENT LAW

A Systematic Exposition

Karl RIESENHUBER

intersentia

Cambridge – Antwerp – Portland

Intersentia Publishing Ltd.
Trinity House | Cambridge Business Park | Cowley Road
Cambridge | CB4 0WZ | United Kingdom
Tel.: +44 1223 393 753 | Email: mail@intersentia.co.uk

Distribution for the UK:
Hart Publishing Ltd.
16C Worcester Place
Oxford OX1 2JW
UK
Tel.: +44 1865 517 530
Email: mail@hartpub.co.uk

Distribution for the USA and Canada:
International Specialized Book Services
920 NE 58th Ave. Suite 300
Portland, OR 97213
USA
Tel.: +1 800 944 6190 (toll free)
Email: info@isbs.com

Distribution for Austria:
Neuer Wissenschaftlicher Verlag
Argentinierstraße 42/6
1040 Wien
Austria
Tel.: +43 1 535 61 03 24
Email: office@nwv.at

Distribution for other countries:
Intersentia Publishing nv
Groenstraat 31
2640 Mortsel
Belgium
Tel.: +32 3 680 15 50
Email: mail@intersentia.be

This book is based on Karl RIESENHUBER, *Europäisches Arbeitsrecht*, 1st edition 2009, published by C.F. Müller, a brand name of the publishing group Hüthig Jehle Rehm, Heidelberg (ISBN 978-3-8114-5607-5).

European Employment Law. A Systematic Exposition
Karl Riesenhuber

© 2012 Intersentia
    Cambridge – Antwerp – Portland
    www.intersentia.com | www.intersentia.co.uk

Artwork on front and back cover: Titian, The Venus of Urbino, 1538, Galleria degli Uffizi (Florence)

ISBN 978-1-78068-080-4
D/2012/7849/78
NUR 825

British Library Cataloguing in Publication Data. A catalogue record for this book is available from the British Library.

To Barbara, Charlotte, Paul,
Konrad, Karl and Elisabeth

SERIES PREFACE

The role of European law is becoming more and more central in comparative law, in the law of the other Member States and as an outstanding model for legal policy. Insiders have known for a long time that in almost all core areas of law, the important spurs to reform have been coming from Europe and that European law increasingly dominates the cornerstones of our legal systems. Therefore, a discussion of European law involves addressing the main problems and guiding principles but, in practical terms, it also increasingly entails raising questions that are threatening to revolutionise national legal traditions and render entire libraries obsolete.

Since 2002, the year marking the introduction of the Euro, a new law of obligations has been in place in Germany, with the old codifications in France and Austria following to a lesser extent. The next years were characterised by unrestricted cross-border mobility of court decisions; re-writing of core areas of company law such as accounting, cross-border mobility, but as well the promulgation of supranational types of company, with some of the largest German enterprises becoming 'European Companies' (SE); and also cross-border crediting of contributions to social security systems becoming a reality. The law on competition and subsidies has been primarily European for a long time and its mighty implementing mechanisms – overriding Heads of State – fill title pages. The same applies to intellectual property law, foreign exchange law, banking and insurance law and environmental law. These have become genuinely European subjects. Then, in the last years, the cross-border arrest warrant fundamentally changed European Criminal Law; anti-discrimination law is all encompassing; there is now a proposal for a European Optional Contract Law (Code); the Lisbon Treaty – though formally not a constitution – installed a new institutional setting strengthening democratic legitimacy and powers of the European Union; and the financial and state debt crises, not even ten years after the introduction of the Euro, triggered measures which considerably strengthened and broadened financial stability schemes at the EU level, from banking law to capital market law and collaboration with respect to systemic risk. The near future will show whether Europe is to have an institutionalised economic collaboration for its political economy ('true economic government') in some way, reflecting the now global importance of the Euro and the responsibility attached to it!

European law – in all legal areas – has long since assumed dimensions that make it absolutely necessary to refer to more than a single book. This series, now beginning its second edition, is structured so as to provide the relevant European complement to a traditional legal area. It offers the internal market package organised in this way, with those areas being chosen for users that have a significant internal market dimension. In comparison with a multi-volume looseleaf work, it has advantages not only in terms of price, but also in that it puts a greater emphasis on classification and limits the material to the essential, which is important in an overflowing area such as European law, of which only very few people manage to preserve an overview.

The dynamic nature of European law is impressive, as its development hurtles along, gathering momentum. There is a need for direction. A serious application of law can no longer focus solely on national transposition. The original, the European guideline, which *de facto* almost always has to be directly applied (even in national legal processes), must be considered. Such direction can best be provided by presenting the contents of European law in context and in the necessary detail – in the present case, up to twelve individual volumes. Some of the volumes have already had considerable success in one national market and are now presented to a pan-European public.

The volumes cover the most important topics in the 'Europeanisation' of law. For practitioners – solicitors and barristers, corporate lawyers, judges or lawyers in state authorities or ministries – who do not wish to turn a blind eye to European law, these volumes provide a reliable treatment of the important problems, with sufficiently detailed references. They provide practitioners with all they need on the EU level, and moreover give comparative law and legal policy insight. As a series, they give an overview of those areas most affected by European law. Likewise, they provide advanced students with material for excellent examination results. Students must study European law seriously as part of their main subject if they really wish to specialise in this in the future and do more than pass their examination with an average result. Works with comparative law and interdisciplinary aspects also prepare students for a possible period of study abroad, help them to analyse law in terms of function and also support studies in related subjects. Thus, IUS COMMUNITATIS makes European substantive law accessible in the form of the classic systematic textbook and specialist work.

All volumes on the applicable law of the Union begin by presenting the necessary tools: in each case, the EC/EU law and the instruments whereby this law enters into the national legal systems are introduced. In all volumes, a thorough description of the EC/EU law rules forms the core of the discussion. However, economic or other interdisciplinary references of significance to the legislation in question are also explained, i.e. what the rules are intended to achieve and, where there are lacunae, the various models that exist and are discussed throughout Europe. European law is, indeed, a law in the making. Each legal area is presented in a logical order, as an organic whole; this implies that the approximated or harmonised law forms only the skeleton or hard nucleus and is supplemented by comparative law explanations where harmonisation is not advanced. In this way, the relationship to national law becomes clearer and the ability of readers to deal with European law will improve, as they are given a coherent picture rather than the fragmentary one often complained of. These are to be textbooks, discussion books and, above all, practical books – sufficiently condensed to contain all the necessary details and yet clear in their outlines. This was the objective we strive for and the challenge. The authors and the editor (Stefan.Grundmann@rewi.hu-berlin.de) thank those who have criticised and inspired us and who may do so in the future.

The entire IUS COMMUNITATIS series owes much to the Thyssen Foundation, which considered the European aspect and in particular the connection with comparative law so important that it generously supported a good number of the volumes. As the editor, I should like to express my deepest thanks.

Berlin, Spring 2012   Stefan Grundmann

AUTHOR'S PREFACE

This volume provides a systematic overview of European employment law: its foundations in primary law and its regulation by secondary legislation. While the book builds upon its German counterpart, *Europäisches Arbeitsrecht* (Heidelberg: C.F. Müller, 2009), it is more than a mere translation. First, the book has been fully updated to cover recent developments. This task alone required substantial revision of the text. Following a well-known proverb (ascribed to *Kahn-Freund*), a week is a long time in employment law. This is certainly also true for EU employment law. Secondly, beyond mere updating, I have attempted to adapt the text to an 'English' readership and take account of current discussions in the English-language literature. Nevertheless, the book cannot mask its author's German background, perspective and methods, nor does it try to. To the contrary, one of my aims was to make this 'Germanic' approach and literature accessible to a broader public.

Much of this book was written during my sabbatical in 2010/11. I am grateful to my university for giving me the time off; to Professor *Richard Buxbaum* who invited me to spend my sabbatical at the University of California at Berkeley School of Law; and to the *Alexander von Humboldt-Foundation* for a research grant. I am especially indebted to *Heike E. Fisher*, LL.M., Palo Alto, who patiently read the whole manuscript and with whom I discussed many details of the book. *Amy Ludlow*, Cambridge, provided a thorough language review and many helpful comments beyond mere linguistic issues. *Ann-Christin Maak* from Intersentia patiently discussed many publication issues with me.

Finally, I would like to thank my assistants at Ruhr-Universität Bochum. Among them, *Stefan Wichary* deserves to take pride of place. He helped me hold the English manuscript together, took care of all the registers and indefatigably helped me keep pace with the most recent legislative and judicial developments. Over the years, many others have provided me with valuable research assistance and have thus left their traces in this book; in particular, I would like to thank *Alexander Jüchser, Sina Krefft, Sandra Rösler, Hans P. Schimmeck, Eva Strippel* and *Jan Szemjonneck*.

Berlin/Bochum, August 2012   *Karl Riesenhuber*

TABLE OF CONTENTS

PART 4. COLLECTIVE EMPLOYMENT LAW

LIST OF ABBREVIATIONS*

AC	Appeal Cases (Law Reports)
AcP	Archiv für die civilistische Praxis (volume [year], page)
ADEA	The Age Discrimination in Employment Act of 1967, codified as Chapter 14 of Title 29 of United States Code, §621
AEntG	Gesetz über zwingende Arbeitsbedingungen für grenzüberschreitend entsandte und für regelmäßig im Inland beschäftigte Arbeitnehmer und Arbeitnehmerinnen (Arbeitnehmer-Entsendegesetz – AEntG) of 20 April 2009 (BGBl. 2009 I, 799), see also AEntG a.F.
AEntG a.F.	Gesetz über zwingende Arbeitsbedingungen bei grenzüberschreitenden Dienstleistungen (Arbeitnehmer-Entsendegesetz) of 26 February 1996 (BGBl. 1996 I, 227), see also AEntG
AG	1. Advocate General at the European Court of Justice; 2. Die Aktiengesellschaft (year, page); 3. Amtsgericht (German Local Court), see also LG, OLG and BGH
AGG	Allgemeines Gleichbehandlungsgesetz of 14 August 2006 (BGBl. 2006 I, 1897)
AiB	Arbeitsrecht im Betrieb (year, page)
alt.	alternative
a.m.	ante meridiem
AöR	Archiv für öffentliches Recht (volume [year], page)
AP	Arbeitsrechtliche Praxis (provision/legal act, number)
Arbeitgeber	Der Arbeitgeber (year, page)
ArbG	Arbeitsgericht (German Labour Court), see also BAG, LAG
ArbRGeg	Das Arbeitsrecht der Gegenwart (year, page)

---

*   For abbreviations of Legal Acts of the European Communities and the European Union used in this book see the table of EU Legislation at page xxxiii, for the list of abbreviated literature see page xxvii.

arg.	argumentum
Ariz. L. Rev.	Arizona Law Review (volume [year], page)
Art.	Article(s)
AuA	Arbeit und Arbeitsrecht (year, page)
AÜG	Gesetz zur Regelung der gewerbsmäßigen Arbeitnehmerüberlassung (Arbeitnehmerüberlassungsgesetz) as amended and promulgated on 3 February 1995 (BGBl. 1995 I, 158)
AuR	Arbeit und Recht (year, page)
AWD	Außenwirtschaftsdienst (year, page)
BAG	Bundesarbeitsgericht (German Federal Labour Court), see also ArbG und LAG
BAGE	the official report series of cases before the Bundesarbeitsgericht (volume, page), see also BAG
BB	Betriebs-Berater (year, page)
BBiG	Berufsbildungsgesetz of 23 March 2005 (BGBl. 2005 I, 931)
BeckRS	Beck-Rechtsprechung (year, number)
BetrVG	Betriebsverfassungsgesetz as amended and promulgated on 25 September 2001 (BGBl. 2001 I, 2518)
BGB	Bürgerliches Gesetzbuch as amended and promulgated on 2 January 2002 (BGBl. 2002 I, 42, 2909, 2003 I, 738)
BGBl.	Bundesgesetzblatt der Bundesrepublik Deutschland (year part, page)
BGH	Bundesgerichtshof (German Federal Court of Justice), see also AG, LG and OLG
BGHZ	the official report series of civil law cases before the Bundesgerichtshof (volume, page), see also BGH
BillBG	Gesetz zur Bekämpfung der illegalen Beschäftigung of 15 December 1981 (BGBl. 1981 I, 1390)
BJIR	British Journal of Industrial Relations (volume [year], page)
BKR	Zeitschrift für Bank- und Kapitalmarktrecht (year, page)
B.L.I.	Business Law International (volume [year], page)
BMW	Bayerische Motorenwerke
BR-Drs.	Bundesrats-Drucksache (document number/year, page), see also BT-Drs.
BT-Drs.	Bundestags-Drucksache (legislative period/ document number, page), see also BR-Drs.

BUrlG	Mindesturlaubsgesetz für Arbeitnehmer (Bundesurlaubsgesetz) of 8 January 1963
BVerfG	Bundesverfassungsgericht (German Federal Constitutional Court)
BVerfGE	the official report series of cases before the Bundesverfassungsgericht (volume, page), see also BVerfG
BWV	Berliner Wissenschaftsverlag
Cambrian L.R.	Cambrian Law Review (year, page)
CEEP	European Centre of Employers and Enterprises
cf.	confer
CFI	Court of First Instance (see Article 220 EC), see also GC
C.F.L.Q	Child and Family Law Quarterly (volume [year], page)
CFSR	Charter of Fundamental Social Rights of Workers
chap.	chapter
ChFR	Charter of Fundamental Rights of the European Union as proclaimed at Strasbourg on 12 December 2007 by the European Parliament, the Council and the Commission and as replaced with effect from 1 December 2009, the date of entry into force of the Treaty of Lisbon (see Article 6(1)(1) TEU), OJ 2010 C 83/389
C.L.J.	Cambridge Law Journal (volume [year], page)
C.L.P.	Current Legal Problems (volume [year], page)
CMLR	Common Market Law Review (volume [year], page)
Co Lawyer	Company Lawyer (volume [year], page)
Colum. J. Eur. L.	Columbia Journal of European Law (volume [year], page)
COM	COM Documents: proposed legislation and other Commission communications to the Council and/or the other institutions, and their preparatory papers. Commission documents for the other institutions (legislative proposals, communications, reports, etc.) ([year] number, page)
Comp. Lab. L.	Comparative Labour Law (volume [year], page) – until 1986, see also Comp. Lab. L. J.
Comp. Lab. L. J.	Comparative Labour Law Journal (volume [year], page) – since 1986, see also Comp. Lab. L.
Comp. Lab. L. & Pol'y J.	Comparative Labour Law Journal & Policy Journal (volume [year], page)

DB	Der Betrieb (year, page)
Der Personalrat	Der Personalrat (year, page)
DGB	Deutscher Gewerkschaftsbund (German Confederation of Trade Unions)
DM	Deutsche Mark (former German currency)
Doc.	Document
DÖV	Die Öffentliche Verwaltung (year, page)
DRdA	Das Recht der Arbeit (year, page)
DrittelbG	Gesetz über die Drittelbeteiligung der Arbeitnehmer im Aufsichtsrat of 18 May 2004 (BGBl. 2004 I, 974)
DStR	Deutsches Steuerrecht (year, page)
Dublin U.L.J.	Dublin University Law Journal (volume [year], page)
DZWIR	Deutsche Zeitschrift für Wirtschafts- und Insolvenzrecht (year, page)
ead.	eadem
eaed.	eaedem
EAEC Treaty	Treaty establishing the European Atomic Energy Community, signed on the 25 March 1957, consolidated version from 1 December 2009, as amended by the Treaty of Lisbon and other preceding treaties, OJ 2010 C 84/1
EAS	Europäisches Arbeits- und Sozialrecht, see the the List of Abbreviated Literature
EAT	Employment Appeal Tribunal
EBLR	European Business Law Review (year, page)
EBOR	European Business Organization Law Journal (volume [year], page)
EWC	European Works Council
EBRG	Gesetz über Europäische Betriebsräte (Europäische Betriebsräte-Gesetz) of 28 October 1996 (BGBl. 1996 I, 1548)
EC	1. European Community; see also EEC 2. Treaty establishing the European Community, consolidated version, as amended by the Treaties of Amsterdam and Nice, OJ 2002 C 325/33; see also EEC, EC Treaty, TEC and TFEU
ECHR	Convention for the Protection of Human Rights and Fundamental Freedoms (European Convention on Human Rights, ECHR) of 4 November 1950
ECJ	European Court of Justice, see also CFI and GC
ECL	European Company Law (volume [year], page)

ECR	European Court Reports (year volume-page), before 1990 all case-law was published in a single volume, now judgments and opinions of the ECJ, together with opinions of the AG are published as volume I and judgments of the CFI or (since amendments by the Treaty of Lisbon) of the GC are published as volume II
ECSA	European Community Shipowners' Associations
ECSR	European Committee of Social Rights
ECtHR	European Court of Human Rights
EC Treaty	Treaty establishing the European Community, for different versions see also EC on the one hand and TEC on the other
ed(s).	editor(s)
edn.	edition
EEC	1. European Economic Community, see also EC and EU; 2. see EEC Treaty
EEC Treaty	Treaty establishing the European Economic Community, signed on the 25 March 1957, see also EC Treaty, EC, TEC und TFEU
EGBGB	Einführungsgesetz zum Bürgerlichen Gesetzbuche as amended and promulgated 21 September 1994 (BGBl. 1994 I, 2494)
E.H.R.L.R.	European Human Rights Law Review (volume [year], page)
Einl.	Einleitung (introduction)
EJIR	European Journal of Industrial Relations (volume [year], page)
EJLL	European Journal of Labour Law (English title of EuZA)
ELJ	European Law Journal (volume [year], page)
ELLJ	European Labour Law Journal (volume [year], page)
E.L. Rep.	European Law Reporter (year, page)
E.L. Rev.	European Law Review (volume [year], page)
ERCL	European Review of Contract Law (volume [year], page)
ERPL	European Review of Public Law (volume [year], page)
ESC	1. European Social Charter of 18 October 1961, see also RESC; 2. Economic and Social Committee (see Article 300 sqq. TEUF)
esp.	especially

ETF	European Transport Workers' Federation
ETUC	European Trade Union Confederation
EU	1. European Union; 2. Treaty on European Union, consolidated version, as amended by the Treaties of Amsterdam and Nice, OJ 2002 C 325/5; see also TEU, TFEU
ECJ Statute	Statute of the Court of Justice of the European Union, as it results from the amendments introduced by the Treaty of Lisbon, OJ 2010 C 83/210
EuGRZ	Europäische Grundrechte-Zeitschrift (year, page)
EuLF	The European Legal Forum – deutsche Ausgabe (year, page)
EuR	Europarecht (year, page)
EuroAS	Informationsdienst Europäisches Arbeits- und Sozialrecht (year, page)
EU Treaty	see EU and TEU
EuZA	Europäische Zeitschrift für Arbeitsrecht (year, page), see also EJLL for the English title of this journal
EuZW	Europäische Zeitschrift für Wirtschaftsrecht (year, page)
EWS	Europäisches Wirtschafts- und Steuerrecht (year, page)
EzA	Entscheidungssammlung zum Arbeitsrecht (provision/legal act number)
FA	Fachanwalt Arbeitsrecht (year, page)
FAZ	Frankfurter Allgemeine Zeitung
Fordham Int. L. J.	Fordham International Law Journal (volume [year], page)
Fordham JCFL	Fordham Journal of Corporate and Financial Law (volume [year], page)
GBP	Great Britain Pound Sterling
GC	General Court (see Art. 254–256 TEUF), see also CFI
Geo. L. J.	Georgetown Law Journal (volume [year], page)
GG	Grundgesetz für die Bundesrepublik Deutschland (the German constitution)
GlBG	(Austrian) Bundesgesetz über die Gleichbehandlung (Gleichbehandlungsgesetz), Austrian BGBl. I 66/2004
GmbHR	GmbH Rundschau (year, page)
GPR	Zeitschrift für Gemeinschaftsprivatrecht (year, page)

Harv. L. Rev.	Harvard Law Review (volume [year], page)
Harv. J. L. & Gender	Harvard Journal of Law & Gender (volume [year], page)
Hofstra Lab. & Emp. L. J.	Hofstra Labor & Employment Law Journal (volume [year], page)
I.C.C.L.R.	International Company and Commercial Law Review (volume [year], page)
ICLQ	International & Comparative Law Quarterly (volume [year], page)
id.	idem
iid.	iidem
IJCLLIR	The International Journal of Comparative Labour Law and Industrial Relations (volume [year], page)
ILJ	Industrial Law Journal (volume [year], page)
ILO	International Labour Organization
Ind. & L.R.Rev.	Industrial and Labour Relations Review (volume [year], page)
IntGesR	Internationales Gesellschaftsrecht (International Company Law)
Int'l Comp. L.Q.	International and Comparative Law Quarterly (volume [year], page)
Int'l Lab.Rev.	International Labour Review (volume [year], page)
Int'l Rev. L. & Econ.	International Review of Law and Economics (volume [year], page)
IPRax	Praxis des Internationalen Privat- und Verfahrensrecht (year, page)
IPRspr.	Die deutsche Rechtsprechung auf dem Gebiete des Internationalen Privatrechts (year, number)
IRJ	Industrial Relations Journal (volume [year], page)
IRLR	Industrial Relations Law Reports ([year], page)
JArbSchG	Gesetz zum Schutz der arbeitenden Jugend (Jugendarbeitsschutzgesetz) of 12 April 1976 (BGBl. 1976 I, 965)
J.B.L.	Journal of Business Law (year, page)
JBl.	Juristische Blätter (year, page)
JITE	Journal of institutional and Theoretical Economics (volume [year], page)
JJZ	Jahrbuch Junger Zivilrechtswissenschaftler (year, page)
J.L. & Econ.	Journal of Law and Economics (volume [year], page)
J.M.H.L.	Journal of Mental Health Law (volume [year], page)
J. Pol. Econ.	Journal of Political Economy (volume [year], page)

JR	Juristische Rundschau (year, page)
J. Soc. Wel. & Fam. L.	Journal of Social Welfare and Family Law (volume [year], page)
JURA	Juristische Ausbildung (year, page)
JuS	Juristische Schulung (year, page)
JZ	JuristenZeitung (year, page)
Konzern	Der Konzern (year, page)
KritV	Kritische Vierteljahresschrift für Gesetzgebung und Rechtswissenschaft (year, page)
KSchG	Kündigungsschutzgesetz as amended and promulgated on 25 August 1969 (BGBl. 1969 I, 1317)
KTS	Konkurs-, Treuhand- und Schiedsgerichtswesen (year, page)
LAG	Landesarbeitsgericht (German Higher Labour Court), see also BAG, ArbG
Leg.Stud.	Legal Studies (volume [year], page)
LG	Landgericht (German Regional Court), see also AG, OLG and BGH
lit.	litera
loc. cit.	loco citato
MgVG	Gesetz über die Mitbestimmung der Arbeitnehmer bei einer grenzüberschreitenden Verschmelzung of 21 December 2006 (BGBl. 2006 I, 3332)
Mich. L. Rev.	Michigan Law Review (volume [year], page)
MitbestG	Gesetz über die Mitbestimmung der Arbeitnehmer (Mitbestimmungsgesetz) of 4 May 1976 (BGBl. 1976 I, 1153)
MJ	Maastricht Journal (volume [year], page)
MJECL	Maastricht Journal of European and Comparative Law (volume [year], page)
MLR	The Modern Law Review (volume [year], page)
MuSchG	Mutterschutzgesetz (= German Maternity Protection Act)
NGO	non-governmental organisation
NJW	Neue Juristische Wochenschrift (year, page)
North Carolina L. Rev.	North Carolina Law Review (volume [year], page)
Nott.L.J.	Nottingham Law Journal (volume [year], page)
No(s).	number(s)
NVwZ	Neue Zeitschrift für Verwaltungsrecht (year, page)
NZA	Neue Zeitschrift für Arbeitsrecht (year, page)
NZA-RR	NZA Rechtsprechungs-Report Arbeitsrecht (year, page)

OGH	Oberster Gerichtshof (Austrian Supreme Court of Justice)
OJ	1. published before 1 February 2003: Official Journal of the European Community (year series document number/page); 2. published since 1 February 2003: Official Journal of the European Union (year series document number/page)
OJLS	Oxford Journal of Legal Studies (volume [year], page)
OLG	Oberlandesgericht (German Higher Regional Court), see also AG, LG and BGH
op. cit.	opus citatum est
p(p).	page(s)
para(s).	paragraph(s)
PersV	Die Personalvertretung (year, page)
p.m.	post meridiem
pt(s).	point(s)
RabelsZ	Rabels Zeitschrift für ausländisches und internationales Privatrecht (volume [year], page)
RdA	Recht der Arbeit (year, page)
Rechtswissenschaft	Rechtswissenschaft – Zeitschrift für rechtswissenschaftliche Forschung (year, page)
Recital	recital to the preamble of a legislative act of the EU
RESC	Revised European Social Charter of 3 May 1996, European Treaty Series – No. 163; see also ESC
RIW	Recht der Internationalen Wirtschaft – Betriebs-Berater International (year, page)
s(s).	section(s)
SAE	Sammlung arbeitsrechtlicher Entscheidungen (year, page)
sc.	scilicet
SCE	Societas Cooperativa Europaea (European Cooperative Company)
SCEAG	Gesetz zur Ausführung der Verordnung (EG) Nr. 1435/2003 des Rates vom 22. Juli 2003 über das Statut der Europäischen Genossenschaft (SCE-Ausführungsgesetz) of 14 August 2006 (BGBl. 2006 I, 1911)
SCEBG	Gesetz über die Beteiligung der Arbeitnehmer und Arbeitnehmerinnen in einer Europäischen Genossenschaft (SCE-Beteiligungsgesetz) of 14 August 2006 (BGBl. 2006 I, 1911, 1917)

SE	Societas Europaea (European Company)
SEAG	Gesetz zur Ausführung der Verordnung (EG) Nr. 2157/2001 des Rates vom 8. Oktober 2001 über das Statut der Europäischen Gesellschaft (SE-Ausführungsgesetz) of 22 December 2004 (BGBl. 2004 I, 3675)
SEBG	Gesetz über die Beteiligung der Arbeitnehmer in einer Europäischen Gesellschaft (SE-Beteiligungsgesetz) of 22 December 2004 (BGBl. 2004 I, 3675, 3686)
SEC	SEC documents: European Commission's documents which cannot be classified in COM or any of the other official series
SGB V	Fünftes Buch Sozialgesetzbuch – Gesetzliche Krankenversicherung – of 20 December 1988 (BGBl. 1988 I, 2477)
SME	small and medium-sized enterprises
SPE	Societas Privata Europaea (European Private Company)
sq.	et sequente (and the following)
sqq.	et sequentes (and the following, plural)
Syracuse J. Int'l L. & Com.	Syracuse Journal of International Law and Commerce (volume [year], page)
TEC	Treaty establishing the European Community, consolidated version, as amended by the Treaty of European Union (Maastricht), OJ 1992 C 224/6; see also EEC, EC Treaty, EC and TFEU
TEU	Treaty on European Union, consolidated version, as it results from the amendments introduced by the Treaty of Lisbon, OJ 2010 C 83/13, see also EU
TFEU	Treaty on the Functioning of the European Union, consolidated version, as it results from the amendments introduced by the Treaty of Lisbon, OJ 2010 C 83/47, see also EEC, EC Treaty, EC and TEC
Tex. L. Rev.	Texas Law Review (volume [year], page)
TVG	Tarifvertragsgesetz as amended and promulgated on 25 August 1969 (BGBl. 1969 I, 1323)
TzBfG	Gesetz über Teilzeitarbeit und befristete Arbeitsverträge (Teilzeit- und Befristungsgesetz) of 21 December 2000 (BGBl. 2000 I, 1966)
U. Chi. L. Rev.	University of Chicago Law Review (volume [year], page)

UK	United Kingdom
UmwG	Umwandlungsgesetz of 28 October 1994 (BGBl. 1994 I, 3210, 1995 I, 428)
UN	United Nations
UNICE	Union of Industrial and Employers' Confederations of Europe
U. Pa. L. Rev.	University of Pennsylvania Law Review (volume [year], page)
VSSR	Vierteljahresschrift für Sozialrecht (year, page)
VVW	Verlag Versicherungswirtschaft
wbl	wirtschaftsrechtliche blätter (year, page)
WIRO	Wirtschaft und Recht in Osteuropa (year, page)
WM	Wirtschafts- und Bankrecht (year, page)
WSI-Mitteilungen	Mitteilungen des Wirtschafts- und Sozialwissenschaftlichen Instituts (year, page)
Yale J. Int.'l L.	Yale Journal of International Law (volume [year], page)
Yale L.J.	The Yale Law Journal (volume [year], page)
YEL	Yearbook of European Law (volume [year], page)
ZAAR	Zentrum für Arbeitsbeziehungen und Arbeitsrecht
ZESAR	Zeitschrift für europäisches Sozial- und Arbeitsrecht (year, page)
ZEuP	Zeitschrift für Europäisches Privatrecht (year, page)
ZfA	Zeitschrift für Arbeitsrecht (year, page)
ZfRV	Zeitschrift für Rechtsvergleichung, Internationales Privatrecht und Europarecht (year, page)
ZGR	Zeitschrift für Unternehmens- und Gesellschaftsrecht (year, page)
ZHR	Zeitschrift für das gesamte Handels- und Wirtschaftsrecht (volume [year], page)
ZIAS	Zeitschrift für ausländisches und internationales Arbeits- und Sozialrecht (year, page)
ZIP	Zeitschrift für Wirtschaftsrecht (year, page)
ZRP	Zeitschrift für Rechtspolitik (year, page)
ZSR	Zeitschrift für Schweizerisches Rechts (volume [year], page)
ZTR	Zeitschrift für Tarifrecht (year, page)
ZVglRWiss	Zeitschrift für vergleichende Rechtswissenschaft (volume [year], page)
ZZPInt	Zeitschrift für Zivilprozess International (volume [year], page)

LIST OF ABBREVIATED LITERATURE*

author, in *AR-Blattei,* SD	Thomas Dietrich/Klaus Neef/Brent Schwab (eds.), *Arbeitsrecht-Blattei, Systematische Darstellungen,* loose-leaf (Heidelberg: C.F. Müller, 2007)
C. Barnard, *EC Employment Law*	Catherine Barnard, *EC Employment Law,* 3rd edn. (Oxford: Oxford University Press, 2006)
B. Bercusson, *European Labour Law*	Brian Bercusson, *European Labour Law and the EU Charter of Fundamental Rights* (Baden-Baden: Nomos, 2006)
R. Blanpain/M. Schmidt /U. Schweibert, *Europäisches Arbeitsrecht*	Roger Blanpain/Marlene Schmidt/Ulrike Schweibert, *Europäisches Arbeitsrecht,* 2nd edn. (Baden-Baden: Nomos, 1996)
author, in C. Calliess/M. Ruffert (eds.), *EUV/AEUV*	Christian Calliess/Matthias Ruffert (eds.), *EUV/AEUV – Das Verfassungsrecht der Europäischen Union mit Europäischer Grundrechtecharta, Kommentar,* 4th edn. (Munich: C.H. Beck, 2011)
H. Collins, *Employment Law*	Hugh Collins, *Employment Law,* 2nd edn. (Oxford: Oxford University Press, 2010)
S. Deakin/G. Morris, *Labour Law*	Simon Deakin/Gillian S. Morris, *Labour Law,* 5th edn. (Oxford and Portland, Oregon: Hart, 2009)
author, in *EAS,* B	Hartmut Oetker/Ulrich Preis (eds.), *Europäisches Arbeits- und Sozialrecht, EAS, part B – Systematische Darstellungen,* loose-leaf (Heidelberg: Forkel, last update: May 2012)
author, in D. Ehlers (ed.), *Europäische Grundrechte und Grundfreiheiten*	Dirk Ehlers (ed.), *Europäische Grundrechte und Grundfreiheiten,* 3rd edn. (Berlin/New York: de Gruyter, 2009)

---

*   Digital resources were last accessed on 1 June 2012.

author, in M. Fuchs/F. Marhold (eds.), *Europäisches Arbeitsrecht*

Maximilian Fuchs/Franz Marhold (eds.), *Europäisches Arbeitsrecht*, 3rd edn. (Vienna/New York: Springer, 2010)

F. Gamillscheg, *Kollektives Arbeitsrecht I*

Franz Gamillscheg, *Kollektives Arbeitsrecht, vol. I: Grundlagen/ Koalitionsfreiheit/ Tarifvertrag/ Arbeitskampf und Schlichtung* (Munich: C.H. Beck, 1997)

F. Gamillscheg, *Kollektives Arbeitsrecht II*

Franz Gamillscheg, *Kollektives Arbeitsrecht, vol. II: Betriebsverfassung*, 6th edn. (Munich: C.H. Beck, 2008)

author, in M. Gebauer/T. Wiedmann (eds.), *Zivilrecht unter europäischem Einfluss*

Martin Gebauer/Thomas Wiedmann, *Zivilrecht unter europäischem Einfluss*, 2nd edn. (Stuttgart: Boorberg, 2010)

author, in E. Grabitz/M. Hilf/M. Nettesheim (eds.), *Das Recht der Europäischen Union*

Martin Nettesheim (ed.), *Das Recht der Europäischen Union*, established by Eberhard Grabitz and continued by Meinhard Hilf, loose leaf (Munich: C.H. Beck, last update: October 2011)

S. Grundmann, *Europäisches Schuldvertragsrecht*

Stefan Grundmann, *Europäisches Schuldvertragsrecht* (Berlin/New York: de Gruyter, 1999)

S. Grundmann, *European Company Law*

Stefan Grundmann, *European Company Law – Organization, Finance and Capital Markets*, 2nd edn. (Antwerpen: Intersentia, 2011)

author, in P. Hanau/H.-D. Steinmeyer/R. Wank (eds.), *Handbuch des europäischen Arbeits- und Sozialrechts*

Peter Hanau/Heinz-Dietrich Steinmeyer/ Rolf Wank (eds.), *Handbuch des europäischen Arbeits- und Sozialrechts* (Munich: C.H. Beck, 2002)

D. Krimphove, *Europäisches Arbeitsrecht*

Dieter Krimphove, *Europäisches Arbeitsrecht*, 2nd edn. (Munich: C.H. Beck, 2001)

author, in B. Kropff/J. Semler (eds.), *Münchener Kommentar zum Aktiengesetz*

Bruno Kropff/Johannes Semler (eds.), *Münchener Kommentar zum Aktiengesetz – volume 9/2: §§329–410 AktG, SE-VO, SEBG, Europäische Niederlassungsfreiheit, Die Richtlinien zum Gesellschaftsrecht*, 2nd edn. (Munich: C.H. Beck/Vahlen, 2006)

S. Lingemann/R. v. Steinau-Steinrück/A. Mengel (eds.)	*Employment and Labor Law in Germany* Stefan Lingemann/Robert von Steinau-Steinrück/Anja Mengel (eds.), *Employment and Labor Law in Germany*, 3rd edn. (Munich: C.H. Beck 2011)
author, in M. Lutter/P. Hommelhoff (eds.), *SE-Kommentar*	Marcus Lutter/Peter Hommelhoff (eds.), *SE-Kommentar: SEVO, SEAG, SEBG, Steuerrecht* (Cologne: Otto Schmidt, 2008)
author, in J. Meyer (eds.), *Charta der Grundrechte der Europäischen Union*	Jürgen Meyer (ed.), *Charta der Grundrechte der Europäischen Union*, 3rd edn. (Baden-Baden: Nomos, 2011)
author, in R. Müller-Glöge/U. Preis/I. Schmidt (eds.), *Erfurter Kommentar*	Rudi Müller-Glöge/Ulrich Preis/Ingrid Schmidt (eds.), *Erfurter Kommentar zum Arbeitsrecht*, established by Thomas Dieterich, Peter Hanau and Günter Schaub, 12th edn. (Munich: C.H. Beck, 2012)
author, in R. Richardi et al. (eds.), *Münchener Handbuch zum Arbeitsrecht*	Reinhard Richardi/Otfried Wlotzke/Hellmut Wißmann/Hartmut Oetker (eds.), *Münchener Handbuch zum Arbeitsrecht*, 3rd edn. (Munich: C.H. Beck, 2009)
author, in F. J. Säcker/R. Rixecker (eds.), *Münchener Kommentar zum BGB*	Franz Jürgen Säcker/Roland Rixecker (eds.), *Münchener Kommentar zum Bürgerlichen Gesetzbuch* – *volume 1: Allgemeiner Teil §§1–240 BGB – ProstG – AGG*, 6th edn. (Munich: C.H. Beck, 2012) – *volume 10: Internationales Privatrecht, Rom I-Verordnung, Rom II-Verordnung, Einführungsgesetz zum Bürgerlichen Gesetzbuche (Art. 1–24)*, 5th edn. (Munich: C.H. Beck, 2010) – *volume 11: Internationales Privatrecht, Internationales Wirtschaftsrecht, Einführungsgesetz zum Bürgerlichen Gesetzbuche (Art. 25 – 248)*, 5th edn. (Munich: C.H. Beck, 2010)

R. A. Posner, *Economic Analysis of Law*

Posner, Richard A., *Economic Analysis of Law,* 7th edn. (Austin et al.: Wolters Kluwer, 2007)

author, in H. W. Rengeling/P. Szczekalla (eds.), *Grundrechte in der Europäischen Union*

Hans-Werner Rengeling /Peter Szczekalla (eds.), *Grundrechte in der Europäischen Union – Charta der Grundrechte und Allgemeine Rechtsgrundsätze* (Cologne/ Munich/Hamburg: Heymanns, 2004)

K. Riesenhuber, *Europäisches Vertragsrecht*

Karl Riesenhuber, *Europäisches Vertragsrecht,* 2nd edn. (Berlin/New York: de Gruyter, 2006)

author, in K. Riesenhuber (ed.), *Europäische Methodenlehre*

Karl Riesenhuber (ed.), *Europäische Methodenlehre – Handbuch für Ausbildung und Praxis,* 2nd edn. (Berlin/ New York: de Gruyter, 2010)

D. Schiek, *Europäisches Arbeitsrecht*

Dagmar Schiek, *Europäisches Arbeitsrecht,* 3rd edn. (Baden-Baden: Nomos, 2007)

M. Schlachter, *Casebook Europäisches Arbeitsrecht*

Monika Schlachter (ed.), *Casebook Europäisches Arbeitsrecht* (Baden-Baden: Nomos, 2005)

M. Schmidt, *Arbeitsrecht der EG*

Marlene Schmidt, *Das Arbeitsrecht der Europäischen Gemeinschaft* (Baden-Baden: Nomos, 2001)

author, in P. Schüren/W. Hamann (eds.), *Arbeitnehmerüberlassungsgesetz*

Peter Schüren/Wolfgang Hamann (eds.), *Arbeitnehmerüberlassungsgesetz Kommentar,* 4th edn. (Munich: C.H. Beck, 2010)

author, in J. Schwarze (ed.), *EU-Kommentar*

Jürgen Schwarze (ed.), *EU-Kommentar,* co-edited by Ulrich Becker, Armin Hatje and Johann Schon, 2nd edn. (Baden-Baden: Nomos, 2008)

author, in R. Streinz (ed.), *EUV/ AEUV*

Rudolf Streinz (ed.), *EUV/AEUV – Vertrag über die Europäisches Union und Vertrag zur Gründung der Europäischen Gemeinschaft,* 2nd edn. (Munich: C.H. Beck, 2011)

R. Streinz, *Europarecht*

Rudolf Streinz, Europarecht, 9th edn. (Heidelberg: C.F. Müller, 2012)

E. Szyszczak, *EC Labour Law*

Erika Szyszczak, EC Labour Law (Harlow/ London/New York: Longman, 2000)

author, in P. J. Tettinger/K. Stern (eds.), *Kölner Gemeinschaftskommentar zur Europäischen Grundrechte-Charta*

Peter J. Tettinger/Klaus Stern (eds.), *Kölner Gemeinschaftskommentar zur Europäischen Grundrechte-Charta* (Munich: C.H. Beck, 2006)

G. Thüsing, *Europäisches Arbeitsrecht*

Gregor Thüsing, *Europäisches Arbeitsrecht* (Munich: C.H. Beck, 2008)

author, in H. von der Groeben/J. Schwarze (eds.), *Kommentar EUV/EGV*

Hans von der Groeben /Jürgen Schwarze (eds.), *Kommentar zum Vertrag über die Europäische Union und zur Gründung der Europäischen Gemeinschaft,* 6th edn. (Baden-Baden: Nomos, 2003)

TABLE OF EU LEGISLATION

The legislative acts are listed in alpha-numerical order of the abbreviations or short titles used in this book.

Abbreviation	Short Title	Official Title	Source
	Brussels I-Regulation, Jurisdiction and Enforcement Regulation	Council Regulation (EC) No 44/2001 of 22 December 2000 on jurisdiction and the recognition and enforcement of judgments in civil and commercial matters	OJ 2001 L 12/1
BoPD	Burden of Proof Directive	Council Directive 97/80/EC of 15 December 1997 on the burden of proof in cases of discrimination based on sex	OJ 1998 L 14/6
CAD	Commercial Agents Directive	Council Directive 86/653/EEC of 18 December 1986 on the coordination of the laws of the Member States relating to self-employed commercial agents	OJ 1986 L 382/17
CBMD	Cross-Border Merger Directive	Directive 2005/56/EC of the European Parliament and of the Council of 26 October 2005 on cross-border mergers of limited liability companies (Text with EEA relevance)	OJ 2005 L 310/1
CFSR	Community Charter of Fundamental Social Rights	Community Charter of Fundamental Social Rights of Workers of 9 December 1989	COM(89) 248 final
ChFR	Charter of Fundamental Rights	Charter of Fundamental Rights of the European Union, solemnly proclaimed on 7 December 2000	OJ 2000 C 364/1, OJ 2007 C 303/1
CMD	Capital Movement Directive	Council Directive 88/361/EEC of 24 June 1988 for the implementation of Article 67 of the Treaty	OJ 1988 L 178/5
CRD 1975	Collective Redundancies Directive 1975	Council Directive 75/129/EEC of 17 February 1975 on the approximation of the laws of the Member States relating to collective redundancies	OJ 1975 L 48/29
CRD	Collective Redundancies Directive	Council Directive 98/59/EC of 20 July 1998 on the approximation of the laws of the Member States relating to collective redundancies	OJ 1998 L 225/16

DPD	Data Protection Directive	Directive 95/46/EC of the European Parliament and of the Council of 24 October 1995 on the protection of individuals with regard to the processing of personal data and on the free movement of such data	OJ 1995 L 281/31
EAD	Equal Access Directive	Council Directive 76/207/EEC of 9 February 1976 on the implementation of the principle of equal treatment for men and women as regards access to employment, vocational training and promotion, and working conditions	OJ 1976 L 39/40
EPD	Equal Pay Directive	Council Directive 75/117/EEC of 10 February 1975 on the approximation of the laws of the Member States relating to the application of the principle of equal pay for men and women	OJ 1975 L 45/19
		Council Directive 79/7/EEC of 19 December 1978 on the progressive implementation of the principle of equal treatment for men and women in matters of social security	OJ 1979 L 6/24
		Council Directive 86/378/EEC of 24 July 1986 on the implementation of the principle of equal treatment for men and women in occupational social security schemes	OJ 1986 L 225/40
ETFD	Equal Treatment Framework Directive	Council Directive 2000/78/EC of 27 November 2000 establishing a general framework for equal treatment in employment and occupation	OJ 2000 L 303/16
EWCD 1994	European Works Council Directive 1994	Council Directive 94/45/EC of 22 September 1994 on the establishment of a European Works Council or a procedure in Community-scale undertakings and Community-scale groups of undertakings for the purposes of informing and consulting employees	OJ 1994 L 254/64
EWCD	European Works Council Directive	Directive 2009/38/EC of the European Parliament and of the Council of 6 May 2009 on the establishment of a European Works Council or a procedure in Community-scale undertakings and Community-scale groups of undertakings for the purposes of informing and consulting employees (Recast)	OJ 2009 L 122/28
FMCD	Free Movement of Citizens Directive	Directive 2004/38/EG of the European Parliament and of the Council of 29 April 2004 on the right of citizens of the Union and their families to move and reside freely within the territory of the Member States amending regulation 1612/68/EEC and repealing Directives 64/221/EEC, 68/360/EEC, 72/194/EEC, 73/148/EEC, 75/34/EEC, 75/35/EEC, 90/364/EEC, 90/365/EEC and 93/96/EEC	OJ 2004 L 158/77

FMWR	Free Movement of Workers Regulation 1612/68	Regulation (EEC) No 1612/68 of the Council of 15 October 1968 on freedom of movement for workers within the Community	OJ 1968 L 257/2
FTWD	Fixed Term Work Directive	Council Directive 1999/70/EC of 28 June 1999 concerning the framework agreement on fixed-term work concluded by ETUC, UNICE and CEEP	OJ 1999 L 175/43
FTWFA	Fixed Term Work Framework Agreement	Framework agreement on fixed-term work concluded by ETUC, UNICE and CEEP	OJ 1999 L 175/43 (Annex to FTWD)
ICFD	Information and Consultation Framework Directive	Directive 2002/14/EC of the European Parliament and of the Council of 11 March 2002 establishing a general framework for informing and consulting employees in the European Community – Joint declaration of the European Parliament, the Council and the Commission on employee representation	OJ 2002 L 80/34
IPD	Insolvency Protection Directive	Council Directive 80/987/EEC of 20 October 1980 on the approximation of the laws of the Member States relating to the protection of employees in the event of the insolvency of their employer	OJ 1980 L 283/23
MPD	Maternity Protection Directive	Council Directive 92/85/EEC of 19 October 1992 on the introduction of measures to encourage improvements in the safety and health at work of pregnant workers and workers who have recently given birth or are breastfeeding (tenth individual Directive within the meaning of Article 16 (1) of Directive 89/391/EEC)	OJ 1992 L 348/1
PLD	Parental Leave Directive	Council Directive 2010/18/EU of 8 March 2010 implementing the revised Framework Agreement on parental leave concluded by BUSINESSEUROPE, UEAPME, CEEP and ETUC and repealing Directive 96/34/EC	OJ 2010 L 68/13
PLD 1996	Parental Leave Directive 1996	Council Directive 96/34/EC of 3 June 1996 on the framework agreement on parental leave concluded by UNICE, CEEP and the ETUC	OJ 1996 L 145/4
PLFA	Parental Leave Framework Agreement	Revised Framework Agreement on parental leave concluded by BUSINESSEUROPE, UEAPME, CEEP and ETUC	OJ 2010 L 68/13 (Annex to PLD)
PoWD	Posting of Workers Directive	Directive 96/71/EC of the European Parliament and of the Council of 16 December 1996 concerning the posting of workers in the framework of the provision of services	OJ 1997 L 18/1

PTWD	Part-Time Work Directive	Council Directive 97/81/EC of 15 December 1997 concerning the Framework Agreement on part-time work concluded by UNICE, CEEP and the ETUC	OJ 1998 L 14/9
PTWFA	Part-Time Work Framework Agreement	Framework Agreement on part-time work concluded by UNICE, CEEP and the ETUC	OJ 1998 L 14/9 (Annex to PTWD)
RAR	Retirement Age Recommen-dation	Council recommendation of 10 December 1982 on the principles of a Community policy with regard to retirement age	
RDD	Race Discrimina-tion Directive	Council Directive 2000/43/EC of 29 June 2000 implementing the principle of equal treatment between persons irrespective of racial or ethnic origin	OJ 2000 L 180/22
	Rome Convention	Convention 80/934/ECC on the law applicable to contractual obligations opened for signature in Rome on 19 June 1980	OJ 1998 C 27/34 (consoli-dated version)
	Rome I-Regulation	Regulation (EC) No 593/2008 of the European Parliament and of the Council of 17 June 2008 on the law applicable to contractual obligations (Rome I)	OJ 2008 L 177/6.
	Rome II-Regulation	Regulation (EC) No 864/2007 of the European Parliament and of the Council of 11 July 2007 on the law applicable to non-contractual obligations (Rome II)	OJ 2007 L 199/40
SCED	SCE-Directive	Council Directive 2003/72/EC of 22 July 2003 supplementing the Statute for a European Cooperative Society with regard to the involvement of employees	OJ 2003 L 207/25
SCER	SCE-Regulation	Council Regulation (EC) No 1435/2003 of 22 July 2003 on the Statute for a European Cooperative Society (SCE)	OJ 2003 L 207/1
SDD	Sex Discrimi-nation Directive	Directive 2006/54/EC of the European Parliament and of the Council of 5 July 2006 on the implementation of the principle of equal opportunities and equal treatment of men and women in matters of employment and occupation (recast)	OJ 2006 L 204/23

SDGS	Sex Discrimi-nation in Access to Goods and Services Directive	Council Directive 2004/113/EC of 13 December 2004 implementing the principle of equal treatment between men and women in the access to and supply of goods and services	OJ 2004 L 373/37
SED	SE-Employee Involvement Directive	Council Directive 2001/86/EC of 8 October 2001 supplementing the Statute for a European company with regard to the involvement of employees	OJ 2001 L 294/22
SER	SE-Regulation	Council Regulation (EC) No 2157/2001 of 8 October 2001 on the Statute for a European company (SE)	OJ 2001 L 294/1
SHFD	Safety and Health Framework Directive	Council Directive 89/391/EEC of 12 June 1989 on the introduction of measures to encourage improvements in the safety and health of workers at work	OJ 1989 L 183/1
SIMD	Services in the Internal Market Directive	Directive 2006/123/EC of the European Parliament and of the Council of 12 December 2006 on services in the internal market	OJ 2006 L 376/36
SPER-P2008	SPE-Regulation-Proposal 2008	Proposal for a Council Regulation on the statute for a European private company	COM(2008) 396 final
SPER-P2009	SPE-Regulation-Proposal 2009	Revised Council Presidency compromise of 27 November 2009 for a Council Regulation on a European Private Company	16115/09, ADD1, DRS 71, SOC 711
SPER-P2011	SPE-Regulation-Proposal 2011	Revised Council Presidency compromise of 23 May 2011 for a Council Regulation on a European Private Company	10611/11, DRS 84, SOC 432
TAWD	Temporary Agency Work Directive	Directive 2008/104/EC of the European Parliament and of the Council of 19 November 2008 on temporary agency work	OJ 2008 L 327/9
TESHD	Temporary Employment Safety and Health Directive	Council Directive 91/383/EEC of 25 June 1991 supplementing the measures to encourage improvements in the safety and health at work of workers with a fixed- duration employment relationship or a temporary employment relationship	OJ 1991 L 206/19
TOD	Takeover Directive	Directive 2004/25/EC of the European Parliament and of the Council of 21 April 2004 on takeover bids	OJ 2004 L 142/12

TUD 1977	Transfer of Undertakings Directive 1977	Council Directive 77/187/EEC of 14 February 1977 on the approximation of the laws of the Member States relating to the safeguarding of employees' rights in the event of transfers of undertakings, businesses or parts of businesses	OJ 1977 L 61/26
TUD 1998	Transfer of Undertakings Directive 1998	Council Directive 98/50/EC of 29 June 1998 amending Directive 77/187/EEC on the approximation of the laws of the Member States relating to the safeguarding of employees' rights in the event of transfers of undertakings, businesses or parts of businesses	OJ 1998 L 201/88
TUD	Transfer of Undertakings Directive	Council Directive 2001/23/EC of 12 March 2001 on the approximation of the laws of the Member States relating to the safeguarding of employees' rights in the event of transfers of undertakings, businesses or parts of undertakings or businesses	OJ 2001 L 82/16
WSD	Written Statement Directive	Council Directive 91/533/EEC of 14 October 1991 on an employer's obligation to inform employees of the conditions applicable to the contract or employment relationship	OJ 1991 L 288/32
WTD	Working Time Directive	Directive 2003/88/EC of the European Parliament and of the Council of 4 November 2003 concerning certain aspects of the organisation of working time	OJ 2003 L 299/9
WTR	Working Time Recommendation	Recommendation of the Council of 22 July 1975 on the principle of the 40-hour week and the principle of four weeks' annual paid holiday	OJ 1975 L 199/32
WTRes	Working Time Resolution	Council Resolution of 18 December 1979 on the adaptation of working time	OJ 1979 C 2/1
YPWD	Young People at Work Directive	Council Directive 94/33/EC of 22 June 1994 on the protection of young people at work	OJ 1994 L 216/12

TABLE OF ECJ CASES

Case Number	Short Title/Parties	Reference	§ para.*
7/56 and 3/57 to 7/57	*Algera*	[1957] ECR 85	**2** 14
14/61	*Hoogovens v. Hohe Behörde*	[1962] ECR 513	**2** 14
25/62	*Plaumann*	[1963] ECR 211	**2** 31
26/62	*van Gend & Loos*	[1963] ECR 3	**1** 67
75/63	*Unger*	[1964] ECR 379	**3** 9
6/64	*Costa v. E.N.E.L.*	[1964] ECR 1253	**3** 49
29/69	*Stauder*	[1969] ECR 419	**2** 14, 39
11/70	*Internationale Handelsgesellschaft*	[1970] ECR 1125	**2** 14
80/70	*Defrenne I*	[1971] ECR 445	**9** 8
5/71	*Schöppenstedt*	[1971] ECR 975	**2** 14
4/73	*Nold*	[1974] ECR 491	**2** 10, 14, 37
152/73	*Sotgiu*	[1974] ECR 153	**3** 24, 33
167/73	*Commission v. France*	[1974] ECR 359	**3** 6
175/73	*Gewerkschaftsbund v. Council*	[1974] ECR 917	**2** 14
18/74	*Allgemeine Gewerkschaft v. Commission*	[1974] ECR 933	**2** 14
33/74	*van Binsbergen*	[1974] ECR 1299	**3** 60
36/74	*Walrave und Koch*	[1974] ECR 1405	**3** 6, 29, 57, 60
41/74	*van Duyn*	[1974] ECR 1337	**3** 6
41/74	*van Duyn*	[1974] ECR 1337	**3** 41
67/74	*Bonsignore*	[1975] ECR 297	**3** 42
36/75	*Rutili*	[1975] ECR 1219	**3** 42
43/75	*Defrenne II*	[1976] ECR 455	**8** 1, 4, 15; **9** 2, 3, 4, 5, 7, 9, 25
118/75	*Watson und Belmann*	[1976] ECR 1185	**3** 6
13/76	*Donà*	[1976] ECR 1333	**3** 29
33/76	*Rewe Zentralfinanz*	[1976] ECR 1989	**1** 66

---

*   Numbers in **bold font style** refer to chapters, numbers in regular font style refer to paragraphs within the chapters.

Case Number	Short Title/Parties	Reference	§ para.*
45/76	Comet	[1976] ECR 2043	1 66
5/77	Tedeschi	[1977] ECR 1555	3 3
30/77	Bouchereau	[1977] ECR 1999	3 42
149/77	Defrenne III	[1978] ECR 1365	2 5; 8 10; 9 6
33/78	Somafer	[1978] ECR 2183	7 13
110/78 and 111/78	van Wesemael	[1979] ECR 35	3 57, 66
120/78	Rewe	[1979] ECR 649	3 43
230/78	Eridania	[1979] ECR 2749	2 14
251/78	Denkavit	[1979] ECR 3369	3 3
25/79	Sanicentral v. Collin	[1979] ECR 3423	7 6
41/79, 121/79 and 769/79	Testa	[1980] ECR 1979	2 14
44/79	Hauer	[1979] ECR 3727	2 10, 11, 14, 37
129/79	Macarthys	[1980] ECR 1275	9 4, 12, 22
149/79	Commission v. Belgium	[1980] ECR 3881	3 23
69/80	Worringham	[1981] ECR 767	9 4, 7, 8, 34
96/80	Jenkins	[1981] ECR 911	8 15, 34; 9 3, 4, 8, 17, 34
279/80	Webb	[1981] ECR 3305	3 57, 60, 61, 63, 66; 9 46, 47, 59, 62; 18 5; 20 32, 34
12/81	Garland	[1982] ECR 359	9 3, 7
15/81	Schul	[1982] ECR 1409	4 48
19/81	Burton	[1982] ECR 554	9 37
53/81	Levin	[1982] ECR 1035	3 6, 9, 10, 12
62/81 and 63/81	Seco	[1982] ECR 223	3 61; 6 1
91/81	Commission v. Italy	[1982] ECR 2133	23 43
115/81 and 116/81	Adoui	[1982] ECR 1665	3 42
318/81	Commission v. CO.DE. MI.	[1985] ECR 3693	5 10
35/82 and 36/82	Morson	[1982] ECR 3723	3 106
165/82	Commission v. United Kingdom	[1983] ECR 3431	9 57
286/82 and 26/83	Luisi and Carbone	[1984] ECR 377	3 58
14/83	von Colson und Kamann	[1984] ECR 1891	1 65, 73; 3 30; 8 64, 66, 67, 68
19/83	Wendelboe	[1985] ECR 457	24 46, 61
59/83	Biovilac	[1984] ECR 4057	2 14
79/83	Harz	[1984] ECR 1921	8 64, 66, 67, 68
107/83	Klopp	[1984] ECR 2971	3 79
135/83	Abels	[1985] ECR 469	24 46, 47, 49, 61

Case Number	Short Title/Parties	Reference	§ para.*
143/83	*Commission v. Denmark*	[1985] ECR 427	**4** 24
180/83	*Moser*	[1984] ECR 2539	**3** 21
184/83	*Hofmann*	[1984] ECR 3047	**9** 62; **20** 9
186/83	*Botzen*	[1985] ECR 519	**24** 49
215/83	*Commission v. Belgium*	[1985] ECR 1039	**23** 13, 14, 43
238/83	*Caisse d'Allocations Familiales v. Meade*	[1984] ECR 2631	**3** 13
284/83	*Nielsen*	[1985] ECR 553	**23** 2, 11
294/83	*Les Verts*	[1986] ECR 1339	**2** 6
41/84	*Pinna*	[1986] ECR 1	**3** 33
105/84	*Danmols Inventar*	[1985] ECR 2639	**24** 13, 49, 75
131/84	*Commission v. Italy*	[1985] ECR 3531	**23** 43
152/84	*Marshall*	[1986] ECR 723	**9** 37
170/84	*Bilka*	[1986] ECR 1607	**8** 34, 36; **9** 8, 17, 22
188/84	*Commission v. France*	[1986] ECR 419	**3** 2; **13** 1
222/84	*Johnston*	[1986] ECR 1651	**1** 66; **8** 54, 76; **9** 38, 57, 60, 62
235/84	*Commission v. Italy*	[1986] ECR 2291	**4** 24; **24** 89, 107
237/84	*Commission v. Belgium*	[1986] ECR 1247	**24** 80, 107
262/84	*Beets-Proper*	[1986] ECR 773	**9** 37
298/84	*Paolo Iorio*	[1986] ECR 247	**3** 21
307/84	*Commission v. France*	[1986] ECR 1725	**3** 22
24/85	*Spijkers*	[1986] ECR 1119	**24** 4, 24, 27, 28
66/85	*Lawrie-Blum*	[1986] ECR 2121	**3** 9, 10, 23, 24
79/85	*Segers*	[1986] ECR 2375	**3** 79
139/85	*Kempf*	[1986] ECR 1741	**3** 9, 12
234/85	*Keller*	[1986] ECR 2897	**2** 14, 37
266/85	*Shenavai*	[1987] ECR 239	**7** 7
26/86	*Deutz and Geldermann*	[1987] ECR 941	**2** 31
80/86	*Kolpinghuis Nijmegen*	[1987] ECR 3969	**1** 72, 74
147/86	*Commission v. Greece*	[1988] ECR 1637	**3** 32
157/86	*Murphy*	[1988] ECR 673	**3** 49
287/86	*Ny Mølle Kro*	[1987] ECR 5465	**24** 33, 44, 65
318/86	*Commission v. France*	[1988] ECR 3559	**9** 43, 56, 57
324/86	*Daddy's Dance Hall*	[1988] ECR 739	**24** 43, 44, 62
22/87	*Commission v. Italy*	[1989] ECR 143	**25** 8, 11, 29
81/87	*Daily Mail*	[1988] ECR 5483	**3** 79, 80, 81, 88

Case Number	Short Title/Parties	Reference	§ para.*
101/87	Bork	[1988] ECR 3057	24 33, 44, 80, 82
144/87 and 145/87	Berg and Busschers	[1988] ECR 2559	24 43, 44, 57, 67, 69
186/87	Cowan	[1989] ECR 195	3 105, 106
C-193/87 and C-194/87	Maurissen	[1990] ECR I-95	2 14
265/87	Schräder	[1989] ECR 2237	2 10, 11, 14
344/87	Bettray	[1989] ECR 1621	3 9, 10, 11
C-349/87	Paraschi	[1991] ECR I-4501	3 7
33/88	Allué I	[1989] ECR 1591	3 24, 33, 34
48/88	Achterberg-Te Riele	[1989] ECR 1963	9 29
68/88	Commission v. Greece	[1989] ECR 2965	1 66; 8 67
109/88	Danfoss	[1989] ECR 3199	8 37, 57; 9 18, 21, 43; 11 37; 16 33
C-145/88	Trofaen	[1989] ECR 3851	14 32
171/88	Rinner-Kühn	[1989] ECR 2743	8 36; 9 7, 17, 22; 16 22
C-175/88	Biehl	[1990] ECR I-1779	3 35
177/88	Dekker	[1990] ECR I-3941	8 66, 69, 93; 9 46, 47, 59
C-179/88	Handels- og Kontorfunktionaerernes Forbund	[1990] ECR I-3979	9 47; 20 26
C-262/88	Barber	[1990] ECR I-1889	8 15; 9 3, 7, 8, 9, 11, 14, 16
C-33/89	Kowalska	[1990] ECR I-2591	9 3, 4, 9, 17, 25
C-106/89	Marleasing	[1990] ECR I-4135	1 73
C-113/89	Rush Portuguesa	[1990] ECR I-1417	3 57, 58, 66; 6 1, 7
C-154/89	Commission v. France	[1991] ECR I-659	3 58
C-180/89	Commission v. Italy	[1991] ECR I-709	3 58
C-184/89	Nimz	[1991] ECR I-297	8 37; 9 3, 10, 22, 25; 16 22
C-198/89	Commission v. Greece	[1991] ECR I-727	3 58
C-221/89	Factortame	[1991] ECR I-3905	3 79
C-260/89	ERT	[1991] ECR I-2925	2 28; 3 48, 65, 72
C-292/89	The Queen v. Immigration Appeal Tribunal, ex parte Antonissen	[1991] ECR I-745	3 6, 16, 17
C-308/89	Cordoniu	[1994] ECR I-1853	2 31
C-312/89	SIDEF-Conforma	[1991] ECR I-1021	14 32
C-332/89	Trafitex	[1991] ECR I-1037	14 32

Case Number	Short Title/Parties	Reference	§ para.*
C-345/89	*Stoeckel*	[1991] ECR I-4047	**9** 35, 58; **20** 9
C-357/89	*Raulin*	[1992] ECR I-1027	**3** 9, 10, 11
C-362/89	*d'Urso*	[1991] ECR I-4105	**24** 1, 3, 46, 49, 57
C-363/89	*Roux*	[1991] ECR I-273	**3** 19
C-3/90	*Bernini*	[1992] ECR I-1071	**3** 9, 10, 11
C-6/90 to C-9/90	*Francovich I*	[1991] ECR I-5357	**1** 75; **25** 32
C-76/90	*Säger*	[1991] ECR I-4221	**3** 63, 66
C-90/90 and C-91/90	*Neu*	[1991] ECR I-3617	**2** 10
C-177/90	*Kühn*	[1992] ECR I-35	**2** 37
C-204/90	*Bachmann*	[1992] ECR I-249	**3** 35, 44
C-300/90	*Commission v. Belgium*	[1992] ECR I-305	**3** 35, 44
C-332/90	*Steen I*	[1992] ECR I-341	**3** 21
C-360/90	*Bötel*	[1992] ECR I-3589	**9** 7, 17, 34
C-27/91	*Union de recouvrement des cotisations de sécurité sociale et d'allocations familiales de la Savoie (URSSAF)*	[1991] ECR I-5531	**3** 35
C-29/91	*Redmond Stichting*	[1992] ECR I-3189	**24** 27, 43, 44, 45
C-109/91	*Ten Oever*	[1993] ECR I-4879	**9** 8
C-110/91	*Moroni*	[1993] ECR I-6591	**8** 15; **9** 16
C-132/91, C-138/91 and C-139/91	*Katsikas*	[1992] ECR I-6577	**2** 14, 15; **24** 71, 73
C-140/91, C-141/91, C-278/91 and C-279/91	*Suffritti*	[1992] ECR I-6337	**25** 32
C-152/91	*Neath*	[1993] ECR I-6935	**9** 8
C-158/91	*Levy*	[1993] ECR I-4287	**9** 35
C-171/91	*Tsiotras*	[1993] ECR I-2925	**3** 6, 16, 17, 20
C-173/91	*Commission v. Belgium*	[1993] ECR 673	**9** 9
C-189/91	*Kirsammer-Hack*	[1993] ECR I-6185	**9** 51
C-200/91	*Coloroll Pension Trustees*	[1994] ECR I-4389	**9** 3, 8, 12, 25
C-206/91	*Poirrez*	[1992] ECR I-6685	**3** 21
C-209/91	*Watson*	[1992] ECR I-5755	**24** 43
C-209/91	*Rask*	[1992] ECR I-5755	**24** 27, 43, 62, 63, 81
C-259/91, C-331/91 and C-332/91	*Allué II*	[1993] ECR I-4309	**3** 33, 34, 44
267/91 and 268/91	*Keck und Mithouard*	[1993] ECR I-6097	**3** 38

Case Number	Short Title/Parties	Reference	§ para.*
C-271/91	*Marshall II*	[1993] ECR I- 4367	8 67, 68
C-314/91	*Weber v. Parliament*	[1993] ECR I-1093	2 6
C-19/92	*Kraus*	[1993] ECR I-1663	3 36, 37, 44, 83
C-91/92	*Faccini Dori*	[1994] ECR I-3325	1 72
C-92/92 and C-326/92	*Phil Collins*	[1993] ECR I-5145	8 5
C-125/92	*Mulox IBC*	[1993] ECR I-4075	5 14; 7 3, 12
C-127/92	*Enderby*	[1993] ECR I-5535	8 57, 58; 9 10, 20, 21
C-272/92	*Spotti*	[1993] ECR I-5185	3 34
C-275/92	*Schindler*	[1994] ECR I-1039	3 62
C-334/92	*Wagner Miret*	[1993] ECR I-6911	25 8, 32; 28 13
C-343/92	*Roks*	[1994] ECR I-571	9 52
C-382/92	*Commission v. United Kingdom*	[1994] ECR I-2435	1 66; 16 44; 23 17; 24 6, 15, 90, 107
C-383/92	*Commission v. United Kingdom*	[1994] ECR I-2479	16 44; 23 17, 18, 32, 43
C-392/92	*Christel Schmidt*	[1994] ECR I-1311	24 31, 35, 81
C-399/92	*Helmig*	[1994] ECR I-5727	9 17
C-408/92	*Avdel Systems*	[1994] ECR I-4435	9 25
C-419/92	*Ingetraut Scholz*	[1994] ECR I-505	3 33, 35
C-421/92	*Habermann-Beltermann*	[1994] ECR I-1657	9 29, 46, 59, 62, 63
C-7/93	*Beune*	[1994] ECR I-4471	9 8
C-13/93	*Minne*	[1994] ECR I-371	9 35
C-28/93	*Van den Akker*	[1994] ECR I-4527	9 25
C-43/93	*Vander Elst*	[1994] ECR I-3803	3 58, 62, 63; 6 1, 7
C-46/93 to C-48/93	*Brasserie du pêcheur, Factortame*	[1996] ECR I-1029	1 75, 76
C-128/93	*Fisscher*	[1994] ECR I-4583	1 74; 9 8
C-132/93	*Steen II*	[1994] ECR I-2715	3 21
C-278/93	*Freers und Speckmann*	[1996] ECR I-1165	8 37; 9 7, 17, 34
C-279/93	*Schumacker*	[1995] ECR I-225	3 33, 35; 9 15
C-280/93	*Germany v. Council*	[1994] ECR I-4973	2 14, 37
C-323/93	*Centre d'Insemination de la Crespelle*	[1994] ECR I-5077	3 3
C-352/93	*Gillespie*	[1996] ECR I-475	9 7, 15, 16, 34; 20 9
C-381/93	*Commission v. France*	[1994] ECR I-5145	3 58
C-384/93	*Alpine Investments*	[1995] ECR I-1141	3 58

Case Number	Short Title/Parties	Reference	§ para.*
C-392/93	*British Telecommunications*	[1996] ECR I-1631	1 75
C-400/93	*Royal Copenhagen*	[1995] ECR I-1275	8 57; 9 13, 15, 21
C-415/93	*Bosman*	[1995] ECR I-4921	2 14; 3 18, 29, 36, 45, 57, 60, 80
C-435/93	*Dietz*	[1996] ECR I-5223	9 3, 8
C-449/93	*Rockfon*	[1995] ECR I-4291	23 6, 7
C-450/93	*Kalanke*	[1995] ECR I-3051	8 53, 54
C-457/93	*Lewark*	[1996] ECR I-243	9 7, 17
C-472/93	*Luigi Spano*	[1995] ECR I-4321	24 49
C-473/93	*Commission v. Luxembourg*	[1996] ECR I-3207	3 22, 23
C-479/93	*Francovich II*	[1995] ECR I-3843	1 75; 25 9, 10
C-5/94	*Hedley Lomas*	[1996] ECR I-2553	1 75
C-13/94	*P v S*	[1996] ECR I-2143	8 32; 9 40
C-22/94	*Irish Farmers*	[1997] ECR I-1809	2 11
C-48/94	*Rygaard*	[1995] ECR I-2745	24 28
55/94	*Gebhard*	[1995] ECR I-4165	3 58, 79, 84
C-84/94	*United Kingdom v. Council*	[1996] ECR 5755	4 3, 20; 13 3, 13; 14 32; 23 39
C-116/94	*Meyers*	[1995] ECR I-2131	9 24, 35; 16 13
C-151/94	*Commission v. Luxembourg*	[1995] ECR I-3685	3 35
C-171/94 and C-172/94	*Merckx and Neuhuys*	[1997] ECR I-1253	24 27, 33, 36, 37, 44, 71, 73, 82, 84
C-178/94 and C-179/94, C-188/94 to C-190/94	*Dillenkofer*	[1996] ECR I-4845	1 75
C-192/94	*El Corte Inglés*	[1996] ECR I-1281	1 72
C-237/94	*O'Flynn*	[1996] ECR I-2617	3 33
C-272/94	*Guiot*	[1996] ECR I-1905	3 66; 6 1
C-278/94	*Commission v. Belgium*	[1996] ECR I-4307	3 33
C-298/94	*Henke*	[1996] ECR I-4989	24 16
C-305/94	*Rotsart de Hertaing*	[1996] ECR I-5927	24 57, 67
C-319/94	*Dethier Equipement*	[1998] ECR I-1061	24 49, 80, 81, 82
C-336/94	*Dafek*	[1997] ECR I-6761	3 35
C-1/95	*Gerster*	[1997] ECR I-5253	8 37; 9 5, 10, 30, 34, 50, 53
C-13/95	*Süzen*	[1997] ECR I-1259	24 22, 27, 28, 29, 37, 44, 45

Case Number	Short Title/Parties	Reference	§ para.*
C-18/95	Terhoeve	[1999] ECR I-345	3 18, 26, 36, 37
C-94/95 and C-95/95	Bonifaci	[1997] ECR I-3969	25 9, 18, 32
C-100/95	Kording	[1997] ECR I-5289	9 50, 53
C-127/95	Norbrook Laboratories	[1998] ECR I-1531	1 75
C-136/95	Thibault	[1998] ECR I-2011	9 36, 62, 63; 20 30
C-168/95	Arcaro	[1996] ECR I-4705	1 72
C-180/95	Draehmpaehl	[1997] ECR I-2195	1 66; 8 58, 66, 67, 68, 69, 92; 9 45
C-235/95	Dumon and Froment	[1998] ECR I-4531	25 21
C-243/95	Hill and Stapleton	[1998] ECR I-3739	9 17, 22, 44
C-299/95	Kremzow	[1997] ECR I-2629	3 21
C-336/95	Pedro Burdalo Trevejo	[1997] ECR I-2115	24 107
C-344/95	Commission v. Belgium	[1997] ECR I-1035	3 17
C-368/95	Familiapress	[1997] ECR I-3689	2 28; 3 48, 72
C-373/95	Maso	[1997] ECR I-4051	25 9, 18, 20, 21, 32
C-383/95	Rutten v. Cross Medical	[1997] ECR I-57	5 14; 7 12
C-398/95	SETTIG	[1997] ECR I-3091	3 58
C-400/95	Larsson	[1997] ECR I-2757	9 47; 20 35
C-409/95	Marschall	[1997] ECR I-6363	8 53, 54
C-15/96	Kalliope Schöning-Kougebetopoulou	[1998] ECR I-47	3 14, 33, 35
C-51/96 and C-191/97	Deliège	[2000] ECR I-2549	3 57
C-66/96	Pedersen	[1998] ECR I-7327	9 7, 16, 36; 20 18, 26, 29, 32, 34
C-67/96	Albany	[1999] ECR I-5751	2 13, 14
C-90/96	Petrie u.a. v. Università degli studi di Verona	[1997] ECR I-6527	3 33, 34
C-117/96	Mosbæk	[1997] ECR I-5017	25 14
C-127/96, C-229/96 and C-74/97	Vidal	[1998] ECR I-8179	24 22, 27, 28, 31
C-129/96	Inter-Environnement Wallonie	[1997] ECR I-7411	1 70
C-158/96	Kohll	[1998] ECR I-1931	3 66
C-162/96	Racke	[1998] ECR I-3655	2 9
C-173/96 and C-247/96	Hidalgo and Ziemann	[1998] ECR I-8237	24 13, 16, 17, 22, 28, 29, 31, 44
C-176/96	Lehtonen und Castors Braine	[2000] ECR I-2681	3 9
C-187/96	Commission v. Greece	[1998] ECR I-1095	3 35; 9 7

Case Number	Short Title/Parties	Reference	§ para.*
C-197/96	*Commission v. France*	[1997] ECR I-1489	9 35
C-207/96	*Commission v. Italy*	[1997] ECR I-6869	9 35
C-249/96	*Grant*	[1998] ECR I-621	8 32; 9 11, 41
C-253 to 258/96	*Kampelmann*	[1997] ECR I-6907	1 66; 12 35, 38, 41
C-261/96	*Palmisani*	[1997] ECR I-4025	1 66
C-264/96	*Imperial Chemical Industries*	[1998] ECR I-4695	3 84
C-326/96	*Levez*	[1998] ECR I-7835	1 66
C-336/96	*Gilly*	[1998] ECR I-2793	8 6
C-348/96	*Calfa*	[1999] ECR I-11	3 42
C-350/96	*Clean Car Autoservice*	[1998] ECR I-2521	3 4, 10, 13, 33, 35, 40
C-369/96 and C-376/96	*Arblade*	[1999] ECR I-8453	3 62, 66, 73; 12 3
C-394/96	*Mary Brown*	[1998] ECR I-4185	9 46, 47; 20 32, 35
C-399/96	*Europièces*	[1998] ECR I-6965	24 49, 71, 74, 85, 88
C-411/96	*Boyle*	[1998] ECR I-6401	9 7, 15, 16; 20 4, 27, 28, 29
C-114/97	*Commission v. Spain*	[1998] ECR I-6717	3 24, 42
C-125/97	*Regeling*	[1998] ECR I-4493	25 16
C-157/97	*Badeck*	[2000] ECR I-1875	8 54, 56
C-167/97	*Seymour-Smith and Perez*	[1999] ECR I-688	9 9, 10, 17, 36, 52
C-185/97	*Coote*	[1998] ECR I-5199	2 25; 8 71; 26 36
C-212/97	*Centros*	[1999] ECR I-1459	3 79, 83, 84, 88
C-215/97	*Bellone*	[1998] ECR I-2191	2 10
C-222/97	*Trummer and Mayer*	[1999] ECR I-1661	3 97
C-240/97	*Spain v. Commission*	[1999] ECR I-6571	2 9, 10
C-250/97	*Lauge*	[1998] ECR I-8738	23 15
C-262/97	*Engelbrecht*	[2000] ECR I-7321	3 49
C-270/97 and C-271/97	*Sievers and Schrage*	[2000] ECR 929	8 4; 9 2
C-273/97	*Sirdar*	[1999] ECR I-7403	9 30, 38, 57
C-281/97	*Krüger*	[1999] ECR I-5127	9 3, 7, 17
C-309/97	*Wiener Gebietskrankenkasse*	[1999] ECR I-2865	9 13, 15
C-321/97	*Andersson und Wåkerås-Andersson*	[1999] ECR I-3551	25 9, 32
C-333/97	*Lewen*	[1999] ECR I-7243	9 3, 7, 17; 20 19, 28, 37; 21 20

Case Number	Short Title/Parties	Reference	§ para.*
C-350/97	*Monsees*	[1999] ECR I-2921	**3** 3
C-424/97	*Haim*	[2000] ECR I-5123	**1** 75
C-49/98, C-50/98, C-52/98 to C-54/98 and C-68/98 to C-71/98	*Finalarte*	[2001] ECR I-7831	**3** 16, 62, 63, 66, 67, 72, 73; **6** 33
C-55/98	*Vestergaard*	[1999] ECR I-7641	**3** 58
C-78/98	*Preston and Fletcher*	[2000] ECR I-3201	**1** 66; **9** 25
C-165/98	*Mazzoleni*	[2001] ECR I-2189	**3** 62, 63, 66, 73; **6** 18
C-190/98	*Graf*	[2000] ECR I-493	**3** 18, 33, 36, 38
C-198/98	*Everson*	[1999] ECR I-8903	**25** 14
C-207/98	*Mahlburg*	[2000] ECR I-549	**9** 46, 47, 59; **20** 35
C-218/98	*Abdoulaye*	[1999] ECR I-5723	**9** 7, 23, 34; **20** 9
C-226/98	*Jørgensen*	[2000] ECR I-2447	**9** 43, 52
C-234/98	*Allen*	[1999] ECR I-8643	**24** 22, 27, 31, 33, 43
C-236/98	*JämO*	[2000] ECR I-2189	**9** 7, 14, 34, 36
C-281/98	*Angonese*	[2000] ECR I-4139	**3** 29, 47, 52, 53; **8** 5
C-285/98	*Kreil*	[2000] ECR I-69	**9** 38, 56, 62
C-302/98	*Sehrer*	[2000] ECR I-4585	**3** 15, 26, 33
C-303/98	*Simap*	[2000] ECR I-7963	**13** 7; **14** 1, 11, 15, 16, 17
C-322/98	*Kachelmann*	[2000] ECR I-7505	**9** 51
C-343/98	*Collino*	[2000] ECR I-6659	**24** 13, 15, 16, 17, 43, 58, 62
C-367/98	*Commission v. Portugal*	[2002] ECR I-4731	**3** 101
C-376/98	*Kommission v. Deutschland*	[2000] ECR I-8419	**4** 8
C-381/98	*Ingmar* v. *Leonard*	[2000] ECR I-9305	**1** 50; **5** 10, 23
C-407/98	*Abrahamsson und Anderson*	[2000] ECR I-5539	**8** 54; **9** 24
C-430/98	*Commission v. Luxemburg*	[1999] ECR I-7395	**28** 86
C-443/98	*Unilever*	[2000] ECR I-7535	**1** 72
C-45/99	*Commission v. France*	[2000] ECR I-3615	**22** 35
C-46/99	*Commission v. France*	[2000] ECR I-4379	**14** 60
C-47/99	*Commission v. Luxembourg*	[1999] ECR I-8999	**22** 35
C-50/99	*Podesta*	[2000] ECR I-4039	**9** 8
C-58/99	*Commission v. Italy*	[2000] ECR I-3811	**3** 101
C-62/99	*bofrost*	[2001] ECR I-2595	**28** 50, 51, 53; **29** 38

1

Case Number	Short Title/Parties	Reference	§ para.*
C-79/99	*Schnorbus*	[2000] ECR I-10997	**9** 30, 61
C-144/99	*Commission v. Kingdom of the Netherlands*	[2001] ECR I-3541	**1** 74
C-164/99	*Portugaia Construções*	[2002] ECR I-787	**3** 62, 63, 66, 67; **6** 33
C-166/99	*Defreyn*	[2000] ECR I-6155	**9** 9
C-172/99	*Oy Liikenne Ab*	[2001] ECR I-745	**24** 17, 31, 44
C-173/99	*BECTU*	[2001] ECR I-4881	**2** 18; **14** 1, 46, 48, 54
C-175/99	*Mayeur*	[2000] ECR I-7755	**24** 16, 17, 113
C-184/99	*Grzelczyk*	[2001] ECR I-6193	**3** 105
C-241/99	*CIG*	[2001] ECR I-5139	**13** 7; **14** 16
C-283/99	*Commission v. Italy*	[2001] ECR I-4363	**3** 40
C-309/99	*Wouters*	[2002] ECR I-1577	**3** 60, 81
C-340/99	*Universaldienst*	[2001] ECR I-4109	**2** 18
C-350/99	*Lange*	[2001] ECR I-1061	**12** 15, 16, 36
C-353/99 P	*Hautala*	[2001] ECR 9565	**2** 18
C-366/99	*Griesmar*	[2001] ECR I-9383	**8** 53; **9** 5, 8, 23, 24, 62; **20** 4, 9
C-379/99	*Pensionskasse für die Angestellten der Barmer Ersatzkasse*	[2001] ECR I-7275	**9** 3, 8
C-381/99	*Brunnhofer*	[2002] ECR I-4961	**8** 15; **9** 3, 7, 13, 14, 15, 20, 21, 22, 43
C-438/99	*Jiménez Melgar*	[2001] ECR I-6915	**9** 35, 46; **20** 3, 32, 34
C-441/99	*Gharehveran*	[2001] ECR I-7687	**25** 7, 23, 32
C-476/99	*Lommers*	[2002] ECR I-2891	**8** 53, 54; **9** 7, 30, 36
C-481/99	*Heininger*	[2001] ECR I-9945	**1** 74
C-483/99	*Commission v. France*	[2002] ECR I-4781	**3** 101
C-493/99	*Commission v. Germany*	[2001] ECR I-8163	**3** 57, 66, 73
C-503/99	*Commission v. Belgium*	[2002] ECR I-4809	**3** 100, 101
C-5/00	*Commission v. Germany*	[2002] ECR I-1305	**13** 25, 26, 43
C-37/00	*Weber*	[2002] ECR I-2013	**7** 3, 12
C-49/00	*Commission v. Italy*	[2001] ECR I-8575	**13** 16, 21, 30, 31, 44
C-50/00 P	*Unión de Pequenos Agricultores*	[2002] ECR I-6677	**2** 31
C-51/00	*Temco Service Industries*	[2002] ECR I-969	**24** 1, 22, 27, 28, 29, 44, 57, 71, 80
C-60/00	*Carpenter*	[2002] ECR I-6279	**2** 28
C-109/00	*Tele Danmark*	[2001] ECR I-6993	**9** 38, 46, 59; **20** 13, 32
C-112/00	*Schmidberger*	[2003] ECR I-5659	**2** 15, 63; **3** 46, 70
C-133/00	*Doyle*	[2001] ECR I-7031	**14** 13

Case Number	Short Title/Parties	Reference	§ para.*
C-164/00	*Beckmann*	[2002] ECR I-4893	**24** 13, 78
C-187/00	*Kutz-Bauer*	[2003] ECR I-2741	**9** 36, 50, 52
C-208/00	*Überseering*	[2002] ECR I-9919	**3** 87, 88, 89, 90
C-320/00	*Lawrence*	[2002] ECR I-7325	**9** 12
C-351/00	*Niemi*	[2002] ECR I-7007	**9** 8
C-437/00	*Pugliese*	[2003] ECR I-3573	**5** 16; **7** 12
C-440/00	*Kühne & Nagel*	[2004] ECR I-787	**28** 46, 52, 56, 87
C-442/00	*Caballero*	[2002] ECR I-11915	**25** 8, 11
C-463/00	*Commission* v. *Spain*	[2003] ECR I-4581	**3** 101, 103
C-473/00	*Cofidis*	[2002] ECR I-10875	**1** 66
C-4/01	*Martin*	[2003] ECR I-12859	**24** 58, 62, 63, 78
C-50/01 and C-84/01	*Barsotti*	[2004] ECR I-2005	**25** 21
C-63/01	*Evans*	[2003] ECR I-1447	**1** 75
C-98/01	*Commission* v. *United Kingdom*	[2003] ECR I-4641	**3** 101
C-125/01	*Pflücke*	[2003] ECR I-9375	**25** 26
C-145/01	*Commission* v. *Italy*	[2003] ECR I-5581	**24** 107
C-160/01	*Mau*	[2003] ECR I-4791	**25** 9, 11
C-167/01	*Inspire Art*	[2003] ECR I-10155	**3** 84, 88, 90
C-186/01	*Dory*	[2003] ECR I-2479	**9** 38
C-201/01	*Walcher*	[2003] ECR I-8827	**25** 16, 23, 24
C-215/01	*Schnitzer*	[2003] ECR I-14847	**3** 58
C-224/01	*Köbler*	[2003] ECR I-10239	**1** 75, 76, 77; **3** 37, 44, 49
C-256/01	*Allonby*	[2004] ECR I-873	**8** 4; **9** 2, 5, 12, 17, 25
C-317/01 and C-369/01	*Abatay*	[2003] ECR I-12301	**3** 59
C-320/01	*Wiebke Busch*	[2003] ECR I-2041	**9** 36, 46, 59, 63; **20** 30
C-340/01	*Abler*	[2003] ECR I-14023	**24** 22, 27, 28, 38, 43, 44, 45
C-342/01	*Merino Gómez*	[2004] ECR I-2605	**8** 65; **9** 36, 48; **14** 46, 49, 54; **20** 28
C-349/01	*ADS*	[2004] ECR I-6819	**28** 50, 54
C-397/01 to C-403/01	*Pfeiffer*	[2004] ECR I-8835	**1** 72, 73; **2** 69; **13** 7, 8; **14** 11, 30
C-405/01	*Colegio de Oficiales de la Marina Mercante Española*	[2003] ECR I-10391	**3** 24

Case Number	Short Title/Parties	Reference	§ para.*
C-413/01	*Ninni-Orasche*	[2003] ECR I-13187	**3** 9, 10
C-425/01	*Commission* v. *Portugal*	[2003] ECR I-6025	**13** 34, 44
C-441/01	*Commission* v. *The Netherlands*	[2003] ECR I-5463	**13** 30, 32, 44
C-465/01	*Commission* v. *Austria*	[2004] ECR I-8291	**3** 32
C-482/01 and C-493/01	*Orfanopoulos und Oliveri*	[2004] ECR I-5257	**3** 48
C-19/02	*Hlozek*	[2004] ECR I-11491	**9** 3, 9, 15
C-25/02	*Rinke*	[2003] ECR I-8349	**8** 4; **9** 2, 3, 53
C-32/02	*Commission* v. *Italy*	[2003] ECR I-12063	**23** 9; **24** 15, 107
C-47/02	*Anker u.a.*	[2003] ECR I-10447	**3** 24
C-55/02	*Commission* v. *Portugal*	[2004] ECR I-9387	**23** 10, 13
C-77/02	*Steinicke*	[2003] ECR I-9027	**9** 10, 36, 52
C-138/02	*Collins*	[2004] ECR I-2703	**3** 1, 9, 17, 19, 108
C-145/02	*Denkavit*	[2005] ECR I-51	**3** 3
C-147/02	*Alabaster*	[2004] ECR I-3101	**9** 7, 15, 16, 34; **20** 9
C-151/02	*Jaeger*	[2003] ECR I-8389	**2** 69; **14** 1, 15, 16, 17, 20, 29, 30
C-184/02	*Spain and Finland* v. *Parliament and Council*	[2004] ECR I-7789	**2** 37
C-196/02	*Vasiliki Nikoloudi*	[2005] ECR I-1789	**8** 36, 57; **9** 12, 13, 18, 42, 45, 50, 52, 53
C-237/02	*Freiburger Kommunalbauten*	[2004] ECR I-3403	**11** 22
C-263/02	*Jégo Quéré*	[2004] ECR I-3425	**2** 31
C-284/02	*Sass*	[2004] ECR I-11143	**9** 3, 10, 30, 46, 48, 62, 63; **20** 30, 35
C-285/02	*Elsner-Lakeberg*	[2004] ECR I-5861	**9** 14, 17
C-309/02	*Radlberger Getränkegesellschaft and Spitz*	[2004] ECR I-11763	**3** 3
C-313/02	*Wippel* v. *Peek & Cloppenburg*	[2004] ECR I-9483	**9** 50; **14** 1, 2; **16** 5, 9, 10, 18
C-335/02	*Commission* v. *Luxembourg*	[2003] ECR I-5531	**13** 44
C-341/02	*Commission* v. *Germany*	[2005] ECR I-2733	**6** 17
C-384/02	*Grøngaard*	[2005] ECR I-9939	**26** 35; **29** 57
C-387/02, C-391/02 and C-403/02	*Berlusconi*	[2005] ECR I-3565	**1** 74
C-425/02	*Delahaye*	[2004] ECR I-10823	**24** 16, 86, 109, 113, 115

Case Number	Short Title/Parties	Reference	§ para.*
C-435/02 and C-103/03	Springer	[2004] ECR I-8663	2 36
C-456/02	Trojani	[2004] ECR I-7573	3 6, 9, 10, 11
C-60/03	Wolff & Müller	[2004] ECR I-9553	3 56, 62, 66, 67, 68, 73; 6 7, 17, 32, 33
C-112/03	Société financière et industrielle du Peloux	[2005] ECR I-3707	7 18
C-173/03	Traghetti	[2006] ECR I-5177	1 75, 77
C-188/03	Junk	[2005] ECR I-885	1 57; 23 10, 18, 19, 21, 32, 36, 38, 40, 44; 26 34
C-191/03	McKenna	[2005] ECR I-7631	9 7, 16, 46, 47; 20 9, 32
C-203/03	Commission v. Austria	[2005] ECR I-935	9 35; 20 4
C-278/03	Commission v. Italy	[2005] ECR I-3747	3 35
C-297/03	Sozialhilfeverband Rohrbach	[2005] ECR I-4305	1 72; 24 108
C-319/03	Briheche	[2004] ECR I-8807	8 53, 54; 9 30
C-333/03	Commission v. Luxembourg	[2004] ECR I-6033	24 107
C-356/03	Mayer	[2005] ECR I-295	20 28, 35
C-411/03	Sevic	[2005] ECR I-10805	3 79, 83, 84; 30 2
C-445/03	Commission v. Luxembourg	[2004] ECR I-10191	3 62
C-470/03	A.G.M.-COS.MET	[2007] ECR I-2749	1 75; 3 2
C-478/03	Celtec	[2005] ECR I-4389	24 57, 61
C-519/03	Commission v. Luxembourg	[2005] ECR I-3067	14 49; 21 11, 17
C-520/03	Valero	[2004] ECR I-12065	25 8
C-540/03	Parliament v. Council	[2006] ECR I-5769	2 14, 18
C-555/03	Warbecq	[2004] ECR I-6041	7 12
C-14/04	Dellas	[2005] ECR I-10253	4 1, 10; 14 1, 2, 18
C-52/04	Personalrat der Feuerwehr Hamburg	[2005] ECR I-7111	13 7; 14 11
C-53/04	Marrosu	[2006] ECR I-7213	17 4, 30, 31, 33
C-109/04	Kranemann	[2005] ECR I-2421	3 9, 10, 12, 35, 39, 44
C-131/04 and C-257/04	Robinson-Steele	[2006] ECR I-2531	14 46, 52, 53, 54, 61
C-132/04	Commission v. Spain	[2006] ECR I-3	13 44
C-144/04	Mangold	[2005] ECR I-9981	1 57, 68, 70, 72; 2 14; 8 10, 11; 11 3, 31, 36, 38; 17 3, 30, 42

Case Number	Short Title/Parties	Reference	§ para.*
C-168/04	*Commission v. Austria*	[2006] ECR I-9041	**3** 62, 65, 66, 73
C-174/04	*Commission v. Italy*	[2005] ECR I-4933	**3** 101
C-180/04	*Vasallo*	[2006] ECR I-7251	**17** 4, 30, 33
C-185/04	*Öberg*	[2006] ECR I-1453	**3** 21, 36, 44; **21** 6
C-196/04	*Cadbury Schweppes*	[2006] ECR I-8031	**3** 79, 83
C-207/04	*Vergani*	[2005] ECR I-7453	**8** 65; **9** 6, 9, 29, 37
C-212/04	*Adeneler*	[2006] ECR I-6057	**1** 70, 73, 74; **17** 4, 30, 31, 32
C-232/04 and C-233/04	*Güney-Görres and Demir*	[2005] ECR I-11237	**24** 27, 39, 45
C-244/04	*Commission v. Germany*	[2006] ECR I-885	**3** 62, 66, 73; **6** 17
C-282/04 and C-283/04	*Commission v. the Netherlands*	[2006] ECR I-9141	**3** 97, 98, 99, 101, 102, 103
C-294/04	*Herrero*	[2006] ECR I-1513	**9** 30, 46, 48, 63; **20** 9, 30, 35
C-428/04	*Commission v. Austria*	[2008] ECR I-3325	**13** 11, 27, 30, 32, 44
C-452/04	*Fidium Finanz*	[2006] ECR I-9521	**3** 57, 62
C-484/04	*Commission v. United Kingdom and Northern Ireland*	[2006] ECR I-7471	**1** 65; **2** 69; **14** 20, 60
C-490/04	*Commission v. Germany*	[2007] ECR I-6095	**3** 62, 65, 66, 72, 73; **6** 29
C-499/04	*Werhof*	[2006] ECR I-2397	**2** 10, 14; **24** 58
C-13/05	*Chacón Navas*	[2006] ECR I-6467	**2** 69; **8** 8, 10; **11** 3, 6, 12, 21, 22, 23, 28
C-17/05	*Cadman*	[2006] ECR I-9583	**8** 4; **9** 2, 18; **11** 34
C-81/05	*Alonso*	[2006] ECR I-7569	**25** 8, 11
C-112/05	*Commission v. Germany*	[2007] ECR I-8995	**3** 97, 100, 104
C-124/05	*Federatie Nederlandse Vakbeweging*	[2006] ECR I-3423	**14** 1, 46, 49, 51, 54; **21** 17
C-127/05	*Commission v. United Kingdom*	[2007] ECR I-4619	**13** 15, 44
C-177/05	*Guerrero Pecino*	[2005] ECR I-10887	**25** 8, 11
C-187/05 to C-190/05	*Agorastoudis*	[2006] ECR I-7775	**23** 2, 4, 10, 13, 15
C-208/05	*ITC*	[2007] ECR I-181	**3** 13, 14, 18, 36, 49, 108
C-270/05	*Athinaïki Chartopoiïa*	[2007] ECR I-1499	**23** 7, 15
C-278/05	*Robins*	[2007] ECR I-1053	**1** 75; **25** 30
C-307/05	*Del Cerro Alonso*	[2007] ECR I-7109	**4** 8, 10, 11; **17** 4, 9, 16

Case Number	Short Title/Parties	Reference	§ para.*
C-341/05	*Laval un Partneri*	[2007] ECR I-11767	**1** 31; **2** 14, 50, 69; **3** 56, 58, 60, 68, 69, 105; **4** 9; **6** 6, 19, 25, 27
C-385/05	*Confédération générale du travail (CGT)*	[2006] ECR I-611	**23** 9; **27** 8
C-392/05	*Alevizos*	[2007] ECR I-3505	**3** 9, 10, 23
C-411/05	*Palacios de la Villa*	[2007] ECR I-8531	**8** 10; **11** 3, 11, 31, 35, 38, 40
C-437/05	*Vorel*	[2007] ECR I-331	**14** 16, 17
C-438/05	*Viking*	[2007] ECR I-10779	**1** 31; **2** 14, 50, 69; **3** 80, 81, 85, 92, 94, 95; **4** 9
C-456/05	*Commission v. Germany*	[2007] ECR I-10517	**11** 34
C-458/05	*Jouini*	[2007] ECR I-7301	**19** 5; **24** 14, 32, 43
C-116/06	*Kiiski*	[2007] ECR I-7643	**9** 36, 46; **13** 9; **20** 4, 11, 12, 25, 27; **21** 16, 17
C-210/06	*Cartesio*	[2008] ECR I-9641	**3** 80, 88, 89
C-226/06	*Commission v. France*	[2008] ECR I-86	**13** 44
C-246/06	*Velasco Navarro*	[2008] ECR I-105	**25** 11
C-267/06	*Maruko*	[2008] ECR I-1757	**11** 6, 43
C-268/06	*Impact*	[2008] ECR I-2483	**1** 65, 71, 73, 74; **4** 12; **15** 16; **16** 14; **17** 9, 19, 45
C-300/06	*Voß*	[2007] ECR I-10573	**9** 17
C-303/06	*Coleman*	[2008] ECR I-5603	**8** 32; **11** 24, 25, 27
C-317/06	*Commission v. Spain*	[2007] ECR I-95	**27** 35
C-319/06	*Commission v. Luxembourg*	[2008] ECR I- 4323	**6** 16, 17, 27, 30; **12** 27
C-320/06	*Commission v. Belgium*	[2007] ECR I-48	**27** 35
C-321/06	*Commission v. Luxembourg*	[2007] ECR I-85	**27** 35
C-327/06	*Commission v. Italy*	[2007] ECR I-22	**27** 35
C-346/06	*Rüffert*	[2008] ECR I-1989	**6** 12, 14, 19, 25
C-350/06 and C-520/06	*Schultz-Hoff*	[2009] ECR I-179	**14** 46, 50, 51, 52, 54, 55, 59
C-381/06	*Commission v. Greece*	[2007] ECR I-112	**27** 35
C-427/06	*Bartsch*	[2008] ECR I-7245	**11** 3, 30
C-460/06	*Paquay*	[2007] ECR I-8511	**8** 66, 67, 68; **9** 46; **20** 32, 34
C-462/06	*Laboratoires Glaxosmithkline*	[2008] ECR I-3965	**7** 8
C-498/06	*Robledillo Núñez*	[2008] ECR I-921	**25** 11, 24

Case Number	Short Title/Parties	Reference	§ para.*
C-506/06	*Mayr*	[2008] ECR I-1017	**9** 46; **20** 11, 32, 33
C-6/07	*Commission* v. *Spain*	[2007] ECR I-174	**25** 32
C-9/07	*Commission* v. *France*	[2007] ECR I-121	**25** 32
C-54/07	*Feryn*	[2008] ECR I-5187	**8** 33, 58, 70; **10** 8
C-55/07 and C-56/07	*Michaeler*	[2008] ECR I-3135	**16** 3, 38
C-94/07	*Raccanelli*	[2008] ECR I-5939	**3** 9, 29, 30, 51, 105
C-306/07	*Andersen*	[2008] ECR I-10279	**4** 24; **12** 37
C-310/07	*Holmqvist*	[2008] ECR I-7871	**25** 14
C-313/07	*Kirtruna*	[2008] ECR I-7907	**24** 60, 81
C-364/07	*Vassilakis*	[2008] ECR I-90	**17** 33
C-378/07 to C-380/07	*Angelidaki*	[2009] ECR I-3071	**2** 69; **8** 89; **17** 30, 31, 33, 42, 45
C-388/07	*Age Concern England*	[2009] ECR I-1569	**8** 36; **11** 11, 31, 34, 35, 38, 40
C-396/07	*Juuri*	[2008] ECR I-8883	**24** 63, 87
C-466/07	*Klarenberg*	[2009] ECR I-803	**24** 40
C-537/07	*Gómez-Limón*	[2009] ECR I-6525	**21** 20, 23, 24
C-555/07	*Kücükdeveci*	[2010] ECR I-365	**2** 14, 28, 41; **8** 11; **11** 3, 50
C-561/07	*Commission* v. *Italy*	[2009] ECR I-4959	**24** 49, 52, 77, 78, 81
C-12/08	*Mono Car Styling*	[2009] ECR I-6653	**1** 73, 74; **23** 1, 2, 41
C-44/08	*AEK* v. *Fujitsu Siemens*	[2009] ECR I-8163	**23** 20, 26, 29, 30
C-63/08	*Pontin*	[2009] ECR I-10467	**1** 66; **9** 46; **20** 32
C-69/08	*Raffaelo Visciano*	[2009] ECR I-6741	**1** 66; **25** 11, 26
C-88/08	*Hütter*	[2009] ECR I-5325	**11** 6, 34, 38
C-116/08	*Meerts*	[2009] ECR I-10063	**21** 17, 20
C-147/08	*Römer*	not yet published in ECR	**11** 3, 6, 43
C-194/08	*Gassmayr*	[2010] ECR I-6281	**9** 16; **14** 53; **20** 19, 20, 28, 29
C 229/08	*Wolf*	[2010] ECR I-1	**11** 6, 29, 44
C-271/08	*Commission* v. *Germany*	[2010] ECR I-7091	**2** 14, 50, 63, 69; **3** 46
C-277/08	*Pereda*	[2009] ECR I-8405	**14** 46, 50, 51
C-323/08	*Rodríguez Mayor*	[2009] ECR I-11621	**23** 12
C-325/08	*Olympique Lyonnais*	[2010] ECR I-2177	**3** 29, 45
C-341/08	*Petersen*	[2010] ECR I-47	**11** 6, 9, 29, 34, 38, 40
C-395/08 and C-396/08	*Bruno and Pettini*	[2010] ECR I-5119	**16** 12, 13, 14, 16, 17, 18, 39
C-405/08	*Holst*	[2010] ECR I-985	**4** 24; **27** 28, 38

Case Number	Short Title/Parties	Reference	§ para.*
C-471/08	*Parviainen*	[2010] ECR I-6533	**14** 53; **20** 19, 20
C-486/08	*Zentralbetriebsrat der Landeskrankenhäuser Tirols*	[2010] ECR I-3527	**14** 46, 54; **16** 21, 27, 28; **17** 6, 16; **21** 20
C-499/08	*Ingeniøreningen i Danmark*	[2010] ECR I-9343	**11** 6, 29, 38
C-45/09	*Rosenbladt*	[2010] ECR I-9391	**11** 37, 38, 40
C-98/09	*Sorge*	[2010] ECR I-5837	**17** 42, 43, 45
C-104/09	*Roca Álvarez*	[2010] ECR I-8661	**9** 62; **21** 16
C-109/09	*Deutsche Lufthansa*	not yet published in ECR	**1** 73; **11** 31; **17** 31, 32, 45
C-151/09	*UGT-FSP*	[2010] ECR I-7591	**24** 31, 98
C-158/09	*Commission v. Spain*	[2010] ECR I-68	**14** 60
C-227/09	*Accardo*	[2010] ECR I-273	**1** 72, 73; **14** 25
C-232/09	*Danosa*	not yet published in ECR	**9** 46; **20** 11, 12, 35
C-242/09	*Albron Catering*	[2010] ECR I-309	**24** 21
C-243/09	*Fuß I*	[2010] ECR I-9849	**1** 71; **2** 25; **14** 27, 57
C-246/09	*Bulicke*	[2010] ECR I-7003	**1** 65; **8** 77, 89
C-250/09	*Georgiev*	not yet published in ECR	**1** 71; **11** 6, 29, 34, 38, 39
C-283/09	*Weryński*	not yet published in ECR	**7** 5
C-307/09	*Vicoplus*	not yet published in ECR	**3** 56; **6** 2, 12
C-356/09	*Kleist*	not yet published in ECR	**9** 37, 42, 45, 56
C-386/09	*Briot*	not yet published in ECR	**24** 80
C-391/09	*Runevič-Vardyn and Wardyn*	not yet published in ECR	**3** 108
C-398/09	*RANI Slovakia*	[2010] ECR I-81	**6** 11
C-428/09	*Union syndicale Solidaires Isère*	[2010] ECR I-9961	**13** 7, 9; **14** 11, 12, 20, 22
C-429/09	*Fuß II*	not yet published in ECR	**1** 76; **14** 27
C-444/09 and C-456/09	*Gavieiro Gavieiro and Iglesias Torres*	not yet published in ECR	**2** 25; **17** 4, 8, 9, 16, 45
C-447/09	*Prigge*	not yet published in ECR	**2** 14, 41, 50; **11** 6, 9, 34, 44
C-463/09	*CLECE*	not yet published in ECR	**24** 37, 41

Case Number	Short Title/Parties	Reference	§ para.*
C-477/09	*Charles Defossez*	not yet published in ECR	25 14
C-519/09	*May*	not yet published in ECR	13 9; 14 12
C-29/10	*Koelzsch*	not yet published in ECR	5 8, 15
C-30/10	*Lotta Andersson*	not yet published in ECR	25 7
C-104/10	*Kelly*	not yet published in ECR	8 61; 9 55
C-108/10	*Scattolon*	not yet published in ECR	24 15, 16, 17, 22, 23, 43, 58, 63
C-149/10	*Chatzi*	[2010] ECR I-8489	21 9, 17
C-151/10	*Dai Cugini v Rijksdienst voor Sociale Zekerheid*	not yet published in ECR	16 12, 39
C-155/10	*Williams*	not yet published in ECR	14 53
C-159/10 and C-160/10	*Fuchs and Köhler*	not yet published in ECR	11 34, 38
C-177/10	*Rosado Santana*	not yet published in ECR	1 66; 17 4, 5, 8, 16, 19
C-214/10	*KHS v. Schulte*	not yet published in ECR	14 46, 51
C-235/10 to C-239/10	*Claes*	not yet published in ECR	23 13
C-258/10	*Grigore*	not yet published in ECR	14 16
C-282/10	*Dominguez*	not yet published in ECR	14 48
C-297/10 and C-298/10	*Hennigs*	not yet published in ECR	11 34, 35, 40
C-310/10	*Agafiţei*	not yet published in ECR	10 4; 11 12
C-313/10	*Jansen*	not yet published in ECR	17 31
C-384/10	*Voogsgeerd*	[2010] ECR I-8471	5 13, 14, 15, 18
C-393/10	*O'Brien*	not yet published in ECR	16 5, 21
C-415/10	*Meister*	not yet published in ECR	8 61, 62
C-435/10	*van Ardennen*	not yet published in ECR	25 26
C-571/10	*Kamberaj*	not yet published in ECR	10 5

Case Number	Short Title/Parties	Reference	§ para.*
C-586/10	*Kücük*	not yet published in ECR	17 30
C-157/11	*Sibilio*	not yet published in ECR	17 4, 6
C-251/11	*Huet*	not yet published in ECR	17 31
C-349/11	*Yangwei*	not yet published in ECR	16 38
C-556/11	*Lorenzo Marténez*	not yet published in ECR	17 9

§1. EUROPEAN EMPLOYMENT LAW: INTRODUCTION, SUBJECT MATTER, SOURCES OF LAW, OVERVIEW

CONTENTS

Bibliography:

J. Basedow, *Von der deutschen zur europäischen Wirtschaftsverfassung* (Tübingen: Mohr Siebeck, 1992); F. Bayreuther, 'Das Grünbuch der europäischen Kommission zum Arbeitsrecht', *NZA* 2007, 371–375; B. Bercusson, 'Maastricht: a Fundamental Change in European Labour Law', *IRJ* 23 (1992), 177–190; B. Bercusson, 'The Dynamic of European Labour Law after Maastricht', *ILJ* 23 (1994), 1–31; R. Birk, 'Der Einfluß des Gemeinschaftsrechts auf das Arbeitsrecht der Bundesrepublik Deutschland', *RIW* 1989, 6–15; R. Birk/E.-G. Erdmann/H. Lampert/G. Muhr, *Europäischer Binnenmarkt und Harmonisierung des Arbeitsrechts* (Mannheim/Vienna/Zurich: Wissenschaftsverlag, 1991); R. Birk, 'Europäisches kollektives Arbeitsrecht – insbesondere der Europäische Betriebsrat', in S. Grundmann (ed.), *Systembildung und Systemlücken in Kerngebieten des Europäischen Privatrechts – Gesellschafts-, Arbeits- und Schuldvertragsrecht* (Tübingen: Mohr Siebeck, 2000), 387–399; T. Blanke, 'Dynamik und Konturen des europäischen Sozialmodells: Warum der Zug nach Europa nicht zu stoppen ist', *NZA* 2006, 1304–1309; W. Blomeyer, 'Der Einfluss der Rechtsprechung des EuGH auf das deutsche Arbeitsrecht', *NZA* 1994, 633–640; S. Borelli, 'Der Arbeitnehmerbegriff im europäischen Recht', *AuR* 2011, 472–476; G. Cavalier/R. Upex, 'The Concept of Employment Contract in European Union Private Law', *ICLQ* 55 (2006), 587–608; H. Collins, 'Justifying European Employment Law', in S. Grundmann/S. Weatherill/W. Kerber (eds.), *Party Autonomy and the Role of Information in the Internal Market* (Berlin/New York: de Gruyter, 2001), 205–224; W. Däubler, 'Auf dem Weg zu einem Europäischen Arbeitsrecht?', in L. Krämer/ H.-W. Micklitz/K. Tonner (eds.), *Recht und diffuse Interessen in der Europäischen Rechtsordnung – Liber amicorum Norbert Reich* (Baden-Baden: Nomos, 1997), 441–458; O. Deinert, *Der europäische Kollektivvertrag – Rechtstatsächliche und rechtsdogmatische Grundlagen einer gemeineuropäischen Kollektivvertragsautonomie* (Baden-Baden: Nomos, 1999); M. Franzen, 'Das Grünbuch der Europäischen Kommission zum Arbeitsrecht', *RIW* 2007, 892–897; M. Franzen, *Privatrechtsangleichung durch die*

Europäische Gemeinschaft (Berlin/New York: de Gruyter, 1999); M. Freedland, 'From the Contract of Employment to the Personal Work Nexus', *ILJ* 35 (2006), 1–29; M. Freedland/N. Kountouris, 'Towards a Comparative Theory of the Contractual Construction of Personal Work Relations in Europe', *ILJ* 37 (2008), 49–74; R. Giesen/L. Eriksen, 'Kündigungsschutz und Arbeitslosenversicherung in Dänemark', *EuZA* 2009, 1–35; S. Grundmann (ed.), *Systembildung und Systemlücken in Kerngebieten des Europäischen Privatrechts – Gesellschafts-, Arbeits- und Schuldvertragsrecht* (Tübingen: Mohr Siebeck, 2000); S. Grundmann, 'Europa- und wirtschaftsrechtliche Grundlagen der Privatrechtsgesellschaft', in K. Riesenhuber (ed.), *Privatrechtsgesellschaft* (Tübingen: Mohr Siebeck, 2007), §5; S. Grundmann, *Europäisches Schuldvertragsrecht – Das europäische Recht der Unternehmensgeschäfte* (nebst Texten und Materialien zur Rechtsangleichung) (Berlin/New York: de Gruyter, 1999) (especially Part 1 and Part 2 §6); S. Grundmann, 'Zum Harmonisierungskonzept im Europäischen Arbeitsrecht', in R. Krause/W. Veelken/K. Vieweg (eds.), *Recht der Wirtschaft und der Arbeit in Europa – Gedächtnisschrift für Wolfgang Blomeyer* (Berlin: Duncker & Humblot, 2004), 71–97; M. Heinze, 'Die Gemeinschaftscharta der sozialen Grundrechte der Arbeitnehmer und die Vertragsrevision des Unionsvertrages 1996', in R. Anzinger/R. Wank (eds.), *Entwicklung im Arbeitsrecht und Arbeitsschutzrecht – Festschrift für Otfried Wlotzke zum siebzigsten Geburtstag* (Munich: C.H. Beck, 1996), 669–682; M. Heinze, 'Europäische Einflüsse auf das nationale Arbeitsrecht', *RdA* 1994, 1–11; M. Heinze, 'Europarecht im Spannungsverhältnis zum nationalen Arbeitsrecht – Von formaler Verdichtung zur offenen Arbeitsrechtsordnung', *ZfA* 1992, 331–359; M. Heinze, 'Zum Einfluß des europäischen Rechts auf das deutsche Arbeits- und Sozialrecht', in O. Due/M. Lutter/J. Schwarze (eds.), *Festschrift für Ulrich Everling* (Baden-Baden: Nomos, 1995), 433–445; B. Hepple, 'The Crisis of EEC Labour Law', *ILJ* 16 (1987), 77–87; B. Hepple/A. Byre, 'EEC Labour Law in the United Kingdom – A New Approach', *ILJ* 18 (1989), 129–143; G. v. Hoyningen-Huene, 'Der Arbeitgeber zwischen Unternehmerfreiheit, Flexibilität und Arbeitnehmerschutz', in H. Konzen et al. (eds.), *Festschrift für Rolf Birk zum siebzigsten Geburtstag* (Tübingen: Mohr Siebeck, 2008), 217–241; B. Jansen, 'Das Arbeits- und Sozialrecht im Zweck- und Kompetenzgefüge der Europäischen Gemeinschaften', *EuR* 1990 Special Issue 2, 5–15; C. Joerges/F. Rödl, 'Informal Politics, Formalised Law and the 'Social Deficit' of European Integration: Reflections after the Judgments of the ECJ in *Viking* and *Laval*', *ELJ* 15 (2009), 1–19; J. Joussen, 'Das Europäische Grünbuch zum Arbeitsrecht vom 22.11.2006 – Eine kritische Würdigung', *ZEuP* 2008, 374–393; A. Junker, 'Arbeitsrecht zwischen Europäisierung und Amerikanisierung', in R. Krause/R. Schwarze (eds.), *Festschrift für Hansjörg Otto* (Berlin: de Gruyter, 2008), 157–171; A. Junker, 'Arbeits- und Sozialrecht in der Europäischen Union', *JZ* 1994, 277–286; A. Junker, 'Der EuGH im Arbeitsrecht – Die schwarze Serie geht weiter', *NJW* 1994, 2527–2528; A. Junker, 'Europäisches individuelles Arbeitsrecht', in S. Grundmann (ed.), *Systembildung und Systemlücken in Kerngebieten des Europäischen Privatrechts – Gesellschafts-, Arbeits- und Schuldvertragsrecht* (Tübingen: Mohr Siebeck, 2000), 357–386; A. Junker, 'Grünbuch Arbeitsrecht – Entwicklungslinien und Perspektiven', in V. Rieble/A. Junker (eds.), *Das Grünbuch und seine Folgen – Wohin treibt das europäische Arbeitsrecht?* (Munich: ZAAR, 2008), 13–26; A. Junker, 'Systembildung und Systemlücken im harmonisierten Arbeitsvertragsrecht', *NZA* 1999, 2–11; D. Kaiser, 'Entzweiung von europäischem und deutschem Arbeitsrecht – Abschied vom Systemdenken?', *NZA* 2000, 1144–1152; R. Käppler, 'Zu den Kompetenzen des Europäischen Gerichtshofs bei der

Rechtsangleichung auf dem Gebiet des Arbeitsrechts', in H.-W. Rengeling (ed.), *Europäisierung des Rechts* (Cologne et al.: Heymanns, 1996), 129–149; J. Kenner, *EU Employment Law – From Rome to Amsterdam and Beyon* (Oxford/Portland, Oregon: Hart, 2003); S. Krebber, 'Der einzelstaatliche Charakter der mitgliedstaatlichen Arbeitsrechte', in V. Rieble/A. Junker (eds.), *Das Grünbuch und seine Folgen – Wohin treibt das europäische Arbeitsrecht?* (Munich: ZAAR, 2008), 33–60; S. Krebber, 'Status and Potential of the Regulation of Labor and Employment Law at the European Level', *Comp. Lab. L. & Pol'y J.* 30 (2009), 875–903; D. Neumann, 'Arbeitsrecht', in K. Langenbucher (ed.), *Europarechtliche Bezüge des Privatrechts*, 2nd edn. (Baden-Baden: Nomos, 2008), §7; L. Nogler, 'Die typologisch-funktionale Methode am Beispiel des Arbeitnehmerbegriffs', *ZESAR* 2009, 461–469; L. Nogler, 'Why do Labour Lawyers Ignore the Question of Social Justice in European Contract Law?', *ELJ* 14 (2008), 483–499; J. Pačić, 'Die Haftung des Arbeitnehmers im Europäischen Rechtsvergleich – Teil I: Schädigung des Arbeitgebers', *EuZA* 2009, 47–68; 'Teil II: Schädigung eines Dritten', *EuZA* 2009, 218–234; D. Pottschmidt, *Arbeitnehmerähnliche Personen in Europa – Die Behandlung wirtschaftlich abhängiger Erwerbstätiger im Europäischen Arbeitsrecht sowie im (Arbeits-) Recht der EU-Mitgliedstaaten* (Baden-Baden: Nomos, 2006); U. Preis, 'Grünbuch und Flexicurity – Auf dem Weg zu einem modernen Arbeitsrecht?', in H. Konzen et al. (eds.), *Festschrift für Rolf Birk zum siebzigsten Geburtstag* (Tübingen: Mohr Siebeck, 2008), 625–642; R. Rebhahn, 'Die Arbeitnehmerbegriffe des Unionsrechts in der neueren Judikatur des EuGH', *EuZA* 2012, 3–34; R. Rebhahn, 'Überlegungen zu weiteren europäischen Mindeststandards zum Arbeitsrecht', *EuZA* 2011, 295–307; R. Rebhahn, 'Arbeitnehmerähnliche Personen – Rechtsvergleich und Regelungsperspektive', *RdA* 2009, 236; R. Rebhahn, *Aktuelle Entwicklungen des Europäischen Arbeitsrechts* (Bonn: Zentrum für Europäisches Wirtschaftsrecht, 2008); R. Rebhahn, 'Der Vorrang der günstigeren Regelung aus rechtsvergleichender Sicht', *EuZA* 2008, 39–67; R. Rebhahn, 'Europäisches Arbeitsrecht', in K. Riesenhuber (ed.), *Europäische Methodenlehre – Handbuch für Ausbildung und Praxis*, 2nd edn. (Berlin: de Gruyter, 2010), §18; H. Reichold, 'Aktuelle Rechtsprechung des EuGH zum Europäischen Arbeitsrecht', *JZ* 2006, 549–556; V. Rieble, *Arbeitsmarkt und Wettbewerb – Der Schutz von Vertrags- und Wettbewerbsfreiheit im Arbeitsrecht* (Berlin et al.: Springer, 1996); V. Rieble/A. Junker (eds.), *Das Grünbuch und seine Folgen – Wohin treibt das europäische Arbeitsrecht?* (Munich: ZAAR, 2008); K. Riesenhuber, *Europäisches Vertragsrecht*, 2nd edn. (Berlin: de Gruyter, 2006); D. Schiek, 'Autonomous Collective Agreements as a Regulatory Device in European Labour Law: How to read Article 139 EC', *ILJ* 34 (2005), 23–56; Marlene Schmidt, 'Perspektiven und Sinn weiterer Regulierung durch Europarecht', *EuZA* 2008, 196–211; M. Shanks, 'Introductory Article: The Social Policy of the European Communities', *CMLR* 14 (1977), 375–383; M. Stein, 'Referenzrahmen eines "European Labour Contract"', in V. Rieble/A. Junker (eds.), *Das Grünbuch und seine Folgen – Wohin treibt das europäische Arbeitsrecht?* (Munich: ZAAR, 2008), 94–100; H.-D. Steinmeyer, 'Der Vertrag von Amsterdam und seine Bedeutung für das Arbeits- und Sozialrecht', *RdA* 2001, 10–22; M. Stoffels, 'Das EU-Grünbuch für ein modernes Arbeitsrecht', *GPR* 2007, 231–235; J. Thau, 'Aktuelle Determinanten Europäischer Sozialpolitik und rechtliche Rahmenbedingungen des Sozialen Dialoges in Europa', in P. Hanau/J. Thau/H. P. Westermann (eds.), *Gegen den Strich – Festschrift für Klaus Adomeit* (Cologne: Wolters Kluwer, 2008), 747–756; G. Thüsing, 'Europa zwischen Flexibility und Security: Versuch einer Positionsbestimmung in einführenden Thesen', *EuZA* 2008, 159–166; M. Uebe,

'Ziele und Perspektiven des Grünbuchs Arbeitsrecht aus der Sicht der Europäischen Kommission', *EuZA* 2008, 167–171; R. Wank, 'Das Grünbuch Arbeitsrecht – Eine Perspektive für das europäische Arbeitsrecht?', *AuR* 2007, 244–249; R. Wank, 'Der Arbeitnehmerbegriff des BAG im Vergleich zum englischen und zum amerikanischen Recht', in P. Hanau et al. (eds.), *Personalrecht im Wandel – Festschrift für Wolfdieter Küttner zum 70. Geburtstag* (Munich: C.H. Beck, 2006), 5–20; R. Wank, 'Die personellen Grenzen des Europäischen Arbeitsrechts: Arbeitsrecht für Nicht-Arbeitnehmer?', *EuZA* 2008, 172–195; M. Weiss, 'Rechtswissenschaft als Motor der Europäisierung des Arbeitsrechts?', in J. Dammann/W. Grunsky/T. Pfeiffer (eds.), *Gedächtnisschrift für Manfred Wolf* (Munich: C.H. Beck, 2011), 761–773; M. Weiss, 'Zur zukünftigen Rolle der Europäischen Union im Arbeitsrecht', in P. Hanau/E. Lorenz/H.-C. Matthes (eds.), *Festschrift für Günther Wiese zum 70. Geburtstag* (Neuwied/Kriftel: Luchterhand, 1998), 633–648; Lord K. W. Wedderburn, 'European Community Law and Workers' Rights – Fact or Fake in 1992?', *Dublin U.L.J.* 13 (1991), 1–35, also reproduced in: id., Labour Law and Freedom (London: Lawrence Wishart, 1995), 247–285; Lord K. W. Wedderburn, 'Inderogability, Collective Agreements, and Community Law', 21 (1992) ILJ 245–264, also reproduced in: id., Labour Law and Freedom (London: Lawrence Wishart, 1995), 212–236; Lord K. W. Wedderburn, 'The Social Charter in Britain – Labour Law and Labour Courts', MLR 54 (1991), 1–47, also reproduced in id., *Employment Rights in Britain and Europe – Selected Papers in Labour Law* (London: Lawrence & Wishart, 1991), 354–416; C. Windbichler, 'Arbeitsrecht und Wettbewerb in der europäischen Wirtschaftsverfassung', *RdA* 1992, 74–84; C. Windbichler, 'Dependent Independence from a Labor Law Perspective', *JITE* 152 (1996) 250–261; C. Windbichler, 'Justifying European Employment Law – Comments', in S. Grundmann/W. Kerber/S. Weatherill (eds.), *Party Autonomy and the Role of Information in the Internal Market* (Berlin/New York: de Gruyter, 2001), 225–229; K. Ziegler, *Arbeitnehmerbegriffe im Europäischen Arbeitsrecht* (Baden-Baden/Munich: Nomos and C.H. Beck, 2011); W. Zöllner, 'Flexibilisierung des Arbeitsrechts', *ZfA* 1988, 265–291; see also the bibliography before paras. 10, 15 and 59.

I. EUROPEAN EMPLOYMENT LAW

1. *The Subject Matter and the Concepts of 'Worker' and 'Employee'*

1. *European* employment law is the employment law embodied in EU primary law and EU secondary legislation. Employment law governs the legal relations between employers and employees.[1]

2. Employment law is commonly defined by the notion of the '**worker**' or '**employee**'. However, the definition of 'worker' varies among the Member States.[2]

---

[1] For a similar approach, see R. Birk, in S. Grundmann (ed.), *Systembildung und Systemlücken in Kerngebieten des Europäischen Privatrechts*, 387 sq. (including also the European Social Charter; on this, see the references in §2 para. 3 below).

[2] See e.g. R. Rebhahn, *RdA* 2009, 236; S. Krebber, in V. Rieble/A. Junker (eds.), *Das Grünbuch und seine Folgen*, 52–57; G. Cavalier/R. Upex, *ICLQ* 55 (2006), 587, 589–600 (UK, F, D); L. Nogler, *ZESAR* 2009, 461–469; R. Wank, *Festschrift für Küttner*, 5–20; K. Ziegler,

Moreover, EU primary law and secondary legislation do not use the concept uniformly. EU law instead contains various different notions of 'worker' or 'employee'.[3]

> In its English language version EU law does not consistently use the terms 'worker' or 'employee'. Whereas the French and German language versions uniformly speak of *travailleur* and *Arbeitnehmer* respectively, the English text sometimes uses the term 'employee', and othertimes the term 'worker'. The former is, for example, used in the Transfer of Undertakings Directive and the directives on information and consultation and employee participation; the latter, for example, in the Collective Redundancies Directive, the Safety and Health Framework Directive and the Maternity Protection Directive. In some jurisdictions, the term 'employee' is used as a specific legal term, referring to a particular category of workers who satisfy certain legal criteria; the term worker, on the other hand, is more colloquial and (consequently) more comprehensive. This book in principle follows the language used in the particular legal act under discussion but will consider both terms to be synonymous.

In interpreting EU employment law, the basic question is whether 'worker' or 'employee' is defined autonomously or rather refers to national definitions in the laws of the Member States.[4] EU law does not provide a uniform answer to this question. It sometimes uses an autonomous concept of 'worker' or 'employee', for example in Article 45 TFEU on the free movement of workers (see §3 paras. 9–12 below) or in the Safety and Health Framework Directive (see §13 paras. 9 sq. below); whereas at other times it refers to national concepts, as in the Transfer of Undertakings Directive (see §24 para. 13 below), to name just one example.

3.   Even where EU law refers to national concepts of 'worker' or 'employee', it often provides a **framework of regulation** which must be observed by the Member States and determines, for example, that part-time or temporary workers must not be excluded from the scope of application. The rules against discrimination in the Part-time Work Directive and the Temporary Agency Work Directive (see §§16, 18 below) have a similar effect. Furthermore, the implementation obligations upon a Member State (see para. 53 below) may impose further requirements with regard to the definition of the worker/employee in national law; the Member States may not arbitrarily exclude particular groups of workers/employees or use a specific concept of worker only for the purpose of implementing a directive

---

Arbeitnehmerbegriffe im Europäischen Arbeitsrecht, 88 sq., 94 sq. See also M. Freedland, *ILJ* 35 (2006), 1–29; id./N. Kountouris, *ILJ* 37 (2008), 49–74.

[3]   See in detail R. Rebhahn, *EuZA* 2012, 3–34 (with an exemplary analysis of the Court's jurisprudence); R. Wank, *EuZA* 2008, 172–195; id., *AuR* 2007, 244, 245–247; id., in P. Hanau/ H.-D. Steinmeyer/R. Wank (eds.), *Handbuch des europäischen Arbeits- und Sozialrechts*, §14 paras. 1–30; K. Ziegler, *Arbeitnehmerbegriffe im Europäischen Arbeitsrecht*; G. Cavalier/R. Upex, *ICLQ* 55 (2006), 587, 601–608; S. Borelli, *AuR* 2011, 472–476.

[4]   On this general issue of interpretation of EU law, see also para. 60.

(see e.g. §23 para. 9, §27 para. 8 below). And finally, we can discern a certain degree of harmonisation in relation to the definition of a worker/employee which has developed as a result of the jurisprudence on free movement of workers.[5]

4.   While EU law does thus not contain a uniform definition of the employee, this does not mean that we cannot sensibly speak of EU employment law. Even where EU law refers to the Member States' laws for a definition of 'worker' (thus accepting some disparities in the personal scope of application of its rules), it still serves the purpose of regulating the legal relationship between employer and employee and can thus be conceived as EU employment law.

5.   In its 2006 Green Paper on EU Employment Law (see para. 40, below), the Commission raised the question whether a uniform concept of worker/employee at the EU level would be desirable.[6] Such harmonisation would, of course, require that the European Union enjoyed the appropriate legislative competence in the first place, which has been doubted by some[7] and affirmed by others.[8] The discussion should distinguish between two possible approaches.[9] A uniform definition of 'worker' could, on the one hand, mean that national concepts of employee *as such* are being unified or harmonised be EU legislation.[10] In other words, the Union would then not only define the term 'employee' for the purposes of its own legislation but also for all internal purposes of the Member States. Such a far-reaching approach does not seem to be warranted and, indeed, a Union competence could hardly be found for such a measure. A uniform definition of 'worker' could, on the other hand, mean that the Union defines 'worker' autonomously for the purpose of determining the personal scope of application of its own legislation. Defining the personal scope of application in detail is indeed a legitimate objective, and the EU legislator has hitherto occasionally used an autonomous definition of 'worker', for example with respect to health and safety (see §13 para. 9 below). Such Union competence is hard to deny, given, in particular, that the central competence in the field of employment law in Art. 153 TFEU (see in detail §4 below) uses the term worker/employee.[11]

---

5   R. Rebhahn, *Aktuelle Entwicklungen des Europäischen Arbeitsrechts*, 4 sq.
6   Commission, Green Paper 'Modernising labour law to meet the challenges of the 21st century', COM(2006) 708 final, 15 sq. See also Recital 87 Services in the Internal Market Directive with elements of a definition.
7   See e.g. F. Bayreuther, *NZA* 2007, 371, 372 sq.; M. Franzen, *RIW* 2007, 892, 893 sq.
8   R. Wank, *AuR* 2007, 244, 245; id., *EuZA* 2008, 172–175.
9   Thus R. Rebhahn, *Aktuelle Entwicklungen des Europäischen Arbeitsrechts*, 5; also A. Junker, in V. Rieble/A. Junker (eds.), *Das Grünbuch und seine Folgen*, 22 sq.
10   On the problems resulting from a definition of general terms of private law in EU law, see generally C.-W. Canaris, 'Der EuGH als zükünftige privatrechtliche Superrevisionsinstanz?', *EuZW* 1994, 417.
11   R. Wank, *EuZA* 2008, 172–175.

Why should things here be different from consumer protection law where the Union uses autonomous concepts as well?[12]

6. **As a matter of policy** the question is, of course, open to debate. However, it would contribute to legal certainty if the EU legislator defined the personal scope of application of all of its own rules. Where the definition is left to the Member States, new distortions to competition may result, thus defeating a central goal of much EU legislation.[13] The jurisprudence of the European Court of Justice on the concept of worker in EU primary law, as well as individual acts of secondary legislation aimed at an approximation of the national laws of the Member States, already provide for the basis of an autonomous definition.[14] On the other hand, there seems no need for far-reaching harmonisation of the definition of 'worker' where purely internal matters of the Member States are concerned.

7. When we define employment law as the law that governs the *legal relations* between employer and employee, this may refer to the **employment contract** or the **employment relationship**. EU employment law often refers to both, apparently with the intention to ensure a broad scope of application. This does not entirely relieve us from the need to distinguish between both concepts. 'Employment *contract*' is the more specific and also the more technical concept. It refers to a specific relationship that is defined by the legal instrument of the contract. The 'employment *relationship*' is therefore the broader and more inclusive concept, encompassing both relationships that are formed by contracts and others of a 'merely' social nature. The concept of an 'employment relationship' may, in particular, also cover the case where the parties have unsuccessfully attempted to create a contractual relationship but acted upon the assumption that there was a contract. Indeed, the purpose of many employee protection rules requires that they be applied irrespective of the validity of the underlying contractual agreement; health and safety regulations in particular.

8. For the sake of convenience, we will in this book often only speak of either the employment contract or the employment relationship when, in substance, we wish to refer to both. Usually, the broader concept of the relationship will be used for this purpose; the EU legislator occasionally pursues the same approach, e.g. in Article 3(1) Insolvency Protection Directive. Where contractual rights are concerned in particular, we will refer to the employment contract.

---

[12] On the consumer definition in EU contract law, see K. Riesenhuber, *Europäisches Vertragsrecht*, §7.

[13] R. Wank, *EuZA* 2008, 172, 175–178 and 187–191; with reservations M. Franzen, *RIW* 2007, 892, 894 sq.

[14] See again R. Wank, *EuZA* 2008, 172, 175–178 and 187–191 (with a proposal for a definition); with reference to provisions of EU employment law and to Recital 87 Services in the Internal Market Directive.

2. Demarcations

a) Third-Country Nationals

9. A separate subject matter which falls outside the scope of this volume concerns the rules on the entry and residence of non-EU citizens for the purpose of employment in the EU. The Union aims to make access to the EU labour market easier for highly qualified workers/employees. The instrument for this is the '**EU Blue Card**' (coined after the US Green Card), which is regulated by the 2009 Blue Card Directive.[15] As a supplementary instrument, in 2010 the Commission submitted a proposal for a directive on conditions of entry and residence of third-country nationals in the framework of an **intra-corporate transfer**.[16] The purpose of the proposed directive is to make intra-corporate transfer of managers, specialists and graduate trainees from third countries easier. At the same time, the EU is fighting illegal employment of third country citizens in the EU, especially through prohibitions of illegal employment.[17] Both issue are primarily regulated by immigration law.

b) Comparative Employment Law[18]

Bibliography (Selection):[19]
R. Birk, 'Arbeitsrecht und Rechtsvergleichung – Die Kontrolle der Einhaltung der Europäischen Sozialcharta', *ZVglRWiss* 100 (2001), 48–61; M. W. Finkin, 'Comparative Labour Law', in: M. Reimann/R. Zimmermann (eds.), *The Oxford Handbook of Comparative Law* (Oxford: Oxford University Press, 2006), 1131–1160; M. Freedland, 'From the Contract of Employment to the Personal Work Nexus', *ILJ* 35 (2006), 1–29; M. Freedland/N. Kountouris, 'Towards a Comparative Theory of the Contractual Construction of Personal Work Relations in Europe', *ILJ* 37 (2008), 49–74; F. Gamillscheg, 'Arbeitsrecht und Rechtsvergleichung', in Göttinger Arbeitskreis (ed.), *Recht im Dienste der Menschenwürde – Festschrift für Herbert Kraus* (Würzburg: Holzner 1964), 95–110; F. Gamillscheg, 'Das Werkzeug der Arbeitsrechtsvergleichung', in H. Bernstein/U. Drobnig/H. Kötz (eds.), *Festschrift für Konrad Zweigert zum siebzigsten Geburtstag* (Tübingen: Mohr Siebeck, 1981), 433–450; F. Gamillscheg, 'Vom Wert der Rechtsvergleichung', *RdA* 1987, 29–32; M. Henssler/A. Braun (eds.), *Arbeitsrecht in*

---

[15] Directive 2009/50/EC of 25 May 2009 on the conditions of entry and residence of third-country nationals for the purposes of highly qualified employment, OJ 2009 L 155/17.

[16] Proposal for a Directive of the European Parliament and of the Council on conditions of entry and residence of third-country nationals in the framework of an intra-corporate transfer, COM(2010) 378 final.

[17] Directive 2009/52/EC of the European Parliament and of the Council of 18 June 2009 providing for minimum standards on sanctions and measures against employers of illegally staying third-country nationals, OJ 2009 L 168/24.

[18] For an excellent introduction, see R. Rebhahn, *ZEuP* 2002, 436–465.

[19] With regard to individual subjects of comparative law, see also the bibliographies in the respective chapters of this book.

Europa, 2nd edn. (Cologne: Otto Schmidt, 2007); B. A. Hepple (ed.), *International Encyclopaedia of Comparative Law, Volume XV: Labour Law* (Tübingen/Dordrecht: Mohr Siebeck/Martinus Nijhoff, since 1976); A. Junker, 'Ausländisches Arbeitsrecht: Strategie und Praxis der Informationsgewinnung', in P. Hanau/J. Thaus/H. P. Westermann (eds.), *Gegen den Strich – Festschrift für Klaus Adomeit* (Cologne: Wolters Kluwer, 2008), 319–330; A. Junker, 'Rechtsvergleichung als Grundlagenfach', *JZ* 1994, 921–928; R. Rebhahn, 'Abfindung statt Kündigungsschutz? – Rechtsvergleich und Regelungsmodelle', *RdA* 2002, 272–291; R. Rebhahn, 'Der Schutz gegen Kündigungen in den EU-Staaten', *ZfA* 2003, 163–235; R. Rebhahn, 'Ziele und Probleme der Arbeitsrechtsvergleichung in Europa', *ZEuP* 2002, 436–465; M. Schlachter, 'Arbeitsrecht und Rechtsvergleichung', *RdA* 1999, 118–124; Lord K. W. Wedderburn, *Employment Rights in Britain and Europe – Selected Papers in Labour Law* (London: Lawrence & Wishart, 1991); Lord K. W. Wedderburn, *Labour Law and Freedom* (London: Lawrence & Wishart, 1995).

10. European employment law, as defined by EU law (see para. 1 above), should be distinguished from 'European employment law' in a comparative sense. Comparative law is traditionally concerned with the comparison of different national legal systems. European employment law could thus be understood as a comparison of the employment laws (plural!) of the Member States of the EU or of European countries in a geographical sense.[20] Such comparison is related to EU law where the directly applicable provisions of EU primary law or EU regulations are concerned or where national laws are determined by EU directives. For a comparative lawyer, EU law is, however, not the primary focus. He or she will instead be concerned with the autonomous national aspects of employment law.

11. Comparative law is of fundamental **importance** and has various different **applications**. The same is true for EU employment law.[21] First of all, comparative law is a discipline of fundamental research in its own right. A functional comparison reveals the substantive questions that underlie disparate national rules and thus enhances our understanding of the issues and contributes to academic teaching.[22] Furthermore, comparative law is an indispensable tool for the legislator. This is true for national legislation and even more so for EU legislation.[23] Moreover, comparative law may contribute to our understanding of EU legislation, in particular where a piece of EU legislation builds upon comparative findings.

---

[20]   To this effect, e.g. R. Rebhahn, *ZEuP* 2002, 436, 450; id., *ZfA* 2003, 163, 164.

[21]   On the functions of comparative law, see e.g. F. Gamillscheg, *Festschrift für Kraus*, 95–110; id., *RdA* 1987, 29–32; M. Schlachter, *RdA* 1999, 118–124. On the 'tools' of comparative law, i.e. materials and resources, see e.g. the – somewhat older – account of F. Gamillscheg, *Festschrift für Zweigert*, 433–450.

[22]   A. Junker, *JZ* 1994, 921–928.

[23]   R. Rebhahn, *ZEuP* 2002, 436, 454, 458 sq.

12. However, it is a matter of debate whether and to what extent comparative law can contribute to the interpretation and judicial development of (national or EU) employment law.[24]

> Comparative considerations appear to be quite common in the practice of the European Court of Justice – as in other international supervisory or judicial bodies. Yet, the Court's decisions do not reveal these considerations. It appears that the comparative findings may serve as a tool for finding the *sedes materiae* of the issue involved, for the historical interpretation (legislative history of the law in question) and perhaps for opening up the panorama of possible interpretations of a given rule.[25] It should not be overlooked, though, that comparative law may prove exceedingly difficult, in particular in the forensic practice of a court. To begin with, the methods of comparative law are far from universally accepted. The choice as to which legal systems are to be compared in particular requires a value judgement, as does the choice (!) of the 'best' (!) of various solutions (as would be necessary in order to provide guidance for the interpretation or judicial development of the law). Certainly, a comparative finding, in particular where it presupposes a value judgement, cannot derogate from the law. Value judgements are for parliament to make, and under the separation of powers, the courts' task is to apply rather than make the law. This does not deny, of course, that judicial development of the law is also a legitimate task of the Court of Justice. But such development has specific requirements (see para. 64 below).

13. Last, but not least, comparative law serves different functions with regard to **fundamental rights** in the EU. Where the Court of Justice establishes fundamental rights as General Principles of EU law (see para. 55 below and §2 paras. 14 sq. below), it relies upon comparative research. And the social rights of the Charter of Fundamental Rights (see §2 paras. 44–61 below) that are relevant in the context of employment law often refer to the Member States' laws.

14. Comparative employment law can be distinguished from the mere description of foreign employment law.[26] Such work is of considerable importance for legal practice, for example for advising clients (e.g. where the parties to an employment contract make a choice of law) or court practice (e.g. where foreign employment law is applicable under conflict rules [see §5 below]).

---

[24]   See only A. Schwartze, in K. Riesenhuber (ed.), *Europäische Methodenlehre*, §4; S. Grundmann/K. Riesenhuber, *JuS* 2001, 529, 533 (inspirational function); R. Rebhahn, *ZEuP* 2002, 436, 454 sq., 456 sq.; M. Schlachter, *RdA* 1999, 118, 120–122; id., *ZfA* 2007, 249, 253 sq. ('helps'); see also the bibliography before para. 59 below.

[25]   See e.g. R. Birk, *ZVglRWiss* 100 (2001), 48–61 on the work of the European Committee of Social Rights, ECSR, with regard to controlling the adherence to the European Social Charter (ESC; see § 2 para. 3 below); at pp. 57 sq. also on the practical difficulties involved.

[26]   See e.g. R. Blanpain (ed.), *International Encyclopedia for Labour Law and Industrial Relations* (The Hague et al.: Kluwer Law International, last update: February 2012); M. Henssler/A. Braun, *Arbeitsrecht in Europa*, 3rd edn. (Cologne: Otto Schmidt, 2011), with country reports structured with regard to specific issues of employment law.

II. SOURCES OF EU EMPLOYMENT LAW[27]

Bibliography:
W. Däubler, 'Instruments of EC Labour Law', in P. Davies et al. (eds.), *European Community Labour Law: Principles and Perspectives – Liber Amicorum Lord Wedderburn* (Oxford: Clarendon, 1996), 151–167; K. Lenaerts/J. A. Gutiérrez-Fons, 'The Constitutional Allocation of Powers and General Principles in EU Law', *CMLR* 47 (2010), 1629–1669; J. Köndgen, 'Die Rechtsquellen des Europäischen Privatrechts', in K. Riesenhuber (ed.), *Europäische Methodenlehre – Handbuch für Ausbildung und Praxis* (Berlin: de Gruyter, 2006), §7.

15. Following our definition of EU employment law, its sources are both the primary and secondary law of the EU, the written law as well as unwritten principles.[28]

A note on citation of legal norms in EU law. Legal Acts of the EU are normally structured and will be cited here by way of Articles (the only exception being the framework agreements concluded by the European social partners which are structured in 'Clauses'). Articles are further subdivided into paragraphs and subparagraphs, sometimes in sentences or lists of items that are structured by Arabic (1., 2., 3., ...) or Roman (i., ii., iii., ...) numbers, letters (a), b), c), ...) indents. This book follows a customary, if in detail ambiguous, mode of citation, referring to both paragraphs and subparagraphs alike by numbers in brackets. Sentences will not usually be specifically referred to, but where they are, the abbreviation 'sent.' will be used. Letters will be referred to by the respective letter in brackets or as 'litera' or 'lit.'. Thus, for example, Article 3(3)(1) Transfer of Undertakings Directive (TUD) refers to Article 3 paragraph 3 subparagraph 1 of that Directive. Article 2(1)(c) TUD refers to Article 2 paragraph 1 letter c) of the Directive. Article 3(3) and (4) refers to Article 3 paragraphs 3 and 4. etc. As in the above example, all legal acts will be referred to by a short title ('Transfer or Undertakings Directive') or an abbreviation thereof ('TUD'). A complete list of the short titles and abbreviations used for legal acts, together with references to the full titles and the official publication details, can be found in Annex 'Table of EU Legislation'; towards the beginning of each chapter, the official title and publication will also be referred to in the references. Where legal acts have been reformed, we will usually – and without any specific reference – refer to the current version of that act. Where an older version is concerned, this will be indicated by a year added to the short title or abbreviation. Thus, the current Transfer of Undertakings Directive will be referred to without any further indication to the year of its enactment. The original 1977 version will be referred to as 'the Transfer of Undertakings Directive 1977' or 'TUD 1977'.

---

[27] See also the exposition on the structure of EU legislation and of decisions of the Court of Justice in K. Riesenhuber, *Europäisches Vertragsrecht*, paras. 14–28.

[28] For an (older) overview of the sources of EU employment law, see W. Däubler, *Liber amicorum Lord Wedderburn*, 151–167.

1. Primary Law

a) The Treaty on European Union and the Treaty on the Functioning of the European Union

16. Despite their constitutional nature, the EU Treaty (TEU) and the Treaty on the Functioning of the European Union (TFEU) are sources of EU employment law which have considerable practical importance. The Treaties initially set out the principles of the economic constitution of the Union in Art. 3(2) and (3) TEU, 119 TFEU: An Internal Market where the fundamental freedoms are ensured, an open market economy with free competition. Since the Treaty of Lisbon of 2009, the economic constitution has been described as a 'highly competitive social market economy, aiming at full employment and social progress, and a high level of protection and improvement of the quality of the environment', Article 3(3)(1) TEU.

17. Beyond mere principles, the **fundamental freedoms** are designed to provide concrete individual rights: freedom of goods, persons, services and capital movement (see in detail §3 below).[29] Of these, free movement of workers has the most obvious importance for EU employment law. Yet, it should not be overlooked that the other fundamental freedoms may also be relevant for employment law and labour relations. Where national employment or labour law infringes upon freedom of services, the freedom of establishment (of the employer) or free movement of capital, it can be subject to a proportionality test. Free movement of goods, can also be relevant in labour and employment cases where, for example, a labour dispute restricts cross-border commerce. Another relevant rule of primary law is the **principle of equal pay** which is contained in Article 157 TFEU (in detail §9 paras. 2–25). Finally, the TFEU contains the EU competence for secondary legislation among which Articles 153–155 on social policy and Article 19 on the prohibition of discrimination are the most important for employment law (in more detail §4).

18. Traditionally, EU primary law did not contain a written catalogue of **fundamental rights** (apart from the fundamental freedoms and the principle of equal pay). It did, however, recognise the 'fundamental rights, as guaranteed by the European Convention for the Protection of Human Rights and Fundamental Freedoms and as they result from the constitutional traditions common to the Member States' as 'general principles' (para. 17) of the Union's law since the Maastricht Treaty (see now Article 6(3) TEU). The 2009 Treaty of Lisbon now incorporates the **Charter of Fundamental Rights of the European Union** of 2000, Article 6(1) TEU. As a consequence, the EU now has several layers of fundamental rights protection.

---

[29] Contrary to G. Thüsing, *EuZA* 2008, 159, 163, the fundamental freedoms may also have a deregulatory effect on employment law.

b)   General Principles of EU Law

19.   Apart from the written provisions of the Treaties, primary law also consists of unwritten rules and principles, which were originally articulated by the Court of Justice and are now largely recognised as customary law. With regard to employment law, the General Principles that the Court has developed on the basis of Article 340(2) TFEU and Article 6(3) TEU (and their predecessors) have been of considerable practical importance (see in detail §2 paras. 15 sq.). Thus, the Court has for example recognised individual property, freedom of contract and freedom of occupation as fundamental rights in the form of General Principles of EU law.

2.   Secondary Legislation

20.   The bulk of EU employment law is to found in secondary legislation. Apart from a number of regulations, most legislation takes the form of directives. The other forms of legal acts enumerated in Article 288 TFEU are of less importance in our context.

a)   Regulations

21.   'A regulation shall have general application. It shall be binding in its entirety and directly applicable in all Member States', Article 288(2) TFEU. A regulation, in other words, has effects similar to those of a national statute. Thus, an employee can rely on the Jurisdiction and Enforcement of Judgments Regulation (see §7 below) just as he can rely upon a national code of civil procedure. An employer may invoke the provisions of the Rome I-Regulation (see §5 below) in the same way as any national statute on conflicts of laws. Apart from these regulations on conflicts of law and jurisdiction, the Free Movement of Workers Regulation, which supplements the fundamental freedom of Article 45 TFEU (see §3 para. 7), is of considerable practical importance. Furthermore, the (proposed) Statutes on the different supranational company types, particularly the SE Statute, also contain provisions of relevance for the employment relationship (see in detail §§29, 32).

b)   Directives

22.   Most of EU employment law is laid down in directives. The table of contents of this treatise reveals the considerable breadth of subjects covered: all of the subjects treated in §§8–31 are regulated by directives.

23.   The directive is a specific form of legislative act of the EU. It 'shall be binding, as to the result to be achieved, upon each Member State to which it is addressed, but shall leave to the national authorities the choice of form and methods', Article 288(3) TFEU. This method of legislation in two steps or levels entails a number of specific questions in regard to the legislation but also in regard to the methods of application of the law. We will address these issues briefly below (paras. 67–77 below).

c) Other Legal Acts

24. Article 288 TFEU further enumerates decisions, recommendations and opinions.[30] These do not play a significant role in EU employment law.

3. *International Treaties*

25. International treaties concluded by the EU can be part of EU law. They are binding on its institutions and on the Member States, Article 216(2) TFEU.[31] They are to be distinguished from international treaties concluded by the Member States which are not as such binding on the EU, even if, as in the case of the European Convention on Human Rights (ECHR), all EU Member States are also members to the international treaty (but see now Article 6(2) sent. 1 TFEU). International conventions concluded by the Member States are not as such part of EU law. Thus, the 1968 Brussels Convention on Jurisdiction and Enforcement of Judgements in civil and commercial matters or the 1980 Rome Convention on the law applicable to contractual obligations were not (formally) part of EU (or then EC) law, irrespective of the fact that they were in many ways interlinked with Union (Community) law. Both conventions have in the meantime been transposed into EU law by way of regulations (§§5, 7).

4. *Collective Agreements*

26. National employment law in some countries recognises collective agreements as a source of law. However, there is, as of yet, no EU law which regulates collective agreements, however. The Commission's considerations on a legal framework for transnational collective agreements are still in their early stages.[32]

27. At the same time the EU social partners – employers' associations and trade unions (see §4 paras. 30 sq.) – and the social partners on the plant level (employers and plant level employee representatives) and the collective agreements concluded by them serve important functions in EU law as well. There is, first of all, involvement of the social partners in the EU legislative process, in particular within the framework of **social dialogue** pursuant to Articles 154 sq. TFEU (§4 paras. 26–41): Framework agreements concluded by the social partners can be

---

30   See only K. Riesenhuber, in J. Basedow/K. Hopt/R. Zimmermann (eds.), *Max Planck Encyclopedia of European Private Law* (Oxford: Oxford University Press, 2012), keyword 'Legal Instruments of the EU (Others)'.

31   The Association Treaties between the EU and third countries are of considerable importance, in particular with regard to employment law, namely issues of free movement of workers. However, these treaties cannot be dealt with in the present book.

32   See M. Schmidt, *EuZA* 2008, 196, 205–211; furthermore O. Deinert, *Der europäische Kollektivvertrag*; R. Schwarze, in *EAS*, B 8100 para. 2; J. Thau, *Festschrift für Adomeit*, 751–755. See also the resolution of the European Parliament of 22 October 2008 on challenges to collective agreements in the EU (2008/2085(INI)), available at www.europarl.europa.eu/oeil/popups/summary.do?id=1054241&t=e&l=en.

transposed into EU law by means of a legal act of the Council. By this token, the European social partners can directly influence the content of EU legislation, and they have repeatedly availed themselves of this opportunity.[33] Furthermore, the national social partners can be entrusted with the **implementation of EU directives** into national law pursuant to Art. 153(3) TFEU (see §4 paras. 24 sq. below).

28. Finally, secondary legislation provides for a specific form of collective agreements. Given the Member States' disparate traditions of employee involvement, the EU Legislator has employed a negotiation model with regard to the European Works Council (§28) and with regard to employee involvement in the European Company (§29): The form and content of employee involvement is largely left for the employer and the employees (as a group) to decide by agreement.

III. THE LEGISLATIVE DEVELOPMENT OF EU EMPLOYMENT LAW – ELEMENTS OF A SYSTEM[34]

1. EU Primary Law and Legislation

29. EU employment law has developed in various phases.[35] The Member States or the (then) Community have repeatedly felt the need to complement economic integration with a 'social dimension'. This, in turn, necessitated the respective legislative competence. The development of EU employment law thus has to be seen in the light of the development of (then) Community competences. More than once, the politics of the day triggered or expedited legislative development.[36] For example, the mass dismissal of employees by the AKZO-Group in 1973 gave

---

[33] Some authors have attempted to use the provision of Article 155(2)(1) Alternative 1 TFEU as a basis for developing collective agreements under EU law; O. Deinert, *ILJ* 32 (2003), 317, 320–324; D. Schiek, *ILJ* 34 (2005), 23–56. Opposed to these approaches R. Birk, 'Vereinbarung der Sozialpartner als Regelungsinstrument in der Europäischen Sozialcharta und im supranationalen Arbeitsrecht', in J. Becker et al. (eds.), *Festschrift für Manfred Rehbinder* (Munich: C.H. Beck, 2002), 3, 11 sq.; H. Buchner, 'Die sozialpolitische Entwicklung der Europäischen Gemeinschaft im Spannungsfeld von hoheitlicher Regelung und tarifautonomer Gestaltung', *RdA* 1993, 193, 200 sq.; P. Hanau, in P. Hanau/H.-D. Steinmeyer/R. Wank (eds.), *Handbuch des europäischen Arbeits- und Sozialrechts*, §19 para. 17; K. Lörcher, 'Der Europäische Gewerkschaftsbund (EGB) und seine Beteiligung am europäischen Arbeitsrecht', *NZA* 2003, 184, 192; S. Smismans, 'The European Social Dialogue between Constitutional and Labour Law', *ELR* 32 (2007), 341, 358–363; J. Thau, *Festschrift für Adomeit*, 747–756.

[34] The following overview only refers to the original enactment of the legal acts, leaving aside subsequent amendments or reforms. See also M. Schmidt, *EuZA* 2008, 196–198; A. Junker, *JZ* 1994, 277–286; id., *NZA* 1999, 2–6; id., in S. Grundmann (ed.), *Systembildung und Systemlücken in Kerngebieten des Europäischen Privatrechts*, 357–386.

[35] G. Thüsing, *EuZA* 2008, 159, 160 ('proceeding in the form of waves, but with a clear objective: progres by means of approximation' – my translation).

[36] B. Jansen, *EuR* 1990 Special Issue 2, 5, 9 ('the priorities of individual proposals are rather determined with regard to practical needs than to programmatic considerations' – my translation).

16

additional impetus for enactment of the Collective Redundancies Directive (§23), the participation of a right-wing populist party in the Austrian government accelerated the enactment of the Race Discrimination Directive (§10) and closure of the *Renault*-plant in Villevoorde, Belgium in 1997 triggered the enactment of the Information and Consultation Framework Directive (§27).

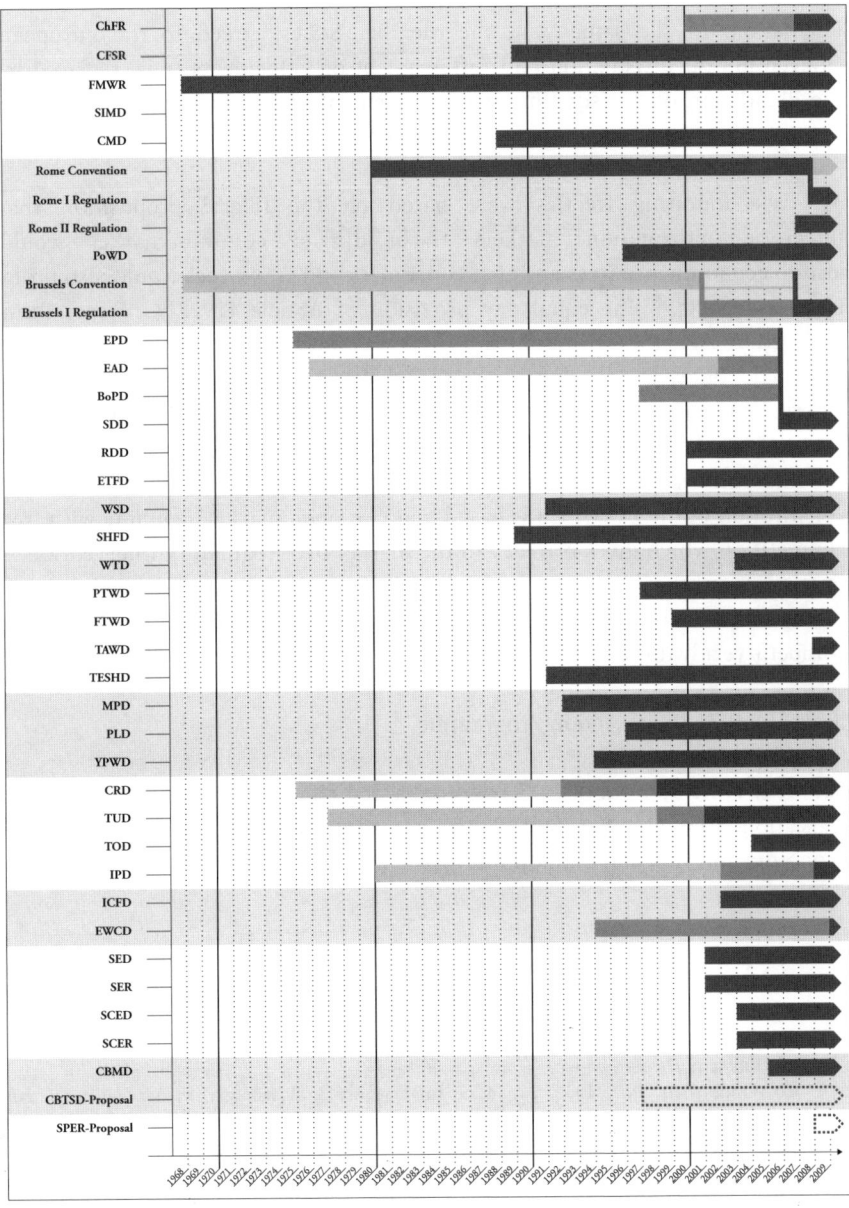

Arrows refer to legislative acts. Different shades of grey indicate reformed or codified versions of the same act (and thus a 'deeper' level of integration). Arrows in frames refer to proposals for legislative acts.

a)   The Liberal Starting Point of the Founding Treaties

30.   For a long time and into the 1970s, the body of EU employment law consisted primarily of the few rules of primary law and a handful of acts of supplementary secondary legislation.[37] In order to effectuate the free movement of workers, the Community enacted the 1968 Free Movement of Workers Regulation. In the same year, the Member States agreed to the European Convention on Jurisdiction and Enforcement of Judgements (now replaced by the Regulation on Jurisdiction and Enforcement of Judgments; see §7) which, *inter alia,* also applies to employment disputes.

31.   The founding treaties were based on the liberal proposition that integration of the national markets – the building of a common market – would lead to economic progress and that consumers and employees would also profit from its effects.[38] The equal pay provision of Article 119 EEC Treaty (now replaced by Art. 157 TFEU) in particular was not motivated by considerations of social policy, but by considerations of competition (see §9 para. 2): The enterprises of a given country should not suffer competitive disadvantage in the common market because they pay women the same wages as men.[39] This liberal starting point is by no means superseded today. It is present in the economic constitution of the EU which is based upon an open market economy with free competition which gives primacy to the market over regulatory intervention.[40] Furthermore, the Treaty is based on the concept that a lesser degree of regulation and lower social costs in individual regions constitute legitimate competitive advantages.[41]

b)   The 1974 Social Action Programme

32.   The Paris Summit of 1972 triggered a first major phase of EU employment legislation. The Member States now agreed to work not only towards an economic and monetary union but also towards coordinated employment and

---

[37]   See e.g. W. Hallstein, *Die Europäische Gemeinschaft* (Berlin: Econ, 1973), 167–176.

[38]   H. Collins, in S. Grundmann/S. Weatherill/W. Kerber (eds.), *Party Autonomy and the Role of Information in the Internal Market,* 212 sq.; A. Junker, *NZA* 1999, 2, 4; id., in S. Grundmann (ed.), *Systembildung und Systemlücken in Kerngebieten des Europäischen Privatrechts,* 359.

[39]   W. Hallstein, *Die Europäische Gemeinschaft,* 167 sq.

[40]   C. Windbichler, *RdA* 1992, 74–84. S. furthermore J. Basedow, *Von der deutschen zur europäischen Wirtschaftsverfassung;* S. Grundmann, in K. Riesenhuber (ed.), *Privatrechtsgesellschaft,* §5; V. Rieble, *Arbeitsmarkt und Wettbewerb,* 42–70; K. Riesenhuber, 'Primärrechtliche Grundlagen der Kapitalmarkttransparenz', in K. Hopt/R. Veil/J. Kämmerer (eds.), *Kapitalmarktgesetzgebung im Europäischen Binnenmarkt* (Tübingen: Mohr Siebeck, 2008), 26–33; see also ECJ Case C-341/05 *Laval un Partneri* [2007] ECR I-11767 paras. 104 sq.; ECJ Case C-438/05 *Viking* [2007] ECR I-10779 paras. 78 sq.

[41]   C. Windbichler, *RdA* 1992, 74, 82.

vocational training policies.[42] The Council concretised this goal in its 1974 social action programme.[43] This action programme was the starting signal for industrious activity of the (then) Community in the field of employment law. In the 1970s, the first sex discrimination directives were enacted (see in detail §9). With the Collective Redundancies Directive (§23) and the Transfer of Undertakings Directive (§24), the Community enacted the first measures for the protection of employees in the case of business restructuring, which, in the Community's observation and anticipation, would become more frequent in the in the future. The Insolvency Protection Directive followed in 1980 (§25).

33. The momentum of this first phase was soon curbed, though. During the course of the economic crisis at the end of the 1970s and beginning of 1980s, social policy projects were put on hold.[44] And the United Kingdom, which had joined the original 'Community of the Six' in 1972 together with Ireland and Denmark, voiced objections against social policy legislation. This was a consequence of the liberal economic perspective which had dominated since the Conservative party had come into power under *Margaret Thatcher* in 1979. During this period, the United Kingdom successfully obstructed a number of legislative proposals in the field of employment law and caused other proposals to be delayed or significantly reduced in their level of protection.[45]

c)   The Community Charter of Fundamental Social Rights and the Action Programme of 1989

34. The call for a 'social dimension' to the Internal Market was raised once again by the Single European Act of 1986.[46] An intensified economic integration, it was argued, had to be accompanied by a complementary social policy. The political agenda found its manifestation in the (misleadingly labelled) Community Charter of Fundamental Social Rights of 1989 (see §2 paras. 54–66, a 'solemn proclamation' of eleven of the now (after the accession of Greece in 1981

---

42   A. Junker, *NZA* 1999, 2, 4 ('a spirit of departure in the area of social policy' – my translation).
43   Council Resolution of 21 January 1974 concerning a social action programme, OJ 1974 C 13/1.
44   M. Heinze, *ZfA* 1992, 331, 334 sq.; M. Shanks, *CMLR* 14 (1977), 375–383.
45   Vgl. auch G. Thüsing, *EuZA* 2008, 159, 160 sq.
46   See e.g. R. Birk et al. (eds.), *Europäischer Binnenmarkt und Harmonisierung des Arbeitsrechts* (Mannheim: Wissenschaftsverlag, 1991); B. Jansen, *EuR* 1990 Special Issue 2, 5, 11 sq. ('Without any social component, the Community runs the danger of no longer being accepted by the citizens, for the fall of the borders will expose differences of employees' rights more clearly than is the case today – the key word is: "social dumping".' – my translation); B. Hepple, *ILJ* 16 (1987), 77–87 (with a sober analysis of the development of EEC employment law so far; suggesting the social dialogue procedure and elaboration on the ESC and the ECHR as promising alternative routes); Lord Wedderburn, *Dublin U.L.J.* 13 (1991), 1–35, also reproduced in id., Labour Law and Freedom (London: Lawrence Wishart, 1995), 247–285; id., MLR 54 (1991), 1–47, also reproduced in id., *Employment Rights in Britain and Europe*, 354–416.

and Spain and Portugal in 1986) twelve Member States – with the sole exception of the United Kingdom. The Community Charter was supplemented by an Action Programme of the Commission, which was also adopted in 1989.[47] While the Community Charter was not a binding legal act, it was nevertheless of considerable importance for the legal development of the following years. In hindsight, this is evidenced by the fact that most of the political goals raised in the Charter have subsequently been achieved by Community measures. Conversely, almost all Community legislation in the field of employment law has since referred to the respective postulation in the Community Charter.

d)   The Maastricht Treaty and the Social Policy Protocol of 1992[48]

35.   However, the legislative competences of the Community proved insufficient to achieve the goals of the Community Charter. The requirement of unanimity for internal market legislation brought on the basis of Article 100 EC (cf. now Article 115 TFEU) proved to be a major obstacle, particularly since the United Kingdom continued to oppose most social policy legislation. Yet, the United Kingdom also objected to the expansion of the Community's legislative powers. The halt could ultimately only be overcome by what came to be known as a 'Multi-speed Europe'. Together with the Maastricht Treaty, eleven of the Member States – all but the United Kingdom – agreed on the Social Policy Protocol (s. also §4 para. 4), which provided for additional competences in the field of social policy and thus allowed for the implementation of the Social Charter. Apart from an expansion of competences, the Social Policy Protocol also provided for a simplified legislative process as well as for the involvement of the social partners by means of consultation and an institutionalised social dialogue.[49] The Social Policy Protocol first introduced the possibility for the social partners to contribute directly to Community legislation by means of framework agreements (see para. 27 above). The European Works Council Directive (§28), the Parental Leave Directive (§21) and the Part-time Work Directive (§16) were enacted on the basis of the Social Policy Protocol.

36.   On the other hand, the Maastricht Treaty also enshrined the **principle of subsidiarity** in the EC Treaty (now Article 5(1) sent. 2, (3) TEU). One could have expected that the principle of subsidiarity would have restricted the extent of Community legislation.[50] Yet, subsequent development has not fulfilled this

---

[47]   Communication from the Commission of 29 November 1989 concerning its Action Programme relating to the Implementation of the Community Charter of Basic Social Rights for Workers, COM(89) 568 final.

[48]   B. Bercusson, *IRJ* 23 (1992), 177–190; id., *ILJ* 23 (1994), 1–31.

[49]   M. Heinze, *Festschrift für Everling*, 440 sq., 444.

[50]   On the subsidiarity principle (arguing for it to be used stringently) M. Heinze, *RdA* 1994, 1–11; id., *Festschrift für Everling*, 433–445.

expectation, and we can observe increasing legislative activity in the area of social policy.

e)   The Amsterdam Treaty of 1997[51]

37. The Amsterdam Treaty introduced new numbering for the Articles of the Treaty (for example, the equal pay provision of the original Article 119 TEC now became Art. 141 EC). In substance, the Treaty provided for a number of institutional changes, in particular a strengthening of the co-decision procedure (now Article 294 TFEU).

> In order to distinguish the different versions of the EC Treaty before and after Amsterdam, the Court of Justice uses different abbreviations. So the EC-Treaty would now be abbreviated EC as opposed to the pre-Amsterdam TEC, the EU-Treaty EU as opposed to the pre-Amsterdam TEU. The Treaty of Lisbon of 2009 (para. 40a below) re-numbered and re-named the Treaties.

38. A significant change with regard to employment law was the integration of the Social Policy Protocol (para. 35 above) into the EC Treaty, thereby also making it binding for the United Kingdom. When in 1997 a labour government under *Tony Blair* succeeded the Conservatives, this paved the way to extend the legal acts based upon the Social Policy Protocol competences to the United Kingdom. The Amsterdam Treaty also introduced a new competence for 'action to combat discrimination' (now Article 19 TFEU). The EU legislator has made extensive use of this new competence since 2000 (see in detail §§8–11).

f)   The Nice Treaty of 2000

39. The Nice Treaty brought about further institutional changes but not the comprehensive reform that many considered necessary with a view to future expansion of the Community. With regard to employment law, the Treaty re-ordered and expanded the competences pursuant to Articles 136 sq. TEC (now Articles 151, 153 TFEU). On the occasion of the Nice conference, the **Charter of Fundamental Rights of the EU** (see para. 34 above and §2 paras. 65–77 below) was solemnly declared, though it was not enacted as part of EU primary law or as binding EU law. The Council adopted the **European Social Agenda**[52] and laid down policy guidelines for the following years. These guidelines were intended to supplement the so-called '**Lisbon Strategy**', which pursued the ambitious goal of making the European Union 'the most competitive

---

[51]   H.-D. Steinmeyer, *RdA* 2001, 10–22; M. Weiss, *Festschrift für Wiese*, 633–648. Generally R. Streinz, *Europarecht*, paras. 49–52.
[52]   European Social Agenda, approved by the Nice European Council meeting on 7, 8 and 9 December 2000, OJ 2001 C 157/4.

and dynamic knowledge-based economy in the world capable of sustainable economic growth with more and better jobs and greater social cohesion'.[53]

g) The 2006 Green Paper

40. In its 2006 Green Paper 'Modernising labour law to meet the challenges of the 21st century',[54] the Commission points towards various avenues for future development. The Commission's approach has received a mixed, mostly critical response.[55] The fundamental idea behind its considerations is summarised in the catchword **Flexicurity**: It aims at achieving greater flexibility together with a high degree of employment security.[56] The instruments of employment law should be developed in a way which gives positive impetus for sustainable growth as well as more and better jobs.[57] This directs attention in particular to atypical employment relations (part-time work, fixed-term work) which are considered to be instruments of flexibility but are at the same time 'precarious' (see in detail §15).[58] The Commission further asks whether 'more convergent definitions of "worker" in EU Directives' were warranted.[59] This issue has attracted particular interest in legal writing and the question has largely been answered in the negative.[60] The negative reaction may, however, partially be due to the fact that a harmonisation of the definition of the worker is often associated with far-reaching harmonisation of the Member States' employment laws as such

---

[53] Lisbon European Council of 23 and 24 March 2003 – Presidency Conclusions No. 5, available at www.europarl.europa.eu/summits/lis1_en.htm.

[54] COM(2006) 708 final; on the considerations of the Commission see also M. Uebe, *EuZA* 2008, 167–171.

[55] With a critical appraisal e.g. F. Bayreuther, *NZA* 2007, 371–375; M. Franzen, *RIW* 2007, 892–897; J. Joussen, *ZEuP* 2008, 374–393; for a summary, see M. Stoffels, *GPR* 2007, 231–235; differentiating G. Thüsing, *EuZA* 2008, 159–166; R. Wank, *AuR* 2007, 244–249; with approval, in particular to the flexicurity-concept U. Preis, *Festschrift für Birk,* 625–642, especially 631.

[56] Commission, Green Paper 'Modernising labour law to meet the challenges of the 21st century', COM(2006) 708 final, 3 sq.; see also the subsequent Opinion of the European Economic and Social Committee on the Communication from the Commission to the European Parliament, the Council, the European Economic and Social Committee and the Committee of the Regions – Towards Common Principles of Flexicurity: More and better jobs through flexibility and security COM(2007) 359 final (with examples for flexicurity from the national legal systems of the Member States 23–25). On this e.g. M. Franzen, *RIW* 2007, 892, 896 sq.; G. v. Hoyningen-Huene, *Festschrift für Birk,* 217–241.

[57] Commission, Green Paper 'Modernising labour law to meet the challenges of the 21st century', COM(2006) 708 final, 3.

[58] It has rightly been pointed out that a legislative competence that is limited to setting minimum standards (Article 153 TFEU) cannot serve as a basis for implementing the flexicurity concept; for while it may set minimum standards with regard to 'security' it cannot impose maximum standards with regard to flexibility; M. Franzen, *RIW* 2007, 892, 897; A. Junker, in A. Junker/V. Rieble (eds.), *Das Grünbuch und seine Folgen,* 21.

[59] Commission, Green Paper 'Modernising labour law to meet the challenges of the 21st century', COM(2006) 708 final, 15 sq.

[60] F. Bayreuther, *NZA* 2007, 371–375; J. Joussen, *ZEuP* 2008, 374, 385, 386 sq., 391–393.

(cf. paras. 2–6 above). After an evaluation of the comments to its Green Paper[61] the Commission has not further pursued the plans promulgated therein.

h)   The 2009 Lisbon Treaty

40a.   The 2009 Lisbon Treaty merged the European Union and the European Community into the 'new' European Union. It also revised the Treaties. The new Treaty on European Union is now referred to with the abbreviation TEU (as opposed to the 'EU' as reference to the Amsterdam version of the Treaty; see para. 37 above). And the previous Treaty establishing the European Community (EC) has been succeeded by the Treaty on the functioning of the European Union (TFEU). The TFEU, in principle and structure, largely follows the EC Treaty, though with significant changes. Thus, the role of the European Parliament has been strengthened; legislative competences have been revised and legislative procedures and majority requirements have been modified (see also §4 below); a provision on the values and goals of the Union has been included (Article 2 TEU; see also §2 below); the Charter of Fundamental Rights was brought into force, Art. 6(1) TEU; see para. 18 above and §2 paras. 16 sqq. below; and not least, the provisions of the Treaties have been renumbered (so, for example, the anti-discrimination provision of Art. 141 EC is now Article 157 TFEU). In the present book, the Lisbon Treaty is referred to unless otherwise indicated.

i)   Recent Development[62]

41.   A number of important legislative projects have been announced towards the end of 2008 and the beginning of 2009, and some have been realised since.[63]

–   Reform of the Working Time Directive has been pursued for a number of years. In April 2009 negotiations in the Conciliation Committee ultimately failed.
–   The Temporary Agency Work Directive was enacted in September 2008 after many years of policy debate.
–   The Maternity Protection Directive is currently under review. The Commission submitted an amendment proposal on 3 October 2008. The details of the reform are controversial, especially the length of maternity leave. See in detail §20 para. 5.

---

[61]   Communication from the Commission 'Outcome of the Public Consultation on the Commission's Green Paper "Modernising labour law to meet the challenges of the 21st century"', COM(2007) 627 final.
[62]   For a good overview, see R. Rebhahn, *Aktuelle Entwicklungen des Europäischen Arbeitsrechts.*
[63]   On the concept as a whole: Communication from the Commission 'Renewed social agenda: Opportunities, access and solidarity in 21st century Europe', COM(2008) 412 final.

- In June 2009 the social partners concluded a new Parental Leave Framework Agreement which was subsequently implemented by the Parental Leave Directive of 8 March 2010.
- The European Works Council Directive has been amended in May 2009; see in detail §28.[64]
- As part of an initiative for small and medium-sized enterprises (SME), referred to as the 'Small Business Act', the introduction of an EU limited liability company (the European Private Company or *Societas Europaea Privata)* and corresponding rules on employee involvement are currently being debated; see §32.
- The *Viking* and *Laval* decisions of the Court of Justice (see in detail §3 paras. 71 and 69 below) have caused considerable uncertainty about the relation of fundamental freedoms (freedom of services, freedom of establishment) on the one hand and fundamental rights (the right to collective action, strike in particular) on the other. While business considered legislative action unnecessary, labour urged the Commission to ensure effective protection of workers' rights on two levels, (a) concerning the right to strike and (b) concerning the rights of posted workers. In 2012, the Commission adopted two proposals addressing these issues.[65] The proposals are controversial even within the Commission, but also in the Member States.

The current phase of development can aptly be described as one of **consolidation** – or standstill.[66] It has been pointed out that this development is due to inherent limits: While Union employment law is focussed upon cross-border issues and the functioning of the internal market, genuine employment protection is a task which falls to the Member States.[67] While there is some room for additional minimum standards in Union law,[68] such development appears to be rather unlikely at present.

j)   A System of European Employment Law?[69]

42.   With regard to EU employment law in particular, it has been asked – or rather questioned – whether there is a common thread, a harmonisation concept,

---

[64]   See M. Schmidt, *EuZA* 2008, 196, 205–207.

[65]   Proposal for a regulation on the exercise of the right to take collective action within the context of the freedom of establishment and the freedom to provide services, COM(2012) 130 final; Proposal for a directive of the European Parliament and of the Council on the enforcement of Directive 96/71/EC concerning the posting of workers in the framework of the provision of services.

[66]   S. Krebber, *Comp. Lab. L. & Pol'y J.* 30 (2009), 875–903.

[67]   S. Krebber, *Comp. Lab. L. & Pol'y J.* 30 (2009), 875, 902 sq.

[68]   See R. Rebhahn, *EuZA* 2011, 295–307 (exploring – from an analytical point of view – where the EU could successfully adopt additional minimum standards in the area of employment [contract] law).

[69]   See the seminal collection of S. Grundmann (ed.), *Systembildung und Systemlücken in Kerngebieten des Europäischen Privatrechts.*

that holds the individual pieces of legislation together; in other words, whether there is a system. While some authors find aspects of an 'inner system' in EU employment law,[70] a majority answer the question in the negative. EU employment law was built 'with no system or concept'.[71]

43. Indeed, it is hard to overlook that social policy in the EU has followed different paths throughout the (almost) sixty years of the Community/Union. More than that, it has radically changed directions, starting from a market-liberal approach and changing to a system of social accommodation or compensation. Apart from such issues of principle, EU legislation has, as we have seen earlier (para. 29), in some instances been influenced by considerations of the politics of the day rather than following a master plan. On the other hand, we can discern an attempt of the Commission and the Council to develop overarching policy concepts, such as in the 1974 Social Action Programme, in the 1989 Action Plan on the Charter of Fundamental Social Rights or recently in the 2006 Green Paper.

44. As a minimum, we can see that EU legislation focuses on a limited number of issues which all have some relevance to the Internal Market: realisation of the fundamental freedoms, the principle of non-discrimination, transparency of working conditions and protection of worker health and safety.[72] More recently, information and consultation of workers and, supplementing legislation in the area of company law, rules on employee participation on the company board, have gained particular attention.

---

[70]　C. Barnard/S. Deakin, 'In Search of Coherence: Social Policy, the Single Market and Fundamental Rights', *ILJ* 2000, 331–345 (considering a combination of 'reflexive law' and fundamental rights as a way to achieve coherence in EU employment law); H. Collins, *Employment Law,* 20 sqq. (discerning 'three key themes …: social inclusion, competitiveness, and citizenship').

[71]　A. Junker, *NJW* 1994, 2527 and 2528 ('without any concept or system'; 'puncutal', 'pointillistic' – my translation); more favourably id., *NZA* 1999, 2, 6–11; D. Kaiser, *NZA* 2000, 1144; S. Krebber, in V. Rieble/A. Junker (eds.), *Das Grünbuch und seine Folgen,* 37; id., *Comp. Lab. L. & Pol'y J.* 30 (2009), 875–903 (895: 'puzzling … No concept, no systematic regulation'); U. Preis, *Festschrift für Birk,* 628; with reservations further H. Reichold, *JZ* 2006, 549; id., 'Neues zum grenzüberschreitenden Betriebsübergang', in H. Konzen et al. (eds.), *Festschrift für Rolf Birk zum siebzigsten Geburtstag* (Tübingen: Mohr Siebeck, 2008), 687.

[72]　S. Grundmann, *Gedächtnisschrift für Blomeyer,* 71–97. Discerning a different concept that had been pursued until the 1990s H. Collins, in S. Grundmann/S. Weatherill/W. Kerber (eds.), *Party Autonomy and the Role of Information in the Internal Market,* 206, 212–216; until then, the Community had largely respected territorial sovereignty; the Collective Redundancies Directive and the Transfer of Undertakings Directive, too, had been nothing more than 'a rag-bag of measures that were motivated more by a desire to impose restrictions on the free movement of capital than an intention to achieve an approximation or uniformity of employment laws'. Safety and Health regulations eliminated a cost factor from competition; the legislation based on the social dialogue (cf. now Articles 155 sq. TFEU) provided for a possibility for (big) employers to extend standards that they already fulfilled to other employers as a uniform cost element (critical to this latter aspect C. Windbichler, ibid. 226 sq.).

45. Furthermore, we can discern that subparts (or subsystems) of employment law are being developed in a principled, in other words, systematic fashion. This was also a concern of the 2006 Green Paper. It is particularly obvious in the area of anti-discrimination law. Here, the legislature has recently codified some of the instruments that had originally been developed by the Court of Justice. With regard to sex discrimination, it has 'codified' existing directives in a new directive, bringing the various pieces of legislation together in a structured manner (§9). We find a similar approach with regard to occupational health and safety, we find a similar approach. Here, the 1989 Framework Directive (§13) constitutes a 'general part' of the law and functioned as the basis for its systematic development. Again, with regard to atypical employment, the Commission had initially pursued a systematic approach, even though, of course, it could ultimately only be realised in a piecemeal fashion (see §§15–19). The development of the Transfer of Undertakings Directive, on the other hand, has not been quite as successful. This may be due to the fact that the legislature has tried to adapt the Court's jurisprudence as closely as possible (rather than attempting a reform). With regard to employee involvement, we can find elements of a system in the increasing number of directives and regulations on the issue. This is true with regard to employee involvement on the shop floor level (through 'works councils' and similar representative bodies) where the EU legislature has developed a 'right to information and consultation', starting from the Community Charter of Fundamental Social Rights and individual rules in the Collective Redundancies Directive and the Transfer of Undertakings Directive, to the European Works Council Directive and the Information and Consultation Framework Directive. The negotiation procedure, first introduced in the Works Council Directive, has now become as a central element of the right of employee involvement in the directives on employee involvement in the European Company and the European Cooperative Company. The legislature has employed the same mechanism in the Cross-Border Merger Directive, the Draft Proposal for a border Transfer of the Registered Office Directive and the Proposal for a European Private Company.

46. If we look at the whole picture, EU employment law can in many respects be considered to constitute a 'coherent whole'; it covers large parts of the regulatory employment law. Irrespective of its considerable breadth, EU employment law constitutes only a small part of all employment law, leaving important areas untouched, such as the general law of employment contracts (with rules on, *inter alia,* the formation of contracts, contractual obligations or employee liability[73]) and the general law of employee involvement on the shop floor or on the board level. Central areas are left to regulation by the Member

---

[73]   See now J. Pačić, *EuZA* 2009, 47–68.

States, such as the issue of continued payment of wages in case of illness (only selectively regulated with regard to maternal leave, §20 paras. 28 sq.) or protection against unfair dismissal[74] (only selectively regulated through the prohibitions against discrimination, §§8–11, the Collective Redundancies Directive and the Transfer or Undertakings Directive, §§23, 24). For lack of competence (Article 153(5) TFEU; see in detail §4 paras. 8–13), pay, the right of association, and the right to strike or the right to impose lock-outs remain for the Member States to regulate, even though the fundamental freedoms exert some influence here, too (§3 paras. 68 sq., 85), and secondary legislation may have an indirect effect as well (see the principle of non-discrimination with regard to atypical employment relations, §15 para. 11).

47. We also have to keep in mind that the Union merely sets **minimum standards** in the field of employment law.[75] For legislation based on Article 153 TFEU, this is mandated by Article 153(2) lit. b), (4) indent 2 TFEU.[76]

48. In contract law, there is considerable debate whether the EU should adopt a European Code of Contract Law. There are only a few voices, though, who propose a **European Employment Code**. Drawing on the experience of EU contract law, where a 'Common Frame of Reference' (CFR) has recently been proposed, a 'European Labour Contract' has been put forward – if only as a 'provocative approach' and 'vision'.[77] Such European Employment Code could be conceived of as a fully-fledged system of rules for employment contracts that the parties can chose as applicable law under conflicts of law rules. It would thus constitute a so-called '28th model', alongside the 27 national legal systems of the Member States. The CFR-approach has encountered considerable difficulty and opposition already in the area of general contract law. With regard to employment contract law, where the aspect of protection and the various interrelationships with social (security) law make matters even more complicated, there would seem to be insurmountable obstacles to such a project at present.[78] Beyond such considerations of feasibility, it may well be doubted whether there is a practical need for a 28th model.

---

[74] In detail R. Rebhahn, *ZfA* 2003, 163–235. Also R. Giesen/L. Eriksen, *EuZA* 2009, 1–35 (Denmark).

[75] M. Heinze, *Festschrift für Everling*, 440–445 (welcoming minimum harmonisation as a harmonisation concept).

[76] In more detail R. Rebhahn, *EuZA* 2008, 39, 47 sq.

[77] M. Stein, in V. Rieble/A. Junker (eds.), *Das Grünbuch und seine Folgen*, 94–100. Cf. also L. Nogler, *ELJ* 14 (2008), 483–499.

[78] Cf. the report of the discussion in V. Rieble/A. Junker (eds.), *Das Grünbuch und seine Folgen*, 101–108.

2. *Excursus: Other Acts of Community Law with Relevance to Employment Law*

49. There are a number of provisions that are not commonly considered part of employment law, but which nonetheless have a formal or inner relationship to it.

50. One example is the **Commercial Agents Directive.**[79] This Directive certainly applies to self-employed persons and also covers commercial agents in the form of legal persons. There is an inner connection with employment law, though, as it is focused on the protection of the commercial agent as the 'weaker party'.[80] The Commercial Agents Directive regulates contractual relations between the commercial agent and the principal. It provides for a general duty of good faith and rights to provision, indemnity and compensation.

51. The **Doorstep Selling Directive**[81] concerns the conclusion of consumer contracts (business to consumer, b2c) outside of business premises in situations where the consumer is not prepared to make contracts and is thus caught 'off guard'. One of the situations covered is the formation of a contract during a visit at the consumer's place of work where the visit does not take place at the express request of the consumer. The directive thus concerns the protection of the individual as a consumer and not as an employee. It does not apply to the conclusion of employment contracts or termination agreements.

52. The **Unfair Terms Directive**[82] protects consumers against unfair terms in consumer contracts. Terms not individually negotiated are deemed to be unfair if, contrary to the requirement of good faith, they cause a significant imbalance in the parties' rights and obligations under the contract. Employment contracts are not within the substantive scope of application of the directive, but national law may subject them to such control.

3. *The Implementation of Directives in the Member States*

53. In considering the legislative development of EU employment law, we could also discuss the national legislation of the Member States where it concerns the implementation of directives. This would, however, exceed the definition of EU

---

[79] Council Directive 86/653/EEC of 18 December 1986 on the coordination of the laws of the Member States relating to self-employed commercial agents, OJ 1986 L 382/17.

[80] See S. Grundmann, *Europäisches Schuldvertragsrecht*, ch. 3.80 (systematising the Commercial Agents Directive as employment law on these grounds). This has, to some extent, been confirmed by ECJ Case C-381/98 *Ingmar* [2000] ECR I-9305.

[81] Council Directive 85/577/EEC of 20 December 1985 to protect the consumer in respect of contracts negotiated away from business premises, OJ 1985 L 372/31.

[82] Council Directive 93/13/EEC of 5 April 1993 on unfair terms in consumer contracts, OJ 1993 L 95/29.

employment law which is being pursued here (para. 1 above). While national implementing legislation is of primary concern to a practitioner, it is merely 'secondary' from an EU perspective. National implementing legislation must conform with the requirements of the directive and can merely specify or supplement it where the directive leaves room for that or specifically so provides. This is not to deny that national implementing measures do not contribute to the development of EU law. The concepts developed by national legislators have repeatedly inspired and influenced EU legislation. And conversely, actual or perceived deficits in the national implementation of directives have, on occasion, contributed to the development of EU employment law. The various requests for preliminary rulings on the sanctions for discrimination provide ample illustration (see §8 paras. 66–70).

54. The present volume focuses exclusively upon EU law and only rarely refers to national implementing measures, mostly only where they have been discussed in a decision of the Court of Justice.[83] Some references to the national laws of the Member States can be found in the footnotes regarding the individual directives and related literature.

IV. THE JUDICIAL DEVELOPMENT OF EU EMPLOYMENT LAW

1. *The Jurisprudence of the European Court of Justice*

55. While the development of the law is primarily a legislative task, it is widely accepted that the courts also perform an important function in this regard (see also para. 64). The European Court of Justice is sometimes even characterised as the 'motor of the development of the law'. This is, of course, a double-edged compliment, and the Court has indeed recently been severely criticised for its sometimes rather bold judicial in(ter)ventions.[84] In the field of employment law in particular, the Court's contributions to the development of the law have often proved to be very controversial. In the mid-1990s, one author spoke of a 'black series' of ECJ-decisions.[85] The Court's jurisprudence has been especially

---

[83] G. Thüsing, *Europäisches Arbeitsrecht*, and P. Hanau/H.-D. Steinmeyer/R. Wank (eds.), *Handbuch des Europäischen Arbeits- und Sozialrechts* have chosen a different conception, presenting the requirements of Community law together with the national implementation measures.

[84] For an emphatically critical perspective, see R. Herzog/L. Gerken, 'Stoppt den Europäischen Gerichtshof', *FAZ* of 8 September 2008, also available at www.cep.eu/fileadmin/user_upload/Pressemappe/CEP_in_den_Medien/Herzog-EuGH-Webseite.pdf. Furthermore e.g. M. Heinze, *ZfA* 1992, 331, 350.

[85] A. Junker, *NJW* 1994, 2527 sq. with regard to the Court's judgements in Paletta, ECJ Case C-206/94 [1996] ECR I-2357 (see also §3), Bötel (cf. §9) and Christel Schmidt (cf. §24); id., *Festschrift für Otto*, 163 sq.; to the same effect W. Blomeyer, *NZA* 1994, 633–640; D. Kaiser,

important for the development of General Principles of law.[86] A positive and widely accepted instance is its recognition of freedom of contract (freedom of occupation, the right to choose one's contract partner/employer) as a basis for recognition of the employee's right to object to the 'transfer' of his employment contract to another employer (see §24 para. 73 below). A further example which has been more critically received is the Court's 'finding' of a General Principle against age discrimination in the infamous *Mangold* case (see §11 para. 50 below).[87] The Court's judgements in *Viking* and *Laval* (see §3 paras. 71 and 69 below), which gave precedence to fundamental economic rights over the fundamental social right of collective action, are highly controversial.[88] With respect to secondary legislation, the anti-discrimination directives in particular have led to considerable judicial activity. In its jurisprudence, the Court has, for example, developed the concept of indirect discrimination which was later adopted by the legislator. Central aspects of the implementation duties of the Member States have also been developed in anti-discrimination cases (see §8 paras. 66–70). The Transfer of Undertakings Directive also triggered a large number of requests for preliminary rulings, and the Court has interpreted the term 'transfer of undertaking' in a long series of judgements. The legislature has repeatedly adopted the Court's jurisprudence in subsequent amendments to existing legislation, occasionally cutting it back. Prominent examples are the 1997 Directive on the Burden of Proof in Cases of Discrimination Based on Sex (§8 paras. 58–62) and the 1998 revision of the Transfer of Undertakings Directive (§24 para. 7).[89]

56. The Court of Justice is sometimes reproached for inadequately taking the specificities of national law into account. While this may be true in some cases, the Court of Justice is not solely to blame. In a dialogue with the ECJ, it is the national courts' responsibility to explain potential systematic or practical problems which may arise from one interpretation or another.[90] By the same token, it is for the Member States to contribute to the proceedings through their own statements (Article 23 ECJ Statute). National courts and Member States often avail themselves of these instruments. The Court's jurisprudence on the employee's right to object to a transfer of his employment relationship can serve as an example (in detail §24 paras. 69–74): Here, the Court initially considered

---

NZA 2000, 1144–1147. More favourably recently A. Junker/O. Aldea, 'Augenmaß im Europäischen Arbeitsrecht – Die Urteile Adeneler und Navas', *EuZW* 2007, 13–17.

[86]   N. Colneric, *EuZA* 2008, 212, 215 sq.

[87]   Justifiying the decision e.g. N. Colneric, *EuZA* 2008, 212, 223–227.

[88]   C. Joerges/F. Rödl, *ELJ* 15 (2009), 1–19 (criticizing a '*de facto* decoupling of the social from the economic constitution' with a view to the limitation to Union legislative competences in Article 153(5) TFEU and suggesting a constitutional 'conflict of laws'); more favourably K. Lenaerts/J. A. Gutiérrez-Fons, *CMLR* 47 (2010), 1629, 1664 sqq.

[89]   Cf. also N. Colneric, *EuZA* 2008, 212, 213–215.

[90]   With a similar approach D. Kaiser, *NZA* 2000, 1144, 1150 sq.

such a right to be incompatible with the Transfer of Undertakings Directive, but later accepted it upon repeated requests for preliminary rulings from German courts.

2. The Jurisprudence of Member States' Courts

57. The Member States' Courts, too, contribute to the on-going development of EU employment law. This is inherent in the mechanism of preliminary rulings (Article 267 TFEU) which institutes a 'dialogue' of national courts and the Court of Justice. However, it is only since the mid-1980s that national courts (and scholars) begun to systematically take EU legislation into account, and even then, the requests for preliminary rulings were often rather selective.[91] The number of references to the Court of Justice has since increased substantially, especially in the area of employment law. There are cases where organisations or private individuals attempt to use EU law as an instrument to pursue political goals, e.g. by instituting or supporting test-cases.[92] Sometimes lower-level national Courts use preliminary references as a lever to overcome established national jurisprudence.[93] Indeed, there have been cases where the highest national court appeared to try to evade the requirements of EU law. In Germany, this has arguably been the case with respect to the Collective Redundancies Directive[94] which was ultimately properly implemented after the Court's decision in the *Junk*-case.[95] On the other hand, it may sometimes be a requirement of judicial restraint that courts first hold back and wait to see how the case law develops until a case which is suitable for reference to the Court of Justice comes up.

58. The obligation under EU law to interpret national law in conformity with the requirements of EU directives (paras. 73 sq. below) implies an obligation upon the national courts to take EU employment law into account in their everyday practice. This obligation has frequently been neglected in the past, but has been broadly discussed in recent years and nowadays seems to be widely adhered to.

---

[91] W. Däubler, in L. Krämer/H.-W. Micklitz/K. Tonner (eds.), *Liber amicorum Reich,* 447.

[92] See the example of ECJ Case C-144/04 *Mangold* [2005] ECR I-9981 and, on the background of the case, J.-H. Bauer/C. Arnold, 'Auf "Junk" folgt "Mangold" – Europarecht verdrängt deutsches Arbeitsrecht', *NJW* 2006, 6 sq. See also B. Hepple/A. Byre, *ILJ* 18 (1989), 129 sqq. ('test case strategy').

[93] Critically (but, in the light of judicial independence, rather misguided) M. Heinze, *ZfA* 1992, 331, 352 sq. ('In particular, it is to be observed with regard to the German labour courts that it seems to have become fashionable in the lower instances to oust German employment law with the tool of EC law and to refer issues of national employment law to the Court of Justice.' – my translation); similarly critically D. Kaiser, *NZA* 2000, 1144.

[94] On the case law of the *Bundesarbeitsgericht* (Federal Labour Court, BAG), see the references in K. Riesenhuber, Case Note, *AP* §17 KSchG 1969 No. 21.

[95] ECJ Case C-188/03 *Junk* [2005] ECR I-885.

V. THE INTERPLAY OF EUROPEAN AND MEMBER STATES' LAW AND ISSUES OF METHODS[96]

Bibliography:

J. Basedow, 'Anforderungen an eine europäische Zivilrechtsdogmatik', in R. Zimmermann (ed.), *Rechtsgeschichte und Privatrechtsdogmatik* (Heidelberg: C.F. Müller, 2000), 79–100; J. Bengoetxea, *The Legal Reasoning of the European Court of Justice: Towards a European Jurisprudence* (Oxford: Oxford University Press, 1993); C.-W. Canaris, 'Die richtlinienkonforme Auslegung und Rechtsfortbildung im System der juristischen Methodenlehre', in H. Koziol/P. Rummel (eds.), *Im Dienste der Gerechtigkeit – Festschrift für Franz Bydlinski* (Vienna/New York: Springer, 2002), 47–103; C.-W. Canaris, 'Gemeinsamkeiten zwischen verfassungs- und richtlinienkonformer Rechtsfindung', in H. Bauer et al. (eds.), *Wirtschaft im offenen Verfassungsstaat – Festschrift für Reiner Schmidt zum 70. Geburtstag* (Munich: C.H. Beck, 2006), 41–60; N. Colneric, 'Die Rolle des EuGH bei der Fortentwicklung des Arbeitsrechts', *EuZA* 2008, 212–227; M. Franzen, *Privatrechtsangleichung durch die Europäische Gemeinschaft* (Berlin/New York: de Gruyter, 1999); S. Grundmann, 'Richtlinienkonforme Auslegung im Bereich des Privatrechts – insbesondere – der Kanon der nationalen Auslegungsmethoden als Grenze?', *ZEuP* 1996, 399–424; S. Grundmann/K. Riesenhuber, 'Die Auslegung des Europäischen Privat- und Schuldvertragsrechts', *JuS* 2001, 529–536; B. Hepple/A. Byre, 'EEC Labour Law in the United Kingdom – A New Approach', *ILJ* 18 (1989), 129–143; C. Herresthal, *Rechtsfortbildung im europarechtlichen Bezugsrahmen – Methoden, Kompetenzen, Grenzen – Dargestellt am Beispiel des Privatrechts* (Munich: C.H. Beck, 2006); C. Hofmann, 'Die Vorwirkung von Richtlinien', in K. Riesenhuber (ed.), *Europäische Methodenlehre – Handbuch für Ausbildung und Praxis*, 2nd edn. (Berlin: de Gruyter, 2010), §16; C. Höpfner, *Die systemkonforme Auslegung – Zur Auflösung einfachgesetzlicher, verfassungsrechtlicher und europarechtlicher Widersprüche im Recht* (Tübingen: Mohr Siebeck, 2008); C. Höpfner/B. Rüthers, 'Grundlagen einer europäischen Methodenlehre', *AcP* 209 (2009), 1–36; J. Joussen, *Die Auslegung europäischen (Arbeits-)Rechts aus deutsch-italienischer Perspektive* (Baden-Baden: Nomos, 2000); J. Kokott, 'Auslegung europäischen oder Anwendung nationalen Rechts? – Grundsätze und Kriterien für die Behandlung arbeitsrechtlicher Streitigkeiten mit europarechtlichem Bezug', *RdA* 2006 Special Supplement to Issue 6, 30–37; H. Konzen, 'Die Wirkung von Richtlinien in der neueren arbeitsrechtlichen Judikatur des EuGH', in H. Konzen et al. (eds.), *Festschrift für Rolf Birk zum siebzigsten Geburtstag* (Tübingen: Mohr Siebeck, 2008), 439–458; B. Kreft, 'Die Auslegung europäischen oder die Anwendung nationalen Rechts – Grundsätze und Kriterien für die Behandlung arbeitsrechtlicher Streitigkeiten mit europarechtlichem Bezug', *RdA* 2006 Special Supplement to Issue 6, 38–45; K. Langenbucher, 'Europarechtliche Methodenlehre', in ead. (ed.), *Europarechtliche Bezüge des Privatrechts*, 2nd edn. (Baden-Baden: Nomos, 2008), §1; M. Lutter, 'Die Auslegung des angeglichenen Rechts', *JZ* 1992, 593–607; J. Neuner, 'Die Rechtsfortbildung', in K. Riesenhuber (ed.), *Europäische Methodenlehre – Handbuch für Ausbildung und Praxis*, 2nd edn. (Berlin: de Gruyter, 2010), §13; J. Neuner,

---

[96] Issues of methods can only be discussed here to the extent necessary for the subsequent exposition of EU employment law.

'Die Vorwirkung von Gesetzen im Privatrecht', in J. Hager et al. (eds.), *Kontinuität im Wandel der Rechtsordnung – Beiträge für Claus-Wilhelm Canaris zum 65. Geburtstag* (Munich: C.H. Beck, 2002), 83–112; J. Neuner, *Die Rechtsfindung contra legem*, 2ⁿᵈ edn. (Munich: C.H. Beck, 2006); M. Pechstein/C. Drechsler, 'Die Auslegung und Fortbildung des Primärrechts', in K. Riesenhuber (ed.), *Europäische Methodenlehre – Handbuch für Ausbildung und Praxis*, 2ⁿᵈ edn. (Berlin: de Gruyter, 2010), §8; R. Rebhahn, 'Europäisches Arbeitsrecht', in K. Riesenhuber (ed.), *Europäische Methodenlehre – Handbuch für Ausbildung und Praxis*, 2ⁿᵈ edn. (Berlin: de Gruyter, 2010), §18; K. Riesenhuber, 'Die Auslegung', in id. (ed.), *Europäische Methodenlehre – Handbuch für Ausbildung und Praxis*, 2ⁿᵈ edn. (Berlin: de Gruyter, 2010), §11; K. Riesenhuber, 'Diskriminierungsverbote im Privatrecht: Europarechtliche Grundlagen', in id. (ed.), *Das Allgemeine Gleichbehandlungsgesetz – Grundsatz- und Praxisfragen* (Berlin: de Gruyter, 2007), 3–36; K. Riesenhuber (ed.), *Europäische Methodenlehre – Handbuch für Ausbildung und Praxis*, 2ⁿᵈ edn. (Berlin: de Gruyter, 2010); K. Riesenhuber/R. Domröse, 'Richtlinienkonforme Rechtsfindung und nationale Methodenlehre – Zugleich eine Besprechung von EuGH, Urt. v. 5.10.2004 – verb. Rs. C-397/01 bis C-403/01 Pfeiffer u.a.', *RIW* 2005, 47–54; K. Riesenhuber/R. Domröse, 'Richtlinienkonforme Auslegung der §§17, 18 KSchG und Rechtsfolgen fehlerhafter Massenentlassungen', *NZA* 2005, 568–570; F. Rosenkranz, 'Die völkerrechtskonforme Auslegung des EG-Sekundärrechts dargestellt am Beispiel des Urheberrechts – Zugleich eine Besprechung von EuGH, Urt. v. 7.12.2006 – C-306/05', *EuZW* 2007, 238–242; W.-H. Roth, 'Die richtlinienkonforme Auslegung', in K. Riesenhuber (ed.), *Europäische Methodenlehre – Handbuch für Ausbildung und Praxis*, 2ⁿᵈ edn. (Berlin: de Gruyter, 2010), §14; A. Röthel, 'Die Konkretisierung von Generalklauseln', in K. Riesenhuber (ed.), *Europäische Methodenlehre – Handbuch für Ausbildung und Praxis*, 2ⁿᵈ edn. (Berlin: de Gruyter, 2010), §12; A. Röthel, 'Vorwirkung von Richtlinien: viel Lärm um Selbstverständliches', *ZEuP* 2009, 34–55; M. Schlachter, 'Methoden der Rechtsgewinnung zwischen EuGH und der Arbeitsgerichtsbarkeit', *ZfA* 2007, 249–275; M. Schlachter, 'Richtlinienkonforme Rechtsfindung – ein neues Stadium im Kooperationsverhältnis zwischen EuGH und den nationalen Gerichten', *RdA* 2005, 115–120; A. Schwartze, 'Die Rechtsvergleichung', in K. Riesenhuber (ed.), *Europäische Methodenlehre – Handbuch für Ausbildung und Praxis*, 2ⁿᵈ edn. (Berlin: de Gruyter, 2010), §4; G. Thüsing, 'Richtlinienkonforme Auslegung und unmittelbare Geltung von EG-Richtlinien im Anti-Diskriminierungsrecht', *NJW* 2003, 3441–3445; S. Vogenauer, *Die Auslegung von Gesetzen in England und auf dem Kontinent – Eine vergleichende Untersuchung der Rechtsprechung und ihrer historischen Grundlagen*, vol. I and II (Tübingen: Mohr Siebeck, 2001) (on the interpretation of EC law, see especially vol. I, chapter 3); S. Vogenauer, 'Gemeineuropäische Methodenlehre – Plädoyer und Programm', *ZEuP* 2005, 234–263; K. Walter, *Rechtsfortbildung durch den EuGH – Eine rechtsmethodische Untersuchung ausgehend von der deutschen und französischen Methodenlehre* (Berlin: Duncker & Humblot, 2009).

Case Law:
ECJ Case 26/62 *van Gend & Loos* [1963] ECR 3; ECJ Case 33/76 *Rewe Zentralfinanz* [1976] ECR 1989; ECJ Case 45/76 *Comet* [1976] ECR 2043; ECJ Case 14/83 *v. Colson und Kamann* [1984] ECR 1894; ECJ Case 222/84 *Johnston* [1986] ECR 1651; ECJ Case 80/86 *Kolpinghuis Nijmegen* [1987] ECR 3969; ECJ Case 68/88 *Kommission* v. *Griechenland*

[1989] ECR 2965; ECJ Case C-106/89 *Marleasing* [1990] ECR I-4135; ECJ Joined Cases C-6/90 to C-9/90 *Francovich u.a.* [1991] ECR I-5357; ECJ Case C-382/92 *Kommission* v. *Vereinigtes Königreich* [1994] ECR I-2435; ECJ Case C-91/92 *Faccini Dori* [1994] ECR I-3325; ECJ Case C-479/93 *Francovich* [1995] ECR I-3843; ECJ Joined Cases C-46/93 to C-48/93 *Brasserie du pêcheur, Factortame* [1996] ECR I-1029; ECJ Case C-192/94 *El Corte Inglés* [1996] ECR I-1281; ECJ Case C-392/93 *British Telecommunications* [1996] ECR I-1631; ECJ Case C-5/94 *Hedley Lomas* [1996] ECR I-2553; ECJ Case C-168/95 *Arcaro* [1996] ECR I-4705; ECJ Joined Cases C-178/94 and C-179/94, C-188/94 to C-190/94 *Dillenkofer u.a.* [1996] ECR I-4845; ECJ Case C-180/95 *Draehmpaehl* [1997] ECR 2195; ECJ Case C-261/96 *Palmisani* [1997] ECR I-4025; ECJ Case C-253 to 258/96 *Kampelmann* [1997] ECR I-6907; ECJ Case C-129/96 *Inter-Environnement Wallonie* [1997] ECR I-7411; ECJ Case C-127/95 *Norbrook Laboratories* [1998] ECR I-1531; ECJ Case C-326/96 *Levez* [1998] ECR I-7835; ECJ Case C-78/98 *Preston* [2000] ECR I- 3201; ECJ Case C-424/97 *Haim* [2000] ECR I-5123; ECJ Case C-443/98 *Unilever*[2000] ECR I-7535; ECJ Case C-473/00 *Cofidis* [2002] ECR I-10875; ECJ Case C-224/01 *Köbler* [2003] ECR I-10239; ECJ Joined Cases C-397/01 to C-403/01 *Pfeiffer* [2004] ECR I-8835; ECJ Case C-297/03 *Sozialhilfeverband Rohrbach* [2005] ECR I-4305; ECJ Case C-144/04 *Mangold* [2005] ECR I-9981; ECJ Case C-173/03 *Traghetti* [2006] ECR I-5177; ECJ Case C-212/04 *Adeneler* [2006] ECR I-6057; ECJ Case C-268/06 *Impact* [2008] ECR I-2483.

59. EU private law raises a number of methodological questions. These cannot be discussed in full detail here. The main issues will instead be addressed briefly to the extent necessary for the purposes of the present volume. Further details can be found in the treatises on methods of EU law.[97]

1. Interpretation and Judicial Development of the Law

60. The interpretation of EU employment law[98] largely follows the same methods which apply to the interpretation of national statutes. Yet, interpretation of EU law also raises a number of specific issues. The first question is whether a term that requires interpretation is to be construed autonomously for EU law or whether it refers to national law.[99] The Court of Justice usually starts from a presumption that the terms used in EU law require an autonomous EU interpretation. An important exception applies with regard to the term 'worker' which – explicitly or implicitly – often refers to the national law of the Member States (see para. 2 above).

---

[97]   M. Franzen, *Privatrechtsangleichung durch die Europäische Gemeinschaft*; K. Langenbucher, in id. (ed.), *Europarechtliche Bezüge des Privatrechts*, §1; K. Riesenhuber (ed.), *Europäische Methodenlehre*.

[98]   The following discussion mainly relates to secondary legislation. On methods of EU primary law, see in more detail M. Pechstein/C. Drechsler, in K. Riesenhuber (ed.), *Europäische Methodenlehre*, §8.

[99]   K. Riesenhuber, in id. (ed.), *Europäische Methodenlehre*, §11 paras. 4–8; see also R. Käppler, in H.-W. Rengeling (ed.), *Europäisierung des Rechts*, 145 sq.

61.   Where a term is to be construed autonomously for EU law, interpretation starts with the wording. It must be kept in mind however, that EU law is being enacted in various **language versions** and that all language versions of EU legislation are equally authentic. On the one hand, this presents an opportunity to confirm an interpretation by reference to another language version. On the other however, other language versions are more likely to raise doubt.

> The **working languages** of the EU – French, English and German – are sometimes considered to be of special importance. In the original 'Community of Six', there was some preponderance of French which remains the working language at the Court of Justice even today. With the accession of England and the subsequent enlargements, the English language has gained certain dominance. These empirical considerations do not, however, warrant methodological conclusions.

62.   Where discrepancies in the different language versions raise doubt, the **legislative materials**, in particular the reasons advanced in the Commission proposal, can often assist interpretation. The Court of Justice, however, attaches decisive weight to the **rationale** of a rule[100] and sometimes 'reinforces' it with the notion of the *effet utile*.

63.   The Court of Justice has often one-sidedly stressed the rationale of employee protection. As a consequence, EU employment law is sometimes criticised as being '**one-dimensional**', taking only employee interests into account and disregarding employer interests.[101] EU employment law as such is, of course, by no means one-dimensional. First, EU legislation cannot be considered in isolation, but only as an (often specific) supplementation of the national employment laws of the Member States. In many instances, national law contains the principle and EU legislation merely provides for an exception. This is why, secondly, the scope of application deserves special attention. As a minimum, the limitations to the scope of application of any employee-protection norm are an expression of countervailing considerations. And finally, the stock of existing EU legislation in the area of employment law increasingly reveals unifying structures and can be conceived of as a system (paras. 43 sq. above), thus allowing courts to interpret it systematically.

---

[100]   K. Riesenhuber, in id. (ed.), *Europäische Methodenlehre*, §11 paras. 40–46; J. Joussen, *Die Auslegung europäischen (Arbeits-)Rechts*, 115–131 *et passim* ('primate of the teleological criterion of interpretation' – my translation).

[101]   M. Franzen, *Privatrechtsangleichung durch die Europäische Gemeinschaft*, 461–465; approvingly A. Junker, *NZA* 1999, 2, 10; D. Kaiser, *NZA* 2000, 1144, 1147. The term 'one-dimensionality' has been coined by F. Schoch, 'Die Europäisierung des Allgemeinen Verwaltungsrechts', *JZ* 1995, 109, 117 sq.

64. As in national law, the **development of the law** is a widely recognised task of the courts beyond interpretation.[102] Principal methodological tools are the analogy and the *teleological reduction,* i.e. the process of restricting a broadly phrased provision in accordance with its purpose. An increasingly broad and dense set of norms provides a sound basis for a systematic-teleological development of the law. Again, we must keep in mind, though, that EU law does not stand on its own, but has to be considered in the context with, and as a complement to, the national law of the Member States. As a consequence, where EU law proves to lack a rule (i.e. there is a *lacuna*), an initial question is whether there is an internal gap in EU law – that requires to be filled on the level of EU law – or whether, from the perspective of EU law, there is an *external* gap that is left for the Member States to fill.[103]

2. Unspecified Sanctions, in Particular in Directives

65. A peculiarity of EU private law is that it will often merely provide for rights or obligations but not for the legal consequences (sanctions) for non-performance or violation. This is particularly the case where directives are concerned, but is also true beyond directives. Such lack of specification should by no means be criticised. On the contrary, it satisfies the requirement of legislative restraint and caution. Determination of the legal consequences is particularly important for a smooth implementation of EU directives into national law. However, where EU law does not specifically define the legal consequences, this does not mean that the Member States are completely free in exercising their discretion. Article 288(3) TFEU imposes a duty of implementation upon the Member States and this implies an obligation to enforce rights and obligations of EU law effectively.[104]

66. The Court of Justice has concretised these obligations with the principle of equivalence and the principle of effectiveness. Pursuant to the **principle of equivalence,** 'Member States must ensure that infringements of Community law are penalised under conditions, both procedural and substantive, which are analogous ['equivalent'; K.R.] to those applicable to infringements of domestic

---

[102] *Bundesverfassungsgericht* (Federal Constitutional Court, BVerfG), *BVerfGE* 89, 155, 209 – Maastricht; *BVerfGE* 75, 223, 242; ECJ, Opinion 1/91 [1991] ECR I-6079 para. 50 – European Economic Area. M. Franzen, *Privatrechtsangleichung durch die Europäische Gemeinschaft,* 575–637; J. Neuner, in K. Riesenhuber (ed.), *Europäische Methodenlehre,* §13; K. Riesenhuber, *System und Prinzipien des Europäischen Privatrechts* (Berlin: de Gruyter, 2003), 29 sq., 65–73.
[103] M. Franzen, *Privatrechtsangleichung durch die Europäische Gemeinschaft,* 605 sq.
[104] See the seminal decision in ECJ Case 14/83 *von Colson und Kamann* [1984] ECR 1891; recently Case C-268/06 *Impact* [2008] ECR I-2483 paras. 39–55; Case C-484/04 *Commission* v. *United Kingdom* [2006] ECR I-7471 paras. 32 sqq.; Case C-246/09 *Bulicke* [2010] ECR I-7003 paras. 22–42.

law of a similar nature and importance'.[105] This principle allows Member States to implement EU norms into their national law in a system-compatible (coherent) way. This will also usually suffice to ensure an effective implementation; EU law trusts that the Member States' laws will work effectively. Furthermore, coherent implementation of EU law is presumed to make the respective rights transparent to the citizens. Following the **principle of effectiveness** Member States must ensure that infringements of EU law are sanctioned under conditions which make the sanction effective, proportionate and dissuasive. They must not be so framed as to make enforcement of EU rights and obligations virtually impossible or excessively difficult.[106] The principle of effectiveness encompasses legal certainty, given that uncertainty may be liable to compromise the effective enforcement of the law.[107] The principle of effectiveness thus supplements the relative measure (relative to 'equivalent' rights and obligations of national origin) by an absolute standard.

3. EU Employment Law and Member States 'Employment Law'

a) The Effect of Primary Law

67. Following the established jurisprudence of the Court of Justice, the fundamental freedoms are, since expiration of the transition period,[108] directly applicable rights for the enjoyment of citizens of the Member States.[109] Every individual can invoke the fundamental freedoms before Member States courts. It is a matter of controversy, though, whether the fundamental freedoms also have horizontal direct effect between private individuals. The Court has accepted horizontal direct effect with regard to the free movement of workers (§3 paras. 28–30).

---

105 ECJ Case C-177/10 *Rosado Santana* 8 September 2011 paras. 89 sqq.; Case C-63/08 *Pontin* [2009] ECR I-10467 paras. 43 sqq.; Case C-180/95 *Draehmpaehl* [1997] ECR I-2195 paras. 29–42; Joined Cases C-253 to 258/96 *Kampelmann* [1997] ECR I-6907 para. 33; Case C-382/92 *Commission* v. *United Kingdom* [1994] ECR I-2435 paras. 26, 55; Case 68/88 *Commission* v. *Greece* [1989] ECR 2965 para. 24; Case 33/76 *Rewe Zentralfinanz* [1976] ECR 1989 para. 5; Case 45/76 *Comet* [1976] ECR 2043 paras. 12 sq. The principle of equivalence does not only apply with regard to substantive rules but also with regard to procedural rules, ECJ Case 222/84 *Johnston* [1986] ECR 1651 paras. 18–20; Case C-261/96 *Palmisani* [1997] ECR I-4025 paras. 32 sq.; Case C-326/96 *Levez* [1998] ECR I-7835 para. 41. See also Case C-78/98 *Preston* [2000] ECR I-3201 paras. 46–63.

106 ECJ Case C-177/10 *Rosado Santana* 8 September 2011 paras. 92 sqq. Which measures are required by the principle of effectiveness is to be determined with regard to the purpose of the legislative act in question, cf. ECJ Case C-473/00 *Cofidis* [2002] ECR I-10875 paras. 32–36; ECJ Case C-382/92 *Commission* v. *United Kingdom* [1994] ECR I-2435 paras. 26, 55.

107 ECJ Case C-69/08 *Raffaelo Visciano* [2009] ECR I-6741 paras. 46–50.

108 Article 8(1) of the EEC Treaty entering into force on 1 January 1958 provided for a transitional period of twelve years.

109 See the seminal decision of ECJ Case 26/62 *van Gend & Loos* [1963] ECR 3, paras 24–27.

68. The principle of equal pay in Article 157 TFEU has also been recognised by the Court of Justice as directly applicable. This means that an individual employee can directly invoke the provision in relation to his employer (in detail §9 paras. 3 sq.). Beyond that, the Court of Justice established the prohibition of age discrimination as a general principle of primary law in its *Mangold*-decision[110] and considered it to be directly applicable between private individuals (§11 para. 50).

b) The Effect of Secondary Legislation: Directives

69. The effect of regulations (Article 288(2) TFEU) is fairly straightforward. They are, as has already been discussed (para. 21 above), binding in their entirety and directly applicable in all Member States, in a manner which is comparable to a national statute. A number of peculiarities of directives as an instrument of a two-step legislative procedure deserve closer attention.

aa) THE DUTY TO IMPLEMENT IN PARTICULAR

70. 'Binding as to [their] result' (see Article 288(3) TFEU), directives requires implementation into the national laws of the Member States. In order for the Member States to accomplish the necessary implementation, directives provides for a specific implementation period. Before the expiry of this implementation period, the directive does not, in principle, have any effect. However, even before expiry of the implementation period, Member States must not do anything that could defeat or frustrate the objectives of the directive.[111] In this sense, directives can have certain legal effects for the Member States both after their entry into force and before expiry of the implementation period.[112]

bb) DIRECT APPLICABILITY

71. Addressed to the Member States who are free to choose the form and method of implementation, directives are not designed to be directly applicable. Yet, where a Member State does not (timely or entirely) fulfil its duty to implement a directive and the purpose of the directive is to create rights against such Member State, it would not seem right to allow the Member State in default to invoke the lack of implementation in its defence. The Court of Justice has thus recognised the direct applicability of directives in such cases, provided that its

---

[110] ECJ Case C-144/04 *Mangold* [2005] ECR I-9981.
[111] ECJ Case C-129/96 *Inter-Environnement Wallonie* [1997] ECR I-7411; Case C-144/04 *Mangold* [2005] ECR I-9981; Case C-212/04 *Adeneler* [2006] ECR I-6057; M. Franzen, *JZ* 2007, 191, 192.
[112] In more detail C. Hofmann, in K. Riesenhuber (ed.), *Europäische Methodenlehre*, §16; J. Neuner, *Festschrift für Canaris*, 105–112.

provisions are 'unconditional and sufficiently precise'.[113] This can be understood as a case of estoppel.

72. A directive cannot, however, have direct effect **against private individuals**: it 'cannot of itself impose obligations on an individual and cannot therefore be relied upon as such against an individual'. A directive cannot, thus, be relied upon between private individuals ('horizontal direct effect'). By the same token, the directive cannot be relied upon against a private individual in the vertical relation between Member State and individual.[114] This latter consideration also applies where the private individual himself relies upon the (improperly implemented) directive against the Member State.[115] It is only with regard to directives that do not grant rights or impose obligations on individuals, and that therefore do not require implementation, that the ECJ has recognised an indirect horizontal effect which places a burden upon private individuals.[116]

cc) The Principle of Interpretation in Conformity with EU Law

73. The direct application of a directive against a Member State (para. 71 above) presupposes that the binding force on the 'Member State' comprises all public authority, including not only the legislature but also the executive. The judiciary, too, is part of the Member States' powers and is as such addressed by the directive and bound by the implementation duties.[117] 'It follows that, in applying the national law and in particular the provisions of a national law specifically introduced in order to implement [a] directive, national courts are required to interpret their national law in the light of the wording and the purpose of the directive in order to achieve the result referred to in

---

113 See recently ECJ Case C-243/09 *Fuß* 14 October 2010 paras. 56 sqq.; Joined Cases C-250/09 and C-268/09 *Georgiev* 18 November 2010 paras. 69 sqq.; Case C-268/06 *Impact* [2008] ECR I-2483 paras. 57–80. For details, see M. Ruffert, in C. Calliess/M. Ruffert, *EUV/AEUV*, Art. 288 AEUV paras. 47–76.

114 On the effects in horizontal relationships, see ECJ Case C-227/09 *Accardo* 21 October 2010 paras. 45 sq.; Joined Cases C-397/01 to C-403/01 *Pfeiffer* [2004] ECR I-8835 paras. 108 sq.; Case C-168/95 *Arcaro* [1996] ECR I-4705 para. 36; Case C-192/94 *El Corte Inglés* [1996] ECR I-1281 para. 16; Case C-91/92 *Faccini Dori* [1994] ECR I-3325 para. 20; contrary to the assessment of some observers the controversial decision in ECJ Case C-144/04 *Mangold* [2005] ECR I-9981 does not depart from these established principles; there the Court bases the 'direct effect' on the general principle against age discrimination (see para. 68 above) rather than on the directive; for a critique, see §11 paras. 47–50 below. On burdening effects in the vertical relation, see ECJ Case 80/86 *Kolpinghuis Nijmegen* [1987] ECR 3969.

115 ECJ Case C-297/03 *Sozialhilfeverband Rohrbach* [2005] ECR I-4305.

116 ECJ Case C-443/98 *Unilever* [2000] ECR I-7535.

117 ECJ Case 14/83 *von Colson und Kamann* [1984] ECR 1891 para. 26 (article-numbering adapted to the Amsterdam Treaty). See also ECJ Joined Cases C-397 to C-403/01 *Pfeiffer* [2004] ECR I-8835 para. 110.

[Article 288(3) TFEU]'.[118] – There is, in other words, a duty placed upon national courts to interpret and develop national law in conformity with EU directives.[119] This duty not only applies where obligations of the Member States are concerned, but also in disputes between private individuals (horizontal relationships).

74. While the principle is widely accepted, its **limits** are rather controversial.[120] The Court hints at the issue when it states that the national court has to interpret national law in light of the wording and purpose of the directive *'as far as possible'*. On the one hand, this indicates that the goal of effectively implementing directives is a high priority. On the other hand, the Court refers to the limits of what is 'possible' which, for every national court, are imposed by national law, particularly constitutional law, and the prevailing legal methodology.[121] The obligation to interpret national law in conformity with Union law 'is limited by the general principles of law, particularly those of legal certainty and non-retroactivity, and that obligation cannot serve as the basis for an interpretation of national law *contra legem*'.[122] Whether or not the principle of interpretation in conformity with EU law may, in the individual case, lead to an interpretation *contra legem* is thus a matter for the national laws of the Member States to determine. Where national law and methods do not prohibit an interpretation or judicial development of the law as such, it thus cannot prohibit the same possibility where EU law is concerned.[123] In Germany, for example, 'the executive and the judiciary by law and justice' (*Gesetz und Recht*), Article 20(3) Basic Law (*Grundgesetz*) and the directive, while not 'law' in this sense, certainly

---

[118] ECJ Case 14/83 *von Colson und Kamann* [1984] ECR 1891 para. 26; Case C-106/89 *Marleasing* [1990] ECR I-4135 para. 8; ECJ Joined Cases C-397 to C-403/01 *Pfeiffer* [2004] ECR I-8835 para. 113; Case C-268/06 *Impact* [2008] I-2483 paras. 93–104; Case C-12/08 *Mono Car Styling* [2009] ECR I-6653 paras. 59–64; ECJ Case C-109/09 *Deutsche Lufthansa* 11 March 2011 paras. 52–56. There cannot, of course, be an obligation to interpret the national law in conformity with *optional* derogations where the Member State has not availed itself of the option in the first place; ECJ Case C-227/09 *Accardo* 21 October 2010 paras. 49 sqq.

[119] W.-H. Roth, in K. Riesenhuber (ed.), *Europäische Methodenlehre*, §14 para. 11; see also ECJ Case C-212/04 *Adeneler* [2006] ECR I-6057 para. 115 (in regard of delayed implementation).

[120] Apart from limitations from the national laws of the Member States, there are also limitations resulting from EU law, in particular from Union Fundamental Rights (ECJ Joined Cases C-387/02, C-391/02 and C-403/02 *Berlusconi* [2005] ECR I-3565 paras. 66–69), the principle of legal certainty (ECJ Case C-144/99 *Commission* v. *Kingdom of the Netherlands* [2001] ECR I-3541), the prohibition of retroactive effect (ECJ Case 80/86 *Kolpinghuis Nijmegen* [1987] ECR 3969 para. 13) and the principle of protection of legitimate expectations (ECJ Case C-128/93 *Fisscher* [1994] ECR I-4583 para. 18; ECJ Case C-481/99 *Heininger* [2001] ECR I-9945 para. 52).

[121] On the *contra legem*-limitation most recently ECJ Case C-212/04 *Adeneler* [2006] ECR I-6057 para. 110; ECJ Case C-268/06 *Impact* [2008] ECR I-2483 paras. 98–100.

[122] ECJ Case C-12/08 *Mono Car Styling* [2009] ECR I-6653 para. 61.

[123] J. Neuner, *Die Rechtsfindung contra legem*, 139–197.

forms part of what is described as 'justice' (*Recht*) within the meaning of that article.[124] The possibility of an interpretation or development of the law *contra legem* thus cannot be excluded *a priori*.[125]

dd) LIABILITY OF THE MEMBER STATES

75. Irrespective of the possibility of direct application of a directive and irrespective of the principle of interpretation in conformity with EU law, there are cases where the Member States do not properly fulfil the requirements of directives. Where a directive is intended to establish rights for individuals, the question arises whether the Member States are liable to the protected persons for a failure to fully implement a directive. State liability is, of course, not restricted to such cases of inadequate implementation of directives, yet it is of considerable practical importance here. Notably, the Court has developed its jurisprudence on EU law state liability in employment cases, namely in the *Francovich*-decisions[126] on the deficient implementation of the Insolvency Protection Directive into Italian law (in detail §25 para. 32 below). Based on (what is now) Article 4(3) TEU and on the principle of *effet utile*, it has recognised a specific state liability of the Member States which it held to be 'inherent to the system of the Treaty'.[127]

76. Prerequisites of such state liability are: '[1] the rule of law infringed must be intended to confer rights on individuals; [2] the breach must be sufficiently serious; and [3] there must be a direct causal link between the breach of the obligation incumbent on the State and the loss or damage sustained by the injured parties.[128] While the Member States may provide for liability under less restrictive conditions, they may not impose additional requirements such as

---

[124] W.-H. Roth, in K. Riesenhuber (ed.), *Europäische Methodenlehre,* §14 paras. 47 sq.

[125] S. Grundmann, *ZEuP* 1996, 399, 412–424; K. Riesenhuber/R. Domröse, *RIW* 2005, 47, 51 sq.; W.-H. Roth, in K. Riesenhuber (ed.), *Europäische Methodenlehre,* §14; apparently also M. Schlachter, *ZfA* 2007, 249, 259–261. More cautiously C.-W. Canaris, *Festschrift für Schmidt,* 41, 58; H. Konzen, *Festschrift für Birk,* 452 sq.

[126] ECJ Joined Cases C-6/90 to C-9/90 *Francovich* [1991] ECR I-5357; ECJ Case C-479/93 *Francovich* [1995] ECR I-3843.

[127] On the further development of the law of state liability see ECJ Joined Cases C-46/93 to C-48/93 *Brasserie du pêcheur, Factortame* [1996] ECR I-1029; ECJ Case C-392/93 *British Telecommunications* [1996] ECR I-1631; ECJ Case C-5/94 *Hedley Lomas* [1996] ECR I-2553; ECJ Joined Cases C-178/94 and C-179/94, C-188/94 to C-190/94 *Dillenkofer* [1996] ECR I-4845; ECJ Case C-127/95 *Norbrook Laboratories* [1998] ECR I-1531; ECJ Case C-424/97 *Haim* [2000] ECR I-5123; ECJ Case C-224/01 *Köbler* [2003] ECR I-10239; ECJ Case C-63/01 *Evans* [2003] ECR I-1447; ECJ Case C-173/03 *Traghetti* [2006] ECR I-5177; ECJ Case C-278/05 *Robins* [2007] ECR I-1053; ECJ Case C-470/03 *A.G.M.-COS.MET* [2007] ECR I-2749.

[128] ECJ Case C-224/01 *Köbler* [2003] ECR I-10239 para. 51; Case C-429/09 25 November 2010 paras. 47 sqq.

---

fault.[129] The procedural requirements for a claim for state liability are, in the absence of provisions of EU law, for the Member States to determine. They must however respect the principles of equivalence and effectiveness (see paras. 66 above).[130] The Member States also determine the remedies which, again, have to be designed so as to ensure effective protection of rights. Where an individual has suffered loss or damage as a result of a breach of EU law, reparation must be commensurate to the loss or damage sustained.[131]

77.   The provisions of a directive are violated where the Member State has not implemented its requirements fully and correctly or where implementation was delayed. However, failures by courts or the administration to fulfil their obligation to interpret and develop national law in conformity with the directive (para. 73), also constitute breaches of this implementation obligation. With regard to the implementation of directives, the requirement of a sufficiently serious breach (above, [2]) has proven to be a considerable obstacle to claimants obtaining relief in practice: National courts must take a number of factors into account, in particular the degree of clarity and precision of the rule infringed, the degree of discretion left to the Member States, whether the infringement was intentional, whether the error of law was excusable or inexcusable, and whether prior action by EU organs induced the breach. Given that directives are binding only as to their results, the Member States often have some discretion for implementation. Directives sometimes provide for different options for example. Where actions of courts are concerned, a violation of EU law will only be regarded as sufficiently serious where the decision is manifestly irreconcilable with the requirements of a directive such as, for example, where the national court manifestly ignored established case law of the Court of Justice.[132]

---

[129]   ECJ Case C-429/09 *Fuß II* 25 November 2010 paras. 65 sqq.
[130]   ECJ Case C-429/09 *Fuß II* 25 November 2010 paras. 72 sqq.
[131]   ECJ Case C-429/09 *Fuß II* 25 November 2010 paras. 92 sqq.; Joined Cases C-46/93 to C-48/93 *Brasserie du pêcheur, Factortame* [1996] ECR I-1029 para. 82.
[132]   ECJ Case C-224/01 *Köbler* [2003] ECR I-10239 para. 56; ECJ Case C-173/03 *Traghetti* [2006] ECR I-5177 paras. 35–45.

PART 1
FOUNDATIONS

§2. FUNDAMENTAL RIGHTS

CONTENTS

I. OVERVIEW AND DEMARCATION

Bibliography:

D. Ehlers (ed.), *Europäische Grundrechte und Grundfreiheiten*, 3rd edn. (Berlin/New York: de Gruyter, 2009); C. Grabenwarter, *Europäische Menschenrechtskonvention,* 4th edn. (Munich: C.H. Beck, 2009); S. Greer, *The European Convention on Human Rights – Achievements, Problems and Prospects* (Cambridge: Cambridge University Press, 2006); T. Lock, 'EU Accession to the ECHR: Implications for the Judicial Review in Strasbourg', *E.L. Rev.* 35 (2010), 777–798; J.P. Jacqué, 'The Accession of the European Union to the European Convention on Human Rigthts and Fundamental Freedoms', *CMLR* 48 (2011), 995–1023; A. Peters, *Einführung in die Europäische Menschenrechtskonvention* (Munich: C.H. Beck, 2003); R. Rebhahn, 'Urteile des EGMR zum Arbeitsrecht', in: H. Barta et al. (eds.), *Analyse und Fortentwicklung im Arbeits-, Sozial- und Zivilrecht – Festschrift für Martin Binder* (Vienna: Linde Verlag, 2010), 795–802; R. Rebhahn, 'Zivilrecht und Europäische Menschenrechtskonvention', *AcP* 210 (2010), 489–554; B. Schneiders, *Die Grundrechte der EU und der EMRK – Das Verhältnis zwischen ungeschriebenen Grundrechten, Grundrechtscharta und Europäischer Menschenrechtskonvention* (Baden-Baden: Nomos, 2010); P.A. Windel, 'Die Bedeutung der Europäischen Menschenrechtskonvention für das Privatrecht', *JR* 2011, 323–327.

1. Fundamental rights that are of relevance for employment law can today be found in various 'collections' at the EU level. However, for a long time, there was no binding catalogue of fundamental rights. The founding Treaties included the fundamental internal market freedoms and certain prohibitions of discrimination, but they did not include a fully-fledged set of fundamental rights. The fundamental rights which were developed by the Court of Justices in the form of 'general principles' of EU law (II. below) were not codified. The Community Charter of Fundamental Social Rights (CFSR) of 1989 is comprehensive, but is merely a 'solemn declaration' and therefore not binding (see IV. below). And the Charter of Fundamental Rights of the European Union (III. below) remained non-binding for some ten years after its proclamation in 2000 before it became part of EU primary law with the 2009 Lisbon Treaty.

2. The co-existence of no less than three sources of fundamental rights as binding law – the Treaties, the Court's jurisprudence on general principles and the Charter of Fundamental Rights – raises intricate questions about their interrelation. The picture becomes even more complicated if we take two other sets of fundamental rights into consideration, the EHCR and the ESC.[1]

3. Fundamental rights are also included in the Convention for the Protection of Human Rights and Fundamental Freedoms (European Convention on Human Rights, ECHR) of 4 November 1950[2] and the European Social Charter (ESC) of 18 October 1961.[3] Both instruments are international treaties drafted by the **Council of Europe**. The Council of Europe is an independent international organisation, which must be distinguished from the European Union.

4. The **European Convention on Human Rights**[4] **(ECHR)** creates fundamental rights of freedom and equality, fundamental rights with regard to judicial procedure as well as fundamental political rights. Of particular relevance for employment law are the prohibition of slavery and forced labour (Article 4 ECHR) the right to respect for private and family life (data protection) (Article 8 ECHR), freedom of expression (Article 10 ECHR), freedom of assembly and association (Article 11 ECHR), the prohibition of discrimination (Article 14 ECHR) as well as the right to individual property (Article 1 Protocol No.1 to the ECHR).[5] Economic rights, such as entrepreneurial freedom and freedom of occupation, are not specifically guaranteed but the right to form trade unions is covered by the general right of association. Rights to take industrial action can only be inferred from the freedom of association to a limited extent; the right to strike, in particular, is not guaranteed comprehensively.[6] The Convention

---

[1]   See J. Kokott/C. Sobotta, *EuGRZ* 2010, 265–271; B. Schneiders, *Die Grundrechte der EU und der EMRK* (2010).

[2]   The Text of the ECHR together with additional information of the Treaty Office of the European Council is available at http://conventions.coe.int/Treaty/Commun/ListeTraites. asp?CM=8&CL=ENG.

[3]   On 1 July 1999, the revised European Social Charter (RESC) entered into force; it incorporates an Additional Protocol of 1988 and modernises the text of the ESC. The text of the ESC and its protocols (including the revision) together with additional material is available at http://conventions.coe.int/Treaty/Commun/ListeTraites.asp?MA=4&CM=7&CL=ENG.

[4]   For an introduction, see the contributions of D. Ehlers/R. Uerpmann-Wittzack/T. Marauhn/B. Wegener/C. Grabenwarter, in D. Ehlers (ed.), *Europäische Grundrechte und Grundfreiheiten*, §§2–6; C. Grabenwarter, *Europäische Menschenrechtskonvention*, 4th edn. (2009); St. Greer, *The European Convention on Human Rights – Achievements, Problems and Prospects* (2006); A. Peters, *Einführung in die Europäische Menschenrechtskonvention* (2003). In general on the relation of the ECHR and private law, see R. Rebhahn, *AcP* 210 (2010), 489–554; P. A. Windel, *JR* 2011, 323–327.

[5]   R. Rebhahn, in: H. Barta/Th. Radner/L. Held/H.-Th. Scharnreitner (eds.), *Festschrift für Martin Binder*, 795–802.

[6]   A. Mair, 'Dimensionen der Koalitionsfreiheit', *ZIAS* 2006, 158–196. See e.g. the recent decisions ECtHR Case 34503/97 *Demir and Baykara* v. *Turkey*, *NZA* 2010, 1425; Case 68959/01 *Enerji Yapi-Yol Sen* v. *Turkey*, *NZA* 2010, 1423; Case 30946/04 *Kaya and Seyhan*; Case 33322/07 Cerikci.

established the European Court of Human Rights (ECtHR, to be distinguished from the EU's European Court of Justice) and thus has its own system of judicial review. All Member States of the EU are also signatories to the ECHR. The EU as such, however, is not, as yet, a member of the ECHR. Accession to the ECHR by the EU raised obstacles from both EU law ECHR perspectives. Prior to the Lisbon Treaty, the EU lacked competence to accede to the Convention.[7] Article 6(2) sent. 1 TEU, which was introduced by the Lisbon Treaty, now imposes an obligation upon the Union – which now forms a legal entity – to accede to the ECHR. The Council adopted a negotiation mandate on 4 June 2010 and negotiations with the Council of Europe are currently under way.[8] The ECHR obstacle to EU accession was that the Convention itself only provided for the accession of states, which appeared to exclude international organisations.[9] In substance, of course, pursuant to Article 6(3) TEU, fundamental rights as guaranteed by the ECHR 'shall constitute general principles of the Union's law' and thus are already part of the EU's legal order (see in more detail paras. 14 sq. below). The reference made by Article 6(3) TEU to the ECHR does not require national courts to apply the provisions of the convention directly.[9a]

5. The **European Social Charter**[10] (ESC) contains a catalogue of social rights, particularly rights for employees, such as a right to work, a right to fair working terms and conditions, a right to safe and healthy working conditions, a right to fair remuneration, a right to freedom of association, a right to collective bargaining (including a right to take collective action). All EU Member States are also signatories of the ESC, but not all have yet ratified the revised version. Again, the EU is not a Member to the Convention. However, Article 151 TFEU refers to the Social Charter of 1961,[11] if only in the context of its statement of objectives. According to that provision, the Union and the Member States should pursue their objectives 'having in mind fundamental social rights such as those set out in the European Social Charter'. The Court of Justice has also occasionally mentioned the Charter.[12] This volume refers to the ESC only in references and does not discuss it in detail.

---

[7] ECJ Opinion 2/94, [1996] ECR I-1783. See also Opinion 1/91 [1991] ECR I-6079.

[8] On the specific issues raised in the negotiations, see T. Lock, *E.L. Rev.* 35 (2010), 777–798; J. P. Jacqué, *CMLR* 48 (2011), 995–1023.

[9] Currently, an obstacle to formal accession of the EU to the ECHR is that it is open only to states. Art. 17 of Protocol No. 14 to the ECHR of 13 May 2004 is intended to provide for a possibility of accession of the Union. However, the protocol has not yet been ratified by Russia (as the 46th of 47 Member States); see http://conventions.coe.int/Treaty/Commun/ChercheSig. asp?NT=194&CM=8&DF=2/18/2009&CL=ENG).

[9a] ECJ Case C-571/10 *Kamberaj* 24 April 2012 paras. 59–63.

[10] For an introduction, see Council of Europe (ed.), *European Social Charta – Short Guide* (Strasbourg: Council of Europe Publishing, 2000); in more detail e.g. D. J. Harris/J. Darcy, *The European Social Charter: the protection of economic and social rights in Europe*, 2nd edn. (New York: Transnational Publishers, 2001); G. Agnelli (ed.), *Die Europäische Sozialcharta* (Baden-Baden: Nomos, 1978); H. Isele, *Die europäische Sozialcharta* (Wiesbaden: Steiner, 1967).

[11] But not to the 1999 revision (cf. note 3 above).

[12] Prominently ECJ Case 149/77 *Defrenne III* [1978] ECR 1365 para. 28.

II. FOUNDATIONS IN PRIMARY LAW: FUNDAMENTAL RIGHTS AND GENERAL PRINCIPLES OF EU LAW

Bibliography:

J. Basedow, *Von der deutschen zur europäischen Wirtschaftsverfassung* (Tübingen: Mohr Siebeck, 1992); J. Basedow, 'Der Grundsatz der Nichtdiskriminierung im europäischen Privatrecht', *ZEuP* 2008, 230–251; R. Birk, 'Arbeitskampf und Europarecht', in H. Oetker/U. Preis/V. Rieble (eds.), *Festschrift 50 Jahre Bundesarbeitsgericht* (Munich: C.H. Beck, 2004), 1165–1178; G.-P. Calliess, 'Die Zukunft der Privatautonomie – Zur neueren Entwicklung eines gemeineuropäischen Rechtsprinzips', in B. Jud et al. (eds.), *Jahrbuch junger Zivilrechtswissenschaftler 2000 – Prinzipien des Privatrechts und Rechtsvereinheitlichung* (Stuttgart et al.: Boorberg, 2001), 85–110; C.-W. Canaris, *Die Bedeutung der iustitia distributiva im deutschen Vertragsrecht* (Munich: C.H. Beck, 1997); C.-W. Canaris, *Grundrechte und Privatrecht – eine Zwischenbilanz –* (Berlin/New York: de Gruyter, 1999); C.-W. Canaris, 'Verfassungs- und europarechtliche Aspekte der Vertragsfreiheit in der Privatrechtsgesellschaft', in P. Badura/R. Scholz, *Festschrift für Peter Lerche zum 65. Geburtstag* (Munich: C.H. Beck, 1993), 873–891; C.-W. Canaris, 'Wandlungen des Schuldvertragsrechts – Tendenzen zu seiner "Materialisierung"', *AcP* 200 (2000), 273–364; W. Däubler, 'Die Koalitionsfreiheit im EG-Recht', in U. Isenhardt/U. Preis (eds.), *Arbeitsrecht und Sozialpartnerschaft – Festschrift für Peter Hanau* (Cologne: Otto Schmidt, 1999), 489–503; A. C. L. Davies, 'One Step Forward, Two Steps Back? The *Viking* and *Laval* Cases in the ECJ', *ILJ* 37 (2008), 126–148; R. A. Epstein, 'In Defense of the Contract at Will', *U. Chi. L. Rev.* 51 (1984), 947–982; C. Estlund, 'An American Perspective on Fundamental Labour Rights', in B. Hepple (ed.), *Social and Labour Rights in a Global Context* (Cambridge: Cambridge University Press, 2002), 192–214; S. Grundmann, 'Europa- und wirtschaftsrechtliche Grundlagen der Privatrechtsgesellschaft', in K. Riesenhuber (ed.), *Privatrechtsgesellschaft* (Tübingen: Mohr Siebeck, 2007), 105–130; S. Grundmann, 'Privatautonomie im Binnenmarkt – Informationsregeln als Instrument', *JZ* 2000, 1133–1143; S. Grundmann/W. Kerber/S. Weatherill, 'Party Autonomy and the Role of Information in the Internal Market – an Overview', in iid. (eds.), *Party Autonomy and the Role of Information in the Internal Market* (Berlin/New York: de Gruyter, 2001), 3–38; K. Lenaerts/J. A. Gutiérrez-Fons, 'The Constitutional Allocation of Powers and General Principles in EU Law', *CMLR* 47 (2010), 1629–1669; E.-J. Mestmäcker, 'Auf dem Wege zu einer Ordnungspolitik für Europa', in id./H. Möller/H.-P. Schwarz (eds.), *Festschrift für Hans von der Groeben* (Baden-Baden: Nomos, 1987), 9–49; E.-J. Mestmäcker, 'Über die normative Kraft privatrechtlicher Verträge', *JZ* 1964, 441–446; E.-J. Mestmäcker, 'Zur Wirtschaftsverfassung in der Europäischen Union', in R. Hasse/J. Molsberger/C. Watrin (eds.), *Ordnung in Freiheit – Festgabe für Hans Willgerodt* (Stuttgart: Fischer Verlag, 1994), 263–292; A. Metzger, *Extra legem, intra ius – Allgemeine Rechtsgrundsätze im Europäischen Privatrecht* (Tübingen: Mohr Siebeck, 2009); P.-C. Müller-Graff, *Privatrecht und Europäisches Gemeinschaftsrecht – Gemeinschaftsprivatrecht*, 2nd edn. (Baden-Baden: Nomos, 1991); J. Neuner, *Privatrecht und Sozialstaat* (Munich: C.H. Beck, 1999); R. Rebhahn, 'Grundfreiheit versus oder vor Streikrecht', *wbl* 2008, 63–69; R. Rebhahn, 'Grundfreiheit vor Arbeitskampf – der Fall Viking', *ZESAR* 2008, 109–117; R. Rebhahn, 'Tarifautonomie aus vergleichender Sicht', *EuZA* 2010, 62–87; K. Riesenhuber,

'Primärrechtliche Grundlagen der Kapitalmarkttransparenz', in K. Hopt/J. Kämmerer/R. Veil (eds.), *Kapitalmarktgesetzgebung im Europäischen Binnenmarkt* (Tübingen: Mohr Siebeck, 2008), 23–59; K. Riesenhuber (ed.), *Privatrechtsgesellschaft* (Tübingen: Mohr Siebeck, 2007); F. Rittner, 'Die wirtschaftsrechtliche Ordnung der EG und das Privatrecht', *JZ* 1990, 838–846; S. Sciarra, 'The Evolution of Collective Bargaining: Observations on a Comparison in the Countries of the European Union', *Comp. Lab. L. & Pol'y J.* 29 (2007–2008), 1–27; E. Steindorff, *EG-Vertrag und Privatrecht* (Baden-Baden: Nomos, 1996); T. Tridimas, *The General Principles of EU Law*, 2nd edn. (Oxford: Oxford University Press, 2006); J. Usher, *General Principles of EC Law* (London/ New York: Longman, 1998); J. Usher, 'Principles Derived from Private Law and the European Court of Justice', *ERPL* 5 (1997), 109–136; C. Windbichler, 'Arbeitsrecht und Wettbewerb in der europäischen Wirtschaftsverfassung', *RdA* 1992, 74–84; U. Zachert, 'Auf dem Weg zu Europäischen Arbeitnehmergrundfreiheiten?', *NZA* 2000, 621–626.

Cases (selection):
ECJ Case 25/62 *Plaumann* [1963] ECR 211; ECJ Case 29/69 *Stauder* [1969] ECR 419; ECJ Case 4/73 *Nold* [1974] ECR 491; ECJ Case 44/79 *Hauer* [1979] ECR 3727; ECJ Case 234/85 *Keller* [1986] ECR 2897; ECJ Case 26/86 *Deutz und Geldermann* [1987] ECR 941; ECJ Case 5/88 *Wachauf* [1989] ECR 2609; ECJ Case C-260/89 *ERT* [1991] ECR I-2925; ECJ Case C-308/89 *Cordoniu* [1994] ECR I-1853; ECJ Case C-280/93 *Deutschland* v. *Rat* [1994] ECR I-4973 – Bananenmarktordnung; ECJ Case C-368/95 *Familiapress* [1997] ECR I-3689; ECJ Case C-67/96 *Albany* [1999] ECR I-5751; ECJ Case C-60/00 *Carpenter* [2002] ECR I-6279; ECJ Case C-50/00 P *Unión de Pequenos Agricultores* [2002] ECR I-6677; ECJ Case C-263/02 P *Jégo Quéré* [2004] ECR I-3425; ECJ Case C-184/02 *Spanien und Finnland* v. *Parlament und Rat* [2004] ECR I-7789; ECJ Joined Cases C-435/02 and C-103/03 *Springer* [2004] ECR I-8663; ECJ Case C-341/05 *Laval un Partneri* [2007] ECR I-11767; ECJ Case C-438/05 *Viking* [2007] ECR I-10779.

1. Originally no Written Catalogue of Fundamental Rights

6. Before the Lisbon Treaty of 2009 became effective, EU primary law, the 'constitution' of the Union,[13] did not contain a written catalogue of fundamental rights. The German Constitutional Court (*Bundesverfassungsgericht*, BVerfG) had particularly criticised this deficiency. In a 1974 decision, the German Court reserved the right to review acts of the (then) European Economic Community in respect of their compatibility with the fundamental rights of the German constitution (the Basic Law, *Grundgesetz*) 'so long as' the Community was not

---

[13] On the EC-Treaty as the Community's (Union's) constitution, see e.g. ECJ Opinion 1/91 [1991] ECR I-6079 para. 21 – Draft agreement between the Community, on the one hand, and the countries of the European Free Trade Association, on the other, relating to the creation of the European Economic Area; ECJ Case C-314/91 *Weber* v. *Parliament* [1993] ECR I-1093 para. 8; ECJ Opinion 2/94 [1996] ECR I-1759 para. 35 – Accession by the Community to the Convention for the Protection of Human Rights and Fundamental Freedoms; ECJ Case 294/83 *Les Verts* [1986] ECR 1339 para. 23; BVerfG, *BVerfGE* 22, 293, 296; I. Pernice, 'Kompetenzabgrenzung im Europäischen Verfassungsverbund', *JZ* 2000, 866, 869–871; R. Streinz/C. Ohler/C. Herrmann, *Der Vertrag von Lissabon zur Reform der EU*, 3rd edn. (Munich: C.H. Beck, 2010), 5 sq.

bound by a catalogue of fundamental rights.[14] In a 1986 decision, the German Court suspended this decision after concluding that the European Court of Justice had by then recognised fundamental rights as general principles of EU law, which were substantially equivalent to those of the German constitution.[15] Indeed, central propositions of fundamental rights can, at least partially, be inferred from written primary law (see 2. below). Not surprisingly for a Union that was originally conceived as – and still remains – an 'Economic Community', this is particularly true for the principles of private autonomy and freedom of contract of which the fundamental freedoms are merely specific expressions with regard to cross-border transactions. Other fundamental rights have been recognised in the Court's jurisprudence as general principles of EU law (see 3. below); Article 6(3) TEU now explicitly refers to this case law.

2. Fundamental Rights as Propositions in EU Primary Law

a) The 'Constitution of the Market' and the 'Social Constitution'[16]

7. From the outset, the central objective of the European Union (formerly European Economic Community) had been economic in nature. 'The Union shall establish an **internal market**', Article 3(3)(1) sent. 1 TEU. In fact, the establishment of a common (internal) market had been the primary purpose of the original EC. The common (internal) market had been regarded as the

---

[14] BVerfG, *BVerfGE* 37, 271, 280 – Solange I. Headnote: 'As long as the integration process of the Community has not advanced to a level where Community law also provides for a catalogue of fundamental rights, adopted by parliament and fully in force, equivalent to that of the Basic Law (Grundgesetz), it remains admissible and is required for a court of the Federal Republic of Germany, after obtaining a decision of the Court of Justice pursuant to Art. 177 of the Treaty [Art. 267 TFEU], to initiate a norm control procedure in the Federal Constitutional Court, if the court considers the provisions relevant to its decision in their interpretation through the Court of Justice to be inapplicable because, and in so far as, they collide with one of the fundamental rights of the Basic Law.' – my translation (German lawyers refer to the decision as 'Solange I' – 'as long as I'-decision.).

[15] BVerfG, *BVerfGE* 73, 339 – Solange II; Headnote 2: 'As long as the European Communities, in particular the case law of the European Court of Justice, in principle guarantee effective protection of fundamental rights against the public powers of the Communities at a level that is generally equivalent to the protection of fundamental rights regarded as indispensable by of the Basic Law, in particular protecting the essence of those rights, the Federal Constitutional Court will not exercise its jurisdiction over the applicability of secondary Community law which serves as a basis for measures of German Courts or administrative bodies in the territory of the Federal Republic of Germany and it will, in other words, not control this law by the measure of the fundamental rights of the Basic Law; references to this effect on the basis of Art. 100(1) Basic Law are thus inadmissible.' – my translation. See also recently BVerfG, *BVerfGE* 102, 147 – Bananenmarktordnung (Common organization of the markets for bananas).

[16] On the economic constitution of the Community with a view to employment law C. Windbichler, *RdA* 1992, 74, 75–78 *et passim*; generally J. Basedow, *Von der deutschen zur Europäischen Wirtschaftsverfassung*; E.-J. Mestmäcker, *Festgabe für Willgerodt*, 263–292; id., *Festschrift für von der Groeben*, 9–49.

---

instrument to achieve other additional objectives, especially 'social' goals such as the protection of consumers and employees. The Lisbon Treaty of 2009 has shifted the emphasis to some extent, and following Article 3(3)(2) sent. 2 TEU, the Union now 'works for … a highly competitive **social market economy**' (German: *soziale Marktwirtschaft*), 'aiming at full employment and social progress, and a high level of protection and improvement of the quality of the environment'. Yet even after Lisbon, the central elements of the internal market remain the 'open market economy with free competition', Articles 119(1), 120 sent. 2, 127(1) sent. 3 TFEU and the guarantee of the fundamental economic freedoms Article 26(2) TFEU: free movement of goods, services, persons and capital (see in detail §3 below).

8. Market economy, competition and the freedom(s) for market actors thus remain the basis of the EU-Treaties.[17] At the same time, the founding treaties are also intended to provide for social protection.[18] From the outset, the establishment of the common market had not only been an objective in itself but also a means for the promotion of social goals.[19] Indeed, the promotion of social objectives is a particular mandate of EU legislation.[20] The attainment of both economic (*Marktverfassung*; 'market constitution') and social objectives (*Sozialverfassung*, 'social constitution') are therefore fundamental to EU private law, and are thus also at the heart of EU employment law.[21]

b) Private Autonomy and Freedom of Contract

9. Following the concept of an open market economy with free competition, EU primary law mandates that EU private law be based upon the principles of private autonomy and freedom of contract.[22] Private autonomy, market economy and competition are mutually dependent.[23] Private autonomy presupposes the existence of a market and leads to competition. Protection of the market against distortion safeguards the market as such and also safeguards freedom of choice

---

[17] S. Grundmann, *JZ* 2000, 1133, 1136 sq.; W. Kluth, 'Die Bindung privater Wirtschaftsteilnehmer an die Grundfreiheiten des EG-Vertrages', *AöR* 122 (1997) 573, 578–581.

[18] J. Neuner, *Privatrecht und Sozialstaat,* 195–201.

[19] ECJ Opinion 1/91 [1991] ECR I-6079 paras. 16–18 – Draft agreement between the Community, on the one hand, and the countries of the European Free Trade Association, on the other, relating to the creation of the European Economic Area.

[20] Especially Art. 114(3), 151, 165, 169 TFEU. J. Neuner, *Privatrecht und Sozialstaat,* 198 sq.

[21] Cf. E. Steindorff, *EG-Vertrag und Privatrecht,* 42–45.

[22] G.-P. Calliess, 'Die Zukunft der Privatautonomie. Zur neueren Entwicklung eines gemeineuropäischen Rechtsprinzips', *JJZ* 2000, 85, 106–110; C.-W. Canaris, *Festschrift für Lerche,* 873, 889 sq.; F. Rittner, *JZ* 1990, 838, 840 sq.; ECJ Case C-162/96 *Racke* [1998] ECR I-3655 para. 49; Case C-240/97 *Spain* v. *Commission* [1999] ECR I-6571 para. 99 – EAGFL.

[23] C.-W. Canaris, *Festschrift für Lerche,* 873, 890; F. Rittner, *JZ* 1990, 838, 839, 841; E. Steindorff, *EG-Vertrag und Privatrecht,* 42; W. Zöllner, *Die Privatrechtsgesellschaft im Gesetzes- und Richterstaat* (Cologne: Otto Schmidt, 1996), 23 sq.

for market actors.[24] The principle of 'self-regulation of his legal relations by the individual pursuant to his own will' – the definition of private autonomy –[25] is the common core of the fundamental freedoms which extend the possibilities of autonomous action beyond the borders of the Member States.[26] Private autonomy has thus rightly been labelled the 'true fundamental freedom'.[27]

10. In some jurisdictions, for example in Germany, the fundamental principles of private autonomy and freedom of contract enjoy constitutional protection as fundamental rights. Apart from the aforementioned inference from the principles of the Union's economic constitution (see paras. 9 sq. above), written EU law does not contain a similar guarantee, and the Court of Justice has not established such guarantee in its case law either.[28] Yet, freedom of contract is no less fundamental in EU law than in national law. Presumably, the Court simply did not feel that it was necessary to declare a fundamental right in this respect. First, the Court had in fact already held that Community fundamental rights did not lag behind the standard of protection in the Member States.[29] The standard phrase of the Court has eventually been incorporated into (what is now) Article 6(3) TEU, pursuant to which fundamental rights 'as they result from the constitutional traditions common to the Member States, shall constitute general principles of the Union's law'.[30] Secondly, the fundamental freedoms of the TFEU are specific expressions of the general principle of freedom of contract for the internal market, and consequently proclamation of the 'general principle' was not necessary.[31] Indeed, the Court of Justice as well as the Court of First

---

24   E.-J. Mestmäcker, *JZ* 1964, 441, 443; C.-W. Canaris, *Die Bedeutung der iustitia distributiva im deutschen Vertragsrecht*, 48; id., *AcP* 200 (2000) 273, 292–295.

25   Thus the famous definition of private autonomy by W. Flume, *Allgemeiner Teil des Bürgerlichen Rechts*, vol. 2: *Das Rechtsgeschäft*, 4th edn. (Berlin: Springer, 1992), §1, 1 – my translation.

26   P.-C. Müller-Graff, *Privatrecht und Europäisches Gemeinschaftsrecht*, 17; id., in S. Grundmann/W. Kerber/S. Weatherill (eds.), *Party Autonomy and the Role of Information in the Internal Market*, 133–150; S. Grundmann, *JZ* 2000, 1133, 1134 sq.; S. Grundmann/W. Kerber/S. Weatherill, in iid. (eds.), *Party Autonomy and the Role of Information in the Internal Market*, 3, 16.

27   P. Mülbert, 'Privatrecht, die EG-Grundfreiheiten und der Binnenmarkt', *ZHR* 159 (1995), 2, 8 – my translation.

28   Assuming that a fundamental right to freedom of contract can already be inferred from the EC-Treaty (now the TFEU) C.-W. Canaris, *Festschrift für Lerche*, 873, 890; id., *AcP* 200 (2000) 273, 363 sq.; D. Coester-Waltjen, 'Constitutional Aspects of Party Autonomy and Its Limits – The Perspective of Law', in S. Grundmann/W. Kerber/S. Weatherill (eds.), *Party Autonomy and the Role of Information in the Internal Market*, 41, 42.

29   ECJ Case 4/73 Nold [1974] ECR 491 paras. 13 sq.; Case 44/79 Hauer [1979] ECR 3727 paras. 13–16; Case 265/87 Schräder [1989] ECR 2237 para. 14.

30   On the general principles of Union law, see also paras. 14 sq. below.

31   P.-C. Müller-Graff, in S. Grundmann/W. Kerber/S. Weatherill (eds.), *Party Autonomy and the Role of Information in the Internal Market*, 133–150; C. Schmidt-Leithoff, 'Gedanken über die Privatrechtsordnungen als Grundlage zum EWG-Vertrag', in M. Löwisch/C. Schmidt-Leithoff/B. Schmiedel (eds.), *Beiträge zum Handels- und Wirtschaftsrecht – Festschrift für Fritz Rittner zum 70. Geburtstag* (Munich: C.H. Beck, 1991), 597, 606. S.a. above para. 9.

Instance presupposes the principle of freedom of contract as a matter of course in their jurisprudence.[32] Thus, the Court of Justice recently stated with regard to the Transfer of Undertakings Directive:

> 'First, the general point should be made that a contract is characterised by the principle of freedom of the parties to arrange their own affairs, according to which, in particular, parties are free to enter into obligations with each other. Under that principle, and in a situation such as the one in the main proceedings where the defendant is not a member of any employers' association and is not bound by any collective agreement, the rights and obligations arising from such an agreement do not therefore apply to it, as a rule. Otherwise (...) the principle that contracts cannot impose obligations on third parties would be infringed.'[33]

In summary therefore, it seems fair to say that the guarantee of private autonomy in EU law does not lag behind that found in the national laws of the Member States.[34]

11. Even if private autonomy and freedom of contract were explicitly recognised as fundamental rights by the Court of Justice, this would not render them free from the restrictions which may be mandated by public policy considerations. Freedom of contract is subject to restrictions similar to those recognised by the Court for the right to property and freedom of trade. Restrictions may be imposed on these rights on grounds of general interest, subject to the principle of proportionality.[35] The same must be true for freedom of contract which, in EU law as in national law, is not an absolute right but must be considered in light of its social function ('*Sozialbindung*').[36]

c)   Prohibitions of Discrimination

12.   Prohibitions of discrimination are also, to a certain extent, already part of primary law.[37] We discuss the details later (see §§8–11 below) and only provide a

---

[32]   ECJ Case C-240/97 *Commission* v. *Spain* [1999] ECR I-6571 para. 99; Case C-215/97 Bellone [1998] ECR I-2191 para. 14 ('principle that the contract is not subject to any formal requirement' as a sub-principle of freedom of contract); CFI Case T-24/90 *Automec* [1992] ECR II-2223 para. 51. See also ECJ Joined Cases C-90/90 and C-91/90 *Neu* [1991] ECR I-3617 para. 13.

[33]   ECJ Case C-499/04 *Werhof* [2006] ECR I-2397 para. 23.

[34]   With regard to German law, see e.g. G.-P. Calliess, *JZ* 2000, 85, 107 ('better protected' – my translation).

[35]   ECJ Case C-22/94 *Irish Farmers* [1997] ECR I-1809 para. 27; Case 265/87 *Schräder* [1989] ECR 2237 para. 15; Case 44/79 *Hauer* [1979] ECR 3727 paras. 17 sq., 32.

[36]   Cf. D. Coester-Waltjen, in S. Grundmann/W. Kerber/S. Weatherill (eds.), *Party Autonomy and the Role of Information in the Internal Market*, 41, 42 sq.; C.-W. Canaris, *Die Bedeutung der iustitia distributiva im deutschen Vertragsrecht*, 119 sq., 127.

[37]   B.-O. Bryde, *RdA* 2003 Special Supplement to Issue 5, 5, 9 sq.

summary here. First, the prohibition of **sex discrimination in respect of pay** pursuant to Article 157 deserves attention. It was already part of the EEC Treaty of 1957. While it had originally been justified by competitive considerations (no disadvantage for companies of countries that enforce equal pay), the Court soon attached a social rationale to it (see in detail §8 para. 4 below with further reference). Secondly, the **fundamental freedoms** contain prohibitions of discrimination, and the Court has recognised horizontal direct effect in some cases (in detail §3 paras. 28–30, 52 sq. below). Third, Article 18 TFEU enshrines a general prohibition of discrimination on grounds of nationality. The provision has only subordinate practical importance as the more specific guarantees of the fundamental freedoms take precedence over the general provision of Article 18 (see §3 para. 105 below). Finally, the specific competence of Article 19 TFEU also implies a special role for the principle of non-discrimination in EU law (see §4 para. 46 and §8 para. 8 below).

d)   Freedom of Association

13.   Freedom of association as a general fundamental right can, to some extent, be inferred from the right of establishment pursuant to Articles 49 sqq., 54 TFEU. The specific rights of employees to form trade unions and of employers to form employer associations, and the rights of such organisations to take collective action and participate in collective bargaining, are not guaranteed as such, but the Treaty contains some references to them.[38] Various aspects of the competence norms contained in Articles 153–155 TFEU presuppose that 'management and labour' form organisations to represent their interests in regulating working conditions: Article 153(3) TFEU thus provides when a Member State may entrust management and labour with the implementation of directives, Article 154 TFEU provides where the Commission has the task of promoting consultation of management and labour, and finally, Article 155 TFEU provides where 'the dialogue between [management and labour] at Union level may lead to contractual relations, including agreements', the so-called 'social dialogue'.[39] Social dialogue cannot of course be compared to collective bargaining in a strict sense, but rather concerns participation of the social partners in the framework of democratic legislation (see in detail §4 paras. 26–41 below). Furthermore, the EU does not have competence to regulate 'pay, the right of association, the right to strike or the right to impose lock-outs', Article 153(5) TFEU. These latter

---

[38]   See also R. Birk, *Festschrift 50 Jahre BAG*, 1165–1178; O. Deinert, 'Partizipation europäischer Sozialpartner an der Gemeinschaftsrechtsetzung', *RdA* 2004, 211, 218 sq.; with caution S. Krebber, in C. Calliess/M. Ruffert (eds.), *EUV/AEUV*, Art. 154 AEUV para. 22.

[39]   Cf. ECJ Case C-67/96 *Albany* [1999] ECR I-5751 paras. 54–64. Similar W. Däubler, *Festschrift für Hanau*, 489, 496.

considerations do not, however, preclude recognition of freedom of association as a general principle of EU law (see para. 13 below).[40]

3.   Fundamental Rights as General Principles of EU Law

14.   Individual fundamental rights can thus already be inferred from primary EU law. Other fundamental rights have been recognised as general principles of EU law in the Court's case law.[41] Articles 340 TFEU and 188(2) EAEC Treaty refer to 'the general principles common to the laws of the Member States' with regard to non-contractual liability. Based on the founding Treaties and on the national laws of the Member States[42], the Court of Justice has also established general principles of EU law in other areas.[43] The provision of Article 6(3) TEU, originally introduced by the 1992 Maastricht Treaty, expressly recognises this jurisprudence: 'Fundamental rights (…) as they result from the constitutional traditions common to the Member States, shall constitute general principles of the Union's law.' The Court has, *inter alia*, recognised individual fundamental rights[44] as well as constitutional principles and principles of administrative law as general principles of EU law.[45] For the purposes of employment law, the **right to property,**[46] **freedom of occupation and**

---

40   M. Fuchs, in id./F. Marhold (eds.), *Europäisches Arbeitsrecht*, 275–277.
41   Pathbreaking ECJ Case 29/69 *Stauder* [1969] ECR 419 para. 7. Recently e.g. ECJ Case C-540/03 *Parliament* v. *Council* [2006] ECR I-5769 paras. 35–37.
42   General Principles of Union law have in most cases been established on the basis of an 'evaluative comparison' of the national legal traditions; see e.g. ECJ Joined Cases 7/56 and 3/57 to 7/57 *Algera* [1957] ECR paras. 85, 118 sq.; AG Lagrange, Opinion in Case 14/61 *Hoogovens* v. *Hohe Behörde* [1962] ECR pts. 513, 570 sq.; AG Roemer, Opinion in Case 5/71 *Schöppenstedt* [1971] ECR pts. 975, 990 sq. (to Art. 215 EWGV/288 EG/340 AEUV); ECJ Case C-341/05 *Laval un Partneri* [2007] ECR I-11767 paras. 90 sq.; S. Grundmann, *Europäisches Schuldvertragsrecht,* §3 paras. 184–186. Critically R. Rebhahn, *ZESAR* 2008, 110–112; also K. Riesenhuber, *System und Prinzipien des Vertragsrechts* (Berlin/New York: de Gruyter, 2003), 33 sq. and note 18.
43   See in detail the treatises of A. Metzger, *Extra legem, intra ius – Allgemeine Rechtsgrundsätze im Europäischen Privatrecht;* T. Tridimas, *The General Principles of EU Law* and J. Usher, *General Principles of EC Law;* D. Ehlers, in D. Ehlers (ed.), *Europäische Grundrechte und Grundfreiheiten,* §14.
44   ECJ Case 11/70 *Internationale Handelsgesellschaft* [1970] ECR 1125 paras. 3 sq.; Case 4/73 *Nold* [1974] ECR 491 paras. 13 sq.; Case 44/79 *Hauer* [1979] ECR 3727 paras. 13–16. See in detail H.-W. Rengeling, *Grundrechtsschutz in der Europäischen Gemeinschaft* (Munich: C.H. Beck, 1993); C. Stumpf, in J. Schwarze (ed.), *EU-Kommentar,* Art. 6 EUV paras. 15–37; T. Tridimas, *The General Principles of EU Law,* 298–369.
45   For an overview, see H.-W. Rengeling, 'Die Entwicklung verwaltungsrechtlicher Grundsätze durch den Gerichtshof der Europäischen Gemeinschaften', *EuR* 1984, 331–360; T. Tridimas, *The General Principles of EU Law,* 370–417; J. Usher, *General Principles of EC Law,* 72–87, 100–120.
46   ECJ Case 44/79 *Hauer* [1979] ECR 3727 paras. 16, 17–30; Joined Cases 41/79, 121/79 and 769/79 *Testa* [1980] ECR 1979 paras. 18–22; Case 59/83 *Biovilac* [1984] ECR 4057 paras. 21 sq. (leaving the question open); Case 265/87 *Schräder* [1989] ECR 2237 para. 15; Case C-280/93 *Germany* v. *Council* [1994] ECR I-4973 para. 78 – Common organization of the markets for bananas; J. Usher, *ERPL* 5 (1993), 109, 123–127; R. Wank, in P. Hanau/H.-D. Steinmeyer/R. Wank (eds.), *Handbuch des europäischen Arbeits- und Sozialrechts,* §13 paras. 6–32.

trade[47] – which comprise the freedom of both employer and employee -, **freedom of association**,[48] the **right to take collective action** and to **collectively bargain**[49] and, last but not least, the **principle of equality**[50] are of particular importance.

15. Based on the Court's mandate to 'ensure that ... the law is observed' (Article 19(1)TEU), the general principles of EU primary law may function as fundamental rights, thus prohibiting interference with an individual's protected sphere by a public authority (legislature, administration and courts) or requiring that a public authority protects an individual. With regard to application of the law, the Court may take general principles into account when interpreting or developing (gap-filling) EU employment law (interpretation in conformity with EU primary law).[51] Take as an example[52] the decision in *Katsikas* where the Court recognised the employee's right to object to the transfer of his employment

---

[47] ECJ Case 4/73 *Nold* [1974] ECR 491 paras. 13 sq.; Case 230/78 *Eridania* [1979] ECR 2749 paras. 20–22, 31; Case 44/79 *Hauer* [1979] ECR 3727 paras. 16, 32; Case 59/83 *Biovilac* [1984] ECR 4057 paras. 22 sq.; Case 265/87 *Schräder* [1989] ECR 2237 paras. 14 sq.; Case 234/85 *Keller* [1986] ECR 2897 para. 8; Joined Cases C-132/91, C-138/91 and C-139/91 *Katsikas* [1992] ECR I-6577 paras. 30–32; Case C-280/93 *Germany* v. *Council* [1994] ECR I-4973 para. 78 – Common organization of the markets for bananas. B.-O. Bryde, *RdA* 2003 Special Supplement to Issue 5, 5, 8 sq.; R. Wank, in P. Hanau/H.-D. Steinmeyer/R. Wank (eds.), *Handbuch des europäischen Arbeits- und Sozialrechts*, §13 paras. 33–43. Cf. also the (non-binding) explanations by the Praesidium of the Convention on Art. 16 ChFR, Dok. CHARTE 4473/00 CONVENT 50, 18 sq., available at www.europarl.europa.eu/charter/pdf/04473_en.pdf.

[48] ECJ Case C-499/04 *Werhof* [2006] ECR I-2397 para. 33; Case C-415/93 *Bosman* [1995] ECR I-4921 para. 79; Case 175/73 *Gewerkschaftsbund* v. *Council* [1974] ECR 917 paras. 14 sq. (unions' right to sue); Case 18/74 *Allgemeine Gewerkschaft* v. *Commission* [1974] ECR 933 paras. 10 sq. (unions' right to sue); Joined Cases C-193/87 and C-194/87 *Maurissen* [1990] ECR I-95 paras. 11–15. See in more detail W. Däubler, *Festschrift für Hanau*, 489–503; R. Wank, in P. Hanau/H.-D. Steinmeyer/R. Wank (eds.), *Handbuch des europäischen Arbeits- und Sozialrechts*, §13 paras. 44–48.

[49] ECJ Case C-271/08 *Commission* v. *Germany* 15 July 2010 paras. 37 sqq.; Case C-341/05 *Laval un Partneri* [2007] ECR I-11767 paras. 90 sq.; Case C-438/05 *Viking* [2007] ECR I-10779 paras. 43 sq.; see already Case C-67/96 *Albany* [1999] ECR I-5751 paras. 54–64; Case C-15/96 *Kalliope Schöning-Kougebetopoulou* [1998] ECR I-47 paras. 29–34 (presupposing a right to collective agreements). R. Birk, *Festschrift 50 Jahre BAG*, 1165–1178; A. C. L. Davies, *ILJ* 37 (2008), 126, 138; C. Schubert, 'Europäische Grundfreiheiten und nationales Arbeitskampfrecht im Konflikt', *RdA* 2008, 289, 292–295; critically with a view to the justification and the scope R. Rebhahn, *wbl* 2008, 63–69; id., *ZESAR* 2008, 109–117. B.-O. Bryde, *RdA* 2003 Special Supplement to Issue 5, 5, 7 (postulating a fundamental right in EU law to freedom of collective bargaining). See also R. Rebhahn, *EuZA* 2010, 62–87 and S. Sciarra, *Comp. Lab. L. & Pol'y J.* 29 (2007–2008), 1–27 (discussing the national traditions and current issues of collective bargaining in comparative perspective).

[50] ECJ Case C-144/04 *Mangold* [2005] ECR I-9981 paras. 73 sqq., Case C-555/07 *Kücükdeveci*, [2010] ECR I-365 para. 22; Case C-447/09 *Prigge* 13 September 2011 para. 38.

[51] Cf. S. Grundmann, *Festschrift für Buxbaum*, 213, 228 sq.

[52] See also ECJ Case C-112/00 *Schmidberger* [2003] ECR I-5659; in that case, an accomodation of free movement of goods and freedom of assembly was at stake, but the same issues may arise in the case of a strike; see the foresight of W. Däubler, *Festschrift für Hanau*, 500 sq.; also M. Fuchs, in id./F. Marhold (eds.), *Europäisches Arbeitsrecht*, 278–280.

contract to a transferee (potentially new employer), arguing that to decide otherwise would violate the employees' fundamental freedom of occupation:[53]

> 'Such an obligation [sc. to continue the employment relationship with the transferee] would jeopardize the fundamental rights of the employee, who must be free to choose his employer and cannot be obliged to work for an employer whom he has not freely chosen.'

While the general principles of Union law thus perform important functions, there is a risk that they may be used by the Court as an instrument of judicial activism, encroaching upon the rights of other EU institutions (horizontal allocation of powers) or the Member States (vertical allocation of powers).[54] This issue is particularly serious as the general principles form part of EU primary law and are thus not open to legislative correction by the EU legislature or national legislatures of the Member States.

III. THE CHARTER OF FUNDAMENTAL RIGHTS

Bibliography:

D. Ashiagbor, 'Economic and Social Rights in the European Charter of Fundamental Rights', *E.H.R.L.R.* 2004, 62–72; R. Blanpain et al., 'Soziale Grundrechte: Vorschläge für die Europäische Union', *KritV* 1995, 452–463; B. Bercusson (ed.), *European Labour law and the EU Charter of Fundamental Rights* (Baden-Baden: Nomos, 2006); N. Bernsdorff, 'Soziale Grundrechte in der Charta der Grundrechte der Europäischen Union', *VSSR* 2001, 1–23; B.-O. Bryde, 'Grundrechte der Arbeit und Europa', *RdA* 2003 Special Supplement to Issue 5, 5–10; C. Calliess, 'Die Charta der Grundrechte der Europäischen Union', *EuZW* 2001, 261–268; C.-W. Canaris, 'Drittwirkung der gemeinschaftsrechtlichen Grundfreiheiten', in H. Bauer et al. (eds.), *Umwelt, Wirtschaft und Recht – Wissenschaftliches Symposium aus Anlaß des 65. Geburtstages von Reiner Schmidt* (Tübingen: Mohr Siebeck, 2002), 29–67; W. Cremer, 'Der programmierte Verfassungskonflikt: Zur Bindung der Mitgliedstaaten an die Charta der Grundrechte der Europäischen Union nach dem Konventsentwurf für eine Europäische Verfassung', *NVwZ* 2003, 1452–1457; W. Däubler, 'EU-Grundrechtecharta und kollektives Arbeitsrecht', *AuR* 2001, 380–384; D. Ehlers (ed.), *Europäische Grundrechte und Grundfreiheiten*, 3rd edn. (Berlin/New York: de Gruyter, 2009); C. Engel, 'The European Charter of Fundamental Rights – A Changed Political Opportunity Structure and its Normative Consequences', *ELJ* 2001, 151–170; U. Everling 'Zur Europäischen Grundrechtscharta und ihren sozialen Rechten', in A. Söllner et al. (eds.), *Gedächtnisschrift für Meinhard Heinze* (Munich: C.H. Beck, 2005), 157–176; W. Frenz/V. Götzkes, 'Ein europäisches Grundrecht der

---

53 ECJ Joined Case C-132/91, C-138/91 and C-139/91 *Katsikas* [1992] ECR I-6577 paras. 30–32; critically R. Birk, 'Der EuGH und das Widerspruchsrecht des Arbeitnehmers beim Betriebsinhaberwechsel nach §613a BGB', *EuZW* 1993, 156, 159.
54 K. Lenaerts/J.A. Gutiérrez-Fons, *CMLRev* 47 (2010), 1629–1669 (allying concern). See also Riesenhuber, *ERCL* 3 (2007), 62–71.

Arbeitnehmerinnen und Arbeitnehmer auf Unterrichtung und Anhörung im Unternehmen? – Zur rechtsdogmatischen Einordnung von Artikel 27 GRCh', *RdA* 2007, 216–218; J. Fudge, 'The New Discourse of Labour Rights: From Social to Fundamental Rights?', *Comp. Lab. L. & Pol'y J.* 29 (2007–2008), 29–66; P. Hanau, 'Die Europäische Grundrechtscharta – Schein und Wirklichkeit im Arbeitsrecht', *NZA* 2009, 1–6; B. Hepple, 'The EU Charter of Fundamental Rights', *ILJ* 30 (2001), 225–231; H. D. Jarass, *EU-Grundrechte* (Munich: C.H. Beck 2005); H. D. Jarass, *Charta der Grundrechte der Europäischen Union – Kommentar* (Munich: C.H. Beck 2010); M. Kenntner, 'Die Schrankenbestimmungen der EU-Grundrechtecharta – Grundrechte ohne Schutzwirkung?', *ZRP* 2000, 423–425; J. Kokott/C. Sobotta, 'Die Charta der Grundrechte der Europäischen Union nach Inkrafttreten des Vertrags von Lissabon', *EuGRZ* 2010, 265–271; J. Lindner, 'Fortschritte und Defizite im EU-Grundrechtsschutz – Plädoyer für eine Optimierung der Grundrechtecharta', *ZRP* 2007, 54–57; J. Lindner, 'Grundrechtsschutz gegen gemeinschaftsrechtliche Öffnungsklauseln – zugleich ein Beitrag zum Anwendungsbereich der EU-Grundrechte', *EuZW* 2007, 71–75; B. Losch/W. Radau, 'Die soziale Verfassungsaufgabe der Europäischen Union', *NVwZ* 2003, 1440–1446; T. Marauhn, 'Die wirtschaftliche Vereinigungsfreiheit zwischen menschenrechtlicher Gewährleistung und privatrechtlicher Ausgestaltung', *RabelsZ* 63 (1999), 537–560; J. Meyer (ed.), *Charta der Grundrechte der Europäischen Union*, 3rd edn. (Baden-Baden: Nomos, 2010); J. Meyer/M. Engels, 'Aufnahme von sozialen Grundrechten in die Europäische Grundrechtecharta?', *ZRP* 2000, 368–371; R. Pitschas, 'Europäische Grundrechte-Charta und soziale Grundrechte', *VSSR* 2000, 207–220; R. Rebhahn, 'Überlegungen zur Bedeutung der Charta der Grundrechte der EU für den Streik und für die Kollektive Rechtsgestaltung', in A. Söllner et al. (eds.), *Gedächtnisschrift für Meinhard Heinze* (Munich: C.H. Beck, 2005), 649–660; R. Rebhahn, 'Zur Bedeutung des Article 30 der Grundrechtecharta der EU betreffend den Kündigungsschutz', in G. Kuras/M. Neumayr/A. Spenling (eds.), *Beiträge zum Arbeits- und Sozialrecht. Festschrift für Peter Bauer, Gustav Maier und Karl Heinz Petrag* (Vienna: Manz, 2004), 283–297; N. Reich, 'Zur Notwendigkeit einer Europäischen Grundrechtsbeschwerde', *ZRP* 2000, 375–378; H.-W. Rengeling/P. Szczekalla (eds.), *Grundrechte in der Europäischen Union – Charta der Grundrechte und Allgemeine Rechtsgrundsätze* (Cologne/Munich/Berlin: Heymanns, 2004); Marlene Schmidt, *Das Arbeitsrecht der Europäischen Gemeinschaften* (Baden-Baden: Nomos, 2001), Chap. 1 paras. 82–115; R. Streinz, *EUV/AEUV – Vertrag über die Europäisches Union und Vertrag zur Gründung der Europäischen Gemeinschaft*, 2nd edn. (Munich: C.H. Beck, 2011); R. Streinz/W. Michl, 'Die Drittwirkung des europäischen Datenschutzgrundrechts Art. 8 GRCh) im deutschen Privatrecht', *EuZW* 2011, 384–388; R. Streinz/C. Ohler/C. Herrmann, *Der Vertrag von Lissabon zur Reform der EU*, 2rd edn. (Munich: C.H. Beck, 2010); P. Tettinger/K. Stern (eds.), *Kölner Gemeinschaftskommentar zur Europäischen Grundrechte-Charta* (Munich: C.H. Beck, 2006); M. Weiss, 'Grundrechtecharta der EU auch für Arbeitnehmer?', *AuR* 2001, 374–378; H. J. Willemsen/A. Sagan, 'Die Auswirkungen der europäischen Grundrechtscharta auf das deutsche Arbeitsrecht', *NZA* 2011, 258–262; U. Zachert, 'Die Arbeitnehmerrechte in einer Europäischen Grundrechtscharta', *NZA* 2001, 1041–1046.

Cases (selection):
ECJ Case C-540/03 *Parliament v. Council* [2006] ECR I-5769.

1. Introduction and Overview

a) The Charter of Fundamental Rights of 2000

16. Notwithstanding that fundamental rights are to some extent already guaranteed by the founding Treaties and by the general principles developed by the Court of Justice, the introduction of a written catalogue of fundamental rights, a charter, remained desirable. Based on its task of adjudication, the Court of Justice can recognise individual fundamental rights only for specific sets of facts. The Court is thus unable to develop them systematically.[55] And fundamental rights developed in this way, through the form of general principles, lack the transparency that a charter ensures.[56]

17. Following a resolution of the European Council adopted at its meeting in Cologne on 3–4 June 1999,[57] the Council, at its summit in October 1999, instituted a body that was entrusted with the task of drafting a charter of fundamental rights. This body called itself 'Convention', and *Roman Herzog* was elected as its president. The Convention took up its work on 17 December 1999 in Brussels and quickly produced a first draft of the charter on 28 July 2000. On 7 December 2000, the **Charter of Fundamental Rights of the European Union** was solemnly proclaimed.[58]

> A written catalogue of fundamental rights raises a host of follow-up questions, especially in a multi-level legal system.[59] Apart from legal questions in a narrow sense, the question has been raised whether codification may trigger a new momentum for social legislation in the EU.[60]

b) The Legal Nature and Binding Effect: From the Charter to the Constitutional Treaty and to the Incorporation into the EU Treaty

18. While the Charter had been solemnly proclaimed in 2000, it took another ten years for it to become binding law,[61] even though a binding document, giving

---

[55] W. Däubler, *AuR* 2001, 380 sq.; M. Weiss, *AuR* 2001, 374; R. Pitschas, *VSSR* 2000, 207, 210; C. Calliess, *EuZW* 2001, 261, 262; U. Zachert, *NZA* 2001, 1041, 1042 (also discussing further motives for a codification of fundamental rights).

[56] U. Zachert, *NZA* 2000, 621, 625; M. Schmidt, *Arbeitsrecht der EG*, I para. 82. See also M. Kenntner, *ZRP* 2000, 423, 424 sq. (with a view to limitations).

[57] Presidency Conclusions No. 44 und 45 – Cologne European Council of 3–4 June 1999, available at www.consilium.europa.eu/ueDocs/cms_Data/docs/pressData/en/ec/kolnen.htm.

[58] On the legislative history e.g. N. Bernsdorff, *VSSR* 2001, 1–23; H. D. Jarass, *EU-Grundrechte*, §1 paras. 18 sqq.; R. Wank, in P. Hanau/H.-D. Steinmeyer/R. Wank (eds.), *Handbuch des europäischen Arbeits- und Sozialrechts*, §13 paras. 130–135; M. Schmidt, *Arbeitsrecht der EG*, I paras. 82–86; M. Weiss, *AuR* 2001, 374, 375; U. Zachert, *NZA* 2001, 1041, 1042.

[59] For a careful analysis, see C. Engel, *ELJ* 2001, 151–170.

[60] See e.g. D. Ashiagbor, *E.H.R.L.R.* 2004, 62–72 (inquiring *inter alia* whether the Charter opens room for 'innovation and judicial activism').

[61] Assuming a certain binding effect even before the formal entry into force ECJ Case C-540/03 *Parliament* v. *Council* [2006] ECR I-5769 para. 38; on this and on other prior effects J. Lindner,

rise to individual rights for EU citizens, had been intended from the outset. In 2004, the Charter was included in the draft **Constitutional Treaty**[62] subject only to minor changes. When, after the negative referenda in France and the Netherlands, the Constitutional Treaty was finally abandoned, it was decided to integrate the Charter into EU primary law via a 'cross-reference'.[63] This was achieved through the Lisbon Treaty which entered into force in December 2010. Article 6(1) TEU now provides:

> 'The Union recognises the rights, freedoms and principles set out in the Charter of Fundamental Rights of the European Union of 7 December 2000, as adapted at Strasbourg, on 12 December 2007, which shall have the same legal value as the Treaties.'

c) Overview: System and Contents of the Charter of Fundamental Rights

19. As the Preamble declares, the Charter 'reaffirms' the rights as they result from the constitutional traditions and international obligations common to the Member States. By way of example, it refers to the European Convention for the Protection of Human Rights and Fundamental Freedoms, the European Social Charter (see para. 5 above) and the Community Charter of Fundamental Social Rights (see paras. 65–77 below). Following the Preamble, the Charter is divided into seven titles. These concern

(I)   dignity,
(II)   freedoms,
(III) equality,
(IV)   solidarity,
(V)   citizens' rights, and
(VI)   justice.
(VII) Title VII contains general principles concerning the interpretation and application of the Charter.

20. Title I contains fundamental provisions that are relevant for employment law: 'Human dignity is inviolable. It must be respected and protected' Article 1 ChFR. Apart from the protection of life (Article 2 ChFR) and physical and mental integrity (Article 3 ChFR), the prohibition of slavery, servitude and forced or compulsory work deserves mention (Article 5 ChFR).[64]

EuZW 2007, 71; C. Calliess, *EuZW* 2001, 261, 267. Previously already AG Alber, Opinion in Case C-340/99 *Universaldienst* [2001] ECR I-4109 pt. 94; AG Tizzano, Opinion in Case C-173/00 *BECTU* [2001] ECR I-4881 pts. 26–28; AG Léger, Opinion in Case C-353/99 P *Hautala* [2001] ECR 9565 pts. 80–83.

62   Treaty establishing a Constitution for Europe, OJ 2004 C 310/1.
63   To the same effect with regard to the Community Charter of Fundamental Social Rights already R. Blanpain et al., *KritV* 1995, 452, 454. With regard to the Charter of fundamental rights advocating an incorporation rather than a mere reference M. Weiss, *AuR* 2001, 374, 378.
64   On the scope of guarantees M. Schmidt, *Arbeitsrecht der EG,* I para. 105.

21.   Among the freedoms of Title II, the following are of particular relevance for employment law:

- the protection of personal data (Article 8 ChFR),
- freedom of thought, conscience and religion (Article 10 ChFR),
- freedom of expression and information (Article 11 ChFR),
- freedom of assembly and of association (Article 12 ChFR),
- right to education (Article 14 ChFR),
- freedom to choose an occupation and right to engage in work (Article 15 ChFR),
- freedom to conduct a business (Article 16 ChFR), and
- the right to property (Article 17 ChFR).

22.   Title III on **equality** contains

- far-reaching prohibitions of discrimination (Article 21 ChFR) and
- a specific provision on the equality of men and women (Article 23 ChFR), with specific reference to 'employment, work and pay'.

23.   Title IV on **solidarity** focuses primarily upon the so-called social fundamental rights with regard to employment and social law, but also addresses environmental protection and consumer protection (in detail paras. 44–61 below).

24.   Title V on **citizens' rights** affects employment law mainly by virtue of its Article 45 on free movement although this does not, however, go beyond the respective fundamental freedom of the TFEU (on which see §3 paras. 4-54 below).

25.   Title VI on **justice** provides *inter alia* for a 'right to an effective remedy and to a fair trial' in Article 47 ChFR. The Court of Justice has used this fundamental right as a (additional) basis for a prohibition of retaliation or victimisation.[65] It also relies on Article 47 as a basis for the principle of effective judicial protection which obliges national courts to effectively protect rights which individuals derive from EU law.[66]

26.   The concluding Title VII contains general provisions. These include, in particular, a definition of the Charter's scope of application (Article 51 ChFR; see para. 28 below) and provisions on limitations (Article 52 Abs. 1 ChFR; see

---

[65]   ECJ Case C-243/09 *Fuß I* 14 October 2010 para. 66; see already Case C-185/97 *Coote* [1998] ECR I-5199 paras. 24 and 27.

[66]   ECJ Joined Cases C-444/09 and C-456/09 *Gavieiro Gavieiro* 22 December 2010 para. 75.

paras. 62–64 below). Article 51(2) ChFR limits of the scope of application with regard to competences, which is important for interpretation of the Charter: 'The Charter does not extend the field of application of Union law beyond the powers of the Union or establish any new power or task for the Union, or modify powers and tasks as defined in the Treaties.' Article 6(1) TEU reaffirms this limitation.

d)   Addressees of the Fundamental Rights

27.   A primary function of EU fundamental rights is to delimit the powers of the **Union** which was hitherto neither bound by the fundamental rights of the Member States nor by those contained in the ECHR.[67] Only Article 6(2) sent. 1 TEU, introduced by the 2009 Treaty of Lisbon, provides for the Union's obligation to accede to the ECHR.

28.   Whether the Charter also provides a standard for the control of genuinely national law is uncertain. Pursuant to Article 51(1) sent. 1 ChFR, the Charter only applies to the **Member States** when they are **implementing Union law.**[68] In its prior case law,[69] the Court of Justice has, however, reviewed national legal acts for their compliance with EU fundamental rights where the action was within the scope of Union law.[70] For example, the Court found that this requirement was satisfied where a Member State relied on the Treaty to define the limitations of fundamental freedoms.[71] Given that the Charter now restricts its scope of application to the Member States '*only* when they are implementing Union law', this should be understood as a restriction to measures which the Member States perform in application of the founding Treaties or secondary legislation (regulations and directives in particular).[72] Omissions in violation of the principle of Union solidarity (Article 4(3) TEU) cannot be regarded as measures 'implementing Union law'.[73] As a consequence, the scope of application of the Charter will, in many areas, remain rather narrow. The right to strike of Article 28 ChFR, for example, has already been labelled a symbolic 'fundamental right without any scope of application'.[74]

---

[67]   J. Lindner, *ZRP* 2007, 54, 55; B. Losch/W. Radau, *NVwZ* 2003, 1440; M. Kenntner, *ZRP* 2000, 368; C. Calliess, *EuZW* 2001, 261.

[68]   J. Kokott/C. Sobotta, *EuGRZ* 2010, 265, 267 sqq.

[69]   For an analysis of the implications of the Court's decision in Case C-555/07 *Kücükdeveci* [2010] ECR I-365, see Editorial Comments, *CMLR* 47 (2010), 1589–1596; G. Thüsing/S. Horler, *CMLR* 2010, 1161–1172.

[70]   ECJ Case C-260/89 *ERT* [1991] ECR I-2925 para. 42; W. Cremer, *NVwZ* 2003, 1452, 1453 sq.

[71]   ECJ Case C-260/89 *ERT* [1991] ECR I-2925 para. 43; Case C-368/95 *Familiapress* [1997] ECR I-3689 para. 24; Case C-60/00 *Carpenter* [2002] ECR I-6279 para. 40; W. Cremer, *NVwZ* 2003, 1452, 1453 sq.

[72]   U. Everling, *Gedächtnisschrift für Heinze,* 164; J. Lindner, *EuZW* 2007, 71, 72; R. Rebhahn, *Gedächtnisschrift für Heinze,* 655–660. S.a. W. Cremer, *NVwZ* 2003, 1452, 1454–1457.

[73]   See in more detail J. Lindner, *EuZW* 2007, 71, 72.

[74]   R. Rebhahn, *Gedächtnisschrift für Heinze,* 559 sq. – my translation; similarly with regard to Art. 30 ChFR id., *Festschrift für Bauer, Maier, Petrag,* 296 sq.

29.   Fundamental rights are thus primarily addressed to the Union and the Member States. In particular, they are not addressed to **private individuals**, even though the wording of some provisions might suggest otherwise. Article 27 ChFR regarding the right to information and consultation can serve as an example. Pursuant to that provision, 'workers or their representatives must, at the appropriate levels, be guaranteed information and consultation' (see in detail paras. 37 sq. below). Such information and consultation can, in the end, only be given ('guaranteed') by the employer. Yet, Article 27 ChFR does not bind the employer but rather the Union and the Member States.[75]

30.   The question whether fundamental rights have a horizontal effect, that is, whether they are binding in relations between private individuals, should be answered in the same way as under national law. German law merely recognises an indirect horizontal effect, mediated through the State's obligation to protect fundamental rights.[76] The same approach has also been suggested with regard to EU fundamental rights,[77] even though the Court of Justice has recognised the horizontal direct effect of fundamental freedoms in a number of cases (see in more detail §3 paras. 28–30, 52 sq., 107 below).[78] Similarly, fundamental rights contained in the Charter should not be directly binding upon private individuals. Yet, the obligation upon both the Union and Member States, to protect fundamental rights can lead to an indirect horizontal effect.[79]

e)   Enforceability

31.   Given its (now) binding nature, the question arises how fundamental rights enshrined in the Charter can be enforced. The Charter does not provide for a special procedure comparable to the 'constitutional complaint' (*Verfassungsbeschwerde*) which is available under German Basic Law (Article 93(1)(4)(a) Basic Law), and a reform to this effect is not in sight.[80] As a consequence, the possibilities for judicial review are limited.

---

[75]   U. Everling, *Festschrift für Heinze,* 157, 172 sq.; more generally with regard to the protective ambit of the provisions of the Charter which relate to third parties, e.g. also Art. 28, 29, 31(2) and 33 ChFR N. Bernsdorff, *VSSR* 2001, 1, 20.

[76]   See e.g. C.-W. Canaris, *Grundrechte und Privatrecht – eine Zwischenbilanz.*

[77]   See e.g. C.-W. Canaris, in H. Bauer/D. Czybulka/W. Kahl/A. Voßkuhle (eds.), *Umwelt, Wirtschaft und Recht,* 29–67; K. Riesenhuber, *Europäisches Vertragsrecht,* paras. 97–128 with further references.

[78]   But see R. Blanpain et al., *KritV* 1995, 452 (458 sq.) (advocating a further-reaching direct effect, especially of social fundamental rights).

[79]   To this effect also H. D. Jarass, *EU-Grundrechte,* §4 paras. 17–20.

[80]   The introduction of such legal remedy has been discussed in the Convention, as well as an amendment of (today's) Art. 263(4) TFEU; see the final report of Group II ((Incorporation

- First, there is the possibility under Article 263(4) TFEU to bring an action against decisions addressed directly to an individual or against an act addressed to the claimant or an act which is of direct and individual concern to him, and against a regulatory act which is of direct concern to him and does not entail implementing measures.[81] Directives and 'normal' regulations, however, are not within the scope of such review pursuant to Article 263(4) TFEU, even if they infringe the rights of an individual.[82]

- Second, an individual can institute proceedings before a national court against provisions implementing a directive or against an act executing a regulation. The national court may then refer the question of compatibility between the EU measure and the Charter to the ECJ by using the preliminary ruling procedure pursuant to Article 267 TFEU. However, an obligation to make such a reference only exists for courts against whose decisions there is no remedy under national law (Article 267(3) TFEU),[83] and even then, there is no way for the parties to enforce this duty to make a reference.[84] (Under German constitutional law, an individual can invoke their fundamental 'right to the lawful judge' [*Recht auf den gesetzlichen Richter;* right to have one's case tried before the judge/court determined by the law] of Article 101(1) Basic Law only when the court's refusal to make a reference is 'objectively arbitrary'.[85])

The procedural protection of fundamental rights under the Charter is thus unsatisfactory, and consideration should be given to adding a mechanism through which individuals could make a 'constitutional complaint'.[86]

---

[81] of the Charter/accession to the ECHR) of the Convention of 22 October 2002, CONV 354/02, S. 15, available at http://register.consilium.europa.eu/pdf/en/02/cv00/cv00354.en02.pdf).

[81] On the issue of a direct and individual concernment, see e.g. ECJ Case 25/62 *Plaumann* [1963] ECR 211; Case 26/86 *Deutz and Geldermann* [1987] ECR 941; Case C-308/89 *Cordoniu* [1994] ECR I-1853 paras. 14 sqq.; W. Cremer, in C. Calliess/M. Ruffert (eds.), *EUV/AEUV,* Art. 263 AEUV paras. 33–53; J. Schwarze, in id. (ed.), *EU-Kommentar,* Art. 230 EG paras. 35–39, 41–47; M. Pechstein, *EU-Prozessrecht* 4th edn. (Tübingen: Mohr Siebeck, 2011), paras. 447–519.

[82] With regard to regulaitons e.g. ECJ Case C-50/00 P *Unión de Pequenos Agricultores* [2002] ECR I-6677, 6735 paras. 42–45; Case C-263/02 *Jégo Quéré* [2004] ECR I-3425 paras. 36 sq.; J. Lindner, *ZRP* 2007, 54, 57; N. Reich, *ZRP* 2000, 375, 376; B. Losch/W. Radau, *NVwZ* 2003, 1440, 1445; C. Calliess, *EuZW* 2001, 261, 267 sq.

[83] See in detail M. Pechstein, *EU-Prozessrecht,* paras. 825–836.

[84] N. Reich, *ZRP* 2000, 375, 376; also B.-O. Bryde, *RdA* 2003 Special Supplement to Issue 5, 5, 10.

[85] BVerfG, *BVerfGE* 19, 38, 43 sq.; *BVerfGE* 75, 223, 234; *BVerfGE* 82, 159, 194–196; N. Reich, *ZRP* 2000, 375, 376; C. Calliess, *EuZW* 2001, 261, 268.

[86] J. Lindner, *ZRP* 2007, 54, 56 sqq.; N. Reich, *ZRP* 2000, 375–378; to the same effect already C. Calliess, *EuZW* 2001, 261, 268; dissenting U. Everling, *Festschrift für Heinze,* 157, 176.

2. Right to Property and Freedom

a) Right to Property

32. The guarantee of a right to property is fundamental for a market economy as well as for a privately organised labour market.[87] While the 'system of property ownership' remains a matter for the Member States, the right to property is guaranteed by Article 17 of the Charter as a matter of Union law: 'Everyone has the right to own, use, dispose of and bequeath his or her lawfully acquired possessions. No one may be deprived of his or her possessions, except in the public interest and in the cases and under the conditions provided for by law,' subject to fair compensation being paid in good time for their loss.' Its scope of protection covers physical property as well as intellectual property (expressly mentioned in Article 17(2)) and other intangible assets (such as private claims).[88]

33. Article 17 ChFR contains a general guarantee of (private) property, Article 17(1) sent. 3 indicates that the right to property requires legal regulation and is thus a fundamental right shaped by the law.[89] Sentence 3 further provides that property may be subject to such restrictions as are necessary (proportionate) on grounds of general interest.[90] In the employment context, the right to individual property, in particular, entails the employer's right to (re-)structure his undertaking according to his wishes and needs, e.g. to transform it into an SE or to merge it with another undertaking.

b) Entrepreneurial Freedom

34. In contrast to, for example, the German constitution, the Charter does not contain a general guarantee of freedom as a 'fall-back right'.[91] Private autonomy and freedom of contract in particular are not guaranteed as such (except to the extent that they can be based on the right to dignity), but only with respect to specific aspects. For the area of employment law, this concerns in particular entrepreneurial freedom (the freedom to conduct a business) on the one hand and occupational freedom on the other.

---

[87] See also C. Calliess, in id./M. Ruffert (eds.), *EUV/AEUV,* Art. 17 ChFR para. 1.

[88] In more detail C. Calliess, in id./M. Ruffert (eds.), *EUV/AEUV,* Art. 17 ChFR paras. 5–9; O. Depenheuer, in P. J. Tettinger/K. Stern (eds.), *Kölner Gemeinschaftskommentar zur Europäischen Grundrechte-Charta,* Art. 17 ChFR paras. 22–38.

[89] C. Calliess, in id./M. Ruffert (eds.), *EUV/AEUV,* Art. 17 ChFR para. 3.

[90] C. Calliess, in C. Calliess/M. Ruffert (eds.), Art. 17 ChFR para. 12; N. Bernsdorff, in J. Meyer (eds.), *Charta der Grundrechte der Europäischen Union,* Art. 17 ChFR para. 21; J. Schwarze, in id. (ed.), *EU-Kommentar,* Art. 17 ChFR para. 5; R. Streinz, in id. (ed.), *EUV/AEUV,* Art. 17 ChFR para. 22. See in detail O. Depenheuer, in P. J. Tettinger/K. Stern (eds.), *Kölner Gemeinschaftskommentar zur Europäischen Grundrechte-Charta,* Art. 17 ChFR paras. 47–60.

[91] With convincing considerations critically J. Lindner, *ZRP* 2007, 54, 56.

35. The **right to conduct a business** is recognised in Article 16 ChFR 'in accordance with Union law and national laws and practices'. The substantive scope covers the freedom of activity of self-employed persons (enterprises, natural as well as legal persons)[92] in all its facets. This comprises the freedom to establish and conduct business as well as the correlating freedom of contract, i.e. the right to conclude contracts with partners of one's own choosing and on the basis of conditions of one's own choosing.[93] The right to conduct a business also entails the right to *discontinue* a business; this must be respected by employment legislation, e.g. in the context of (collective) redundancies.

c) Freedom of Occupation and a Right to Work

36. Article 15(1) ChFR provides that 'Everyone has the right to engage in work and to pursue a freely chosen or accepted occupation'.[94] The personal scope covers 'everyone'. Pursuant to paragraph 3, this includes 'nationals of third countries who are authorised to work in the territories of the Member States', in other words subject to admission to the labour market of the Union.[95] The broad wording would also cover legal entities,[96] and they indeed enjoyed protection under the previous case law of the Court of Justice on the 'freedom to exercise a trade or profession'.[97] Yet, their activity will usually be protected by the specific Article 16 ChFR.[98] Employees in civil service are also protected, albeit with the

---

[92] C. Calliess, in id./M. Ruffert (eds.), *EUV/AEUV,* Art. 16 ChFR para. 3; N. Bernsdorff, in J. Meyer (eds.), *Charta der Grundrechte der Europäischen Union,* Art. 16 ChFR para. 16; J. Schwarze, in id. (ed.), *EU-Kommentar,* Art. 16 ChFR para. 4; R. Streinz, in id. (ed.), *EUV/ AEUV,* Art. 16 ChFR para. 7.

[93] C. Calliess, in id./M. Ruffert (eds.), *EUV/AEUV,* Art. 16 ChFR paras. 1 sq.; R. Streinz, in id. (ed.), *EUV/AEUV,* Art. 16 ChFR para. 6; H.-J. Blanke, in P. J. Tettinger/K. Stern (eds.), *Kölner Gemeinschaftskommentar zur Europäischen Grundrechte-Charta,* Art. 16 ChFR paras. 9–11.

[94] This largely conforms to the wording of No. 4 CCFR, although the ChFR does not emphasise the restriction 'according to the regulations governing each occupation'. On the CCFR, see paras. 65–77 below.

[95] M. Ruffert, in C. Calliess/M. Ruffert (eds.), *EUV/AEUV,* Art. 15 ChFR para. 9; R. Streinz, in id. (ed.), *EUV/AEUV,* Art. 15 ChFR paras. 11, 15; critically N. Bernsdorff, *VSSR* 2001, 1 (19), who (at note 91) refers to the limited wording of Art. 153(1) lit. g) TFEU ('conditions of employment').

[96] J. Schwarze, in id. (ed.), *EU-Kommentar,* Art. 15 ChFR para. 3.

[97] J. Schwarze, in id. (ed.), *EU-Kommentar* (ed.), Art. 15 ChFR para. 3; H.-J. Blanke, in P. J. Tettinger/K. Stern (eds.), *Kölner Gemeinschaftskommentar zur Europäischen Grundrechte-Charta,* Art. 15 ChFR para. 36. S. e.g. ECJ Joined Cases C-435/02 and C-103/03 *Springer* [2004] ECR I-8663 paras. 58 sq.

[98] To the same effect H. D. Jarass, *Charta der Grundrechte der EU,* Art. 15 GRCh para. 9. Strictly against an application of Art. 15 ChFR to legal entities M. Ruffert, in C. Calliess/M. Ruffert (eds.), *EUV/AEUV,* Art. 15 ChFR para. 8; with a differentiating approach N. Bernsdorff, in J. Meyer (eds.), *Charta der Grundrechte der Europäischen Union,* Art. 15 ChFR para. 19 (if the legal entity pursues an economic activity that, by its nature, could also be pursued by a natural person).

---

exception of those falling under the provision of Articles 45(4) and 51 TFEU, who thus cannot be affected by restrictive acts of the EU (see §3 para. 22 below).[99]

37. The substantive scope of protection of freedom of profession has, in the Court's previous case law,[100] not been outlined in much detail.[101] In contrast to entrepreneurial freedom, which is specifically guaranteed by Article 16, Article 15 ChFR only protects dependent (as opposed to self-employed) work.[102] Similar to free movement of workers (§3 para. 12 below), freedom of occupation does not presuppose that employment is intended only to earn a living. The pursuit of an occupation requires an element of continuity. Article 15(2) ChFR incorporates free movement of workers (Articles 45 sqq. TFEU) as well as freedom of establishment and services (Articles 49 sqq. and 56 sqq. TFEU), though without any extension or restriction of the previous scope of protection.[103] Free movement of workers in Article 45 sqq. TFEU remains in force and is the *lex specialis* with regard to cross-border professional activity.[104]

d)   Freedom of Association

38. Article 12(1) ChFR provides that 'Everyone has the right … to freedom of association at all levels, in particular in … trade union … matters, which implies the right of everyone to form and to join trade unions for the protection of his or her interests'.[105] The right to form and join trade unions is not only a 'positive' freedom, but also includes the 'negative' component of staying away from a union.[106] The right to negotiate and conclude collective agreements and the right

---

99   M. Ruffert, in C. Calliess/M. Ruffert (eds.), *EUV/AEUV,* Art. 15 ChFR para. 7; R. Streinz, in id. (ed.), *EUV/AEUV,* Art. 15 ChFR para. 11; H.-J. Blanke, in P. J. Tettinger/K. Stern (eds.), *Kölner Gemeinschaftskommentar zur Europäischen Grundrechte-Charta,* Art. 15 ChFR para. 35.

100   Cf. e.g. ECJ Case 4/73 *Nold* [1974] ECR 491 paras. 12–15; Case 44/79 *Hauer* [1979] ECR 3750 paras. 31 sq.; Case 234/85 *Keller* [1986] ECR 2897 paras. 8–18; Case C-177/90 *Kühn* [1992] ECR I-35 paras. 16 sq.; Case C-280/93 *Germany* v. *Council,* [1994] ECR I-4973 paras. 78, 81–87 – Common organization of the markets for bananas; ECJ Case C-184/02 *Spain and Finland* v. *Parliament and Council* [2004] ECR I-7789 paras. 51–60.

101   H.-P. Folz, in C. Vedder/W. Heintschel von Heinegg (eds.), *Europäisches Unionsrecht – Handkommentar* (Baden-Baden: Nomos, 2012), Art. 15 GR-Charta para. 3.

102   H. D. Jarass, *Charta der Grundrechte der EU,* Art. 15 GRCh para. 4 and Art. 16 GRCh para. 8; M. Ruffert, in C. Calliess/M. Ruffert (eds.), *EUV/AEUV,* Art. 15 ChFR para. 4; apparently also R. Streinz, in id. (ed.), *EUV/AEUV,* Art. 15 ChFR paras. 7 sq.; differently H.-W. Rengeling/P. Szczekalla (eds.), *Grundrechte in der Europäischen Union,* §20 para. 780; J. Schwarze, in id. (ed.), *EU-Kommentar,* Art. 15 ChFR para. 3; H.-J. Blanke, in P. J. Tettinger/K. Stern (eds.), *Kölner Gemeinschaftskommentar zur Europäischen Grundrechte-Charta,* Art. 15 ChFR para. 25.

103   R. Streinz, in id. (ed.), *EUV/AEUV,* Art. 15 ChFR para. 14; U. Zachert, *NZA* 2001, 1041, 1044.

104   M. Ruffert, in C. Calliess/M. Ruffert (eds.), *EUV/AEUV,* Art. 15 ChFR paras. 26 sq.

105   In more detail W. Däubler, *AuR* 2001, 380, 383; s.a. id., *Festschrift für Hanau,* 489–503; to ECHR T. Marauhn, *RabelsZ* 63 (1999), 537–560.

106   Cf. M. Ruffert, in C. Calliess/M. Ruffert (eds.), *EUV/AEUV,* Art. 12 ChFR para. 15; N. Bernsdorff, in J. Meyer (eds.), *Charta der Grundrechte der Europäischen Union,*

to take collective action are specifically guaranteed in Article 28 ChFR (see paras. 50 sq.below).

e)   Right to Protection of Personal Data

39.   As part of the protection of privacy (see Article 7 ChFR), Article 8 ChFR provides for 'the right to the protection of personal data concerning him or her'.[107] The provision is based upon former Article 286(1) EC, today's Article 16(1) TFEU. Details of the right to data protection are regulated at the EU level in the Data Protection Directive[108] and the Directive on Privacy and Electronic Communication.[109,110] The right to data protection can be of considerable practical impact in the area of employment law:[111] Article 8 ChFR may be instrumental in the interpretation of the data protection directives. It can also be interpreted as imposing a duty on the Union and on the Member States to ensure adequate data protection, thus exerting an indirect horizontal effect. In the context of fundamental freedoms, Article 8 ChFR may constitute a limitation (see also §3 paras. 46, 48, 69 sqq. below).

3.   Equality

40.   Title III contains equality rights, starting with the general principle that 'Everyone is equal before the law', (Article 20 ChFR). In the employment context, the fundamental right to non-discrimination (Article 21 ChFR), equality between men and women (Article 23 ChFR) and the integration of persons with disabilities are of particular importance. The principle of equality and the prohibition of discrimination can rightly be considered one of the cornerstones of EU law and, indeed, the Union. The specific manifestations of the fundamental principle will be discussed in detail in §§8–11 below.

41.   Pursuant to Article 21 ChFR, 'any discrimination based on any ground such as sex, race, colour, ethnic or social origin, genetic features, language,

---

Art. 12 ChFR para. 18; M. Knecht, in J. Schwarze (ed.), *EU-Kommentar*, Art. 12 ChFR para. 8; R. Streinz, in id. (ed.), *EUV/AEUV*, Art. 12 ChFR para. 9.

[107]   See already ECJ Case 29/69 *Stauder* [1969] ECR 419.

[108]   Directive 95/46/EC of the European Parliament and of the Council of 24 October 1995 on the protection of individuals with regard to the processing of personal data and on the free movement of such data, OJ 1995 L 281/31.

[109]   Directive 2002/58/EC of the European Parliament and of the Council of 12 July 2002 concerning the processing of personal data and the protection of privacy in the electronic communications sector, OJ 2002 L 201/37.

[110]   On the normative background, see explanations by the Praesidium of the Convention to Art. 8 ChFR, Dok. CHARTE 4473/00 CONVENT 50, 11; available at www.europarl.europa.eu/charter/pdf/04473_en.pdf; T. Kingreen, in C. Calliess/M. Ruffert (eds.), Art. 8 ChFR paras. 2–8.

[111]   R. Streinz/W. Michl, *EuZW* 2011, 384, 385–388.

religion or belief, political or any other opinion, membership of a national minority, property, birth, disability, age or sexual orientation shall be prohibited'. The provision draws upon Article 19 TFEU and expands the list of forbidden grounds recognised therein. Since adoption of the Charter, the Court of Justice, in its *Mangold*-decision, has recognised the prohibition of age-discrimination as a general principle of (then) Community law (see para. 14 above). In its subsequent judgments in *Kücükdeveci* and *Prigge*, it has confirmed this jurisprudence, now with reference to Article 21 ChFR.[112]

42. Among the prohibitions of discrimination, equality of men and women has historically figured particularly prominently in Community law (and still does today in Union law). The 1957 EEC Treaty already required equal pay for men and women (Article 119 EEC) – albeit motivated by competitive considerations – and the Court of Justice has subsequently developed it as a social right. Community legislation supplements and extends the principle. See in detail §§8, 9 below.

43. While Article 21 ChFR provides for a prohibition of disability discrimination, Article 26 of the Charter describes integration of persons with disabilities as a fundamental right. The 2000 Equal Treatment Framework Directive requires employers to make 'reasonable accommodations' for disabled persons; see in more detail §11 paras. 27 sq. below.

4. Social Fundamental Rights of Workers

a) Introduction

44. Under the heading of 'solidarity', the Charter contains a catalogue of so-called 'fundamental social rights'. They were the subject of particular debate in the Convention's deliberations.[113] There was doubt whether the disparate traditions of the Member States could be unified. Another concern was that the recognition of social rights could impose excessive financial burdens upon the Member States.[114] Those arguing in favour of social rights postulated an 'indivisibility' of

---

[112] ECJ Case C-555/07 *Kücükdeveci* [2010] ECR I-365 para. 22; Case C-447/09 *Prigge* 13 September 2011 para. 38 ('The prohibition of all discrimination on grounds, *inter alia*, of age is incorporated in Article 21 of the Charter of Fundamental Rights of the European Union ..., which, from 1 December 2009, has the same legal status as the treaties.').

[113] N. Bernsdorff, *VSSR* 2001, 1–23; B.-O. Bryde, *RdA* 2003 Special Supplement to Issue 5, 5, 7 sq.; W. Frenz/V. Götzkes, *RdA* 2007, 216; B. Losch/W. Radau, *NVwZ* 2003, 1440, 1442; S. Krebber, in C. Calliess/M. Ruffert (eds.), Art. 27 ChFR para. 2; J. Meyer/M. Engels, *ZRP* 2000, 368–371; R. Wank, in P. Hanau/H.-D. Steinmeyer/R. Wank (eds.), *Handbuch des europäischen Arbeits- und Sozialrechts*, §13 para. 141; M. Weiss, *AuR* 2001, 374, 375, 377; U. Zachert, *NZA* 2001, 1041, 1042.

[114] U. Everling, *Festschrift für Heinze*, 157, 161.

political and social rights.[115] Further, they pointed out that the Community Charter of Fundamental Social Rights (see paras. 65–77 below) had already been recognised in Article 151 TFEU.[116] The final result is a compromise. Social rights were included in the Charter, but their scope of protection is only weak and they have not been designed as claims (*Leistungsrechte*) against the Member States or the Union.[117] In many instances, the Charter does not provide for autonomous guarantees, but rather refers the question of whether and to what extent protection should be granted, to the law of the Union and the Member States. As the legislative materials indicate, social rights have often been construed by way of 'reverse engineering', starting from the *acquis communautaire*.[118] Thus, the comments in relation to Article 8 ChFR on the protection of personal data state that the article 'is based on' (what is now) Article 16 TFEU and the Data Protection Directive.[119]

b)   Personal Scope of Protection

45.   Articles 27, 28, 30 and 31 ChFR protect exclusively employees, whereas Articles 29, 33 and 34 ChFR protect everybody. The Charter does not define the concept of '**worker**'. Teleological considerations of an effective protection of fundamental rights point towards an autonomous definition for which the Court's case law on the free movement of workers (see §3 paras. 9–12 below) could be relevant.[120]

46.   Nationals of **third countries** are expressly only entitled to social security benefits and social advantages; Article 34(2) ChFR protects 'everyone residing and moving legally within the European Union'.[121] By *argumentum e contrario*, the other social rights can only be invoked by nationals of the Member States.[122]

---

[115]   Cf. Commission (ed.), Report of the Expert Group on Fundamental Rights, 'Affirming Fundamental Rights in the European Union – Time to Act' (1999), 17, available at http://ftp. infoeuropa.eurocid.pt/database/000038001-000039000/000038827.pdf; J. Meyer/M. Engels, *ZRP* 2000, 368, 369. This consideration has also been incorporated in the Preamble, cf. pt. 2 of the Preamble pursuant to which human dignity, freedom, equality and solidarity are indivisible; B. Losch/W. Raudau, *NVwZ* 2003, 1440, 1442, 1445.

[116]   S. Krebber, in C. Calliess/M. Ruffert (eds.), *EUV/AEUV*, Art. 27 ChFR para. 3. See also R. Pitschas, *VSSR* 2000, 207, 214–220.

[117]   See (critically) C. Calliess, *EuZW* 2001, 261, 264 sq.

[118]   See also B. Hepple, *ILJ* 30 (2001), 225 (227: 'The charge that the Charter creates "new rights" can be readily rebutted.').

[119]   Directive 95/45/EC on the protection of individuals with regard to the processing of personal data and on the free movement of such data, OJ 1995 L 281/31.

[120]   H. Lang, in P. J. Tettinger/K. Stern (eds.), *Kölner Gemeinschaftskommentar zur Europäischen Grundrechte-Charta*, Art. 27 ChFR para. 21; Art. 30 ChFR para. 4; H. Jarass, *EU-Grundrechte*, §29 para. 3.

[121]   For a critical analysis, see M. Weiss, *AuR* 2001, 374, 377.

[122]   For a dissenting view see H. Jarass, *EU-Grundrechte*, §29 para. 3; H. Lang, in P. J. Tettinger/K. Stern (eds.), *Kölner Gemeinschaftskommentar zur Europäischen Grundrechte-Charta*, Art. 27 ChFR para. 21.

c) Substantive Scope of Application

aa) THE RIGHT TO INFORMATION AND CONSULTATION

47. Article 27 ChFR creates a 'right' to information and consultation[123] but this right takes the form only of a principle which is cast in rather vague terms, referring to secondary legislation and the Member States' laws for its precise details. The provision merely covers the right to information and consultation but not the more far-reaching aspect of employee participation at the board level (which, in EU law, is a clearly distinct issue; see §26 para. 1 below).[124]

48. Workers and their representatives must be informed and consulted 'at the appropriate levels' and 'in good time'. The right is, however, guaranteed only 'in the cases and under the conditions provided for by Union law and national laws and practices'. Article 27 ChFR is thus a mere reference to existing law and does not autonomously determine its scope of protection.[125] It neither requires that further rights to information and consultation are adopted nor that the *status quo* be maintained.[126] However, as a minimum, a core of information and consultation rights seems to be indispensable.[127]

49. The *acquis communautaire* of rights to information and consultation is rather well developed, though Article 153(1) lit. e), (2) TFEU (see §4 para. 16 below) provides for a Union competence for harmonisation in this area. Rights to information had initially been laid down in specific directives for specific employment issues (Collective Redundancies Directive, Transfer of Undertakings Directive, Safety and Health Framework Directive; see in detail §§13, 23–26 below). More recently, EU legislation has addressed rights to information and consultation as such (Information and Consultation Framework Directive, European Works Council Directive, SE-Directive, SCE-Directive; see in detail §§27–29 below).

---

[123] See already Art. 21 RESC (see para. 3 above) and No. 17, 18 CFSR (para. 75 below).

[124] See also U. Zachert, *NZA* 2001, 1041, 1045; S. Krebber, in C. Calliess/M. Ruffert (eds.), *EUV/ AEUV*, Art. 27 ChFR para. 15; H. Lang, in P. J. Tettinger/K. Stern (eds.), *Kölner Gemeinschaftskommentar zur Europäischen Grundrechte-Charta*, Art. 27 ChFR paras. 18 sq., 26. Critically also M. Weiss, *AuR* 2001, 374, 376.

[125] To the same effect U. Everling, *Gedächtnisschrift für Heinze*, 173; W. Frenz/V. Götzkes, *RdA* 2007, 216, 217; S. Krebber, in C. Calliess/M. Ruffert (eds.), *EUV/AEUV*, Art. 27 ChFR paras. 10–14; see also W. Däubler, *AuR* 2001, 380, 384 ('of little value' – my translation).

[126] S. Krebber, in C. Calliess/M. Ruffert (eds.), *EUV/AEUV*, Art. 27 ChFR para. 12; apparently also R. Streinz, in id. (ed.), *EUV/AEUV*, Art. 27 ChFR para. 2; H. Lang, in P. J. Tettinger/K. Stern (eds.), *Kölner Gemeinschaftskommentar zur Europäischen Grundrechte-Charta*, Art. 27 ChFR para. 25; s.a. N. Bernsdorff, *VSSR* 2001, 1, 17.

[127] W. Frenz/V. Götzkes, *RdA* 2007, 216, 218 (arg. e Art. 1 ChFR, human dignity, arguing that undertakings were obliged to provide for some form of information and consultation); differently S. Krebber, in C. Calliess/M. Ruffert (eds.), *EUV/AEUV*, Art. 27 ChFR para. 12.

bb) Right of Collective Bargaining and Action

50. Employers and employees have the right to negotiate and conclude collective agreements and to pursue their interests in case of conflict by way of collective action, which includes strike action.[128] Again, these rights are only guaranteed 'in accordance with Union law and national laws and practices', Article 28 ChFR.[129] There is, of course, no specific secondary legislation in this area. Article 153(5) TFEU specifically excludes 'the right of association, the right to strike or the right to impose lock-out' (and thus also the right of collective bargaining[130]) from the Union's legislative competence. Moreover, Article 51(2) ChFR explicitly states that it does not extend competences (see para. 26 above).[131] As a consequence, the rights of Article 28 ChFR are primarily determined by the laws of the Member States.[132] The limitation contained in Article 153(5) TFEU does not exempt collective action from EU law. Fundamental freedoms and the prohibitions of discrimination in particular, may therefore limit this fundamental right.[133] Beyond that, the rights of collective bargaining and action do not seem to have any practical importance in the context of implementation of Union law, Article 51(1) ChFR.[134]

51. Article 28 ChFR supplements the freedom of association contained in Article 12(1), in respect of collective bargaining and action.[135] In relation to the right of information and consultation contained in Article 27 ChFR, Article 28 is more specific where collective agreements are concerned. Article 28 also covers collective agreements on the shop floor level.[136] Going beyond the national laws of some of the Member States, Germany in particular, the right to collective

---

[128] ECJ Case 447/09 *Prigge* 13 September 2011 para. 47; Case C-271/08 *Commission* v. *Germany* 15 July 2010 paras. 37 sqq.

[129] See already Art. 6 ESC; No. 12–14 CFSR. On freedom of association, see para. 38 above. On the interpretation in more detail R. Rebhahn, *Gedächtnisschrift für Heinze*, 649–660.

[130] To the same effect S. Krebber, in C. Calliess/M. Ruffert (eds.), *EUV/AEUV*, Art. 153 EG para. 12; apparently also E. Eichenhofer, in R. Streinz (ed.), *EUV/AEUV*, Art. 153 AEUV para. 13; dissenting R. Rebhahn/ M. Reiner, in J. Schwarze (ed.), *EU-Kommentar*, Art. 137 EG paras. 50, 56.

[131] Critically M. Weiss, *AuR* 2001, 374, 377.

[132] U. Everling, *Gedächtnisschrift für Heinze*, 157, 173 sq. ('limited value' – my translation); S. Krebber, in C. Calliess/M. Ruffert (eds.), *EUV/AEUV*, Art. 28 ChFR paras. 3 sq. ('superfluous' – my translation); R. Streinz, in id. (ed.), *EUV/AEUV*, Art. 28 ChFR para. 5. More optimistically W. Däubler, *AuR* 2001, 380, 383 sq.; S. Rixen, in P. J. Tettinger/K. Stern (eds.), *Kölner Gemeinschaftskommentar zur Europäischen Grundrechte-Charta*, Art. 28 ChFR para. 22.

[133] ECJ Case 447/09 *Prigge* 13 September 2011 paras. 47 sq.; Case C-438/05 *Viking* [2007] ECR I-10779 para. 44; Case C-341/05 *Laval un Partneri* [2007] ECR I-11767 para. 91.

[134] R. Rebhahn, *Gedächtnisschrift für Heinze*, 655–660.

[135] For details, see S. Rixen, in P. J. Tettinger/K. Stern (eds.), *Kölner Gemeinschaftskommentar zur Europäischen Grundrechte-Charta,* Art. 28 ChFR paras. 13 sq.

[136] S. Krebber, in C. Calliess/M. Ruffert (eds.), *EUV/AEUV,* Art. 28 ChFR para. 5; H. D. Jarass, *Charta der Grundrechte der EU*, Art. 28 GRCh para. 6.

---

action is not only guaranteed as an instrument to resolve conflicts in collective bargaining situations, but more generally, as an instrument to resolve *conflicts of interests*.[137]

cc) RIGHT OF ACCESS TO PLACEMENT SERVICES

52. Everyone has the right of access to free placement services, Article 29 ChFR.[138] 'Everyone' includes those seeking employment as well as those offering employment. 'Access' means that the placement services will make a genuine effort to find or place an employee. Placement services can be publicly or privately organised,[139] and the right to access does not entail a right to access each and every placement service. There is no obligation placed upon the State to institute placement services.[140]

53. The possibilities for the Union to contribute to the guaranteeing of this right are limited. The Union does not have the competence to institute placement services of its own.[141] Pursuant to Article 153(1) lit. h) TFEU, the Union may only 'support and complement the activities of the Member States' in 'the integration of persons excluded from the labour market'.[142]

dd) PROTECTION IN THE EVENT OF UNJUSTIFIED DISMISSAL

54. Every worker has the right to protection against unjustified dismissal, Article 30 ChFR.[143] However, once again, the right is guaranteed only 'in accordance with Union law and national laws and practices'. The Charter does not, in other words, make any commitment of its own.[144] 'Dismissal' is the

---

[137] U. Zachert, *NZA* 2001, 1041, 1045; R. Streinz, in id. (ed.), *EUV/AEUV*, Art. 28 ChFR para. 6; S. Rixen, in P. J. Tettinger/K. Stern (eds.), *Kölner Gemeinschaftskommentar zur Europäischen Grundrechte-Charta*, Art. 28 ChFR para. 10; H. D. Jarass, *Charta der Grundrechte der EU*, Art. 28 GRCh para. 7. On the limitation to conflicts between employer- and employee-interest M. Holoubek, in J. Schwarze (ed.), *EU-Kommentar*, Art. 28 ChFR para. 20.

[138] See already Art. 1 No. 3 ESC; No. 6 CFSR. With this, the Charter goes beyond the traditions of the Member States; S. Krebber, in C. Calliess/M. Ruffert (eds.), *EUV/AEUV*, Art. 27 ChFR para. 4; R. Streinz, in id. (ed.), *EUV/AEUV*, Art. 29 ChFR para. 2, H. Lang, in P. J. Tettinger/K. Stern (eds.), *Kölner Gemeinschaftskommentar zur Europäischen Grundrechte-Charta*, Art. 29 ChFR paras. 3 sq.

[139] S. Krebber, in C. Calliess/M. Ruffert (eds.), *EUV/AEUV*, Art. 29 ChFR para. 4; E. Riedel, in J. Meyer (eds.), *Charta der Grundrechte der Europäischen Union*, Art. 29 ChFR para. 8.

[140] N. Bernsdorff, *VSSR* 2001, 1 (19) therefore considers a guarantee of participation in existing institutions, free of discrimination, to be at the heart of the provision. See also F. Ross, in J. Schwarze (ed.), *EU-Kommentar*, Art. 29 ChFR para. 2 with further references.

[141] S. Krebber, in C. Calliess/M. Ruffert (eds.), *EUV/AEUV*, Art. 153 AEUV para. 19.

[142] S. Krebber, in C. Calliess/M. Ruffert (eds.), *EUV/AEUV*, Art. 29 ChFR para. 5.

[143] In more detail R. Rebhahn, *Festschrift für Bauer, Maier, Petrag*, 283–297. On the regulatory environment S. Krebber, in C. Calliess/M. Ruffert (eds.), *EUV/AEUV*, Art. 30 ChFR para. 1.

[144] As the recent decision of ECJ Case C-323/08 *Rodríguez Mayor* [2009] ECR I-11621 paras. 58 sq. illustrates.

termination of the contract by the employer.[145] From a teleological perspective, termination by the employee must equally be covered where it has been induced by the employer. By the same token, Article 30 ChFR also covers the circumvention of protection against unfair dismissal by means of fixed-term employment. Protection does not necessarily mean that the employee must be reinstated into his employment position. Protection may also be achieved through compensation.[146]

55. Union law contains protection against unfair dismissal in the Collective Redundancies Directive (§23), in the Transfer of Undertakings Directive (§24), the Anti-Discrimination Directives (§§8–11), the Parental Leave Directive (§21), the Part-time Work Directive (§16), the Fixed-term Work Directive (§17), the Maternity Protection Directive (§20), the Safety and Health Framework Directive (§13), the Information and Consultation Framework Directive (§27), and the Insolvency Protection Directive (§25).[147]

56. Special protection against 'dismissal for a reason connected with **maternity**' is provided for in Article 33(2) ChFR. Given that the provision distinguishes between maternity leave and parental leave, the protection against dismissal on grounds of maternity is concerned with the specific need for protection of pregnant women, women who have recently given birth or who are breastfeeding.[148]

ee) Right to Fair and Just Working Conditions

57. Contrary to its promising title, Article 31 ChFR is concerned with 'fair and just' working conditions in only a limited sense since it deals only health, safety and dignity as well as working time.[149] In particular, the provision does not address the issue of a 'fair exchange', i.e. 'fair remuneration'.[150] In EU law, the

---

[145] In more detail R. Rebhahn, *Festschrift für Bauer, Maier, Petrag,* 288 sq.

[146] R. Rebhahn, *RdA* 2002, 272, 291; J. Lindner, *RdA* 2005, 166–170.

[147] R. Rebhahn, *Festschrift für Bauer, Maier, Petrag,* 292–297 (speaking of a 'fundamental right without scope of application' – my translation – given the limited regulation in Union law). See also U. Everling, *Gedächtnisschrift für Heinze,* 157, 173.

[148] '"Maternity" covers the period from conception to weaning.', explanations by the Praesidium of the Convention to Art. 33 ChFR, Dok. CHARTE 4473/00 CONVENT 50, 31; available at www.europarl.europa.eu/charter/pdf/04473_en.pdf.

[149] The explanations by the Praesidium of the Convention to Art. 31 ChFR refer to the Safety and Health Directive with regard to paragraph 1 and to the Working Time Directive with regard to paragraph 2; Dok. CHARTE 4473/00 CONVENT 50, 29; available at www.europarl.europa.eu/charter/pdf/04473_en.pdf.

[150] Differently U. Everling, *Gedächtnisschrift für Heinze,* 173, who suggests to establish the necessary restrictions by a requirement of implementation. In favour of a fundamental right to fair remuneration as well as fair employment conditions (beyond mere protection of safety and health) R. Blanpain et al., *KritV* 1995, 452 (458). On No. 4 CFSR see also para. 72 below.

interests protected in Article 31 ChFR are addressed by the Safety and Health Framework Directive, various individual supplementing directives (see §13 below) and by the Working Time Directive (see §14 below).

58. The provision is supplemented by Article 32 ChFR on the protection of young people and by Article 33(2) ChFR on maternity protection. Despite its ambiguous wording, Articles 31–33 ChFR do not give rise to individual rights for employees against their employers, but rather constitute a general mandate of the Union (again, though, without extending the Union's competences; see para. 26 above).[151]

ff)   PROHIBITION OF CHILD LABOUR AND PROTECTION OF YOUNG PEOPLE AT WORK

59. Child labour is prohibited. Employment of young people (age limit: minimum school-leaving age) must be adapted to their development and to their special needs for protection, Article 32 ChFR. They must be protected from economic exploitation and any work likely to harm their safety, health or physical, mental, moral or social development or to interfere with their education. In Union law, these concerns are addressed in the Young People at Work Directive (see §22 below).

gg)   PROTECTION OF FAMILY AND PROFESSIONAL LIFE

60. Article 33 ChFR concerns the protection of family and professional life. Paragraph 1 is a matter of social law as it does not refer to the employment relation as such when it postulates 'legal, economic and social protection'.[152] Paragraph 2 guarantees protection against dismissal and maternity leave for new mothers and parental leave following the birth or adoption of a child. In EU law, the Maternity Protection Directive (see §20 below) and the Parental Leave Directive (see §21 below) address these issues.

hh)   SOCIAL SECURITY AND SOCIAL ASSISTANCE

61. The Union 'recognises and respects' the 'entitlement to social security benefits and social services providing protection' in a non-conclusive list of 'emergencies'. By way of example, the provision refers to maternity, illness, industrial accidents, dependency, old age, and loss of employment. The provision merely states a principle and does not contain a rule, given that it refers to the

---

[151]   Generally N. Bernsdorff, *VSSR* 2001, 1, 20. It seems doubtful whether Art. 31 ChFR can also establish an individual right to have laws enacted. Opposed to that U. Everling, *Festschrift für Heinze*, 157, 173.

[152]   See also B. Losch/W. Raudau, *NVwZ* 2003, 1440, 1442.

entitlement 'in accordance with the rules laid down by Union law and national laws and practices'.[153] Paragraph 2 provides for a specific equality right with regard to social benefits.[154]

5. Limitations

62. The Charter does not pursue a differentiated approach to limitations. There are, in other words, no specific rules of limitations for each individual right (as is, for example, the case in German constitutional law). Instead, Article 52 ChFR provides for a **general clause** on limitations, applicable to all fundamental rights. The specificities of individual fundamental rights can thus only be addressed by way of a purposive (teleological) interpretation.[155]

63. Formally, a limitation of fundamental rights must be provided for **by law**, Article 52(1) sent. 1 ChFR. In EU legislation, regulations and directives are the respective instruments (but not decisions or recommendations).[156] In substance, limitations may be made on grounds of a **general interest** recognised by the Union or to protect the **rights and (fundamental) freedoms of others**.[157] In any case, the **essence** of the rights and freedoms must be respected and limitations are subject to the principle of **proportionality**, Article 52(1) sent. 2 ChFR.[158]

64. Where the rights of the Charter correspond to rights of the ECHR, 'the meaning and scope of those rights shall be the same as those laid down by the said Convention', Article 52(3) sent. 1 ChFR. This reference also includes the **limitations of the ECHR**; but the Charter may provide for more extensive protection of rights, Article 52(3) sent. 2 ChFR.[159] With regard to employment

---

153   R. Streinz, in id. (ed.), *EUV/AEUV*, Art. 34 ChFR para. 5. But see also A. Nußberger, in P. J. Tettinger/K. Stern (eds.), *Kölner Gemeinschaftskommentar zur Europäischen Grundrechte-Charta*, Art. 34 ChFR paras. 53 sq.

154   In more detail S. Krebber, in C. Calliess/M. Ruffert (eds.), *EUV/AEUV*, Art. 34 ChFR paras. 6–13; A. Nußberger, in P. J. Tettinger/K. Stern (eds.), *Kölner Gemeinschaftskommentar zur Europäischen Grundrechte-Charta*, Art. 34 ChFR paras. 101–103.

155   For a critical perspective with a view to effective protection of fundamental rights M. Kenntner, *ZRP* 2000, 423, 425; R. Wank, in P. Hanau/H.-D. Steinmeyer/R. Wank (eds.), *Handbuch des europäischen Arbeits- und Sozialrechts*, §13 para. 148.

156   C. Calliess, *EuZW* 2001, 261, 264.

157   ECJ Case C-271/08 *Commission v. Germany* [2010] ECR I-7091 paras. 43 sq.; Case 112/00 *Schmidberger* [2003] ECR I-5659. U. Zachert, *NZA* 2001, 1041, 1043; W. Däubler, *Festschrift für Hanau*, 500 sq.; see also M. Fuchs, in id./F. Marhold (eds.), *Europäisches Arbeitsrecht*, 278–280.

158   ECJ Case C-271/08 *Commission v. Germany* [2010] ECR I-7091 paras. 43 sq., 52 ('fair balance'). See also T. v. Danwitz, in P. J. Tettinger/K. Stern (eds.), *Kölner Gemeinschaftskommentar zur Europäischen Grundrechte-Charta*, Art. 52 ChFR paras. 39–44.

159   C. Calliess, *EuZW* 2001, 261, 264; cf. also the final report of Group II (Incorporation of the Charter/accession to the ECHR) of the European Convention 22 October 2002, CONV 354/02, p. 7; available at http://register.consilium.europa.eu/pdf/en/02/cv00/cv00354.en02.

---

law, the limitations of the right to form a trade union pursuant to Article 11(2) ECHR may be of practical importance.

IV. THE COMMUNITY CHARTER OF FUNDAMENTAL SOCIAL RIGHTS

Bibliography:

B. Bercusson, 'The European Community's Charter of Fundamental Social Rights of Workers', *MLR* 1990, 624–642; R. Blanpain et al., 'Soziale Grundrechte: Vorschläge für die Europäische Union', *KritV* 1995, 452–463; H. Buchner, 'Das deutsche Arbeits- und Sozialrecht unter dem Einfluss der Europäischen Gemeinschaft', *VSSR* 1992, 1–32; W. Däubler, 'Soziale Mindeststandards in der EG – eine realistische Perspektive?', in R. Birk (ed.), *Die soziale Dimension des europäischen Binnenmarktes* (Baden-Baden: Nomos, 1989), 49–71; B. Hepple, 'The Implementation of the Community Charter of Fundamental Social Rights', *MLR* 53 (1990), 643–654; M. Heinze, 'Die Gemeinschaftscharta der sozialen Grundrechte der Arbeitnehmer und die Vertragsrevision des Unionsvertrages 1996', in R. Anzinger/R. Wank (eds.), *Entwicklungen im Arbeitsrecht und Arbeitsschutzrecht – Festschrift für Otfried Wlotzke* (Munich: C.H. Beck, 1996), 669–682; U. Preis/M. Gotthardt, 'Arbeitsrecht als Gegenstand des Gemeinschaftsrechts – Das Europäische Arbeitsrecht', in H. Oetker/U. Preis (eds.), *Europäisches Arbeits- und Sozialrecht, EAS, part B – Systematische Darstellungen*, loose-leaf (Heidelberg: Forkel, last update: July 2000), B 1100 para. 35; S. J. Silvia, 'The Social Charter of the European Community: A Defeat for European Labor', *Ind. & L.R.Rev.* 44 (1990–91), 626–643; P. Watson, 'The Community Social Charter', *CMLR* 1991, 37–68; Lord K. W. Wedderburn, *The Social Charter, European Company and Employment Rights – An Outline Agenda* (London: The Institute of Employment Rights, 1990); Lord K. W. Wedderburn, 'The Social Charter in Britain – Labour Law and Labour Courts', *MLR* 54 (1991), 1–47; M. Weiss, 'Zur zukünftigen Rolle der Europäischen Union im Arbeitsrecht', in P. Hanau/E. Lorenz/H. Matthes (eds.), *Festschrift für Günther Wiese* (Neuwied/Kriftel: Luchterhand, 1998), 633–648; O. Wlotzke, 'EG-Binnenmarkt und Arbeitsrechtsordnung – Eine Orientierung', *NZA* 1990, 417–423; M. Zuleeg, 'Eine neue Gemeinschaftscharta der sozialen Grundrechte?', *AuR* 1995, 429 sq.; M. Zuleeg, 'Der Schutz sozialer Rechte in der Rechtsordnung der Europäischen Gemeinschaft', *EuGRZ* 1992, 329–334.

1. Introduction and Overview

65. The Community Charter of Fundamental Social Rights of Workers (CFSR) is part of the foundations of EU employment law.[160] Adopted on 9 December 1989

---

pdf. On the scope of this 'transfer clause' T. v. Danwitz, in P. J. Tettinger/K. Stern (eds.), *Kölner Gemeinschaftskommentar zur Europäischen Grundrechte-Charta*, Art. 52 ChFR paras. 56–60.

[160] Community Charter of the Fundamental Social Rights of Workers of 9 December 1989; see also the drafts by Commission, COM(89) 248 final and COM(89) 471 final.

by eleven of the then twelve Member States (without the UK)[161] as a 'solemn declaration', the Community Charter contains what can be called a 'programmatic summary' of fundamental social rights (Title 1, No. 1–26; in detail 3. below) together with provisions on the 'Implementation of the Charter' (No. 27–30; see paras. 69 sq. below). After the change of government in the UK in 1997 (see §1 para. 38 above), the UK gave up its resistance against the Community Charter,[162] and the Amsterdam Treaty introduced a reference to it in Article 151 TFEU.[163] With a view to a prompt implementation of the Community Charter, the Commission quickly adopted an action programme on 29 November 1989 (i.e. before the Charter itself was adopted).[164]

66. Today, the Community Charter is in many respects obsolete, given that the Charter of Fundamental Rights also contains an extensive catalogue of fundamental social rights (see para. 47–61 above). It has, however, given substantial impetus to the development of EU employment law, and numerous acts of secondary legislation refer to it (see e.g. Recital 6 ETFD, Recital 7 PTWD, Recital 7 FTWD, Recitals 5 and 6 MPD, Recital 3 PLD, Recital 2 ICFD). The development and content of the Community Charter shall thus be briefly described.

2.   History, Legal Status and Legal Effects

67. When the 1987 Single European Act, which was primarily focused on the realisation of the internal market and thus economic objectives, was adopted, some voices raised the issue of a **social dimension of the internal market**: What would the effects of the establishment and completion of the internal market be on the social rights and interests of, in particular, workers (see already §1 para. 33 above)?[165] Some pointed to the stimulating effects of the internal market upon the labour market. Others were concerned that it might lead to a lowering of social (employee) protection standards ('social dumping').[166] In consequence, the Community Charter of Fundamental Social Rights, establishing social rights and interests, was created as a counterweight to the Single European Act with its economic focus.

---

[161]   On the British response to the Charter, see Lord Wedderburn, *The Social Charter, European Company and Employment Rights*, 7 sq. See also D. Schiek, *Europäisches Arbeitsrecht*, 58; O.Wlotzke, *NZA* 1990, 417, 421.

[162]   O. Schulz, *Grundlagen und Perspektiven einer Europäischen Sozialpolitik* (Cologne: Heymanns, 2003) 99 sq., 111, 116 sq.

[163]   R. Blanpain et al., *KritV* 1995, 452, 454, had favoured a reference in Art. 6(2) EU-Treaty.

[164]   Communication from the Commission concerning its Action Programme relating to the Implementation of the Community Charter of Basic Social Rights for Workers, COM(89) 568 final. See also B. Hepple, *MLR* 53 (1990), 643–654 (discussing issues of implementation).

[165]   In more detail W. Däubler, in R. Birk (ed.), *Die soziale Dimension des europäischen Binnenmarktes*, 49–71; see also Zuleeg, *EuGRZ* 1992, 329.

[166]   See e.g. the exposition in H.-D. Steinmeyer, in P. Hanau/H.-D. Steinmeyer/R. Wank (eds.), *Handbuch des europäischen Arbeits- und Sozialrechts*, §11 paras. 43–49; W. Däubler, in R. Birk (ed.), *Die soziale Dimension des europäischen Binnenmarktes*, 53 sq.

68.   Social fundamental rights were, however, by no means uncontroversial among the Member States – as the reluctance of the United Kingdom to participate amply proves. The controversy has affected both the content and the legal nature of the Community Charter.[167] In substance, it largely contains programmatic and repetitive statements (reiterating pre-existing EU primary law). Formally, the Community Charter, irrespective of its name, is not a legal act of the (then) Community (cf. Article 288 TFEU) and, given the abstention of the UK, is not even an instrument of all Member States. Instead, the Community Charter constitutes no more than a 'solemn declaration' without binding effect,[168] a 'political declaration of intent',[169] a 'working programme'.[170] It has nonetheless developed legal relevance, certainly since the Amsterdam Treaty, but it is primarily its political importance which should not be underestimated.

69.   The Community Charter's **legal status** (and relevance) is controversial. Given that the Community Charter itself is not binding, the 'fundamental rights' set forth in its first Title do not constitute directly applicable subjective rights.[171] Indeed, Title II regarding the 'implementation of the Charter' considers it 'particularly the responsibility of the Member States' to guarantee the rights of the Charter (No. 27 CFSR). The Commission is merely 'invited … to submit … initiatives which fall within its powers, as provided for in the Treaties' (No. 28 CFSR). The fundamental rights of the Community Charter cannot, as a whole, be regarded as general principles of EU law,[172] even though that may be the case with regard to some of its propositions (see para. 14

---

[167]   See e.g. B. Bercusson, *MLR* 1990, 624–642 (discussing selected issues in comparison of the various drafts).

[168]   Cf. e.g. M. Fuchs, in id./F. Marhold (eds.), *Europäisches Arbeitsrecht,* 21; R. Wank, in P. Hanau/H.-D. Steinmeier/R. Wank (eds.), *Handbuch des europäischen Arbeits- und Sozialrechts,* §13 para. 96; H. Konzen, 'Der europäische Einfluß auf das deutsche Arbeitsrecht nach dem Vertrag über die Europäische Union', *EuZW* 1995, 39, 40 ('solemn press release' – my translation).

[169]   M. Fuchs, in id./F. Marhold (eds.), *Europäisches Arbeitsrecht,* 21 – my translation; E. Eichenhofer, in R. Streinz (ed.), *EUV/AEUV,* Art. 150 AEUV para. 23; M. Zuleeg, *EuGRZ* 1992, 329, 330 sq.; W. Däubler, 'Instruments of EC Labour Law', in P. Davies et al. (eds.), *European Community Labour Law: Principles and Perspectives – Liber Amicorum Lord Wedderburn* (Oxford: Clarendon, 1996), 151, 159 ('declaration of good intent').

[170]   M. Zuleeg, *AuR* 1995, 429 – my translation. Also in this respect, the Charter suffers from its indeterminate wording; see W. Däubler, in R. Birk (ed.), *Die soziale Dimension des europäischen Binnenmarktes,* 67 ('classic example of the art of diplomatic-ambiguous drafting'; the draftsmen had followed the principle 'much ado about nothing' – my translations).

[171]   R. Rebhahn/M. Reiner, in J. Schwarze (ed.), *EU-Kommentar,* Art. 136 EG para. 10.

[172]   To this effect, though, M. Weiss, *Festschrift für Wiese,* 633, 635. Considering it as an aid for the interpretation M. Heinze, *Festschrift für Wlotzke,* 669, 670; B. Hepple, *MLR* 53 (1990), 643, 644; R. Wank, in P. Hanau/H.-D. Steinmeyer/R. Wank (eds.), *Handbuch des europäischen Arbeits- und Sozialrechts,* §13 para. 108; R. Rebhahn/M. Reiner, in J. Schwarze (ed.), *EU-Kommentar,* Art. 136 EG para. 10.

---

above). The jurisprudence of the Court of Justice is somewhat equivocal, though. In some decisions, the Court has referred to the Community Charter in order to emphasise the particular importance of an act of secondary legislation.[173] In the context of its recognition of a right to take collective action, the Court has recently referred to the Community Charter and considered it as one of the 'instruments developed by [the] Member States at Community level or in the context of the European Union'.[174] Notwithstanding its non-binding nature, the Community Charter may thus be used as a tool for the interpretation of secondary legislation, for example in the context of historical or teleological interpretation. It should however be observed that even the reference in Article 151 TFEU merely assigns limited weight to the Community Charter, stating that the social *objectives* of the Union have been formulated with a view to ('having in mind') the Community Charter (see also §4 para. 8 below).[175]

70. The **political dimension** of the Community Charter far outweighs its legal relevance.[176] It has thus been considered as the 'initial spark for an expansion of the social dimension of the internal market'.[177] The Commission has willingly accepted the invitation to contribute to the implementation of the Charter and produced an action programme on 29 November 1989, even before the Charter itself was adopted (see para. 61 above). This action programme has since been largely implemented. From today's perspective, the Community Charter can to a large extent be read as an overview of the 'programme and objectives of EU employment law'.[178]

---

[173]   See e.g. ECJ Joined Cases C-378/07 to C-380/07*Angelidaki* [2009] ECR I-3071 paras. 112; Case C-484/04 *Commission* v. *United Kingdom and Northern Ireland* [2006] ECR I-7471 para. 35; Case C-13/05 *Chacon Navas* [2006] ECR I-6467 para. 11; Joined Cases C-397/01 to C-403/01 *Pfeiffer* [2004] ECR I-8835 para. 91; Case C-151/02 *Jaeger* [2003] ECR I-8389 para. 47.

[174]   ECJ Case C-341/05 *Laval un Partneri* [2007] ECR I-11767 paras. 90 sq.; Case C-438/05 *Viking* [2007] ECR I-10779 paras. 43 sq.; Case C-271/08 *Commission* v. *Germany* [2010] ECR I-7091 para. 37; critically R. Rebhahn, *ZESAR* 2008, 109, 110.

[175]   U. Preis/M. Gotthardt, in *EAS*, B 1100 para. 35. Too far-reaching E. Eichenhofer, in R. Streinz (ed.), *EUV/AEUV*, Art. 151 AEUV para. 23 ('Status of a comprehensive competence in the field of social policy, legitimating measures of the Community' – my translation). Contrary to M. Weiss, *Festschrift für Wiese*, 42 (with regard to the European Social Charter), jurisdiction of the Court of Justice cannot be established on the basis Art. 151 TFEU.

[176]   B. Bercusson, *European Labour Law*, 139–141.

[177]   R. Birk, in R. Richardi/O. Wlotzke (eds.), *Münchener Handbuch zum Arbeitsrecht*, 2nd edn. (Munich: C.H. Beck, 2000), §18 para. 81 – my translation. See also Lord Wedderburn, *The Social Charter, European Company and Employment Rights*, 65 ('a remarkable signpost of social progress').

[178]   S. Grundmann, *Europäisches Schuldvertragsrecht*, §6 para. 28.

3. *Workers' Social Fundamental Rights*

71. The fundamental rights in the Charter are arranged in twelve sections which concern the following issues:[179]

[1]   freedom of movement (No. 1–3),
[2]   employment and remuneration (No. 4–6),
[3]   improvement of living and working conditions (No. 7–9),
[4]   social protection (No. 10),
[5]   freedom of association and collective bargaining (No. 11–14),
[6]   vocational training (No. 15),
[7]   equal treatment for men and women (No. 16),
[8]   information, consultation and participation for workers (No. 17–18),
[9]   health protection and safety at the workplace (No. 19),
[10] protection of children and adolescents (No. 20–23),
[11] elderly persons (No. 24–25), and
[12] disabled persons (No. 26).

72. To some extent, the propositions contained in the Community Charter **only repeat** what the TFEU expressly provides for, for example with regard to free movement of workers. With regard to the principle of equality, the Community Charter even lags behind the current state of primary law (Article 19 TFEU) and secondary legislation (see §§8–11) as it only addresses sex discrimination. In some areas, however, the Charter is particularly far-reaching, for example where, in addition to freedom to choose and engage in an occupation (No. 4 CFSR), it includes a right to 'fair remuneration' and defines this as 'a wage sufficient to enable them to have a decent standard of living' (No. 5 indent 1 CFSR).

73. With regard to the improvement of living and working conditions, No. 7 CFSR in effect deviates from the primacy of the internal market (cf. Article 3(3)(1) TFEU), when it requires that '[t]he completion of the internal market must lead to an improvement in the living and working conditions of workers in the European Community'. In substance, however, the provision merely addresses limited objectives of protection:

–   an approximation of national laws governing duration and organisation of work time and atypical forms of employment (No. 7(1) CFSR);
–   the development of certain aspects of employment regulations such as procedures for collective redundancies and bankruptcies (No. 7(2) CFSR);

---

[179]   For details see e.g. P. Watson, *CMLR* 1991, 37, 49 sqq.

- a right to a weekly rest period and to annual paid leave (No. 8 CFSR); and
- determination of the conditions of employment in laws, in a collective agreement or in an employment contract.

74.   The Community Charter recognises a **right of association** (No. 11 CFSR) and the **right to negotiate and conclude collective agreements** (No. 12 CFSR) as well as the right to resort to **collective action**, particularly strike action, in cases of conflicts of interest (No. 13 CFSR).

75.   The right to **information, consultation and the participation of workers** is emphasised with regard to

- companies and groups of companies with establishments or companies in several EU Member States (No. 17(2) CFSR);
- restructuring or merger of undertakings (No. 18 indent 2 CFSR); and
- cases of collective redundancy procedures (No. 18 indent 3 CFSR).

76.   With respect to **health protection and safety at the workplace**, the Community Charter postulates the worker's right to enjoy 'satisfactory health and safety conditions in his working environment' (No. 19(1) CFSR). It stresses 'the need for the training, information, consultation and balanced participation of workers as regards the risks incurred and the steps taken to eliminate or reduce them' (No. 19(2) CFSR).

77.   The fundamental social rights are thus rather broadly phrased, and in some respects the Community Charter goes far beyond other sources of EU law, especially for example in respect of fair remuneration.[180] At the same time, the catalogue is by no means comprehensive. While the Community Charter deals with some details such as the seizure and transfer of wages (No. 5 indent 3 CFSR), other important issues, such as economic protection in the event of a worker's illness, are not addressed.[181]

---

[180]   For an opposite view, see M. Weiss, *Festschrift für Wiese*, 635 (criticising the 'fragmentary' character).

[181]   H.-D. Steinmeyer, in P. Hanau/H.-D. Steinmeyer/R. Wank (eds.), *Handbuch des europäischen Arbeits- und Sozialrechts*, §11 para. 59.

§3. FUNDAMENTAL FREEDOMS

CONTENTS

I. OVERVIEW: FUNDAMENTAL FREEDOMS WITH RELEVANCE FOR EMPLOYMENT LAW

1. Next to the fundamental rights discussed in §2, the fundamental internal market freedoms set out in the TFEU are a second central component of EU employment law, which are largely independent of any harmonisation of conflicts of law rules or substantive law. Since the end of the transition period,[1] the fundamental freedoms are directly applicable individual rights. Individuals can invoke the fundamental freedoms directly in court proceedings and thereby render inapplicable conflicting national law of the Member States. Moreover, the fundamental freedoms also play a significant role in the interpretation and control of secondary Union law.[2]

---

[1] Article 8(1) of the EEC Treaty which entered into force on 1 January 1958 provided for a transitional period of twelve years.

[2] ECJ Case C-138/02 *Collins* [2004] ECR I-2703 paras. 60–63.

2. The free movement of workers is of obvious relevance for employment law, but freedom of services, establishment and free movement of capital should also be considered.[3] The various freedoms impact upon employment law in different ways, though. Free movement for workers is primarily an individual right which is enjoyed by employees against excessive restrictions placed upon cross-border work. However, the economic freedoms also have protective effects for employers. Freedom of services and freedom of establishment protect the employer against restrictions of his – temporary or permanent – activity in other Member States. The employer's right may, however, be limited to the extent necessary to protect employees. Free movement of capital – in our context – protects investors. Again, employee interests may justify limits to the investor's freedom.

3. The fundamental freedoms may not apply where the Union has already enacted secondary legislation. To the extent that secondary legislation conclusively regulates a certain area, there is no recourse to the fundamental freedoms.[4] Where secondary legislation conclusively provides for restrictions to fundamental freedoms, there is no recourse to Member States' law.[5] Secondary legislation thus takes precedence of application over the fundamental freedoms.[6] Yet, that secondary legislation must also conform with primary law, in particular the fundamental freedoms (see para. 50 below).

II. FREEDOM OF MOVEMENT FOR WORKERS

Bibliography:
C. Barnard, *The Substantive Law of the EU: The Four Freedoms*, 3rd edn. (Oxford: Oxford University Press, 2010); U. Battis/A. Ingold/K. Kuhnert, 'Zur Vereinbarkeit der "6+5"-Spielregel der FIFA mit dem Unionsrecht', *EuR* 2010, 3–30; U. Becker, 'Arbeitnehmerfreizügigkeit', in D. Ehlers (ed.), *Europäische Grundrechte und Grundfreiheiten*, 3rd edn. (Berlin/New York: de Gruyter, 2009), §9; C.-W. Canaris, 'Drittwirkung der gemeinschaftsrechtlichen Grundfreiheiten', in H. Bauer et al. (eds.),

---

3   Furthermore, free movement of goods may also be relevant to employment law; see e.g. ECJ Case 188/84 *Commission v. France* [1986] ECR 419 (prohibition of the import of German wood processing machines to France justified as they did not satisfy the national provisions of employee protection; see now Directive 98/37/EC of the European Parliament and of the Council of 22 June 1998 on the approximation of the laws of the Member States relating to machinery, OJ 1998 L 207/1); ECJ Case C-470/03 *A.G.M.-COS.MET* [2007] ECR I-2749. On both decisions, see D. Schiek, *Europäisches Arbeitsrecht*, 165.

4   ECJ Case C-309/02 *Radlberger Getränkegesellschaft and Spitz* [2004] ECR I-11763 para. 53; Case C-145/02 *Denkavit* [2005] ECR I-51 para. 22.

5   ECJ Case 251/78 *Denkavit* [1979] ECR 3369 para. 14; Case 5/77 *Tedeschi* [1977] ECR 1555 para. 35; Case C-323/93 *Centre d'Insemination de la Crespelle* [1994] ECR I-5077 para. 31; Case C-350/97 *Monsees* [1999] ECR I-2921 para. 24.

6   T. Kingreen, in C. Calliess/M. Ruffert (eds.), Art. 34–36 AEUV para. 18.

Umwelt, Wirtschaft und Recht – Wissenschaftliches Symposium aus Anlaß des 65. Geburtstages von Reiner Schmidt (Tübingen: Mohr Siebeck, 2002), 29–67; M. Coester/W. Denkhaus, 'Die Verordnung zur Freizügigkeit der Arbeitnehmer', in H. Oetker/U. Preis (eds.), *Europäisches Arbeits- und Sozialrecht, EAS, part B – Systematische Darstellungen,* loose-leaf (Heidelberg: Forkel, last update: October 1999), B 2100; D. Ehlers (ed.), *Europäische Grundrechte und Grundfreiheiten,* 3rd edn. (Berlin/New York: de Gruyter, 2009); M. Franzen, *Privatrechtsangleichung durch die Europäische Gemeinschaft* (Berlin/ New York: de Gruyter, 1999), §§4–6 (118–243); M. Fuchs, 'Arbeitsmigration im Spannungsfeld von nationalstaatlicher und europarechtlicher Regelung', in H. Konzen et al. (eds.), *Festschrift für Rolf Birk* (Tübingen: Mohr Siebeck, 2008), 115–133; N. Görlitz, *Struktur und Bedeutung der Rechtsfigur der mittelbaren Diskriminierung im System der Grundfreiheiten* (Baden-Baden: Nomos, 2005); S. Grundmann, *Europäisches Schuldvertragsrecht* (Berlin/New York: de Gruyter, 1999), part 1 paras. 53–104; H.-J. Hellwig/C. Behme, 'Gemeinschaftsrechtliche Probleme der deutschen Unternehmensmitbestimmung', *AG* 2009, 261–278; H.-J. Hellwig/C. Behme, 'Gemeinschaftsrechtswidrigkeit und Anwendungsvorrang des Gemeinschaftsrechts in der deutschen Unternehmensmitbestimmung', *ZIP* 2010, 871–874; W. Kluth, 'Die Bindung privater Wirtschaftsteilnehmer an die Grundfreiheiten des EG-Vertrages – Eine Analyse am Beispiel des Bosman-Urteils des EuGH', *AöR* 122 (1997), 557–582; E. Kocher, 'Arbeitnehmerfreizügigkeit und Berufsfreiheit – Ablaufen der Übergangsfristen am 1.5.2011 – aktuelle Rechtsprechung – Rückzahlung von Aus- und Weiterbildungskosten', *GPR* 2011, 132–138; T. Körber, *Grundfreiheiten und Privatrecht* (Tübingen: Mohr Siebeck, 2004), part 2 (55–376); R. Langer, 'Primärrechtliche Regelungen der Dienstleistungsfreiheit, Niederlassungsfreiheit und Freizügigkeit der Arbeitnehmer – Unter besonderer Berücksichtigung der Übergangsregelungen in den Beitrittsverträgen', *NZA* 2005 Supplement 2 to Issue 21, 83–87; H. Parpart, *Die unmittelbare Bindung Privater an die Personenverkehrsfreiheiten im europäischen Gemeinschaftsrecht – Eine Darstellung der Arbeitnehmerfreizügigkeit, Niederlassungs- und Dienstleistungsfreiheit* (Munich: C.H. Beck, 2003); K. Preedy, *Die Bindung Privater an die europäischen Grundfreiheiten. Zur sogenannten Drittwirkung im Europarecht* (Berlin: Duncker & Humblot, 2005); R. Resch, 'Arbeitnehmerfreizügigkeit und Diskriminierungsverbot für Amateurjugendmannschaftssportler', *ZESAR* 2009, 214–220; V. Rieble/C. Latzel, 'Inlandsmitbestimmung als Ausländerdiskriminierung bei Standortkonflikten', *EuZA* 2011, 145–170; S. Roloff, *Das Beschränkungsverbot des Art 39 EG (Freizügigkeit) und seine Auswirkungen auf das nationale Arbeitsrecht* (Berlin: Duncker & Humblot, 2003); U. Runggaldier/G.-P. Reissner, 'Die Freizügigkeit der Arbeitnehmer im EG-Vertrag', in H. Oetker/U. Preis (eds.), *Europäisches Arbeits- und Sozialrecht, EAS, part B – Systematische Darstellungen,* loose-leaf (Heidelberg: Forkel, last update: May 2008), B 2000; C. Teichmann, 'Europäisierung der deutschen Mitbestimmung', *ZIP* 2009 Supplement to Issue 48, 10–17; C. Teichmann, 'Europäisierung der deutschen Mitbestimmung durch Nichtanwendung des Gesetzes?', *ZIP* 2010, 874–875; R. Wank, 'Die Entwicklung der Dienstleistungs- und Niederlassungsfreiheit in der EU – die Rechtslage in Germany', *NZA* 2005 Supplement 2 to Issue 21, 88–97; R. Wank, 'Die personellen Grenzen des Europäischen Arbeitsrechts: Arbeitsrecht für Nicht-Arbeitnehmer?', *EuZA* 2008, 172–195.

Cases (Selection):
ECJ Case 41/74 *van Duyn* [1974] ECR 1337; ECJ Case 36/74 *Walrave und Koch* [1974] ECR 1405; ECJ Case 13/76 *Donà* [1976] ECR 1333; ECJ Case 30/77 *Bouchereau* [1977] ECR 1999; ECJ Case 53/81 *Levin* [1982] ECR 1035; ECJ Joined Cases 115/81 and 116/81 *Adoui* [1982] ECR 1665; ECJ Case 66/85 *Lawrie-Blum* [1986] ECR 2121; ECJ Case C-3/90 *Bernini* [1992] ECR I-1071; ECJ Case C-415/93 *Bosman* [1995] ECR I-4921; ECJ Case C-15/96 *Kalliope Schöning-Kougebetopoulou* [1998] ECR I-47; ECJ Case C-176/96 *Lehtonen und Castors Braine* [2000] ECR I-2681; ECJ Case C-281/98 *Angonese* [2000] ECR I-4139; ECJ Case C-224/01 *Köbler* [2003] ECR I-10239; ECJ Case C-405/01 *Colegio de Oficiales de la Marina Mercante Española* [2003] ECR I-10391; ECJ Case C-413/01 *Ninni-Orasche* [2003] ECR I-13187; ECJ Case C-138/02 *Collins* [2004] ECR I-2703; ECJ Joined Cases C-482/01 and C-493/01 *Orfanopoulos und Oliveri* [2004] ECR I-5257; ECJ Case C-456/02 *Trojani* [2004] ECR I-7573; ECJ Case C-109/04 *Kranemann* [2005] ECR I-2421; ECJ Case C-185/04 *Öberg* [2006] ECR I-1453; ECJ Case C-208/05 *ITC* [2007] ECR I-181; ECJ Case C-392/05 *Alevizos* [2007] ECR I-3505; ECJ Case C-94/07 *Raccanelli* [2008] ECR I-5939; ECJ Case C-325/08 *Olympique Lyonnais* [2010] ECR I-2177.

4. 'Freedom of movement for workers shall be secured within the Union', Article 45(1) TFEU. 'Article 45(1) states, in general terms, that freedom of movement for workers is to be secured within the Community. Under Article 45(2) and (3), such freedom of movement is to entail the abolition of any discrimination based on nationality between workers of the Member States as regards employment, remuneration and other conditions of work and employment, and to entail the right, subject to limitations justified on grounds of public policy, public security or public health, to accept offers of employment actually made, to move freely within the territory of Member States for that purpose, to stay in a Member State in order to be employed there under the same conditions as nationals of that State and to remain there after such employment.'[7]

1.   Introduction: The Regulatory System[8]

5.   One of the central objectives of the Union is to establish and ensure an **internal market**, Article 26 TFEU. This internal market 'shall comprise an area without internal frontiers in which the free movement of goods, persons, services and capital is ensured in accordance with the provisions of the Treaties'. Freedom of movement for workers is, in other words, a component of the internal market. While Articles 45 sqq. TFEU concern the freedom of movement for workers, freedom of establishment in Article 49 TFEU and the freedom to provide services in Article 56 TFEU are related to activities of the self-employed and companies (see in detail paras. 55–74 and 78–95 below).

---

7   ECJ Case C-350/96 *Clean Car Autoservice* [1998] ECR I-2521 para. 18; the numbering of the Articles has been adapted to that of the Lisbon Treaty.

8   For a good overview of the regulatory framework as a whole, see M. Fuchs, *Festschrift für Birk*, 115–133.

6. Free movement of workers prohibits any direct or indirect **discrimination** on grounds of nationality between workers of the Member States in regard to employment, remuneration and other conditions of work and employment, Article 45(2) TFEU. It grants workers access to all Member States of the Union for **all phases of employment**: job seeking, employment, and a right to remain in the territory of a Member State after having been employed there. The scope of protection does thus not cover free movement as such, but rather freedom of movement for workers in their capacity as workers.[9] The bottom line of the prohibition of discrimination is that workers from one Member States are entitled to work in another Member State under the same conditions as nationals of the host Member State. The right to free movement of workers does not require any implementation or legislation by the Union or its Member States.[10] Article 45 TFEU 'has a direct effect in the legal orders of the Member States and confers on individuals rights which the national courts must protect'.[11]

7. Article 45 is complemented by two provisions which confer **competence** upon the Union (see also §4 para. 43). Article 46 TFEU authorises the Union to issue directives or regulations regarding measures to bring about freedom of movement for workers. Article 48 TFEU authorises the Union to adopt such measures in the field of social security as are necessary to provide freedom of movement for workers. This includes such issues as the recognition of employment times abroad, e.g. for the purposes of unemployment or pension insurance.[12] Finally, the Member States 'shall encourage the exchange of young workers'.

8. The predecessor of Article 46 TFEU has, in particular, served as a basis for the enactment of the **Free Movement of Workers Regulation** (FMWR) of 1968.[13] It fleshes out the prohibition on discrimination pursuant to Article 45(2) TFEU with regard to access to employment, placement services and conditions of employment including remuneration and dismissal. The **Free Movement of**

---

9   Cf. ECJ Case C-171/91 *Tsiotras* [1993] ECR I-2925 para. 9; Case C-292/89 *The Queen* v. *Immigration Appeal Tribunal* [1991] ECR I-745 (expulsion admissible if job search has been unsuccessful); but see Case 53/81 *Levin* [1982] ECR 1035 paras. 19–23 (limited reviewability: irrelevance of other motives). On the right of residence pursuant to Article 21 TFEU (and its limitations) see e.g. Case C-456/02 *Trojani* [2004] ECR I-7573 paras. 30–46.

10 ECJ Case 167/73 *Commission* v. *France* [1974] ECR 359 paras. 35–41/42; Case 36/74 *Walrave und Koch* [1974] ECR 1405 paras. 16/19; Case 118/75 *Watson und Belmann* [1976] ECR 1185 paras. 11/12.

11 ECJ Case 41/74 *van Duyn* [1974] ECR 1337.

12 See e.g. ECJ Case C-349/87 *Paraschi* [1991] ECR I-4501.

13 Regulation (EEC) No 1612/68 of the Council of 15 October 1968 on freedom of movement for workers within the Community, OJ 1968 L 257/2. On the Regulation, see e.g. M. Coester/W. Denkhaus, in *EAS*, B 2100.

Citizens Directive[14] sets out, in greater detail, the limitations provided for in Article 45(3) on grounds of public policy, public security or public health in regard to the grounds for limitations, procedures and the right to remain.

2.   Scope of Application

a)   Personal Scope of Protection

aa)   THE DEFINITION OF WORKER

9.   Article 45 TFEU protects the freedom of movement for 'workers'.[15] This term is not uniformly defined in the legal systems of the Member States. Based on the purpose of the provision, which requires a uniform definition, independent of the rules in the Member States, the Court has **defined** the term **autonomously**.[16] It applies a broad interpretation, significantly exceeding that found in many Member States. A **worker** is defined as a person who, for a certain period of time performs services – an economic activity – for and under the direction of another in return for which he receives remuneration. In more detail: 'any person who pursues activities which are real and genuine, to the exclusion of activities on such a small scale as to be regarded as purely marginal and ancillary (...). The essential feature of an employment relationship is (...) that for a certain period of time a person performs services for and under the direction of another person in return for which he receives remuneration'.[17]

---

[14]   Directive 2004/38/EC of the European Parliament and of the Council of 29 April 2004 on the right of citizens of the Union and their family members to move and reside freely within the territory of the Member States amending Regulation (EEC) No 1612/68 and repealing Directives 64/221/EEC, 68/360/EEC, 72/194/EEC, 73/148/EEC, 75/34/EEC, 75/35/EEC, 90/364/EEC, 90/365/EEC and 93/96/EEC, OJ 2004 L 158/77, Corrigendum in OJ 2004 L 229/35.

[15]   A separate issue to be distinguished from this determination of the scope of application is whether others – the employer or an employment agency – can invoke the freedom of movement of 'their employee; see paras. 13 sq. below.

[16]   ECJ Case 75/63 *Unger* [1964] ECR 379 order 1; Case 53/81 *Levin* [1982] ECR 1035 para. 11; Case 139/85 *Kempf* [1986] ECR 1741 para. 15; Case 66/85 *Lawrie-Blum* [1986] ECR 2121 para. 16; Case 344/87 *Bettray* [1989] ECR 1621 para. 11; Case C-357/89 *Raulin* [1992] ECR I-1027 para. 10; Case C-3/90 *Bernini* [1992] ECR I-1071 para. 14.

[17]   ECJ Case C-94/07 *Raccanelli* [2008] ECR I-5939 para. 33; Case C-392/05 *Alevizos* [2007] ECR I-3505 para. 67; Case C-109/04 *Kranemann* [2005] ECR I-2421 para. 12; Case C-456/02 *Trojani* [2004] ECR I-7573 para. 15; Case C-138/02 *Collins* [2004] ECR I-2703 para. 26; Case C-413/01 *Ninni-Orasche* [2003] ECR I-13187 paras. 23 sq.; Case C-176/96 *Lehtonen und Castors Braine* [2000] ECR I-2681 para. 45; Case C-3/90 *Bernini* [1992] ECR I-1071 para. 14; Case C-357/89 *Raulin* [1992] ECR I-1027 para. 10; Case 344/87 *Bettray* [1989] ECR 1621 para. 12; Case 66/85 *Lawrie-Blum* [1986] ECR 2121 para. 17. For a detailed analysis oft he elements of the definition of worker see U. Runggaldier/G.-P. Reissner, in *EAS*, B 2000 paras. 26–52.

10. The **nature of the employment relationship** under national law, whether involving a private law contract or public law status, is irrelevant.[18] Thus, **civil servants** can qualify as 'workers' within the meaning of Article 45 TFEU, as can persons in atypical employment relationships (*'sui generis'*), i.e. not only permanent workers, but also seasonal workers,[19] frontier workers, part-time[20] and fixed term workers.[21] **Trainee teachers in preparatory service** who teach and receive remuneration are 'workers', irrespective of the special nature of their employment;[22] the same is true for trainee lawyers in preparatory service.[23] Notwithstanding the potentially lower degree of productivity or a small(er) number of working hours, the **apprentice** is a worker within the meaning of Article 45 so long as he receives remuneration.[24] Even when a person is employed for the purpose of rehabilitation (but then there is possibly no 'economic activity'; para. 12)[25] or as a director of a limited company (provided he works under the direction of another person), he may, depending upon the circumstances of the individual case, be considered to be a 'worker'.[26]

11. The services rendered must be '**effective and genuine activities**' and not activities 'on such a small scale as to be purely marginal and ancillary'.[27] A person who is employed for the sole purpose of rehabilitation or reintegration into society (in this case: drug addicts) does not qualify as 'worker'.[28]

12. The services must be rendered in exchange for **remuneration**. The amount of remuneration is not decisive.[29] It does not matter whether the income is below

---

18   ECJ Case C-456/02 *Trojani* [2004] ECR I-7573 para. 16; Case C-357/89 *Raulin* [1992] ECR I-1027 para. 10.

19   ECJ Case C-357/89 *Raulin* [1992] ECR I-1027 ('oproepcontract', on-call contract).

20   ECJ Case 53/81 *Levin* [1982] ECR 1035 paras. 14 sq.; Case C-357/89 *Raulin* [1992] ECR I-1027 para. 13.

21   ECJ Case C-413/01 *Ninni-Orasche* [2003] ECR I-13187 para. 25; even if the period employment is relatively short compared to the period of the stay as a whole, paras. 28–30.

22   ECJ Case 66/85 *Lawrie-Blum* [1986] ECR 2121 paras. 17–22.

23   ECJ Case C-109/04 *Kranemann* [2005] ECR I-2421 paras. 13–18.

24   ECJ Case 66/85 *Lawrie-Blum* [1986] ECR 2121 paras. 19–21; Case C-3/90 *Bernini* [1992] ECR I-1071 paras. 14–16.

25   ECJ Case C-392/05 *Alevizos* [2007] ECR I-3505 para. 68; Case 344/87 *Bettray* [1989] ECR 1621 para. 16.

26   ECJ Case C-350/96 *Clean Car Autoservice* [1998] ECR I-2521; M. Franzen, in R. Streinz (ed.), *EUV/AEUV*, Art. 45 AEUV para. 19; H. Wißmann, in R. Müller-Glöge/U. Preis/I. Schmidt (eds.), *Erfurter Kommentar,* Art. 45 AEUV para. 11.

27   ECJ Case C-357/89 *Raulin* [1992] ECR I-1027 paras. 10, 13; Case C-3/90 *Bernini* [1992] ECR I-1071 para. 14.

28   ECJ Case 344/87 *Bettray* [1989] ECR 1621 paras. 17 sq. But see also ECJ Case C-456/02 *Trojani* [2004] ECR I-7573 paras. 17–24 (performance of various jobs for the salvation army in return for benefits in kind and some pocket money may constitute 'effective and genuine activities').

29   ECJ Case C-109/04 *Kranemann* [2005] ECR I-2421 para. 17 (maintenance allowance for trainee lawyers in preparatory service).

the level that a Member State defines as the subsistence level[30] or whether the income as such (without any assistance from public funds) suffices to earn a living.[31]

bb) PROTECTED PERSONS

13. Article 45 TFEU first of all protects **workers**[32] of the **Member States**.[33] However, it is established in the Court's case law that other groups of persons can also rely upon the freedom of movement for workers. **Relatives** enjoy derivative protection under the Free Movement of Workers Regulation (Articles 10–12). An **employer** who intends to employ a national of another Member State as a worker can invoke Article 45 TFEU.[34] The Court argues that the wording of Article 45 TFEU does not indicate otherwise and that the purpose of the provision requires such an interpretation since this would enhance the *effet utile* of free movement. By the same token, a **recruitment agency** can rely upon the free movement of workers.[35]

14. These latter issues require further discussion. It is unclear whether the employer and the recruitment agency can invoke their own subjective right (such as a 'passive' right to free movement of workers) or whether they must rely upon the employee's right. With regard to the recruitment agency, the relationship between free movement of workers and the freedom to provide services requires clarification.[36]

b) Temporary Connection with the Employment Relationship

15. Whether someone qualifies as a 'worker' depends on the employment relationship. The scope of protection is not, however, limited to the term of the

---

30   ECJ Case 53/81 *Levin* [1982] ECR 1035 paras. 6–18.
31   ECJ Case 139/85 *Kempf* [1986] ECR 1986 1741.
32   On the temporal limitations – protection of persons who are looking for a job or who are retired – see para. 15 below.
33   ECJ Case 238/83 *Caisse d'Allocations Familiales* v. *Meade* [1984] ECR 2631 para. 7. Workers of third countries can only invoke the right to free movement if this has been agreed in an association treaty with that third country or provided for in secondary legislation on the basis of Article 79(2)(b) TFEU. On free movement rights of third country nationals, see A. Wiesbrock, 'Free movement of third-country nationals in the European Union: the illusion of inclusion', *E.L. Rev.* 35 (2010), 455–475; U. Forsthoff, in E. Grabitz/M. Hilf/M. Nettesheim (eds.), *Das Recht der Europäischen Union*, Art. 45 AEUV paras. 32–44, 124 sq. On the transitional provisions on the occasion of the accession of new Member States, see U. Runggaldier/G.-P. Reissner, in *EAS*, B 2000 paras. 65–73.
34   ECJ Case C-350/96 *Clean Car Autoservice* [1998] ECR I-2521 paras. 19–23; Case C-208/05 *ITC* [2007] ECR I-181 para. 23. Generally, U. Forsthoff, in E. Grabitz/M. Hilf/M. Nettesheim (eds.), *Das Recht der Europäischen Union*, Art. 45 AEUV paras. 47–52.
35   ECJ Case C-208/05 *ITC* [2007] ECR 2007 I-181 paras. 24–26.
36   See also ECJ Case C-208/05 *ITC* [2007] ECR I-181 paras. 54–62.

employment relationship. It covers a period before an employment relationship is established and it lasts after the employment relationship has ended. The decisive criterion is whether the period in question is 'intrinsically linked to the objective status of worker'.[37] Freedom of movement for workers thus includes the right 'to **accept offers** of employment actually made', Article 45(3)(a) TFEU and the right to go to a Member State to **seek** an open position on one's own initiative (see in detail para. 17 below). And even after employment has ended, the worker has a right to **remain** in the Member State (see in detail para. 20 below).

c)   Protected Activities

16.   Article 45 TFEU does not define the scope of protection of the freedom of movement for workers in full detail. Paragraph 1 describes it in general as freedom of movement. This clause is, to some extent, defined in more detail by the prohibition on discrimination in paragraph 2 and the – non-exhaustive –[38] enumeration of individual rights in paragraph 3. The Court has considered **access to the labour market of the host Member State** to be the hallmark of freedom of movement for workers. Posted workers are thus not protected under Article 45 TFEU but enjoy the protection of the (employer's) freedom to provide services (see paras. 55 sq., 64 and 73 sq. below).[39]

17.   The individual rights of paragraph 3 cover, first, the right to **accept offers of employment actually made** (lit. a). Freedom of movement would, however, largely be ineffective if employees could not seek, and apply for, open positions on their own initiative. The Court has thus recognised the employee's right to access another Member State, to move freely within that Member State's territory and to stay there for the purpose of **seeking employment**.[40] Following the intended purpose of free movement of workers (which does not provide for a general right to free movement; see para. 5 above), the worker must be actively seeking employment and must have 'genuine chances of being engaged'. The Member States must allow the worker a reasonable period of time in which to seek employment. The Court has deemed a period of three months to be too

---

[37]   ECJ Case C-302/98 *Sehrer* [2000] ECR I-4585 para. 30 (concerning pension).
[38]   Cf. ECJ Case C-292/89 *Antonissen* [1991] ECR I-745 para. 13; Case C-171/91 *Tsiotras* [1993] ECR I-2925 para. 8.
[39]   ECJ Joined Cases C-49/98, C-50/98, C-52/98 to C-54/98 and C-68/98 to C-71/98 *Finalarte* [2001] ECR I-7831 paras. 19–23. Approvingly S. Krebber, 'Die Vereinbarkeit von Entsenderichtlinie und Arbeitnehmer-Entsendegesetz mit der Dienstleistungsfreiheit und Freizügigkeit des EGV', in C. Weber et al. (eds.), *Jahrbuch Junger Zivilrechtswissenschaftler 1997* (Stuttgart: Boorberg, 1998), 129, 139 sq.; critically R. Rebhahn, 'Entsendung von Arbeitnehmern in der EU – Arbeitsrechtliche Fragen zum Gemeinschaftsrecht', *DRdA* 1999, 173, 181 sq.; V. Rieble/J. Lessner, 'Arbeitnehmer-Entsendegesetz, Nettolohnhaftung und EG-Vertrag', *ZfA* 2002, 29, 44–47.
[40]   ECJ Case C-292/89 *Antonissen* [1991] ECR I-745 para. 13; Case C-171/91 *Tsiotras* [1993] ECR I-2925 para. 8.

short in light of the purposes of Article 45 TFEU.[41] An expulsion after six month is compatible with free movement of workers if the worker has not found a position and cannot prove that he is continuing to seek employment and has a genuine chance of being engaged.[42]

18. The Court has also recognised a 'right to leave [one's] State of origin'.[43] While Article 45 TFEU does not expressly include such a right, it presupposes it in substance as the corollary of the right to enter another Member State.

19. The worker has the right to stay in a Member State in order to **pursue employment**. The right of residence is thus conferred directly by the Treaty and is not dependent upon a residency permit being issued by the host Member State.[44]

20. Finally, Article 45 TFEU gives the worker a **right to remain** in the host Member State after employment has ended. The details are set forth in Article 17 of the Free Movement of Citizens Directive (see para. 8 above). The right to remain is intended to enable the worker to remain in a familiar social environment after termination of his employment or after his retirement. It requires that the person has previously been employed as a worker in that Member State and consequently does not apply when a worker becomes permanently unable to perform a job while seeking employment in a host Member State.[45]

d)   Connection to the Internal Market

21. The regulatory context and purpose of the free movement of workers (see para. 5 above) require that there is a connection to the internal market.[46] In other words, Article 45 TFEU does not apply to situations which are **wholly internal** to a Member State.[47] A person who has never resided or worked in

---

41   ECJ Case C-344/95 *Commission* v. *Belgium* [1997] ECR I-1035.

42   ECJ Case C-138/02 *Collins* [2004] ECR I-2703 para. 37; Case C-292/89 *Antonissen* [1991] ECR I-745 para. 16; Case C-171/91 *Tsiotras* [1993] ECR I-2925 para. 13.

43   ECJ Case C-208/05 *ITC* [2007] ECR I-181 paras. 32–34; Case C-18/95 *Terhoeve* [1999] ECR I-345 para. 38; Case C-415/93 *Bosman* [1995] ECR I-4921 paras. 95 sq.; Case C-190/98 *Graf* [2000] ECR I-493 para. 22.

44   Cf. ECJ Case C-138/02 *Collins* [2004] ECR I-2703 para. 40; Case C-363/89 *Roux* [1991] ECR I-273 para. 9.

45   ECJ Case C-171/91 *Tsiotras* [1993] ECR I-2925 paras. 17–19.

46   Where there is a sufficiently close connection of the employment relationship to Community territory, free movement of workers is considered to apply also with regard to extra-Community cases; see in detail U. Runggaldier/G.-P. Reissner, in *EAS*, B 2000 paras. 16–18; U. Forsthoff, in E. Grabitz/M. Hilf/M. Nettesheim (eds.), *Das Recht der Europäischen Union*, Art. 45 AEUV paras. 12–14.

47   ECJ Case 180/83 *Moser* [1984] ECR 2539 order 2; Case 298/84 *Paolo Iorio* [1986] ECR 247; Case C-332/90 *Steen I* [1992] ECR I-341. On occupation with international organisations, in particular the EU: ECJ Case C-185/04 *Öberg* [2006] ECR I-1453 para. 12.

---

another Member State (different from his Member State of residence) cannot rely on the free movement provisions.[48] It is a matter of national law of the Member States whether any resulting discrimination of its own nationals should be considered unlawful.[49]

> The Court, for example, points out that imprisonment – as any other deprivation of liberty – may impede the person from exercising his right to free movement. Yet, a 'purely hypothetical prospect of exercising that right does not establish a sufficient connection with Community law to justify the application of Community provisions'.[50]

e) Exception: Public Service

22. The provisions of Article 45(1)-(3) TFEU do not apply to employment in public service, Article 45(4) TFEU. This exception is intended to reserve a core of public powers for the Member States. The fact that this exception is intended to protect the interests of the Member States could suggest that they should also be entitled to determine what constitutes public service. The Court has, however, taken a different view and **interpreted** the term 'public service' **autonomously**, reasoning that it was central to the scope of the freedom of movement for workers (*effet utile*).[51]

23. As an exception from the general rule, the Court has construed the term narrowly.[52] It has employed a **functional concept** of 'public service'. Article 45(4) TFEU 'removes from the ambit of Article 45(1) to (3) a series of posts which involve direct or indirect **participation in the exercise of powers** conferred by public law and duties designed to **safeguard the general interest of the state** or of other public authorities. Such posts in fact presume on the part of those occupying them the existence of a special relationship of allegiance to the state and reciprocity of rights and duties which form the foundation of the bond of nationality. On the other hand, the exception contained in Article 48(4) does not apply to posts which, whilst coming under the state or other organisations

---

[48] ECJ Case C-206/91 *Poirrez* [1992] ECR I-6685 paras. 10–12.
[49] ECJ Case C-132/93 *Steen II* [1994] ECR I-2715 paras. 9 sq.
[50] ECJ Case C-299/95 *Kremzow* [1997] ECR I-2629 para. 16 (however, on the review with regard to fundamental rights).
[51] ECJ Case C-473/93 *Commission v. Luxembourg* [1996] ECR I-3207 paras. 26 sq.; Case 307/84 *Commission v. France* [1986] ECR 1725 para. 12.
[52] ECJ Case 66/85 *Lawrie-Blum* [1986] ECR 2121 para. 26; Case C-473/93 *Commission v. Luxembourg* [1996] ECR I-3207 para. 33. See also K. Riesenhuber, in id. (ed.), *Europäische Methodenlehre*, §11 paras. 61–66 (with a critical assessment in regard of the methodological background).

governed by public law, still do not involve any association with duties belonging to the public service properly so called.'[53]

24. A trainee teacher in preparatory service does not fulfil these narrow conditions, even where he is employed in public service.[54] The same is true for foreign language assistants.[55] The positions of masters and chief mates on merchant ships flying a Member State's flag may not be reserved to that State's citizens where the special powers conferred by public law upon workers in these employment positions – such as penal or disciplinary powers – in practice represent only a very minor part of their activities.[56] Private security activities are not part of public service.[57] A Member State cannot invoke the exception of Article 45(4) TFEU once it has employed a foreign national in a position of public service.[58]

3. Infringements

25. Freedom of movement is infringed where an addressee of the provision (a) below) interferes with the scope of protection (b) below).

a) Addressees

aa) MEMBER STATES

26. Freedom of movement for employees is primarily addressed to the **Member States**. Both the host and home Member States are bound. The host Member State must not impede access to its labour market and the Member State of origin must not hamper an individual's freedom to leave the country (see para. 18 above).[59]

bb) THE UNION

27. The Union is also an addressee of freedom of movement for workers. The factual situation may however be different here, in particular where the Union

---

53   ECJ Case 149/79 *Commission* v. *Belgium* [1980] ECR 3881 order 1 (emphasis added; numbering of the Articles adapted to that of the Lisbon Treaty); Case C-392/05 *Alevizos* [2007] ECR I-3505 para. 69; Case 66/85 *Lawrie-Blum* [1986] ECR 2121 para. 27.
54   ECJ Case 66/85 *Lawrie-Blum* [1986] ECR 2121 para. 28.
55   ECJ Case 33/88 *Allué I* [1989] ECR 1591.
56   ECJ Case C-405/01 *Colegio de Oficiales de la Marina Mercante Española* [2003] ECR I-10391; Case C-47/02 *Anker u.a.* [2003] ECR I-10447.
57   ECJ Case C-114/97 *Commission* v. *Spain* [1998] ECR I-6717 para. 33.
58   ECJ Case 152/73 *Sotgiu* [1974] ECR 153 para. 4; Case 33/88 *Allué I* [1989] ECR 1591 para. 8.
59   ECJ Case C-18/95 *Terhoeve* [1999] ECR I-345 paras. 25–29; Case C-302/98 *Sehrer* [2000] ECR I-4585 paras. 29, 33.

sets uniform or harmonised standards for all Member States: Where a certain standard – such as a special professional training requirement – may constitute an obstacle to free movement if it is introduced by a single Member State, it may well enhance free movement if implemented as a common standard by the Union. The obligation of the Union is also different in terms of theoretical construction.[60]

cc) PRIVATE INDIVIDUALS

28.   It is a matter of controversy whether Article 45 TFEU is directly applicable not only in relation to the Member States and the Union but also between private individuals. In other words, do the fundamental freedoms have a **direct horizontal effect?** In German **legal writing**, the prevailing opinion is that horizontal direct effect should not be recognised. Fundamental freedoms merely exert an indirect effect upon private individuals, mediated by the Member States' obligation to ensure their effective operation.[61] Indeed, the wording of the fundamental freedoms as well as their limitations pursuant to the Treaty, indicate that they are directed against public authorities and not private individuals. From a systematic perspective, the Treaty already specifically addresses the issue of private power in its provisions on competition in Articles 101–106 TFEU.

29.   The **Court of Justice** has, however, decided differently in relation to the prohibition of discrimination, initially with regard to collective regulation by private associations – sports associations in particular – in the area of employment and services.[62] The Court argues that horizontal direct effect is required in order to secure the *effet utile*. For example, it has reviewed the rules of a cycling association (*Union Cycliste Internationale*) which required that in medium distance cycling championships behind motorcycles, 'the pacemaker must be of the same nationality as the stayer' pursuant to Article 45 TFEU.[63] The Court also subjected transfer rules in the area of football to control under the free movement of workers.[64] More recently, the Court considered recruitment

---

[60]   T. Körber, *Grundfreiheiten und Privatrecht*, 81–95 with further references; see also U. Forsthoff, in E. Grabitz/M. Hilf/M. Nettesheim (eds.), *Das Recht der Europäischen Union*, Art. 45 AEUV paras. 131–136.

[61]   See in detail T. Körber, *Grundfreiheiten und Privatrecht*, part 4 (631–819); further C.-W. Canaris, *Festschrift für Reiner Schmidt*, 29–67; K. Riesenhuber, *Europäisches Vertragsrecht*, paras. 694–697 with further references.

[62]   ECJ Case 36/74 *Walrave und Koch* [1974] ECR 1405 paras. 14/15–20/24; Case 13/76 *Donà* [1976] ECR 1333 para. 17/18; Case C-415/93 *Bosman* [1995] ECR I-4921 paras. 83 sq.; Case C-325/08 *Olympique Lyonnais* [2010] ECR I-2177 paras. 30 sq.

[63]   ECJ Case 36/74 *Walrave und Koch* [1974] ECR 1405.

[64]   ECJ Case C-415/93 *Bosman* [1995] ECR I-4921 paras. 92 sqq.; Case C-325/08 *Olympique Lyonnais* [2010] ECR I-2177 paras. 27 sqq. For a discussion, see K. Pijetlovic, 'Another Classic

requirements of individual employers which were of a discriminatory nature or effect (such as a specific, locally obtained language certificate) and found them to be incompatible with Article 45 TFEU.[65]

30. If one accepts horizontal direct effect of the freedom of movement for workers, then Article 45 TFEU also constitutes a rule of private law. Article 45 TFEU does not specify the legal implications of a violation by private individuals but gives the Member States some discretion regarding its implementation.[66] Article 45 TFEU may thus function as a prohibition in contract or in tort law, depending upon the relevant national law.[67] Yet, the Member States' discretion regarding implementation is limited, as in the case of implementation of directives. Here too, the sanctions must satisfy the principles of equivalence and effectiveness (see §1 para. 66 above).[68]

b)   Restrictions

aa)   DISCRIMINATION

31. Freedom of movement for workers entails 'the abolition of any discrimination based on nationality between workers of the Member States as regards employment, remuneration and other conditions of work and employment', Article 45(2) TFEU.

i.   Direct Discrimination

32. First, the prohibition of discrimination covers direct discrimination on grounds of nationality. The Court found direct discrimination in a case where only **Austrian nationals** were eligible to serve on workers' chambers and works councils.[69] Similarly, the exclusion of nationals from other Member States from

---

of EU Sports Jurisprudence: Legal Implications of Olympique Lyonnaise v Olivier Bernard and Newcastle UFC (C-325/08)', *E.L. Rev.* 35 (2010), 857–868.

[65]   ECJ Case C-281/98 *Angonese* [2000] ECR I-4139; further Case C-94/07 *Raccanelli* [2008] ECR I-5939 paras. 40–46. For a critical discussion of the *Angonese*-decision see R. Streinz/S. Leible, 'Die unmittelbare Drittwirkung von Grundfreiheiten', *EuZW* 2000, 459–467; R. Lane/N. Shuibhne, 'Case C-281/98, Roman Angonese v. Cassa die Risparmio di Bolzano SpA, Judgement of 6 June 2000', *CMLR* 37 (2000), 1237, 1243–1247; approvingly A. Lengauer, 'Drittwirkung von Grundfreiheiten – Eine Besprechung der Rs C-281/98, Angonese', *ZfRV* 2001, 57, 64. For a critical discussion of *Raccanelli*, see C. Birkemeyer, 'Die unmittelbare Drittwirkung der Grundfreiheiten', *EuR* 2010, 662–677.

[66]   ECJ Case C-94/07 *Raccanelli* [2008] ECR I-5939 para. 50.

[67]   Hinting at the latter ECJ Case C-94/07 *Raccanelli* [2008] ECR I-5939 para. 51 ('non-contractual liability').

[68]   This in indicated in ECJ Case C-94/07 *Raccanelli* [2008] ECR I-5939 para. 50, where the Court refers to its decision in Case 14/83 *von Colson* und *Kamann* [1984] ECR 1891.

[69]   ECJ Case C-465/01 *Commission v. Austria* [2004] ECR I-8291.

employment as teachers at '*frontistiria*' (schools for the preparation to university in Greece) and private music and dance schools constitutes direct discrimination.[70] In contrast, employee involvement rules that deny active and/ or passive voting rights to workers of the undertaking who are **employed abroad** (in other Member States) do not overtly discriminate on grounds of nationality. However, given that such rules will, in all probability, overwhelmingly affect foreign nationals, they are, however, indirectly discriminatory.[71]

ii.   Indirect Discrimination

33.   Article 45(2) TFEU further prohibits indirect ('covert') discrimination.[72] Indirect discrimination occurs where seemingly neutral, i.e. non-discriminatory criteria have a **discriminatory effect**. This is the case where, e.g. 'a provision of national law (…) is intrinsically liable to affect migrant workers more than national workers and if there is a consequent risk that it will place the former at a particular disadvantage. It is not necessary to find that the provision in question does in practice affect a substantially higher proportion of migrant workers. It is sufficient that it is liable to have such an effect.'[73] For a finding of indirect discrimination, it is sufficient that there is a 'real risk' that the seemingly neutral provision puts migrant workers at a disadvantage.[74] A *prima facie* case of discrimination thus established is, however, overturned (and not only justified) where the neutral criterion is based upon **objective considerations** which are unrelated to the nationality of the employees concerned and **proportionate** to a legitimate purpose pursued by the national law.[75]

> The theoretical construction of indirect discrimination is rather controversial and the Court's jurisprudence is inconsistent. While some cases support the view submitted above, others refer to 'objective considerations' as a type of justification.[76]

---

[70]   ECJ Case 147/86 *Commission v. Greece* [1988] ECR 1637.
[71]   V. Rieble/C. Latzel, *EuZA* 2011, 145, 151 sq.; H.-J. Hellwig/C. Behme, *AG* 2009, 261–278; iid. *ZIP* 2010, 871–874; C. Teichmann, *ZIP* 2009 Supplement to Issue 48, 10–17; id., ZIP 2010, 874–875.
[72]   ECJ Case 152/73 *Sotgiu* [1974] ECR 153 para. 11; Case 41/84 *Pinna* [1986] ECR 1 para. 23; Case 33/88 *Allué I* [1989] ECR 1591 para. 11; Joined Cases C-259/91, C-331/91 and C-332/91 *Allué II* [1993] ECR I-4309 para. 11; Case C-419/92 *Ingetraut Scholz* [1994] ECR I-505 para. 7; Case C-279/93 *Schumacker* [1995] ECR I-225 para. 26; Case C-278/94 *Commission v. Belgium* [1996] ECR I-4307 para. 27; Case C-350/96 *Clean Car Autoservice* [1998] ECR I-2521 para. 27; Case C-190/98 *Graf* [2000] ECR I-493 para. 14.
[73]   ECJ Case C-278/94 *Commission v. Belgium* [1996] ECR I-4307 para. 20; Case C-237/94 *O'Flynn* [1996] ECR I-2617 paras. 20 sq.
[74]   ECJ Case C-302/98 *Sehrer* [2000] ECR I-4585.
[75]   ECJ Case C-350/96 *Clean Car Autoservice* [1998] ECR I-2521 para. 31; Case C-15/96 *Kalliope Schöning-Kougebetopoulou* [1998] ECR I-47 para. 21. See also N. Görlitz, *Struktur und Bedeutung der Rechtsfigur der mittelbaren Diskriminierung im System der Grundfreiheiten*, 67–70.
[76]   ECJ Case C-237/94 *O'Flynn* [1996] ECR I-2617 paras. 19 sq., 24 sq.; Case C-90/96 *Petrie u.a. v. Università degli studi di Verona* [1997] ECR I-6527 para. 56.

34. An **example** of indirect discrimination is where **language assistants,** who were predominantly (75%) foreign nationals, were being placed at a disadvantage in comparison to other lecturers, in only being offered temporary employment contracts for example.[77] The Court has thus considered a fixed-term contract, specifically designed for language assistants only, to be incompatible with Article 45(2) TFEU.[78] It has not recognised the universities' interest in ensuring up-to-date instruction to be a valid justification.[79]

35. Similarly, linking a privilege to a residence requirement, may also be considered to be indirectly discriminatory.[80] The same is true where employment as director of a company requires residency in that country.[81] Again, there may be indirect discrimination where employment in other Member States is not counted to the same extent for purposes of granting a benefit or imposing a disadvantage; examples include the following cases:

- recruitment proceedings or labour evaluations did not take previous employment in other Member States into account;[82]
- professional (here: teaching) experience in other Member States was not taken into account (to the same degree);[83]
- certificates and similar documents to prove the personal status are not attributed the same evidential value if issued by the competent authorities of other Member States (in proceedings determining the entitlements so social security benefits of a migrant worker who is a EU national);[84]
- the deductibility of sickness and invalidity insurance contributions and pensions and life assurance contributions is made conditional on those contributions being paid in the Member State levying the tax;[85]
- the right to reimbursement of travel expenses for a journey to a practical training assignment in another Member State is limited to the amount

---

[77] ECJ Case 33/88 *Allué I* [1989] ECR 1591 paras. 11 sq. See also ECJ Case C-90/96 *Petrie u.a.* v. *Università degli studi di Verona* [1997] ECR I-6527 paras. 55 sq. (teaching license of language assistants).

[78] ECJ Case 33/88 *Allué I* [1989] ECR 1591; Joined Cases C-259/91, C-331/91 and C-332/91 *Allué II* [1993] ECR I-4309; Case C-272/92 *Spotti* [1993] ECR I-5185 para. 18.

[79] ECJ Case C-272/92 *Spotti* [1993] ECR I-5185 paras. 19–21 with further references.

[80] ECJ Case C-279/93 *Schumacker* [1995] ECR I-225 para. 29; Case C-151/94 *Commission* v. *Luxembourg* [1995] ECR I-3685 paras. 13–15.

[81] ECJ Case C-350/96 *Clean Car Autoservice* [1998] ECR I-2521.

[82] ECJ Case C-419/92 *Ingetraut Scholz* [1994] ECR I-505 para. 11; Case C-187/96 *Commission* v. *Greece* [1998] ECR I-1095; see also ECJ Case C-15/96 *Kalliope Schöning-Kougebetopoulou* [1998] ECR I-47.

[83] ECJ Case C-278/03 *Commission* v. *Italy* [2005] ECR I-3747 order 2.

[84] ECJ Case C-336/94 *Dafek* [1997] ECR I-6761 paras. 9–13.

[85] ECJ Case C-204/90 *Bachmann* [1992] ECR I-249 paras. 8–13; Case C-300/90 *Commission* v. *Belgium* [1992] ECR I-305 para. 9; (justification with considerations of the coherence of the tax-system possible, though).

incurred in respect of the domestic stretch of the journey, while all the travel costs would be reimbursed if the same activity had been carried out on national territory;[86] and

- residents and nationals of other Member States are being treated differently with respect to income taxation,[87] for example by applying a more unfavourable calculation basis for the social security contributions for foreign trainee workers.[88]

bb) OTHER RESTRICTIONS

36. Apart from the prohibition of discrimination – which has dominated the case law –, the Court has also derived from Article 45 TFEU a prohibition on imposing other restrictions. 'Provisions which preclude or deter a national of a Member State from leaving his country of origin in order to exercise his right to freedom of movement (...) constitute an obstacle to that freedom even if they apply without regard to the nationality of the workers concerned.'[89] Freedom of movement for workers precludes 'any national measure [that], even though it is applicable without discrimination on grounds of nationality, is liable to hamper or to **render less attractive** the exercise by Community nationals, including those of the Member State which enacted the measure, of fundamental freedoms guaranteed by the Treaty.'[90] The Court argues that such a prohibition upon other restrictions is necessary in light of teleological considerations and in order to give the freedom of movement for workers, which serves the goal of facilitating any employment activity within Union territory, its practical effect (*effet utile*). Measures which create a restriction which is capable of discouraging job-seekers from looking for work in another Member States, are thus incompatible with Article 45 TFEU.[91]

37. A requirement that an employee must pay higher social security levies (without a corresponding right to better benefits or services) if he takes up employment in another Member State, also constitutes a restriction to free

---

[86]   ECJ Case C-109/04 *Kranemann* [2005] ECR I-2421.
[87]   ECJ Case C-175/88 *Biehl* [1990] ECR I-1779; Case C-279/93 *Schumacker* [1995] ECR I-225; Case C-151/94 *Commission* v. *Luxembourg* [1995] ECR I-3685 (forfeiture of taxes paid in excess for temporary residents).
[88]   ECJ Case C-27/91 *Union de recouvrement des cotisations de sécurité sociale et d'allocations familiales de la Savoie (URSSAF)* [1991] ECR I-5531.
[89]   ECJ Case C-415/93 *Bosman* [1995] ECR I-4921 para. 96; Case C-190/98 *Graf* [2000] ECR I-493 paras. 18, 21.
[90]   ECJ Case C-19/92 *Kraus* [1993] ECR I-1663 para. 32 (here: recognition of a academic degree earned in another Member State; emphasis added); Case C-185/04 *Öberg* [2006] ECR I-1453 para. 16.
[91]   ECJ Case C-208/05 *ITC* [2007] ECR I-181 para. 36; Case C-18/95 *Terhoeve* [1999] ECR I-345 para. 39; Case C-415/93 *Bosman* [1995] ECR I-4921 para. 94.

movement.[92] Similarly, it must not be made excessively difficult and costly to obtain recognition of an academic grade which was attained in another Member State.[93] It is an obstacle to free movement when periods of employment in another Member States are not taken into account for the calculation of seniority bonuses; such practices could discourage residents from making use of their right to free movement.[94]

38. An issue which has been raised in relation to the free movement of goods is how such a broad prohibition of restrictions, can be limited sensibly in light of the purpose of free movement.[95] With respect to free movement of goods, the Court of Justice has introduced the distinction between product requirements and 'certain selling arrangements'. In principle, the Court only subjects the former category to a proportionality test since they are considered to be 'measures having an equivalent effect'.[96] 'Certain selling arrangements' in contrast, are presumptively lawful and therefore fall outside the scope of the Treaty provisions on freedom of goods (provided the do not work discriminatorily). With regard to free movement for workers, two comparable strategies can be discerned. On the one hand, the Court's decisions on restrictions to free movement often concern impediments to the right to leave one's home Member State. These impediments affect access to the labour market of other Member States (**obstacles to market access**) and not only conditions of employment.[97] On the other hand, the Court has, on occasion, regarded **uncertain and indirect** impediments as insufficient to be regarded as liable to hinder freedom of movement for workers.[98] The impediments at issue in these cases were considered to lack the necessary connection to free movement and cross-border activity. Thus, the Court found no restriction in an Austrian law which denies the worker a right to compensation upon termination of his employment if he himself gives notice (in this case: in order to take up employment in another Member State) when those provisions grant him a right to such compensation if the contract ends without the termination being at his own initiative or attributable to him. The Court considered that when giving notice, the employee would not take into consideration that he would 'lose' a

---

92   ECJ Case C-18/95 *Terhoeve* [1999] ECR I-345 para. 39.
93   ECJ Case C-19/92 *Kraus* [1993] ECR I-1663 para. 32.
94   ECJ Case C-224/01 *Köbler* [2003] ECR I-10239 para. 74.
95   Om more details see U. Forsthoff, in E. Grabitz/M. Hilf/M. Nettesheim (eds.), *Das Recht der Europäischen Union,* Art. 45 AEUV paras. 188–227, 273–288.
96   ECJ Joined Cases 267/91 and 268/91 *Keck und Mithouard* [1993] ECR I-6097 para. 16.
97   M. Franzen, in R. Streinz (ed.), *EUV/AEUV,* Art. 45 AEUV para. 90 with further references. See also U. Forsthoff, in E. Grabitz/M. Hilf/M. Nettesheim (eds.), *Das Recht der Europäischen Union,* Art. 45 AEUV paras. 274–288 (discussing different categories of cases).
98   Critical of this instrument (but not of the objective of restraining review) M. Pechstein, 'Reisekostenerstattung eines Rechtsreferendars zu einem selbst gewählten ausländischen Dienstort', *JZ* 2005, 943 sq.

right to compensation, for this right did not only depend upon the worker remaining in service with his employer but also on his employment being terminated without his initiative or fault. This prospect was 'too uncertain and indirect a possibility for legislation to be capable of being regarded as liable to hinder freedom of movement for workers'.[99]

39. It remains uncertain, though, whether the prohibition of restrictions upon freedom of movement for employees needs to be delimited in this way and whether these criteria are appropriate for that purpose. From a practical perspective, market access cases have not gained significant importance in the Court's jurisprudence on restrictions to freedom of movement for workers; in many instances, such 'restrictions' will at the same time constitute discrimination.[100] The prohibition of restrictions will thus usually be relevant only for cases of *exit from market*. Here, a demarcation does indeed seem necessary, but it is doubtful whether criteria such as the 'uncertain and indirect effect' are suitable for that purpose. It has been suggested that the distinction between intrusion and benefit could be useful in this context.[101]

4. Justification of Infringements

a)   Justifications

aa)   ORDRE PUBLIC: PUBLIC POLICY, PUBLIC SECURITY AND PUBLIC HEALTH

40. An **express derogation (justification)** is the *ordre public*-reservation provided for in the introductory sentence of Article 45(3) TFEU with regard to public policy, public security and public health. The *ordre public*-reservation is fleshed out in the Free Movement of Citizens Directive (see para. 7 above). Although the list of aspects of freedom of movement for workers in paragraph 3 provides only examples and is not exhaustive, on the basis of its purpose, the *ordre public*-reservation, is a **general justification** for infringements of the freedom of movement for workers, irrespective of its systematic location. It is also applicable to violations of the prohibition of discrimination of paragraph 2.[102]

---

[99]   ECJ Case C-190/98 *Graf* [2000] ECR I-493 paras. 24 sq.
[100]   See e.g. the cases of infringement considered by the Court in ECJ Case C-224/01 *Köbler* [2003] ECR I-10239 paras. 73 sq.
[101]   M. Pechstein, *JZ* 2005, 943 sq. with a critical review of ECJ Case C-109/04 *Kranemann* [2005] ECR I-2421.
[102]   See e.g. for the case of a direct discrimination ECJ Case C-283/99 *Commission* v. *Italy* [2001] ECR I-4363 para. 26; for the case of indirect discrimination ECJ Case C-350/96 *Clean Car Autoservice* [1998] ECR I-2521 paras. 39 sq. To the same effect U. Becker, in D. Ehlers (ed.), *Europäische Grundrechte und Grundfreiheiten*, §9 para. 47; U. Forsthoff, in E. Grabitz/M. Hilf/M. Nettesheim (eds.), *Das Recht der Europäischen Union*, Art. 45 AEUV para. 416. Differentiating (not with regard to cases of direct discrimination) W. Brechmann, in C. Calliess/M. Ruffert (eds.), *EUV/AEUV,* Art. 45 AEUV paras. 46, 95; H. Schneider/N. Wunderlich, in J. Schwarze (ed.), *EU-Kommentar,* Art. 39 EG para. 117.

41. In light of the central importance of the fundamental freedoms, the Court of Justice has construed the *ordre public*-reservation **autonomously** and **narrowly**. This is comparable to the reservation with regard to public administration (see para. 23 above): Here too, the purpose of the rule advocates a certain discretion for the Member States to determine the content of *ordre public*,[103] but at the same time the necessity of a uniform determination for the Union requires an autonomous definition, subject to full review by the Court of Justice.[104]

42. Justification on grounds of public policy require a 'genuine and sufficiently serious threat' affecting 'one of the fundamental interests of society'.[105] Purely economic interests do not qualify as a sufficient justification and *ordre public*-grounds cannot be invoked for economic purposes.[106] A threat to the *ordre public* cannot be defined abstractly but must be established in each individual case and with regard to the **personal behaviour of the person concerned**.[107] On these considerations, an 'automatic' expulsion because of drug offences is irreconcilable with Article 45 TFEU[108] as is a deportation ordered for the purpose of deterring other aliens.[109] Similarly, the *ordre public*-reservation cannot be construed as a general exception for whole economic sectors (such as the private security sector) but rather constitutes a specific exception for the purpose of allowing Member States to refuse access to their territory or residency therein to persons whose access or residency would in itself constitute a danger for public policy, public security or public health.[110]

bb) UNWRITTEN LIMITATION TO THE PROHIBITION OF RESTRICTIONS: MANDATORY REQUIREMENTS OF PUBLIC INTEREST

43. Given that the prohibition of restrictions (see paras. 36–39 above) leads to a rather broad scope of protection of the freedom of movement for workers, the (written) justifications for infringements provided for in the TFEU need to be supplemented. As with other fundamental freedoms, infringements can be justified if they are necessary (proportionality) to achieve mandatory

---

[103]   ECJ Case 41/74 *van Duyn* [1974] ECR 1337 para. 18.
[104]   ECJ Case 41/74 *van Duyn* [1974] ECR 1337 paras. 18 sq.
[105]   ECJ Case 36/75 *Rutili* [1975] ECR 1219 order 3; Case 30/77 *Bouchereau* [1977] ECR 1999 paras. 33/35; Joined Cases 115/81 and 116/81 *Adoui* [1982] ECR 1665.
[106]   Article 27(1)(2) Free Movement of Citizens Directive 2004/38/EC.
[107]   Article 27(2) Free Movement of Citizens Directive 2004/38/EC. Cf. Case 30/77 *Bouchereau* [1977] ECR 1999 paras. 27–30.
[108]   ECJ Case C-348/96 *Calfa* [1999] ECR I-11 (the proportionality of an expulsion *for life-time* thus did not need to be discussed).
[109]   ECJ Case 67/74 *Bonsignore* [1975] ECR 297 order 3.
[110]   ECJ Case C-114/97 *Commission* v. *Spain* [1998] ECR I-6717 para. 42.

requirements of public interest (*Cassis* formula).[111] This justification does *not* apply, though, in relation to direct discrimination. As regards indirect discrimination, the Court's case law is not quite consistent; it sometimes considers 'objective grounds' as overturning a finding of indirect discrimination, and other times as justifying it (para. 33 above).

44. By way of **example**, the following considerations have been accepted as mandatory requirements of public interest in the Court's case law:[112]

- the cohesion of the applicable tax system;[113]
- measures intended to ensure the proper management of universities;[114] and
- the need to protect the public from misleading use of academic titles which have not been awarded according to the rules laid down in the country in which the holder of the title intends to make use of it.[115]

Here too, considerations of a purely economic nature do not justify infringements of freedom of movement for workers (see also para. 42 above).[116]

45. As we have seen above (paras. 28 sqq.), the Court considers free movement of workers to have horizontal effect between private individuals, e.g. a private organisation or an individual employer on the one hand and an employee on the other. This jurisprudence also has repercussions for the justification of infringements with the fundamental freedom. Thus, for example in *Bosman,* the Court considered that '[i]n view of the considerable social importance of sporting activities and in particular football in the Community, the aims of maintaining a balance between clubs by preserving a certain degree of equality and uncertainty as to results and of encouraging the recruitment and training of young players must be accepted as legitimate'.[117]

46. It also emerges from recent case law that conflicting (apparently: EU-)[118] **fundamental rights** (see §2 above) can constitute limitations to fundamental

---

[111] ECJ Case 120/78 *Rewe* [1979] ECR 649 para. 9 – Cassis de Dijon.
[112] See also ECJ Case C-224/01 *Köbler* [1003] ECR I-10239 para. 83.
[113] ECJ Case C-204/90 *Bachmann* [1992] ECR I-249 paras. 23–28; Case C-300/90 *Commission* v. *Belgium* [1992] ECR I-305 paras. 14–21.
[114] ECJ Joined Cases C-259/91, C-331/91 and C-332/91 *Allué II* [1993] ECR I-4309 para. 15.
[115] ECJ Case C-19/92 *Kraus* [1993] ECR I-1663 para. 35.
[116] ECJ Case C-185/04 *Öberg* [2006] ECR I-1453 paras. 21, 23; Case C-109/04 *Kranemann* [2005] ECR I-2421 para. 34.
[117] ECJ Case C-415/93 *Bosman* [1995] ECR I-4921 para. 106; see also Case C-325/08 *Olympique Lyonnais* [2010] ECR I-2177 para. 39. See also B. Eichel, 'Transferentschädigungen für Berufsfußballspieler – Neue Erkenntnisse für die Behandlung des Sports im Europarecht durch "Bosman II"?', *EuR* 2010, 685, 691 sq.
[118] The case law is somewhat unclear; in *Schmidberger* Austria had invoked the national fundamental rights and the ECHR; the Court, however, at least as a starting point, considers

freedoms immanent to the Treaty.[119] This has, however, not yet had any practical relevance with regard to freedom of movement for workers (but see with regard to freedom of services paras. 70 sq. and freedom of establishment para. 85). If a fundamental freedom and fundamental right conflict, the conflicting positions need to be accommodated proportionately.[120]

b)   Limits to Justification

47.   A general limitation to both written and unwritten justifications is the **principle of proportionality.** Justifications on grounds of mandatory reasons of public interest need in particular to be limited to what is necessary. Thus, it may, for example, be legitimate to require a certain level of language skills from applicants. Yet, it exceeds the limit of necessary requirements to demand a specific certificate for that purpose which is difficult to obtain for non-residents.[121]

48.   Furthermore, limitations 'must be interpreted in the light of the general principles of law and in particular of fundamental rights'.[122] EU fundamental rights may thus function as an additional barrier to the justification of infringements of fundamental freedoms or, in a term coined by German constitutional law doctrine, 'limitation-limitations' (*Schranken-Schranken*). For example, the expulsion of a job-seeking national of another Member State who has been repeatedly convicted of drug and violent offences constitutes an infringement of the freedom of movement for workers but may, in principle, be justified on grounds of public policy. The consideration may, however, be different if the person concerned is married to a resident of that country and three children were born of that marriage. In this latter case, the fundamental right to protection of the family must also be taken into account.[123]

---

fundamental rights as general principles of Community law; ECJ Case C-112/00 *Schmidberger* [2003] ECR I-5659 paras. 71–75. Following the approach taken here D. Ehlers, in id. (ed.), *Europäische Grundrechte und Grundfreiheiten*, §7 para. 98 and §14 para. 13, with further references. For a different approach, see M. A. Dauses, in id. (ed.), *Handbuch zum EU-Wirtschaftsrecht* (Munich: C.H. Beck, 2010), chapter C I para. 256 (fundamental rights of the national laws of the Member States as mandatory requirements of public interest to the extent that they are recognised at the Community level).

[119]   See the seminal decision in ECJ Case C-112/00 *Schmidberger* [2003] ECR I-5659. Further ECJ Case C-271/08 *Commission* v. *Germany* [2010] ECR I-7091 paras. 37 sqq.

[120]   ECJ Case C-271/08 *Commission* v. *Germany* [2010] ECR I-7091 paras. 43 sq., 52 ('fair balance').

[121]   ECJ Case C-281/98 *Angonese* [2000] ECR I-4139 para. 44.

[122]   ECJ Case C-260/89 *ERT* [1991] ECR I-2925 para. 43; Case C-368/95 *Familiapress* [1997] ECR I-3689 para. 24; Case C-60/00 *Carpenter* [2002] ECR I-6279 para. 40.

[123]   ECJ Joined Cases C-482/01 and C-493/01 *Orfanopoulos und Oliveri* [2004] ECR I-5257 paras. 97 sq.

5. *Consequences of an Infringement of the Freedom of Movement for Workers*

49. Where the national law or another measure of a **Member State** is incompatible with the freedom of movement for workers, an interpretation in conformity with the fundamental freedom should be considered. '[I]t is for the national court, to the full extent of its discretion under national law, to interpret and apply domestic law in conformity with the requirements of Community law'.[124] Where an interpretation in conformity with Union law is not possible, the national court must 'apply Union law in its entirety and protect rights which it confers on individuals, disapplying, if necessary, any contrary provision of domestic law'.[125] Union law thus has a precedence of application. Contravening national law is not void but must be left unapplied if the full protection of EU law so requires.[126] In the case of discrimination, this will normally require an 'adaptation to the top', in other words, the victim of discrimination is to be granted the advantages hitherto withheld from him and relieved from the disadvantages hitherto burdened upon him. Depending on the situation, the Member State may be liable to the protected person or group if there has been a sufficiently serious violation of EU law.[127]

50. EU law or a measures of the **Union** may also violate freedom of movement for workers. In that case, too, the first port of call is an interpretation in conformity with primary law. Where this is not possible, the legal act which is incompatible with fundamental freedoms is void. This can be judicially determined in the proceedings according to Articles 263 and 264 TFEU or in a preliminary ruling pursuant to Article 267(1)(b) TFEU.

51. The legal consequences of a violation of fundamental freedoms by a **private individual** are largely unclear. Given that general private law is (still) a domain of the Member States, the details must be left to them. Where a contractual obligation is incompatible with the fundamental freedoms, it may be void or unenforceable as in the case of illegality or immorality. Otherwise, there may be liability in tort.[128]

---

[124] ECJ Case C-208/05 *ITC* [2007] ECR I-181 para. 68; to the same effect already ECJ Case C-262/97 *Engelbrecht* [2000] ECR I-7321 para. 38; Case 157/86 *Murphy* [1988] ECR 673 para. 11. See on details S. Leible/R. Domröse, in K. Riesenhuber (ed.), *Europäische Methodenlehre*, §9.

[125] ECJ Case C-208/05 *ITC* [2007] ECR I-181 para. 69; Case C-262/97 *Engelbrecht* [2000] ECR I-7321 para. 40; Case 157/86 *Murphy* [1988] ECR 673 para. 11.

[126] Cf. the seminal decision in ECJ Case 6/64 *Costa* v. *E.N.E.L.* [1964] ECR 1253.

[127] Thus e.g. ECJ Case C-224/01 *Köbler* [2003] ECR I-10239. See also the references in §1 paras. 75 sq. above.

[128] Cf. ECJ Case C-94/07 *Raccanelli* [2008] ECR I-5939 paras. 50 sq.

6. *The Example of the Angonese-Case*[129]

52. A private employer from the province of Bolzano, Italy made application for a vacant position conditional upon the applicant obtaining a certain certificate of bilingualism (in Italian and German). Mr. Angonese, who was perfectly bilingual, did not have such a certificate and his application was therefore not considered. The required certificate was only issued by the public authorities of the province of Bolzano after an examination. Participation in this examination is difficult for non-residents of Bolzano. For residents of the province of Bolzano, on the other hand, it is usual to obtain the certificate as a matter of course for employment purposes. 'Obtaining the Certificate is viewed as an almost compulsory step as part of normal training.'[130] Requiring the certificate was permitted but not mandatory pursuant to the applicable collective agreement.

53. The Court of Justice considered this requirement that applicants prove their language skills exclusively through a diploma issued only in one particular province of a Member State to be incompatible with Article 45 TFEU. The Court's judgement is based upon the direct horizontal effect of Article 45 TFEU.[131]

54. It seems preferable to consider indirect horizontal effect of freedom of movement for workers; this approach may lead to the same result. If a language certificate is being regarded 'as an almost compulsory step as part of normal training' this may indicate that employers in that region generally make the certificate a requirement for application. Such pervasive practice in effect means that the labour market of that region may be almost sealed off from non-residents. An empirical finding of such a pervasive practice is a proper reason for requiring the Member State – all state powers including courts and administration – to effectively protect the fundamental freedoms. Indeed, it would amount to a positive infringement if the Member State stands on the side-lines in view of practices which have such discriminatory effect. It is a matter of discretion of the Member State (and its powers) to determine the proper instruments of protection. Union law merely requires that it effectively protect the fundamental freedoms.

---

[129] ECJ Case C-281/98 *Angonese* [2000] ECR I-4139.
[130] ECJ Case C-281/98 *Angonese* [2000] ECR I-4139 para. 6.
[131] ECJ Case C-281/98 *Angonese* [2000] ECR I-4139 paras. 30–36.

III. FREEDOM TO PROVIDE SERVICES – OVERVIEW

Bibliography:[132]

C. Barnard, '"British Jobs for British Workers": The Lindsey Oil Refinery Dispute and the Future of Local Labour Clauses in an Integrated EU Market', *ILJ* 38 (2009), 245–277; J. Busche, 'Freizügigkeit der Dienstleistungen', in H. Oetker/U. Preis (eds.), *Europäisches Arbeits- und Sozialrecht, EAS, part B – Systematische Darstellungen*, loose-leaf (Heidelberg: Forkel, last update: October 2002), B 2400; T. v. Danwitz, 'Die Rechtsprechung des EuGH zum Entsenderecht – Bausteine für eine Wirtschafts- und Sozialverfassung der EU', *EuZW* 2002, 237–244; P. Davies, 'Market Integration and Social Policy in the Court of Justice', *ILJ* 24 (1995), 49–77; P. Davies, 'Posted Workers – Single Market or protection of national labour law systems?', *CMLR* 34 (1997), 571–602; P. Davies, 'The Posted Workers Directive and the EC Treaty', *ILJ* 31 (2002), 298–306; R. Eklund, 'A Swedish Perspective on Laval', Comp. Lab. L. & Pol'y J. 29 (2007–2008), 551–571; E. Eichenhofer, 'Dienstleistungsfreiheit und Mindestlohn', ZESAR 2007, 53–57; A. Feuerborn, 'Grenzüberschreitender Einsatz von Fremdfirmenpersonal', in H. Oetker/U. Preis (eds.), *Europäisches Arbeits- und Sozialrecht, EAS, part B – Systematische Darstellungen*, loose-leaf (Heidelberg: Forkel, last update: August 2003), B 2500; M. Franzen, 'Kurzzeitige Arbeitnehmerentsendung und Dienstleistungsfreiheit', *IPRax* 2002, 186–191; M. Fuchs, 'Arbeitsmigration im Spannungsfeld von nationalstaatlicher und europarechtlicher Regelung', in H. Konzen et al. (eds.), *Festschrift für Rolf Birk* (Tübingen: Mohr Siebeck, 2008), 115–133; R. Giesen, 'Posting: Social Protection of Workers vs. Fundamental Freedoms?', *CMLR* 40 (2003), 143–158; A. Junker, 'Arbeitnehmerentsendung aus deutscher und europäischer Sicht', *JZ* 2005, 481–488; T. Kienle/A. Koch, 'Grenzüberschreitende Arbeitnehmerüberlassung – Probleme und Folgen', *DB* 2001, 922–927; H. Konzen, 'Europäische Dienstleistungsfreiheit und nationaler Arbeitnehmerschutz', *NZA* 2002, 781–783; M. Kort, 'Die Bedeutung der europarechtlichen Grundfreiheiten für die Arbeitnehmerentsendung und die Arbeitnehmerüberlassung', *NZA* 2002, 1248–1254; S. Krebber, 'Die Vereinbarkeit von Entsenderichtlinie und Arbeitnehmer-Entsendegesetz mit der Dienstleistungsfreiheit und Freizügigkeit des EGV', in C. Weber et al. (eds.), *Jahrbuch Junger Zivilrechtswissenschaftler 1997 – Europäisierung des Privatrechts – Zwischenbilanz und Perspektiven* (Stuttgart et al.: Boorberg, 1997), 129–156; E. Pache, 'Dienstleistungsfreiheit', in D. Ehlers (ed.), *Europäische Grundrechte und Grundfreiheiten*, 3rd edn. (Berlin: de Gruyter, 2009), §11; M. Schlachter, 'Grenzüberschreitende Dienstleistungen: Die Arbeitnehmerentsendung zwischen Dienstleistungsfreiheit und Verdrängungswettbewerb', *NZA* 2002, 1242–1248; W. Schrammel, 'Dienstleistungsfreiheit und Sozialdumping', *EuZA* 2009, 36–46; R. Wank, 'Die Entwicklung der Dienstleistungs- und Niederlassungsfreiheit in der EU: die Rechtslage in Germany', *NZA* 2005 Supplement 2 to Issue 21, 88–97.

---

[132] See also the bibliography on freedom of establishment, before para. 78 below. Focussing on issues of labour law rather than on substance of EU law, many contributions deal with both, freedom to provide services and freedom of establishment; this is true in particular with regard to the discussions of the Court's judgements in *Viking* and *Laval*.

Cases (Selection):
ECJ Case 33/74 *van Binsbergen* [1974] ECR 1299; ECJ Joined Cases 110/78 and 111/78 *van Wesemael* [1979] ECR 35; ECJ Case 279/80 *Webb* [1981] ECR 3305; ECJ Joined Cases 286/82 and 26/83 *Luisi and Carbone* [1984] ECR 377; ECJ Case C-113/89 *Rush Portuguesa* [1990] ECR I-1417; ECJ Case C-260/89 *ERT* [1991] ECR I-2925; ECJ Case C-76/90 *Säger* [1991] ECR I-4221; ECJ Case C-43/93 *Vander Elst* [1994] ECR I-3803; ECJ Case C-381/93 *Commission* v. *France* [1994] ECR I-5145; ECJ Case C-55/98 *Vestergaard* [1999] ECR I-7641; ECJ Joined Cases C-369/96 and C-376/96 *Arblade* [1999] ECR I-8453; ECJ Case C-165/98 *Mazzoleni* [2001] ECR I-2189; ECJ Case C-493/99 *Commission* v. *Germany* [2001] ECR I-8163; ECJ Joined Cases C-49/98, C-50/98, C-52/98 to C-54/98 and C-68/98 to C-71/98 *Finalarte* [2001] ECR I-7831; ECJ Case C-164/99 *Portugaia Construções* [2002] ECR I-787; ECJ Case C-60/00 *Carpenter* [2002] ECR I-6279; ECJ Case C-60/03 *Wolff & Müller* [2004] ECR I-9553; ECJ Case C-445/03 *Commission* v. *Luxemburg* [2004] ECR I-10191; ECJ Case C-244/04 *Commission* v. *Germany* [2006] ECR I-885; ECJ Case C-168/04 *Commission* v. *Austria* [2006] ECR I-9041; ECJ Case C-452/04 *Fidium Finanz* [2006] ECR I-9521; ECJ Case C-490/04 *Commission* v. *Germany* [2007] ECR I-6095; ECJ Case C-341/05 *Laval un Partneri* [2007] ECR I-11767.

55. Freedom of services, establishment and capital do not need to be described in full detail here. We will instead merely provide a general outline with regard to their relevance for employment law. Freedom of services is primarily relevant with regard to the posting of workers and temporary agency work.[133]

56. Today, issues of posting of workers are primarily governed by the Posting of Workers Directive (see §6 below) which had to be implemented into national law by 16 December 1999. This directive itself must be interpreted in light of the freedom to provide services.[134]

1. Scope of Application[135]

57. Following the broad definition of Article 57 TFEU, 'services shall be considered to be "**services**" within the meaning of the Treaties where they are normally provided for remuneration, in so far as they are not governed by the provisions relating to freedom of movement for goods, capital and persons.' Freedom to provide services is, in this sense, designed as a catch-all provision among the fundamental freedoms:[136] it covers all 'services' (*prestations*,

---

[133] The Court of Justice has not reviewed posting of workers issues in the light of free movement of workers, given that posted workers do not intend to access the labour market of the host Member State; see para. 16 above with further references.

[134] ECJ Case C-341/05 *Laval un Partneri* [2007] ECR I-11767 para. 61; Case C-60/03 *Wolff & Müller* [2004] ECR I-9553 paras. 25–27, 45, 85, 86–111.

[135] On the transition period following the Union's East enlargement, see ECJ Case C-307/09 *Vicoplus* 10 February 2011.

[136] J. Busche, in *EAS*, B 2400 para. 12; W. Kluth, in C. Calliess/M. Ruffert (eds.), *EUV/AEUV*, Art. 57 AEUV para. 6 ('residual freedom' – my translation). But see ECJ Case C-452/04 *Fidium Finanz* [2006] ECR I-9521 paras. 31–33 (no subsidiarity of freedom of services).

Leistungen) not governed by other fundamental freedoms.[137] Services thus include rather disparate subjects such as construction work,[138] the work of agencies for the provision of manpower[139] or of fee-charging employment agencies[140] and legal advice. Only cross-border services are covered; purely internal cases are outside the scope of protection. Article 57 TFEU presupposes that the services are normally, if not in every single instance, provided for remuneration.[141]

58. Freedom to provide services protects both, the 'active freedom' of the person providing services as well as the 'passive freedom' of the person receiving services.[142] Services can be provided in the Member State of the service recipient or in that of the person rendering them; the service provider may go to the Member State of the recipient or the recipient may come to the Member State where the service provider is established.[143] Following the Court's case law, freedom to provide services also covers cases where the services are rendered in another Member State but both the person providing services and the recipient are established in the same Member State.[144] Freedom to provide services entails the right to go to another Member State for the purpose of providing or receiving services, for example in the case of construction work, Article 57(3) TFEU. As services do not have to be rendered in person, the person providing services also has the right to use employees to provide services and, for that purpose, have them accompany him to another Member State or post them to work in another Member State.[145] The temporal limitation of the stay in the other Member State distinguishes the freedom to provide services from the freedom of establishment (para. 76 below).[146]

---

[137] On the issue of ostensible self-employment R. Wank, *NZA* 2005 Supplement 2 to Issue 21, 88, 91.

[138] ECJ Case C-113/89 *Rush Portuguesa* [1990] ECR I-1417.

[139] ECJ Case 279/80 *Webb* [1981] ECR 3305 paras. 8–10; Case C-493/99 *Commission* v. *Germany* [2001] ECR I-8163 para. 18. On the issue of cross-border temporary agency work in the light of the fundamental freedoms, see T. Kienle/A. Koch, *DB* 2001, 922–927.

[140] ECJ Joined Cases 110/78 and 111/78 *van Wesemael* [1979] ECR 35 para. 7.

[141] ECJ Case 36/74 *Walrave und Koch* [1974] ECR 1405 para. 4/10; Case C-415/93 *Bosman* [1995] ECR I-4921 paras. 73–76; Joined Cases C-51/96 and C-191/97 *Deliège* [2000] ECR I-2549 para. 41.

[142] ECJ Joined Cases 286/82 and 26/83 *Luisi and Carbone* [1984] ECR 377 para. 10.

[143] ECJ Joined Cases 286/82 and 26/83 *Luisi and Carbone* [1984] ECR 377 para. 10; Case C-384/93 *Alpine Investments* [1995] ECR I-1141 para. 20.

[144] ECJ Case C-381/93 *Commission* v. *France* [1994] ECR I-5145 para. 15; Case C-55/98 *Vestergaard* [1999] ECR I-7641 para. 19. See also the tourist guide cases, Case C-198/89 *Commission* v. *Greece* [1991] ECR I-727; Case C-154/89 *Commission* v. *France* [1991] ECR I-659; Case C-180/89 *Commission* v. *Italy* [1991] ECR I-709; Case C-398/95 *SETTG* [1997] ECR I-3091.

[145] ECJ Case C-341/05 *Laval un Partneri* [2007] ECR I-11767 para. 56; Case C-113/89 *Rush Portuguesa* [1990] ECR I-1417 paras. 11 sq.; Case C-43/93 *Vander Elst* [1994] ECR I-3803 paras. 17–21; S. Krebber, in C. Weber et al. (eds.), *Jahrbuch Junger Zivilrechtswissenschaftler* 1997, 129, 147.

[146] ECJ Case 55/94 *Gebhard* [1995] ECR I-4165 para. 26; Case C-215/01 *Schnitzer* [2003] ECR I-14847 paras. 26–32. See also A. Randelzhofer/U. Forsthoff, in E. Grabitz/M. Hilf/M. Nettesheim (eds.), *Das Recht der Europäischen Union*, Art. 57 AEUV paras. 41–43.

59. Freedom to provide services protects those rendering and receiving services. Beyond that, it would be consequential, following the Court's jurisprudence on freedom of movement for workers (see paras. 13 sq. above), to consider it as also protecting (posted) **employees**, with the effect that they, too, can invoke the fundamental freedom of Article 57 TFEU in court proceedings.[147]

2. Infringements

60. Since expiry of the transitional period, freedom to provide services is a directly applicable right.[148] It is binding upon the Member States, the Union and, following the Court's jurisprudence,[149] private individuals.[150] Private individuals must respect freedom of movement for services in particular where they have a collective regulatory power, e.g. where collective agreements or collective action of trade unions are concerned.

61. Freedom of services contains a **prohibition of discrimination** which is, however, only imperfectly expressed by Article 57(3) TFEU. Here too, the Treaty prohibits any direct or indirect discrimination (cf. paras. 32–35 above).[151]

62. Furthermore, Article 56(1) TFEU prohibits **restrictions on** the freedom to provide services. 'It is settled case-law that Article 49 EC requires not only the elimination of all discrimination against service providers on the ground of their nationality but also the abolition of any restriction, even if it applies without distinction to national providers of services and to those of other Member States, when it is liable to prohibit or otherwise impede the activities of a service provider established in another Member State where it lawfully provides similar services'.[152]

---

147 With hints to this effect ECJ Joined Cases C-317/01 and C-369/01 *Abatay* [2003] ECR I-12301. R. Wank, NZA 2005 Supplement 2 to Issue 21, 88, 92 ('annex-freedom'), 93 sq. ('derivative right to free movement' – my translations).

148 ECJ Case 33/74 *van Binsbergen* [1974] ECR 1299 paras. 20/23 and 24/26; Case 279/80 *Webb* [1981] ECR 3305 para. 13; Case C-341/05 *Laval un Partneri* [2007] ECR I-11767 para. 97. See above Fn. 1.

149 ECJ Case C-341/05 *Laval un Partneri* [2007] ECR I-11767 para. 98; Case C-309/99 *Wouters* [2002] ECR I-1577 para. 120; Case C-415/93 *Bosman* [1995] ECR I-4921, paras. 83 sq.; Case 36/74 *Walrave and Koch* [1974] ECR 1405 paras. 17 sq.

150 See also U. Bernitz/N. Reich, 'Case No. A 268/04, The Labour Court, Sweden (Arbetsdomstolen) Judgment No. 89/09 of 2 December 2009, Laval un Partneri Ltd. v. Svenska Byggnadsarbetareförbundet et al.', CMLR 48 (2011), 603–623 (discussing the decision in *Laval* of the Swedish Labour Court which awarded *Laval* damages for breach of the freedom to provide services as a fundamental right directly applicable between private parties).

151 ECJ Joined Cases 62/81 and 63/81 *Seco [1982]* ECR 223 para. 8; Case 279/80 *Webb* [1981] ECR 3305 para. 14.

152 ECJ Case C-490/04 *Commission v. Germany* [2007] ECR I-6095 para. 63; Case C-452/04 *Fidium Finanz* [2006] ECR I-9521 para. 46; Case C-168/04 *Commission v. Austria* [2006] ECR I-9041 para. 36; Case C-244/04 *Commission v. Germany* [2006] ECR I-885 para. 30; Case C-60/03 *Wolff & Müller* [2004] ECR I-9553 para. 31; Case C-164/99 *Portugaia Construções* [2002] ECR I-787 para. 16; Case C-165/98 *Mazzoleni* [2001] ECR I-2189 para. 22; Joined Cases

In other language versions of this judgement, the broad scope of Article 56 is expressed even more clearly since a restriction is found where measures are liable to **render** the exercise of freedom of movement **less attractive**. For example, it constitutes a restriction upon freedom of services where the posting of workers to another Member State requires a work permit for the employees.[153]

63.   From the wording of Article 57(3) TFEU, it appears that the provision of services in another Member State requires the person providing services to observe all 'conditions as are imposed by that State on its own nationals'. Yet, this would result in a double burden (as the service provider must also observe the conditions of his home Member State) and would thus certainly make the provision of services in another Member State less attractive. Indeed, to require that a person rendering services in the host Member State observe all conditions imposed by that State on its own nationals would in effect put him in a position similar to that of opening a branch establishment. This would in practice render freedom to provide services ineffective (*effet utile*).[154] On the basis of these considerations, the Court has interpreted Article 57(3) TFEU as a mere prohibition of discrimination rather than a justification for the application of domestic law to nationals of other Member States rendering services in the host Member State.[155] Even a selective application of national law of the host Member State is subject to control on its restrictive effect, given that it could be liable to render the provision of services less attractive where additional costs or administrative or economic burdens result from it.[156] Accommodation of the countervailing interests – application of the host Member State's law on the one hand and freedom to provide services on the other – is considered only in the justification of the restriction.

64.   In the context of employment law, this is of practical importance with regard to the **posting of workers**. If, for example, a construction company of one Member State ('home Member State') temporarily posts its workers to another Member State ('host Member State'), the employment relationship will, under

---

C-49/98, C-50/98, C-52/98 to C-54/98 and C-68/98 to C-71/98 *Finalarte* [2001] ECR I-7831 para. 28; Joined Cases C-369/96 and C-376/96 *Arblade* [1999] ECR I-8453 para. 33; Case C-275/92 *Schindler* [1994] ECR I-1039 para. 43.

[153]   ECJ Case C-168/04 *Commission* v. *Austria* [2006] ECR I-9041 paras. 39–42; Case C-445/03 *Commission* v. *Luxembourg* [2004] ECR I-10191 para. 24; Case C-43/93 *Vander Elst* [1994] ECR I-3803 para. 15.

[154]   ECJ Case C-164/99 *Portugaia Construções* [2002] ECR I-787 para. 17; Joined Cases C-49/98, C-50/98, C-52/98 to C-54/98 and C-68/98 to C-71/98 *Finalarte* [2001] ECR 2001 I-7831 para. 29; Case C-165/98 *Mazzoleni* [2001] ECR I-2189 para. 23; Case C-43/93 *Vander Elst* [1994] ECR I-3803 para. 17; Case C-76/90 *Säger* [1991] ECR I-4221 para. 13.

[155]   ECJ Case 279/80 *Webb* [1981] ECR 3305 para. 16.

[156]   ECJ Case C-164/99 *Portugaia Construções* [2002] ECR I-787 para. 18; Joined Cases C-49/98, C-50/98, C-52/98 to C-54/98 and C-68/98 to C-71/98 *Finalarte* [2001] ECR 2001 I-7831 para. 30; Case C-165/98 *Mazzoleni* [2001] ECR I-2189 para. 24.

conflict of laws principles, still be governed by the laws of the home Member State (see in detail §5 below). The question then is whether the host Member State may require that its employment protection rules, e.g. on minimum wage, also be applied. Application of the host Member State's law is initially a restriction of the company's freedom to provide services. Doing business in other Member States, the company would have to observe different employment standards with every new posting of workers. The question thus is whether such restriction of the freedom of services can be justified.

3. Justification of Infringements

65. Infringements of the freedom of services – discrimination as well as restrictions – can be justified by the *ordre public*-reservation of Article 52 TFEU to which Article 62 TFEU refers (see paras. 40–42 above).[157] This is the only available justification for *discrimination*.[158]

66. *Restrictions* may further be justified by **mandatory requirements of public interests**. This justification is, however, restricted to cases where the public interest in question is not yet satisfied by the laws and regulations of the home Member State of the person providing services (the issue of 'double burdens').[159] Economic goals, and particularly the protection of domestic enterprises, do not constitute accepted public interests.[160] But the Court considers the **protection of employees** to be a legitimate public interest.[161] As to the issue of double burdens, this entails an inquiry not only as to whether the issue of employee protection is

---

[157] ECJ Case C-168/04 *Commission v. Austria* [2006] ECR I-9041 para. 64 ('only if there is a genuine and sufficiently serious threat to a fundamental interest of society').

[158] ECJ Case C-490/04 *Commission v. Germany* [2007] ECR I-6095 para. 86; Case C-260/89 *ERT* [1991] ECR I-2925 para. 24. Details are controversial; cf. E. Pache, in D. Ehlers (ed.), *Europäische Grundrechte und Grundfreiheiten*, §11 paras. 67 sq., 70.

[159] ECJ Case C-490/04 *Commission v. Germany* [2007] ECR I-6095 para. 64; Case C-168/04 *Commission v. Austria* [2006] ECR I-9041 para. 36; Case C-244/04 *Commission v. Germany* [2006] ECR I-885 paras. 31, 44; Case C-60/03 *Wolff & Müller* [2004] ECR I-9553 para. 34; Joined Cases C-49/98, C-50/98, C-52/98 to C-54/98 and C-68/98 to C-71/98 *Finalarte* [2001] ECR 2001 I-7831 para. 31; Case C-165/98 *Mazzoleni* [2001] ECR I-2189 para. 25; Joined Cases C-369/96 and C-376/96 *Arblade* [1999] ECR I-8453 para. 34; Case C-76/90 *Säger* [1991] ECR I-4221 para. 15; Case 279/80 *Webb* [1981] ECR 3305 para. 17; Joined Cases 110/78 and 111/78 *van Wesemael* [1979] ECR 35 paras. 24–30.

[160] Joined Cases C-49/98, C-50/98, C-52/98 to C-54/98 and C-68/98 to C-71/98 *Finalarte* [2001] ECR 2001 I-7831 para. 39; Case C-158/96 *Kohll* [1998] ECR I-1931 para. 41.

[161] ECJ Case C-490/04 *Commission v. Germany* [2007] ECR I-6095 para. 70; Case C-168/04 *Commission v. Austria* [2006] ECR I-9041 para. 47; Case C-60/03 *Wolff & Müller* [2004] ECR I-9553 para. 35; Case C-164/99 *Portugaia Construções* [2002] ECR I-787 para. 20; Case C-493/99 *Commission v. Germany* [2001] ECR I-8163 para. 20; Joined Cases C-49/98, C-50/98, C-52/98 to C-54/98 and C-68/98 to C-71/98 *Finalarte* [2001] ECR 2001 I-7831 para. 33; Case C-165/98 *Mazzoleni* [2001] ECR I-2189 para. 27; Joined Cases C-369/96 and C-376/96 *Arblade* [1999] ECR I-8453 para. 36; Case C-272/94 *Guiot* [1996] ECR I-1905 para. 16; Case C-113/89 *Rush Portuguesa* [1990] ECR I-1417 para. 18; Case 279/80 *Webb* [1981] ECR 3305 para. 19.

as such already covered by national law but also whether the provisions of the host Member State offer better protection than those of the home Member State (e.g. a higher minimum wage).[162]

67. With regard to the posting of workers, a specific problem lies in the fact that national laws, in particular the German Law on Posting of Workers (*Arbeitnehmerentsendegesetz*), have often been overtly justified by the consideration that national companies needed to be protected against foreign competitors ('*Billigkonkurrenz*') (see §6 para. 33 below). Protection of the national economy can, however, by no means constitute a legitimate public interest under the TFEU. In the relevant cases, the Court has been rather generous, mandating that the national courts examine whether, irrespective of the insufficient legislative motivation, the law in question could *objectively* be justified by legitimate public interests.[163] As a matter of internal market policy, this seems to be misguided; the Member States should be expected not to pursue objectives that are incompatible with the internal market in the first place.

68. In a recent judgement, the Court has taken a noteworthy and – from an internal market-perspective – even fatal turn. Instead of referring to the protection of posted employees it considered 'the protection of the workers of the host State against possible social dumping' to constitute an overriding reason of public interest.[164] In substance, this supports a protectionist approach pursuant to which the protection of the national economy may constitute a reason for the justification of infringements of fundamental freedoms.

69. Finally, conflicting **fundamental rights** may also justify an infringement of the freedom of services. In the Court's case law, namely its *Laval* decision, this has, in particular, been recognised with regard to the right to strike (the right to take collective action; see §2 paras. 13, 50 sq.; regarding trade unions as addressees of the fundamental freedoms, see para. 60 above).[165] The fact that the right to strike is, pursuant to Article 153(5) TFEU, outside the regulatory competence of the EU (see §4 paras. 13 sq.), means Member States are competent to legislate in this field, but it does not exempt it from application of the

---

Critically M. Franzen, *IPRax* 2002, 186, 189 sq. (concluding at p. 190: 'acknowledgement of an incomplete internal market' – my translation).

[162] Against this approach with convincing considerations S. Krebber, in C. Weber et al. (eds.), *Jahrbuch Junger Zivilrechtswissenschaftler 1997*, 129, 151 sq.

[163] Particularly far-reaching (after an almost provocative reference by the *Bundesarbeitsgericht* [Federal Labour Court, BAG]) ECJ Case C-60/03 *Wolff & Müller* [2004] ECR I-9553 paras. 18 sq., 38 sq. See also Case C-164/99 *Portugaia Construções* [2002] ECR I-787 paras. 25 sq.; Joined Cases C-49/98, C-50/98, C-52/98 to C-54/98 and C-68/98 to C-71/98 *Finalarte* [2001] ECR 2001 I-7831 paras. 38–41; P. Davies, *ILJ 31 (2002), 298, 302*; R. Giesen, *CMLR* 40 (2003), 143, 157.

[164] ECJ Case C-341/05 *Laval un Partneri* [2007] ECR I-11767 para. 103; see also para. 113. To the same effect already Case C-60/03 *Wolff & Müller* [2004] ECR I-9553 para. 41.

[165] ECJ Case C-341/05 *Laval un Partneri* [2007] ECR I-11767 paras. 86–111.

fundamental freedoms.[166] A measure of industrial action against a company posting workers in another Member State may thus constitute a restriction of freedom of services ('liable to render less attractive') and be subject to proportionality control.[167]

70. The **theoretical foundation** of this accommodation of fundamental freedoms and fundamental rights is rather uncertain in many respects.[168] The Court seems to assume that the fundamental right in question is one of Union law and not of the Member States' laws.[169] The conflict between fundamental freedoms and fundamental rights can be compared to a collision of fundamental rights, a case well known from national constitutional law theory.[170] Yet, the Court indicates that it tries to incorporate this case in its usual conception of justifications when it considers the protection of fundamental rights as a legitimate public interest. Fundamental rights may also be invoked as justification by private organisations (whom the Court also considers addressees of fundamental rights); where administrative and judicial measures are in question, the issue would be whether they were under an obligation to protect the fundamental rights.

71. The Court's decisions in *Laval* and *Viking* (see para. 95 below) have caused considerable concern that the scope of collective action as established in the national laws of the Member States could be changed one way or another. Unions, in particular, were concerned that the right to strike could be unduly constrained. The Commission has recently adopted a proposal for a regulation on the exercise of the right to take collective action within the context of the freedom of establishment and the freedom to provide services.[171] It aims at establishing a relationship of 'mutual respect' of the fundamental freedoms on the one hand and the fundamental rights to collective action on the other. The proposal further provides for dispute resolution mechanisms and 'alert mechanisms'. In initial reactions, both sides of industry have expressed discontent with the proposal. While business considers the proposal unnecessary and *ultra vires* (Article 153(5) TFEU!), labour holds that the protection of the right to strike does not go far enough.

72. Here too, justifications are subject to '**limitation-limitations**'. First of all, they have to be interpreted in light of EU fundamental rights (see para. 48

---

166   Thus already R. Birk, *Festschrift 50 Jahre Bundesarbeitsgericht*, 1165, 1167.
167   ECJ Case C-341/05 *Laval un Partneri* [2007] ECR I-11767. Critically with regard to the interference with the national social model e.g. R. Eklund, *Comp. Lab. L. & Pol'y J.* 29 (2007–2008), 551, 564 sqq.
168   Critically R. Rebhahn, *wbl* 2008, 63, 67 sq.; id., *ZESAR* 2008, 109, 113–116.
169   Cf. ECJ Case C-112/00 *Schmidberger* [2003] ECR I-5659 paras. 71–75.
170   Thus, e.g., C. *Schubert*, *RdA* 2008, 289, 293 sq. Contra R. Birk, *Festschrift 50 Jahre Bundesarbeitsgericht*, 1165, 1171–1177 (on the basis of a concept of obligations of protection).
171   Proposal for a regulation on the exercise of the right to take collective action within the context of the freedom of establishment and the freedom to provide services, COM(2012) 130 final.

above).[172] Secondly, all justifications, written as well as unwritten, are limited by the principle of proportionality: The restriction must be suitable and necessary for the pursuit of a legitimate objective. Where the restrictions result from the application of employee protection laws of the host Member State, the burden on the employer, in the form of costs and administrative efforts, needs to be weighed against the additional protection awarded to the employee.[173]

4. Practical Consequences: Posting of Workers[174]

73. As a **practical result**, this means that a host Member State may extend application of its national employee protection laws, e.g. on minimum wages or minimum paid leave, to employees posted in the context of the provision of services, provided that such laws offer an additional protection and the principle of proportionality is observed. This is true even with regard to areas of the law that are already subject to minimum harmonisation by the EU, such as paid leave (Working Time Directive, see §14 below).[175] The Court argues that the Working Time Directive merely provides for a minimum period of paid leave. 'It is therefore for each Member State to determine the period of paid leave which is necessary in the public interest.'[176] Freedom to provide services is thus no obstacle to the extension of national provisions on a minimum period of paid leave, and a Member State may even consider a minimum period of 30 days to be necessary in the (public) interest of employee protection.[177] There are four remaining outermost **limits**:

(1) the prohibition of discrimination which is only limited by the *ordre public-* reservation;[178]

(2) the requirement of a *genuine benefit* for the posted employees;[179]

---

[172]　ECJ Case C-260/89 *ERT* [1991] ECR I-2945 para. 43; Case C-368/95 *Familiapress* [1997] ECR I-3689 para. 24; Case C-60/00 *Carpenter* [2002] ECR I-6279 para. 40.

[173]　ECJ Case C-490/04 *Commission* v. *Germany* [2007] ECR I-6095 para. 46; Joined Cases C-49/98, C-50/98, C-52/98 to C-54/98 and C-68/98 to C-71/98 *Finalarte* [2001] ECR 2001 I-7831 para. 50.

[174]　Apart from the two issues discussed in the following, that of ostensible self-employment is of considerable practical importance in the context of freedom of services. In particular during transitional periods where workers of new Member States did not enjoy full freedom of movement for workers, a circumvention under the cover so being self-employed had to be considered, see R. Wank, *NZA* 2005 Supplement 2 to Issue 21, 88, 91.

[175]　Also critical M. Franzen, *IPRax* 2002, 186, 189 sq.

[176]　Joined Cases C-49/98, C-50/98, C-52/98 to C-54/98 and C-68/98 to C-71/98 *Finalarte* [2001] ECR 2001 I-7831 para. 58.

[177]　Joined Cases C-49/98, C-50/98, C-52/98 to C-54/98 and C-68/98 to C-71/98 *Finalarte* [2001] ECR 2001 I-7831 paras. 57 sq. Critically, but consenting with the outcome, R. Giesen, *CMLR* 40 (2003), 143, 155–157.

[178]　See e.g. ECJ Case C-490/04 *Commission* v. *Germany* [2007] ECR I-6095 paras. 83–86; also Case C-493/99 *Commission* v. *Germany* [2001] ECR I-8163 paras. 14–24.

[179]　The ECJ applies a concrete-individual measure, looking at the advantages for the individual worker, not at the advantages of workers as a whole; ECJ Case C-60/03 *Wolff & Müller* [2004]

(3) the limitation that the protected interest must not already be safeguarded by the rules to which the service provider is subject in the Member State in which it is established (the issue of double burdens);[180] and

(4) the principle of proportionality;[181] here as well, the Court requires a comparative examination: the application of the law of the host Member State may be disproportionate where the protected interest has already been addressed by a similar or more advantageous provision of the national law of the home Member State.[182] This requires a balancing of the burdens upon the employer and the interests of the employee.

It cannot be overlooked that the comparative examination in particular (which is left for the national courts to carry out!) will pose considerable difficulty in practice and is bound to lead to *disparate application* of the national laws on posting of workers, depending upon the level of protection in the employee's home Member State.[183]

74. As a matter of regulatory policy in the internal market, the extension of national employment law to posted workers, as approved by the Court of Justice, is rather controversial and problematic. The EU has adopted the Posting of Workers Directive to pursue its goal of establishing, as a minimum, a level of transparency for service providers from other Member States. See in detail §6 below and regarding the precedence of application of directives, see para. 56 above.

5.   *Appendix: The Services in the Internal Market Directive*

Bibliography:
A. Hatje, 'Die Dienstleistungsrichtlinie – Auf der Suche nach dem liberalen Mehrwert – Auch eine Herausforderung für die Rechtsanwaltschaft?', *NJW* 2007, 2357–2363; M. Körner, 'EU-Dienstleistungsrichtlinie und Arbeitsrecht', *NZA* 2007, 233–238; M. Schlachter, 'Der Commissionsentwurf für eine Richtlinie über Dienstleistungen im Binnenmarkt', *GPR* 2003/04, 245–249; M. Schlachter/C. Ohler (eds.), *Europäische Dienstleistungsrichtlinie – Handkommentar* (Baden-Baden: Nomos, 2008).

ECR I-9553 para. 40 ('Moreover, the dispute in the main proceedings itself appears to confirm that Paragraph 1(a) of the AEntG is of protective intent.').

[180] ECJ Case C-244/04 *Commission v. Germany* [2006] ECR I-885 paras. 48–51; Joined Cases C-369/96 and C-376/96 *Arblade* [1999] ECR I-8453 paras. 48–55. See also P. *Davies, CMLR* 34 (1997), 571, 594 sq.

[181] ECJ Case C-168/04 *Commission v. Austria* [2006] ECR I-9041 paras. 48–53; ECJ Case C-244/04 *Commission v. Germany* [2006] ECR I-885 paras. 41, 45; ECJ Case C-493/99 *Commission v. Germany* [2001] ECR I-8163 paras. 21 sq.

[182] ECJ Case C-165/98 *Mazzoleni* [2001] ECR I-2189 paras. 30–35.

[183] For a critical appraisal, see P. *Davies, ILJ 31 (2002), 298, 304;* R. Giesen, *CMLR* 40 (2003), 143, 152.

75. At the end of 2006, the Services in the Internal Market Directive (SIMD)[184] was enacted. We shall only briefly introduce this directive as it explicitly leaves labour law unaffected. The Services in the Internal Market Directive is the result of a long and **controversial legislative process.**[185] Its objective is to facilitate free movement of services. It was initially considered to establish the country of origin principle, that is the principle that a service provider should be allowed to pursue his activity in other Member States subject (only) to the rules and regulations of his Member State of origin ('home Member State') and under the supervision of the supervisory authorities of his home Member State.[186] This approach failed, however, due to resistance from the Member States as well as the European Parliament. Part of this resistance was based upon employment law considerations, particularly a concern that the state of origin-principle could foster 'social dumping' in respect of posted employees or ostensibly self-employed service providers.[187] Conversely, the Court's jurisprudence which recognises employee protection as a 'mandatory requirement of public interest' and the Posting of Workers Directive, were considered sensible instruments of regulation and protection.

76. The **directive** as finally **enacted**[188] contains first, procedural requirements that are intended to simplify administrative rules for cross-border services and establish a single reference person for any admission procedures ('one-stop-shop', Article 5–8 and 22–46 SIMD). Secondly, there are provisions on freedom of establishment of service providers; they largely follow the Court's jurisprudence, Article 9–15 SIMD. Finally, the directive contains provisions on freedom of services, Article 16–21 SIMD. These no longer include the state-of-origin principle; in addition, the directive provides for a number of important exceptions. It is important to note, though, that the 'mandatory requirements of public interest' justifying infringement of freedom of services have been narrowly defined, Article 16(3) SIMD.

77. The directive explicitly leaves **labour law** unaffected, Article 1(6) and Recitals 14, 15, 90 SIMD.[189] Recital 15 SIMD further expounds that the directive respects the exercise of fundamental rights recognised in the Charter of Fundamental Rights of the EU, reconciling them with the freedom of establishment and the freedom of services. As we have already discussed (see

---

[184] Directive 2006/123/EC of the European Parliament and of the Council of 12 December 2006 on services in the internal market, OJ 2006 L 376/36.

[185] For a summary, see A. Hatje, *NJW* 2007, 2357; on the Commission's proposal M. Schlachter, *GPR* 2003/04, 245–249.

[186] In more detail A. Hatje, *NJW* 2007, 2357, 2360–2362; see also M. Körner, *NZA* 2007, 233, 234.

[187] Cf. M. Körner, *NZA* 2007, 233, 234 sq.

[188] For an overview, see A. Hatje, *NJW* 2007, 2357, 2359–2362.

[189] For a critical view of the exclusion of employment law see M. Körner, *NZA* 2007, 233, 235 sq.

paras. 70 sq. above), this can be important for the law of industrial action to which Recital 15 explicitly refers. In addition, certain aspects of cross-border provision of services have been explicitly excluded from the directive's scope of application. This is true for the services of temporary work agencies, Article 2(2)(e) SIMD. Furthermore, the Posting of Workers Directive takes precedence over the Services in the Internal Market Directive, Article 3(1)(a) SIMD. Issues covered by the former have been explicitly excluded from the freedom of services in Article 16 SIMD; cf. Article 17(2) SIMD. The legislator also wanted to leave the Court's jurisprudence on posting of workers untouched. Pursuant to Recital 82 SIMD, the provisions of the Directive should not preclude the application by a Member State of rules on employment conditions, provided that they are necessary and proportionate. Unlike the model proposed in an earlier draft, supervisory competence is no longer divided between the home Member State and the host Member State but lies exclusively in the hands of the latter, Article 31(1) SIMD.[190]

IV. FREEDOM OF ESTABLISHMENT – OVERVIEW

Bibliography:[191]
K. Apps, Damages claims against trade unions after Viking and Laval, *E.L. Rev.* 34 (2009), 141–154; J. Bartsch, *Mitbestimmung und Niederlassungsfreiheit* (Berlin: Logos, 2006); B. Bercusson, 'The Trade Union Movement and the European Union: Judgment Day', *ELJ* 13 (2007), 279–308; R. Birk, 'Arbeitskampf und Europarecht', in H. Oetker/U. Preis/V. Rieble (eds.), *Festschrift 50 Jahre Bundesarbeitsgericht* (Munich: C.H. Beck, 2004), 1165–1178; S. Braun, *Die Sicherung der Unternehmensmitbestimmung im Lichte des europäischen Rechts* (Baden-Baden: Nomos, 2005); J. Dammann, 'Freedom of Choice in European Corporate Law', *Yale J. Int.'l L.* 29 (2004), 477–544; J. Dammann, 'The Future of Codetermination After Centros: Will German Corporate Law Move Closer to the US Model?', *Fordham JCFL* 8 (2003) 607–686; A. C. L. Davies, 'One Step Forward, Two Steps Back The Viking and Laval Cases in the ECJ', *ILJ* 37 (2008), 126–148; H. Eidenmüller (ed.), *Ausländische Kapitalanlagegesellschaften im deutschen Recht* (Munich: C.H. Beck, 2004); H. Eidenmüller, 'Mobilität und Restrukturierung von Unternehmen im Binnenmarkt – Entwicklungsperspektiven des europäischen Gesellschaftsrechts im Schnittfeld von Gemeinschaftsgesetzgeber und EuGH', *JZ* 2004, 24–33; H. Eidenmüller/G. Rehm, 'Niederlassungsfreiheit versus Schutz des inländischen Rechtsverkehrs: Konturen des europäischen Internationalen Gesellschaftsrechts', *ZGR* 2004, 159–188; U. Forsthoff, *Niederlassungsfreiheit für Gesellschaften – Europarechtliche Grenzen für die Erstreckung deutschen (Mitbestimmungs-)Rechts* (Baden-Baden: Nomos, 2006); M. Franzen, 'Niederlassungsfreiheit, internationales Gesellschaftsrecht und Unternehmensmitbestimmung', *RdA* 2004, 257–263; M. Franzen, 'Standortverlagerung und Arbeitskampf', *ZfA* 2005, 315–351; F. Hendrickx, 'Beyond Viking and Laval:

---

[190] M. Schlachter, in M. Schlachter/C. Ohler (eds.), *Europäische Dienstleistungsrichtlinie*, vor Art. 19 DLRL para. 1.

[191] From the company law literature, see only S. Grundmann, *European Company Law*, §25 before para. 1.

The Evolving European Context', *Comp. Lab. L. & Pol'y J.* 35 (2011), 1055–1077; M. Henssler, 'Mitbestimmungsrechtliche Konsequenzen einer Sitzverlegung innerhalb der Europäischen Union – Inspirationen durch "Inspire Art"', in A. Söllner et al. (eds.), *Gedächtnisschrift für Meinhard Heinze* (Munich: C.H. Beck, 2005), 333–355; H. Hirte/T. Bücker, *Grenzüberschreitende Gesellschaften – Praxishandbuch für ausländische Kapitalgesellschaften mit Sitz im Inland* (Cologne et al.: Carl Heymanns, 2005); C. Joerges/F. Rödl, 'Informal Politics, Formalised Law and the 'Social Deficit' of European Integration: Reflections after the Judgments of the ECJ in *Viking* and *Laval*', *ELJ* 15 (2009), 1–19; A. Junker, 'Sechsundsiebzig verweht – Die deutsche Mitbestimmung endet in Europa', *NJW* 2004, 728–730; A. Junker, 'Standortverlagerung und Niederlassungsfreiheit – Das Rosella-Verfahren vor dem EuGH', *EWS* 2007, 49–55; A. Junker, 'Unternehmensmitbestimmung in Deutschland – Anpassungsbedarf durch internationale und europäische Entwicklungen', *ZfA* 2005, 1–44; C. Kerwer, 'Von Lokführern, solidarischen Druckern und Nürnberger Haushaltsgeräten: Neue Tendenzen im Arbeitskampfrecht', *EuZA* 2008, 335–354; E.-M. Kieninger, *Wettbewerb der Privatrechtsordnungen im Europäischen Binnenmarkt – Studien zur Privatrechtskoordinierung in der Europäischen Union auf den Gebieten des Gesellschafts- und Vertragsrechts* (Tübingen: Mohr Siebeck, 2002); O. Kisker, *Unternehmensmitbestimmung bei Auslandsgesellschaft mit Verwaltungssitz in Germany* (Baden-Baden: Nomos, 2007); K. Lenaerts/J. A. Gutiérrez-Fons, 'The Constitutional Allocation of Powers and General Principles in EU Law', *CMLR* 47 (2010), 1629–1669; R. Lubitz, *Sicherung und Modernisierung der Unternehmensmitbestimmung* (Munich: ZAAR, 2005); M. Lutter (ed.), *Europäische Auslandsgesellschaften in Germany* (Cologne: Otto Schmidt, 2005); T. Müller-Bonanni, 'Mitbestimmung', in H. Hirte/T. Bücker (eds.), *Grenzüberschreitende Gesellschaften* (Cologne et al.: Carl Heymanns, 2006), 479–497; T. Müller-Bonanni, 'Unternehmensmitbestimmung nach "Überseering" und "Inspire Art"', *GmbHR* 2003, 1235–1239; W. Paefgen, 'Auslandsgesellschaften und Durchsetzung deutscher Schutzinteressen nach Überseering"', *DB* 2003, 487–492; G. Orlandini, 'Trade Union Rights and Market Freedoms: The European Court of Justice Sets Out the Rules', *Comp. Lab. L. & Pol'y J.* 29 (2007–2008), 573–603; R. Rebhahn, 'Grundfreiheit versus oder vor Streikrecht', *wbl* 2008, 63–69; R. Rebhahn, 'Grundfreiheit vor Arbeitskampf – der Fall Viking', *ZESAR* 2008, 109–117; M. Rehberg, 'Arbeits- und Sozialrecht', in H. Eidenmüller (ed.), *Ausländische Kapitalanlagegesellschaften im deutschen Recht* (Munich: C.H. Beck, 2004), §6; W.-H. Roth, 'From Centros to Überseering: Free Movement of Companies, Private International Law, and Community Law', *ICLQ* 52 (2003), 177–208; W.-H. Roth, 'Unternehmensmitbestimmung und internationals Gesellschaftsrecht', in A. Söllner et al. (eds.), *Gedächtnisschrift für Meinhard Heinze* (Munich: C.H. Beck, 2005), 709–729; M. Schlachter, 'Die Verhältnismäßigkeit von Arbeitskampfmaßnahmen gegen grenzüberschreitende Standortverlagerungen', in H. Konzen et al. (eds.), *Festschrift für Rolf Birk* (Tübingen: Mohr Siebeck, 2008), 809–821; C. Schubert, 'Europäische Grundfreiheiten und nationales Arbeitskampfrecht im Konflikt – Zugleich eine Besprechung der Entscheidungen des EuGH v. 11.12.2007 – Rs. C-438/05 – Viking und v. 18.12.2007 – Rs. C-341/05 – Laval', *RdA* 2008, 289–299; E. Schwark, 'Globalisierung, Europarecht und Unternehmensmitbestimmung im Konflikt', *AG* 2004, 173–180; C. Teichmann, 'Gesellschaftsrecht im System der Europäischen Niederlassungsfreiheit', *ZGR* 2011, 639–689; G. Thüsing, 'Deutsche Unternehmensmitbestimmung und europäische Niederlassungsfreiheit', *ZIP* 2004, 381–388; G. Thüsing, 'Europäische Perspektiven der deutschen Unternehmensmitbestimmung', in V. Rieble (ed.), *Zukunft der Unternehmensmitbestimmung* (Munich: ZAAR, 2004), 95–113 (also published in *ZIP* 2004, 381–388); C. Tietje, 'Niederlassungsfreiheit', in D. Ehlers (ed.), *Europäische Grundrechte und Grundfreiheiten,* 3rd edn. (Berlin: de Gruyter, 2009), §10; E. Vaccaro, 'Transfer of Seat and Freedom of Establishment in European Company Law', *EBLR* 2005, 1348–1365; R. Wank, 'Die Entwicklung der Dienstleistungs- und Niederlassungsfreiheit in der EU – Die Rechtslage in Germany', *NZA* 2005 Supplement 2 to Issue 21, 88–97; G. Weidmann, *Die Anwendung des Mitbestimmungsgesetzes 1976 in Fällen mit Auslandsbezug* (Baden-Baden: Nomos, 2007); C. Windbichler/G. Bachmann, 'Corporate Governance und Mitbestimmung als "wirtschaftsrechtlicher ordre public"', in K. Mock/H. Westermann (eds.), *Festschrift für Gerold Bezzenberger* (Berlin/New York: de Gruyter, 2000), 797–805.

Cases (Selection):
ECJ Case 79/85 *Segers* [1986] ECR 2375; ECJ Case 81/87 *Daily Mail* [1988] ECR 5483; ECJ Case 55/94 *Gebhard* [1995] ECR I-4165; ECJ Case C-212/97 *Centros* [1999] ECR I-1459; ECJ Case C-208/00 *Überseering* [2002] ECR I-9919; ECJ Case C-167/01 *Inspire Art* [2003] ECR I-10155; ECJ Case C-411/03 *Sevic* [2005] ECR I-10805; ECJ Case C-196/04 *Cadbury Schweppes,* [2006] ECR I-8031; ECJ Case C-438/05 *Viking* [2007] ECR I-10779.

78. While freedom of services is of practical importance in the field of employment for the posting of employees, the practical importance of the freedom of establishment lies in its effect upon employee involvement and collective action which is taken against attempts to relocate firms.

1.   Scope of Application

79. Restrictions on the freedom of establishment which are imposed upon nationals of a Member State in the territory of another Member State are prohibited, Article 49(1) sent. 1 TFEU. Pursuant to Articles 49–54 TFEU, freedom of establishment is the **free movement of the self-employed**, which encompasses both natural and legal persons ('companies or firms' within the meaning of Article 54(2) TFEU), Article 54(1) TFEU.[192] Freedom of establishment protects the taking up and pursuit of a self-employed economic activity in the territory of another Member State through a fixed establishment[193] under the laws and regulations that apply in the host Member State to its own nationals: formation and management of enterprises including the cross-border merger[194] (Article 49(2) TFEU) as well establishment of agencies, branch offices[195] or subsidiaries (Article 49(1) sent. 2 TFEU).[196] 'Establishment' thus does not require

---

[192]   See e.g. ECJ Case C-212/97 *Centros* [1999] ECR I-1459 para. 19; Case 55/94 *Gebhard* [1995] ECR I-4165 para. 23; Case 79/85 *Segers* [1986] ECR 2375 para. 12.

[193]   ECJ Case C-221/89 *Factortame* [1991] ECR I-3905.

[194]   ECJ Case C-411/03 *Sevic* [2005] ECR I-10805 paras. 17–19.

[195]   ECJ Case C-212/97 *Centros* [1999] ECR I-1459 paras. 17 sq., 20; Case 79/85 *Segers* [1986] ECR 2375 para. 13.

[196]   ECJ Case 55/94 *Gebhard* [1995] ECR I-4165 para. 23. See also Case 81/87 *Daily Mail* [1988] ECR 5483 para. 17; Case C-196/04 *Cadbury Schweppes* [2006] ECR I-8031 para. 41.

that a company has to relocate its seat from one Member State to another (see agencies, branch offices, subsidiaries), and a company can have more than one 'establishment' in this sense.[197] 'The concept of establishment within the meaning of the Treaty is therefore very broad, allowing a Community national to participate, on a stable and continuous basis, in the economic life of a Member State other than his state of origin and to profit therefrom, thus contributing to economic and social development within the Community in the sphere of activities as self-employed persons'.[198] The element of time ('stable and continuous basis') distinguishes freedom of establishment from freedom of services which is characterised by temporary cross-border activity (see para. 58 above).[199]

80. Unlike the freedom of movement for workers (see para. 18 above), freedom of establishment does not 'as [Union] law now stands' to a full extent comprise the freedom to leave the home Member State.[200] National law can thus restrict a company from moving to another Member State while maintaining the legal form of its home Member State. Matters are different, though, with regard to cross-border transformation into a legal entity recognised by the host Member State.

2. Infringements

81. Since expiry of the transitional period, freedom of establishment is directly applicable.[201] It is addressed to the Member States, the Union and, following the Court of Justice,[202] to private individuals, particularly where they exert collective regulatory power.[203]

82. If the fundamental freedoms are directly applicable to trade unions and if collective action may constitute an infringement of fundamental freedoms, the question of sanctions arises. Trade unions maybe liable in damages under national law.[204]

---

[197] ECJ Case 55/94 *Gebhard* [1995] ECR I-4165 para. 24; Case 107/83 *Klopp* [1984] ECR 2971 para. 19.

[198] ECJ Case 55/94 *Gebhard* [1995] ECR I-4165 para. 25.

[199] G. Bröhmer, in C. Calliess/M. Ruffert (eds.), *EUV/AEUV*, Art. 49 AEUV paras. 12 sq.; M. Schlag, in J. Schwarze (ed.), *EU-Kommentar*, Art. 43 EG para. 16.

[200] ECJ Case C-210/06 *Cartesio* [2008] ECR I-9641 paras. 99–124. Left open and only vaguely addressed in Case C-438/05 *Viking* [2007] ECR I-10779 para. 69; Case C-415/93 *Bosman* [1995] ECR I-4921 para. 97; Case 81/87 *Daily Mail* [1988] ECR 5483 para. 16. See also U. Forsthoff, in E. Grabitz/M. Hilf/M. Nettesheim (eds.), *Das Recht der Europäischen Union*, Art. 49 AEUV paras. 116 sq.; S. Grundmann, *European Company Law*, §25 para. 37; P.-C. Müller-Graff, in R. Streinz (ed.), *EUV/AEUV*, Art. 48 EG para. 17.

[201] ECJ Case 81/87 *Daily Mail* [1988] ECR 5483 para. 15; Case C-438/05 *Viking* [2007] ECR I-10779 para. 68. See para. 1 above.

[202] ECJ Case C-438/05 *Viking* [2007] ECR I-10779 paras. 33, 57–59, 61; Case C-309/99 *Wouters* [2002] ECR I-1577 para. 120. See also the analysis of horizontal effect and the Member States duties to protect fundamental freedoms by A. Junker, *EWS* 2007, 49, 52–55.

[203] For a critical perspective see e.g. M. Schlachter, *Festschrift für Birk*, 809, 818 sq.

[204] K. Apps, *E.L. Rev.* 34 (2009), 141–154; U. Bernitz/N. Reich, *CMLR 48* (2011), 603–623.

83. The wording of Article 49 TFEU indicates that it includes both a **prohibition of discrimination** – the right to pursue an activity in another Member State 'under the conditions laid down for its own nationals' (Article 49(2) TFEU, equality with residents) – as well as a **prohibition of restrictions**. As is the case for freedom of movement for workers (see para. 36 above), freedom of establishment also precludes 'any national measure ... that ..., even though it is applicable without discrimination on grounds of nationality, is liable to hamper or to render less attractive the exercise by Community nationals ... of fundamental freedoms guaranteed by the Treaty'.[205] And here too, the central objective is ensuring access to the markets of other Member States.[206] For example, it constitutes a restriction of the freedom of establishment if a Member State refuses registration of a branch office of a company with a registered seat in another Member State.[207] Similarly, the Court found a restriction in national legislation that refused registration of cross-border mergers while enabling internal mergers.[208]

3. Justification of Infringements

84. Infringements of the freedom of establishment can be justified on the written grounds of Article 52(1) TFEU: public policy, public security, public health. This is the only justification for direct discrimination.[209] Apart from that, Member States can make taking up and pursuing self-employed activity dependent on compliance with special provisions regarding, for example, organisation, qualification, professional regulations, supervision and liability to the extent that such requirements are necessary on **mandatory grounds of public interest**. As in the case of other fundamental freedoms, such restrictions have to satisfy four requirements (the so-called *Gebhard*-formula):[210]

(1) they must be applied in a non-discriminatory manner;
(2) they must be justified by imperative requirements in the general interest;
(3) they must be suitable for securing the attainment of the objective which they pursue;
(4) and they must not go beyond what is necessary in order to attain it.

---

[205] ECJ Case C-19/92 *Kraus* [1993] ECR I-1663 para. 32. Further e.g. Case C-196/04 *Cadbury Schweppes*, [2006] ECR I-8031 para. 48.

[206] C. Teichmann, *ZGR* 2011, 639–689 (pointing out that this purpose is also the inherent limitation of the fundamental freedom of establishment).

[207] ECJ Case C-212/97 *Centros* [1999] ECR I-1459 paras. 21 sq.

[208] ECJ Case C-411/03 *Sevic* [2005] ECR I-10805 paras. 20–23.

[209] AG Tizzano, Opinion in Case C-411/03 *Sevic* [2005] ECR I-10805 pt. 55. Considering a justification on mandatory requirements of public interest of a direct discrimination ECJ Case C-264/96 *Imperial Chemical Industries* [1998] ECR I-4695 para. 29.

[210] ECJ Case C-167/01 *Inspire Art* [2003] ECR I-10155 para. 133; Case C-212/97 *Centros* [1999] ECR I-1459 para. 34; Case 55/94 *Gebhard* [1995] ECR I-4165 para. 37.

Here too, the Court of Justice has recognised **employee protection** as a mandatory requirement of public interest.[211]

85. Furthermore, conflicting **fundamental rights** may justify an infringement of the freedom of establishment.[212] In the case of labour disputes in particular, recourse may be made to the fundamental right to take collective action (see also paras. 70 sq. above). The limitation of freedom of establishment by fundamental rights is, however, subject to the principle of proportionality (limitation-limitation) (see paras. 47 sq. and 72 above).[213]

4. Practical Consequences

a) Cross-border Transfer of Seat – Proportionality Test for Employee Participation

86. Freedom of establishment does not as such raise any employment law issues of importance. Following conflict of laws rules, the employment relations of those employed in an establishment will normally be governed by the law of the Member State of that establishment (see in detail §6 below). Employee involvement on the shop level (works councils) will also be governed by the law of the Member State in which the establishment (plant, workshop) is located.[214] This is compatible with Article 49 TFEU, which merely guarantees the right to take up and pursue an activity in a Member State 'under the conditions laid down for its own nationals'. The issue of a **cross-border transfer of the registered seat of companies** raises specific questions with regard to **employee involvement**, though.

87. Discussion of this issue requires that we look initially at the **underlying conflict of laws rules** on the cross-border transfer of seat.[215] National companies[216] are always formed pursuant to national company laws. Conflict of laws rules determine the applicable law, the *lex societatis*. There are two

---

[211] ECJ Case C-411/03 *Sevic* [2005] ECR I-10805 para. 28.

[212] ECJ Case C-438/05 *Viking* [2007] ECR I-10779 para. 77.

[213] For a critical discussion, see A. C. L. Davies, *ILJ* 37 (2008), 126, 141–145.

[214] M. Schlachter, in R. Müller-Glöge/U. Preis/I. Schmidt (eds.), *Erfurter Kommentar*, Art. 3, 8, 9 Rom I-VO para. 29; H. Oetker, in R. Richardi et al. (eds.), *Münchener Handbuch zum Arbeitsrecht*, §11 para. 129; each with further references.

[215] On the following in detail H. Eidenmüller/G. Rehm, *ZGR* 2004, 159–188; H. Eidenmüller (ed.), *Ausländische Kapitalgesellschaften im deutschen Recht*; H. Hirte/T. Bücker (ed.), *Grenzüberschreitende Gesellschaften*; S. Grundmann, *European Company Law*, §25 paras. 15 sqq., 25 sqq.; J. Dammann, *Yale J. Int.'l L.* 29 (2004), 477–544; see also ECJ Case C-208/00 *Überseering* [2002] ECR I-9919 para. 4.

[216] We do not consider here the supra-national company types of the SE, the SCE and – in preparation – the SPE. For the SE and the SPE, formation is largely governed by the SE-Regulation, though not entirely independently of the national laws of the Member States. There are specific provisions with regard to the transfer of the registered office.

competing approaches in the Member States' international company laws, the 'company seat principle' (*Sitztheorie*) and the 'incorporation principle' (*Gründungstheorie*).[217]

- Following the **incorporation principle** the company is subject to the law of the state in which it was incorporated and in which its *registered seat* is registered. Only this formal aspect matters, even if the company subsequently transfers its actual centre of administration to another state.

- Pursuant to the **company seat principle**, the *actual centre of administration* determines the applicable law[218] and there cannot be a discrepancy between the actual centre of administration and the registered seat. If the company subsequently transfers its actual seat of administration into another state, this will, under the company seat principle, be considered to be a dissolution, given that the actual seat and the registered seat must not diverge. If the law of the new location follows the company seat principle as well, it cannot recognise the status as a legal entity either as it has been dissolved. As a practical result, the company needs to be newly incorporated.[219]

88. The obstacles for a cross-border transfer of seat resulting from the company seat principle – dissolution and denial of the status as a legal entity – constitute an infringement of the freedom of establishment.[220] It is true that freedom of establishment only covers the right to take up and pursue an economic activity in another Member State 'under the conditions laid down for its own nationals'. Given that freedom of establishment is explicitly granted to companies as well (Article 54(2) TFEU), their *legal existence* cannot be challenged or called into question at the border: 'Such a measure is tantamount to an outright negation of the freedom of establishment conferred on companies by Articles [49 and 54 TFEU]'.[221] While the principle of company seat pursues legitimate interests

---

[217] On this with comparative references E.-M. Kieninger, *Wettbewerb der Privatrechtsordnungen im Europäischen Binnenmarkt,* 106–169. See also on the cross-border transfer of the registered office §31 below.

[218] In more detail P. Kindler, in F. J. Säcker/R. Rixecker (eds.), *Münchener Kommentar zum BGB,* IntGesR paras. 420–425.

[219] Cf. ECJ Case C-208/00 *Überseering* [2002] ECR I-9919 paras. 4 sq. In detail on the company seat principle under German law P. Kindler, in F. J. Säcker/R. Rixecker (eds.), *Münchener Kommentar zum BGB,* IntGesR paras. 420–425.

[220] ECJ Case C-167/01 *Inspire Art* [2003] ECR I-10155; Case C-208/00 *Überseering* [2002] ECR I-9919; before that already ECJ Case C-212/97 *Centros* [1999] ECR I-1459 (branch establishment). 'As Community law now stands', freedom of establishment only offers protection against obstacles to moving into a Member State of a company but not against obstacles of moving out of a Member State; ECJ Case C-210/06 *Cartesio* [2008] ECR I-9641; left open in ECJ Case 81/87 *Daily Mail* [1988] ECR 5483; in *Überseering* and *Inspire Art* the Court 'distinguished' *Daily Mail*. See in detail S. Grundmann, *European Company Law,* §25 paras. 23 sqq.

[221] ECJ Case C-208/00 *Überseering* [2002] ECR I-9919 para. 93.

(protection of creditors etc.)[222], it goes beyond what is necessary for this purpose. It is thus incompatible with the freedom of establishment to deny a company the status as legal entity when it moves its administrative seat to a different Member State. Mandatory requirements of public interests can be satisfied by *procedural* instruments but they must not (in practice) prohibit transfer of the company seat (maintaining the identity of the legal person) as such.

89. This can also have **consequences for employee participation.**[223] In common with rules regarding the organisation of the company, employee participation is also governed by the applicable company law.[224] A company which is lawfully incorporated in another Member State thus carries its regime of employee involvement with it when its seat is transferred to another Member State. As the cross-border transfer of the company seat cannot be denied by the host Member State, and as there is thus no need to incorporate the company afresh, the law of employee involvement of the host Member State does not apply. As a consequence, there may be a danger for Member States with a high level of employee involvement that their national law on employee participation will be circumvented.

90. While the national law may not prevent the cross-border transfer of the company seat as such, it can still invoke **mandatory requirements** of public interest with regard to the conditions of such transfer.[225] In particular, we can consider a provision of conflict of laws of a Member State pursuant to which the national law on employee participation also applies to foreign companies taking their seat in the territory of that state, irrespective of the fact that other issues, legal capacity in particular, are governed by the law of another Member State.[226] As such regulation also constitutes a restriction of the freedom of

---

[222] On this issue P. Kindler in F. J. Säcker/R. Rixecker (eds.), *Münchener Kommentar zum BGB,* IntGesR paras. 421–423.

[223] See already the argument of the Federal Republic of Germany in ECJ Case C-208/00 *Überseering* [2002] ECR I-9919 para. 89. On the consequences to employee participation (though before the decision of ECJ Case C-210/06 *Cartesio* [2008] ECR I-9641; see above para. 83), see W.-H. Roth, *Gedächtnisschrift für Heinze,* 709, 712–717.

[224] M. Franzen, *RdA* 2004, 257, 258; A. Junker, *ZfA* 2005, 1, 5 sq.; P. Kindler, in F. J. Säcker/R. Rixecker (eds.), *Münchener Kommentar zum BGB,* IntGesR paras. 590 sq.

[225] The only other way of justification as protection against abuse does not apply; on this see also A. Junker, *ZfA* 2005, 1, 8–10.

[226] Favouring this approach already under the current *lex lata* M. Franzen, *RdA* 2004, 257, 258–260 (analogical Art. 34 EGBGB); M. Henssler, *Gedächtnisschrift für Heinze,* 343–347; R. Lubitz, *Sicherung und Modernisierung der Unternehmensmitbestimmung,* 61–78; G. Weidmann, *Die Anwendung des Mitbestimmungsgesetzes 1976 in Fällen mit Auslandsbezug,* 23–57; *de lege lata* negatively O. Kisker, *Unternehmensmitbestimmung bei Auslandsgesellschaft mit Verwaltungssitz in Germany,* 155–171; W. Paefgen, *DB* 2003, 487, 491 sq.; W.-H. Roth, *Gedächtnisschrift für Heinze,* 709, 726–728; J. Bartsch, *Mitbestimmung und Niederlassungsfreiheit,* 132–155; S. Braun, Die *Sicherung der Unternehmensmitbestimmung im Lichte des europäischen Rechts,* 161–172. See also ECJ Case C-167/01 *Inspire Art* [2003] ECR I-10155.

---

establishment,[227] its compatibility with EU law depends upon whether such extension of the law of employee participation is required in the public interest.[228] As in the case of freedom of services (and other fundamental freedoms), **protection of employees** constitutes a legitimate public interest.[229] The decisive question is thus whether the application of the national laws of the host Member State regarding employee participation is **necessary**[230] or whether the protection provided by the laws of the Member State of origin is already sufficiently. This question cannot be countered with the argument that employee involvement on the shop floor level already satisfies employee interests, because employee involvement on the board level pursues a different objective.[231] Yet extension of national law regarding employee participation is not necessary where the company is subject to equivalent employee participation under the laws of its Member State of origin.[232] Furthermore, the extension of a *mandatory* employee participation (such as is provided by German law) should be considered disproportionate, given that a *negotiation model* such as provided by the SE Employee Involvement Directive (see §29 below) constitutes a less intrusive means for the achievement of the same purpose.[233]

---

[227] ECJ Case C-167/01 *Inspire Art* [2003] ECR I-10155 paras. 99–104.

[228] ECJ Case C-167/01 *Inspire Art* [2003] ECR I-10155 paras. 132 sq. On the further issues of transparency and consistency – which have priority over the issue of proportionality, convincingly W.-H. Roth, *Gedächtnisschrift für Heinze*, 709, 719–723.

[229] ECJ Case C-208/00 *Überseering* [2002] ECR I-9919 para. 92. See also ECJ Case C-167/01 *Inspire Art* [2003] ECR I-10155 para. 132. With regard to employee participation critically A. Junker, *ZfA* 2005, 1, 10–13 (however with considerations of proportionality); C. Windbichler/G. Bachmann, *Festschrift für Bezzenberger*, 797–805.

[230] Affirmatively e.g. J. Dammann, *Fordham JCFL* 8 (2003) 607–686; M. Franzen, *RdA* 2004, 258, 262 sq.; P. Kindler, in F. J. Säcker/R. Rixecker (eds.), *Münchener Kommentar zum BGB*, IntGesR para. 596; C. Teichmann, *ZGR* 2011, 639, 673 sq. (arguing, with regard to nominee companies, that application of employee participation rules did not hamper access to the market in the first place); G. Thüsing, in V. Rieble (ed.), *Zukunft der Unternehmens-mitbestimmung*, §3 paras. 11–22 (also reproduced in *ZIP* 2004, 381, 383–387); apparently also E.-M. Kieninger, *Wettbewerb der Privatrechtsordnungen im Europäischen Binnenmarkt*, 138 sq., 219–221; G. Weidmann, *Die Anwendung des Mitbestimmungsgesetzes 1976 in Fällen mit Auslandsbezug*, 103–121. Negatively H. Eidenmüller, *JZ* 2004, 26, 28 sq. (with respect to employee involvement on the shop level, in any case where the law of incorporation does not provide for similar employee participation); similarly H. Eidenmüller/G. Rehm, *ZGR* 2004, 159, 184 sq.; A. Junker, *ZfA* 2005, 1, 13–15; T. Müller-Bonanni, *GmbHR* 2003, 1235, 1237 sq.; id., in H. Hirte/T. Bücker (ed.), *Grenzüberschreitende Gesellschaften*, §14 paras. 20–22; E. Schwark, *AG* 2004, 173, 178; with doubt also W. Paefgen, *DB* 2003, 487, 491 sq. Differentiating M. Rehberg, in H. Eidenmüller (ed.), *Ausländische Kapitalgesellschaften im deutschen Recht*, §6 (accepting the possibility of justification in general, but subject to a proportionality test in each individual case with respect to the law of employee participation in the home Member State).

[231] W.-H. Roth, *Gedächtnisschrift für Heinze*, 709, 725; S. Braun, *Die Sicherung der Unternehmensmitbestimmung im Lichte des europäischen Rechts*, 189 sq., with doubt though at 191 sq.; R. Lubitz, *Sicherung und Modernisierung der Unternehmensmitbestimmung*, 89.

[232] M. Franzen, *RdA* 2004, 257, 262 sq.; R. Lubitz, *Sicherung und Modernisierung der Unternehmensmitbestimmung*, 89.

[233] U. Forsthoff, *Niederlassungsfreiheit für Gesellschaften*, 208–228; M. Henssler, *Gedächtnis-schrift für Heinze*, 353–355; O. Kisker, *Unternehmensmitbestimmung bei Auslandsgesellschaft*

91. The preceding discussion merely concerns the cross-border transfer of the *actual centre of administration*. This is to be distinguished from the cross-border transfer of the *registered seat*. The latter cannot be achieved without dissolution and re-incorporation under either the incorporation principle or the company seat principle.[234] In other words: The incorporation principle does not allow for a company to change the applicable law irrespective of the registered seat. This should not amount to an infringement of free establishment though, because any restrictive effect does not so much result from the Member States' laws than from a lack of (harmonising Union) regulation. Consequently, the Commission has long considered harmonising measures in this field; see in more detail §31 paras. 2 sq. below.

b) Collective Action against Relocation of Firms

92. Freedom of establishment can also be affected where employees or trade unions take collective action to protest against or prevent the relocation of firms. Such facts were at issue in the Court's judgement in the *Viking*-case.[235]

> The vessel *Rosella* of the Finnish ferry operator *Viking* plied the Route between Helsinki (Finland) and Tallinn (Estonia). The *Rosella* was running at a loss as a result of direct competition from Estonian vessels operating on the same route with lower wage costs. As an alternative to selling the vessel, Viking sought in October 2003 to reflag it by registering it in either Estonia or Norway, in order to be able to enter into a new collective agreement with a trade union established in one of those States. In opposition to these plans, ITF, the International Transport Workers' Federation, sent a letter to its affiliates asking them to refrain from entering into negotiations with Viking. One of the principal ITF policies is its 'Flag of Convenience' ('FOC') policy. The primary objectives of this policy are, on the one hand, to establish a genuine link between the flag of the ship and the nationality of the owner and, on the other, to protect and enhance the conditions of seafarers on FOC ships. ITF considers a vessel to be registered under a flag of convenience where the beneficial ownership and control of the vessel is found to lie in a State other than the State of the flag. In accordance with the ITF policy, only trade unions established in the state of beneficial ownership have the right to conclude collective agreements covering the vessel concerned. The FOC campaign is enforced by boycotts and other actions of solidarity amongst workers.

---

mit *Verwaltungssitz in Germany*, 185–205; C. Teichmann, 'Gestaltungsfreiheit in Mitbestimmungsvereinbarungen', *AG* 2008, 797, 798; id., *ZGR* 2011, 639, 674. Disapprovingly W.-H. Roth, *Gedächtnisschrift für Heinze*, 709, 726.

[234]   On the perspective of German law *Oberlandesgericht* (Higher Regional Court, OLG) Munich, *BB* 2007, 2247–2248.

[235]   ECJ Case C-438/05 *Viking* [2007] ECR I-10779. See e.g. A. Junker, *EWS* 2007, 49–55; M. Schlachter, *Festschrift für Birk*, 809–821; on the evaluation of the issue under German law M. Franzen, *ZfA* 2005, 315–351; C. Kerwer, *EuZA* 2008, 335, 344–349.

93. The relocation of a firm falls within the scope of application of freedom of establishment which, in principle, prohibits restrictions against leaving a Member State and against entering a Member State (see paras. 79 sq. above). Following the Court's jurisprudence, unions are also addressees of the freedom of establishment if they resort to collective action (see para. 81 above).[236] The Court reasons that the *effet utile* requires this because collective regulation of employment conditions in essence, has the same effect as regulation by law. Collective measures such as boycott or strike against relocation with the objective of maintaining present employment conditions are liable to make the exercise of freedom of establishment less attractive (or even futile) and thus constitute a restriction that requires justification.[237]

94. The mere fact that the right to collective action is an established EU fundamental right does not exempt such action from scrutiny arising from the fundamental freedoms. Similarly, the limitation of the Union's competences in Article 137(5) TFEU does not restrict control pursuant to fundamental rights (see para. 70 above).[238] Countervailing rights – fundamental freedoms and fundamental rights – must be balanced at the justification stage. The right to take collective action to protect employee interests has been recognised as an EU fundamental right and, following the Court of Justice, constitutes a legitimate interest that may justify a restriction of fundamental freedoms (see para. 69 above). This presupposes, however, that the collective measure is necessary for the protection of employee interests (proportionality).[239] This is not the case where the measure is aimed at preventing the exercise of freedom of movement,[240] where, for example, ship-owners are prevented from registering their vessels in a state other than that of which the beneficial owners of those vessels are nationals.[241]

95. The policy issues are similar to those raised by the issue of posting of workers (see paras. 73 sq. above). In the *Viking*-case, the Finnish union justified its position by arguing that Finnish jobs needed to be protected.[242] As the *Laval*-case (on freedom of services) illustrates, the issues are largely governed by the

---

[236] Differently R. Birk, *Festschrift 50 Jahre Bundesarbeitsgericht*, 1165, 1172 (conception of obligations of protection); also critically R. Rebhahn, *wbl* 2008, 63, 65.

[237] Critically G. Orlandini, *Comp. Lab. L. & Pol'y J.* 29 (2007–2008), 573, 590 sqq. (distinguishing between 'rules' and 'facts' as obstacles to free movement).

[238] ECJ Case C-438/05 *Viking* [2007] ECR I-10779 paras. 33–55. Critically R. Rebhahn, *wbl* 2008, 63, 69; C. Joerges/F. Rödl, *ELJ* 15 (2009), 1–19.

[239] The proportionality test – and its concretisation, 'soft' or 'hard' – has received particular and critical attention; see e.g. A. C. L. Davies, *ILJ* 37 (2008), 126–148; G. Orlandini, *Comp. Lab. L. & Pol'y J.* 29 (2007–2008), 573, 595 sqq.; more favourably, K. Lenaerts/J.A. Gutiérrez-Fons, *CMLR* 47 (2010), 1629, 1664 sqq.

[240] M. Schlachter, *Festschrift für Birk*, 809, 816 sq.

[241] ECJ Case C-438/05 *Viking* [2007] ECR I-10779 para. 88.

[242] ECJ Case C-438/05 *Viking* [2007] ECR I-10779 para. 15.

Posting of Workers Directive. This Directive is, of course, itself rather controversial, given its protectionist approach (see §6 paras. 4 sqq. below). *Viking* and *Laval* have triggered a new policy debate based on the consideration that the decisions interfered with the national 'social models' or changed the pre-existing 'European social model'. This has led some commentators and, notably, trade unions to call for a reform of the Posting of Workers Directive.[243]

V. FREE MOVEMENT OF CAPITAL – OVERVIEW

Bibliography:

C. Armbrüster, 'Golden Shares und die Grundfreiheiten des EG-Vertrags – EuGH, NJW 2002, 2303, 2305, 2306', *JuS* 2003, 224–227; S. Grundmann/F. Möslein, 'Die Goldenen Shares Grundsatzentscheidungen des Europäischen Gerichtshofs', *BKR* 2002, 758–765; S. Grundmann/F. Möslein, 'Die Goldene Aktie – Staatskontrollrechte in Europarecht und wirtschaftspolitischer Bewertung', *ZGR* 2003, 317–366; S. Grundmann/F. Möslein, 'Die Goldene Aktie und der Markt für Unternehmenskontrolle im Rechtsvergleich – insbesondere Staatskontrollrechte, Höchst- und Mehrfachstimmrechte sowie Übernahmeabwehrmaßnahmen', *ZVglRWiss* 102 (2003), 289–345; F. Möslein, 'Kapitalverkehrsfreiheit und Gesellschaftsrecht – Zugleich Besprechung EuGH vom 28.9.2006 – Rs. C-282 und 283/04', *ZIP* 2007, 208–215; G. Spindler, 'Deutsches Gesellschaftsrecht in der Zange zwischen Inspire Art und Golden Shares?', RIW 2003, 850–858; P. v. Wilmowsky, 'Freiheit des Kapital- und Zahlungsverkehrs', in D. Ehlers (ed.), Europäische Grundrechte und Grundfreiheiten, 3rd edn. (Berlin: de Gruyter, 2009), §12.

Cases (Selection):

ECJ Joined Cases 286/82 and 26/83 *Luisi and Carbone* [1984] ECR 377; ECJ Case C-58/99 *Commission* v. *Italy* [2000] ECR I-3811; ECJ Case C-367/98 *Commission* v. *Portugal* [2002] ECR I-4731 – Golden Share I; ECJ Case C-483/99 *Commission* v. *France* [2002] ECR I-4781 – Golden Share II; ECJ Case C-503/99 *Commission* v. *Belgium* [2002] ECR I-4809 – Golden Share III; ECJ Case C-463/00 *Commission* v. *Spain* [2003] ECR I-4581 – Golden Share IV; ECJ Case C-98/01 *Commission* v. *United Kingdom* [2003] ECR I-4641 – Golden Share V; ECJ Case C-174/04 *Commission* v. *Italy* [2005] ECR I-4933 – Golden Share VI; ECJ Joined Cases C-282/04 and C-283/04 *Commission* v. *The Netherlands* [2006] ECR I-9141 – Golden Share VII; ECJ Case C-112/05 *Commission* v. *Germany* [2007] ECR I-8995 – Volkswagen-Act.

96. The free movement of capital may affect employment law in a similar way to the freedom of establishment. Where restrictions to free movement of capital result from employment regulation, the latter will be subjected to a proportionality test.

---

[243] Cf. e.g. F. Hendrickx, *Comp. Lab. L. & Pol'y J.* 35 (2011), 1055–1077.

1. Scope of Application

97. Free movement of capital is not defined in the TFEU. In general terms, its scope of protection can be described as 'the unilateral transfer of real or monetary capital, in other words transactions that result in monetary claims or debt'.[244] The Court of Justice found reference points for a definition in the 1988 Capital Movement Directive.[245,246] Capital movement includes, *inter alia,* direct investments, operations in securities normally dealt in on the capital market and operations in units of collective investment undertakings.[247]

98. '"Movements of capital" for the purposes of [Article 63(1) TFEU]', the Court says, 'include in particular direct investments in the form of participation in an undertaking through the holding of shares which confers the possibility of effectively participating in its management and control ('direct' investments) and the acquisition of shares on the capital market solely with the intention of making a financial investment without any intention to influence the management and control of the undertaking ('portfolio' investments).'[248]

---

[244]   M. Sedlaczek, in R. Streinz (ed.), *EUV/AEUV,* Art. 60 AEUV para. 20 – my translation.

[245]   Council Directive 88/361/EEC of 24 June 1988 for the implementation of Article 67 of the Treaty, OJ 1988 L 178/5.

[246]   See the seminal decision in ECJ Case C-222/97 *Trummer and Mayer* [1999] ECR I-1661 paras. 20 sq.; e.g. Case C-112/05 *Commission* v. *Germany* [2007] ECR I-8995 para. 18 – Volkswagen-Act; ECJ Joined Cases C-282/04 and C-283/04 *Commission* v. *Niederlande* [2006] ECR I-9141 para. 19. On case law see only S. Grundmann, 'Europäisches Kapitalmarktrecht', ZSR 115 (1996), 103, 106.

[247]   Annex I of the Capital Movement Directive 88/361/EWG (no. 245) contains a 'nomenclature of the capital movements' which is divided into the following main categories:
I. Direct Investments
II. Investments in Real Estate
III. Operations in Securites Normally Dealt in on the Capital Market
IV. Operations in Units of Collective Investment Undertakings
V. Operations in Securities and other Instruments Normally Dealt in on the Money Market
VI. Operations in Current and Deposit Accounts with Financial Institutions
VII. Credits Related to Commercial Transactions or to the Provision of Services in Which a Resident is Participating
VIII. Financial Loans and Credits
IX. Sureties, other Guarantees and Rights of Pledge
X. Transfers in Performance of Insurance Contracts
XI. Personal Capital Movements
XII. Physical Import and Export of Financial Assets
XIII. Other Capital Movements.

[248]   ECJ Joined Cases C-282/04 and C-283/04 *Commission* v. *The Netherlands* [2006] ECR I-9141 para. 19 (references removed).

2. Infringements

99. In common with the other fundamental freedoms, the Court has inferred not only a **prohibition of discrimination** from the free movement of capital but also a **prohibition of other restrictions**. With regard to direct investments and portfolio investments, the Court has, for example, considered that 'national measures must be regarded as "restrictions" within the meaning of [Article 63(1) TFEU] if they are **likely** to prevent or limit the acquisition of shares in the undertakings concerned or **to deter investors** of other Member States from investing in their capital'.[249]

3. Justification of Infringements

100. Infringements of capital movement can, first, be justified on the written grounds of Article 65(1)(a) TFEU, public policy and public security; this is the only available justification for direct discrimination.[250] The Court has, for example, recognised the safeguarding of energy supplies in the event of a crisis as a public security ground under this provision.[251] Beyond the written grounds infringements may also be justified by mandatory requirements of public interest.[252] Here, too, the principle of proportionality limits the limitations (limitation-limitation).[253]

4. Practical Consequences. Proportionality Test of Employee Participation

101. Free movement of capital may affect employee participation in a similar way to the freedom of services discussed above (para. 73). In its **golden shares-case law**,[254] the Court has applied a proportionality test to the special rights under national law and the rules about the election of board members of a

---

[249] ECJ Joined Cases C-282/04 and C-283/04 *Commission v. The Netherlands* [2006] ECR I-9141 para. 20.

[250] This appears to be the predominant opinion; see M. Sedlaczek, in R. Streinz (ed.), *EUV/AEUV,* Art. 65 AEUV para. 52; A. Glaesner, in J. Schwarze (ed.), *EU-Kommentar,* Art. 56 EG paras. 22–24. Differently P. v. Wilmowsky, in D. Ehlers (ed.), *Europäische Grundrechte und Grundfreiheiten,* §12 para. 12.

[251] ECJ Case C-503/99 *Commission v. Belgium* [2002] ECR I-4809 para. 46.

[252] ECJ Case C-112/05 *Commission v. Germany* [2007] ECR I-8995 para. 72 – Volkswagen-Act.

[253] ECJ Case C-112/05 *Commission v. Germany* [2007] ECR I-8995 para. 73 – Volkswagen-Act.

[254] ECJ Case C-367/98 *Commission v. Portugal* [2002] ECR I-4731 – Golden Share I; Case C-483/99 *Commission v. France,* ECR [2002], I-4781 – Golden Share II; Case C-503/99 *Commission v. Belgium* [2002] ECR I-4809 – Golden Share III; Case C-463/00 *Commission v. Spain* [2003] ECR I-4581 – Golden Share IV; Case C-98/01 *Commission v. United Kingdom* [2003] ECR I-4641 – Golden Share V; also see ECJ Case C-174/04 *Commission v. Italy* [2005] ECR I-4933 – Golden Share VI; Joined Cases C-282/04 and C-283/04 *Commission v. The Netherlands* [2006] ECR I-9141 – Golden Share VII. See also ECJ Case C-58/99 *Commission v. Italy* [2000] ECR I-3811.

company pursuant to the company's articles of incorporation (inter alia).[255] Employee participation entails comparable privileges.

102. *Golden shares* is a term used to describe cases where a legislative act (statute, regulation) or shareholder's resolution[256] grants special rights or privileges in a private company to a state or a state institution as a shareholder.[257] This is often the case in the course of privatisation of hitherto public or publicly owned enterprises. The special rights or privileges will usually be attached to certain shares; thus 'golden shares'. They may concern different kinds of shareholder rights, e.g. voting rights of influence on the composition of the group of shareholders or of company organs and the influence may be established in different ways, e.g. by an approval requirement or a veto. With such rights, a state tries to maintain a certain degree of influence on enterprises which are considered to be of national importance even after their privatisation. This is, for example, of practical importance with regard to energy supply or postal services.

103. The Court of Justice has reviewed provisions on golden shares only in light of the right to free movement of capital and indicated that the result would not be different if they were considered under the freedom of establishment provisions.[258] Public privileges infringe upon the free movement of capital as they are liable to prevent or deter from direct investment or portfolio investment in the companies concerned.[259] In the context of golden shares, the Court has, for example, accepted the interest in guaranteeing universal postal services as mandatory requirements of public interest.[260] Given that employee protection has been recognised as legitimate public interest in the jurisprudence on freedom of services and freedom of establishment, the same should apply in the present context of free movement of capital.

104. The *golden shares*-jurisprudence can be applied to the issue of employee participation. Employee participation also entails that a third party (the employees and/or their representatives) are granted a special right, the right to

---

[255] On the golden shares-issue, see only S. Grundmann/F. Möslein, *BKR* 2002, 758–765; iid., *ZGR* 2003, 317–366; F. Möslein, *ZIP* 2007, 208–215; C. Armbrüster, *JuS* 2003, 224–227.

[256] ECJ Joined Cases C-282/04 and C-283/04 *Commission* v. *The Netherlands* [2006] ECR I-9141 with a note by F. Möslein, *ZIP* 2007, 208, 209.

[257] In more detail S. Grundmann/F. Möslein, *ZGR* 2003, 317, 322–325; iid., *BKR* 2002, 758, 759 sq.

[258] See e.g. ECJ Joined Cases C-282/04 and C-283/04 *Commission* v. *The Netherlands* [2006] ECR I-9141 paras. 42–44. See also S. Grundmann/F. Möslein, *BKR* 2002, 758, 760 sq. (pointing to the convergence of different fundamental freedoms).

[259] ECJ Joined Cases C-282/04 and C-283/04 *Commission* v. *The Netherlands* [2006] ECR I-9141 paras. 19 sq., 23–30.

[260] ECJ Joined Cases C-282/04 and C-283/04 *Commission* v. *The Netherlands* [2006] ECR I-9141 paras. 37 sq. Also see ECJ Case C-463/00 *Commission* v. *Spain* [2003] ECR I-4581 para. 70 (considering a justification on grounds of banking services in the public interest).

---

elect some board members. Such privilege can make investment in the companies affected less attractive and thus constitutes an infringement of free movement of capital.[261] The question therefore is whether the national rules on employee participation are necessary for the purpose of protecting employees (as a legitimate public interest).[262] The Court's case law with regard to freedom of services (see para. 66 above) indicates that such justification is indeed possible but that the national legislation may in individual cases be incompatible with the requirements of proportionality.[263]

VI. THE GENERAL PROHIBITION OF DISCRIMINATION ON GROUNDS OF NATIONALITY AND THE EU CITIZENS' RIGHT TO FREE MOVEMENT

Bibliography:
R. Domröse/P. Kubicki, 'Das unionsbürgerliche Freizügigkeitsrecht und der Zugang zu sozialen Leistungen des Herkunftsstaates', *EuR* 2008, 873–891; S. Kadelbach, 'Die Unionsbürgerrechte', in D. Ehlers (ed.), *Europäische Grundrechte und Grundfreiheiten*, 3rd edn. (Berlin: de Gryuter, 2009), §19; T. Kingreen, 'Verbot der Diskriminierung wegen der Staatsangehörigkeit', in D. Ehlers (ed.), *Europäische Grundrechte und Grundfreiheiten*, 3rd edn. (Berlin: de Gryuter, 2009), §13; M. Rossi, 'Das Diskriminierungsverbot nach Art. 12 EGV', *EUR* 2000,197–217; A. Wiesbrock, 'Free movement of third-country nationals in the European Union: the illusion of inclusion', *E.L. Rev.* 35 (2010), 455–475.

Cases (Selection):
ECJ Case C-391/09 *Runevič-Vardyn and Wardyn* 12 May 2011.

1. The General Prohibition of Discrimination on Grounds of Nationality

105. Article 18(1) TFEU contains a general prohibition of discrimination on grounds of nationality. This is the principle underlying the specific prohibitions of discrimination in the provisions on fundamental freedoms.[264] Article 18(1) only applies 'without prejudice to any special provisions contained [in the Treaties]'; it is, in other words, subordinate to the special provisions.[265] The provision can have practical effect in employment-related cases, too, for example

---

[261] Cf. ECJ Case C-112/05 *Commission* v. *Germany* [2007] ECR I-8995 paras. 59–69 – Volkswagen-Act. See also F. Möslein, *ZIP* 2007, 208, 213.

[262] The justification of the Volkswagen-Act already did not satisfy the criterion of suitability; ECJ Case C-112/05 *Commission* v. *Germany* [2007] ECR I-8995 paras. 74–76 – Volkswagen-Act.

[263] To this effect already S. Grundmann/F. Möslein, *ZGR* 2003, 317, 350 sq.; iid., *ZVglRWiss* 102 (2003) 289, 341–344 (with a comparative survey).

[264] ECJ Case C-94/07 *Raccanelli* [2008] ECR I-5939 para. 45; Case C-341/05 *Laval un Partneri* [2007] ECR I-11767 paras. 54 sq.

[265] ECJ Case 186/87 *Cowan* [1989] ECR 195 para. 14.

where the limits of the employment related time period (see para. 15 above) are exceeded. This may be the case where a student seeks employment or applies for state benefits in the host Member State.[266] In the Court's case law, Article 18 may sometimes be relevant if the question referred to the Court does not refer to the fact that the person concerned is a worker.

106. The prohibition of discrimination in Article 18(1) TFEU protects natural and legal persons with nationality of or their seat in the Member States.[267] With regard to its subject matter, the prohibition is restricted to the scope of the TFEU. The Court of Justice has construed this requirement broadly. A case merely needs to have points of contact with EU law.[268] This does not necessarily require that the Union also has the relevant legislative competence. The reservation with regard to public administration pursuant to Article 45(4) TFEU is considered inapplicable to the general norm of Article 12(1) TFEU.[269] In common with the fundamental freedoms, the provision of Article 18(1) TFEU presupposes a cross-border aspect and does not apply to purely internal cases.[270]

107. The prohibition of discrimination is addressed to the Member States and the Union. Whether it is also binding upon private individuals is a matter of controversy.[271] It prohibits direct and indirect discrimination. Indirect discrimination presupposes that neutral criteria with a discriminatory effect are not justified on objective grounds.

---

[266] See e.g. ECJ Case C-184/99 *Grzelczyk* [2001] ECR I-6193; in more detail R. Domröse/P. Kubicki, *EuR* 2008, 873–891.

[267] Whether citizens of third countries are protected is controversial; teleological considerations argue against that; T. Kingreen, in D. Ehlers (ed.), *Europäische Grundrechte und Grundfreiheiten,* §13 para. 5; with doubt A. v. Bogdandy, in E. Grabitz/M. Hilf/M. Nettesheim (eds.), *Das Recht der Europäischen Union,* Art. 18 AEUV paras. 31 sq. See also M. Holoubek, in J. Schwarze (ed.), *EU-Kommentar,* Art. 12 EG para. 27 with references to the Court's jurisprudence.

[268] ECJ Joined Cases 35/82 and 36/82 *Morson* [1982] ECR 3723 paras. 14–16; Case 186/87 *Cowan* [1989] ECR 195 para. 10.

[269] M. Rossi, *EUR* 2000, 197, 208.

[270] See also M. Holoubek, in J. Schwarze (ed.), *EU-Kommentar,* Art. 12 EG paras. 19–21.

[271] K. Riesenhuber, *Europäisches Vertragsrecht,* paras. 100 sq.; for a merely indirect effect M. Holoubek, in J. Schwarze (ed.), *EU-Kommentar,* Art. 12 EG paras. 34–36; M. Zuleeg, in H. von der Groeben/J. Schwarze, Art. 12 EG para. 17; apparently also R. Streinz, in id. (eds.), *EUV/AEUV,* Art. 18 AEUV para. 43 (but with reference to the *Angonese*-decision). In principle favouring a direct effect in A. v. Bogdandy, in E. Grabitz/M. Hilf/M. Nettesheim (eds.), *Das Recht der Europäischen Union,* Art. 18 AEUV paras. 26–28 (though with the limitation that this should not affect the freedom to conclude a contract); differentiating A. Epiney, in C. Calliess/M. Ruffert (eds.), *EUV/AEUV,* Art. 18 AEUV para. 44 (only in case of private collective regulation).

2. *The EU Citizens' Right to Free Movement*

108. Finally, Article 21 TFEU supplements the fundamental freedoms by granting a right of free movement to EU citizens.[272] Pursuant to that provision, every Union citizen (Article 20(1) sent. 2 TFEU: nationals of the Member States)[273] has the right to move and reside freely in the territory of the Member States, subject to the limitations and conditions laid down in the Treaties and by the implementing measures.[274] Similar to Article 18 TFEU, Article 21 states the general rule, of which the fundamental freedoms are specific expressions.[275] Unlike the fundamental freedoms, the citizens' right to free movement under Article 21 TFEU does not presuppose economic activity.

109. As a right to free movement, Article 21(1) TFEU covers both, the freedom to enter another Member State and to leave a Member State. It further comprises a prohibition of discrimination. The provision of Article 21(1) TFEU is also inapplicable to purely internal cases and thus does not prohibit discrimination by a Member State against its own nationals. With regard to justification of infringements, Article 21(1) TFEU refers to such limitations as are contained in the Treaty and the measures adopted to give them effect. This in particular covers limitations on grounds of public policy, public security and public health as they are recognised in Articles 45(3) and 52(1) TFEU, and as they are specified in the Free Movement of Citizens Directive. As a limitation to limitations, the EU fundamental rights and the principle of proportionality must be respected. The essence of the right conferred by Article 21(1) TFEU must not be undermined.[276]

---

[272] Beyond the concrete right to free movement, the Court also uses the Union citizenship as an additional argument in its interpretation e.g. of the freedom of movement for workers; see e.g. ECJ Case C-138/02 *Collins* [2004] ECR I-2703 paras. 60 sq., 63, 73.

[273] On free movement rights of third country nationals, see A. Wiesbrock, *E.L. Rev.* 35 (2010), 455–475.

[274] See e.g. ECJ Case C-391/09 *Runevič-Vardyn and Wardyn* 12 May 2011.

[275] See e.g. ECJ Case C-208/05 *ITC* [2007] ECR I-181 paras. 64 sq.

[276] A. Hatje, in J. Schwarze (ed.), *EU-Kommentar*, Art. 18 EG para. 15 with further references.

§4. LEGISLATIVE COMPETENCES

CONTENT

Bibliography:
M. Bell/R. Whittle, 'Between Social Policy and Union Citizenship: The Framework Directive on Equal Treatment in Employment', *E.L. Rev.* 27 (2002), 677–691; B. Bercusson, 'Maastricht: a Fundamental Change in European Labour Law', *IRJ* 23 (1992), 177–190; B. Bercusson, 'The Dynamic of European Labour Law after Maastricht', *ILJ* 23 (1994), 1–31; R.

Birk, 'Die Gesetzgebungszuständigkeit der Europäischen Gemeinschaft im Arbeitsrecht', *RdA* 1992, 68–73; R. Birk, 'Vereinbarungen der Sozialpartner als Regelungsinstrumente in der Europäischen Sozialcharta und im supranationalen Arbeitsrecht', in J. Becker et al. (eds.), *Recht im Wandel seines sozialen und technologischen Umfeldes – Festschrift für Manfred Rehbinder* (Munich/Bern: C.H. Beck and Stämpfli, 2002), 3–15; H. Buchner, 'Die sozialpolitische Entwicklung der Europäischen Gemeinschaft im Spannungsfeld von hoheitlicher Regelung und tarifautonomer Gestaltung', *RdA* 1993, 193–203; W. Däubler, 'Die Koalitionsfreiheit im EG-Recht', in U. Isenhardt/U. Preis (eds.), *Arbeitsrecht und Sozialpartnerschaft – Festschrift für Peter Hanau* (Cologne: Otto Schmidt, 1999), 489–503; B. Fitzpatrick, 'Straining the Definition of Health and Safety?', *ILJ* 26 (1997), 115–135; M. Heinze, 'Europarecht im Spannungsverhältnis zum nationalen Arbeitsrecht – Von formaler Verdichtung zur offenen Arbeitsrechtsordnung', *ZfA* 1992, 331–359; M. Heinze, 'Europäische Einflüsse auf das nationale Arbeitsrecht', *RdA* 1994, 1–11; A. Höland, 'Partnerschaftliche Setzung von Recht in der Europäischen Gemeinschaft', *ZIAS* 1995, 425–451; R. Käppler, 'Zu den Kompetenzen des Europäischen Gerichtshofs bei der Rechtsangleichung auf dem Gebiet des Arbeitsrechts', in H.-W. Rengeling (ed.), *Europäisierung des Rechts* (Cologne/Berlin/Bonn/Munich: Heymanns, 1996), 129–149; J. Kenner, 'A distinctive legal basis for social policy? The Court of Justice answers a 'delicate' question', *E.L. Rev.* 22 (1997), 579–586; H. Konzen, 'Der europäische Einfluss auf das deutsche Arbeitsrecht nach dem Vertrag über die Europäische Union', *EuZW* 1995, 39–50; R. Langner, 'Kompetenzen in der Europäischen Union auf dem Gebiet der Gleichbehandlung', *ZIAS* 1998, 178–189; F. Lecomte, 'Embedding Employment Rights in Europe', *Colum. J. Eur. L.* 17 (2010–2011), 1–22; R. Rebhahn, 'Der Vorrang der günstigeren Regelung aus rechtsvergleichender Sicht', *EuZA* 2008, 39–67; U. Runggaldier, 'Inhalt und Reichweite des Art. 13 EGV sowie der darauf gestützten Maßnahmen zur Bekämpfung von Diskriminierungen', in P. Hanau/J. Thaus/H. Westermann (eds.), *Gegen den Strich – Festschrift für Klaus Adomeit* (Cologne: Wolters Kluwer, 2008), 645–659; A. Seifert, 'Arbeitsrechtliche Sonderregeln für kleine und mittlere Unternehmen – Zur Auflösung des Spannungsverhältnisses von Mittelstands- und Arbeitnehmerschutz', *RdA* 2004, 200–210; H.-D. Steinmeyer, 'Der Vertrag von Amsterdam und seine Bedeutung für das Arbeits- und Sozialrecht', *RdA* 2001, 10–22; B. Veit, 'Die Kompetenzen der Europäischen Gemeinschaften (EG) auf dem Gebiet des Arbeitsrechts', *ZTR* 1990, 56–66; L. Waddington, 'Testing the Limits of the EC Treaty Article on Non-discrimination', *ILJ* 28 (1999), 133–151; R. Wank, 'Arbeitsrecht nach Maastricht', *RdA* 1995, 10–26; P. Watson, 'Social Policy after Maastricht', *CMLR* 30 (1993), 481–513; M. Weiss, 'Die Bedeutung von Maastricht für die EG-Sozialpolitik', in W. Däubler/M. Bobke/K. Kehrmann (eds.), *Arbeit und Recht – Festschrift für Albert Gnade* (Cologne: Bund-Verlag, 1992), 583–596; M. Weiss, 'Zur zukünftigen Rolle der Europäischen Union im Arbeitsrecht', in P. Hanau/E. Lorenz/H. Matthes (eds.), *Festschrift für Günther Wiese* (Neuwied/Kriftel: Luchterhand, 1998), 633–648; B. Zwanziger, 'Zur Zuständigkeit der Europäischen Gemeinschaft auf dem Gebiet des Arbeitsrechts', *AuR* 1995, 430–438; For references on the social dialogue, see the specific bibliography before para. 26 below.

Cases (Selection):
ECJ Case C-84/94 *United Kingdom* v. *Council* [1996] ECR 5755; ECJ Case C-14/04 *Dellas* [2005] ECR I-10253; ECJ Case C-307/05 *Del Cerro Alonso* [2007] ECR I-7109; ECJ Case C-268/06 *Impact* [2008] I-2483; ECJ Case C-306/07 *Andersen* [2008] I-10279.

I. INTRODUCTION AND OVERVIEW

1. Competences formally define whether the Union may legislate in the area of employment law. Competences also sometimes define which forms of action (regulation, directive) are at the Union's disposal in a given legal field. They may also be relevant for the interpretation of legal acts which are based upon them, particularly for interpretation in conformity with primary law.[1]

1. The Principle of Conferral

2. 'The limits of Union competences are governed by the **principle of conferral**. Under the principle of conferral, the Union shall act only within the limits of the competences conferred upon it by the Member States in the Treaties to attain the objectives set out therein', Article 5(1) sent. 1, (2) TEU.[2] In contrast to a national state, the Union does not have comprehensive legislative powers. Its competence is limited to those areas where power has been conferred upon it by the Treaties. We will therefore discuss the most important competences in the employment law field. In this context, the details of the legislative process[3] or the general limitations to EU legislation as they result, in particular, from the principle of subsidiarity (Article 5(3) TEU) and the principle of proportionality (Article 5(4) TEU), will not be addressed.[4]

2. The Development of EU Competences[5]

3. The **founding treaty of the EEC** did not provide for any competence in the area of employment law, leaving aside the competence with regard to the freedom of movement for workers (now Article 46 TFEU; para. 43 below). 'The Treaty has a neo-liberal tradition: economic policy as social policy.'[6] Legislation in the field of employment law could thus only be based upon the competence for harmonisation for the purposes of the common market pursuant to Article 100 EEC (today Article 114 TFEU; see paras. 48–50 below). It was the 1986 Single European Act that first introduced a specific competence in the field of health and safety in employment, through Article 118a TEC[7] (cf. today's Article 153 TFEU).

---

[1]   See e.g. ECJ Case C-14/04 *Dellas* [2005] ECR I-10253 paras. 38 sq. (concerning the WTD).

[2]   See in more detail R. Birk, *RdA* 1992, 68 and 70; R. Streinz, *Europarecht*, paras. 498 sq.

[3]   See in detail R. Streinz, *Europarecht*, paras. 500–520.

[4]   Specifically emphasised by M. Heinze, *RdA* 1994, 1–11; more reservedly B. Zwanziger, *AuR* 1995, 430–438.

[5]   See also §1 paras. 5, 17, 29, 35 sq., 38. On the development up to the 1992 Maastricht Treaty R. Wank, *RdA* 1995, 10, 11 sq.

[6]   H. Konzen, *EuZW* 1995, 39, 40 (my translation); R. Wank, *RdA* 1995, 10, 11.

[7]   See ECJ Case C-84/94 *United Kingdom* v. *Council* [1996] ECR 5755; J. Kenner, *E.L. Rev.* 22 (1997), 579–586. On the development see R. Opfermann, 'Das EG-Recht und seine Auswirkungen auf das deutsche Arbeitsschutzrecht', in R. Anzinger/R. Wank (eds.), *Entwicklungen im Arbeitsrecht und Arbeitsschutzrecht – Festschrift für Otfried Wlotzke*, 732–736; B. Veit, *ZTR* 1990, 56–66, and §13 para. 3 below.

4.   With the 1992 Maastricht Treaty, the **Social Policy Protocol** brought about an important extension of competences.[8] The protocol was intended to provide the necessary competence for implementation of the Community Charter of Fundamental Social Rights (CFSR; §2 paras. 65–77 above).[9] It contains far-reaching competences, partly based upon the majority principle. The United Kingdom had not participated in the Community Charter (§2 para. 65) and did not sign the Social Policy Protocol either. Enacted as a separate convention of eleven of the twelve Member States in the form of a protocol to the EC Treaty (cf. Article. 51 TEU), the Social Policy Protocol was nonetheless part of Community law, albeit in a complicated and controversial way.[10] Still, it became the model for the rules now enshrined in the TFEU and served as a basis for a number of important pieces of EU employment legislation, such as the Parental Leave Directive (§21), the European Works Council Directive (§28) and the Part-time Work Directive (§16).

5.   The 1997 **Amsterdam Treaty** incorporated the Social Policy Protocol into the EC Treaty in an only slightly modified form as Article 137, effective as of 1 May 1999; Article 118 TEC was merged with the new provision. The Amsterdam Treaty also introduced a new competence to 'combat discrimination' (found today in Article 19 TFEU), and a specific competence with a view to ensuring full equality between men and women in the area of employment. Furthermore, the new competences of Articles 67 and 81(2)(b) TFEU, which allow an approximation of conflict of laws (see §5 below), were added to the Treaty.

6.   The 2000 **Nice Treaty** introduced changes to Article 19 TFEU and thereby simplified certain procedures. The competence contained in Article 153 TFEU was expanded in some respects and certain procedures were also simplified. The wording of Article 155 TFEU was modified. The 2009 **Lisbon Treaty** brought about a renumbering of the Treaty and strengthened the rights of the European Parliament. The special role of the social partners, management and labour, is emphasised in Article 152 TFEU.

---

[8]   See M. Heinze, *ZfA* 1992, 331–359; P. Watson, *CMLR* 30 (1993), 481–513.

[9]   See the Preamble to the Social Policy Protocol: 'that eleven Member States (…) wish to continue along the path laid down in the 1989 Social Charter'. R. Birk, 'Vereinbarungen der Sozialpartner im Rahmen des Sozialen Dialogs und ihre Durchführung', *EuZW* 1997, 453, 455 ('instrument for the realisation of the Community Charter of Fundamental Social Rights' – my translation).

[10] See in more detail R. Wank, *RdA* 1995, 10, 15–18; also A. Höland, *ZIAS* 1995, 425, 427 sq.

3.   Overview of the EU Competences

7. Today, the *status quo* of EU competences in the field of employment is structured as follows:

–   Article 153 TFEU includes the central competence in the field of social policy. It is supplemented by the rules on participation of management and labour in EU legislation pursuant to Article 154 sq. TFEU ('social dialogue').
–   Further competences for individual areas of regulation in employment or with relevance to employment law are bestowed:
    •   to bring about freedom of movement for workers, Article 46 TFEU;
    •   to ensure application of the principle of equal opportunities of men and women, Article 157(3) TFEU;
    •   to combat discrimination, Article 19(1) TFEU;
    •   to enhance and intensify judicial cooperation in civil matters, Articles 67(4) and 81(2)(c) TFEU; and
    •   to approximate laws which have as their object, or directly affect, the establishment and functioning of the internal market, Article 114 and 115 TFEU.
–   Finally, Article 352 TFEU contains a supplementary competence.

4.   Areas Excluded from EU Regulation

8. Certain areas, which are politically sensitive, have **specifically been excluded** from Union competence in Article 153(5) TFEU: pay, the right of association, the right to strike and the right to impose lock-outs. These are **autonomous terms**[11] which must be interpreted with a view to the purpose of the rule and the system of primary law. The European Social Charter (ESC, §2 para. 3 above) and the Community Charter of Fundamental Social Rights referred to in Article 151(1) TFEU may provide guidance for interpretation.[12] Given that the exceptions of Article 153(5) demarcate the boundary between the competences of the EU and Member States, and given that this demarcation bears elements of a compromise, teleological considerations do not require or justify a narrow interpretation. However, the Court of Justice has decided differently, relying on the formal consideration that exceptions are to be narrowly interpreted.[13] The case at hand illustrates that this interpretive maxim

---

[11]   S. Krebber, in C. Calliess/M. Ruffert (eds.), *EUV/AEUV*, Art. 153 AEUV para. 10; R. Rebhahn/M. Reiner, in J. Schwarze (ed.), *EU-Kommentar*, Art. 137 EG para. 56.

[12]   S. Krebber, in C. Calliess/M. Ruffert (eds.), *EUV/AEUV*, Art. 153 AEUV para. 12.

[13]   ECJ Case C-307/05 *Del Cerro Alonso* [2007] ECR I-7109 para. 39. Critically M. Bieder/S. Diekmann, 'Verbot der Diskriminierung befristet Beschäftigter bei der Gewährung von Dienstalterszulagen', *EuZA* 2008, 515, 518 sq.

is misguided:[14] Following the principle of conferral (para. 2 above), EU competence is the *exception* and not the rule. It is controversial whether the limitation to EU competences pursuant to Article 153(5) TFEU also applies to other competences such as Articles 81, 114, and 115 TFEU. There are good reasons to support this view, since the limitation could otherwise be easily circumvented.[15] If one were to favour a narrow interpretation, following the Court's jurisprudence, this might however lead to a different result.

9.   The Court has, however, rightly argued that the limitations of Article 153(5) TFEU only draw the line between the legislative competences of the EU and the Member States. They do not exempt national (and private) measures falling within those limitations from the scrutiny of EU law.[16] In particular, national (and private) measures in this area must still respect the fundamental freedoms. A strike or boycott aimed at preventing a company from relocating to another Member State is not exempt from control under freedom of establishment or freedom to provide services because of Article 153(5) TFEU (see §3 paras. 69, 94 above).

10.   The limitations contained in Article 153(5) TFEU first exclude **pay** from EU competence.[17] The reason behind this exception is that the determination of pay falls within the traditional domain of the (national) social partners.[18] Furthermore, the founding fathers of the Treaty did not want to give the EU competence to specify minimum wages, given that the economic circumstances in the Member States were (and still are) too disparate. Pay is to be construed broadly, in a similar way to the interpretation of Article 157 TFEU.[19] When the Member States – as parties to the Treaty – introduced the new provision of Article 153(5), they were aware of Article 157 as it had been interpreted in the Court's case law. It can thus be assumed that this shaped their understanding of the term 'pay'.

---

[14]   See with regard to secondary legislation K. Riesenhuber, in id. (ed.), *Europäische Methodenlehre*, §11 paras. 61–66.

[15]   To this effect see also ECJ Case C-376/98 *Kommission v. Deutschland* [2000] ECR I-8419 para. 79 (on Article 129a(4) indent 1 TEC, today Article 168(5) TFEU). P. Hanau, in P. Hanau/ H.-D. Steinmeyer/R. Wank (eds.), *Handbuch des europäischen Arbeits- und Sozialrechts*, §19 para. 14. Differently R. Rebhahn/M. Reiner, in J. Schwarze (ed.), *EU-Kommentar*, Art. 137 EG para. 56.

[16]   ECJ Case C-341/05 *Laval un Partneri* [2007] ECR I-11767 paras. 86–88; Case C-438/05 *Viking* [2007] ECR I-10779 paras. 39–41.

[17]   Cf. ECJ Case C-14/04 *Dellas* [2005] ECR I-10253 paras. 38 sq. (concerning the WTD).

[18]   ECJ Case C-307/05 *Del Cerro Alonso* [2007] ECR I-7109 para. 40; E. Eichenhofer, in R. Streinz (ed.), *EUV/AEUV*, Art. 137 paras. 32 sq.

[19]   To the same effect S. Krebber, in C. Calliess/M. Ruffert (eds.), *EUV/AEUV*, Art. 153 AEUV para. 11; R. Rebhahn/M. Reiner, in J. Schwarze (ed.), *EU-Kommentar*, Art. 137 EG para. 57.

11. The scope of the exclusion of pay is a matter of controversy: Does it also prevent *indirect regulation* of pay, as it results from prohibitions of discrimination such as those contained in the Part-time Work Directive, the Fixed Term Work Directive and the Temporary Agency Work Directive (§§16–18)? Some answer the question in the affirmative, arguing that a prohibition of discrimination in regard of pay, too, is a regulation of pay.[20] Others construe the purpose of the exclusion more narrowly, as merely prohibiting a Union-wide minimum wage, but not rules against discrimination.[21] A third opinion draws further distinctions, arguing that indirect regulation through a prohibition of discrimination is excluded from the EU's competence where it involves a value judgement with regard to the *tertium comparationis* (equal treatment with other employees of the temporary work agency or those of the user-undertaking).[22]

12. The broad interpretation advanced by the first opinion may be doubted in light of systematic and teleological considerations. Given that numerous measures of employee protection have an indirect effect upon pay – for example working time and on-call duty or transfer of undertakings – such broad interpretation of the exclusion regarding pay would severely curtail EU competence, which is discernibly incompatible with the intention of the Treaty. This would be especially true if the exclusions of Article 153(5) TFEU also applied to other competences (see para. 8 above). As the drafters of Article 153(5) TFEU knew, Community legislation had also hitherto encompassed directives with (indirect) relevance to pay, particularly prohibitions of discrimination. Furthermore, the principle of equality is of fundamental importance in EU law (see in more detail §2 para. 12; §8 para. 4). One could thus expect that it would be specifically emphasised if the competence did not include such indirect regulation of pay through a prohibition of discrimination. Especially with regard to part-time work and fixed-term work, the prohibition of discrimination also serves as a protection against indirect discrimination of women who constitute

---

[20] S. Krebber, in C. Calliess/M. Ruffert (eds.), *EUV/AEUV*, Art. 153 AEUV para. 11; M. Schmidt, *NZA* 1998, 576, 578 sq.

[21] Thus now ECJ Case C-307/05 *Del Cerro Alonso* [2007] ECR I-7109 paras. 39–42. W. Däubler, *Festschrift für Hanau*, 498; P. Hanau, in P. Hanau/H.-D. Steinmeyer/R. Wank (eds.), *Handbuch des europäischen Arbeits- und Sozialrechts*, §19 para. 16. See also N. Busby/D. Christie, 'Regulation of Temporary Agency Work in the European Union', *Cambrian L.R.* 2005, 15, 24 sq.; T. Raab, 'Europäische und nationale Entwicklungen im Recht der Arbeitnehmerüberlassung', *ZfA* 2003, 389, 413 sq.; G. Thüsing, 'Europäische Impulse im Recht der Arbeitnehmerüberlassung', *DB* 2002, 2218, 2220.

[22] R. Wank, 'Der Richtlinienvorschlag der EG-Kommission zur Leiharbeit und das "Erste Gesetz für moderne Dienstleistungen am Arbeitsmarkt"', *NZA* 2003, 14, 17 sq.; id., *RdA* 2003, 1, 10; similarly T. Raab, *ZfA* 2003, 389, 413 sq.; U. Klebeck, *Gleichstellung der Leiharbeitnehmer als Verfassungsverstoß* (Baden-Baden: Nomos, 2004), 205 sq.; see also V. Rieble/U. Klebeck, 'Lohngleichheit für Leiharbeit', *NZA* 2003, 23, 26. See also O. Bertram, 'Die AÜG-Reform im Spiegel des EG-Richtlinienentwurfs zur Leiharbeit', *ZESAR* 2003, 205, 214 sq.; G. Thüsing, *DB* 2002, 2218, 2220.

---

the majority of part-time workers and, in some areas, of fixed-term workers. Directives prohibiting [sex] discrimination have originally been based on (what is now) Article 115 TFEU (see paras. 48–50 below). In sum, an interpretation of the exclusion of 'pay' which leaves room for such indirect regulation as results, for example, from a prohibition of discrimination, has stronger arguments on its side. Such interpretation is compatible with the purpose of the provision, given that the essence of determination of pay remains in the hands of the (national) social partners (collective bargaining agreements) and of the Member States (minimum wage). These national parties are merely restricted in that their regulation of pay must be free of discrimination.[23] Contrary to the third opinion (para. 11 at the end), there is no need for an exception with regard to temporary agency work. While it is true that the prohibition of discrimination requires a value judgement here, this value judgement does not concern pay but rather the system of temporary agency work.

13.   The **right of association** denotes regulations on the formation, dissolution and activity and membership of, employee associations (trade unions) and employers.[24] 'The right to **strike** and to impose **lock-outs**' refers to the entire body of law on industrial action, including rules on strikes which have not been authorised by a trade union.[25] The law regarding collective agreements is inherently linked to the right of association and may consequently also be reserved for the Member States.[26] Yet, except for the right to strike and the right to impose lock-outs, the law regarding collective agreements is not specifically exempted in Article 153(5) TFEU, even though language used in other EU legislation (e.g. in Article 28 ChFR) refers to it specifically.[27]

II.   SOCIAL POLICY, ARTICLES 153–155 TFEU

1.   Overview and System

14.   Title X of the Treaty on the Functioning of the European Union entitled 'Social Policy' establishes the competence of the EU in the field of employment law. Article 151(1) TFEU underscores the objectives in this area,[28] referring to the European Social Charter (§2 para. 3) and to the Community Charter of

---

[23]   Thus now ECJ Case C-268/06 *Impact* [2008] ECR I-2483 paras. 105–133.

[24]   S. Krebber, in C. Calliess/M. Ruffert (eds.), *EUV/AEUV*, Art. 153 AEUV para. 12.

[25]   S. Krebber, in C. Calliess/M. Ruffert (eds.), *EUV/AEUV*, Art. 153 AEUV para. 12; R. Rebhahn/M. Reiner, in J. Schwarze (ed.), *EU-Kommentar*, Art. 137 EG para. 59.

[26]   S. Krebber, in C. Calliess/M. Ruffert (eds.), *EUV/AEUV*, Art. 153 AEUV para. 12.

[27]   R. Rebhahn/M. Reiner, in J. Schwarze (ed.), *EU-Kommentar*, Art. 137 EG para. 58.

[28]   Differently F. Lecomte, *Colum. J. Eur. L.* 17 (2010–2011), 1–22 (arguing that Article 151 TFEU hat 'metamorphosed' from a programmatic into a substantive rule).

Fundamental Social Rights (§2 paras. 65–77): 'the promotion of employment, improved living and working conditions, so as to make possible their harmonisation while the improvement is being maintained, proper social protection, dialogue between management and labour, the development of human resources with a view to lasting high employment and the combating of exclusion'. The Union does not solely pursue these goals through the approximation of the laws of the Member States. Union and Member States first of all 'believe that such a development will ensue not only from the functioning of the internal market, which will favour the harmonisation of social systems', Article 151(3) TFEU. Where the Union and the Member States take measures towards these objectives, they 'take account of the diverse forms of national practices, in particular in the field of contractual relations, and the need to maintain the competitiveness of the Union's economy', Article 151(2) TFEU.

15. Apart from stating the objectives in Article 151 TFEU, Title X – to the extent relevant here – includes a competence for supporting related activities of the Union in Article 153 TFEU (2. below) and provisions regarding the participation of the social partners – management and labour – in the legislative process (3. below).

2.   *The Supplementary Competence of Article 153 TFEU*

a)   Overview and System

16. Article 153 TFEU, initially introduced into the Treaty by the Amsterdam revision, and slightly amended by the Nice revision, incorporates and further develops the provisions of the Social Policy Protocol (para. 4 above). The competence relates to the objectives of Article 151 TFEU (para. 14 above) and enables the Union to **support and supplement** the activities of the Member States in the areas covered by paragraph 1.

17. Article 153 TFEU is not easy to understand because it addresses **four separate issues**:

(1) the objects of the supplementary competence, paragraphs 1, 4 and 5;
(2) the measures at the Union's disposal, i.e. regulations, directives and other measures, paragraph 2;
(3) the applicable procedures, paragraph 2; and
(4) the possibility of entrusting the national social partners – management and labour – with the implementation of directives, paragraph 3.

Paragraph 3 thus concerns different issues and will be discussed later (paras. 25 sq. below). Paragraphs 4 and 5 determine the limitations on the EU's competences, some of which we discussed earlier (paras. 8–13 above). The remaining provisions become clearer if we distinguish them as follows:

Subject	Measure	Procedure
(a) improvement in particular of the **working environment** to protect workers' health and safety	(a) **measures designed to encourage** cooperation between Member States through initiatives aimed at – improving knowledge, – developing exchanges of information and best practices, – promoting innovative approaches and evaluating experiences (b) **directives** as minimum requirements	Procedure of **Article 294 TFEU (qualified majority in the Council)** after consultation with the Economic and Social Committee and the Committee of Regions
(b) **working conditions**		
(c) **social security** and social protection of workers		**unanimously** upon a proposal by the Commission and after consultation with the European Parliament, the Economic and Social Committee and the Committee of Regions
(d) protection of workers where their **employment contract is terminated**		
(e) the **information and consultation** of workers		Procedure of **Article 294 TFEU (qualified majority in the Council)** after consultation with the Economic and Social Committee and the Committee of Regions
(f) representation and **collective defence of the interests of workers and employers**, including co-determination, subject to paragraph 5		**unanimously** upon a proposal by the Commission and after consultation with the European Parliament, the Economic and Social Committee and the Committee of Regions
(g) conditions of employment for **third-country nationals** legally residing in Union territory		
(h) **integration of persons excluded from the labour market**, without prejudice to Article 166		Procedure of **Article 294 TFEU (qualified majority in the Council)** after consultation with the Economic and Social Committee and the Committee of Regions
(i) **equality between men and women** with regard to labour market opportunities and treatment at work		
(j) the combating of **social exclusion**	Measures to **encourage** cooperation between Member States (as above)	
(k) **modernisation of social protection systems** without prejudice to point (c)		

18. If we look at the differentiated options of action and procedure in paragraph 2 and the list of excluded subjects in paragraph 5, we can discern a **graded system** with regard to the political sensitivity of the matters at issue.[29]

Gradation	Subjects of Regulation
Area of harmonisation (majority requirement)	(a) improvement in particular of the **working environment** to protect workers' health and safety (b) **working conditions** (e) **information and consultation** of workers (h) **integration of persons excluded from the labour market**, without prejudice to Article 166 (i) **equality between men and women** with regard to labour market opportunities and treatment at work
Area of limited harmonisation (unanimity requirement)	(c) **social security** and social protection of workers (d) protection of workers upon termination of their **employment contracts** (f) representation and **collective defence of the interests of workers and employers,** including co-determination, subject to paragraph 5 (g) conditions of employment for **third-country nationals** legally residing within Union territory
Area of 'encouragement'	(j) the combating of **social exclusion** (k) **modernisation of social protection systems** without prejudice to point (c)
Reserved subjects	**pay, the right of association, the right to strike, the right to impose lock-outs**

b)   Individual Areas of Regulation

19. The demarcation of the different areas of regulation is thus of central importance in order to maintain the balancing of interests which was intended by the draftsmen. As is the case in respect of matters which are reserved for the Member States (paras. 8–13 above), the terms of the Treaty require an **autonomous interpretation.**[30]

20. One of the most important areas of Union competence in the employment field is the protection of workers' **health and safety**, which is covered by Article 153(1)(a) TFEU (see §13). In considering the **working environment**, the Court has given the competence a broad meaning, 'embracing all factors, physical or otherwise, capable of affecting the health and safety of the worker in his working environment, including in particular certain aspects of the

---

[29]   For a critical appraisal, see M. Weiss, *Festschrift für Wiese*, 639 ('not thought through').
[30]   R. Rebhahn/M. Reiner, in J. Schwarze (ed.), *EU-Kommentar*, Art. 137 EG para. 21.

organization of working time'.[31] The issues covered by **working conditions** mentioned in lit. b) are rather unclear, given that this term could theoretically be interpreted so as to cover employment law as a whole.[32] Following a systematic interpretation of Article 153 'employment conditions' cannot cover 'pay' or any of the other matters which are mentioned in paragraph 1. The language used in the Community Charter of Fundamental Social Rights also suggests a narrow interpretation:[33] apart from health and safety (already covered by lit. a)), 'working conditions' refers to issues of working time in a broad sense (including paid leave). **Information and consultation** of workers signifies employee involvement, except for employee co-determination (see lit. f)).[34] There already exists a wide range of EU legislation pertaining to these issues (see §§26–28). **Equality between men and women** with regard to labour market opportunities and treatment at work does not only affect the prohibition of discrimination pursuant to Article 157(1) and (2) TFEU and in the relevant secondary legislation, but more generally affects equal opportunities. Article 157(3) TFEU provides for a similar competence (see paras. 44 sq. below).

21. Protection of workers where their employment contract is terminated covers the law of unfair dismissal in a broad sense, including general protection as well as specific provisions for the protection of particular categories of employees (mothers, young people, disabled people) as it may be attained by prohibitions of termination, notice periods, compensation rights and protection in cases of fixed-term employment.[35] **Representation and collective defence of the interests of workers and employers, including co-determination** must be read together with the exclusions of paragraph 5 on the one hand, and with the specific provisions on information and consultation of lit. e) on the other. Litera f) therefore primarily concerns employee co-determination on the workshop level and on the board level.[36]

22. The predecessor of Article 153 TFEU in Article 118a TEC, which was primarily focused on health and safety of workers, served as a basis for a number of directives, in particular the Safety and Health Framework Directive (§13), the Working Time Directive (§14), the Maternity Protection Directive (§20) and the Young People at Work Directive (§22). The Social Policy Protocol, which

---

[31] ECJ Case C-84/94 *United Kingdom* v. *Council* [1996] ECR 5755 paras. 14 sq. (concerning the WTD); on this, see B. Fitzpatrick, *ILJ* 26 (1997), 115–135.

[32] See H.-D. Steinmeyer, *RdA* 2001, 10, 14 ('catch-all provision'); R. Wank, *RdA* 1995, 10, 19.

[33] To the same effect R. Rebhahn/M. Reiner, in J. Schwarze (ed.), *EU-Kommentar*, Art. 137 EG para. 36. Differently H. Buchner, *RdA* 1993, 193, 196.

[34] H.-D. Steinmeyer, *RdA* 2001, 10, 16.

[35] More narrowly R. Rebhahn/M. Reiner, in J. Schwarze (ed.), *EU-Kommentar*, Art. 137 EG para. 44 who allocate protection of special categories of employees against unfair dismissal to lit. c) and the protection of fixed-term employees to lit. b).

[36] S. Krebber, in C. Calliess/M. Ruffert (eds.), *EUV/AEUV*, Art. 153 AEUV para. 20.

constitutes the second root of today's Article 153 TFEU, served as a basis for the European Works Council Directive (§28). The Information and Consultation Framework Directive was already enacted on the basis of Article 137 TEC, the immediate predecessor of Article 153 TFEU.

c)   Implementation Standards

23.   Article 153(2)(b) TFEU not only determines the scope of Union competence but also sets standards for the directives which are based upon this provision. These standards are also relevant for the interpretation of directives which are based upon Article 153 TFEU. The competence merely serves as a basis for **minimum requirements.**[37] This is re-emphasised in paragraph 4, pursuant to which provisions adopted on the basis of Article 153 TFEU shall not prevent the Member States from maintaining or introducing more stringent protective measures. Furthermore, the minimum requirements adopted in this economically important area should be **implemented gradually,** Article 153(2)(b) TFEU. This restriction is intended to address the fact that the employment laws of the Member States have rather disparate levels of protection. Gradual implementation thus serves the interests of economically weaker Member States and their enterprises. Finally, directives which are based upon Article 153 TFEU 'shall avoid imposing administrative, financial and legal constraints in a way which would hold back the creation and development of **small and medium-sized undertakings**', Article 153(2)(b) TFEU. This provision 'lays down a substantive obligation, compliance with which is subject to review by the Community judicature at the instance of any interested party which brings the appropriate action'.[38]

d)   Participation of the Social Partners in the Implementation of Directives

24.   The Member States can entrust implementation of directives which are based upon Article 153(2) TFEU[39] to the social partners – management and labour – upon their joint request, Article 153(3).[40] Assigning implementation to the social partners certainly does not relieve the **Member States** of their **responsibility** towards the Union.[41] The Member States must ensure that the

---

[37]   In more detail R. Rebhahn, *EuZA* 2008, 39, 47 sq.

[38]   CFI Case T-135/96 *UEAPME* v. *Council* [1998] ECR II-2335 para. 80. See also A. Seifert, *RdA* 2004, 200, 203 sq.

[39]   The Lisbon Treaty further allows for the implementation of Council decisions pursuant to Article 155 TFEU by the social partners.

[40]   The possibility as such had been recognised in the Court's jurisprudence even before the formal recognition in the Treaty: ECJ 143/83 *Commission* v. *Denmark* [1985] ECR 427 para. 8; Case 235/84 *Commission* v. *Italy* [1986] ECR 2291 para. 20; Case C-306/07 *Andersen* [2008] ECR I-10279 paras. 24–29; Case C-405/08 *Holst* [2010] ECR I-985 paras. 34–45.

[41]   M. Heinze, *ZfA* 1997, 505, 511 sq.; A. Höland, *ZIAS* 1995, 425, 438 sq.

social partners have, by means of agreement, taken the steps necessary to ensure correct implementation of the directives by the end of the implementation period. The Member States must also guarantee that such implementing measures satisfy the requirements of the directive in the future. If implementation by the social partners proves to be deficient, it is thus the Member States who will be subjected to proceedings under Article 258 TFEU[42] or claims for damages.

25. The provision of paragraph 3 has been added to the Treaty with a view to individual Member States such as Denmark and Belgium, where the regulation of employment is largely left to collective agreements by the social partners.[43] It does not have practical relevance in Member States such as Germany where the competence of the social partners varies between sectors and regions and where there are consequently no all-encompassing collective agreements.[44]

3.   Social Dialogue pursuant to Articles 154 and 155 TFEU

Bibliography:

C. Arnold, 'Die Stellung der Sozialpartner in der europäischen Sozialpolitik', *NZA* 2002, 1261–1268; S. Arnold, *Der Sozial Dialog nach Art. 139 EG – Eine Analyse unter besonderer Berücksichtigung der Legitimation des Ratsbeschlusses nach Art. 139 Abs. 2 S. 1 Alt. 2 EG* (Baden-Baden: Nomos, 2008); R. Birk, 'Vereinbarungen der Sozialpartner im Rahmen des Sozialen Dialogs und ihre Durchführung', *EuZW* 1997, 453–459; G. Britz/Marlene Schmidt, 'Die institutionalisierte Mitwirkung der Sozialpartner an der Rechtsetzung der Europäischen Gemeinschaft', *EuR* 1999, 467–498 = G. Britz/Marlene Schmidt, 'The Institutionalised Participation of Management and Labour in the Legislative Activities of the European Community: A Challenge to the Principle of Democracy under Community Law', *ELJ* 6 (2000), 45–71; W. Däubler, 'Europäische Tarifverträge nach Maastricht', *EuZW* 1992, 329–336; H.-G. Dederer, 'Durchführung von Vereinbarungen der europäischen Sozialpartner – Korporative Ausübung von Rechtsetzungsgewalt und ihr demokratisches Defizit', *RdA* 2000, 216–222; O. Deinert, *Der europäische Kollektivvertrag – Rechtstatsächliche und rechtsdogmatische Grundlagen einer gemeineuropäischen Kollektivvertragsautonomie* (Baden-Baden: Nomos, 1999); O. Deinert, 'Modes of Implementing European Collective Agreements and their Impact on Collective Autonomy', *ILJ* 23 (2003), 317–325; O. Deinert, 'Partizipation europäischer Sozialpartner an der Gemeinschaftsrechtsetzung', *RdA* 2004, 211–226; J. Dötsch, 'Vereinbarungen der Europäischen Sozialpartner', *AuA* 1998, 262–264; W. Goos, 'Sozialer Dialog und Arbeitgeberverbände', in H. Oetker/U. Preis (eds.), *Europäisches Arbeits- und Sozialrecht, EAS, part B – Systematische Darstellungen*, loose-leaf (Heidelberg: Forkel, last

---

42   Cf. again ECJ Case 143/83 *Commission v. Denmark* [1985] ECR 427; Case 235/84 *Commission v. Italy* [1986] ECR 2291.

43   See also R. Birk, *Festschrift für Rehbinder*, 3, 14 see note 26.

44   R. Birk, *Festschrift für Rehbinder*, 3, 13; H. Buchner, *RdA* 1993, 193, 200 sq.; S. Krebber, in C. Calliess/M. Ruffert (eds.), *EUV/AEUV*, Art. 153 AEUV para. 36; H. Konzen, *EuZW* 1995, 39, 46 sq.

update: October 1999), B 8110; W. Goos, 'Tarifautonomie in Europa – Chancen und Risiken', in H. Konzen et al. (eds.), *Festschrift für Rolf Birk* (Tübingen: Mohr Siebeck, 2008), 135–149; B. Hepple, *European Social Dialogue – Alibi or Opportunity?* (London: Institute of Employment Rights, 1993); M. Heinze, 'Die Rechtsgrundlagen des sozialen Dialogs auf Gemeinschaftsebene', *ZfA* 1997, 505–521; M. Heinze, 'Europarecht im Spannungsverhältnis zum nationalen Arbeitsrecht – Von formaler Verdichtung zur offenen Arbeitsrechtsordnung', *ZfA* 1992, 331–359; K. Langenbucher, 'Zur Zulässigkeit parlamentsersetzender Normgebungsverfahren im Europarecht', *ZEuP* 2002, 265–286; K. Lörcher, 'Der Europäische Gewerkschaftsbund (EGB) und seine Beteiligung am europäischen Arbeitsrecht', *NZA* 2003, 184–194; R. Parrish, 'Social Dialogue in European Professional Football', *ELJ* 17 (2011), 213–229; St. Peers, 'Non-Regression Clauses: The Fig Leaf has Fallen', *ILJ* 39 (2010), 436–443; O. Ricken, 'Der soziale Dialog im EG-Vertrag als Zielvorgabe für die Europäische Betriebsverfassung', *DB* 2000, 874–878; A. Röthel, 'Europäische Rechtsetzung im sozialen Dialog – Zur Richtlinie 1999/70/EG über befristete Arbeitsverhältnisse', *NZA* 2000, 65–69; D. Schiek, 'Autonomous Collective Agreements as a Regulatory Device in European Labour Law: How to read Article 139 EC', *ILJ* 34 (2005), 23–56; G. Schnorr, 'Kollektivverträge in einem integrierten Europa', *DRdA* 1994, 193–198; R. Schwarze, 'Legitimation kraft virtueller Repräsentation', *RdA* 2001, 208–218; R. Schwarze, 'Sozialer Dialog im Gemeinschaftsrecht', in H. Oetker/U. Preis (eds.), *Europäisches Arbeits- und Sozialrecht, EAS, part B – Systematische Darstellungen,* loose-leaf (Heidelberg: Forkel, last update: March 2012), B 8100; S. Smismans, 'The European Social Dialogue between Constitutional and Labour Law', *E.L. Rev.* 32 (2007), 341–364; B. Waas, 'Der soziale Dialog auf europäischer Ebene', *ZESAR* 2004, 443–451; M. Weiss, 'Der soziale Dialog als Katalysator koordinierter Tarifpolitik in der EG', in M. Heinze/A. Söllner (eds.), *Arbeitsrecht in der Bewährung – Festschrift für Otto Rudolf Kissel* (Munich: C.H. Beck, 1994), 1253–1267; M. Weiss, 'Transnationale Kollektivvertragsstrukturen in der EG: Informalität oder Verrechtlichung?', in H. Konzen et al. (eds.), *Festschrift für Rolf Birk* (Tübingen: Mohr Siebeck, 2008), 957–975; A. Wisskirchen, 'Der soziale Dialog in der Europäischen Gemeinschaft', in J. Arnold (ed.), *Die Arbeitsgerichtsbarkeit – Festschrift zum 100jährigen Bestehen des Deutschen Arbeitsgerichtsverbandes* (Neuwied/Kriftel/Berlin: Luchterhand, 1994), 653–677; see also the bibliography before para. 1 above as well as the references collected by the commission at http://ec.europa.eu/employment_social/social_dialogue/docs_de.htm.

Cases (Selection):
CFI Case T-135/96 *UEAPME* v. *Council* [1998] ECR II-2335.

a) Basic Principles

26. 'The Commission shall have the task of promoting the consultation of management and labour at Union level and shall take any relevant measure to facilitate their dialogue by ensuring balanced support for the parties', Articles 154(1) and 152(1) TFEU.[45] '**Social dialogue**' refers to the exchange of

---

45 On the development of European social dialogue, starting from the colloquies as Val Duchesse see e.g. S. Arnold, *Der Soziale Dialog nach Art. 139 EG*, 25–31; M. Fuchs, in M. Fuchs/F. Marhold (eds.), *Europäisches Arbeitsrecht*, 11–14; M. Heinze, *ZfA* 1997, 505–509;

opinions between employers' and employees' associations, i.e. the 'social partners' (see Articles 152(1) and 154(1) TFEU; in the English version, the latter provision refers to 'management and labour'; see also paras. 30 sq.) on social issues. Such social dialogue occurs in two distinct manners in the TFEU.

- For one thing, social dialogue refers to an exchange of opinions between the social partners in an '**informal**' and general sense. The Commission has the task of promoting such social dialogue. And this informal dialogue may also lead to 'contractual relations' within the meaning of Article 155(1) TFEU. To the extent that such informal dialogue leads to agreements, these will be implemented 'in accordance with the procedures and practices specific to management and labour and the Member States', Article 155(2) alt. 1 TFEU. However, this procedure is of little practical importance and outside our present context of *EU legislation.*[46]
- Apart from that, Articles 154(2)-(4) and 155 TFEU provide for a **formal social dialogue** which allows for the **participation of the social partners in the Union's legislative procedures** through consultation, statements and proposals, which gives the social partners an opportunity to exert a formative influence upon EU law-making. It is this latter form of social dialogue that will be exclusive focus of the discussions that follow.[47]

27. For some time now, the social partners have also been involved in the Union's social policy in the context of the so-called **Tripartite Summit for Growth and Employment**. The purpose of these consultation processes is to ensure 'that there is a continuous concertation between the Council, the Commission and the social partners'.[48] Since the Lisbon Treaty the Tripartite Summit has been recognised in Article 152(2) TFEU as contributing to social dialogue.

28. Participation of the social partners in the legislative process serves different **objectives**. First, the legislature makes use of the expertise of the social partners

---

B. Hepple, *European Social Dialogue – Alibi or Opportunity?*, 12–19; R. Wank, *RdA* 1995, 10, 19–21; M. Weiss, *Festschrift für Kissel*, 1253, 1258–1262; auch W. Goos, *Festschrift für Birk*, 140–145. The newly introduced provision of Article 152(1) TFEU should not imply any substantial changes or expansions, R. Rebhahn, in J. Schwarze (ed.), *EU-Kommentar*, Art. 138 EG para. 13.

[46] See e.g. R. Birk, *Festschrift für Rehbinder*, 3, 11 sq.; H. Buchner, *RdA* 1993, 193, 200 sq.; P. Hanau, in P. Hanau/H.-D. Steinmeyer/R. Wank (eds.), *Handbuch des europäischen Arbeits- und Sozialrechts*, §19 para. 17; K. Lörcher, *NZA* 2003, 184, 192; R. Rebhahn, in J. Schwarze (ed.), *EU-Kommentar*, Art. 139 EG paras. 11–14; S. Smismans, *E.L. Rev.* 32 (2007), 341, 358–363; M. Weiss, *Festschrift für Kissel*, 253–1267. But see also O. Deinert, *ILJ* 23 (2003), 317, 320–324; D. Schiek, *ILJ* 34 (2005), 23–56.

[47] The development of Community law is outlined by O. Deinert, *RdA* 2004, 212–216.

[48] Council Decision 2003/174/EC of 6 March 2003 establishing a Tripartite Social Summit for Growth and Employment, OJ 2003 L 70/31.

who are closer to the needs of employers and employees as their constituents.[49] Their participation in legislation, secondly, conveys an element of 'closeness to citizens' (*Bürgernähe*) and with it an element of democratic legitimation. Finally, where the social partners influence or mould the content of employment legislation, this can be regarded as a manifestation of the principle of subsidiarity.[50]

29. However, the way in which social dialogue is designed in Articles 154(4) and 155 TFEU raises questions of **democratic legitimation**. Where agreements of the social partners are implemented by way of Council decision, i.e. in the form of a legal act, this does **not require participation of the European Parliament** (see para. 40 below). The 2009 Lisbon Treaty merely introduced an obligation to inform the European Parliament, Article 155(2)(1) sent. 2 TFEU. Some scholars consider these legislative procedures to be incompatible with the principle of democracy.[51] Others seek to establish the necessary democratic legitimacy in other ways. For example, legitimacy can be found in the decisive role of the Council, which itself enjoys indirect democratic legitimacy.[52] Another approach is to establish specific requirements for the recognition of organisations as social partners so as to increase the legitimacy of the social partners themselves.[53,54]

b) Social Partners

30. In a general sense, employers and their organisations on the one hand and employee organisations on the other, can be defined as social partners. The TFEU uses the term in different contexts and with different meanings. If Article 153(3) TFEU provides for the possibility of entrusting the social partners with the implementation of directives into national law, it refers to organisations of the Member States; the definition of the term is also left to the Member States. On the other hand, it is a matter of EU law – and autonomous interpretation – to

---

[49]   A. Höland, *ZIAS* 1995, 425, 426.

[50]   With special emphasis of the aspect of subsidiarity O. Deinert, *RdA* 2004, 211, 217 sq.; critically C. Arnold, *NZA* 2002, 1261, 1267 sq.; M. Heinze, *ZfA* 1992, 331, 336–338, 355.

[51]   C. Arnold, *NZA* 2002, 1261–1268; S. Arnold, *Der Soziale Dialog nach Art. 139 EG*; H.-G. Dederer, *RdA* 2000, 216–222; critically also M. Weiss, *Festschrift für Wiese*, 639 sq.

[52]   G. Britz/M. Schmidt, *EuR* 1999, 467, 487–490 (measured against the Union law principle of democracy); K. Langenbucher, *ZEuP* 2002, 265, 278 sq.; R. Schwarze, in *EAS*, B 8100 para. 64; id., *RdA* 2002, 208, 217 sq.; P. Hanau, in P. Hanau/H.-D. Steinmeyer/R. Wank (eds.), *Handbuch des europäischen Arbeits- und Sozialrechts*, §19 para. 9; differently H.-G. Dederer, *RdA* 2000, 216, 218–220; C. Arnold, *NZA* 2002, 1261, 1265–1268.

[53]   A similar model can be found in Spanish employment law where collective agreements can have a further reaching *erga omnes*-effect; see B. Gutiérrez-Solar Calvo, 'Die Entsendung von Arbeitnehmern nach Spanien', *RdA* 2001, 350, 352.

[54]   Critically G. Britz/M. Schmidt, *EuR* 1999, 467, 490 sq.; 491–497; also R. Schwarze, *RdA* 2002, 208, 217 sq.

define the 'social partners' eligible for participation in EU legislation through the social dialogue of Articles 154(2)-(4), and 155 TFEU.[55] Given their (potential) participation in EU law-making (Article 155(2) TFEU; para. 29 above), **representativeness** is an indispensible requirement[56] in two ways: representativeness with regard to the represented group (employers, employees) and with regard to the Member States of the EU.[57] Following the requirements formulated by the Commission,[58] the organisations should

(1) be cross-industry or relate to specific sectors or categories and be organised at the European level;

(2) consist of organisations which are themselves an integral and recognised part of the Member States' social partner structures and with the capacity to negotiate agreements, and which are representative of all Member States, to the extent possible; and

(3) have adequate structures to ensure their effective participation in the consultation process.

31. The general organisations of employers and employees are widely considered to satisfy these requirements.[59] They include:

– the *Confederation of European Business* (**BUSINESSEUROPE**, see www.businesseurope.eu), previously the Union of Industrial and Employers' Confederations of Europe (**UNICE**),

– the European Centre of Employers and Enterprises providing Public Services (**CEEP**; see www.ceep.eu), and

– the European Trade Union Confederation (**ETUC**, see www.etuc.org).[60]

---

[55]   S. Krebber, in C. Calliess/M. Ruffert (eds.), *EUV/AEUV*, Art. 154 AEUV paras. 7–9; see also S. Arnold, *Der Soziale Dialog nach Art. 139 EG*, 33–38.

[56]   CFI Case T-135/96 *UEAPME* v. *Council* [1998] ECR II-2335 paras. 88–90; H. Konzen, *EuZW* 1995, 39, 46; R. Birk, *EuZW* 1997, 453, 455; G. Britz/M. Schmidt, *EuR* 1999, 467, 494 sq.; H. Buchner, *RdA* 1993, 193, 202 sq.; R. Rebhahn, in J. Schwarze (ed.), *EU-Kommentar*, Art. 138 EG paras. 6, 9; approvingly also R. Schwarze, *RdA* 2002, 208, 218.

[57]   S. Krebber, in C. Calliess/M. Ruffert (eds.), *EUV/AEUV*, Art. 154 AEUV para. 15 (though critically with regard to [a] the exclusion of participation of the European Parliament and [b] the requirement of representativity as developed by the CFI; loc. cit., Art. 155 AEUV paras. 25, 28); see also R. Rebhahn, in J. Schwarze (ed.), *EU-Kommentar*, Art. 138 EG para. 9.

[58]   Communication concerning the application of the Agreement on social policy presented by the Commission to the Council and to the European Parliament, COM(93) 600 final; Communication from the Commission adapting and promoting the social dialogue at Community level, COM(98) 322 final. Critically S. Krebber, in C. Calliess/M. Ruffert (eds.), *EUV/AEUV*, Art. 154 AEUV paras. 19–22.

[59]   K. Langenbucher, *ZEuP* 2002, 265, 266 sq. Critically C. Arnold, *NZA* 2002, 1261, 1266. See also the proceedings of CFI Case T-135/96 *UEAPME* v. *Council* [1998] ECR II-2335.

[60]   In more detail K. Lörcher, *NZA* 2003, 184–194.

Apart from these umbrella organisations, there is a large number of cross-sector and sector-specific European organisations which the Commission involves in social dialogue.[61]

c)   Consultation of the Social Partners

32.   The social partners are initially involved in the legislative process through a consultation right.[62] 'Before submitting proposals in the social policy field, the Commission shall consult management and labour on the possible direction of Union action', Article 154(2) TFEU. If, after the consultation, the Commission considers Union action advisable, it consults with the social partners again on the content of the envisaged proposal. The social partners then have the opportunity to submit their opinion or recommendation to the Commission, Article 153(3) TFEU.

d)   Social Dialogue to Reach Agreement

33.   In addition to the consultation right, the social partners have the opportunity to actively participate in the legislative proceedings by concluding a framework agreement which can then, upon the Commission's proposal, be implemented by a Council decision. In effect, the social partners can thus write the text of a directive which, of course, must be endorsed by the Council in order to become effective.

aa)   Initiation and Execution of the Process

34.   The process can be initiated pursuant to Article 154(4) TFEU after the social partners have been consulted regarding a proposal of the Commission. It is in this way and thus in connection with a Commission proposal that the social partners may, by unilateral notification to the Commission, initiate social dialogue pursuant to Article 155 TFEU. The social partners thus negotiate with the knowledge of the Commission's considerations of what constitutes a fair balancing of interests – a process that can be compared to *bargaining in the shadow of the law*.[63] The Commission's proposal will usually influence the expectations of the social partners and also constitute the basis for the

---

[61]   See the overview in the Communication from the Commission 'Partnership for change in an enlarged Europe – Enhancing the contribution of European social dialogue' of 12 August 2004, annex 5, COM(2004) 557 final, 24 sq. (b).

[62]   See M. Heinze, *ZfA* 1997, 505, 513 sq. On the legal consequences of a violation of Article 154(2) or (3) TFEU R. Rebhahn, in J. Schwarze (ed.), *EU-Kommentar*, Art. 138 EG para. 5.

[63]   B. Bercusson, *IRJ* 23 (1992), 177, 185; id., *ILJ* 23 (1994), 1, 20 sqq. See also the seminal article by R. Mnookin/L. Kornhauser, 'Bargaining in the Shadow of the Law', *Yale L.J.* 88 (1979), 950–997.

Commission's decision whether or not to propose the enactment of an agreement reached by the social partners.

35. The social partners can also **initiate** the proceedings **autonomously,** without there being a Commission proposal under Article 154(3) TFEU. This is certainly true for the 'informal' social dialogue outside legislative proceedings pursuant to Article 155(2) and 153 TFEU (para. 26 above), but should also be recognised in our context.[64]

36. The **duration of negotiations** – from the initiation to the conclusion of an agreement – is limited to nine months but may be extended if the social partners and the Commission jointly so decide. This provision ensures that social dialogue cannot obstruct legislative proceedings – as could easily be the case where controversial subjects are concerned. In light of Article 153(5) TFEU, **collective action** is not permitted in this context.[65]

bb) THE AGREEMENT

37. 'Should management and labour so desire, the dialogue between them at Union level may lead to contractual relations, including agreements', (**freedom of contract**), Article 155(1) TFEU. It follows from the nature of the matters at issue and the requirements for legislative proceedings, that the agreement be concluded in writing (cf. Article 155(2) TFEU: 'signatory parties'). It is unclear, however, which rules (laws) govern the conclusion and effectiveness of the agreement, given that the law of collective agreements is not harmonised (let alone unified).[66]

38. In substance, the agreement must respect the limitations which are placed upon the EU's competences in Article 153 TFEU if the agreement is intended to be implemented by Council decision pursuant to Article 155(1)(1) sent. 1 alt. 2 TFEU.[67] The agreement can thus only cover matters which are listed in Article 153(1)(a)-(i) TFEU.

---

[64] As here O. Deinert, *RdA* 2004, 211 sq.; M. Heinze, *ZfA* 1997, 505, 515 sq.; S. Krebber, in C. Calliess/M. Ruffert (eds.), *EUV/AEUV*, Art. 155 AEUV para. 1; R. Schwarze, in *EAS*, B 8100 para. 67; S. Smismans, *E.L. Rev.* 32 (2007), 341, 343, 352; differently R. Birk, *EuZW* 1997, 453, 455, 458; critically also M. Weiss, *Festschrift für Birk,* 963.

[65] R. Birk, *EuZW* 1997, 453, 454 sq.; E. Eichenhofer, in R. Streinz (ed.), *EUV/AEUV,* Art. 139 para. 9; S. Krebber, in C. Calliess/M. Ruffert (eds.), *EUV/AEUV,* Art. 155 AEUV para. 8.

[66] S. Krebber, in C. Calliess/M. Ruffert (eds.), *EUV/AEUV,* Art. 155 AEUV paras. 5 sq. See also W. Däubler, *EuZW* 1992, 329, 331 sq.; E. Eichenhofer, in R. Streinz (ed.), *EUV/AEUV,* Art. 139 EG para. 8.

[67] R. Rebhahn, in J. Schwarze (ed.), *EU-Kommentar,* Art. 139 EG para. 4.

cc) IMPLEMENTATION OF THE AGREEMENT

39. The agreement can be implemented in accordance 'with the procedures and practices specific to management and labour and the Member States'; this is a matter of national law.[68] Furthermore, as far as matters covered by Article 153 TFEU are concerned, the agreement may (1) upon joint request of the signatory parties and (2) on a proposal by the Commission (3) be implemented by a Council decision. The Commission is considered to be obliged to make a requisite proposal if the social partners so request[69] and may, in any case, not make substantial changes or amendments (*argumentum e* Article 154(2) and (3) TFEU: this would trigger a new right to consultation and lead to a never-ending procedural spiral).[70] The Council, on the other hand, should be allowed to make changes or amendments as it would be inconsistent to hold it more strictly bound with regard to proposals of the social partners than with regard to autonomous proposals of the Commission (cf. Article 193(1) TFEU).[71] The majority requirements for the Council are the same as set forth in Article 153(2) TFEU. In principle, its decisions require a qualified majority but where one of the more 'sensitive' subjects of Article 153(1)(c), (d), (f) and (g) is concerned, the Council decides unanimously. The Council decisions can, in general, take any of the legal forms provided for in Article 288 TFEU.[72] In the present context, the 'decision' must take the form of a directive given that decisions,

---

68 In more detail R. Schwarze, in *EAS,* B 8100 paras. 53–60. See for example: Communication from the Commission to the Council and the European Parliament transmitting the European framework agreement on harassment and violence at work of 8 November 2007, COM(2007) 686 final; Framework agreement on inclusive labour markets of 25 March 2010, available at www.etuc.org/a/7076; Framework agreement on work-related stress of 8 October 2004, available at www.etuc.org/a/529; Report by the European Social Partners of 18 June 2008 on Implementation of the European Autonomous Framework Agreement on Work-Related Stress, available at www.etuc.org/IMG/pdf_Final_Implementation_report. pdf; Framework agreement on telework of 16 December 2002, available at www.etuc. org/a/579.

69 M. Heinze, *ZfA* 1997, 505, 517–520; also A. Höland, *ZIAS* 1995, 425, 442–445; K. Langenbucher, *ZEuP* 2002, 265, 271 sq. (recognising a right of withdrawal in analogy to Article 250(2) EC [Art. 293 TFEU]); E. Eichenhofer, in R. Streinz (ed.), *EUV/AEUV,* Art. 139 EG paras. 18–20. Differently G. Britz/M. Schmidt, *EuR* 1999, 467, 477 sq.; R. Rebhahn, in J. Schwarze (ed.), *EU-Kommentar,* Art. 139 EG para. 7; R. Schwarze, in *EAS,* B 8100 para. 71; S. Smismans, *E.L. Rev.* 32 (2007), 341, 350.

70 See S. Arnold, *Der Soziale Dialog nach Art. 139 EG,* 118–121; M. Heinze, *ZfA* 1997, 505, 518 sq.; A. Höland, *ZIAS* 1995, 425, 445; K. Langenbucher, *ZEuP* 2002, 265, 270 sq.; R. Schwarze, in *EAS,* B 8100 para. 72; H.-D. Steinmeyer, *RdA* 2001, 20, 21.

71 M. Heinze, *ZfA* 1997, 505, 519 sq.; K. Langenbucher, *ZEuP* 2002, 265, 272 and 279. Differently S. Arnold, *Der Soziale Dialog nach Art. 139 EG,* 122–127; B. Bercusson, *European Labour Law,* 548; G. Britz/M. Schmidt, *EuR* 1999, 467, 478; A. Höland, *ZIAS* 1995, 425, 445; R. Schwarze, in *EAS,* B 8100 para. 77; S. Smismans, *E.L. Rev.* 32 (2007), 341, 343; M. Weiss, *Festschrift für Birk,* 961; R. Rebhahn, in J. Schwarze (ed.), *EU-Kommentar,* Art. 139 EG para. 7.

72 M. Heinze, *ZfA* 1997, 505, 517; A. Höland, *ZIAS* 1995, 425, 446 sq. Differently R. Rebhahn, in J. Schwarze (ed.), *EU-Kommentar,* Art. 139 EG para. 4.

---

recommendations and opinions (Article 288(4) and (5) TFEU) have no binding force and given that Article 153(2)(b) TFEU rules out the form of a regulation.[73]

40. The process of social dialogue does not provide for participation by the **European Parliament**.[74] The Lisbon Treaty merely introduced a right for Parliament to be informed, Article 155(2)(1) sent. 2 TFEU. The bottom line is that the social partners may effectively exclude the Parliament from participation by requesting to initiate the process under Article 155.[75] This is unsatisfactory on the one hand, yet on the other, can be considered part and parcel of the design of social dialogue, in respecting the autonomy of the social partners.

41. So far, the European Works Council Directive (§28), the Part-time Work Directive (§16) and the Parental Leave Directive have been drawn up using the social dialogue process. They were subsequently implemented by the Council under (what is now) Article 155 TFEU. Apart from these legislative acts, there are a number of sector-specific agreements.[76]

III. FURTHER COMPETENCES WITH RELEVANCE TO EMPLOYMENT LAW

42. The TFEU also contains a number of other competences for specific areas which have proved to be relevant for employment law.

1. Freedom of Movement for Workers, Article 46 TFEU

43. Article 46 TFEU confers upon the Union a specific competence for measures required to bring about freedom of movement for workers. It enables the European Parliament and the Council to adopt directives and regulations using the ordinary legislative procedure (Article 294 TFEU) after consulting the Economic and Social Committee. The predecessor of Article 46 TFEU was a basis for the Free Movement of Workers Regulation (see §3 para. 7 above).

---

[73] See S. Arnold, *Der Soziale Dialog nach Art. 139 EG*, 79–102; O. Deinert, *ILJ* 23 (2003), 317, 318 sq.; R. Schwarze, in *EAS*, B 8100 para. 76; similarly G. Britz/M. Schmidt, *EuR* 1999, 467, 475.

[74] CFI Case T-135/96 *UEAPME v. Council* [1998] ECR II-2335 paras. 88 sq. Critically e.g. M. Heinze, *ZfA* 1997, 505, 520. On the issue of legitimation, see already para. 29 above.

[75] Critically E. Eichenhofer, in R. Streinz (ed.), *EUV/AEUV*, Art. 139 EG para. 13; S. Krebber, in C. Calliess/M. Ruffert (eds.), *EUV/AEUV*, Art. 154 AEUV para. 36 and Art. 155 AEUV para. 28.

[76] See the examples in Communication from the Commission to the Council and the European Parliament transmitting the European framework agreement on harassment and violence at work of 8 November 2007, COM(2007) 686 final, 16. Recently Council Directive 2009/13/EC of 16 February 2009 implementing the Agreement concluded by the European Community Shipowners' Associations (ECSA) and the European Transport Workers' Federation (ETF) on the Maritime Labour Convention, 2006, and amending Directive 1999/63/EC, OJ 2009 L 124/30.

2. Ensuring the Principle of Equal Opportunities and Equal Treatment of Men and Women, Article 157(3) TFEU

44. Despite Article 153(1)(i) already covering this issue,[77] Article 157(3) TFEU also empowers the European Parliament and Council to adopt measures to ensure application of the principle of equal opportunity and equal treatment of men and women in matters of employment and occupation. This includes equal pay for equal work or work of equal value, using the ordinary legislative procedures of Article 294 TFEU after consulting the Economic and Social Committee. In relation to the competence of Article 19 TFEU (para. 46 below), Article 157(3) TFEU is the *lex specialis.*

45. The competence, first introduced by the 1997 Amsterdam Treaty, has thus far had only little practical relevance. The revision of the Sex Discrimination in Working Conditions Directive (§8 paras. 8 sq., 16) (which had originally been adopted on the basis of the predecessor of Article 352 TFEU) was based on (what is now) Article 157(3) TFEU, as was codification of the law in this field in the Sex Discrimination Directive of 2006 (cf. §8 para. 19).

3. Combating Discrimination, Article 19(1) TFEU

46. Article 19 TFEU, a special competence to combat discrimination, was originally introduced by the 1997 Amsterdam Treaty.[78] It enables the Council, acting unanimously in accordance with a special legislative procedure and after obtaining the consent of the European Parliament, to take 'appropriate action' – i.e. not only action in the form of the legal acts of Article 288 TFEU but also programmes or resolutions – to combat discrimination on grounds of sex, race or ethnic origin, religion or belief, disability, age or sexual orientation. Until revision of the Amsterdam Treaty, the competence merely required that Parliament was consulted, but its consent was not required.

47. The EU has based the Race Discrimination Directive (§10) and the Anti-Discrimination Framework Directive (§11)[79] on (what is now) Article 19 TFEU. Outside the field of employment, the Sex Discrimination in Access to Goods and Services Directive has been adopted on the basis of Article 19 TFEU (see also §8 paras. 26–63).

---

[77] On the (problematic) relationship between these provisions see E. Eichenhofer, in R. Streinz (ed.), *EUV/AEUV*, Art. 141 EG para. 22; S. Krebber, in C. Calliess/M. Ruffert (eds.), *EUV/AEUV*, Art. 157 AEUV para. 89.

[78] On the development see R. Langner, *ZIAS* 1998, 178–189. On the relationship with Article 153 TFEU, see M. Bell/R. Whittle, 'Between social policy and Union citizenship: the Framework Directive on equal treatment in employment', *E.L. Rev.* 27 (2002), 677–691.

[79] For a critical appraisal, see M. Bell/R. Whittle, *E.L. Rev.* 27 (2002), 677–691.

4. Approximation of Law for the Internal Market, Article 114, 115 TFEU

48. Article 115 TFEU (former Article 100 TEC) and Article 114 TFEU (originally added to the Treaty by the Single European Act as Article 100a TEC) empower the Union to adopt measures for the approximation of the laws of the Member States which have as their objective the establishment and functioning of the internal market and which directly affect the internal market. Both competences are not restricted to any area of law or policies of the Union and thus, in principle, also extend to legislation in the employment law field. The focus here however is upon the establishment and functioning of the internal market, rather than social policy.[80] Central to these competences are thus the realisation of the fundamental freedoms (see Article 26(2) TFEU) and the avoidance of distortions of competition. As to procedures, Article 115 TFEU requires unanimity in the Council but merely consultation of the European Parliament and the Economic and Social Committee, while legal acts based upon Article 114 TFEU are enacted with qualified majority in the ordinary legislative procedure (of Article 294 TFEU) and after consultation of the Economic and Social Committee.

49. Pursuant to its second paragraph, Article 114(1) TFEU can**not**, however, serve as a basis for provisions relating to the **free movement** of persons and for provisions controlling the **rights and interests of employed persons**. This is to be understood as a comprehensive exclusion. The only exception is protection of safety and health of employees, which Article 114(4) TFEU presupposes to be suitable for legislation under this competence norm.

50. The predecessor of Article 115 TFEU has been the basis for the Sex Discrimination in Pay Directive (§8 para. 15; §9 paras. 26 sqq.), the Collective Redundancies Directive (§23), the Transfer of Undertakings Directive (§24), the Insolvency Protection Directive (§25) and the Written Statement Directive (§12).[81]

5. Judicial Cooperation in Civil Matters, Article 81 TFEU

51. The 1997 Amsterdam Treaty introduced the new objective of building an area of freedom, security and justice in Europe and inserted a new chapter into the Treaty for this purpose, (what is now) Title V with Articles 67–89 TFEU. With regard to private law, employment law in particular, competence in the field of judicial cooperation in civil matters in Article 81 TFEU is of interest.

---

[80] ECJ Case 15/81 *Schul* [1982] ECR 1409 para. 33.
[81] For a critical perspective see R. Käppler, in H.-W. Rengeling (ed.), *Europäisierung des Rechts*, 136–140.

Following Article 81(2)(c) TFEU, the competence extends, in particular, to measures aimed at ensuring 'the compatibility of the rules applicable in the Member States concerning conflict of laws and of jurisdiction'.[82] The provision – at last – establishes a Union competence for **conflict of laws** (international private law) and **international procedure**. It should be noted, however, that Denmark as well as the United Kingdom and Ireland have declared a reservation to this competence (see also §5 para. 5).[83]

52. The predecessor of Article 81(2)(c) TFEU served as a basis for the Jurisdiction and Recognition of Judgements Regulation (§7) as well as for the Rome I- and Rome II-Regulations (§5).

6.   The Supplementary Competence of Article 352 TFEU

53. Finally, the supplementary competence of (today's) Article 352 TFEU has also been used in the area of employment. It enables the Council (acting unanimously, upon a proposal from the Commission and after obtaining the consent of the European Parliament [which, before the Lisbon Treaty merely had to be consulted]) to adopt 'appropriate measures' 'if action by the Union should prove necessary, within the framework of the policies defined in the Treaties, to attain one of the objectives set out in the Treaties, and the Treaties have not provided the necessary powers'.[84] This competence should only be used cautiously, as it would otherwise threaten to disrupt the differentiated system of Union competences.[85] Article 352(3) TFEU now clarifies that the provision may not be used for harmonisation of the Member States' laws in cases where the Treaty excludes such harmonisation (as is the case, e.g., in Article 153(2)(1)(a) TFEU); this *proviso* is likely to further limit the practical relevance of the competence.[86]

54. The original Sex Discrimination in Working Conditions Directive (§8 para. 16) was based on the predecessor to Article 352 TFEU. It has been recently used as a basis for the SE-Employee Involvement Directive (§29 paras. 1–61) and the SCE-Employee Involvement Directive (§29 paras. 62–66).

---

[82]   Newly introduced to Article 81(2)(g) TFEU is a competence for the development of alternative methods of dispute resolution which may, in particular, be relevant in the employment area.

[83]   See Protocol on the position of Denmark annexed to he Treaty on European Union and to the Treaty establishing the European Community, OJ 1997 C 340/101 and – updated by the Treaty of Lisbon – OJ 2010 C 83/299; Protocol on the position of the United Kingdom and Ireland annexed to he Treaty on European Union and to the Treaty establishing the European Community, OJ 1997 C 340/99 and – updated by the Treaty of Lisbon – OJ 2010 C 83/299.

[84]   ECJ Case Opinion 2/94 *EMRK* [1996] ECR I-1759 para. 29.

[85]   On this, see e.g. H. Konzen, *EuZW* 1995, 39, 43 sq.

[86]   M. Geiss, in J. Schwarze (ed.), *EU-Kommentar,* Art. 308 EG para. 37.

PART 2
CONFLICT OF LAWS

§5. CONFLICT OF LAWS – THE ROME I AND ROME II-REGULATIONS

CONTENTS

Bibliography:

C. v. Bar, *Internationales Privatrecht – Zweiter Band – Besonderer Teil* (Munich: C.H. Beck, 1991); C. v. Bar/P. Mankowski, *Internationales Privatrecht – Erster Band – Allgemeine Lehren*, 2nd edn. (Munich: C.H. Beck, 2003); R. Birk, 'Das Internationale Arbeitsrecht der Bundesrepublik Deutschland', *AcP* 46 (1982), 384–420; R. Birk, 'Die Bedeutung der Parteiautonomie im internationalen Arbeitsrecht', *RdA* 1989, 201–207; M. Bogdan, 'Rome I Regulation on the Law Applicable to Contractual Obligations and the Choice of Law by the Parties', *NIPR* 2009, 407–410; M. Franzen, 'Anknüpfung von Arbeitsverträgen im französischen internationalen Privatrecht', *IPRax* 1999, 278–280; M. Franzen, 'Die Lohnwucherrechtsprechung des BAG als Eingriffsnorm im Sinne von Art. 9 Rom I-VO bzw. §2 Nr. 1 AEntG?', *ZESAR* 2011, 101–107; M. Franzen, 'Vertragsstatut und zwingende Bestimmungen im internationalen Arbeitsrecht', *IPRax* 2003, 239–243; F. Gamillscheg, 'Ein Gesetz über das internationale Arbeitsrecht', *ZfA* 1983, 307–373; F. Gamillscheg, 'Intereuropäisches Arbeitsrecht – Zu zwei Vorschlägen der EWG zum Internationalen Arbeitsrecht', *RabelsZ* 37 (1973), 284–316; M. Giuliano/P. Lagarde, 'Report on the Convention on the law applicable to contractual obligations', *OJ* 1980 C 282/1–50; B. Hepple, 'Conflict of Laws on Employment Relationships in the EEC', in K. Lipstein (ed.), *Harmonisation of Private International Law by the EEC* (London: Institute of Advanced Legal Studies, 1978); A. Junker, *Arbeitnehmereinsatz im Ausland – Anzuwendendes Recht und Internationale Zuständigkeit* (Munich: ZAAR, 2007); A. Junker, 'Arbeitsverträge', in F. Ferrari/S. Leible (eds.), *Ein neues Internationales Vertragsrecht für Europa – Der Vorschlag für eine Rom I-Verordnung* (Jena: Jenaer Wissenschaftliche Verlagsgesellschaft, 2007), 111–127; A. Junker, 'Das Internationale Arbeitsrecht im Spiegel der Rechtsprechung', in H. Oetker/U. Preis/V. Rieble (eds.), *Festschrift 50 Jahre Bundesarbeitsgericht* (Munich: C.H. Beck, 2004), 1197–1218; A. Junker, 'Der sogenannte "räumliche Geltungsbereich" des Kündigungsschutzgesetzes', in B. Dauner-Lieb et al. (eds.), *Festschrift für Horst Konzen 2006* (Tübingen: Mohr Siebeck, 2006), 367–389; A. Junker, 'Der Teilzeitanspruch des deutschen Arbeitsrechts: Keine Eingriffsnorm nach europäischem IPR', *EuZA* 2009, 88–98; A. Junker, 'Die "zwingenden Bestimmungen" im neuen internationalen Arbeitsrecht', *IPRax* 1989, 69–75; A. Junker, 'Die einheitliche europäische Auslegung nach dem EG-Schuldvertragsübereinkommen', *RabelsZ* 55 (1991), 674–696; A. Junker, 'Die freie Rechtswahl und ihre Grenzen – Zur veränderten Rolle der Parteiautonomie im Schuldvertragsrecht', *IPRax* 1993, 1–10; A. Junker, 'Gewöhnlicher Arbeitsort und vorübergehende Entsendung im Internationalen Privatrecht', in S. Lorenz et al. (eds.), *Festschrift für Andreas Heldrich* (Munich: C.H. Beck, 2005), 719–739; A. Junker, 'Internationale Zuständigkeit und anwendbares Recht in Arbeitssachen – Eine Einführung für die Praxis', *NZA* 2005, 199–205; A. Junker, *Internationales Arbeitsrecht im Konzern* (Tübingen: Mohr Siebeck, 1992); A. Junker, 'Internationales Arbeitsrecht in der geplanten

Rom-I-Verordnung', *RIW* 2006, 401–408; O. L. Knöfel, 'Kommendes Internationales Arbeitsrecht – Der Vorschlag der Kommission der Europäischen Gemeinschaften vom 15.12.2005 für eine "Rom I"-Verordnung', *RdA* 2006, 269–281; O. L. Knöfel, 'Aufhebungsverträge im Internationalen Privat- und Prozessrecht', *ZfA* 2006, 397–434; S. Krebber, 'Conflict of Laws in Employment in Europe', *Comp. Lab. L. & Pol'y J.* 21 (2000), 501–541; S. Krebber, 'Die Bedeutung von Entsenderichtlinie und Arbeitnehmer-Entsendegesetz für das Arbeitskollisionsrecht', *IPRax* 2001, 22–28; S. Krebber, 'Individualarbeitsrecht als Arbeitsmarktrecht und Anknüpfung des Arbeitsverhältnisstatuts', in H. Konzen et al. (eds.), *Festschrift für Rolf Birk* (Tübingen: Mohr Siebeck, 2008), 477–494; S. Krebber, *Internationales Privatrecht des Kündigungsschutzes bei Arbeitsverhältnissen* (Baden-Baden: Nomos, 1997); H. Kronke, 'Europäische Vereinheitlichung des Arbeitskollisionsrechts als Wirtschafts- und Sozialpolitik', *RabelsZ* 45 (1981), 301–316; J. Kropholler, *Internationales Privatrecht*, 6th edn. (Tübingen: Mohr, 2006); P. Mankowski, 'Employment Contracts under Article 8 of the Rome I Regulation', in F. Ferrari/S. Leible (eds.), *Rome I Regulation: The Law Applicable to Contractual Obligations in Europea* (Munich: Sellier, 2009), 171–216; D. Martiny, 'Neuanfang im Europäischen Internationalen Vertragsrecht mit der Rom I-Verordnung, *ZEuP* 2010, 747–782; R. Plender/M. Wilderspin, *The European Private International Law of Obligations,* 3rd edn. (London: Sweet & Maxwell, 2009), chapter 1–15; C. Reithmann/D. Martiny (eds.), *Internationales Vertragsrecht*, 7th edn. (Cologne: Otto Schmidt, 2010); K. Riesenhuber, 'Die konkludente Rechtswahl im Arbeitsvertrag – Indizien für einen "realen Rechtswahlwillen" und ihr Gewicht –', *DB* 2005, 1571–1576; W.-H. Roth, 'Europäische Kollisionsrechtsvereinheitlichung – Überblick – Kompetenzen – Grundfragen', *EWS* 2011, 314–328; M. Schlachter, 'Fortentwicklung des Kollisionsrechts der Arbeitsverträge', in S. Leible (ed.), *Das Grünbuch zum Internationalen Vertragsrecht – Beiträge zur Fortentwicklung des Europäischen Kollisionsrechts der vertraglichen Schuldverhältnisse* (Munich: Sellier, 2004), 155–165; M. Schlachter, 'Grenzüberschreitende Arbeitsverhältnisse', *NZA* 2000, 57–64; G. Thüsing, 'Rechtsfragen grenzüberschreitender Arbeitsverhältnisse – Grundlagen und Neuigkeiten im Internationalen Arbeitsrecht', *NZA* 2003, 1303–1312; P. Winkler v. Mohrenfels/A. Block/A. Block, 'Abschluss des Arbeitsvertrages und anwendbares Recht', in H. Oetker/U. Preis (eds.), *Europäisches Arbeits- und Sozialrecht, EAS, part B – Systematische Darstellungen,* loose-leaf (Heidelberg: Forkel, last update: August 2010), B 3000; W. Wurmnest, 'Das neue Internationale Arbeitsvertragsrecht der Rom I-Verordnung; Europäische Zeitschrift für Arbeitsrecht', *EuZA* 2009, 481–499; see also the references before para. 37 below on the Rome II-Regulation.

Cases (Selection):
ECJ Case C-381/98 *Ingmar* v. *Leonard* [2000] ECR I-9305; ECJ Case C-29/10 *Koelzsch* 15 March 2011; ECJ Case C-384/10 *Voogsgeerd* 15 December 2011.

I. ISSUES, DEVELOPMENTS, COMPETENCE AND OVERVIEW

1. Private international law or conflict of law rules determine which national law applies in a case with connections to a foreign country. Private international

law rules continue to be of high practical importance in Europe as the national laws of the Member States are far from unified. EU employment law merely covers regulatory aspects of employment law and even here, central issues such as protection against unfair dismissal and sick pay have not been touched upon. Furthermore, the most commonly used legal form for the approximation of laws by introduction of minimum standards through directives leaves considerable leeway in the implementation process to maintain or introduce more stringent standards of protection. For the time being, national employment laws of the Member States thus remain disparate. Consequently, the question of which national law applies in a cross-border case will often be decisive.

2. Where the national legal systems remain disparate, unification of private international law is a **fundamental desideratum**. Divergent conflict of law rules cause legal uncertainty in respect of the applicable law and cause a danger that the same set of facts may be judged differently depending on which (national!) private international law reigns.[1] Unsurprisingly, the call for a unified private international law in Europe had already been raised in the early days of the EEC, particularly with regard to contract law as an area of central importance for the internal market.[2] Yet, there was doubt as to whether the EEC had the legislative competence to regulate private international law.

3. Consequently, conflict of law rules were initially enacted outside Community law proper in the form of the 1980 Convention on the Law Applicable to Contractual Obligation (the **Rome Convention**)[3].[4] The Convention was not a Community instrument in one of the forms of (today's) Article 288 TFEU nor was it adopted under the former Article 293 EC. The Rome Convention instead constituted an independent international treaty. However, at the same time, the Convention had always been devised as a complementary instrument to EC law and in many ways had a close relationship with the Community. The Convention was originally initiated by the Community and the

---

[1] See e.g. the case discussed by M. Franzen, *IPRax* 1999, 278–280.

[2] With regard to employment law, the initial proposals primarily aimed at promoting free movement: Commission, Proposal for a Regulation of the Council on the provisions on conflict of laws on employment relationships within the Community, OJ 1972 C 49/26 (not available in English; German text reproduced with explanatory comments in *RabelsZ* 37 (1973), 585–593); Amended proposal for a Regulation of the Council on the provisions on conflict of laws on employment relationships within the Community, COM(75) 653 final. On these proposals see F. Gamillscheg, *RabelsZ* 37 (1973), 284–316; on the development H. Kronke, *RabelsZ* 45 (1981), 301–316.

[3] 1980 Rome Convention on the law applicable to contractual obligations (consolidated version), OJ 1998 C 27/34.

[4] On the legislative history, see M. Giuliano/P. Lagarde, OJ 1980 C 282/1, 4–8; D. Martiny, in F. J. Säcker/R. Rixecker (eds.), *Münchener Kommentar zum BGB*, Vorbemerkung zu Art. 1 Rom I-VO, paras. 1 sqq.; id., *ZEuP* 2010, 747 sqq.; R. Plender/M. Wilderspin, *The European Private International Law of Obligations*, paras. 1.007–1.013.

Commission gave advice and support during the drafting process; only EC Member States could accede to the Rome Convention and all EC Member States were required to do so. In substance, the Rome Convention contained mechanisms to be adapted to Community law and its development.[5]

4. The issue of competence was resolved by the 1997 Amsterdam Treaty which introduced the new provision of (what is now) Article 81(2)(c) TFEU, enabling the Union to adopt measures aimed at ensuring 'the compatibility of the rules applicable in the Member States concerning conflict of laws and of jurisdiction' (see §4 para. 5 above).[6] Based on this new competence, the Rome Convention was 'converted into a Community instrument' in 2008, the **Rome I-Regulation**[7].[8] It entered into force on 24 July 2008 and applies to contracts concluded after 17 December 2009, Articles 28 sq. Rome I-Regulation.[9] The new competence also paved the way for the unification of other areas of private international law. The **Rome II-Regulation**[10] on the law applicable to non-contractual obligations[11] was enacted in 2007 and entered into force on

---

5   See e.g. K. Riesenhuber, *Europäisches Vertragsrecht*, paras. 46–48.

6   On this provision and its limits W.-H. Roth, *EWS* 2011, 314, 316 sqq.; M. Rossi, in C. Calliess/M. Ruffert (eds.), *EUV/AEUV*, Art. 81 AEUV paras. 17 sqq.; M. Graßhof in J. Schwarze, Art. 66 EG para. 27; on the predecessors, see also S. Leible, in R. Streinz (ed.), *EUV/AEUV*, Art. 81 AEUV paras. 29–32; S. Leible/A. Staudinger, 'Art. 65 EGV im System der EG-Kompetenzen', *EuLF* 2000, 222, 229 sq.

7   Regulation (EC) No 593/2008 of the European Parliament and of the Council of 17 June 2008 on the law applicable to contractual obligations (Rome I), OJ 2008 L 177/6.

8   On the development from the Rome Convention to the Rome I-Regulation, see Commission, Green paper on the conversion of the Rome Convention of 1980 on the law applicable to contractual obligations into a Community instrument and its modernisation, COM(2002) 654 final; Commission, Proposal for a Regulation of the European Parliament and the Council on the law applicable to contractual obligations (Rome I), COM(2005) 650 final. See also A. Junker, in F. Ferrari/S. Leible (eds.), *Ein neues Internationales Vertragsrecht für Europa*, 111–127 (discussing the proposal of 2005); D. Martiny, 'Europäisches Internationales Vertragsrecht vor der Reform', *ZEuP* 2003, 590–618; D. Martiny, in F. J. Säcker/R. Rixecker (eds.), *Münchener Kommentar zum BGB*, Vorbemerkung zu Art. 1 Rom I-VO paras. 12 sqq.; Max-Planck-Institute for Foreign Private and Private International Law, 'Comments on the European Commission's Green Paper on the conversion of the Rome Convention of 1980 on the law applicable to contractual obligations into a Community instrument and its modernization', *RabelsZ* 68 (2004), 1–118. For a brief survey of the new Regulation, see M. Bogdan, *NIPR* 2009, 407–410.

9   On the intertemporal scope W. Wurmnest, *EuZA* 2009, 481, 486.

10   Regulation (EC) No 864/2007 of the European Parliament and of the Council of 11 July 2007 on the law applicable to non-contractual obligations (Rome II), OJ 2007 L 199/40. For an introduction, see e.g. A. Junker, 'Das Internationale Privatrecht der Straßenverkehrsunfälle nach der Rom II-Verordnung', *JZ* 2008, 169–178; O. L. Knöfel, 'Internationales Arbeitskampfrecht nach der Rom II-Verordnung', *EuZA* 2008, 228–250; S. Leible/M. Lehmann, 'Die neue EG-Verordnung über das auf außervertragliche Schuldverhältnisse anzuwendende Recht ("Rom II")', *RIW* 2007, 721–735.

11   On the legislative history in more detail A. Junker, 'Die Rom II-Verordnung: Neues Internationales Deliktsrecht auf europäischer Grundlage', *NJW* 2007, 3675, 3676; O. L. Knöfel, *EuZA* 2008, 228, 232–234; R. Plender/M. Wilderspin, *The European Private International Law of Obligations*, paras. 17.001–17.005.

---

11 January 2009. It applies to events giving rise to damage which occur after the date of its entry into force, Articles 31 sq. Rome II-Regulation.[12] While the Rome I-Regulation also covers the **international private law of employment contracts**, the Rome II-Regulation merely contains a specific provision which is relevant to labour law, namely concerning damages caused by industrial action.

5.   The following discussion focuses exclusively upon the Rome I- and Rome II-Regulations, leaving aside the 1980 Rome Convention (even though publications related to the Convention will be referred to given its genetic connection with the Rome I-Regulation). However, it should be noted that the Rome Convention not only remained in force until the Rome I-Regulation became effective. Pursuant to a Protocol to the Amsterdam Treaty[13] **Denmark** does not participate in the measures of Title IV TFEU (cf. Article 69 TFEU) and these include the Rome I-Convention. **Ireland** and the **United Kingdom** had originally made similar reservations but have subsequently agreed to accept the Rome I-Regulation.[14]

6.   In the area of employment law, the law on posting of employees – with its foundations in the freedom of services (§3 paras. 55–77) and the Posting of Workers Directive (§6 below) – is part of the **regulatory context** of the Rome I- and Rome II-Regulations.[15] As *lex specialis,* the Posting of Workers Directive also takes precedence over the Rome I-Regulation (see para. 9 below). Starting from the general rule that the employment relation of a posted employee will normally be governed by the law of his home country, the Court has accepted that the host Member State may extend its employee protection laws to him and the Posting of Workers Directives makes that mandatory for a 'core' of employee protection. The bottom line is that employee protection laws of the host Member State have the effect of 'overriding mandatory provisions' within the meaning of Article 9 Rome I-Regulation (see paras. 28 sqq. below).[16]

---

[12]   On the temporal scope J. v. Hein, 'Europäisches Internationales Deliktsrecht nach der Rom II-Verordnung', *ZEuP* 2009, 6, 10–12; P. Winkler v. Mohrenfels/A. Block, in *EAS,* B 3000 paras. 13–16; R. Plender/M. Wilderspin, *The European Private International Law of Obligations,* paras. 17.015–17.020.

[13]   Article 2 of the Protocol on the Position of Denmark in the Annex to the Treaty on European Union and to the Treaty Establishing the European Community, OJ 1997 C 341/101 and – in the version oft he Lisbon Treaty – OJ 2006/C 321 E/01.

[14]   See the Commission Opinion on the request from the United Kingdom to accept Regulation (EC) No 593/2008 of the European Parliament and the Council of 17 June 2008 on the law applicable to contractual obligations (ROME I), COM(2008) 730 final; Articles 2, 3 and 4 of the Protocol annexed to the Treaty on European Union and to the Treaty establishing the European Community – Protocol on the position of Denmark, OJ 2006 C 321 E/201 and the Protocol on the Position of the United Kingdom and of Ireland, OJ 2006 C 321 E/198.

[15]   On other aspects of the regulatory context in private international law S. Krebber, *Comp. Lab. L. & Pol'y J.* 21 (2000), 501–542.

[16]   See e.g. S. Krebber, *IPRax* 2001, 22–28 (criticising the incoherence of the PWD with regard to private international employment law).

II.   PRIVATE INTERNATIONAL LAW OF EMPLOYMENT CONTRACTS IN THE ROME I-REGULATION

1.   *Scope of Application and Principles of Interpretation*

a)   Scope of Application

7.   The Rome I-Regulation applies to contractual obligations with connections to the laws of several states, Article 1(1) Rome I-Regulation.[17] To establish a connection to another state, the pure choice of foreign law under Article 3(3) Rome I-Regulation is sufficient (even if all other elements relevant to the situation at the time of the choice are located in one and the same other country). As a *loi uniforme* the Regulation covers any contractual relationship which is to be considered by a Court of one of the Member States, irrespective of whether it is related to the EU and to the Member States and irrespective of whether it leads to the application of the law of one of the Member States.[18] The law specified by the Rome I-Regulation should also be applied where it is the law of a third country, Article 2 Rome I Regulation.

b)   Interpretation

8.   The 1980 Rome Convention specifically prescribed that in the interpretation and application of its provisions, 'regard shall be had to their international character and to the desirability of achieving uniformity in their interpretation and application', Article 18 Rome Convention.[19] This is a general rule of interpretation for uniform laws;[20] A similar provision is contained in Article 7(1) Convention on the International Sale of Goods for example. In contrast, the Rome I-Regulation does not specifically require uniform interpretation. Such provision was dispensable, given that the autonomous interpretation of EU law is a generally recognised maxim of interpretation (see §1 para. 60 above).

---

[17]   In more detail D. Martiny, in F. J. Säcker/R. Rixecker (eds.), *Münchener Kommentar zum BGB*, Art. 1 Rom I-VO paras. 5 sqq. The exceptions of Article 1(2)-(4) Rome I-Regulation are of limited relevance only for employment law; see also para. 32 below on capacity.

[18]   D. Martiny, in F. J. Säcker/R. Rixecker (eds.), *Münchener Kommentar zum BGB*, Art. 2 Rom I-VO para. 3; W. Wurmnest, *EuZA* 2009, 481, 483.

[19]   See also ECJ Case C-29/10 *Koelzsch* 15 March 2011 para. 32 (and para 33 on the systematic interpretation with the Brussels Convention).

[20]   J. Kropholler, *Internationales Einheitsrecht* (Tübingen: Mohr Siebeck, 1975), 240–243; see also U.P. Gruber, *Methoden des internationalen Einheitsrechts* (Tübingen: Mohr Siebeck, 2004), 69 and 80–86.

c)   Special Conflict Rules

9.   The Rome I-Regulation contains what we may consider the 'general' rules of private international contract law of the EU. There are, however, a number of 'special' rules contained in particular regulations and directives. The Regulation does not affect these, Article 23 Rome I-Regulation. As *leges speciales* they take precedence over the rules of the Regulation. In the area of employment law, this is of practical relevance only for the Posting of Workers Directive (see para. 6 above and §6 below), see Recital 34 Preamble Rome I-Regulation.[21]

2.   Determination of Applicable Law

a)   Foundations and Principles

10.   There are two countervailing principles at the heart of the private international law of employment contracts of the Rome I-Regulation, the principle of **freedom of choice** as a sub-principle of private autonomy and freedom of contract versus the **protection of the employee** as the 'weaker party'.[22] Freedom of choice is the fundamental principle which underpins the Regulation.[23] With regard to its 'classical' scope of application in international private law of contracts, the Regulation is almost 'universally recognised',[24] and it is no accident that this rule is located at the head of the rules in Article 3.[25] Even where, as is the case with regard to employment contracts, countervailing principles come into play, freedom of choice is not completely side-lined but it is rather only adjusted proportionately, that is, to the extent necessary. Freedom of choice also applies with regard to employment contracts and is merely supplemented by the **principle of favourability**, which gives room for mandatory

---

[21]   See D. Martiny, in F. J. Säcker/R. Rixecker (eds.), *Münchener Kommentar zum BGB*, Art. 8 Rom I-VO paras. 116 sqq.

[22]   D. Martiny, in F. J. Säcker/R. Rixecker (eds.), *Münchener Kommentar zum BGB*, Art. 8 Rom I-VO para. 1; R. Plender/M. Wilderspin, *The European Private International Law of Obligations,* para. 11.001.

[23]   C. v. Bar, *Internationales Privatrecht II*, paras. 412–415; R. Birk, *RdA* 1989, 201–207; F. Gamillscheg, *ZfA* 1983, 307, 317–327; A. Junker, *IPRax* 1993, 1–10; M. Giuliano/P. Lagarde, OJ 1980, C 282/1, 15; C. Morse, 'The EEC Convention on the Law Applicable to Contractual Obligations', *YEL* 2 (1982) 107, 116 ('cardinal principle'); see also ECJ Case C-381/98 *Ingmar* v. *Leonard* [2000] ECR I-9305 para. 15; Case 318/81 *Commission* v. *CO.DE.MI.* [1985] ECR 3693 paras. 20 sq.; AG Slynn, Opinion in Case 318/81 *Commission* v. *CO.DE.MI.* [1985] ECR 3693, 3697 sq. See also para 45 below.

[24]   A. Junker, *IPRax* 1993, 1–4; J. Kropholler, *Internationales Privatrecht*, §52 II and §40; s.a. ECJ Case C-381/98 *Ingmar* v. *Leonard* [2000] ECR I-9305 para. 15.

[25]   On the Rome Convention, see M. Giuliano/P. Lagarde, OJ 1980, C 282/1, 15 sq.; B. v. Hoffmann, 'Inländische Sachnormen mit zwingendem internationalem Anwendungsbereich', *IPRax* 1989, 261, 262; S. Grundmann, 'Europäisches Vertragsrechtsübereinkommen, EWG-Vertrag und §12 AGBG', *IPRax* 1992, 1 sq.

---

legal employment protection provisions that would have been applicable in the absence of a choice (see c) below).[26] Furthermore, 'overriding mandatory provisions' and the *ordre public* will prevail over a choice of law (see d) below). The scope of the applicable law will be discussed at the end (see f) below). First, though, we have to determine when the specific rules on 'individual employment contracts' apply.

b)   Employment Contracts and Employment Relationships

11.   The provision of Article 8 Rome I-Regulation applies to 'individual employment contracts'; this conforms with the terminology used by the Brussels I-Regulation (see §7 para. 7 below).[27] The restriction to **individual** contracts indicates that collective agreements (on a sectorial level or a company level) are not covered.[28] Unlike (the German version of) the Rome Convention, the Rome I-Regulation does not specifically refer to 'employment relationships'. This should not be construed as a change in substance though.[29] It already follows from Article 12(1)(e) Rome I-Regulation that invalid employment contracts which have been executed will still be covered.[30]

12.   The central test for the scope of application of Article 8 Rome I-Regulation is the characterisation as *employment* contract with an *employee*. For private international law purposes, the qualification of a legal relationship as an employment contract does not depend upon a national conception, but must rather follow an autonomous definition (see para. 8 above).[31] The Court's jurisprudence on the concept of a worker in Article 45 TFEU can serve as a starting point.[32] **Employee** then is a person who, for a certain period of time,

---

[26]   Critically e.g. S. Krebber, *Festschrift für Birk,* 477–494 (proposing a further reaching application of the law of the relevant labour market *de lege ferenda* but also *de lege lata* as internationally mandatory norms). On other mechanisms of protection, see the discussion of A. Junker, *Internationales Arbeitsrecht im Konzern,* 87–96.

[27]   On the qualification of the termination agreement see O. L. Knöfel, *ZfA* 2006, 397–434 (independent qualification under Articles 3 sq. Rome I-Regulation).

[28]   A. Junker, *RIW* 2006, 401, 402; M. Giuliano/P. Lagarde, OJ 1980 C 282/1, 25; W. Wurmnest, *EuZA* 2009, 481, 485. See also R. Plender/M. Wilderspin, *The European Private International Law of Obligations,* paras. 11.003–11.009; P. Winkler v. Mohrenfels/A. Block, in *EAS,* B 3000 para. 49.

[29]   W. Wurmnest, *EuZA* 2009, 481, 484.

[30]   A. Junker, *RIW* 2006, 401, 402; D. Martiny, in F. J. Säcker/R. Rixecker (eds.), *Münchener Kommentar zum BGB,* Art. 8 Rom I-VO para. 21; P. Winkler v. Mohrenfels/A. Block, in *EAS,* B 3000 para. 50. See already M. Giuliano/P. Lagarde, OJ 1980 C 282/1, 25; F. Gamillscheg, *ZfA* 1983, 307, 332.

[31]   P. Winkler v. Mohrenfels/A. Block, in *EAS,* B 3000 para. 52 with further references; critically R. Plender/M. Wilderspin, *The European Private International Law of Obligations,* paras. 11.010–11.024 (favouring the definition of the *lex causae;* – 'bootstrap-solution').

[32]   H. Oetker, in R. Richardi et al. (eds.), *Münchener Handbuch zum Arbeitsrecht,* §11 para. 8; U. Magnus, 'Englisches Kündigungsrecht auf deutschem Schiff – Probleme des

performs services for and under the direction of another person in return for which he receives remuneration (see §3 paras. 9–12 above).

c) Determination of the Applicable Law in Detail

aa) Objective Determination of the Applicable Law[33]

13. Where the parties did not make a choice of law, the applicable law must be determined by reference to objective criteria, Article 8(2)-(4) Rome I-Regulation.[34] The three paragraphs stand in **hierarchical order**.[35] Article 8(2) contains the general rule: the applicable law is the law of the country in which the employee habitually carries out his work. This provision is to be broadly construed. Article 8(3), in contrast, provides for a subsidiary criterion which only applies *where the law cannot be determined pursuant to paragraph 2:* the law of the country where the place of business which engages the employee is situated. This provision is to be narrowly construed. Finally, Article 8(4) contains an exception; see para. 19 below.

14. The primary criterion for the determination is the place *in which* the employee *habitually carries out his work,* failing that the place *from which* he habitually carries out his work: the **habitual place of work** (*lex loci laboris*).[36] In order to demarcate the scope of the provisions of paragraphs (2) and (3), the Court, in *Voogsgeerd,* has distinguished between 'factors which characterise the actual employment' and 'factors which relate to the conclusion of the contract': 'the factors characterising the employment relationship ... namely the place of actual employment, the place where the employee received instructions or to where he must report before discharging his tasks, are relevant for the determination of the law applicable to that employment relationship in that, when those places are located in the same country, the court seized may take the

---

internationalen Seearbeitsrechts', *IPRax* 1991, 382, 384; A. Junker, *Internationales Arbeitsrecht im Konzern,* 169–173; P. Winkler v. Mohrenfels/A. Block, in *EAS,* B 3000 para. 59; B. Rudisch, in D. Czernich/H. Heiss (eds.), *Kommentar zum Römischen Übereinkommen über das auf vertragliche Schuldverhältnisse anzuwendende Recht* (Vienna: Orac, 1999), Art. 6 EVÜ paras. 6–7; C. v. Bar/P. Mankowski, *Internationales Privatrecht I,* §7 para. 172; D. Martiny, in C. Reithmann/D. Martiny (eds.), *Internationales Vertragsrecht,* para. 1872; J. Kropholler, *Internationales Privatrecht,* §52 VI 1; A. Junker, *NZA* 2005, 199, 204; D. Martiny, in F. J. Säcker/R. Rixecker (eds.), *Münchener Kommentar zum BGB,* Art. 8 Rom I-VO para. 17. Critically O. L. Knöfel, *RdA* 2006, 269, 271 sq.

[33] P. Winkler v. Mohrenfels/A. Block, in *EAS,* B 3000 paras. 96–104 (discussing different categories of cases).

[34] On the system A. Junker, *Festschrift für Heldrich,* 719–722.

[35] ECJ Case C-384/10 *Voogsgeerd* 15 December 2011 paras. 34 sq. (on the Rome Convention).

[36] A. Junker, *Festschrift für Heldrich,* 726 sq.; id., *RIW* 2006, 401, 406. Cf. with regard to the corresponding terminus in Article 5(1)(1) Brussels-Convention ECJ Case C-383/ 95 *Rutten* v. *Cross Medical* [1997] ECR I-57; Case C-125/92 *Mulox* [1993] ECR I-4075.

view that the situation falls within the scope of Article 6(2)(a) of the Rome Convention [now: Article 8(2) Rome I-Regulation]'.[37] Such factors 'cannot also be relevant to the application of Article 6(2)(b) of the Rome Convention [now Article 8(3) Rome I-Regulation'.[38] This interpretation allows for a formal delineation of the two paragraphs and thus contributes to legal certainty.

15.   The second variant of Article 8(2) – the place *'from which'* the employee habitually carries out his work, sometimes referred to as the 'base rule' or the 'flight attendant-clause', allows the – hitherto controversial -[39] attribution of employment relations of 'personnel working on board aircraft, if there is a fixed base from which work is organised and where the personnel perform other obligations in relation to the employer (registration, safety checks)'.[40] As the Court indicates in a decision concerning the Rome Convention, the second variant may also apply in the case of a lorry driver in the international transport sector.[41]

16.   The fact that an employee is **temporarily posted abroad** does not change his *habitual* place of work, Article 8(2) sent. 2 Rome I-Regulation. Recital 36 of the Preamble provides: 'As regards individual employment contracts, work carried out in another country should be regarded as temporary if the employee is expected to resume working in the country of origin after carrying out his tasks abroad. The conclusion of a new contract of employment with the original employer or an employer belonging to the same group of companies as the original employer should not preclude the employee from being regarded as carrying out his work in another country temporarily.'[42] The decisive factor is

---

37   ECJ Case C-384/10 *Voogsgeerd* 15 December 2011 para. 40.
38   ECJ Case C-384/10 *Voogsgeerd* 15 December 2011 para. 44.
39   M. Franzen, *IPRax* 2003, 239–243; A. Junker, *Festschrift für Heldrich*, 727–732; id., *Festschrift 50 Jahre Bundesarbeitsgericht*, 1207–1210; D. Martiny, in F. J. Säcker/R. Rixecker (eds.), *Münchener Kommentar zum BGB*, Art. 8 Rom I-VO para. 52; G. Thüsing, *NZA* 2003, 1303, 1305 sq. See also W. Wurmnest, *EuZA* 2009, 481, 495–497.
40   Commission, Proposal for a Regulation of the European Parliament and the Council on the Law Applicable to Contractual Obligations (Rome I) of 15 May 2005, COM(2005) 650 final, 4.2 comments on Article 6 (p. 8). O. L. Knöfel, *RdA* 2006, 269, 274. See also P. Mankowski, in F. Ferrari/S. Leible (eds.), *Rome I Regulation*, 171, 177–181. On the lack of a special rule for seamen see ibid., 199 sq. and W. Wurmnest, *EuZA* 2009, 481, 497 sq.
41   ECJ Case C-29/10 *Koelzsch* 15 March 2011 para. 46. Judging the case under the Rome Convention, the Court advocates a broad interpretation of the criterion 'country in which the employee habitually carries out his work' (Article 6(2)(a) Rome Convention): the country 'in which or from which, in the light of all the factors which characterise that activity, the employee performs the greater part of his obligations towards his employer'. Approving case note by P. Mankowski/O. L. Knöfel, *EuZA* 2011, 521–536. Further ECJ Case C-384/10 *Voogsgeerd* 15 December 2011 paras. 37 sqq.
42   Cf. on this latter case the Court's judgement in ECJ Case C-437/00 *Pugliese* [2003] ECR I-3573 (on the Brussels I-Regulation; though with a different reasoning). See also O. L. Knöfel, *RdA* 2006, 269, 274.

thus not time alone but rather the intention of the parties: whether or not there is an intention to return or to recall the employee (*animus retrahendi*).[43]

17. Given that the habitual place of work may change over the course of the employment relationship if an employee is sent to work in another country on a more than temporary basis, so too, may the **applicable law change**.[44] This potential to change the applicable law also follows from the fact that the employment relationship may develop a closer connection with another country over time (para. 19) and from the possibility of a subsequent choice of law.

18. Where the applicable law cannot be determined on the basis of the habitual place of work, the law of the country where the **place of business**[45] **through which the employee was engaged**[46] is located applies, Article 8(3) Rome I-Regulation. The provision may apply to field installation workers, flight attendants or aircraft pilots who do not perform their work at a single 'habitual' place or who perform their work in an area outside state territories (provided there is no place from which they habitually perform their work, para. 14).[47] It is debated whether 'engaged' refers to the conclusion of the employment contract or to integration within the workforce.[48] While the wording hints at the former, teleological considerations of employee protection point towards the latter, given that the place of the conclusion of the contract can easily be manipulated, thus *de facto* giving the employer a chance to unilaterally determine the applicable law. On the basis of these considerations, it has been suggested that the 'place of business…' 'should thus denote a place of business which did not merely act as a mail-box, but was actively engaged in the engagement of the employee'.[49] The Court's decision in *Voogsgeerd* now suggests that the 'engagement' can only be determined with a view to the elements and circumstances of the actual

---

[43] A. Junker, *RIW* 2006, 401, 407; M. Schlachter, in S. Leible (ed.), *Das Grünbuch zum Internationalen Vertragsrecht*, 157 sq.; W. Wurmnest, *EuZA* 2009, 481, 492 sq. See also P. Winkler v. Mohrenfels/A. Block, in *EAS*, B 3000 paras. 103 sq.; H. Oetker, in R. Richardi et al. (eds.), *Münchener Handbuch zum Arbeitsrecht*, §11 para. 31.

[44] P. Winkler v. Mohrenfels/A. Block, in *EAS*, B 3000 para. 61.

[45] On the interpretation of the 'place of business', see ECJ Case C-384/10 *Voogsgeerd* 15 December 2011 paras. 53 sqq.

[46] See in more detail M. Schlachter, in R. Müller-Glöge/U. Preis/I. Schmidt (eds.), *Erfurter Kommentar*, Art. 3, 8, 9 Rom I-VO para. 14.

[47] O. L. Knöfel, *RdA* 2006, 269, 276 sq.; W. Wurmnest, *EuZA* 2009, 481, 495–497. The qualification of this latter case is, however, controversial, given that it could be attributed to the state where the aircraft is registered; see the references in note 39 above.

[48] Conclusion of the contract: M. Schlachter, *NZA* 2000, 57, 70; P. Winkler v. Mohrenfels/A. Block, in *EAS*, B 3000 para. 110; integration into the workforce: A. Junker, *Festschrift 50 Jahre Bundesarbeitsgericht*, 1204; D. Martiny, in F. J. Säcker/R. Rixecker (eds.), *Münchener Kommentar zum BGB*, Art. 8 Rom I-VO para. 65; P. Mankowski, in F. Ferrari/S. Leible (eds.), *Rome I Regulation*, 171, 193–196; W. Wurmnest, *EuZA* 2009, 481, 491.

[49] R. Plender/M. Wilderspin, *The European Private International Law of Obligations*, para. 11.053.

conclusion of the contract. In contrast, the integration of the employee into the workforce is a factor related to the actual employment relationship and can thus not be considered in the interpretation of Article 8(3);[50] see para. 18 above.

19. The two basic rules of paragraphs 2 and 3 of Article 8 are conceived as conclusive alternatives: either there is a habitual place of work (then paragraph 2 applies) or not (then paragraph 3 applies), *tertium non datur*.[51] Article 8(4) Rome I-Regulation thus does not contain a catch-all provision but merely an **exception clause** which allows for a deviation from the basic rules. 'Where it appears from the circumstances as a whole that the contract is **more closely connected** with a country other than that indicated in paragraphs 2 or 3, the law of that other country shall apply.' The relevant circumstances may include the nationality of the parties, the language of the contract or the currency in which the remuneration is to be paid.[52]

bb) CHOICE OF LAW

i. Choice of Law as a Rule

20. Private autonomy is the basic principle that underlies freedom of contract in substantive law and freedom of choice in private international contract law. Choice of law enables the parties to choose a (national) legal system as a whole – and to exclude the application of another legal system as a whole, including its mandatory provisions. In the Rome I-Regulation a choice of law is the primary factor for the determination of the applicable law, Article 3(1) sent. 1 and Article 8(1) sent. 1 Rome I-Regulation. This is true not only for contracts in general, but also for employment contracts in particular. 'Choice of law' is a separate contract between the parties, to be distinguished theoretically from the substantive employment contract (cf. Article 10(1) Rome I-Regulation), even though both agreements may be made at the same time and stipulated in a single document.

21. Choice of law can be made **explicitly or implicitly**. An implicit choice must, however, 'be … clearly demonstrated by the terms of the contract or the circumstances of the case', Article 3(1) Rome I-Regulation.[53] This wording has been amplified in comparison with the Rome Convention (which merely required that the choice be 'demonstrated with reasonable certainty'). It emphasises that an implicit choice still requires a *(subjective) choice*, even though it may be determined using *objective factors*. Rather than the 'objective interests'

---

50 ECJ Case C-384/10 *Voogsgeerd* 15 December 2011 paras. 34 sqq.
51 A. Junker, *Festschrift für Heldrich*, 720 sq.; R. Plender/M. Wilderspin, *The European Private International Law of Obligations*, para. 11.053.
52 A. Junker, *Festschrift 50 Jahre Bundesarbeitsgericht*, 1204 sq. See also P. Winkler v. Mohrenfels/A. Block, in *EAS*, B 3000 para. 113.
53 C. v. Bar, *Internationales Privatrecht II*, para. 468; K. Riesenhuber, *DB* 2005, 1571–1576.

of the parties or a 'well understood' intent,[54] it is their subjective intention and an actual choice that need to be ascertained.[55] There are a number of 'indications', though, that play a prominent role in court practice:

- an agreement of jurisdiction (see Recital 12 of the Preamble; in employment contracts, such agreement is, however, admissible only under the narrow conditions of Article 21 Brussels I-Regulation; §7 para. 18);
- reference to (and integration of the contract into) a national law or a national collective agreement;
- the language of the contract; and
- the place in which the contract was concluded and the nationality of the parties.[56]

22. A choice of law may be made **initially** (before or together with the conclusion of the substantive contract) or **subsequently**,[57] it may also be changed later, even in court proceedings (for example by a behaviour that indicates a choice of law), Article 3(2) sent. 1 Rome I-Regulation (but see with regard to formal validity sent. 2!). It may relate to the **contract as a whole, or separable parts** thereof (so-called *dépeçage*), Article 3(2) sent. 3 Rome I-Regulation.[58] Such a choice for parts of the contract is of little practical importance in employment law[59], but it may be advisable with regard to pension agreements or a non-compete provision.[60]

23. The parties may also make a choice of law where the employment relationship and all elements relevant to it are located in a country other than the country whose law has been chosen at the time when the choice was made. In this case, however, the choice cannot derogate from the (internally) mandatory provisions of the law of that country, Article 3(3) Rome I-Regulation;[61] otherwise national laws – here, of employment protection – could all too easily be circumvented. Similarly, Article 3(4) Rome I-Regulation protects mandatory provisions of or determined by EU law against circumvention.[62]

---

[54] M. Giuliano/P. Lagarde, OJ 1980 C 282/1, 17; M. Franzen, *IPRax* 1999, 278, 279.

[55] A. Junker, *RIW* 2006, 401, 403.

[56] C. v. Bar, *Internationales Privatrecht II*, paras. 469–472.

[57] *Bundesgerichtshof* (Federal Court of Justice, BGH), *IPRspr.* 1996, No. 33.

[58] Details are controversial; see e.g. S. Krebber, *Comp. Lab. L. & Pol'y J.* 21 (2000), 501, 523 sq.; R. Plender/M. Wilderspin, *The European Private International Law of Obligations*, paras. 6.044–6.054; M. Schlachter, in R. Müller-Glöge/U. Preis/I. Schmidt (eds.), *Erfurter Kommentar*, Art. 3, 8, 9 Rom I-VO para. 4 with further references.

[59] A. Junker, *NZA* 2005, 199, 204.

[60] R. Birk, *RdA* 1989, 201, 205 sq.; O. L. Knöfel, *RdA* 2006, 269, 277.

[61] M. Schlachter, *NZA* 2000, 57, 62; P. Winkler v. Mohrenfels/A. Block, in *EAS,* B 3000 para. 67.

[62] This conforms with the rationale of ECJ Case C-318/98 *Ingmar* v. *Leonard* [2000] ECR I-9305 (on the Sales Agent Directive).

ii.   More favourable Provisions of Employee Protection

24.   Freedom of choice is however limited with regard to employment contracts. It may not result in depriving the employee of the protection afforded to him by internally mandatory provisions under the law that would have been applicable in the absence of a choice of law (see paras. 13–16 above), Article 8(1) sent. 2 Rome I-Regulation. This area is not open to the parties' choice or, in other words, their choice of law will be 'corrected'.[63] Put another way: Mandatory provisions of the law applicable in the absence of a choice of law that are specifically designed for employee protection will be applied irrespective of the choice of law to the extent that they are **more favourable** for the employee than those of the law chosen by the parties.[64] The general law against unfair dismissal, rules for the protection of disabled people or mothers have been regarded as such mandatory provisions of employee protection.[65]

25.   The standards of protection which apply in the absence of a choice of law pursuant to Article 8(2)-(4) Rome I-Regulation are considered as **minimum standards** which apply subject to a **comparison of favourability**.[66] 'If the law applicable pursuant to [paragraphs 2–4] grants employees protection which is greater than that resulting from the law chosen by the parties, the result is not that the choice of this law becomes completely without effect. On the contrary, in this case the law which was chosen continues in principle to be applicable. In so far as the provisions of the law applicable pursuant to paragraph 2 give employees better protection than the chosen law, for example by giving a longer period of notice, these provisions set the provisions of the chosen law aside and are applicable in their place.'[67] Whether a provision is more favourable (provides better protection) is to be determined concretely with regard to individual issues of employment (functional approach).[68] The courts thus neither make a comprehensive comparison of the legal systems as a whole nor a specific comparison with regard to individual norms ('picking raisins') but rather compare groups of norms on a given issue.[69]

---

[63]   D. Martiny, in F. J. Säcker/R. Rixecker (eds.), *Münchener Kommentar zum BGB*, Art. 8 Rom I-VO paras. 32 sq.

[64]   R. Birk, *RdA* 1989, 201, 205 sq.; A. Junker, *IPRax* 1989, 69, 72; D. Martiny, *ZEuP* 2003, 590, 605 sq.

[65]   D. Martiny, in F. J. Säcker/R. Rixecker (eds.), *Münchener Kommentar zum BGB*, Art. 8 Rom I-VO para. 37; P. Winkler v. Mohrenfels/A. Block, in *EAS*, B 3000 para. 77.

[66]   A. Junker, *IPRax* 1989, 69, 71 sq.; Bundesarbeitsgericht (Federal Labour Court, BAG), *BAGE* 63, 17, 24 sq.; BAG, *IPRax* 1994, 123, 126.

[67]   M. Giuliano/P. Lagarde, OJ 1980 C 282/1, 25.

[68]   D. Martiny, in F. J. Säcker/R. Rixecker (eds.), *Münchener Kommentar zum BGB*, Art. 8 Rom I-VO paras. 40 sq.; S. Krebber, *Comp. Lab. L. & Pol'y J.* 21 (2000), 501, 528 sq.; M. Schlachter, *NZA* 2000, 57, 61. See also H. Oetker, in R. Richardi et al. (eds.), *Münchener Handbuch zum Arbeitsrecht*, §11 paras. 25 sq.

[69]   R. Birk, *RdA* 1989, 201, 206; P. Winkler v. Mohrenfels/A. Block, in *EAS*, B 3000 paras. 72 sq.

26. While the purpose of this favourability test is plausible, the instrument can prove to be problematic in practice. The law chosen by the parties will be supplemented by other rules. Given that the favourability test requires difficult value judgements, it is hard to determine the applicable law in advance. This results in legal uncertainty. In addition, supplementing the chosen law with rules that are extraneous to it leads to a 'virtual' regime that neither of the parties wanted and which may be imbalanced.[70]

d) Overriding Mandatory Provisions and Public Policy (*ordre public*)

aa) Overriding Mandatory Provisions

27. In the application of the law thus determined (either by the parties' choice or, in the absence thereof, objectively), mandatory provisions of another country may be given effect pursuant to Article 9 Rome I-Regulation. As in the case of the favourability rule of Article 8(1) (paras. 21 sqq. above), here too mandatory provisions are applied. While the more favourable provisions referred to in Article 8(1) sent. 2 are internally or *nationally mandatory* provisions, Article 9 Rome I-Regulation concerns **internationally mandatory provisions**. Mandatory provisions of this nature do not only prevail over a choice of law but also prevail over the objectively determined applicable law.

28. The purpose of this restriction to freedom of choice, and to the scope of the objective determination of the applicable law, can be inferred from the definition of Article 9(1) Rome I-Regulation. 'Overriding mandatory provisions are provisions the respect for which is regarded as crucial by a country for safeguarding its public interests, such as its political, social or economic organisation, to such an extent that they are applicable to any situation falling within their scope, irrespective of the law otherwise applicable to the contract under this Regulation.' Yet the details as to how to determine overriding mandatory rules are rather unclear.[71] Indications – but not necessary requirements – for the internationally mandatory character of a norm can be found in their public law nature or the fact that a provision is enforced by criminal law.[72] The objective of regulating economic or social policy as opposed to the purpose of merely balancing private interests may be an argument in

---

[70] For a critical assessment e.g. R. Birk, *RdA* 1989, 201 (206) ('Legal certainty is severely impaired and the outcome of judicial decisions can hardly be predicted at all.' – my translation).

[71] R. Birk, *RdA* 1989, 201, 207; A. Junker, *Festschrift 50 Jahre Bundesarbeitsgericht*, 1210–1214; M. Schlachter, in R. Müller-Glöge/U. Preis/I. Schmidt (eds.), *Erfurter Kommentar*, Art. 3, 8, 9 Rom I-VO paras. 19 sqq.; A. Junker, *Internationales Arbeitsrecht im Konzern*, 286–292; J. Kropholler, *Internationales Privatrecht*, §52 IX.

[72] Rightly critically S. Krebber, *Comp. Lab. L. & Pol'y J.* 21 (2000), 501, 533 sq.

favour of a mandatory nature;[73] as can a provision's purpose to protect an institution rather than only groups or individuals.[74] With regard to employment law in particular, the enforcement by a public agency or a provision relating to public law may indicate an internationally mandatory nature.[75] Irrespective of controversies in regard to the fundamentals, a core of overriding mandatory provisions is widely recognised. This encompasses regulatory norms such as export bans, foreign exchange regulations and provisions regarding the protection of the market and competition.[76] In the area of *employment law* courts have – rather extensively – considered provisions on sick pay, the protection of pregnant workers and women[77] or provisions on mass dismissal as overriding mandatory norms.[78] In contrast, the general law against unfair dismissal is not internationally mandatory, given that it merely balances the interests of the contract parties.[79] A right to reduce working hours to part-time is also concerned with private interests of the parties and promotes public interests only as a by-product.[80] On minimum wage legislation, see the Posting of Workers Directive (§6 below).[81]

29. The applicable law, first, does not restrict the application of overriding mandatory provisions of the **law of the forum**, Article 9(2) Rome I-Regulation. Overriding mandatory provisions of the **country where the contractual obligations** are to be or have been **performed** *may be given* effect in so far as they render performance of the contract unlawful, Article 9(3) Rome I-Regulation. This latter case thus requires a discretionary decision of the national court.[82]

---

73   A. Junker, *IPRax* 2000, 65, 70 sq.; J. Kropholler, *Internationales Privatrecht*, §52 IX 1; D. Martiny, in F. J. Säcker/R. Rixecker (eds.), *Münchener Kommentar zum BGB*, Art. 9 Rom I-VO para. 13; *BAGE* 63, 17, 30–32; BAG, *IPRax* 1994, 123, 128; critically E. Jayme, 'Zum internationalen Geltungswillen der europäischen Regeln über den Handelsvertreterausgleich', *IPRax* 2001, 190, 191.

74   J. Basedow, 'Wirtschaftskollisionsrecht', *RabelsZ* 52 (1988) 8, 27–31.

75   A. Junker, *Festschrift 50 Jahre Bundesarbeitsgericht*, 1213 sq.

76   J. Kropholler, *Internationales Privatrecht*, §52 IX 2, 3; D. Martiny, in F. J. Säcker/R. Rixecker (eds.), *Münchener Kommentar zum BGB*, Art. 9 Rom I-VO paras. 58 sqq.

77   BAG, *BAGE* 100, 130.

78   M. Schlachter, in R. Müller-Glöge/U. Preis/I. Schmidt (eds.), *Erfurter Kommentar*, Art. 3, 8, 9 Rom I-VO paras. 21 sq.; partly critically M. Franzen, *IPRax* 2003, 239, 242 sq.; A. Junker, *Internationales Arbeitsrecht im Konzern*, 283–293; id., 'Der Teilzeitanspruch des deutschen Arbeitsrechts: Keine Eingriffsnorm nach europäischem IPR', *EuZA* 2009, 88, 94 sq.; P. Winkler v. Mohrenfels/A. Block, in *EAS*, B 3000 paras. 151–153. See also D. Martiny, 'Europäisches Internationales Vertragsrecht in Erwartung der Rom I-Verordnung', *ZEuP* 2008, 97, 105 sq.

79   D. Martiny, in F. J. Säcker/R. Rixecker (eds.), *Münchener Kommentar zum BGB*, Art. 8 Rom I-VO paras. 104 sqq., 115; differently S. Krebber, *Internationales Privatrecht des Kündigungsschutzes bei Arbeitsverhältnissen*, 304–316.

80   BAG, *NZA* 2008, 761; in this respect approvingly A. Junker, *EuZA* 2009, 88, 93–96.

81   On minimum wages established in the individual case on the basis of the general contract law provisions on immorality, see M. Franzen, *ZESAR* 2011, 101–107.

82   See also W.-H. Roth, *EWS* 2011, 314, 326 sq. (advocating an interpretation in conformity with the duty to solidarity of Article 4(3) TEU).

As paragraph 3 sent. 2 explains, '[i]n considering whether to give effect to those provisions, regard shall be had to their nature and purpose and to the consequences of their application or non-application.'

bb)   Reservation of Public Policy (*ordre public*)

30.   The *ordre public*-derogation in Article 21 Rome I-Regulation leaves room to take into consideration the fundamental values of the law of the forum. The application of the law specified pursuant to Articles 3 and 8 Rome I-Regulation may be refused (only!) 'if such application is manifestly incompatible with the public policy (*ordre public*) of the forum'. Article 8(1) and 9 Rome I-Regulation leave little room for this *proviso* in the area of employment law, though.

e)   Exclusion of Renvoi

31.   The applicable law pursuant to the provisions discussed above would, without any qualification, also include the respective country's private international law. However, if the private international law follows different principles to the Rome I-Regulation, it could refer the case back or refer to the law of a third country (*renvoi*), leading to a potentially endless line of references. This would be incompatible with the requirement of legal certainty and would render the enforcement of the law exceedingly difficult for the parties concerned. Where the applicable law is determined by a choice of law, a *renvoi* would thwart freedom of choice. Article 20 Rome I-Regulation therefore provides that the application of the law specified by the Regulation, as a rule, refers to the law in force in the country without its rules of private international law.

f)   Scope of the Applicable Law

aa)   General Rule

32.   Pursuant to the non-exhaustive list contained in Article 12(1) Rome I-Regulation, the law applicable to an employment contract pursuant to Articles 3 and 8 governs the interpretation of the contract, performance of the obligations arising from it, consequences of a breach, ways of extinguishing obligations, prescription and limitation of actions as well as the consequences of the contract being void.

bb)   Consent and Material Validity, Form, Capacity

33.   Existence and material validity of the (employment) contract are determined by the law which would govern it if the contract or term were valid,

Article 10(1) Rome I-Regulation (exception in paragraph 2). The same is true with regard to the agreement on the choice of law, Article 3(5) Rome I-Regulation.

34. Regarding the **form** it will, in any case, be sufficient if the agreement satisfies the formal requirement of the law which governs the contract in substance, Article 11(1) and (2) Rome I-Regulation. Where the parties are in the same country at the time that the contract was concluded, is the contract will be formally valid if it fulfils the formal requirements of that country; where the parties are in different countries at the time of conclusion, it is formally valid if it satisfies the law of either of the countries.[83] The rules are of little practical relevance with regard to employment contracts since they are not normally subject to formal requirements. The provision of Article 11(3) Rome I-Regulation on **unilateral acts** such as notice of termination is more problematic. A unilateral act relating to a contract is formally valid if it satisfies the formal requirements of (1) the law which governs or would govern the contract in substance, or (2) the law of the country where the act was done, or (3) the law of the country where the person by whom it was done had his habitual residence at that time. The latter alternatives could open the door for a circumvention of requirements as to contractual form (e.g. for notice of termination).[84]

35. Issues of **capacity** are in principle not governed by the Regulation, Article 1(2)(a) and (f) Rome I-Regulation. Article 13 contains a narrowly limited exception to that rule, based upon the protection of good faith.[85] It concerns the case where the parties, when forming the contract, were in the same country and had capacity under the law of that country but (one of them) did not have capacity under the law of another country. In that situation, lack of capacity under the other country's law cannot be invoked unless the other party to the contract knew or should have known (negligence) of that incapacity at the time of conclusion of the contract.

cc)   EVIDENCE

36. Issues of evidence are governed by the law of the forum (*lex fori*). The law governing the contract under the Regulation is, however, applicable with regard to *presumptions* and the *burden of proof*, Article 18(1) Rome I-Regulation.

---

[83]   On the problematic application in employment cases A. Junker, *IPRax* 1993, 1 (5) ('principle of unfavourability' – my translation).

[84]   Textbook example: In order to evade formalities required by French law, the French employer terminates the contract of a Germany employee working in France by making a phone call from Germany. On such cases (with different remedial proposals) S. Krebber, *Comp. Lab. L. & Pol'y J.* 21 (2000), 501, 529 sq.; M. Schlachter, *NZA* 2000, 57, 63.

[85]   See e.g. M. Giuliano/P. Lagarde, OJ 1980 C 282/1, 34.

III. PRIVATE INTERNATIONAL LAW OF TORTS IN INDUSTRIAL ACTION

Bibliography:

F. Dorssement/A. van Hoeke, 'Collective action in Labour Conflicts under the Rome II Regulation (Part I)', *ELLJ* 2 (2011), 48–75; J. v. Hein, 'Europäisches Internationales Deliktsrecht nach der Rom II-Verordnung', *ZEuP* 2009, 6–33; C. W. Hergenröder, *Der Arbeitskampf mit Auslandsberührung* (Berlin: Duncker & Humblot, 1987); C. W. Hergenröder, 'Internationales Arbeitskampfrecht', in H. Konzen et al. (eds.), *Festschrift für Rolf Birk* (Tübingen: Mohr Siebeck, 2008), 197–215; A. Junker, 'Die Rom II-Verordnung: Neues Internationales Deliktsrecht auf europäischer Grundlage', *NJW* 2007, 3675–3682; T. Kadner Graziano, 'Das auf außervertragliche Schuldverhältnisse anzuwendende Recht nach der Rom II-Verordnung', *RabelsZ* 73 (2009), 1–77; O. L. Knöfel, 'Internationales Arbeitskampfrecht nach der Rom II-Verordnung', *EuZA* 2008, 228–250; S. Leible/M. Lehmann, 'Die neue EG-Verordnung über das auf außervertragliche Schuldverhältnisse anzuwendende Recht ("Rom II")', *RIW* 2007, 721–735; R. Plender/M. Wilderspin, *The European Private International Law of Obligations*, 3rd edn. (London: Sweet & Maxwell, 2009), chapter 16 and 23; G. Wagner, 'Die neue Rom II-Verordnung', *IPRax* 2008, 1–17; see also the bibliography before para. 1 above.

1. Introduction

37. Private international law of industrial action is increasingly important in an increasingly internationally connected economic and employment environment. Industrial action in one country can be directed against, or affect, a company in another country where, for example, dock workers refuse to unload a foreign ship.[86] The Rome II-Regulation does not comprehensively regulate private international law of industrial disputes[87] but merely covers a rather small and isolated segment: tort liability of employers, employees and their organisations for damages resulting from collective action.[88] The provision was only introduced into the Regulation at a fairly late stage in the legislative process, upon a proposal of the European Parliament.[89] 'The platitudinous proposition of the provision is not so much owed to an actual regulatory need but rather to the wish of interested circles in the European Parliament to get their foot in the door to collective labour law.'[90]

---

[86]   O. L. Knöfel, *EuZA* 2008, 228 sq.

[87]   See A. Junker, in F. J. Säcker/R. Rixecker (eds.), *Münchener Kommentar zum BGB*, Art. 9 Rom II-VO paras. 11 sqq.; id., *Internationales Arbeitsrecht im Konzern*, 465–507; C.W. Hergenröder, *Der Arbeitskampf mit Auslandsberührung*.

[88]   O. L. Knöfel, *EuZA* 2008, 228, 234. See in general A. Junker, in F. J. Säcker/R. Rixecker (eds.), *Münchener Kommentar zum BGB*, Art. 9 Rom II-VO para. 11.

[89]   In detail on the legislative history O. L. Knöfel, *EuZA* 2008, 228, 232–234; F. Dorssement/A. van Hoeke, *ELLJ* 2 (2011), 48, 49 sqq.; R. Plender/M. Wilderspin, *The European Private International Law of Obligations*, paras. 23.001–23.005.

[90]   A. Junker, *NJW* 2007, 3675, 3680 – my translation.

38. As a matter of **competence**, the provision of Article 9 should not be questioned despite the exclusions contained in Article 153(5) TFEU which encompass collective action (strike, lock-out). This is also true irrespective of the standpoint submitted above (§4 para. 8) pursuant to which the reservation of competence applies not only to legislation based upon Article 153, but also to legislation based upon other competences of the Treaty.[91] The Rome II-Regulation merely regulates the applicable law and not the law of collective action as such (see Recital 28 of the Preamble). However, the limitation placed upon the Union's competences in this field should still be kept in when interpreting the provision.

2. The Law Applicable to Liability for Damages caused by Industrial Action

a) Scope of Application

39. The Rome II-Regulation applies to **non-contractual obligations** in civil and commercial matters with a connection to the law of different Member States, Article 1(1).[92] Non-contractual obligations result from torts (including *culpa in contrahendo*), unjustified enrichment and *negotiorum gestio,* (cf. Article 2(2) Rome II-Regulation). The Regulation is universally applicable, meaning that the law specified by the Regulation is applicable irrespective of whether or not it is the law of a Member State, Article 3 Rome II-Regulation.

b) General Rule for Torts: Law of the Country where Damage Occurred

40. Pursuant to the general rule of Article 4(1) Rome II-Regulation, the law of the country where the damage occurred (*locus damni*) applies to non-contractual obligations arising from tort, irrespective of where the underlying event or indirect consequences occur.[93] The 'place of the consequences' is decisive rather than the 'place of the action'. The rationale behind this rule is that it better protects the victim.

c) Special Rule for Torts Caused by an Industrial Action: Law of the Country where Action Occurred

41. The conflicts rule for the liability of workers, employers or their organisations for damages caused by an industrial action (pending or carried out) is different. Pursuant to Article 9 Rome II-Regulation, the law of the place where the action is to be or has been taken applies: the *lex loci delicti commissi*. The consideration

---

[91] To the same effect A. Junker, *NJW* 2007, 3675, 3680.
[92] In more detail S. Leible/M. Lehmann, *RIW* 2007, 721, 722–724.
[93] See in more detail J. v. Hein, *ZEuP* 2009, 6, 16 sq.; T. Kadner Graziano, *RabelsZ* 73 (2009), 1, 13–19; S. Leible/M. Lehmann, *RIW* 2007, 721, 724–727; R. Plender/M. Wilderspin, *The European Private International Law of Obligations*, paras. 18.007–18.040.

behind this exception is that injunctive proceedings (see Article 15(d) Rome II-Regulation; para. 44 below) play a prominent role in this area. Prevention is more important than compensation. For these purposes, the law of the place where the action is intended to be taken is more appropriate given that injunctive relief will often be sought in the courts of this country for which their own national law is more easily accessible. The parties will usually look at the law applicable at the place of action as a measure for their behaviour (see also Recital 27 Rome II-Regulation).[94] Another argument in favour of the law of the country where the action is intended to be or has been taken is the fact that it relates to – or may depend upon – the private international law of industrial action.[95] Collective action which is lawful under the law applicable to industrial action should not be subjected to an additional, potentially disparate, control of lawfulness.[96]

42. The Regulation does not determine what constitutes **industrial action**; instead the term refers to the national laws of the Member States, (Recital 27 Rome II-Regulation).[97] This is partly due to the disparity between national laws on industrial action. It is also due to the limitation in the Union's competences (para. 38 above) as the provision could otherwise have repercussions on the substantive law of industrial action.

d) Exceptions

43. There are a number of exceptions to the general rule that the law of the country where the tortious act occurred applies.

aa) COMMON HABITUAL RESIDENCE OF THE TORTFEASOR AND THE VICTIM

44. The general rule of Article 9 Rome II-Regulation only applies 'without prejudice to Article 4(2)'.[98] Where the (alleged) tortfeasor and the (perceived) victim have a common habitual residence at the time when the damage occurs, the law of this country applies (*lex domicilii communis*). In such cases, the law of the country of common habitual residence appears to be more appropriate and, conversely, the law where the tortious act occurred appears to be rather 'accidental'.[99]

---

[94] O. L. Knöfel, *EuZA* 2008, 228, 235 sq.; A. Junker, in F. J. Säcker/R. Rixecker (eds.), *Münchener Kommentar zum BGB*, Art. 9 Rom II-VO paras. 2 sq.

[95] A. Junker, in F. J. Säcker/R. Rixecker (eds.), *Münchener Kommentar zum BGB*, Art. 9 Rom II-VO para. 3.

[96] T. Kadner Graziano, *RabelsZ* 73 (2009), 1, 58 sq.

[97] Thus also (if critically) S. Leible/M. Lehmann, *RIW* 2007, 721, 731. Differently F. Dorssement/A. van Hoeke, *ELLJ* 2 (2011), 48, 63 sqq.; R. Plender/M. Wilderspin, *The European Private International Law of Obligations*, paras. 23.008 sq. (favouring an autonomous interpretation).

[98] See in detail T. Kadner Graziano, *RabelsZ* 73 (2009), 1, 18 sq.

[99] Cf. A. Junker, in F. J. Säcker/R. Rixecker (eds.), *Münchener Kommentar zum BGB*, Art. 9 Rom II-VO para. 30.

bb) Choice of Law

45. The parties may also choose the applicable law in respect of the private international law of torts.[100] With regard to damages caused by industrial action, this would perhaps only be practical in the case provided for in Article 14(1)(a) Rome II-Regulation, which allows for a choice of law after the event giving rise to damage occurred. The parties may choose the law explicitly or implicitly. In the latter case, however, the choice must be 'demonstrated with reasonable certainty by the circumstances of the case' (note that the wording differs from that of Article 3(1) Rome I-Regulation; see para. 21 above).

cc) Ordre public-Reservation

46. Finally, there is also an *ordre public*-derogation in the private international law of torts. The application of a provision of the law of any country specified by the Regulation may be refused (only) if such application is manifestly incompatible with the public policy of the forum, Article 26 Rome II-Regulation.

e) Scope of the Applicable Law

47. The applicable law covers tort law, which is given a comprehensive meaning, (see in detail Article 15 Rome II-Regulation). This includes the basis for liability (violation of a protected right or legally protected interest, causation, imputation of liability, fault and vicarious liability) as well as exclusions or restrictions of liability. It also covers issues of damages and their calculation, injunctive relief and remedial action. The burden of proof is also determined by the applicable law, Article 22 Rome II-Regulation.

f) Implications for Issues of the Employment Contract?

48. Article 9 Rome II-Regulation only directly determines the law applicable to torts caused by industrial action. Industrial action may also affect the employment contract, though, e.g. an employee's right to remuneration. Here, too, the question of the applicable law arises: should these issues be determined by the law that, pursuant to Articles 3 and 8 Rome I-Regulation, governs the employment contract in general or rather, as in Article 9 Rome II-Regulation, the law of the country where the industrial action occurred? Scholars argue in favour of the latter solution, given the inherent connection of the contract law questions with those of the legality of industrial action.[101]

---

[100] See in detail J. v. Hein, *ZEuP* 2009, 6, 19–23; T. Kadner Graziano, *RabelsZ* 73 (2009), 1, 5–13.

[101] H. Oetker, in R. Richardi et al. (eds.), *Münchener Handbuch zum Arbeitsrecht*, §11 para. 127; See already R. Birk, *RabelsZ* 48 (1982), 384, 398; C. W. Hergenröder, *Der Arbeitskampf mit Auslandsberührung* (Berlin: Duncker & Humblot, 1987), 306 sqq.; A. Junker, *Internationales Arbeitsrecht im Konzern*, 491–493.

§6. THE POSTING OF WORKERS DIRECTIVE

CONTENT

Bibliography:

C. Barnard, '"British Jobs for British Workers": The Lindsey Oil Refinery Dispute and the Future of Local Labour Clauses in an Integrated EU Market', *ILJ* 38 (2009), 245–277; F. Bayreuther, 'Anmerkung zu EuGH v. 24.1.2002 – Rs. C-164/99 *Portugaia Construções,* Slg. 2002, I-787', *BB* 2006, 627–628; D. Beisiegel/W. Mosbacher/E. Lepante, 'Vergleich des deutschen Arbeitnehmerentsendegesetzes mit seinem französischen Pendant', *JZ* 1996, 668–670; R. Birk, 'Entsende-Richtlinie und Konzern', *ZIAS* 1995, 481–488; B. Boemke, 'EU-Osterweiterung und grenzüberschreitende Arbeitnehmerüberlassung', *BB* 2005,

266–272; B. Borgmann, 'Kollisionsrechtliche Aspekte des Arbeitnehmer-Entsendegesetzes', *IPRax* 1996, 315–320; B. Cornelissen, 'Die Entsendung von Arbeitnehmern innerhalb der Europäischen Gemeinschaft und die soziale Sicherheit', *RdA* 1996, 329–330; J. Cremers/J. E. Dølvic/G. Bosch, 'Posting of workers in the single market: attempts to prevent social dumping and regime competition in the EU', *IRJ* 38 (2007), 524–541; T. v. Danwitz, 'Das neugefasste Arbeitnehmer-Entsendegesetz auf dem Prüfstand: Europa- und verfassungsrechtliche Schranken einer Neuorientierung im Arbeitsrecht', *RdA* 1999, 322–327; T. v. Danwitz, 'Die Rechtsprechung des EuGH zum Entsenderecht – Bausteine für eine Wirtschafts- und Sozialverfassung der EU', *EuZW* 2002, 237–244; W. Däubler, 'Der Richtlinienvorschlag zur Entsendung von Arbeitnehmern – ein Mittel zur Abwehr von sozialem Dumping?', *EuZW* 1993, 370–374; W. Däubler, 'Die Entsende-Richtlinie und ihre Umsetzung in das deutsche Recht', *EuZW* 1997, 613–618; W. Däubler, 'Posted Workers and Freedom to Supply Services', *ILJ* 27 (1998), 264–268; P. Davies, 'Posted Workers – Single Market or Protection of National Labour Law Systems?', *CMLR* 34 (1997), 571–602; P. Davies, 'The Posted Workers Directive and the EC Treaty', *ILJ* 31 (2002), 298–306; O. Deinert, 'Arbeitnehmerentsendung im Rahmen der Erbringung von Dienstleistungen innerhalb der Europäischen Union – Rechtsprobleme der Sonderanknüpfung eines "harten Kerns" arbeitsrechtlicher Vorschriften des Arbeitsortes', *RdA* 1996, 339–352; Editorial, 'The Auf Wiedersehen Directive', *E.L. Rev.* 20 (1995), 29–30; E. Eichenhofer, 'Arbeitsbedingungen bei Entsendung von Arbeitnehmern', *ZIAS* 1996, 55–82; A. Feuerborn, 'Grenzüberschreitender Einsatz von Fremdfirmenpersonal', in H. Oetker/U. Preis (eds.), *Europäisches Arbeits- und Sozialrecht, EAS, part B – Systematische Darstellungen*, loose-leaf (Heidelberg: Forkel, last update: August 2003), B 2500; A. Feuerborn, 'Erstreckung der Normwirkung tarifvertraglicher Regelungen auf ausländische Arbeitgeber', *SAE* 2004, 138–144; M. Franzen, 'Arbeitskollisionsrecht und sekundäres Gemeinschaftsrecht – Die EG-Entsende-Richtlinie', *ZEuP* 1997, 1055–1074; M. Franzen, 'Gleicher Lohn für gleiche Arbeit am gleichen Ort'? – Die Entsendung von Arbeitnehmern aus EU-Staaten nach Deutschland', *DZWIR* 1996, 89–100; M. Franzen, 'Kurzzeitige Arbeitnehmerentsendung und Dienstleistungsfreiheit', *IPRax* 2002, 186–199; A. R. Ganesh, 'Appointing Foxes to Guard Henhouses: The European Posted Workers' Directive', *Colum.J.Eur.L* 15 (2008), 123–142; L. Gerken/M. Löwisch/V. Rieble, 'Der Entwurf eines Arbeitnehmer-Entsendegesetzes in ökonomischer und rechtlicher Sicht', *BB* 1995, 2370–2375; B. Gutiérrez-Solar Calvo, 'Die Entsendung von Arbeitnehmern nach Spanien', *RdA* 2001, 350–353; P. Hanau, *Rechtsgutachten zur Rechtsstellung über die Grenzen entsandter und verliehener Arbeitnehmer in der EG* (Tübingen: Mohr-Siebeck, 1992); P. Hanau, 'Der Vorschlag für eine Richtlinie des Rates der Europäischen Gemeinschaft über die Entsendung von Arbeitnehmern im Rahmen der Erbringung von Dienstleistungen aus deutscher Sicht', in R. Blanpain/M. Weiss (eds.), *The Changing Face of Labour Law and Industrial Relations – Liber amicorum for Clyde W. Summers* (Baden-Baden: Nomos, 1993), 194–215; P. Hanau, 'Das Arbeitnehmer-Entsendegesetz', *NJW* 1996, 1369–1373; P. Hanau, 'Lohnunterbietung ("Sozialdumping") durch Europarecht', in O. Due/M. Lutter/J. Schwarze (eds.), *Festschrift für Ulrich Everling* (Baden-Baden: Nomos, 1995), 415–431; F. A. Hayek, *The Road to Serfdom – Text and Documents – The Definitive Edition* (Chicago: The University of Chicago Press, 2007); A. Junker, 'Arbeitnehmerentsendung aus deutscher und europäischer Sicht', *JZ* 2005, 481–488; A. Junker/J. Wichmann, 'Das Arbeitnehmer-Entsendegesetz – doch ein Verstoß gegen Europäisches Recht?', *NZA* 1996, 505–512; C. Kilpatrick, 'Laval's Regulatory Conondrum:

Collective Standard-Setting and the Court's New Approach to Posted Workers', *E.L. Rev.* 34 (2009), 844–865; E. Kocher, 'Mindestlöhne und Tarifautonomie – Festlegung allgemeiner Mindestentgelte durch Verbindlicherklärung nach AEntG?', *NZA* 2007, 600–604; F. Koenigs, 'Lohngleichheit am Bau? – Zu einem Arbeitnehmer-Entsendegesetz', *DB* 1995, 1710–1711; F. Koenigs, 'Rechtsfragen des Arbeitnehmer-Entsendegesetzes und der EG-Entsenderichtlinie', *DB* 1997, 225–231; E. Kolehmainen, 'The Directive Concerning the posting of Workers: Synchronization of the Functions of National Legal Systems', *Comp. Lab. L. & Pol'y J.* 20 (1998), 71–104; M. Körner, 'EU-Dienstleistungsrichtlinie und Arbeitsrecht', *NZA* 2007, 233–238; M. Kort, 'Die Bedeutung der europarechtlichen Grundfreiheiten für die Arbeitnehmerentsendung und die Arbeitnehmerüberlassung', *NZA* 2002, 1248–1254; S. Krebber, 'Die Vereinbarkeit von Entsenderichtlinie und Arbeitnehmer-Entsendegesetz mit der Dienstleistungsfreiheit und Freizügigkeit des EGV', in C. Weber et al. (eds.), *Jahrbuch Junger Zivilrechtswissenschaftler 1997 – Europäisierung des Privatrechts – Zwischenbilanz und Perspektiven* (Stuttgart et al.: Boorberg, 1997), 129–156; S. Krebber, 'Die Bedeutung von Entsenderichtlinie und Arbeitnehmer-Entsendegesetz für das Arbeitskollisionsrecht', *IPRax* 2001, 22–28; M. Löwisch, 'Der Entwurf einer Entsende-Richtlinie der EU in rechtlicher Sicht', in K. A. Bettermann et al. (eds.), *Festschrift für Albrecht Zeuner* (Tübingen: Mohr Siebeck, 1994), 91–99; M. Pechstein/P. Kubicki, 'Dienstleistungsfreiheit im Baugewerbe für polnische Handwerker', *EuZW* 2004, 167–172; O. Philipp, 'Entsende-Richtlinie besser umsetzen', *EuZW* 2006, 708–709; S. Piffl-Pavelec, 'Entsendung von Arbeitnehmern im Rahmen der Dienstleistungsfreiheit (Richtlinien-Entwurf)', *DRdA* 1995, 292–297; R. Rebhahn, 'Entsendung von Arbeitnehmern in der EU – arbeitsrechtliche Fragen zum Gemeinschaftsrecht', *DRdA* 1999, 173–186; V. Rieble, *Arbeitsmarkt und Wettbewerb – Der Schutz von Vertrags- und Wettbewerbsfreiheit im Arbeitsrecht* (Berlin et al.: Springer, 1996); V. Rieble/J. Lessner, 'Arbeitnehmer-Entsendegesetz, Nettolohnhaftung und EG-Vertrag', *ZfA* 2002, 29–89; M. Schlachter, 'Grenzüberschreitende Dienstleistungen: Die Arbeitnehmerentsendung zwischen Dienstleistungsfreiheit und Verdrängungswettbewerb', *NZA* 2002, 1242–1248; B. Schwab, 'Das Arbeitnehmer-Entsendegesetz – Eine Zwischenbilanz', *NZA-RR* 2004, 1–6; M. Selmayr, 'Die gemeinschaftsrechtliche Entsendungsfreiheit und das deutsche Entsendegesetz', *ZfA* 1996, 615–658; R. Singer/T. C. Büsing, 'Arbeitnehmer-Entsendegesetz – Dienstleistungsfreiheit – Mindestlohn', *SAE* 2003, 35–39; B. Steck, 'Geplante Entsende-Richtlinie nach Maastricht ohne Rechtsgrundlage?', *EuZW* 1994, 140–142; B. Waas, 'Neues zur Gemeinschaftsrechtskonformität des Arbeitnehmer-Entsendegesetzes – Urteil des Europäischen Gerichtshofs vom 18.7.2007 – Kommission/Bundesrepublik Deutschland', *EuZA* 2008, 367–374; R. Wank/U. Börgmann, 'Die Einbeziehung ausländischer Arbeitnehmer in das deutsche Urlaubskassenverfahren', *NZA* 2001, 177–186; see also the references in §3 before para. 55 on the freedom to provide services.

Cases:

ECJ Joined Cases 62/81 and 63/81 *Seco* [1982] ECR 223; ECJ Case C-113/89 *Rush Portuguesa* [1990] ECR I-1417; ECJ Case C-43/93 *Vander Elst* [1994] ECR I-3803; ECJ Case C-272/94 *Guiot* [1996] ECR I-1905; ECJ Case C-369/96 *Arblade* [1999] ECR I-8453; ECJ Case C-165/98 *Mazzoleni* [2001] ECR I-2189; ECJ Joined Cases C-49/98, C-50/98, C-52/98 to C-54/98 and C-68/98 to C-71/98 *Finalarte* [2001] ECR I-7831; ECJ Case C-164/99 *Portugaia Construções* [2002] ECR I-787; ECJ Case C-60/03 *Wolff & Müller* [2004] ECR I-9553; ECJ Case C-341/02 *Commission v. Germany* [2005] ECR I-2733; ECJ Case C-244/04 *Commission v. Germany*

[2006] ECR I-885; ECJ Case C-168/04 *Commission v. Austria* [2006] ECRI-9041; ECJ Case C-490/04 *Commission v. Germany* [2007] ECR I-6095; ECJ Case C-341/05 *Laval un Partneri,* [2007] ECR I-11767; ECJ Case C-346/06 *Rüffert* [2008] ECR I-1989; ECJ Case C-319/06 *Commission v. Luxembourg* [2008] ECR I- 4323; ECJ Case C-398/09 *RANI Slovakia* [2010] ECR I-81; ECJ Case Joined Cases C-307/09 to C-309/09 *Vicoplus* 10 February 2011.

I.   ISSUES, OVERVIEW, COMPETENCE, REGULATORY CONTEXT

1.   Issues[1]

1.   After Portugal became a Member of the (then) European Communities on 1 January 1986, the Portuguese company Rush Portuguesa entered into a subcontract with a French business for the construction of a railway line in the west of France. For that purpose it brought its Portuguese employees from Portugal. However, in France, by virtue of the exclusive right conferred by the French Labour Code, only the *Office national d'immigration* may recruit nationals of third countries. After establishing that Rush Portuguesa had not complied with the requirements of the Labour Code regarding the activities of employed persons performed in France by nationals of non-member countries, the Director of the *Office national d'immigration* notified Rush Portuguesa of a decision by which he required payment of a 'special contribution' that an employer employing foreign workers in breach of the provisions of the Labour Code is liable to pay. In preliminary proceedings the Court of Justice had to examine whether it was compatible with European law to subject the exercise of freedom of services to special conditions such as the use of local personnel, the requirement of a special work permit for the service provider's employees or the payment of a fee to the national immigration office.[2] While the Court answers these questions in the negative, 'in response to the concern expressed in this connection by the French Government' the Court goes on to say in an *obiter dictum*[3]

> 'that Community law does not preclude Member States from extending their legislation, or collective labour agreements entered into by both sides of industry, to any person who is employed, even temporarily, within their territory, no matter in which country the employer is established'.[4]

---

1   For an (older) introduction, see M. Selmayr, *ZfA* 1996, 615–658.

2   ECJ Case C-113/89 *Rush Portuguesa* [1990] ECR I-1417; on the Services in the Internal Market Directive, see in more detail §3 paras. 55-77. The Treaties on the conditions of the accession of Spain and Portugal merely contained special provisions on the free movement of workers but not on the free movement of services.

3   See also P. Davies, *ILJ* 31 (2002), 298, 300: 'In *Rush Portuguesa* the Court, committing a basic error of the craft of judicial decision-making, answered a question which was not necessary for its decision'.

4   ECJ Case C-113/89 *Rush Portuguesa* [1990] ECR I-1417 para. 18; to the same effect already Joined Cases 62 and 63/81 *Seco* [1980] ECR 223 para. 14; and subsequently Case C-43/93

2. The case illustrates the posting of workers issue in the context of freedom of services (even beyond the specific circumstances of the accession). The *obiter dictum* of the Court has triggered the enactment of national posting of workers laws by many Member States[5] and ultimately also the 1996 Posting of Workers Directive (PoWD)[6] (cf. Recital 12 PoWD).[7] Where there are wage differences between the Member States of the internal market, businesses in labour-intensive sectors from low-wage countries are in a position to make (significantly) lower bids than their competitors from high-wage countries: Their employees will, in the absence of a choice of law, usually work under the conditions of the home countries, either because that is the habitual place of work (which will not be affected by a temporary posting abroad) or because this is the place of business where the employee has been engaged (see §5 paras. 13–19 above).[8] In effect, this leads to the **country of origin principle**.

3. The Posting of Workers Directive levels this competitive advantage in so far as it makes a 'hard core' of protective employment rules (Recital 13 Preamble PoWD) of the host Member State applicable to workers posted from abroad: This 'hard core' includes, in particular, minimum wage and minimum paid annual holidays. As a technical matter, the Directive in effect supplements the rules of private international law on employment contracts: An internationally mandatory character, comparable to that of the 'overriding mandatory rules' of Article 9 Rome I-Regulation (§5 paras. 24–26 above), is attributed to the respective protective rules.[9] The **principle of the place of work** prevails over the country of origin principle. As a practical result, the principle 'equal pay at the same place of work' applies.[10]

Vander Elst [1994] ECR I-3803 para. 23 (work permits); Case C-272/94 *Guiot* [1996] ECR I-1905 (loyalty stamps and bad-weather stamps).

[5]   P. *Davies, CMLR* 34 (1997), 571, 585–591; D. *Beisiegel/W. Mosbacher/E. Lepante, JZ* 1996, 668–670.

[6]   Directive 96/71/EC of the European Parliament and of the Council of 16 December 1996 concerning the posting of workers in the framework of the provision of services, OJ 1997 L 18/1.

[7]   On the legislative history, see e.g. P. Hanau, *Liber amicorum Summers*, 194–215.

[8]   See in more detail M. Schlachter, *NZA* 2002, 1242, 1243–1245; O. *Deinert, RdA* 1996, 339, 340–347. See also T. v. Danwitz, *EuZW* 2002, 237, 238; H. Konzen, 'Europäische Dienstleistungsfreiheit und nationaler Arbeitnehmerschutz', *NZA* 2002, 781 sq.; Bundesregierung, Explanation to proposal for an *Arbeitnehmer-Entsendegesetz* (German Law on Posting of Workers, AEntG), *BT-Drs.* 13/2414, S. 8. On the accession of Poland (primarily with a view to free movement of services) also M. Pechstein/P. Kubicki, *EuZW* 2004, 167–172; ECJ Joined Cases C-307/09 to C-309/09 *Vicoplus* 10 February 2011.

[9]   M. Franzen, *Privatrechtsangleichung durch die Europäische Gemeinschaft* (Berlin/New York: de Gruyter, 2010), 227 sq. On the relation of the Directive to the conflict-of-laws rules of the Rome Convention see id., *ZEuP* 1997, 1055, 1065–1070.

[10]   M. Schlachter, *NZA* 2002, 1242, 1245.

2. Policy Discussion

4. The Directive is rather controversial as a matter of policy.[11] There are only few commentators who consider it to be founded on sound economic policy.[12] The prevailing opinion criticises the Directive from a regulatory policy perspective.[13] Competitors from low-wage countries should be allowed to use their cost-advantage in competition, just as competitors from other countries may use their lead in terms of, for instance, know-how.[14] Indeed, Attorney General *Verloren van Themaat* considered this a basic principle:

> 'It is one of the fundament al features of the Common Market, which is to be attained inter alia by the freedom to provide services, that when providing services in another Member State any employer may in principle make use of the cost advantages existing in his country, including lower wage costs, under the conditions of undistorted competition which constitute another objective of the Treaty.'[15]

And there are areas where it is indeed possible and admissible to play off a low-wage advantage.[16] This is the case where, e.g., textiles are being produced in a low-wage country and exported to other Member States under the free movement of goods and its country of origin principle. It is moreover permissible in the field of services (and desirable under the concept of the internal market) for a competitor to take advantage of a wage differential with regard to services rendered in his home Member State; for example where bed linen and towels of the Berlin Hotel *Adlon* are shipped to neighbouring Poland for cleaning.

---

[11] The underlying economic issues are, of course, by no means novel; see e.g. F. A. Hayek, *The Road to Serfdom*, 226 sqq. (first published in 1944).

[12] But see W. Däubler, *EuZW* 1993, 370, 371 (avoid a 'segmentation of the labour market' and 'tensions beteween local and foreign workers' – my translations); T. v. Danwitz, *EuZW* 2002, 237–244; differentiating R. Rebhahn, *DRdA* 1999, 173, 176–180. P. *Davies, CMLR* 34 (1997), 571, 598–602 a justification of which he is not convinced himself and which proves to be unsatifsfactory; he points out that, outside the construction sector, the Directive was originally intended to apply only to postings of more than three months and this would have been easier to justify (592, 601 sq.). See also J. Cremers/J. Dølvic/G. Bosch, *IRJ* 38 (2007), 524–541 (referring to the principle of equality which, however, merely raises the question but does not give an answer).

[13] See in detail L. Gerken/M. Löwisch/V. Rieble, *BB* 1995, 2370–2375.

[14] O. *Deinert, RdA* 1996, 339, 349.

[15] Opinion of AG P. VerLoren van Themaat, Joined Cases 62/81 and 63/81 *Seco* [1982] ECR 223, 239, 244.

[16] L. Gerken/M. Löwisch/V. Rieble, *BB* 1995, 2370 ('What is specific about the construction sector is not the special need for protection but rather the fact that regulators can easily extend protection to the workers concerned, given that construction sites cannot be transferred abroad.' – my translation); F. Koenigs, *DB* 1995, 1710; M. Kort, *NZA* 2002, 1248, 1253; V. Rieble, *Arbeitsmarkt und Wettbewerb,* paras. 330 sqq. Differently R. Rebhahn, *DRdA* 1999, 173, 185 sq., arguing that special treatment of human capital could be justified with the value judgements underlying Article 45 TFEU.

5. The Directive is double-edged in respect of the interests of employees. It seems to focus upon posted workers. However, as a matter of governance, the Directive's mechanism appears ill-fitted, given that both the legislator and the social partners of the host Member State are in a conflict of interest if they set the standard of 'protection' for posted workers.[17] At first sight the Directive seems to be advantageous, given that posted workers benefit from higher minimum wages or minimum paid holidays. Yet, they will only benefit from the higher level of protection if their employer gets the job in the first place ('more rights, but no jobs' [*Michael Portillo*])[18].[19] Levelling out the labour costs substantially decreases their employer's prospects of success. As a consequence, the beneficiaries may rather be the businesses of the (prospective) host Member State and their employees – who are being protected against competitive pressure from low-wage Member States. Indeed, national laws on posting of workers have sometimes been expressly justified by reference to protecting national economy and employment, in other words by considerations of **protectionism**. To castigate low-wage offers as '**social dumping**' and an objectionable competitive practice,[20] is not a valid justification for such protectionism. 'Dumping' refers to the case where an offer is made below its standard value in the country of origin, but that is not the case where posted workers receive their customary national wage.[21]

6. However, the Court of Justice has recently come to a different position. It has justified the extension of protective rules pursuant to Article 3(1) PoWD by reference to ensuring 'fair competition' (see already §3 para. 67 above).[22] This would seem to presuppose that using a labour-cost advantage constitutes unfair competition in the internal market (even though this is perhaps only with regard to posting of workers).

3.   Conformity with EU Primary Law and Competence

7. Evaluation of the Directive under EU law is no less controversial, starting with its compatibility with the **fundamental freedoms**, and free movement of

---

17   Cf. A. R. Ganesh, *Colum.J.Eur.L.* 15 (2008), 123–142 (suggesting an amendment of the Directive so as to give posted workers 'voice' in the rule-making of the host Member State).

18   Cf. Editorial, *E.L. Rev.* 20 (1995), 129, 130.

19   V. *Rieble/J. Lessner*, ZfA 2002, 29, 69, 73 sq.

20   Thus, however W. Däubler, 'Ein Antidumping-Gesetz für die Bauwirtschaft', *DB* 1995, 726–731; differently though id., *EuZW* 1993, 370.

21   L. Gerken/M. Löwisch/V. Rieble, *BB* 1995, 2370 and 2373 sq.; P. Hanau, *Festschrift für Everling*, 416; V. Rieble, *Arbeitsmarkt und Wettbewerb*, para. 288; M. Selmayr, *ZfA* 1996, 615, 643. In substance also E. Eichenhofer, *ZIAS* 1996, 55, 62 sq. (who, however, speaks of 'social dumping' at p. 57).

22   ECJ Case C-341/05 *Laval un Partneri* [2007] ECR I-11767 paras. 74 sq.

services in particular.[23] This question is also relevant for the issue of competence. If the protective rules of the host Member State are extended to posted workers, this means that the employer must not only take the law of his home Member State into account (country of origin principle) but is additionally bound by the law of the host Member State: In providing services abroad, the employer is subject to two legal systems.[24] And the employment conditions change with every posting to another Member State. The extension of national employment law to posted workers is certainly liable to render the provision of cross-border services less attractive and thus constitutes an infringement of the freedom of services.[25] In a line of cases following *Rush Portuguesa,* the Court has, however, accepted that such infringement is justified where it is necessary (principle of proportionality) for the protection of workers (see in detail §3 para. 66 above). On the basis of this jurisprudence, it is safe to assume that the Court considers the Posting of Workers Directive to be compatible with the freedom to provide services.[26] The Court has, indeed, repeatedly interpreted the Directive without calling its compatibility with EU primary law into question.[27] It has, however, limited its effect somewhat by interpreting the Directive's provisions 'in the light' of the freedom of services, in other words in conformity with primary law.[28]

8.   The **competence** for the Directive is also debated.[29] The legislature based the Directive on the coordinating competence of (what is today) Articles 53(1) and 62 TFEU which allowed for a majority decision (against the votes of Portugal and England).[30] The legislature apparently expected that the legal certainty

---

23   See in detail S. Grundmann, *Europäisches Schuldvertragsrecht,* §3.60 paras. 7–10; S. Krebber, in C. Weber et al. (eds.), *Jahrbuch Junger Zivilrechtswissenschaftler 1997,* 129–156; V. *Rieble/J. Lessner, ZfA* 2002, 29–89. See further B. Gutiérrez-Solar Calvo, *RdA* 2001, 350–353, H. Konzen, *NZA* 2002, 781–783; M. Kort, *NZA* 2002, 1248–1254. The Court has never discussed the compatibility of the Directive or national laws on posting of workers with the free movement of *workers;* given that the posted workers do not enter into employment relationships in the host Member State, free movement of workers is not affected; E. Eichenhofer, *ZIAS* 1996, 55, 60 sq.; A. Junker, *JZ* 2005, 481, 482; S. Krebber, in C. Weber et al. (eds.), *Jahrbuch Junger Zivilrechtswissenschaftler 1997,* 129, 138–140, 149; differently L. Gerken/M. Löwisch/V. Rieble, *BB* 1995, 2370, 2372 sq.; V. *Rieble/J. Lessner, ZfA* 2002, 29, 44–47; see also R. Rebhahn, *DRdA* 1999, 173, 181 sq., 185. Cf. ECJ Case C-113/89 *Rush Portuguesa* [1990] ECR I-1417 paras. 9 sq., 13–18; Case C-43/93 *Vander Elst [1994]* ECR I-3803 para. 21.

24   This problem is only slightly ameliorated by the cooperation on information pursuant to Article 4 PoWD (see paras. 29 sq. below; see in particular Article 4(3) PoWD).

25   M. Franzen, *ZEuP* 1997, 1055, 1063, speaks of an intentional aggravation of market access.

26   To the same effect also W. Däubler, *EuZW* 1997, 613, 614.

27   To the same effect A. Junker, *JZ* 2005, 481, 488 (though with the reservation: 'with substantial strain by the Court of Justice' – my translation).

28   ECJ Case C-60/03 *Wolff & Müller* [2004] ECR I-9553 paras. 30–45; see also paras. 31 sq. below. See further Article 3(10) PoWD where the duty to implement the directive in conformity with primary law is highlighted specifically.

29   See in detail the discussion by S. Grundmann, *Europäisches Schuldvertragsrecht,* §3.60 paras. 13–18.

30   Cf. P. Hanau, *NJW* 1996, 1369, 1372 sq.

---

resulting from the legal approximation (cf. Recital 6 Preamble PoWD) would facilitate cross-border transactions.[31] Yet, with its concept of double employment standards and a number of far-reaching options for implementation, the Directive may in fact make only a limited contribution to legal certainty.[32] Critics further argue that legal certainty alone does not open the door to the Union having legislative competence.[33] Furthermore, the Directive would impede rather than facilitate cross-border trade, given that it did not lead to any approximation of substantive law but instead only to an extension of the disparity between national laws.[34] At the same time, it would not have been possible to base the Directive on the former Article 118a TEC, for this provision merely opened up a competence for the 'working environment' (§4 para. 22 above).[35] (This is different in the provision's successor in Article 153 TFEU!), Moreover, the Directive could not have been based upon Article 100 TEC (today's Article 115 TFEU) either, for this provision required unanimity.

4.   Reform Discussions

9. The Commission's report on the implementation of the directive[36] and the Court's judgements in *Laval* and *Rüffert* triggered a policy debate and reform discussion. While business organisations and most Member States do not consider reform of the Directive necessary, Unions have urged amendments, in particular with regard to effective implementation and enforcement of the Directive. On March 21, 2012, the Commission adopted a proposal for a Directive concerning the enforcement of the provision applicable to the posting of workers in the framework of the provision of services.[37] While leaving the substance of the Posting of Workers Directive untouched, the proposed directive 'aims to improve, enhance and reinforce the way in which this Directive is implemented, applied

---

[31] With a view to the degree of discretion recognised by the European Court of Justice R. Wank/U. Börgmann, *NZA* 2001, 177, 180. See also Commission, The implementation of Directive 96/71/EC in the Member States, COM(2003) 458 final, 7 sq.

[32] See also P. *Davies, CMLR* 34 (1997), 571, 592 sq.

[33] S. Grundmann, *Europäisches Schuldvertragsrecht,* §3.60 para. 15.

[34] E. Eichenhofer, *ZIAS* 1996, 55, 74 sq.; M. Franzen, *ZEuP* 1997, 1055, 1059–1061; S. Grundmann, *Europäisches Schuldvertragsrecht,* §3.60 para. 16; F. Koenigs, *DB 1997,* 225, 227–230; V. *Rieble/J. Lessner, ZfA* 2002, 29, 49 sq.; M. Selmayr, *ZfA* 1996, 615; B. Steck, *EuZW* 1994, 140–142; see also M. Löwisch, *Festschrift für Zeuner,* 91, 92. Differently W. Däubler, *EuZW* 1997, 613, 614; P. Hanau, *NJW* 1996, 1369, 1373 (relying on the 'general principle of the place of work' – my translation).

[35] E. Eichenhofer, *ZIAS* 1996, 55, 76–79; M. Franzen, *ZEuP* 1997, 1055, 1061 sq.

[36] Report from the Commission services on the implementation of Directive 96/71/EC of the European Parliament and of the Council of 16 December 1996 concerning the posting of workers in the framework of the provision of services, available (together with other material on posting of workers) at http://ec.europa.eu/social/main.jsp?catId=471&langId=en.

[37] Proposal for a Directive oft he European Parliament and oft he Council on the Enforcement of Directive 96/71/EC Concerning the Posting of Workers in the Framework of the Provision of Services, COM(2012) 131 final.

and enforced in practice across the European Union by establishing a general common framework of appropriate provisions and measures for better and more uniform implementation, application and enforcement of the Directive, including measures to prevent any circumvention or abuse of the rules'.[38] For this purpose, the proposal provides for more precise definitions, additional information requirements, rules on administrative cooperation and, with regard to subcontracting of construction works, for joint and several liability.

5. Regulatory Context

10. The regulatory context is, first, determined by the freedom to provide services as interpreted in the Court's jurisprudence on posted workers (§3 para. 64). As a conflict of laws rule, the Directive supplements the private international law on employment contracts pursuant to the Rome I-Regulation (§5 paras. 7–36 above). There is no further secondary legislation on posted workers, apart from a special rule in the Written Statement Directive (§12 paras. 26–29). The Services in the Internal Market Directive (see §3 paras. 75–77 above) explicitly does not affect labour law (Article 1(6) SIMD) and is subsidiary to the Posting of Workers Directive (Article 3(1)(a) SIMD).[39] With regard to third-country nationals, in 2010 the Commission proposed a directive on intra-corporate transfers.[40] However, this proposal is mainly concerned with issues of entry and residence in the EU Member States and family reunion and only touches upon the issue of employment conditions in this context (see Article 5 of the proposal).

II. SCOPE OF APPLICATION

1. Personal Scope of Application

11. The **personal** scope of application covers undertakings established in a Member State, Article 1(1) PoWD. With regard to undertakings from third countries, the Directive provides for a minimum standard as they may not be treated more favourably than those established in a Member State, Article 1(4) PoWD;[41] they should not enjoy any competitive advantage.[42] Seagoing personnel of merchant navies are excluded, Article 1(2) PoWD.

---

[38]   COM(2012) 131 final sub 3.1.
[39]   See e.g. M. Körner, *NZA* 2007, 233, 236 sq.
[40]   Proposal for a Directive of the European Parliament and of the Council on conditions of entry and residence of third-country nationals in the framework of an intra-corporate transfer, COM(2010), 378 final.
[41]   On the background S. Piffl-Pavelec, *DRdA* 1995, 292, 294. The provision cannot justify preferential treatment of national undertakings *vis-à-vis* undertakings from other Member States; ECJ Case C-398/09 *RANI Slovakia* [2010] ECR I-81 paras. 40–51.
[42]   See also Proposal for a Directive of the European Parliament and of the Council on conditions of entry and residence of third-country nationals in the framework of an intra-corporate

2. Substantive Scope of Application

12. In substance, the Directive – in accordance with its competence basis (para. 8 above) – applies to the posting of workers in connection with the **transnational provision of services,** Article 1(1) PoWD.[43] The Directive thus does not apply where an employee is sent abroad in the context of work provided only for his employer, e.g. where a sales agent or a truck driver works in another country.[44] The directive covers three instances of posting of workers, Article 1(3) PoWD:

(a) **posting of workers** under a contract concluded between the undertaking making the posting and the party for whom the services are intended (lit. a)),[45]
(b) posting of workers **within a group of companies** (lit. b)),[46] and
(c) posting of workers in the context of **temporary agency work** ('hiring out') (lit. c)). The Court of Justice has defined this case in more detail:

> 'the hiring-out of workers, within the meaning of Article 1(3)(c) of Directive 96/71, is a service provided for remuneration in respect of which the worker who has been hired out remains in the employ of the undertaking providing the service, no contract of employment being entered into with the user undertaking. It is characterised by the fact that the movement of the worker to the host Member State constitutes the very purpose of the provision of services effected by the undertaking providing the services and that that worker carries out his tasks under the control and direction of the user undertaking'.[47]

All cases presuppose that there is an employment relationship between the undertaking making the posting and the worker during the period of posting.[48] Where, in the context of freedom of movement for workers, an employment relationship with an employer in the *host Member State* is concluded, this will, pursuant to conflict of laws rules, normally lead to the applicability of the law of that country (Article 8 Rome I-Regulation; see §5 paras. 13–19 above).

13. The definition of a **worker** follows the law of the Member State to whose territory the worker is posted, Article 2(2) PoWD. This is in line with the general

---

transfer, COM(2010), 378 final.

[43] ECJ Joined Cases C-307/09 to C-309/09 *Vicoplus* 10 February 2011 para. 43. S. Krebber, in C. Weber et al. (eds.), *Jahrbuch Junger Zivilrechtswissenschaftler 1997,* 129, 133.
[44] P. *Davies, CMLR* 34 (1997), 571, 576.
[45] See e.g. ECJ Case C-346/06 *Rüffert* [2008] ECR I-1989 para. 19.
[46] In greater detail on the issues as they relate to groups of companies see R. Birk, *ZIAS* 1995, 481–488 (discussing the draft Directive); further M. Franzen, *ZEuP* 1997, 1055, 1057; M. Löwisch, *Festschrift für Zeuner,* 91, 93.
[47] ECJ Joined Cases C-307/09 to C-309/09 *Vicoplus* 10 February 2011 paras. 42–51.
[48] ECJ Joined Cases C-307/09 to C-309/09 *Vicoplus* 10 February 2011 para. 44.

purpose of the Directive, given that it is concerned with the extension of the protective rules of that country.[49] This may be important where the issue of disguised employment (*Scheinselbständigkeit*) is being judged differently in different Member States.[50] A *posted* worker is a worker who, for a limited period, carries out his work in the territory of a Member State other than the State in which he normally works, Article 2(1) PoWD. Adopting a literal interpretation, this would not cover a worker who has been engaged only for the time of his 'posting' abroad. This may be justified on teleological considerations if in such a case the law of the host Member State applies under Article 8(2) sent. 1 alt. 1 Rome I-Regulation, given that this is the habitual place of work.[51] If, however, the law of the home Member State applied on the basis that the contract was more closely connected to that country (Article 8(4) Rome I-Regulation, §5 para. 19),[52] there would be a gap in the Posting of Workers Directive, which may be filled by analogy or by an *argumentum a fortiori*.

III. EXTENSION OF NATIONAL TERMS AND CONDITIONS OF EMPLOYMENT TO POSTED WORKERS

1. Overview

14. Article 3 PoWD contains the Directive's central mechanism of protection. The provision first contains a mandatory extension of protective rules (Article 3(1)-(7); paras. 15–23 below) and then an optional extension of employee protection to posted workers (Article 3(8) subparagraphs 2 and 3, (9), (10) PoWD; see paras. 24–28 below). Whether national rules should be applied to posted workers depends upon two variables: the different terms and conditions concerned and the sources of those terms and conditions.[53] Where terms and conditions are regulated by collective agreements, the directive further distinguishes between the construction sector, as defined in the annex, and other sectors. As a consequence, the system of rules is rather complicated. It can be summarised in the form of a table:

---

[49]   P. Davies, *CMLR* 34 (1997), 571, 577.
[50]   On this issue, see already P. Hanau, *NJW* 1996, 1369, 1373 (submitting a solution on the basis of the definition of a 'worker' of Article 39 TEC [Art. 45 TFEU]).
[51]   S. Grundmann, *Europäisches Schuldvertragsrecht*, §3.60 para. 19.
[52]   M. Schlachter, *NZA* 2002, 1242, 1244.
[53]   Cf. ECJ Case C-346/06 *Rüffert* [2008] ECR I-1989 paras. 23–31.

Application of terms and conditions of employment to posted workers	Terms and conditions of employment covered	Sources of law (in a broad sense) covered
Mandatory*	Terms and conditions of employment pursuant to Article 3(1) PoWD a) maximum work periods and minimum rest periods b) minimum paid annual holidays c) minimum rates of pay, including overtime rates; this point does not apply to occupational retirement pension schemes d) the conditions of hiring-out of workers, in particular the supply of workers by temporary employment undertakings e) health, safety and hygiene at work f) protective measures with regard to the terms and conditions of employment of pregnant women or women who have recently given birth, of children and of young people g) equality of treatment between men and women and other provisions on non-discrimination	– law, regulation or administrative provision, Article 3(1) indent 1 PoWD – collective agreements or arbitration awards which have been declared universally applicable (see Article 3(8) PoWD) in the construction sector (as defined in the Annex PoWD), Article 3(1) indent 2 PoWD
Optional		in the absence of a system for declaring collective agreements or arbitration awards to be of universal application – collective agreements or arbitration awards which are generally applicable to all similar undertakings in the geographical area and in the profession or industry concerned and/or – collective agreements which have been concluded by the most representative employers' and labour organizations at national level and which are applied throughout national territory in the *construction sector* (as defined in the Annex), Article 3(8) subparagraphs 2 and 3 PoWD
		collective agreements or arbitration awards within the meaning of paragraph 8 and concerning *activities other than those referred to in the Annex,* Article 3(10) indent 2 PoWD
	terms and conditions of employment regarding matters other than those referred to in the first subparagraph of paragraph 1 in the case of public policy provisions, Article 3(10) indent 1 PoWD	[not defined by the directive, but in practice only law, regulation or administrative provision]
	terms and conditions which apply to temporary workers, Article 3(9) PoWD	[not defined by the directive]

* The prerequisites with regard to the terms and conditions covered (column 2) and the sources (column 3) are cumulative.

2. Mandatory Guarantee of a 'Hard Core' of Protective Rules

15. Certain employee protection rules, in particular with regard to pay and working time, must be extended to posted workers where they are more favourable than those of the applicable law (of the home state) (paras. 16–19 below). There are only a few exceptions from this general mandatory principle which apply to the following narrowly defined cases: the initial assembly of goods (Article 3(2)), a short-term posting (para. 22) and on the ground that the work to be performed is not significant (para. 23).

a) General Rule

16. The Member States *must* extend a '**hard core**' (cf. Recital 13 of the Preamble PoWD) of mandatory terms and conditions of employment to workers posted to their territory, Article 3(1) PoWD.[54] Pursuant to the exhaustive list[55] contained in subparagraph 1, these include provisions regarding

(d) working time (maximum work periods, minimum rest periods and paid holiday leave), lit. a) and b);
(e) minimum rates of pay including overtime rates, lit. c);
(f) the conditions of hiring-out of workers, lit. d);
(g) health and safety and the protection of special groups of employees (pregnant women or women who have recently given birth, children and young people), lit. g); and
(h) anti-discrimination, lit. g).

The 'hard core' thus does *not* cover important areas, most notably unfair dismissal protection, sick pay (except as provided for the specific groups of workers of lit. g)) or the law of employee involvement. This is in line with the – usually – temporary nature of posting workers (even though this is perhaps not entirely convincing in respect of the exclusion of sick pay).[56]

17. Thus the majority of terms and conditions which are covered, are already regulated by EU law, at least by way of a framework or minimum standards.[57] In many instances, this 'hard core' of protective rules will also be rendered mandatory as a matter of international law under the Rome I-Regulation (overriding mandatory rules, Article 9 Rome I-Regulation; see §5 paras. 27–29

---

[54] On aspects of social security see P. Hanau, *NJW* 1996, 1369, 1371.
[55] ECJ Case C-319/06 *Commission* v. *Luxembourg* [2008] ECR I- 4323 para. 26.
[56] E. Kolehmainen, *Comp. Lab. L. & Pol'y J.* 20 (1998), 71, 85 sq.
[57] Suffice it to refer to the Table of Contents of the present book here.

above).[58] The main exception remains **pay**.[59] It is thus with regard to minimum wages that the Directive is of the greatest practical importance. Supplementary occupational retirement pension schemes are, however, specifically excluded. What constitutes *minimum rates of pay* is to be determined by the host Member State, Article 3(1)(2) PoWD. Allowances which are specific to the posting will be considered to be part of the minimum wage, unless they are paid to reimburse expenses actually incurred on account of the posting (e.g. expenditure on travel, board and lodging), Article 3(7)(2) PoWD.[60] The Directive merely requires – and allows – that the Member States extend their *minimum* wages to posted workers; both legislative intent and the purpose of the regulation do not justify the extension of other rules on pay such as an automatic adjustment of rates of pay other than minimum wages.[61]

18. The aforementioned terms and conditions are only to be extended to posted employees where they are laid down in specific sources of law: **law**, regulation or administrative provisions or **collective agreements** or arbitration awards which have been **declared universally applicable**, although the latter only with regard to the construction sector (as defined in the Annex), Article 3(1) PoWD.[62] The rationale behind this restriction is that foreign employers should only be bound by such rules as are also binding for employers of the host Member State due to their general, abstract nature.[63] Collective agreements or arbitration awards which have been 'declared universally applicable' must be observed by all undertakings, within a particular geographical area or profession or industry, Article 3(8)(1) PoWD.[64,65] This distinction as to sources of law and sectors is important for the practical result:[66] Where, as is the case in Germany, minimum wages are not determined by law, the directive requires their extension to posted workers only with regard to the construction sector but not for other services such as private security services;[67] the regulation of such cases is left to the Member States (see paras. 24–28 below).

---

58   S. Krebber, in C. Weber et al. (eds.), *Jahrbuch Junger Zivilrechtswissenschaftler 1997*, 129, 134; id., *IPRax* 2001, 22, 26.

59   Cf. ECJ Case C-244/04 *Commission* v. *Germany* [2006] ECR I-885 para. 61; Case C-60/03 *Wolff & Müller* [2004] ECR I-9553 para. 28.

60   ECJ Case C-341/02 *Commission* v. *Germany* [2005] ECR I-2733: insufficient implementation because allowances and supplements not been taken into account as constituent components of minimum pay.

61   ECJ Case C-319/06 *Commission* v. *Luxembourg* [2008] ECR I- 4323 paras. 47–55.

62   Article 3(10) indent 2 PoWD leaves it to the Member States to include other sectors as well.

63   A. Feuerborn, in *EAS*, B 2500 para. 114.

64   This is, e.g., often the case in Spain due to an *erga omnes*-effect of collective agreements; see in detail B. Gutiérrez-Solar Calvo, *RdA* 2001, 350, 352.

65   Not all Member States provide for the instrument of declaring a collective agreement universally applicable; paragraphs 8 subparagraphs 2 and 3 provide for alternative solutions eligible for these Member States; see also para. 25 below.

66   See also A. Junker, *JZ* 2005, 481, 483; S. Piffl-Pavelec, *DRdA* 1995, 292, 294.

67   See the case of ECJ Case C-165/98 *Mazzoleni* [2001] ECR I-2189.

19. The rules of Article 3(1)-(6) PoWD do not prevent the application of **more favourable terms and conditions**, Article 3(7)(1) PoWD. This latter provision seems to be primarily directed at more favourable conditions of the applicable law, i.e. (normally) the law of the home state (Article 8(2) Rome I-Regulation); this interpretation fits with the exposition in subparagraph 2 regarding allowances specific to the posting. The minimum standards of the host Member State are, in other words, only extended to posted workers to the extent that they are more favourable than those of the applicable law. Article 3(7) does not allow for the extension to posted workers of protective rules that *exceed* the legislative minimum level of protection, such as may be contained in collective agreements.[68] While a central purpose of the directive is to ensure a minimum standard of protection to posted workers, it also aims to define a reliable minimum standard for the undertaking which is making the posting.[69]

b)   General and Optional Exceptions

20. There are a number of exceptions, some of which are optional for Member States, to the general rule. These exceptions can, to some extent, be explained on the basis of teleological considerations.[70] However, these exceptions only concern minimum wages and minimum paid holidays. There are no exceptions to the extension of other terms and conditions of employment, the so-called 'hard core' (Recital 14 Preamble PoWD), which includes, most notably, safety and health.

21. The provisions on minimum wages and minimum paid holidays do not apply with regard to **initial assembly and first installation** of goods, Article 3(2) PoWD. This exception is, however, narrowly construed and only applies where four further conditions are fulfilled, namely that (1) the assembly or installation is an integral part of a contract for the supply of goods and (2) necessary in order to start using the supplied goods, (3) carried out by the skilled or specialist worker of the supplier, (4) and the posting does not exceed eight days.

22. After consultation with the social partners, the Member States may provide for an exception of the extension of minimum pay to posted workers where the posting is only for a **short term** of **not more than one month**,[71] Article 3(3) PoWD. This option may, however, only be used with regard to the *posting of workers* (in the narrow sense of Article 1(3)(a) and (b)) but not with regard to *temporary agency work* (in the meaning of Article 1(3)(c)), which will often also

---

[68]   ECJ Case C-341/05 *Laval un Partneri* [2007] ECR I-11767 paras. 79 sq.; Case C-346/06 *Rüffert* [2008] ECR I-1989 paras. 32–34 with approving case-note by M. Franzen/C. Richter, *CMLR* 2010, 537–554.

[69]   To the same effect see R. Rebhahn, *DRdA* 1999, 173, 177.

[70]   For an evaluation of the exceptions, see also P. Davies, *CMLR* 34 (1997), 571, 583 sq.

[71]   On the calculation of the period, see Article 3(6) PoWD.

be short-term only. If the national law of the Member States so provides, a collective bargaining agreement which has been declared universally applicable (Article 3(3) PoWD) may return to the general rule that the minimum wage be extended to posted workers even where the posting does not exceed one month, Article 3(4) alt. 2 PoWD.

23. Finally, Member States have the option not to extend the provisions on minimum pay and minimum paid holiday to posted workers where the amount of **work to be done is not significant**, Article 3(5)(1) PoWD. As it is an extension of their own national laws, determination of the criteria for work to be considered as falling with the definition of insignificant is left to the Member States (subparagraph 2). This optional exception also only applies to posted workers and not temporary agency work as defined in Article 1(3)(c) PoWD.

3.   Optional Supplementation of Protection

24. While the extension of protective rules of the host Member States is *mandatory* cases falling within Article 3(1) PoWD (para. 16 above), Article 3(8) subparagraphs 2 and 3, (9) and (10) PoWD give the Member States an *option* to extend their national employment protection laws to posted employees.

a)   Lack of a System for Declaring Collective Agreements Universally Applicable

25. If national law does not provide for a system for declaring collective agreements or arbitration awards to be of universal application within the meaning of Article 3(8)(1) PoWD (not the case in Germany)[72] (see above para. 18),[73] these Member States[74] may apply certain collective agreements to posted workers: (a) collective agreements which are generally applicable to all similar undertakings in the geographical area and in the profession or industry concerned;[75] or (b) collective agreements which have been concluded by the most representative employers' and labour organisations at national level and which are applied throughout national territory, Article 3(8) subparagraphs 2 and 3 PoWD.[76] Again, this only applies with regard to the central rules of protection listed in Article 3(1) PoWD and, as can be inferred from the

---

[72]   See §5 Tarifvertragsgesetz (TVG, Collective Agreement Act), bilingual German-English version in S. Lingemann/R. v. Steinau-Steinrück/A. Mengel (eds.), *Employment and Labour Law in Germany*, Part II, XI. Cf. also ECJ Case C-346/06 *Rüffert* [2008] ECR I-1989 para. 28.

[73]   ECJ Case C-346/06 *Rüffert* [2008] ECR I-1989 para. 27.

[74]   Following a different view, this option is open to all Member States; thus apparently P. Davies, *CMLR* 34 (1997), 571, 580 sq.

[75]   Different from subparagraph 1 (see para. 18 above) subparagraphs 2 and 3 refer to the factual dissemination not to the legal applicability.

[76]   On this ECJ Case C-341/05 *Laval un Partneri* [2007] ECR 2007 I-11767 paras. 65–71.

systematic context with Article 3(1) and (8)(1), only with regard to the construction sector as defined in the annex.

b) Terms and Conditions for Temporary Agency Work

26. Member States may provide that placement agencies must guarantee temporary agency workers (Article 1(3)(c) PoWD) the same terms and conditions which apply to temporary workers in the Member State where the work is carried out, Article 3(9) PoWD.

c) Stricter Working Conditions on Public Policy Reasons

27. The Member States – but not the social partners –[77] may extend national protective rules to posted workers even outside the 'hard core' defined in Article 3(1) PoWD, where they qualify as public policy provisions. However, this is conditional upon those national rules applying equally to national undertakings and undertakings of other states. In substance, this takes up the *ordre public* express derogation in relation to freedom of services (Articles 62 and 52 TFEU, see §3 para. 65 above). The Member States may be granted a degree of discretion as to what constitutes 'public policy' but the limits must be determined by EU law, as otherwise the scope of protection afforded by the Directive would be at the full discretion of the Member States. The Court of Justice has interpreted the exception narrowly (as in the jurisprudence on the fundamental freedoms).[78]

d) Universally Applicable Collective Agreements in other Sectors

28. Finally, the Member States may extend to posted workers the terms and conditions of employment defined in universally applicable (Article 3(8)(1) PoWD) or equivalent (Article 3(8) subparagraphs 2 and 3) collective agreements in sectors *other* than the construction sector, Article 3(10) indent 2 PoWD.[79] Again, equal treatment of national undertakings and undertakings from other states is required.

4. *'Cooperation on Information'*

29. The practical result of the Directive is that service providers who, in a cross-border provision of services, post their workers in another Member State must comply with certain protective terms and conditions of employment of the

---

[77] ECJ Case C-341/05 *Laval un Partneri* [2007] ECR 2007 I-11767 paras. 83 sq.

[78] ECJ Case C-319/06 *Commission* v. *Luxembourg* [2008] ECR I- 4323 paras. 29–33, 48–55. On teleologcial considerations to the same effect already R. Rebhahn, *DRdA* 1999, 173, 177 sq.

[79] P. Davies, *CMLR* 34 (1997), 571, 518 sq.; critically Kilpartrick, *E.L. Rev.* 34 (2009), 844, 849.

host Member State as defined by the Directive (Article 3(1) PoWD) and as it has been implemented by the particular Member State. Merely the need to obtain the relevant information about the applicable protective rules is a considerable obstacle. The legislature was well aware of that and thus required the Member States to 'cooperate on information', Article 4 PoWD.[80] For this purpose, the Member States must provide for 'liaison offices' (paragraph 1) and the public authorities responsible for monitoring terms and conditions of employment referred to in Article 3 PoWD are required to cooperate (paragraph 2). Furthermore, information on the terms and conditions of employment within Article 3 must be made generally available (paragraph 3).[81]

30. The Court of Justice has interpreted the system of cooperation thus installed also as a limitation on other instruments of exchange of information. The requirement for the undertaking making the posting to appoint an ad hoc-representative in the host Member State thus proved to be a disproportionate infringement upon freedom of services.[82]

IV. SANCTIONS AND JUDICIAL ENFORCEMENT

31. Member States are responsible for the enforcement of the protective rules which must be extended to posted workers, Article 5 PoWD. Member States are, however, bound to observe their general implementation duties (see §1 paras. 64 sq.).[83] It is a specific requirement that the posted worker must be given the right to institute proceedings for the enforcement of the terms and conditions of employment guaranteed in Article 3 in the Member State where he was posted, Article 6 PoWD. This supplements the jurisdictions provided for in the Jurisdiction and Enforcement Regulation which would normally lead to the courts of the workers' home Member State having jurisdiction (residence, habitual place of work, place of business through which the employee was engaged; see §7 paras. 10–15 below).[84]

---

80 The requirement to translate certain employment documents into the language of the host Member State (§2(3) German Law on Posting of Workers [Arbeitnehmerentsendegesetz, AEntG], is not incompatible with the duty to cooperate; ECJ Case C-490/04 *Commission* v. *Germany* [2007] ECR I-6095 para. 78).

81 On deficiencies of the cooperation, see Commission Recommendation of 31 March 2008 on enhanced administrative cooperation in the context of the posting of workers in the framework of the provision of services, OJ 2008 C 85/1.

82 ECJ Case C-319/06 *Commission* v. *Luxembourg* [2008] ECR I- 4323 paras. 85–95.

83 As a practical matter, enforcement is of essential relevance; it appears that posted workers sometimes do not even receive the pay as agreed under the law of their home Member State; cf. P. Davies, *CMLR* 34 (1997) 571, 575.

84 M. Franzen, *ZEuP* 1997, 1055, 1071 sq. See also P. Davies, *CMLR* 34 (1997), 571, 577–579.

32. With regard to sanctions and enforcement (Article 5 PoWD), the Court has accepted that the Member States have 'a wide margin of appreciation', but has also emphasised that, they are bound to observe the fundamental freedoms, particularly freedom of services, when exercising their discretion (see §3 paras. 56–77 above).[85] On the basis of these considerations, the Court has held that a national requirement for a construction undertaking which subcontracts with another undertaking for construction works to provide liability as guarantor for the latter's obligation to pay minimum wages or contributions to a joint scheme for parties of a collective agreement, is incompatible with Article 5 PoWD, as interpreted in the light of Article 56 TFEU.[86]

V.   IMPLEMENTATION

33. German implementation of the Directive required amendment of the pre-existing German Law on Posting of Workers (*Arbeitnehmer-Entsendegesetz*, AEntG)[87].[88] In its explanatory statement to the original act, the German legislator candidly – as an English observer says, 'with its customary commitment to honesty and transparency' –[89] argued that the law was required for the protection of the national economy.[90] The Court of Justice – upon persistent preliminary references – considered the law to be compatible with the freedom to provide services, arguing that even though the subjective statement of purposes might be insufficient, it was the objective purpose of the law that mattered.[91] The Court merely objected to individual aspects of the German law where a legal or factual discrimination of service providers from other Member

---

[85]   ECJ Case C-60/03 *Wolff & Müller* [2004] ECR I-9553 para. 30.

[86]   ECJ Case C-60/03 *Wolff & Müller* [2004] ECR I-9553 paras. 31–45.

[87]   Gesetz über zwingende Arbeitsbedingungen bei grenzüberschreitenden Dienstleistungen (Arbeitnehmer-Entsendegesetz, AEntG) of 26 February 1996 (BGBl. 1996 I, 227), last amended by statute of 21 December 2007 (BGBl. 2007 I, 3140).

[88]   On this see e.g. P. Hanau, *NJW* 1996, 1369–1373; A. Feuerborn, in *EAS*, B 2500 paras. 121–133; A. Junker/J. Wichmann, *NZA* 1996, 505–512; B. Schwab, *NZA-RR* 2004, 1–6; M. Selmayr, *ZfA* 1996, 615, 637–642; B. *Borgmann, IPRax* 1996, 315–320; W. Däubler, *EuZW* 1997, 613, 616 sq. On the implementation in Spain B. Gutiérrez-Solar Calvo, *RdA* 2001, 350–353; on the implementation in the United Kingdom, see P. Davies, *ILJ* 31 (2002), 298. 299 sq. For a survey, see Commission, The implementation of Directive 96/71/EC in the Member States, COM(2003) 458 final, 7. See also J. Cremers/J. E. Dølvic/G. Bosch, *IRJ* 38 (2007), 524–541.

[89]   P. Davies, *ILJ* 31 (2002), 298, 302.

[90]   Bundesregierung, Explanation to proposal for an *Arbeitnehmer-Entsendegesetz* (German Law on Posting of Workers, AEntG), BT-Drs. 13/2414, 6 sq. A. Junker, *JZ* 2005, 481, 487: 'This justification is honest but it bears a risk.' – my translation.

[91]   ECJ Case C-60/03 *Wolff & Müller* [2004] ECR I-9553 paras. 18 sq., 38 sq.; Case C-164/99 *Portugaia Construções* [2002] ECR I-787 paras. 25 sq.; Joined Cases C-49/98, C-50/98, C-52/98 to C-54/98 and C-68/98 to C-71/98 *Finalarte* [2001] ECR I-7831 paras. 38–41. See also P. Davies, *ILJ* 31 (2002), 298, 302. See already §3 para. 67 above.

States was involved.[92] The law was reformed in 2009.[93] Its purpose is now highlighted in §1 AEntG. In addition to the construction sector seven other sectors have been included as falling within the protective scope of the Act, with the consequence that collective agreements in those sectors may, by declaring their terms universally applicable, be extended to posted workers.

---

[92]   ECJ Case C-164/99 *Portugaia Construções* [2002] ECR I-787 paras. 31–35 (and previously already A. Junker/J. Wichmann, *NZA* 1996, 505, 511 sq.); Joined Cases C-49/98, C-50/98, C-52/98 to C-54/98 and C-68/98 to C-71/98 *Finalarte* [2001] ECR 2001 I-7831 paras. 76–83. Further with regard to the calculation of minimum wage Case C-341/02 *Commission* v. *Germany* [2005] ECR I-2733.

[93]   Gesetz über zwingende Arbeitsbedingungen für grenzüberschreitend entsandte und für regelmäßig im Inland beschäftigte Arbeitnehmer und Arbeitnehmerinnen (Arbeitnehmer-Entsendegesetz – AEntG) of 20 April 2009 (BGBl. 2009 I, 799), last amendment by Article 25 Law of 20 December 2011 (BGBl. 2011 I, 2854).

§7. THE BRUSSELS I-REGULATION ON JURISDICTION AND THE RECOGNITION AND ENFORCEMENT OF JUDGMENTS

CONTENTS

Bibliography:

V. Behr, 'Internationale Zuständigkeit in Individualarbeitsrechtsstreitigkeiten im Europäischen Verfahrensrecht', in R. Krause/W. Veelken/K. Vieweg (eds.), *Recht der Wirtschaft und der Arbeit in Europa – Gedächtnisschrift für Wolfgang Blomeyer* (Berlin: Duncker & Humblot, 2004), 15–42; R. Bosse, *Probleme des europäischen Internationalen Arbeitsprozessrechts* (Frankfurt a.M. et al.: Lang, 2007); W. Däubler, 'Die internationale Zuständigkeit der deutschen Arbeitsgerichte – Neue Regeln durch die Verordnung (EG) Nr. 44/2001', *NZA* 2003, 1297–1302; M. Franzen, 'Internationale Gerichtsstandsvereinbarungen in Arbeitsverträgen zwischen EuGVÜ und autonomem internationalen Zivilprozeßrecht', *RIW* 2000, 81–88; R. Geimer, 'EuGVVO', in R. Zöller (founding ed.), *Zivilprozessordnung*, 27th edn. (Cologne: Otto Schmidt, 2009); P. Gottwald, 'EuGVVO', in T. Rauscher/P. Wax/J. Wenzel (eds.), *Münchener Kommentar zur Zivilprozessordnung*, 3rd edn. (Munich: C.H. Beck, 2008); R. Hausmann, 'Die Revision des Brüsseler Übereinkommens von 1968 – Teil I: Internationale Zuständigkeit', *EuLF* 2000/01, 40–49; B. Hess, *Europäisches Zivilprozessrecht* (Heidelberg: C.F. Müller, 2010); R. Hüßtege, 'EuGVVO', in H. Thomas/H. Putzo (eds.), *Zivilprozessordnung*, 32nd edn. (Munich: C.H. Beck, 2011); P. Jenard, Report on the Convention on jurisdiction and the enforcement of judgments in civil and commercial matters (signed at Brussels, 27 September 1968), OJ 1979 C 59/1–151; A. Junker, *Arbeitnehmereinsatz im Ausland – Anzuwendendes Recht und Internationale Zuständigkeit* (Munich: ZAAR, 2007); A. Junker, 'Die internationale Zuständigkeit deutscher Gerichte in Arbeitssachen', *ZZPInt* 3 (1998), 179–202; A. Junker, 'Gewöhnlicher Arbeitsort und vorübergehende Entsendung im Internationalen Privatrecht', in S. Lorenz et al. (eds.), *Festschrift für Andreas Heldrich* (Munich: C.H. Beck, 2005), 719–739; A. Junker, 'Internationale Zuständigkeit in Arbeitssachen nach der Brüssel I-Verordnung', in B. Bachmann et al. (eds.),

Grenzüberschreitungen – Beiträge zum Internationalen Verfahrensrecht und zur Schiedsgerichtsbarkeit – Festschrift für Peter Schlosser (Tübingen: Mohr Siebeck, 2005), 299–319; A. Junker, 'Internationale Zuständigkeit und anwendbares Recht in Arbeitssachen', *NZA* 2005, 199–205; A. Junker, 'Vom Brüsseler Übereinkommen zur Brüsseler Verordnung – Wandlungen des Internationalen Zivilprozessrechts', *RIW* 2002, 569–577; A. Junker, 'Zuständigkeit und anwendbares Recht in Arbeitssachen', *NZA* 2005, 199–205; S. Krebber, 'Gerichtsstand des Erfüllungsortes bei mehreren, aber aufeinander abgestimmten Arbeitsverhältnissen', *IPRax* 2004, 309–315; J. Kropholler, *Europäisches Zivilprozessrecht, Kommentar zu EuGVO und Lugano-Übereinkommen*, 8th edn. (Frankfurt a.M.: Recht und Wirtschaft, 2005); D. Leipold, 'Einige Bemerkungen zur Internationalen Zuständigkeit in Arbeitssachen', in R. Krause/W. Veelken/K. Vieweg (eds.), *Recht der Wirtschaft und der Arbeit in Europa – Gedächtnisschrift für Wolfgang Blomeyer* (Berlin: Duncker & Humblot, 2004), 143–164; P. Mankowski, 'Der gewöhnliche Arbeitsort im Internationalen Privat- und Prozeßrecht', *IPRax* 1999, 332–338; P. Mankowski, 'Europäisches Internationales Arbeitsprozessrecht – Weiteres zum gewöhnlichen Arbeitsort', *IPRax* 2003, 21–28; H.-W. Micklitz/P. Rott, 'Vergemeinschaftung des EuGVÜ in der Verordnung (EG) Nr. 44/2001', *EuZW* 2001, 325–334 and 2002, 15–24; T. Rauscher (ed.), *Europäisches Zivilprozess- und Kollisionsrecht (EuZPR/EuIPR) – Kommentar, volume 1: Brüssel I-VO, LugÜbk 2007* (Munich: Sellier, 2011); T. Rauscher, 'Arbeitnehmerschutz – ein Ziel des Brüsseler Übereinkommens', in R. Geimer (ed.), *Wege zur Globalisierung des Rechts – Festschrift für Rolf A. Schütze* (Munich: C.H. Beck 1999), 695–710; G. Thüsing, 'Rechtsfragen grenzüberschreitender Arbeitsverhältnisse – Grundlagen und Neuigkeiten im Internationalen Arbeitsrecht', *NZA* 2003, 1303–1312.

Cases (still on the Brussels Convention):
ECJ Case 14/76 *De Bloos* v. *Bouyer* [1976] ECR 1497; ECJ Case 25/79 *Sanicentral* v. *Collin* [1979] ECR 3423; ECJ Case 133/81 *Ivenel* v. *Schwab* [1982] ECR 1891; ECJ Case 266/85 *Shenavai* [1987] ECR 239; ECJ Case 32/88 *Six Constructions* [1989] ECR 341; ECJ Case C-125/92 *Mulox IBC* [1993] ECR I-4075; ECJ Case C-383/95 *Rutten* [1997] ECR I-57; ECJ Case C-412/98 *Group Josi* v. *UGIC* [2000] ECR I-5925; ECJ Case C-37/00 *Weber* [2002] ECR I-2013; ECJ Case C-437/00 *Pugliese* [2003] ECR I-3573; ECJ Case C-462/06 *Laboratoires Glaxosmithkline* [2008] ECR I-3965.

I.   INTRODUCTION

1.   In addition to the employee protection afforded by the conflict of laws rules (§§5, 6 above) and the substantive protection provided by rules on formation, content and termination of employment contracts (§§8–25 below), '**jurisdictional employee protection**', through the rules on the competent courts for actions related to employment, are of central practical importance. Substantive protection is of little value if its enforcement in court is exceedingly difficult. In particular, an employee may be intimidated by the prospect of having to assert his rights in a Member State which is foreign and unfamiliar to him. And conversely, the defence of his rights may be equally difficult if he is being sued in a foreign country.

2. The **Brussels I-Regulation**[1] provides for detailed rules on 'jurisdiction and the recognition and enforcement of judgments in civil and commercial matters' (as its official title indicates). In common with the Rome I-Regulation, the Brussels I-Regulation was preceded by a convention of the Member States. Once the Union's competence had been established in Article 81(2)(a) TFEU (see §4 para. 52 above), the Convention was turned into a '**Community instrument**' in the form of a regulation (Article 288(2) TFEU). As a regulation it is directly applicable in all Member States (in effect comparable to a national law).

3. For most Member States (with the exception of Denmark, cf. Article 1(3) and Recital 21 sq. of Brussels I-Regulation), the regulation replaces the European Convention on Jurisdiction and the Enforcement of Judgements in Civil and Commercial Matters that had been adopted in Brussels in 1968 (thus also known as 'Brussels Convention').[2] Unlike the Brussels I-Regulation, the Brussels Convention had not been a Community instrument but was rather an international treaty of the Member States. It was not until the 1997 Amsterdam Treaty introduced the new competence of (what is now) Article 81(2)(a) TFEU into the (then) EC Treaty that the Convention could be converted into a Community instrument. The original Brussels Convention did not contain any specific provisions for actions arising from employment relations. However, the Court of Justice developed the jurisdiction of the place of performance of the obligation so as to serve the special needs of employment relations, construing the 'place of performance of the obligation' as the place where the characteristic obligation, i.e. the work, was to be performed (while it would otherwise look at the place of performance of the specific obligation in question).[3] This jurisdiction applied to both actions brought by the employee and the employer. Therefore in effect, the Court already established the jurisdiction of the habitual place of work as the regular jurisdiction for actions arising from the employment relationship, even under the 1968 Brussels Convention. In 1989, the Convention was amended accordingly.[4]

4. Special rules for the **protection of employees** are now included in Section 5 of Chapter II of the Brussels I-Regulation. The Regulation protects the employee by providing him with the additional jurisdiction of the habitual place of work or, in the absence of that, the jurisdiction of the place where the business which

---

[1] Council Regulation (EC) No 44/2001 of 22 December 2000 on jurisdiction and the recognition and enforcement of judgments in civil and commercial matters, OJ 2001 L 12/1.

[2] On the changes to the Brussels-Convention V. Behr, *Gedächtnisschrift für Blomeyer*, 19–22.

[3] ECJ Case C-125/92 *Mulox IBC* [1993] ECR I-4075 paras. 25 sq.; Case C-37/00 *Weber* [2002] ECR I-2013 para. 43.

[4] On the development of the Court's jurisprudence under the Brussels Convention, see in more detail V. Behr, *Gedächtnisschrift für Blomeyer*, 22–27; A. Junker, *ZZPInt* 3 (1989), 179–202; id., *Festschrift für Schlosser*, 300 sq.; D. Leipold, *Gedächtnisschrift für Blomeyer*, 144–146; T. Rauscher, *Festschrift für Schütze*, 695–710.

engaged him is located (in addition to the general jurisdiction of the Member State where he is domiciled) for actions brought against the employer – the 'active process' (from the employee's perspective). On the other hand, for actions brought by the employer against the employee – the 'passive process' – the courts of the Member States where the employee is domiciled, in principle, have exclusive jurisdiction. These rules are intended to allow for an easy and affordable enforcement or defence of rights by the employee. At the same time, the jurisdiction is intended to serve the interests of an expedient and efficient procedure, giving jurisdiction to courts that are close by and which can (more) easily familiarise themselves with the relevant circumstances of the case.

5. The Brussels I-Regulation is one of a number of European regulations and conventions in the area of civil procedure. The **regulatory environment** includes, first, the Lugano Convention with the EFTA-States that extends the provisions of the Brussels Convention with minor adaptations to Norway, Iceland and Switzerland.[5] Other EU legislation on civil procedure may also be relevant, notwithstanding the absence of any specific rules for employment disputes. These include in particular:

- the Brussels II-Regulation[6] on jurisdiction and the recognition and enforcement of judgments in matrimonial matters and in matters of parental responsibility for children of both spouses;
- the Regulation on the Service of Judicial and Extrajudicial Documents in Civil or Commercial Matters;[7]
- the Regulation on Cooperation between the Courts of the Member States in the Taking of Evidence in Civil or Commercial Matters;[8] and
- the Regulation on Insolvency Proceedings.[9]

---

[5]   R. Geimer, in R. Zöller (ed.), *Zivilprozessordnung*, Art. 1 EuGVVO paras. 16–18; H.-W. Micklitz/P. Rott, *EuZW* 2001, 325 sq.

[6]   Council Regulation (EC) No 1347/2000 of 29 May 2000 on jurisdiction and the recognition and enforcement of judgments in matrimonial matters and in matters of parental responsibility for children of both spouses, OJ 2000 L 160/19.

[7]   Council Regulation (EC) No 1348/2000 of 29 May 2000 on the service in the Member States of judicial and extrajudicial documents in civil or commercial matters, OJ 2000 L 160/37.

[8]   Council Regulation (EC) No 1206/2001 of 28 May 2001 on cooperation between the courts of the Member States in the taking of evidence in civil or commercial matters, OJ 2001 L 174/1. See the recent (employment) Case C-283/09 *Weryński* 17 February 2011 (concerning payment of an advance or reimbursement of costs paid to witnesses examined).

[9]   Council regulation (EC) No 1346/2000 of 29 May 2000 on insolvency proceedings, OJ 2000 L 160/1; on this regulation, see H. Eidenmüller, 'Europäische Verordnung über Insolvenzverfahren und zukünftiges deutsches internationales Insolvenzrecht', *IPRax* 2001, 2–15; S. Leible/A. Staudinger, 'Die Europäische Verordnung über Insolvenzverfahren', *KTS* 2000, 533–575.

Apart from that, Article 6 PoWD provides for a special – non-exclusive – jurisdiction for actions for the enforcement of the rights extended to posted workers pursuant to Article 3 PoWD (see §6 para. 31 above).[10]

II. SCOPE OF APPLICATION

6. The Regulation applies to civil and commercial matters only. **Civil matters** include matters related to employment contracts.[11] Matters of public law are not governed by the Regulation.[12] Social security is specifically excluded, Article 1(2)(c) Brussels I-Regulation. Claims resulting from (public) unemployment insurance or (public) accident insurance are not to be brought under the Regulation's jurisdictions, even if they are employment related. On the other hand, the fact that a lawsuit also involves issues of public or social security law does not exclude it from the scope of application of the Regulation. Where, for example, in an action against unfair dismissal, the employee argues that he was not obligated to perform a task required by his employer as it was illegal under public law, this is still a civil matter.

III. THE JURISDICTIONS OF ARTICLE 18–21 BRUSSELS I-REGULATION

1. Overview and System

7. The Brussels I-Regulation provides for special jurisdictions for individual contracts of employment in Articles 18–21. '**Contracts of employment**' and 'employee' ('worker') are defined here in the same way as in Article 45 TFEU (see §3 paras. 9–12 above).[13] A **worker** is a person who for a certain period of time performs services for and under the direction of another in return for which he receives remuneration.[14] The restriction to **individual** employment contracts excludes disputes over collective agreements for which the special protection of Articles 18–21 does not seem to be necessary (having regard to the 'location' of

---

[10]   V. Behr, *Gedächtnisschrift für Blomeyer*, 40 sq.; B. Gaul, 'Neues im Arbeitsförderungsrecht nach dem Ersten SGB III-Änderungsgesetz', *NJW* 1998, 644 (648); A. Junker, *Festschrift für Schlosser*, 305 sq.; J. Kropholler, *Europäisches Zivilprozessrecht*, Art. 19 para. 14.

[11]   ECJ Case 25/79 *Sanicentral* v. *Collin* [1979] ECR 3423.

[12]   See in detail P. Mankowski, in T. Rauscher (ed.), *EuZPR/EuIPR*, Art. 1 Brüssel I-VO paras. 2g-4d; B. Hess, *Europäisches Zivilprozessrecht*, §6 paras. 4–12.

[13]   P. Mankowski, in T. Rauscher (ed.), *EuZPR/EuIPR*, Art. 18 Brüssel I-VO para. 3; also P. Gottwald, in T. Rauscher/P. Wax/J. Wenzel (eds.), *Münchener Kommentar zur Zivilprozessordnung*, Art. 18 EuGVVO para. 2; B. Hess, *Europäisches Zivilprozessrecht*, §6 para. 104. See also V. Behr, *Gedächtnisschrift für Blomeyer*, 32 sq.

[14]   On the concept of worker/employee cf. ECJ Case 266/85 *Shenavai* [1987] ECR 239 (architect's contract). A. Junker, *Festschrift für Schlosser*, 302; M. Schmidt, *Arbeitsrecht der EG*, 118 sq.

the subject matter and the professional actors involved).[15] Again, a dispute arising from an individual employment contract may, however, also involve questions related to collective agreements that determine the content of the contract. That is, e.g., the case where the employee brings a suit for a Christmas bonus determined by a collective agreement. Here Articles 18–21 Brussels I-Regulation apply, even if formation and validity of the collective agreement may be in issue.

8. With regard to the wording, the system and the legislative history of these provisions, the Court of Justice has interpreted the jurisdictions of Section 5 to be **exclusive**, foreclosing recourse to the general jurisdiction, except for the cases which are specifically referred to in Article 18.[16] Teleological considerations, particularly the purpose of employee protection, would not justify a different interpretation. For if one were to allow for recourse to the general jurisdictions of the regulation for the benefit of the employee, the same would have to apply to his disadvantage. Therefore, an employee could not rely upon the provision of Article 6(1) Brussels I-Regulation (pursuant to which one of a number of defendants may be sued in the place where *any one* of them is domiciled if the claims are closely connected), if he wanted to bring an action against two businesses in their capacities as his employer, which are located in different Member States. Recourse to the general jurisdictions remains open, of course, where the dispute between the parties to the employment contract is not about claims arising from the employment contract. This can be of practical importance in respect of claims in tort which the employer or the employee may institute in the courts at the place where the harmful event occurred (at the plaintiff's choice the place where the action was taken or the place where the damage occurred)[17], Article 5(3) Brussels I-Regulation.[18]

2. The Various Jurisdictions

9. For the purpose of protecting the employee, the provisions of Section 5 provide for different jurisdictions depending upon whether the employee brings an action ('**active process**'; below a)) or is being sued by the employer ('**passive process**'; below b)). This distinction is adapted to the different needs of protection. To ensure that these jurisdictions are not being circumvented, there

---

[15]   A. Junker, *Festschrift für Schlosser*, 301 sq.

[16]   ECJ Case C-462/06 *Laboratoires Glaxosmithkline* [2008] ECR I-3965 paras. 17–33. To the same effect already V. Behr, *Gedächtnisschrift für Blomeyer*, 28–30; P. Gottwald, in T. Rauscher/P. Wax/J. Wenzel (eds.), *Münchener Kommentar zur Zivilprozessordnung*, Art. 18 EuGVVO para. 4. See also D. Leipold, *Gedächtnisschrift für Blomeyer*, 162 sq.

[17]   See e.g. S. Leible, in T. Rauscher (ed.), *EuZPR/EuIPR*, Art. 5 Brüssel I VO para. 85 with further references.

[18]   V. Behr, *Gedächtnisschrift für Blomeyer*, 29; A. Junker, *NZA* 2005, 199 (203); id., *Festschrift für Schlosser*, 307 sq.

are also limits to agreements conferring jurisdiction (prorogation). However, where an employee appears in court, this court has jurisdiction (c) below).

a)   Jurisdiction for Actions brought against the Employer

10.   Pursuant to the general rule of Article 2 Brussels I-Regulation, a person domiciled in a Member State may be sued in that Member State (**jurisdiction of the domicile**). Article 19(1) reiterates this rule with regard to employers. Whether a party is domiciled in a Member State should be determined by the internal law of that state, Article 59(1). A *company or other legal person or association of natural or legal persons* is domiciled at the place where it has (a) its statutory seat or (b) its central administration or (c) its principal place of business, Article 60(1). In this respect, the Regulation itself makes the determination and not the national law of the state in which the seat is located.

11.   In addition, an employee has the right to sue the employer in one of two alternative jurisdictions, namely, the jurisdiction of the habitual place of work or that of the place where the business that engaged the employee is or was situated. The rationale behind these rules is that the employee may not have any relation to the state where the employer is domiciled, for example, where a German employee has been engaged by an English employer to perform work in France.

12.   Pursuant to Article 19(2)(a) Brussels I-Regulation, an employer domiciled in a Member State may also be sued in the courts of the place where the employee habitually carries out work or where he last did so. The **jurisdiction of the habitual place of work** will usually be easily and affordably accessible for the employee. At the same time, considerations of expedience and efficiency argue in favour of the jurisdiction of the habitual place of work as it will be easier for the courts of that state to become familiar with the relevant facts and circumstances.[19] The term 'habitual place of work' is autonomously defined in EU law.[20] The habitual place of work is the place where the employee, following the agreement of the parties, predominantly carries out his work.[21] The amount of time spent at different places is of considerable relevance, but it is not the only decisive factor. Apart from that, qualitative criteria may be considered such as the 'nature or importance' of an activity. For example, the

---

[19]   See on these purposes – employee protection and efficiency – ECJ Case C-437/00 *Pugliese* [2003] ECR I-3573 paras. 17 sq.; Case C-37/00 *Weber* [2002] ECR I-2013 paras. 39 sq. with note by P. Mankowski, *IPRax* 2003, 21–28. A. Junker, *Festschrift für Schlosser,* 308 sq.

[20]   V. Behr, *Gedächtnisschrift für Blomeyer,* 33 sq.; A. Junker, *Festschrift für Schlosser,* 309 sq.

[21]   For lack of jurisdiction, the Court has not decided where flight attendants have their habitual place of work: ECJ Case C-555/03 *Warbecq* [2004] ECR I-6041.

office from which an employee prepares his travel activity and to which she returns afterwards will usually be her habitual place of residence,[22] even if she only spends a relatively small amount of time there. Only *one* place can be the 'habitual place of work'.[23] While the wording would allow for a different view, the purpose of the Regulation mandates this interpretation, as its purpose is to avoid competing competences of different courts. When Article 19(2)(a) Brussels I-Regulation refers to the place where the employee habitually carries out his work *or the last place where he did so*,[24] this could indicate that an employee whose habitual place of work has changed has a choice between different jurisdictions. A more consistent interpretation, however, seems to be that the legislature wanted to clarify that the jurisdiction of the habitual place of work is also available after the employment relationship has been terminated.

13. There are cases where the employee does not habitually carry out his work in a single place (or state)[25], for example where his task is to assemble or install machines at varying places. In such cases, the jurisdiction of the habitual place of work cannot apply. Instead, Article 2(2)(b) Brussels I-Regulation provides for the jurisdiction of the **place where the business that engaged the employee is situated**. If the business has been subsequently relocated, the employee may also choose the place where the business that engaged him *was* located.[26] 'Business' (*Niederlassung, établissement*) refers to 'a place of business which has the appearance of permanency, such as the extension of a parent body, has a management and is materially equipped to negotiate business with third parties'.[27] Whether 'engaged' refers to the conclusion of the contract or to integration within the workforce is controversial (for discussion of the same controversy with regard to Article 8 Rome I-Regulation, see §5 para. 18 above).[28]

---

[22] ECJ Case C-125/92 *Mulox IBC* [1993] ECR I-4075 para. 26; Case C-383/95 *Rutten* [1997] ECR I-57 para. 25.

[23] ECJ Case C-125/92 *Mulox IBC* [1993] ECR I-4075 paras. 21, 23; Case C-383/95 *Rutten* [1997] ECR 1997 I-57 para. 18; Case C-37/00 *Weber* [2002] ECR I-2013 para. 55.

[24] See e.g. A. Junker, *Festschrift für Schlosser*, 312 sq. with further references.

[25] Following the wording and purpose of the provision, 'state' should be interpreted as state and not as Member State; consequently, an occupation in varying third states can also be covered; A. Junker, *Festschrift für Schlosser*, 314.

[26] V. Behr, *Gedächtnisschrift für Blomeyer*, 38.

[27] ECJ Case 33/78 *Somafer* [1978] ECR 2183 para. 12. W. Däubler, *NZA* 2003, 1297, 1298; K. Thorn, 'Termingeschäfte an Auslandsbörsen und internationale Schiedsgerichtsbarkeit', *IPRax* 1997, 98 sq.

[28] W. Däubler, *NZA* 2003, 1297 (1300); P. Mankowski, in T. Rauscher (ed.), *EuZPR/EuIPR*, Art. 19 Brüssel I-VO para. 19.

14. The special rules of Section 5 only apply 'without prejudice to ... point 5 of Article 5' (Article 18(1) Brussels I-Regulation); the employee may thus also bring actions in respect of disputes arising out of the operation of a branch, agency or establishment against an employer[29] who is domiciled in a Member State at the **place in which** the branch, agency or **establishment is located.**

15. The jurisdictions of Articles 19 and 5(5) Brussels I-Regulation presuppose that the employer is domiciled (Articles 59 sq.) in a Member State. This is not necessarily the case. Where the employer is domiciled in a **third country** but has a branch, agency or establishment in a Member State, he will be deemed to be domiciled in this Member State for the purpose of disputes arising out of the operation of the branch, agency or establishment, Article 18(2) Brussels I-Regulation (**fiction of domicile**). The employer can, following the general rule contained in Article 19(1), be sued in that Member State.[30] This provision may, for instance, be relevant for an action of an air pilot or a flight attendant against a foreign airline.[31]

b) Jurisdiction for Actions brought against the Employee

16. For actions against the employee, the state where the employee is domiciled in principle has exclusive jurisdiction (**jurisdiction of the domicile**), Article 20(1) Brussels I-Regulation. The employee should not be forced to defend himself against lawsuits in the courts of other Member States.[32] In particular, an employee cannot be sued at the habitual place of work or the place where the business which engaged him is located. Considerations of expediency and efficiency which support the jurisdiction of the habitual place of work for actions of the employee have been considered to be less important here.[33]

17. There are only three exceptions to the general rule of Article 20(1) Brussels I-Regulation. First, an employer who is being sued by an employee at one of the jurisdictions contained in Articles 18 sq. can bring a counter-claim in the same jurisdiction. In this case, considerations of expediency and efficiency prevail, and it is also not considered to be excessively burdensome for the employee to defend himself against a counter-claim in the same court where he brought a

---

29 Not applicable in actions brought against the employee; V. Behr, *Gedächtnisschrift für Blomeyer*, 39 sq.; A. Junker, *NZA* 2005, 199 (203).
30 See in more detail V. Behr, *Gedächtnisschrift für Blomeyer*, 30 sq.; A. Junker, *Festschrift für Schlosser*, 304 sq.; D. Leipold, *Gedächtnisschrift für Blomeyer*, 159.
31 See e.g. BAG, *BAGE* 100, 130.
32 Critically A. Junker, *NZA* 2005, 199 (202); id., *Festschrift für Schlosser*, 316.
33 Critically V. Behr, *Gedächtnisschrift für Blomeyer*, 26 sq. and 36 sq.; A. Junker, *Festschrift für Schlosser*, 315–317.

claim in the first place. Further exceptions may result from an agreement of jurisdiction or where an employee appears in the court of a different jurisdiction:

c)   Agreements of Jurisdiction (Prorogation) and Jurisdiction established by Appearance in Court

18.   If the jurisdictions of Section 5 Brussels I-Regulation serve the specific purpose of protecting the employee, the parties may not deviate from these jurisdictions without further justification as this could jeopardise the protective purpose. While **agreements of jurisdiction** are generally admissible pursuant to the principle of freedom of contract, Article 21 Brussels I-Regulation restricts their scope with regard to disputes arising from individual employment contracts.[34] Apart from the general formal requirements of Article 23 which also apply, a valid agreement of jurisdiction presupposes that either it has been entered into only after the dispute arose or it merely gives the employee the option to bring proceedings in courts in addition to those indicated in Section 5. In the former case, the employee can well assess the importance and consequences of the agreement and will often have had legal advice,[35] and in the latter he does not need any protection as the prorogation unilaterally favours him.[36]

19.   Similar considerations apply with regard to the jurisdiction of the court where the employee appears, Article 24 Brussels I-Regulation.[37] As in the case of a prorogation after the dispute has arisen, the employee is in a position to assess the consequences and importance of such action himself. One can expect an employee to either know or enquire about the consequences of his appearance in court. In an active process, the employee himself chose the court, and in a passive process, the mere fact that he is being sued in a 'foreign' place constitutes sufficient warning.

---

[34]   On the preceding provisions of the Brussels Convention M. Franzen, *RIW* 2000, 81–88.

[35]   M. Franzen, *RIW* 2000, 81 sq.; A. Junker, *NZA* 2005, 199 (201); P. Mankowski, in T. Rauscher (ed.), *EuZPR/EuIPR*, Art. 21 Brüssel I-VO para. 3.

[36]   Cf. on the parallel issues with regard to insurance matters under Article 12(2) Brussels Convention ECJ Case C-112/03 *Société financière et industrielle du Peloux* [2005] ECR I-3707.

[37]   To the same effect R. Geimer, in R. Zöller (ed.), *Zivilprozessordnung*, Art. 24 EuGVVO paras. 1 sq.; P. Gottwald, in T. Rauscher/P. Wax/J. Wenzel (eds.), *Münchener Kommentar zur Zivilprozessordnung*, Art. 21 EuGVVO para. 1; A. Staudinger, in T. Rauscher (ed.), *EuZPR/EuIPR*, Art. 24 Brüssel I-VO para. 11; differently P. Mankowski, in T. Rauscher (ed.), *EuZPR/EuIPR*, Art. 18 Brüssel I-VO para. 2b (only against the employer).

PART 3
INDIVIDUAL EMPLOYMENT LAW

CHAPTER 1

ANTI-DISCRIMINATION LAW

§8. THE PRINCIPLE OF EQUALITY AND PROHIBITIONS OF DISCRIMINATION – GENERAL PART: SOURCES OF LAW AND INSTRUMENTS OF PROTECTION

CONTENTS

Bibliography:

K. Adomeit, 'Spanisches und deutsches Gleichbehandlungsrecht und gemeinsame Probleme der Umsetzung europäischer Direktiven', in H. Konzen et al. (eds.), *Festschrift für Rolf Birk zum siebzigsten Geburtstag* (Tübingen: Mohr Siebeck, 2007), 1–9; K. Adomeit/J. Mohr, 'Die mittelbare Diskriminierung als Instrument überindividueller Verhaltenssteuerung – Zugleich Besprechung von BAG v. 22.4.2010 – 6 AZR 966/08', *RdA* 2011, 102–108; K. Adomeit/J. Mohr, *Kommentar zum Allgemeinen Gleichbehandlungsgesetz* (Stuttgart et al.: Boorberg, 2007); I. Ayres/J. Brown, 'Mark(et) ing Non-Discrimination: Privatizing ENDA with a Certification Mark', 104 (2005–2006)

Mich. L. Rev., 1639–1712; M. Barbera, 'Not the same? The Judicial Role in the New Community Anti-Discrimination Law Context', *ILJ* 31 (2002), 82–91; C. Barnard, 'The Principle of Equality in the Community Context: *P, Grant, Kalanke* and *Marshall:* Four Uneasy Bedfellows?', *C.L.J.* 57 (1998), 352–373; C. Barnard/B. Hepple, 'Substantive Equality', *C.L.J.* 59 (2000), 562–585; J. Basedow, 'Der Grundsatz der Nichtdiskriminierung im europäischen Privatrecht', *ZEuP* 2008, 230–251; J.-H. Bauer/B. Göpfert/S. Krieger, *Allgemeines Gleichbehandlungsgesetz – Kommentar* (Munich: C.H. Beck, 2006); G. S. Becker, *The Economics of Discrimination*, 2nd edn. (Chicago/London: The University of Chicago Press, 1971); G. S. Becker, *The Economic Approach to Human Behavior*, (Chicago/London: The University of Chicago Press, 1976) (Part 2); M. Bell, 'Article 13 EC: The European Commission's Anti-Discrimination Proposals', *ILJ* 29 (2000), 79–84; M. Bell, 'Beyond European Labour Law? Reflections on the EU Racial Equality Directive', *ELJ* 8 (2002), 384–399; M. Bell/L. Waddington, 'More Equal than Others: Distinguishing European Union Equality Directives', *CMLR* 38 (2001), 587–611; M. Bell/L. Waddington, 'Reflecting on inequalities in European equality law', *E.L. Rev.* 28 (2003), 349–369; D. E. Bernstein, *You Can't Say That! – The Growing Threat to Civil Liberties from Antidiscrimination Laws* (Washington D.C.: Cato Institute, 2003); T. Bezzenberger, 'Ethnische Diskriminierung, Gleichheit und Sittenordnung im bürgerlichen Recht', *AcP* 196 (1996), 395–434; R. Blanpain, 'Equality of Treatment in Employment', in B. Hepple (ed.), *International Encyclopaedia of Comparative Law, Volume XV: Labour Law* (Tübingen: Mohr Siebeck, 1990), Chapter 10; W. Blomeyer, 'Der Einfluß der Rechtsprechung des EuGH auf das deutsche Arbeitsrecht', *NZA* 1994, 633–640; C.-W. Canaris, *Die Bedeutung der iustitia distributiva im deutschen Vertragsrecht* (Munich: C.H. Beck, 1997); H. Collins, 'Discrimination, Equality, and Social Inclusion', *MLR* 66 (2003), 16–43; W. Däubler/M. Bertzbach (eds.), *Allgemeines Gleichbehandlungsgesetz – Handkommentar*, 2nd edn. (Baden-Baden: Nomos, 2008); M. Diller/J. Kern/R. Zeh, 'AGG-Archiv: Die Schlussbilanz', *NZA* 2009, 1386–1391; J. J. Donohue, 'Is Title VII Efficient?', *U. Pa. L. Rev.* 134 (1986), 1141–1431; J. J. Donohue, 'Further Thoughts on Employment Discrimination: A Reply to Judge Posner', *U. Pa. L. Rev.* 136 (1987), 523–551; J. J. Donohue, 'Prohibiting Sex Discrimination in the Workplace: An Economic Perspective', *U. Chi. L. Rev.* 56 (1989), 1337–1368; O. Doyle, 'Direct Discrimination, Indirect Discrimination and Autonomy', *OJLS* 27 (2007), 537–553.; M. Driessen-Reilly/B. Driessen, 'Don't Shoot the Messenger: A Look at Community Law Relating to Harassment in the Workplace', *E.L. Rev.* 28 (2003), 493–507; R. Dworkin, *A Matter of Principle* (Oxford: Oxford University Press, 1986); R. Dworkin, *Taking Rights Seriously*, (Cambridge, MA: Harvard University Press, 1977); R. A. Epstein, *Forbidden Grounds – The Case Against Employment Discrimination Law* (Cambridge, Massachusetts/London, England: Harvard University Press, 1995); R. A. Epstein, *Equal Opportunity or More Opportunity? – The Good Thing about Discrimination* (London: Civitas, 2002); R. A. Epstein, *Simple Rules for a Complex World* (Cambridge, MA/London: Harvard University Press, 1995), 170–193; L. Fastrich, 'Gleichbehandlung und Gleichstellung', *RdA* 2000, 65–81; S. Fredman, 'Combating Racism with Human Rights: The Right to Equality', in ead./P. Alston/G. Búrca (eds.), *Discrimination and Human Rights – The case of Racism* (Oxford: Oxford University Press, 2001); S. Fredman, *Discrimination Law,* 2nd edn. (Oxford: Oxford University Press, 2011); S. Fredman, 'European Community Discrimination Law: A Critique', *ILJ* 21 (1992), 119–134; S. Fredman, 'Equality: A New Generation?', *ILJ* 30 (2001), 145–168; M. Friedman, *Capitalism and Freedom* (Chicago:

The University of Chicago Press 1962/2002), Ch. VII; M. Friedman/R. D. Friedman, *Free to Choose – A Personal Statement* (San Diego/New York/London: Harncourt, 1980/1990); F. Gamillscheg, 'Die mittelbare Diskriminierung der Frau im Arbeitsleben', in O. Martinek (ed.), *Arbeitsrecht und soziale Grundrechte, Festschrift für Hans Floretta zum 60. Geburtstag* (Vienna: Manz, 1983), 171–185; J. Gardner, 'Liberals and Unlawful Discrimination', *OJLS* 9 (1989) 1–22; J. Gardner, 'Private Activities and Personal Autonomy: At the Margins of Anti-discrimination Law', in B. Hepple/E. M. Szyszczak (eds.), *Discrimination: The Limits of the Law?* (London: Mansell, 1992), 148–171; J. Gardner, 'Discrimination as Injustice', *OJLS* 16 (1996) 367; J. Gardner, 'On the Grounds of her Sex(uality)', *OJLS* 18 (1998), 167–187; N. Görlitz, *Struktur und Bedeutung der Rechtsfigur der mittelbaren Diskriminierung im System der Grundfreiheiten* (Baden-Baden: Nomos, 2005); E. Guild, 'European developments. The EC directive on race discrimination: surprises, possibilities and limitations', *ILJ* 29 (2000), 416–423; P. Hanau/U. Preis, 'Zur mittelbaren Diskriminierung wegen des Geschlechts', *ZfA* 1988, 177–207; B. Hepple, 'Equality and Discrimination', in P. Davis et al. (eds.), *European Community Labour Law: Principles and Perspectives, Liber Amicorum Lord Wedderburn* (Oxford: Clarendon Press 1996), 237–259; B. Hepple, 'The Aims of Equality Law', *C.L.P.* 61 (2008), 1–22; B. Hepple/M. Coussey/C. Tufyal, *Equality: A New Framework* (Oxford: Hart Publishing, 2000); B. Hepple/E. M. Szyszczak (eds.), *Discrimination: The Limits of Law* (London/New York: Mansell, 1992); E. Herrmann, 'Die Abschlussfreiheit – ein gefährdetes Prinzip', *ZfA* 1996, 19–68; E. Howard, 'An Opportunity Missed ? Comment on Römer', *E.L. Rev.* 36 (2011), 589–599; E. Howard, 'The European Year of Equal Opportunities for All – 2007: Is the EU Moving Away From a Formal Idea of Equality?', *ELJ* 14 (2008), 168–185; G. Hueck, *Der Grundsatz der gleichmäßigen Behandlung im Privatrecht* (Munich/Berlin: C.H. Beck, 1958); S. Huster, 'Gleichheit im Mehrebenensystem: Die Gleichheitsrechte der Europäischen Union in systematischer und kompetenzrechtlicher Hinsicht', *EuR* 2010, 325–337; J. Isensee (ed.), *Vertragsfreiheit und Diskriminierung* (Berlin: Duncker & Humblot, 2007); S. Issacharoff, 'Contractual Liberties in Discriminatory Markets', *Tex. L. Rev.* 70 (1992), 1219–1259; S. Issacharoff/J. Nelson, 'Discrimination with a Difference: Can Employment Discrimination Law Accommodate the Americans with Disabilities Act?', *North Carolina L. Rev.* 79 (2001), 307–358; C. Jolls, 'Antidsicrimination and Accomodation', *Harv. L. Rev.* 115 (2001), 642–699; S. Kamanabrou, 'Europarechtskonformer Schutz vor Benachteiligungen bei Kündigungen', *RdA* 2007, 199–207; C. Kirchner, 'Zivilrechtlicher Diskriminierungsschutz: ein ökonomischer Ansatz', in S. Leible/M. Schlachter (eds.), *Diskriminierungsschutz durch Privatrecht* (Munich: Sellier, 2006), 37–52; K. Koch/A. Nguyen, 'Das Verbot der mittelbaren Diskriminierung – Gleiches Recht für alle? – Das Verbot der mittelbaren Diskriminierung in der höchstrichterlichen Rechtsprechung', *EuR* 2010, 364–377; E. Kocher, 'Vom Diskriminierungsverbot zum "Mainstreaming"', *RdA* 2002, 167–173; G. Krause, 'Antidiskriminierungsrecht und Kundenpräferenzen', in P. Hanau/J. Thau/H. P. Westermann (eds.), *Gegen den Strich – Festschrift für Klaus Adomeit* (Cologne: Luchterhand, 2008), 377–393; S. Krebber, 'Das arbeitsrechtliche Diskriminierungsverbot als Regelungsvorbild?', in S. Leible/M. Schlachter (eds.), *Diskriminierungsschutz durch Privatrecht* (Munich: Sellier, 2006), 93–121; S. Krebber, 'The Social Rights Approach of the European Court of Justice to Enforce European Employment Law', *Comp. Lab. L. & Pol'y J.* 27 (2006), 377–403; S. B. Lahuerta, 'Race Equality and TCN's [Third Country Nationals; KR], or How to Fight Discrimination with a Discriminatory Law', *ELJ* 15 (2009), 738–756; W. Landes, 'The Economics of Fair Employment Laws', *J. Pol. Econ.* 76 (1968), 507–552; M. Le Friant, 'Das Prinzip der Nichtdiskriminierung im französischen Recht: Zum Stand der Debatte', *NZA* 2004, 49–59; M. Le Friant, 'Rechtstechniken im Kampf gegen Diskriminierungen: Die Lage in Frankreich', *AuR* 2003, 51–56; S. Leible/M. Schlachter (eds.), *Diskriminierungsschutz durch Privatrecht* (Munich: Sellier, 2006); T. Lobinger, 'Vertragsfreiheit und Diskriminierungsverbote – Privatautonomie im modernen Zivil- und Arbeitsrecht', in J. Isensee (ed.), *Vertragsfreiheit und Diskriminierung* (Berlin: Duncker & Humblot, 2007), 99–180; M. Lorenz, 'Schwieriger Weg zur Lohnangleichung von Männern u. Frauen', in R. Anzinger/R. Wank (eds.), *Entwicklungen im Arbeitsrecht und Arbeitsschutzrecht – Festschrift für Otfried Wlotzke* (Munich: C.H. Beck, 1996) 45–82; C. A. MacKinnon, *Feminism Unmodified – Discourses on Life and Law* (Cambridge, MA: Harvard University Press, 1987); C. McCrudden 'The Effectiveness of European Equality Law: National Mechanisms for Enforcing Gender Equality Law in the Light of European Requirements', *OJLS* 13 (1993), 320–367; M. Mahlmann, 'Gerechtigkeitsfragen im Gemeinschaftsrecht', in U. Rust et al. (eds.), *Gleichbehandlungsrichtlinien der EU und ihre Umsetzung in Deutschland – Loccumer Protokolle 40/03* (Rehburg Loccum: Evangelische Akademie Loccum, 2003) 47–72; J. Neuner, 'Diskriminierungsschutz durch Privatrecht', *JZ* 2003, 57–66; J. Neuner, 'Protection against Discrimination in European Contract Law', *ERCL* 2006, 35–50; J. Neuner, *Privatrecht und Sozialstaat* (Munich: C.H. Beck, 1999); J. Neuner, 'Vertragsfreiheit und Gleichbehandlungsgrundsatz', in S. Leible/M. Schlachter (eds.), *Diskriminierungsschutz durch Privatrecht* (Munich: Sellier, 2006) 73–91; C. O'Brien, 'Equality's False Summits: New Varieties of Disability Discrimination, "Excessive" Equal Treatment and Economically Constricted Horizons', *E.L. Rev.* 36 (2011), 26–50; S. Peers, 'Supremacy, Equality and Human Rights: Comment on Kücükdeveci', *E.L. Rev.* 35 (2010), 849–856; H. M. Pfarr/K. Bertelsmann, *Diskriminierung im Erwerbsleben – Ungleichbehandlung von Frauen und Männern in der Bundesrepublik Deutschland* (Baden-Baden: Nomos, 1989); E. Picker, 'Antidiskriminierungsprogramme im freiheitlichen Privatrecht', in E. Lorenz (ed.), *Karlsruher Forum 2004: Haftung wegen Diskriminierung nach derzeitigem und zukünftigem Recht* (Karlsruhe: VVW, 2004), 7–115; M. Pilgerstorfer/S. Forshaw, 'Transferred Discrimination in European Law', *ILJ* 37 (2008), 384–393; R. A. Posner, 'An Economic Analysis of Sex Discrimination Laws', *U. Chi. L. Rev.* 56 (1989), 1311–1335; R. A. Posner, *Economic Analysis of Law*, 8th edn. (Austin et al.: Wolters Kluwer, 2011), §11.10, §27; R. A. Posner, 'The Efficiency and the Efficacy of Title VII', *U. Pa. L. Rev.* 136 (1987), 513–521; U. Preis/K. Mallossek, 'Überblick über das Recht der Gleichbehandlung von Frauen und Männern im Gemeinschaftsrecht', in H. Oetker/U. Preis (eds.), *Europäisches Arbeits- und Sozialrecht, EAS, part B – Systematische Darstellungen*, loose-leaf (Heidelberg: Forkel, last update: December 1995), B 4000; R. Rebhahn (ed.), *Kommentar des Gleichbehandlungsgesetzes* (Vienna/New York: Springer, 2005); R. Rebhahn/C. Kietaibl, 'Mittelbare Diskriminierung und Kausalität', *Rechtswissenschaft* 2010, 373–396; K. Riesenhuber, 'Privatautonomie und Diskriminierungsverbote', in id./Y. Nishitani (eds.), *Wandlungen oder Erosion der Privatautonomie? – Deutsch-japanische Perspektiven des Vertragsrechts* (Berlin: de Gruyter, 2007), 19–61; K. Riesenhuber (ed.), *Das Allgemeine Gleichbehandlungsgesetz – Grundsatz- und Praxisfragen* (Berlin: de Gruyter, 2007); K. Riesenhuber, 'Das Verbot der Diskriminierung aufgrund der Rasse oder der ethnischen Herkunft sowie aufgrund des Geschlechts beim Zugang zu und der Versorgung mit Gütern und Dienstleistungen', in S.

Leible/M. Schlachter (eds.), *Diskriminierungsschutz durch Privatrecht* (Munich: Sellier, 2006), 123–140; K. Riesenhuber, 'Case-Note: ECJ of 22 November 2005 – Case C-144/04 – Mangold', *ERCL* 3 (2007), 62–71; K. Riesenhuber, 'Diskriminierungsverbote im Arbeitsrecht der Vereinigten Staaten', *RdA* 1993, 36–44; K. Riesenhuber, '"Mangold" verabschiedet', in P. Hanau/J. T. Thau/H.P. Westermann (eds.), *Gegen den Strich – Festschrift für Klaus Adomeit* (Cologne: Wolters Kluwer 2008), 631–644; K. Riesenhuber/ J.-U. Franck, 'Verbot der Geschlechtsdiskriminierung im Europäischen Vertragsrecht', *JZ* 2004, 529–538; U. Rust et al. (eds.), *Gleichbehandlungsrichtlinien der EU und ihre Umsetzung in Deutschland – Loccumer Protokolle 40/03* (Rehburg Loccum: Evangelische Akademie Loccum, 2003); M. Sargeant (ed.), *Discrimination Law* (London/New York/ Boston: Pearson Longman, 2004); D. Schiek (ed.), *Allgemeines Gleichbehandlungsgesetz* (Munich: Sellier, 2007); D. Schiek, 'A new Framework on equal treatment of persons in EC law?', *ELJ* 8 (2002), 290–314; D. Schiek, *Differenzierte Gerechtigkeit – Diskriminierungsschutz und Vertragsrecht* (Baden-Baden: Nomos, 2000); D. Schiek, 'Gleichbehandlungsrichtlinien der EU – Umsetzung im deutschen Arbeitsrecht', *NZA* 2004, 873–884; D. Schiek/V. Chege (eds.), *European Union Non-Discrimination Law – Comparative Perspectives on Multidimensional Equality Law* (London/New York: Routledge Cavendish, 2009); D. Schiek/A. Lawson (eds.), *European Union Non-Discrimination Law and Intersectionality – Investigating the Triangle of Racial, Gender and Disability Discrimination* (Farnham, Surrey/Burlington, VT: Ashgate, 2011); M. Schlachter, 'Benachteiligung wegen besonderer Verbindung statt Zugehörigkeit zu einer benachteiligten Gruppe – Der Diskriminierungsbegriff des EuGH in der Entscheidung Coleman v. 17.7.2008 – C-303/06', *RdA* 2010, 104–109; M. Schlachter, 'Das Arbeitsrecht im Allgemeinen Gleichbehandlungsgesetz', *ZESAR* 2006, 391–399; M. Schlachter, *Wege zur Gleichberechtigung – Vergleich des Arbeitsrechts der Bundesrepublik Deutschland und der Vereinigten Staaten* (Munich: C.H. Beck, 1993); B. Schmidt am Busch, 'Grundsatz der Gleichbehandlung von Männern und Frauen im Bereich der sozialen Sicherheit (Richtlinie 79/7/EWG)', in H. Oetker/U. Preis (eds.), *Europäisches Arbeits- und Sozialrecht, EAS, part B – Systematische Darstellungen*, loose-leaf (Heidelberg: Forkel, last update: June 1996), B 4300; I. Scholten, *Diskriminierungsschutz im Privatrecht? – Beweis- und verfahrensrechtliche Probleme der Umsetzung der Richtlinie 2000/43/EG* (Cologne/ Berlin/Bonn/Munich: Heymanns, 2004); S. J. Schwab, 'Employment Discrimination', in K. G. Dau-Schmidt/S. D. Harris/O. Lobel (eds.), *Labor and Employment Law and Economics – Encyclopedia of Law and Economics*, 2nd edn. (Cheltenham, UK/ Northampton, MA: Edward Elgar Publishing, 2009), 296–319; R. Singer, 'Vertragsfreiheit und Antidiskriminierung – zur rechtspoltischen, verfassungs- und europarechtlichen Kritik am Allgemeinen Gleichbehandlungsgesetz', in P. Hanau/J. T. Thau/H.P. Westermann (eds.), *Gegen den Strich – Festschrift für Klaus Adomeit* (Cologne: Wolters Kluwer, 2008), 703–717; I. Solanke, 'Putting Race and Gender Together: A New Approach to Intersectionality', *MLR* 72 (2009), 723–749; A. Somek, 'A Constitution for Antidiscrimination: Exploring the Vanguard Moment of Community Law', *ELJ* 5 (1999), 243–271; C. R. Sunstein, 'Why Markets Don't Stop Discrimination', in id. (ed.), *Free Markets and Social Justice* (New York/Oxford: Oxford University Press, 1997), 151–166; E. M. Szyszczak, 'Antidiscrimination Law in the European Community', *Fordham Int.L.J.* 32 (2009), 624–659; G. Thüsing, 'Das Arbeitsrecht der Zukunft? – Die deutsche Umsetzung der Anti-Diskriminierungsrichtlinien im internationalen Vergleich', *NZA* 2004 Special Supplement to issue 22, 3–16; G. Thüsing, 'Der Fortschritt des

Diskriminierungsschutzes im Europäischen Arbeitsrecht – Anmerkungen zu den Richtlinien 2000/43/EG und 2000/78/EG', *ZfA* 2001, 397–418; G. Thüsing, 'Gedanken zur Effizienz arbeitsrechtlicher Diskriminierungsverbote', *RdA* 2003, 257–264; G. Thüsing, in F.-J. Säcker/R. Rixecker (eds.), *Münchener Kommentar zum BGB, volume 1: Allgemeiner Teil §§1–240 BGB – ProstG – AGG*, 6th edn. (Munich: C.H. Beck, 2012); M. Trebilcock, *The Limits of Freedom of Contract* (Cambridge, MA/London: Harvard University Press, 1994), chapter 9; A.-S. Vandenberghe, 'The Economics of Non-Discrimination', in R. Schulze (ed.), *Non-Discrimination in European Private Law* (Tübingen: Mohr Siebeck, 2011), 9–26; L. Waddington, 'Art. 13 EC: Setting Priorities in the Proposal for a Horizontal Employment Directive', *ILJ* 29 (2000), 176–181; L. Waddington, 'Future prospects for EU equality law: lessons to be learnt from the proposed Equal Treatment Directive', *E.L. Rev.* 36 (2011), 163–184; L. Waddington, 'Taking stock and looking forward: the Commission Green Paper on Equality and Non-Discrimination in an Enlarged European Union', *ILJ* 33 (2004), 367–273; L. Waddington, 'Testing the Limits of the EC Treaty Article on Non-discrimination', *ILJ* 28 (1999), 133–151; R. Wank, 'Diskriminierung in Europa – Die Umsetzung der europäischen Antidiskriminierungsrichtlinien aus deutscher Sicht', *NZA* 2004 Special Supplement to issue 22, 16–26; A. Waughray, 'Cast Discrimination: A Twenty-First Century Challenge for UK Anti-Discrimination Law?', *MLR* 72 (2009), 723–749; U. Wendeling-Schröder, 'Grund und Grenzen gemeinschaftsrechtlicher Diskriminierungsverbote im Zivil- und Arbeitsrecht', *NZA* 2004, 1320–1323; U. Wendeling-Schröder/A. Stein (eds.), *Allgemeines Gleichbehandlungsgesetz – Kommentar* (Munich: C.H. Beck, 2008); R. Whittle, 'Disability Discrimination and the Amsterdam Treaty', *E.L. Rev.* 23 (1998), 50–58; H. Wiedemann, *Die Gleichbehandlungsgebote im Arbeitsrecht* (Tübingen: Mohr Siebeck, 2001); H. Wiedemann, 'Probleme der Gleichberechtigung im europäischen und deutschen Arbeitsrecht', in R. Wendt/W. Höfling/U. Karpen (eds.) – *Staat Wirtschaft Steuern, Festschrift für Karl Heinrich Friauf zum 65. Geburtstag* (Heidelberg: C.F. Müller, 1996), 135–154; H. Wißmann, 'Mittelbare Geschlechtsdiskriminierung: iudex calculat', in R. Anzinger/R. Wank (eds.), *Entwicklung im Arbeitsrecht und Arbeitsschutzrecht – Festschrift für Otfried Wlotzke* (Munich: C.H. Beck, 1996), 807–834; W. Zöllner, 'Gleichberechtigung und Gleichstellung der Geschlechter', in W. Schwarz et al. (eds.), *Möglichkeiten und Grenzen der Rechtsordnung – Festschrift für Rudolf Strasser* (Vienna: Manz, 1983), 223–240; see also the bibliographies to specific topics below, before paras. 53, 58, 63, 76, 81 and 86 as well as the bibliographies to the various legal acts in the area of anti-discrimination in §§9–11 below.

Cases (Selection):

ECJ Case 43/75 *Defrenne II* [1976] ECR 455; ECJ Case 96/80 *Jenkins* [1981] ECR 911; ECJ Case 170/84 *Bilka* [1986] ECR 1607; ECJ Case C-249/96 *Grant,* [1998] ECR I-621; ECJ Case 171/88 *Rinner-Kühn* [1989] ECR 2743; ECJ Case C-262/88 *Barber* [1990] ECR I-1889; ECJ Case 177/88 *Dekker* [1990] ECR 3941; ECJ Case C-172/92 *Enderby* [1993] ECR I-5535; ECJ Case C-13/94 *P v S* [1996] ECR I-2143; ECJ Case C-25/02 *Rinke* [2003] ECR I-8349; ECJ Case C-144/04 *Mangold* [2005] ECR I-9981; ECJ Case C-54/07 *Feryn* [2008] ECR I-5187; ECJ Case C-303/06 *Coleman* [2008] ECR I-5603; ECJ Case C-388/07 *Age Concern England* [2009] ECR I-1569.

I. INTRODUCTION

1. The prohibition on discrimination can rightly be considered to be fundamental to EU law.[1] For the Member States and the Union, not distinguishing on grounds of nationality is a core aspect of the fundamental freedoms and, indeed, the concept of the internal market (see already §2 above). With regard to employment law – or private law in general – only one aspect of the principle of non-discrimination was included in the Founding Treaties, which was based upon considerations of fair competition: the principle of equal pay for men and women. The Community (now Union) has since richly developed this field, starting with its 1970s secondary legislation on sex discrimination and expanding to different forms of discrimination and to different areas of life and law since 2000.

2. Based upon elaborate legislation, anti-discrimination law, more than all other parts of EU employment law (or even EU private law), has been the object of extensive jurisprudence by the Court of Justice. More than in other areas of EU employment law, there is a need to focus upon the basic structures of anti-discrimination law. The present chapter presents an overview of the entire body of anti-discrimination law in three steps. After a brief discussion of the foundations of anti-discrimination law in primary EU law (below II.[2]), we will review its legislative development (III. below). Following that, we will discuss the instruments of EU anti-discrimination law as they are now rather uniformly being used in secondary legislation (IV. below). The subsequent chapters (§§9–11) will then address questions which are specific to the individual prohibitions of discrimination. These will predominantly relate to the respective 'forbidden grounds' of distinction, the obligation of 'reasonable accommodation' upon employers in respect of protected staff groups and the grounds for justification. However, before we embark upon that, let us have a look at the foundations of anti-discrimination law in EU primary law.

3. Anti-discrimination law has a large number of **theoretical foundations**, which remain controversial.[3] Is the principle of non-discrimination well founded

---

[1]   ECJ Case 43/75 *Defrenne II* [1976] ECR 455 para. 12 (with regard to Article 141 EC).

[2]   See e.g. I. Solanke, *MLR* 72 (2009), 723–749 (advocating (a) the creation of an open-ended, non-exhaustive list of forbidden grounds of discrimination based on the concept of 'stigma' and (b) a 'social framework analysis').

[3]   For a comparative discussion see M. Schlachter, *Wege zur Gleichberechtigung*; M. Schmidt-Kessel, 'Fremde Erfahrungen mit zivilrechtlichen Diskriminierungsverboten', in S. Leible/M. Schlachter (eds.), *Diskriminierungsschutz durch Privatrecht*, 53–71; K. Riesenhuber, *RdA* 1993, 36–44. On the historical development, see e.g. K. Adomeit, in id./J. Mohr (eds.), *Kommentar zum Allgemeinen Gleichbehandlungsgesetz*, Einl. AGG paras. 1–105.

from a social and regulatory policy perspective?[4] More specifically, with regard to economic theory: Can the market cure discrimination (and if so, under what conditions),[5] are anti-discrimination laws warranted in general, do they work effectively and efficiently, do such laws give the right incentives and do they have undesired side-effects?[6] Should the objective be equal treatment, equal opportunity, 'equalisation' or something else?[7] How can the principle of non-discrimination be justified in a liberal society[8] and how does it relate to other fundamental principles of the legal system, particularly the paramount principle of private autonomy (freedom of contract)?[9] How can the redistributive

---

[4]   See on the one hand R. A. Epstein, *Forbidden Grounds* (critically reviewed by S. Issacharoff, *Tex. L. Rev.* 70 (1992), 1219–1259); M. Lorenz, *Festschrift für Wlotzke*, 45–82; on the other hand – with different positions – T. Bezzenberger, *AcP* 196 (1996), 395–434; C. Kirchner, in S. Leible/M. Schlachter (eds.), *Diskriminierungsschutz durch Privatrecht*, 37–52; S. Krebber, in S. Leible/M. Schlachter (eds.), *Diskriminierungsschutz durch Privatrecht*, 93–121; J. Neuner, *JZ* 2003, 57–66; id., *ERCL* 2006, 35–50; id., in S. Leible/M. Schlachter (eds.), *Diskriminierungsschutz durch Privatrecht*, 73–91; D. Schiek, *Differenzierte Gerechtigkeit*; G. Thüsing, *RdA* 2003, 257–264; M. Trebilcock, *The Limits of Freedom of Contract*, 188–213; H. Wiedemann, *Die Gleichbehandlungsgebote im Arbeitsrecht.*

[5]   G. S. Becker, *The Economics of Discrimination*; C. R. Sunstein, *Free Markets and Social Justice*, 151–166.

[6]   For a survey of the economic literature, see S. Schwab, in K. G. Dau-Schmidt/S. D. Harris/O. Lobel (eds.), *Labor and Employment Law and Economics*, 296–319; A.-S. Vandenberghe, in R. Schulze (ed.), *Non-Discrimination in European Private Law*, 9–26. Further e.g. W. Landes, *J.Pol. Econ.* 76 (1968), 507–552; J. J. Donohue, *U. Pa. L. Rev.* 134 (1986), 1141–1431; id., *U. Pa. L. Rev.* 136 (1987), 523–551; id., *U. Chi. L. Rev.* 56 (1989), 1337–1368; R. A. Posner, *U. Pa. L. Rev.* 136 (1987), 513–521; id. *U. Chi. L. Rev.* 56 (1989), 1311–1335 (concluding at p. 1334: 'What has been the net effect of the cascade of laws and lawsuits aimed at eliminating sex discrimination in employment? This is maddeningly difficult to say, but it is possible that women as a whole have not benefited and have in fact suffered.').

[7]   C. Barnard, *C.L.J.* 57 (1998), 352–373; H. Collins, *MLR* 66 (2003), 16–43 ('the aim of social inclusion'); L. Fastrich, *RdA* 2000, 65–81; S. Fredman, in ead./P. Alston/G. Búrca (eds.), *Discrimination and Human Rights,* 14–22; E. Howard, *ELJ* 14 (2008), 168–185 (discerning a move from formal to substantive equality in EU law and policy); C. Jolls, *Harv. L. Rev.* 115 (2001), 642–699 (discussing, *inter alia,* accommodation elements in standard anti-discrimination norms); W. Zöllner, *Festschrift für Strasser,* 223–240. See also S. Fredman, *ILJ* 21 (1992), 119–134 (discussing 'the male norm', 'equality and difference', 'neutrality', equality and the market order and 'individualism'). For a feminist perspective on the, see C.A. MacKinnon, *Feminism Unmodified,* 32 sqq.

[8]   O. Doyle, *OJLS* 27 (2007), 537–553; J. Gardner, *OJLS* 9 (1989), 1–22 (discussing justification of direct discrimination by the harm principle and of indirect discrimination as redistribution and relating both instances to the concept of autonomy); id., *OJLS* 16 (1996), 367; id., *OJLS* 18 (1998), 167–187.

[9]   J. Basedow, *ZEuP* 2008, 230–251; C.-W. Canaris, *Die Bedeutung der iustitia distributiva im deutschen Vertragsrecht*; W. Däubler, in id./M. Bertzbach (eds.), *Allgemeines Gleich-behandlungsgesetz*, Einl. AGG paras. 8–11 and 68–75; E. Herrmann, *ZfA* 1996, 19–68; T. Lobinger, in J. Isensee, (ed.), *Vertragsfreiheit und Diskriminierung*, 99–180; M. Mahlmann, in U. Rust et al. (eds.), *Gleichbehandlungsrichtlinien der EU und ihre Umsetzung in Deutschland*, 47–72; E. Picker, in E. Lorenz (ed.), *Karlsruher Forum 2004*, 7–115; R. Rebhahn, in id. (ed.), *Kommentar des Gleichbehandlungsgesetzes*, Einl. GlBG paras. 25–42; K. Riesenhuber, in id./Y. Nishitani (eds.), *Wandlungen oder Erosion der Privatautonomie?*, 19–61; W. Zöllner, *Festschrift für Strasser*, 223 sq. On equality as a principle of private law – distinct from the provisions on

burdens involved, in particular in 'equalisation' norms such as 'reasonable accommodation' be justified?[10] Are the prohibitions of discrimination based upon a concept of individual or collective justice,[11] upon economic considerations or upon considerations of social policy?[12] Is the objective procedural or substantive justice?[13] On a more technical level, are the distinctions between the various prohibitions of discrimination as they exist, e.g., with regard to 'reasonable accommodations', grounds for justification and, in their details, also with regard to definitions and sanctions, due to different substantive issues or do they rather reflect political compromise?[14] Is there, or should there, be a hierarchy of prohibitions of discrimination (so that, for example, disability outranks sex)?[15] The present context does not provide room to discuss these issues in detail although some will be addressed in their systematic context in the following sections.

II. FOUNDATIONS IN EU PRIMARY LAW[16]

1. Prohibitions of Discrimination in EU Primary Law

4. EU primary law – the Treaties – already contains prohibitions of discrimination. There is, first of all, the **prohibition of sex discrimination in regard of pay** in Article 157 TFEU. The prohibition – in its basic form – was

---

equality of men and women or other anti-discrimination laws – see the pathbreaking monograph by G. Hueck, *Der Grundsatz der gleichmäßigen Behandlung im Privatrecht.*

[10] C.-W. Canaris, *Die Bedeutung der iustitia distributiva im deutschen Vertragsrecht*; S. Issacharoff/J. Nelson, *North Carolina L. Rev.* 79 (2001), 307–358.

[11] M. Bell/L. Waddington, *E.L. Rev.* 28 (2003), 349, 350–358; C. McCrudden, *OJLS* 13 (1993), 320, 326–328; R. Rebhahn, in id. (ed.), *Kommentar des Gleichbehandlungsgesetzes*, Einl. GlBG paras. 31–33. See also D. Schiek, *ELJ* 8 (2002), 290, 302–308.

[12] W. Däubler, in id./M. Bertzbach (eds.), *Allgemeines Gleichbehandlungsgesetz*, Einl. AGG paras. 195–238 (on the 'concept of equality of the EU anti-discrimination directives' [my translation]).

[13] C. Barnard/B. Hepple, *C.L.J.* 59 (2000), 562–585; M. Barbera, *ILJ* 31 (2002), 82–91; S. Fredman, *ILJ* 30 (2001), 145, 154–157.

[14] On different approaches e.g. M. Bell/L. Waddington, *E.L. Rev.* 28 (2003), 349, 358–368; iid., *CMLR* 2001, 587–611.

[15] See e.g. (who find a particular strength of the protection from sex discrimination in comparison to the protection from race discrimination) M. Bell/L. Waddington, *CMLR* 2001, 587–611; iid., *E.L. Rev.* 28 (2003), 349–369; S. Fredman, *ILJ* 30 (2001), 145–168; D. Schiek, *ELJ* 8 (2002), 290, 299–302, 308 sq.; L. *Waddington, ILJ* 29 (2000), 176–181. With a view to third country nationals S.B. Lahuerta, *ELJ* 15 (2009), 738–756 (advocating protection of third party nationals under Article 18 TFEU and by means of a broad interpretation of the RDD).

[16] See S. Huster, *EuR* 2010, 325–337 (discussing the principle of equality in a multi-level system, in particular with regard to competences, the role of the principle in EU law and the relations of the general principle to individual prohibitions of discrimination). For a survey, see also D. Schiek, in ead. (ed.), *Allgemeines Gleichbehandlungsgesetz*, Einl. AGG paras. 24–27; E. Szyszczak, *Fordham Int.L.J.* 32 (2009), 624–659.

already part of the 1957 EEC Treaty in Article 119, thus even predating the US-American Civil Rights Act 1964.[17] However, it was not based upon considerations of civil rights, but was rather included into the constitution of the economic community because the principle of equal pay for men and women was, at that time, already effectively established in French law and France was concerned that its businesses would be at a disadvantage in comparison with businesses from other Member States where that was not the case (and women provided 'cheap labour'):[18] The prohibition of discrimination may entail economic burdens for businesses! However, the Court soon also ascribed a 'social' rationale to (today's) Article 157 TFEU.[19] 'This double aim, which is at once economic and social, shows that the principle of equal pay forms part of the **foundations of the Community**' (see also §9 para. 2).[20] Building on this, the Court has finally recognised the prohibition of sex discrimination as a **Union fundamental right**, which also binds the Union itself.[21] Today, the rationale for non-discrimination which is based upon social considerations and considerations of fundamental rights is in the foreground.[22]

5. Secondly, the **fundamental freedoms** – free movement of goods, freedom of movement for workers, freedom of establishment, freedom to provide services and free movement of capital – also contain prohibitions of discrimination (see §3 above).[23] Indeed, Advocate General Jacobs has called the prohibition of discrimination on grounds of nationality 'the single most important principle of Community law. It is the *leitmotiv* of the EEC Treaty'.[24] Thus, pursuant to Article 45(2) TFEU, freedom of movement for workers entails 'the abolition of any discrimination based on nationality between workers of the Member States

---

[17] The EU development – legislation and jurisprudence – still lagged behind the US development which was triggered by the specific issues of race relations and the civil rights movement; for a survey of the US-American development see L. M. Friedman, *American Law in the 20th Century* (New Haven/London: Yale University Press, 2002), 280–348. R. Blanpain, in B. Hepple (ed.), *International Encyclopaedia of Comparative Law, Volume XV: Labour Law,* Chapter 10 still provides a good comparative survey of the development in different countries.

[18] On this purpose ECJ Case 43/75 *Defrenne II* [1976] ECR 455 paras. 8, 11 (already with a hint of the additional social purpose); Joined Cases C-270/97 and C-271/97 *Sievers and Schrage,* [2000] ECR 929 paras. 53–57. On the historical background S. Deakin/G. Morris, *Labour Law,* 520 sq.; U. Preis/K. Mallossek, in *EAS,* B 4000 para. 5; U. Rust, in H. v. d. Groeben/ J. Schwarze (eds.), *Kommentar EUV/EGV,* Art. 141 EG para. 5; V. Rieble, *Arbeitsmarkt und Wettbewerb* (Berlin: Springer, 1996), 89 sq.

[19] W. Däubler, in id./M. Bertzbach (eds.), *Allgemeines Gleichbehandlungsgesetz,* Einl. AGG paras. 211 sq. ('from economic consideration to the principle of equality' – my translation).

[20] ECJ Case 43/75 *Defrenne II* [1976] ECR 455 para. 12; Case C-17/05 *Cadman* [2006] ECR I-9583 para. 28; Joined Cases C-270/97 and C-271/97 *Sievers und Schrage* [2000] ECR I-929 paras. 53–57; Case C-256/01 *Allonby* [2004] ECR I-873 para. 65.

[21] ECJ Case C-25/02 *Rinke* [2003] ECR I-8349 paras. 25–27.

[22] ECJ Joined Cases C-270/97 and C-271/97 *Sievers und Schrage* [2000] ECR I-929 para. 57.

[23] D. Ehlers, in id. (ed.), *Europäische Grundrechte und Grundfreiheiten,* §7 paras. 20–27.

[24] AG Jacobs, Opinion in Joined Cases C-92/92 and C-326/92 *Phil Collins* [1993] ECR I-5145 pt. 9.

as regards employment, remuneration and other conditions of work and employment' (see in detail §3 para. 31 above). The other fundamental freedoms comprise similar provisions. They are initially addressed to the Member States and the Union, but in its *Angonese*-decision[25], the Court assigned a far-reaching horizontal effect to the prohibition of discrimination in the context of free movement of workers (see in detail §3 paras. 52–54).

6.   Finally, Article 18 TFEU provides for a general prohibition of discrimination on grounds of nationality for Union citizens. The practical importance of the provision is, however, limited as it is subsidiary to the fundamental freedoms ('without prejudice to any special provisions contained' in the Treaty).[26] It does not figure prominently in the Court's jurisprudence. Whether Article 18 TFEU also applies 'horizontally' between private individuals is a matter of debate (see in detail §3 para. 107).

7.   These prohibitions of discrimination contained in EU primary law – including also the original equal pay provision of (today's) Article 157 TFEU – do not primarily pursue social policy goals but rather have the establishment and functioning of the internal market as their objective. They can thus also be termed **internal market related prohibitions of discrimination**.[27]

2.   EU Competences

8.   **Article 19(1) TFEU**, which was originally introduced by the 1997 Amsterdam Treaty, provides for a **specific competence** in the field of anti-discrimination, pursuant to which the Council acting unanimously may, after obtaining consent of the European Parliament, take measures to combat discrimination on grounds of sex, race and ethnic origin, religion and belief, disability, age or sexual orientation (see in detail §4 paras. 46 sq. above). The provision is yet another expression of the underlying principle of non-discrimination, although it does not as such lay down a prohibition.[28] On the basis of **Article 18(2) TFEU**, the Council may, in the normal legislative procedure of Article 294 TFEU, adopt rules designed to prohibit discrimination on grounds of nationality. With regard to sex discrimination, since the Amsterdam reform **Article 157(3) TFEU** provides for a specific competence. This competence used recently for the so-called 'codification' of directives against sex discrimination (see para. 19 below).

---

25   ECJ Case C-281/98 *Angonese* [2000] ECR I-4139.
26   Cf. ECJ Case C-336/96 *Gilly* [1998] ECR I-2793 para. 37; M. Holoubek, in J. Schwarze (ed.), *EU-Kommentar*, Art. 12 EG para. 8.
27   J. Basedow, *ZEuP* 2008, 230, 234–236.
28   See in detail AG Geelhoed, Opinion in Case C-13/05 *Chacón Navas* [2006] ECR I-6467 pts. 46–56. Further L. Waddington, *ILJ* 28 (1999), 133, 147–150.

9. Large parts of EU anti-discrimination law – especially in the area of employment law – are older, though, and have been based upon general competences. Thus, the 1975 Equal Pay Directive was enacted on the basis of Article 100 EEC Treaty (Article 115 TFEU). The primary objective then is, as was the case with the original Article 157 TFEU (para. 4 above), to avoid distortions in competition. The 1976 Sex Discrimination in Working Conditions Directive was based upon the supplementary competence of Article 235 EEC-Treaty (Article 352 TFEU). The 1997 Burden of Proof in Sex Discrimination Directive was originally adopted upon the basis of the 1992 Social Policy Protocol to the Maastricht Treaty (see §4 para. 4 above; the subsequent extension to the United Kingdom was based upon Article 100 EEC-Treaty).

3. The Principle of Equality as a General Principle of EU Law

10. Taken together, these rules of primary law form a comparatively tight net of prohibitions of discrimination, even though it is not arranged systematically and is not without its gaps. The Court sometimes speaks of the principle of equality as a general principle of EU (primary) law.[29] It has, however, for the most part, not drawn practical conclusions from this characterisation,[30] but rather used the *topos* of a general principle as an additional argument. The general principle of equality has therefore been termed a **hermeneutic principle** which may be helpful as an additional argument for a teleological and systematic interpretation of non-discrimination law, but which must be distinguished from an operative principle with a substantive regulatory content or an optimization requirement.[31]

11. The *Mangold* decision[32] (on this see §11 para. 50 below) and its progeny provide for an important – and controversial – exception. In that case, the plaintiff claimed he had been discriminated against on grounds of age by his employer. At the relevant time of the case, the implementation period of the Equal Treatment Framework Directive (see para. 24 below) had not yet expired. As the case concerned the 'horizontal relationship' between private individuals, the Directive could not have been directly applicable anyway (see §1 para. 72 above). In a bold move, the Court asserted that the prohibition of age discrimination did not flow from the Directive but rather from a general

---

[29] See e.g. ECJ Case C-13/05 *Chacón Navas* [2006] ECR I-6467 paras. 55 sq.; ECJ Case C-144/04 *Mangold* [2005] ECR I-9981 paras. 74–78.

[30] See e.g. ECJ Case 149/77 *Defrenne III* [1978] ECR 1365 paras. 25–33.

[31] J. Basedow, *ZEuP* 2008, 230, 234–245. To the same effect also AG Geelhoed, Opinion in Case C-13/05 *Chacón Navas* [2006] ECR I-6467 pts. 46–56; AG Mazák, Opinion in Case C-411/05 *Palacios de la Villa* [2007] ECR I-8531 pts. 79–100, 105–139. Differently S. Krebber, *Comp. Lab. L. & Pol'y J.* 27 (2006), 377–403, who considers the decision to be part of the Court's 'social rights approach'; critically K. Riesenhuber, *Festschrift für Adomeit*, 641 sq.

[32] ECJ Case C-144/04 *Mangold* [2005] ECR I-9981.

principle of EU law which the Directive presupposed: The Directive 'merely gives expression to, but does not lay down, the principle of equal treatment in employment and occupation, and (...) the principle of non-discrimination on grounds of age is a general principle of European Union law in that it constitutes a specific application of the general principle of equal treatment'. As part of EU primary law, the general principle was directly applicable, taking supremacy over incompatible national legislation which consequently had to be disapplied. The only requirement was that the national rules in question fall within the scope of Community (now: Union) law. That was the case in *Mangold* as the case was not only related to the Equal Treatment Framework Directive but also to the Fixed-Term Directive (the implementation period of which had already expired). While a subsequent judgement appeared to retreat from *Mangold,* the Court reaffirmed it in *Kücükdeveci.*[33]

12.   There is nothing in the judgements that provides for a distinction between age discrimination and discrimination on other grounds. Furthermore, as the Court infers the general principle against age discrimination from the common constitutional traditions of the Member States, it seems uncertain whether general principles against discrimination can be limited to the grounds listed in Article 19(1) TFEU (what about nationality discrimination – in general, and with respect to third country nationals?). And on the basis of similar considerations, the argument in *Mangold* could also be applied where other general principles or fundamental rights are concerned.[34] Technically, *Mangold* is concerned with the direct applicability of a general principle (against age discrimination) but not with the direct (horizontal) applicability of the Directive. In effect, though, this jurisprudence leads to a direct (horizontal) application of directives where the essence of the subject matter is determined by fundamental rights. The general principle of EU primary law is – in an obscure way –[35] related to EU secondary legislation, in the case at hand: the Equal Treatment Framework Directive. While the general principle provides for the prohibition of discrimination, the Directive regulates all the details, such as the definition of discrimination, grounds for justification or sanctions and enforcement. It is unclear, whether and to what extent the general principle of non-discrimination already determines these details or whether the legislature is free to shape them according to its own value judgements. Could the Directive, for example, provide that only direct discrimination is prohibited but not indirect discrimination or discrimination

---

[33]   ECJ Case C-555/07 *Kücükdeveci* [2010] ECR I-365. Case note by G. Thüsing/S. Horler, *CMLR* 2010, 1161–1172 (critical with regard to the extension of the scope of the general principle and the resulting horizontal effect); P. Fischinger, *ZEuP* 2011, 203–216.
[34]   Thus indeed S. Peers, *E.L. Rev.* 35 (2010), 849, 855 sq.; E. Howard, *E.L. Rev.* 36 (2011), 589, 593 sq.; A. Seifert, *ZESAR* 2010, 802, 808. Critically H. J. Willemsen/A. Sagan, *NZA* 2011, 258, 261.
[35]   See also P. Fischinger, *ZEuP* 2011, 203, 206 sq.

by association? How much leeway is left for the legislature to make choices of social policy – as are often involved in anti-discrimination law?

III. OVERVIEW OF DEVELOPMENT AND CURRENT STATE OF EU ANTI-DISCRIMINATION LAW

13. Starting from this basis in EU primary law, the legislature has, in a first strand of development, further developed the prohibition of sex discrimination in the employment sector.[36] It was only after the specific competence of Article 19 TFEU had been introduced into the Treaty that the prohibition of discrimination was further developed, in two respects: in regard to the prohibited grounds of distinction and the substantive scope of application (beyond employment issues).

1. The Prohibition of Sex Discrimination in the Employment Sector

a) Development by Individual Directives

14. Sex discrimination in employment is particularly elaborately regulated. The individual provisions have, over time, been shaped by the extensive jurisprudence of the Court of Justice and, have also been revised, to some extent, by the legislature.

15. – Development began with the 1975 **Equal Pay Directive** (EPD),[37] which fleshes out the prohibition of discrimination in Article 119 EEC (Article 157 TFEU) and was intended to ensure the full implementation of that Treaty provision.[38] The directive did not play a very prominent role in judicial practice, due to the fact that the prohibition of discrimination was, at least in its core, already included in Article 119 EEC (157 TFEU). The Court has often preferred to base its decisions directly upon Article 119 EEC.[39]

---

[36] On the development K. Adomeit, in id./J. Mohr (eds.), *Kommentar zum Allgemeinen Gleichbehandlungsgesetz*, Einl. AGG paras. 132–234; U. Preis/K. Mallossek, in *EAS*, B 4000 paras. 2–51.

[37] Council Directive 75/117/EEC of 10 February 1975 on the approximation of the laws of the Member States relating to the application of the principle of equal pay for men and women, OJ 1975 L 45/19.

[38] See also ECJ Case 43/75 *Defrenne II* [1976] ECR 455 paras. 53/55.

[39] See e.g. ECJ Case C-381/99 *Brunnhofer* [2002] ECR I-4961 para. 29; Case C-262/88 *Barber* [1990] ECR I-1889 para. 11; Case 96/80 *Jenkins* [1981] ECR 911 para. 22. See also Case C-110/91 *Moroni* [1993] ECR I-6591 paras. 21–26.

16. – The **Equal Access Directive** (EAD), which was originally enacted in 1976[40] and then revised in 2002[41], extends the prohibition of sex discrimination to access to employment, vocational training and promotion, and working conditions.

17. – Two directives provide for equality of men and women in the area of **social security**, one with regard to the statutory systems,[42] and the other with regard to occupational social security schemes.[43] We will not discuss these directives here (see also §9 paras. 27, 30–33).

18. – The 1997 **Burden of Proof Directive**[44] (BoPD) supplements the prohibitions of discrimination by shifting the burden of proof in favour of the perceived victim of discrimination (see in detail paras. 58–62 below).

b)   Consolidation by the Sex Discrimination Directive

19. The co-existence of a number of different directives in the area of sex discrimination in employment led to complexity and a lack of transparency which bore the danger of inconsistent development. To improve the clarity of the law in this field, the legislature has recently integrated the individual directives into one comprehensive directive, the 2006 **Sex Discrimination Directive**[45] (SDD) in a so-called 'codification'. This new directive had to be implemented into the national laws of the Member States by 15 August 2008, and, became

---

[40]   Council Directive 76/207/EEC of 9 February 1976 on the implementation of the principle of equal treatment for men and women as regards access to employment, vocational training and promotion, and working conditions, OJ 1976 L 39/40. On the legislative history J. Eichinger, in *EAS*, B 4200 paras. 1–4.

[41]   Directive 2002/73/EC of the European Parliament and of the Council of 23 September 2002 amending Council Directive 76/207/EEC on the implementation of the principle of equal treatment for men and women as regards access to employment, vocational training and promotion, and working conditions, OJ 2002 L 269/15. On this directive, see I. Hadeler, 'Die Revision der Gleichbehandlungsrichtlinie 76/207/EWG – Umsetzungsbedarf für das deutsche Arbeitsrecht', *NZA* 2003, 77–81; U. Rust, 'Änderungsrichtlinie 2002 zur Gleichbehandlungs-richtlinie von 1976', *NZA* 2003, 72–77.

[42]   Council Directive 79/7/EEC of 19 December 1978 on the progressive implementation of the principle of equal treatment for men and women in matters of social security, OJ 1979 L 6/24; on this directive, see in detail B. Schmidt am Busch, in *EAS*, B 4300.

[43]   Council Directive 86/378/EEC of 24 July 1986 on the implementation of the principle of equal treatment for men and women in occupational social security schemes, OJ 1986 L 225/40.

[44]   Council Directive 97/80/EC of 15 December 1997 on the burden of proof in cases of discrimination based on sex, OJ 1997 L 14/6. Extended to the United Kingdom by Council Directive 98/52/EC of 13 July 1998 on the extension of Directive 97/80/EC on the burden of proof in cases of discrimination based on sex to the United Kingdom of Great Britain and Northern Ireland, OJ 1998 L 205/66. On the legislative history M. Schlachter, 'Richtlinie über die Beweislast bei Diskriminierung', *RdA* 1998, 321, 322 sq.

[45]   Directive 2006/54/EC of the European Parliament and of the Council of 5 July 2006 on the implementation of the principle of equal opportunities and equal treatment of men and women in matters of employment and occupation (recast), OJ 2006 L 204/23.

effective on 15 August 2009. The individual directives comprised therein were thus repealed, Articles 33 sq. SDD. In the sections that follow, we will deal exclusively with the new Sex Discrimination Directive and refer to the older texts only where the context so requires.[46]

20. There are a number of provisions that form part of the **regulatory environment** of prohibitions against sex discrimination in European employment law. First and directly sex-related, there is the Maternity Protection Directive (§20). Other directives have an indirect relation to sex, such as the Part Time Work Directive (§16) and the Fixed Term Work Directive (§17), both of which provide for specific prohibitions of discrimination of the respective groups of employees. And finally the Parental Leave Directive (§21) *inter alia* also aims to achieve equal opportunity for men and women in employment.

21. Looking beyond the area of sex discrimination in employment, there is also Directive 2004/113/EC (SDGS) implementing the principle of equal treatment between men and women in the access to and supply of goods and services. It establishes a prohibition of discrimination applicable 'to all persons who provide goods and services, which are available to the public irrespective of the person concerned'. The Directive thus covers large parts of **general contract law.**[47]

2. Prohibition of Further Grounds of Discrimination

22. Based on the new competence of Article 19 TFEU (para. 8 above), two directives which were enacted in 2000 signify the introduction of a **new generation** of EU prohibitions of discrimination.[48] This new generation is characterised by an expansion of the prohibited grounds of discrimination as well as of the scope of application. Starting with these directives, the EU legislator has also begun to regulate issues of enforcement, matters which were hitherto largely left to the discretion of the Member States.

a) The Race Discrimination Directive

23. The Race Discrimination Directive[49] (RDD) prohibits discrimination on grounds of race or ethnic origin. To some extent, the Directive was intended to

---

46   A **synopsis** can be found in Annex II SDD.
47   K. Riesenhuber, in S. Leible/M. Schlachter (eds.), *Diskriminierungsschutz durch Privatrecht*, 127; id./J.-U. Franck, *JZ* 2004, 529, 529 sq.; iid., 'Das Verbot der Geschlechtsdiskriminierung beim Zugang zu Gütern und Dienstleistungen', *EWS* 2005, 245.
48   M. Bell, *ILJ* 29 (2000), 79–84; id., *ELJ* 8 (2002), 384–399; S. Fredman, *ILJ* 30 (2001), 145–168.
49   Council Directive 2000/43/EC of 29 June 2000 implementing the principle of equal treatment between persons irrespective of racial or ethnic origin, OJ 2000 L 180/22.

set an example against xenophobia.[50] The Directive not only introduces a new forbidden ground of distinction but it also extends the scope of application. For while it applies to employment and a large number of related issues (Article 3(a)-(g)), it also applies to access to and supply of goods and services (Article 3(h)), in other words general contract law.[51]

b) The Equal Treatment Framework Directive

24. The Equal Treatment Framework Directive[52] (ETFD) was enacted shortly after the Race Discrimination Directive. It prohibits discrimination on a number of other grounds:

– religion or belief
– disability
– age and
– sexual orientation.

Its scope of application is, however, restricted to the area of employment and occupation (it does not cover general contract law). The Commission has, however, proposed a directive that is intended to implement the principle of equal treatment between persons irrespective of religion or belief, disability, age or sexual orientation outside the labour market.[53]

3. Future Issues

25. The list of prohibited grounds in the directives is **exhaustive**.[54] The Court thus felt unable to accommodate a claim of 'discrimination on grounds of socio-professional category or place of work' under either the Race Discrimination Directive or the Equal Treatment Framework Directive. Similarly, EU law does not prohibit 'caste discrimination' as such.[55] While the concept of 'associative' disability discrimination (para. 32 below) offers reflexive protection for relatives of disabled persons, EU law does not prohibit discrimination against 'carers' of disabled persons *per se*.[56]

---

[50] On the legislative history e.g. C. Brown, 'The Race Directive: Towards Equality for All the Peoples of Europe?', *YEL* 21 (2002), 195, 197–204.

[51] On the contract law aspects, see e.g. K. Riesenhuber, *Europäisches Vertragsrecht*, paras. 414–425.

[52] Council Directive 2000/78/EC of 27 November 2000 establishing a general framework for equal treatment in employment and occupation, OJ 2000 L 303/16.

[53] Commission, Proposal for a Council Directive on implementing the principle of equal treatment between persons irrespective of religion or belief, disability, age or sexual orientation, COM(2008) 426 final. L. Waddington, *E.L. Rev.* 36 (2011), 163–184.

[54] ECJ Case C-310/10 *Agafiţei* 7 July 2011 paras. 31–36.

[55] A. Waughray, *MLR* 72 (2009), 723–749 (discussing caste discrimination under Indian, international and UK law).

[56] Cf. O'Brien, *E.L. Rev.* 36 (2011), 26–50.

26. An issue which is attracting increasing discussion is that of 'multiple discrimination'.[57] It was initially raised in regard to discrimination against women from black and minority ethnic backgrounds but may be relevant beyond. Existing EU legislation does not specifically regulate multiple discrimination, but the 2000-Directives mention the issue in regard to the multiple discrimination of women: 'In implementing the principle of equal treatment, the Community should, in accordance with Article 3(2) of the EC Treaty, aim to eliminate inequalities, and to promote equality between men and women, especially since women are often the victims of multiple discrimination' (Recital 3 ETFD; similarly Recital 14 RDD). However, the 2006 codification of the sex discrimination directives did not take up the issue. The existing directives are, however, not mutually exclusive and a violation of the principle of equality may be based upon a claim of discrimination on more than one ground, e.g. race, religion and disability (so-called 'additive approach'). Based on a concept originally developed in feminist sociology, 'intersectionality' is being considered as a separate issue where discrimination on two grounds (e.g. sex and race) amounts to more than an addition of the discrimination on either ground. It may even occur where discrimination on either ground separately cannot be separately established.

IV. INSTRUMENTS OF EU ANTI-DISCRIMINATION LAW

27. The instruments of protection in EU Anti-Discrimination law – as developed in *secondary legislation* –[58] now, after the 2006 codification of prohibitions of sex discrimination, follow a fairly coherent system. From a structural perspective, there are three questions involved, (1) the prohibition of discrimination, (2) grounds for justification and (3) issues of enforcement and accompanying measures.

1. *The Prohibition of Discrimination – The Principle of Equal Treatment*

Provisions: Article 4, 5 und 14 SDD, Article 2(1) RDD, Article 2(1) ETFD, Article 4(1) SDGS

28. The legislator now addresses the prohibited behaviour as part of the 'principle of equal treatment'. The principle of equal treatment provides 'that

---

[57] See e.g. I. Solanke, *MLR* 72 (2009), 723–749; D. Schiek, *CMLR* 2011, 777–799; D. Schiek/ V. Chege (eds.), *European Union Non-Discrimination Law – Comparative Perspectives on Multidimensional Equality Law*.

[58] The prohibition of discrimination of Article 157 TFEU largely follows the same rules, even though the wording of the provision is not as detailed with regard to the legal consequences of a violation and the complementary measures of protection. It should be noted that the status of primary law leads to special effects in relation to the national laws of the Member States (supremacy); see also §9 para. 25.

there shall be no direct or indirect discrimination', in other words, that any direct or indirect discrimination is prohibited.[59] Direct and indirect discrimination are then legally defined.

29. It is rather unclear why the legislator does not clearly express the prohibition of discrimination but instead hides it behind rather obscure phrasing, such as in Article 1 ETFD, pursuant to which the purpose is 'to lay down a general framework for combating discrimination'. This defect of drafting technique[60] has led to an uncertainty in the Court of Justice whether the Directive contains a prohibition of discrimination at all or rather presupposes its existence as a general principle of Union law (see in more detail §11 paras. 3, 50 below).

a)   Direct Discrimination

Provisions: Article 2(1)(a) SDD, Article 2(1)-(4) EAD, Article 1 EPD, Article 2(2)(a) RDD, Article 2(2)(a) ETFD, Article 2(a), (b) SDGS.

30.   Direct discrimination occurs where a person is treated less favourably than another is, has or would be treated in a comparable situation on one of the prohibited grounds (sex, ethnic origin, age, ...).[61] The disparate treatment is directly based on one of the prohibited grounds (sex, ethnic origin, age, ...).[62] The definition follows the concept of a comparable person, comparing one person's treatment with that of another. But this is supplemented by a **hypothetical element** ('would be treated').[63]

31.   The prohibition of direct discrimination thus has the following elements:

(1)   a person is treated less favourably than another is, has been or would be in a comparable situation
(2)   causation ('on grounds of')
(3)   one of the prohibited grounds.

---

[59]   See the systematisation developed by J. Neuner, in S. Leible/M. Schlachter (eds.), *Diskriminierungsschutz durch Privatrecht*, 84 sqq.
[60]   W. Zöllner, 'Altersgrenzen beim Arbeitsverhältnis jetzt und nach Einführung eines Verbots der Altersdiskriminierung', in R. Richardi/H.Reichold (eds.), *Altersgrenzen und Alterssicherung im Arbeitsrecht: Wolfgang Blomeyer zum Gedenken* (Munich: C.H. Beck, 2003), 517, 526 sq.
[61]   H. Wiedemann, *Die Gleichbehandlungsgebote im Arbeitsrecht*, 29–31.
[62]   On the development of the Court's jurisprudence see L. Waddington/M. Bell, *CMLR* 38 (2001), 587, 591 sq.
[63]   See D. Schiek, *NZA* 2004, 873, 874; R. Wank, *NZA* 2004 Special Supplement to Issue 22, 16, 21 sq.

32. The directives prohibit discrimination *'on grounds of'* the designated characteristic. It will normally be the victim of discrimination who possesses the relevant protected characteristic. Yet the wording of the prohibitions of discrimination does not necessarily[64] require that such a restriction be imposed. In light of the social policy objectives pursued by the Equal Treatment Framework Directive, the Court in *Coleman* has interpreted the concept of direct discrimination as also covering **associative discrimination:**[65] on these facts, where a worker was treated less favourably because of the disability of her child. This decision raises a number of questions. Precisely what form of association is required?[66] Which rules apply? The Court's reasoning does not seem to be restricted to the case of discrimination on grounds of disability or to the specifics of the Equal Treatment Framework Directive.[67] Furthermore, the Court's reasoning seems to be capable of supporting other instances of 'transferred discrimination', such as cases where a protected characteristic is being attributed to the victim notwithstanding the fact that he does not possess it ('attribution').[68] *Coleman* concerned a case of direct discrimination and harassment. It is uncertain whether protection will be extended to cases of indirect associative discrimination.[69] The Court specifically noted that the obligation to provide 'reasonable accommodation' only applies with regard to 'persons with disabilities' and cannot be extended to third parties associated with them.[70] Similarly, positive action should also be limited to members of the protected group.

---

[64] M. Schlachter, *RdA* 2010, 104–109 rightly points out that while the wording of the ETFD is rather open, not requiring that the person who is discriminated against is the bearer of the relevant characteristic (e.g. disability), this is different in the RDD ('one person is treated less favourably … on grounds of racial or ethnic origin'; *'eine Person auf Grund* ihrer [!] *Rasse oder ethnischen Herkunft'*) and in the SDD ('one person is treated less favourably on grounds of sex').

[65] ECJ Case C-303/06 *Coleman* [2008] ECR I-5603 paras. 34–55. For a thorough discussion, see M. Schlachter, *RdA* 2010, 104–109. The issue of associative or transferred discrimination had already been referred to the ECJ in Case C-249/96 *Grant* [1998] ECR I-621 para. 11 (question 3); the Court, considering all six referred questions together and discussing its decision in Case C-13/94 *P v S* [1996] ECR I-2143, held at para. 42: 'The Court considered that such discrimination was in fact based, essentially if not exclusively, on the sex of the person concerned. That reasoning, which leads to the conclusion that such discrimination is to be prohibited just as is discrimination based on the fact that a person belongs to a particular sex, is limited to the case of a worker's gender reassignment and does not therefore apply to differences of treatment based on a person's sexual orientation.'

[66] M. Schlachter, *RdA* 2010, 104, 108 sq.

[67] S. Deakin/G. Morris, *Labour Law*, 531; M. Schlachter, *RdA* 2010, 104, 108 sq.

[68] M. Pilgerstorfer/S. Forshaw, *ILJ* 37 (2008), 384, 392 sq.

[69] O'Brien, *E.L. Rev.* 36 (2011), 26–50 (advocating protection against indirect associative discrimination and direct protection of carers and criticizing an economic approach to anti-discrimination law where non-discrimination as a 'social good' is being weighed against economic goods).

[70] ECJ Case C-303/06 *Coleman* [2008] ECR I-5603 paras. 42 sq.

33. In its *Feryn* decision, the Court ruled that there could be direct discrimination even where there is **no victim of discrimination**. This seems a rather broad interpretation of direct discrimination, even under the concept of a hypothetical comparison. The director of the Feryn company announced that he was looking to recruit fitters but that the company could not employ 'immigrants' because its customers were reluctant to give them access to their private residences for the works to be undertaken. Notwithstanding that no foreign applicants were in fact rejected, the Court held that this was a case of direct discrimination.[71] This decision is difficult to reconcile with the wording of the definition of direct discrimination and with the conception of the Directive as a protection of individual rights. The decision may be explained by reference to the social policy *objectives* of the Directive. The Court argued that the company director's remarks could have dissuaded potential candidates from applying.

b)   Indirect Discrimination

Provisions: Article 2(1)(d) SDD, Article 2(2) indent 2 EAD, Article 1 EPD, Article 2(2) BoPD, Article 2(2)(b) RDD, Article 2(2)(b) ETFD, Article 2(b) SDGS

34. Indirect discrimination occurs where an apparently neutral provision, criterion or practice would put persons falling within the protected groups at a particular disadvantage compared with persons outside that group. In other words a provision, criterion or practice is indirectly discriminatory where it has a disparate impact[72] upon the protected group.[73] A subjective element, discriminatory intent in particular, is not required.[74]

---

[71]   ECJ Case C-54/07 *Feryn* [2008] ECR I-5187 paras. 22–28. Approvingly R. Krause, *CMLR* 2010, 917–931.

[72]   On the origins in US-American anti-discrimination law K. Riesenhuber, *RdA* 1993, 36, 36 sq.; H. Wiedemann, *Festschrift für Friauf,* 136 sq.

[73]   See the seminal decisions ECJ Case 96/80 *Jenkins* [1981] ECR 911 paras. 10–13; Case 170/84 *Bilka* [1986] ECR 1607 paras. 29–31. On the concept, its development and justification W. Blomeyer, *NZA* 1994, 633, 638 ('a vehicle for the nivellation of many other differences in employment law' – my translation); O. Doyle, *OJLS* 27 (2007), 537–553; N. Görlitz, *Struktur und Bedeutung der Rechtsfigur der mittelbaren Diskriminierung im System der Grundfreiheiten,* 29–35; M. Lorenz, *Festschrift für Wlotzke,* 60–63; K. Koch/A. Nguyen, *EuR* 2010, 364–377; R. Rebhahn/C. Kietaibl, *Rechtswissenschaft* 2010, 373–396. A legal definition has first been introduced by the 1997 Burden of Proof Directive (see para 18 above); see M. Schlachter, *RdA* 1998, 321, 323. The concept can be traced to the jurisprudence of the US Supreme Court on Title VII of the Civil Rights Act 1964 starting with *Griggs* v. *Duke Power,* 401 U.S. 424 (1965). See also K. Riesenhuber, *RdA* 1993, 36, 37; M. Schlachter, *Wege zur Gleichberechtigung,* 76–82; H. Wiedemann, *Die Gleichbehandlungsgebote im Arbeitsrecht,* 31–34.

[74]   M. Schlachter, in R. Müller-Glöge/U. Preis/I. Schmidt (eds.), *Erfurter Kommentar,* Art. 141 EG para. 17; H. Wiedemann, *Festschrift für Friauf,* 138.

35. Such disparate impact may, in particular (but not exclusively, see Recital 15 RDD), be **established** by using statistical data.[75] While the Burden of Proof Directive required proof that 'a substantially higher proportion of the members of one sex' were disadvantaged (Article 2(2) BoPD), this is no longer the case in more recent directives. Pursuant to the Race Discrimination Directive, it suffices to show that the criterion etc. would put persons of the protected group 'at a particular disadvantage' (Article 2(2)(b) and Recital 15 RDD, Article 2(2)(b) and Recital 15 ETFD) and thus alleviates proof.[76]

36. As the prohibition of indirect discrimination is based upon *neutral* criteria (etc.), there is a danger that legitimate objectives pursued by such criteria may be defeated. In order to avoid disruption, it is a (negative) element of the prohibition of indirect discrimination as such (and not only an element of justification) that the neutral criteria cannot be justified as **necessary to achieve a legitimate objective**, Article 2(b) RDD and Article 2(2)(b) ETFD die Rechte.[77] Indirect discrimination is, in other words, only established where a two-step test is satisfied:[78] Neutral criteria must have a discriminatory effect *and* these criteria must not be necessary to achieve a legitimate goal.[79] What is at stake here is thus not the justification of *discrimination* but the justification of *neutral criteria*.[80] The bottom line effect is similar, though, as justification of the criteria exempts the discrimination.

---

[75] H. Wiedemann, *Festschrift für Friauf,* 138 sq.; K. Adomeit/J. Mohr, *RdA* 2011, 102–108.

[76] E. Guild, *ILJ* 29 (2000), 416, 420; D. Schiek, *NZA* 2004, 873, 875; id., *ELJ* 8 (2002), 290, 296; M. Schlachter, 'Altersgrenzen angesichts des gemeinschaftlichen Verbots der Altersdiskriminierung', in R. Richardi/H.Reichold (eds.), *Altersgrenzen und Alterssicherung im Arbeitsrecht: Wolfgang Blomeyer zum Gedenken* (Munich: C.H. Beck, 2003), 355, 358 sq.; M. Schmidt/D. Senne, 'Das gemeinschaftsrechtliche Verbot der Altersdiskriminierung und seine Bedeutung für das deutsche Arbeitsrecht', *RdA* 2002, 80, 83; B. Waas, 'Die neue EG-Richtlinie zum Verbot der Diskriminierung aus rassischen oder ethnischen Gründen im Arbeitsverhältnis', *ZIP* 2000, 2151, 2153; L. Waddington/M. Bell, *CMLR* 38 (2001), 587, 592–594.

[77] On Articles 2(2)(b), 6(1) ETFD ECJ Case C-388/07 *Age Concern England* [2009] ECR I-1569 para. 66; on Article 119 EEC (Article 141 EC/157 TFEU) Case 170/84 *Bilka* [1986] ECR 1607 para. 36; Case 171/88 *Rinner-Kühn* [1989] ECR 2743 para. 14; on the EAD Case C 196/02 *Vasiliki Nikoloudi* [2005] ECR I-1789 para. 48.

[78] On this two-step test D. Schiek, *NZA* 2004, 873, 874 sq.; M. Schlachter, in R. Müller-Glöge/U. Preis/I. Schmidt (eds.), *Erfurter Kommentar,* Art. 141 EG para. 18; id., *ZESAR* 2006, 391, 395; R. Wank, in P. Hanau/H.-D. Steinmeyer/R. Wank (eds.), *Handbuch des europäischen Arbeits- und Sozialrechts,* §16 paras. 43–46. See also F. Gamillscheg, *Festschrift für Floretta,* 179 sq.

[79] Article 2(1)(b) SDD, Article 2(2)(b) RDD, Article 2(2)(b)(i) ETFD, Article 2(b) SDGS. Pursuant to Article 2(2)(b)(ii) ETFD, also the measures mandated by national law to eliminate disadvanteges for disabled persons are recognised as legitimate aims. See also H. Wiedemann, *Festschrift für Friauf,* 143 sq.

[80] K. Riesenhuber/J.-U. Franck, *EWS* 2005, 245, 247; D. Schiek, *NZA* 2004, 873 (874 sq.); differently I. Scholten, *Diskriminierungsschutz im Privatrecht?,* 40–42.

37. Take for **example** a reward for 'flexibility' which, as a matter of social fact, female employees cannot as easily provide as their male counterparts, due family and household responsibilities. The facially neutral criterion of flexibility thus has a discriminatory effect in fact upon female employees. An employer may 'justify the remuneration of such adaptability by showing it is of importance for the performance of specific tasks entrusted to the employee'.[81] However, a mere 'generalisation concerning certain categories of worker' such as the allegation of a 'special link between length of service and acquisition of a certain level of knowledge or experience' are insufficient for this justification.[82] It should be noted that Union law provides for the legal framework of this test but that it is for the national courts to apply it to individual cases.[83]

c)   Harassment[84]

Provisions: Article 2(1)(c) SDD, Article 2(2) indent 3 EAD, Article 2(3) RDD, Article 2(3) ETFD

38. Beginning with the new generation of directives of 2000 (para. 22 above), the prohibition of discrimination was extended to also cover harassment. The subsequent revisions of the sex discrimination directives provide for a specific prohibition of sexual harassment (paras. 44 sq. below). Harassment could be considered unlawful as such, comparable to a special tort, irrespective of discrimination.[85] Yet, there is good reason to consider it a special form of discrimination, given that harassment as such may lead to the exclusion of individuals or groups. On the basis of the same considerations, it seems well-founded to define harassment with regard to a 'hostile environment'.

39. While harassment can be a particularly nasty form of behaviour, its prohibition is especially prone to encroach upon civil liberties, and free speech in particular.[86] It is particularly here that anti-discrimination laws run the danger of leading to 'political correctness' and thus the stifling of free expression. For example, Matthias Matussek in his book on *Das katholische Abenteuer* ('The Adventure of Being Catholic') indicates that being catholic is not particularly

---

[81]   ECJ Case 109/88 *Danfoss* [1989] ECR 3199 para. 22 (with regard to Article 119 EEC).
[82]   ECJ Case C-1/95 *Gerster* [1997] ECR I-5253 paras. 35–41 (with regard to the EAD); Case C-184/89 *Nimz* [1991] ECR I-297 paras. 13 sq. (with regard to Article 119 EEC).
[83]   See e.g. ECJ Case C-1/95 *Gerster* [1997] ECR I-5253 paras. 35–41 (on the EAD); Case C-278/93 *Freers und Speckmann* [1996] ECR I-1165 paras. 24–30 (on Article 119 EEC).
[84]   Protection against harassment is not a general protection against mobbing; advocating further EU legislation M. Driessen-Reilly/B. Driessen, *E.L. Rev.* 28 (2003), 493–507.
[85]   Favouring a tort concept G. Thüsing, *ZfA* 2001, 397, 411 sq.
[86]   D. E. Bernstein, *You Can't Say That!*.

popular in the German weekly DER SPIEGEL for which he works.[87] What about jokes about the Pope in the newsroom? Or, in some jobs it is not uncommon to have a radio on playing music. Rock and roll lyrics are, from today's perspective, notorious for describing traditional and out-dated role-models. (Take Ray Charles's 'I've got woman': '… she knows a woman's place is right there now in her home'.) Some of the rap lyrics that one hears are outright sexist.

40. Harassment is **unwanted conduct** which is related to one of the prohibited grounds where it fulfils two cumulative prerequisites.[88] It occurs with the purpose or effect

(1) of violating the dignity of a person and
(2) of creating an intimidating, hostile, degrading, humiliating or offensive environment (hereinafter simply referred to as hostile environment).[89]

41. Whether conduct is **unwanted** is determined by the victim's perception.[90] This does not mean, however, that only conduct that continues after objection could be considered unwanted. The fact that a conduct is subjectively unwanted can also be established without any utterance of the victim. It can be based merely upon the usual standards of behaviour *in the respective social environment*[91] and can thus even be found where it first occurred. It is unclear whether harassment requires intent. With regard to discrimination as such, which can also be considered a tort, the Court has interpreted the requirements of the Directive in a formal and verbatim way and as such has rejected a requirement of fault (see para. 69). The characterisation as 'unwanted' does not imply a fault requirement either, given that it is not only conduct which continued after objection (and thus pursued with at least conditional intent) that may be considered unwanted. A requirement of intent would also run counter to the protective intentions of the law in this field, since it would privilege persons with a dull sense of decency. Overly restricting individual freedom can be prevented by, on the one hand, adopting a narrow interpretation of the other requirements (violation of dignity, hostile environment) and on the other, by taking into account the usual standards of behaviour (in the respective social

---

[87]　M. Matussek, *Das katholische Abenteuer – Eine Provokation*, 2nd edn. (Munich: Deutsche Verlagsanstalt, 2011), 45.

[88]　Differently R. Nickel, 'Handlungsaufträge zur Bekämpfung von ethnischen Diskriminierungen in der neuen Gleichbehandlungsrichtlinie 2000/43/EG', *NJW* 2001, 2668, 2670 (with regard to Directive 2000/43/EC).

[89]　On the origins of this criterion in US American law G. Thüsing, *ZfA* 2001, 397, 412. This is not, as R. Nickel, *NJW* 2001, 2668, 2670 argues with regard to the RDD, a liability for a hostile environment.

[90]　Differently I. Hadeler, *NZA* 2003, 77, 78 sq.

[91]　To the same effect G. Thüsing, in F. J. Säcker/R. Rixecker (eds.), *Münchener Kommentar zum BGB*, §3 AGG para. 57.

environment). A suggestive joke may be acceptable in one environment but not in another.

42. A **violation of dignity** occurs where a remark or behaviour is degrading or disparaging. As the prohibition covers intentional behaviour as well as behaviour which has 'the effect' of violating dignity, 'well-intended' jokes may also be prohibited. They will, however, not necessarily lead to a hostile environment. Note, however, that the requirements of 'harassment' are fulfilled where the conduct gives rise to a degrading or humiliating environment. It thus constitutes harassment where the employer causes other employees to behave similarly by his derogatory remarks.

43. The legislature considered that the prohibition of harassment in the Race Discrimination Directive and the Equal Treatment Framework Directive required further elaboration and explicitly left it to the Member States to provide accordingly, Article 2(3) sent. 2 RDD and Article 2(3) ETFD. The same should apply with regard to the definition of harassment in the Sex Discrimination Directive, even though this is not explicitly expressed, Article 2(1)(c) SDD. The EU legislature may have thought that national implementation laws could concretise the prohibition of harassment by way of example. As a matter of course, the Member States may not lag behind the requirements of the Directives.

d)   Sexual Harassment

Provisions: Article 2(1)(d) SDD, Article 2(2) indent 4 EAD

Bibliography:
C. A. MacKinnon, *Sexual Harassment of Working Women* (New Haven/London: Yale University Press, 1979).

44. In addition to harassment, the Sex Discrimination Directive specifically prohibits sexual harassment. Sexual harassment is different from 'simple' harassment in that it applies only with regard to **unwanted behaviour of a sexual nature**. It can occur in the form of verbal, non-verbal or physical conduct. Sexual harassment further requires that a violation of dignity is being intended or effected. Other than in respect of 'simple' harassment, the creation of a hostile environment is considered to be part of the violation of dignity ('in particular when creating a hostile environment') and, in other words, not a separate (cumulative) requirement. This seems rather inconsistent but may be justified on the ground that sexual harassment is particularly nasty (and should thus be prohibited on the basis of more easily satisfied requirements). Secondly, the legislature may have presumed that sexual harassment will regularly involve creating a degrading environment.

45. As with 'simple' harassment, the **unwanted** conduct does not require the victim's explicit objection. Confrontation with obscene pictures or objects will be unwanted as such. And as with 'simple' harassment, sexual harassment does not require **intent**.[92]

e)   Instruction to Discriminate

Provisions: Article 2(2)(b) SDD, Article 2(4) EAD, Article 2(4) RDD, Article 2(4) ETFD, Article 2(d) SDGS

46. Discrimination also includes 'instruction to discriminate'. This specific prohibition prevents the principal from hiding behind an employee or agent, or the organisation (e.g. an employer's association) behind its members.

47. Other issues of participation are not explicitly addressed. **Vicarious liability** could be of practical importance,[93] for example where the employer does not prevent his employees from harassing others. Such behaviour of employees may not always be imputed to the employer and therefore characterised as harassment by the employer. A requirement of vicarious liability may, however, be inferred from the general duties to implement the Directive with regard to the principles of equivalence and effectiveness (on these see §1 para. 66).

2.   Justification

a)   Justification in the strict sense

Provisions: Article 14(2) SDD, Article 2(6) EAD, Article 4 RDD, Article 4–6 ETFD, Article 4(5) SDGS

48. The prohibition of discrimination thus defined is supplemented by grounds of justification which have a common structure but differ in their detail depending upon the prohibited ground at issue, since the justifications reflect the different issues between the various grounds which are at stake.

49. The grounds for justification in the area of employment are rather uniformly structured, albeit with some possibilities for variation on account of the options which are given to the Member States. Thus, the Member States may provide that a distinction on grounds of sex or race and ethnic origin does not constitute discrimination where such characteristic constitutes a '**genuine and**

---

[92]   For a different view see I. Hadeler, *NZA* 2003, 77, 78; G. Thüsing, in F. J. Säcker/R. Rixecker (eds.), *Münchener Kommentar zum BGB*, §3 AGG paras. 65 sq.

[93]   K. Riesenhuber, in S. Leible/M. Schlachter (eds.), *Diskriminierungsschutz durch Privatrecht*, 139 sq.

determining occupational requirement'.[94] This can, however, only justify discrimination with regard to *access* to employment and not with regard to conditions of employment and pay.

50. The *Feryn* case (see para. 33 above) raises the issue whether **customer preferences** provide a justification for an employer's discrimination (even though the question was not explicitly referred to the Court).[95] *Feryn* argued 'that it could not employ "immigrants" because its customers were reluctant to give them access to their private residences for the period of the works'. Similarly, customers of a gynaecologist, a shop for women's wear, of a battered women's shelter or a women's bookstore may expect female employees; customers of an Indian restaurant may expect Indian waiters (and an Indian chef?). The issue has received close attention in US American law, and section 5(2) of the UK Race Relations Act 1976 provides for a differentiated catalogue of justifications. While we may not like the customers' preferences, they will often not be unlawful. The customers are not addressees of EU anti-discrimination law. Indeed, in many ways, different preferences are the essence of a free society and a market economy. The employer behaves rationally if he accommodates his customers' preferences. A discriminatory intent cannot be assumed. He merely obeys the laws of the market (although this may not be true to the same extent in the case of the women's bookstore or the [authentic] Indian restaurant). At the same time, it cannot be overlooked that taking account of customer preferences may not only perpetuate societal prejudice (which, as such, could be considered tolerable in an open society) but may also be abused (as a pretext) and may thwart anti-discrimination policy. The Court in *Feryn* did not rule on the issue. The determination whether an occupational requirement is 'genuine and determining' involves a value judgement. This leaves room for distinction between different groups of cases depending upon whether the accommodation of customer preferences appears to be legitimate or not.[96] The legitimacy may, in particular, be grounded in the customers' fundamental rights (such as in the case of the gynaecologist) or in the employers' fundamental rights (such as in the case of the Indian restaurant). An additional factor in determining the legitimacy of an employer's actions may be whether the specific offer concerned (massage for women or Indian restaurant) may, in an open market, be matched by

---

94   See R. Wank, *NZA* 2004 Special Supplement to Issue 22, 16, 22–24; H. Wiedemann, *Die Gleichbehandlungsgebote im Arbeitsrecht*, 45–52.

95   On the issue, e.g. E. Picker, in E. Lorenz (ed.), *Karlsruher Forum 2004*, 36 sq., 76 sq.; R. Krause, *Festschrift für Adomeit*, 377–393; R. A. Epstein, *Forbidden Grounds*, 299–309; C. Sunstein, in id. (ed.), *Free Markets and Social Justice*, 151, 153 sq. See also C. Jolls, *Harv. L. Rev.* 115 (2001), 642–699 (discussing the parallel of 'accommodation' of employee interests in customer preference-cases and in other cases requiring 'reasonable accommodation' such as disability discrimination cases).

96   See e.g. R. Krause, *Festschrift für Adomeit*, 388–392.

respective other offers (massage for men; Italian restaurant), thereby presumptively creating job opportunities for the different groups concerned.[97]

51. The **justification of age discrimination** is specifically regulated. Age discrimination may particularly be justified by employment policy, labour market and vocational training objectives, Article 6(1) ETFD (see in detail §11 paras. 33–40). Justification of different treatment on grounds of **disability** is limited by the requirement of '**reasonable accommodation**', Article 5 ETFD (see in detail §11 paras. 27 sq.). The grounds for justification also differ in other respects; different treatment does not in all cases indicate unlawfulness.[98] The different accommodations of interests that are discernible from the differentiated approach appear to be well-founded on substantive considerations.[99] Some consider variations in the law on justification to express differences in the 'weight' which is assigned to the different grounds of prohibited discrimination.[100]

52. With regard to *general contract law* only the directive on sex discrimination provides the possibility for justification where the difference in treatment is necessary to achieve a legitimate objective, Article 4(5) SDGS.[101] The Race Discrimination Directive only provides for a ground of justification with regard to employment but not with regard to general contract law.[102] Distinctions are thus admissible only outside the scope of application or, in regard to indirect discrimination, where discriminatory effects of (legitimate and proportionate) neutral criteria are concerned.

b)   Positive Action (Affirmative Action)

Provisions: Article 157(4) TFEU, Article 3 SDD, Article 2(8) EAD, Article 5 RDD, Article 7 ETFD, Article 6 SDGS

Bibliography:
N. Colneric, 'Frauenförderung nach der Kalanke-Entscheidung des EuGH', *ArbRGeg* 1997, 69–94; C. McCrudden, 'A Comparative Taxonomy of "Positive Action" and

---

[97]   Thüsing, in F. J. Säcker/R. Rixecker (eds.), *Münchener Kommentar zum BGB*, §8 AGG para. 20.
[98]   M. Schlachter, in R. Richardi/H.Reichold (eds.), *Altersgrenzen und Alterssicherung im Arbeitsrecht: Wolfgang Blomeyer zum Gedenken*, 355, 367.
[99]   D. König, 'Das Verbot der Altersdiskriminierung – ein Diskriminierungsverbot zweiter Klasse?', in C. Gaitanides/S. Kadelbach/G. Rodriguez Iglesias (eds.), *Europa und seine Verfassung: Festschrift für Manfred Zuleeg zum siebzigsten Geburtstag*, 341, 352.
[100]   D. Schiek, *ELJ* 8 (2002), 290, 301 sq.; M. Schmidt/D. Senne, *RdA* 2002, 80, 89 (criticising that the prohibition of age discrimination had been made a 'second-class fundamental right' and considering whether this deficit could be remedied with the instruments of the Charter of Fundamental Rights). See also the references in n. 15 above.
[101]   K. Riesenhuber/J.-U. Franck, *EWS* 2005, 245–251.
[102]   Article 4 RDD only concerns the area of employment law; see I. Scholten, *Diskriminierungsschutz im Privatrecht?*, 38–40.

"Affirmative Action" Policies', in R. Schulze (ed.), *Non-Discrimination in European Private Law* (Tübingen: Mohr Siebeck, 2011), 157–180; M. Rosenthal, *Affirmative Action and Justice – A Philosophical and Constitutional Inquiry* (New Haven/London: Yale University Press, 1991); M. Sachs, 'Frauenquoten wieder vor dem EuGH', *RdA* 1998, 129–142; D. Schiek, '"Kalanke" und die Folgen – Überlegungen zu EG-rechtlichen Anforderungen an betriebliche Gleichstellungspolitik', *AuR* 1996, 128.

Cases (Selection):
ECJ Case C-450/93 *Kalanke* [1995] ECR I-3051; ECJ Case C-409/95 *Marschall* [1997] ECR I-6363; ECJ Case C-157/97 *Badeck* [2000] ECR I-1875; ECJ Case C-407/98 *Abrahamsson und Anderson* [2000] ECR I-5539; ECJ Case C-476/99 *Lommers* [2002] ECR I-2891; ECJ Case C-319–03 *Briheche* [2004] ECR I-8807.

53. All anti-discrimination directives today allow for positive action to be taken, as does Article 157(4) TFEU: measures aimed at promoting a disadvantaged group. Such positive action is of special practical importance with regard to disabled people; see in more detail §11 paras. 27 sq.[103] While the provision on positive action in the Equal Access Directive of 1976 was aimed at 'promoting equal opportunity', recent directives have shifted the emphasis to the rather more ambitious goal of 'ensuring full equality'.[104] Positive action is not concerned with the compensation of concrete individual disadvantages of individuals but rather with the removal of disadvantages faced by a protected group as a matter of social fact.[105] For the purpose of promoting a disadvantaged group (e.g. women), another group (e.g. men) may be disadvantaged. While the goal is widely accepted, the moral evaluation of affirmative action measures is controversial.[106] For EU anti-discrimination law, the Court of Justice has consistently given an unequivocal evaluation though: Positive action is a form of

---

[103] See H. Wiedemann, *Die Gleichbehandlungsgebote im Arbeitsrecht,* 40–44. See also the seminal case in US-American law *Regents of the University of California v. Bakke,* 438 U.S. 265 (1978).

[104] See also E. Howard, *ELJ* 14 (2008), 168, 174 sqq. ECJ Case C-450/93 *Kalanke* [1995] ECR I-3051 para. 23, had still criticised a national regulation on the consideration: 'Furthermore, in so far as it seeks to achieve equal representation of men and women in all grades and levels within a department, such a system substitutes for equality of opportunity as envisaged in Article 2(4) the result which is only to be arrived at by providing such equality of opportunity.'

[105] ECJ Case C-319–03 *Briheche* [2004] ECR I-8807 paras. 22, 25, 31; Case C-476/99 *Lommers* [2002] ECR I-2891 para. 32; Case C-450/93 *Kalanke* [1995] ECR I-3051 paras. 18 sq.; Case C-409/95 *Marschall* [1997] ECR I-6363 para. 26.

[106] See e.g. H. Collins, *MLR* 66 (2003), 16–43 (on the basis of the 'aim of social inclusion'); R. Dworkin, *Taking Rights Seriously,* 223–239 (based on the conception of equality as a 'right to treatment as an equal, which is the right ... to be treated with the same respect and concern as anyone else'); id., *A Matter of Principle,* 293 sqq.; R. A. Epstein, *Forbidden Grounds,* 412–437. For a survey, see S. Fredman, *Discrimination Law,* 233–237; M. Trebilcock, *The Limits of Freedom of Contract,* 206 sq., 209–211.

discrimination.[107] The provisions allowing Member States to take positive action therefore constitute optional **grounds for justification** for the Member States.[108]

54. Since it constitutes a restriction upon the individual right to equal treatment, positive action is permitted only within narrow limits.[109] It **presupposes** that the measure in question is intended to ensure full equality and the prevention of, or compensation for, disadvantages linked to the prohibited grounds of discrimination. 'Positive' action means taking active countermeasures ('affirmative action'). The determination as to which positive measures should be taken is a question of policy and does not depend upon the evaluation of individual members of the promoted group.[110] A measure that restricts the autonomy of the 'protected' group (e.g. by limiting their choices) can, however, hardly constitute prevention or compensation for disadvantages. As a restriction of individual rights, positive measures are only admissible where the principle of proportionality is satisfied, even though the principle has not been expressly included within the respective rules.[111] The Court has thus objected to positive measures that automatically and unconditionally give priority to members of the promoted group.[112] Even in the context of positive action, applications must be subject to an 'objective assessment which takes account of the specific situations of all candidates'.[113]

---

[107] See e.g. ECJ Case C-366/99 *Griesmar* [2001] ECR I-9383 paras. 39–58 (Article 141 EC/157 TFEU); Case C-450/93 *Kalanke* [1995] ECR I-3051 para. 16 (EAD).

[108] S. Krebber, in C. Calliess/M. Ruffert (eds.), *EUV/AEUV*, Art. 157 AEUV para. 74; M. Sachs, *RdA* 1998, 129 (130 sq.); G. Thüsing, *ZfA* 2001, 397 (415); expressing doubt D. Schiek, *E.L. Rev.* 8 (2002), 290 (298).

[109] ECJ Case C-450/93 *Kalanke* [1995] ECR I-3051 para. 21; M. Sachs, *RdA* 1998, 129, 134 sq.

[110] Mistakable M. Schlachter, in R. Richardi/H. Reichold (eds.), *Altersgrenzen und Alterssicherung im Arbeitsrecht: Wolfgang Blomeyer zum Gedenken*, 355, 367.

[111] ECJ Case C-319–03 *Briheche* [2004] ECR I-8807 paras. 24, 27 sq., 31; Case C-476/99 *Lommers* [2002] ECR I-2891 para. 39 (on the EAD); Case C-407/98 *Abrahamsson und Anderson* [2000] ECR I-5539 para. 55 (on Article 141(4) EC); Case 222/84 *Johnston* [1986] ECR 1651 para. 38. See also J. Mohr, *Schutz vor Diskriminierungen* (Berlin: Duncker & Humblot, 2004), 320–323; K. Riesenhuber/J.-U. Franck, *JZ* 2004, 529, 535; also G. Thüsing, *ZfA* 2001, 397, 415.

[112] ECJ Case C-319–03 *Briheche* [2004] ECR I-8807 paras. 23 sq.; Case C-450/93 *Kalanke* [1995] ECR I-3051 para. 22. N. Colneric, *ArbRGeg* 1997, 69, 89 sq.; M. Sachs, *RdA* 1998, 129, 135 sq.

[113] ECJ C-319–03 *Briheche* [2004] ECR I-8807 paras. 23 sq.; Case C-407/98 *Abrahamsson und Anderson* [2000] ECR I-5539 paras. 43, 52 sq.; Case C-157/97 *Badeck* [2000] ECR I-1875 paras. 22 sq.; Case C-409/95 *Marschall,* [1997] ECR I-6363 paras. 32 sq. To the same effect with regard to favouring female employees in giving their children access to subsidised nursery schemes Case C-476/99 *Lommers* [2002] ECR I-2891 paras. 39–48. For a critical discussion of this approach with a view to the US-Supreme Court's *Bakke*-decision Dworkin, *A Matter of Principle*, chap. 14 (denouncing the right to be judged on one's merits and as an individual – both of which seem to be behind the ECJ's judgements too – as 'catch phrases').

55. Only **the Member States** may take positive measures.[114] The social partners or contract partners are thus excluded. The wording and purpose of the provisions on positive action in the directives require that such rules must, in their essential features, be determined by the Member States.[115] What is at stake in substance, is a derogation of the principle of equality on social policy considerations of the common good. The common good cannot, however, be pursued by individuals without central coordination. Positive action may be introduced or maintained. There is, however, no obligation for the individual to take such measures. Despite the general 'prohibition of regression' (see para. 88 below), Member States are not obliged to maintain measures of positive action either. Such measures are, by their very nature, only temporary and must, as measures of social policy, be flexible and adaptable to the changing circumstances.

56. The Court of Justice seems to distinguish between positive action in a narrow sense and neutrally worded selection criteria that benefit the promoted group (in the concrete case: women) (indirect discrimination of men), for example where abilities and experiences gained from work at home for the family are taken into account for the evaluation of candidates. The Court considered this to be covered by Article 3 Sex Discrimination Directive without any further justification.[116] This is not convincing, though, if one accepts – with the Court of Justice – that positive measures infringe upon the individual right to equality. While the prohibition of indirect discrimination may allow for a justification of such neutral criteria (para. 36 above), a proportionality test must still be satisfied.

3. Enforcement of Rights and Accompanying Measures

57. The prohibitions of discrimination are supplemented by provisions on sanctions and enforcement as well as a prohibition of so-called victimisation. Rules on enforcement were not very elaborate in the sex discrimination directives of the 1970s. However, beginning with the 2000 Race Discrimination Directive, this changed and the EU legislature structured this aspect of anti-discrimination law as well.[117]

---

[114] But see R. Epstein, *Forbidden Grounds*, 413–421 (advocating full admissibility of affirmative action-programs in the private sphere – based on freedom of contract and absent any prohibition of discrimination).

[115] M. Schlachter, in R. Richardi/H.Reichold (eds.), *Altersgrenzen und Alterssicherung im Arbeitsrecht: Wolfgang Blomeyer zum Gedenken*, 355, 364 sq.; id., in R. Müller-Glöge/ U. Preis/I. Schmidt (eds.), *Erfurter Kommentar*, Art. 141 EG paras. 28; G. Thüsing, *RdA* 2001, 319, 324.

[116] ECJ Case C-158/97 *Badeck* [2000] ECR I-1875 paras. 31 sq.

[117] M. Bell, *ELJ* 8 (2002), 384, 390–393.

a)   Burden of Proof and Information

Provisions: Article 19 SDD, Article 4 BoPD, Article 8 RDD, Article 10 ETFD, Article 9
SDGS

Bibliography:

C. Bergwitz, 'Die neue EG-RL zur Beweislast bei geschlechtsbedingter Diskriminierung',
DB 1999, 94–99; H. Prütting, 'Beweisrecht und Beweislast im arbeitsgerichtlichen
Diskriminierungsprozess', in H. Oetker/U. Preis/V. Rieble (eds.), *Festschrift 50 Jahre
Bundesarbeitsgericht* (Munich: C.H. Beck, 2004), 1311–1327; A. Röthel, 'Beweislast und
Geschlechterdiskriminierung – Zur Umsetzung der Richtlinie 97/80/EG', *NJW* 1999,
611–614; M. Schlachter, 'Richtlinie über die Beweislast bei Diskriminierung', *RdA* 1998,
321–326; P. A. Windel, 'Der Beweis diskriminierender Benachteiligungen', *RdA* 2007,
1–8; P. A. Windel, 'Aktuelle Beweisfragen im Antidiskriminierungsprozess', *RdA* 2011,
193-.

Cases (Selection):

ECJ Case C-127/92 *Enderby* [1993] ECR I-5535; ECJ Case 109/88 *Danfoss* [1989] ECR
3199; ECJ Case C-400/93 *Royal Copenhagen* [1995] ECR I-1275; ECJ Case C-460/06
Paquay [2007] ECR I-8511; ECJ Case C-54/07 *Feryn* [2008] ECR I-5187; ECJ Case
C-104/10 *Kelly* 21 July 2011; ECJ Case C-415/10 *Meister* 12 January 2012.

58.   With regard to the prohibition of discrimination in employment, the 1997
Burden of Proof Directive, following the jurisprudence of the Court of
Justice,[118] provided for a shift of the burden of proof in favour of the (alleged)
victim of discrimination.[119] Similar rules are today a standard part of the
supplementary provisions. When the alleged victim of discrimination
establishes facts on the basis of which it may be presumed that there has been
direct or indirect discrimination (including harassment or instruction to
discriminate)[120],[121] it is for the alleged wrongdoer to prove that there has been
no breach of the principle of equal treatment.[122] This means, in other words,
that the alleged victim must merely establish the prerequisites of discrimination

---

[118]   ECJ Case 109/88 *Danfoss* [1989] ECR 3199 paras. 12–15; Case C-127/92 *Enderby* [1993] ECR
I-5535 paras. 13 sq.; Case C-400/93 *Royal Copenhagen* [1995] ECR I-1275 para. 24. See also
Case C-196/02 *Nikoloudi* [2005] ECR I-1789 para. 69. I. Scholten, *Diskriminierungsschutz im
Privatrecht?*, 82–84.

[119]   C. Bergwitz, *DB* 1999, 94–99; H. Prütting, *Festschrift 50 Jahre BAG*, 1311–1327; A. Röthel,
NJW 1999, 611, 612; M. Schlachter, *RdA* 1998, 321–326; I. Scholten, *Diskriminierungsschutz
im Privatrecht?*, 80–85; R. Wank, in P. Hanau/H.-D. Steinmeyer/R. Wank (eds.), *Handbuch
des europäischen Arbeits- und Sozialrechts,* §16 para. 277; P. A. Windel, *RdA* 2007, 1, 2 sq.

[120]   I. Scholten, *Diskriminierungsschutz im Privatrecht?*, 80 sq.

[121]   E.g. the public declaration not to hire foreigners; ECJ Case C-54/07 Feryn [2008] ECR I-5187
paras. 30–33.

[122]   P. A. Windel, *RdA* 2011, 193, 196: the shift of the burden of proof covers both the 'less
favourable treatment' and, where applicable, the employer's motive.

to a lower degree of probability, rather than provide full proof.[123] The **burden of proof** then **shifts** to the alleged wrongdoer. This allocation of the burden of proof is intended to ensure the effective enforcement of the principle of equality.[124] It can also be justified by reference to considerations of victim protection as well as ensuring that the burden of proof is allocated according to spheres of responsibility.[125] Where discrimination may be presumed from the facts, the employer is in a better position to allay suspicion. From a policy perspective, it should not be overlooked, though, that the provision has a restrictive effect upon individual freedom and is bound to lead to greater bureaucratisation.[126] It forces the employer to document and disclose his motivations.

59. The burden of proof applies with regard to **judicial proceedings** as well as proceedings involving other competent authorities (in particular the 'equality bodies', see para. 86 below). The Member States may exempt the application of the burden or proof-rules in procedures where the court or competent body investigates the facts; this is in line with the purpose of the rule. The more recent directives explicitly exempt criminal proceedings (Article 8(3) RDD, Article 10(3) ETFD and Article 19(5) SDD); this exception is based on considerations of the protection of fundamental rights (presumption of innocence, Article 48(1) ChFR); consequently, this exception must also apply even if this has not explicitly been provided (as in the former Article 4 BoPD).

60. The **basis** for shifting the burden of proof is that a person who considers himself wronged because the principle of equal treatment has not been applied, establishes facts from which a discrimination may be presumed.[127] The legal consequence is a **reversal of the burden of proof** and not merely an alleviation of the standard of proof. It is then for the alleged wrongdoer to prove that the principle of equal treatment has not been violated.

61. The burden of proof is an aspect of the general issue of **information**. The provisions on the burden of proof do not specifically address that issue or require the Member States to implement provisions that entitle persons who consider themselves wronged by discrimination to information about, e.g., the applicant

---

123   M. Schlachter, *RdA* 1998, 321, 324; P. A. Windel, *RdA* 2007, 1, 2 with further references.

124   Cf. already ECJ Case C-127/92 *Enderby* [1993] ECR I-5535 para. 14.

125   M. Schlachter, in *EAS*, B 4100 paras. 52 sq.; ead., *RdA* 1998, 321; H. Wiedemann, *Die Gleichbehandlungsgebote im Arbeitsrecht*, 92–94; ECJ Case C-180/95 *Draehmpaehl* [1997] ECR I-2195 para. 36 ('… it is for the employer, who has in his possession all the applications submitted, to adduce proof …').

126   K. Riesenhuber/J.-U. Franck, *JZ* 2004, 529 (532); iid., *EWS* 2005, 245, 250.

127   R. Wank, in P. Hanau/H.-D. Steinmeyer/R. Wank (eds.), *Handbuch des europäischen Arbeits- und Sozialrechts*, §16 paras. 277.

pool. At the same time, such a right may flow from the general implementation duties upon a Member State, namely the principle of effectiveness (on which see §1 paras. 65 sq.). As the Court puts it, 'it cannot be ruled out that a refusal of disclosure by the defendant, in the context of establishing such facts [sc. 'facts from which it may be presumed that there has been direct or indirect discrimination'], could risk compromising the achievement of the objective pursued by [the Burden of Proof Directive] and thus depriving, in particular, Article 4(1) thereof of its effectiveness'.[128] Where, however, the national law, following the principle of effectiveness, provides for a right to information, it should also take into account the rules of EU law on confidentiality.[129] These include the Personal Data Directive,[130] the Privacy and Electronic Communications Directive[131] and Article 8 ChFR.

62. In *Meister,* the Court went one step further. While it confirmed that the employer is not, as a matter of Union law, under an obligation to provide information to the applicant who suspects that he or she has been discriminated against, it added that the employer's refusal to grant access to information may be one of the factors establishing facts from which it may be presumed that there has been discrimination.[132] This means, in other words, that also the employer's subsequent behaviour, after the application procedure has been completed, may be taken into account with regard to a shift of the burden of proof. As a consequence, the employer has an incentive to provide applicants who consider themselves wronged with a certain amount of objective justification.

b)   Sanctions

Bibliography:
R. Abele, 'Schadensersatz wegen geschlechtsbezogener Diskriminierung eines Stellenbewerbers', *NZA* 1997, 641–643; G. Annuß, 'Grundfragen der Entschädigung bei unzulässiger Geschlechtsdiskriminierung', *NZA* 1999, 738–744; I. Ayres/J. G. Brown, 'Mark(et)ing Nondiscrimination: Privatizing ENDA with a Certification Mark', *Mich.*

---

[128]   ECJ Case C-104/10 *Kelly* 21 July 2011 paras. 38 sq. AG Mengozzi, Opinion in Case C-415/10 *Meister* 12 January 2012 pts. 20–24. On the issue and its background in German civil procedure law, see P. A. Windel, *RdA* 2011, 193, 199.

[129]   ECJ Case C-104/10 *Kelly* 21 July 2011 paras. 55 sq.

[130]   Directive 95/46/EC of the European Parliament and of the Council of 24 October 1995 on the protection of individuals with regard to the processing of personal data and on the free movement of such data, OJ 1995 L 281/31.

[131]   Directive 2002/58/EC of the European Parliament and of the Council of 12 July 2002 concerning the processing of personal data and the protection of privacy in the electronic communications sector (Directive on privacy and electronic communications), OJ 2002 L 201/37, as amended by Directive 2009/136/EC of the European Parliament and of the Council of 25 November 2009, OJ 2009 L 337/11.

[132]   ECJ Casae C-415/10 *Meister* 12 January 2012 paras. 43 sqq.

L. Rev. 104 (2006), 1639–1712; I. Ayres/J. G. Brown, 'Privatizing Employment Protections', *Ariz. L. Rev.* 49 (2007), 587–598; M. Benecke/G. Kern, 'Sanktionen im Antidiskriminierungsrecht: Möglichkeiten und Grenzen der Umsetzung der Europäischen Richtlinien im deutschen Recht', *EuZW* 2005, 360–364; J. Busche, 'Effektive Rechtsdurchsetzung und Sanktionen bei Verletzung richtliniendeterminierter Diskriminierungsverbote', in S. Leible/M. Schlachter (eds.), *Diskriminierungsschutz durch Privatrecht* (Munich: Sellier, 2006), 159–177; N. Colneric, 'Voller Schadensersatz bei geschlechtsbedingter Diskriminierung', *ZEuP* 1995, 646–654; E. Herrmann, 'Die Abschlussfreiheit – ein gefährdetes Prinzip', *ZfA* 1996, 19–68; T. Hoppe, 'Europäischer Schutz vor sexueller Diskriminierung beim Zugang zur Arbeit', *ZEuP* 2002, 78–95; S. Kamanabrou, 'Rechtsfolgen unzulässiger Benachteiligung im Antidiskriminierungsrecht', *ZfA* 2006, 327–345; W. Koberski, 'Gleichbehandlung und Diskriminierung unter besonderer Berücksichtigung der Gleichstellung von Mann und Frau', in K. Schmidt (ed.), *Arbeitsrecht und Arbeitsgerichtsbarkeit – Festschrift zum 50-jährigen Bestehen der Arbeitsgerichtsbarkeit in Rheinland-Pfalz* (Neuwied/Kriftel: Luchterhand, 1999), 503–519; N. Reich, 'Effective Private Law Remedies in Discrimination Cases', in R. Schulze (ed.), *Non-Discrimination in European Private Law* (Tübingen: Mohr Siebeck, 2011), 57–79; K. Riesenhuber, 'Nicht-spezifizierte Rechtsfolgen im Europäischen Vertragsrecht', in Klaus-C. Clavée/W. Kahl/R. Pisal (eds.), *Festschrift 10 Jahre Brandenburgisches Oberlandesgericht* (Baden-Baden: Nomos, 2003), 161–178; M. Schlachter, 'Anforderungen der Gleichbehandlungsrichtlinien an ein wirksames Sanktions-Instrumentarium', in U. Rust et al. (eds.), *Gleichbehandlungsrichtlinien der EU und ihre Umsetzung in Deutschland – Loccumer Protokolle 40/03* (Rehburg Loccum: Evangelische Akademie Loccum, 2003), 239–253; H. Schlieman, 'Gleichberechtigung bei der Begründung von Arbeitsverhältnissen – eine (fast) unendliche Geschichte von Europa und Michel', in P. Hanau/F. Heither/J. Kühling (eds.), *Richterliches Arbeitsrecht – Festschrift für Thomas Dieterich* (Munich: C.H. Beck, 1999), 569–583; B. Steinbrück, 'Geldentschädigung bei ethnischen Diskriminierungen – Punitive damages als zivilrechtliche Sanktion?', *JURA* 2004, 439–446; M. Stoffels, ''Grundprobleme der Schadensersatzverpflichtung nach §15 Abs. 1 AGG', *RdA* 2009, 204–215; G. Wagner, 'Prävention und Verhaltenssteuerung durch Zivilrecht – Anmaßung oder legitime Aufgabe?', *AcP* 206 (2006), 352–476.

63. As is often the case in EU private law, the anti-discrimination directives do not specify the legal consequences of a violation of the principle of equal treatment. Still, the general obligation to transpose a directive as highlighted in the directives (declaratorily) provided for a framework of requirements (§1 paras. 64 sq.). Furthermore, more recent directives provide, to some extent, for specific sanctions.

aa)   SPECIFIC SANCTIONS

i.   Compensation or Reparation (Damages)

Provisions: Article 18 SDD, Article 6(2) EAD, Article 8(2) SDGS

64.   Only the Sex Discrimination Directive contains a specific obligation to introduce a claim for 'real and effective compensation or reparation (...) for the loss and damage sustained by a person injured as a result of discrimination on grounds of sex'. Such a claim must be devised 'in a way which is dissuasive and proportionate to the damage suffered'.[133] The claim for damages may not be subject to a **prior upper limit**, 'except in cases where the employer can prove that the only damage suffered by an applicant as a result of discrimination (...) is the refusal to take his/her job application into consideration'. This provision effectively codifies the Court's prior case law (see para. 68 below). At the same time, to some extent, it curtails the Member States' freedom to choose between sanctions in private law or public law[134] as had hitherto been recognised by the Court of Justice.[135]

ii.   Nullity of Discriminatory Agreements[136]

Provisions: Article 23(b) SDD, Article 3(2)(b) EAD, Article 4 EPD, Article 14(b) RDD, Article 16(b) ETFD, Article 13(b) SDGS

65.   Another specified sanction is that legal acts in violation of the principle of equal treatment shall be declared null and void or must be amended.[137] This sanction covers 'individual or collective agreements, internal rules of undertakings or rules governing independent occupations and professions and workers' and employers' organisations or any other arrangements'. The wording indicates that the legislature intended it to comprehensively cover all private legal acts.

---

[133]   Differently e.g. S. Kamanabrou, *ZfA* 2006, 327, 329 sq. (following Recital 18 Directive 2002/73 [not Recital 34 SDD] the legislature only intended to adopt the Court's previous jurisprudence which also included the Member State's freedom to decide whether they wanted to provide for monetary compensation or not). On the calculation of monetary compensation (with comparative considerations) B. Steinbrück, *JURA* 2004, 439–446.

[134]   Still differently Article 15 RDD, Article 17 ETFD. Also Article 14 SDGS requires payment of damages as a sanction; see K. Riesenhuber, in S. Leible/M. Schlachter (eds.), *Diskriminierungsschutz durch Privatrecht*, 123, 135; differently E. Picker, in E. Lorenz (ed.), *Karlsruher Forum 2004*, 19; M. Benecke/G. Kern, *EuZW* 2005, 360, 363.

[135]   ECJ Case 14/83 *v. Colson and Kamann* [1984] ECR 1891 paras. 15–18. See also Case 79/83 *Harz* [1984] ECR 1921 para. 18.

[136]   The Member States are further obliged to remove discriminatory provisions of law, Article 23(a) SDD, Article 5(2)(a) EAD, Article 3 EPD, Article 14(a) RDD, Article 16(a) ETFD, Article 13(a) SDD; see e.g. ECJ Case C-207/04 *Vergani* [2005] ECR I-7453 paras. 25 sq.

[137]   See e.g. ECJ Case C-342/01 *Merino Gómez* [2004] ECR I-2605 para. 40. Cf. also J. Basedow, *ZEuP* 2008, 230, 238–240; S. Kamanabrou, *ZfA* 2006, 327, 328, 331 sq.

bb)   Non-specified Sanctions

Provisions: Article 25 SDD, Article 8d EAD, Article 15 RDD, Article 17 ETFD, Article 14 SDGS

Cases (Selection):
ECJ Case 79/83 *Harz* [1984] ECR 1921; ECJ Case 14/83 *v. Colson and Kamann* [1984] ECR 1891; ECJ Case C-271/91 *Marshall II* [1993] ECR I- 4367; ECJ Case C-180/95 *Draehmpaehl* [1997] ECR I-2195; ECJ Case C-54/07 *Feryn* [2008] ECR I-5187.

i.   General

66.   Apart from these few specified provisions, sanctions are for the Member States to determine. Sanctions must comply with the principles of equivalence and effectiveness as they follow from the obligation to transpose directives (see §1 para. 66 above).[138] The directives re-emphasise the obligations to transpose directives (which already follow from EU primary law). In accordance with the Court's jurisprudence, 'penalties' (*Sanktionen, sanctions*) 'must be effective, proportionate and dissuasive'.[139] They 'may comprise the payment of compensation to the victim'.[140]

ii.   Member States' Sanctions in the Court's Jurisprudence

67.   The **obligations to implement** the directives have played a prominent role with regard to the transposition of the anti-discrimination directives.[141] With regard to the 1976 Equal Access Directive (see now Article 25 SDD), the Court initially established that the Member States have a duty to employ measures that are sufficiently effective to ensure equal access to employment for men and women. However, it is left to the Member States to choose between different solutions which are suitable for achieving this objective.[142] As such, the measures

---

[138]   ECJ Case C-460/06 *Paquay* [2007] ECR I-8511 para. 44.

[139]   From the Court's jurisprudence, see ECJ Case 14/83 *v. Colson and Kamann* [1984] ECR 1891 paras. 22–25; Case 79/83 *Harz* [1984] ECR 1921 para. 23; Case 177/88 *Dekker* [1990] ECR I-3941 para. 23; Case C-180/95 *Draehmpaehl* [1997] ECR I-2195 paras. 24 sq.; Case C-460/06 *Paquay* [2007] ECR I-8511 para. 45; S. Busche, in S. Leible/M. Schlachter (eds.), *Diskriminierungsschutz durch Privatrecht*, 159–177; M. Benecke/G. Kern, *EuZW* 2005, 360–364; I. Scholten, *Diskriminierungsschutz im Privatrecht?*, S. 54–57; M. Schlachter, in U. Rust et al. (eds.), *Gleichbehandlungsrichtlinien der EU und ihre Umsetzung in Deutschland*, 239–244.

[140]   Discussing the various implementation schemes (criminal and private law) T. Hoppe, *ZEuP* 2002, 78–95.

[141]   See e.g. N. Colneric, *ZEuP* 1995, 646–654; W. Koberski, *Festschrift 50 Jahre Arbeitsgerichtsbarkeit Rheinland-Pfalz*, 503–519; H. Schlieman, *Festschrift für Dieterich*, 569–583.

[142]   ECJ Case 14/83 *von Colson und Kamann* [1984] ECR 1891 para. 18; Case 79/83 *Harz* [1984] ECR 1921 para. 18.

may be **of private law or of public law**[143] (but see para. 64 above with regard to compensation). Consequently, the directives do not require that the employer be forced to enter into an employment contract with a candidate who has been discriminated against.[144] In their choice of suitable sanctions, the Member States must observe the principle of equivalence (§1 para. 66 above), though, pursuant to which infringements of Union law are penalised under conditions, both procedural and substantive, which are analogous to those applicable to infringements of domestic law of a similar nature and importance.[145] In the case of termination on grounds of pregnancy in particular, which is also prohibited by Article 10 Maternity Protection Directive, the principle of equivalence may require that the sanctions for a breach of the principle of equal treatment must not be less than those of maternity protection law.[146]

68. The Court has derived further requirements from the principle of effectiveness (§1 para. 66) pursuant to which a sanction must guarantee real and effective judicial protection[147] and have a deterrent effect. If a Member State chooses compensation as a sanction, it must be 'adequate, in that it must enable the loss and damage actually sustained as a result of the discriminatory dismissal to be made good in full'.[148] Compensation which is merely symbolic – such as reimbursement for the costs of application (e.g. postage and travel expenses) – is insufficient.[149] This also has implications for any **upper limits** to compensation. Thus, damages for a discriminatory *termination* may not be subject to a prior upper limit as this would impede adequate compensation for the damages sustained in an individual case.[150] Compensation is insufficient if it does not include interest for the period from the accrual of the claim until actual payment;[151] this is a requirement of both full compensation and effective deterrence (as the discriminator would otherwise have an incentive to delay payment). When calculating the compensation for discrimination in hiring,

---

[143] The Court decided differently, though, in the case of a discriminatory dismissal where equality could only be restored by reinstating the victim or compensating the damage; ECJ Case C-271/91 *Marshall II* [1993] ECR I- 4367 para. 25.

[144] ECJ Case 14/83 *v. Colson and Kamann* [1984] ECR 1891, 1907 para. 19; Case 79/83 *Harz* [1984] ECR 1921 para. 19.

[145] ECJ Case C-460/06 *Paquay* [2007] ECR I-8511 paras. 50–52; Case 68/88 *Commission* v. *Greece* [1989] ECR 2965 para. 24; Case C- 180/95 *Draehmpaehl* [1997] ECR I-2195 para. 9.

[146] ECJ Case C-460/06 *Paquay* [2007] ECR I-8511 para. 51.

[147] ECJ Case 14/83 *v. Colson and Kamann* [1984] ECR 1891 para. 23; Case 79/83 *Harz* [1984] ECR 1921 para. 23.

[148] ECJ Case C-460/06 *Paquay* [2007] ECR I-8511 paras. 46, 49; Case C-271/91 *Marshall II* [1993] ECR I-4367 para. 25.

[149] ECJ Case C-180/95 *Draehmpaehl* [1997] ECR I-2195 para. 27; Case 14/83 *v. Colson and Kamann* [1984] ECR 1891, 1907 para. 23; Case 79/83 *Harz* [1984] ECR 1921 para. 23.

[150] ECJ Case C-271/91 *Marshall II* [1993] ECR I-4367 para. 30; with a note by N. Colneric, *ZEuP* 1995, 646–654.

[151] ECJ Case C- 271/91 *Marshall II* [1993] ECR I-4367 para. 32.

causation may be taken into account. A prior upper limit is thus admissible if the unsuccessful applicant would not have obtained the vacant position, even without discrimination in the selection process; where, however, the applicant would have been hired but for the discrimination, compensation may not be so limited.[152] It is in line with the purpose of the principle of equality and also compatible with the relevant spheres of responsibility that the burden of proof is on the employer to show that the unsuccessful applicant would not have been hired because the applicant who was hired instead had superior qualifications.[153] The Court also dismissed a '**cumulative upper limit**', as would apply where a plurality of applicants claim compensation, as incompatible with the requirements of real and effective legal protection. Again, such upper limit would not guarantee full reparation in the individual case. Furthermore, such cumulative upper limit could deter a victim of discrimination from claiming his or her rights.[154]

69. A compensation claim cannot be subject to a requirement of employer's **fault** under the applicable law.[155] Where a Member State opts for a sanction forming part of the rules on civil liability (see para. 67 above), any infringement of the prohibition of discrimination must make the infringer fully liable without further requirements.[156]

70. In a case of 'direct discrimination without a victim' (para. 33 above), the Court considered that the sanction 'may include a finding of discrimination by the court or the competent administrative authority in conjunction with an adequate level of publicity' (cost to be borne by the perpetrator).[157] The sanction may also take the form of a prohibitive injunction ordering the employer to cease the discriminatory practice and, where appropriate, a fine, or they may take the form of an award of 'damages' to the entity bringing the claim.[158]

---

[152] ECJ Case C-180/95 *Draehmpaehl* [1997] ECR I-2195 para. 37.
[153] ECJ Case C-180/95 *Draehmpaehl* [1997] ECR I-2195 para. 36.
[154] ECJ Case C-180/95 *Draehmpaehl* [1997] ECR I-2195 para. 40.
[155] ECJ Case C-177/88 *Dekker* [1990] ECR I-3979 para. 24; Case C-180/95 *Draehmpaehl* [1997] ECR I-2195 paras. 17–19. S. Kamanabrou, *ZfA* 2006, 327, 330 sq.
[156] ECJ Case C-177/88 *Dekker* [1990] ECR I- 3979 para. 26.
[157] Such 'publicity' and the employer's obligation to pay the costs raise further questions including issues of the fundamental rights of the employer; the German implementation legislation does not provide an adequate basis for these measures; J.F. Lindner, 'Staatliches "Anprangern" des Arbeitgebers wegen Verstoßes gegen das AGG?', *RdA* 2009, 45–48.
[158] ECJ Case C-54/07 *Feryn* [2008] ECR I-5187 paras. 36–39.

c) 'Victimisation'

Provisions: Article 24 SDD, Article 5 EPD, Article 7 EAD, Article 9 RDD, Article 11 ETFD, Article 10 SDGS

Bibliography:

M. Benecke, 'Umfang und Grenzen des Maßregelungsverbots und des Verbots der „Viktimisierung" – Der Konflikt nach dem Konflikt', *NZA* 2011, 481–486; M. Connolly, 'Victimising Third Parties: The Equality Directives, the European Convention on Human Rights, and EU General Principles', *E.L. Rev.* 35 (2010), 822–836; M. Dougan, 'The Equal Treatment Directive: Retaliation, Remedies and Direct Effect', *E.L. Rev.* 24 (1999), 664–673; D. Faulenbach, *Das arbeitsrechtliche Maßregelungsverbot (§612a BGB)* (Heidelberg: C.F. Müller, 2005); G. Thüsing, 'Anwendungsbereich und Regelungsgehalt des Maßregelungsverbots gem. §612a BGB', *NZA* 1994, 728–732; F. Wilken, *Regelungsgehalt des Maßregelungsverbots gem. §612a BGB* (Berlin: Duncker & Humblot, 2001).

Cases (Selection):
ECJ Case C-185/97 *Coote* [1998] ECR I-5199.

71. The directives also impose an obligation upon the Member States to protect employees against adverse treatment by the employer as a reaction to a complaint that the principle of equal treatment has been violated. This treatment is given the rather obscure term, 'victimisation'. A prohibition of victimisation, albeit of limited scope, was already included in the 1975 and 1976 sex discrimination directives. In substance, the prohibition of victimisation follows from the prohibition of discrimination as a matter of course. Indeed, the Court of Justice has deduced the same principle from the general obligation to implement the principle of equal treatment.[159]

72. The rules on victimisation require that

(1) employees and – in some specifically emphasised instances – employee representatives
(2) must be protected against adverse treatment (in particular dismissal) by the employer
(3) which arises as a reaction (a) to a complaint [within the undertaking] or (b) to any [legal] proceedings aimed at enforcing compliance with the principle of equal treatment.[160]

---

[159] Cf. ECJ Case C-185/97 *Coote* [1998] ECR I-5199 paras. 20–27; differently, though, AG Mischo in his Opinion in this Case, pts. 23 sqq. (who pointed to the limited wording of the Article 7 EAD). See also M. Dougan, *E.L. Rev.* 24 (1991), 664–673.

[160] The wording of the Race Discrimination Directive is broader ('individual' instead of 'employee'; qualifications in brackets not included). This difference appears to be owed to the broader scope of application which is not restricted to the area of employment.

73. When, pursuant to such provision, *'employees'* are protected, this may, under the open wording of the provision, not only cover the employees who have claimed their rights under the anti-discrimination directives but also their fellow-employees (of the same employer) who have, e.g., supported a claimant morally by expressing sympathy.[161] The prohibition protects employees against retaliation in reaction to a *'complaint'* or the institution of 'any *legal proceedings* aimed at enforcing compliance with the principle of equal treatment'. The wording does not restrict the protected behaviour to instances where the complaint or proceedings were *justified or successful.* To the contrary, the wording focuses upon the intention ('aimed at'). Indeed, a broad reading is also supported on the basis of purposive considerations. Retaliation because of an unjustified complaint or the unjustified initiation of proceedings is unlawful; national law may (only) provide for protection against frivolous proceedings or other abuse.[162] This broad protection is, however, limited to the two enumerated instances of (1) internal complaints and (2) legal proceedings. If the employee refuses to perform work on the erroneous belief that he was discriminated against, he may lose his pay. The (justified or unjustified) allegation of discrimination is, in other words, not a free ticket for the employee.

d)   Dissemination of Information

Provisions: Article 30 SDD, Article 7 EPD, Article 8 EAD, Article 10 RDD, Article 12 ETFD

74. In order to give effect to the principle of equal treatment, the directives require Member States to ensure that the national implementing measures, together with legal provisions which are already in force, are brought to the attention of all persons concerned by all suitable means. Regarding the prohibition of discrimination in employment, this may include information at the workplace.

75. The provisions of Article 21(3) and (4) SDD can also be mentioned in this context. Member States shall encourage employers to promote equal treatment and employers shall be encouraged to provide employees and their

---

[161]   M. Connolly, *E.L. Rev.* 35 (2010), 822–836 (discussing (1) a broad interpretation of the directives, (2) grounding protection of third parties on general principles of EU law; and suggesting a legislative amendment of the directives).

[162]   Differently (with regard to the German implementation legislation) M. Benecke, *NZA* 2011, 481, 482 and 484; U. Preis, in R. Müller-Glöge/U. Preis/I. Schmidt (eds.), *Erfurter Kommentar,* §612a BGB para. 5; R. Richardi/P. Fischinger, in J. v. Staudinger (founding ed.), *Kommentar zum Bürgerlichen Gesetzbuch mit Einführungsgesetz und Nebengesetzen* (Berlin: Sellier/de Gruyter, 2011), §612a BGB para. 19; G. Thüsing, in F. J. Säcker/R. Rixecker (eds.), *Münchener Kommentar zum BGB,* §16 AGG para. 9. With a tendency to the position taken here M. Schlachter, in R. Müller-Glöge/U. Preis/I. Schmidt (eds.), Erfurter Kommentar, §16 AGG para. 1.

representatives with appropriate information on equal treatment for men and women in the business; see para. 85 below.

e) Enforcement: Access to Courts and Authorities

Bibliography:
M. Gotthardt, 'Die Vereinbarkeit der Ausschlussfristen für Entschädigungsansprüche wegen geschlechtsbedingter Benachteiligung (§611a Abs. 4 BGB, §61b Abs. 1 ArbGG) mit dem europäischen Gemeinschaftsrecht', *ZTR* 2000, 448–455; E. Kocher, 'Die Rechtsdurchsetzung nach dem AGG', in K. Riesenhuber (ed.), *Das Allgemeine Gleichbehandlungsgesetz – Grundsatz- und Praxisfragen* (Berlin: de Gruyter, 2007), 55–75; E. Kocher, 'Instrumente der effektiven Rechtsdurchsetzung II – "Verbandsklagerecht" der Richtlinien', in U. Rust et al. (eds.), *Gleichbehandlungsrichtlinien der EU und ihre Umsetzung in Deutschland – Loccumer Protokolle 40/03* (Rehburg Loccum: Evangelische Akademie Loccum, 2003), 301–319; H. Pfarr/E. Kocher, 'Kollektivverfahren im Arbeitsrecht – Arbeitnehmerschutz und Gleichberechtigung durch Verfahren', *NZA* 1999, 358–365.

aa) DEFENCE OF RIGHTS

Provisions: Article 17(1), (3) SDD, Article 2 EPD, Article 6(1) EAD, Article 7(1) RDD, Article 9(1) ETFD, Article 8(1), (4) SDGS

Cases (Selection):
ECJ Case C-246/09 *Bulicke* 8 July 2010.

76.   Member States must ensure that **judicial or administrative procedures** are available to (perceived) victims of discrimination.[163] Administrative proceedings may include, in particular, those before the 'equality bodies' (para. 86). Administrative proceedings may be designed as an alternative to proceedings in court (different in Article 2 EPD). The national law of the Member States may provide for preceding **conciliation procedures**.

77.   Procedures may be instituted even after the relationship, in which the discrimination is alleged to have occurred, has ended. This is indeed a requirement of individual protection as an individual's sense of grievance and degradation may still be ongoing. Furthermore, the (perceived) victim may often only find the courage to bring proceedings after the (employment) relationship has ended (irrespective of the protection that the prohibition of victimisation affords him). This provision also reflects the social policy goal of combating discrimination in the long run, although **general time limits** (preclusion, prescription) also apply here, Article 17(3) SDD, Article 5(4) EAD, Article 7(3)

---

[163]   ECJ Case 222/84 *Johnston* [1986] ECR 1651 para. 20 (discussing an exemption from the principle of equal treatment not subject to judiical control).

RDD and Article 9(3) ETFD.[164] Procedures do, however, have to satisfy the implementation principles of equivalence and effectiveness.[165]

bb)   INVOLVEMENT OF ANTI-DISCRIMINATION ORGANISATIONS

Provisions: Article 17(2) SDD, Article 6(3) EAD, Article 7(2) RDD, Article 9(2) ETFD, Article 8(3) SDGS

78.   All of the anti-discrimination directives now provide for the involvement of 'associations, **organisations and other legal entities**' (hereinafter 'organisations') which have a legitimate interest in ensuring that the provisions of this Directive are complied with.[166] Member States must ensure that such organisations may engage, either on behalf or in support of the complainant, with his approval, in any judicial or administrative procedure provided for the enforcement of obligations under the directives. The directives do not require a right of action for the organisations as such[167] or a class action. Involvement of organisations is intended to alleviate some of the difficulties which are associated with the individual enforcement of rights, as may result from the fact that such proceedings may be expensive and emotionally difficult for the individual.

79.   Member States have a wide discretion for determining which organisations have a **legitimate interest** in ensuring that the provisions of the directives are complied with. These may (but do not have to)[168] include employer associations and trade unions and also organisations founded specifically for this purpose. In defining the legitimate interest, Member States must ensure that organisations can be effectively involved. National law may make it a requirement that an organisation has significant 'weight' or 'power' but it may also require specific (e.g. democratic or pluralistic or legal) organisational structures.

80.   Apart from the 'legitimate interest' of the organisation, its involvement also requires that the aggrieved person **consents** in the individual case ('approval').[169] While this requirement restricts involvement of organisations,

---

[164]   See also M. Gotthardt, *ZTR* 2000, 448–455.
[165]   ECJ Case C-246/09 *Bulicke* 8 July 2011 paras. 22–42. Approving case notes P. Fischinger, 'Europarechtskonformität des §15 Abs. 4 AGG?', *NZA* 2010, 1048–1052; S. Kolbe, 'Fristen für Entschädigungsansprüche des Diskriminierungsopfers', *EuZA* 2011, 65–73.
[166]   See the seminal contribution, founded on a comparative discussion procedural protection against discrimination, of P. Rädler, *Verfahrensmodelle zum Schutz vor Rassendiskriminierung*; id., *ZRP* 1997, 5–9.
[167]   Thus R. Nickel, *NJW* 2001, 2668, 2671.
[168]   For a different perspective see E. Kocher, 'Instrumente einer Europäisierung des Prozessrechts Zu den Anforderungen an den kollektiven Rechtsschutz im Antidiskriminierungsrecht', *ZEuP* 2004, 260, 267 sq.
[169]   K. Riesenhuber/J.-U. Franck, *JZ* 2004, 529, 533. See also E. Kocher, *ZEuP* 2004, 260–275; I. Scholten, *Diskriminierungsschutz im Privatrecht?*, 194–198. Critically C. Brown, *YEL* 21 (2002), 195, 219.

Member States may not dispense with it in their implementation by relying upon the minimum standard clause, as it also serves the interests of the aggrieved individual. It is not a requirement, though, that the aggrieved person be a member of the organisation.[170]

f)   Social Dialogue and Dialogue with Non-Governmental Organisations

Bibliography:
O. Deinert, 'Sozialer Dialog und Zielvereinbarungen als Wege zur Antidiskriminierung', in U. Rust et al. (eds.), *Gleichbehandlungsrichtlinien der EU und ihre Umsetzung in Deutschland – Loccumer Protokolle 40/03* (Rehburg Loccum: Evangelische Akademie Loccum, 2003), 381–403; D. König, 'Umsetzung im Dialog und Anforderungen an den Mitgliedstaate Deutschland', in U. Rust et al. (eds.), *Gleichbehandlungsrichtlinien der EU und ihre Umsetzung in Deutschland – Loccumer Protokolle 40/03* (Rehburg Loccum: Evangelische Akademie Loccum, 2003), 355–375.

81.   The anti-discrimination directives further impose some 'soft' obligations upon the Member States to **promote** social dialogue (dialogue between the social partners) and dialogue with non-governmental organisations (NGOs). In a similarly soft way, Member States are required to 'encourage' employers to promote equal treatment. What these provisions have in common is that Member States are merely under an obligation to 'promote' or to 'encourage'. The aim of these mechanisms is to have private persons (social partners, employers) promote the goals of the directives through their own actions, be it unilaterally or in collaboration. These mechanisms are intended to ensure that private parties adopt the goals of the directives as their own. This cannot be forced.[171] Such procedural, long-term instruments are considered to be part of what is being called *gender mainstreaming*.[172]

aa)   Social Dialogue

Provisions: Article 21(1), (2) SDD, Article 8b EAD, Article 11 RDD, Article 13 ETFD

82.   The anti-discrimination directives in employment law uniformly require Member States to *promote* dialogue between social partners.[173] The **purpose** of such social dialogue should be to foster equal treatment. The directives give

---

170   E. Kocher, *ZEuP* 2004, 260, 266.
171   D. König, in U. Rust et al. (eds.), *Gleichbehandlungsrichtlinien der EU und ihre Umsetzung in Deutschland*, 355 sq.
172   E. Kocher, *RdA* 2002, 167–173 (see p. 171: 'Gender mainstreaming can be defined as a [re-] organisation, improvement, development and evaluation of all decision-making processes with a view to equal treatment of men and women.' – my translation).
173   Articles 11(1) RDD, 13 ETFD speak of employers and employees.

several examples of **instruments** that may be used for this purpose (and the employment of which Member States should encourage):

- monitoring of practices in the workplace,
- monitoring of collective agreements,
- codes of conduct,
- research, and
- exchange of experience and good practice.

83. Member States are further required to encourage the social partners to conclude **agreements laying down anti-discrimination rules** in the fields of the respective directives. However, the legislator emphasises the autonomy of both the Member States and the social partners. The obligation of the Member States is restricted to such measures as are consistent with national traditions and practice. And their encouragement of the social partners should be 'without prejudice to their autonomy' and only relating to subjects 'which fall within the scope of collective bargaining'. The content of such anti-discrimination agreements is also left to the autonomy of the social partners but must 'respect the provisions of this Directive and the relevant national implementing measures'. Such agreements will thus rather be of an affirmative or declaratory nature.

bb) DIALOGUE WITH NON-GOVERNMENTAL ORGANISATIONS

Provisions: Article 22 SDD, Article 8c EAD, Article 12 RDD, Article 14 ETFD, Article 11 SDGS

84. Apart from social dialogue which is specific to the employment sector, Member States are further obliged to promote dialogue with the respective non-governmental organisations (NGOs) that have a legitimate interest in contributing to the 'fight' against discrimination.[174] Unlike with the social partners, the goal is a dialogue between the NGOs and the Member States. Such dialogue need not have any specific objectives. Instead, the purpose is to appreciate the NGOs as partners in a dialogue and thus to promote their activity and, more generally, an awareness of the principle of non-discrimination within the Member States.

cc) THE EMPLOYERS' OBLIGATION TO PROMOTE AND INFORM

Provisions: Article 21(3), (4) SDD, Article 8c(3), (4) EAD

85. Finally, we can also consider the employers' obligation to promote and inform as it is now provided for in Article 21(3) and (4) SDD. Member States

---

[174] On the practical relevance see M. Bell, *ELJ* 8 (2002), 384, 393–398.

should encourage employers to promote the equal treatment of men and women in a planned and systematic way. Employers should be encouraged to provide employees and their representatives with information regarding equal treatment of men and women in the business at regular intervals. Such information may provide an overview of the percentages of men and women at different levels of the organisation and possible measures to improve the situation. What is at stake here, is not so much the subjective rights of individual employees, but rather the creation of an environment that enhances knowledge and awareness of equal treatment and how it might be achieved. Where the information includes statistics on the percentages of men and women (which is, of course, not mandatory), such data may assist individual employees in proving a claim for (indirect) discrimination (see para. 35 above).

g)   Equality Bodies

Bibliography:
P. Rädler, 'Gesetze gegen Rassendiskriminierung', *ZRP* 1997, 5–9; P. Rädler, *Verfahrensmodelle zum Schutz vor Rassendiskriminierung* (Berlin et al.: Springer, 1999).

Provisions: Article 20 SDD, Article 8a EAD, Article 13 RDD, Article 12 SDGS

86. The Sex Discrimination Directive and the Race Discrimination Directive (but not the Equal Treatment Framework Directive) require Member States to designate one or more 'bodies' for the promotion of equal treatment without discrimination on grounds of sex and race respectively.[175] '**Bodies**' as a generic term (and as opposed to 'public bodies' to which the legislator otherwise frequently refers) covers public and private bodies alike. Even where private entities are entrusted with the tasks of equality bodies, responsibility remains with the Member States to ensure that they fulfil their tasks under the Directive. The **task** of the equality bodies is 'the promotion, analysis, monitoring and support of equal treatment'. More specifically they may

–   provide independent assistance to victims of discrimination in pursuing their complaints about discrimination;
–   conduct independent surveys concerning discrimination;
–   publish independent reports and make recommendations on any issue relating to such discrimination; and
–   at the appropriate level exchange available information with corresponding European bodies such as any future European Institute for Gender Equality.

---

[175]   P. Rädler, *Verfahrensmodelle zum Schutz vor Rassendiskriminierung*; id., *ZRP* 1997, 5–9.

h)   Further Options and Obligations of the Member States

Provisions: Article 27 SDD, Article 8e EAD, Article 6 RDD, Article 8 ETFD

aa)   MINIMUM STANDARD CLAUSE

87.   The anti-discrimination directives merely provide for minimum standards. The Member States may introduce or maintain provisions with more stringent requirements for the protection of the principle of equal treatment than those included in the standards of the directives.

bb)   NON-REGRESSION CLAUSE

88.   In addition, the directives provide that their implementation shall 'under no circumstances be sufficient grounds for a reduction in the level of protection'. While the concern is understandable, the details of the 'prohibition of regression' are unclear, as are its limits.[176]

89.   As to the **limits**, the prohibition of regression is not intended to provide for a petrification of any more favourable rules of national law. Article 27(2) SDD now takes this concern into account by limiting the prohibition so as to be 'without prejudice to the Member States' right to respond to changes in the situation by introducing laws, regulations and administrative provisions which differ from those in force on the notification of this Directive'. Beyond that, the Member States should be free to pursue a different policy and/or system of protection, e.g. upon re-consideration of the matter on the occasion of implementation of the directive or after a new government has been elected. The Court of Justice has limited the scope of the prohibition of regression by linking it to the respective directive's scope of application.[177]

4.   *Protection against Abusive Discrimination Claims*

90.   Anti-discrimination law appears to be particularly prone to abusive claims. An archive, installed by a German law firm, aimed to collect material so as to facilitate proof of abuse (but had to be closed in 2009 on grounds of data protection). The operators report a considerable number of cases where 'applicants' had (often successfully) tried to take advantage of discriminatory job advertisements even though they did not have any serious interest in the position

---

[176]   For a (critical) survey see S. Peers, 'Non-Regression Clauses: The Fig Leaf has Fallen', *ILJ* 39 (2010), 436–443.

[177]   ECJ Case C-246/09 *Bulicke* 8 July 2011 paras. 43–47; see also Joined Cases C-378/07 to C-380/07 *Angelidaki* [2009] ECR I-3071 para. 126.

offered.[178] EU anti-discrimination law does not address the issue of abusive discrimination claims but rather leaves it to the national laws of the Member States. They may apply their general provisions against abuse or provide for specific measures. These must comply with the general implementation obligations, particularly with the principles of equivalence and effectiveness. The issue is particularly sensitive. On the one hand, there is a risk that the collection of allegedly abusive claims may lead to the stigmatisation of plaintiffs and have a deterrent effect. On the other hand, it is a serious criminal offence for a person who has no interest in the position advertised to claim damages for discrimination. Furthermore, the allegation of discriminatory behaviour, too, may lead to stigmatisation. The provisions on the burden of proof make it particularly difficult for the employer to prove his 'innocence'.

V. IMPLEMENTATION OF ANTI-DISCRIMINATION DIRECTIVES

91. In Germany,[179] the 2006 General Equal Treatment Act (*Allgemeines Gleichbehandlungsgesetz*, AGG) now provides for a comprehensive law implementing the anti-discrimination directives.[180] The implementation of the Race Discrimination Directive and the Equal Treatment Framework Directive had been delayed[181] and proved insufficient in individual respects.[182] For example, the issue of dismissal has been exempted from its scope of application

---

[178] M. Diller/J. Kern/R. Zeh, *NZA* 2009, 1386–1391.

[179] See the commentaries by K. Adomeit/J. Mohr (eds.), *Kommentar zum Allgemeinen Gleichbehandlungsgesetz*, J.-H. Bauer/B. Göpfert/S. Krieger (eds.), *Allgemeines Gleichbehandlungsgesetz – Kommentar*, D. Schiek (ed.), *Allgemeines Gleichbehandlungsgesetz*, G. Thüsing, in F. J. Säcker/R. Rixecker (eds.), *Münchener Kommentar zum BGB, volume I*, AGG, and U. Wendeling-Schröder/A. Stein (eds.), *Allgemeines Gleichbehandlungsgesetz – Kommentar*; M. Schlachter, *ZESAR* 2006, 391–399; G. Thüsing, *NZA* 2004 Special Supplement to Issue 22, 3–16; R. Wank, *NZA* 2004, Special Supplement to Issue 22, 16–26. On the implementation in **other Member States** K. Adomeit, *Festschrift für Birk*, 1–9 (Spain); I. Asscher-Vonk/M. Schlachter, 'Verbot der Diskriminierung wegen Alters in den Niederlanden und Deutschland', *RIW* 2005, 503–511 (prohibition of age discrimination in the Netherlands); M. LeFriant, 'Das Prinzip der Nichtdiskriminierung im französischen Recht: Zum Stand der Debatte', *NZA* 2004 Supplement to issue 22, 49–59 (France); ead., 'Rechtstechniken im Kampf gegen die Diskriminierungen: Die Lage in Frankreich', *AuR* 2003, 51–56 (France); R. Rebhahn, *Kommentar des Gleichbehandlungsgesetzes* (Austria); M. Sargeant (ed.), *The Law on Age Discrimination in the EU* (Alphen aan den Rijn: Kluwer, 2008) (age discrimination; with country reports); H. Wiedemann/G. Thüsing, 'Der Schutz älterer Arbeitnehmer und die Umsetzung der Richtlinie 2000/78/EG', *NZA* 2002, 1234, 1235 sq. (age discrimination).

[180] BGBl. I 2006, 1897; bilingual German-English version in S. Lingemann/R. v. Steinau-Steinrück/A. Mengel, *Employment and Labour Law in Germany*, Part II, II.

[181] ECJ Case C-329/04 *Commission v. Germany*, OJ 2005 C 143/13 (operative part of the judgment), with written reasons reproduced in *BeckRS* 2005, 70308.

[182] On implementation deficits AGG J.-H. Bauer/B. Göpfert/S. Krieger (eds.), *Allgemeines Gleichbehandlungsgesetz – Kommentar*, Einl. AGG paras. 43; G. Thüsing, in F. J. Säcker/

altogether (on the incorrect consideration that it was sufficiently covered by the Protection Against Unfair Dismissal Act [Kündigungsschutzgesetz, KSchG][183]) contrary to the requirements of the directives.[184] The claim for damages under §§15(1) sent. 2, 21(2) sent. 2 AGG presupposes fault, contrary to the Court's jurisprudence (see para. 69 above).[185]

VI. THE EXAMPLE OF THE *DRAEHMPAEHL*-CASE[186]

92. In 1994, Herr Draehmpaehl applied for a post advertised in the 'Hamburger Abendblatt' (a daily newspaper) which read as follows:

'We are seeking an experienced female assistant in our sales management department. If you can get along with the chaotic members of a sales-orientated firm, are willing to make them coffee, get little praise and can work hard, you are the right person for us. We need someone who is able to work on the computer and think with and for others. If you can really face this challenge, we await your application with documents giving full information. But do not say we have not warned you…'

The business, Urania neither replied to Mr Draehmpaehl's letter nor did they return the documents accompanying his application. Claiming that he was the best qualified applicant for the position and that he had suffered discrimination on grounds of sex in the hiring process, Mr Draehmpaehl brought a lawsuit in the *Arbeitsgericht* Hamburg for compensation amounting to three-and-a-half months' earnings. The *Arbeitsgericht* took the view that Mr Draehmpaehl had been discriminated against by Urania on the grounds of his sex since the job advertisement was formulated in terms which were not neutral and was clearly addressed to women. The Court also found that there were no clear grounds which would justify an exception and concluded that Urania was in principle

---

R. Rixecker (eds.), *Münchener Kommentar zum BGB*, Einl AGG para. 25; R. Singer, *Festschrift für Adomeit*, 703–717.

[183] Kündigungsschutzgesetz of 25 August 1969 (BGBl. 1969 I, 1317); bilingual German-English version in S. Lingemann/R. v. Steinau-Steinrück/A. Mengel (eds.), *Employment and Labor Law in Germany*, Part II, V.

[184] See in more detail R. Domröse, 'Krankheitsbedingte Kündigung als Verstoß gegen das Verbot der Diskriminierung wegen einer Behinderung in Beschäftigung und Beruf?', *NZA* 2006, 1320, 1323–1325; S. Kamanabrou, 'Europarechtskonformer Schutz vor Benachteiligungen bei Kündigungen', *RdA* 2007, 199–207. See also D. Schiek/ I. Horstkötter, 'Kündigungsschutz via Diskriminierungsverbot', *NZA* 1998, 863–868.

[185] M. Schlachter, in R. Müller-Glöge/U. Preis/I. Schmidt (eds.), *Erfurter Kommentar*, §15 AGG paras. 1 sq.; ead., *ZESAR* 2006, 391, 397 sq.; G. Thüsing, in F. J. Säcker/R. Rixecker (eds.), *Münchener Kommentar zum BGB*, §15 AGG paras. 33 sq.; M. Stoffels, *RdA* 2009, 204, 210 sq.; differently W.-D. Walker, *NZA* 2009, 5, 6 sq. See also G. Annuß, *NZA* 1999, 738, 742 (expressing doubt on grounds of constitutional law).

[186] ECJ Case C-180/95 *Draehmpaehl* [1997] ECR I-2195. On this e.g. R. Abele, *NZA* 1997, 641–643; G. Annuß, *NZA* 1999, 738–744.

bound to pay compensation damages to the plaintiff. There was doubt, however, whether Urania had acted intentionally or negligently (as German law then required for damages). Furthermore, compensation was restricted by several rules, an upper limit of three months' salary and, where there were several applicants who had been discriminated against, a cumulative upper limit of six months' salary for all victims. In a preliminary ruling, the *Arbeitsgericht* referred the question to the Court of Justice whether these restrictions where compatible with the Equal Access Directive (now Sex Discrimination Directive).

93. With regard to the requirement of fault, the Court, following its earlier jurisprudence in *Dekker,*[187] considered that while the Directive provides for certain exceptions and justifications, it does not make liability conditional upon any requirement of fault. Article 6 EAD (Article 17 SDD) rather presupposed that breach of the prohibition of discrimination was in itself sufficient to render the employer fully liable without any possibility of invoking the grounds of exemption provided for by domestic law. Beyond these – rather formal – considerations the Court argued that a requirement of fault would compromise the practical effectiveness (*effet utile*) of the prohibition of discrimination. It was thus incompatible with the requirements of the directive. As the Court clarified in *Draehmpaehl,* this holds true even where fault covers both intent and negligence and even if proof of fault is presumed (and proof thus not excessively difficult) under the applicable national law.

94. The Court's evaluation of upper limits to liability is based upon the requirements of an effective implementation of the Directive.[188] If a Member State chooses to sanction breach of the prohibition of discrimination by the award of compensation, that compensation must be adequate relative to the damage sustained. Upper limits are incompatible with these requirements where the applicant would have been hired but for the discrimination. Matters are different, however, where the employer can prove that the applicant would not have been appointed to the vacant position since the applicant appointed had superior qualifications. In this latter case, an upper limit of three months' salary would not be inadequate. A ceiling of six months' salary on the aggregate amount of compensation for all applicants harmed by discrimination, on the other hand, would be irreconcilable with the requirements of effective implementation. Given that such a mechanism might lead to the award of reduced compensation it could have the effect of dissuading applicants who had been discriminated against from asserting their rights. Such sanction would, in other words, not have a deterrent effect.

---

[187] ECJ Case 177/88 *Dekker* [1990] ECR 1990, 3941.
[188] The Court further (paras. 28–30) refers to the principle of equivalence which is not discussed in the above summary.

§9. PROHIBITION OF SEX DISCRIMINATION

CONTENT

I. INTRODUCTION AND OVERVIEW

1. The prohibition of sex discrimination still rests on several sources of law, even after the 'codification' of various directives in the 2006 Sex Discrimination Directive (see §8 para. 19). First, there is the prohibition of sex discrimination in respect of pay in EU primary law. Secondly, there are the prohibitions of sex discrimination which are found in secondary legislation. The provisions overlap with regard to pay. Despite the common subject-matter of these provisions and the common regulatory concepts which are used, the state of this legislation necessitates discussion which differentiates between the different sources of law (II., III. below). The prohibition of sex discrimination in primary EU law is an unalterable datum for the European legislature and takes priority in its application over the laws of the Member States[1] (see also §1 paras. 67 sq.). From a policy perspective, it would also seem preferable to lay the prohibition of sex discrimination with regard to pay entirely in the hands of the legislature. There are historical reasons for the exceptional position of this specific prohibition, which, otherwise, is not warranted in substance (§8 para. 4), particularly since the Charter of Fundamental Rights entered into force (§2 para. 18). The status as primary law bears the disadvantage that changes necessitated for economic or policy reasons (e.g. with regard to positive action!) can only be achieved through the cumbersome procedure of an amendment of the Treaty. Furthermore, the plurality of legal sources addressing the same subject matter does not add to transparency and renders application of the law rather more difficult.

---

[1]   See e.g. M. Schlachter, in R. Müller-Glöge/U. Preis/I. Schmidt (eds.), *Erfurter Kommentar,* Art. 157 AEUV paras. 2 sq.; id., in *EAS,* B 4100 paras. 4 sq.

II. THE PROHIBITION OF SEX DISCRIMINATION WITH REGARD TO PAY IN EU PRIMARY LAW

Bibliography (Selection):

C. Barnard/B. Hepple, 'Indirect Discrimination: Interpreting Seymour-Smith', *C.L.J.* 58 (1999), 399–412; L. Fastrich, 'Gleichbehandlung und Gleichstellung', *RdA* 2000, 65–81; T. Fuchs, 'Gemeinschaftsrechtswidrige Gleich- oder Ungleichbehandlung im Rahmen von Art. 141 EG', *EuR* 2008, 697–702; T. Huep, 'Die zeitliche Reichweite des geschlechtsbezogenen Entgeltgleichheitsgrundsatzes im deutschen und europäischen Arbeitsrecht', *RdA* 2001, 325–333; M. Kort, 'Zur Gleichbehandlung im deutschen und europäischen Arbeitsrecht, insbesondere beim Arbeitsentgelt teilzeitbeschäftigter Betriebsratsmitglieder', *RdA* 1997, 277–284; M. Lorenz, 'Schwieriger Weg zur Lohnangleichung von Männern u. Frauen', in R. Anzinger/R. Wank (eds.), *Entwicklungen im Arbeitsrecht und Arbeitsschutzrecht – Festschrift für Otfried Wlotzke* (Munich: C.H. Beck, 1996), 45–82; H. M. Pfarr, 'Gleichbehandlung von Männern und Frauen im Arbeitsverhältnis', *AR-Blattei*, SD 800.2; H. M. Pfarr, 'Mittelbare Diskriminierung von Frauen – Die Rechtsprechung des EuGH', *NZA* 1986, 585–589; V. Rieble, 'Entgeltgleichstellung der Frau', *RdA* 2011, 36–46; M. Schlachter, 'Grundsatz des gleichen Entgelts nach Art. 119 EG-Vertrag und der Richtlinie 75/117/EWG', in H. Oetker/U. Preis (eds.), *Europäisches Arbeits- und Sozialrecht, EAS, part B – Systematische Darstellungen*, loose-leaf (Heidelberg: Forkel, last update 1998), B 4100; M. Schlachter, *Wege zur Gleichberechtigung – Vergleich des Arbeitsrechts der Bundesrepublik Deutschland und der Vereinigten Staaten* (Munich: C.H. Beck, 1993); R. Winter, *Gleiches Entgelt für gleichwertige Arbeit – Ein Prinzip ohne Praxis* (Baden-Baden: Nomos, 1998); W. Zöllner, 'Gleichberechtigung und Gleichstellung der Geschlechter', in W. Schwarz et al. (eds.), *Möglichkeiten und Grenzen der Rechtsordnung – Festschrift für Rudolf Strasser* (Vienna: Manz, 1983), 223–240; see also the bibliograhy to §8.

Cases (Selection):

ECJ Case 80/70 *Defrenne I* [1971] ECR 445; ECJ Case 43/75 *Defrenne II* [1976] ECR 455; ECJ Case 149/77 *Defrenne III* [1978] ECR 1365; ECJ Case 129/79 *Macarthys* [1980] ECR 1275; ECJ Case 69/80 *Worrigham* [1981] ECR 767; ECJ Case 96/80 *Jenkins* [1981] ECR 911; ECJ Case 12/81 *Garland* [1982] ECR 359; ECJ Case 170/84 *Bilka* [1986] ECR 1607; ECJ Case 171/88 *Rinner-Kühn* [1989] ECR 2743; ECJ Case 109/88 *Danfoss* [1989] ECR 3199; ECJ Case C-262/88 *Barber* [1990] ECR I-1889; ECJ Case C-33/89 *Kowalska* [1990] ECR I-2591; ECJ Case C-184/89 *Nimz* [1991] ECR I-297; ECJ Case C-360/90 *Bötel* [1992] ECR I-3589; ECJ Case C-109/91 *Ten Oever* [1993] ECR I-4879; ECJ Case C-172/92 *Enderby* [1993] ECR I-5535; ECJ Case C-110/91 *Moroni* [1993] ECR I-6591; ECJ Case C-152/91 *Neath* [1993] ECR I-6935; ECJ Case C-200/91 *Coloroll Pension Trustees* [1994] ECR I-4389; ECJ Case C-408/92 *Avdel Systems* [1994] ECR I-4435; ECJ Case C-7/93 *Beune* [1994] ECR I-4471; ECJ Case C-28/93 *Van den Akker* [1994] ECR I-4527; ECJ Case C-128/93 *Fisscher* [1994] ECR I-4583; ECJ Case C-399/92 *Helmig* [1994] ECR I-5727; ECJ Case C-400/93 *Royal Copenhagen* [1995] ECR I-1275; ECJ Case C-457/93 *Lewark* [1996] ECR I-243; ECJ Case C-352/93 *Gillespie* [1996] ECR I-475; ECJ Case C-278/93 *Freers and Speckmann* [1996] ECR I-1165; ECJ Case C-435/93 *Dietz* [1996] ECR I-5223; ECJ Case C-1/95 *Gerster* [1997] ECR I-5253; ECJ Case C-249/96 *Grant* [1998] ECR I-621; ECJ Case

C-243/95 *Hill and Stapleton* [1998] ECR I-3730; ECJ Case C-411/96 *Boyle* [1998] ECR I-6401; ECJ Case C-167/97 *Seymour-Smith u. Perez* [1999] ECR I-688; ECJ Case C-309/97 *Wiener Gebietskrankenkasse* [1999] ECR I-2865; ECJ Case C-281/97 *Krüger* [1999] ECR I-5127; ECJ Case C-218/98 *Abdoulaye* [1999] ECR I-5723; ECJ Case C-333/97 *Lewen* [1999] ECR I-7243; ECJ Case C-270/97 and C-271/97 *Sievers and Schrage* [2000] ECR I-929; ECJ Case C-236/98 *JämO* [2000] ECR I-2189; ECJ Case C-78/98 *Preston and Fletcher* [2000] ECR I-3201; ECJ Case C-50/99 *Podesta* [2000] ECR I-4039; ECJ Case C-381/99 *Brunnhofer* [2001] ECR I-4961; ECJ Case C-407/98 *Abrahamsson and Anderson* [2000] ECR I-5539; ECJ Case C-379/99 *Pensionskasse für die Angestellten der Barmer Ersatzkasse* [2001] ECR I-7275; ECJ Case C-366/99 *Griesmar* [2001] ECR I-9383; ECJ Case C-320/00 *Lawrence* [2002] ECR I-7325; ECJ Case C-351/00 *Niemi* [2002] ECR I-7007; ECJ Case C-256/01 *Allonby* [2004] ECR I-873; ECJ Case C-147/02 *Alabaster* [2004] ECR I-3101; ECJ Case C-285/02 *Elsner-Lakeberg* [2004] ECR I-5861; ECJ Case C-19/02 *Hlozek* [2004] ECR I-11491; ECJ Case C-196/02 *Vasiliki Nikoloudi* [2005] ECR I-1789; ECJ Case C-191/03 *McKenna* [2005] ECR I-7631; ECJ Case C-207/04 *Vergani* [2007] ECR I-7453; ECJ Case C-17/05 *Cadman* [2006] ECR I-9583; ECJ Case C-227/04 *Lindorfer* [2007] ECR I-6767 (on the Staff Regulations of officials of the European Communities); ECJ Case C-300/06 *Voß* [2007] ECR I-10573; ECJ Case C-46/07 *Commission v. Italy* [2008] ECR I-151; ECJ Case C-194/08 *Gassmayr* [2012] ECR I-6281.

1. Overview and Purpose

2. 'Each Member State shall ensure that the principle of equal pay for male and female workers for equal work or work of equal value is applied', Article 157(1) TFEU. The provision was originally included in the (then: EEC-) Treaty with the purpose of avoiding competitive disadvantages for undertakings from those Member States where the principle of equal pay was already effectively enforced. The Court has held that the provision is also has a social rationale and considered that this double objective – economic and social – demonstrated that the provision was part of the '**foundations of the Community**' (now: Union) (see also §8 para. 4).[2] Building upon this, the Court has recognised the prohibition of sex discrimination as an EU fundamental right which is also binding upon the Union itself.[3] This has been recently confirmed by the entry into force of the Charter of Fundamental Rights (§2 para. 18). Today, the social purpose and characterisation of the provision as a fundamental right are considered to be rather more important than the provision's original economic rationale.[4]

---

[2]   ECJ Case 43/75 *Defrenne II* [1976] ECR 455 para. 12; Case C-17/05 *Cadman* [2006] ECR I-9583 para. 28; Joined Cases C-270/97 and C-271/97 *Sievers and Schrage* [2000] ECR 929 paras. 53–57; Case C-256/01 *Allonby* [2004] ECR I-873 para. 65.

[3]   ECJ Case C-25/02 *Rinke* [2003] ECR I-8349 paras. 25–27.

[4]   ECJ Joined Cases C-270/97 and C-271/97 *Sievers and Schrage* [2000] ECR 929 para. 57.

2.   Addressees

3.   Article 157 TFEU is, as its wording shows, first of all addressed to Member States (and the same has been true for its predecessors, starting with Article 119 EEC Treaty). Furthermore, there is no doubt that the provision, which the Court considers expresses a fundamental principle of EU law, is also binding upon the Union itself.[5] Beyond that, the Court has, in its seminal *Defrenne II* decision, held that (today's) Article 157 TFEU has **horizontal direct effect**, that is, that it also binds private parties,[6] i.e. the parties to an employment contract as well as the social partners.[7] Next to the employer, third parties involved in the execution of his obligations, such as trustees for the administration of a pension fund, may also be bound by the prohibition contained in Article 157 TFEU. Conversely, the provision may also entitle third parties, e.g. surviving dependants of the employee, in respect of pension rights.[8]

4.   Initially, the Court considered that the prohibition of *direct* discrimination was merely horizontally applicable, as it did not require further concretisation.[9] In later decisions, however, the Court extended the direct applicability of Article 157 TFEU to private individuals in relation to the prohibition of indirect discrimination.[10]

3.   Scope of Application

a)   Personal Scope of Application: Worker

5.   The scope of application of Article 157 TFEU is denoted by the term 'pay for workers' which encompasses the personal aspect of the employment

---

[5]   ECJ Case C-25/02 *Rinke* [2003] ECR I-8349 paras. 25–27.

[6]   ECJ Case 43/75 *Defrenne II* [1976] ECR 455 paras. 4, 6–40. Further Case C-262/88 *Barber* [1990] ECR I-1889 paras. 37 sq.; Case 12/81 *Garland* [1982] ECR 359 paras. 14 sq.; Case 96/80 *Jenkins* [1981] ECR 911 para. 17.

[7]   ECJ Case C-19/02 *Hlozek* [2004] ECR I-11491 para. 43; Case C-284/02 *Sass* [2004] ECR I-11143 para. 25; Case C-379/99 *Pensionskasse für die Angestellten der Barmer Ersatzkasse* [2001] ECR I-7275 para. 17; Case C-381/99 *Brunnhofer* [2001] ECR I-4961 para. 32; Case C-333/97 *Lewen* [1999] ECR I-7243 para. 26; Case C-281/97 *Krüger* [1999] ECR I-5127 para. 20; Case C-200/91 *Coloroll Pension Trustees* [1994] ECR I-4389 para. 26; Case C-184/89 *Nimz* [1991] ECR I-297 para. 11; Case C-33/89 *Kowalska* [1990] ECR I-2591 para. 12.

[8]   ECJ Case C-379/99 *Pensionskasse für die Angestellten der Barmer Ersatzkasse* [2001] ECR I-7275 paras. 19–23; Case C-435/93 *Dietz* [1996] ECR I-5223 paras. 30 sq.; Case C-200/91 *Coloroll Pension Trustees* [1994] ECR I-4389 paras. 20–23. M. Schlachter, in R. Müller-Glöge/U. Preis/I. Schmidt (eds.), *Erfurter Kommentar*, Art. 157 AEUV paras. 4 sq.

[9]   ECJ Case 43/75 *Defrenne II* [1976] ECR 455 paras. 16/20, 21/24; Case 129/79 *Macarthys* [1980] ECR 1275 para. 15; Case 69/80 *Worrigham* [1981] ECR 767 para. 23.

[10] ECJ Case C-33/89 *Kowalska* [1990] ECR I-2591 para. 18; Case 96/80 *Jenkins* [1981] ECR 911 paras. 17 sq. (with the qualification that the national court must be 'able, using the criteria of equal work and equal pay, without the operation of Community or national measures, to establish … discrimination').

---

relation and the substantive aspect of remuneration. The provision covers employers in both the private and public sectors.[11] Only workers (and, in certain cases, their relatives or legal successors) can rely upon Article 157 TFEU.[12] The term **worker** must be construed autonomously with regard to Union law[13] and the term has the same scope as under Article 45 TFEU: A worker is a person who, for a certain period of time, performs services for and under the direction of another in return for which he receives remuneration (see in detail §3 paras. 9–12 above).[14] In line with the purpose of the provision, the term also extends to civil servants,[15] although self-employed persons are not covered.[16]

b)   Substantive Scope of Application: Pay

6.   The substantive scope of application is delineated by reference to **pay** (for workers).[17] This covers 'the ordinary basic or minimum wage or salary and any other consideration, whether in cash or in kind, which the worker receives directly or indirectly, in respect of his employment, from his employer', Article 157(2)(1) TFEU. Pay is thus **construed broadly**.

7.   Apart from basic salary, pay also covers any salary supplement, bonus, allowance or extra pay,[18] including e.g. sick pay,[19] benefits paid during maternity leave[20] or compensation received for loss of earnings due to attendance at training courses imparting the information necessary for performing staff committee functions.[21] Pay covers consideration in cash as well as in kind, e.g. special travel facilities for active or retired railroad

---

[11]   ECJ Case 43/75 *Defrenne II* [1976] ECR 455 paras. 21/24; Case C-1/95 *Gerster* [1997] ECR I-5253 para. 18.

[12]   ECJ Case C-256/01 *Allonby* [2004] ECR I-873 paras. 43, 62.

[13]   ECJ Case C-256/01 *Allonby* [2004] ECR I-873 paras. 65 sq.

[14]   ECJ Case C-256/01 *Allonby* [2004] ECR I-873 paras. 67 sq.

[15]   ECJ Case C-366/99 *Griesmar* [2001] ECR I-9383 para. 31; Case C-1/95 *Gerster* [1997] ECR I-5253 para. 18.

[16]   ECJ Case C-256/01 *Allonby* [2004] ECR I-873 para. 68.

[17]   ECJ Case 149/77 *Defrenne III* [1978] ECR 1365 paras. 19/23. This does not include tax benefits as these are not being granted by the employer; ECJ Case C-207/04 *Vergani* [2005] ECR I-7453 paras. 22 sq.

[18]   ECJ Case C-381/99 *Brunnhofer* [2001] ECR I-4961 para. 34; Case C-236/98 *JämO* [2000] ECR I-2189 paras. 39–42 (supplement for inconvenient working hours); Case C-187/98 *Commission v. Greece* [1999] ECR I-7713 para. 41 (family and marriage allowance).

[19]   ECJ Case C-191/03 *McKenna* [2005] ECR I-7631 para. 29; Case C-66/96 *Pedersen* [1998] ECR I-7327 para. 32; Case 171/88 *Rinner-Kühn* [1989] ECR 2743.

[20]   ECJ Case C-147/02 *Alabaster* [2004] ECR I-3101 paras. 43 sq.; Case C-411/96 *Boyle* [1998] ECR I-6401 para. 38; Case C-352/93 *Gillespie* [1996] ECR I-475 para. 14. See also Case C-218/98 *Abdoulaye* [1999] ECR I-5723 paras. 13–15 (allowance for pregnant women going on maternity leave).

[21]   ECJ Case C-278/93 *Freers and Speckmann* [1996] ECR I-1165 paras. 16–19; Case C-457/93 *Lewark* [1996] ECR I-243 paras. 20–23; Case C-360/90 *Bötel* [1992] ECR I-3589 paras. 11–15. With doubt M. Kort, *RdA* 1997, 277, 282 (not 'work').

employees or their families.[22] It also includes special benefits, such as a Christmas bonus, even if paid on a voluntary basis and irrespective of whether it is paid mainly or exclusively as an incentive for future work or loyalty to the business or both.[23] Pursuant to the wording of Article 157(2) TFEU ('receives'), it does not matter whether payment is made pursuant to a legal duty or voluntarily.[24]

8. Contributions paid directly to the trustees of a **retirement benefits scheme** which are included in the calculation of the gross salary payable to the employee constitute pay.[25] The same is true for an occupational pension,[26] the right to join an occupational pension scheme[27] and a survivor's pension paid to relatives of the deceased employee.[28] The fact that payment is made after termination of the employment relationship or, in the case of a survivor's pension, after the death of the employee to a third person does not affect its nature as pay.[29] On the other hand, pay does not include social security schemes or benefits, in particular retirement pensions, which are directly governed by legislation and not subject to the agreement of the parties to the employment contract.[30]

---

[22]   ECJ Case 12/81 *Garland* [1982] ECR 359 paras. 5–9. But see Case C-476/99 *Lommers* [2002] ECR I-2891 para. 27 (denying the categorisation of a nursery place as pay); differently S. Krebber, in C. Calliess/M. Ruffert (eds.), *EUV/AEUV*, Art. 157 AEUV paras. 22 sqq.

[23]   ECJ Case C-333/97 *Lewen* [1999] ECR I-7243 paras. 19–21; Case C-281/97 *Krüger* [1999] ECR I-5127 paras. 15–17.

[24]   ECJ Case C-262/88 *Barber* [1990] ECR I-1889 para. 19; Case 12/81 *Garland* [1982] ECR 359 para. 10; Case 69/80 *Worrigham* [1981] ECR 767 para. 16; Case 43/75 *Defrenne II* [1976] ECR 455 para. 19.

[25]   ECJ Case 69/80 *Worrigham* [1981] ECR 767 paras. 14 sq. But see on the issue of different employer contributions on grounds of factors of actuarial mathematics Case C-200/91 *Coloroll Pension Trustees* [1994] ECR I-4389 paras. 72–82; Case C-152/91 *Neath* [1993] ECR I-6935 paras. 28–33 ('the funding arrangements chosen to secure the periodic payment of the pension' fall outside the scope of Article 157 TFEU); see now Recital 15 SDD.

[26]   ECJ Case 170/84 *Bilka* [1986] ECR 1607 para. 27. Furhter Case C-366/99 *Griesmar* [2001] ECR I-9383 para. 27 (civil servants' pension); Case C-7/93 *Beune* [1994] ECR I-4471 paras. 21–46 (pension system in the public service); Case C-50/99 *Podesta* [2000] ECR I-4039 (supplementary retirement pension).

[27]   ECJ Case C-435/93 *Dietz* [1996] ECR I-5223 paras. 12–16; Case C-128/93 *Fisscher* [1994] ECR I-4583 paras. 10–14.

[28]   ECJ Case C-200/91 *Coloroll Pension Trustees* [1994] ECR I-4389 paras. 18 sq.; Case C-109/91 *Ten Oever* [1993] ECR I-4879 paras. 8–13.

[29]   ECJ Case C-379/99 *Pensionskasse für die Angestellten der Barmer Ersatzkasse* [2001] ECR I-7275 para. 18; Case C-7/93 *Beune* [1994] ECR I-4471 para. 21; Case C-152/91 *Neath* [1993] ECR I-6935 para. 28; Case 96/80 *Jenkins* [1981] ECR 911 para. 12.

[30]   ECJ Case C-351/00 *Niemi* [2002] ECR I-7007 paras. 39 sq. (and paras. 45, 47 on the criteria for demarcation); Case C-262/88 *Barber* [1990] ECR I-1889 para. 22; Case 170/84 *Bilka* [1986] ECR 1607 paras. 15–22; Case 80/70 *Defrenne I* [1971] ECR 445 paras. 7/12.

9. Benefits paid **after termination of an employment relationship** can constitute a form of 'deferred remuneration', and thus qualify as pay.[31] Compensation granted to a worker in connection with his redundancy[32] or a 'bridging allowance'[33] constitute pay, even where such compensation is determined by the law or a court.[34] In contrast, a tax concession for compensation to workers of a certain age does not qualify as pay (as it is not granted by the employer).[35]

10. Classification into **salary grades** is related to pay where a 'system of practically automatic salary classification based on rules relating to length of service' is at stake.[36] In contrast, where classification is not linked to remuneration, but rather concerns access to career advancement, it may only be subject to scrutiny under the rules of the Sex Discrimination Directive (para. 35 below).[37] In the case of termination of the contract of employment, it depends upon what is at issue: Where compensation (= pay) is concerned, Article 157 TFEU applies, but where the employee seeks re-employment, this falls into the scope of the Sex Discrimination Directive.[38]

4. *The Prohibition of Discrimination*

a) Prohibited Ground of Distinction: Sex

11. Sex may not be a ground for distinction. Article 157 TFEU thus not only protects women but men alike. Male employees have, in particular, brought actions based upon discrimination arising from different retirement ages in violation of Article 157 TFEU.[39] In light of the wording (compare with Article 19 TFEU) and historical development of Article 157 TFEU, sex is to be distinguished

---

31 ECJ Case C-33/89 *Kowalska* [1990] ECR I-2591 para. 9; Case C-173/91 *Commission* v. *Belgium* [1993] ECR 673 paras. 12–22 (additional redundancy payment for employees over 60 who receive unemployment benefits); Case C-166/99 *Defreyn* [2000] ECR I-6155 paras. 26, 35.
32 ECJ Case C-262/88 *Barber* [1990] ECR I-1889 para. 13; Case C-167/97 *Seymour-Smith and Perez* [1999] ECR I-688 paras. 23–23.
33 ECJ Case C-19/02 *Hlozek* [2004] ECR I-11491 paras. 37–39 ('bridging allowance' based on a social plan); Case C-33/89 *Kowalska* [1990] ECR I-2591 paras. 8–11.
34 ECJ Case 43/75 *Defrenne II* [1976] ECR 455 para. 40; Case C-262/88 *Barber* [1990] ECR I-1889 para. 17.
35 ECJ Case C-207/04 *Vergani* [2007] ECR I-7453 paras. 22 sq.
36 ECJ Case C-184/89 *Nimz* [1991] ECR I-297 paras. 9 sq.; Case C-172/92 *Enderby* [1993] ECR I-5535 para. 21.
37 ECJ Case C-1/95 *Gerster* [1997] ECR I-5253 para. 24. Also Case C-77/02 *Steinicke* [2003] ECR I-9027 para. 51 (scheme of part-time work for older employees with pecuniary implycations); see also Case C-284/02 *Sass* [2004] ECR I-11143 paras. 30 sq.
38 ECJ Case C-167/97 *Seymour-Smith and Perez* [1999] ECR I-688 paras. 35–37.
39 See in parcitular ECJ Case C-262/88 *Barber* [1990] ECR I-1889.

from sexual orientation.[40] To exclude same sex partners from travel concessions that are granted to spouses or partners of the opposite sex does not violate Article 157 TFEU.[41]

b) Discrimination

aa) EVALUATION BASIS: COMPARABLE FACTS

12. Any examination of discrimination begins with the determination of comparable facts. This is easy where the worker at issue can be compared with another worker in the business.[42] Beyond that, a comparison raises intricate questions.[43] Different pay may be an expression of different preferences, different working conditions (atmosphere, size of the business, job security, family-friendliness), different bargaining situations, different collective agreements etc. The Court has held that a comparison with a former employee is a suitable basis for the determination of discrimination; here, however, the national court may have to inquire whether the difference in pay between workers occupying the same post at different periods in time may be explained by factors unrelated to any discrimination on grounds of sex.[44] On the other hand, the Court did not allow for a comparison with a **hypothetical person** ('concept of a hypothetical male/female worker') under Article 157 TFEU, originally on the ground that the direct application of the provision was limited,[45] and subsequently on the categorical consideration that where there was no actual comparable worker of the other sex in the same company, now or in the past, 'the essential criterion for ascertaining that equal treatment exists in the matter of pay cannot be applied'.[46] Where all employees are of the same sex (which, of course, may only rarely be the case without discrimination), there is no room for a claim of pay discrimination under Article 157 TFEU.[47] The prohibition of discrimination with respect to pay is not an instrument to bring about 'fair remuneration' as such. This is why its

---

[40] See also J. Gardner, 'On the Grounds of her Sex(uality)', *OJLS* 18 (1998),167–187 (arguing the distinction as a matter of principle).

[41] ECJ Case C-249/96 *Grant* [1998] ECR I-621. Critical H. Collins, *Employment Law,* 57 sq.

[42] ECJ Case 129/79 *Macarthys* [1980] ECR 1275 para. 10.

[43] For a detailed analysis, see V. Rieble, *RdA* 2011, 36–46 (emphasising individual preferences, private autonomy of the contract partners and collective autonomy of the social partners as determening factors for pay).

[44] ECJ Case 129/79 *Macarthys* [1980] ECR 1275 paras. 11 sq.

[45] ECJ Case 129/79 *Macarthys* [1980] ECR 1275 paras. 14 sq. ('indirect and disguised discrimination').

[46] ECJ Case C-200/91 *Coloroll Pension Trustees* [1994] ECR I-4389 paras. 102 sq. Approvingly S. Krebber, in C. Calliess/M. Ruffert (eds.), *EUV/AEUV,* Art. 157 AEUV para. 51 (*argumentum:* no general right to 'fair' remuneration); for a critical discussion, see H. Collins, *Employment Law,* 88–90.

[47] ECJ Case C-256/01 *Allonby* [2004] ECR I-873 para. 74. But see Case C 196/02 *Vasiliki Nikoloudi* [2005] ECR I-1789 paras. 26–29 (in adequate cases, an employee of the opposite sex with comparable work may be used for comparison).

application in principle presupposes a comparable worker of the *same employer.* '[W]here (...) the differences identified in the pay conditions of workers performing equal work or work of equal value cannot be attributed to a single source, there is no body which is responsible for the inequality and which could restore equal treatment.'[48]

13. Judicial control of discrimination in pay does not, however, presuppose that the person compared performs the **same work**. The comparison may also be based upon **work of equal value**.[49] Following a formula established by the Court of Justice, it must be determined 'whether, taking account of a number of factors such as the nature of the work, the training requirements and the working conditions, those persons can be considered to be in a comparable situation'.[50] Classification in the same job category under a collective agreement is not itself sufficient for that purpose and has merely indicative value and needs to be confirmed on concrete factors.[51] 'It is therefore necessary to ascertain whether, when a number of factors are taken into account, such as the nature of the activities actually entrusted to each of the employees in question in the case, the training requirements for carrying them out and the working conditions in which the activities are actually carried out, those persons are in fact performing the same work or comparable work.'[52] It is for the national courts to apply this test to the circumstances of the individual case.

bb)   Forms and Determination of Discrimination

14. The comparable facts thus established form the basis for the determination whether unequal treatment occurred. On the basis of the teleological consideration of effective enforcement of the prohibition of discrimination, the Court has also determined the **method of comparison** at the level of Union law:[53] The central question is not whether remuneration, when compared overall by taking all consideration paid to the workers into account, are equal ('the bottom line'). Instead, the principle of equal pay applies to *each aspect of remuneration* granted to men and women. This entails a special **principle of transparency** as the comparison of individual aspects of remuneration will only

---

[48]   ECJ Case C-320/00 *Lawrence* [2002] ECR I-7325 para. 18; Case C-256/01 *Allonby* [2004] ECR I-873 paras. 45 sq. and 82 sq. (the case may have concerned a transfer of undertaking under the Transfer or Undertakings Directive, though).

[49]   ECJ Case C 196/02 *Vasiliki Nikoloudi* [2005] ECR I-1789 paras. 26–29.

[50]   ECJ Case C-381/99 *Brunnhofer* [2001] ECR I-4961 para. 43; Case C-309/97 *Wiener Gebietskrankenkasse* [1999] ECR I-2865 paras. 17 sq.; Case C-400/93 *Royal Copenhagen* [1995] ECR I-1275 para. 33.

[51]   ECJ Case C-381/99 *Brunnhofer* [2001] ECR I-4961 paras. 44–47.

[52]   ECJ Case C-381/99 *Brunnhofer* [2001] ECR I-4961 para. 48.

[53]   ECJ Case C-381/99 *Brunnhofer* [2001] ECR I-4961 para. 35; Case C-262/88 *Barber* [1990] ECR I-1889 para. 34.

be possible where the individual components (basic pay, bonuses, gratifications, non-pecuniary benefits etc.) are being disclosed.[54] A lack of transparency may lead to a shift in the burden of proof (see para. 21 below).

15. Equal pay without discrimination on grounds of sex thus entails, pursuant to Article 157(2)(2) TFEU, that

(a) pay for the same *work at per unit rates* shall be calculated on the basis of the same unit of measurement[55] and

(b) pay for *work in time increments* shall be the same for the same job.[56]

Discrimination occurs where different rules are being applied to comparable situations or where the same provision is being applied to different situations.[57] Following established jurisprudence, Article 157 TFEU prohibits both direct and indirect discrimination.

i.   Direct Discrimination

16. Direct discrimination occurs where **sex is the ground for differentiation**. The prohibition of direct discrimination had particular practical relevance with regard to different retirement ages for men and women,[58] which had traditionally been considered justified with regard to the burdens upon women in their roles as mothers. A distinction with regard to **pregnancy** or the aspects of **motherhood** which are specifically related to sex (in particular giving birth and breastfeeding) has also been considered direct discrimination under Article 157 TFEU (and the legislator has recently followed suit in Article 2(2)(c) SDD; see para. 46 below; on the admissibility of specific protection of pregnant women and parents, see paras. 63 sqq. below).[59] Thus, an employer may not deny a female employee a pay raise on the ground that she had been on maternity leave at the relevant time (see

---

54   ECJ Case C-285/02 *Elsner-Lakeberg* [2004] ECR I-5861 para. 15; Case C-236/98 *JämO* [2000] ECR I-2189 para. 43; Case C-262/88 *Barber* [1990] ECR I-1889 para. 33.

55   See e.g. ECJ Case C-400/93 *Royal Copenhagen* [1995] ECR I-1275 paras. 12–14, 20–22.

56   Differences is performance may well be taken into account in a system of work paid at time rates, but this will usually require an evaluation of the performance and a corresponding assignment of tasks; ECJ Case C-381/99 *Brunnhofer* [2001] ECR I-4961 paras. 76–79.

57   ECJ Case C-147/02 *Alabaster* [2004] ECR I-3101 para. 45; Case C-309/97 *Wiener Gebietskrankenkasse* [1999] ECR I-2865 para. 15; Case C-411/96 *Boyle* [1998] ECR I-6401 paras. 39–42; Case C-352/93 *Gillespie* [1996] ECR I-475 para. 16; Case C-279/93 *Schumacker* [1995] ECR I-225 para. 30. See also Case C-19/02 *Hlozek* [2004] ECR I-11491 paras. 44–50 (taking into account of different legal retirement ages as a factor for the risks resulting from dismissal does not constitute discrimination).

58   ECJ Case C-110/91 *Moroni* [1993] ECR I-6591 paras. 10–19; Case C-262/88 *Barber* [1990] ECR I-1889.

59   Cf. also the development in U.S.-American law: *Geduldig* v. *Aiello* 417 U.S. 484 (1974); *General Electric* v. *Gilbert* 429 U.S. 415 (1976); *AT&T* v. *Hulteen* U.S. Sup Ct. 04–16–87 Pregnancy Discrimination Act 1978 (effectively reversing the Supreme Court's judgements in *Geduldig* and *Gilbert*).

also §20 para. 35).[60] However, as the situation of a worker on maternity leave differs from that of an active employee, she does not have a right to continued full remuneration.[61] Direct discrimination also occurs where continued pay is lower for times of absence due to pregnancy-related illness than for times of absence due to other illness.[62] Yet, a provision pursuant to which continued pay can be reduced in cases of pregnancy-related illness as in any other case of illness has not been considered discriminatory by the court 'as Community law stands at present' (*inter alia* with regard to Article 11(2) and (3) Maternity Protection Directive).[63]

ii.   Indirect Discrimination

17.   Indirect (or disguised) discrimination occurs where facially neutral criteria have a **discriminatory effect** based upon sex. This can be proven, in particular, on the basis of statistics.[64] Such discriminatory effect may result especially from the facially neutral criterion of **part-time work**, given that it is predominantly women who work part-time (similarly with regard to persons in minor employment)[65] (see also para. 50 below). The Court of Justice has considered this issue in a long series of cases[66] and found indirect discrimination to be established in the following cases:

– unequal pay for part-time workers;[67]
– the exclusion of part-time workers from continued payment of wages in the event of illness,[68] from a severance grant upon termination of employment,[69] from an occupational pension scheme[70] or a Christmas bonus[71];

---

[60]   ECJ Case C-147/02 *Alabaster* [2004] ECR I-3101 paras. 47–49; Case C-411/96 *Boyle* [1998] ECR I-6401 paras. 39–42; Case C-352/93 *Gillespie* [1996] ECR I-475 paras. 21 sq.

[61]   ECJ Case C-194/08 *Gassmayr* [2010] ECR I-6281 paras. 78 sqq.; Case C-191/03 *McKenna* [2005] ECR I-7631 para. 50; Case C-147/02 *Alabaster* [2004] ECR I-3101 para. 46; Case C-352/93 *Gillespie* [1996] ECR I-475 para. 20.

[62]   ECJ Case C-66/96 *Pedersen* [1998] ECR I-7327 paras. 33–37.

[63]   ECJ Case C-191/03 *McKenna* [2005] ECR I-7631 paras. 57–62; similarly, setting off times of pregnancy-related illness against the total number of paid sick-leave cannot be objected, paras. 63–68.

[64]   On the requirements of proof, see in more detail ECJ Case C-167/97 *Seymour-Smith and Perez* [1999] ECR I-688 paras. 58–62; Case C-256/01 *Allonby* [2004] ECR I-873 paras. 74 sq. For a critical discussion, see C. Barnard/B. Hepple, *C.L.J.* 58 (1999), 399–412.

[65]   ECJ Case C-281/97 *Krüger* [1999] ECR I-5127 para. 26.

[66]   For an overview of this caselaw, see E. Traversa, 'The Protection of Part-Time Workers in the Case Law of the Courtof Justice of the European Communities', *IJCLLIR* 19 (2003), 219–241.

[67]   ECJ Case 96/80 *Jenkins* [1981] ECR 911 para. 13 (The employer had previously paid women less than men, then changed the system, now providing for equal rates for both sexes but for 10% lower rates for part-time employees; all part-time employees were women).

[68]   ECJ Case 171/88 *Rinner-Kühn* [1989] ECR 2743.

[69]   ECJ Case C-33/89 *Kowalska* [1990] ECR I-2591 para. 13.

[70]   ECJ Case 170/84 *Bilka* [1986] ECR 1607 paras. 29 sq.

[71]   ECJ Case C-333/97 *Lewen* [1999] ECR I-7243 paras. 34–42; Case C-281/97 *Krüger* [1999] ECR I-5127 paras. 26–29.

- lower compensation for staff committee members employed on a part-time basis for their participation in training courses for staff committee members in relation to the time of such training (not in relation to their working hours);[72]
- a higher obligation to work extra hours, relative to the normal working hours;[73]
- a generally lower level of pay for extra hours (applicable for both, full-time and part-time employees) which has the effect that part-time workers on balance receive a lower pay than full-time workers would in the same working time;[74] and
- where part-time workers are adversely affected upon conversion to full-time work.[75]

The Court has left it to the national courts to examine whether the neutral criteria are necessary in order to achieve a legitimate objective.

18. Not every disparate effect resulting from facially neutral criteria constitutes discrimination. The decisive question is whether the criterion is **necessary** on **objective grounds**, i.e. on grounds which are independent of sex. This is, for example, the case with flexibility or training. Both criteria are traditionally (though, perhaps, increasingly less so) more difficult for women to satisfy than for men, given the role of females with regard to child-rearing. Yet, they are unobjectionable where flexibility or training is necessary for specific tasks.[76] Similarly, the Court considers experience which enables the worker to perform his duties better, to be a legitimate aspect of pay policy. Recourse to the criterion of length of service is considered appropriate to attain that objective as 'length of service goes hand in hand with experience, and experience generally enables the worker to perform his duties better'.[77]

---

[72] ECJ Case C-278/93 *Freers and Speckmann* [1996] ECR I-1165 paras. 22–24; Case C-457/93 *Lewark* [1996] ECR I-243 paras. 26–30; Case C-360/90 *Bötel* [1992] ECR I-3589 paras. 15–21. Approving note by J. Shaw, 'Works Council in German Enterprises and Article 119 EC', *ELR* 22 (1997), 256–262; critically M. Kort, *RdA* 1997, 277 (281–284); M. Schlachter, in *EAS*, B 4100 paras. 21–23.

[73] ECJ Case C-285/02 *Elsner-Lakeberg* [2004] ECR I-5861 paras. 12–17. Differently with regard to the overtime-pay Case C-399/92 *Helmig* [1994] ECR I-5727 paras. 23–31.

[74] ECJ Case C-300/06 *Voß* [2007] ECR I-10573 paras. 34–38; critically T. Fuchs, *EuR* 2008, 697–702.

[75] ECJ Case C-243/95 *Hill and Stapleton* [1998] ECR I-3739 paras. 24–34.

[76] ECJ Case 109/88 *Danfoss* [1989] ECR 3199 paras. 21–23.

[77] ECJ Case C-17/05 *Cadman* [2006] ECR I-9583 paras. 34 sq., 39 (and paras. 37 sq. on the limits); Case 109/88 *Danfoss* [1989] ECR 3199 para. 24. More restrictive though (on the EAD) Case C-196/02 *Nikoloudi* [2005] ECR I-1789 para. 55 (depending on the circumstances of the individual case).

19. The theory of indirect discrimination is rather unclear with respect to Article 157 TFEU where this prohibition is not defined in more detail by the legislator (with regard to secondary legislation, see §8 paras. 34–37 above). In particular, the Court has failed to define the role of 'necessary objective grounds': It sometimes considers the discriminatory effect to establish a *prima facie* case of discrimination which can then be refuted (para. 18 above). However, in other cases, the Court refers to the justification of discrimination thus established (see also para. 22 below).

cc)   BURDEN OF PROOF

20.   Under Article 157 TFEU, too, the general rule is that the burden of proof lies on the person alleging the respective facts.[78] Consequently, it is in principle for the worker (alleged victim of discrimination) who brings proceedings against his employer to prove the existence of discrimination.

21.   However, the burden of proof may shift when a worker who appears to be the victim of discrimination would otherwise not have any effective means of enforcing the principle of equal pay.[79] This is particularly the case where the employer uses a system of remuneration which wholly lacks transparency and the worker demonstrates, with data from a large number of employees, that the average income for women is less than that for men. It is then for the employer to prove that there is no discrimination.[80]

c)   Justification

aa)   JUSTIFICATION IN A STRICT SENSE

22.   The Court of Justice uses a (largely) uniform approach and formula with regard to the justification of direct,[81] as well as indirect, discrimination.[82] The employer must establish that a difference in treatment was based upon **objective**

---

[78]   ECJ Case C-381/99 *Brunnhofer* [2001] ECR I-4961 para. 52; Case C-172/92 *Enderby* [1993] ECR I-5535 para. 13.

[79]   ECJ Case C-381/99 *Brunnhofer* [2001] ECR I-4961 para. 53; Case C-400/93 *Royal Copenhagen* [1995] ECR I-1275 para. 24; Case C-172/92 *Enderby* [1993] ECR I-5535 para. 14.

[80]   ECJ Case C-381/99 *Brunnhofer* [2001] ECR I-4961 paras. 54 sq.; Case C-172/92 *Enderby* [1993] ECR I-5535 para. 14; Case 109/88 *Danfoss* [1989] ECR 3199 paras. 12 sq. M. Schlachter, in *EAS,* B 4100 para. 54.

[81]   See e.g. ECJ Case C-381/99 *Brunnhofer* [2001] ECR I-4961 para. 62. Differently M. Schlachter, in *EAS,* B 4100 para. 39.

[82]   It should not be overlooked, though, that both cases are to be distinguished analytically and with regard to the underlying value judgements; see also §8 paras. 30–37 and paras. 16–19 above.

factors which are unrelated to sex.[83] These grounds must correspond to a *real need* of the business, be *appropriate* for achieving certain objectives and *necessary* to that end.[84] Within this framework, the determination whether the different treatment or impact is so justified is left to the national court.[85]

bb)   POSITIVE MEASURES

23.   'With a view to ensuring full equality in practice between men and women in working life', Article 157(4) TFEU allows Member States (but not the EU, the social partners or individual employers) to maintain or adopt 'measures providing for specific advantages in order to make it easier for the underrepresented sex' (i.e. not only women!) 'to pursue a vocational activity or to prevent or compensate for disadvantages in professional careers'. Given that a benefit to one sex will usually[86] entail discrimination against the other, Article 157(4) TFEU constitutes a special ground for **justification**.[87] The provision would, in principle, also justify discrimination in pay, but that does not appear to be of practical relevance;[88] its scope of application goes beyond the limited realm of pay discrimination.

24.   Justification presupposes 'specific advantages' for the purpose of making it easier for the underrepresented sex to pursue a vocational activity or preventing or compensating for disadvantages in professional careers. As the Court held, measures to make vocational *activity* easier have to occur while the beneficiary is still in active employment and cannot justify pension benefits.[89] Related to a specific purpose, the measures must further satisfy the **principle of proportionality**: They must not exceed what is necessary to achieve the (limited) purposes.[90]

---

[83]   ECJ Case C-381/99 *Brunnhofer* [2001] ECR I-4961 para. 66; Case C-243/95 *Hill and Stapleton* [1998] ECR I-3739 para. 34; Case C-184/89 *Nimz* [1991] ECR I-297 paras. 13 sq.; Case 129/79 *Macarthys* [1980] ECR 1275 para. 12.

[84]   ECJ Case C-381/99 *Brunnhofer* [2001] ECR I-4961 para. 67; Case 171/88 *Rinner-Kühn* [1989] ECR 2743 paras. 13 sq.; Case 170/84 *Bilka* [1986] ECR 1607 para. 36.

[85]   See e.g. ECJ Case C-243/95 *Hill and Stapleton* [1998] ECR I-3739 para. 35.

[86]   Where the facts are comparable! Matters are different where the benefit is, e.g., intended to compensate disadvantages flowing from maternity leave; Case C-366/99 *Griesmar* [2001] ECR I-9383 para. 41; Case C-218/98 *Abdoulaye* [1999] ECR I-5723 paras. 18–21.

[87]   S. Krebber, in C. Calliess/M. Ruffert (eds.), *EUV/AEUV*, Art. 157 AEUV para. 74.

[88]   M. Schlachter, in R. Müller-Glöge/U. Preis/I. Schmidt (eds.), *Erfurter Kommentar*, Art. 157 AEUV para. 31.

[89]   ECJ Case C-366/99 *Griesmar* [2001] ECR I-9383 paras. 64 sq. But see also Case C-116/94 *Meyers* [1995] ECR I-2131 para. 22 (with countervailing considerations with regard to acces to employment under the EAD (now SDD).

[90]   ECJ Case C-407/98 *Abrahamsson and Anderson* [2000] ECR I-5539 para. 55.

d)   Sanctions

25.   In view of the primacy of Union law, a clause which is incompatible with Article 157 TFEU, whether in a statute, a collective or an individual agreement, must not be applied.[91] In many cases, this is only the first step to establish full equality of treatment, in particular where such a clause does not penalise the disadvantaged sex but rather benefits the advantaged sex. In such cases, the group placed at a disadvantage has a right to obtain the same benefits (levelling up).[92] At the same time, a new provision or regulation may, in a non-discriminatory way, reduce advantages of the persons previously favoured for the future.[93]

III.   THE SEX DISCRIMINATION DIRECTIVE

Bibliography:

H. Buchner, 'Gleichbehandlungsgebot und Mutterschutz', in F. Farthmann et al. (eds.), *Arbeitsgesetzgebung und Arbeitsrechtsprechung – Festschrift für Eugen Stahlhacke* (Neuwied/Kriftel/Berlin: Luchterhand, 1995), 83–100; J. Eichinger, 'Grundsatz der Gleichbehandlung hinsichtlich des Zugangs zur Beschäftigung, zur Berufsausbildung und zum beruflichen Aufstieg sowie in Bezug auf die Arbeitsbedingungen (Richtlinie 76/207/EWG)', in H. Oetker/U. Preis (eds.), *Europäisches Arbeits- und Sozialrecht, EAS, part B – Systematische Darstellungen,* loose-leaf (Heidelberg: Forkel, last update: January 1999), B 4200; L. Fastrich, 'Gleichbehandlung und Gleichstellung', *RdA* 2000, 65–81; F. Gamillscheg, 'Die mittelbare Diskriminierung der Frau im Arbeitsleben', in O. Martinek (eds.), *Arbeitsrecht und soziale Grundrechte, Festschrift für Hans Floretta zum 60. Geburtstag* (Vienna: Manz, 1983), 171–185; I. Hadeler, 'Die Revision der Gleichbehandlungsrichtlinie 76/207/EWG – Umsetzungsbedarf für das deutsche Arbeitsrecht', *NZA* 2003, 77–81; P. Hanau/U. Preis, 'Zur mittelbaren Diskriminierung wegen des Geschlechts', *ZfA* 1988, 177–207; S. Issacharoff/E. Rosenblum, 'Women and the Workplace: Accomodating the Demands of Pregnancy', *Colum. L. Rev.* 94 (1994), 2154–2221; W. Paul, 'Einstellung Schwangerer bei Beschäftigungsverboten nach dem Mutterschutzgesetz', *DB* 2000, 974–978; U. Rust, 'Änderungsrichtlinie 2002 zur Gleichbehandlungsrichtlinie von 1976', *NZA* 2003, 72–77; R. Scholz, 'Frauen an die Waffe kraft Europarechts? – Zum Verhältnis von Art. 12a Abs. 4 S. 2 GG zur

---

[91]   ECJ Case C-256/01 *Allonby* [2004] ECR I-873 para. 77; Case C-184/89 *Nimz* [1991] ECR I-297 paras. 19 sq.

[92]   See the seminal decision in ECJ Case 43/75 *Defrenne II* [1976] ECR 455 para. 14/15; established case law: Case C-28/93 *Van den Akker* [1994] ECR I-4527 paras. 15–17; Case C-408/92 *Avdel Systems* [1994] ECR I-4435 paras. 15–17; Case C-200/91 *Coloroll Pension Trustees* [1994] ECR I-4389 paras. 31 sq.; Case C-184/89 *Nimz* [1991] ECR I-297 para. 18; Case C-33/89 *Kowalska* [1990] ECR I-2591 para. 19. On national limitation periods (which are admissible within the limits of the implementation obligations) Case C-78/98 *Preston and Fletcher* [2000] ECR I-3201. M. Schlachter, in *EAS*, B 4100 para. 58.

[93]   ECJ Case C-200/91 *Coloroll Pension Trustees* [1994] ECR I-4389 para. 33.

EU-Gleichbehandlungsrichtlinie', *DÖV* 2000, 417–420; M. Schulte Westenberg, 'Aktuelles vom EuGH zur Kündigung wegen Schwangerschaft', *NJW* 2003, 490–492; K. Stürmer, 'Bewerbung und Schwangerschaft', *NZA* 2001, 526–530; G. Thüsing, 'Zulässige Ungleichbehandlung weiblicher und männlicher Arbeitnehmer – Zur Unverzichtbarkeit i.S. des §611 a Abs. 1 Satz 2 BGB', *RdA* 2001, 319–325; see also the references in §8 before paras. 1, 53, 58, 63, 74, 81, 86 and before para. 2 above.

Cases (Selection):
ECJ Case 184/83 *Hofmann* [1984] ECR 3047; ECJ Case 222/84 *Johnston* [1986] ECR 1651; ECJ Case 152/84 *Marshall I* [1986] ECR 723; ECJ Case 318/86 *Commission v. France* [1988] ECR 3559; ECJ Case 177/88 *Dekker* [1990] ECR 3941; ECJ Case 179/88 *Handels- og Kontorfunktionaererenes Forbund* [1990] ECR I-3979; ECJ Case C-345/89 *Stoeckel* [1991] ECR I-4047; ECJ Case C-189/91 *Kirsammer-Hack* [1993] ECR I-6185; ECJ Case C-421/92 *Habermann-Beltermann* [1994] ECR I-1657; ECJ Case C-116/94 *Meyers* [1995] ECR I-2131; ECJ Case C-32/93 *Webb* [1994] ECR I-3567; ECJ Case C-450/93 *Kalanke* [1995] ECR I-3051; ECJ Case C-13/94 *P v. S* [1996] ECR I-2413; ECJ Case C-400/95 *Larsson* [1997] ECR I-2757; ECJ Case C-1/95 *Gerster* [1997] ECR I-5253; ECJ Case C-100/95 *Kording* [1997] ECR I-5289; ECJ Case C-136/95 *Thibault* [1998] ECR I-2011; ECJ Case C-394/96 *Mary Brown* [1998] ECR I-4185; ECJ Case C-66/96 *Pedersen* [1998] ECR I-7327; ECJ Case C-273/97 *Sirdar* [1999] ECR I-7403; ECJ Case C-285/98 *Kreil* [2000] ECR I-69; ECJ Case C-207/98 *Mahlburg* [2000] ECR I-549; ECJ Case C-157/97 *Badeck* [2000] ECR I-1875; ECJ Case C-226/98 *Jørgensen* [2000] ECR I-2447; ECJ Case C-79/99 *Schnorbus* [2000] ECR I-10997; ECJ Case C-109/00 *Tele Danmark* [2001] ECR I-6993; ECJ Case C-476/99 *Lommers* [2002] ECR I-2891; ECJ Case C-320/01 *Wiebke Busch* [2003] ECR I-2041; ECJ Case C-187/00 *Kutz-Bauer* [2003] ECR I-2741; ECJ Case C-77/02 *Steinicke* [2003] ECR I-9027; ECJ Case C-342/01 *Merino Gómez* [2004] ECR I-2605; ECJ Case C-319/03 *Briheche* [2004] ECR I-8807; ECJ Case C-313/02 *Wippel* [2004] ECR I-9483; ECJ Case C-284/02 *Sass* [2004] ECR I-11143; ECJ Case C-196/02 *Nikoloudi* [2005] ECR I-1789; ECJ Case C-207/04 *Vergani* [2005] ECR I-7453; ECJ Case C-294/04 *Herrero* [2006] ECR I-1513; ECJ Case C-116/06 *Kiiski* [2007] ECR I-7643; ECJ Case C-460/06 *Paquay* [2007] ECR I-8511; ECJ Case C-506/06 *Mayr* [2008] ECR I-1017; ECJ Case C-63/08 *Pontin* [2009] ECR I-10467; ECJ Case C-104/09 *Roca Álvarez* [2010] ECR I-8661; ECJ Case C-232/09 *Danosa* 11 November 2010; ECJ Case C-356/09 *Kleist* 18 November 2010; ECJ Case C-104/10 *Kelly* 21 July 2011; ECJ Case C-415/10 *Meister* 19 April 2012 (on which, see §8 para. 62).

1. Survey and Purpose

26. 'On grounds of clarity', the Sex Discrimination Directive (SDD) brings together the provisions of a number of individual directives in one text (so-called codification), arranging the prohibition of sex discrimination with regard to the respective issues (§8 para. 19). For the most part, the new Directive merely restates, and sometimes summarises, the previous provisions as they had been interpreted by the Court of Justice. Older judgements that had been made on the basis of the individual directives are thus also still relevant for the new directive.

27. The fact that sex discrimination is the subject of primary law and secondary legislation is one of the reasons that regulation in this field remains rather lacking in transparency, even after the codification. Another is that the new Directive does not regulate the subject in a coherent and systematic fashion. It is true that the Directive arranges instruments of protection in a 'general part' towards the end of the Directive and contains definitions (as well as a statement of purpose and a provision on positive measures) in another general part located at its beginning. Yet the issue of equal pay is dealt with in two provisions, Articles 4 and 14(1)(c) SDD. The area of occupational social security systems is addressed in a separate chapter. And the Court's jurisprudence has not been comprehensively codified.

28. The **purpose** of the Directive is 'to ensure the implementation of the principle of equal opportunities and equal treatment of men and women in matters of employment and occupation', Article 1(1)SDD.

2. Addressees

29. The Sex Discrimination *Directive* is (by its nature) addressed to the Member States, Article 288(3) TFEU. The Member States are in particular under an obligation to remove any discriminatory laws, regulations and administrative provisions, Article 23(a) SDD.[94] The Directive is not directly applicable to private individuals;[95] the sole exception is the case where a *Member State* assumes the role of a private actor, i.e. where it acts as an employer (see in more detail §1 paras. 71 sq. above).

3. Scope of Application

a) Personal Scope of Application

30. The Sex Discrimination Directive – similar to its predecessors in the individual directives -[96] pursues the purpose of ensuring the equal treatment of men and women not in general, but only in their roles as employees. The personal scope of application has, however, only partly been regulated explicitly (in Article 6 with regard to the occupational systems of social security which is not discussed here; see also para. 34). But further support for this proposition can be inferred from the statement of purpose in Article 1 SDD and the provisions on the substantive scope of application. Furthermore, the term **'worker'** that

---

[94]   See e.g. ECJ Case C-207/04 *Vergani* [2005] ECR I-7453 paras. 25 sq.
[95]   S.a. ECJ Case C-421/92 *Habermann-Beltermann* [1994] ECR I-1657 paras. 8–10 (obligation to interpretation of national law in conformity with the directive).
[96]   ECJ Case 48/88 *Achterberg-Te Riele* [1989] ECR 1963 paras. 11 sq.

delineates the personal scope of application is not defined. It should, however, be **autonomously** construed. The Court has also autonomously construed the same term in the prohibition of sex discrimination contained in Article 157 TFEU, which to some extent determines the prohibition in secondary legislation (para. 5 above). It would not make sense to take a less comprehensive approach with regard to the Directive. Furthermore, the autonomous definition is based upon the consideration that the prohibition of discrimination as a fundamental right would not allow for disparate application in the Member States. The term 'worker' is thus to be interpreted autonomously as in Article 157 TFEU (para. 5 above), following the same definition as established with regard to freedom of movement for workers in Article 45 TFEU: A worker is a person who, for a certain period of time, performs services for and under the direction of another in return for which he receives remuneration. As the introductory sentence of Article 14(1) SDD confirms, this comprises employment relations in the public sector.[97]

31. Unfortunately, the Court did not engage in a more detailed analysis of the scope(s) of application in *Danosa,* where it held that a **member of a company's Board of Directors** should be protected against discriminatory dismissal on grounds of sex (pregnancy). The Court seems to hold that the case could be covered by the Sex Discrimination Directive (or, on the specific facts, its predecessor). Indeed, the Court also held that a member of a company's Board of Directors can be considered to be a 'worker' within the meaning of the Maternity Protection Directive (see §20 para. 12). Yet the Court avoids a definite decision but rather points out that, in any case, the board member may be covered by Directive 86/613.[98]

b) Substantive Scope of Application

32. **In substance**, the Directive covers three areas (Article 1(2) SDD):

(1) access to employment, including promotion, and to vocational training;
(2) terms and conditions of employment, including pay; and
(3) occupational social security systems.

---

[97] ECJ Case C-294/04 *Herrero* [2006] ECR I-1513 para. 35; Case C-284/02 *Sass* [2004] ECR I-11143 para. 25; Case C-319–03 *Briheche* [2004] ECR I-8807 para. 18; Case C-476/99 *Lommers* [2002] ECR I-2891 para. 25; Case C-79/99 *Schnorbus* [2000] ECR I-10997 para. 28; Case C-273/97 *Sirdar* [1999] ECR I-7403 para. 18; Case C-1/95 *Gerster* [1997] ECR I-5253 para. 18.

[98] Council Directive 86/613/EEC of 11 December 1986 on the Application of the Principle of Equal Treatment between Men and Women Engaged in an Activity, including Agriculture, in a Self-employed Capacity, and on the Protection of Self-employed Women During Pregnancy and Motherhood, OJ 1986 L 359/56.

33. However, the **outer system** of the Directive follows a different order. Following general provisions, there is an introductory chapter on equal pay (Article 4 SDD).[99] The subsequent chapter is dedicated to equal treatment in occupational social security systems (Article 5–13 SDD). And finally, the issue of access to, and conditions of, employment are addressed (Article 14–16 SDD). This rather obscure ordering of subject-matter seems to be owed to two circumstances. First, the legislator has little room to shape the prohibition of discrimination in pay as it is largely determined by primary law in Article 157 TFEU. Secondly (and partly connected to the first point), the other subjects – access to, and conditions of, employment and occupational systems of social security – have previously been regulated in independent directives. The present account follows the chronology of the employment relation; the subject of occupational systems of social security will not be discussed.

aa) PAY

34. The substantive scope of application initially covers pay, Articles 4 and 14(1)(c) SDD. **Pay** is to be defined here as in Article 157 TFEU (para. 6 above); the legislator has adopted the definition contained in Article 157(2) TFEU and Article 2(1)(e) SDD, and also refers to it in Article 14(2)(c).[100] The equal pay provision also applies to the case where a job classification system is used for determining pay, Article 4(2) SDD;[101] based upon the Court's jurisprudence on Article 157 TFEU (para. 10), this is a merely declaratory provision.

bb) ACCESS TO EMPLOYMENT

35. The scope of the Directive also covers **access to employment**, which includes **promotion**, Article 14(1)(b) SDD. This comprises in particular selection criteria and the conditions for hiring and promotion. Access to employment is not only concerned with the initial hiring but also where the renewal of a fixed term contract is at issue.[102] Sex-related **prohibitions of employment** also affect access to employment, e.g. a (general, legislative) prohibition of night work for

---

[99]   In addition to Article 157 TFEU, the Directive prohibits sex discrimination with regard to pay twice as pay is also covered by the 'employment conditions' in Article 14(1)(c) SDD.

[100]   ECJ Case C-147/02 *Alabaster* [2004] ECR I-3101 para. 41; Case C-236/98 *JämO* [2000] ECR I-2189 para. 38; Case C-218/98 *Abdoulaye* [1999] ECR I-5723 para. 14; Case C-352/93 *Gillespie* [1996] ECR I-475 paras. 11–15; Case C-360/90 *Bötel* [1992] ECR I-3589 paras. 11–15; Case 69/80 *Worringham* [1981] ECR 767 para. 21. See also Case 96/80 *Jenkins* [1981] ECR 911 paras. 20 sq.; Case C-278/93 *Freers and Speckmann* [1996] ECR I-1165.

[101]   For a distinction of a quasi-automatic promotion from promotion on the basis of merit ECJ Case C-1/95 *Gerster* [1997] ECR I-5253 paras. 21–24.

[102]   ECJ Case C-438/99 *Jiménez Melgar* [2001] ECR I-6915 paras. 41, 47.

women[103] or a (general) prohibition of female labour in the underground mining industry.[104] A wage subsidy in the form of a 'family credit', the aim of which is to keep poorly paid workers employed by ensuring that families do not find themselves worse off in work than they would be if they were not working, concerns access to employment as it provides an incentive to take up work.[105]

cc) CONDITIONS OF WORK

36. The term **conditions of work** in Article 2(1)(c) has been broadly construed by the Court. It covers, e.g., a worker's right to occupation under his contract (and thus conversely the statutory right of an employer to send home a woman who is pregnant, although not unfit for work, without paying her salary in full when he considers that he cannot provide work for her);[106] a reduction or restructuring of working hours;[107] rules on the conditions for returning to work from parental leave;[108] the right of an employee to have his performance assessed every year;[109] the determination of when paid annual leave is to be taken;[110] the making available to employees, by their employer, of nursery places at their place of work;[111] or reinstatement after unfair dismissal (as opposed to the right to compensation because of unfair dismissal which constitutes pay and is subject to Article 157 TFEU/Articles 4 and 14(1)(a) SDD).[112]

37. The Directive explicitly includes **dismissal** in the conditions of employment. This term should also be broadly construed;[113] it encompasses all prerequisites and consequences of the termination of employment. All forms of

---

103 ECJ Case C-345/89 *Stoeckel* [1991] ECR I-4047. The Directive also prohibits discrimination with regard to the exceptions from the general admissibility of night work; Case C-13/93 *Minne* [1994] ECR I-371 para. 13. See also Case C-207/96 *Commission* v. *Italy* [1997] ECR I-6869; Case C-197/96 *Commission* v. *France* [1997] ECR I-1489; Case C-158/91 *Levy* [1993] ECR I-4287.

104 ECJ Case C-203/03 *Commission* v. *Austria* [2005] ECR I-935 paras. 45–49.

105 ECJ Case C-116/94 *Meyers* [1995] ECR I-2131 paras. 17–22; otherwise the wage subsidy would have to be considered an 'employment condition' as it is inherently linked with the employment relationship; paras. 23 sq.

106 ECJ Case C-66/96 *Pedersen* [1998] ECR I-7327 paras. 51–59.

107 ECJ Case C-77/02 *Steinicke* [2003] ECR I-9027 paras. 49 sq.; Case C-187/00 *Kutz-Bauer* [2003] ECR I-2741 paras. 44 sq.; Case C-236/98 *JämO* [2000] ECR I-2189 paras. 59 sq.

108 ECJ Case C-320/01 *Wiebke Busch* [2003] ECR I-2041 para. 38; Case C-116/06 *Kiiski* [2007] ECR I-7643 paras. 53–56 (interruption of child-care leave).

109 ECJ Case C-136/95 *Thibault* [1998] ECR I-2011 para. 27.

110 ECJ Case C-342/01 *Merino Gómez* [2004] ECR I-2605 para. 36.

111 ECJ Case C-476/99 *Lommers* [2002] ECR I-2891 paras. 26 sq.

112 ECJ Case C-167/97 *Seymour-Smith and Perez* [1999] ECR I-688 paras. 36 sq. Critically C. Barnard/B. Hepple, *C.L.J.* 58 (1999), 399, 404 sq.

113 ECJ Case C-207/04 *Vergani* [2005] ECR I-7453 para. 27; Case C-356/09 *Kleist* 18 November 2010 para. 26 ('covers an age limit set for the compulsory dismissal of workers pursuant to an employer's general policy concerning retirement, even if the dismissal involves the grant of a retirement pension').

termination are covered: expiry of a contractual term (e.g. age limit),[114] notice of termination, consensual resolution[115] or an employee reaching retirement age.[116]

c) No Exceptions

38. The Directive does not expressly provide for any derogations from its scope, and the Court has refused to establish them by way of judicial legal development. In particular, it has not accepted a derogation with regard to **public security and public policy**, which are recognised as exceptions, e.g., to freedom of movement for workers in the TFEU (Article 45(3) TFEU, see §3 paras. 40–42 above)[117].[118] Consequently, the relevant issues can only be dealt with at the level of justification and are thus subject to the principle of proportionality. Small and medium-sized businesses are also covered by the Directive, without any alleviation.[119]

4. The Prohibition of Discrimination

a) The Prohibited Ground of Distinction: Sex

39. The prohibited ground for differentiation, here as in Article 157 TFEU, is **sex**. Therefore, the Directive does not only prohibit discrimination against women.

40. The Court has held discrimination on grounds of **transsexuality** to be a case of sex discrimination.[120] In its reasoning, the Court refers to the fundamental importance of the prohibition of discrimination, its recognition as a fundamental right and the requirement of protecting the dignity of the person. Discrimination on grounds of transsexuality was based 'essentially if not exclusively' on the sex of the person: 'Where a person is dismissed on the ground that he or she intends to undergo, or has undergone, gender reassignment, he or she is treated unfavourably by comparison with persons of the sex to which he or she was deemed to belong before undergoing gender reassignment.' It may well be doubted whether this interpretation was in line with the original intention of

---

114   ECJ Case 262/84 *Beets-Proper* [1986] ECR 773 para. 36.
115   ECJ Case C-207/04 *Vergani* [2005] ECR I-7453 para. 27; Case 152/84 *Marshall* [1986] ECR 723 para. 34; Case 19/81 *Burton* [1982] ECR 554 para. 9.
116   ECJ Case 152/84 *Marshall* [1986] ECR 723 paras. 32–38.
117   See also Article 30, 46, 58, 64, 296 and 297 EG/36, 52, 65, 346 and 347 AEUV.
118   ECJ Case C-186/01 *Dory* [2003] ECR I-2479 paras. 31 sq.; Case C-285/98 *Kreil* [2000] ECR I-69 paras. 15–18; Case C-273/97 *Sirdar* [1999] ECR I-7403 paras. 16–19; Case 222/84 *Johnston* [1986] ECR 1651 paras. 26 sq.
119   ECJ Case C-109/00 *Tele Danmark* [2001] ECR I-6993 para. 37. Critically F. Gamillscheg, *Festschrift für Floretta*, 179.
120   ECJ Case C-13/94 *P* v. *S* [1996] ECR I-2413 paras. 16–23.

the legislator (of the 1976 Equal Access Directive).[121] Yet the legislator has affirmed the Court's decision in the 2006 Sex Discrimination Directive, as Recital 3 SDD indicates.

41. Discrimination on grounds of **sexual orientation** (see also para. 11 above) is not prohibited by the Sex Discrimination Directive,[122] but is now covered by the 2000 Equal Treatment Framework Directive (§11 below).

b)   Discrimination

aa)   BASIS OF THE EVALUATION: COMPARABLE FACTS

42. Determination of the comparability of situations does not require that a worker of the opposite sex performs the same work for the same employer.[123] While this is not explicitly expressed in the Sex Discrimination Directive, the Court has also allowed for a comparison to be made based upon work of equal value (as in Article 157 TFEU, see para. 13 above).[124]

43. The object of the comparison (here as pursuant to Article 157 TFEU, see para. 14 above) is not an overall assessment of the conditions of access, pay or employment. Rather, **the various elements** of the provisions governing a professional activity must be individually evaluated, in so far as they are separable.[125] Consequently, a **principle of transparency** applies with regard to the individual conditions of employment.[126] A lack of transparency as to those conditions, particularly systems of remuneration, may shift the burden of proof to the employer.[127]

bb)   FORMS AND DETERMINATION OF DISCRIMINATION

44. The **prohibition of discrimination** contained in Articles 4(1) and 14(1) SDD prohibits both direct and indirect[128] discrimination as defined in Article 2(1)(a) and (b) SDD (on the definitions, see §8 paras. 30–37 above). The prohibition of

---

[121]   For a critical perspective see G. Thüsing, in F. J. Säcker/R. Rixecker (eds.), *Münchener Kommentar zum BGB*, §1 AGG para. 89.

[122]   ECJ Case C-249/96 *Grant* [1998] ECR I-621.

[123]   See also ECJ Case C-356/09 *Kleist* 18 November 2010 paras. 32 sqq. (comparability affirmed in a case of discriminatory dismissal irrespective of the fact that female workers of 60–65 have social cover by virtue of a statutory retirement pension whereas their male counterparts do not).

[124]   ECJ Case C-196/02 *Vasiliki Nikoloudi* [2005] ECR I-1789 paras. 27–29.

[125]   ECJ Case C-226/98 *Jørgensen* [2000] ECR I-2447 paras. 27–36.

[126]   ECJ Case C-381/99 *Brunnhofer* [2001] ECR I-4961 paras. 35 sq.; Case 318/86 *Commission v. France* [1988] ECR 3559 paras. 26 sq.

[127]   ECJ Case 109/88 *Danfoss* [1989] ECR 3199 paras. 12–16.

[128]   See e.g. ECJ Case C-243/95 *Hill and Stapleton* [1998] ECR I-3730 (part-time work).

indirect discrimination pursuant to Article 2(1)(b) presupposes that the neutral criteria (which have a discriminatory effect upon one sex) cannot be objectively justified as a necessary means to achieve a legitimate objective and thus differs from the definition established by the Court in its jurisprudence regarding Article 157 TFEU (para. 17 above; see also §8 paras. 31 sq.).

i.   Direct Discrimination

45.   Employment laws have traditionally contained a large number of overtly discriminatory provisions which are aimed at protecting women. These include, for example, prohibitions on night-work for women in working-time regulations, higher exposure levels for men in occupational health and safety provisions[129] and different retirement ages for men and women.[130] Nowadays, **direct discrimination** on grounds of sex (Article 2(1)(a) SDD; §8 paras. 26–28 above) is primarily of practical importance in cases of careless job advertisements.[131] It can also constitute *direct* discrimination if a class of workers (in the case at hand: cleaners) is being treated less favourably.[132]

46.   Direct discrimination sometimes occurs where the distinction is not directly related to sex, but to a sex-specific (and thus not neutral) attribute such as **pregnancy or motherhood**, Article 2(2)(c) and Recital 23 SDD.[133] With regard

---

[129]   See e.g. S. Deakin/G. Morris, *Labour Law*, para. 4.94.

[130]   Case C-356/09 *Kleist* 18 November 2010 paras. 28 sqq.

[131]   See e.g. ECJ Case C-180/95 *Draehmpaehl* [1997] ECR I-2195 ('We are seeking an experienced female assistant in our sales management department. If you can get along with the chaotic members of a sales-orientated firm, are willing to make them coffee, get little praise and can work hard, you are the right person for us. We need someone who is able to work on the computer and think with and for others. If you can really face this challenge, we await your application with documents giving full information. But do not say we have not warned you...').

[132]   ECJ Case C-196/02 *Nikoloudi* [2005] ECR I-1789 para. 36.

[133]   ECJ Case C-232/09 *Danosa* 11 November 2010 paras. 59 sqq., 65 sqq.; Case C-63/08 *Pontin* [2009] ECR I-10467 paras. 71 sqq. (restriction of remedies available to pregnant employees to an action for nullity and reinstatement with the exclusion of an action for damages); Case C-506/06 *Mayr* [2008] ECR I-1017 paras. 46–52 (dismissal on account of an upcoming pregnancy by way of in-vitro fertilisation before the implantation of the fertilised ovum); Case C-460/06 *Paquay* [2007] ECR I-8511 paras. 29, 40; Case C-116/06 *Kiiski* [2007] ECR I-7643 paras. 53–56; Case C-294/04 *Herrero* [2006] ECR I-1513 para. 38; Case C-191/03 *McKenna* [2005] ECR I-7631 para. 47; Case C-284/02 *Sass* [2004] ECR I-11143 para. 36; Case C-320/01 *Wiebke Busch* [2003] ECR I-2041 para. 39; Case C-438/99 *Jiménez Melgar* [2001] ECR I-6915 paras. 41, 47; Case C-109/00 *Tele Danmark* [2001] ECR I-6993 para. 25; Case C-207/98 *Mahlburg* [2000] ECR I-549 para. 20; Case C-394/96 *Mary Brown* [1998] ECR I-4185 para. 16; Case C-421/92 *Habermann-Beltermann* [1994] ECR I-1657 para. 15; Case C-32/93 *Webb* [1993] ECR I-3567 para. 19; Case 177/88 *Dekker* [1990] ECR 3941 para. 12. Codifying this case law, the legislator has for one thing taken care of the theoretical concerns against considering pregnancy related discrimination as sex discrimination; and it has also clarified that the aim is 'equalisation' rather than equal treatment; on both issues see L. Fastrich, *RdA* 2000, 65, 78–81 *et passim;* also G. Thüsing, *Europäisches Arbeitsrecht,* §3 paras. 47 sq.

to hiring, such criterion will also be considered to be directly discriminatory where women exclusively apply for a position.[134]

47. Similarly, a **pregnancy-related inability to work** is sex-related and cannot be compared to an inability to work on grounds of illness that may affect both sexes.[135] Whether an employer who is looking for a temporary substitute for his pregnant employee may refuse a pregnant applicant can consequently only be a question of justification (and is thus subject to a proportionality test). Any direct sanction (such as a warning or dismissal) for a pregnancy-related inability to work and any indirect consequence for times of absence due to pregnancy (or maternity leave)[136] constitute discrimination.[137] The Court has, however, drawn a line with regard to pathological conditions caused by pregnancy or childbirth that arise after the end of maternity leave.[138] It is a matter for maternity protection laws (for which the Maternity Protection Directive provides a minimum standard; §20) to protect women against such risks. Beyond the framework of maternity protection, pregnancy-related illnesses will be treated just like any other sex-specific illness: The prohibition of discrimination does not require any special allowance as long as men and women are subject to formally equal rules (e.g. with regard to illness).

48. Direct discrimination further occurs where an employee is being treated less favourably because she is relying upon pregnancy or maternity protection laws (see also para. 63).[139] The Court has therefore found discrimination where the time of maternity leave was not counted towards a qualifying period,[140] irrespective of whether it applied to promotion in an existing employment relationship or to hiring for a new employment relationship.[141] It also constitutes discrimination if an employee is prevented from taking annual leave during a period other than the period of her maternity leave.[142] This case-law, in effect,

---

[134] ECJ Case 177/88 *Dekker* [1990] ECR 3941 para. 17.
[135] ECJ Case C-207/98 *Mahlburg* [2000] ECR I-549 paras. 21–27; Case C-394/96 *Mary Brown* [1998] ECR I-4185 paras. 21 sq.; Case C-32/93 *Webb* [1993] ECR I-3567 paras. 24 sq. See also Case 177/88 *Dekker* [1990] ECR 3941 paras. 23–25.
[136] With regard to maternity protection, Article 10 contains a special provision on victimisation; see §20 para. 35 below.
[137] ECJ Case C-394/96 *Mary Brown* [1998] ECR I-4185 para. 27, expressly renouncing its previous jurisprudence on absence from work in Case C-400/95 *Larsson* [1997] ECR I-2757 paras. 22–24.
[138] ECJ Case C-191/03 *McKenna* [2005] ECR I-7631 para. 52; Case C-394/96 *Mary Brown* [1998] ECR I-4185 para. 26; Case C-400/95 *Larsson* [1997] ECR I-2757 paras. 13–20 (rejecting a distiction between illnesses occuring during and after pregnancy or maternity leave); Case 179/88 *Handels- og Kontorfunktionaererernes Forbund* [1990] ECR I-3979 paras. 15–18.
[139] ECJ Case C-294/04 *Herrero* [2006] ECR I-1513 paras. 38 sq.; Case C-342/01 *Merino Gómez,* [2004] ECR I-2605 para. 37.
[140] ECJ Case C-284/02 *Sass* [2004] ECR I-11143 paras. 35 sq.
[141] ECJ Case C-294/04 *Herrero* [2006] ECR I-1513 paras. 41 sq.
[142] ECJ Case C-342/01 *Merino Gómez* [2004] ECR I-2605 para. 38.

supplements the Maternity Protection Directive with a comprehensive protection against retribution (see also §20 para. 35).

49. The legislator has also codified the Court's case law – largely on Article 157 TFEU (para. 16 above) – regarding maternity leave in Article 15 SDD. A woman is entitled to return to her job or to an equivalent position after her maternity leave on terms which are no less favourable to her. She has a right to benefit from any improvement in working conditions to which she would have been entitled during her absence.

ii. Indirect Discrimination

50. 'It is settled case-law that a national measure involves indirect discrimination where, although worded in neutral terms, it works to the disadvantage of a much higher percentage of women than men'[143] (see now Article 2(1)(b) SDD and on this §8 paras. 34–37 above).[144] Here as well, unfavourable treatment of **part-time workers** is a central case of indirect discrimination against women (see already para. 17 above), e.g. where only full-time employees have access to a position as 'established member of staff'.[145] Regarding employment which is based upon the principle of 'work on demand' – where the employer would seek services according to workload and the employee had a right to refuse the offer without any justification – on the one hand, and other (full-time or part-time) employees on the other, the Court flatly denied any (basis for) discrimination, reasoning that the situation of the former group was not analogous to that of the latter.[146]

51. The Court did not find any discrimination in a national provision – which aimed to protect **small businesses** – which does not take into account part-time employees (working not more than ten hours per week or 45 hours per month) when determining whether or not a business must apply the system of protection against unfair dismissal. Such provision would not specifically disadvantage part-time employees which may be employed by small businesses as well as others.[147] A national provision pursuant to which, for the purpose of a **selection process on the basis of social criteria** in the context of dismissal on economic grounds, full-time workers are not to be compared with part-time workers, has

---

[143] ECJ Case C-196/02 *Nikoloudi* [2005] ECR I-1789 para. 44; Case C-313/02 *Wippel* [2004] ECR I-9483 para. 43; Case C-100/95 *Kording* [1997] ECR I-5289 para. 16; Case C-1/95 *Gerster* [1997] ECR I-5253 para. 30; Case C-187/00 *Kutz-Bauer* [2003] ECR I-2741 paras. 48–50 (discriminatory impact of the requirements for a right to old-age part-time work).

[144] See also the survey in P. Hanau/U. Preis, *ZfA* 1988, 193–206.

[145] ECJ Case C-196/02 *Nikoloudi* [2005] ECR I-1789 paras. 43–47; Case C-100/95 *Kording* [1997] ECR I-5289 paras. 16–19 (exemption from tax advisor examination).

[146] ECJ Case C-313/02 *Wippel* [2004] ECR I-9483 paras. 64 sq.

[147] ECJ Case C-189/91 *Kirsammer-Hack* [1993] ECR I-6185 paras. 20–34.

been held to be discriminatory; yet, it can – in the context of a margin of appreciation that is enjoyed by national legislators in the area of social policy – be considered justified as a necessary instrument in order to achieve a legitimate objective of social policy.[148]

52. **Objective factors** that may be used to justify neutral criteria with a discriminatory effect can, e.g., be found in objectives of employment policy such as the increase in hiring.[149] Their concretisation is left to the Member States who enjoy wide discretion in this area.[150] Although *budgetary considerations* may underlie a Member State's choice of social policy, they cannot in themselves constitute an objective of that policy and cannot therefore justify sex discrimination.[151]

53. A longer **waiting period** (length of service requirement) for the promotion of part-time workers cannot be justified by reference to a general statement about the interrelation of length of professional activity and skills, abilities, knowledge or experience. Instead, justification requires an evaluation of relevance of experience for the respective activity with regard to the length of service requirement and the concrete goal in the individual case.[152] It is for the employer to prove the extent to which professional experience is relevant for the concrete activity and that part-time workers are generally slower than full-time employees in acquiring the relevant abilities, knowledge or experience.[153] The discriminatory effect resulting from the requirement, determined by EU law, that general medical training must include a number of periods of full-time training, has been considered justified as it enhances the free movement of doctors and contributes to a high level of public health in the Union; the Court also considers that the EU legislator, also enjoys a wide margin of appreciation.[154]

iii. Harassment and Sexual Harassment

54. Harassment and sexual harassment are defined as discrimination, as is instruction to discriminate, Article 2(1)(c) and (d), (2)(a) and (b) SDD (see already §8 paras. 44–47).

---

[148]   ECJ Case C-322/98 *Kachelmann* [2000] ECR I-7505 paras. 23–34.
[149]   ECJ Case C-77/02 *Steinicke* [2003] ECR I-9027 paras. 61 sq.; Case C-187/00 *Kutz-Bauer* [2003] ECR I-2741 para. 56.
[150]   ECJ Case C-187/00 *Kutz-Bauer* [2003] ECR I-2741 para. 55; Case C-167/97 *Seymour-Smith and Perez* [1999] ECR I-688 para. 74.
[151]   ECJ Case C-196/02 *Nikoloudi* [2005] ECR I-1789 para. 53; Case C-77/02 *Steinicke* [2003] ECR I-9027 paras. 66 sq.; Case C-187/00 *Kutz-Bauer* [2003] ECR I-2741 paras. 59 sq.; Case C-226/98 *Jørgensen* [2000] ECR I-2447 para. 39; Case C-343/92 *Roks* [1994] ECR I-571 paras. 35 sq.
[152]   ECJ Case C-196/02 *Nikoloudi* [2005] ECR I-1789 paras. 55 sq., 61 sq.; Case C-100/95 *Kording* [1997] ECR I-5289 paras. 20–26.
[153]   ECJ Case C-1/95 *Gerster* [1997] ECR I-5253 paras. 39–41.
[154]   ECJ Case C-25/02 *Rinke* [2003] ECR I-8349 paras. 37–42.

cc)   BURDEN OF PROOF

55. The reversal of the burden of proof for the benefit of persons who can establish facts from which discrimination may be presumed, (which the Court has established on teleological grounds under Article 157 TFEU) is explicitly provided for in secondary legislation, Article 19 SDD (see §8 paras. 58–62 above). Following the Court's jurisprudence, a lack of transparency in employment conditions may also justify shifting the burden of proof; see para. 43 above. Following the Court's case law, the provision on burden of proof in the sex discrimination directives does not imply an obligation upon the employer to disclose information to a person who considers him- or herself wronged by discrimination (e.g. on the applicant pool), but the implementation obligations (principle of effectiveness) may require a duty of disclosure; see already §8 para. 71 above).[155]

c)   Justification

aa)   JUSTIFICATION IN A STRICT SENSE

56. The Directive provides only for an optional ground for justification with regard to **access to employment**, Article 14(2) SDD. In other words, the optional ground of justification is not available in relation to conditions of employment, including pay, or dismissal.[156] The national law of the Member States may provide that different treatment, based upon sex or on an attribute related to sex, does not constitute discrimination where, by reason of the nature of the particular occupational activities or the context in which they are carried out, such attribute constitutes a **genuine and determining occupational requirement** which is necessary to achieve a legitimate objective (see also Recital 19 SDD).[157] Such occupational requirements must be related to *particular activities* and cannot, in other words, justify a global exclusion of, e.g., women from military positions involving the use of arms.[158] Consequentially, here too, a **requirement of transparency** applies: occupational

---

[155]   ECJ Case C-104/10 *Kelly* 21 July 2011 paras. 38 sq. On the issue and its background in German civil procedure law, see P. A. Windel, *RdA* 2011, 193, 199.

[156]   ECJ Case C-356/09 *Kleist* 18 November 2010 paras. 38 sqq. rejected the suggestion that different pensionable ages for men and women established under national law pursuant to Article 7(1)(a) Directive 79/7 could justify directly discriminatory dismissal as prohibited by (today's) Article 14(1)(c) SDD.

[157]   See in more detail G. Thüsing, *RdA* 2001, 319–325.

[158]   ECJ Case C-285/98 *Kreil* [2000] ECR I-69 para. 27; critical on the basis of considerations of constitutional law R. Scholz, *DÖV* 2000, 417–420. The Court has not objected against a German law maintaining the general duty of military to men (while giving women a right to access military service), reasoning that this issue of military organisation of national defence was not subject to Union law; Case C-186/01 *Dory* [2003] ECR I-2479 paras. 35–41.

requirements must be defined in a transparent way, open to the scrutiny of the court.[159]

57. With regard to the Royal Marines, the 'point of the arrow head' of the British armed forces, intended to be the first line of attack, the Court has, for example, recognised the 'interoperability' rule, established for the purpose of ensuring combat effectiveness, as a **legitimate goal**: All members of the corps including chefs are trained and required to serve as front-line commandos; this would justify the total exclusion of women.[160] The specific nature of the post of warden and the conditions under which prison officers carry out their activities justify reserving such posts primarily for men in male prisons and primarily for women in female prisons.[161] Similarly, the context of certain police activities, particularly in a situation characterised by serious internal disturbances, may be such that the sex of police officers constitutes a determining factor for carrying them out.[162] Furthermore, reconciliation of the principle of equal treatment with the 'principle of respect for private life'[163] may also be found here; it may, for example, justify an exception for employment in private households (but not a general exception for small businesses!).[164]

58. Protection of women against the unlawful action of third parties – e.g. attack at night on the way home from work – does not, on these normative considerations, constitute a legitimate goal; it is for the state to guard against such risk.[165] A general principle of excluding women from nightwork is thus incompatible with the Directive; at best, an exclusion with regard to specific activities could be justified.[166]

59. Based upon normative considerations, the Court has, in principle, not accepted restrictions regarding a woman's ability to work on grounds of **pregnancy or motherhood**. This is because such restrictions may occur on factual or legal (prohibition to work) grounds as justification for unequal treatment, even where the employee is unable to perform essential duties of the employment relationship. An inability to work on grounds of pregnancy thus

---

159 ECJ Case 318/86 *Commission* v. *France* [1988] ECR 3559 paras. 26 sq.
160 ECJ Case C-273/97 *Sirdar* [1999] ECR I-7403 paras. 29–31.
161 ECJ Case 318/86 *Commission* v. *France* [1988] ECR 3559 paras. 11–18.
162 ECJ Case 222/84 *Johnston* [1986] ECR 1651 paras. 36 sq.; this is subject to doubt, though, if protection of the female police officers should be recognised as objective ground; see para 58 below.
163 ECJ Case 165/82 *Commission* v. *United Kingdom* [1983] ECR 3431 para. 13.
164 ECJ Case 165/82 *Commission* v. *United Kingdom* [1983] ECR 3431 paras. 14 sq.
165 ECJ Case C-345/89 *Stoeckel* [1991] ECR I-4047 paras. 15–17.
166 ECJ Case C-345/89 *Stoeckel* [1991] ECR I-4047 paras. 19 sq.

cannot justify dismissal;[167] this is even true where a woman was initially recruited to replace another employee during the latter's maternity leave.[168] The Court had held this to be the case with regard to employment for an indefinite period, but subsequently accepted it in relation to fixed term employment (in the case: six months).[169] Again, where (on a contract for an indefinite period) a woman has been specifically hired for night work and a prohibition of night work for pregnant women temporarily prevents her from performing her contract, this cannot justify her dismissal.[170] Financial burdens resulting from maternity protection rules cannot justify discrimination of protected workers either;[171] this, of course, already follows from the purpose of maternity protection.

60.   The occupational qualifications must be *appropriate* and *necessary* for the legitimate purpose (**principle of proportionality**).[172]

bb)   POSITIVE MEASURES

61.   Regarding the admissibility of positive measures, Article 3 SDD refers to the provision of Article 157(4) (para. 23 above) with regard to the whole substantive scope of application of the Directive (i.e. not only with regard to pay!). The Court's jurisprudence mainly concerns positive measures with regard to access to employment. The Court has developed criteria for the evaluation of positive action, predominantly with regard to quotas for women: They must not provide for an automatic and absolute priority and must leave room for an objective assessment which takes the specific situation of all candidates into account (in more detail §8 para. 54 above). With a view to equal opportunity, the Court has accepted the preferential treatment of men who had undertaken military duty (indirect discrimination of women if they are not subject to military duty) as a legitimate positive measure.[173]

---

[167]   ECJ Case C-320/01 *Wiebke Busch* [2003] ECR I-2041 paras. 41–43; Case C-207/98 *Mahlburg* [2000] ECR I-549 para. 27; Case C-421/92 *Habermann-Beltermann* [1994] ECR I-1657 paras. 24 sq.

[168]   ECJ Case C-32/93 *Webb* [1993] ECR I-3567 paras. 26–28.

[169]   ECJ Case C-109/00 *Tele Danmark* [2001] ECR I-6993 paras. 30–33. Critically e.g. G. Thüsing, *Europäisches Arbeitsrecht*, §3 paras. 47–49.

[170]   ECJ Case C-421/92 *Habermann-Beltermann* [1994] ECR I-1657 paras. 23–25.

[171]   ECJ Case C-320/01 *Wiebke Busch* [2003] ECR I-2041 para. 44; Case C-109/00 *Tele Danmark* [2001] ECR I-6993 para. 28; Case 177/88 *Dekker* [1990] ECR 3941 para. 12.

[172]   See also ECJ Case 2022/84 *Johnston* [1986] ECR 1651 para. 38.

[173]   ECJ Case C-79/99 *Schnorbus* [2000] ECR I-10997 paras. 43–46.

5. Specific Protection of Pregnancy, Motherhood and Fatherhood

62. As in the 1976 Equal Access Directive, the Sex Discrimination Directive also makes a reservation for the specific protection of women in respect of **pregnancy and maternity**, Article 28(1) SDD.[174] This reservation – as well as the provisions of the Maternity Protection Directive (§20) – takes account of the special need of protection of (expectant) mothers. At the same time, this purpose also limits the reservation: It is concerned with the specific protection of the physical condition of the woman and the protection of the special relationship between a mother and the unborn and newborn child.[175] Provisions for the protection of women against any other higher risks or in their capacity as parents (a capacity which both male and female workers may have!) cannot be justified under this provision.[176] Thus, for example, national legislation which excluded fathers from 'breastfeeding leave' (or restricted their access to it) while, in fact, such leave was not conditional on the mother in fact breastfeeding the child, could not be justified as specific protection of the mother on account of her biological condition.[177]

63. When the prohibition allows for special protection of pregnant women or women who have recently given birth, this implies that they should not be disadvantaged if they make use of such protection ('**victimisation**').[178] This follows from the purpose of the protective rules, but also from the prohibition of discrimination, since unfavourable treatment because of pregnancy or motherhood constitutes direct discrimination on grounds of sex, Article 2(2)(c) SDD (see para. 46 above).[179] Article 15 SDD specifically provides for return from maternity leave. Part of the general scheme of protection is a 'right to lie in self-defence': 'Since the employer may not take the employee's pregnancy into consideration for the purpose of applying her working conditions, she is not obliged to inform the employer that she is pregnant.'[180] Her silence or lie cannot be considered to constitute deceit under national law as any

---

[174]   ECJ Case C-284/02 *Sass* [2004] ECR I-11143 paras. 32 sq.; Case C-366/99 *Griesmar* [2001] ECR I-9383 para. 43; Case C-136/95 *Thibault* [1998] ECR I-2011 para. 25; Case 184/83 *Hofmann* [1984] ECR 3047 paras. 25 sq. For a (comparative) discussion of the policy issues (mere anti-discrimination laws insufficient; some form of accommodation needed) from a US perspective, see S. Issacharoff/E. Rosenblum, *Colum. L. Rev.* 94 (1994), 2154–2221.
[175]   ECJ Case C-104/09 *Roca Álvarez* [2010] ECR I-8661 para. 27; Case C-366/99 *Griesmar* [2001] ECR I-9383 para. 43; Case C-285/98 *Kreil* [2000] ECR I-69 para. 30; Case C-421/92 *Habermann-Beltermann* [1994] ECR I-1657 para. 21; Case C-32/93 *Webb* [1994] ECR I-3567 paras. 20 sq.; Case 222/84 *Johnston* [1986] ECR 1651 para. 44.
[176]   ECJ Case C-366/99 *Griesmar* [2001] ECR I-9383 para. 44.
[177]   ECJ Case C-104/09 *Roca Álvarez* [2010] ECR I-8661 paras. 26 sqq.
[178]   ECJ Case C-294/04 *Herrero* [2006] ECR I-1513 paras. 38 sq.; Case C-284/02 *Sass* [2004] ECR I-11143 paras. 35 sq.; Case C-136/95 *Thibault* [1998] ECR I-2011 para. 26.
[179]   ECJ Case C-136/95 *Thibault* [1998] ECR I-2011 paras. 29–32.
[180]   ECJ Case C-320/01 *Wiebke Busch* [2003] ECR I-2041 para. 40.

---

misapprehension of the employer cannot, on normative grounds, constitute a relevant error.[181]

64.   Member States may also recognise a right to **paternity leave** and **adoption leave**, Article 16 SDD. Member States have discretion about whether or not to provide for such a right in their national law but if they do so, they are bound to grant employees who make use of it special protection. Member States must thus take the necessary steps to protect working men and women against dismissal arising from their exercise of these rights. They must ensure that, at the end of such leave, workers are entitled to return to their jobs or to equivalent posts on terms and conditions which are no less favourable to them, and to benefit from any improvement in working conditions to which they would have been entitled during their absence. Paternity leave and adoption leave should thus be protected in a similar way to maternity leave, if the Member States chose to introduce them. The – somewhat unusual – rule which leaves introduction of paternity leave and adoption leave to the Member States but at the same time establishes special requirements if such leave is introduced, thus constitutes a specific prohibition of discrimination.

IV.   THE EXAMPLE OF THE *BARBER* CASE

65.   Douglas Harvey Barber had been employed by the Guardian Royal Exchange Assurance Group ('the Guardian'). He was a member of the pension fund established by the Guardian, a non-contributory scheme wholly financed by the employer. That scheme, which was a 'contracted-out' scheme, that is to say it was approved under the Social Security Pensions Act 1975, involved the contractual waiver by members of the earnings-related part of the State pension scheme, for which the scheme in question was a substitute. Under the Guardian's pension scheme, the normal pensionable age was fixed for the category of employees to which Mr Barber belonged at 62 for men and at 57 for women. That difference was equivalent to that which exists under the State social security scheme, where the normal pensionable age is 65 for men and 60 for women. Members of the Guardian's pension fund were entitled to an immediate pension upon attaining the normal pensionable age provided for by that scheme. Entitlement to a deferred pension payable at the normal pensionable age was also conferred upon members of the fund who were at least 40 years old and had completed 10 years' service with the Guardian when the employment relationship was terminated. Pursuant to the conditions of employment, members of the pension fund were entitled to an immediate

---

[181]   ECJ Case C-320/01 *Wiebke Busch* [2003] ECR I-2041 para. 49; Case C-421/92 *Habermann-Beltermann* [1994] ECR I-1657 para. 25.

pension subject to having attained the age of 55 for men or 50 for women in the event of redundancy. Staff who did not fulfil those conditions received certain cash benefits calculated on the basis of their years of service and a deferred pension payable at the normal pensionable age.

66. Mr Barber was made redundant on 31 December 1980 at the age of 52. The Guardian paid him the cash benefits provided for in his severance terms: the statutory redundancy payment and an *ex gratia* payment. He would have been entitled to a retirement pension beginning on his 62nd birthday. It is undisputed that a woman in the same position as Mr Barber would have received an immediate retirement pension as well as the statutory redundancy payment and that the total value of those benefits would have been greater than the amount paid to Mr Barber. Mr Barber instituted proceedings in the industrial relations tribunals as he considered himself to be discriminated against on grounds of sex. The Court of Appeal stayed the proceedings and referred the question whether this was a violation of the prohibition of sex discrimination to the Court of Justice.

67. The Court considered both the severance payment and the retirement pension to constitute pay and thus evaluated them under Article 157 TFEU.

- The compensation granted to a worker in connection with his redundancy constitutes 'a form of pay to which the worker is entitled in respect of his employment, which is paid to him upon termination of the employment relationship, which makes it possible to facilitate his adjustment to the new circumstances resulting from the loss of his employment and which provides him with a source of income during the period in which he is seeking new employment'. The fact that such compensation is not based upon contractual agreement but has been paid (a) under a statutory obligation or (b) voluntarily is irrelevant, as such payment is made by the employer owing to the employment relationship.
- As regards the pension, the Court emphasised that the concept of pay in Article 157 TFEU 'cannot encompass social security schemes or benefits, in particular retirement pensions, directly governed by legislation without any element of agreement within the undertaking or the occupational branch concerned, which are compulsorily applicable to general categories of workers'. Where however, (1) the scheme is the result of an agreement between the employer and the employee or of a unilateral decision taken by the employer; (2) it is wholly financed by the employer or by both employers and workers without any contribution being made by the public authorities; (3) it is not compulsorily applicable to general categories of workers but only to workers employed by certain businesses; and (4) the benefits granted under the scheme are greater than those paid by the statutory scheme, it constitutes 'pay' within

the meaning of Article 157 TFEU, irrespective of the fact that it replaces the statutory pension system. It is also irrelevant that the pension fund is being administered by trustees who are formally independent of the employer, as Article 157 TFEU also applies to benefits 'paid indirectly' by the employer.

68. If the pension in question falls into the scope of application of Article 157 TFEU, the different pensionable ages for men and women constitute a case of direct discrimination. It was irrelevant, in the Court's view, that these age limits were equivalent to those of the statutory retirement ages. Furthermore, the Court did not leave any room for an overall assessment of the benefits received by men and women but reaffirmed that the principle of equal pay applies to each of the elements of remuneration. An overall assessment would be difficult to conduct by the courts and was liable to diminish the effectiveness of Article 157 TFEU; the provision requires 'genuine transparency, permitting effective review'. As the prohibition of discrimination was, following established case law, directly applicable also between private individuals, it follows that Mr Barber had a right to have his pension 'levelled up' effective as of the day of his redundancy.

69. It is easy to imagine that this judgement threatened to bring about fatal consequences. A large number of employees in the United Kingdom were members of such pension systems which had hitherto not been considered to constitute 'pay' and which usually contained age limits which had now been considered discriminatory. The Commission and the United Kingdom thus asked the Court to limit the **temporal effects** of the judgement. The Court allowed this request but at the same time emphasised the restrictive formal and substantive prerequisites for such limitation. A restriction of that kind may be permitted by the Court only in the actual judgment which gives the ruling on the interpretation requested. It further requires that the persons concerned could reasonably rely upon a different legal position. This was the case here as secondary legislation had also supported the view that Article 157 TFEU did not apply to such pension schemes. Due to a disposition in reliance upon that view, the (normal) retroactive effect of the judgement threatened to retroactively upset the financial balance of many similarly structured pension schemes. The Court thus ruled that 'the direct effect of Article 119 of the Treaty may not be relied upon in order to claim entitlement to a pension with effect from a date prior to that of this judgment, except in the case of workers or those claiming under them who have before that date initiated legal proceedings or raised an equivalent claim under the applicable national law'.[182]

---

[182] This temporal limitation has, however, lead to a series of further references for preliminary rulings to the Court of Justice; see the overview in C. Barnard, *EC Employment Law*, 522–526; more generally on the limitation of temporal effects C. Waldhoff, *Rückwirkung von EuGH-Entscheidungen* (Bonn: Zentrum für Europäisches Wirtschaftsrecht, 2006).

§10. RACE DISCRIMINATION DIRECTIVE

CONTENT

Bibliography:

S. Baer, 'Recht gegen Fremdenfeindlichkeit und andere Ausgrenzungen', *ZRP* 2001, 500–504; M. Bell, 'Beyond European Labour Law? Reflections on the EU Racial Equality Directive', *ELJ* 8 (2002), 384–399; T. Bezzenberger, 'Ethnische Diskriminierung, Gleichheit und Sittenordnung im bürgerlichen Recht', *AcP* 196 (1996), 395–434; C. Brown, 'The Race Directive: Towards Equality for All the Peoples of Europe?', *YEL* 21 (2002), 195–227; S. Fredman (ed.), *Discrimination and Human Rights – The case of Racism* (Oxford: Oxford University Press, 2001); E. Guild, 'The EC Directive on Race Discrimination: Surprises, Possibilities and Limitations', *ILJ* 29 (2000), 416–423; N. Högenauer, *Die europäischen Richtlinien gegen Diskriminierung im Arbeitsrecht – Analyse, Umsetzung und Auswirkung der Richtlinien 2000/43/EG und 2000/78/EG im deutschen Arbeitsrecht* (Hamburg: Kovač, 2002); T. Jones, 'The Race Directive: Redefining Protection from Discrimination in EU Law', *E.H.R.L.R.* 5 (2003), 515–526; S. McInerney, 'Bases for Action against Race Discrimination in E.U. law', *E.L. Rev.* 27 (2002), 72–79; S. McInerney, 'Equal Treatment between Persons irrespective of Racial or Ethnic Origin: A Comment', *E.L. Rev.* 25 (2000), 317–323; R. Nickel, 'Handlungsaufträge zur Bekämpfung von ethnischer Diskriminierung in der neuen Gleichbehandlungsrichtlinie 2000/43/EG', *NJW* 2001, 2668–2672; P. Rädler, 'Gesetze gegen Rassendiskriminierung', *ZRP* 1997, 5–9; P. Rädler, *Verfahrensmodelle zum Schutz vor Rassendiskriminierung* (Heidelberg/New York/Berlin: Springer, 1999); D. Schiek, 'Diskriminierung wegen "Rasse" oder "ethnischer Herkunft" – Probleme bei der Umsetzung der RL 2000/43/EG', *AuR* 2003, 44–51; I. Scholten, *Diskriminierungsschutz im Privatrecht? – Beweis- und verfahrensrechtliche Probleme der Umsetzung der Richtlinie 2000/43/EG* (Cologne et al.: Heymanns, 2004); G. Thüsing, 'Der Fortschritt des Diskriminierungsschutzes im Europäischen Arbeitsrecht – Anmerkungen zu den Richtlinien 2000/43/EG und 2000/78/EG', *ZfA* 2001, 397–418; G. Thüsing, 'Handlungsbedarf im Diskriminierungsrecht – Die Umsetzungserfordernisse auf Grund der Richtlinien 2000/78/EG und 2000/43/EG', *NZA* 2001, 1061–1064; B. Waas, 'Die neue EG-Richtlinie zum Verbot der Diskriminierung aus rassischen oder ethnischen Gründen im Arbeitsverhältnis', *ZIP* 2000, 2151–2155; see also the bibliography to §8.

Cases:

ECJ Case C-329/04 *Commission* v. *Germany,* [unpublished, available at curia.europa.eu]; ECJ Case C-335/04 *Commission* v. *Austria* [unpublished, available at curia.europa.eu]; ECJ Case C-54/07 *Feryn* [2008] ECR I-5187; ECJ Case C-391/09 *Runevič-Vardyn and Wardyn* 12 May 2011; ECJ Case C-310/10 *Agafiţei* 7 July 2011.

I. OVERVIEW AND PURPOSE

1. The Race Discrimination Directive (RDD) prohibits discrimination on grounds of race or ethnic origin in employment and related areas, as well as with regard to access to and supply of goods and services, i.e. in general contract law. The purpose of the Directive is 'to lay down a framework for combating discrimination on the grounds of race or ethnic origin', Article 1 RDD. The legislator considered that the Directive contributes to the protection of the principle of equality as a **fundamental right**, (Recitals 2 and 3 RDD), and also serves as an **instrument to attain other – also economical – purposes**, including 'a high level of employment and of social protection, the raising of the standard of living and quality of life, economic and social cohesion and solidarity', (Recital 9 sent. 1 RDD).[1] In contrast to the Sex Discrimination Directive, the fundamental rights-rationale predominates. Some consider the Directive to be an expression of emerging *European Social Law* or as a substantive manifestation of Union citizenship.[2]

II. SCOPE OF APPLICATION

1. Personal Scope of Application

2. The personal scope of application is not expressly determined in the Directive. However, the provision on the substantive scope of application in Article 3 RDD (para. 3 below) reveals that (a) the legislator intended an autonomous delineation of the personal scope of application by **Union law** and (b) the scope of application is to be **construed broadly**, as in the Sex Discrimination Directive (§9 para. 30). Thus, the Directive applies 'to all persons, as regards both the public and private sectors, including public bodies' (Article 3(1) introductory sentence RDD) and thus also covers employees in the

---

[1]   S. McInerney, *E.L. Rev.* 27 (2002), 72–79.
[2]   M. Bell, *ELJ* 8 (2002), 384, 386, 390 with further references.

civil service. As the Directive also applies to access to (and thus consequently also to conditions of) self-employment, the issue of 'disguised employment' is irrelevant here. If the purpose of the prohibition of discrimination is to protect fundamental rights (see para. 1 above), the Directive should be given a broad scope of application (see also Recital 13 RDD: nationals of third countries).

2. Substantive Scope of Application

3. As far as employment is concerned,[3] the substantive scope of application covers:

– **access to employment** including **promotion**, Article 3(1)(a) RDD,
– the employment itself and **working conditions**, Article 3(1)(c) RDD, which includes
– **dismissal** and
– **pay**.

It is apparent that the legislator has drafted the provisions on the scope of application in line with the sex-discrimination directives (now codified in the 2006 Sex Discrimination Directive). Consequently, its terms should be construed in the same way (see in more detail §9 paras. 34–37 above).

III. PROHIBITION OF DISCRIMINATION

1. Prohibited Grounds of Distinction: Race and Ethnic Origin

4. The prohibited grounds of distinction are – exhaustively enumerated –[4] race and ethnic origin.[5] The term 'race' is controversial as it was 'race-theories' that tried to establish or justify distinctions on grounds of race. The legislator has made it clear that the use of this term does not imply an acceptance of these theories, which attempt to determine the existence of separate human races, (Recital 6 RDD).[6] Linguistically, **race** refers to the origin or the tribe; **ethnicity** to a people or a tribe, more generally to a group of people who share a common

---

3   On the scope of application in contract law, pursuant to Article 3(1)(h) RDD. see
     K. Riesenhuber, *Europäisches Vertragsrecht*, para. 419.
4   See also ECJ Case C-310/10 *Agafiţei* 7 July 2011 paras. 31–36 ('exhaustive list'; does not cover
     'discrimination on grounds of socio-professional category or place of work').
5   See also S. B. Lahuerta, *ELJ* 15 (2009), 738–756 (advocating a broad interpretation so as to
     ensure the protection of third country nationals).
6   In detail G. Thüsing, in F. J. Säcker/R. Rixecker (eds.), *Münchener Kommentar zum BGB*, §1
     AGG para. 52; R. Nickel, *NJW* 2001, 2668, 2670.

heritage and culture.[7] The Sinte, the Romani or the Sorbs form ethnic groups in this sense.[8] The 'East-Germans' (those stemming from the former German Democratic Republic), on the other hand, are not an ethnic group.[9]

5.   The Directive does not cover differences in treatment which are based upon nationality (Article 3(2) RDD),[10] despite the fact that **nationality** is often strongly linked with ethnic origin.[11] As Recital 13 RDD indicates, this exception is intended to exempt provisions on the entry and residence of third-country nationals and their access to employment and occupation. This purpose suggests that a narrow interpretation should be taken,[12] pursuant to which reference to nationality may well be considered prohibited ethnic discrimination while it is still compatible with the Directive to reject an applicant on the ground that he does not have a valid residence permit.

6.   Furthermore, the Directive does not prohibit discrimination on grounds of **religion**, which again, may be closely linked to ethnic origin.[13] This issue is, however, directly addressed in the Equal Treatment Framework Directive (§11).

2.   Discrimination

7.   The Directive prohibits direct and indirect discrimination. Harassment and instruction to discriminate are also defined as discrimination, Article 2 RDD.

8.   **Direct discrimination** may also be found where an ethnic group is not overtly addressed but referred to by using a physical or cultural characteristic which is specific to that group, e.g. where unfavourable treatment uses criteria such as colour of skin, texture of the hair or hairstyle.[14] In its *Feryn* decision, the Court of Justice held that there was direct discrimination where the employer publicly announced that applicants of foreign origin would not be employed,

---

[7]   In more detail I. Scholten, *Diskriminierungsschutz im Privatrecht*, 19–22; G. Thüsing, in F. J. Säcker/R. Rixecker (eds.), *Münchener Kommentar zum BGB*, §1 AGG paras. 52–55; D. Schiek, *AuR* 2003, 44 sq.

[8]   See G. Thüsing, in F. J. Säcker/R. Rixecker (eds.), *Münchener Kommentar zum BGB*, §1 AGG para. 55 with further examples.

[9]   Cf. the Case of the Labour Court (*Arbeitsgericht*, ArbG) Stuttgart, *NZA-RR* 2010, 344 = *BeckRS* 2010, 68846.

[10]   See ECJ Case C-571/10 *Kamberaj* 24 April 2012 paras. 59–63.

[11]   T. Bezzenberger, *AcP* 196 (1996), 395, 412–415.

[12]   Thus – with different emphasis – R. Nickel, *NJW* 2001, 2668, 2670; I. Scholten, *Diskriminierungsschutz im Privatrecht*, 15–17; similarly (but critical) C. Brown, *YEL* 21 (2002), 195, 209 sq.

[13]   C. Brown, *YEL* 21 (2002), 195, 204 sq.; E. Guild, *ILJ* 29 (2000), 416, 418.

[14]   Cf. D. Schiek, *AuR* 2003, 44, 45.

irrespective of the fact that no actual victim of discrimination was identified (see already §8 para. 33 above).[15]

9. Other criteria may be prohibited because of their disparate impact (**indirect discrimination**), e.g. height. The use of such criteria may, of course, be justified by objective criteria unrelated to discrimination, subject to a proportionality test.

3. Justification

10. The national law of the Member States may provide for a justification for differences in treatment on grounds of race or ethnic origin only 'in very limited circumstance' (Recital 18 RDD) where, by reason of the nature of the particular occupational activity, or the context in which it is carried out, such characteristic constitutes a **genuine and determining occupational requirement**, Article 4 RDD. The justification further requires that the characteristic is *necessary* (proportionality) in order to achieve a *legitimate purpose*. Textbook examples are the waiter in a Chinese restaurant or the actor for the role of Othello.[16] Yet, these examples merely indicate that what is at stake are the limits to **entrepreneurial freedom**, e.g. the owner's freedom to consider 'authenticity' part of his business concept[17] (Does this also apply to the cook? Does it justify the exclusion of, say, Japanese applicants by the Chinese restaurant?) or the director's freedom to consider authenticity part of his artistic concept. In Germany, pizzerias are often run by Tamil people, and in *Kenneth Branagh's* movie version of 'Much Ado about Nothing', *Denzel Washington* plays the part of Don Pedro of Aragon. Given that entrepreneurial freedom is also a fundamental right, it is the balancing between these conflicting fundamental rights which is at stake in these cases.

---

[15]   ECJ Case C-54/07 *Feryn* [2008] ECR I-5187 paras. 22–28.
[16]   T. Jones, *E.H.R.L.R.* 5 (2003), 515, 521; G. Thüsing, in F. J. Säcker/R. Rixecker (eds.), *Münchener Kommentar zum BGB*, §8 AGG para. 23. See also D. Schiek, *AuR* 2003, 44, 47 sq.
[17]   Cf. Section 5(2)(c) Race Relation Act 1976 [UK].

§11. THE EQUAL TREATMENT FRAMEWORK DIRECTIVE (RELIGION, BELIEF, DISABILITY, AGE AND SEXUAL ORIENTATION)

CONTENT

Bibliography:

I. Asscher-Vonk/M. Schlachter, 'Verbot der Diskriminierung wegen Alters in den Niederlanden und Deutschland – Die Umsetzung der EG-Rahmenrichtlinie gegen Diskriminierung 2000/78/EG', *RIW* 2005, 503–511; J. Basedow, 'Der Grundsatz der Nichtdiskriminierung im europäischen Privatrecht', *ZEuP* 2008, 230–251; J.-H. Bauer/C. Arnold, 'Verbot der Altersdiskriminierung – Die Bartsch-Entscheidung des EuGH und ihre Folgen', *NJW* 2008, 3377–3383; M. Bell/R. Whittle, 'Between Social Policy and Union Citizenship: The Framework Directive on Equal Treatment in Employment', *E.L. Rev.* 27 (2002), 677–691; D. W. Belling, 'Umsetzung der Antidiskriminierungsrichtlinie im

Hinblick auf das kirchliche Arbeitsrecht', *NZA* 2004, 885–889; R. Birk, 'Altersdiskriminierung im Arbeitsrecht – kollisionsrechtlich betrachtet', in J. Basedow et al. (eds.), *Private Law in the International Arena – Liber Amicorum Kurt Siehr* (The Hague: T.M.C. Asser Press, 2000) 45–60; M. Böhm, 'Umfang und Grenzen eines europäischen Verbots der Altersdiskriminierung im deutschen Recht', *JZ* 2008, 324–330; C. Brors, 'Die Sozialauswahl nach der Reform des KSchG und im Rahmen der Richtlinie 2000/78/EG', *AuR* 2005, 41–45; M. Connolly, 'Forced Retirement, Age Discrimination and the *Heyday Case*', *ILJ* 2009, 233–241; C. Daugherty Rasnic/R. Resch, 'Altersdiskriminierung nach amerikanischem Recht', *ZIAS* 2010/2011, 274–292; R. Domröse, 'Krankheitsbedingte Kündigung als Verstoß gegen das Verbot der Diskriminierung wegen einer Behinderung in Beschäftigung und Beruf? – Besprechung von EuGH, Urt. v. 11.7.2006 – Rs. C-13/05 Chacón Navas', *NZA* 2006, 1320–1325; M. Grünberger, 'Altersdiskriminierung und Abfindungsansprüche', *EuZA* 2011, 171–187; S. D. Harris/M. A. Stein, 'Workplace Disability', in K. G. Dau-Schmidt/S. D. Harris/O. Lobel (eds.), *Labor and Employment Law and Economics – Encyclopedia of Law and Economics,* 2nd edn. (Cheltenham, UK/ Northampton, MA, 2009), 342–360; M. Henssler/K. Tillmanns, 'Altersdiskriminierung in Tarifverträgen', in H. Konzen et al. (eds.), *Festschrift für Rolf Birk zum siebzigsten Geburtstag* (Tübingen: Mohr Siebeck, 2008), 179–196; D. Hosking, 'Great Expectations: Protection from Discrimination because of Disability in Community Law', *E.L. Rev.* 31 (2006), 667–689; J. Joussen, 'Die Folgen der europäischen Diskriminierungsverbote für das kirchliche Arbeitsrecht', *RdA* 2003, 32–39; E. Kocher, 'Neujustierung des Verhältnisses zwischen EuGH und nationalen Arbeitsgerichten – oder ein Ausrutscher? – Zugleich Besprechung des Urteils EuGH v. 16. 10. 2007 – Rs. C-411/05 – Palacios de la Villa', *RdA* 2008, 238–241; D. König, 'Das Verbot der Altersdiskrminierung – Ein Diskriminierungsverbot zweiter Klasse?', in C. Gaitanides/S. Kadelbach/G. C. Rodriguesz Iglesias (eds.), *Europa und seine Verfassung – Festschrift für Manfred Zuleeg* (Baden-Baden: Nomos, 2005), 341–361; M. Körner, 'Europäisches Verbot der Altersdiskriminierung in Beschäftigung und Beruf', *NZA* 2005, 1395–1398; S. Krebber, 'The Social Rights Approach of the European Court of Justice to Enforce European Employment Law', *Comp. Lab. L. & Pol'y J.* 27 (2006), 377–403; P. M. Kummer, *Umsetzungsanforderungen der neuen arbeitsrechtlichen Antdiskriminierungsrichtlinie (RL 2000/78/EG)* (Frankfurt a.M.: Peter Lang, 2003); J. Mohr, 'Altersdifferenzierungen im Sozialplan nach deutschem und europäischem Recht – Zugleich ein Beitrag zur (teleologischen) Auslegung von Sozialplänen', *RdA* 2010, 44–54; J. Mohr, *Schutz vor Diskriminierungen im Europäischen Arbeitsrecht – Die Rahmenrichtlinie 2000/78/EG vom 27. November 2000 – Religion, Weltanschauung, Behinderung, Alter oder sexuelle Ausrichtung – Darstellung der methodischen Grundlagen und Auslegung insbesondere des Anwendungsbereichs Arbeitsentgelt – unter Berücksichtigung der aktuellen Rechtsprechung zur Geschlechtergleichheit* (Berlin: Duncker & Humblot, 2003); E. Muir, 'Enhancing the Effects of Community Law on National Employment Policies: The Mangold Case', *E.L. Rev.* 31 (2006), 879–891; M. Pilgerstorfer/S. Forshaw, 'Transferred Discrimination in European Law', *ILJ* 37 (2008), 384–393; M. Plum, *Tendenzschutz im europäischen Arbeitsrecht* (Berlin: Duncker & Humblot, 2011); T. Polloczek, *Altersdiskriminierung im Licht des Europarechts* (Baden-Baden: Nomos, 2008); U. Preis, 'Verbot der Altersdiskriminierung als Gemeinschaftsgrundrecht', *NZA* 2006, 401–410; R. A. Posner, *Ageing and Old Age* (Chicago: University of Chicago Press, 1997); H. Reichold, 'Europa und das deutsche kirchliche Arbeitsrecht – Auswirkungen der Antidiskriminierungs-Richtlinie 2000/78/EG auf kirchliche Arbeitsverhältnisse', *NZA* 2001, 1054–1060; V. Rieble/A. Zedler, 'Alterdiskrimminierung in Tarifverträgen', *ZfA* 2006, 273–303; K. Riesenhuber, 'Case-Note: ECJ of 22 November 2005 – Case C-144/04 – Mangold', *ERCL* 3 (2007), 62–71; K. Riesenhuber, '"Mangold" verabschiedet', in P. Hanau/J. T. Thau/H. P. Westermann (eds.), *Gegen den Strich – Festschrift für Klaus Adomeit* (Cologne: Wolters Kluwer, 2008), 631–644; M. Rohe, 'Schutz vor Diskriminierung aus religiösen Gründen im Europäischen Arbeitsrecht – Segen oder Fluch?', in R. Krause/W. Veelken/K. Vieweg (eds.), *Recht der Wirtschaft und der Arbeit in Europa – Gedächtnisschrift für Wolfgang Blomeyer* (Berlin: Duncker & Humblot, 2004), 217–244; M. Sargeant (ed.), *The Law on Age Discrimination in the EU* (Alphen aan den Rijn: Kluwer, 2008); D. Schiek, 'Age Discrimination Before the ECJ – Conceptual and Theoretical Issues', *CMLR* 2011, 777–799; D. Schiek, 'A New Framework on Equal Treatment of Persons in EC Law', *ELJ* (2002) 290–314; D. Schiek, 'The ECJ Decision in Mangold: A Further Twist on Effects of Directives and Constitutional Relevance of Community Equality Legislation', *ILJ* 35 (2006), 329–341; M. Schlachter, 'Altersgrenzen angesichts des gemeinschaftsrechtlichen Verbots der Altersdiskriminierung', in R. Richardi/H. Reichold (eds.), *Altersgrenzen und Alterssicherung im Arbeitsrecht – Wolfgang Blomeyer zum Gedenken* (Munich: C.H. Beck, 2003), 355–373; M. Schlachter, 'Gemeinschaftsrechtliche Grenzen der Altersbefristung', *RdA* 2004, 352–358; Marlene Schmidt/D. Senne 'Das gemeinschaftsrechtliche Verbot der Altersdiskriminierung und seine Bedeutung für das deutsche Arbeitsrecht', *RdA* 2002, 80–89; P. Skidmore, 'EC Framework Directive on Equal Treatment in Employment: Towards a Comprehensive Community Anti-Discrimination Policy?', *ILJ* 30 (2001), 126–132; R. Streinz/C. Herrmann, 'Der Fall Mangold – eine "kopernikanische Wende im Europarecht"?', *RdA* 2007, 165–169; F. Temming, *Altersdiskriminierung im Arbeitsleben – Eine rechtsmethodische Analyse* (Munich: C.H. Beck, 2008); G. Thüsing, 'Der Fortschritt des Diskriminierungsschutzes im Europäischen Arbeitsrecht – Anmerkungen zu den Richtlinien 2000/43/EG und 2000/78/EG', *ZfA* 2001, 397–418; G. Thüsing, 'Handlungsbedarf im Diskriminierungsrecht – Die Umsetzungserfordernisse auf Grund der Richtlinien 2000/78/EG und 2000/43/EG', *NZA* 2001, 1061–1064; L. Vickers, 'Freedom of Religion and the Workplace: The Draft Employment Equality (Religion or Belief) Regulations 2003', *ILJ* 32 (2003), 23–36; L. Waddington, 'Art. 13 EC: Setting Priorities in the Proposal for a Horizontal Employment Directive', *ILJ* 29 (2000), 176–181; R. Waltermann, 'Bemerkungen zu den Rechtssachen Mangold und Palacios de la Villa', in H. Konzen et al. (eds.), *Festschrift für Rolf Birk zum siebzigsten Geburtstag* (Tübingen: Mohr Siebeck, 2008), 915–928; C. Weber, 'Das Verbot altersbedingter Diskriminierung nach der Richtlinie 2000/78/EG – eine neue arbeitsrechtliche Dimension', *AuR* 2002, 401–405; K. Wells, 'The Impact of the Framework Employment Directive on UK Disability Discrimination Law', *ILJ* 32 (2003), 253–273; R. Whittle, 'The Framework Directive for equal treatment in employment and occupation: an analysis from a disability rights perspective', *E.L. Rev.* 27 (2002), 303–326; H. Wiedemann/G. Thüsing, 'Der Schutz älterer Arbeitnehmer und die Umsetzung der Richtlinie 2000/78/EG', *NZA* 2002, 1234–1242; W. Zöllner, 'Altersgrenzen beim Arbeitsverhältnis jetzt und nach Einführung des Verbots der Altersdiskriminierung', in R, Richardi/H, Reichold (eds.), *Altersgrenzen und Alterssicherung im Arbeitsrecht – Wolfgang Blomeyer zum Gedenken* (Munich: C.H. Beck, 2003), 517–533; see also the bibliography to §8.

Cases:

ECJ Case C-144/04 *Mangold* [2005] ECR I-9981; ECJ Case C-43/05 *Commission* v. *Germany* [2006] ECR I-33; ECJ Case C-133/05 *Commission* v. *Austria* [2006] ECR I-36; ECJ Case C-13/05 *Chacon Navas* [2006] ECR I-6467; ECJ Case C-411/05 *Palacios de la Villa* [2007] ECR I-323; ECJ Case C-267/06 *Maruko* [2008] ECR I-1757; ECJ Case C-303/06 *Coleman* [2008] ECR I-5603; ECJ Case C-427/06 *Bartsch* [2008] ERC I-7245; ECJ Case C-388/07 *Age Concern England* [2009] ECR I-1569; ECJ Case C-88/08 *Hütter* [2009] ECR I-5325; ECJ Case C-229/08 *Wolf* [2010] ECR I-1; ECJ Case C-341/08 *Petersen* [2010] ECR I-47; ECJ Case C-555/07 *Kücükdeveci* [2010] ECR I-365; ECJ Case C-246/09 *Bulicke* [2010] ECR I-7003 (on which, see §8 para. 76); ECJ Case C-499/08 *Ingeniøreningen i Danmark* [2010] ECR I-9343; ECJ Case C-45/09 *Rosenbladt* [2010] ECR I-9391; ECJ Case C-250/09 *Georgiev* 18 November 2010; ECJ Case C-109/09 *Deutsche Lufthansa* 10 March 2010; ECJ Case C-147/08 *Römer* 10 May 2010; ECJ Case C-310/10 *Agafiţei* 7 July 2011; ECJ Joined Cases C-159/10 and C-160/10 *Fuchs and Köhler* 21 July 2011; ECJ Joined Cases C-297/10 and C-298/10 *Hennigs* 8 September 2011; ECJ Case C-447/09 *Prigge* 13 September 2011; ECJ Case C-415/10 *Meister* 19 April 2012 (on which, see §8 para. 62).

I. OVERVIEW AND PURPOSE

1. The purpose of the Equal Treatment Framework Directive (ETFD)[1] is 'to lay down a general framework for combating discrimination on the grounds of religion or belief, disability, age or sexual orientation as regards employment and occupation', Article 1 ETFD. The legislator considers the Directive to contribute to the prohibition of discrimination as a **fundamental right**, (Recitals 1 and 4–6 ETFD), but it has also justified the Directive as an **instrument** to attain **further objectives**: a high level of employment and social protection, raising the standard of living and the quality of life, economic and social cohesion and solidarity, and free movement of persons, (Recital 11 ETFD).[2]

2. Particularly with regard to discrimination on grounds of disability, it is not only equal treatment that is at stake but rather **'equalisation'**[3] similar to the case of discrimination on grounds of pregnancy and maternity (see §9 para. 17). Recital 17 refers directly to the Court's jurisprudence pursuant to which differences in the treatment of women on grounds of their pregnancy-related (factual or legal) inability to work constitutes discrimination when it provides that the Directive 'does not require the recruitment, promotion, maintenance in employment or training of an individual who is not competent, capable and available to perform the essential functions of the post concerned or to undergo the relevant training'. Consequently, the prohibition does not require the

---

[1] Council Directive 2000/78/EC of 27 November 2000 establishing a general framework for equal treatment in employment and occupation, OJ 2000 L 303/16.

[2] J. Mohr, *Schutz vor Diskriminierungen im Europäischen Arbeitsrecht,* 188–192.

[3] On the concepts, see L. Fastrich, 'Gleichbehandlung und Gleichstellung', *RdA* 2000, 65–81.

employer to take religious rest times into account.[4] As regards discrimination of disabled workers, this only applies 'without prejudice to the obligation to provide reasonable accommodation for people with disabilities' (Recital 17 ETFD) as required by Article 5 (see para. 22 below). Within the obligation to make reasonable accommodations – which is in turn limited by the principle of proportionality – the prohibition of discrimination thus requires equalisation. In other words, the rejection of a disabled applicant constitutes discrimination where his abilities can be compensated by making reasonable accommodations.

3. In its' (in-) famous *Mangold* decision[5], the Court has called both the content and relevance of the Equal Treatment Framework Directive into question. The Court considered that the Directive merely provided a '**framework**' for the application of the prohibition of (age) discrimination which existed independent of the Directive as a general principle of primary law. Rather than determining the prohibition of discrimination itself, the Directive presupposes the prohibition's existence. The sole point of reference for this view can be found in the title of the Directive and in Article 1 ETFD. At the same time, the legislative history (Recital 12 ETFD), its wording (Article 2(1) ETFD) and teleological considerations support the opposite view, namely that the **directive** itself **lays down the prohibition of discrimination**.[6] The *Mangold* decision has met with substantial and well-reasoned opposition from several Attorneys General.[7] While a subsequent ruling indicated that the Court might not adhere to it in the future,[8] in *Kücükdevic* the Court argued along the lines of *Mangold* once again.[9]

---

[4]   G. Thüsing, *NZA* 2001, 1061, 1062 sq.

[5]   ECJ Case C-144/04 *Mangold* [2005] ECR I-9981.

[6]   See e.g. M. Körner, *NZA* 2005, 1395, 1396 sq.; E. Muir, *E.L. Rev.* 31 (2006), 879–891; U. Preis, *NZA* 2006, 401, 404–406; V. Rieble/A. Zedler, *ZfA* 2006, 273, 280–282; K. Riesenhuber, *ERCL* 3 (2007), 62, 66–70; R. Streinz/C. Herrmann, *RdA* 2007, 165–169. Differently M. Böhm, *JZ* 2008, 324–330; S. Krebber, *Comp. Lab. L. & Pol'y J.* 27 (2006), 377–403; D. Schiek, *ILJ* 35 (2006), 329–341; F. Temming, *Altersdiskriminierung im Arbeitsleben*, 393–404; R. Waltermann, *Festschrift für Birk*, 916–921. See also AG Jääskinen, Opinion in Case C-147/08 *Römer* 15 July 2010 pts. 125–134; E. Howard, *E.L. Rev.* 36 (2011), 589–599 (arguing that the prohibition of discrimination on grounds of sexual orientation flows for the general principle of equality in EU law).

[7]   AG Geelhoed, Opinion in Case C-13/05 *Chacón Navas* [2006] ECR I-6467 pts. 46–56; AG Mazák, Opinion in Case C-411/05 *Palacios de la Villa* [2008] ECR I-8531 pts. 79–100, 105–139; differentiating AG Sharpston, Opinion in Case C-427/06 *Bartsch* [2008] ECR I-7245 pts. 28–66.

[8]   ECJ Case C-13/05 *Chacon Navas* [2006] ECR I-6467 paras. 53–57; see also H. Reichold/M. Heinrich, 'Zur Kündigung eines Arbeitsvertrages wegen Krankheit und deren mögliche Wertung als Diskriminierung wegen Behinderung', *JZ* 2007, 196, 198; K. Riesenhuber, *Festschrift für Adomeit*, 631–644.

[9]   ECJ Case C-555/07 *Kücükdeveci* [2010] ECR I-365. Case notes: J. Joussen, *ZESAR* 2010, 185–192; U. Preis/F. Temming, *NZA* 2010, 185–198; D. Schiek, *ELLJ* 1 (2010), 368–379; G. Thüsing/S. Horler, *CMLR* 2010, 1161–1172 (critical with regard to the extension of the scope of the general principle and the resulting horizontal effect).

II. SCOPE OF APPLICATION

4. The provisions on the scope of application have the same wording as those of the Race Discrimination Directive (§10).

1. Personal Scope of Application

5. Here too, there is no explicit provision on the personal scope of application. Again, though, it can be assumed that the personal scope is to be determined autonomously in EU law. It covers private employment relationships as well as those in the public sector including civil service (see in more detail §10 para. 2 above).[10]

2. Substantive Scope of Application

6. As far as the field of employment is concerned,[11] the substantive scope of application is delineated in the same way as in the Race Discrimination Directive (§10 para. 3).[12] It comprises

– **access to employment**[13] including **promotion**, Article 3(1)(a) ETFD, as well as
– **employment and working conditions**, Article 3(1)(c) ETFD,[14] including
– **dismissal**[15] (or, in case of a fixed term, automatic termination)[16] and
– **pay** (within the broad meaning of Article 157 TFEU).[17]

It is clearly discernible that the legislator followed the wording of the sex discrimination directives (today the 2006 Sex Discrimination Directive). Consequently, the provisions should be construed in the same way (see §9 paras. 34–37 above).

The Court does not always place great emphasis upon the analytical distinction between the different areas of the substantive scope once it is apparent that a case falls within the scope of the Directive. Thus, it considered a

---

[10] D. König, *Festschrift für Zuleeg*, 346.
[11] For the scope of application otherwise, see P. Skidmore, *ILJ* 30 (2001), 126, 127 sq. and, for example, ECJ Case C-341/08 *Petersen* [2010] ECR I-47 paras. 32 sq. (practice as panel dentist).
[12] See further J. Mohr, *Schutz vor Diskriminierungen im Europäischen Arbeitsrecht*, 214–225.
[13] ECJ Case C 229/08 *Wolf* [2010] ECR I-1 paras. 26 sq.
[14] ECJ Case C-250/09 *Georgiev* 18 November 2010 paras. 29 sq. (compulsory retirement).
[15] ECJ Case C-499/08 *Ingeniøreningen i Danmark* 12 October 2010 para. 21. See also ECJ Case C-13/05 *Chacon Navas* [2006] ECR I-6467 paras. 36 sq.
[16] ECJ Case 447/09 *Prigge* 13 September 2011 para. 41.
[17] ECJ Case C-267/06 *Maruko* [2008] ECR 2008 I-1757 paras. 40–48; Case C-147/08 *Römer* 10 May 2011 paras. 32 sqq. (concerning supplementary retirement pensions); AG Villalón, Opinion in Joined Cases C-124/11, C-125/11 and C-143/11 *Dittrich* 28 June 2012 (grant of assistance to employees as 'pay').

provision that excluded accreditation of any professional experience acquired before the age of 18 for the purposes of grading contractual staff as 'relating to the conditions for access to employment, recruitment and pay, within the meaning of Article 3(1)(a) and (c) of Directive 2000/78'.[18] While the accreditation was potentially relevant for pay, the provision is first and foremost an 'employment condition'.

3. Exceptions and Options for Exception

7.   With regard to the prohibition of sex discrimination, the Court has, in a number of cases, been asked to permit exceptions with regard to public security and public policy but (rightly) felt that the directives did not leave any room for that or for any judicial development to that effect (§9 para. 38). The Equal Treatment Framework Directive contains two provisions that take this issue into account.

8.   Member States have the **option** to provide that the prohibitions on grounds of *disability* and *age* do not apply to the **armed forces**, Article 3(4) and Recital 19 ETFD.[19] Without such exception, (here too) distinctions based upon age or disability would have to be justified as necessary for attaining legitimate aims (see Recital 18 ETFD) in the same way as we have discussed with regard to sex discrimination (women in the armed forces, §9 para. 56 above). The optional exception, in other words, allows for the Member States to avoid judicial control in respect of the legitimate aim and proportionality of the distinction.

9.   In addition, the Equal Treatment Framework Directive does not affect 'measures laid down by national law which, in a democratic society, are necessary for **public security** (such as air traffic safety)[20], the maintenance of **public order** and the prevention of criminal offences, the **protection of health**[21] and the **protection of the rights and freedoms** of others', Article 2(5) ETFD.[22] Notwithstanding the location of this provision after the prohibition of discrimination in the Directive, it constitutes an exception from the substantive scope of application as it is not only concerned with a justification of discrimination but rather provides that *the Directive* shall be without prejudice to such measures.[23] With regard to the limited and only optional exception for the armed forces (see para. 8 above) and in light of the limited grounds for

---

[18]   ECJ Case C-88/08 *Hütter* [2009] ECR I-5325 para. 35.

[19]   D. König, *Festschrift für Zuleeg*, 349.

[20]   ECJ Case 447/09 *Prigge* 13 September 2011 para. 58.

[21]   ECJ Case C-341/08 *Petersen* [2010] ECR I-47 paras. 49 sqq.

[22]   See in more detail D. König, *Festschrift für Zuleeg*, 347 sq. Critically P. Skidmore, *ILJ* 30 (2001), 126, 129 sq.

[23]   The Court's analysis in ECJ Case C-341/08 *Petersen* [2010] ECR I-47 paras. 47 sqq. remains rather nebulous. Discussing a (discriminatory) age limit, it considers both, Article 6(1) and Article 2(5), in the context of justification.

justification in Article 4(1), this exception to the scope of application should be **narrowly construed**.[24] The Court's case law suggests that the provision will not be interpreted as narrowly as the comparable provision of Article 2(2) Safety and Health Framework Directive, Article 2(5) which only applies to emergency services and the like.[25] Here as well, though, a **proportionality** test applies ('necessary').[26] The proportionality test includes, in particular, an inquiry into the consistency of the national regulation.[27] The Court has accepted that the Member States may **delegate** their competence for adopting measures within the meaning of Article 2(5) to the social partners. They may not, however, leave the determination entirely to the social partners. The authorisation of the social partners must be 'sufficiently precise so as to ensure that those measures fulfill the requirements set out in Article 2(5)'.[28]

10. The substantive scope of application does not cover differences of treatment based upon **nationality** and is without prejudice to provisions and conditions relating to the entry into and residence of third country nationals and stateless persons in the territory of the Member States, Article 3(2) ETFD. It does not apply to payments of any kind made by state schemes including **social security** and social protection schemes, Article 3(3) ETFD. These exceptions may well be doubted if one considers the prohibitions of discrimination to be based upon fundamental rights (para. 1 above).[29]

11. There is no exception from the substantive scope of application for **small and medium sized undertakings**.[30] Their interests can be taken into account, though, where 'reasonable accommodations are at stake' (para. 28 below). When Recital 14 ETFD states that the Directive shall be without prejudice to 'national provisions laying down **retirement ages**', this only pertains to retirement ages in social legislation. The Recital cannot constitute an exception from the scope of application as there is no corresponding provision in the operative part of the directive.[31]

---

[24] ECJ Case 447/09 *Prigge* 13 September 2011 para. 56; Case C-341/08 *Petersen* [2010] ECR I-47 para. 60.

[25] ECJ Case C-341/08 *Petersen* [2010] ECR I-47 paras. 49 sqq. For a broader construction (including, e.g., age limits for the police forces, prison guards or aviation safety officers) also D. König, *Festschrift für Zuleeg*, 347 sq.; M. Schlachter, *Gedächtnisschrift für Blomeyer*, 356.

[26] ECJ Case 447/09 *Prigge* 13 September 2011 para. 63; Case C-341/08 *Petersen* [2010] ECR I-47 paras. 53 sqq. D. König, *Festschrift für Zuleeg*, 348.

[27] ECJ Case C-341/08 *Petersen* [2010] ECR I-47 paras. 53 sqq.

[28] ECJ Case 447/09 *Prigge* 13 September 2011 paras. 61–64.

[29] Very critically P. Skidmore, *ILJ* 30 (2001), 126, 127 sq.

[30] This differs from US-American law (ADEA); see e.g. R. Birk, *Liber Amicorum Siehr*, 49; H. Wiedemann/G. Thüsing, *NZA* 2002, 1234, 1236.

[31] ECJ Case C-411/05 *Palacios de la Villa* [2007] ECR I-323 paras. 44–47; Case C-388/07 *Age Concern England* [2009] ECR I-1569 para. 25; E. Kocher, *RdA* 2008, 238, 239. Differently AG Mazák, Opinion in Case C-411/05 *Palacios de la Villa* [2007] ECR 2007 I-323 pts. 51–67.

III. PROHIBITION OF DISCRIMINATION

12. The Framework Directive prohibits any direct or indirect discrimination on grounds of – in an exhaustive list –[32] religion or belief, disability, age or sexual orientation, Article 1 ETFD. Harassment and instruction to discriminate are also considered discrimination, Article 2 ETFD (see §8 para. 38 above). The prohibited grounds of distinction are not defined in the Directive, and the text does not refer to national law for their concretisation. In light of the purpose of the Directive, the terms should be construed **autonomously**.[33] In the following, we will first (1.) discuss the prohibited grounds of distinction together with additional specific rules and then (2.) consider the general option for justification based upon occupational requirements.

1. Prohibited Grounds of Distinction and Specific Rules

a) Religion and Belief

aa) THE PROHIBITED GROUND OF DISTINCTION

13. Religion is faith and its confession.[34] The substantive configuration is irrelevant, as is membership in a religious community or a church or its organisation. The mere negation of credence (atheism) is not a religion but may constitute 'belief' (see para. 14 below). It is thus prohibited to discriminate against Buddhists, Christians, Hindus, Jews, Muslims, etc. Whether sects constitute 'religions' within the meaning of the Directive is a matter of controversy;[35] this question is of practical relevance, e.g., with regard to Scientology. The wording of the text could indicate a narrow interpretation as sects are not commonly regarded as religions. But the purpose of the prohibition of discrimination, on the other hand, points in the other direction. If sects are not considered to be religions, they should still be regarded as 'belief'. As a practical result, it constitutes direct discrimination, and thus requires justification under Article 4 ETFD, if an employer in a job interview asks the applicant about membership of the 'Church of Scientology'.

---

[32] See also ECJ Case C-310/10 *Agafiţei* 7 July 2011 paras. 31–36 ('exhaustive list'; does not cover 'discrimination on grounds of socio-professional category or place of work').

[33] Thus for the term 'disability' ECJ Case C-13/05 *Chacon Navas* [2006] ECR I-6467 paras. 40–42.

[34] For a closer examination of the contours of this debate see G. Thüsing, in F. J. Säcker/R. Rixecker (eds.), *Münchener Kommentar zum BGB*, §1 AGG paras. 61–66. See also id., *ZfA* 2001, 397, 405; J. Mohr, *Schutz vor Diskriminierungen im Europäischen Arbeitsrecht*, 201; *Bundesarbeitsgericht* (Federal Labour Court, BAG), *BAGE* 79, 319, 338.

[35] Question raised by G. Thüsing, *ZfA* 2001, 397, 405, with reference to disparate evaluations under national laws.

14. **Belief** constitutes a unity of ideas which concern the position of humankind in the world.[36] The legislator has placed belief in a specific context with religion (which other prohibited grounds lack; see also Article 4(2)(1)) and has thus expressed that it considers both grounds to be similar or equivalent. Belief thus presupposes a certain coherence and wholeness of ideas which give meaning to life.[37]

15. The exclusion of differences in treatment on grounds of **nationality** can have particular relevance for religion and belief, Article 3(2) ETFD. We have already discussed these issues in relation to race discrimination (see §10 para. 5 above).

bb) PROTECTION OF ORGANISATIONS WITH ETHOS BASED UPON RELIGION OR BELIEF

16. Within narrow limits, the national laws of the Member States may justify discrimination on grounds of religion and belief, on two levels. First, religion or belief may constitute a legitimate occupational requirement for activities carried out in public or private organisations the ethos of which is based upon religion or belief (including, of course, churches), Article 4(2)(1) ETFD. Secondly, and beyond that, these organisations may require their employees to behave loyally, Article 4(2)(2) ETFD.

17. Under the national law of the Member States, a difference in treatment based upon religion or belief can be considered justified[38] where occupational activities within churches and other organisations with an ethos based upon religion or belief are concerned.[39] The substantive requirement which must be fulfilled is that, by reason of the nature of these activities or the context in which they are carried out, a person's religion or belief constitutes a genuine, legitimate and justified occupational requirement, having regard to the organisation's

---

[36] For the German *Weltanschauung* M. Waite (ed.), *Oxford Dictionary and Thesaurus*, 2nd edn. (Oxford/New York: Oxford University Press, 2007). See G. Thüsing, in F. J. Säcker/R. Rixecker (eds.), *Münchener Kommentar zum BGB*, §1 AGG paras. 68–73 (proposing a more contured legal definition).

[37] Thus with regard to Article 4 GG D. Jarrass/B. Pieroth, *Grundgesetz*, 11th edn. (Munich: C.H. Beck, 2011), Art. 4 GG para. 8.

[38] While the wording of Article 4(2)(1) ETFD suggests that it concerns an exception of the prohibition of discrimination ('shall not constitute discrimination'), its systematic location and its substantive reference to paragraph 1 indicate that it rather provides for a special justification.

[39] On the organisations covered, see M. Plum, *Tendenzschutz im europäischen Arbeitsrecht*, 216 sqq. Given that 'church' constitutes a narrower term that is covered by the broader term 'organisation', the latter should be construed narrowly as referring to specific institution; organisations in a broader sense can only rely on Article 4(1) ETFD. Critically from a policy perspective M. Rohe, *Gedächtnisschrift für Blomeyer*, 227 sq. (concerning restaurants or grocery stores).

ethos. This wording refers to the general justification contained in Article 4(1) ETFD. In substance, it provides that religion or belief may constitute a legitimate occupational qualification for occupational activities within an organisation. Yet, here as well, the employer must justify the requirements concretely and specifically with regard to a certain activity.[40] A proportionality test also applies.[41]

18. Justification pursuant to Article 4(2)(1) sent. 1 ETFD merely concerns distinctions on grounds of religion or belief and cannot 'justify **discrimination on another ground**' (sent. 2), e.g. sexual orientation. This raises the question of what applies when the principles of a religion or belief require taking other grounds of distinction, such as sexual orientation, into account. Following the purpose of the exception, this should also be justifiable, for otherwise religion or belief would be subject to far-reaching control by the state.[42]

19. Further (formal) restrictions follow from the fact that the Member States may merely **maintain** such grounds of justification but may not newly introduce them: Only Member States whose national legislation or national practices provided for such justification at the time that the Directive was adopted may maintain such legislation or incorporate the respective practice into new legislation. The justification must also satisfy any other requirements of Union law or national constitutional law as a matter of course, Article 4(2)(1) sent. 2 ETFD.

20. It may also constitute direct discrimination on grounds of religion or belief if an employer requires his employees to behave loyally to a religion or belief or if he warns or dismisses employees for acting disloyally. However, churches and equivalent organisations (para. 13 above) should be allowed to demand such loyalty. As employers they may 'require individuals working for them to act in good faith and with loyalty to the organisation's ethos', Article 4(2)(2) ETFD.[43] Loyalty does not require a positive creed or confession but 'only' demands respect. A person cannot work for a church's social institution and at the same time speak derogatorily of the church. This **claim to loyalty** may justify discrimination on grounds of religion or belief and also discrimination on other grounds, e.g. sexual orientation.[44]

---

[40] J. Joussen, *RdA* 2003, 32, 36 sq. (arguing – to far-reaching – the definition of 'certain activities' by the churches should not be subject to judicial control).

[41] To the same effect H. Reichold, *NZA* 2001, 1054, 1059 sq.

[42] J. Joussen, *RdA* 2003, 32, 36–38; J. Mohr, *Schutz vor Diskriminierungen im Europäischen Arbeitsrecht*, 203; more restrictive D. W. Belling, *NZA* 2004, 885, 886 sq.; L. Vickers, *ILJ* 32 (2003), 23, 31 sq.; M. Plum, *Tendenzschutz im europäischen Arbeitsrecht*, 235 sqq.

[43] See M. Plum, *Tendenzschutz im europäischen Arbeitsrecht*, 237 sqq.

[44] G. Thüsing, in F. J. Säcker/R. Rixecker (eds.), *Münchener Kommentar zum BGB*, §9 AGG para. 21. Differently J. Joussen, *RdA* 2003, 32, 36–38 (who seems to consider Article 4(2)(2) ETFD to constitute the general norm and thus as to resolve a contradiction to subparagraph 1).

b)   Disability

aa)   THE PROHIBITED GROUND OF DISTINCTION

21.   Disability is a personal limitation based upon a physical, mental or psychological impairment. It is here in particular that the details of the definition and delimitation cause difficulties.[45] This is partially due to the fact that a disability is not only defined by a physical, mental or psychological limitation but also by the (resulting) impairment and that the latter is, to some extent, determined by changing social perceptions. The **Court** has construed disability 'as referring to a limitation which results in particular from physical, mental or psychological impairments and which hinders the participation of the person concerned in professional life'.[46] Based upon teleological considerations, this can be further concretised: **Disability** presupposes

(1) A physical, mental or psychological defect.

The defect must be, to a certain extent, permanent or long-standing (*argumentum e* Article 5 and Recital 16 ETFD).[47] This restriction is warranted with regard to the prohibition of discrimination as it is primarily of importance in respect of unalterable characteristics. The defect must be evaluated having regard to the relevant age group. The Directive provides for a specific prohibition of discrimination with regard to age. For example, the loss of strength of an older person is not a disability.

(2) Disability is characterised by an impairment which hinders the participation of the person concerned in social or professional life. With regard to loss of hair, dandruff or body height (which may be lasting and atypical for the respective age), this will usually not be the case. An HIV-infection without symptoms[48] is also not a disability in this sense.

---

[45]   On the disparity of national definitions of disability D. Hosking, *E.L. Rev.* 31 (2006), 667, 680 sq.; G. Thüsing, *ZfA* 2001, 397, 401 sq.

[46]   ECJ Case C-13/05 *Chacon Navas* [2006] ECR I-6467 para. 43; with an approving case note by H. Reichold/M. Heinrich, *JZ* 2007, 196 (197). Similarly already AG Geelhoed, Opinion in Case C-13/05 *Chacon Navas* [2006] ECR I-6467 pts. 76 sq.: 'Disabled people are people with serious functional limitations (disabilities) due to physical, psychological or mental afflictions. From this two conclusions can be drawn:
– the cause of the limitations must be a health problem or physiological abnormality which is of a long-term or permanent nature;
– the health problem as cause of the functional limitation should in principle be distinguished from that limitation.'
Similarly already J. Mohr, *Schutz vor Diskriminierungen im Europäischen Arbeitsrecht*, 205. Critically against against a 'medical model' as opposed to a 'social model' of disability K. Wells, *ILJ* 32 (2003), 253, 255–263.

[47]   ECJ Case C-13/05 *Chacon Navas* [2006] ECR I-6467 para. 45.

[48]   Question raised by G. Thüsing, *ZfA* 2001, 397, 402 (with reference to the disparate national laws); on further border-line cases J. Mohr, *Schutz vor Diskriminierungen im Europäischen Arbeitsrecht,* 205.

22. Drawing the line still remains difficult. This is particularly true for deficiencies that can occur at different degrees such as hearing or sight impairments or obesity. Whether a characteristic qualifies as a disability has practical relevance because the Directive not only contains a ('negative') prohibition of discrimination but also requires ('positive') 'reasonable accommodation' to be provided for disabled persons, Article 5 ETFD. Critical cases require the examination of their specific details. As is the case with regard to the concretisation of general clauses,[49] the competence for **judicial control** is **divided** between the Court of Justice and the Member States' courts. The Court of Justice merely controls the framework of the term while its application in the individual case is a matter for the national courts.[50]

23. It follows from both the wording and purpose of the provision that **sickness** is to be distinguished from disability. An impairment of the (physical, mental or psychical) health is only one factor to determine discrimination but not as such a disability.[51] For it to constitute disability, it must also satisfy the a temporal element (certain duration) and constitute an impairment which hinders participation in professional life (para. 21).

24. As can be inferred from Articles 5 and 7(2) ETFD, the legislator was primarily concerned with the protection of *disabled employees*. The Court of Justice went beyond that and has also held that the disparate treatment of a non-disabled employee on grounds of the **disability of his child** is prohibited ('associative discrimination'; see §8 para. 32 and para. 25 below).[52] In its reasoning, the Court refers to the social policy goals of the Directive and the requirement of the *effet utile*. This concept offers reflexive protection for carers of disabled persons.[53]

bb) DIRECT AND INDIRECT DISCRIMINATION

25. Direct discrimination occurs where a person is being treated less favourably than another on grounds of disability.[54] Associative discrimination

---

49   With regard to the Unfair Terms in Consumer Contracts Directive ECJ Case C-237/02 *Freiburger Kommunalbauten* [2004] ECR I-3403; see K. Riesenhuber, *Europäisches Vertragsrecht*, para. 633.
50   Similarly AG Geelhoed, Opinion in Case C-13/05 *Chacon Navas* [2006] ECR I-6467 pt. 67; R. Domröse, *NZA* 2006, 1320, 1320 sq. ('framework-concept in Community law' – my translation).
51   ECJ Case C-13/05 *Chacon Navas* [2006] ECR I-6467 paras. 44–46 with approving note by H. Reichold/M. Heinrich, *JZ* 2007, 196, 197; see already AG Geelhoed, Opinion in Case C-13/05 *Chacon Navas* [2006] ECR I-6467 pts. 78–80. R. Domröse, *NZA* 2006, 1320, 1321 sq.
52   ECJ Case C-303/06 *Coleman* [2008] ECR I-5603 paras. 34–55, with approving case notes by M. Pilgerstorfer/S. Forshaw, *ILJ* 37 (2008), 384–393; F. Welti, 'Gleichbehandlung in Beschäftigung und Beruf – Unmittelbare Diskriminierung wegen einer Behinderung', *ZESAR* 2009, 147–151.
53   See also O'Brien, *E.L. Rev.* 36 (2011), 26–50 (advocating further protection).
54   R. Whittle, *E.L. Rev.* 27 (2002), 303, 306 sq.

which occurs, for instance, where the parent of a disabled child is treated less favourably, has also been considered to constitute direct discrimination (see §8 para. 32 above).[55] A standard (textbook) example of **indirect discrimination** on grounds of disability[56] is the requirement of a driver's licence.[57] A recent reference for a preliminary ruling raises the question whether it constitutes indirect disability discrimination to calculate redundancy compensation in a social plan with regard to the retirement age if, on account of a lower retirement age for disabled workers (60 as opposed to the regular retirement age of 65), this may lead to lower compensation awards for members of this group.[57a]

26. The Directive provides for a specific restriction with regard to indirect discrimination in Article 2(b)(ii) ETFD. If the employer is under a duty, under national legislation, to take 'appropriate measures' (see para. 28 below) in order to eliminate disadvantages caused by the (neutral) provision, criterion or practice in question, there is no indirect discrimination. For example, where the employer is required to provide a driver for a disabled person, the requirement of a driver's licence cannot be considered to be indirectly discriminatory. The exception only refers to appropriate measures required by national legislation and only to the employer's duty, not to the actual practice. This seems to be based upon the assumption that disabled applicants will know of such obligations and will thus not hesitate to apply for a position irrespective of the requirements which would (otherwise) have a discriminatory effect. To the extent that the employer voluntarily provides measures to compensate for any provisions, criteria or measures with a discriminatory effect, there is no discrimination in the first place.

cc)   REASONABLE ACCOMMODATION FOR DISABLED PERSONS

27. With regard to disabled persons (but not with regard to people associated with them; see §8 paras. 25, 32 above)[58], the Directive requires *employers*[59] not only 'negatively' not to discriminate. Was this not the case, effective integration of disabled persons would not be achieved where distinctions could be justified as necessary occupational qualifications, Article 4 ETFD; see para. 44 below. Therefore to some extent, Article 5 ETFD requires employers to provide for an equalisation of disabled persons, more specifically to provide for reasonable

---

[55]   ECJ Case C-303/06 *Coleman* [2008] ECR I-5603 paras. 34–55.
[56]   See also R. Whittle, *E.L. Rev.* 27 (2002), 303, 308–310 (pointing out specific difficulties of indirect discrimination on grounds of disability, given that disabled persons are not a homogenous group).
[57]   R. Whittle, *E.L. Rev.* 27 (2002), 303, 307.
[57a]   See AG Sharpston, Opinion in Case C-152/11 *Odar* v. *Baxter* 12 July 2012.
[58]   ECJ Case C-303/06 *Coleman* [2008] ECR I-5603 paras. 42 sq.
[59]   But not the other addressees of the Directive, e.g. training supervisors or public authorities; R. Whittle, *E.L. Rev.* 27 (2002), 303, 315.

accommodation to enable them to participate in professional life.[60] Technically, the provision can be implemented as a separate prohibition of discrimination, as a supplementation of the prohibition of direct and indirect discrimination or as a restriction upon the grounds of justification. The Directive largely leaves the issue open.[61]

28. Under this provision measures are considered appropriate where they are suitable and necessary to enable a person with a disability to have access to occupation, promotion or training. Examples which the legislator had in mind include adapting premises and equipment, patterns of working time, the distribution of tasks, or training or integration resources (Recital 20 ETFD).[62] There is a limit, though, where the employer can show that such measures would impose a **disproportionate burden** upon him. This is also the safety valve which allows for an accommodation of the needs of small and medium sized enterprises (Recital 21 ETFD). A disproportionate burden may result from the costs of the measure. Costs that are already compensated for within the framework of the Member State's disability policy (directly or indirectly, e.g. by way of a tax break) cannot be taken into account, Article 5 sent. 2 ETFD. The proportionality test remains difficult, though, as the relevant purpose is unclear.[63] Arguably, it would have been preferable for the legislator to install a definite standard of burden such as, e.g., an increase of 10% in labour costs or similar.[64]

c) Age

aa) The Prohibited Ground of Distinction

29. The wording, the recitals and the purpose of the Directive reveal that the prohibition of **age discrimination**[65] was not intended as a protection of the

---

[60] On the *conceptual background*, see S. Issacharoff/J. Nelson, *North Carolina L. Rev.* 79 (2001), 307–358 (emphasizing the redistributive element of accommodation requirements; criticising the open-textured character of the 'reasonable accomodation'-standard and the implied delegation of assessment from parliament to courts and the fact that the cost-bearer is chosen at random); C. Jolls, 'Antidiscrimination and Accommodation', *Harv. L. Rev.* 115 (2001), 642–699. The *efficiency* of such duty to accommodate is controversial; see R. A. Posner, *Economic Analysis of Law*, §11.10(4); S. D. Harris/M. A. Stein, in K. G. Dau-Schmidt/S. D. Harris/O. Lobel (eds.), *Labor and Employment Law and Economics*, 342–360; all with further references.

[61] Cf. L. Waddington, *ILJ* 29 (2000), 176, 177 sq. (considering, more narrowly, failure to make reasonable accommodations a 'third and separate form of discrimination'); R. Whittle, *E.L. Rev.* 27 (2002), 303, 311–315.

[62] D. Hosking, *E.L. Rev.* 31 (2006), 667, 683 sq.

[63] See already (if *obiter*) AG Geelhoed, Opinion in Case C-13/05 *Chacon Navas* [2006] ECR I-6467 pt. 83.

[64] Cf. S. Issacharoff/J. Nelson, *North Carolina L. Rev.* 79 (2001), 307–358.

[65] See in detail F. Temming, *Altersdiskriminierung im Arbeitsleben* (making use of insight of gereontological research). For a comprehensive discussion (with regard to US-American law),

elderly but as a protection against discrimination on grounds of age (see also Article 6(1)(a) ETFD: 'young people').[66] While unfavourable treatment of older workers may be the more pressing social problem, the provisions do not provide for any such restriction. Young people must not be treated unfavourably because of their age, either. An age limit may thus be subject to a proportionality test both where it functions as a maximum age and as a minimum age. For example, an age limit of 68 years for panel dentists or for professors constitutes direct age discrimination,[67] as does a maximum age for hiring for the fire services.[68,69] Similarly, a national provision that deprives workers of severance pay on the ground that they are entitled to draw an old age pension – which, by its nature, is subject to a minimum age – is directly discriminatory on grounds of age.[70]

30. The *Bartsch* case raised the question whether discrimination on grounds of the **'relative age'** was also prohibited.[71] Pursuant to an **age gap clause** in a pension scheme, a surviving spouse was not entitled to a survivor's pension if he or she was more than 15 years younger than the deceased employee. It was thus not the 'absolute age' but rather the 'relative age' – in relation to the deceased spouse – that provided the ground for distinction. The Court did not have to answer the question as the implementation period for the Directive had not expired at the relevant time. However, Attorney General *Sharpston* had considered the question in her Opinion and argued that there was age discrimination in violation of the Directive's prohibition.[72] Others consider this to be a case of indirect discrimination of older employees.[73]

---

see R. A. Posner, *Aging and Old Age* (with a discussion of issues of discrimination in chap. 13; arguing at p. 319 sqq. that '[t]he age discrimination law [sc. the 1967 Age Discrimination in Employment Act as amended] is at once inefficient, regressive, and harmful to the elderly').

66   G. Annuß, 'Das Verbot der Altersdiskriminierung als unmittelbar geltendes Recht', *BB* 2006, 325; D. König, *Festschrift für Zuleeg*, 341 sq.; G. Thüsing, in F. J. Säcker/R. Rixecker (eds.), *Münchener Kommentar zum BGB*, §1 AGG paras. 86 sq.; M. Schlachter, *Gedächtnisschrift für Blomeyer*, 357; H. Wiedemann/G. Thüsing, *NZA* 2002, 1234, 1236; W. Zöllner, *Gedächtnisschrift für Blomeyer*, 527. Differently and critically J. Mohr, *Schutz vor Diskriminierungen im Europäischen Arbeitsrecht*, 207 sq. The US-American 1967 Age Discrimination in Employment Act (as amended), in contrast, protects employees 40 years and older; see C. Daugherty Rasnic/R. Resch, *ZIAS* 2010/2011, 274, 275.

67   ECJ Case C-341/08 *Petersen* [2010] ECR I-47 paras. 34 sq.; Case C-250/09 *Georgiev* 18 November 2010 paras. 31 sq. Approving case note by C. Krois, 'Altersgrenzen für Universitätsprofessoren', *EuZA* 2011, 351–361.

68   ECJ Case C 229/08 *Wolf* [2010] ECR I-1 paras. 28 sq.

69   For a discussion of the economic rationale of a mandatory retirement age, see R. A. Posner, *Ageing and Old Age,* 322 sqq., 349 sqq.; id., *Economic Analysis of Law*, §11.10(3).

70   ECJ Case C-499/08 *Ingeniøreningen i Danmark* 12 October 2010 paras. 23 sq. Approving case note by R. Giesen, 'Diskriminierender Ausschluss einer Entlassungsabfindung wegen Anspruchs auf vorgezogene Altersrente', *EuZA* 2011, 383–395; M. Grünberger, *EuZA* 2011, 171–187.

71   ECJ Case C-427/06 *Bartsch* [2008] ECR I-7245.

72   AG Sharpston, Opinion in Case C-427/06 *Bartsch* [2008] ECR I-7245 pts. 100–106.

73   J.-H. Bauer/C. Arnold, *NJW* 2008, 3377 (3380).

31.   Direct age discrimination[74] occurs where **age limits** apply, e.g. with regard to remuneration, promotion or termination of the employment relationship (as to the scope of application, see also para. 11 above, as to justification, see para. 40 below).[75] The prohibition of age discrimination has also been of practical relevance in regard to the fixed-term employment of older employees: A provision of German law that facilitated fixed-term employment of employees of over 52 years of age constituted age discrimination; the justification on grounds of employment policy (reduction of old age unemployment) did not meet the proportionality test (see paras. 39 and 49 below).[76]

32.   Indirect age discrimination[77] may be at work where provisions or conditions relate to the **age of service** or the **period of employment with the company.**[78] Whether such criteria may be justified by the pursuit of legitimate goals would, following the Court's case law on sex discrimination (§9 para. 18), depend upon the purpose pursued by these criteria and whether they are suitable and necessary in the individual case.[79]

bb)   JUSTIFICATION OF AGE DISCRIMINATION ON GROUNDS OF PUBLIC INTEREST[80]

33.   Following the general provision of Article 4(1) ETFD, age discrimination may be justified by **occupational requirements,** in other words on grounds related to the individual employment relation and the individual employee (see para. 44 below).[81] Article 6 ETFD provides the Member States with the additional

---

74   See also R. A. Posner, *Ageing and Old Age,* 320 sqq. (on 'animus discrimination' – which is, of course, not identical with direct discrimination -; arguing that discrimination of employees 40 years and older is unlikely, given the average age of the decision makers and competitive pressures for rational behaviour in private markets); referring to J. H. Ely, *Democracy and Distrust – A Theory of Judicial Review* (Cambridge, MA/London: Harvard University Press, 1980), 160 sq. On the merits and demerits of 'statistical discrimination', see R. A. Posner, op. cit., 322 sqq. (in particular: saving information costs).

75   ECJ Case C-411/05 *Palacios de la Villa* [2007] ECR I-323 para. 51; Case C-388/07 *Age Concern England* [2009] ECR I-1569 para. 34; Case C-141/11 *Hörnfeldt* 5 July 2012.

76   ECJ Case C-144/04 *Mangold* [2005] ECR I-9981. See also Case C-109/09 *Deutsche Lufthansa* 10 March 2011 (preliminary ruling on the compatibility with the ETFD refused as it proved after analysis of the issue in the light of the FTWD).

77   From a comparative perspective, the prohibition of indirect age discrimination is not a matter of course; cf. H. Wiedemann/G. Thüsing, *NZA* 2002, 1234, 1236.

78   See in more detail V. Rieble/A. Zedler, *ZfA* 2006, 273, 283–286, 294–299 (discussing also other groups of cases such as performance-based pay, seniority-based pay, protection of earnings; directly discriminatory: old-age time-off; prolonged paid leave for older employees; preferential treatment of older employees with regard to dismissal).

79   See in more detail V. Rieble/A. Zedler, *ZfA* 2006, 273, 283–286.

80   See D. Schiek, *CMLR* 2011, 777–799 (analysing the effect of the less strict standard of scrutiny under Article 6 ETFD with a view to cases of multiple or intersectional discrimination).

81   Special consideration to age bears the risk that the employer may be guided by stereotypes, in particular where a general assessment of a group (of cases) is being made; critically on the basis of insight of gerontological research F. Temming, *Altersdiskriminierung im Arbeitsleben,* 41–61.

possibility of justifying age discrimination on grounds of **public interest** (Recital 25 ETFD). The provision allows for the justification of any form of discrimination including that caused by 'positive measures' (cf. Article 7) to prevent or compensate disadvantages of a group.[82]

34. The optional justification is limited to the pursuit of '**legitimate aims**' which the ensuing list of examples ('including') concretises as grounds of **public interest**[83] **in the area of employment and occupation:**

- employment policy,
- labour market and
- vocational training.[84]

Thus, for example, the Court has accepted the 'objective ... to **share** out among the generations **employment opportunities** in the profession of panel dentist' as a legitimate aim within the meaning of Article 6(1) ETFD.[85] Similarly, 'the aim of establishing an **age structure** that balances the young and older civil servants in order to **encourage recruitment** and promotion of young people, to improve personnel management and thereby to prevent possible disputes concerning employees' fitness to work beyond a certain age, while at the same time seeking to provide high-quality justice services, can constitute a legitimate aim of employment and labour market policy'.[86] '**Rewarding experience** that enables a worker to perform his duties better is, as a general rule, a legitimate aim of wages policy'.[87] Again, the aim of **protecting established rights** and avoiding hardship for a transitional period (during which a discriminatory system of pay is being replaced by a non-discriminatory system) might constitute a legitimate aim.[88] These examples illustrate that the Court considers the justification of Article 6(1) ETFD to be public interest oriented in a wider sense when it accepts such aims as a 'balanced age structure'. Indeed, in *Fuchs and Köhler*, the Court has made this

---

[82] D. König, *Festschrift für Zuleeg*, 350.

[83] ECJ Case C-388/07 *Age Concern England* [2009] ECR I-1569 paras. 45 sq., 49; Case C-88/08 *Hütter* [2009] ECR I-5325 para. 41; Case 447/09 *Prigge* 13 September 2011 para. 81. M. Schlachter, *Gedächtnisschrift für Blomyer*, 368; H. Wiedemann/G. Thüsing, *RdA* 2002, 1234, 1237 sqq.; M. Connolly, *ILJ* 38 (2009), 233–241; differently D. König, *Festschrift für Zuleeg*, 349 (considering that Article 6 would also allow for the accommodation of individual interests such as the employer's interest in a balanced age structure of his workforce).

[84] On the concretisation in German law M. Henssler/K. Tillmanns, *Festschrift für Birk*, 183–187.

[85] ECJ Case C-341/08 *Petersen* [2010] ECR I-47 paras. 65 sqq. See also ECJ Case C-250/09 *Georgiev* 18 November 2010 paras. 45 sq.

[86] ECJ Joined Cases C-159/10 and C-160/10 *Fuchs and Köhler* 21 July 2011 para. 50.

[87] ECJ Joined Cases C-297/10 and C-298/10 *Hennigs* 8 September 2011 para. 71; Case C-17/05 *Cadman* [2006] ECR I-9583 para. 34; Case C-88/08 *Hütter* [2009] ECR I-5325 para. 47.

[88] ECJ Joined Cases C-297/10 and C-298/10 *Hennigs* 8 September 2011 paras. 88 sqq. (referring to the freedom of establishment-case of ECJ Case C-456/05 *Commission v. Germany* [2007] ECR I-10517 paras. 63 and 65).

understanding explicit and maintained that 'the aims that may be considered "legitimate" within the meaning of Article 6(1) ETFD are aims having a public interest nature distinguishable from purely individual reasons particular to the employer's situation, such as cost reduction or improving competitiveness'.[89] Even further, the Court accepted in the same decision that, where a Member State pursues a legitimate aim of public interest, this is not called into question by the fact that it also serves this aim, e.g., issues of cost reduction.

35. Contrary to Article 4 ETFD, Article 6 ETFD cannot be used as a justification on grounds based upon the **individual employment relationship** of the parties. Furthermore, the provision only allows for a justification that is essentially determined by the **Member States 'law'** for individual employers are not in a position to define and pursue a public interest (such as employment policy).[90] It is thus problematic in the context of Article 6 ETFD if the national legislator does not directly determine public policy with regard to age but merely provides for a framework that allows employers to take age into account, e.g. in their selection of employees to be dismissed. The Court has accepted the determination of legitimate aims by **collective agreement**, though, given that Article 18 ETFD allows for the implementation of the Directive by the social partners. However, the social partners do not enjoy a broader discretion than the Member States in this field.[91]

36. Whether or not an aim pursued by a Member State is 'legitimate' is subject to **control by Union law** by the Court of Justice. If, however, a provision is plausibly intended to serve one of the enumerated purposes, the Court will not, as its *Mangold* decision indicates, question it.[92] Judicial control by the Court of Justice is generally limited because the pursuit of public interest involves political decision by the Member States and Article 6 is intended to leave room for exercise of that political discretion (cf. Recital 25 ETFD). In particular, the exemplary enumeration of legitimate aims cannot be interpreted as imposing binding value judgments upon the Member States regarding the States' employment policies. It would be going too far to assume that, by naming three examples of legitimate aims, the EU legislator intended to restrict the social policy of the Member States which often involves complex evaluations and value judgements. Thus, the 'promotion of integration of older workers' in lit. a) cannot

---

89   ECJ Joined Cases C-159/10 and C-160/10 *Fuchs and Köhler* 21 July 2011 para. 52.
90   ECJ Case C-388/07 *Age Concern England* [2009] ECR I-1569 paras. 43 sq. See also Case C-411/05 *Palacios de la Villa* [2007] ECR I-323 paras. 53–66. To the same effect M. Schlachter, *Gedächtnisschrift für Blomyer*, 368; J. Mohr, *Schutz vor Diskriminierungen im Europäischen Arbeitsrecht*, 276; see also M. Henssler/K. Tillmanns, *Festschrift für Birk*, 184 sq. With a critical assessment of *Palacios* E. Kocher, *RdA* 2008, 238–241.
91   ECJ Joined Cases C-297/10 and C-298/10 *Hennigs* 8 September 2011 paras. 62 sqq.
92   ECJ Case C-144/04 *Mangold* [2005] ECR I-9981 paras. 58–60.

be interpreted as limiting the admissibility of part-time work programmes for older employees.[93]

37. The **choice of means** employed to pursue the respective social policies is left to the Member States but is subject to proportionality control (see para. 38 below). Pursuant to an exemplary (not exhaustive, 'among others')[94] list, such instruments may include:

(1) **Special conditions on access** to employment and occupation or on employment and occupation (in a broad sense, including dismissal and remuneration conditions) in order to promote the vocational integration of young people, older workers and persons with responsibilities of care for family members, lit. a). Easing the admissibility of part-time work for older workers with the objective of reducing old age unemployment is an example (which was in issue in *Mangold*; the critical point is proportionality). Another example is the protection of older employees in the case of dismissal for operational reasons.[95]

(2) Provisions on **minimum age**, professional experience or seniority in services for access to employment or certain advantages linked to employment, lit. b). Think, for example, of longer times of paid leave for older employees[96] or bonuses or benefits for professional experience[97] or loyalty to the firm.[98]

(3) Provisions on a **maximum age** for recruitment which is based upon the training requirements for the position in question or the need for a reasonable period of employment before retirement; lit. c). For example, one may think of a maximum age of 52 for the first appointment as a university professor or of 28 for entry into the fire brigade.

The list is non-exhaustive and the Member States enjoy a margin of discretion in their implementation which allows them to provide for further examples. The Court has, e.g., held that Article 6(1) ETFD does not preclude a national provision under which clauses (in individual or collective agreements) on automatic termination of employment contracts, on the ground that the employee has reached the age of retirement, are considered to be valid.[99]

---

[93] Differently M. Schmidt/D. Senne, *RdA* 2002, 80, 86.
[94] ECJ Case C-45/09 *Rosenbladt* [2010] ECR I-9391 para. 40 ('the list is merely a guide'; Member States have a discretion in the implementation of Article 6 ETFD).
[95] To the same effect C. Brors, *AuR* 2005, 41, 43.
[96] D. König, *Festschrift für Zuleeg*, 350.
[97] M. Schmidt/D. Senne, *RdA* 2002, 80, 87 sq. Cf. also ECJ Case 109/88 *Danfoss* [1989] ECR 3199.
[98] M. Schmidt/D. Senne, *RdA* 2002, 80, 88 sq.
[99] ECJ Case C-45/09 *Rosenbladt* [2010] ECR I-9391 para. 53. The provision in question was §10(5) AGG (*Allgemeines Gleichbehandlungsgesetz*; the German General Law on Equal Treatment) pursuant to which permissible differences of treatment on grounds of age

38. The means (para. 37) are, however, subject to a proportionality test of whether they are '**appropriate and necessary**' for the achievement of the legitimate aim (para. 34) pursued. That test includes an inquiry into the **consistency** of the national regulation.[100] Judicial control leaves the Member States – or, where they are involved in the implementation, the social partners –[101] a *broad discretion*,[102] as the instruments of employment and labour market policy are usually difficult to assess in respect of their effects. The Court has rightly recognised that the Member States 'must have the possibility available of altering the means used to attain a legitimate aim of public interest, for example by adapting them to changing circumstances in the employment situation in the Member State concerned'.[103] The Court insists, though, that 'that discretion cannot have the effect of frustrating the implementation of the principle of non-discrimination on grounds of age'.[104] While it appears to readily accept the 'appropriateness' of a national measure in the public interest ('not appear to be manifestly inappropriate for attaining the legitimate employment policy objective pursued'), it has, in recent cases, scrutinised the 'necessity' in considerable detail.[105]

39. In *Mangold,* the Court objected to a provision in German law which authorised, without restriction, the conclusion of fixed-term contracts of employment once the worker had reached the age of 52.[106] The Court accepted that the provision served the legitimate aim of enhancing the integration of older workers in the labour market and that authorising fixed-term contracts was a suitable means for that aim. But it considered the general authorisation of fixed-term work, without consideration of the previous employment situation of the worker, to be disproportionate as it effectively excluded a group of workers from the regular labour market (see also §17 para. 43 with regard to the Fixed-Term Employment Directive). The German legislator responded to the judgement by making it an additional requirement that the employee had been unemployed for

---

included *inter alia*: 'An agreement which provides for the termination of the employment relationship without notice of termination at a date when the employee may claim an old-age pension; this shall be without prejudice to Paragraph 41 of the SGB VI.'

100 Cf. ECJ Case C-88/08 *Hütter* [2009] ECR I-5325 paras. 46 sq.
101 ECJ Case C-45/09 *Rosenbladt* [2010] ECR I-9391 para. 69.
102 ECJ Case C-144/04 *Mangold* [2005] ECR I-9981 para. 63; Case C-411/05 *Palacios de la Villa* [2007] ECR I-323 paras. 67 sq.; Case C-88/08 *Hütter* [2009] ECR I-5325 para. 45; Case C-341/08 *Petersen* [2010] ECR I-47 paras. 69 sqq.; Case C-250/09 *Georgiev* 18 November 2010 para. 50; Joined Cases C-159/10 and C-160/10 *Fuchs and Köhler* 21 July 2011 paras. 61 sqq.; 80 sqq. Critically F. Temming, *Altersdiskriminierung im Arbeitsleben*, 473–484.
103 ECJ Case C-411/05 *Palacios de la Villa* [2007] ECR I-323 para. 70; Joined Cases C-159/10 and C-160/10 *Fuchs and Köhler* 21 July 2011 para. 54.
104 ECJ Case C-499/08 *Ingeniøreningen i Danmark* 12 October 2010 para. 33; Case C-388/07 *Age Concern England* [2009] ECR I-1569 para. 51.
105 ECJ Case C-499/08 *Ingeniøreningen i Danmark* 12 October 2010 paras. 34 sq. (appropriateness) and paras. 36–47 (!) (necessity).
106 Differently M. Schlachter, *RdA* 2004, 352, 356 (arguing for the Member States' discretion also with regard to the proportionality test).

at least the previous four months before taking up the fixed-term position. In *Georgiev,* the Court distinguished such general alleviation of fixed-term work for older employees from national legislation, pursuant to which a professor may continue working beyond the age of 65 only by means of fixed-term one-year contracts, renewable at most twice.[107] Such legislation may be justified under Article 6(1) ETFD.

40. *Palacios de la Villa* concerned a Spanish provision, pursuant to which compulsory retirement clauses in collective agreements were regarded as lawful where such clauses provided as sole requirements that workers must have reached retirement age, set at 65 by the national legislation, and must fulfil the social security conditions for entitlement to draw a contributory retirement pension.[108] The Court accepted as a legitimate aim the justification of the provision on grounds of labour market policy, irrespective of the fact that this justification was kept in rather general terms and that it had only been mentioned in vague terms in the legislative proceedings. In regard to the proportionality test, the Court recognised a 'broad discretion' of the Member States and, as to the necessity, merely applied a plausibility control ('does not appear unreasonable'). It did not consider the provision to be unreasonable given that the legitimate expectations of workers were safeguarded by the requirement that they are entitled to draw a pension. This latter aspect, however, was not considered in the recent *Hörnfeldt*-judgement.[108a] In *Age Concern England* and *Rosenbladt,* the Court has confirmed the general admissibility of automatic termination clauses in national law.[109] In *Petersen* the age limit failed the justification test as the national law proved to be incoherent.[110] In *Hennings,* the Court considered pay steps based upon age in a collective agreement. While it considered that this mechanism – directly discriminatory on grounds of age – could, in principle, be justified by reference to the legitimate aim of rewarding professional experience, it found the system in question to go beyond what was appropriate and necessary for that end.[111]

d)   Sexual Orientation

41. Discrimination on grounds of sexual orientation is not covered by the prohibitions of sex discrimination in Article 157 TFEU or in the sex-discrimination directives (§9 para. 11). The literal meaning of sexual orientation would refer to a person's preference in the choice of their sexual partner, but the

---

[107]   ECJ Case C-250/09 *Georgiev* 18 November 2010 paras. 57 sqq.

[108]   ECJ Case C-411/05 *Palacios de la Villa* [2007] ECR I-323 paras. 52–73; approvingly R. Waltermann, *Festschrift für Birk,* 924–928; critically E. Kocher, *RdA* 2008, 238, 240.

[108a]   ECJ-Case C-141/11 *Hörnfeldt* 5 July 2012.

[109]   ECJ Case C-388/07 *Age Concern England* [2009] ECR I-1569; Case C-45/09 *Rosenbladt* [2010] ECR I-9391 with approving note by J. Joussen, *ZESAR* 2011, 201–208.

[110]   ECJ Case C-341/08 *Petersen* [2010] ECR I-47.

[111]   ECJ Joined Cases C-297/10 and C-298/10 *Hennigs* 8 September 2011 paras. 53 sqq.

language used refers more broadly to the choice of a partner. Even though the legislator may have had a prohibition of discrimination of homosexuals in mind, as this may constitute a particular social problem, the prohibition also covers discrimination of **heterosexuals**.[112] Thus, discrimination against the father of a family or of a mother may constitute indirect discrimination on grounds of sexual orientation. The legislator did not however intend the Directive to affect national laws on **marital status** and the benefits dependent thereon (Recital 22 ETFD). The prohibition also extends to sexual orientations that are unwelcome in society such as adult sexual attraction for children or animals.[113] The Court has considered **transsexuality** to be an issue of sex and is thus covered by Article 157 TFEU. The legislator has recently affirmed this in the 2006 Sex Discrimination Directive (Recital 3 SDD; see §9 para. 40). This indicates that the legislator did not consider transsexuality to be an issue of sexual orientation.

42. The Commission distinguishes sexual orientation from **sexual behaviour**.[114] 'Sexual behaviour' in general and sexual harassment (as prohibited by the Sex Discrimination Directive, §9 para. 54) may be grounds for distinction. While specific sexual behaviour may be linked to sexual orientation, it may nonetheless be a legitimate ground for distinction as long as it is the behaviour (rather than the orientation) to which is being referred.

43. In *Maruko*, the Court found direct discrimination on grounds of sexual orientation if a survivor's benefit granted under an occupational pension scheme was granted to the surviving spouse but not to the surviving partner in a same sex life partnership formed under German Law on Registered Life-Partnerships.[115] The Court reasoned that Article 2(2)(a) ETFD presupposes less favourable treatment than another person in a *comparable situation*. 'In that regard, it should be pointed out that [...], first, it is required not that the situations be identical, but only that they be comparable and, second, the assessment of that comparability must be carried out not in a global and abstract manner, but in a specific and concrete manner in the light of the benefit concerned.'[116] It held that the same-sex life-partnership under German law was

---

112 G. Thüsing, in F. J. Säcker/R. Rixecker (eds.), *Münchener Kommentar zum BGB*, §1 AGG para. 89.

113 Critically with regard to potential inconsistencies with (German) criminal law G. Thüsing, in F. J. Säcker/R. Rixecker (eds.), *Münchener Kommentar zum BGB*, §1 AGG para. 88. Differently (only 'bi-, homo- and heterosexual forms' of orientation) – P. M. Kummer, *Umsetzungsanforderungen der neuen arbeitsrechtlichen Antidiskriminierungsrichtlinie (RL 2000/78/EG)*, 79–83.

114 Commission, Proposal of 25 November 1999 for a Council Directive establishing a general framework for equal treatment in employment and occupation, COM(99) 565 final, comments on Article 1.

115 ECJ Case C-267/06 *Maruko* [2008] ECR I-1757. Confirmed by ECJ Case C-147/08 *Römer* 10 May 2011 paras. 42 sqq.

116 ECJ Case C-147/08 *Römer* 10 May 2011 para. 42.

largely aligned to marriage. If the widow of a worker and the surviving partner of a worker were placed in a comparable situation, it constituted direct discrimination on grounds of sex to exclude the latter from survivor's benefits. Arguably, the contrary would be more convincing: If one considers, as the Court seems to, that the position of a same-sex partner is not as such comparable to that of a spouse, then it is for the Member States to determine the extent of equalisation. If a Member State opted for a partial equalisation, this must be accepted and cannot be used as a ground to further extend the equalisation.

2. The General Ground for Justification: Occupational Requirements

44. Apart from the specific justifications provided with regard to discrimination on grounds of religion and belief (paras. 16–20), disability (paras. 27 sq.) and age (paras. 33–40), Article 4(1) ETFD contains a (optional) general ground for justification, the substance of which will now already be familiar from other directives (see §8 para. 49). Direct or indirect discrimination on grounds of religion or belief, disability, age or sexual orientation may – 'in very limited circumstances' – be justified if the discriminatory criterion constitutes a genuine and determining occupational requirement for the specific occupational activities concerned. The provision must be narrowly construed.[117] The requirement has to be necessary for the attainment of a legitimate aim. For example, we can think of age limits for fire fighters, policemen, air traffic controllers or bus drivers.[118] Indeed, the Court agreed that 'the concern to ensure the operational capacity and proper functioning of the professional fire service constitutes a legitimate objective within the meaning of Article 4(1) of the Directive'; it accepted that 'the possession of especially high physical capacities may be regarded as a genuine and determining occupational requirement within the meaning of Article 4(1) of the Directive for carrying on the occupation of a person in the intermediate career of the fire service'.[119]

45. The issue of age limits is of practical relevance for **air pilots**.[120] *Lufthansa* airlines and the competent air pilots union had agreed on an age limit of 60 years for the automatic retirement of pilots. The Court was asked to consider whether this direct age discrimination could be justified under Article 2(5), 4(1) or 6 ETFD. The Court accepted that air traffic safety was a legitimate aim under Article 2(5) ETFD (as part of 'public security') and under Article 4(1). Possessing particular

---

[117] ECJ Case 447/09 *Prigge* 13 September 2011 para. 72.
[118] D. König, *Festschrift für Zuleeg*, 348; R. Wank, 'Diskriminierung in Europa – Die Umsetzung der europäischen Antidiskriminierungsrichtlinien aus deutscher Sicht', *NZA* 2004 Special Supplement to issue 22, 16, 22–24; H. Wiedemann/G. Thüsing, *NZA* 2002, 1234, 1237.
[119] ECJ Case C 229/08 *Wolf* [2010] ECR I-1 paras. 39 sq.
[120] See the examples from German case law LAG Hessen, *NZA-RR* 2003, 648 (651); BAG, *BAGE* 100, 292, 299 sq. Based on a strict proportionality test critically F. Temming, *Altersdiskriminierung im Arbeitsleben*, 614 sq. with further references.

physical capabilities may be considered as a 'genuine and determining occupational requirement' within the meaning of Article 4(1). As, however, national and international authorities considered that pilots have the physical capability to act as pilot until the age of 65 (even if, between 60 and 65, they do so only as a member of a crew in which the other pilots are younger than 60), the age limit of 60 was disproportionate. The defence of Article 6(1) ETFD was not available as under this provision, exclusively social policy objectives such as those related to employment policy, labour market or vocational training could be considered legitimate aims. – The Court thus accepts a rather broad interpretation of 'public security' within the meaning of Article 2(5) while strictly limiting the justification under Article 6. This is of considerable practical importance as the exception of Article 2(5) applies with regard to all prohibited grounds, whereas the defence of Article 6 is only available in cases of age discrimination. The narrow proportionality test does not appear to leave any leeway for taking entrepreneurial decisions into account. In other words, it would not have helped *Lufthansa* to argue that being a particularly safe airline was part of its business and marketing concept; indeed, it is doubtful whether the Court would have accepted this as a legitimate aim under Article 4(1) in the first place. Finally, the fact that the age limit had been agreed in a collective agreement, concluded in the exercise of collective bargaining autonomy of the social partners, did not help either. While the Court agreed that the right to collective negotiation was protected under Article 28 ChFR (see §2 paras. 50 sq. above), this could not trump the prohibition of discrimination in the Directive, as contained in Article 16(1)(b) ETFD.

46. There is no justification for **harassment**. The lawfulness of an 'instruction to discriminate' depends upon the lawfulness of the discrimination itself.

IV. THE EXAMPLE OF THE *MANGOLD* CASE

47. On 26 June 2003, Mr Mangold, then 56 years old, concluded a contract which took effect on 1 July 2003 with Mr Helm, a practising lawyer. §5 of that contract provided that:

'1. The employment relationship shall start on 1 July 2003 and last until 28 February 2004.

2. The duration of the contract shall be based on the statutory provision which is intended to make it easier to conclude fixed-term contracts of employment with older workers (the provisions of the fourth sentence, in conjunction with those of the fourth sentence, of Paragraph 14(3) of the TzBfG ...), since the employee is more than 52 years old.

3. The parties have agreed that there is no reason for the fixed term of this contract other than that set out in paragraph 2 above. All other grounds for limiting the

term of employment accepted in principle by the legislature are expressly excluded from this agreement.'

The provisions of the Law on Part-Time and Fixed-Term Employment (*Gesetz über Teilzeitarbeit und befristete Arbeitsverträge,* TzBfG),[121] to which the agreement refers, allowed for fixed-term employment contracts to be concluded without need of an objective requirement, the fulfilment of which would otherwise be required. The relevant provision aimed to enhance the prospects of older employees on the labour market.[122] In bringing his action, Herr Mangold *inter alia* claimed that the fixed-term agreement of §5 of the contract was incompatible with the prohibition of age discrimination contained in the Equal Treatment Framework Directive. The *Arbeitsgericht* (Labour Court, AG) Munich referred the question to the Court of Justice for a preliminary ruling.[123]

48.   Fixed-term employment without objective justification constitutes direct discrimination on grounds of age contrary to the prohibition of Article 2 ETFD. Such discrimination could, however, be justified under Article 6(1) ETFD which specifically mentions 'the setting of special conditions on access to employment (...), employment and occupation, including dismissal and remuneration conditions, for (...) older workers (...) in order to promote their vocational integration'. Promotion of the integration of older employees thus constitutes a legitimate public interest, capable of justifying discrimination.

49.   The means employed (here: authorising fixed-term employment without a requirement of objective justification), however, must be appropriate and necessary for achieving that aim. The Member States enjoy broad discretion in their choice of the measures capable of attaining their objectives in the field of social and employment policy, given that an evaluation of economic policy is required. This margin for discretion was exceeded in the present case: The provision of the Law on Part-Time and Fixed-Term Employment provided that workers of 52 years of age and above – irrespective of whether and for how long they had hitherto been unemployed – could be offered (even repeatedly) part-time contracts without any restriction or control. As a consequence, this large group of workers was liable to be effectively excluded from the regular labour

---

[121]   Bilingual German-English version in S. Lingemann/R. v. Steinau-Steinrück/A. Mengel, *Employment and Labour Law in Germany,* Part II, III.

[122]   The provision had also previously been controversial as a matter of policy; see e.g. U. Preis, *NZA* 2006, 401, 401 sq. with further references.

[123]   Other questions referred to the ECJ concerned the compatibility with the Fixed-Term Work Directive (see also §17). For a discussion of the *Mangold* decision, see e.g. U. Preis, *NZA* 2006, 401–410; K. Riesenhuber, *ERCL* 3 (2007), 62–71. The case appears to have been construed with a view to forcing a preliminary ruling; see in detail J.-H. Bauer, 'Ein Stück aus dem Tollhaus: Altersbefristung und der EuGH', *NZA* 2005, 800, 801 sq.; this leads to interesting procedural issues of admissibility.

market, 'when it has not been shown that fixing an age threshold, as such, regardless of any other consideration linked to the structure of the labour market in question or the personal situation of the person concerned, is objectively necessary to the attainment of the objective'. The means were thus not proportionate to the aim pursued and could not be justified under Article 6(1) ETFD.

50. This part of the judgement largely met with support. Yet, the Court's ensuing statements with regard to the temporal effect of the Directive triggered a vigorous debate. The facts of the *Mangold* case took place at a time when the implementation period of the Equal Treatment Framework Directive had not yet expired. The Court therefore considered whether the Directive could have an effect even before expiry of the implementation period (as has been previously occasionally recognised (see §1 para. 70 above))[124] but ultimately had recourse to a different line of argument. The Court reasoned that the Equal Treatment Framework Directive merely laid down a 'framework' to combat discrimination and did not, as such, prohibit discrimination but rather presupposed the pre-existence of the prohibition of discrimination. Indeed, the Court argued, the prohibition of age discrimination already constitutes a general principle of primary Union law (see §1 para. 68 above). This could be inferred from international treaties and the constitutional traditions common to the Member States. As a general principle of primary Union law, the prohibition of discrimination was applicable independent of the Directive and therefore expiry of the implementation period. On this latter point, the decision met with fierce opposition from legal writers as well as from Attorneys General. In Germany, the Court's 'invention' of a general principle against age discrimination even led to a reference to the *Bundesverfassungsgericht* (German Federal Constitutional Court, BVerfG) on the ground that the Court of Justice may have exceeded its jurisdictional powers.[125] While the Court of Justice had indicated in a subsequent judgement that it would not adhere to *Mangold*,[126] the Court later expressly confirmed the decision.[127]

---

[124]   On the issue of prior effects of directives, see e.g. C. Hofmann, in K. Riesenhuber (ed.), *Europäische Methodenlehre*, §16.

[125]   BVerfG, *BVerfGE* 126, 286 = *NJW* 2010, 3422 – Honeywell.

[126]   See the references note 8 above.

[127]   ECJ Case C-555/07 *Kücükdeveci* [2010] ECR I-365.

CHAPTER 2

INDIVIDUAL INFORMATION RIGHTS

§12. WRITTEN STATEMENT DIRECTIVE

CONTENT

Bibliography:

R. Birk, 'Das Nachweisgesetz zur Umsetzung der Richtlinie 91/533/EWG in das deutsche Recht', *NZA* 1996, 281–290; J. Clark/M. Hall, 'The Cinderella Directive? Employee Rights to Information about Conditions applicable to their Contract or Employment Relationship', *ILJ* 21 (1992), 106–118; S. Deakin, 'Social Norms, Information, and the Employment Relationship: The Role of Legal Regulation', in S. Grundmann/W. Kerber/S.

Weatherill (eds.), *Party Autonomy and the Role of Information in the Internal Market* (Berlin/New York: de Gruyter, 2001), 371–392; B. Friese, 'Der Nachweis der wesentlichen Regelungen des Arbeitsvertrages', in H. Oetker/U. Preis (eds.), *Europäisches Arbeits- und Sozialrecht, EAS, part B – Systematische Darstellungen,* loose-leaf (Heidelberg: Forkel, last update: March 2010), B 3050; J. Kenner, 'Statement or Contract? – Some Reflections on the EC Employment Information (Contract or Employment Relationship) Directive after *Kampelmann*', *ILJ* 28 (1999), 205–231; U. Preis, 'Nachweisgesetz – lästige Förmelei oder arbeitsrechtliche Zeitbombe?', *NZA* 1997, 10–17; K. Riesenhuber, 'Nachweispflichten: Ansprüche auf Information über Vertragsbedingungen im Europäischen und deutschen Vertragsrecht', in H. P. Westermann/K. Mock (eds.), *Festschrift für Gerold Bezzenberger zum 70. Geburtstag am 13. März 2000* (Berlin/New York: de Gruyter, 2000), 721–743; R. Schwarze, 'Praktische Handhabung und dogmatische Einordnung des Nachweisgesetzes', *ZfA* 1997, 43–66; T. Sigeman, 'Zur Umsetzung der Nachweis-Richtlinie in nationales Recht', *RdA* 2001 Special Supplement to issue 5, 39–45; R. Wank, 'Das Nachweisgesetz', *RdA* 1996, 21–24.

Cases:

ECJ Joined Cases C-253/96 to C-258/96 *Kampelmann* [1997] ECR I-6907; ECJ Case C-350/99 *Lange* [2001] ECR I-1076; ECJ Case C-319/06 *Commission* v. *Luxembourg* [2008] ECR I-4323; ECJ Case C-306/07 *Andersen* [2008] ECR I-10279; CFI Case T-333/99 *X* v. *EZB* [2001] ECR II-3021.

I.   ISSUES, OVERVIEW, COMPETENCE, REGULATORY CONTEXT

1.   EU employment law does not include provisions on the formation of the employment contract. The prohibitions of discrimination merely restrict the freedom to choose the contract partner. There is no requirement as to form for the formation of the employment contract, either. The Written Statement Directive (WSD)[1], however, is (primarily) related to the formation of the employment relationship. As a rule, it requires the employer to notify the employee in writing of the essential aspects of the employment contract within a period of two months after commencement of employment.

2.   The Directive, which is also intended to implement No. 9 of the Community Charter of Fundamental Social Rights (Recital 6 WSD; on the CCFR, see §2 paras. 16 sqq. above), was enacted against the background of a labour market that had become increasingly opaque with new forms of work and new types of employment relationship (Recital 1 WSD). The Member States had reacted differently to the resulting diversity of types of employment relationship

---

[1]   Council Directive 91/533/EEC of 14 October 1991 on an employer's obligation to inform employees of the conditions applicable to the contract or employment relationship, OJ 1991 L 288/32.

(Recitals 2, 3 WSD). The legislator intended the Directive to counteract the ensuing regulatory disparity.

3. Following the example of UK legislation,[2] the Written Statement Directive employs the tool of information. The legislator thus neither interferes with the freedom to choose one's contract partner nor with the freedom to determine the content of the contract. The intention is not to reduce the diversity in forms of work, but rather to make the choices transparent. The obligation to inform is intended to protect the individual employee (Recitals 2 and 7 WSD), to make enforcement of his rights easier and to foster a relationship of confidence and trust;[3] it also contributes to transparency of the labour market (Recital 2 WSD).[4] In contrast to a common purpose in EU consumer law, information is not intended to enable the addressee to make a rational contract decision (the written statement is to be given only after the formation of the contract!). This is, indeed, rather less important in relation to employment contracts as the average (or: model) employee will usually not be able to make a choice between competing offers and as the law and collective agreements largely ensure fair contract terms.

4. If the Directive is regarded as a regulation of new types of employment relationship (para. 2), it is closely connected to the various directives on **atypical employment relationships** (§§15–19). With its specific requirement to notify posted employees, it is also related to the Posting of Workers Directive (§6).

II.   SCOPE OF APPLICATION

5. The scope of application is largely determined by Article 1(1) WSD, paragraph 2, which gives Member States options to provide for certain exceptions. The rules are rather opaque (also in other language versions) and raise a disproportionate number of issues of interpretation – which, however, have not thus far led to any difficulty in practical application.

1.   Personal and Substantive Scope of Application

6. The Written Statement Directive applies '[1] to every paid employee having a contract or employment relationship [2] defined by the law in force in a Member

---

2   J. Kenner, *ILJ* 28 (1999), 205–231.
3   Cf. H. Collins, *Employment Law*, 109 sq. (avoid misunderstandings, promote confidence and trust).
4   See also ECJ Joined Cases C-369/96 and C-376/96 *Arblade* [1999] ECR I-8453 para. 68. K. Riesenhuber, *Festschrift für Bezzenberger*, 725 sq.; id., *Europäisches Vertragsrecht*, paras. 518–521.

State and/or governed by the law in force in a Member State', Article 1(1) WSD (numbering added). Reference to the 'employee having a contract or employment relationship' describes the same fact twice as the terms are mutually referential. Employee is the debtor of the characteristic obligation of an employment contract or relationship. It can be assumed that the legislator intended to ensure that the Directive also applies where the employment contract has not been effectively concluded but the parties have still entered into a ('factual') employment relationship.

7.   Interpretation of the term 'employee' is controversial. The Directive neither provides for a definition, nor refers to national definitions. The purpose of the approximation of national laws is an argument in favour of an **autonomous** definition,[5] given that a central objective was to comprehensively cover the disparate forms of work. This objective could be seriously hampered if the definition of 'employee' were left to the Member States. The wording also indicates an autonomous definition when Article 1(1) refers to employment relationships 'defined by the law in force in a Member State and/or governed by the law in force in a Member State', for the latter alternative would be obsolete if the Directive only covered employment relationships defined by national law.[6]

8.   For an autonomous definition, we can refer to the concept of **employee** developed in the Court's jurisprudence on freedom of movement for workers, Article 45 TFEU (§3 paras. 9–12 above). A worker is a person who, for a certain period of time, performs services for and under the direction of another in return for which he receives remuneration. This also covers employees in the public service including civil servants (*argumentum e* Article 45(4) TFEU; see §3 paras. 22–24).[7] Part-time employees and casual employees are also covered, as is revealed by the optional exceptions contained in Article 1(2) WSD (paras. 10–12 below).

9.   Both the wording and the substance of the second requirement, that the contract or employment relationship must be defined and/or governed by the law of a Member State, are rather unclear. It appears that the legislator intended to ensure that the obligation to notify the employee would also apply where a relationship would be considered employment under national law ('defined') but

---

5   To the same effect see G. Thüsing, *Europäisches Arbeitsrecht*, §8 paras. 6 sq.; differently R. Wank, *RdA* 1996, 21, 22; left open by F. Marhold, in M. Fuchs/F. Marhold (eds.), *Europäisches Arbeitsrecht*, 78 sq.; M. Schmidt, *Arbeitsrecht der EG*, III para. 301. If one were to follow the opposing view, this would still not justify exempting individual groups of employees such as executive employees from the scope of application; differently R. Wank, *RdA* 1996, 21, 22.

6   G. Thüsing, *Europäisches Arbeitsrecht*, §8 para. 6.

7   Differently R. Birk, *NZA* 1996, 281, 286; R. Wank, *RdA* 1996, 21, 22; with doubt also F. Marhold, in M. Fuchs/F. Marhold (eds.), *Europäisches Arbeitsrecht*, 78.

not be governed by it under the conflict of law rules, as may be the case where the parties make a choice of law, Articles 3 and 8 Rome I-Regulation (see §5 paras. 20–23 above).[8] This would ensure that the obligation to notify the employee also applies where the law of a third country is applicable. However, the comparison of favourability under Article 8 Rome I-Regulation ensures the application of more favourable employee protection rules.

2.   Optional Exceptions

10.   An obligation to inform as an instrument of protection reveals that the legislator did not intend to diminish the variety of forms of work. In order not to disturb the flexibility of the labour market (see Recital 8 WSD), Article 1(2) WSD provides for a number of optional exceptions from the scope of application.

11.   Member States may exclude employment relationships which are for a fixed **total duration** (of up to one month) or a limited number of **working hours** (up to eight hours per week) only, lit. a). While the first exception seems plausible, this is rather different in regard to the second, as it also applies to on-going part-time employment. It does not seem convincing that the requirement of a written statement would be excessively costly or burdensome in this latter case. In addition, the ensuing disadvantage for part-time employment relationships amounts to indirect discrimination against women (§9 para. 17).

12.   A second optional exception concerns causal work or employment 'of a specific nature', lit. b). However, both exceptions presuppose that the non-application is justified on 'objective grounds'. **Casual work** is not to be equated with fixed-term work as the latter is covered by lit. a). It further requires a lack of regularity. Examples could be ancillary work or seasonal work.[9] Activities **of a specific nature** are not rare. As the requirement of 'objective grounds' indicates, the 'specific nature' must be considered with regard to the requirement of a written statement. One could perhaps think of employees in private households (non-professional employer). Or one might consider work in the civil service where confidentiality requirements provide an obstacle to documentation of the conditions of employment (*James Bond*). Article 1(2)(b) WSD cannot justify an exception with regard to a group of employees such as executive staff, though,[10] as the activities of executive employees differ considerably; they can neither be considered 'special' in total nor could such global exception be justified on objective grounds.

---

8   R. Birk, *NZA* 1996, 281, 285; G. Thüsing, *Europäisches Arbeitsrecht*, §8 para. 8.

9   To the same effect R. Wank, *RdA* 1996, 21, 22 (German implementation incompatible with the requirements of the Directive).

10   Differently W. Däubler, 'EG-Arbeitsrecht auf dem Vormarsch', *NZA* 1992, 577, 578; also R. Wank, *RdA* 1996, 21, 22.

III.   OBLIGATION TO PROVIDE INFORMATION

1.   Introduction

13.   In its general rule which is contained in Article 2, the Written Statement Directive requires the employer to give the employee a statement of his conditions of employment. Article 3 determines the means of information (see 2.b) below). Articles 4 and 5 provide for supplementary obligations to include information in the cases of posting of workers and of any subsequent change to working conditions. Sanctions have largely been left open (Articles 6 and 8 WSD) and are thus for Member States to determine, subject to the obligations that follow from the general duty to implement the Directive.

14.   The provisions of the Written Statement Directive thus appear to be clear enough. Issues of interpretation arise from the fact that the legislator has not only set up a catalogue of details about which the employer must inform the employee in Article 2(2) WSD, but has supplemented it by a general clause in paragraph 1 of that Article. How both provisions relate to each other, however, has not been thought through.

2.   The General Information Requirement

a)   Content

15.   Article 2(1) WSD states the basic rule: The employer is obliged to notify the employee of the essential aspects of the employment contract or employment relationship. This general clause is supplemented by a catalogue of minimum data in paragraph 2. The relationship between the general clause and the catalogue is clear from the wording of the provision; the catalogue merely contains minimum data and does not relieve the employer from providing any additional information on essential conditions that are not covered by the catalogue.[11] That makes sense, given that the legislator started from the premise that the variety of forms of work lead to a multiplicity of different conditions of employment. As a matter of policy, the general clause may still be subject to

---

[11]   ECJ Case C-350/99 *Lange* [2001] ECR I-1061 paras. 20–23 (concerning the employer's right to require overtime work); *Bundesarbeitsgericht* (Federal Labour Court, BAG), *BAGE* 100, 225, 232; K. Linde/V. Lindemann, 'Der Nachweis tarifvertraglicher Ausschlussfristen', *NZA* 2003, 649, 650; R. Müller-Glöge, 'Zur Umsetzung der Nachweisrichtlinie in nationales Recht', *RdA* 2001 Special Supplement to issue 5, 46, 47; M. Schmidt, *Arbeitsrecht der EG*, III paras. 306–318; T. Sigeman, *RdA* 2001 Special Supplement to issue t 5, 39, 42. The question had previously been controversial; of the same opinion as here already S. Grundmann, *Europäisches Schuldvertragsrecht*, §3.20 para. 10; differently R. Wank, in P. Hanau/H.-D. Steinmeyer/R. Wank (eds.), *Handbuch des europäischen Arbeits- und Sozialrechts*, §18 para. 24; id., *RdA* 1996, 21, 23.

criticism as it imposes a substantial burden upon the employer (who bears the onus of evaluating which conditions – outside the catalogue – are 'essential') and as it is prone to provoking conflict about whether the obligation has been properly performed. This adds to legal uncertainty and litigation risks – which are difficult to assess for the employee.

16. The determination of which aspects of the employment relation are 'essential' proves difficult. The rephrasing by the Court of Justice is not of much help when it considers that the obligation 'concerns all the aspects of the contract or employment relationship which are, by virtue of their nature, essential elements'.[12] Certainly, the *essentialia negotii* should be considered essential, i.e. the contracting parties, the employee's obligations and the remuneration. Beyond that, the catalogue of Article 2(2) WSD gives some guidelines. The obvious obligations such as the employee's duty of loyalty may be essential but do not have to be specifically emphasised.[13] Drafting practises can also be considered to be indicative, given that the parties, when entering into a written contract, will usually spell out what they consider to be essential. In light of the purpose of the general clause to cover the essential conditions of any new form of work which may come up after the Directive's enactment (para. 15), the catalogue of paragraph 2 can be considered to be exhaustive for the large number of 'normal' employment relationships. It is only with regard to exceptional cases that additional conditions must be included.

17. The **catalogue** of Article 2(2) WSD provides for ten individual aspects (lit. a)-j)) which can be arranged into three groups. The first group (lit. a)-e)) covers such data as will usually be individually determined: the personal data of the parties, the place of work, the particulars of the work assigned to the employee, the commencement of the contract and, where applicable, the duration of the employment relationship. The second group (lit. f)-i)) relates to conditions which will often be covered by law or collective agreement (amount of paid leave, notice periods, remuneration, working time); the information can be supplemented by a reference to law or collective agreement, Article 2(3) WSD (see para. 18 below). The third group, applicable collective agreements (lit. j)), as such merely requires a reference in the contract.

18. Instead of giving the information of lit. f)-i) specifically, the employer may refer to the respective laws, regulations, administrative or statutory provisions, or collective agreements governing those particulars, Article 2(3) WSD. This

---

12 ECJ Case C-350/99 *Lange* [2001] ECR I-1061 para. 21, with a critical case note by H. Reichold, 'Zur Unterrichtungspflicht bezüglich der Regelung von Überstunden in Arbeitsverträgen', *JZ* 2001, 1026, 1027.

13 CFI Case T-333/99 *X* v. *EZB* [2001] ECR II-3021 paras. 81–83.

provision – which is central for the determination of the rights and obligations of the parties – delimits the responsibilities of employer and employee to secure information and makes it easier for the employer to show compliance with the information requirements. It is also an expression of the principle of individual responsibility pursuant to which it is for each private individual to know his rights. It is not the employer's responsibility to teach the employee.[14] Still, the employer's obligation under Article 2(3) WSD is not properly fulfilled by a global reference. Instead, the reference must be individualised for the respective subjects ('particular points').[15]

19. There is controversy, stemming from the UK's implementing measures, about whether the employer's obligation to provide information only relates to **contractual** or also covers **statutory terms and conditions**.[16] The interest behind the debate appears to be the question whether, where the parties have not agreed on any of the 'essential aspects' of the employment contract or relationship, a court is entitled to imply a respective term.[17] The wording of the Directive indicates that it does not distinguish between different sources of the 'essential aspects'. If, pursuant to Article 2(3) WSD, the employer can give the required information by reference to 'the laws, regulations and administrative or statutory provisions or collective agreements governing those particular points', this presupposes that the written statement also covers terms and conditions which do not have a contractual basis. However, the Directive merely creates an obligation for the employer to *inform* about certain matters but not an obligation on both employer and employee to *agree* upon them. If a written statement – correctly or mistakenly – does not give information on one or more of the items of 'essential aspects', nor refers to legislation on this point, then the statement is incorrect (on sanctions, see paras. 33 sqq. below). It cannot be inferred, though, that the parties have failed to reach (a necessary or required) agreement, much less that they have agreed on a specific contractual term.

b)   Means of Information

20. Article 3 WSD – an ill-drafted provision – regulates the 'means of information'; additional requirements follow from the purpose of the obligation to provide information in Article 2 WSD. The provision of Article 3 WSD is not easily understood, probably because the European legislator also wanted to

---

14   K. Riesenhuber, *Europäisches Vertragsrecht*, paras. 492–504 and 902–904.
15   R. Wank, *RdA* 1996, 21, 23.
16   S. Deakin/G. Morris, *Labour Law*, paras. 4.22 sq.
17   C. Barnard, *EC Employment Law*, p. 607, indicates that '[s]ome Continental commentators suggest that the obligation to inform the employee of the essential aspects of the contracts indicates that all these aspects must have been agreed for the relationship to have been formed correctly' (though without providing a reference for that view).

respect the disparate national legal traditions and establish minimum requirements for the form of the written statement.

21. With regard to the **form** of information, Article 3(1) WSD does not necessarily require a separate document if there is a written employment contract, a letter of engagement or one or more written documents such as an exchange of letters. In the latter case, where the information is provided in several documents, one of them must include the details of Article 2(2)(a), (b), (c), (d), (h) and (i) WSD as otherwise a defragmentation would be liable to thwart the objective of the written statement. Where none of these documents has been provided, Article 3(2)(1) WSD requires a separate written statement, signed by the employer (email does not suffice; for some sectors rather misguided from today's perspective). Where the documents of paragraph 1 only cover part of the required information, they must be supplemented by a signed written statement covering the remaining information, Article 3(2)(2) WSD.

22. Irrespective of the form, the written statement must be provided **no later than two months** after commencement of the employment. This time-frame leaves the employer with enough time and is sufficiently close to the time of the formation of the contract for the employee to check its accuracy. In line with its purpose, the written statement must be provided **spontaneously**, without any request being made from the employee (which the employee might hesitate to make).[18] Other time limits apply in special circumstances: Where the employment relationship comes to an end before the two-month period has expired, the written statement is to be provided upon the termination at the employment relationship.[19] Where an employee is required to work in a country other than the Member State whose law governs the employment relationship, the written statement must be 'in his possession before his departure', Article 4(1) WSD (see also paras. 26–29 below). Information about any **change** to the essential conditions of employment must be provided 'at the earliest opportunity and not later than one month after the date of [their] entry into effect', Article 5 WSD.

23. The directive does not include any requirements regarding the **wording or arrangement** of the written statement. They follow from the purpose of the obligation to provide information about the 'essential' conditions. The written statement must be drafted and arranged in a clear and comprehensible manner (principle of transparency). The essential information must not be obscured by an excess of details.

---

[18] K. Riesenhuber, *Festschrift für Bezzenberger,* 741; id., *Europäisches Vertragsrecht,* para. 515.
[19] For a different view see B. Friese, in *EAS,* B 3050 para. 50 (see note 131).

24. Article 3 WSD again raises the issue of minimum contents of the written statement that has already been addressed in the discussion of Article 2 WSD. Both paragraphs of Article 3 only refer to the catalogue in Article 2(2) WSD and not to the general clause. This is, however, a mere drafting error that can be explained from the legislative history. In other words, information on essential aspects of the employment relationship (Article 2(1)), which is not covered by the catalogue in Article 2(2) WSD, should be provided in the form and within the time limits of Article 3 WSD.

3. Special Obligations to Provide Information

25. The Directive requires a special written statement where an employee is obliged to work in another country, or where the essential conditions of employment have changed.

a) Posting of Employees ('Expatriate Employees')

26. Article 4 WSD applies in certain cases of posting of workers (see also §6 on the Posting of Workers Directive): Where the employee is required to work in a country other than the Member State whose law governs the employment contract (paragraph 1) for more than one month (paragraph 3).

27. The law applicable to the employment contract is determined by Article 8 Rome I-Regulation (see in detail §5 paras. 13–19). Where the parties have not made a choice of law, this will normally be the law of the country of the habitual place of work or, in the absence of a habitual place of work, the law of the country where the business through which the employee was engaged is located, and in exceptional cases the law of the country with which the contract as a whole is more closely connected. A temporary posting of employees does not change the applicable law. Yet, overriding mandatory provisions of the host country may, under certain conditions, also be extended to posted workers (see in detail §5 paras. 24–26). Furthermore, the Posting of Workers Directive provides for the extension of protective rules of the host Member State to posted workers. At the same time, however, both the Posting of Workers Directive (§6 para. 19) and the freedom to provide services (§3 paras. 73 sq.) limit the possibilities of extending protective rules of the host Member State to posted workers. The Court of Justice has considered the extension of the obligation to provide information on the employment conditions under the law of the host Member State to posted workers to be incompatible with both the Posting of Workers Directive and freedom to provide services.[20] The obligation to provide information on employment conditions is not part of the 'hard core' of protective rules of

---

[20]   ECJ Case C-319/06 *Commission* v. *Luxembourg* [2008] ECR I-4323.

Article 3(1)(1) PWD. And as the employer already has an obligation to provide a written statement with the relevant information under the applicable law, the extension of essentially the same obligation under the law of the host Member State would lead to a double burden with no additional protection for the employee and would thus be disproportionate.

28. As regards posting of workers, Article 4(1) WSD – systematically a supplementation of Article 2(1) and (2) WSD – provides for additional **minimum data** to be provided with the written statement. Again, the catalogue is not exhaustive ('at least'). The written statement must provide information on: (a) the duration of the employment abroad; (b) the currency to be used for the payment of remuneration; (c) the benefits in cash or in kind attendant on the employment abroad (e.g. a separation allowance, accommodation or flights home); (d) the conditions governing the employee's repatriation. The information required under lit. b) and c) may, again, be supplemented by a reference to the applicable law or collective agreement governing those particular issues, Article 4(2) WSD.

29. In the case of a posting of employees, the written statement – including the conditions of employment of both Article 2(1) and (2) and Article 4(1) (Article 4(1) refers to Article 3(1) which again refers to Article 2!) – must be provided so as to be in the possession of the employee **before his departure**.

b)   Change of Conditions

30. If the written statement is to provide the employee with reliable information, it follows that it needs to be amended when the conditions of employment change, Article 4 WSD. The written statement is to be given 'at the earliest opportunity not later than a month after the date of entry into effect of the change in question'.

31. The wording of Article 5 WSD only refers to a change in the details enumerated in Article 4(2) WSD (likewise Article 3(1) and (2) WSD; para. 24 above). This raises the question whether a change in essential conditions outside the catalogue also triggers an obligation to provide information. In light of the purpose of the provision, the question should be answered in the affirmative. The narrow wording of Article 4(2) WSD seems to be due to a drafting error.

32. A written statement is not required where merely the laws, regulations, administrative or statutory provisions or the collective agreements referred to in the written statement pursuant to Articles 2(3), 4(2) WSD have changed, Article 5(2) WSD. This is teleologically sound, given that the Directive considers the employee responsible to inform himself about the laws, collective agreements etc. (para. 18 above). The same applies where a law or collective agreement referred to in the written statement[21] is being replaced by a new law or collective agreement.[22]

4. Sanctions

33. The Written Statement Directive does not contain specific provisions on the effects of a written statement that has been provided or sanctions for the employer's breach of the obligation to provide a written statement. To the contrary, pursuant to Article 6, the Directive expressly 'shall be without prejudice' to the Member States' laws concerning the form of the employment contract or relationship, proof as regards the existence and content of the employment contract or relationship and the relevant procedural rules. Article 8 WSD provides that the Member States' laws shall enable employees who consider themselves wronged by a failure to comply with the obligation to provide a written statement to pursue their claims by judicial process; however, Article 8 does not provide for sanctions in substantive law either, but merely expresses the character of the obligation to provide a written statement as an individual right of the employee. This is not as such a deficit of the Directive, but is rather a characteristic of the legal instrument of a 'directive', for the issue of sanctions often determines the legal nature of the rights and obligations. Consequently, it is of central importance to the Member States to make this determination for themselves, so as to be able to properly implement the requirements of the Directive.

34. As we have already discussed earlier (§1 paras. 65 sq. above), the duty to implement the Directive entails a framework of further obligations that is also relevant for the design of legal consequences of performance or breach of obligations determined by the Directive. Pursuant to the principle of equivalence, the Member States must ensure that rights and obligations determined by EU law will be enforced under conditions equivalent to those applicable to rights under domestic law of a similar nature. Pursuant to the principle of effectiveness, the Member States must ensure that rights and obligations determined by EU law remain effective in practice.

a) Effects of a Written Statement Provided by the Employer

35. These implementation duties, first, apply with regard to the effects of a written statement provided by the employer. If one of its purposes is to assure the employee of his rights, then he must be able to use the written statement as proof

---

[21] This requirement had not been fulfilled in BAG, NZA 2004, 102, 104.
[22] For a different perspective see B. Friese, in *EAS,* B 3050 para. 56.

in judicial proceedings. The Directive does not determine the legal nature and weight to be attributed to the written statement in judicial proceedings; it does not require a specific rule of evidence such as a reversal of the burden of proof or *prima facie* evidence. But if follows from the principle of equivalence, that national law must give the written statement referred to in Article 2(1) 'such evidential weight as to allow it to serve as factual proof of the essential aspects of the contract of employment or employment relationship, enjoying such presumption as to its correctness as would attach, in domestic law, to any similar document drawn up by the employer and communicated to the employee'.[23] Since the Directive does not itself lay down any rules of proof or procedure (Article 6 indents 2, 3 (para. 33)), it does not require national law to consider the written statement as full and irrefutable proof of the correctness of its contents. The employer may, under national law, therefore be allowed to bring any evidence to the contrary by showing that the information in the written statement is incorrect.[24] As the written statement unilaterally serves the protection of the employee, the Directive does not require that the *employer* must be able to rely upon the notification in judicial proceedings. More generally, on these purposive considerations, it would require a specific justification (e.g. in contract law) for the employee to be bound by the written statement (be that in the form of a contractual obligation or in the form of an onus of proof).[25]

b)   Sanctions for a Failure to Provide a Written Statement

36.   The duty to implement also provides for a framework of sanctions for non-performance of the obligation to provide a written statement. In any case, national law may not provide that conditions favourable to the employee would be ineffective if they were not contained in the written statement; that would be incompatible with the purpose of the Directive.[26] It would seem obvious that a failure to provide a written statement should lead to consequences in judicial proceedings, be that in the form of an aggravation of the employer's burden of proof or an alleviation of the employee's burden of proof. Again, the details of such procedural consequences cannot be determined by the Directive, Article 6 indents 2 and 3 WSD. 'Where an employer fails to comply with his obligation under the [Written Statement] Directive to provide information, the Directive does not require the national court to apply, or refrain from applying, principles of national law under which the proper taking of evidence is deemed to have been obstructed where a party to the proceedings has not complied with his legal obligations to

---

23   ECJ Joined Cases C-253/96 to C-258/96 *Kampelmann* [1997] ECR I-6907 para. 33.
24   ECJ Joined Cases C-253/96 to C-258/96 *Kampelmann* [1997] ECR I-6907 paras. 32–34.
25   On the binding effect upon the employee, see J. Kenner, *ILJ* 28 (1999), 205, 207–213.
26   ECJ Case C-350/99 *Lange* [2001] ECR I-1061 paras. 27 sq.

provide information'[27].[28] A practical difficulty will be to ensure that the employer provides the written statement *spontaneously.* Private law sanctions, such as a right to specific performance or damages, will arguably not be sufficient for that purpose.

5. Enforcement

37. The law of the Member States must enable employees to pursue the rights determined by the Directive in court, Article 8(1) WSD. It may provide that access to judicial proceedings is subject to a failure of the employer to provide the written statement within a period of 15 days upon the employee's request, Article 8(2) subparagraph 1 WSD. On teleological considerations, this latter formality does not apply to the written statement for expatriate employees or for employees with a temporary employment relationship or for employees not covered by a collective agreement relating to the employment relationship, Article 8(2)(2) WSD.[29]

IV. IMPLEMENTATION

38. **Germany** has implemented the Written Statement Directive by the Written Statement Law (*Nachweisgesetz,* NachwG)[30] after a delay of three years.[31] In regard to the civil service – where the state acts as employer – the directive was held to be directly applicable in the interim period after the implementation period had expired.[32] The implementation appears to conform with the requirements of the Directive. The German legislator has only cautiously used the optional exception of Article 1(2) WSD (see §1 NachwG).[33] The obligations to provide a written statement have correctly been implemented in §§2, 3 NachwG.[34]

---

[27] ECJ Case C-350/99 *Lange* [2001] ECR I-1061 paras. 31–35.

[28] Differently M. Schmidt, *Arbeitsrecht der EG,* III para. 325.

[29] See ECJ Case C-306/07 *Andersen* [2008] ECR I-10279 paras. 31–38 and paras. 39–54.

[30] Gesetz über den Nachweis der für ein Arbeitsverhältnis geltenden wesentlichen Bedingungen of 20 July 1995 (BGBl. 1995 I, 946); bilingual German-English version in S. Lingemann/R. v. Steinau-Steinrück/A. Mengel (eds.), *Employment and Labour Law in Germany,* Part II, XXIV.

[31] For a survey on the implementation in Germany, see B. Friese, in *EAS,* B 3050 paras. 6 sq.; R. Müller-Glöge, *RdA* 2001 Special Supplement to issue 5, 46–56; G. Thüsing, *Europäisches Arbeitsrecht,* §8 paras. 16–18; R. Wank, in P. Hanau/H.-D. Steinmeyer/R. Wank (eds.), *Handbuch des europäischen Arbeits- und Sozialrechts,* §18 paras. 9–36; R. Wank, *RdA* 1996, 21–24. On the implementation in Germany, Denmark, Norway, Sweden and the UK T. Sigeman, *RdA* 2001 Special Supplement to issue 5, 39–45; on the implementation in the UK J. Kenner, *ILJ* 28 (1999), 205–231.

[32] ECJ Joined Cases C-253/96 to C-258/96 *Kampelmann* [1997] ECR I-6907 paras. 36–47.

[33] Critically with regard to the original (broader) exceptions R. Wank, *RdA* 1996, 21, 22.

[34] On the initial deficit, see ECJ Joined Cases C-253/96 to C-258/96 *Kampelmann* [1997] ECR I-6907 para. 44.

39. The NachwG did not specify the legal consequences of performance or non-performance of the obligation to provide a written statement, either. While the restraint of the European legislator can be justified as being in line with the nature of a directive (para. 33), the restraint of the German legislator proved to be rather ill-advised, leading to considerable legal uncertainty, particularly since similar obligations had hitherto been unknown in German civil law or civil procedure.[35] The issue of legal consequences was thus subject to extensive debate in academic writing and judicial decisions. As the law now stands,[36] an employee can invoke the written statement in court proceedings in order to prove the agreement; whether this will lead to a reversal of the burden of proof or only amounts to (weaker) *prima facie* evidence is controversial.[37] If the employer does not (fully and correctly) notify the employee of the conditions of employment, this will not lead to invalidity for lack of form under the Civil Code (§125 BGB).[38] The employer may still rely upon any agreed conditions of employment even if he failed to include them in the written notification; this will not be regarded as an abuse of law *per se*.[39] If the employee relies upon conditions of employment which he cannot prove because they have not been included in the written statement, it is a matter for the courts to take the employer's non-performance into their consideration of part of the evidence.[40] While the Federal Labour Court (*Bundesarbeitsgericht*, BAG) has not accepted a right to damages under tort law (§823(2) BGB), such liability may arise under contract law rules (§280(1) BGB, violation of an ancillary obligation).[41] This can be of practical importance where the notification did not inform the employee about an applicable limitation period of a collective agreement. For the proof of causation that such claim for damages presupposes, the employee may rely upon a presumption that he would have acted upon the information.[42]

---

[35]   To the same effect R. Wank, *RdA* 1996, 21, 24.

[36]   Overview B. Friese, in *EAS*, B 3050 paras. 59–73.

[37]   R. Krause, in *AR-Blattei*, SD 220.2.2 paras. 233–235; U. Preis, *NZA* 1997, 10, 12; C. Bergwitz, 'Beweislast und Nachweisgesetz', *RdA* 1999, 188, 192 sq.; B. Friese, in *EAS*, B 3050 para. 64; R. Müller-Glöge, *RdA* 2001 Special Supplement to issue 5, 46, 51 sq.

[38]   BAG, *AP* BBiG §4 Nr. 1 (under II 2. a).

[39]   BAG, *EzA* NachwG §2 Nr. 4; BAG, *BAGE* 101, 75, 80; BAG, *ZTR* 2003, 87; BAG, *NZA* 2004, 102, 104.

[40]   C. Bergwitz, 'Die Bedeutung des Nachweisgesetzes für die Darlegungs- und Beweislast beim Arbeitsvertrag', *BB* 2001, 2316; id., *RdA* 1999, 188, 193 sq.; R. Birk, *NZA* 1996, 281, 289; K. Franke, 'Bedeutung des Nachweisgesetzes für die Darlegungs- und Beweislast im arbeitsgerichtlichen Verfahren', *DB* 2000, 274–278; H.-W. Friedrich/T. Kloppenburg, 'Vergütungskorrektur und Nachweisrecht', *RdA* 2001, 293, 303 sq.; R. Krause, in *AR-Blattei*, SD 220.2.2 paras. 249–261; R. Müller-Glöge, *RdA* 2001 Special Supplement to issue 5, 46, 52 sq.; U. Preis, *NZA* 1997, 11, 13; R. Richardi, 'Formzwang im Arbeitsverhältnis', *NZA* 2001, 57, 60; R. Schwarze, *ZfA* 1997, 43, 64 sq.

[41]   BAG, *BAGE* 101, 75, 80–83; BAG, *ZTR* 2003, 87; R. Krause, in *AR-Blattei*, SD 220.2.2 para. 262; R. Müller-Glöge, *RdA* 2001 special supplement to issue 5, 46, 53 sq.; U. Preis, *NZA* 1997, 11, 12 sq.; R. Richardi, *NZA* 2001, 57, 60.

[42]   BAG, *BAGE* 101, 75, 81 sq.; critically B. Friese, in *EAS*, B 3050 paras. 70 sq.

40. In the **United Kingdom,** a right to a written statement was introduced as early as 1963. The legislation was repeatedly amended. The Trade Union Reform and Employment Rights Act (TURERA) 1993 (s. 26 with Schedule 4) brought the law in line with the requirements of the Directive. Today, the Employment Rights Act (ERA) 1996[43] (ss. 1 sqq.) is the relevant implementing legislation.[44]

V. THE EXAMPLE OF THE *KAMPELMANN* CASE[45]

41. Mr. Kampelmann was notified in writing by his employer, the Landschaftsverband Lippe-Westfalen ('Landschaftsverband'), of his compensation level and category of activity. Some years later, he applied for promotion to a higher level. The Landschaftsverband refused his application on the ground that the previous assessment of his category of activity had been incorrect and that his work in fact corresponded to a lower category which did not qualify him for a higher compensation level in accordance with the applicable collective agreements. Mr. Kampelmann then applied to the Arbeitsgericht (Labour Court) for a declaration establishing reclassification of his activities at a higher level. This application was dismissed on the ground, essentially, that the applicant had not provided proof that he had the necessary length of service at the required compensation level and category of activity to qualify for advancement to a higher compensation level on the basis of satisfactory service, as sought. The Landschaftsverband's previous classification was considered irrelevant. When Mr. Kampelmann applied to the *Landesarbeitsgericht* (Higher Labour Court, LAG) Hamm, that court stayed the proceedings and referred questions to the Court of Justice concerning the legal consequences of a written statement provided by the employer.

42. At the outset, the Court of Justice considered that the Directive, pursuant to its Article 6, is without prejudice to national laws concerning the burden of proof. While the Directive thus does not explicitly require a sanction in respect of the burden of proof, the question remained whether Article 6 WSD was further intended to delimit the Member States' duty to implement the Directive to the effect that they would, under no circumstances, require such sanction. In light of the purpose of the Directive, the Court gave priority to the general implementation duty over the specific provision of Article 6. The objectives of the Directive could not be effectively achieved if a written statement provided by the employer did not have any relevance in regard of proof. The national courts 'must therefore apply and interpret their national rules on the burden of proof in

---

[43] Available at www.legislation.gov.uk/ukpga/1996/18/contents.
[44] For a survey, see S. Deakin/G. Morris, *Labour Law,* paras. 4.14 sqq.
[45] ECJ Joined Cases C-253/96 to C-258/96 *Kampelmann* [1997] ECR I-6923.

the light of the purpose of the Directive, giving the notification referred to in Article 2(1) such evidential weight as to allow it to serve as factual proof of the essential aspects of the contract of employment or employment relationship, enjoying such presumption as to its correctness as would attach, in domestic law, to any similar document drawn up by the employer and communicated to the employee' (para. 33).

43. In an unusual interplay, the principle of effectiveness thus requires that the written statement may be used for the purpose of proof in judicial proceedings. The principle of equivalence then determines how the written statement may be used: The courts must give it the same evidential weight as they would any similar document drawn up by the employer and communicated to the employee under national law.

CHAPTER 3

WORKERS' SAFETY AND HEALTH

§13. THE SAFETY AND HEALTH FRAMEWORK DIRECTIVE

CONTENT

Bibliography:

R. Birk, 'Die Rahmenrichtlinie über die Sicherheit und den Gesundheitsschutz am Arbeitsplatz – Umorientierung des Arbeitsschutzes und bisherige Umsetzung in den Mitgliedstaaten der Europäischen Union', in R. Anzinger/R. Wank (eds.), *Entwicklungen im Arbeitsrecht und Arbeitsschutzrecht – Festschrift für Otfried Wlotzke* (Munich: C.H.

Beck, 1996), 645–667; H. Brandes, *System des europäischen Arbeitsschutzrechts* (Frankfurt a.M. et al.: Lang, 1999); R. F. Eberlie, 'The New Health and Safety Legislation of the European Community', *ILJ* 19 (1990), 81–97; M. G. Faure/L. Tilindyte, 'Effective Enforcement of Occupational Health and Safety Regulation: An Economic Approach', *ELLJ* 1 (2010), 346–367; V. Howes, 'Workers Involvement in Health and Safety Management and Beyond: The UK Case', *IJCLLIR* 23 (2007), 245–265; W. Kohte, 'Arbeitsschutzrahmenrichtlinie', in H. Oetker/U. Preis (eds.), *Europäisches Arbeits- und Sozialrecht, EAS, part B – Systematische Darstellungen*, loose-leaf (Heidelberg: Forkel, last update: August 1998), B 6100; W. Kohte, 'Der Beitrag der ESC zum europäischen und deutschen Arbeitsschutzrecht', in H. Konzen et al. (eds.), *Festschrift für Rolf Birk* (Tübingen: Mohr Siebeck, 2008), 417–437; W. Kohte, 'Die Umsetzung der Richtlinie 89/391 in den Mitgliedstaaten', *ZIAS* 1999, 85–118; M. Koll, 'Die Beurteilungen von Gefährdungen am Arbeitsplatz und ihre Dokumentation nach der EG-Rahmenrichtlinie Arbeitsschutz', in R. Anzinger/R. Wand (eds.), *Entwicklungen im Arbeitsrecht und Arbeitsschutzrecht – Festschrift für Otfried Wlotzke* (Munich: C.H. Beck, 1996), 701–711; K. Kreizberg, 'Einzelrichtlinien zur Arbeitsschutzrahmenrichtlinie', in H. Oetker/U. Preis (eds.), *Europäisches Arbeits- und Sozialrecht, EAS, part B – Systematische Darstellungen*, loose-leaf (Heidelberg: Forkel, last update: April 2011), B 6200; A. Neal, 'The European Framework Directive on the Health and Safety of Workers: Challenges for the United Kingdom?', *IJCLLIR* 6 (1990), 80–117; R. Opfermann, 'Das EG-Recht und seine Auswirkungen auf das deutsche Arbeitsschutzrecht', in R. Anzinger/R. Wank (eds.), *Entwicklungen im Arbeitsrecht und Arbeitsschutzrecht – Festschrift für Otfried Wlotzke* (Munich: C.H. Beck, 1996), 729–767; R. Wank, 'Technischer Arbeitsschutz in der EU im Überblick', in H. Oetker/U. Preis (eds.), *Europäisches Arbeits- und Sozialrecht, EAS, part B – Systematische Darstellungen*, loose-leaf (Heidelberg: Forkel, last update: May 2009), B 6000; R. Wank/U. Börgmann, *Deutsches und europäisches Arbeitsschutzrecht – eine Darstellung der Bereiche Arbeitsstätten, Geräte- und Anlagensicherheit, Gefahrstoffe und Arbeitsorganisation mit Abdruck der einschlägigen EG-Richtlinien* (Munich: C.H. Beck, 1992); K. Wheat, 'Mental Health in the Workplace (1) – 'Stress' Claims and Workplace Standards and the European Framework Directive on Health and Safety at work', *J.M.H.L.* 11 (2006), 53–65; O. Wlotzke, 'Das neue Arbeitsschutzgesetz zeitgemäßes Grundlagengesetz für den betrieblichen Arbeitsschutz', *NZA* 1996, 1017–1024.

Cases:

ECJ Case 188/84 *Commission* v. *France*, [1986] ECR 419; ECJ Case C-84/94 *United Kingdom* v. *Council* [1996] ECR I-5755 (WTD); ECJ Case C-303/98 *Simap* [2000] ECR I-7963 (WTD); ECJ Case C-241/99 *Confederación Intersindical Galega (CIG)* [2001] ECR I-5139; ECJ Case C-49/00 *Commission* v. *Italy* [2001] ECR I-8575; ECJ Case C-5/00 *Commission* v. *Germany* [2002] ECR I-1305; ECJ Case C-441/01 *Commission* v. *The Netherlands* [2003] ECR I-5463; ECJ Case C-335/02 *Commission* v. *Luxembourg* [2003] ECR I-5531; ECJ Case C-425/01 *Commission* v. *Portugal* [2003] ECR I-6025; ECJ Joined Cases C-397/01 to C-401/01 *Pfeiffer* [2004] ECR I-8835; ECJ Case C-52/04 *Personalrat der Feuerwehr Hamburg* [2005] ECR I-7111; ECJ Case C-132/04 *Commission* v. *Spain* [2006] ECR I-3; ECJ Case C-428/04 *Commission* v. *Austria* [2008] ECR I-3325; ECJ Case C-127/05 *Commission* v. *United Kingdom* [2007] ECR I-4619; ECJ Case C-226/06 *Commission* v. *France* [2008] ECR I-86; ECJ Case C-428/09 *Union syndicale Solidaires Isère* 14 October 2010; ECJ Case C-519/09 *May* 7 April 2011.

I. ISSUES, OVERVIEW, COMPETENCE, REGULATORY CONTEXT

1. 'For the most part, European employment law is industrial safety legislation.'[1] The particular relevance of this field of law lies in its protection of the fundamental value of bodily integrity – safety and health – of workers; it is thus concerned with the protection of a fundamental right.[2] As industrial safety is costly (see also para. 24), it is also of central importance from a competition perspective. National safety and health legislation may impede cross-border transactions (protection of employees as a mandatory requirement of public policy).[3] Approximation of national safety and health legislation eliminates this competition dimension[4] and at the same time counteracts undesirable distortions of competition or a 'race to the bottom' (decreasing standards of protection at the expense of employees; this is sometimes [inappropriately] labelled 'social dumping'). The approximation of national laws in the area of safety and health of workers is fairly broad and detailed and cannot be discussed here in its entirety.[5] Rather than introduce the large number of individual legislative acts, we will focus upon the Safety and Health Framework Directive (SHFD)[6] which provides the central mechanisms of protection and serves as a basis for further special directives. It has aptly been called the '**basic law of industrial safety**' (*Grundgesetz des betrieblichen Arbeitsschutzes*).[7] Apart from that, we will discuss a small number of specific directives which are of considerable practical importance and theoretical interest in the following chapters: The Working Time Directive (§14), the Temporary Employment Safety and Health Directive (§19) as well as the Maternity Protection Directive (§20) and the Young People at Work Directive (§22) (the latter two of which are also characterised by an element of 'social' protection).

2. The **Safety and Health Framework Directive** imposes obligations upon both employers and employees which are aimed at improving safety and health at all workplaces in both the public and private sectors, including also vocational training. The scope of the employer's obligation is determined by a number of general principles – priority of safety and health over economic considerations

---

1   R. Birk, *Festschrift für Wlotzke*, 645, 667 (my translation).
2   Cf. W. Kohte, *Festschrift für Birk*, 417–437.
3   ECJ Case 188/84 *Commission v. France* [1986] ECR 419.
4   For a comparative survey see R. Wank/U. Börgmann, *Deutsches und europäisches Arbeitsschutzrecht*, 149–157.
5   See in more detail R. Wank/U. Börgmann, *Deutsches- und europäisches Arbeitsschutzrecht*; H. Brandes, *System des europäischen Arbeitsschutzrechts*; and the contributions of R. Wank (good survey at *EAS*, B 6000), W. Kohte, K. Kreizberg and N. F. Kollmer in *EAS*, B 6000–6400.
6   Council Directive 89/391/EEC of 12 June 1989 on the introduction of measures to encourage improvements in the safety and health of workers at work, OJ 1989 L 183/1.
7   O. Wlotzke, *NZA* 1990, 417, 419 (my translation); id., *NZA* 1996, 1017, 1024. Approvingly e.g. R. Birk, *Festschrift für Wlotzke*, 645, 662; A. Bücker/K. Feldhoff/W. Kohte, *Vom Arbeitsschutz zur Arbeitsumwelt*, 82; R. Wank/U. Börgmann, *Deutsches- und europäisches Arbeitsschutzrecht*, 87.

and early prevention – as well as a duty to evaluate and react appropriately to risk, a delimitation of grounds for exculpation and a duty to introduce protective and preventive services. There are additional specific requirements for particular emergencies, a duty to maintain certain documentation as well as obligations to inform, instruct and cooperate. The employee also bears a responsibility to take care of his own health and safety and that of persons affected by his acts. The Safety and Health Framework Directive is without prejudice to more specific directives which supplement it.

3.   The **development**[8] of European safety and health legislation, its fundamental rules in the Safety and Health Framework Directive in particular, started with the introduction of a new (then:) Community **competence**: Article 118a EEC (now part of Article 153 TFEU), introduced by the 1987 Single European Act. This provided for a clear Community competence and thus allowed for more dynamic development of the law in this field than was hitherto possible on the basis of Article 100 EEC (today's Article 115 TFEU); see §4 para. 3 above.[9] A central aspect of Article 118a was that it allowed directives to be passed on grounds of social policy (rather than on considerations of internal market). The new competence is also the nucleus for the concept of the working environment (see already §4 para. 17).[10]

4.   The Safety and Health Framework Directive is the centrepiece of European industrial safety legislation. It sets forth the principles and concepts for the whole area of industrial safety. While its official title does not designate the directive as such, it is a '**framework directive**' in substance.[11] Article 16(1) SHFD provides the basis for a number of **individual ('daughter') directives**, particularly in the areas listed (non-exhaustively; '*inter alia*') in the annex.[12] The Framework Directive remains applicable in addition to the individual Directives, except where the latter contain more stringent or more specific provisions, Article 16(3) SHFD.[13] As a consequence, a '**general part**' (constituted by the Framework Directive) and a '**special part**' (constituted by the individual Directives) of

---

[8]   For the recent development see Communication from the Commission to the European Parliament, the Council, the European Economic and Social Committee and the Committee of the Regions – Improving quality and productivity at work: Community strategy 2007–2012 on health and safety at work, COM(2007) 62 final.

[9]   *R. Birk, Festschrift für Wlotzke*, 657; R. F. Eberlie, *ILJ* 19 (1990), 81, 85–91; R. Opfermann, *Festschrift für Wlotzke*, 732–736, 757 sq.; R. Wank, in *EAS*, B 6000 paras. 5–17.

[10]   See ECJ Case C-84/94 *United Kingdom v. Council*, [1996] ECR I-5755 paras. 14 sq. (interpreting the new competition broadly).

[11]   R. Birk, *Festschrift für Wlotzke*, 662; M. Koll, *Festschrift für Wlotzke*, 701.

[12]   'Purely technical adjustments' to the individual directives may be made under the simplified procedure of Article 17 SHFD.

[13]   W. Däubler/M. Kittner/K. Lörcher, *Internationale Arbeitsordnung und Sozialordnung*, 2nd edn. (Cologne: Bund, 1994), 1194.

European industrial safety legislation emerged.[14] The total stock now provides for a '"*corpus Europaeicum*" of industrial safety legislation (...) of enormous breadth and considerable scope'.[15] Individual directives have been enacted on the basis of Article 16(1) SHFD on the following matters:[16]

(1)   workplace,[17]
(2)   work equipment,[18]
(3)   personal protective equipment,[19]
(4)   manual handling of loads,[20]
(5)   display screen equipment,[21]
(6)   carcinogens or mutagens,[22]
(7)   biological agents,[23]
(8)   temporary or mobile construction sites,[24]

---

14   H. Brandes, *System des europäischen Arbeitsschutzrechts*, 95–100, 106–108.

15   R. Birk, *Festschrift für Wlotzke*, 645 (my translation).

16   See in more detail K. Kreizberg, in *EAS*, B 6200; R. Wank, in P. Hanau/H.-D. Steinmeyer/ R. Wank (eds.), *Handbuch des europäischen Arbeits- und Sozialrechts*, §18 para. 442; R. Wank, in *EAS*, B 6000 paras. 24–43 (discussing also the implementation in Germany); R. Opfermann, *Festschrift für Wlotzke*, 759–764 and 764–766.

17   Council Directive 89/654/EEC of 30 November 1989 concerning the minimum safety and health requirements for the workplace (first individual directive within the meaning of Article 16(1) of Directive 89/391/EEC), OJ 1989 L 393/1.

18   Directive 2001/45/EC of the European Parliament and of the Council of 27 June 2001 amending Council Directive 89/655/EEC concerning the minimum safety and health requirements for the use of work equipment by workers at work (second individual Directive within the meaning of Article 16(1) of Directive 89/391/EEC) (Text with EEA relevance), OJ 2001 L 195/46.

19   Council Directive 89/656/EEC of 30 November 1989 on the minimum health and safety requirements for the use by workers of personal protective equipment at the workplace (third individual directive within the meaning of Article 16(1) of Directive 89/391/EEC), OJ 1989 L 393/18; cf. as a technical supplementation Directive 89/686/EWG of the Council of 21 December 1989, OJ 1989 L 399/18 (as repeatedly amended).

20   Council Directive 90/269/EEC of 29 May 1990 on the minimum health and safety requirements for the manual handling of loads where there is a risk particularly of back injury to workers (fourth individual Directive within the meaning of Article 16(1) of Directive 89/391/EEC), OJ 1990 L 156/9.

21   Council Directive 90/270/EEC of 29 May 1990 on the minimum safety and health requirements for work with display screen equipment (Fifth individual Directive within the meaning of article 16(1) of Directive 87/391/EEC), OJ 1990 L 156/14.

22   Directive 2004/37/EC of the European Parliament and of the Council of 29 April 2004 on the protection of workers from the risks related to exposure to carcinogens or mutagens at work (Sixth individual Directive within the meaning of Article 16(1) of Council Directive 89/391/ EEC) (codified version) (Text with EEA relevance), OJ 2004 L 158/50.

23   Directive 2000/54/EC of the European Parliament and of the Council of 18 September 2000 on the protection of workers from risks related to exposure to biological agents at work (seventh individual directive within the meaning of Article 16(1) of Directive 89/391/EEC), OJ 2000 L 262/21.

24   Council Directive 92/57/EEC of 24 June 1992 on the implementation of minimum safety and health requirements at temporary or mobile construction sites (eighth individual Directive within the meaning of Article 16(1) of Directive 89/391/EEC), OJ 1989 L 40/12.

(9)   safety and health signs at work,[25]

(10) pregnancy and maternity protection (§20),

(11) mineral-extracting industries through drilling,[26]

(12) surface and underground mineral-extracting industries,[27]

(13) fishing vessels,[28]

(14) chemical agents,[29]

(15) explosive atmospheres,[30]

(16) physical agents (vibration),[31]

(17) physical agents (noise),[32]

(18) physical agents (electromagnetic fields),[33]

(19) physical agents (artificial optical radiation).[34]

---

[25]   Council Directive 92/58/EEC of 24 June 1992 on the minimum requirements for the provision of safety and/or health signs at work (ninth individual Directive within the meaning of Article 16(1) of Directive 89/391/EEC), OJ 1992 L 245/23.

[26]   Council Directive 92/91/EEC of 3 November 1992 concerning the minimum requirements for improving the safety and health protection of workers in the mineral-extracting industries through drilling (eleventh individual Directive within the meaning of Article 16(1) of Directive 89/391/EEC), OJ 1992 L 348/9.

[27]   Council Directive 92/104/EEC of 3 December 1992 on the minimum requirements for improving the safety and health protection of workers in surface and underground mineral-extracting industries (twelfth individual Directive within the meaning of Article 16(1) of Directive 89/391/EEC), OJ 1992 L 404/10.

[28]   Council Directive 93/103/EC of 23 November 1993 concerning the minimum safety and health requirements for work on board fishing vessels (thirteenth individual Directive within the meaning of Article 16(1) of Directive 89/391/EEC), OJ 1993 L 307/1.

[29]   Council Directive 98/24/EC of 7 April 1998 on the protection of the health and safety of workers from the risks related to chemical agents at work (fourteenth individual Directive within the meaning of Article 16(1) of Directive 89/391/EEC), OJ 1998 L 131/11.

[30]   Directive 1999/92/EC of the European Parliament and of the Council of 16 December 1999 on minimum requirements for improving the safety and health protection of workers potentially at risk from explosive atmospheres (15th individual Directive within the meaning of Article 16(1) of Directive 89/391/EEC), OJ 2000 L 23/57 (*corrigendum* OJ 2000 L 131/11).

[31]   Directive 2002/44/EC of the European Parliament and of the Council of 25 June 2002 on the minimum health and safety requirements regarding the exposure of workers to the risks arising from physical agents (vibration) (sixteenth individual Directive within the meaning of Article 16(1) of Directive 89/391/EEC) – Joint Statement by the European Parliament and the Council, OJ 2002 L 177/13.

[32]   Directive 2003/10/EC of the European Parliament and of the Council of 6 February 2003 on the minimum health and safety requirements regarding the exposure of workers to the risks arising from physical agents (noise) (Seventeenth individual Directive within the meaning of Article 16(1) of Directive 89/391/EEC), OJ 2003 L 42/38.

[33]   Directive 2004/40/EC of the European Parliament and of the Council of 29 April 2004 on the minimum health and safety requirements regarding the exposure of workers to the risks arising from physical agents (electromagnetic fields) (18th individual Directive within the meaning of Article 16(1) of Directive 89/391/EEC), OJ 2004 L 159/1 (*corrigendum* OJ 2004 184/1).

[34]   Directive 2006/25/EC of the European Parliament and of the Council of 5 April 2006 on the minimum health and safety requirements regarding the exposure of workers to risks arising from physical agents (artificial optical radiation) (19th individual Directive within the meaning of Article 16(1) of Directive 89/391/EEC), OJ 2006 114/38.

5. In addition to these individual Directives which are based upon Article 16(1) SHFD, there are a number of other directives that form part of the regulatory context: The Temporary Employment Safety and Health Directive (§19) and the Young People at Work Directive (§22) provide for specific protection for certain groups of workers. The legislator has also based the Working Time Directive (§14) upon health and safety considerations.

II. SCOPE OF APPLICATION

6. Articles 2 and 3 SHFD provide for a broad personal and substantive scope of application.[35]

7. As to **substantive** scope, the Directive applies to all sectors of activity, both public and private, Article 2(1) SHFD.[36] A non-exhaustive list refers to 'industrial, agricultural, commercial, administrative, service, educational, cultural, leisure, etc.' activities. There are only a few exceptions. They apply where characteristics peculiar to specific public service activities (to be determined by the Member States), such as the armed forces or the police, or to certain specific activities in the civil protection services inevitably conflict with the Directive, Article 2(2)(1) SHFD. The Member States enjoy discretion in determining the scope of the exceptions, subject to judicial control by the Court of Justice. The exceptions must not render the intended protection of the Directive 'illusory' (principle of effectiveness, §1 para. 66). The Court has interpreted the exception narrowly and restricted it to 'what is strictly necessary in order to safeguard the interests which it allows the Member States to protect'.[37] It refers to 'certain specific public service activities intended to uphold public order and security, which are essential for the proper functioning of society'.[38] The exception does not exclude whole areas or sectors – such as emergency services *as such* – but rather only *specific activities*.[39] With regard to activities thus excluded, the health and safety of workers must still be 'ensured as far as possible in the light of the objectives', Article 2(2)(2) SHFD.

---

[35] H. Brandes, *System des europäischen Arbeitsschutzrechts*, 100–106; W. Kohte, in *EAS*, B 6100 para. 30; R. Wank/U. Börgmann, *Deutsches- und europäisches Arbeitsschutzrecht*, 88.

[36] A. Neal, *IJCLLIR* 6 (1990), 80, 82.

[37] ECJ Joined Cases C-397/01 to C-401/01 *Pfeiffer* [2004] ECR I-8835 para. 54; Case C-52/04 *Personalrat der Feuerwehr Hamburg* [2005] ECR I-7111 para. 61.

[38] ECJ Case C-303/98 *Simap*, [2000] ECR I-7963 para. 36; Case C-428/09 *Union syndicale Solidaires Isère* 14 October 2010 para. 24. See also ECJ Case C-241/99 *CIG* [2001] ECR I-5139. See also the discussion in M. Schlachter, *Casebook Europäisches Arbeitsrecht*, Case 16.

[39] ECJ Joined Cases C-397/01 to C-401/01 *Pfeiffer* [2004] ECR I-8835 para. 53.

8. The Court's decision in *Pfeiffer*[40] illustrates the Directive's scope of application as well as the interplay between the Framework Directive and the individual Directives. The case concerned maximum working hours within the Working Time Directive (see §14 para. 27). This directive refers to the Safety and Health Framework Directive to determine its scope of application (Article 1(4) WTD). The Court was asked to decide whether the activity of emergency workers, performed as part of emergency medical services, was excluded from the scope of the Directive under Article 2(2) SHFD. The Court answered the question in the negative. It argued that the exception should be narrowly construed and did not exclude civil protection services as such but solely certain specific activities of those services. The exceptions had to be restricted to what was strictly necessary. Other than in the case of civil protection services in a strict sense, the activities of emergency workers such as paramedics and doctors on ambulance crews were largely foreseeable and capable of being planned and organised. The exception thus did not apply on the basis of these teleological considerations.

9. The **personal scope** of application is determined by the terms 'worker' and 'employer'. The definitions in Article 3(a) and (b) SHFD are, however, rather less helpful, given that they are (partially) cross-referential. A **worker** is a person who is employed by an employer, an employer is a person who has an employment relationship with the worker (and has responsibility for the undertaking or establishment). It is unclear whether the term 'worker' should be **autonomously** construed. The rather unhelpful definition which is provided (if it may be called a definition) and the fact that the legislator did not give any substantive clue for the term's construction, e.g. by referring to the definition used for Article 45 TFEU, argue against an autonomous definition. Considerations of the internal market (avoid distortion of competition) and social policy argue in favour of a uniform construction of the personal scope.[41] The wide definition given by the Court in the context of the free movement of workers (§3 paras. 9–12 above) also works well for the present purposes; the form of employment is irrelevant with regard to health and safety.[42] In addition, the Directive provides a framework for the definition in a number of

---

[40] ECJ Joined Cases C-397/01 to C-401/01 *Pfeiffer* [2004] ECR I-8835 paras. 47–63.

[41] W. Kothe, in *EAS*, B 6000 para. 30. See also ECJ Case C-116/06 *Kiiski* [2007] ECR I-7643 paras. 23 sq. (the case concerns the MPD and thus one of the individual directives to the SHFD; here too, the Court assumes an autonomous concept); Case C-337/10 *Neidel* 3 May 2012 paras. 19–26.

[42] ECJ Case C-519/09 *May* 7 April 2011 para. 21; Case C-428/09 *Union syndicale Solidaires Isère* 14 October 2010 paras. 27 sq. See also W. Kothe, in *EAS*, B 6100 para. 31 (arguing for an even wider determination of the concept of worker, relying on considerations of the legislative history); to the same effect O. Wlotzke, *NZA* 1996, 1017, 1019.

provisions: Part-time workers and temporary agency workers[43] are 'workers' within the meaning of the Directive, as are trainees and apprentices,[44] Article 3(a) SHFD. Employees in the **civil services** are also covered, as can be inferred from the provision on the substantive scope of protection (para. 7 above).[45] The single (and rather ill-founded) exception is that for domestic servants.[46]

10. The Directive does not only provide for obligations for the benefit of the employer's *own* workers but also workers from outside undertakings engaged in work in his undertaking whom the employer must adequately inform (para. 35 below).

11. The **employer** is not only characterised by his employment relationship with the employee but also by his responsibility for the undertaking or establishment. This follows, somewhat self-referentially, from the Directive specifically aiming to impose this responsibility upon the employer. At the same time, an ('artificial') assigning of both functions to different persons cannot lead to an exception from the Directive's scope of application. It is part of the Member States' obligation to implement the Directive effectively to ensure that its scope of application may not be circumvented. In line with the purpose of the Directive (protection of health and safety of employees), **small and medium size enterprises** are not excluded from its scope of application. However, the Directive accommodates their interests in some individual respects: in regard to the documentation obligations (Article 9(2) SHFD, para. 26 below), emergency measures (Article 8(1), para. 27 below),[47] protective and preventive services (Article 7(7) SHFD, para. 30), and employee involvement (Article 10(1) SHFD, para. 32 below).[48]

---

[43] B. Gaul/G. Schoenen, 'Aktuelle Aspekte des Rechts der Europäischen Union', AuA 1995, 113, 116; further A. Bücker/K. Feldhoff/W. Kohte, *Vom Arbeitsschutz zur Arbeitsumwelt*, 90 sq. (pointing out, though, that Articles 6(4) and 10(2) SHFD provide for specific rules for the issues involved).

[44] R. Wank/U. Börgmann, *Europäisches Arbeitsschutzrecht*, 88.

[45] ECJ Case C-519/09 *May* 7 April 2011 paras. 21, 24 sq. G. Märtins, 'Arbeitsschutz und Unfallverhütung im öffentlichen Dienst', ZTR 1992, 223, 267. On the direct applicability of the respective directives, see e.g. B. Gaul, 'Praktische Konsequenzen aus der Nichtumsetzung der EU- Arbeitsschutzrichtlinien', *AuR* 1995, 445 sq.

[46] On the background, see W. Kohte, in *EAS*, B 6100 para. 34.

[47] See also ECJ Case C-428/04 *Commission* v. *Austria* [2008] ECR I-3325 paras. 58–67: Article 8(2)(1) SHFD does not allow for a general exception for small or medium-sized undertakings.

[48] A. Neal, *IJCLLIR* 6 (1990), 80, 85.

III. EMPLOYERS' OBLIGATIONS

12. The duties of employers can be divided into three categories: prevention of risks, information and instruction of employees and employee involvement.[49] Underlying these individual duties is the principle of employer responsibility.

1. The Principle of Employer Responsibility

13. Pursuant to the **general rule** of Article 5(1) SHFD, the employer has a duty to ensure the safety and health of workers in every aspect related to work ('principle of responsibility of the employer').[50] The general clause expresses the fundamental importance of health and safety protection and the employer's responsibility, in that it requires the employer to do more than just execute individual duties. In light of the paramount importance of employee health protection and the ever-changing risks and possibilities to prevent those dangers to employees, it does not appear unreasonable to impose such far-reaching and burdensome obligations upon the employer.

14. The Directive merely sets out a framework for the **limits to the employer's responsibility**, Article 5(2)-(4) SHFD. Where the employer uses external protective and preventive services (Article 7 SHFD, para. 30 below) this does not discharge him from his responsibility, Article 5(2) SHFD. Neither can workers' health and safety obligations (Article 13 SHFD, para. 37 below) affect the principle of employer responsibility, Article 5(3) SHFD. This latter aspect should not be incompatible with a national rule of contributory negligence pursuant to which an employee's claim for damages may be reduced where he acted negligently himself, as long as it does not provide for the automatic exclusion of liability. Member States may further provide for an exclusion or limitation of employer responsibility where incidents result from 'unusual and unforeseeable circumstances, beyond the employers' control, or to exceptional events, the consequences of which could not have been avoided despite the exercise of all due care', i.e. in cases of **force majeure**, Article 5(4) SHFD.[51]

15. The Directive does not require Member States to introduce **civil liability** of employers. The principle of employer responsibility may also be sanctioned, e.g. by criminal law, perhaps in combination with compensation based upon taxes or

---

[49]   See also the systematisation by A. Neal, *IJCLLIR* 6 (1990), 80, 84.

[50]   This conforms to the broad interpretation that the Court has given to the term 'health' in Article 118a EG (cf. today's Article 153 AEUV): ECJ Case C-84/94 *United Kingdom* v. *Council* [1996] ECR I-5755 para. 15.

[51]   W. Kohte, in *EAS*, B 6100 para. 24; see also C. Barnard, *EC Employment Law*, 553 (considering a broad construction as 'a more general defence based on proportionality').

insurance.[52] Furthermore, it does not require the introduction of a '**no-fault liability**'. The Court convincingly argued that neither the wording nor the systematic context of paragraphs 2 and 3 demand strict liability, or even the *optional* limitation of responsibility in cases of *force majeure* can justify the reverse argument that the Directive requires strict liability.[53] A clause in the British implementing legislation, pursuant to which the employer had to ensure the health and safety of employees 'so far as is reasonably practicable', thus satisfied the requirements of the Directive.

2. Prevention of Risks

16. The principle of employer responsibility is concretised by individual obligations which are imposed upon him. The central obligation is to **take the measures necessary** to ensure employee health and safety, and is laid down in Article 6(1) SHFD. It includes

–   avoiding occupational risks,
–   information and instruction, and
–   providing appropriate organisations and the necessary means.

The employer must further ensure that the measures taken in the interest of health and safety protection will be adjusted in light of changing circumstances and are aimed at a constant improvement of working conditions. Safety and health protection thus has a *dynamic element* that allows for adaptation over time.[54]

a) General Principles of Prevention

17. The obligation to prevent risks is concretised in the Directive by a list of principles in Article 6(2) SHFD. The primary obligation is to avoid risks (lit. a)) and to combat risks at their source (lit. c)). Risks that cannot be avoided must be evaluated (lit. b)). Dangerous elements must be replaced by non-dangerous or less dangerous ones (lit. f)). Prevention also includes giving appropriate instructions to workers (lit. i)). This must all be continuously updated in line with technical progress (lit. e)).

18. Prevention requires '**adapting work to the individual**' (lit. d)); the French language version is more illustrative: 'adapter le travail à l'homme' (German: '*Berücksichtigung des Faktors "Mensch" bei der Arbeit*'). This applies particularly

---

[52]   Cf. ECJ Case C-127/05 *Commission* v. *United Kingdom* [2007] ECR I-4619.
[53]   ECJ Case C-127/05 *Commission* v. *United Kingdom* [2007] ECR I-4619 paras. 39–51.
[54]   O. Wlotzke, *NZA* 1996, 1017, 1019, 1020; cf. also ECJ Case C-49/00 *Commission* v. *Italy* [2001] ECR I-8575 para. 13.

to workplace design and organisation as well as the choice of work equipment and working and production methods. Monotonous work or work at a predetermined work-rate should be alleviated and its negative effect upon health should be reduced.

19. In sum, prevention should aim to achieve a 'coherent overall prevention policy which covers technology, organization of work, working conditions, social relationships and the influence of factors related to the working environment' (lit. g)). The employer is thus obliged to pursue a systematic – one could say: 'holistic' – approach. He should give collective protective measures priority over individual protective measures (lit. h)).

b)   Specific Risk Prevention Obligations

20.   Article 6(3) and other provisions further concretise specific obligations to prevent risks.

aa)   RISK EVALUATION

21.   These obligations first include risk evaluation, Articles 6(3)(a) and 9(1)(a) SHFD. The employer must **evaluate** the risks to employee health and safety and must document such evaluation. This evaluation concerns – in a non-exhaustive list –[55] '*inter alia*' the choice of work equipment, the chemical substances or preparations used and the fitting-out of work places. It already follows from Article 6(1) (and also Article 9(1)(b)) SHFD that the employer must also **act** upon his findings and draw appropriate conclusions. Paragraph 3 further concretises this obligation: To the extent necessary, the employer must improve the level of protection afforded to workers. The concept of a 'coherent overall prevention policy' of paragraph 2(g) (para. 19 above) recurs since individual preventive measures must be 'integrated into all the activities of the undertaking and/or establishment and at all hierarchical levels', paragraph 3(a) indent 2.

bb)   CHOICE, INSTRUCTION AND TRAINING OF WORKERS

22.   Other obligations concern choice and instruction of workers. The employer must take the worker's *capabilities* as regards safety and health into consideration when he **assigns a task** to a worker, Article 6(3)(b) SHFD. He must further ensure that only workers who have received **adequate instruction** have access to areas with serious and specific dangers, lit. d).

---

[55]   ECJ Case C-49/00 *Commission* v. *Italy* [2001] ECR I-8575 paras. 12 sq.

23.   Beyond that, the employer is obliged to ensure that employees receive adequate **safety and health training**: at the beginning of the employment or in connection with a transfer or change of job as well as when new work equipment or technology is introduced.[56] Such training must be specifically tailored to the employee's workstation or job. It must be adapted to take account of new or changed risks and must be repeated if necessary. Training should be broadly construed and may include practical instruction as well as continued education. Training 'may not be at the workers' expense or at that of the workers 'representatives' (no disadvantage and no costs) and must take place during working hours, Article 12(4) SHFD; this is in line with the respective spheres of responsibility. When the employer is further held responsible for the qualification of employees from outside undertakings or establishments engaged in work in his undertaking or establishment (Article 12(2) SHFD; e.g. cleaning or maintenance personnel), this concerns, on the one hand, protection of those employees against specific risks, and on the other, protection of the employer's own employees against improper behaviour of the former.

c)   Costs

24.   Measures related to safety, hygiene and health at work may, under no circumstances, require that workers make a financial contribution, Article 6(5) SHFD.[57] The provision is only negative. It thus leaves it to the Member States to allocate costs between the employer, another private party or the State. Costs will typically fall to the employer as part of his entrepreneurial sphere of responsibility. Article 6(5) SHFD can also be understood as an expression of the principle that improvement of workers' safety, health and hygiene should not be subordinated to purely economic considerations, Recital 13 SHFD.

3.   *Documentation*

25.   The obligation to document certain health and safety measures pursuant to Article 9 SHFD is an innovative supplementary instrument of protection, which is intended to reinforce prevention.[58] The employer must be in possession of an **assessment of risks** to health and safety at work,[59] keep a **list of** the more serious occupational **accidents** and draw up reports on occupational accidents suffered by his workers for the responsible authorities. Such documentation will assist the workers 'representatives who have specific responsibility for the worker health

---

[56]   W. Kohte, in *EAS*, B 6100 para. 92.
[57]   For a critical perspective, see A. Neal, *IJCLLIR* 6 (1990), 80, 85. On the protection of small and medium-sized undertakings, see para. 11 above.
[58]   See in detail M. Koll, *Festschrift für Wlotzke*, 701–711; O. Wlotzke, *NZA* 1996, 1017, 1020.
[59]   Cf. ECJ Case C-5/00 *Commission* v. *Germany* [2002] ECR I-1305 paras. 25 sq.

and safety (Article 3(c) SHFD; see para. 34 below), the employees' representatives (see Article 10(3)(a) SHFD) and the responsible authorities as a basis for the performance of their work.

26. It is for the Member States to determine the details of the documentation obligations for the different categories of undertakings 'in the light of the nature of the activities and size of the undertakings'. They may not, however, entirely exempt small enterprises from these duties.[60]

4. First Aid, Fire-Fighting and Evacuation of Workers

27. Article 8 SHFD provides for special organisational duties and rights of employees in cases of emergencies[61] with regard to first aid, fire-fighting and evacuation. The employer should take the necessary steps so as to be prepared for emergencies, particularly by drawing up an evacuation plan and establishing contact with external services such as ambulance and fire-fighters. In addition, an employer must designate the workers required to implement first aid, fire-fighting and evacuation procedures, and ensure that they receive adequate equipment and training, Articles 8(2), 12(3) SHFD.[62]

28. In an emergency, the employer must **inform the workers** who are exposed to serious and imminent danger as soon as possible of the risks involved and the steps to be taken as regards protection, Article 8(3) SHFD. He has to **take action** and give instructions to enable workers to stop work and leave the workplace and proceed to a place of safety in an event of serious, imminent and unavoidable danger. The employer must refrain from asking workers to resume work while the danger is on-going. Workers who leave their workplace in the event of serious, imminent and unavoidable danger may not be placed at a disadvantage because of their action, Article 8(4) SHFD.

29. Similar rules apply where employees, in a situation of serious and imminent danger to their own safety or that of other persons, **act on their own authority** where the immediate superior cannot be contacted, Article 8(5) SHFD. Again, their actions shall not place them at any disadvantage, unless they acted carelessly or negligently. This latter restriction aims to prevent the abuse of emergency mechanisms.

---

[60] ECJ Case C-5/00 *Commission* v. *Germany* [2002] ECR I-1305 paras. 35–37.

[61] R. Wank/U. Börgmann, *Europäisches Arbeitsschutzrecht,* 91 sq.

[62] See also ECJ Case C-428/04 *Commission* v. *Austria* [2008] ECR I-3325 paras. 58–67: Article 8(2)(1) SHFD is mandatory and does not allow for an exception for small or medium-sized undertakings.

5. Protective and Preventive Services

30. An employer's organisational obligations are supplemented by the obligation to designate workers or enlist external persons for protective and preventive services, Article 7 SHFD.[63] Their task is to carry out activities related to the protection and prevention of occupational risks for the undertaking or establishment, Article 7(1) SHFD. The employer should primarily designate competent personnel from his workforce for such protective and preventive services; (only) if such protective and preventive services cannot be organised within the undertaking or establishment for lack of competent personnel,[64] the employer must[65] enlist competent external services or persons, Article 7(3) SHFD (he owes a special obligation to inform such outside personnel, Article 7(4)). Member States may – 'in the light of the nature of the activities and the size of the undertaking' – provide that the employer himself may take responsibility for the preventive and protective measures, Article 7(7) SHFD.

31. The persons in charge of the protective and preventive services must have the capabilities and means necessary to perform their tasks, Article 7(5) SHFD; details are left to be determined by the Member States, Article 7(8) SHFD.[66] Workers who perform this function are entitled to appropriate training, Article 12(3) SHFD. They should be allowed adequate time to enable them to fulfil their obligations and may not be placed at a disadvantage because of their activities, Article 7(2) SHFD. The provision of Article 6(5) SHFD on costs also applies here (para. 24 above).

6. Employee Involvement: Information and Consultation

32. The employer's substantive obligations are supplemented by provisions on employee involvement (see also §28 below): information (Article 10 SHFD) and consultation (Article 11 SHFD).[67] '[T] the 11th and 12th recitals in the preamble to the Directive show that the objectives of the latter include a dialogue and balanced participation between employers and workers with a view to adopting

---

[63]   In greater detail, see W. Kohte, in *EAS*, B 6100 paras. 69–75.
[64]   This constitutes a hierarchy established by the Directive, ECJ Case C-441/01 *Commission v. The Netherland* [2003] ECR I-5463; Case C-428/04 *Commission v. Austria* [2008] ECR I-3325 paras. 49–54.
[65]   ECJ Case C-49/00 *Commission v. Italy* [2001] ECR I-8575 para. 23: not only optional!
[66]   This determination is not only an option open to the Member States but their duty under the Directive, they may not delegate it to the employer; ECJ Case C-49/00 *Commission v. Italy* [2001] ECR I-8575 paras. 35–37.
[67]   For a comparative discussion, see V. Howes, *IJCLLIR* 23 (2007), 245–265.

the measures necessary for the protection of workers against accidents at work and occupational diseases'.[68]

33. The **workers and/or their representatives** receive information on risks and the measures taken for their prevention, Article 10(1) SHFD. The employer consults the workers and/or their representatives and allows them to participate in discussions about all questions relating to safety and health at work, Article 11(1) SHFD, as well as in the planning and introduction of new technologies, Article 6(3)(c) SHFD. 'Consultation' comprises the right to be heard, the right to make proposals and 'balanced participation in accordance with national laws and/or practices'.[69]

34. The **workers and workers' representatives with specific responsibility** for worker health and safety (Article 3(c) SHFD)[70] also have access to certain documents which must be drawn up by the employer (para. 25 above), Article 10(3) SHFD. They have a specific right to be consulted (or involved) in certain health and safety issues, Article 11(2) SHFD, and to submit proposals to the employer with regard to the prevention of risks or the removal of sources of danger, Article 11(3) SHFD. The representatives must get adequate time off work without loss of pay, Article 11(5) SHFD, and may not be placed at a disadvantage because of their activities, Article 11(4) SHFD. Where the employer enlists **external services** or persons to provide protective and preventive services (para. 30 above), he must give them the relevant information, Articles 7(4) and 10(2) SHFD.

35. The employer is further obliged to give adequate information about health and safety issues as well as emergency measures to the employers of workers from any **outside undertakings or establishments** engaged in work in his undertaking or establishment. This information must be passed on to the workers in question, Article 10(2) SHFD.

36. The Directive finally addresses the issue of an **appeal to the competent authority** (*whistleblowing*) in the context of employee involvement, Article 11(6) SHFD. The employees and their representatives are entitled – in accordance with national laws and practices –[71] to appeal to the authorities responsible for health and safety protection at work when they consider that the measures taken and the means employed by the employer are inadequate to ensure health and safety

---

68 ECJ Case C-428/04 *Commission* v. *Austria* [2008] ECR I-3325 para. 74; Case C-441/01 *Commission* v. *The Netherlands* [2003] ECR I-5463 para. 39.
69 Critically R. F. Eberlie, *ILJ* 19 (1990), 81, 96 (too vague).
70 Their determination – by way of selection, election or appointment or the like – is a matter of the national law of the Member States, ECJ Case C-425/01 *Commission* v. *Portugal* [2003] ECR I-6025.
71 R. Wank/U. Börgmann, *Deutsches und europäisches Arbeitsschutzrecht*, 142 sq.

at work. Workers' representatives must be given an opportunity to submit their observations during inspection visits by the competent authorities, i.e. an opportunity to attend such visits and to speak to the representatives of the authorities. It is a matter for the laws of the Member States to determine – within the limits of their implementation obligations (§1 paras. 65 sq.) – the details of a right to appeal to the competent authorities. Member States may, for example, provide for a principle of proportionality (appeal to authority only after the employer has been informed without success; cf. Article 13(2)(d) SHFD).[72] While this is not specifically mentioned in the Directive, the right to appeal to the competent authorities also implies a right not to be placed at a disadvantage because of such an appeal.

IV. WORKERS' OBLIGATIONS

37.   Effective protection against health and safety risks will often also presuppose the cooperation and active participation of the employee. The Directive therefore also provides for workers' responsibilities. While health and safety at work still remains the employer's responsibility (Article 5(1) SHFD), the Directive imposes the benchmark of a **responsible employee** and cooperation between employer and employee by introducing workers' obligations in Article 13.[73]

38.   Pursuant to the **general clause** of Article 13(1) SHFD, every employee is responsible to take care, as far as possible, of his own safety and health and that of other persons affected by his acts or omissions at work. This responsibility is 'in accordance with [the worker's] training and the instructions given by his employer'. Such a qualification has three inferences. First, this qualification re-emphasises the primary responsibility of the employer (para. 13 above) who must also give instruction and provide for training (para. 23 above). Secondly, instruction and training also determine the scope of the employee's obligations. Finally, this does not mean that the worker only had to do what he was instructed to do. Just as 'work to rule' does not satisfy the obligation to work under the employment contract, instruction and training do not strictly limit the employee's responsibility (cf. also Article 8(5)(2) SHFD).

39.   The **individual obligations** of the employee under Article 13(2) SHFD fall into three groups: The obligation to minimise risks by correct use of the elements

---

[72]   O. Wlotzke, *RdA* 1992, 85, 95; id. *NZA* 1996, 1017, 1022.
[73]   A. Bücker/K. Feldhoff/W. Kohte, *Vom Arbeitsschutz zur Arbeitsumwelt*, 83; W. Kohte, in *EAS*, B 6100 para. 84 (speaking of a cooperative – as opposed to a patriarchic – character of EU safety and health legislation); see also O. Wlotzke, *NZA* 1996, 1017, 1022. Critically on the comparatively low level of burden placed on the employee A. Neal, *IJCLLIR* 6 (1990), 80, 82 sq.

of the workplace (lit. a)-c)), the obligation to give notice about any dangerous situation (lit. d) and obligations to cooperate with the employer and health and safety worker representatives (lit. e), f)).

40. These obligations are imposed primarily upon the employee, but not exclusively, in his own interest. They also serve the protection of fellow employees, the employer (who may equally be exposed to workplace risks and who also has an interest in avoiding risks in light of his own obligations; see the case of Article 13(2)(d)) and any other persons who may be affected (visitors, passers-by). The Directive does not require the imposition of any liability towards third persons or the employer upon the employee (see also para. 15). The national law of the Member States may sanction the employee's non-performance with disadvantages such as a loss or reduction of his rights.

41. The workers' obligations are an essential part of the system of industrial safety under the Directive: The intended protection cannot be achieved effectively without worker participation and cooperation. Consequently, Member States cannot rely upon the minimum standard clause of Article 1(3) SHFD to reduce the workers' obligations; this would not lead to a 'more favourable protection'.

V. SANCTIONS

42. The Directive does not specify any sanctions for non-performance of its obligations but leaves these for the Member States to determine – in the framework of their implementation obligations, Article 4 SHFD (see §1 paras. 65 sq. above; see also para. 15). This leaves room for the Member States to dovetail the Directive's requirements into their national employment law, the law of employment contracts and employee involvement. Economic analysis suggests that Member States may not rely exclusively upon private enforcement but will need to employ a mixture of public enforcement measures (as well) which should encompass proactive as well as reactive inspections.[74]

VI. IMPLEMENTATION

43. The Directive had to be implemented into national law by 31 December 1992, Article 18(1) SHFD. In **Germany**, implementation was considerably

---

[74]   M. G. Faure/L. Tilindyte, *ELLJ* 1 (2010), 346–367.

delayed, but eventually came about with the 'Law on the Implementation of the Safety and Health Framework Directive and other Directives on Industrial Safety' (*Gesetz zur Umsetzung der EG-Rahmenrichtlinie Arbeitsschutz und weiterer Arbeitsschutzrichtlinien*)[75] which entered into force on 21 August 1996.[76] Article 1 contains the Law on Safety and Health at Work (*Arbeitsschutzgesetz, ArbSchG*)[77], which basically provides for a 'one to one' transposition of the Directive.[78] The Commission successfully challenged the exemption of small size enterprises from the obligation to provide documentation which was provided for in the original Act.[79]

44. Several **other Member States**[80] also did not implement the Directive in time or correctly.[81] In the **United Kingdom**, the Directive was implemented by the Health and Safety at Work Act 1974[82] and the Management of Health and Safety at Work Regulations 1999.[83]

---

75   BGBl. 1996 I, 1246.

76   On the implementation in Germany, see R. Wank, in P. Hanau/H.-D. Steinmeyer/R. Wank (eds.), *Handbuch des europäischen Arbeits- und Sozialrechts*, §18 paras. 451–454; M. Fuchs, in M. Fuchs/F. Marhold, *Europäisches Arbeitsrecht*, 394 sq.; O. Wlotzke, *NZA* 1996, 1017–1024; R. Opfermann, *Festschrift für Wlotzke*, 729–767.

77   Gesetz über die Durchführung von Maßnahmen des Arbeitsschutzes zur Verbesserung der Sicherheit und des Gesundheitsschutzes der Beschäftigten bei der Arbeit of 7 August 1996, also available at www.gesetze-im-internet.de/arbschg/index.html.

78   R. Wank, in P. Hanau/H.-D. Steinmeyer/R. Wank (eds.), *Handbuch des europäischen Arbeits- und Sozialrechts*, §18 para. 452; O. Wlotzke, *NZA* 1996, 1017–1024.

79   ECJ Case C-5/00 *Commission v. Germany* [2002] ECR I-1305 (on the documentation; see para. 26 above).

80   On the implementation in other Member States, see R. Birk, *Festschrift für Wlotzke*, 645 sqq.; W. Kohte, *ZIAS* 1999, 95–118.

81   ECJ Case C-49/00 *Commission v. Italy* [2001] ECR I-8575; Case C-441/01 *Commission v. The Netherlands* [2003] ECR I-5463; Case C-335/02 *Commission v. Luxembourg* [2003] ECR I-5531; Case C-132/04 *Commission v. Spain* [2006] ECR I-3. See also the – unfounded – challenge of the implementation in Portugal, ECJ Case C-425/01 *Commission v. Portugal* [2003] ECR I-6025; ECJ Case C-428/04 *Commission v. Austria* [2008] ECR I-3325; ECJ Case C-226/06 *Commission v. France* [2008] ECR I-86.

82   Available at www.legislation.gov.uk/ukpga/1974/37/contents. See also ECJ Case C-127/05 *Commission v. United Kingdom* [2007] ECR I-4619 and para. 15 above.

83   SI 1999/3242; available at www.legislation.gov.uk/uksi/1999/3242/contents/made. For a survey, see S. Deakin/G. Morris, *Labour Law*, para. 4.95.

§14. THE WORKING TIME DIRECTIVE

CONTENT

Bibliography:

C. Abeln/M. Repey, 'Die Revision der Arbeitszeitrichtlinie und der Bereitschaftsdienst der Ärzte', *AuR* 2005, 20–22; N. Addnett/S. Hardy, 'Reviewing the Working Time Directive: Rationale, Implementation and Case Law', *IRJ* 32 (2001), 114–125; R. Anzinger, 'Das Bereithalten zur Arbeit am Beispiel des ärztlichen Bereitschaftsdienstes – ¼ kann denn Schlafen Arbeit sein?', in W. Kohte/H.-J. Dörner/R. Anzinger (eds.), *Arbeitsrecht im sozialen Dialog – Festschrift für Hellmut Wißmann* (Munich: C.H. Beck, 2005), 3–14; W. Balze, 'Arbeitszeit und Urlaub', in H. Oetker/U. Preis (eds.), *Europäisches Arbeits- und Sozialrecht, EAS, part B – Systematische Darstellungen,* loose-leaf (Heidelberg: Forkel, last update: February 2011), B 3100; W. Balze, 'Die Richtlinie über die Arbeitszeitgestaltung', *EuZW* 1994, 205–208; C. Barnard/S. Deakin/R. Hobbs, 'Opting Out of the 48 Hour-Week: Employer Necessity or Individual Choice? An Empirical Study of the Operation of Article 18(1)(b) of the Working Time Directive in the UK', *ILJ* 32 (2003), 223–252; A. L. Bogg, 'The Right to Paid Annual Leave in the Court of Justice: the Eclipse of Functionalism', *E.L. Rev.* 12 (2006), 892–905; M. Diller, 'Fortschritt oder Rückschritt? – das neue Arbeitszeitrecht', *NJW* 1994, 2726–2728; J. Fairhurst, 'SIMAP – Interpreting the Working Time Directive', *ILJ* 30 (2001), 236–243; M. Fenski, 'Urlaubsrecht im Umbruch? – Urlaub im Spannungsfeld zwischen internationalem, europäischem und deutschem Recht', *DB* 2007, 686–691; B. Fitzpatrick, 'Straining the Definition of Health and Safety?', *ILJ* 26 (1997), 115–135; R. Glaser/H. Lüders, '§7 BUrlG auf dem Prüfstand des EuGH', *BB* 2006, 2690–2694; M. Gray, 'A Recalcitrant Partner: The UK Reaction to the Working Time Directive', *YEL* 17 (1998), 323–362; L. Hey/P. Cooke, 'Implementation of the Working Time Directive', *C.C.L.R.* 9 (1998), 164–169; R. Hornung-Draus, 'Zur Revision der Arbeitszeitrichtlinie – die Position der Arbeitgeber', *EuroAS* 2004, 107–108; J. Kenner, 'Re-evaluating the Concept of Working Time: An Analysis of Recent Case Law', *IRJ* 35 (2004), 588–601; K. Lörcher, 'Die Arbeitszeitrichtlinie der EU', *AuR* 1994, 49–51; K. Lörcher, 'Rückschritte im Sozialbereich – Ein neuer Kommissionsansatz? – Zum Vorschlag der Kommission zur Änderung der Arbeitszeitrichtlinie 2003/88/EG', *EuroAS* 2005, 16–18; G. Moffat, 'Competition, Competitiveness and Re-Regulating the Labour Market: The Working Time Directive', *Nott.L.J.* 6 (1997), 45–68; F. v. Prondzynski, 'Council Directive 93/104/EG Concerning Certain Aspects of the Organization of Working Time', *ILJ* 23 (1994), 92–95; L. E. Ramsey, 'The Working Time Directive', *E.L. Rev.* 19 (1994), 528–535; U. Reim, 'Die Neuregelungen im Arbeitszeitgesetz zum 1.1.2004', *DB* 2004, 186–190; M. Schlachter (ed.), *Casebook Europäisches Arbeitsrecht* (Baden-Baden: Nomos, 2005), Case No. 16; H. Schliemann, 'Bereitschaftsdienst im EG-Recht', *NZA* 2006, 1009–1014; G. Thüsing, 'Zu den Grenzen richtlinienkonformer Auslegung – Irritationen und Hinweise in der Rechtssache Pfeiffer', *ZIP* 2004, 2301–2305; D. Ulber, 'Die Vereinbarkeit der Neuregelung des Arbeitszeitgesetzes mit dem Europarecht und dem Grundgesetz', *ZTR* 2005, 70–82; W. Wahlers, 'Die Arbeitszeitrichtlinie (Richtlinie 2003/88/EG) im Meinungsstreit zwischen Kommission und Parlament – Eine Zwischenbilanz', *ZTR* 2005, 515–521; G. Zeppenfeld, *Das europäische Arbeitszeitrecht und seine Umsetzung – unter besonderer Berücksichtigung der EU-Arbeitszeitrichtlinie 93/104/EG* (Frankfurt a.M.: private print, 1999).

Cases:

ECJ Case C-84/94 *United Kingdom* v. *Council* [1996] ECR I-5755; ECJ Case C-303/98 *Simap* [2000] ECR I-7963; ECJ Case C-173/99 *BECTU* [2001] ECR I-4881; ECJ Case C-241/99 *CIG* [2001] ECR I-5139; ECJ Case C-133/00 *Bowden* [2001] ECR I-7031; ECJ Case C-151/02 *Jaeger*

[2003] ECR I-8389; ECJ Joined Cases C-397/01 to C-430/01 *Pfeiffer* [2004] ECR I-8835; ECJ Case C-342/01 *Merino Gómez* [2004] ECR I-2605; ECJ Case C-52/04 *Personalrat der Feuerwehr Hamburg* v. *Leiter der Feuerwehr Hamburg* [2005] ECR I-7111; ECJ Case C-14/04 *Dellas* [2005] ECR I-10253; ECJ Joined Cases C-131/04 and C-257/04 *Robinson-Steele* [2006] ECR I-2531; ECJ Case C-124/05 *Federatie Nederlandse Vakbeweging* [2006] ECR I-3423; ECJ Case C-484/04 *Commission* v. *United Kingdom* [2006] ECR I-7471; ECJ Case C-437/05 *Vorel* [2007] ECR I-331; ECJ Joined Cases C-350/06 and C-520/06 *Schultz-Hoff* [2009] ECR I-179; ECJ Case C-277/08 *Pereda* [2009] ECR I-8405; ECJ Case C-158/09 *Commission* v. *Spain* [2010] ECR I-68; ECJ Case C-486/08 *Zentralbetriebsrat der Landeskrankenhäuser Tirols* [2010] ECR I-3527; ECJ Case C-243/09 *Fuß I* [2010] ECR I-9849; ECJ Case C-428/09 *Union syndicale Solidaires Isère* [2010] ECR I-9961; ECJ Case C-227/09 *Accardo* [2010] ECR I-10273; ECJ Case C-429/09 *Fuß II* 25 November 2010; ECJ Case C-258/10 *Grigore* 4 March 2011; ECJ Case C-519/09 *May* 7 April 2011; ECJ Case C-155/10 *Williams* 15 September 2011; ECJ Case C-214/10 *KHS* v. *Schulte* 22 November 2011; ECJ Case C-282/10 *Dominguez* 24 January 2012.

I. ISSUES, OVERVIEW, COMPETENCE, REGULATORY CONTEXT

1. Overview

1. The harmonisation of national laws on working time by the Working Time Directive (WTD)[1] aims to improve the **safety and health of workers** by prescribing minimum rest periods, adequate breaks, a weekly maximum working time and paid annual leave.[2] The Court has considered this protection to be a '*social right*' of the employees.[3] In setting minimum standards, the Directive prevents a 'race to the bottom' and partially eliminates working hours as a factor of competition.

2. The Directive sets minimum standards for the organisation of working time and related issues of employee protection for almost all employment relationships (with very few exceptions).[4] First, it initially regulates daily and weekly rest periods, i.e. issues of working time in a narrow sense. It additionally also

---

[1] Directive 2003/88/EC of the European Parliament and of the Council of 4 November 2003 concerning certain aspects of the organisation of working time, OJ 2003 L 299/9.

[2] ECJ Case C-124/05 *Federatie Nederlandse Vakbeweging* [2006] ECR I-3423 para. 26; Case C-173/99 *BECTU* [2001] ECR I-4881 para. 38; Case C-14/04 *Dellas* [2005] ECR I-10523 para. 41. On the purpose of the Directive, also with economic considerations N. Addnett/S. Hardy, *IRJ* 32 (2001), 114, 117–119.

[3] ECJ Case C-313/02 *Wippel* [2004] ECR I-9483 para. 47; Case C-173/99 *BECTU* [2001] ECR I-4881 para. 38; Case C-151/02 *Jaeger* [2003] ECR I-8389 para. 46; Case C-303/98 *Simap* [2000] ECR I-7963 para. 49.

[4] Article 15 WTD; cf. also ECJ Case C-313/02 *Wippel* [2004] ECR I-9483 para. 46. More favourable national provisions in one are (maximum of 44 working hours per week) cannot justify the reduction of protection in another area (on-call duty only partially taken into account); ECJ Case C-14/04 *Dellas* [2005] ECR I-10253.

provides for minimum standards on annual leave ('annual working time'). The Directive does not address issues of remuneration (and could not do so given the limits to the Union's competence in Article 153(5) TFEU), even though they are closely related to the regulation of working time.[5] The rules on working time are supplemented by additional protective rules on night work and shift work, as well as on patterns of work.

3. The Directive provides for relatively strict standards, but it gives the Member States or the social partners the opportunity to ensure the necessary degree of **flexibility** by defining reference periods and by availing themselves of optional exceptions, so as to be able to adapt the general standards to the specific requirements of individual sectors or regions.[6] While some consider the scope of Member State discretion to be too narrowly tailored,[7] others criticise the legislator would thus take away with one hand the protection that it had given with the other.[8] The particulars are to be found in the – rather casuistic – provisions of Article 16, 17 and 22 WTD which cannot be discussed in detail here.[9]

2. Legislative History and Competence

4. The enactment of the Working Time Directive is closely related to two other subjects. It is rooted in a **1975 Council Recommendation**[10] which pursued two central objectives:

– limitation of the weekly working time to 40 hours without a reduction in earnings (with optional exceptions for specific sectors and the civil service) and
– the 'principle of four weeks annual paid holiday'.

A **1979 Council Resolution**[11] considers the subject of working time in a broader context. It addresses three subjects:

– working time (Nos. 2, 6, 7),
– flexible retirement (No. 3), and
– part-time work and temporary work (Nos. 4, 5).

---

5 ECJ Case C-14/04 *Dellas* [2005] ECR I-10253 paras. 37–39.
6 M. Schmidt, 'Perspektiven und Sinn weiterer Regulierung durch Europarecht', *EuZA* 2008, 196, 201 sq. ('classic example of a flexible regulation' – my translation).
7 Cf. C. Barnard, *EC Employment Law*, 597 sq.
8 J. Kenner, *IRJ* 35 (2004), 588, 599 sq.
9 For survey of Article 17, see W. Balze, in *EAS*, B 3100 paras. 67–73; C. Barnard, *EC Employment Law*, 592–598; G. Moffat, *Nott.L.J.* 6 (1997), 45, 59 sq.
10 Recommendation of the Council of 22 July 1975 on the principle of the 40-hour week and the principle of four weeks' annual paid holiday (75/457/EEC), OJ 1975 L 199/32.
11 Council Resolution of 18 December 1979 on the adaptation of working time, OJ 1980 C 2/1.

The Working Time Directive was the first measure to implement these objectives. Separate directives have been enacted on part-time work and fixed-term work (§§16, 17 and 19). In addition, a 1982 Council Recommendation addresses the issue of retirement ages.[12]

5.　The Working Time Directive had **originally been enacted in 1993,** by majority vote (with abstention by the United Kingdom), and was based upon the new competence of Article 118a EEC (cf. today Article 153 TFEU; in more detail §4 paras. 16–22 above).[13] In its proposal of 1990, the Commission retreated from its more ambitious proposal of 1983.[14] The United Kingdom in particular had strongly opposed the Directive and insisted upon more flexible arrangements; regulation of working time had traditionally been a subject matter for collective agreements within individual sectors or establishments, rather than for the legislator, in the UK.[15]

6.　Whether working time regulations do, indeed, contribute to the protection of safety and health of employees had been – and still is – a matter of controversy.[16] Again, it was the United Kingdom that expressed doubt in this regard. Its ensuing action before the Court of Justice was, however, for the most part unsuccessful. In light of its reference to the 'working environment', the Court broadly interpreted the Union's competence in Article 118a EEC (cf. Article 153 TFEU) (see in more detail §4 para. 20 above; but see also para. 32 below with regard to Sunday rest).[17]

7.　The **changes and amendments of 2000 and 2003** have reduced some of the exceptions from the scope of application and consolidated the provisions in light of the Court's jurisprudence. The controversial issue of on-call duty (as, in particular, performed by medical doctors) which the Court of Justice had qualified as working time (para. 16 below) was, however, left untouched.

12　Council Recommendation of 10 December on the Principles of a Community Policy with Regard to Retirement Age (82/857/EEC), OJ 1982 L 357/27; Opinion of the European Parliament OJ 1982, C 267/71; Opinion Economic and Social Committee, OJ 1982 C 178/30; for a brief discussion, see R. Blanpain/M. Schmidt/U. Schweibert, *Europäisches Arbeitsrecht,* 285.

13　Council Directive 93/104/EC of 23 November 1993 concerning certain aspects of the organization of working, OJ 1993 L 307/18.

14　On the development, see in more detail G. Moffat, *Nott.L.J.* 6 (1997), 45, 49–61.

15　S. Deakin/G. Morris, *Employment Law,* paras. 4.75 sq.; M. Gray, *YEL* 17 (1998), 323, 324–326; F. v. Prondzynski, *ILJ* 23 (1994), 92–95.

16　Cf. N. Addnett/S. Hardy, *IRJ* 32 (2001), 114, 117–119; M. Gray, *YEL* 17 (1998), 323, 327–329.

17　ECJ Case C-84/94 *United Kingdom* v. *Council* [1996] ECR I-5755. On the decision e.g. B. Fitzpatrick, *ILJ* 26 (1997), 115–135; M. Gray, *YEL* 17 (1998), 323–362.

3. Plans for Reform

8. The Commission initiated more far-reaching reform in its 2004 proposal,[18] which was amended after the 2005 opinion of the European Parliament[19].[20] This proposal addresses four areas:

- regulation of on-call duty that allows for the recognition of qualitative elements;
- review of the reference periods for maximum working time (Commission proposal: extension from four to twelve months);
- review of the opt-out provision (Commission proposal: maintain it in principle); and
- provision on the compatibility between work and family.

The Council and Parliament are in dispute about the reform. A central issue is whether the inactive part of on-call duty should be defined as working time. Given that both sides intend to leave room for some discretion of the Member States or social partners, the key issue is what should be the default rule or, in other words, who should bear the burden of disposition. In respect of the other reform issues, Commission and Council lean towards broader discretion for the Member States and social partners.

9. The Council had reached a **Common Position** on 15 September 2008.[21] The Parliament then proposed changes with an absolute majority of votes (Article 294(7)(c) TFEU).[22] In its opinion of 4 February 2009, the Commission

---

[18] Opinion of the European Economic and Social Committee on the Proposal for a Directive of the European Parliament and of the Council amending Directive 2003/88/EC concerning certain aspects of the organisation of working, COM(2004) 607 final (cf. OJ 2004 C 322/10); see e.g. K. Lörcher, EuroAS 2005, 16–18 (critically); D. Ulber, ZTR 2005, 70, 82; W. Wahlers, ZTR 2005, 515–521.

[19] Commission, Proposal European Parliament and of the council amending Directive 2003/88/EC concerning certain aspects of the organisation of working time, COM(2005) 246 final, OJ 2005 C 146/13; W. Wahlers, ZTR 2005, 515, 521.

[20] Cf. H. Schliemann, NZA 2006, 1009–1014; C. Abeln/M. Repey, AuR 2005, 20–22; R. Anzinger, Festschrift für Wißmann, 14; M. Fuchs, in M. Fuchs/F. Marhold (eds.), Europäisches Arbeitsrecht, 296 sq., 298 sq.; G. Thüsing, Europäisches Arbeitsrecht, §7 para. 39; id., EuZA 2008, 159, 163 sq. See also R. Hornung-Draus, EuroAS 2004, 107–108.

[21] Common Position (EC) No 23/2008 of 15 September 2008 adopted by the Council, acting in accordance with the procedure referred to in Article 251 of the Treaty establishing the European Community, with a view to the adoption of a Directive of the European Parliament and of the Council amending Directive 2003/88/EC concerning certain aspects of the organisation of working time, OJ 2008 C 254 E/26.

[22] Proposal for a Directive of the European Parliament and of the Council amending Directive 2003/88/EC concerning certain aspects of the organisation of working time, COM(2004) 607 final.

signalled a readiness to make concessions.[23] Nevertheless, the negotiations in the Conciliation Committee in April 2009 ultimately failed, mainly because the Parliament insisted on a definite date for expiry of the opt-out clause. In 2010, the Commission initiated the social-dialogue consultation procedures pursuant to Articles 154 sq. TFEU.[24] The social partners initially could not agree on the subjects for negotiations. While the employer side aimed at a codification of the Court's case law, unions insisted on a more comprehensive review. Ultimately, the social partners entered into negotiations on 8 December 2011.

4. Regulatory Context

10. The Working Time Directive is supplemented by a number of special provisions, with those that address road traffic – driving time for lorry drivers – having the greatest practical importance.[25] The Maternity Protection Directive (§20) and the Young People at Work Directive (§22) contain special provisions (*inter alia*) with regard to working time for the respective groups of employees. With a view to its purpose, as well as its configuration in substance, the Working Time Directive is further closely linked to the Safety and Health Framework Directive, even though it has not been enacted as an 'individual directive' under Article 16(1) SHFD. Finally, the Court's jurisprudence on sex discrimination in a prohibition of night work (see §9 paras. 35 and 58 sq. above) and on national prohibitions of Sunday work as a measure having an equivalent effect (see para. 32 below), is also part of the general subject of working time.[26]

---

23   Opinion of the Commission of 4. February 2009 pursuant to Article 251 (2), third subparagraph, point (c) of the EC Treaty on the European Parliament's amendments to the Council's common position regarding the proposal for a Directive of the European Parliament and of the Council amending Directive 2003/88/EC concerning certain aspects of the organisation of working time amending the proposal of the Commission pursuant to Article 250 (2) of the EC Treaty, COM(2009) 57 final.

24   See Communication from the Commission to the European Parliamnet, the Council, the European Economic and Social Committee and the Committee of the Regions Reviewing the Working Time Directive (Second-phase consultation of the social partners at European Level under Article 154 TFEU, COM(2010) 801 final.

25   Directive 2002/15/EC of the European Parliament and of the Council of 11 March 2002 on the organisation of the working time of persons performing mobile road transport activities, OJ 2002 L 80/35; Council Regulation (EEC) No 3820/85 of 20 December 1985 on the harmonization of certain social legislation relating to road transport, OJ 1985 L 370/1; *corrigendum* OJ 1986 L 206/36. See now Proposal for a Directive of the European Parliament and of the Council amending Directive 2002/15/EC on the organisation of the working time of persons performing mobile road transport activities, COM(2008) 650 final.

26   See also F. Marhold, in M. Fuchs/F. Marhold (eds.), *Europäisches Arbeitsrecht*, 150–153.

II. SCOPE OF APPLICATION

11. 'The Court has ... held ... that this basic directive must ... be taken to be broad in scope'.[27] – The Working Time Directive principally has the same scope of application as the Safety and Health Framework Directive (§13 paras. 7 sq.):[28] It applies to all public and private sectors of activity with the exception of 'specific public service activities', which are subject to special regulations also with regard to working time, Article 1(3) WTD with Article 2 SHFD. As has been discussed in the context of the Safety and Health Framework Directive (above §13 para. 7), this latter exception is, following the Court's jurisprudence, narrowly defined, applying only to specific activities of civil protection in a narrow sense.[29] The normal activity of emergency medical services, fire-fighters or medical doctors in the health sector is thus not covered.[30]

12. The **personal** scope of application extends to **workers**. Again, the term 'worker' is not defined. Pursuant to Article 1(4) WTD, the provisions of the Safety and Health Framework Directive apply. Thus, **'worker'** should be **autonomously** defined for the purposes of the Directive, following the definition developed by the Court in regard of freedom of movement for workers (see §13 para. 9 above with further references).[31] Referring to its jurisprudence on freedom of movement for workers, the Court has defined 'worker' as a person who, for a certain period of time, performs services for and under the direction of another person in return for which he receives remuneration.[32] The *sui generis* legal nature of a given employment relationship under national law does not affect this autonomous definition of Union law. It also covers workers employed on a fixed-term basis.

13. Of the considerable number of exceptions from the scope of application[33] provided for in the original 1993 directive, the 2003 revision only maintained the **exception** for seafarers. Apart from that – e.g. with regard to doctors in training – there are no global exceptions anymore but instead only differentiated

---

27 ECJ Case C-428/09 *Union syndicale Solidaires Isère* [2010] ECR I-9961.
28 ECJ Case C-303/98 *Simap* [2000] ECR I-7963 paras. 30 sq.; Joined Cases C-397/01 to C-430/01 *Pfeiffer* [2004] ECR I-8835 para. 48; Case C-52/04 *Personalrat der Feuerwehr Hamburg* [2005] ECR I-7111 para. 38.
29 Recently ECJ Case C-428/09 *Union syndicale Solidaires Isère* [2010] ECR I-9961 para. 24.
30 ECJ Case C-337/10 *Neidel* 3 May 2012 paras. 21 sq. See the references at §13 paras. 7 sq. above on the Safety and Health Framework Directive.
31 ECJ Case C-337/10 *Neidel* 3 May 2012 paras. 20–25; Case C-519/09 *May* 7 April 2011 para. 21; Case C-428/09 *Union syndicale Solidaires Isère* [2010] ECR I-9961 paras. 27 sq. Differently G. Thüsing, *Europäisches Arbeitsrecht*, §7 para. 10.
32 ECJ Case C-337/10 *Neidel* 3 May 2012 paras. 20–25; Case C-428/09 *Union syndicale Solidaires Isère* [2010] ECR I-9961 paras. 28, 30 sq.
33 On the exception for street traffic in the original Directive 93/104/EG see ECJ Case C-133/00 *Doyle* [2001] ECR I-7031.

optional exceptions in individual respects, Articles 17, 18 and 22 WTD. The optional derogation contained in Article 17(1) WTD 'on account of the specific characteristics of the activity concerned, the duration of the working time is not measured and/or predetermined or can be determined by the workers themselves' is of considerable practical importance. The legislature particularly considered the work of managing executives, family workers and workers officiating at religious ceremonies in churches and religious communities.

III. WORKING TIME

14.   The Directive initially regulates working time in a narrow sense, i.e. the daily and weekly working hours. The provisions presuppose a definition of working time.

1.   Definitions

a)   Working Time and Rest Periods

15.   The central terms are defined in Article 2 WTD. Defined by the Union legislator and essential for the achievement of the purposes of the directive, they must be autonomously construed.[34] Pursuant to Article 2(1) WTD, '**working time**' means 'any period during which the worker [1] is working, [2] at the employer's disposal and [3] carrying out his activity or duties, in accordance with national laws and/or practice' [numbering added]. Pursuant to No. 2, '**rest period**' means any period which is not working time.

b)   The Classification of On-Call Duty

16.   This dichotomy of working time and rest periods leads to practical difficulty. In general, it is rather unsatisfactory, as it does not allow for qualitative differentiations.[35] The problem became particularly clear in regard to the classification of on-call duty. The Court of Justice attempted to integrate such specific forms of working time into the system of the Directive in accordance with the wording and purpose of Article 2(1) WTD.[36] It ruled that time spent **on-call** by doctors should be regarded as **working time** in its entirety if they are required to be at their place of work (hospital, …).[37] Even where the doctor is not

---

[34]   ECJ Case C-151/02 *Jaeger* [2003] ECR I-8389 paras. 58 sq. To the same effect (but without a discussion) ECJ Case C-303/98 *Simap* [2000] ECR I-7963 paras. 47–52.

[35]   R. Anzinger, *Festschrift für Wißmann*, 3–14; see also R. Wank, case note to Case C-303/98 *Simap*, in *EAS*, part C, Art. 2 RL 93/104/EWG Nr. 1, 41, 45–49.

[36]   ECJ Case C-303/98 *Simap* [2000] ECR I-7963 paras. 47–50; Case C-437/05 *Vorel* [2007] ECR I-331. See already W. Balze, *EuZW* 1994, 205, 206.

[37]   This also applies to other medical and nursing staff: ECJ Case C-241/99 *CIG* [2001] ECR I-5139 para. 27. See also ECJ Case C-258/10 *Grigore* 4 March 2011 paras. 42 sqq. (concerning forest ranger's wardenship duties).

actually 'working' and the first of the three criteria of Article 2(1) WTD is thus not fulfilled,[38] he is still at his employer's disposal (criterion 2). And being 'on-call' is also part of the 'duties' a doctor carries out (criterion 3). The Court's qualification of on-call duty as working time is thus, at least to some extent, covered by the wording of the Directive. The Court further justifies it on the basis of the teleological consideration[39] that the Directive is intended to safeguard safety and health of workers by guaranteeing them minimum breaks and rest periods. This purpose could be jeopardised if time during which the worker must be personally present was not counted as working time.[40]

17. On-call duty where the doctor is required to be at his workplace, must be distinguished from **on-call duty** where the doctor must **merely be contactable** but is otherwise free to dispose of his time and pursue his own interests. If the doctor merely has to be contactable at all times when on-call, then only time linked to the **actual provision of primary health care services** must be regarded as working time; otherwise, such periods will be regarded as rest periods.[41]

18. The Court thus refers to an easily discernible and teleologically founded criterion. Still, its decision remains unsatisfactory for several reasons. This is first of all because the crude dichotomy of working time and rest periods does not do justice to the variety of working time models developed in practice. While the Court's qualification is convincing on the basis of the dichotomy, the cases do not fit squarely into these forms. It does not seem adequate to consider time where the worker 'must merely be contactable' to be a rest period, nor is it justified to consider the (various and disparate forms of) on-call duty at the workplace (with degrees of actual working time from 10–90%) to be working time. What is required in substance is a (one or more) middle category which allows the disparate qualitative burdens and restrictions to be taken into account.[42] Many Member States have, for lack of such a middle category, availed themselves of the optional exception contained in Article 22 WTD which, under certain circumstances, allows for a derogation to the maximum weekly working time (Article 6 WTD) by the parties (see paras. 30 sq. below).

---

[38] ECJ Case C-303/98 *Simap* [2000] ECR I-7963 para. 48 considers the first criterion to be fulfilled as well ('It is not disputed that during periods of duty on call under those rules, the first two conditions are fulfilled.').

[39] Critically on account of the arid reasoning R. Wank, case note to Case C-303/98 *Simap*, in *EAS*, part C, Art. 2 RL 93/104/EWG Nr. 1 paras. 41, 45–49.

[40] ECJ Case C-151/02 *Jaeger* [2003] ECR I-8389 paras. 63, 92.

[41] ECJ Case C-303/98 *Simap* [2000] ECR I-7963 para. 50; Case C-151/02 *Jaeger* [2003] ECR I-8389 para. 51; Case C-437/05 *Vorel* [2007] ECR I-331.

[42] To this effect also J. Kenner, *IRJ* 35 (2004), 588, 600. Cf. also ECJ Case C-14/04 *Dellas* [2005] ECR I-10253 paras. 43, 47.

19. Attempts to reform the Directive, which were initiated in 2004 (para. 8 above), were aimed at producing a legislative solution to the issue of on-call duty. The Common Position of 15 September 2008 ('CP'; para. 9) intended to insert two new definitions into the Directive, namely a definition of 'on-call time' (Article 2(1a) CP) and a definition of 'inactive part of on-call time' (Article 2(1c) CP). This latter 'period during which the on-call worker is on-call within the meaning of point 1a but is not required by his employer to actually carry out his activity or duties' should, in principle, not constitute working time, Article 2a(1) sent. 1 CP. The national laws of the Member States were to be allowed to provide otherwise, though; in addition, they would have been given the opportunity to calculate the inactive time on the basis of an average number of working hours or a proportion of on-call time, Articles 2a(1)(2) and (2) CP. For the calculation of the daily or weekly maximum working hours, inactive time of on-call duty would not be taken into account unless a collective agreement or national legislation provided otherwise, Article 2a(3) CP. Conversely, the period during which the employee actually carries out his activity or duties during on-call time should always be regarded as working time, Article 2a(4) CP. This would effectively reverse the Court's jurisprudence. Yet, it is not quite correct to say that this model would *reduce* employee protection. The reform would rather be the *first* legislative regulation of on-call duty, retrieving the issue from the judiciary back to legislation (where it properly belongs). This should be welcomed in the first place. For even if one considered that the original Directive intended to cover the issue of on-call duty at all (rather than leaving it to the Member States!), the Court's categorisation was still rather improvised and unsatisfactory in substance. The regulation of on-call duty is, however, the focal point for the controversy between Commission and Council on the one hand, and Parliament on the other (see paras. 8 sq. above).

2. Daily Working Time

20. Daily working time is determined by Articles 3 and 4 WTD. The Court has characterised these periods as 'rules of European Union social law of particular importance from which every worker must benefit as a minimum requirement necessary to ensure the protection of his health and safety'.[43] They provide for

- a *minimum daily rest period* of 11 consecutive hours per 24-hour period, Article 3 WTD, and
- a *rest break* where the working day is longer than six hours, Article 4 WTD.[44]

---

[43] ECJ Case C-428/09 *Union syndicale Solidaires Isère* [2010] ECR I-9961 para. 36.

[44] See also ECJ Case C-484/04 *Commission* v. *United Kingdom* [2006] ECR I-7471 para. 38 (provisions on rest periods 'constitute rules of Community social law of particular importance from which every worker must benefit as a minimum requirement necessary to ensure protection of his safety and health'). On the organisation C. Barnard, *EC Employment Law*, 580 (rest periods have to be determined *ex ante*, and downtime thus cannot retrospectively qualified as rest period); cf. also ECJ Case C-151/02 *Jaeger* [2003] ECR I-8389 para. 95.

There is thus a *maximum daily working time* of (24 – 11 =) 13 hours. This maximum working time applies to every individual worker ('every worker') rather than to the respective occupation with an individual employer. Even where a worker works for more than one employer, the maximum daily working time must not exceed 13 hours.[45]

21. The **details of rest breaks** remain decentralised: They shall be laid down in collective agreements or, failing that, national legislation of the Member States, Article 4 WTD. The precedence of collective regulation also applies in countries such as Germany where there are no industry-wide, multi-employer agreements.[46]

22. **Exceptions** to the maximum daily working time and rest breaks may be provided for pursuant to Articles 17 and 18 WTD.[47] 'As exceptions to the European Union system for the organisation of working time', the Court has narrowly interpreted the provisions of Articles 17 sq. WTD.[48]

3. Weekly Working Time

23. The weekly working time is determined by two elements, the weekly rest period (somewhat simplified: 'the weekend', but see para. 26 below!), Article 5 WTD, and the maximum weekly working time, Article 6 WTD.

a) Weekly Rest Period

24. The weekly rest period is an uninterrupted rest period of 24 hours plus the 11 hours' daily rest of Article 3 WTD, Article 5 WTD, in other words **35 hours**. The composite provision makes it clear that the daily rest period is not to be merged with the weekly rest period. Pursuant to Article 5(2) WTD, this link may be cut and the weekly rest period of only 24 hours may be applied where objective, technical or work organisation conditions so justify. An example would be the change from the late shift (e.g. on a Saturday until 20 p.m.) to the early shift (e.g. Monday from 6 a.m.: rest period of only 32 hours).[49]

25. The weekly rest period need not necessarily be strictly observed. Member States may determine a – limited – **reference period of up to 14 days** during which the requirements for rest periods must, *on* average, be fulfilled,

---

[45] Thus rightly W. Balze, in *EAS*, B 3100 para. 111 n. 323.

[46] Cf. H. Günther, 'Gemeinsamer Standpunkt verabschiedet', *Bundesarbeitsblatt* 10 (1993), 17, 20 (also company agreements).

[47] M. Schmidt, *Arbeitsrecht der EG*, Part II para. 74.

[48] ECJ Case C-428/09 *Union syndicale Solidaires Isère* [2010] ECR I-9961 para. 40.

[49] W. Balze, *EuZW* 1994, 205, 207; H. Günther, *Bundesarbeitsblatt* 10 (1993), 17, 18.

Article 16(a) WTD. Articles 17 sq. WTD provide for optional exceptions for further cases.[50]

26. The exceptions of Articles 16 sq. WTD, here and in other cases, enable Member States to determine **reference periods**. This allows employers greater flexibility in the organisation of working time. While the limits remain the same, they do not have to be observed strictly in every single instance, but rather only on average during the reference period. Instead of granting the worker 24 hours of rest (in addition to the daily rest period) every week, the parties to the employment relationship may, pursuant to the applicable national law, agree upon a rest period of 48 hours every two weeks.

b)   Maximum Working Time

27. In principle, the Directive provides for a maximum working time of **48 hours**, Article 6(b) WTD. 'That maximum limit on average weekly working time constitutes a rule of European Union social law of particular importance from which every worker must benefit as a minimum requirement intended to ensure protection of his safety and health'.[51] More specifically, the average working time for each seven-day period, including overtime, must not exceed 48 hours. Again, following the purpose of the provision, working hours with different employers have to be added up.[52]

28. For determining the average working time, Member States may provide for a **reference period** of up to four months, Article 16(b)(1) WTD. Periods of paid annual leave and sick leave shall not be included or shall be neutral in the calculation of the average, Article 16(b)(2) WTD.

29. **Derogations** by law or collective agreement may only be provided for pursuant to Article 17(1) WTD with regard to activities where the duration of the working time is not measured or predetermined and pursuant to Article 17(5) WTD for doctors in training.[53]

30. Beyond that, the provision of Article 22(1) WTD – which had originally been inserted into the Directive upon instigation of the United Kingdom – allows for an **optional derogation** from Article 6 WTD **by agreement** of the

---

[50]   On the interpretation of Articles 17 sq. WTD, see ECJ Case C-227/09 *Accardo* [2010] ECR I-10273 paras. 30 sqq.

[51]   ECJ Case C-243/09 *Fuß I* [2010] ECR I-9849 para. 33; Case C-429/09 *Fuß II* 25 November 2010 paras. 33, 49, 79.

[52]   Expressly provided for in Art. 4(b) Directive 2002/15/EG (see para. 10 above with note 25).

[53]   ECJ Case C-151/02 *Jaeger* [2003] ECR I-8389 para. 83.

parties.[54] Initially, the provision had been used predominantly in the UK,[55] but other Member States have also availed themselves of it since the Court's *SIMAP*-decision on on-call duty (paras. 16–19 above).[56] In light of the purpose of the Directive, the Court has narrowly construed this possibility for individual derogation, requiring not only that every individual employee consent to the derogation, but also that his consent is expressly and freely given.[57] A mere reference to a provision in a collective agreement did not satisfy these requirements.[58]

31. The Common Position of 15 September 2008 ('CP'; see para. 9 above) further curtailed the optional derogation in Article 22. Article 22(1) CP initially emphasised the 'general principle' that 'the maximum weekly working time in the European Union is 48 hours'; the option not to apply Article 6 required instead that the Member States take the necessary measures to ensure the effective protection of worker safety and health. Furthermore, Article 22(2) CP also reinforced the procedural safeguards, providing, in particular, that the worker's consent to work longer hours was void if it had been given at the conclusion of the contract or during the first four weeks of the employment relationship (i.e. after taking up work).

32. Article 5 WTD originally provided for a second paragraph – introduced on the instigation of Germany[59] and later removed by Directive 2000/34 – which provided that the minimum weekly rest period should, in principle, include **Sunday**. The Court has, however, declared the provision void as it could not be based on the competence of Article 118a EEC (cf. today's Article 153 TFEU).[60] Sunday is no more closely related to safety and health of workers than any other work day. While the competence allows for the legislator to respect any religious or cultural peculiarities of individual Member States, it could not be used as a basis to prescribe them in a binding fashion for all Member States. National

---

54   For a critical perspective see J. Kenner, *IRJ* 35 (2004), 588, 590–592.
55   C. Barnard/S. Deakin/R. Hobbs, *ILJ* 32 (2003), 223–252 (p. 224: 'the individual opt-out is in widespread use and is regarded, in preference to other derogations, as the most convenient and effective mechanism for avoiding the 48-hour limit on weekly working time'); the authors consider the possibility of an opt out to be the main reason why the Directive's goals have been watered down in the implementation in the United Kingdom.
56   C. Barnard, *EC Employment Law*, 588–591; J. Kenner, *IRJ* 35 (2004), 588, 595–599 (referring to resulting counter-intentional effects). S.a. ECJ Case C-151/02 *Jaeger* [2003] ECR I-8389 paras. 84 sq.
57   ECJ Joined Cases C-397/01 to C-430/01 *Pfeiffer* [2004] ECR I-8835 para. 84. See also C. Barnard, *EC Employment Law*, 590 sq.
58   ECJ Joined Cases C-397/01 to C-430/01 *Pfeiffer* [2004] ECR I-8835 paras. 75–86.
59   The provision had been introduced on account of Germany and was held (in the Council) not to be binding (applicable only 'in principle'); see also W. Balze, *EuZW* 1994, 205, 207; H. Günther, *Bundesarbeitsblatt* 10 (1993), 17, 18.
60   ECJ Case C-84/94 *United Kingdom* v. *Council* [1996] ECR I-5755 para. 37.

prohibitions of Sunday work may constitute measures having an equivalent effect to quantitative restrictions within the meaning of Article 34 TFEU (free movement of goods) and are thus subject to a proportionality test.[61]

IV. SPECIAL WORKING TIMES AND FORMS OF WORK, NIGHT WORK IN PARTICULAR

1. Overview

33. Chapter 3 of the Directive contains special provisions for night work, shift work and patterns of work, in other words special working times and special forms of work which (a) deviate from the usual working conditions and (b) may entail specific risks or strain for workers. The legislature responded to these special features with a package of protective measures which are primarily aimed at night work, address only certain aspects of shift work and provide only a framework for the regulation of patterns of work.

34. Only the provisions on **night work** are carved out in more detail:

- Article 8 regulates the length of night work,
- Article 9 a right to a health assessment,
- Article 10 the protection of certain categories of workers,
- Article 11 notification of the competent authorities, and
- Article 12 measures for safety and health protection.

35. The provision of Article 12 on safety and health protection also applies to **shift work** which is, however, not otherwise regulated any further. With regard to **patterns of work**, Article 13 WTD merely provides for the general principle of adapting work to the worker.

2. Length of Night Work

36. Article 8 WTD is located at the intersection of provisions on the organisation of working time (chapter 2) and those on night work, shift work and patterns of work (chapter 3). It contains specific provisions for the **organisation of working time** with regard to night work. While it is thus formally part of chapter 3, the substance of Article 8 WTD is part of the provisions on working time proper.

---

61 On the prohibition of Sunday work ECJ Case C-145/88 *Trofaen* [1989] ECR 3851; Case C-312/89 *SIDEF-Conforma* [1991] ECR I-1021; Case C-332/89 *Trafitex* [1991] ECR I-1037.

37.   The provision applies to **night work** which, in turn, is defined by the term 'night worker'. A night worker is a worker who works during 'night time' as defined in Article 2(3) WTD as either at least three hours of his daily working time or a certain proportion (defined, at the Member States' choice, by national law or collective agreement) of his annual working time, Article 2(4) WTD.[62]

38.   For a night worker, the normal working time must not exceed an average of eight hours in any 24-hour period, Article 8(1)(a) WTD. The provision merely applies to the normal working time and leaves room for exceptions in special circumstances. Further, it only requires determination of a certain average. It is for the Member States to determine the reference period for this average. They can either, after consultation with the social partners, determine the reference period by law or leave the determination to a collective agreement of the social partners, Article 16(c)(1) WTD. If the minimum weekly rest period of Article 5 WTD falls within the reference period, it must not be included in the calculation of the average. The discretion thus opened up by the provision of lit. c) becomes particularly obvious if compared to that of lit. b), on the reference period for the regular weekly maximum hours.

39.   For a separate group of work – to be determined by the national law of the Member States – which involves special hazards or heavy physical or mental strain, the maximum hours for night work is absolutely and strictly limited to eight hours. Both determinations – hazardous or 'heavy' work – may also be delegated to the social partners, pursuant to Article 8(2) WTD.

3.   Health Assessment and Transfer of Night Workers to Day Work

40.   Night workers are entitled to a **health assessment** before taking up night work and at regular intervals thereafter, Article 9(1)(a) WTD. The assessment must be offered without any costs to the employee (*argumentum e silencio*) and it must comply with medical confidentiality, (paragraph 2). It may be conducted within the national health system, (paragraph 3). It is a matter of controversy whether the worker may waive his right to a medical assessment or refuse to undergo it. The wording is not unequivocal.[63] In favour of a mere right (and not an obligation), it might be argued that it is primarily the worker's health that is at

---

[62]   With references to the implementation in Germany: W. Balze, in *EAS*, B 3100 para. 163.

[63]   See L. E. Ramsey, *E.L. Rev.* 19 (1994), 528, 533 (arguing for a mere right with regard to the English language version); to the same effect G. Thüsing, *Europäisches Arbeitsrecht*, §7 para. 28. The French language version (*bénéficient*) rather hints at an obligation on the employee; C. Klein, 'Die Bestimmung über Nachtarbeit, Schichtarbeit und Arbeitsrhythmus', *DRdA* 1994, 293, 294.

stake. Yet, the assessment may also be of relevance for other persons such as fellow workers or third persons (think of medical doctors or lorry drivers). The safety and health of these groups should not be at the worker's disposal. If one were to follow a different interpretation, effective transposition would require the national law of the Member States to ensure effective protection against abuse.

41. In a second strand, Article 9 WTD provides for the employer's obligation to transfer the night worker to day work if he suffers from health problems recognised as being connected with the fact that he performs night work. This obligation is, however, **narrowly confined**, first of all in its prerequisites:

- It requires proof of causation between night work and the health problems. While night work does not have to be the sole cause, such proof may not always be easy to provide.[64]
- It further requires 'health problems' which is narrowly construed, as otherwise the requirement for causation would lose its meaning. Other than is sometimes the case in safety and health directives, health is to be distinguished from 'well-being'.

The obligation to transfer the employee is thus not related to abstract prevention, but requires concrete proof of danger or damage.

42. Secondly, the employer's obligation is not absolute but only applies 'whenever possible'. 'Possibility' first presupposes that the worker concerned is fit for work in a daytime position. Furthermore, where the employer does not have an open position for day work, nor a right to order another employee to make the reverse change from day work to night work,[65] the transfer will only be possible where another worker is willing to swap. The employer is under no obligation to hire another worker (whom he would not need otherwise) so as to satisfy the wish to transfer.

4.   Safety and Health Protection for Night Workers and Shift Workers

43. Night workers and shift workers[66] may be exposed to specific risks to safety and health; Article 12 WTD requires Member States to take adequate

---

64 Such difficulty of proof have been a reason for the enactment of the Directive's provisions more generally; cf. W. Balze, *EuZW* 1994, 205, 206.
65 This is to be determined by the national laws. With regard to German law, see U. Preis, in R. Müller-Glöge/U. Preis/I. Schmidt (eds.), *Erfurter Kommentar*, §611 BGB para. 656 and §106 GewO para. 19.
66 For the definition, cf. Article 2(3)-(6) WTD and the discussion at para. 37 above with regard to night-work.

precautions. As a minimum, the protective and preventive measures for the protection of their safety and health must be **equivalent** to those afforded to other workers and must be available at all times. This amounts to a prohibition of discrimination, an instrument of protection also employed with regard to other atypical employment relations (see in more detail §§15–19 below). This part of the provision is worded so precisely ('at all times') that it does not leave any room for balancing with economic interests.[67] All protection afforded during 'day work' must be provided for night workers in an equivalent manner. In addition, Article 12(1) WTD sets forth a specific duty to provide for such prevention and protection as is appropriate to the nature of night or shift work. The obvious example is adequate lighting for night work. This obligation goes beyond adaptation of the usual ('day time') measures and may require specific ('night time') measures to be taken.

5. *Pattern of Work*

44. Article 13 WTD merely imposes a rather 'soft' obligation upon the employer in regard to patterns of work.[68] An employer who intends to organise work according to a certain pattern must *'take account* of the general principle of **adapting work to the worker** *with a view,* in particular, to alleviating monotonous work and work at a predetermined work-rate'. Somewhat more precisely, the Directive mentions (but does not strictly require) breaks during work time, as a measure to be taken into account. The general concept is in line with that of the Safety and Health Framework Directive, which first introduced the principle of adapting work to the worker (see §13 para. 18 above). It is rather doubtful, though, whether the provision of Article 13 WTD adds anything in substance.

6. *Derogations and Exceptions*

45. The Member States or social partners may, pursuant to Articles 17 and 18 WTD, only deviate from the provisions on the length of night work. The other provisions, which do not concern the organisation of working time but directly relate to the prevention of risks and the protection of safety and health are not subject to derogations or exceptions.

---

[67]   R. Wank, in P. Hanau/H.-D. Steinmeyer/R. Wank (eds.), *Handbuch des europäischen Arbeits- und Sozialrechts,* §18 para. 312.
[68]   In the same direction W. Balze, *EuZW* 1994, 205, 208.

V. PAID ANNUAL LEAVE

1. Overview

46. On the basis of systematic and teleological considerations, the Court of Justice has considered the right to paid annual leave to constitute a 'particularly **important principle of Community [Union] social law**'.[69] The competence of Article 118a EEC (see now Article 153 TFEU), the Community Charter of Fundamental Social Rights (§2 para. 73) and the fact that the right to paid annual leave has been provided for in a strict way, not allowing for any derogations or exceptions, indicate that the legislator considered this right to be particularly important. The distinguished position of the right to paid annual leave has led to Article 7 WTD, in combination with the implementation obligations of the Member States, having a number of **further effects**: In light of the paramount importance of paid annual leave, the Court has curtailed the discretion of the Member States in respect of implementation (see para. 66). Conversely, the Court has left little room for **individual responsibility of the employee** which, for example, the Dutch legislator had intended to emphasise[70]; its jurisprudence is sometimes criticised as paternalistic.[71]

2. Annual Leave

47. The national law of the Member States must provide for **minimum**[71a] **annual leave** of four weeks, Article 7(1) WTD.

48. **Conditions** for entitlement to, and granting of, such leave, such as a waiting period or deference to business necessities, are to be determined by the Member States, albeit within the framework of their implementation obligations (§1 paras. 65 sq.). In light of the special importance of paid annual leave (para. 46) which the Directive provides without any exceptions (para. 56), the Court considered national rules, under which a worker does not begin to accrue rights to paid annual leave until he has completed a minimum period of 13 weeks' uninterrupted employment with the same employer, to be

---

[69] ECJ Case C-214/10 *KHS* v. *Schulte* 22 November 2011 para. 23; Case C-486/08 *Zentralbetriebsrat der Landeskrankenhäuser Tirols* [2010] ECR I-3527 paras. 28 sqq.; Case C-277/08 *Pereda* [2009] ECR I-8405 para. 18; Joined Cases C-350/06 and C-520/06 *Schultz-Hoff* [2009] ECR I-179 para. 22; Case C-342/01 *Merino Gómez* [2004] ECR I-2605 para. 29; Case C-124/05 *Federatie Nederlandse Vakbeweging* [2006] ECR I-3423 para. 28; Joined Cases C-131/04 and C-257/04 *Robinson-Steele* [2006] ECR I-2531 para. 48; Case C-173/99 *BECTU* [2001] ECR I-4881 paras. 36–47.

[70] ECJ Case C-124/05 *Federatie Nederlandse Vakbeweging* [2006] ECR I-3423 para. 17.

[71] A. L. Bogg, *E.L. Rev.* 31 (2006), 892–905.

[71a] ECJ Case C-337/10 *Neidel* paras. 33–37; Case C-282/10 *Dominguez* 24 January 2012 paras. 48–50.

incompatible with the Directive.[72] For certain sectors where workers are usually employed for shorter periods, the rule was liable to effectively defeat the right to paid annual leave.[73] It would, in other words, lead to an exception to the scope of application, contrary to the provision of Article 1(3) WTD, pursuant to which the Directive is applicable to all sectors and in particular, without exclusion of part-time work. The Court has, more generally, restricted the Member States' freedom to determine the 'conditions for entitlement to, and granting of' paid leave to the mere determination of modalities ('how'), which do not as such affect the right to paid leave. They may thus provide for a waiting period for the exercise of the right to paid leave,[74] but not for the existence of such a right.

49. Given that annual leave and **maternity leave** (Article 8 MLD, see §20 below) pursue different purposes, the respective times of leave may not be 'set off' against each other In other words, annual leave and maternity leave require separate times off work.[75] The prohibition of discrimination requires that the worker must be able to take her annual leave at another time outside of the maternity leave.[76] More generally, the Court of Justice has held that 'a period of leave guaranteed by Community law cannot affect the right to take another period of leave guaranteed by that law'.[77]

50. Two countervailing considerations come into play where the worker stays away from work because of sickness ('**sick leave**'). On the one hand, the worker should have his annual leave during a given year (annually); on this consideration he should have the opportunity to take annual leave even while he is sick. On the other hand, the worker will only have a chance to recover from work and relax if he is healthy (vacation is no good if you're sick); on this consideration he should not have to, or even be entitled to, take annual leave for the time of his sickness. However, sick leave is not regulated at the level of EU law. Furthermore, Article 7(1) WTD expressly leaves the determination of the conditions to the Member States. On the basis of these considerations, the Court came to the conclusion that both would be admissible under Article 7 WTD: (1) to grant workers a right to annual leave even if they are sick and (2) to deny such right,

---

[72] ECJ Case C-173/99 *BECTU* [2001] ECR I-4881 paras. 36–53. See also ECJ Case C-282/10 *Dominguez* 24 January 2012 paras. 17 sqq. (condition on a minimum period of ten days' or one month's actual work during the reference period incompatible with Article 7).

[73] Cf. ECJ Case C-173/99 *BECTU* [2001] ECR I-4881 para. 27: The members of BECTU, the union that initiated the proceedings, are predominantly employed on a short-term basis of often less than 13 weeks.

[74] G. Thüsing, *Europäisches Arbeitsrecht*, §7 para. 23.

[75] ECJ Case C-342/01 *Merino Gómez* [2004] ECR I-2605 paras. 28–32.

[76] ECJ Case C-342/01 *Merino Gómez* [2004] ECR I-2605 paras. 37 sq.

[77] ECJ Case C-519/03 *Commission v. Luxembourg* [2005] ECR I-3067 para. 33; Case C-124/05 *Federatie Nederlandse Vakbeweging* [2006] ECR I-3423 para. 24.

the latter, however, only under the condition that 'the worker in question has the opportunity to exercise the right conferred by that directive during another period'.[78]

51. The *proviso* that the worker should have an opportunity to exercise the right to annual leave during another period addresses the issue of the temporal limitations of the right to annual leave, which is often regulated in the form of (limited) **transfer times** (the possibility to 'transfer' leave from one year to another for a limited period). Such transfer times are also part of the 'conditions for entitlement to and granting of' annual leave'. They may determine that the right to annual leave expires entirely after a certain period of time.[79] It is then for the employee to claim his right to leave in time. The Court has drawn a line, though, where the worker does **not have the opportunity** to go on annual leave, in particular where he is prevented from doing so by long-lasting sickness that continues beyond the end of the transfer period determined by national law. To deny or terminate a right to annual leave in such a case would not only affect the 'conditions' of annual leave, but the right as such; that would be incompatible with Article 7(1) WTD (see para. 48 above).[80] Indeed, it must be considered that the need for recovery and recreation does not cease where a worker has been on sick leave for the whole year (or until the end of a transfer period) and was thus unable to take his annual leave.[81] Yet it should also be considered that the need for recovery and recreation does not add up in a linear fashion over the years.[82] To uphold the worker's right to annual leave unconditionally would thus overprotect the worker and place considerable burden upon the employer. The employer could only limit this burden by terminating the employment relationship. The Court has recognised these conflicting interests and held that 'a worker who is unfit for work for several consecutive years and who is prevented by national law from taking his paid annual leave during that period cannot have the right to accumulate, without any limit, entitlements to paid annual leave acquired during that period'.[83] On the basis of these considerations, it has accepted as compatible with Article 7(1) WTD a carry-over period of 15 months

---

[78]   ECJ Joined Cases C-350/06 and C-520/06 *Schultz-Hoff* [2009] ECR I-179 paras. 27–31; Case C-277/08 *Pereda* [2009] ECR I-8405 para. 19; Case C-78/11 *ANGED* v. *FASGA* 21 June 2012 paras. 19 sqq.

[79]   ECJ Joined Cases C-350/06 and C-520/06 *Schultz-Hoff* [2009] ECR I-179 paras. 34 sq., 42 sq.; Case C-214/10 *KHS* v. *Schulte* 22 November 2011 para. 26.

[80]   ECJ Joined Cases C-350/06 and C-520/06 *Schultz-Hoff* [2009] ECR I-179 paras. 43–52; Case C-277/08 *Pereda* [2009] ECR I-8405 paras. 23 sqq.; Case C-337/10 *Neidel* 3 May 2012 paras. 27–32; Case C-78/11 *ANGED* v. *FASGA* 21 June 2012 paras. 20 sqq. To the same effect already AG *Trstenjak*, Opinion in Case C-350/06 *Schultz-Hoff* [2009] ECR I-179 pt. 47.

[81]   Cf. ECJ Case C-124/05 *Federatie Nederlandse Vakbeweging* [2006] ECR I-3423 para. 30.

[82]   See also G. Thüsing, *Europäisches Arbeitsrecht*, §7 para. 24; R. Glaser/H. Lüders, *BB* 2006, 2690–2694.

[83]   ECJ Case C-214/10 *KHS* v. *Schulte* 22 November 2011 para. 34.

in a collective agreement on the expiry of which the right to paid annual leave lapses (even) where this carry-over period limited the accumulation of entitlements to paid leave of a worker who is unfit for work for several consecutive reference periods.[84] Where the employment relationship ends and the worker did not have a chance to take the annual leave to which he is entitled, it is in line with Article 7(2) WTD (see in more detail para. 54 below) and the purpose of the right to annual leave to grant him an entitlement to allowance in lieu.[85]

3. Paid Leave: Pay During the Time of Annual Leave

52. Every worker has a right to *paid* annual leave. The Court of Justice has also construed this element having regard to the special importance of the right to annual leave and has interpreted it to mean that the remuneration is to be paid continuously during the time of annual leave.[86] The right to annual leave and payment on that account are 'two aspects of a single right'.[87] This is in line with the wording of Article 7(1) WTD and is well-founded on the basis of teleological considerations, if the rationale of the provision is to ensure that the worker does in fact take his annual leave. The right to pay is to ensure that the worker continues to receive the same income during his leave, for there would otherwise be a risk that he would hesitate to go on leave.[88] This interpretation finds further support in the general prohibition to replace annual leave by an allowance in lieu in Article 7(2) WTD as the division of leave and pay would have a similar effect.[89]

53. This basic concept of paid annual leave leads to concrete consequences for the **composition of pay**.

(1) Holiday pay (the remuneration paid in respect of annual leave) must, in principle, be determined as analogous to normal remuneration.[90] Where

---

[84] ECJ Case C-214/10 *KHS* v. *Schulte* 22 November 2011 para. 44. But see ECJ Case C-337/10 *Neidel* 3 May 2012 paras. 38–43 (transfer period of nine months too short).

[85] ECJ Case C-337/10 *Neidel* 3 May 2012 paras. 38–43; see also (if rather implicitly) Joined Cases C-350/06 and C-520/06 *Schultz-Hoff* [2009] ECR I-179 paras. 54–56.

[86] ECJ Joined Cases C-131/04 and C-257/04 *Robinson-Steele* [2006] ECR I-2531 paras. 48–50. Critically A.L. Bogg, *E.L. Rev.* 31 (2006), 892–905 (criticising the interpretation as paternalistic as it was not covered by the purpose of Article 7 and as disproportionate; preferring an examination of the individual case which would leave room for a distinction of individual and collective agreements).

[87] ECJ Joined Cases C-131/04 and C-257/04 *Robinson-Steele* [2006] ECR I-2531 para. 58; Joined Cases C-350/06 and C-520/06 *Schultz-Hoff* [2009] ECR I-179 para. 60.

[88] Critically A.L. Bogg, *E.L. Rev.* 31 (2006), 892, 900–902 (arguing that, with a proper design of the default, there was no market failure or otherwise need of protection of employees).

[89] ECJ Joined Cases C-131/04 and C-257/04 *Robinson-Steele* [2006] ECR I-2531 para. 60.

[90] ECJ Case C-155/10 *Williams* 15 September 2011 paras. 15–31.

normal remuneration is composed of various parts, holiday pay must cover all these parts, and must therefore also include supplementary allowances relating to the status of the employee (e.g. with regard to seniority, length or services or professional qualifications).[91] On the other hand, components of pay which are designed to cover specific expenses (e.g. costs connected with time spent away from home) need not be included in the calculation of holiday pay. Where normal remuneration contains variable parts, the calculation of holiday pay should be based upon an average, which is determined over a representative reference period.

(2) Holiday pay must be paid out **during the time of annual leave**. Thus, a so-called **rolled-up holiday pay**, pursuant to which holiday pay is paid as an additional sum which is added to regular pay and paid out in small instalments over the course of the year,[92] is incompatible with Article 7(1) WTD, as this would mean that the employee did not continuously receive pay during his annual leave.[93]

The Court has held that the Directive does not, in principle, preclude 'sums additional to remuneration payable for work done which have been paid, transparently and comprehensibly, as holiday pay, from being set off against the payment for specific leave'. It has, at the same time, emphasised, though, that the Member States are required to ensure that practices incompatible with the Directive will not be continued. It appears that the UK Working Time Regulations have not been amended so as to explicitly designate rolled-up holiday pay as unlawful; UK courts appear to continue to allow for a set-off.[94] While this may be acceptable in relation to older contracts, concluded before the *Robinson-Steele*-judgement, it would be incompatible with the Directive to allow for a set-off as an on-going practice. This would not ensure that practices incompatible with the Directive will not be continued and thus violates the UK's implementation duties.

(3) Holiday pay as an **additional pay**: It is not in line with the requirements of Article 7 WTD to just *formally* designate part of the remuneration as holiday pay. Where the parties have agreed upon a certain remuneration for the work done (without holidays), they may not later stipulate that the same amount should also serve, in part, as holiday pay. Again, this would, in effect, mean that the worker did not receive pay during his period of annual

---

[91] ECJ Case C-155/10 *Williams* 15 September 2011 para. 27 referring by analogy to Case C-471/08 *Parviainen* [2010] ECR I-6533 para. 73 and to Case C-194/08 *Gassmayr* [2010] ECR I-6281 para. 65 (on the MPD; see §20 para. 21).

[92] On the background in British employment law and the economic relevance C. Barnard, *EC Employment Law*, 582–585; A. L. Bogg, *E.L. Rev.* 31 (2006), 892, 893; S. Deakin/G. Morris, *Labour Law*, para. 4.82.

[93] ECJ Joined Cases C-131/04 and C-257/04 *Robinson-Steele* [2006] ECR I-2531 paras. 53–63.

[94] See e.g. *Lyddon v Englefield Brickwork Ltd* [2008] *IRLR* 198 EAT. See S. Deakin/G. Morris, *Labour Law*, para. 4.82.

leave and it is thus incompatible both with Article 7 WTD also the prohibition of regression in Article 23 WTD.[95]

4. *The Prohibition of an Allowance in lieu of Annual Leave*

54. 'A worker must normally be entitled to actual rest'.[96] Pursuant to the principle of Article 7(2) WTD, annual leave may not be replaced by a payment in lieu. The Court has construed this provision strictly, and there is only a single exception to it, which applies in the case of termination of the employment relationship, Article 7(2) WTD.[97] The prohibition is intended to ensure that the worker actually takes his annual leave as a period of rest so that the purpose of protecting his safety and health will be effectively achieved.[98] Even a national provision that would merely give the worker an incentive to have his annual leave replaced by an allowance in lieu is thus incompatible with the Directive.[99] The Court, e.g., considered a Dutch provision, pursuant to which the worker could have those parts of his annual leave that he had not used in a given year replaced by a payment in lieu in the following year, to be incompatible with the Directive.[100] This case is to be distinguished, though, from a **transfer** of unused periods of leave to the following year (see para. 51 above). The Member States may provide for such transfer period as part of their national 'conditions for the entitlement to and the granting of' annual leave. They may, in principle, also provide for a termination of the right to annual leave at the end of such a transfer period,[101] as this does not compromise the intended protection of safety, health and recreation.[102] For limitations, see para. 51 above.

55. The Directive does not expressly determine the **calculation of a payment in lieu**, yet it indirectly regulates the issue with the concept of 'paid annual leave' (para. 52 above). Given that this concept is based upon the consideration that pay should be continued during the leave period, it implies that regular remuneration should also form the basis for the calculation of a payment in lieu.[103]

---

[95] ECJ Joined Cases C-131/04 and C-257/04 *Robinson-Steele* [2006] ECR I-2531 paras. 51 sq.
[96] ECJ Case C-486/08 *Zentralbetriebsrat der Landeskrankenhäuser Tirols* [2010] ECR I-3527 para. 31.
[97] ECJ Case C-337/10 *Neidel* 3 May 2012 paras. 27–32. See also H. Günther, *Bundesarbeitsblatt* 10 (1993), 17, 19.
[98] ECJ Case C-173/99 *BECTU* [2001] ECR I-4881 para. 44; Case C-342/01 *Merino Gómez* [2004] ECR I-2605 para. 30; Joined Cases C-131/04 and C-257/04 *Robinson-Steele* [2006] ECR I-2531 para. 60.
[99] ECJ Case C-124/05 *Federatie Nederlandse Vakbeweging* [2006] ECR I-3423 para. 32.
[100] ECJ Case C-124/05 *Federatie Nederlandse Vakbeweging* [2006] ECR I-3423 paras. 25–35; Fenski, *DB* 2007, 686, 688 sq.
[101] ECJ Joined Cases C-350/06 and C-520/06 *Schultz-Hoff* [2009] ECR I-179 paras. 34 sq., 42 sq.
[102] Cf. ECJ Case C-124/05 *Federatie Nederlandse Vakbeweging* [2006] ECR I-3423 para. 30.
[103] ECJ Joined Cases C-350/06 and C-520/06 *Schultz-Hoff* [2009] ECR I-179 paras. 57–61.

5. No Reference Periods or Exceptions

56. Article 7 WTD is the only one of the provisions on working time in Articles 3–8 WTD in regard to which Article 16 WTD does not allow for a reference period. Annual leave of four weeks may, in other words, not be replaced by a bi-annual leave of eight weeks. Articles 17 and 18 WTD do not allow for exceptions or derogations either.

VI. SANCTIONS

57. The Directive does not specifically provide for sanctions which must, therefore, be derived from the general implementation duties, in particular the principles of equivalence and effectiveness (see §1 para. 66 above). In light of the fundamental right to effective judicial protection in Article 47 ChFR, the Court has inferred a prohibition of **victimisation** from the Directive.[104] The employer may not compulsorily transfer an employee to another service on the ground that he has requested compliance with the maximum working time requirement of Article 6 WTD. Violation of Article 6 WTD as such triggers this prohibition, and the fact that the employee has not suffered any detriment is irrelevant in that regard.

VII. IMPLEMENTATION

58. The original Working Time Directive 93/104/EEC had to be implemented into national law by 23 November 1996. The codification of Directive 2003/88/EC entered into force on 2 August 2004, leaving the implementation periods of the original Directive unaffected, Article 27 WTD.

59. In **Germany**, working time is regulated by the Act on Working Time (*Arbeitszeitgesetz*, ArbzG) of 1 July 1994, which had originally been drafted in the same period as Directive 93/104/EEC.[105] Following the *SIMAP* decision of the Court of Justice (see para. 16 above), the Federal Labour Court held that the provisions of the Act relating to the classification of on-call duty, were incompatible with the Directive. However, the Court felt unable to interpret the Act so as to conform to the Directive's requirements, given its unequivocal wording.[106] The legislature made the necessary amendments with the Act on Reforms of the Labour Market (*Gesetz zu Reformen am Arbeitsmarkt*) of

---

[104]   ECJ Case C-243/09 *Fuß I* [2010] ECR I-9849 paras. 64 sqq.
[105]   R. Wank, in R. Müller-Glöge/U. Preis/I. Schmidt (eds.), *Erfurter Kommentar*, §1 ArbZG para. 2.
[106]   BAG, *NZA* 2003, 742, 749.

24 December 2003,[107] which changed or repealed a number of provisions of the Act on Working Time.[108] The Federal Vacation Act (*Bundesurlaubsgesetz, BUrlG*)[109] transposes the provisions on paid annual leave. Recently, the jurisprudence of the Federal Labour Court on the expiry of the right to annual leave in the case where the worker cannot take his annual leave due to sickness, proved to be incompatible with the requirements of the Directive (para. 51 above).[110]

60. Implementation in France, Spain and the United Kingdom[111] was delayed or defective in individual respects.[112]

VIII. THE EXAMPLE OF THE *ROBINSON-STEELE* CASE[113]

61. Mr *Robinson-Steele* worked for R. D. Retail Services Ltd ('Retail Services') between 19 April 2002 and 19 December 2003. Retail Services provides the services of its workers to large undertakings in the retail sector. The workers provide shop-fitting and shelf-stacking services. Mr Robinson-Steele worked either day shifts of 12 hours each over five days or night shifts also of 12 hours each over four days, continuously throughout that period of employment except for one week of leave over the Christmas period in 2002, for which he was not separately paid.

62. His contractual terms varied during his period of employment. Beginning on 29 June 2003, he worked pursuant to a contract entitled 'Terms of Engagement for Temporary Workers'. The relevant terms of the contract provide: 'Entitlement to payment for leave accrues in proportion to the amount of time worked continuously by the Temporary Worker on Assignment during the leave year. The Temporary Worker agrees that payment in respect of the entitlement to paid

---

107   BGBl. 2003 I, 3002 sqq.
108   BGBl. 1994 I, 1170; also available at www.gesetze-im-internet.de/arbzg/index.html; bilingual German-English version in S. Lingemann/R. v. Steinau-Steinrück/A. Mengel, *Employment and Labour Law in Germany*, Part II, XIV. R. See Anzinger, *Festschrift für Wißmann*, 3–14; U. Reim, *DB* 2004, 186–190; D. Ulber, *ZTR* 2005, 70–82.
109   *Mindesturlaubsgesetz für Arbeitnehmer (Bundesurlaubsgesetz)*, BGBl. 1963 I p. 2 as amended; also available at http://bundesrecht.juris.de/burlg/BJNR000020963.html; bilingual German-English version in S. Lingemann/R. v. Steinau-Steinrück/A. Mengel, *Employment and Labour Law in Germany*, Part II, VI.
110   ECJ Joined Cases C-350/06 and C-520/06 *Schultz-Hoff* [2009] ECR I-179.
111   S. Deakin/G. Morris, *Labour Law*, paras. 4.76–4.90; L. Hey/P. Cooke, *I.C.C.L.R.* 9 (1998), 164–169 (United Kingdom); N. Addnett/S. Hardy, *IRJ* 32 (2001), 114, 119–121 (various Member States).
112   ECJ Case C-46/99 *Commission* v. *France* [2000] ECR I-4379; Case C-484/04 *Commission* v. *United Kingdom* [2006] ECR I-7471; ECJ Case C-158/09 *Commission* v. *Spain* [2010] ECR I-68.
113   ECJ Joined Cases C-131/04 and C-257/04 *Robinson-Steele* [2006] ECR I-2531.

leave shall be made together with and in addition to the Temporary Worker's hourly rate at 8.33% of his hourly rate.' Mathematically, an 8.33% (= 1/12) leave pay element does produce the correct sum to reflect one week's pay after the worker has worked continuously for three months on the alternating day and night shift pattern in question.

63. Mr Robinson-Steele received his wages on a weekly basis. His rate of remuneration was GBP 6.25 per hour for day shift work and GBP 7.75 per hour for night shift work. His pay slips bore the words: 'Pay rate includes compensation for hols [holidays] & sick days'.

64. On 14 January 2004, he applied to the Employment Tribunal in Leeds, in which he stated that he had worked for Retail Services for 20 months and that, as regards annual holiday pay, the company had paid him only 'rolled-up holiday pay'. That meant in most cases that no leave was taken because it was not paid for immediately before, or after it was taken, or while it was being taken. The Employment Tribunal stayed the proceedings and referred the question whether such agreement on rolled-up holiday pay was compatible with the requirements of the Working Time Directive to the Court of Justice.

65. The Working Time Directive does not expressly address the question of when holiday pay must be paid. It merely provides that every worker is entitled to a minimum of four weeks of paid holiday. The conditions for the entitlement to, and the granting of, holiday are for the Member States to determine, Article 7(1) WTD. These conditions, in principle, also include the time at which holiday pay must be paid.

66. However, the discretion thus left to the Member States is restricted by the general principles of implementation of Union law. In particular, the conditions may not be framed so as to endanger the right to annual holiday, for which the Directive makes unconditional provision as an important social right. Furthermore, it must be kept in mind that the Directive provides for a right to *paid* annual leave, thus conceiving the right to annual leave and the right to pay during this time as 'two aspects of a single right'. Remuneration during the period of annual leave should place the worker in a financial situation which is similar to that when he performs his work. Teleologically, this serves as to give proper effect to the right to annual leave: If the worker did not continuously receive his pay during his time of annual leave, although his expenses are (presumably) the same, he would have an incentive not to take his annual leave or might use it for the purpose of working elsewhere so as to meet his material needs. This legislative intent can also be inferred from the fact that holiday pay can only be replaced by an allowance in lieu in one exceptional case (termination of the employment relationship). In a normal situation, the legislature wanted to avoid the worker 'liquidating' his right to annual leave.

67.   Rolled-up holiday pay could, as the case at hand illustrates, have the consequence that workers would not make use of their right to annual leave. Such agreement is thus incompatible with the requirements of the Directive and may not be upheld by the national laws of the Member States.

CHAPTER 4
ATYPICAL FORMS OF EMPLOYMENT

§15. ATYPICAL FORMS OF EMPLOYMENT – OVERVIEW AND GENERAL PART

CONTENT

Bibliography:

E. Albin, 'Labour Law in a Service World', *MLR* 73 (2010), 959–984; W. Balze, 'Arbeitszeit, Urlaub und Teilzeitarbeit', in H. Oetker/U. Preis (eds.), *Europäisches Arbeits- und Sozialrecht, EAS, part B – Systematische Darstellungen*, loose-leaf (Heidelberg: Forkel, last update: February 2011), B 3100 paras. 242–300; F. Becker/P. Bader, 'Der Vorschlag der EG-Kommission für eine Richtlinie des Rates zur Regelung der Leiharbeitsverhältnisse und befristeter Arbeitsverträge – Darstellung und Kritik', *RdA* 1983, 1–18; R. Blanpain (ed.), *Temporary Work and Labour Law* (Deventer/Boston: Kluwer, 1993); A. Feuerborn, 'Grenzüberschreitender Einsatz von Fremdfirmenpersonal', in H. Oetker/U. Preis (eds.), *Europäisches Arbeits- und Sozialrecht, EAS, part B – Systematische Darstellungen*, loose-leaf (Heidelberg: Forkel, last update: August 2003), B 2500; B. Hepple, *Working Time – A New Legal Framework?* Employment Paper No 3 (London: Institute for Public Policy Resarch, 1991); B. A. Hepple/B. W. Napier, 'Temporary Workers and the Law', *ILJ* 7 (1978), 84–99; M. Jeffery, 'The Commission Proposals on 'Atypical Work': Back to the Drawing Board … Again', *ILJ* 24 (1995), 296–299; A. Junker, 'Grünbuch Arbeitsrecht – Entwicklungslinien und Perspektiven', in V. Rieble/A. Junker (eds.), *Das Grünbuch und seine Folgen – Wohin treibt das europäische Arbeitsrecht?* (Munich: ZAAR, 2008), 13–26;

A. Junker, 'Arbeitsrecht zwischen Markt und gesellschaftspolitischen Herausforderungen – Differenzierung nach Unternehmensgröße – Familiengerechte Strukturen, Gutachten B zum 65. Deutschen Juristentag', in Ständige Deputation des Deutschen Juristentages (ed.), *Verhandlungen des fünfundsechzigsten Juristentages* (Munich: C.H. Beck, 2004); S. Krebber, 'Der einzelstaatliche Charakter der mitgliedstaatlichen Arbeitsrechte', in V. Rieble/A. Junker (eds.), *Das Grünbuch und seine Folgen – Wohin treibt das europäische Arbeitsrecht?* (Munich: ZAAR, 2008), 33–60; M. Lembke, 'Die "Hartz-Reform" des Arbeitnehmerüberlassungsgesetzes', *BB* 2003, 98–104; K. Lörcher, 'Ungeschützte Arbeitsverhältnisse – Die Richtlinienentwürfe der Europäischen Gemeinschaften zu den "atypischen Arbeitsverhältnissen"', *Der Personalrat* 1991, 73–83; D. Lutz, 'Schutz der Teilzeitarbeitsverhältnisse und der befristeten Arbeitsverhältnisse', *DRdA* 1994, 538–541; A. Neal, 'Atypical Workforms and European Labour Law', *RdA* 1992, 115–120; T. Prinz, 'Europäische Rahmenvereinbarung über Telearbeit', *NZA* 2002, 1268–1270; T. Schmechel, 'Die Rolle des Betriebsrats bei der Einführung und Durchführung von Telearbeit', *NZA* 2004, 237–241; Marlene Schmidt, *Teilzeitarbeit in Europa – Eine Analyse der gemeinschaftsrechtlichen Regelungsbestrebungen auf vergleichender Grundlage des englischen und des deutschen Rechts* (Baden-Baden: Nomos, 1995); Marlene Schmidt, *Die Richtlinienvorschläge der Kommission der Europäischen Gemeinschaften zu den atypischen Arbeitsverhältnissen* (Baden-Baden: Nomos, 1992); R. Wank, 'Atypische Arbeitsverhältnisse', *RdA* 1992, 103–114; R. Wank, 'Das Grünbuch Arbeitsrecht – Eine Perspektive für das europäische Arbeitsrecht?', *AuR* 2007, 244–249; R. Wank, 'Die personellen Grenzen des Europäischen Arbeitsrechts: Arbeitsrecht für Nicht-Arbeitnehmer?', *EuZA* 2008, 172–195; U. Zachert, 'Erosion des Normalarbeitsver-hältnisses in Europa', *BB* 1990, 565–568; see further the bibliographies to §§16–19.

I.   ISSUES

1.   A number of directives regulate **atypical forms of employment**, i.e. those that deviate from the model of the standard employment relationship: fixed-term employment, part-time employment and temporary agency work.[1] Some authors speak of '*precarious*' employment relationships,[2] thereby emphasising the specific need for protection of the workers concerned. Yet, it should not be overlooked that the needs for protection vary between the different types of atypical employment.[3] In addition, regulation is not only concerned with the

---

[1]   M. Jeffery, 'Not Really Going to Work? Of the Directive on Part-Time Work, "Atypical Work" and Attempts to Regulate It', *ILJ* 27 (1998), 193, 205–208; A. Neal, *RdA* 1992, 115, 116 sq., 117 sq. (criticising the term 'atypical' employment as lacking contour and as being rather diffuse with regard to the issues involved). On the development in the UK with some comparative references, see B. A. Hepple/B. W. Napier, *ILJ* 7 (1978), 84–99. See also the stimulating and inspiring contribution by E. Albin, *MLR* 73 (2010), 959–984 (discussing the implications of the change to a 'service world' for labour law – which offers new perspectives on 'atypical' employment relations).

[2]   See e.g. G. Thüsing, *Europäisches Arbeitsrecht*, §4 para. 2 *et passim*.

[3]   Thus rightly A. Junker, in V. Rieble/ A. Junker (eds.), *Das Grünbuch und seine Folgen,* 15, 16 and 18.

protection of employees; the example of temporary agency work illustrates that one of the concerns is also to ensure the admissibility of such forms of employment in the interests of the parties as well as of employment policy (see §18 para. 2 below). The common denominator of the employment relationships in question is their deviation from the typical (model) employment relationship. The Green Paper 'Modernising labour law to meet the challenges of the 21st century' also refers to 'those engaged in working arrangements differing from the standard contractual model'.[4] Union law does **not** (attempt to) regulate atypical employment relationships **comprehensively** (and, indeed, this would not even be possible, given freedom of contract and the ensuing freedom to define types of contracts) but rather, regulates only partially. Thus, even homework or telework have not been regulated at the Union level, despite their relevance to the internal market;[5] the same is true with regard to seasonal work or on-call work.[6]

2. Atypical employment relationships have become **increasingly important** in recent decades.[7] There are various reasons for this. The main factors appear to be a flexibilisation of the organisation of work and a 'feminisation' of the workforce.[8] Furthermore, the Member States and the Union have considered atypical forms of employment as an instrument for the promotion of employment. Atypical employment relationships may provide a chance for (re-) entry into the employment market after a longer period of unemployment (e.g. following child-rearing or sickness). Atypical employment relationships can alleviate the transition to a standard employment contract. At the same time, there are specific risks and needs for protection which are inherent in atypical employment relationships. Thus, there is a risk of atypical workers being treated less favourably than 'normal' workers. Because of a lack of continuity in

---

4   Commission, Green Paper 'Modernising labour law to meet the challenges of the 21st century' of 22 November 2011, COM(2006) 708 final, 7; see §1 para. 40 above.

5   But see the (voluntary) framework agreement (concluded outside the social dialogue of Articles 154 sq. TFEU) of the European social partners on telework of 2002 (*RdA* 2002, 55; available at www.etuc.org/a/579; see e.g. T. Prinz, *NZA* 2002, 1268–1270; T. Schmechel, *NZA* 2004, 237–241; also the reference by M. Weiss, 'Transnationale Kollektivvertragsstrukturen in der EG: Informalität oder Verrechtlichung?', in H. Konzen et al. (eds.), *Festschrift für Rolf Birk* (Tübingen: Mohr Siebeck, 2008), 957, 963 sq.

6   Critically e.g. A. Neal, *RdA* 1992, 115 sq.; also G. Thüsing, *Europäisches Arbeitsrecht*, §4 para. 1.

7   A. Neal, *RdA* 1992, 115 sq.; S. Krebber, in V. Rieble/A. Junker (eds.), *Das Grünbuch und seine Folgen*, 16–24 (with comparative references; finding a development from employee-protection to employment market regulation).

8   A. Neal, *RdA* 1992, 115, 116 ('feminisation of the workforce'); N. Busby/D. Christie, 'The Regulation of Temporary Agency Work in the European Union', *Cambrian L.R.* 2005, 15–28 (quoting M. Castells, *The Internet Galaxy: Reflections on the Internet, Business and Society* (Oxford: Oxford University Press 2001), 95: 'the "organisation man" is out, the "flexible woman" is in'); A. Junker, *Arbeitsrecht zwischen Markt und gesellschaftspolitischen Herausforderungen*, B 98-B 104.

employment, there is a danger that atypical workers may be excluded from continued training or education and thus be excluded from the regular labour market. This may trigger a downward spiral ('low skill bad job trap').[9]

3.   In light of these issues, the regulation of atypical employment in Union law pursues **various purposes**.[10] First, there is protection against sex discrimination. If and to the extent that women are predominantly being employed in fixed-term or part-time relationships, less favourable treatment of such atypical workers may imply indirect discrimination of women (§9 paras. 17 and 50 above).[11] Second, specific additional measures are required for the protection of atypical employees, particularly with regard to safety and health but also with regard to their occupational advancement. Third, the legislator also pursues objectives of occupational policy (integration into the labour market); this is particularly clear with regard to temporary agency work which should not be unduly restricted by the Member States. Finally, one could think of an internal market rationale, especially with regard to the area of temporary agency work which is usually more heavily regulated; here, uniform standards could help to facilitate cross-border activity (see §18 para. 5 below). However, this latter purpose is only inadequately addressed by the directives, the Services in the Internal Market Directive in particular specifically excludes temporary agency work from its scope (Article 2(2)(e) SIMD; see also §3 paras. 75–77 above).

II.   STATUS QUO, DEVELOPMENT AND COMPETENCES

1.   *Overview*

4.   Today, there are **four directives** which address issues of atypical employment relationships:

- the Part-Time Work Directive (PTWD, §16),
- the Fixed-Term Work Directive (FTWD, §17)
- the Temporary Agency Work Directive (TAWD, §18), and
- the Temporary Employment Safety and Health Directive (TESHD, §19).

All four directives share a **common root**.

---

[9]   L. Zappala, 'The Temporary Agency Workers' Directive: An Impossible Agreement? ', *ILJ* 32 (2003), 310, 314.

[10]   For a different view see C. Barnard, *EC Employment Law*, 469 sqq. (considering regulation of atypical employment relationships as an aspect of family friendly policies).

[11]   See also M. Schmidt, *Teilzeitarbeit in Europa*, 49–80.

2. Legislative Development and Competences

5. The legislative development of the relevant directives is closely connected with the development of the (then:) Community's competences. The Community had already undertaken to regulate atypical employment relationships in the 1980s.[12] After the 1974 Council Resolution concerning the social action programme[13], the 1979 Council Resolution on the adaptation of working time[14], and the 1980 Resolution of the Parliament on employment and the adaptation of working time,[15] a number of proposals for directives were put forward: on voluntary part-time work[16] as well as on 'temporary work' (i.e. temporary agency work) and fixed-term work.[17] The proposals, which were based upon Article 100 EEC (Article 115 TFEU)[18] were, however, opposed by the United Kingdom and Denmark and ultimately failed, given the requirement of unanimous voting.[19]

6. The 1989 **Community Charter of Fundamental Social Rights** (§2 paras. 65–77) picked up the subject of atypical employment relationships again.

---

12 On the development up to the 1990 proposals M. Schmidt, *Die Richtlinienvorschläge der Kommission der Europäischen Gemeinschaften zu den atypischen Arbeitsverhältnissen*; R. Wank, *RdA* 1992, 103–114; U. Zachert, *BB* 1990, 565–568. Also M. Jeffery, *ILJ* 24 (1995), 296–299; id., 'Not Really Going to Work? Of the Directive on Part-Time Work, "Atypical Work" and Attempts to Regulate It', *ILJ* 27 (1998), 193, 190–204; M. Schmidt, *Teilzeitarbeit in Europa*, 271–346. Specifically with regard to temporary agency work Commission, Proposal for a Directive oft he European Parliament and the Council on working conditions for temporary workers, COM(2002) 149 final, OJ 2002 C 203/1, 8–11; A. Feuerborn, in *EAS*, B 2500 paras. 91–104; T. Raab, 'Europäische und nationale Entwicklungen im Recht der Arbeitnehmerüberlassung', *ZfA* 2003, 389, 396; B. Riederer von Paar, in P. Schüren/W. Hamann (eds.), *Arbeitnehmerüberlassungsgesetz*, Einl. AÜG paras. 5561–561, 604; J. Treber, 'Sozialer Dialog in der Europäischen Union und Gleichbehandlung bei Teilzeitarbeit – Die Richtlinie des Rates zu der von UNICE, CEEP und EGB geschlossenen Rahmenvereinbarung über Teilzeitarbeit', *ZTR* 1998, 250, 252 sq.; G. Schnorr, 'Die gewerbsmäßige Arbeitnehmerüberlassung – Analyse des Rechtszustands in den Mitgliedstaaten der Europäischen Gemeinschaften und Vorschläge einer Rechtsangleichung', *RdA* 1972, 191–209.

13 Council Resolution of 21 January 1974 concerning a social action programme, OJ 1974 C 13/1, 3 ('to protect workers hired through temporary employment agencies and to regulate the activities of such firms with a view to eliminating abuses therein').

14 Council Resolution of 18 December 1979 on the adaptation of working time, OJ 1980 C 2/1.

15 Resolution of the Parliament of 17 September 1981 on employment and the adaptation of working time, OJ 1981 C 260/54.

16 Proposal for a Council Directive on Voluntary Part-time Work of 22 December 1981, COM(81) 775 final, OJ 1982 C 62/7. Amended Proposal for a Council Directive on Voluntary Part-time Work of 5 January 1983, COM(82) 830 final, OJ 1983 C 18/5.

17 Proposal for a Council Directive concerning Temporary Work of 7 May 1982, COM(82) 155 final, OJ 1982 C 128/2; see in detail F. Becker/P. Bader, *RdA* 1983, 1–18 (also reproducing the proposal). Amended Proposal for a Council Directive Concerning the Supply of Workers by Temporary Employment Businesses and Fixed-Duration Contracts of Employment of 6 April 1984, OJ 1984 C 133/1.

18 The competence had been controversial; see C. Rolfs, in *EAS*, B 3200 para. 7; F. Becker/P. Bader, *RdA* 1983, 1, 10 (doubting the relevance for the internal market).

19 See in more detail M. Schmidt, *Teilzeitarbeit in Europa*, 283–285.

With regard to 'fair remuneration', the Charter expressed the objective that 'workers subject to terms of employment other than an open-ended full-time contract shall receive an equitable reference wage' ('in accordance with arrangements applying in each country') (No. 5 CCFR). The Charter further aims to improve living and working conditions 'as regards in particular the duration and organisation of working time and forms of employment other than open-ended contracts, such as fixed-term contracts, part-time working, temporary work and seasonal work' (No. 7 CCFR).

7.   The Commission subsequently presented a package of **three proposals for directives in 1990,** which all concerned the regulation of temporary work.[20] The order of the proposed directives was based upon the respective competences:

–   Directive regarding working conditions, based upon Article 100 EEC (Article 115 TFEU),[21]
–   Directive regarding distortion of competition,[22] based upon Article 100a EEC (Article 114 TFEU), and
–   Directive regarding an improvement in safety and health, based upon Article 118a EEC (Article 153 TFEU).[23]

Only the last of these three proposals was eventually enacted (see §19 below, Temporary Employment Safety and Health Directive). The other proposals, again, did not clear the hurdle of the unanimity requirement, given the United Kingdom's resistance.[24]

8.   It was not until the **Social Policy Protocol to the 1997 Maastricht Treaty** (§4 para. 4 above) – to which the United Kingdom was not a part – came into effect that a suitable competence was established for further legislation. This was the legal basis for the 1997 **Part-Time Work Directive** (§16).[25] The Directive's substantive regulation was rather modest though, and critical observers submit

---

[20]   See B. Hepple, *Working Time – A New Legal Framework?*, 20 sqq.; K. Lörcher, *Der Personalrat* 1991, 73–83; D. Lutz, *DRdA* 1994, 538–541.
[21]   Proposal for a Council Directive on Certain Employment Relationships with regard to Working Conditions, COM(90) 228 final, OJ 1990 C 224/4.
[22]   Proposal for a Council Directive on Certain Employment Relationships with regard to Distortions of Competition, COM(90) 228 final, OJ 1990 C 224/6. Amendment to the Proposal for a Council Directive on Certain Employment Relationships with regard to Distortions of Competition, COM(90) 533 final, OJ 1990 C 305/8.
[23]   Proposal for a Council Directive Supplementing the Measures to Encourage Improvements in the Safety and Health at Work of Temporary Workes, COM(90) 228 final, OJ 1990 C 224/8.
[24]   M. Jeffery, *ILJ* 24 (1995), 296, 298 sq.; S. Deakin/G. Morris, *Labour Law,* para. 3.58 (see also para. 3.52, pointing out that the provision on the prevention of abuse in the FTWA 'signifies a radical departure from the traditional position in UK law').
[25]   On the negotiations of the social partners I. Kaufmann, 'Die europäische Sozialpartnervereinbarung über befristete Arbeitsverträge', *AuR* 1999, 332, 332 sq.

that the Commission may have been interested in a successful test of the social dialogue procedure rather than the substance of the regulation as such.[26] After the Labour Party came into power in the United Kingdom in 1998, the scope of the Part-Time Work Directive was extended by Directive 98/23/EG,[27] based upon Article 100 EEC (Article 115 TFEU), so as to also cover the UK. The 1999 **Fixed-Term Work Directive**[28] (§17 below) was also enacted through the social dialogue procedure (which had, meanwhile, been incorporated into the Treaty by the 1997 Amsterdam Treaty; cf. now Article 155 TFEU).

9.   While the social partners had thus concluded framework agreements on part-time work and fixed-term work by using the social dialogue procedure in (what is now) Article 155 TFEU, negotiations over a framework agreement for temporary agency work failed. The negotiations had been difficult from the outset, as the employer side aimed for liberalisation, while the employee side insisted upon further regulation (including a limitation to temporary agency work) and an improvement of employee protection. A critical issue was whether the prohibition of discrimination should be based upon a comparison with the employees of the temporary-work agency or those of the user undertaking.[29] The underlying cause for differences lay in the disparate regulatory systems of the Member States. The evaluation of the needs for protection changes depending upon whether the temporary agency worker is employed by the temporary-work agency only for the duration of his work assignment with the user undertaking, or permanently, with the consequence that he will also be paid in any interim period between two assignments. After the negotiations between the social partners failed in May 2001, the Commission presented a first proposal for a directive in March 2002[30] and, after consultation with the Economic and Social Committee and the Parliament, a second, amended proposal was produced in November 2002.[31] The proposal built upon the negotiations with the social

---

[26]   J. Kreimer-de Fries, 'EU-Teilzeitvereinbarung – kein gutes Omen für die Zukunft der europäischen Verhandlungsebenen', *AuR* 1998, 314, 316 sq.

[27]   Council Directive 98/23/EC of 7 April 1998 on the extension of Directive 97/81/EC on the framework agreement on part-time work concluded by UNICE, CEEP and the ETUC to the United Kingdom of Great Britain and Northern Ireland, OJ 1998 L 131/10.

[28]   Council Directive 1999/70/EC of 28 June 1999 concerning the framework agreement on fixed-term work concluded by ETUC, UNICE and CEEP, OJ 1999 L 175/43.

[29]   E. L. Jones, 'Temporary Agency Labour: Back to Square One?', *ILJ* 31 (2002), 183, 184 sq., 187 (unions aimed at equal treatment with the employees of the user undertaking, employers preferred leaving the issue for the Member States or the [national] social partners to decide).

[30]   Commission, Proposal for a Directive of the European Parliament and the Council on working conditions for temporary workers, COM(2002) 149 final, OJ 2002 C 203/1. On the proposal, see e.g. G. Thüsing, 'Europäische Impulse im Recht der Arbeitnehmerüberlassung – Zum Entwurf einer Richtlinie des Europäischen Parlaments und des Rates über die Arbeitsbedingungen von Leiharbeitnehmern – KOM(2002) 149 endgültig', DB 2002, 2218–2223.

[31]   Commission, Amended proposal for a Directive of the European Parliament and the Council on working conditions for temporary workers, COM(2002) 701 final.

partners and further developed their concepts with regard to the controversial issues. The objective was to establish temporary agency work as, to promote its acceptance and use and, at the same time, ensure minimum standards of protection for workers. To achieve these goals, the Directive was to lay down a uniform framework for temporary agency work in the EU. After the proposal had been put on hold for a number of years, as the Council could not reach an agreement,[32] the Council finally agreed on a common position on 15 September 2008,[33] which was the basis for the enactment of the Temporary Agency Work Directive (TAWD)[34] on 19 November 2008.

III.   COMMON DEFINITIONS AND CONCEPTS

10.   In substance, we can distinguish the Temporary Employment Health and Safety Directive on the one hand and the Part-Time Work Directive, the Fixed Term Work Directive and the Temporary Agency Work Directive on the other. The Temporary Employment Health and Safety Directive, which was the first to be enacted, contains a number of definitions which the legislator (or the social partners, as applicable) have also used in subsequent regulation (part-time work, fixed term work, temporary agency work).

11.   The central instrument of protection employed by the Part-Time Work Directive, the Fixed-Term Work Directive and the Temporary Agency Work Directive is a **prohibition of discrimination** ('principle of equal treatment'). It prohibits any discrimination of such atypical workers in comparison with workers in 'regular' employment. In other words, the prohibition of discrimination does not protect the workers in respect of their personal characteristics, but rather as members of a specific group of workers. It prohibits less favourable treatment in comparison with workers in standard employment relationships. The application of this prohibition to part-time and fixed term workers is straightforward. As regards temporary agency work, the question of proper comparison arises: Should the comparator standard be the

---

[32]   See in more detail press release IP/03/796 of 3 June 2003, available at http://europa.eu/rapid/pressReleasesAction.do?reference=IP/03/796&format=PDF&aged=1&language=EN&guiLanguage=en. Two aspects proved problematic, the deregulation (general admissibility of temporary agency work) on the one hand and the reference point for the prohibition of discrimination on the other (on this latter point, see the text in the following paragraphs); N. Busby/D. Christie, 'The Regulation of Temporary Agency Work in the European Union', *Cambrian L.R.* 2005, 15, 26 sq.

[33]   Common Position (EC) No 24/2008 adopted by the Council on 15 September 2008 with a view to the adoption of Directive 2008/.../EC of the European Parliament and of the Council of... on temporary agency work, OJ 2008 C 254 E/36.

[34]   Directive 2008/104/EC of the European Parliament and of the Council of 19 November 2008 on temporary agency work, OJ 2008 L 327/9.

workers of the temporary-work agency or those of the user undertaking? This issue posed a considerable obstacle for the approximation of national laws, given the different systems of protection traditionally pursued by the Member States.

12. Other protective instruments include provisions aimed at facilitating a change from an atypical employment relationship to a 'standard' employment relationship. These are, however, rather 'soft' in nature, taking the form of information rules (information about open positions) or of an appeal to the good-will of the employer.

IV. SPECIFICALLY: EQUAL PAY AND LEGISLATIVE COMPETENCES

13. The principle of discrimination entails a specific issue of Union competences. As a preliminary aspect, there is an issue of interpretation: Is the prohibition of discrimination *intended* to also cover discrimination in regard of pay. And, if that is the case: Did the Community (Union) have the *competence* for such (indirect) regulation of pay.

14. The issue of interpretation is controversial with regard to the Part-Time Work Directive and the Fixed Term Work Directive; in each case, the prohibition of discrimination is related to 'employment conditions'. The term may well cover remuneration but it is also open to another interpretation. The prohibition of discrimination in the Temporary Agency Work Directive, however, unequivocally also covers pay, Articles 2(1)(f) and 5(2) TAWD.

15. *Sedes materiae* of the issue of competences is Article 2(2) Social Policy Protocol and its successor in Article 153(5) TFEU. Pursuant to these provisions, the competence for EU legislation based upon Article 153 TFEU or the social dialogue procedure of Article 155 TFEU, does not apply to pay (see in more detail §4 paras. 8, 10 above). The issue of whether Articles 153 and 155 TFEU empower the Union to also regulate pay discrimination can also impact the interpretation of the Directives (interpretation in conformity with primary law; s. §4 para. 1 above).

16. Some authors already deny that the Union has competence to prohibit discrimination in respect of pay under Articles 153 or 155 TFEU. Article 153(5) TFEU not only prohibits the direct regulation of pay, they argue, but also any indirect regulation through a prohibition of discrimination. Others argue that Article 153(5) TFEU merely prohibits the establishment of a Union-wide minimum wage.[35] An intermediary position distinguishes between whether a prohibition can be applied without any additional value judgement: While this was true with regard to part-time work and fixed-term work (comparison with the normal open-ended, full-term employment relationship), it was not true with regard to temporary agency work (value judgement whether the measure for comparison is the temporary-work agency's workers or those of the user undertaking); Article 153(5) TFEU left such value judgement to the Member States.[36] We have already addressed this issue in our discussion of competences (§4 paras. 11 sq.). The better arguments are in favour of a Union competence for the indirect regulation of pay. This is also true with regard to temporary agency work. If the Union legislator requires a comparison of the temporary agency workers with the workers of the user undertaking, it merely opts for one of several *systems* of temporary agency work. This is the gist of its value judgement, rather than the determination of pay.

V. REGULATORY CONTEXT

17.   The prohibitions of **sex discrimination** in primary law and secondary legislation (§9 above; see also para. 3 above) are part of the regulatory environment of the regulation of atypical employment relationships (less favourable treatment of part-time workers as indirect discrimination against women). The prohibition of discrimination on grounds of nationality as embodied, in particular, by the freedom of movement for workers, also has a practical impact upon atypical employment relations (§3 para. 35; less favourable treatment of language assistants as indirect discrimination of foreign nationals). The Directives on atypical employment relationships, however, protect the workers concerned irrespective of sex and nationality; the scope of protection is instead more general and independent. The Equal Treatment Framework Directive with its prohibition of age discrimination provides for supplementary regulation of fixed term employment (§11 paras. 31, 37 above); it is of considerable practical relevance given that e.g. retirement ages or an alleviation of the restrictions of fixed-term work for older workers are used as instruments of labour market policy (cf. Article 6 ETFD). With regard to industrial safety, the broad range of EU directives on health and safety are also part of the regulatory environment (§13).

18.   Other directives regulate, or refer to, temporary agency work in individual respects. The Posting of Workers Directive provides for the regulation of cross-

---

[35]   Thus also ECJ Case C-268/06 *Impact* [2008] ECR I-2483 paras. 105–133 (on the Fixed-Term Work Directive).

[36]   See in detail and with references §4 para. 12 above.

border temporary agency work (§6 paras. 12, 22 sq., 26 above). In respect of their personal scope of application, several directives provide that while the term 'worker' must be determined by national law, atypical workers may not be excluded from its scope (see e.g. the Transfer of Undertakings Directive; §24 para. 14). Temporary agency work is a special form of services and is thus covered by the freedom of services; restrictions to cross-border temporary agency work services may, however, be justified on mandatory grounds of public policy (e.g. employee protection) within the limits of proportionality (§3 paras. 65–72). The Services in the Internal Market Directive does not regulate atypical employment relationships, and temporary agency work is specifically excluded, Article 2(2)(e) SIMD (see para. 3 above).

19.   Finally, the Written Statement Directive (§12 above) can also be considered to be part of the regulatory context of the regulation of atypical forms of employment. The Directive was originally triggered by the observation that the flexibilisation of employment was leading to new (atypical) forms of employment. While the Directive applies to all employees, it specifically serves the purpose of providing transparency as to the non-standardised conditions of atypical employment relationships.

§16. THE PART-TIME WORK DIRECTIVE

CONTENT

Bibliography:

W. Balze, 'Arbeitszeit, Urlaub und Teilzeitarbeit', in H. Oetker/U. Preis (eds.), *Europäisches Arbeits- und Sozialrecht, EAS, part B – Systematische Darstellungen,* loose-leaf (Heidelberg: Forkel, last update: February 2011), B 3100 paras 242–300; C. Barnard/B. Hepple, 'Substantive Equality', *C.L.J.* 59 (2000), 562–585; N. Busby, 'The Part-Time Workers (Prevention of Less Favourable Treatment) Regulations 2000: Righting a Wrong or out of Proportion', *J.B.L.* 2001, 344–356; W. Däubler, 'Das geplante Teilzeit- und Befristungsgesetz', *ZIP* 2000, 1961–1969; W. Däubler, 'Das neue Teilzeit- und Befristungsgesetz', *ZIP* 2001, 217–225; H. F. Eisemann et al., 'Der Anspruch auf Teilzeitarbeit und seine gerichtliche Durchsetzung in den Niederlanden, Frankreich, Großbritannien, Schweden, Dänemark und der Bundesrepublik Deutschland', *RdA* 2004, 129–141; M. Jeffery, 'Not Really Going to Work? Of the Directive on Part-Time Work, "Atypical Work" and Attempts to Regulate It',

ILJ 27 (1998), 193–213; M. Kliemt, 'Der neue Teilzeitanspruch', *NZA* 2001, 63–71; P. A. Köhler, 'Teilzeitarbeit in Schweden', *EuroAS* 2001, 217–224; J. Kreimer-de Fries, 'EU-Teilzeitvereinbarung – kein gutes Omen für die Zukunft der europäischen Verhandlungsebenen', *AuR* 1997, 314–317; A. McColgan, 'Missing the Point? The Part-time Workers (Prevention of Less Favourable Treatment) Regulations 2000 (SI 2000, No 1551)', *ILJ* 29 (2000), 260–267; U. Preis/M. Gotthardt, 'Neuregelung der Teilzeitarbeit und befristeten Arbeitsverhältnisse', *DB* 2000, 2065–2074; R. Richardi/G. Annuß, 'Gesetzliche Neuregelung von Teilzeitarbeit und Befristung', *BB* 2000, 2201–2205; K. Riesenhuber, 'Anspruch auf Teilzeitbeschäftigung nach §15b BAT?', *NZA* 1995, 56–63; C. Rolfs, 'Das neue Recht der Teilzeitarbeit', *RdA* 2001, 129–143; Marlene Schmidt, 'Die neue EG-Richtlinie zur Teilzeitarbeit', *NZA* 1998, 576–582; Marlene Schmidt, *Teilzeitarbeit in Europa – Eine Analyse der gemeinschaftsrechtlichen Regelungsbestrebungen auf vergleichender Grundlage des englischen und des deutschen Rechts* (Baden-Baden: Nomos, 1995); Michael Schmidt, *Die Richtlinienvorschläge der Kommission der Europäischen Gemeinschaften zu den atypischen Arbeitsverhältnisse* (Baden-Baden: Nomos, 1991); J. E. Thurman/G. Trah, 'Part-time work in international perspective', *ILR* 129 (1990), 23–40; G. Thüsing, 'Das Verbot der Diskriminierung wegen Teilzeit und Befristung nach §4 TzBfG – Aktuelles und Grundsätzliches zu einer Rechtsfigur *sui generis*', *ZfA* 2002, 249–273; J. Treber, 'Sozialer Dialog in der Europäischen Union und Gleichbehandlung bei Teilzeitarbeit – Die Richtlinie des Rates zu der von UNICE, CEEP und EGB geschlossenen Rahmenvereinbarung über Teilzeitarbeit', *ZTR* 1998, 250–257; H. P. Viethen, 'Richtlinie der EG zur Teilzeitarbeit', *EuroAS* 2002, 51–56; R. Wank, 'Atypische Arbeitsverhältnisse', *RdA* 1992, 103–114; U. Zachert, '"Erosion des Normalarbeitsverhältnisses" in Europa', *BB* 1990, 565–568; See further the bibliography to §15.

Cases:

ECJ Case C-313/02 *Wippel* v. *Peek & Cloppenburg* [2004] ECR I-9483; ECJ Joined Cases C-55/07 and C-56/07 *Michaeler* [2008] ECR I-3135; ECJ Case C-486/08 *Zentralbetriebsrat der Landeskrankenhäuser Tirols* [2010] ECR I-3527; ECJ Joined Cases C-395/08 and C-396/08 *Bruno and Pettini* [2010] ECR I-5119; ECJ Case C-151/10 *Dai Cugini* v *Rijksdienst voor Sociale Zekerheid* 7 April 2011; ECJ Case C-349/11 *Yangwei* 9 December 2011; ECJ Case C-393/10 *O'Brien* 1 March 2012.

I. ISSUES AND OVERVIEW[1]

1. Part-time work is an important instrument for the **flexible organisation of working time**. It enables the employer to hire workers in accordance with the specific needs of his undertaking. For workers, part-time work may help accommodate professional interests with personal needs such as the

---

[1] See also the overview in §15 above, in particular with regard to the legislative history and EU competences. On the development of part-time work regulation in particular (with comparative references) U. Zachert, *BB* 1990, 565–568; J. E. Thurman/G. Trah, *ILR* 129 (1990), 23–40.

compatibility of occupational and family life.[2] While both sides *may* have an interest in part-time work, their interests may also conflict in a given case, particularly with regard to the allocation of working hours during the work day and a subsequent change in the number of working hours or their allocation during the work day.

2. Notwithstanding the positive aspects of part-time work, full-time work is still the standard form of employment and part-time work thus remains **atypical** and – with regard to the needs of the worker for protection – 'precarious' (see §15 para. 1 above). In practice, part-time workers often do not enjoy equal treatment in comparison with full-term employees (absolutely or pro rata temporis), e.g., with regard to pay, promotion or access to facilities of the undertaking or establishment etc. Traditionally, it has been predominantly women who have worked part-time, often because they would shoulder the larger part of child-rearing and housework. Less favourable treatment of part-time workers thus often implies indirect discrimination against women (§9 paras. 17, 50 above).[3]

3. The Part-Time Work Directive (PTWD)[4] merely serves to implement the Part-Time Work Framework Agreement (PTWFA) of the European Social Partners of 6 June 1997, which is annexed to it and which contains the substantive provisions.[5] The PTWD/PTWFA is not primarily aimed at the realisation of the internal market but rather pursues **social policy** objectives. It is intended to promote part-time work as a desirable form of employment.[6] Given that predominantly women work part-time, it also serves as an instrument to combat sex discrimination and to reconcile professional and family life. The Framework Agreement merely provides for **minimum standards** (cf. Article 2(5) Social Policy Protocol, today's Article 153(4) TFEU; Preamble PTWFA). Its central regulation is the **prohibition of discrimination** contained in Clause 4 PTWFA, which is supplemented – where appropriate – by the principle of pro rata temporis. Other provisions which aim to promote part-time work through several different instruments (Clause 5 PTWFA) take the form of more of an appeal than strictly binding obligations.[7] They merely require the employer to give consideration to the needs of (part-time) workers.

---

2   For a discussion in context, see H. Collins, *Employment Law,* 91–95.

3   For an overview, see M. Schmidt, *Teilzeitarbeit in Europa,* 49–80.

4   Council Directive 97/81/EC of 15 December 1997 concerning the Framework Agreement on part-time work concluded by UNICE, CEEP and the ETUC, OJ 1998 L 14/9.

5   On the competence and the mechanism of implementation of framework agreements of the social partners see §4 paras. 33–41 above.

6   ECJ Joined Cases C-55/07 and C-56/07 *Michaeler* [2008] ECR I-3135 paras. 21 sq.

7   M. Jeffery, *ILJ* 27 (1998), 193, 195–199 (doubting that the Directive reaches its objectives). From a union perspective critically with regard to the low level of employee protection J. Kreimer-de Fries, *AuR* 1997, 314–317.

Even with regard to information, the provision merely requires the employer to 'give consideration'. Only the prohibition of termination in Clause 5(2) PTWFA imposes a more stringent obligation upon the employer, albeit of limited reach. The prohibition of discrimination of Clause 4 PTWFA also particularly serves the purpose of preventing sex discrimination, where (and as long as) predominantly women work part-time. The Framework Agreement, however, goes beyond that: While the prohibition of sex discrimination could cover less favourable treatment only as indirect discrimination against women, the Directive 'upgrades' the prohibition of discrimination against part-time workers, as an object of protection in itself. Part-time work is being promoted autonomously and independently of its relationship to the professional activity of women.

4.   The Health and Safety in Temporary Employment Directive provides for **supplementary regulation** in the field of industrial safety (§19 below). The Fixed Term Directive (§17 below) and the Temporary Agency Work Directive (§18 below) in many ways correlate with the Part-Time Work Directive. Part-time work and fixed-term work are often considered to be related subjects of regulation (e.g., in Germany, they are regulated in a single act). Temporary agency work is in some jurisdictions regarded as a form of part-time work. A common denominator of all three types of employment is that they are conceived as atypical (or 'precarious') employment relationships and it is, in many cases, predominantly women who are employed in these ways. The instruments of protection of the three directives are consequently similar in many ways (even though there are some distinctive features as well).

II.   SCOPE OF APPLICATION AND DEFINITIONS

5.   The Framework Agreement applies to part-time workers. Only the aspect of part-time work, and not the term '**worker**', is autonomously defined in Clause 3 No. 1 PTWFA. It is for national law to determine who qualifies as a **worker**.[8] Clause 2(1) PTWFA refers to part-time workers 'who have an employment contract or employment relationship as defined by the law, collective agreement or practice in force *in each Member State*'; see also Recital 16 PTWD. The Member State's discretion is, however, limited by the implementation principles and the principle of effectiveness. An exclusion of certain groups of employees must not be arbitrary and may not be justified on purely formal considerations. This requires that 'the nature of the employment relationship concerned is substantially different from the relationship between

---

[8]   ECJ Case C-313/02 *Wippel* v. *Peek & Cloppenburg* [2004] ECR I-9483 para. 40; ECJ Case Case C-393/10 *O'Brien* 1 March 2012 paras. 28–33.

employers and their employees which fall within the category of "workers" under national law'.[9]

6. An employee is a **part-time worker** if his normal hours of work are less than the normal hours of work of a comparable full-time worker. For the purpose of this definition, 'normal hours of work' are calculated on a weekly basis or on average over a period of employment of up to one year.

7. A **comparable full-time worker** is a worker in *the same establishment*, having the same type of employment contract or relationship, who is engaged in *similar*[10] *work* or occupation. For comparison purposes, seniority, qualification and skills should be considered as well as 'other considerations'. Where there is no comparable full-time worker in the same establishment, the comparison must be made on a normative or hypothetical basis. The position of a hypothetical worker under the applicable collective agreements and laws should be considered.

8. Such hypothetical comparison is of primary importance with regard to the prohibition of discrimination (paras. 13–24 below). Hypothetical comparison is **critical** where it implies an equalisation of the workers in question with those of *another establishment*. There is, in principle, no reason why one employer should not treat his part-time workers (or his full-time workers, for that matter) less favourably than *another employer* treats his full-time workers.[11] The hypothetical comparison should thus be made with regard to hypothetical workers of the same employer, but not as a comparison of workers of different employers, i.e. on the scale of the labour market. The burden of proof is particularly high for workers in these circumstances.

9. In the case of a 'part-time worker working according to need' whose working hours are determined by requests of the employer, subject to the worker's right to refuse, the Court of Justice did not find that the criteria of a 'comparable full-time worker' were met (and thus did not find discrimination).[12]

10. The personal scope of application is **not** limited by a **threshold working time**.[13] The Member States (after consultation with the social partners) or social

---

9   ECJ Case C-393/10 *O'Brien* 1 March 2012 paras. 34 sqq.; AG Kokott, Opinion in Case C-393/10 *O'Brien* 17 November 2011 pt. 53.

10 This alleviates the finding (or testing) of discrimination where there are no full-time workers performing identical work; G. Thüsing, *ZfA* 2002, 249, 255 sq.

11 G. Thüsing, *ZfA* 2002, 249, 257; id., *Europäisches Arbeitsrecht*, §4 para. 18.

12 ECJ Case C-313/02 *Wippel* v. *Peek & Cloppenburg* [2004] ECR I-9483 paras. 61 sq.

13 The 1990 proposals, with a view to the resulting costs, had limited the scope of application to workers with an average weekly working time of eight hours; K. Lörcher, 'Ungeschützte Arbeitsverhältnisse – Die Richtlinienentwürfe der Europäischen Gemeinschaften zu den

partners may, however, exclude **casual workers** from the terms of the Framework Agreement.[14] Casual work may, for example, cover seasonal work during Christmas sales.[15]

11. Issues of **social security** are excluded from its substantive scope of application.[16] In paragraph 3 of the Preamble to the Framework Agreement, the social partners refer to the national legislation of the Member States. They support the Council's desire to make social security systems 'more employment-friendly' by 'developing social protection systems capable of adapting to new patterns of work and of providing appropriate protection to people engaged in such work'.

III.   THE PRINCIPLE OF EQUAL TREATMENT

12. The core of the Framework Agreement is the prohibition of discrimination (1) which is being supplemented by the principle of pro rata temporis (2). The Member States may – as a restriction to equal treatment – make access to particular conditions of employment subject to specific factors unrelated to part-time work (3). The Court of Justice has interpreted Article 4 PTWFA 'as articulating a **principle of European Union social law** which cannot be interpreted restrictively'.[17]

1.   *The Prohibition of Discrimination*

a)   Scope of Application

13. The prohibition of discrimination applies to the **employment conditions** of part-time workers. The term 'employment conditions' is central to the Framework Agreement's scope of application and must thus be autonomously determined. As in other areas of EU employment law, the term must be construed broadly,[18] so as to refer to any conditions of the employment contract or relationship.[19] Employment conditions include, for example, the duration and organisation of working time or leave and participation in advanced training

---

"atypischen Arbeitsverhältnissen"', *Der Personalrat* 1991, 73, 80 (critically); R. Wank, *RdA* 1992, 103, 106.

[14]   Cf. ECJ Case C-313/02 *Wippel* v. *Peek & Cloppenburg* [2004] ECR I-9483 para. 38.

[15]   H. P. Viethen, *EuroAS* 2002, 51, 53.

[16]   On the 1990 proposals, see *Wank*, RdA 1992, 103, 106 sq. ('The focus of the proposals is on equal treatment with regard to social security.').

[17]   ECJ Joined Cases C-395/08 and C-396/08 *Bruno and Pettini* [2010] ECR I-5119 para. 32; Case C-151/10 *Dai Cugini* v *Rijksdienst voor Sociale Zekerheid* 7 April 2011 para. 36.

[18]   W. Balze, in *EAS*, B 3100 para. 260; M. Schmidt, *NZA* 1998, 576, 578. See e.g. ECJ Case C-116/94 *Meyers* [1995] ECR I-2131 (concerning sex discrimination).

[19]   See now ECJ Joined Cases C-395/08 and C-396/08 *Bruno and Pettini* [2010] ECR I-5119 para. 32.

courses (see also Clause 5(3)(d) PTWFA). They also cover issues such as the eligibility as employee representatives.[20]

14. It is a matter of controversy whether **pay** is an employment condition within the meaning of Clause 4(1) PTWFA because the provision of Article 2(6) Social Policy Protocol (now Article 153(5) TFEU; see §4 paras. 10–12 and §15 paras. 13–16 above) specifically excludes pay from the Union's legislative competence. This exclusion should not, however, be construed so as to prohibit any regulation with regard to pay; in particular, it does not apply to 'indirect regulation' through a prohibition of discrimination.[21] The competence thus does not require the exclusion of pay from Article 4(1) PTWFA, and the broad concept of 'employment conditions' also covers pay.[22] The Court has interpreted the provision so as to cover 'pay' in the broad sense established in its jurisprudence on Article 157 TFEU, and concluded that 'the term "employment conditions" within the meaning of Clause 4(1) of the framework agreement covers pensions which depend on an employment relationship between worker and employer, excluding statutory social security pensions, which are determined less by that relationship than by considerations of social policy'.[23]

15. Another controversial issue is whether the conditions of **termination** fall within the scope of the prohibition of discrimination. The wording of Clause 4(1) PTWFA is not unequivocal. European anti-discrimination law usually refers to the 'employment and working conditions, including dismissals' (see e.g. Article 14(1)(c) SDD; see also §9 para. 37, §10 para. 3, §11 para. 6 above). This could indicate that 'employment conditions' is meant in its broader sense, which would include the conditions of dismissal. However, the legislator otherwise explicitly expressed an intention to cover dismissals. Moreover, the social partners, in full knowledge of this drafting technique and deviating from previous drafts, have not specifically mentioned dismissals in the final Framework Agreement. Furthermore, the Commission based its preceding proposal for a directive on Article 2(1) Social Policy Protocol ('working conditions') rather than on

---

[20] Cf. the Commissions application in the infringement proceedings C-204/04 *Commission* v. *Germany,* OJ 2004 C 201/7 (concerning the exclusion from eligibility for election to staff committees of part-time workers); the Commission abandoned its action after the national provisions had been amended; cf. ECJ Case C-204/04 *Commission* v. *Germany,* OJ 2006 C 154/12 (tenor).

[21] For a more detailed discussion, see §4 paras. 11 sq. above with further references. With regard to the PTWD in particular H. P. Viethen, *EuroAS* 2002, 51, 53 sq.; differently C. Rolfs, in *EAS,* B 3200 para. 14; M. Schmidt, *NZA* 1998, 576, 578 sq.; R. Wank, in P. Hanau/H.-D. Steinmeyer/R. Wank (eds.), *Handbuch des europäischen Arbeits- und Sozialrechts,* §18 para. 257.

[22] On the Fixed-Term Work Directive now ECJ Case C-268/06 *Impact* [2008] ECR I-2483 paras. 105–133 (also with regard to pension benefits).

[23] ECJ Joined Cases C-395/08 and C-396/08 *Bruno and Pettini* [2010] ECR I-5119 paras. 27–51. Critically W. Balze, in *EAS,* B 3100 para. 261.

Article 2(3) Social Policy Protocol ('protection of workers where their employment contract is terminated') (the latter requiring unanimity!).[24] In the light of these systematic considerations, the legislative history and the Union's competences, Clause 4(1) PTWFA should be construed so as not to cover termination.[25]

b) Content

16. 'The prohibition on discrimination laid down in that provision is simply a specific expression of one of the fundamental principles of European Union law, namely the general principle of equality'.[26]

aa) THE PROHIBITION OF DISCRIMINATION

17. Part-time workers must not be treated less favourably than comparable full-time workers solely because they work part-time. The test is whether

- a part-time worker within the meaning of Clause 3 No. 1 PTWFA (paras. 5, 10 above)
- is treated less favourably
- than a comparable full-time worker within the meaning of Clause 3 No. 2 PTWFA
- solely because he works part-time.

For example, the Court considered a national provision, pursuant to which periods not worked by 'vertical-cyclical part-time workers' were disregarded in calculating the **qualifying period for a retirement pension** solely because they were working part-time, to be discriminatory (subject, of course, to justification on objective grounds).[27] Under *vertical-cyclical part-time* arrangements, the employee only works during certain weeks or certain months of the year, on full or reduced hours.

18. The wording of this provision differs from that of the established prohibitions of discrimination in EU employment (and contract) law. In particular, the Framework Agreement does not establish a 'principle of equal

---

[24]   See also J. Treber, *ZTR* 1998, 250, 255 (inconclusive).

[25]   To the same effect W. Balze, in *EAS,* B 3100 para. 262.

[26]   ECJ Joined Cases C-395/08 and C-396/08 *Bruno and Pettini* [2010] ECR I-5119 para. 58.

[27]   ECJ Joined Cases C-395/08 and C-396/08 *Bruno and Pettini* [2010] ECR I-5119 paras. 56–68; approving case not by C. Hießl, *ZESAR* 2011, 82–86; J. Joussen, 'Willkürkontrolle oder "negative Willkürprüfung"?', *EuZA* 2011, 97–110. See also the different analysis of AG Sharpston, Opinion in Joined Cases C-395/08 and C-396/08 *Bruno and Pettini* [2010] ECR I-5119 pts. 90 sqq. (different treatment (a) as between the vertical-cyclicyl part-time workers and horizontal part time workers to the disadvantage of the former, and (b) between horizontal part-time workers and full-time workers, to the disadvantage of full-time workers; discussing a solution under the general principle of non-discrimination).

treatment' which would prohibit direct and indirect discrimination.[28] The wording instead indicates that the prohibition merely extends to direct discrimination. As one can assume that the social partners and the Commission were well aware of the difference, this appears to be a deliberate decision.[29] It also makes sense, given that the prohibition of discrimination is supplemented by the principle of pro rata temporis of paragraph 2, which should largely exclude indirect discrimination.

19. Furthermore, the prohibition only prohibits any *less favourable* treatment. It does not, in other words, object to **more favourable** treatment of part-time workers[30] but, of course, does not require it, either. Yet, the prohibition of sex discrimination may restrict more favourable treatment of part-time workers to the extent that it would amount to indirect discrimination against men.[31]

20. Unlike other directives, the Part-Time Work Directive does not contain a provision on 'victimisation' (retaliation) which would protect workers against adverse treatment as a reaction to the exercise of their rights.[32] An explicit provision is not necessary, either. For one thing, the prohibition of discrimination teleologically includes a prohibition of adverse treatment (see §8 paras. 71 sq. above). For another, any adverse treatment of a part-time worker because of his invocation of rights under the Directive would constitute discrimination on grounds of part-time work.[33]

bb) JUSTIFICATION

21. The prohibition of discrimination is subject to justification on '**objective grounds**' (*raisons objectives, sachliche Gründe*). The grounds for justification can be specified by analogy to the established rules of EU anti-discrimination law.[34]

---

28 Differently W. Balze, in *EAS*, B 3100 para. 257 with reference to ECJ Case C-313/02 *Wippel* [2004] ECR I-9483 paras. 54–56; to the effect also ECJ Joined Cases C-395/08 and C-396/08 *Bruno and Pettini* [2010] ECR I-5119 paras. 58. The general principle referred to in the decision does not necessarily imply, though, that both forms of discrimination, direct and indirect, are prohibited. As here J. Oppertshäuser, in M. Gebauer/T. Wiedmann (eds.), *Zivilrecht unter europäischem Einfluss,* chap. 19 para. 85.

29 Differently H. P. Viethen, *EuroAS* 2002, 51, 54. With doubt concerning the lack of regulation of indirect discrimination G. Thüsing, *ZfA* 2002, 249, 259 sq.

30 H. P. Viethen, *EuroAS* 2002, 51, 54. More narrowly (based on the general principle of equality) G. Thüsing, *ZfA* 2002, 249, 258 sq.

31 R. Richardi/G. Annuß, *BB* 2000, 2201.

32 The 'prohibition of termination' of §5(2) PTWFA (see para. 36 below) does not concern the termination on account of part-time work but the termination on account of the worker's refusal to transfer from part-time work to full-time work or vice versa.

33 Cf. with regard to the prohibition of retaliation of §5 TzBfG U. Preis, in R. Müller-Glöge/U. Preis/I. Schmidt (eds.), *Erfurter Kommentar,* §5 TzBfG paras. 1 sq.

34 Similarly now ECJ Case C-486/08 *Zentralbetriebsrat der Landeskrankenhäuser Tirols* [2010] ECR I-3527 paras. 41–47. See already M. Schmidt, *NZA* 1998, 576, 577. With doubt J. Oppertshäuser, in M. Gebauer/T. Wiedmann (eds.), *Zivilrecht unter europäischem Einfluss,* chap. 19 para. 88.

In order to justify less favourable treatment solely on grounds of part-time work, the employer must establish that the distinction was necessary in order to achieve a legitimate purpose. Determination of a 'legitimate' purpose requires an evaluation with regard to the purposes of the Part-Time Work Directive and the EU legal system.[35] The requirement that the distinction must be 'necessary' refers to the principle of proportionality. Following the Court's jurisprudence, the requirement of objective grounds relates to the individual employment relationship rather than abstract, general norms such as the formal designation of a position. Instead, 'that concept requires the unequal treatment at issue to respond to a genuine need, be appropriate for achieving the objective pursued and be necessary for that purpose'.[36]

22.   Examples can be found in the Court's jurisprudence on sex discrimination. Thus, a distinction between full-time workers and part-time workers may be justified where there is a concrete link between the nature of work performed and the experience gained from the performance of that work upon completion of a certain number of working hours.[37] Distinctions may also be justified in regard to differences in qualifications, work performance or professional experience.[38]

23.   The wording of Clause 4(1) PTWFA ('unless') already hints at the **burden of proof**: It is for the employer to submit and prove any objective grounds. This is appropriate, given that the relevant grounds fall within the employer's sphere of knowledge. Details of the burden of proof are, however, part of the 'arrangements for the application' which, pursuant to paragraph 3, are for the Member States (or the national social partners) to determine (see para. 24 below).

c)   Arrangements for the Application

24.   Arrangements for the application of the prohibition of discrimination (as well as of the principle of pro rata temporis) are for the Member States and/or the social partners to determine. Examples include rules of procedure and the burden of proof (but see also para. 23 above), sanctions, collective actions or state supervision. With regard to **sanctions** and judicial protection in particular, the general implementation principles apply, namely the principles of equivalence and the effectiveness.

---

[35]   Consequently, discriminatory features cannot constitute objective grounds; M. Schmidt, *NZA* 1998, 576, 577.

[36]   ECJ Case Case C-393/10 *O'Brien* 1 March 2012 para. 64.

[37]   ECJ Case C-184/89 *Nimz* [1991] ECR I-297 para. 14; cf. also Case 171/88 *Rinner-Kühn* [1993] ECR I-5534 paras. 13–15.

[38]   G. Thüsing, *ZfA* 2002, 249, 264–272; H. P. Viethen, *EuroAS* 2002, 51, 54.

2. The Principle of Pro Rata Temporis

a) Scope of Application

25. 'Where appropriate', part-time workers should be treated in accordance with the principle of pro rata temporis, Clause 4(2) PTWFA. The reference to the 'appropriateness' does not imply that the scope of application of the principle is left to the Member States;[39] Member States merely regulate the 'arrangements for the application' (para. 30 below). Rather, the imprecise term of 'appropriateness' should be defined in light of the purpose of the provision. Application of the principle of pro rata temporis is 'appropriate' where benefits are (or, in any case, may be from a normative perspective) measured with regard to time. As a minimum, this presupposes that such benefits can be divided so that they can be granted based on time (working hours).[40] This should, e.g., also be the case with regard to childcare.[41] Indivisible benefits such as *access* to institutions of the undertaking or establishment (e.g., cafeteria or library) cannot be granted pro rata temporis.[42] With regard to indivisible benefits, the prohibition of discrimination of Clause 4(1) PTWFA applies.

26. Divisible benefits will often have an element of **pay**.[43] Following the opinion para. 14 above, this is no obstacle to the application of the Directive or the principle of pro rata temporis. The length of annual leave may, e.g., be considered to be a divisible benefit outside pay. Here, application of the principle of pro rata temporis is not only possible (as the case of termination of employment during the course of a given year illustrates) but also *appropriate,* given that annual leave is, by definition, ('annual'!) and is granted based upon (working) time (see only Article 7 WTD, §14 paras. 46–56 above).

b) Content

27. The principle of pro rata temporis means the calculation of benefits proportionate to (working) time. It expresses a central concern of justice if we understand the principle of equality to mean that essentially similar facts should be treated similarly and that essentially dissimilar facts should be treated differently according to the measure of their difference. The principle does not only mean that part-time workers are entitled to equal treatment compared to full-time workers, based upon their working time. It also means that part-time

---

39 Differently H. P. Viethen, *EuroAS* 2002, 51, 55 (for the Member States to determine).

40 M. Schmidt, *NZA* 1998, 576, 577; W. Balze, in *EAS,* B 3100 para. 266.

41 Differently W. Balze, in *EAS,* B 3100 para. 266.

42 C. Rolfs, in *EAS,* B 3200 para. 18; R. Wank, in P. Hanau/H.-D. Steinmeyer/R. Wank (eds.), *Handbuch des europäischen Arbeits- und Sozialrechts,* §18 para. 258.

43 Cf. the overview of specific aspects in U. Preis, in R. Müller-Glöge/U. Preis/I. Schmidt (eds.), *Erfurter Kommentar,* §4 TzBfG paras. 59 sq.

---

employment relationships differ from the 'normal' full-time employment only in respect of working time. For **example**, a part-time worker has a right to annual leave proportionate to his working time.[44]

28. Conversely, the Court held that it is incompatible with the principle of pro rata temporis to reduce an employee's right to annual leave which has already accumulated as a full-time worker, on the ground that he has reduced his working hours from full-time to part-time.[45] The Court has based its finding on the principle of pro rata temporis of Clause 4(2) PTWFA; arguably, the prohibition of discrimination of Clause 4(1) PTWFA would have been the more appropriate basis.

29. While the prohibition of discrimination of paragraph 1 means – negatively – that part-time workers may not be treated less favourably, except for objective reasons. The principle of pro rata temporis means – positively – that part-time workers should enjoy equal treatment compared to full-time workers, proportionate to the relative working time.

c)   Arrangements for the Application

30. Member States and/or the social partners also determine the arrangements for the application of the principle of pro rata temporis, Clause 4(3) PTWFA. They may, in particular, wish to define the central criterion of 'appropriateness' (even though this will still be subject to control by the Court of Justice; see para. 25 above). And, again, they may determine sanctions as well as procedural arrangements.

3.   *Consideration of Periods of Service, Time Worked or Earnings Qualifications*

31. Clause 4(4) PTWFA gives Member States the option to determine certain criteria as grounds for distinction with regard to access to 'particular conditions of employment'.[46] National law may, in other words, provide for a **general exemption** from the prohibition of discrimination.[47] Member States (after

---

[44]   ECJ Case C-486/08 *Zentralbetriebsrat der Landeskrankenhäuser Tirols* [2010] ECR I-3527 para. 33.

[45]   ECJ Case C-486/08 *Zentralbetriebsrat der Landeskrankenhäuser Tirols* [2010] ECR I-3527 para. 32; critical case note – with further discussion of the complex issues underlying the reference – D. Rief, *ZESAR* 2010, 427–430.

[46]   For a critical perspective see M. Jeffery, *ILJ* 27 (1998), 193, 195 sq.

[47]   Differently W. Balze, in *EAS*, B 3100 para. 265 (Member States may provide for particular conditions only on objective grounds).

consultation with the social partners) and/or the social partners may make access to particular conditions of employment subject to

- a period of service,
- time worked or
- earnings qualifications (*Lohn- und Gehaltsbedingungen, conditions de salaire*).

While the relevance of a period of service and time worked is rather obvious for the prohibition of discrimination, it is fairly unclear how the criterion of 'earnings qualifications' could constitute a requirement for access to particular conditions of employment (to the disadvantage of part-time workers). The provision appears to refer to the level of earnings which will (following the principle of pro rata temporis) usually be lower for part-time workers than for full-time workers.

32. The term **'particular conditions of employment'** should be broadly construed as in Clause 4(1) PTWFA. The question of whether pay constitutes a 'condition of employment' (see para. 14 above) is less problematic in the present context. Following the approach favoured here, pay is a condition of employment and may thus be exempted based upon the option contained in Clause 4(4) PTWFA. Even if the opposite view is taken, pay is not covered by the prohibition of discrimination of Clause 4(1) PTWFA in the first place and the optional exemption is thus irrelevant.

33. Formally, exercise of the exemption requires that the Member States (after consultation with the social partners) or social partners do so by way of a national measure. In substance, the exemption presupposes a justification based upon **objective reasons**. This contrasts with the Court's jurisprudence on indirect sex discrimination, pursuant to which the period of service could generally constitute a ground for distinction. The Court reasons that 'length of service goes hand in hand with experience and since experience generally enables the employee to perform his duties better', consequently 'the employer is free to reward it without having to establish the importance it has in the performance of specific tasks entrusted to the employee'.[48] Under the optional justification of Clause 4(4) PTWFA, the burden of justification is more specific.

34. Such general exemption of grounds for differentiation is liable to defeat the central purpose of the prohibition of discrimination. Thus, where a Member State avails itself of this option, it is required to periodically **review** the exemption, e.g., every five years, in light of the principle of non-discrimination.

---

[48] ECJ Case 109/88 *Danfoss* [1989] ECR 3199 para. 24; on this issue, see §9 para. 18.

IV. PROMOTION OF PART-TIME WORK

35. Beyond the principle of equal treatment (III. above), the social partners have also agreed upon provisions concerning the promotion of part-time work. With the exception of the prohibition to terminate (see para. 36 below), these provisions merely take the form of an appeal.[49] In particular, they do not provide for a right to switch to part-time work or, conversely, to full-time work.

1. Specific Prohibition of Retaliation: Prohibition of Termination

36. Clause 5(2) PTWFA specifically prohibits victimisation but goes beyond that and further expresses the – self-evident – principle that a worker cannot be forced to transfer from full-time to part-time work or *vice versa*. Understood in this way, one can justifiably speak of a 'principle of voluntariness'[50] which is also indicated by Clause 1(2) PTWFA. This is, however, nothing but an instance of the general principle of 'contract commitment' (*pacta sunt servanda*) which applies to both parties to the employment contract, employer and worker alike: If the parties have agreed on full-time work, none of them can unilaterally change the agreement to part-time work. Clause 5(2) PTWFA does not however express this principle; it merely expresses the prohibition of victimisation that follows from it, and here only with regard to termination. A refusal to transfer from full-time work to part-time work or *vice versa* does not *as such* constitute a reason for termination. This is certainly an important aspect, but only part of the whole picture. The provision goes on to explicitly state that a termination on other reasons 'such as may arise from the operational requirements of the establishment concerned' remains possible.[51] Where the development of business operations or a restructuring of the undertaking has reduced the employer's demand for part-time workers, this may well justify the termination of the contracts of part-time workers.

37. The provision not only expresses the principle of contract commitment but it also defines the limits to protection. In particular, it does **not** provide for a **right to transfer to part-time work**. The national law of the Member States may, however, provide for such right for workers (not the employer) as a more stringent measure of protection, Article 6(5) Social Policy Protocol (Article 153(4) TFEU (see para. 3 above).

---

49   M. Jeffery, *ILJ* 27 (1998), 193, 196 sq.

50   Thus, however, M. Schmidt, *NZA* 1998, 567, 580 sq. (without, though, relating the principle back to the principle of freedom of contract and individual autonomy and – wrongly – considering §5(3)(a)-(c) PTWFA an expression of the same principle; against this approach, see para. 43 below.

51   M. Kliemt, *NZA* 2001, 63, 69; C. Rolfs, *RdA* 2001, 129, 131 sq.

2. Identification, Review and Elimination of Obstacles

38. The Member States and social partners 'should', for their respective spheres of responsibility, identify and review obstacles which may limit opportunities for part-time work in their legal systems or autonomous regulations. Such obstacles 'should' be eliminated, Clause 5(1) PTWFA. This (soft) obligation only applies 'in the context of Clause 1 of this Agreement', i.e. with regard to the **conditions of employment**, including pay (see para. 14 above).[52] Irrespective of the rather 'soft' wording of the provision, the Court of Justice has inferred an obligation of the Member States from it, subject to judicial review. The Court of Justice held that the obligation under national law to send part-time work contracts to a supervisory authority was incompatible with the provision of Clause 5(1) PTWFA, and in particular was not justifiable as a measure to combat illegal employment as this objective could be achieved by less intrusive means.[53] On the other hand, the Court considered that the obligation to preserve and publish the contracts and working hours of part-time was justifiable under Clause 5(1).[54]

39. In another decision, the Court held that a Member State had violated its obligation under Clause 5(1) if the application of national law violated the prohibition of Clause 4(1) and this was, under the concrete circumstances of the case at hand, liable to discourage the category of workers concerned from taking part-time employment.[55] The decision is not entirely clear at this point, but it seems that it takes more than a mere violation of the prohibition to trigger Clause 5(1) PTWFA. It appears that a chilling effect is also required:[56] 'Those factors, taken together, tend to make part-time work less attractive for that category of workers'. This is rather surprising: Despite only providing for a 'soft' duty, Clause 5(1) seems to go beyond a mere additional sanction of the prohibition of discrimination. A second disconcerting aspect of the judgement is that the Court seems to base its conclusion upon the fact that *application* of the law may have a discouraging effect for *a certain category of workers of a certain employer*: Among the decisive factors, it considers the fact that the 'difference in treatment is accentuated by the fact that vertical-cyclical part-time work is the sole form of part-time work offered to Alitalia cabin crew'. But Clause 5(1) PTWFA is concerned with 'obstacles of a legal or administrative nature'. And third, the Court 'invents' a surprising sanction: 'Clauses 1 and 5(1) of the agreement would have to be interpreted as also precluding such legislation.' Given that Clause 1 is a mere statement of purpose and Clause 5(1) PTWFA is rather softly worded, this

---

[52]   Differently M. Schmidt, *NZA* 1998, 567, 580.
[53]   ECJ Joined Cases C-55/07 and C-56/07 *Michaeler* [2008] ECR I-3135 paras. 21–29.
[54]   ECJ Case C-349/11 *Yangwei* 9 December 2011.
[55]   ECJ Joined Cases C-395/08 and C-396/08 *Bruno and Pettini* [2010] ECR I-5119 paras. 76–81.
[56]   For a different approach see ECJ Case C-151/10 *Dai Cugini v Rijksdienst voor Sociale Zekerheid* 7 April 2011 para. 54.

seems to be a rather strong consequence. Its meaning is, again, not entirely clear, though: As the framework agreement has been adopted in the form of a directive, it certainly cannot invalidate, derogate or even render inapplicable contravening national law (except where the vertical relation of the employee and the Member State is concerned; see §1 paras. 71 sq. above).

3. Promotion of Part-Time Work and Part-Time Workers

40. There are various factual obstacles – which may be unobjectionable as a matter of law – that are liable to render part-time work less attractive. This concerns issues such as the transfer from one form of employment to the other, access to part-time work, particularly qualified and managerial positions, and the lack of promotion of part-time workers, especially with regard to professional development. Clause 5(3) PTWFA addresses these issues without, however, effectively regulating them.

41. Employers should, 'as far as possible', facilitate a transfer from full-time work to part-time work (and *vice versa*). For this purpose, they are required to 'give consideration to'

- requests by workers to transfer from full-time to part-time work that becomes available in the establishment, lit. a);
- requests by workers to transfer from part-time to full-time work or to increase their working time should the opportunity arise, lit. b);
- timely information on the availability of part-time and full-time positions in the establishment in order to facilitate transfers from full-time to part-time or vice versa, lit. c);
- measures to facilitate access to part-time work at all levels of the enterprise, including skilled and managerial positions, lit. d); and
- measures to facilitate access by part-time workers to vocational training to enhance career opportunities and occupational mobility, lit. d).

42. Again, this amounts to little more than an appeal or the expression of a general commitment to part-time work.[57] The central concern of the social partners appears to have been to fully respect **entrepreneurial freedom** to organise one's business (Article 16 ChFR; cf. §2 paras. 9 sqq., 34 sqq. above). There is nothing in these provisions that could force the employer to provide for a part-time position or a full-time position, as the case may be. The employer does not have to justify the organisation of his workforce (part-time or full-time).

---

[57] Similarly G. Thüsing, *Europäisches Arbeitsrecht,* §4 para. 22; further reaching M. Schmidt, *NZA* 1998, 576, 580 (far-reaching duties of implementation); internally inconsistent H. P. Viethen, *EuroAS* 2002, 51, 55.

43. It has been suggested that these latter provisions should be considered to be an expression of a 'principle of voluntariness', pursuant to which 'part-time work should always be performed voluntarily' (presumably: by the worker).[58] This does not seem to capture the rationale of the provision or provide for a helpful systematisation. If Clause 5(3)(a)-(c) PTWFA expresses an element of voluntariness, then it is the voluntariness of the employer rather than that of the worker which is at issue. This provision (other than the prohibition of victimisation in paragraph 2; see para. 36 above) is not concerned with the worker's freedom from coercion or his protection against a disregard of his private autonomy. To speak of a 'principle of voluntariness' incorrectly suggests that all that matters are the needs and wishes of the worker; instead, Clause 5(3)(a)-(c) PTWFA is concerned with the employer's entrepreneurial freedom.

V. INFORMATION OF WORKERS' REPRESENTATIVES

44. Finally, the employer's obligation to provide information to worker representatives is also formulated in rather 'soft' terms. The employer should 'give consideration to the provision of appropriate information to existing bodies representing workers about part-time working in the enterprise', Clause 5(3)(e) PTWFA.[59] When the provision speaks of *existing* bodies representing workers, it clearly refers to the Court's jurisprudence on the Collective Redundancies Directive and the Transfer of Undertakings Directive, both of which the Court has interpreted to oblige Member States to install worker representations where none existed (see §23 para. 17 and §24 para. 90 below).[60] The Part-Time Work Framework Agreement is not intended to give rise to a similar obligation.

45. Altogether, the employers' obligations to provide information are not very far-reaching. This deviates from the 'information model' which is otherwise employed in EU private law and employment law. The comparable provisions in the Fixed-Term Work Framework Agreement, which was concluded two years later, are somewhat more extensive, though still rather restrained (Clauses 6, 7 FTWFA, §17 paras. 35 sq. below). One may expect that the social partners will eventually align the provisions of the Part-Time Work Frame Work Agreement with those of the Fixed Term Work Framework Agreement.

---

[58]   M. Schmidt, *NZA* 1998, 567, 580.

[59]   The weakness of the provision results from its scope ('As far as possible, employers should give consideration') and not – as M. Schmidt, *NZA* 1998, 576, 581, suggests – from the vagueness of its wording ('appropriate information').

[60]   ECJ Case C-382/92 *Commission* v. *United Kingdom* [1994] ECR I-2435 paras. 8–31; Case C-383/92 *Commission* v. *United Kingdom* [1994] ECR I-2479 paras. 9–23. See also M. Schmidt, *NZA* 1998, 576, 581.

VI. IMPLEMENTATION

46. Implementation into **German Law**[61] was achieved by the Act on Part-Time Work and on Fixed Term Work (*Teilzeit- und Befristungsgesetz*, TzBfG), which also serves to implement the Fixed Term Work Directive (§17). In many respects, it goes beyond the requirements of the Directive(s).[62] The prohibition of discrimination and the principle of pro rata temporis are laid down in Clause 4(1) TzBfG. The obligations to promote part-time work and provide information are set forth in §§6 sq., 10 TzBfG. Going beyond the requirements of the Directive, §8 TzBfG provides for a – limited right to reduction of working hours in §8 TzBfG. Pursuant to §9 TzBfG, the employer must give preference to an employee's wish to extend working hours if he has a vacant position. §5 TzBfG provides for a general prohibition of victimisation, §11 TzBfG for a specific prohibition of termination.

47. In the **United Kingdom** the Directive was implemented by the Part-Time Workers (Prevention of Less Favourable Treatment) Regulations 2000.[63] Regulation 2 defines full-time workers, part-time workers and the concept of comparable full-time worker in some detail. The pro rata temporis principle is considered to be a tool of analysis for determining whether there has been less favourable treatment. The principle is more far-reaching than the Directive, since Regulation 5(3) provides that it applies 'unless it is inappropriate'. An interesting element of enforcement is the employee's right to receive a written statement of reasons for less favourable treatment in Regulation 6. Regulation 7 spells out the prohibition of dismissal of Article 5(2) PTWFA in more detail and expands its scope.

---

[61] BGBl. 2000 I, 1966; also available at www.gesetze-im-internet.de/tzbfg/index.html; bilingual German-English version in S. Lingemann/R. v. Steinau-Steinrück/A. Mengel (eds.), *Employment and Labor Law in Germany*, Part II, III. For an overview, see W. Balze, in *EAS*, B 3100 para. 298; C. Rolfs, *RdA* 2001, 129–143; R. Wank, in P. Hanau/H.-D. Steinmeyer/R. Wank (eds.), *Handbuch des europäischen Arbeits- und Sozialrechts*, §18 paras. 235–250; further U. Preis/M. Gotthardt, *DB* 2000, 2065–2074. On the implementation in other Member States, see H. F. Eisemann et al., *RdA* 2004, 129–141; N. Busby, *J.B.L.* 2001, 344–356. See also B. Waas, 'Gesetzlicher Anspruch auf Teilzeitbeschäftigung in den Niederlanden', *NZA* 2000, 583–585.

[62] This is true in particular with the (limited) right to transfer to part-time work. Critically M. Kliemt, *NZA* 2001, 63–71; critically on the general tendency to over-implement EU directives G. Thüsing, *Europäisches Arbeitsrecht*, §4 para. 23.

[63] SI 2000/1551, available at www.legislation.gov.uk/uksi/2000/1551/contents/made. For an overview, see S. Deakin/G. Morris, *Labour Law*, para. 3.58; A. McColgan, *ILJ* 29 (2000), 260–267.

§17. THE FIXED-TERM WORK DIRECTIVE

CONTENT

Bibliography:

C. Barnard/B. Hepple, 'Substantive Equality', *C.L.J.* 59 (2000) 562–585; J.-H. Bauer, 'Befristete Arbeitsverträge unter neuen Vorzeichen – Teil 1: Europarechtliche Vorgaben und Befristungen ohne Sachgrund', *BB* 2001, 2473–2477; J.-H. Bauer, 'Neue Spielregeln für Teilzeitarbeit und befristete Arbeitsverträge', *NZA* 2000, 1039–1043; M. Bieder/S. Diekmann, 'Verbot der Diskriminierung befristet Beschäftigter bei der Gewährung von Dienstalterszulagen', *EuZA* 2008, 515–525; R. Blanpain, 'Fixed-term Employment Contracts: The Exception or the Rule?', *IJCLLIR* 24 (2008), 123–131; L. Corazza, 'Hard Times for Hard Bans: Fixed-Term Work and So-Called Non-Regression Clauses in the Era of Flexicurity', *ELJ* 2011, 385–402; L. Corazza/L. Nogler, 'Die "weiche" Wirkung des Verschlechterungsverbotes in EU-Richtlinien', *ZESAR* 2011, 58–64; W. Däubler, 'Das geplante Teilzeit- und Befristungsgesetz', *ZIP* 2000, 1961–1969; W. Däubler, 'Das neue Teilzeit- und Befristungsgesetz', *ZIP* 2001, 217–225; H. J. Desmond, 'Fixed-term Contracts – Regulating "Atypical" Working', *Denning L.J.* 15 (2000), 43–66; S. Engblom, 'Fixed-term-at-Will: The New Regulation of Fixed-term Work in Sweden', *IJCLLIR* 34 (2008), 133–150; S. Greiner, 'Auslegung von Absenkungsverboten in Richtlinien und Reichweite der richtlinienkonformen Auslegung', *EuZA* 2011, 74–84; P. Hanau, 'Was ist wirklich neu in der Befristungsrichtlinie?', *NZA* 2000, 1045; W. Hromadka, 'Befristete und bedingte Arbeitsverhältnisse neu geregelt', *BB* 2001, 621–627 and 674–677; I. Kaufmann, 'Die europäische Sozialpartnervereinbarung über befristete Arbeitsverträge', *AuR* 1999, 332–335; K. Kröger, *Die Befristung von Arbeitsverträgen in Frankreich, Großbritannien und Deutschland – Ein Systemvergleich nach der Richtlinie 99/70 EG* (Hamburg: Dr. Kovač, 2008); P. Lorber, 'Regulating Fixed-term Work in the United Kingdom: A Positive Step towards Workers' Protection?', *IJCLLIR* 15 (1999), 121–135; A. McColgan, 'The Fixed-Term Employees (Prevention of Less Favourable Treatment) Regulations 2002: fiddling while Rome burns?', *ILJ* 32 (2003), 194–199; J. Murray, 'Normalising Temporary Work', *ILJ* 28 (1999), 269–275; A. Numhauser-Henning, 'Fixed-term Work in Nordic Labour Law', *IJCLLIR* 18 (2002) 429–458; U. Preis/M. Gotthard, 'Das Teilzeit- und Befristungsgesetz', *DB* 2001, 145–152; U. Preis/M. Gotthardt, 'Neuregelung der Teilzeitarbeit und befristeten Arbeitsverhältnisse', *DB* 2000, 2065–2074; R. Richardi/G. Annuß, 'Gesetzliche Neuregelung von Teilzeitarbeit und Befristung', *BB* 2000, 2201–2205; C. Rolfs, 'Befristung des Arbeitsvertrags', in H. Oetker/U. Preis (eds.), *Europäisches Arbeits- und Sozialrecht, EAS, part B – Systematische Darstellungen*, loose-leaf (Heidelberg: Forkel, last update: February 2001), B 3200; C. Rolfs/S. E. de Groot, 'Die Befristung von Arbeitsverträgen in der Rechtsprechung des EuGH', *ZESAR* 2009, 5–13; A. Röthel, 'Europäische Rechtsetzung im sozialen Dialog – Zur Richtlinie 1999/70/EG über befristete Arbeitsverhältnisse', *NZA* 2000, 65–69; M. Schlachter, 'Gemeinschaftsrechtliche Grenzen der Altersbefristung', *RdA* 2004, 352–358; Michael Schmidt, *Die Richtlinienvorschläge der Kommission der Europäischen Gemeinschaften zu den atypischen Arbeitsverhältnisse* (Baden-Baden: Nomos, 1991); M. Tiraboschi, 'Glancing at the Past: An Agreement for the Markets of the XXIst Century', *IJCLLIR* 15 (1999), 105–119; R. Wank, 'Atypische Arbeitsverhältnisse', *RdA* 1992, 103–114; R. Wank, 'Befristung von Arbeitsverträgen', in P. Hanau/H.-D. Steinmeyer/R. Wank (eds.), *Handbuch des europäischen Arbeits- und Sozialrechts* (Munich: C.H. Beck, 2002), §18 VI; R. Wank/U. Börgmann, 'Der Vorschlag für eine Richtlinie des Rates über befristete Arbeitsverträge', *RdA* 1999, 383–389 (also reproducing the proposal); L. Zappala, 'Abuse of Fixed Term Employment Contracts and Sanctions in the Recent ECJ's Jurisprudence', *ILJ* 35 (2006), 439–444; see further the bibliography to §15.

Cases:

ECJ Case C-144/04 *Mangold* [2005] ECR I-9981; ECJ Case C-212/04 *Adeneler* [2006] ECR I-6057; ECJ Case C-53/04 *Marrosu* [2006] ECR I-7213; ECJ Case C-180/04 *Vasallo* [2006] ECR I-7251; ECJ Case I-7/05 *Del Cerro Alonso* [2007] ECR I-7109; ECJ Case C-268/06 *Impact* [2008] ECR I-2483; ECJ Case C-364/07 *Vassilakis* [2008] ECR I-90; ECJ Case C-306/07 *Andersen* [2008] ECR I-10279; ECJ Joined Cases C-378/07 to C-380/07 *Angelidaki* [2009] ECR I-3071; ECJ Case C-486/08 *Zentralbetriebsrat der Landeskrankenhäuser Tirols* [2010] ECR I-3527; ECJ Joined Cases C-162/08 to C-164/08 *Lagoudakis* [2009] ECR I-195 (order pursuant to Article 104(3) ECJ Rules of Procedure, referring to *Angelidaki*); ECJ Case C-519/08 *Koukou* [2009] ECR I-65 (order pursuant to Article 104(3) ECJ Rules of Procedure, referring to *Adeneler, Marrosu, Vassalo, Del Cerro Alonso, Vassilakis, Angelidaki*); ECJ Case C-98/09 *Sorge* [2010] ECR I-5837; ECJ Joined Cases C-444/09 and C-456/09 *Gavieiro Gavieiro and Iglesias Torres* 22 December 2010; ECJ Case C-3/10 *Affatato* OJ 2011 C 30/11 (order pursuant to Article 104(3) ECJ Rules of Procedure, referring to *Adeneler, Marrosu, Vassalo, Vassilakis, Angelidaki, Kokou*); ECJ Case C-20/10 *Vino* OJ 2011 C 63/14 (order pursuant to Article 104(3) ECJ Rules of Procedure, referring to *Mangold, Angelidaki, Sorge, Kokou*); ECJ Case C-272/10 *Verkizi-Nikolakaki* OJ 2011 C 120/3 (order pursuant to Article 104(3) ECJ Rules of Procedure, referring to *Adeneler, Angelidaki, Vassilakis, Kokou*); ECJ Case C-109/09 *Deutsche Lufthansa* 10 March 2011; ECJ Case C-273/10 *Montoya Medina* OJ 2011 C 186/10 (order pursuant to Article 104(3) ECJ Rules of Procedure, referring to *Del Cerro Alonso, Impact, Gavieiro Gavieiro and Iglesias Torres*); ECJ Case C-177/10 *Rosado Santana* 8 September 2011; ECJ Case C-586/10 *Kücük* 26 January 2012; ECJ Case C-157/11 *Sibilio* 15 March 2012; ECJ Case C-556/11 *Lorenzo Marténez* OJ 2012 C-133/13 (order pursuant to Article 104(3) ECJ Rules of Procedure, referring to *Del Cerro Alonso*); ECJ Case C-251/11 *Huet* 8 March 2012.

I. ISSUES AND OVERVIEW[1]

1. Fixed-term employment contracts are used primarily as an instrument to preserve the employer's **flexibility**. The contract terminates without the need for a dismissal (which will often be restricted by a requirement of cause). Employees will not usually have an interest in fixed-term contracts, given that an employment contract for an indefinite period of time will usually leave them with the possibility to terminate subject only to any applicable notice periods.[2] Fixed-term employment may, however, serve the **interests of employees** as a group where it makes employers more inclined to hire. A fixed-term position may also provide the employee with a chance to distinguish himself and qualify for further employment – be that in the current position or a different position. Fixed-term employment is thus also considered to be an instrument of occupational policy. Fixed-term employment relations may facilitate (re-)

---

[1] See also the overview in §15 above.
[2] See also J. Murray, *ILJ* 28 (1999), 269, 274; P. Lorber, *IJCLLIR* 15 (1999), 121, 126 sq.

integration into the labour market, e.g. after a period of unemployment or another discontinuity, for example a break to raise children, especially for women and older employees.

2. There are, however, certain **disadvantages and risks** inherent in fixed-term employment relationships. Especially in the case of recurrent fixed-term positions, there is a risk of protections against unfair dismissal being circumvented. In addition, workers in atypical employment relationships, such as fixed-term positions, often experience less favourable treatment than their counterparts in open-ended positions. Sometimes predominantly members of a group protected by anti-discrimination laws are employed on a fixed-term basis: In some countries significantly more women then men are in fixed-term positions (see also Recital 9 FTWFA);[3] sometimes a higher percentage of older workers are hired on a fixed-term basis;[4] foreign language assistants who tend to be foreign nationals, have traditionally only been employed for a limited period (see §3 para. 34 above). In such cases, less favourable treatment of employees in fixed-term positions may also constitute indirect discrimination of the workers as members of the protected group.

3. The Fixed-Term Work Framework Agreement of the EU social partners addresses these issues (Clause 1 FTWFA). The Fixed-Term Work Directive (FTWD)[5] implements the Framework Agreement pursuant to Article 155(2) TFEU. The social partners start from the premise that employment contracts for an indefinite period are the 'general form' of employment, which contributes to the quality of life of the workers concerned and improves their performance (Recital 6 FTWFA).[6] Irrespective of that, they consider fixed-term employment relationships as admissible in principle, even without any positive justification; their intention is thus to prevent abuse of this form of employment rather than disinhibiting its use altogether.[7] Thus, an initial agreement to work under a fixed-term contract should be unobjectionable. Only successive fixed-term employment

---

[3]   See European Commission, *The social situation in the European Union 2003*, 159, available at http://epp.eurostat.ec.europa.eu/cache/ITY_OFFPUB/KE-AG-03-001/EN/KE-AG-03-001-EN.PDF; Eurostat, *The life of women and men in Europe – A statistical portrait*, press release 32/2007 of 5 March 2007, 4, available at http://epp.eurostat.ec.europa.eu/cache/ITY_OFFPUB/KS-80-07-135/EN/KS-80-07-135-EN.PDF; the discrepancy is, of course, not as stark as in the case of part-time work.

[4]   M. Bieder/S. Diekmann, *EuZA* 2008, 515, 521.

[5]   Council Directive 1999/70/EC of 28 June 1999 concerning the framework agreement on fixed-term work concluded by ETUC, UNICE and CEEP, OJ 1999 L 175/43.

[6]   Cf. ECJ Case C-212/04 *Adeneler* [2006] ECR I-6057 para. 61; Case C-109/09 *Deutsche Lufthansa* 10 March 2011 para. 30.

[7]   Here the provision differs fundamentally from the 1982 proposal (see §15 para. 5 above) pursuant to which fixed-term employment would have been admissible only in a defined number of cases; see J. Murray, *ILJ* 28 (1999), 269, 271 sqq.

contracts are subject to control.[8] However, the Framework Agreement only contains a rather limited number of regulations, and these often only provide a regulatory framework. At the core of the Framework Agreement is the **prohibition of discrimination** in Clause 4 FTWFA. This prohibition is supplemented by a mandate for the Member States to **prevent abuse** through certain measures, Clause 5 FTWFA. Employers are required to inform fixed-term workers about vacant positions which are for an indefinite period and to facilitate their access to professional training and development, Clause 6 FTWFA.

II. SCOPE OF APPLICATION

4. The Framework Agreement applies to fixed-term workers, Clause 2(1) FTWFA. For the term 'worker', the social partners refer to the national law of the Member States; yet, the implementation obligations and the *effet utile* provide for a framework[9] that considerably narrows any leeway for national definitions of 'worker'. An exclusion of certain groups of employees must not be arbitrary and may not be justified on purely formal considerations.[10] In particular, the Court held that, as the wording of Clause 2(1) FTWFA is without any limitation and as Clause 2(2) FTWFA only provides for clearly defined exceptions (see para. 6 below), the Framework Agreement must be interpreted so as to apply to employment relationships in the **private and public sectors**.[11] Consequently, the Court has held that the FTWFA is applicable to 'all workers providing remunerated services in the context of a fixed-term employment relationship linking them to their employer'.[12] It 'can apply also' to employment relationships concluded with public authorities and other public-sector bodies.[13] Subsequently, the Court ruled that the Framework Agreement 'must be interpreted (...) as applying to employment contracts and relationships concluded with the public authorities and other public-sector bodies'.[14]

---

[8]   ECJ Case C-144/04 *Mangold* [2005] ECR I-9981 paras. 40–43; P. Lorber, *IJCLLIR* 15 (1999), 121, 125; L. Zappala, *ILJ* 35 (2006), 439, 440.

[9]   For a different view see *M. Bieder/S. Diekmann, EuZA* 2008, 515, 517.

[10] ECJ Case C-157/11 *Sibilio* 15 March 2012 para. 49; the Court accepted, however, that persons performing socially useful services for the public administration, under national laws, collective agreements and practices, do not necessarily have to be regarded as workers.

[11] ECJ Case C-307/05 *Del Cerro Alonso* [2007] ECR I-7109 paras. 25–29; Case C-53/04 *Marrosu* [2006] ECR I-7213 paras. 38–42; Case C-180/04 *Vasallo* [2006] ECR I-7251 para. 32; ECJ Joined Cases C-444/09 and C-456/09 *Gavieiro Gavieiro and Iglesias Torres* 22 December 2010 paras. 38–45.

[12] ECJ Case C-307/05 *Del Cerro Alonso* [2007] ECR I-7109 para. 28; Case C-177/10 *Rosado Santana* 8 September 2011 para. 40.

[13] ECJ Case C-212/04 *Adeneler* [2006] ECR I-6057 paras. 54 sqq.; Case C-53/04 *Marrosu* [2006] ECR I-7213 paras. 39 sqq.; Case C-180/04 *Vassallo* [2006] ECR I-7251 paras. 32 sqq.; Case C-307/05 *Del Cerro Alonso* [2007] ECR I-7109 para. 25.

[14] ECJ Case C-177/10 *Rosado Santana* 8 September 2011 paras. 49 sqq.

5. Only the definition of **fixed-term** is autonomous (Clause 3(1) FTWFA); the provision follows that of Article 1(1) Temporary Employment Health and Safety Directive (see §19 para. 5 below). A fixed-term occupation is characterised by the fact that its end is determined by objective conditions.[15] In a non-exhaustive ('such as') list, the social partners provide the examples of 'reaching a specific date, completing a specific task or the occurrence of a specific event'. The 'objective condition' may be certain or uncertain and thus cover time limitations or conditions in a narrow sense.[16] Pursuant to the purpose of the Framework Agreement, it does not however include the termination of an indeterminate contract by termination notice. A worker may still rely upon the protection afforded by the Directive after he has become a full-time employee; this may be relevant, e.g., in regard of the calculation of periods of service.[17]

6. The Member States (after consultation with the social partners) or social partners **may exclude** two groups of employment relationships from the scope of the Framework Agreement (Clause 2(2) FTWFA): initial vocational training and apprenticeship schemes as well as employment relationships which have been concluded within the framework of a specific public or publicly-supported training, integration and vocational retraining programme.[18] In both groups of cases, the reason for the temporary limitation of the employment relationship lies in its inherent purpose, and the optional exception indicates that the social partners recognised the purpose as legitimate. The brevity of fixed-term employment – e.g. six months or 'casual work' – does not as such justify an exception from the Framework Agreement.[19]

III.   PRINCIPLE OF EQUAL TREATMENT

7. At the heart of the Framework Agreement lies the 'principle of non-discrimination' pursuant to Clause 4 FTWFA. It covers three distinct provisions:

- the prohibition of discrimination in paragraph 1,
- the principle of pro rata temporis in paragraph 2 and
- a specific provision on period-of-service qualifications in paragraph 4.

---

[15] Reference to an 'employment contract or relationship entered into *directly* between an employer and a worker' aims at excluding temporary agency work; see Preamble Paragraph 4 and General Considerations Recital 4 FTWFA; S. Deakin/G. Morris, *Labour Law*, para. 3.52.

[16] To the same effect C. Rolfs, in *EAS*, B 3200 para. 11.

[17] ECJ Case C-177/10 *Rosado Santana* 8 September 2011 paras. 41 sqq.

[18] See ECJ Case C-157/11 *Sibilio* 15 March 2012 paras. 52 sqq. (Member State's discretion to exclude from the scope employees performing socially useful work for the government).

[19] Cf. ECJ Case C-486/08 *Zentralbetriebsrat der Landeskrankenhäuser Tirols* [2010] ECR I-3527 paras. 36–47.

Arrangements for the application of clause 4 are left for the Member States to decide. Given that the provisions partially overlap, their relationship to each other needs to be determined.

1.   The Prohibition of Discrimination[20]

a)   Scope of Application

8.   In substance, the prohibition of discrimination applies to **employment conditions**. The term 'employment conditions' is central to the scope of application and must thus be autonomously determined. As in other areas of EU employment law, the term must be broadly construed[21] so as to refer to any conditions of the employment contract or relationship. Employment conditions thus include, for example, the duration and organisation of working time or leave; participation in advanced training courses; or the conditions to qualify for promotion[22] (see also Clause 6 FTWFA).

9.   As **pay** is excluded from the legislative measures under Article 153(5) TFEU (see §4 para. 10 above), it is controversial whether remuneration is still one of the employment conditions to which the prohibition of discrimination applies. Many authors answer the question in the negative.[23] Yet, there are stronger reasons in favour of an interpretation of Article 153(5) TFEU that only excludes direct regulation of pay, such as would occur in the determination of a minimum wage. The reservation does not apply to the indirect regulation of pay, for example a prohibition of discrimination that also affects pay (see in more detail and with references §4 paras. 11 sq. above). Therefore, the prohibition of discrimination in Clause 4(1) PTWFA should be interpreted so as to also apply to pay as a (central) condition of employment.[24] With a view to the broad definition of pay in Article 157 TFEU, the Court also considered pensions[25] or a

---

[20]   The prohibition is directly applicable as against the Member States (public employer); see ECJ Joined Cases C-444/09 and C-456/09 *Gavieiro Gavieiro and Iglesias Torres* 22 December 2010 paras. 68–90.

[21]   On the analogous provision of Clause 4(1) PTWFA W. Balze, in *EAS*, B 3100 para. 260.

[22]   ECJ Case C-177/10 *Rosado Santana* 8 September 2011 paras. 46 sq.

[23]   C. Rolfs, in *EAS*, B 3200 para. 14; R. Wank/U. Börgmann, *RdA* 1999, 383, 384; R. Wank, in P. Hanau/H.-D. Steinmeyer/R. Wank (eds.), *Handbuch des europäischen Arbeits- und Sozialrechts*, §18 para. 257. See also M. Schmidt, 'Die neue EG-Richtlinie zur Teilzeitarbeit', *NZA* 1998, 576, 578 sq. (on the respective provision of Article 2(6) Social Policy Protocol). Differently H. Nielebock, 'Die neuen gesetzlichen Regelungen zur befristeten Beschäftigung', *AiB* 2001, 75, 76.

[24]   ECJ Case C-307/05 *Del Cerro Alonso* [2007] ECR I-7109 paras. 43 sqq.; Case C-268/06 *Impact* [2008] ECR I-2483 paras. 106–133; ECJ Case C-556/11 *Lorenzo Marténez* OJ 2012 C-133/13 (concerning a continued education-bonus); S. Deakin/G. Morris, *Labour Law,* para. 3.52; C. Rolfs/S. E. de Groot, *ZESAR* 2009, 5, 9.

[25]   ECJ Case C-268/06 *Impact* [2008] ECR I-2483 paras. 131–133.

length-of-service increment[26] to be part of employment conditions within the meaning of Clause 4(1) FTWFA.

b)   Content

aa)   PROHIBITION OF DISCRIMINATION

10.   Fixed-term workers must not be treated less favourably than comparable permanent workers solely because they have a fixed-term contract. The test is whether

- a fixed-term worker within the meaning of Clause 3(2) FTWFA (para. 5 above)
- is treated less favourably
- than a comparable permanent worker within the meaning of Clause 3(2) PTWFA (see para. 11 below)
- solely because he has a fixed-term contract.

11.   A 'comparable permanent worker' is a worker in the same establishment, engaged in the same or similar work or occupation with an employment contract or relationship of indefinite duration. When evaluating comparability, due regard must be given to qualifications and skills. Where there is no actual comparable worker in the same establishment, the comparison should be conducted in a normative or hypothetical manner. In such cases, reference must be made to the applicable collective agreement, or where there is no applicable collective agreement, in accordance with national law, collective agreements or practice. (On the issue of a hypothetical comparison, see also §16 paras. 7–9.)

12.   The wording of this provision differs from that of the established prohibitions of discrimination in EU employment (and contract) law. In particular, the Framework Agreement does not establish a 'principle of equal treatment' that would prohibit direct and indirect discrimination. Instead, the wording indicates that the prohibition merely extends to direct discrimination. As one can suppose that the social partners and the Commission were well aware of the difference, this appears to be a deliberate decision. It also makes sense, given that the prohibition of discrimination is supplemented by the principle of pro rata temporis of paragraph 2, which should largely exclude indirect discrimination.

13.   Furthermore, the prohibition only prohibits any *less favourable* treatment. It does not, in other words, preclude **more favourable** treatment of part-time

---

[26]   ECJ Joined Cases C-444/09 and C-456/09 *Gavieiro Gavieiro and Iglesias Torres* 22 December 2010 para. 50.

workers but, of course, does not require it either. Yet, the prohibition of sex discrimination may restrict more favourable treatment of part-time workers to the extent that it would amount to indirect discrimination against men.

14. Unlike other directives, the Fixed-Term Work Directive does not contain a provision on 'victimisation' (retaliation) which would protect workers against adverse treatment as a reaction to the exercise of their rights. An explicit provision is not necessary either: The prohibition of discrimination teleologically includes a prohibition of adverse treatment (see §8 paras. 71 sq. above). In addition, any adverse treatment of a part-time worker because he has invoked his rights under the Directive would constitute discrimination on grounds of part-time work.[27]

bb) JUSTIFICATION

15. The prohibition of discrimination is restricted by the possibility of a justification on '**objective grounds**' (*raisons objectives, sachliche Gründe*). The justification can be specified by analogy to the established rules of EU anti-discrimination law. In order to justify less favourable treatment solely on grounds of fixed-term work, the employer must establish that the distinction was necessary in order to achieve a legitimate purpose. Determination of a 'legitimate' purpose requires an evaluation with regard to the purposes of the Fixed-Term Work Directive and the EU legal system.[28] The requirement that the distinction must be 'necessary' refers to the principle of proportionality.

16. In line with this general conception, the Court has interpreted the requirement of 'objective grounds' 'as referring to **precise and concrete circumstances characterising a given activity**, which are therefore capable, in that particular context, of justifying the use of successive fixed-term employment contracts. Those circumstances may result, in particular, from the specific nature of the tasks for the performance of which such contracts have been concluded and from the inherent characteristics of those tasks or, as the case may be, from pursuit of a legitimate social-policy objective of a Member State'.[29] **Budgetary consideration** (such as the aim of 'rigorous personnel management') cannot justify discrimination.[30] The Court has further supplemented the requirement of

---

[27]   Cf. for the prohibition of retaliation in §5 TzBfG U. Preis, in R. Müller-Glöge/U. Preis/I. Schmidt (eds.), *Erfurter Kommentar*, §5 TzBfG paras. 1 sq.

[28]   Consequently, discriminatory features cannot constitute objective grounds; thus with regard to the PTWD M. Schmidt, *NZA* 1998, 576, 577.

[29]   ECJ Case C-307/05 *Del Cerro Alonso* [2007] ECR I-7109 paras. 52 sq., 56; Joined Cases C-444/09 and C-456/09 *Gavieiro Gavieiro and Iglesias Torres* 22 December 2010 para. 55; M. Bieder/S. Diekmann, *EuZA* 2008, 515–525.

[30]   ECJ Case C-486/08 *Zentralbetriebsrat der Landeskrankenhäuser Tirols* [2010] ECR I-3527 paras. 45 sq.

'precise and concrete circumstances' by a principle of **transparency**, so as to enable judicial control. The unequal treatment at issue must be 'justified by the existence of precise and concrete factors, characterising the employment condition to which it relates, in the specific context in which it occurs and on the basis of objective and transparent criteria in order to ensure that that unequal treatment in fact responds to a genuine need, is appropriate for achieving the objective pursued and is necessary for that purpose'.[31] Thus understood in a concrete, individual fashion, a justification needs to be given in every single case; abstract, general distinctions in laws or collective agreements cannot satisfy this requirement.[32] Objective grounds must be established

> 'by the existence of precise and specific factors, characterising the employment condition to which it relates, in the particular context in which it occurs and on the basis of objective and transparent criteria in order to ensure that that unequal treatment in fact meets a genuine need, is appropriate for achieving the objective pursued and is necessary for that purpose. Those factors may result, in particular, from the specific nature of the tasks for the performance of which fixed-term contracts have been concluded and from the inherent characteristics of those tasks or, as the case may be, from pursuit of a legitimate social-policy objective of a Member State.'[33]

The mere temporary nature of the employment relationship cannot as such constitute an objective ground which justifies disparate treatment.

17.   Training opportunities offered by the employer (an issue only partially regulated by Clause 6(2) FTWFA) can serve to illustrate the issues. An employer may restrict his offer for training for special new software to permanent workers if the fixed-term workers will not be able to use the program with a view to the prospective termination of their employment. Similarly, the employer may limit access to regular computer courses (e.g. a refresher-course in word processing for secretaries) based upon a minimum term of employment; while such course may well also be useful for a holiday substitute worker, generally offering courses to temporary workers would be excessively burdensome for the employer.

18.   The wording of Clause 4(1) FTWFA ('unless') already hints at the **burden of proof**: It is for the employer to submit and prove any objective grounds. This is appropriate, given that the relevant grounds fall within the employer's sphere of knowledge. Details of the burden of proof are, however, part of the 'arrangements for the application' that, pursuant to paragraph 3, are for the Member States (or the national social partners) to determine (see para. 19 below).

---

[31]   ECJ Case C-307/05 *Del Cerro Alonso* [2007] ECR I-7109 para. 58; Case C-486/08 *Zentralbetriebsrat der Landeskrankenhäuser Tirols* [2010] ECR I-3527 paras. 42–44.
[32]   ECJ Case C-307/05 *Del Cerro Alonso* [2007] ECR I-7109 para. 57.
[33]   ECJ Case C-177/10 *Rosado Santana* 8 September 2011 para. 73.

c)   Arrangements for the Application

19.   Arrangements for the application of the prohibition of discrimination (as well as of the principle of pro rata temporis) are for the Member States and/or the social partners to determine.[34] Examples include rules of procedure and the burden of proof (but see also para. 21 above), sanctions, collective actions or state supervision. With regard to **sanctions** and judicial protection in particular, the general implementation principles apply, namely the principles of equivalence and effectiveness.[35] The Court has, for example, accepted that a two-month time limit for bringing actions may, in principle, be considered to be compatible with these implementation obligations.[36]

2.   *The Principle of Pro Rata Temporis*

a)   Scope of Application

20.   'Where appropriate', fixed-term workers should be treated in accordance with the principle of pro rata temporis.[37] The reference to the 'appropriateness' does not imply that the scope of application of the principle is left to the Member States; Member States merely regulate the 'arrangements for the application' (para. 24 below). 'Appropriateness' must be defined in light of the purpose of the provision. Application of the principle of pro rata temporis is 'appropriate' where benefits are (or, in any case, may be from a normative perspective) measured on the basis of time. As a minimum, this presupposes that such benefits can be divided so that they can be granted in respect of time (working hours).[38] Indivisible benefits such as *access* to institutions of the undertaking or establishment (e.g. cafeteria or library) cannot be granted pro rata temporis.[39] The prohibition of discrimination in Clause 4(1) PTWFA applies with respect to indivisible benefits.

21.   Divisible benefits will often be characterised as **pay**.[40] Following the view put forward in para. 9 above, this is no obstacle to the application of the Directive

---

[34]   See ECJ Case C-268/06 *Impact* [2008] ECR I-2483 paras. 66 sq. ('Such arrangements cannot therefore in any way relate to the actual substance of that principle' 'they cannot therefore limit the existence or restrict the scope of that principle'.).

[35]   ECJ Case C-177/10 *Rosado Santana* 8 September 2011 paras. 89 sqq.

[36]   Ibid. paras. 93 sqq.

[37]   C. Rolfs, in *EAS*, B 3200 para. 18 (considering the provision to be 'more than unclear' – my translation).

[38]   M. Schmidt, *NZA* 1998, 576, 577.

[39]   C. Rolfs, in *EAS*, B 3200 para. 18; R. Wank, in P. Hanau/H.-D. Steinmeyer/R. Wank (eds.), *Handbuch des europäischen Arbeits- und Sozialrechts*, §18 para. 258.

[40]   Cf. the overview of specific aspects in U. Preis, in R. Müller-Glöge/U. Preis/I. Schmidt (eds.), *Erfurter Kommentar*, §4 TzBfG paras. 59 sq.

or the principle of pro rata temporis. The length of annual leave may, e.g., be considered to be a divisible benefit outside pay. Here, application of the principle of pro rata temporis is not only possible (as the case of termination of employment during the course of a given year illustrates) but also *appropriate,* given that annual leave is by definition ('annual'!) granted with regard to (working) time (see only Article 7 WTD, §14 paras. 46–56 above).

b)   Content

22.   The principle of pro rata temporis means the calculation of benefits proportionate to (working) time. It expresses a central concern of justice if we understand the principle of equality to mean that essentially similar facts should be treated similarly and that essentially dissimilar facts should be treated differently according to the measure of their difference. The principle does not only mean that part-time workers are entitled to equal treatment compared to full-time workers, based upon their working time. It also means that part-time employment relationships differ from the 'normal' full-time employment only in respect of working time. For **example**, a part-time worker has a right to annual leave proportionate to his working time.

23.   While the prohibition of discrimination in paragraph 1 means – negatively – that part-time workers may not be treated less favourably, except for objective reasons, the principle of pro rata temporis means – positively – that part-time workers should be treated equally compared to full-time workers, proportionate to the relative working time. For the delimitation of both principles, see also para. 29 below.

c)   Arrangements for the Application

24.   Member States and/or the social partners also determine the arrangements for the application of the principle of pro rata temporis, Clause 4(3) PTWFA. Member States may, in particular, wish to define the central criterion of 'appropriateness' (even though this will still be subject to control by the Court of Justice; see para. 20 above). And, again, they may determine sanctions as well as procedural arrangements.

3.   *Period of Service Qualifications*

25.   The wording of Clause 4(4) FTWFA regarding period of service qualifications (*Betriebszugehörigkeitszeiten, critères de périodes d'ancienneté*) is somewhat complicated. It could perhaps be 'translated' as follows:

Where particular conditions of employment are conditional upon certain periods of employment, the same periods apply for fixed-term workers and permanent workers unless different length-of-service qualifications are justified on objective grounds.

26. In other words, where (certain) periods of service are a prerequisite for benefits from the employer, fixed-term workers and permanent workers are to be treated equally in a formal way.[41] The provision thus contains a concretisation of the prohibition of discrimination or the principle of pro rata temporis for a specific issue. The principle of **formal equality**, which will in many instances work to the disadvantage of fixed-term workers, is being declared appropriate. A different approach may be taken only as an exception and only where it is justified on objective grounds.[42]

27. The provision can, in particular, be relevant with regard to pension expectancies. If, of course, one considered pay to be excluded from the scope of application (see paras. 9, 21 above), pension expectancies would not be covered in the first place.

28. Systematically, the provision can be understood as a concretisation or clarification of the rules contained in paragraphs 1 and 2. Its location, after paragraph 3 on the arrangements for application, seems to be misplaced. Arrangements for application by the Member States and/or the social partners may also be necessary in respect of periods of qualification. The systematic position of paragraphs 3 and 4 seems to be due to a drafting error.

*4.   The Relationship between the Prohibition of Discrimination and the
       Principle of Pro Rata Temporis*

29. The preceding considerations lead to a coherent system of rules in Clause 4. Paragraph 1 provides for the fundamental, but only negative, prohibition of discrimination. Where a benefit is divisible and this seems appropriate (in light of the Framework Agreement), the principle of pro rata temporis applies. Both rules do not object to making the same periods of service a prerequisite for certain conditions of employment for both 'normal' and fixed-term employees. Details as to application are determined by the Member States and/or the social partners.

---

[41]   S. Deakin/G. Morris, *Labour Law,* para. 3.52 ('prohibits laws which count continuity of employment differently according to whether employment is fixed term or permanent'). This distinguishes the provision from that of Article 4(4) PTWFA; on this latter provision, see §16 paras. 31–34 above.

[42]   The exceptional nature of the provision – and thus the implicit regulation of burden of proof – becomes particularly apparent in comparison with §4(4) PTWFA.

IV. MEASURES TO PREVENT ABUSE

30. Pursuant to Recital 6 FTWFA, the social partners consider that employment contracts for an indefinite duration are the 'general' form of employment relationships, which is advantageous for the quality of life of the workers concerned (see para. 3 above). Consequently, the social partners seek to prevent abuse of fixed-term employment such as can occur, in particular, by the use of **successive fixed-term employment contracts**. It is the repetitive use of fixed-term contracts, rather than their initial use, which is therefore subject to control.[43] While such prevention against abuse conformed with the regulatory policy of some Member States, such as Germany, it 'signifies a radical departure from the traditional position in UK law, which was to impose no restrictions upon the rights of the parties to agree successive fixed-term employment contracts'.[44] Clause 5 FTWFA provides for a framework for measures to prevent abuse to be taken by the Member States; it contains no more than a 'minimal consensus'.[45] Where there are no equivalent measures[46] to prevent abuse, Member States must adopt at least one of the three measures:

(1)   objective reasons justifying the renewal of such contracts or relationships;

(2)   the maximum total duration of successive fixed-term employment contracts or relationships;[47] and/or

(3)   the number of renewals of such contracts or relationships.

On the basis of teleological considerations, the Court has construed the term **'objective reasons'** within the meaning of Clause 5(1)(a) FTWFA 'as referring to precise and concrete circumstances characterising a given activity, which are therefore capable in that particular context of justifying the use of successive fixed-term employment contracts. Those circumstances may result, in particular, from the specific nature of the tasks for the performance of which such contracts

---

[43]   ECJ Case C-144/04 *Mangold* [2005] ECR I-9981 paras. 40–43; ECJ Joined Cases C-378/07 to C-380/07 *Angelidaki* [2009] ECR I-3071 para. 90. C. Rolfs/S. E. de Groot, *ZESAR* 2009, 5, 6 sq.

[44]   S. Deakin/G. Morris, *Labour Law*, para. 3.52.

[45]   C. Rolfs, in *EAS*, B 3200 para. 20 – my translation.

[46]   ECJ Joined Cases C-378/07 to C-380/07 *Angelidaki* [2009] ECR I-3071 paras. 68–77 (at para. 76: 'any national legal measure whose purpose, like that of the measures laid down by that clause, is to prevent effectively the misuse of successive fixed-term employment contracts or relationships'. Clause 5 FTWA in substance contains an open catalogue of instruments for the prevention of abuse. The Court has, however, restricted the criterion of 'equivalent' measures by the implementation duties (equivalence and effectiveness); ECJ Case C-53/04 *Marrosu* [2006] ECR I-7213 paras. 49–56; Case C-180/04 *Vasallo* [2006] ECR I-7251 paras. 34–41. See also M. Schlachter, *RdA* 2004, 352, 353.

[47]   See e.g. the example of the new Regulation of fixed-term work in Sweden; see S. Engblom, *IJCLLIR* 34 (2008), 133–150 (critical with regard to the effectiveness of the prevention of abuse). Also Belgium and the Netherlands use time-limits; see R. Blanpain, *IJCLLIR* 24 (2008), 123–131.

have been concluded and from the inherent characteristics of those tasks or, as the case may be, from pursuit of a legitimate social-policy objective of a Member State'.[48] A Greek regulation that authorised recourse to successive fixed-term employment contracts in a general and abstract manner did not satisfy these requirements; the Court considered it to be 'of a purely formal nature'.[49] Similarly, even where the letter of the national law requires precise and concrete circumstances in which successive fixed-term employment contracts or relationships, that national law may be considered to be incompatible with the Directive if, 'in reality, the needs covered by those provisions are not in fact of a temporary nature but are, on the contrary, "fixed and permanent"'.[50] On the other hand, where there is an actual need for replacement staff, 'the mere fact that an employer may have to employ temporary replacements on a recurring, or even permanent, basis and that those replacements may also be covered by the hiring of employees under employment contracts of indefinite duration does not mean that there is no objective reason under clause 5(1)(a) of the FTWFA or that there is abuse within the meaning of that clause'.[51] The Court has, in other words, recognised the employer's entrepreneurial freedom to organise his firm according to his own discretion.

31. Member States enjoy a margin of **discretion** in the choice of (one of the catalogued or equivalent) measures and their configuration.[52] They should take the needs of **specific sectors** (e.g. art, sciences, and construction) and **specific categories of workers** into account.[53] The Member States' discretion is fettered by the general implementation principles (§1 paras. 65 sq. above) which require equivalence and effectiveness, the latter including transparency, of the prevention of abuse.[54] Thus, the Directive does not require that the Member States convert fixed-term contracts that have reached a certain duration into

---

[48] ECJ Case C-212/04 *Adeneler* [2006] ECR I-6057 paras. 69 sq.; Joined Cases C-378/07 to C-380/07 *Angelidaki* [2009] ECR I-3071 paras. 96–107.

[49] ECJ Case C-212/04 *Adeneler* [2006] ECR I-6057 paras. 71–74 approving note by M. Franzen, 'Zum maßgeblichen Zeitpunkt für den Beginn der Pflicht zur richtlinienkonformen Auslegung bei verspäteter Richtlinienumsetzung', *JZ* 2007, 191, 193.

[50] ECJ Joined Cases C-378/07 to C-380/07 *Angelidaki* [2009] ECR I-3071 paras.101, 103 sq.

[51] ECJ Case C-586/10 *Kücük* 26 January 2012 sentence 2 of the rule and para. 56.

[52] ECJ Joined Cases C-378/07 to C-380/07 *Angelidaki* [2009] ECR I-3071 paras. 79–82; Case C-109/09 *Deutsche Lufthansa* 10 March 2011 paras. 35–37. Pre-existing equivalent measures to prevent abuse do not prevent Member States from adopting one of the measures listed in Article 5(1) FTWFA; see ECJ Joined Cases C-378/07 to C-380/07 *Angelidaki* [2009] ECR I-3071 paras. 79–82.

[53] ECJ Case C-53/04 *Marrosu* [2006] ECR I-7213 para. 48 considers the possibility of providing for specific rules for the 'public sector'; perhaps too far-reaching. AG Jääskinen, Opinion in Case C-313/10 *Jansen* 15 September 2011 pts. 51 sqq., argues, though, that in regard of the objective grounds a distinction between the private and public sectors could not be justified. Also budgetary considerations could not constitute objective grounds; loc. cit.

[54] ECJ Joined Cases C-378/07 to C-380/07 *Angelidaki* [2009] ECR I-3071 paras. 83–86; Case C-53/04 *Marrosu* [2006] ECR I-7213 paras. 51–53.

contracts for an indefinite period; yet, if the national law so provides, the Member States must ensure that, in the course of such conversion, the conditions of the employment contract are not materially downgraded to the employee's detriment.[55]

32. The detail is for the Member States (after consultation with the social partners) or social partners to determine. In particular, they may define the circumstances under which two or more fixed-term contracts are to be regarded as **successive** and the conditions under which they should be regarded as **relationships of an indefinite duration**. Again, the Member States must however still respect the general obligations of implementation.[56] Under these principles, the Court has, for example, objected to a national definition under which fixed-term employment contracts could be regarded as successive only in so far as they were not separated by a period of time longer than 20 working days.[57] Indeed, this definition amounted to an invitation to circumvent the rules and was thus liable to compromise the goal of worker protection.[58]

33. This issue of when an employment relationship should be regarded as of an indefinite duration already addresses the issue of **sanctions** or, more broadly, legal consequences which the Framework Agreement intended to leave for the Member States to decide.[59] That makes sense and is in line with the general approach of the European legislator: The issue of sanctions is of particular importance for the smooth implementation of the Agreement into pre-existing national legal systems and should thus be left to the Member States. Yet, the Member States must ensure an equivalent and effective transposition of the rights and obligations determined by the Directive (framework agreement) (see §1 para. 66 above).[60] Despite the suggestive wording of Clause 5(2)(b) FTWFA, pursuant to which the Member States 'shall determine under what conditions fixed-term employment contracts or relationships … shall be deemed to be contracts or relationships of indefinite duration', Member States are not obliged to use such fiction as a sanction. They may also consider other effective sanctions such as a right to damages or compensation or supervisory sanctions or a penalty.[61]

---

55   ECJ Case C-251/11 *Huet* 8 March 2012 paras. 38 sqq.; see also ECJ Case C-212/04 *Adeneler* [2006] ECR I-6057 para. 91.
56   See also ECJ Case C-109/09 *Deutsche Lufthansa* 10 March 2011 paras. 40–50.
57   ECJ Case C-212/04 *Adeneler* [2006] ECR I-6057 paras. 76–89.
58   To the same effect M. Franzen, *JZ* 2007, 191, 193.
59   Cf. ECJ Joined Cases C-378/07 to C-380/07 *Angelidaki* [2009] ECR I-3071 paras. 145, 159 sq., 182 sqq.; ECJ Case C-364/07 *Vassilakis* [2008] ECR I-90 para. 123. C. Rolfs, in *EAS*, B 3200 para. 25.
60   ECJ Case C-53/04 *Marrosu* [2006] ECR I-7213 paras. 51–53; Case C-180/04 *Vasallo* [2006] ECR I-7251 paras. 36–38.
61   ECJ Case C-53/04 *Marrosu* [2006] ECR I-7213 para. 55; Case C-180/04 *Vasallo* [2006] ECR I-7251 para. 40; critically L. Zappala, *ILJ* 35 (2006), 439, 443 sq.

V. INFORMATION

1. Information for Individual Workers

34. In order both to enable fixed-term workers to transfer to an employment relationship of indefinite duration and to ensure equal opportunity in the application process, the employer is obliged to inform fixed-term workers about vacancies which become available in the undertaking or establishment, Clause 6(1) FTWFA. He is not, however, obliged to create new positions of indefinite duration or to favour fixed-term workers over external applicants.[62] Here too, though, the prohibition of discrimination of Clause 4(1) FTWFA applies, e.g. where a fixed-term worker applies for a promotion. The information may be provided by way of a general announcement located at a suitable place (which will also be visited by fixed-term workers) in the undertaking or establishment.

2. Information for Workers' Representatives

35. The employer's obligation to inform the workers' representatives in Clause 7(3) FTWFA is phrased rather vaguely. Such an obligation may well make good sense, e.g. in order to give the representatives an opportunity to take care of the interests of fixed-term workers and to safeguard their rights. It fits in well with the system of information and consultation in EU law, given that the EU legislator also employs collective information duties in other areas (see also §26 below).

36. The definition of 'information' is rather vague: 'appropriate information … about fixed-term work in the undertaking'. This merely requires the employer to give information about the fact that the undertaking uses fixed-term workers and details about the extent of its use. In any case, the information is without bite, given that the clause obliges the employer merely to *give consideration* to the provision of appropriate information'. In other words, it merely constitutes a form of soft law.[63]

VI. SUPPLEMENTARY PROVISIONS

1. Access to Training Opportunities

37. It is often difficult for fixed-term workers to keep pace with the development of occupational requirements. Their employment prospects in general and the

---

[62]　A demand to this effect, voiced by ETUC, was not followed by the legislature; see I. Kaufmann, *AuR* 1999, 332, 334; R. Wank/U. Börgmann, *RdA* 1999, 383, 385.

[63]　R. Wank, in P. Hanau/H.-D. Steinmeyer/R. Wank (eds.), *Handbuch des europäischen Arbeits- und Sozialrechts*, §18 para. 267.

chance to obtain a position for an indefinite duration may thus deteriorate: If a worker has been in fixed-term positions, perhaps repeatedly and with different employers, he will often not find the time for advanced training or professional development. The employer has little interest in investing in fixed-term workers and, indeed, his distinguishing between permanent and fixed-term workers may be justified on objective grounds in such case (see paras. 15–18 above). Clause 6(2) FTWFA seeks to counteract these difficulties for fixed-term workers to some extent. Employers should, 'as far as possible', *facilitate* access by fixed-term workers to appropriate training opportunities to enhance their skills, career development and occupational mobility. The provision thus requires positive action by the employer, but only to a limited extent ('facilitate'). The employer may, of course, not make access to training opportunities excessively burdensome. Beyond that, he must facilitate the participation of fixed-term workers. This does not mean, though, that he would have to neglect his own entrepreneurial interests. Furthermore, the employer is not obliged to bear the costs of such occupational training. Clause 6(2) FTWFA cannot be interpreted as establishing a right to training for fixed-term workers.[64]

2. Calculation of the Threshold for the Constitution of Workers' Representations

38. Finally, fixed-term workers have to be taken into consideration in calculating the threshold above which workers' representative bodies may be constituted in the undertaking, Clause 7(1) FTWA. The provision can be interpreted as a consequential execution of giving effect to the prohibition of discrimination in respect of worker representation (see also Clause 7(2) FTWFA). In addition, if fixed-term workers are to be taken into consideration for the thresholds just as permanent workers, the employer does not have any incentive to hire the former in order to avoid employee involvement and, the system of employee involvement will thus also be protected.

39. Fixed-term workers must be taken into consideration in calculating the thresholds above which workers' representatives under Union law (European Works Council) or national law of the Member States must be established. The details of the calculation (e.g. the reference date, the formation of average values etc.) are left for the Member States to determine, as are the arrangements for the application (Clause 7(2) FTWFA). The reference to Clause 4(1) FTWFA in paragraph 2 clarifies that the prohibition of discrimination also applies here. This may e.g. be relevant with regard to the right to vote or stand for election.

---

[64] For a different view see I. Kaufmann, *AuR* 1999, 332, 334.

3. Information for Representatives of Fixed-Term Workers

40. Rather than regulating collective information, Clause 7(3) FTWFA refers the issue to the employer who is merely required to 'give consideration to' the provision of information on fixed-term work to workers' representatives. See already paras. 35 sq. above.

4. Prohibition of Regression

41. Implementation of the Framework Agreement may not constitute valid grounds for reducing the general level of protection afforded to workers in the field of the agreement, Clause 8(3) FTWFA. The basic intention of this so-called non-regression clause is understandable, particularly in light of the minimum harmonisation approach of EU employment law (see Article 153(4) indent 2 TFEU). Yet it raises intricate issues of competence, policy and interpretation. The non-regression clause cannot be interpreted to mean that just any lowering of the level of protection is prohibited; that would lead to a (partial) petrification of the legal system (though some authors euphemistically speak of 'crystallisation'). Strictly understood, the prohibition of regression could prevent even such restrictions as are required on grounds of coherence, and it would also prevent the Member States from switching from one system of protection to another.

42. While the Court has interpreted the provision broadly,[65] it has also taken account of countervailing considerations.[66] The Court considers the **scope** of the non-regression clause to extend to all measures related to the objective of the Directive, even where they go beyond the Directive's actual rules. Thus, neither the Directive/Framework Agreement, nor the non-regression clause, is limited to workers who have entered into successive fixed-term employment contracts (even though that is the focus of Article 5(1) FTWFA). Whether there is a **'reduction'** of the level of protection cannot be assessed in isolation, but must be determined in light of the whole of national law relating to fixed-term employment contracts.[67] '[I]n order for that reduction to be caught by the prohibition laid down by clause 8(3) of the agreement, it must, first, be connected to the "implementation" of the Framework Agreement and, second, relate to the

---

[65] ECJ Joined Cases C-378/07 to C-380/07 *Angelidaki* [2009] ECR I-3071 paras. 109–113.

[66] Critically L. Corazza, *ELJ* 2011, 385–402 (arguing that the Court's broad construction led to a *de facto* ineffectiveness of the non-regression clause); also L. Corazza/L. Nogler, *ZESAR* 2011, 58–64.

[67] ECJ Joined Cases C-378/07 to C-380/07 *Angelidaki* [2009] ECR I-3071 paras. 116–121, 124; ECJ Case C-98/09 *Sorge* [2010] ECR I-5837 para. 34. Approving case not S. Greiner, 'Auslegung von Absenkungsverboten in Richtlinien und Reichweite der richtlinienkonformen Auslegung', *EuZA* 2011, 74–84.

"general level of protection" afforded to fixed-term workers.'[68] The clause does not prohibit a reduction of protection as such; it applies only in the context of **'implementation'**, both as an object and as an activity. As regards 'implementation' as an object of comparison, this does not refer to the original implementing measure but covers 'all domestic measures intended to ensure that the objective pursued by the directive may be attained, including those which, after transposition in the strict sense, add to or amend domestic rules previously adopted'.[69] As regards 'implementation' as an activity, a national measure will not be considered to be implementing, where it is unconnected and pursues a different objective.[70] Finally, the non-regression clause is concerned with the **'general level'** of protection: 'only a reduction on a scale likely to have an effect overall on national legislation relating to fixed-term employment contracts is liable to be covered by clause 8(3) PTWFA'.[71] This may, for example, not be the case where the reduction only applies to a certain group of workers (e.g. temporary replacements) who do not represent a significant proportion of all temporary workers.[72] The Court thus takes an overall view, pursuant to which an improvement in some areas can offset reduction in others.

43. In *Mangold*, the national court, as well as the German government, convincingly argued that a gradual lowering of the age from which fixed-term contracts could be concluded, without a requirement of 'objective reasons', had not been triggered by the implementation of the Directive, but rather by the need to promote employment of older workers in Germany. The Court held that a regulation that lowered the level of protection on grounds of employment policy and independent of the implementation of the Framework Directive was unobjectionable.

44. Clause 8(3) PTWFA cannot have direct effect as it does not give individuals a right that is 'sufficiently clear, precise and unconditional'. National courts do, though, have an obligation under Article 288(3) TFEU to interpret their law to the greatest possible extent in conformity with the requirements of the non-regression clause.[73]

---

68 ECJ Case C-144/04 *Mangold* [2005] ECR I-9981 para. 52; Joined Cases C-378/07 to C-380/07 *Angelidaki* [2009] ECR I-3071 para. 126.
69 ECJ Case C-144/04 *Mangold* [2005] ECR I-9981 para. 51; Joined Cases C-378/07 to C-380/07 *Angelidaki* [2009] ECR I-3071 para. 131.
70 ECJ Case C-144/04 *Mangold* [2005] ECR I-9981 paras. 52 sq.; Joined Cases C-378/07 to C-380/07 *Angelidaki* [2009] ECR I-3071 para. 133.
71 ECJ Joined Cases C-378/07 to C-380/07 *Angelidaki* [2009] ECR I-3071 para. 140; ECJ Case C-98/09 *Sorge* [2010] ECR I-5837 para. 42.
72 ECJ Case C-98/09 *Sorge* [2010] ECR I-5837 paras. 43 sq.
73 ECJ Case C-98/09 *Sorge* [2010] ECR I-5837 paras. 49–55. Critically L. Corazza, *ELJ* 2011, 385, 395 sqq. (arguing that other means of enforcement would not work effectively).

VII. IMPLEMENTATION[74,75]

45. In **Germany,** the Directive has been implemented – together with the Part-Time Work Directive (§16 para. 46) by the Act on Part-Time Work and on Fixed-Term Work (*Teilzeit- und Befristungsgesetz,* TzBfG)[76] of 21 December 2000.[77,78] §4(2) sent. 1 and 2 TzBfG provide for the prohibition of discrimination and the principle of pro rata temporis. As a measure to prevent abuse, §14 TzBfG provides for the requirement of objective reasons for the agreement of a fixed-term employment relationship.[79] Even though the provision takes the form of a general clause ('objective reasons'), it should satisfy the implementation obligations.[80] An earlier version of the act contained a provision that facilitated the agreement of fixed-term employment with older workers on grounds of occupational policy (reduce old age unemployment) (See §11 paras. 31, 47–49).[81] After the Court of Justice objected to the provision on the ground that it was disproportionate to the aim pursed, the legislator corrected it and brought it into conformity with the Directive.[82] §18 TzBfG deals with information on permanent positions; in conformity with the Directive, the provision must be interpreted as relating to positions in the whole undertaking.[83] §19 TzBfG

---

[74]   On issues of direct effect (public employees!), interpretation of national law in conformity with the Directive and state liability, see ECJ Joined Cases C-378/07 to C-380/07 *Angelidaki* [2009] ECR I-3071 paras. 191–212; Case C-98/09 *Sorge* [2010] ECR I-5837 paras. 49–55. On the question of whether national courts are under an obligation to give the Directive retrospective effect, see ECJ Case C-268/06 *Impact* [2008] ECR I-2483 paras. 93–104; Joined Cases C-444/09 and C-456/09 *Gavieiro Gavieiro and Iglesias Torres* 22 December 2010 paras. 91–99; ECJ Case C-109/09 *Deutsche Lufthansa* 10 March 2011 paras. 50–56.

[75]   On the Member States' obligation under Article 2(3) FTWD to include, into the implementation laws, a reference to the Directive, see ECJ Joined Cases C-444/09 and C-456/09 Gavieiro Gavieiro and Iglesias Torres 22 December 2010 paras. 59–67.

[76]   BGBl. 2000 I, 1966; also available at www.gesetze-im-internet.de/tzbfg/index.html; bilingual German-English version in S. Lingemann/R. v. Steinau-Steinrück/A. Mengel (eds.), Employment and Labor Law in Germany, Part II, III.

[77]   See in detail C. Rolfs, in *EAS*, B 3200 paras. 33–45; R. Wank, in P. Hanau/H.-D. Steinmeyer/R. Wank (eds.), *Handbuch des europäischen Arbeits- und Sozialrechts,* §18 paras. 268–284;. J. Oppertshäuser, in M. Gebauer/T. Wiedmann (eds.), *Zivilrecht unter europäischem Einfluss,* chap. 19 paras. 209–212. On the alterations in comparison to previous legislation P. Hanau, 'Was ist wirklich neu in der Befristungsrichtlinie?', *NZA* 2000, 1045. See also M. Franzen, *JZ* 2007, 191–194.

[78]   On the implementation in other Member States see K. Kröger, *Die Befristung von Arbeitsverträgen in Frankreich, Großbritannien und Deutschland,* 151–166 (France, United Kingdom); see also text with note 84 below; S. Engblom, *IJCLLIR* 34 (2008), 133–150 (Sweden); A. Numhauser-Henning, *IJCLLIR* 18 (2002), 429–458 (Nordic countries; Denmark, Finland, Norway, Sweden); R. Blanpain, *IJCLLIR* 24 (2008), 123–131.

[79]   On the compatibility with the Direcitve M. Franzen, *JZ* 2007, 191, 193.

[80]   To the same effect G. Thüsing, *Europäisches Arbeitsrecht,* §4 para. 29; with doubt, though, C. Rolfs, in *EAS,* B 3200 para. 37.

[81]   See further G. Thüsing, *Europäisches Arbeitsrecht,* §4 paras. 30–35.

[82]   Gesetz zur Verbesserung der Beschäftigungschancen älterer Menschen of 19 April 2007, BGBl. 2007 I, 538.

[83]   Rightly C. Rolfs, in *EAS,* B 3200 para. 42.

concerns access to occupational training; it satisfies the – rather vague – requirements of the Directive. In the **United Kingdom**, the Directive was implemented by the Fixed-Term Employees (Prevention of Less Favourable Treatment) Regulations 2002.[84]

---

[84] SI 2002/2043. For an overview see S. Deakin/G. Morris, *Labour Law,* para. 3.52; P. Lorber, *IJCLLIR* 15 (1999), 121, 127–135; A. McColgan, *ILJ* 32 (2003), 194–199 (critical with regard to the scope of application and the effectiveness of the measures to prevent abuse); see also H. J. Desmond, *Denning L.J.* 15 (2000), 43–66 (discussing the law before the implementation of the Directive).

§18. THE TEMPORARY AGENCY WORK DIRECTIVE

CONTENT

Bibliography:

W. Behrens/J. Richter, 'Leiharbeit/Arbeitnehmerüberlassung (Temporary Agency Work) – EIAS-Tagung am 10./11. 2002', *NZA* 2003, 87–89; O. Bertram, 'Die AÜG-Reform im Spiegel des EG-Richtlinienentwurfs zur Leiharbeit', *ZESAR* 2003, 205–214; N. Busby/D. Christie, 'The Regulation of Temporary Agency Work in the European Union', *Cambrian L. R.* 2005, 15–28; N. Contouris/R. Horton, 'The Temporary Agency Work Directive – Another Broken Promise?', *ILJ* 38 (2009), 329–338; A. Davies, 'The Implementation of the Directive on Temporary Agency Work in the UK: A missed Opportunity', *ELLJ* 2 (2010), 303–327; J. Dirzus, *Zeitarbeit in den Niederlanden – Eine Beschreibung der Zeitarbeit unter besonderer Berücksichtigung hochqualifizierter Zeitarbeitnehmer* (Tönning/ Lübeck/Marburg: Der Andere Verlag, 2006); A. Feuerborn, *Die soziale Sicherung von Leiharbeitnehmern und vergleichbaren Arbeitnehmergruppen in Italien* (Berlin: Duncker & Humblot, 1993); A. Feuerborn, 'Grenzüberschreitender Einsatz von Fremdfirmenpersonal', in H. Oetker/U. Preis (eds.), *Europäisches Arbeits- und Sozialrecht, EAS, part B – Systematische Darstellungen*, loose-leaf (Heidelberg: Forkel, last update: August 2003), B 2500; S. Flämig, *Arbeitnehmerüberlassung im internationalen Konzern – Eine rechtsvergleichende Untersuchung am Beispiel der Länder Niederlande, Japan und USA* (Aachen: Shaker, 2003); M. Franzen, 'Grenzüberschreitende Arbeitnehmerüberlassung – Überlegungen aus Anlass der Herstellung vollständiger Arbeitnehmerfreizügigkeit zum 1.5.2011', *EuZA* 2011, 452–473; M. Fuchs, 'Das Gleichbehandlungsgebot in der Leiharbeit nach der neuen Leiharbeitsrichtlinie', *NZA* 2009, 57–63; F. B. J. Grapperhaus, 'A twist of the equality logic: The Directive on Working Conditions for Temporary Agency Workers and Dutch Law', *ELLJ* 1 (2010), 406–413; A. Guamán, 'Temporary Agency Work Directive and Its Transposition in Spain', *ELLJ* 1 (2010), 414–421; P. Humblet, 'Leiharbeit in Belgien–Employment through temporary staff agencies in Belgium: A brief outline', *EuroAS* 2002, 183–190; E. L. Jones, 'Temporary Agency Labour: Back to Square One?', *ILJ* 31 (2002), 183–190; T. Kienle/A. Koch, 'Grenzüberschreitende Arbeitnehmerüberlassung – Probleme und Folgen', *DB* 2001, 922–927; U. Klebeck, *Gleichstellung der Leiharbeitnehmer als Verfassungsverstoß* (Baden-Baden: Nomos, 2004); M. Kort, 'Die Bedeutung der europarechtlichen Grundfreiheiten für die Arbeitnehmerentsendung und die Arbeitnehmerüberlassung', *NZA* 2002, 1248–1254; M. Lembke, 'Die "Hartz-Reform" des Arbeitnehmerüberlassungsgesetzes', *BB* 2003, 98–104; L. W. Mitlacher/J. Burgess, 'Temporary Agency Work in Germany and Australia: Contrasting Regulatory Regimes and Policy Changes', *IJCLLIR* 23 (2007), 401–431; J. Naderhirn, 'Der Richtlinienvorschlag der Kommission zur Leiharbeit', *ZESAR* 2003, 258–265 (with references to the legal situation in Austria); W. Nienhüser/W. Matiaske, 'Der "Gleichheitsgrundsatz" bei Leiharbeit-Entlohnung und Arbeitsbedingungen von Leiharbeitern im europäischen Vergleich', *WSI-Mitteilungen* 2003, 466–473; T. Raab, 'Europäische und nationale Entwicklungen im Recht der Arbeitnehmerüberlassung', *ZfA* 2003, 389–446; T. Reineke, *Das Recht der Arbeitnehmerüberlassung in Spanien und Deutschland und sein Verhältnis zu der geplanten europäischen Regelung* (Frankfurt a.M.: Peter Lang, 2005); V. Rieble/U. Klebeck, 'Lohngleichheit für Leiharbeit', *NZA* 2003, 23–29; V. Rieble/S. Vielmeier, 'Umsetzungsdefizite der Leiharbeitsrichtlinie', *EuZA* 2011, 474–504; G. Schnorr, 'Die gewerbsmäßige Arbeitnehmerüberlassung – Analyse des Rechtszustands in den Mitgliedstaaten der Europäischen Gemeinschaften und Vorschläge einer Rechtsangleichung', *RdA* 1972, 191–209; P. Schüren/R. Wank, 'Die neue

Leiharbeitsrechtslinie und ihre Umsetzung in deutsches Recht', *RdA* 2011, 1–12; G. Thüsing, 'Europäische Impulse im Recht der Arbeitnehmerüberlassung – Zum Entwurf einer Richtlinie des Europäischen Parlaments und des Rates über die Arbeitsbedingungen von Leiharbeitnehmern – KOM(2002) 149 endgültig –', *DB* 2002, 2218–2223; B. Waas, 'Temporary Agency Work in Germany: Reflections on Recent Developments', *IJCLLIR* 19 (2003), 387–404; B. Waas, 'Die Richtlinie des Europäischen Parlaments und des Rates über Leiharbeit', *ZESAR* 2009, 207–213; R. Wank, 'Der Richtlinienvorschlag der EG-Kommission zur Leiharbeit und das "Erste Gesetz für moderne Dienstleistungen am Arbeitsmarkt"', *NZA* 2003, 14–23; R. Wank, 'Leiharbeit in Deutschland aus arbeitsrechtlicher Sicht', *EuroAS* 2002, 167–174; R. Wank, 'Neuere Entwicklungen im Arbeitnehmerüberlassungsrecht', *RdA* 2003, 1–11; U. Zachert, 'Kündigungsschutz, Befristung und Leiharbeit in Europa', *WSI-Mitteilungen* 2004, 132–137; L. Zappala, 'The Temporary Agency Workers' Directive: An Impossible Agreement?', *ILJ* 32 (2003), 310–317; see also the bibliography to §15.

Cases:

ECJ Case 35/70 *Manpower* [1970] ECR 1251 (social security); ECJ Joined Cases 110/78 and 111/78 *van Wesemael* [1979] ECR 35 (freedom to provide services); ECJ Case 279/80 *Webb* [1981] ECR 3305 (freedom to provide services); ECJ Joined Cases C-369/96 and C-376/96 *Arblade* [1999] ECR I-8453 (freedom to provide services); ECJ Case C-493/99 *Commission* v. *Germany* [2001] ECR I-8163 (freedom to provide services); ECJ Case C-202/97 *Fitzwilliam Executive Search* [2002] ECR I-883 (social security); ECJ Case C-242/09 *Albron Catering* [2010] ECR I-10309 (on the TUD).

I. ISSUES, OVERVIEW[1]

1. Temporary Agency Work is characterised by a triangle of legal relations between the temporary-work agency, the worker and the user undertaking. There are considerable differences between national regulations of temporary agency work in respect of fundamental systematic issues as well as the details, but the basic structures are the same.[2] There is, in principle, initially a

---

[1] See also the overview in §15 above.

[2] For an introduction (on the basis of German law and with comparative references) see e.g. R. Wank, *RdA* 2003, 1–11 (p. 3 identifying two basic models: [1] one related to the user-undertaking where the temporary-work agency functions as a form of employment agency and where its contract with the worker is for the limited time of the assignment with the user undertaking only; and [2] one related to the temporary-work agency where the worker is employed for an indefinite period and where the agency also bears the risk of not being able to 'hire out' the worker between to assignments). For further comparative references, see N. Busby/D. Christie, *Cambrian L.R.* 2005, 15, 16–18; L. W. Mitlacher/J. Burgess, *IJCLLIR* 23 (2007), 401–431 (Germany, Australia); B. Riederer von Paar, in P. Schüren/W. Hamann (eds.), *Arbeitnehmerüberlassungsgesetz*, Einl. AÜG paras. 624–640 (EC member states); B. Waas, *IJCLLIR* 19 (2003), 387, 395 sq. (The Netherlands); F. Becker/P. Bader, 'Der Vorschlag der EG-Kommission für eine Richtlinie des Rates zur Regelung der Leiharbeitsverhältnisse und befristeten Arbeitsverträge – Darstellung und Kritik', *RdA* 1983, 1, 9; A. Feuerborn, *Die soziale Sicherung von Leiharbeitnehmern und vergleichbaren Arbeitnehmergruppen in Italien;*

---

contractual relationship between the temporary-work agency and the worker, normally a – fixed-term or permanent – employment relationship.[3] On the basis of a contract with the user undertaking, the temporary-work agency assigns the worker to perform work under the supervision and direction of the user undertaking for a limited period of time; this is sometimes called a 'split' employer position.

2. Temporary agency work may be of **interest for employers**, particularly small and medium sized enterprises,[4] because it allows them to satisfy a temporary need for workers, e.g. where they have more work for a limited period or where they need a specialist for a limited period of time, such as for the implementation of new software (cf. Recital 9 TAWD). Employers sometimes also use temporary agency workers as an alternative for a training period, giving them an opportunity to get to know the worker with a view to establishing a permanent employment relationship. The flexibility of temporary agency work can also be in the **interest of the worker**,[5] particularly where it assists in balancing family and professional life (cf. Recital 11 TAWD). As regards **occupational policy**, the Union for considers temporary agency work to be an instrument for the promotion of occupational reintegration:[6] an employee may, after an initial period of temporary agency work, find an opportunity for permanent employment with the user undertaking ('sticking effect').[7] Furthermore, given the growth of the temporary agency work sector,[8] there is potential for the creation of new jobs. The Commission even spoke of temporary agency work as a 'key factor' of legislation for the creation of more

---

P. Humblet, *EuroAS* 2002, 183–190 (Belgium); G. Thüsing, *DB* 2002, 2218, 2222 sq. (France and United Kingdom); R. Wank, *RdA* 1992, 103, 110; id., *EuroAS* 2002, 167, 170 sq.; U. Zachert, *WSI-Mitteilungen* 2004, 132–137; see also the references in Commission, Proposal for a Directive of the European Parliament and the Council on working conditions for temporary workers, COM(2002) 149 final, 5. For an older overview, see G. Schnorr, *RdA* 1972, 193, 197–200.

[3]   But see S. Deakin/G. Morris, *Labour Law,* paras. 3.35 and 3.53, on the qualification of the contract relationship between agency and worker under UK law.

[4]   On the employers' interests, see also U. Klebeck, *Gleichstellung der Leiharbeitnehmer als Verfassungsverstoß,* 13–18; V. Rieble/U. Klebeck, *NZA* 2003, 23 sq.; R. Wank, *RdA* 2003, 1, 4 sq.; id., in R. Müller-Glöge/U. Preis/I. Schmidt (eds.), *Erfurter Kommentar,* Einleitung AÜG para. 1.

[5]   See also R. Wank, *RdA* 2003, 1, 4.

[6]   R. Wank, *RdA* 2003, 1, 5; T. Raab, *ZfA* 2003, 398, 402; B. Waas, *IJCLLIR* 19 (2003), 387–404. V. Rieble/U. Klebeck, *NZA* 2003, 23 sq. consider temporary agency work primarily to be an 'employment policy for the integration of low-qualified workers with a below-average level of productivity' – my translation.

[7]   U. Klebeck, *Gleichstellung der Leiharbeitnehmer als Verfassungsverstoß,* 18–20; with reservations R. Wank, *AuR* 2007, 244, 247 ('sticking effect' only happened in a limited number of cases); see also U. Zachert, *WSI-Mitteilungen* 2004, 132, 135 sq. ('bridging function or revolving door-effect?'; my translation) with statistical data for individual countries.

[8]   Commission, Proposal for a Directive of the European Parliament and the Council on working conditions for temporary workers, COM(2002) 149 final, 3 ('first proposal').

and better jobs.[9] It thus aims to achieve greater acceptance of temporary agency work.[10]

3. Thus, the initial ('social') **need for regulation** lies in the removal of unjustified limitations of temporary agency work so as to enable it to reach its potential.[11] Beyond that, the need for regulation predominantly arises from the interests of workers. This primarily concerns equal treatment of temporary agency workers with workers in comparable standard employment relationships. While one might expect that temporary agency workers would receive higher remuneration given the specific risks they bear, their actual pay is estimated to be some 20–40% less than that of comparable 'regular' workers.[12] These figures must be read with the facts that temporary-work agencies charges a fee for their services and that a significant percentage of temporary agency workers are low-qualified, in mind. Another problematic issue can be access to professional training.[13] Temporary agency work bears the risk that neither the temporary-work agency nor the user undertaking feels responsible for the professional training of the workers concerned, as long as there is a constant influx of 'fresh' (qualified) workers.[14] With regard to the transition of temporary agency workers to a permanent employment relationship with the user undertaking, the interests of both 'employers' are potentially at conflict where the agency does not want to let go of the workers (whom they may have specifically trained) or, in any case, not without any reward for their effort. These interests cannot be denied, even if one is to put the interests of workers in the foreground. Finally, specific questions about the representation of workers are raised in the case of a split-employer. Issues about the protection of health and safety are already covered by the 1991 Temporary Employment Health and Safety Directive (§19 below).

---

9   Ibid., 6.

10   The interests of employers and workers proved to be irreconcilable in the legislative process, though; see in more detail E. L. Jones, *ILJ* 31 (2002), 183–190; and already §15 para. 9 above.

11   See e.g. on the restrictive regulatory tradition of Italy A. Feuerborn, *Die soziale Sicherung von Leiharbeitnehmern und vergleichbaren Arbeitnehmergruppen in Italien*.

12   Commission, Proposal for a Directive of the European Parliament and the Council on working conditions for temporary workers, COM(2002) 149 final, 7 ('first proposal'); see also Neunter Bericht der Bundesregierung über Erfahrungen bei der Anwendung des AÜG sowie über die Auswirkungen des BillBG (Ninth Report of the Federal Government on the Experience with the Application of the Temporary Agency Wort Act and the Act on Combatting Illegal Employment), *BT-Drs.* 14/4220, 15 (referring to information from the German Federation of Unions [*Deutscher Gewerkschaftsbund*, DGB)); W. Nienhüser/W. Matiaske, *WSI-Mitteilungen* 2003, 466–473. See also T. Raab, *ZfA* 2003, 389, 394 sq.

13   Commission, Proposal for a Directive of the European Parliament and the Council on working conditions for temporary workers, COM(2002) 149 final, 7 sq. ('first proposal').

14   A special regulatory issue results from the fact that there is some indication that while equal pay may raise the income of temporary agency workers to equal that of workers employed directly by the user undertaking, it also effects a deterioration of their chances of receiving training, perhaps because employers try to save money at this end; W. Nienhüser/W. Matiaske, *WSI-Mitteilungen* 2003, 466–473.

4.   The 2008 **Temporary Agency Work Directive** (TAWD)[15] is intended to balance these employee and split-employer interests.[16] The Directive was the subject of a Commission proposal as early as 2002[17], which was finally[18] adopted on 19 November 2008. The Temporary Agency Work Directive employs similar instruments of protection as the preceding Directives on Part-Time Work (§16) and Fixed-Term Work (§17), in particular equal treatment and information. The principle of equality raises specific questions here, though.

5.   Beyond questions of social and occupational policy, **cross-border temporary agency work** raises specific issues which are genuinely related to the **internal market**.[19] Differences in the national laws on temporary agency work, as regards its admissibility and the instruments of protection,[20] may result in considerable restrictions to cross-border agency work. The freedom to provide services cannot eliminate these obstacles altogether, for the Court of Justice has accepted that national instruments of protection are, in principle, justified on grounds of employee protection (see in general §3 para. 66 above).[21] The Directive addresses this internal market issue only to a very limited extent, namely by providing for the general admissibility of temporary agency work (on grounds of occupational policy). The Services in the Internal Market Directive does not address the issue either (Article 2(2)(e) SIMD; see §3 para. 77 above). Consequently, temporary-work agencies are faced with regulatory disparity between the Member States, e.g. with regard to admission or supervision.

II.   SCOPE OF APPLICATION

6.   The **substantive scope** of application of the Temporary Agency Work Directive is determined by the definition of temporary agency work. The

---

[15]   Directive 2008/104/EC of the European Parliament and of the Council of 19 November 2008 on temporary agency work, OJ 2008 L 327/9.

[16]   On the legislative history, see already §15 para. 9 above; specifically for the TAWD, see M. Fuchs, *NZA* 2009, 57 sq. See also G. Schnorr, *RdA* 1972, 191–209. For a critical assessment of the Directive adopted, see N. Contouris/R. Horton, *ILJ* 38 (2009), 329, 338 sq. ('What emerges is a regulatory instrument that seeks to remove any remaining stigma, restriction or prohibition, associated with temporary agency work without providing for a sufficiently protective, equitable and fair regulatory framework.').

[17]   Commission, Amended Proposal for a Directive of the European Parliament and the Council on working conditions for temporary workers, COM(2002) 701 final.

[18]   After a Common Position had been agreed upon on 15 September 2008; OJ 2008 C 254 E/36.

[19]   B. Riederer von Paar, in P. Schüren/W. Hamann (eds.), *Arbeitnehmerüberlassungsgesetz,* Einl. AÜG paras. 535–553.

[20]   Cf. the references in note 2 above.

[21]   ECJ Case 279/80 *Webb* [1981] ECR 3305. T. Kienle/A. Koch, *DB* 2001, 922–927; A. Feuerborn, in *EAS,* B 2500 paras. 65–67; B. Riederer von Paar, in P. Schüren/W. Hamann (eds.), *Arbeitnehmerüberlassungsgesetz,* Einl. AÜG paras. 547–551.

definition established by the preceding Temporary Employment Health and Safety Directive (§19 para. 5 below) is followed: Temporary agency work is characterised by an employment[22] contract or relationship between the temporary-work agency and the worker in order to assign him to work temporarily[23] under the supervision and direction of the user undertaking, Article 1(1) TAWD.[24] As regards the agency and the user undertaking, the scope is broadly defined and extends to **public and private** undertakings which pursue an economic activity,[25] irrespective of whether they are operating for profit, Article 1(2) TAWD.[26] Member States *may* **exclude** employment relationships concluded under a specific public or publicly supported vocational training, integration or retraining programme.

7. The **personal scope** of application protects *workers* as they are defined by the national laws of the Member States, Article 3(1)(a) and (2)(1) TAWD.[27] On the basis of teleological considerations, as well as in light of the Directives on part-time work and fixed term work (§§16, 17 above), Member States may not exclude workers from the scope of protection on the ground that they work part-time or are engaged for a fixed period, Article 3(2)(2) TAWD. As the Directive also applies to public undertakings, this further narrows the scope for implementation; see the Court's jurisprudence on the Fixed-Term Work Directive, §17 para. 4 above.

III. REMOVAL OF PROHIBITIONS AND RESTRICTIONS

8. As a general rule, temporary agency work is to be regarded as admissible; prohibitions and restrictions must be justified on grounds of general interest, Article 4(1) TAWD.[28] This does not affect national requirements with regard to registration, licensing, certification, financial guarantees or monitoring of temporary-work agencies, though, Article 4(4) TAWD.[29] In line with the Court's

---

[22] The characterisation as 'employment' raises difficulties in UK law; S. Deakin/G. Morris, *Labour Law*, paras. 3.35 and 3.53.

[23] This criterion raises the question whether the Directive also covers permanent assignment; teleological considerations and the legislative history suggest an affirmative answer; V. Rieble/S. Vielmeier, *EuZA* 2011, 474, 486 sqq.

[24] The Directive does not expressly cover the 'hiring out' of workers within a group of undertakings; some authors argue that on purposive considerations this case should be covered as well; S. Flämig, *Arbeitnehmerüberlassung im internationalen Konzern*, 59 sq.

[25] V. Rieble/S. Vielmeier, *EuZA* 2011, 474, 477 sqq.

[26] In this respect critically R. Wank, *NZA* 2003, 14, 16. See also G. Thüsing, *DB* 2002, 2218, 2222.

[27] N. Contouris/R. Horton, *ILJ* 38 (2009), 329, 330.

[28] See also L. Zappala, *ILJ* 32 (2003), 310, 312 sq.

[29] On the respective issue in the draft directive differently J. Naderhirn, *ZESAR* 2003, 258, 260. Critically with a view to cross-border temporary agency work T. Kienle/A. Koch, *DB* 2001, 922, 923 sq.

---

jurisprudence on freedom of services (§3 paras. 66–68), the general interests include 'in particular' (but are not limited to) the protection of temporary agency workers, the requirements of safety and health, the need to ensure the proper functioning of the labour markets and the prevention of abuse.[30] As Recital 20 clarifies, the Directive's provisions on restrictions or prohibitions on temporary agency work 'are without prejudice to national legislation or practices that prohibit workers on strike being replaced by temporary agency workers'. Even though this is not expressly stated, prohibitions or restrictions to the general admissibility of temporary agency work must not go beyond what is necessary for the general interest pursued (principle of proportionality). The Member States must review any restrictions by 5 December 2011 (the end of the implementation period) in order to verify whether they are justified on grounds of public interest, Article 4(2) TAWD. Unlike the proposal, the Directive does not expressly state that any unjustified restrictions must be removed; yet, that already follows from the general provision of paragraph 1.[31] The Directive as enacted also addresses the review of restrictions in **collective agreements** which – on grounds of the protection of the right to collective bargaining – may be left to the social partners, Article 4(3) TAWD. As the social partners are not addressees of the Directive, it remains the duty of the Member States to ensure that the social partners effectively remove any unjustified restrictions to temporary agency work. Given that the only justification for maintaining restrictions are grounds of general interest, it would seem difficult to justify restrictions in collective agreements. The social partners, when concluding collective agreements, pursue their individual interests (even if they are those of collectives) rather than the general interest.

IV. THE PRINCIPLE OF EQUAL TREATMENT

1. The Principle

9. The 'principle of equal treatment' is the central instrument of protection of the Directive.[32] 'The basic working and employment conditions of temporary agency workers shall be, for the duration of their assignment at a user undertaking, at least those that would apply if they had been recruited directly by that undertaking to occupy the same job', Article 5(1) TAWD.[33] Unlike in

---

[30] See e.g. on the prohibition of temporary agency work in the construction sector Federal Constitutional Court (*Bundesverfassunggericht,* BVerfG), *BVerfGE* 77, 84, 107.
[31] The Council thus considered an express provision unnecessary; see the explanatory notes of the Council to the Common Position, OJ 2008 C 254 E/42 to 2.2.
[32] For a detailed account of the development, see M. Fuchs, *NZA* 2009, 57–63.
[33] V. Rieble/U. Klebeck, *NZA* 2003, 23–29 (raising general objections against equal treatment of temporary agency workers with workers employed directly be the user undertaking).

the proposal,[34] the principle is formulated in absolute terms, which does not allow for a justification of less favourable treatment on objective grounds. Paragraphs (2)-(4) provide for optional exceptions, though (see paras. 15 sqq. below).

10. As a matter of economic policy, the principle of equal treatment of the two groups of workers – temporary agency workers and the workers recruited directly by the user undertaking – is controversial.[35] Critics object that it would deprive temporary agency work of its economic basis, given that the temporary-work agency must cover its costs and also needs to make a profit. Consequently, the principle of equal treatment is liable to give away the opportunities of temporary agency work as an instrument of occupational policy.

2. Scope of Application

11. The '**basic working and employment conditions**' to which the principle of equal treatment applies are defined as the working and employment conditions laid down by binding abstract, general provisions ('legislation, regulations, administrative provisions, collective agreements and/or other binding general provisions')[36] in force in the user undertaking relating to **working time** ('the duration of working time, overtime, breaks, rest periods, night work, holidays and public holidays') and **pay**, Article 3(1)(f) TAWD.[37] These terms are central to determining the scope of the principle of equality; it can be anticipated that the Court will construe them broadly. For the definition of pay, the jurisprudence to Article 157 TFEU can be drawn upon.[38]

12. The legislator specifically emphasised that, in the application of the principle of equal treatment of Article 5(1)(1) TAWD, the rules on (a) the protection of pregnant and nursing mothers, of children and young workers as well as (b) those on equal treatment of men and women and measures to combat discrimination 'must be complied with', Article 5(1)(2) TAWD. The meaning and purpose of this qualification in subparagraph 2 – which only relates to the application of the principle of equal treatment of subparagraph 1 – is rather unclear. It appears that it was intended to be a clarification. Yet the rules of

---

34   Article 5(1) of the first proposal, COM(2002) 149 final, 23.
35   See e.g. V. Rieble/U. Klebeck, *NZA* 2003, 23–29; B. Waas, *IJCLLIR* 19 (2003), 387, 398–404.
36   Still differently in Article 3(1)(d) of the first proposal, COM(2002) 149 final: 'd) "basic working and employment conditions": working and employment conditions relating to; i) the duration of working time, rest periods, night work, paid holidays and public holidays; ii) pay; iii) work done by pregnant women and nursing mothers, children and young people; iv) action taken to combat discrimination on the grounds of sex, race or ethnic origin, religion or beliefs, disabilities, age or sexual orientation.'
37   See in more detail T. Raab, *ZfA* 2003, 389, 403 sqq.
38   See also N. Contouris/R. Horton, *ILJ* 38 (2009), 329, 334 sq. (submitting a similar approach).

worker protection referred to are applicable and binding in their own right, and each has its own demarcation as to the scope of application. Article 5(1)(2) TAWD should not be read as a restriction of the respective scopes of application. It may be understood as a supplementation of the scopes of application of the respective legislation or collective agreement, providing that temporary agency workers are included.

13. The restriction that follows from the definition of the 'basic working and employment conditions' is essential for the scope of the specific principle of equal treatment for temporary agency workers: Unlike the initial proposal,[39] the Directive is not concerned with equal treatment on a concrete, individual level but rather on an abstract, general level ('general provisions') with regard to working time and pay. The instrument employed here can thus be compared to that of the Posting of Workers Directive (§6 paras. 3, 16–19) rather than to that of the Directives on Part-Time and on Fixed-Term Work (§16 paras. 17–19, §17 paras. 10–13).[40] On the Union competence for such (indirect) regulation of pay in the light of Article 153(5) TFEU, see §4 paras. 10–12, §15 paras. 13–16 above.

14. The principle of equal treatment sets only a **minimum standard**. It does not prevent more favourable treatment of temporary agency workers as may be justified with a view to the characteristics of such work (no permanent position, higher expenses).[41]

3. Optional Exceptions

15. The Directive provides for three (optional) exceptions to the general principle of equal treatment of the two groups of workers – temporary agency workers and the workers directly recruited by the user undertaking – which are modelled on provisions in the national law of the Member States but which are, at the same time, all well-founded on purposive considerations.

a) Compensation of Lower Pay through a Permanent Employment Contract with Continued Remuneration

16. Member States may derogate from the principle of equal treatment with regard to *pay* (not in general!) if the worker has a *permanent* contract with the

---

[39]   Article 5(1) with Article 3(1)(d) of the first proposal, COM(2002) 149 final, 22, 23; in accordance with the concrete-individual comparison there established, Article 3(1)(b) of the first proposal contained a definition of comparable workers which Article 5(5) of the proposal supplemented by a provision on the possibility of a hypothetical comparison.

[40]   See V. Rieble/U. Klebeck, *NZA* 2003, 23 sq. (also drawing a comparison to the case of posted workers; though with regard to the first proposal of COM(2002) 149 final).

[41]   Differently V. Rieble/U. Klebeck, *NZA* 2003, 23, 26.

temporary-work agency and continues to be paid during the time between two assignments, Article 5(2) TAWD.[42] This derogation is based upon objective reasons given that less favourable treatment of temporary agency workers compared to the workers who were recruited directly by the user undertaking is being compensated by the security of continued pay. The provision does not expressly require that remuneration between two assignments is at the same level as that earned during assignments, and this is moreover not required on the basis of teleological considerations either. Member States may well allow for a reduction in remuneration during the time between assignments, which reflects the decreased expenditure and increase in free time on the one hand, and the needs of the worker on the other.

17. This optional exception is of particular relevance in Member States that follow a system of temporary agency work where the 'temporary' worker has a permanent contract with the agency. In such a case, the principle of equal treatment with the workers of the user-undertaking does not fit coherently but rather leads to excessive burdens of the temporary-work agency (which has to adjust the remuneration for every new assignment and also covers the risk that the worker may not be used for a period between two assignments) on the one hand and a doubling of protection of the worker (who takes the advantage of permanent employment – and pay – as well as equal treatment with the workers of the user-undertaking) on the other.

b) Less Favourable Treatment in Collective Agreements while Respecting the Overall Protection of Temporary Agency Workers

18. Secondly, the Member States may give social partners the option to establish arrangements concerning the working and employment conditions (working time and pay; see para. 11 above) of temporary agency workers, which may differ from those that would apply pursuant to the principle of equal treatment, Article 5(3) TAWD. This (optional) exception finds its justification in the collective bargaining process, which leads to a presumption of fairness of the collective agreement.[43] As an outermost safeguard, the legislator has supplemented this procedural safeguard by a substantive safeguard requiring the collective agreement to respect 'the overall protection of temporary agency

---

[42] L. Zappala, *ILJ* 32 (2003), 310, 315, suggests that the principle of equal treatment should only be suspended for the time between two assignments; but the starting point that exceptions should be construed narrowly is ill-founded, such restriction is not covered by the wording of Article 5(2) TAWD and it is not supported by teleological considerations either.

[43] On the presumption of fairness, see e.g. M. Löwisch/V. Rieble, *Tarifvertragsgesetz*, 2nd edn. (Munich: Vahlen, 2004), Grundl. para. 48, §1 paras. 1–8; H. Wiedemann, in id. (ed.), *Tarifvertragsgesetz*, 7th edn. (Munich: C.H. Beck, 2007), Einl. para. 221. Critically L. Zappala, *ILJ* 32 (2003), 310, 315 sq.

workers'. Whether this latter safeguard constitutes a mere 'program' ('respect', 'overall protection'), or a judicially enforceable standard, is controversial. While some consider the provision to provide for judicial control,[44] others point out that this interpretation would be incompatible with the limitation of competences in Article 153(5) TFEU and amount to censorship in violation of the freedom of collective bargaining as a fundamental right, pursuant to Article 28 ChFR.[45]

c)   Optional Exception for Member States in which there is no System for Declaring Collective Agreements Universally Applicable

19.   A last (optional) exception was introduced into the Directive only through the Common Position of 2008. It applies to Member States which do not have a system in law for declaring collective agreements universally applicable, Article 5(4) TAWD. The provision is aimed, in particular, at implementation in the UK and Ireland.[46] The respective Member States may derogate from the principle of equal treatment in paragraph 1 by law; this may include, in particular, a qualifying period for equal treatment. Such derogation must, however, be based upon a collective agreement and may only be introduced after consultation with the social partners. The apparent aim of this option is to establish the same conditions for all Member States. The optional exception for collective agreements (see para. 18 above) opens up the possibility for some Member States to make such agreements universally applicable. Where, for lack of a system of making collective agreements universally applicable, that is not possible, the respective Member States should be able to reach the same result by law under paragraph 4. As a bottom line, the provision amounts to the introduction a system of making collective agreements universally applicable to those Member States in its (limited) scope.

d)   No Exception for Short-term Temporary Agency Work

20.   An option not to apply the principle of equal treatment to the two groups of workers – temporary agency workers and the workers recruited directly by the user undertaking – in respect of pay for an assignment of up to six weeks has been deleted in the Common Position. This option was of considerable economic importance. It was well-founded upon teleological considerations given that in a long-term relationship (such as an employment relationship) the temporary and directly recruited workers can only be regarded as substantially equal after some

---

[44]   See e.g. M. Fuchs, *NZA* 2009, 57, 61–63. Cf. also T. Raab, *ZfA* 2003, 389, 409 sq.
[45]   See e.g. V. Rieble/S. Vielmeier, *EuZA* 2011, 474, 498 sqq.
[46]   See N. Contouris/R. Horton, *ILJ* 38 (2009), 329, 332 sq. (criticizing that qualifying periods may render the principle of equality largely ineffective); B. Waas, *ZESAR* 2009, 207, 212.

time has elapsed.[47] The fact that the specific optional exception has been deleted does not mean that the social partners could not provide for a similar exception under Article 5(3) and (4) TAWD; to the contrary, the Council expressly considered this to be admissible.[48]

e)   Prevention of Misuse

21.   Finally, Article 5(5) provides for the Member States' obligation to take appropriate measures to prevent misuse of this article. The content and purpose of this provision, as well as its systematic location, are difficult to understand; this seems to be due to a drafting error. The prevention of misuse apparently aims at the provisions of paragraphs 2–4 rather than that of paragraph 1, for how could the principle of equal treatment be misused?! The preceding proposal for a directive provided for a similar provision against misuse in the context of the optional exception for short-term assignments (see para. 20). Indeed, where the principle of equal treatment does not apply to short-term assignments, there is a danger that the protection of temporary agency worker could be circumvented by the use of successive short-term assignments. There may also be potential for abuse in respect of the other exceptions, but this requires control of the implementation laws, rather than control of their application.[49] With regard to the optional exceptions of paragraphs 2 and 4, such control follows from the Member States' obligations of implementation; paragraph 3 expressly provides for the control of collective agreements ('respect the overall protection of temporary agency workers').

V.   EQUAL OPPORTUNITY WITH REGARD TO ACCESS TO PERMANENT EMPLOYMENT

22.   The principle of equal treatment is supplemented by a number of provisions that are concerned with equal opportunity for temporary agency workers, particularly with regard to access to permanent and high-quality employment relationships, both at the user undertaking or more generally. Even though the legislator considers temporary agency work to be admissible in principle, it still wants to promote mobility of temporary agency workers to the 'regular labour market'. Indeed, this also contributes to the acceptance of temporary agency work: Entering the market for temporary agency work is not a one way street. The Directive takes account of the countervailing interest of the temporary-work agencies (that they do not lose their workers) by protecting the agency's financial interests.

---

[47]   Critically e.g. L. Zappala, *ILJ* 32 (2003), 310, 316.
[48]   See the explanatory notes of the Council to the Common Position, OJ 2008 C 254 E/42 to 2.2.
[49]   Similarly B. Waas, *ZESAR* 2009, 207, 212.

1. No Prohibitions of Transfer

23. The temporary agency worker may not be prohibited or prevented from entering into an employment contract with the user undertaking. A contract clause that prohibits the conclusion of such contract or effectively prevents it (such as a penalty clause) should be declared null and void, Article 6(2)(1) TAWD. This merely leaves unaffected provisions under which temporary-work agencies receive reasonable compensation for services rendered to the user undertaking for the assignment, recruiting and training of the worker, subparagraph 2. This means that transfer fees ('temp-to-perm-fees') are in principle admissible, but only for a defined set of purposes and are thus subject to a test of reasonableness.[50] The *temporary agency worker* may not, in any case, be charged any fees in exchange for being recruited by a user undertaking or for concluding a contract of employment with the user undertaking after carrying out an assignment in that undertaking, Article 6(3) TAWD.[51]

24. The provision does not, of course, justify the temporary agency worker breaching his employment contract with the agency. It goes without saying that the worker must honour his employment contract with the agency. Only an excessively long duration or notice period may be objectionable if it has the effect of preventing a transfer.

2. Equal Opportunity with the Workers of the User Undertaking: Information about Vacant Positions

25. Temporary agency workers must be informed about vacant positions in the user undertaking so as to give them an equal opportunity to obtain a permanent position as the workers of the user undertaking, Article 6(1) TAWD. The provision does not require the temporary agency workers to be informed individually; instead, such information may be provided by a general announcement in a suitable place in the user undertaking.

3. Access to Training in the Temporary-Work Agency and in the User Undertaking

26. In an ever-changing working environment, continued training is central to enhancing the employment opportunities of every worker. For temporary agency workers, access to training opportunities is particularly important. The Directive

---

[50] L. Zappala, *ILJ* 32 (2003), 310, 313 sq. (with a critical evaluation). See also T. Raab, *ZfA* 2003, 389, 422 (considering also a transfer fee to be incompatible with Article 6(2)(1) Draft TAWD; subparagraph (2) of the provision, however, argues against this position).

[51] See T. Raab, *ZfA* 2003, 389, 422 sq.

only imposes rather soft obligations. Member States shall take 'suitable measures' in order to improve the access of temporary agency workers to training facilities in the temporary-work agencies 'even in the periods between their assignments in order to enhance their career development and employability'. Similarly, they should take suitable measures to improve access to training for user undertakings' workers.[52]

27.   There are good reasons for both the obligation and its soft wording. In many cases, neither the temporary-work agency nor the user undertaking has an incentive to train temporary agency workers. In many cases, the user undertaking uses temporary agency work to 'buy' specific know-how for a limited period of time (rather than building up know-how itself). The agency, on the other hand, can rely upon having a constant influx of well-trained workers in many areas. Where an employer does not hire workers permanently and where it does not pay them between assignments, it will not be concerned with their employability.

4.   Access to Amenities or Collective Facilities

28.   Temporary agency workers have a right to access the amenities or collective facilities in the user undertaking; the Part-Time Work Directive and the Fixed-Term Work Directive provide for similar rights. One can think of the undertakings' cafeteria, child-care or transportation. In substance, this right is a special expression of the right to equal treatment. It also provides for a special justification for exceptions on objective grounds. The child care of the user undertaking may refuse to take care of the temporary agency worker's children if, under its pedagogic concept, they cannot be integrated into the group for the short period of the assignment.

VI. REPRESENTATION OF TEMPORARY AGENCY WORKERS

1.   Counting Temporary Agency Workers for the Calculation of Thresholds

29.   With respect to representation, too, temporary agency workers are in a position between the temporary-work agency on the one hand and the user undertaking on the other. The Directive only addresses one of the issues involved, namely whether and in which undertaking temporary agency workers will be counted for the threshold above which bodies representing workers must

---

[52]   L. Zappala, *ILJ* 32 (2003), 310, 314 (criticising the soft wording with a view to the danger of opportunistic behaviour of the employer).

be established.[53] Other issues, such as the right of the temporary agency worker to vote or stand for election[54] or the right of workers' representatives to be involved in decisions concerning temporary agency work, are left for the Member states to regulate.

30. Temporary agency workers are counted **in the temporary-work agency** for the purposes of calculating the threshold above which bodies representing workers are to be formed under Union law (EWCD, CRD, TUD; see §28), national law or collective agreements, Article 7(1) TAWD. Member States *may* provide that temporary agency workers should be counted **in the user undertaking** in the same way as if they were workers employed directly for the same period of time by the user undertaking, Article 7(2) TAWD. If they do so, they must also provide for the temporary agency workers to be counted in the temporary-work agency, Article 7(3) TAWD.

2. Information about the Use of Temporary Agency Workers

31. The Directive does not autonomously regulate information and consultation. Instead it 'upgrades' pre-existing provisions on information on the employment situation in the undertaking: When providing such information, the user undertaking must include 'suitable' information on the use of temporary agency workers, Article 8 TAWD.[55] Other – more stringent – provisions on information and consultation, in particular those of the Information and Consultation Framework Directive (§27 below), are left unaffected by this provision.

VII. IMPLEMENTATION

32. The Directive must be implemented into national law by 5 December 2011, Article 11 TAWD.[56] In **Germany**, the Directive has been implemented by a reform of the (pre-existing) Act on Temporary Agency Work (*Arbeitnehmerüberlassungsgesetz*, AÜG).[57] In the **United Kingdom**, the Directive has been implemented by the Agency Workers Regulations 2010.[58]

---

[53] See T. Raab, *ZfA* 2003, 389, 438.

[54] See also R. Wank, *RdA* 2003, 1, 6.

[55] See also T. Raab, *ZfA* 2003, 389, 444 sq.; G. Thüsing, *DB* 2002, 2218, 2221.

[56] For **other Member States**, see F. B. J. Grapperhaus, *ELLJ* 1 (2010), 406–413 (Netherlands); A. Guamán, *ELLJ* 1 (2010), 414–421 (Spain).

[57] M. Fuchs, *NZA* 2009, 57, 61–63 (discussing the need of implementation measures in Germany with regard to the principle of equal treatment); P. Schüren/R. Wank, *RdA* 2011, 1–12; see also B. Waas, *ZESAR* 2009, 207–213.

[58] Available at www.legislation.gov.uk/uksi/2010/93/contents/made. On the implementation process, see also N. Contouris/R. Horton, *ILJ* 38 (2009), 329–338.

§19. THE TEMPORARY WORK HEALTH AND SAFETY DIRECTIVE

CONTENT

Bibliography:
W. Balze, 'Überblick zum sozialen Arbeitsschutz in der EU', in H. Oetker/U. Preis (eds.), *Europäisches Arbeits- und Sozialrecht, EAS, part B – Systematische Darstellungen,* loose-leaf (Heidelberg: Forkel, last update: August 1998), B 5000; W. Däubler, 'EG-Arbeitsrecht auf dem Vormarsch', *NZA* 1992, 577–585; R. Wank/U. Börgmann, *Deutsches und Europäisches Arbeitsschutzrecht* (Munich: C.H. Beck, 1992); O. Wlotzke, 'Das neue Arbeitsschutzgesetz zeitgemäßes Grundlagengesetz für den betrieblichen Arbeitsschutz', *NZA* 1996, 1017–1024; see further the bibliography to §§13 and 15.

Cases:
ECJ Case C-458/05 *Jouini* [2007] ECR I-7301 (concerning the TUD).

I.   ISSUES, OVERVIEW, COMPETENCE, REGULATORY CONTEXT

1.   Since the 1980s, **temporary work** – the term is used here to refer to temporary agency work and fixed-term work (see in detail para. 5 below) – has become increasingly important. Some fields of work proved to pose specific risks to the **safety and health** of temporary workers (Recital 4 TWSHD).[1] As they work at the establishment for a limited period of time only, temporary workers will

---

[1]   W. Balze, in *EAS*, B 5000 para. 12; critically R. Wank, *RdA* 1992, 103, 109.

initially not be familiar with the specific dangers of their workplace. There is a risk that the employer may not take the necessary risk prevention measures in light of the effort and costs, relative to the short period of their employment. An employer might also understate specific risks – such as an exposure to toxics – as being irrelevant for the limited duration of a temporary worker's employment.

2. The 1991 Temporary Work Safety and Health Directive[2] takes account of these specific risks, if only for fixed-term and temporary agency workers and, in its the substantive regulations, with an emphasis on temporary agency work. It aims for the equal treatment of atypical workers and workers in 'regular' employment relationships (Article 2(1) TWSHD). The central **instruments of protection** are information and equal treatment. Temporary workers must be informed about the specific risks of their occupation and, where necessary, receive specific training (Articles 3 and 4 TWSHD). As for health and safety, temporary workers must be afforded the same level of protection as other workers at the user undertaking (Article 2(2) TWSHD). In addition, Member States may specify that temporary workers may not be used or be used only under special medical supervision in respect of certain work (Article 5 TWSHD).

3. The Directive is thus a specific part of the general law of industrial safety. As such, it could – after a lengthy legislative process –[3] be based upon the competence for regulation of the working environment contained in Article 118a EEC (now merged in Article 153 TFEU, see §4 para. 5 above).

4. Even though the Directive is not technically an 'individual directive' for the purposes of the Safety and Health Framework Directive (§13 paras. 4 sq.; cf. Recital 6 TWSHD)[4], the legislator still referred to the protective instruments of this latter Directive. Information and equal treatment have also become the model for subsequent directives on atypical work: the Part-Time Work Directive, the Fixed-Term Work Directive and the Temporary Agency Work Directive (§§16–18).

II. SCOPE OF APPLICATION

5. The scope of application is restricted to fixed-term and temporary agency workers, Article 1 TWSHD. The uniformity in regulation for fixed-term and

---

2   Council Directive 91/383/EEC of 25 June 1991 supplementing the measures to encourage improvements in the safety and health at work of workers with a fixed- duration employment relationship or a temporary employment relationship, OJ 1991 L 206/19.
3   R. Wank, 'Atypische Arbeitsverhältnisse', *RdA* 1992, 103, 104 sqq.
4   R. Wank, in P. Hanau/H.-D. Steinmeyer/R. Wank (eds.), *Handbuch des europäischen Arbeits- und Sozialrechts*, §18 para. 926, speak of a 'supplementary directive' to the Safety and Health Framework Directive.

temporary workers may be due to the fact that the model of French law considers both as instances of work of a limited duration.[5] In substance, this scope of application seems to be well devised as it is precisely the limited time of work in a specific working environment that leads to certain health and safety risks. The Directive does not define the term 'employment relationship' – or that of the worker or employee – but rather refers to the concepts of the Member States. A **fixed-term** (or fixed-duration) contract is characterised as a contract the end of which is established by objective conditions such as – in a non-exhaustive list of examples – reaching a specific date, completing a specific task or the occurrence of a specific event. The specific emphasis in Article 1(1) TWSHD upon the contract being concluded directly between the employer and the worker, aims to distinguish fixed-term work from temporary agency work (see also §17 para. 4 above). **Temporary agency work** is characterised by an employment relationship between the temporary-work agency and the worker, in the course of which the worker is assigned to work under the supervision and direction of user-undertakings, Article 1(2) TWSHD (see also §18 para. 1 above).[6]

6.   **Part-time work** is not covered.[7] Here too, there may be specific risks in respect of the worker's health and safety. Yet, the risks are – following the legislator's plausible demarcation – structurally different here: Unlike a temporary worker – fixed-term worker or temporary agency worker -, the part-time worker is permanently employed. It may thus be assumed that he will be familiar with the specific risks of the undertaking or establishment. The legislator thus considered that the general laws on industrial safety were sufficient to take account of the protection needs of part-time workers.[8]

III.   INSTRUMENTS OF PROTECTION

1.   Equal Treatment

7.   The central aim of the Directive is equal treatment of temporary workers and the other workers of the user undertaking with regard to the protection of safety and health, Article 2(1) TWSHD. Corresponding to this objective, the Directive provides for a right to equal treatment, Article 2(2) TWSHD: The fact

---

[5]   R. Wank, *RdA* 1992, 103, 104; following the French model, the worker concludes a fixed-term contract with the temporary work agency for the time of the assignment only.

[6]   Cf. ECJ Case C-458/05 *Jouini* [2007] ECR I-7301 para. 36 (concerning the TUD).

[7]   See B. Riederer von Paar, in P. Schüren/W. Hamann (eds.), *Arbeitnehmerüberlassungsgesetz*, Einl. AÜG para. 563. The European Parliament had requested an extension to all atypical employment relationships; cf. OJ 1990 C 305/12.

[8]   M. Jeffrey, 'The Commission Proposals on "Atypical Work": Back to the Drawing-Board... Again', *ILJ* 24 (1995), 296, 297.

that the employment relationship is of a 'temporary' nature (fixed-term and temporary agency work) 'cannot justify different treatment with respect to working conditions inasmuch as the protection of safety and health at work are involved'. Temporary workers must, in particular, have access to personal protective equipment in the same way as 'regular' workers. The Directive expressly – if only declaratorily – emphasises that the protective rules of the Safety and Health Framework Directive, and the individual directives adopted upon its basis, 'apply in full' to temporary workers, Article 2(3) TWSHD.

2. Information and Training

8. Fixed-term workers and temporary agency workers have a right to be **informed** by the undertaking or establishment making use of their services about the risks they face before taking up an activity, Article 3(1) TWSHD. The information, in particular, must cover any special occupational qualifications or skills, required special medical supervision, and must 'state clearly' any increased specific risks as defined by national legislation, that the job may entail.

9. In the cases referred to in Article 3 TWSHD – i.e. where the work requires specific qualifications or skills or entails specific risks – the obligation to provide information is supplemented by the further obligation to provide sufficient **training**, Article 4 TWSHD. This refers to instructions that enable the worker to control risks to the greatest possible extent.[9] The obligation to provide training supplements the related obligation under Article 12 SHFD (see §13 para. 23 above). The Directive does not expressly state who is obliged to provide such training but it would seem plausible that it should be the person who is also required to provide the information under Article 3: The user-undertaking is responsible for the provision of training, only it would know the specific detailed requirements of the work.

3. Prohibition of Temporary Work and Special Medical Supervision

10. Certain activities can be considered too dangerous to be entrusted to temporary workers. Cleaning personnel in nuclear power plants may be an example. Originally, the (then) Community legislator intended to define these areas mandatorily for all Member States.[10] However, in its enacted form, the Directive leaves this determination to the Member States, who may prohibit temporary workers from being used for certain work which would be particularly dangerous to their safety and health, particularly for certain work which requires

---

[9]   W. Däubler, *NZA* 1992, 577, 579.
[10]   See Article 6 of the Commission's Proposal for a Council Directive supplementing the measure to encourage improvements in the safety and health at work of temporary workers, COM (90) 228 final, OJ 1990 C 224/8.

medical supervision, Article 5(1) TWSHD. If the Member States do not avail themselves of this opportunity, they *have to* ensure that temporary workers, who are used for work which requires special medical supervision, 'are provided with appropriate special medical surveillance' (paragraph 2) which may extend beyond the end of the employment relationship (paragraph 3).

4.   Specific Measures of Protection for Temporary Agency Work

11.   Temporary agency work in particular bears the risk that the different levels of responsibility (temporary-work agency, user undertaking) will not cooperate. The Directive does not regulate the issue of responsibility as such (see Article 8(1) TWSHD), but it provides for supplementary rules with regard to two specific issues.

12.   The first concerns information and training of the temporary agency worker. Here, the agency and the user undertaking should cooperate in the *selection of employees.* The user undertaking must define the profile of worker needed and the temporary work agency must select an appropriate worker. In order to enable the agency to make this choice, the user undertaking must submit the required qualifications to the agency. It is thus obliged to specify to the temporary employment business the occupational **qualifications** required and the specific **features** of the job to be filled, Article 7(1)(1) TWSHD. Member States may provide that these details have to appear in the contract of assignment between the agency and the user undertaking, Article 7(2) TWSHD. The agency has to bring these facts to the attention of the worker, Article 7(1)(2) TWSHD. The worker is thus also enabled to assess his own qualification himself; industrial safety cannot work effectively without the cooperation of the worker (see also §13 paras. 37–41).

13.   Secondly, for the duration of the assignment, the user undertaking is **responsible** for the conditions governing performance of the work which are connected with safety, hygiene and health at work, Article 8 TWSHD.

5.   Informational Requirements for the Benefit of Persons Carrying out Protective and Preventive Services

14.   Article 6 SHWD supplements these instruments of protection by imposing an obligation to inform the services or persons designated under Article 7 SHFD to carry out activities related to protection from, and prevention of, occupational risks (cf. §13 para. 30 above) arising from the assignment of temporary workers. This obligation arises to the extent necessary for these services or persons to be able to adequately carry out their protection and prevention activities for all the workers in the undertaking and/or establishment.

IV. IMPLEMENTATION

15. In **Germany**, the Directive has been implemented by the Act on Temporary Agency work (*Arbeitnehmerüberlassungsgesetz*, AÜG) and the Act on Industrial Safety (*Arbeitsschutzgesetz*, ArbSchG).[11] In the UK, the Directive was originally implemented by the Management of Health and Safety Regulations 1992.[12]

---

[11] B. Riederer von Paar, in P. Schüren/W. Hamann (eds.), *Arbeitnehmerüberlassungsgesetz*, Einl. AÜG paras. 575 sq.; R. Wank, in P. Hanau/H.-D. Steinmeyer/R. Wank (eds.), *Handbuch des europäischen Arbeits- und Sozialrechts*, §18 paras. 939–946; see also R. Opfermann, 'Das EG-Recht und seine Auswirkungen auf das deutsche Arbeitsschutzrecht', in R. Anzinger/R. Wank (eds.), *Festschrift für Wlotzke* (Munich: C.H. Beck, 1996), 729, 764 sq.; R. Wank, *RdA* 1992, 103, 111 sq.; O. Wlotzke, *NZA* 1996, 1017–1024.

[12] SI 1992/20151, regulations 10 and 13, original version available at www.legislation.gov.uk/ uksi/1992/2051/contents/made. The 1992 Regulations have been replaced by the Management of Safety and Health Regulations 1999, SI 1999/3242; see regulations 12 and 15; available at www.legislation.gov.uk/uksi/1999/3242/contents/made.

CHAPTER 5

PROTECTION OF SPECIFIC
GROUPS OF WORKERS

§20. THE MATERNITY PROTECTION DIRECTIVE

CONTENT

Bibliography:

N. Burrows, 'Maternity Rights in Europe – An Embryonic Legal Regime', *YEL* 11 (1991), 273–293; E. Caracciolo Di Torella, 'Recent Developments in Pregnancy and Maternity Rights', *ILJ* 28 (1999), 276–282; D. Coester-Waltjen, *Mutterschutz in Europa – Der Schutz der erwerbstätigen Frau während der Schwangerschaft und Mutterschaft in den Mitgliedstaaten der Europäischen Gemeinschaft* (Munich: Schweitzer, 1986) (also Euro. Dok. V/1829/84-EN, Brussels 1984/85); V. Cromack, 'The E.C. Pregnancy Directive – Principle or Pragmatism?', *J. Soc. Wel. & Fam. L.* 15 (1993), 261–272; E. Ellis, 'Protection of Pregnancy and Maternity', *ILJ* 22 (1993), 63–67; E. Herrmann, 'Abschluss eines befristeten Arbeitsvertrags mit einer schwangeren Arbeitnehmerin', *SAE* 2003, 125–134; J. Joussen, 'Das neue Mutterschutzgesetz', *NZA* 2002, 702–706; A. Junker, 'Arbeitsrecht zwischen Markt und gesellschaftspolitischen Herausforderungen – Differenzierung nach Unternehmensgröße – Familiengerechte Strukturen – Gutachten B zum 65. Deutschen Juristentag', in Ständige Deputation des Deutschen Juristentages (ed.), *Verhandlungen des fünfundsechzigsten Deutschen Juristentages* (Munich: C.H. Beck, 2004); S. Klein-Jahns, 'Mutterschutz und Erziehungsurlaub', in H. Oetker/U. Preis (eds.), *Europäisches Arbeits- und Sozialrecht, EAS, part B – Systematische Darstellungen,* loose-leaf (Heidelberg: Forkel, last update: January 1999), B 5100; M. Kossens, 'Änderung des Jugendarbeitsschutz- und des Mutterschutzgesetzes', *RdA* 1997, 209–212; M. Lenz, 'Änderungen im Mutterschutzrecht', *NJW* 1997, 1491–1492.; K. Lörcher, 'EG-Mutterschutzrichtlinie verabschiedet', *AuR* 1993, 54–55; H. Marburger, 'Änderungen des Mutterschutzrechts', *BB* 1997, 521–524; C. McGlynn, 'Ideologies of Motherhood in European Community Sex Equality Law', *ELJ* 6 (2000), 29–44; D. Muffat-Jeandet, 'Protection of Pregnancy and Maternity', *ILJ* 20 (1991), 76–79; K. Nebe, *Betrieblicher Mutterschutz ohne Diskriminierungen: Die RL 92/85 und ihre Konsequenzen für das deutsche Mutterschutzrecht* (Baden-Baden: Nomos, 2006); M. Reiner, 'Schwanger oder nicht schwanger: Die Rechtssache Mayr', *EuZA* 2009, 79–87; H.-H. Sowka, 'Änderungen im Mutterschutzrecht und im Jugendarbeitsschutzrecht', *NZA* 1997, 296–298; H.-H. Sowka, 'Mutterschutzrichtlinienverordnung', *NZA* 1997, 927–928; J. T. Thau, 'Novelliertes Mutterschutzrecht – für das Arbeitsleben von großer Bedeutung', *AuA* 1997, 213–215; M. Wynn, 'Pregnancy Discrimination: Equality, Discrimination or Reconciliation?', *MLR* 62 (1999), 435–447; J. Zmarzlik, 'Überblick über die EG-Mutterschutz-Richtlinie und ihre Umsetzung', *DB* 1994, 96–97; see also the bibliography to §9.

Cases:

ECJ Case 184/83 *Hofmann* [1984] ECR 3047; ECJ Case C-179/88 *Handels- og Kontorfunktionaererernes Forbund* [1990] ECR I-3979; ECJ Case C-345/89 *Stoeckel* [1991] ECR I-4047; ECJ Case C-32/93 *Webb* [1994] ECR I-3567; ECJ Case C-342/93 *Gillespie* [1996] ECR I-475; ECJ Case C-400/95 *Larsson* [1997] ECR I-2757; ECJ Case C-136/95 *Thibault* [1998] ECR I-2011; ECJ Case C-394/96 *Mary Brown* [1998] ECR I-4185; ECJ Case C-411/96 *Boyle* [1998] ECR I-6401; ECJ Case C-66/96 *Pedersen* [1998] ECR I-7327; ECJ Case C-218/98 *Abdoulaye* [1999] ECR I-5723; ECJ Case C-333/97 *Lewen* [1999] ECR I-7243; ECJ Case C-207/98 *Mahlburg* [2000] ECR I-549; ECJ Case C-438/99 *Jiménez Melgar* [2001] ECR I-6915; ECJ Case C-109/00 *Tele Danmark* [2001] ECR I-6993; ECJ Case C-366/99 *Griesmar* [2001] ECR I-9383; ECJ Case C-320/01 *Wiebke Busch* [2003]

ECR I-2041; ECJ Case C-342/01 *Merino Gómez* [2004] ECR I-2605; ECJ Case C-147/02 *Alabaster* [2004] ECR I-3101; ECJ Case C-284/02 *Sass* [2004] ECR I-11143; ECJ Case C-356/03 *Mayer* [2005] ECR I-295; ECJ Case C-203/03 *Commission* v. *Austria* [2005] ECR I-935; ECJ Case C-191/03 *McKenna* [2005] ECR I-7631 (with a good summary of the development oft he Court's jurisprudence at paras. 40–54); ECJ Case C-294/04 *Herrero* [2006] ECR I-1513 (on sex discrimination); ECJ Case C-116/06 *Kiiski* [2007] ECR I-7643; ECJ Case C-460/06 *Paquay* [2007] ECR I-8511; ECJ Case C-506/06 *Mayr* [2008] ECR I-1017; ECJ Case C-63/08 *Pontin* [2009] ECR I-10467; ECJ Case C-471/08 *Parviainen* [2010] ECR I-6533; ECJ Case C-194/08 *Gassmayr* [2010] ECR I-6281; ECJ Case C-104/09 *Roca Álvarez* [2010] ECR I-8661; ECJ Case C-232/09 *Danosa* [2010] 11 November 2011.

I.   ISSUES, OVERVIEW, COMPETENCE, REGULATORY CONTEXT

1.   Issues

1.   Pregnant women, women who have recently given birth and women who are breastfeeding are in special need of protection as workers. This initially involves protection of safety and health of the mother and her unborn or recently born child. Protection from dangerous substances or radiation and from excessive physical strain is particularly important. Around the (prospective) time of birth, special regard should be given to the fragility of the expectant mother. Beyond that, it is desirable to assist pregnant women by making it easy for them to schedule their ante-natal appointments.

2.   Development and Overview

2.   In EU employment law,[1] protection of pregnant women and women who have recently given birth (hereinafter also 'maternity protection') evolved initially as part of sex discrimination law (see §9 paras. 46–49, 59, 62–64 above and para. 35 below).[2] Similarly, the Community Charter of Fundamental Social Rights of 1989 (§2 paras. 65–70 above) addresses maternity protection only within the framework of equal treatment for men and women, namely as part of the promotion of work and family life balance (No. 17(3) CFSR).[3] Only the 2000

---

[1]   For a survey on the legislative history, see N. Burrows, *YEL* 11 (1991), 273, 285–293; E. Ellis, *ILJ* 22 (1993), 63–65; K. Nebe, *Betrieblicher Mutterschutz ohne Diskriminierungen,* 103–111. On the comparative background before the enactment, see D. Coester-Waltjen, *Mutterschutz in Europa.*

[2]   Some authors today treat it as part equality law; see e.g. S. Deakin/G. Morris, *Labour Law,* paras. 6.105 sqq.

[3]   Similarly in the Commission's Communication of 29 November 1989 concerning its Action Programme relating to the Implementation of the Community Charter of Basic Social Rights for Workers, COM(89) 568 final, 36 sq.

Charter of Fundamental Social Rights considers both the protection of family and professional life and maternity protection as such (Article 33(2) ChFR; see §2 paras. 58, 60 above). However, as early as 1990, the Commission published an initial proposal for a maternity protection directive.[4] While the proposal met with much support, it was criticised by the United Kingdom as being too far-reaching and resource-intensive. But the Commission was reluctant to compromise upon the level of maternity protection in the proposed directive. The Directive which was finally enacted in 1992 provides for a lower standard of protection than initially envisaged; in particular, the time of maternity leave was reduced from 16 to 14 weeks – a standard that was already widely applied throughout the Member States.

3.   The Maternity Protection Directive (MPD)[5] provides for the protection of **pregnant women and women who have recently given birth** in their capacity as workers and in relation to the employer. The Directive supplements the Safety and Health Framework Directive and substantially extends its scope of protection. The Maternity Protection Directive uses **three principal instruments of protection**. *First,* the women concerned are protected from activities that entail specific risks. For this purpose, the Directive requires the employer to assess risks (Article 4) and take appropriate action based upon this assessment (Article 5): The employer has a duty to avoid exposing the relevant group of women to risks which are identified by the assessment, preferably by adjusting their working conditions and hours or, where that is not possible, by moving them to another job or granting them leave. Exposure of the protected workers to certain risks is prohibited altogether (Article 6). And in certain cases, the protected women are not obliged to perform night work (Article 7). *Secondly,* the protected workers have a right to maternity leave (Article 8) and, within limits, time off for antenatal medical assessments (Article 9). The Directive provides for a (limited) right to continued payment or an entitlement to an 'adequate allowance' (i.e. social benefits) (Article 11) during maternity leave and times of work which fall within Articles 5–7 and 8. *Thirdly,* the Directive includes a prohibition of dismissal (Article 10). All these provisions are merely **minimum standards** (Article 188a(2) EEC [see today Article 153(2)(1)(b) TFEU], Recital 1

---

[4]   Commission, Proposal for a Council directive of 11 September 1990 concerning the protection at work of pregnant women or women who have recently given birth, COM(90) 406 final, OJ 1990 C 281/3. Commission, Amendment to the proposal for a Council Directive of 18 January 1991 concerning measures to encourage improvements in the safety and health of pregnant workers, women workers who have recently given birth and women who are breastfeeding, COM(90) 692 final, OJ 1991 C 25/3.

[5]   Council Directive 92/85/EEC of 19 October 1992 on the introduction of measures to encourage improvements in the safety and health at work of pregnant workers and workers who have recently given birth or are breastfeeding (tenth individual Directive within the meaning of Article 16(1) of Directive 89/391/EEC), OJ 1992 L 348/1.

MPD).[6] Furthermore, Article 1(3) MPD prohibits regression in the level of protection ('standstill clause').

4. The Directive pursues several **purposes**. It aims to protect the health and safety of pregnant and nursing workers, and workers who have recently given birth.[7] It protects the relationship between the mother and her newly born child, by preventing its disruption by the mother's professional obligations.[8] The Directive also serves to protect against sex discrimination. And finally, it contributes to the balancing of family and professional life.

5. A **Commission Proposal** of 3 October 2008[9] aims to amend the Maternity Protection Directive to further promote the balancing of work and family life. Following this proposal, maternity leave should be extended from 14 to 18 weeks (the Commission refers to a 'modest increase'), six of which must be taken after childbirth, the remaining (non-compulsory) twelve may be freely allocated by the worker. Following the Court's decision in *Paquay* (para. 32), the prohibition of dismissal in Article 10 should be extended so as to also apply to 'any preparations for dismissal'; the special requirement to give grounds for dismissal should be extended. Instead of the 'adequate allowance' provided for in respect of pay during maternity leave and other periods of leave associated with maternity by the current Directive (para. 29), the proposal suggests an allowance equivalent to the worker's full salary, with an option given to Member States to lay down a ceiling which is not lower than sick pay. And finally, there are a number of provisions related to the prohibition of sex discrimination which are already addressed in the 2006 Sex Discrimination Directive: The determination that less favourable treatment on account of pregnancy or maternity leave constitutes sex discrimination; a right to return to one's old job; rules on burden of proof; and provisions on victimisation similar to those of the Sex Discrimination Directive. The Commission considers that the financial burdens which result from these extended maternity rights are affordable. It argues that, for one thing, extended maternity leave would probably lead mothers to have less recourse to parental leave, thus giving employers, small and medium sized enterprises in particular, greater certainty as to the length of a mother's absence. Furthermore, the Commission points out that the issue of who bears the costs is for the Member States to decide. The Commission proposal was met with general support in the European Parliament. However, Parliament

---

6   Cf. ECJ Case C-438/99 *Jiménez Melgar* [2001] ECR I-6915 para. 37.
7   ECJ Case C-203/03 *Commission* v. *Austria* [2005] ECR I-935 para. 44.
8   ECJ Case C-116/06 *Kiiski* [2007] ECR I-7643 paras. 46, 50; Case C-366/99 *Griesmar* [2001] ECR I-9383 para. 43; Case C-411/96 *Boyle* [1998] ECR I-6401 para. 61.
9   Commission, Proposal for a Directive of the European Parliament and of the Council of 3 October 2008 amending Council Directive 92/85/EEC on the introduction of measures to encourage improvements in the safety and health at work of pregnant workers and workers who have recently given birth or are breastfeeding, COM(2008) 637 final.

favours even more stringent rules, advocating, in particular, 20 weeks of fully paid maternity leave. While the Council, in principle, also favours an improvement in the standards of maternity protection, it insists that the Directive should only provide for minimum standards. The Council meeting of 1–2 December 2011 could not endorse the proposals of the Commission and Parliament. In particular, 'it has become crystal clear that the period of 20 weeks of maternity leave with full pay is unacceptable to the Council'.[10]

6.   The proposal is closely linked to the Commission's endeavour to give *self-employed women* and their spouses and partners (recognised under national law) a right to maternity (parental) benefits (so as to enable maternity [parental] leave). This recently led to the adoption of the Directive on the application of the principle of equal treatment between men and women engaged in an activity in a self-employed capacity.[11] It is further linked to an endeavour to enhance work and family life balance by the introduction of new forms of family-related leave, such as paternity leave, adoption leave, filial leave and care leave.[12] The new models of family-related leave could become the subject of a new framework agreement which the social partners have been negotiating since September 2008 (see §21 para. 4 below).

7.   It was not just the contents of the Directive, but also the issue of Union competence, which has been controversial during legislative proceedings.[13] As the proposal did not only contain provisions on health and safety, but also included provisions on the protection of the economic interests of workers (compensation during periods of absence), it was doubtful whether it could legitimately be based upon Article 118a EEC (today merged into Article 153 TFEU). However, protection of economic interests may well be considered necessary and complementary to the provisions on leave, as many workers might be deterred from taking leave of absence if there was no economic security (cf. the Court's jurisprudence on the right to paid annual leave, §14 paras. 52 sqq.).

---

[10]   Press Release 17943/11, available at www.consilium.europa.eu/uedocs/cms_data/docs/pressdata/en/lsa/126530.pdf, p. 10. See in more detail Council, Interinstitutional File 2008/0193 (COD), available at http://register.consilium.europa.eu/pdf/en/11/st17/st17029.en11.pdf.

[11]   Directive 2010/41/EU of the European Parliament and of the Council of 7 July 2010 on the application of the principle of equal treatment between men and women engaged in an activity in a self-employed capacity and repealing Council Directive 86/613/EEC, OJ 2010 L 180/1.

[12]   Commission, Communication of 3. October 2008 to the European Parliament, the Council, the European Economic and Social Committee and the Committee of the Regions – A better work-life balance: stronger support for reconciling professional, private and family life, COM(2008) 635 final, pp. 6–8.

[13]   With doubt e.g. N. Burrows, *YEL* 11 (1991), 273, 287 sq. See also D. Muffat-Jeandet, *ILJ* 20 (1991), 76, 77 sq.

3. Regulatory Context

8. The substance of the Maternity Protection Directive is connected to a number of other areas of EU employment law regulation. Article 1(1) MPD indicates that it is an individual directive under the **Safety and Health** Framework Directive (Article 15, 16 SHFD, see in detail §13 para. 4 above) (see also Recitals 7 and 8 MPD).[14] Consequently, where the Maternity Protection Directive's provisions are not more stringent or specific than the Safety and Health Framework Directive, the latter Directive applies subordinately within the scope of the Maternity Protection Directive,[15] Article 1(2) MPD and Article 16(3) SHFD. Going beyond industrial safety in a narrow sense, the Maternity Protection Directive also protects the **economic interests** of relevant workers, by regulating compensation for times of leave and protection against dismissal. The provisions on working time, night work and leave in particular, supplement those of the **Working Time Directive**. Following the Commission's proposals, the Working Time Directive will also in future aim to promote a better balance between work and family life (§14 para. 8). The **Parental Leave Directive** (§21) also contributes to this goal.[16]

This development is arguably double-edged. The specific protection of mothers tends to be diluted in this context as pregnancy, birth and the mother-child-relationship are being put on the same level as other private matters.

9. There has long been a close connection between the Maternity Protection Directive and the **Sex Discrimination Directive** (§9; cf. Recital 9 MPD); the amendment proposed by the Commission (para. 5 above) would reinforce this connection. Following the Court's jurisprudence that has been recently confirmed by the legislature, less favourable treatment on grounds of pregnancy constitutes direct discrimination on grounds of sex (§9 paras. 16, 46–49). Special protection of women is, however, ambivalent,[17] as the Court's jurisprudence on night work also illustrates.[18] Provisions on the protection of women – privileges

---

[14] Article 16(1) with the Annex SHFD does not expressly mention maternity protection (and it does not fit easily in the System of the list of 'areas' and 'work places' listed in the Annex); the list is not conclusive, though ('*inter alia*'); see also N. Burrows, *YEL* 11 (1991), 273, 287.

[15] R. Blanpain/M. Schmidt/U. Schweibert, *Europäisches Arbeitsrecht*, 239; W. Däubler/ M. Kittner/K. Lörcher, *Internationale Arbeitsordnung und Sozialordnung*, 2nd edn. (Cologne: Bund, 1994), 1288.

[16] Commission, Communication to the European Parliament, the Council, the European Economic and Social Committee and the Committee of the Regions of 3 October 2008 – 'A better work-life balance: stronger support for reconciling professional, private and family life', COM(2008) 635 final.

[17] C. McGlynn, *ELJ* 6 (2000), 29–44, considers the Court's jurisprudence to be based on 'traditional' conceptions of roles of mothers and fathers and as adhering to the 'dominant ideology of motherhood', thus not fully exploiting the potential of prohibitions of discrimination.

[18] See the seminal decision of ECJ Case C-345/89 *Stoeckel* [1991] ECR I-4047.

as well as burdens – take precedence over the principle of equal treatment, Article 28 SDD. In other areas, case law illustrates that the protection against discrimination and maternity protection can be supplementary. For example, the Maternity Protection Directive presupposes the existence of an employment relationship and does not afford protection before its conclusion.[19] Furthermore, the prohibition against dismissal under the Maternity Protection Directive does not grant any protection against non-renewal of a fixed-term engagement on grounds of pregnancy (para. 32 below). In both cases, the Sex Discrimination Directive steps in (§9 para. 35 above). In respect of **compensation during maternity leave** (pay within the meaning of Article 157 TFEU, §9 para. 6 above), the Court (ruling on a case before the expiry of the implementation period for the MPD), decided that the equal pay provisions of Article 157 TFEU and Articles 4 and 14(1)(c) SDD (§9 para. 16 above) did not contain any criteria as to the level of remuneration. However, the purpose of the provisions required that compensation may not be so low as to imperil the purpose of maternity leave, albeit that the provisions cannot serve as a basis for a right to continued full remuneration.[20] If the worker becomes entitled to a pay raise during her maternity leave, she must benefit from that pay rise by it being taken into account in the calculation of maternity compensation and it being paid upon her return to work.[21] Benefits for female workers do not constitute unlawful discrimination where they are granted as compensation for the disadvantages flowing from maternity leave. Male and female workers are not 'substantially equal' in this respect and thus need not be treated equally.[22]

II. SCOPE OF APPLICATION

10. The Directive does not explicitly define its scope of application. For most provisions (different, e.g., for Article 4(2) MPD), the Directive's scope of application can be inferred from the **definitions** contained in Article 2 MPD and from the provisions of the Safety and Health Protection Directive (§13 paras. 6–11).

11. As its title indicates, the Directive protects not only pregnant workers and workers who have recently given birth, but also workers who are breastfeeding. However, in respect of this latter group, only the provisions contained in

---

[19]   Cf. ECJ Case C-294/04 *Herrero* [2006] ECR I-1513 paras. 26–32, 41.

[20]   ECJ Case C-191/03 *McKenna* [2005] ECR I-7631 para. 50; Case C-147/02 *Alabaster* [2004] ECR I-3101 para. 46; Case C-352/93 *Gillespie* [1996] ECR I-475 para. 20.

[21]   ECJ Case C-147/02 *Alabaster* [2004] ECR I-3101 paras. 47–49; Case C-352/93 *Gillespie* [1996] ECR I-475 paras. 21 sq.

[22]   ECJ Case C-366/99 *Griesmar* [2001] ECR I-9383 para. 41 (differently with regard to child-rearing; para. 56); Case C-218/98 *Abdoulaye* [1999] ECR I-5723 paras. 18–21. See also Case 184/83 *Hofmann* [1984] ECR 3047 paras. 25 sq.

Articles 4–7 MPD on the prevention of risks are relevant. For the definition of a pregnant worker, Article 2 refers to the word's natural everyday meaning[23] and the Court of Justice has considered the term to be autonomous in Union law.[24] The definitions of 'workers who have *recently* given birth' and 'workers who are *breastfeeding*' require a temporal determination[25] – the Directive leaves this determination to be made by reference to the national laws of the Member States. In all instances, whether or not the worker **informs** the employer of her condition is decisive; protection is not imposed upon her.[26] This is true even where the worker's circumstances are obvious.[27] Only the duty to inform pursuant to Article 4(2) MPD which expressly also applies to 'workers likely to be in one of the situations referred to in Article 2' irrespective of such information. Member States may provide for more stringent protection, Article 1(3) MPD. However, the Court of Justice has taken a **different position**, and without analysing the provisions of the Directive more closely but having direct recourse to what it considered the purpose of the Directive, has held: 'If, without having been formally informed by the worker in person, the employer learns of her pregnancy, it would be contrary to the spirit and purpose of Directive 92/85 to interpret the provisions of Article 2(a) of that Directive restrictively and to deny the worker concerned the protection against dismissal provided for under Article 10.'[28]

12.   The term '**worker**' is not defined as such but it is part of the terms 'pregnant worker', 'worker who has recently given birth' and 'worker who is breastfeeding'. This indicates that the legislature did not intend to define the term *en passant*. However, since the Maternity Protection Directive is an individual directive under the Safety and Health Framework Directive, the term 'worker' should be interpreted in the same way as under the Framework Directive, i.e. **autonomously** (see §13 para. 9 above). The Court has also taken this position, albeit without any discussion of the issue as such.[29] Following the Court's **definition** – here as in Article 45 TFEU on the free movement of workers (§3 paras. 9–12 above) – '[t]he essential feature of an employment relationship is

---

23   But see with regard to the beginning of pregnancy in the case of in-vitro fertilisation ECJ Case C-506/06 *Mayr* [2008] ECR I-1017 and para. 33 below.

24   M. Reiner, *EuZA* 2009, 79, 81 sq.; AG Colomer, Opinion in Case C-506/06 *Mayr* [2008] ECR I-1017 pt. 28.

25   These cases are not determined by 'biological facts' but rather by a value judgement; differently S. Klein-Jahns, in *EAS*, B 5100 para. 13.

26   Cf. ECJ Case C-116/06 *Kiiski* [2007] ECR I-7643 para. 33. Differently K. Nebe, *Betrieblicher Mutterschutz ohne Diskriminierungen*, 140–147.

27   To the same effect S. Klein-Jahns, in *EAS*, B 5100 para. 13. Differently S. Grundmann, *Europäisches Schuldvertragsrecht*, 3.45 para. 10.

28   ECJ Case C-232/09 *Danosa* 11 November 2010 paras. 55.

29   ECJ Case C-116/06 *Kiiski* [2007] ECR I-7643 paras. 23 sq.; Case C-232/09 *Danosa* 11 November 2010 paras. 39.

that, for a certain period of time, a person performs services for and under the direction of another person, in return for which he receives remuneration'.[30] The Court also refers to a **relationship of subordination**.[31] It is irrelevant that the relationship is considered to be *sui generis* under national law:[32] In the case at hand, the Court considered a *worker on parental leave* (Clause 3 PLFA, §21 paras. 25–28) to be a worker. Similarly, the fact that national law considers a person to be *self-employed*, does not meant that she cannot be a worker within the meaning of the Maternity Protection Directive. In a bold move, the Court ruled that even **a member of a capital company's Board of Directors** may, under the principles outlined above, be considered to be a worker within the Directive.[33] In respect of the 'relationship of subordination', the Court highlighted that a member of a Board of Directors may be removed by a decision of the company's shareholders. As in the Safety and Health Framework Directive, there is also an **exception** to the Directive's scope of application in respect of domestic servants (Article 3(a) SHFD, §13 para. 9).[34]

13. The Directive does not provide for any restrictions upon the scope of the Directive in respect of **employers**. In particular, no distinction is drawn between the public and private sectors or on the basis of the size of the undertaking (such as an exception for small enterprises).[35] This appears sensible in light of the Directive's purpose to protect the health and safety of workers.

III. PROTECTION AGAINST RISKY ACTIVITIES

1. Overview and Guidelines

14. The Maternity Protection Directive provides for a graded system of protection against hazards to pregnant workers and workers who have recently given birth or who are breastfeeding within Articles 4–7. At the outset, the employer is under general obligations of assessment, information and risk avoidance under Article 4 MPD. Where assessment reveals concrete risks to

---

[30] ECJ Case C-116/06 *Kiiski* [2007] ECR I-7643 para. 25; Case C-232/09 *Danosa* 11 November 2010 para. 39.

[31] Case C-232/09 *Danosa* 11 November 2010 paras. 44 sqq.

[32] ECJ Case C-116/06 *Kiiski* [2007] ECR I-7643 para. 26; confirmed by ECJ Case C-232/09 *Danosa* 11 November 2010 para. 40.

[33] ECJ Case C-232/09 *Danosa* 11 November 2010 paras. 42 sqq. Critical case note by C. Schubert, 'Kündigungsschutz für die Geschäftsführerin einer Kapitalgesellschaft während der Schwangerschaft – Gesundheitsschutz und Diskriminierungsschutz', *EuZA* 2011, 362–371 (365: distinction between the right to direction under the employment contract and under company law).

[34] J. Zmarzlik, *DB* 1994, 96, 97.

[35] ECJ Case C-109/00 *Tele Danmark* [2001] ECR I-6993 para. 37.

safety and health, Article 5 obliges the employer to take the necessary measures. Article 6 provides for a prohibition of exposure in certain cases of abstract risk. And finally, Article 7 on night-work relates to a special type of risk.

15. These specific provisions are preceded by Article 3 MPD which entrusts the Commission with the task of drawing up **guidelines** on the assessment of chemical, physical and biological agents and industrial processes which are considered to be hazardous for the safety or health of protected workers. These guidelines should serve as a basis for the assessment which the employer must conduct under Article 4.[36] The provision is particularly relevant as it provides for a **wide definition of health** in paragraph 1 subparagraph 2, which includes both mental and physical fatigue and stress.

2.   Assessment

16. The employer is under an obligation to conduct an assessment of risks under two conditions: where the protected worker is subject to (1) a specific risk of (2) exposure to the agents, processes and working conditions contained in the non-exhaustive list in Annex I MPD, Article 4(1) MPD. The employer must bear the risks and costs resulting from the indeterminate term of a 'specific risk' and from the non-exhaustive character of the list in Annex I; this is in line with the entrepreneurial risk and with principles of strict liability. The Commission's guidelines (Article 3) and amendments to Annex I (which may be adopted in a facilitated procedure under Article 13)[37] may alleviate these burdens.

17. Assessment of risks means that the employer must appraise the nature, degree and duration of exposure with regard to the worker's specific activities in order to evaluate any health and safety risks and any possible effect upon the worker's pregnancy or breastfeeding. The employer must then decide what measures should be taken, Article 4(1) MPD. Pregnant workers, workers who have recently given birth and workers who are breastfeeding, as well as workers who are likely to be in one of these situations as well as their representatives,[38] must be informed about the results of the employer's assessment and the health and safety measures which are to be taken, Article 4(2) MPD.

---

[36]   Commission, Communication of 5 October 2000 on the Guidelines on the assessment of the chemical, physical and biological agents and industrial processes considered hazardous for the safety or health of pregnant workers and workers who have recently given birth or are breastfeeding, COM(2000) 466 final.

[37]   This procedure has not yet been used.

[38]   R. Wank, in P. Hanau/H.-D. Steinmeyer/R. Wank (eds.), *Handbuch des Europäischen Arbeits- und Sozialrechts*, §18 para. 914.

3. Avoidance of Risks

18. Building on the assessment of Article 4 MPD, Article 5 imposes an incremental obligation upon the employer to take the required action where assessment reveals a risk to safety or health or an effect upon the pregnancy or breastfeeding of the protected group of workers. In order of intensity of interference for the employer and the worker, the employer

(1) must initially **adjust working conditions** and/or working time so as to avoid risks for the workers, Article 5(1);
(2) where that is not technically and/or objectively feasible or cannot reasonably be required on duly substantiated grounds: secondly **move** the worker concerned **to another job**, Article 5(2); and
(3) where that is not possible either, **grant** the worker **leave**.

The hierarchy of measures to be taken by the employer indicates that the worker's interest in pursuing her occupation is also protected. Therefore, a Danish regulation, pursuant to which the employer could grant a pregnant worker leave on a reduced wage independently of her ability to work when the employer considered that he cannot provide work for her, could not be based upon this provision.[39]

19. While these risk prevention measures serve to protect the health and safety of the worker (and her child), Article 11(1) MPD provides for a supplementary provision on the protection of **economic interests** in the cases of, *inter alia*, Article 5 MPD:[40] Employment rights arising from the employment contract, which also include the maintenance of a payment to, and/or entitlement to an adequate allowance for, the protected workers, must be ensured in accordance with national legislation and/or national practice. Consequently, e.g. for the calculation of service periods, annual leave or bonuses (which do not presuppose active performance at the time of their being granted)[41], the protected workers must be treated as if they had continued working on their original jobs.[42] This is of particular relevance with regard to **remuneration**, where the worker is moved to a lower paid job or is granted leave. As the Court emphasises, maintenance of pay plays a different role in the present context of a temporary adjustment of the working conditions (Article 5(1) and (2)) than in the context of maternity leave

---

[39] ECJ Case C-66/96 *Pedersen* [1998] ECR I-7327 paras. 57 sq.; the national provision also violated the prohibition of sex discrimination; see §9 para. 36 above.
[40] The provisions of Article 11(1)-(3) MPD are unconditional and sufficiently precise and may, consequently, be directly applied as against the Member States; ECJ Case C-194/08 *Gassmayr* [2010] ECR I-6281 paras. 43–53.
[41] On Article 11(2) MPD ECJ Case C-333/97 *Lewen* [1999] ECR I-7243 paras. 29, 31.
[42] S. Klein-Jahns, in *EAS,* B 5100 para. 40.

(Article 8 MPD).[43] Article 11(1) does not however provide for the full maintenance of remuneration ('a payment' not 'the pay'!). Instead, the provision leaves room for a reduction as well as for a replacement by adequate compensation through social benefits.[44] The determination of what is 'adequate' is left to national legislation and practice (*argumentum e* Article 11(3)). Implementation of the Directive may not, however, have the effect of lowering the level of protection afforded to workers, Article 1(3) MPD. Member States may make entitlement to pay or the allowance conditional upon the worker fulfilling eligibility criteria for such benefits under national law (Article 11(4)(1) MPD), in particular the requirement of a minimum period of previous employment of up to (a maximum of) twelve months (subparagraph 2). While the details of continued pay or adequate compensation are thus left for the Member States to determine, their discretion is limited by the objectives of Article 11(1) as well as the duties of implementation (principles of equivalence and effectiveness; §1 para. 66), which are subject to scrutiny by the Court of Justice.[45] In particular, the Member States may not render the economic protection of the relevant workers 'illusory'.

20. The Court has inferred quite detailed requirements from the objectives of the provision. Thus, where an employee is transferred to another position, her pay cannot be less than that paid to other employees in that position.[46] With regard to **allowances**, the Court draws a distinction between such allowances which relate to the employee's *professional status* such as her seniority, length of service and professional qualification on the one hand, and allowances which are dependent upon the employee's *performance*, on the other. While the employee, in principle, remains entitled to status-based allowances, Member States may come to a different conclusion in respect of performance-based allowances.[47]

4. Prohibitions of Work

21. The Directive further provides for certain prohibitions of exposure for pregnant workers and workers who are breastfeeding, which are differentiated with regard to specific risks, Article 6 with Annex II MPD. Cases falling within

---

[43] ECJ Case C-471/08 *Parviainen* [2010] ECR I-6533 paras. 38 sqq. Approving case note C. Höpfner, 'Zur Vergütung von Arbeitnehmerinnen während eines schwangerschaftsbedingten Arbeitsplatzwechsels', *EuZA* 2011, 223–232.

[44] ECJ Case C-471/08 *Parviainen* [2010] ECR I-6533 para. 49; Case C-194/08 *Gassmayr* [2010] ECR I-6281 paras. 60 sqq.-76; case notes F. Donath, *ZESAR* 2011, 134–138 (critically on policy considerations); K. Nebe, 'Arbeitsentgelt bei mutterschutzbedingter Umsetzung', *ZESAR* 2011, 10–17 (largely approvingly).

[45] ECJ Case C-471/08 *Parviainen* [2010] ECR I-6533 paras. 55 sq.

[46] ECJ Case C-471/08 *Parviainen* [2010] ECR I-6533 para. 58.

[47] ECJ Case C-471/08 *Parviainen* [2010] ECR I-6533 paras. 60 sq.; Case C-194/08 *Gassmayr* [2010] ECR I-6281 paras. 60 sqq.-76 (maintenance of average pay with the exception of on-call duty allowances is compatible with Article 11(1) MPD).

Annex II are comparatively narrowly defined. They had been controversial in the legislative proceedings, and this is probably one of the reasons why an adaptation of Annex II using the facilitated procedure contained in Article 13 MPD is not possible here.

22. Article 6 MPD refers to the 'assessment' and thus to Article 4 (though without expressly mentioning the norm). This implies that the rules on assessment and information contained in Article 4 also apply here. Only the provisions of Article 5 on the avoidance of risks are replaced by the prohibitions of work. Furthermore here, the Directive also requires that the workers' rights, including their right to pay, must be maintained Article 11(1) and (4) (see para. 19 above).

5.   Night Work

23. Pregnant women and women who have recently given birth or who are breastfeeding are not generally prohibited from working at night. For a period following childbirth, the protected workers are **not**, however, **obliged** to perform **night work** within the meaning of Article 2(3) WTD, if they submit a medical certificate stating that avoidance of night work is necessary for their safety and health.[48] There are no specific assessment and information duties, given that the facts of night work are sufficiently clearly defined and given that the concrete risks are individually assessed by a doctor.

24. In such a case, the employer is obliged to transfer the worker to daytime work or, where that is not technically or objectively feasible or cannot reasonably be required on duly substantiated grounds, to grant her leave from work or extension of maternity leave, Article 7(2) MPD. Once again, the Directive requires that the workers' rights, including their right to pay, must be maintained Article 11(1) and (4) (see para. 19 above).

IV.   MATERNITY LEAVE AND TIME OFF FOR ANTE-NATAL EXAMINATIONS

1.   Maternity Leave

a)   Leave

25. The protected workers (Article 2 MPD) have a right to maternity leave. The Court of Justice considers maternity leave to be '**a particularly important mechanism of protection under employment law**'. It takes account of

---

[48]   K. Lörcher, *AuR* 1993, 54.

fundamental changes in the living conditions of the women during this period, which constitute 'a legitimate ground on which they could suspend their employment, without the public authorities or employers being allowed in whatever way to call the legitimacy of that ground into question'.[49] Maternity leave pursues the dual objective of protecting the woman's physical health and protecting the special relationship between a mother and her child during the last weeks of pregnancy and the time immediately after birth. Time off work should prevent the relationship from being disturbed by the multiple burdens which result from employment.[50]

26. Maternity leave should be granted for a continuous **period of 14 weeks**, Article 8(1) MPD.[51] Member States may offer twelve of these weeks to protected workers as a *right* which they may or may not use, but two weeks must be made obligatory, Article 8(2) MPD.[52] The allocation of both periods before and after delivery is for the Member States to determine, Article 8(1) MPD.[53]

27. The purpose of a continuous period of 14 weeks' leave is not only to protect the health of the worker, but is also to give her an opportunity to take care of her child without also being burdened by employment. On the basis of these considerations, a clause in an employment contract, pursuant to which the worker must definitely terminate maternity leave if she wants to avail herself of **sick leave** in that period, is incompatible with Article 8 MPD.[54] On the other hand, as the purpose of protecting the worker against double burdens is an abstract underlying consideration, rather than a prerequisite for the right to maternity leave, this right is not excluded where, in a given case, the worker does not have to bear such double burden in the first place, e.g., where she is on **parental leave**.[55] In other words: The fact that the employee is on parental leave does not preclude her right to maternity leave. Finally, since **annual leave** (Article 7 WTD, §14 paras. 46–56) and maternity leave pursue different objectives, one may not be 'set off' against the other. Where maternity leave coincides with that of a company holiday, the worker's right to annual leave under Article 7(1) WTD does not cease to exist.[56] The worker must be granted an opportunity to take annual leave at another time.

---

[49]   ECJ Case C-116/06 *Kiiski* [2007] ECR I-7643 para. 49.
[50]   ECJ Case C-116/06 *Kiiski* [2007] ECR I-7643 paras. 46, 50.
[51]   The length of maternity leave had hitherto been left for the Member States to determine; the Equal Access Directive provided for a prohibition of discrimination, though; see ECJ Case C-179/88 *Handels- og Kontorfunktionaerernes Forbund* [1990] ECR I-3979 para. 15.
[52]   Maternity leave had previously often been only optional: D. Coester-Waltjen, *Mutterschutz in Europa*, 16–18.
[53]   ECJ Case C-66/96 *Pedersen* [1998] ECR I-7327 paras. 45–54.
[54]   ECJ Case C-411/96 *Boyle* [1998] ECR I-6401 paras. 55–66.
[55]   ECJ Case C-116/06 *Kiiski* [2007] ECR I-7643 paras. 30 sq.
[56]   ECJ Case C-342/01 *Merino Gómez* [2004] ECR I-2605 paras. 28–32.

b)   Protection of Economic Interests – particularly Continued Payment of
      Wages

28.   Article 11(2) and (3) MPD protect the economic interests of workers during
their maternity leave.[57,58] During maternity leave, Member States must
guarantee the protection of (other) rights arising from the employment contracts
of protected workers (No. 2(a)) and the maintenance of payment and/or
entitlement to an adequate allowance (No. 2(b)). **Protection of (other) rights**
connected with the employment contract requires that the period of maternity
leave be taken into account as normal working time e.g. for the purposes of
calculating length of service, rights to annual leave,[59] accrual of pension rights,[60]
or bonuses (which do not require the worker to be in active employment at the
time of award).[61]

29.   **Maintenance of payment** or entitlement to allowance does not require that
the worker receive her full remuneration.[62] Rather, it only ensures *'a'* payment
and/or an *'adequate'* allowance. The details (debtor, financing etc.) are for the
Member States to determine.[63] For the purposes of Article 11(2) MPD (but not
of No. 1), the **adequacy** of the allowance is defined in further detail in No. 3.
While the wording of provision No. 3 only applies to allowances, the Court has
also applied it to maintenance of payment. Such an interpretation is convincing,
since Article 11 MPD was designed to propose maintenance of pay and
entitlement to an allowance as equivalent options for implementation. Pursuant
to No. 3, pay or allowance must be at least equivalent to the amount of sick pay
under national legislation. The Directive only ensures this minimum and does
not, in other words, require that maternity pay/allowance be *higher* than sick
pay. Member States are free to determine a ceiling, provided, however, that such
ceiling does not have a discriminatory effect and put protected workers in a less
favourable position than a worker on sick leave.[64] Maternity pay or allowance

---

[57]   The provisions of Article 11(1)-(3) MPD are unconditional and sufficiently precise and may,
        consequently, be directly applied as against the Member States; ECJ Case C-194/08 *Gassmayr*
        [2010] ECR I-6281 paras. 43–53.
[58]   The Commission's proposal provided for substantially more far-reaching economic rights;
        COM(1990) 406 final, OJ 1990 C 281/3. See N. Burrows, YEL 11 (1991), 273, 290 sq.
[59]   ECJ Case C-411/96 *Boyle* [1998] ECR I-6401 paras. 68 sq. In the Case C-356/03 *Mayer* [2005]
        ECR I-295, the implementation period of the Maternity Protection Directive had not yet been
        expired (para. 33).
[60]   ECJ Case C-411/96 *Boyle* [1998] ECR I-6401 paras. 82 sq.
[61]   ECJ Case C-333/97 *Lewen* [1999] ECR I-7243 paras. 29, 31.
[62]   Cf. ECJ Case C-194/08 *Gassmayr* [2010] ECR I-6281 paras. 77–91 (maintenance of average pay
        with the exception of on-call duty allowances is compatible with Article 11(2), (3) MPD).
[63]   S. Klein-Jahns, in *EAS*, B 5100 para. 31. Further limitations may follow from ILO-
        Conventions No. 3 and 103 (requiring public funding).
[64]   To the same effect see also ECJ Case C-66/96 *Pedersen* [1998] ECR I-7327 paras. 38–41
        (without, however, objecting to Article 11(3) MPD; see para. 39).

may also be made dependent upon a preceding minimum period of service of up to twelve month, Article 11(4) MPD (see also para. 19 above). *Contractually agreed payments* which exceed the minimum required under Article 11(3) MPD may be made subject to additional prerequisites; that is unobjectionable under Article 11(3) MPD as well as under Article 157 TFEU.[65]

c)   Protection Against Less Favourable Treatment

30.   The provisions on maternity leave in the Maternity Protection Directive are supplemented by two provisions in the **Sex Discrimination Directive** (see §9 paras. 46, 62 sq. above). First, under Article 2(2)(c) SDD, any less favourable treatment in connection with pregnancy or maternity constitutes discrimination (see also para. 35 below).[66] Secondly, Article 15 SDD gives the worker a right to return to her job or an equivalent post on terms and conditions which are no less favourable to her.[67] Furthermore, she is entitled to benefit from all improvements in working conditions to which she would have been entitled but for her absence.

2.   *Time Off for Ante-natal Examinations*

31.   Pregnant workers must be granted time off work without loss of pay in order to attend ante-natal examinations, if such examinations *have to*[68] take place during working hours, Article 9 MPD. Given that the prerequisites are fairly narrow and that ante-natal examinations usually only take a limited amount of time, the right to continued pay seems justifiable.

V.   PROTECTION AGAINST LESS FAVOURABLE TREATMENT

1.   *Prohibition of Dismissal*

32.   The **dismissal** of protected workers (para. 11 above; requirement of information!) is, in principle, prohibited from the start of pregnancy[69] to the

---

[65]   ECJ Case C-66/96 *Pedersen* [1998] ECR I-7327 paras. 30–44; Case C-411/96 *Boyle* [1998] ECR I-6401 paras. 30–36 (clause in an employment contract which makes the payment, during the period of maternity leave of pay higher than the statutory payments in respect of maternity leave conditional on the worker's undertaking to return to work after the birth of the child for at least one month).

[66]   ECJ Case C-294/04 *Herrero* [2006] ECR I-1513 paras. 38 sq.; Case C-284/02 *Sass* [2004] ECR I-11143 paras. 32–36; Case C-136/95 *Thibault* [1998] ECR I-2011.

[67]   Cf. also ECJ Case C-320/01 *Wiebke Busch* [2003] ECR I-2041.

[68]   Employee bears the burden of proof; S. Klein-Jahns, in *EAS*, B 5100 para. 38.

[69]   On the 'beginning of pregnancy' in casea of in-vitro fertilisation see para. 33 above with further references.

end of maternity leave – the latter being determined by the national laws of the Member States implementing Article 8(1) MPD[70] (but not during any additional period of breastfeeding that may extend beyond the 14 weeks of maternity leave).[71] The legislator intended this prohibition to take account of 'the harmful effects which the risk of dismissal may have on the physical and mental state of women who are pregnant, have recently given birth or are breastfeeding, including the particularly serious risk that pregnant women may be prompted voluntarily to terminate their pregnancy'[72] (see also Recital 15 MPD). The provision prohibits dismissal but, on teleological considerations, also mere preparation for dismissal, such as the employer advertising a worker's job.[73] The prohibition of dismissal also applies to fixed-term employment relationships,[74] but it does not cover **non-renewal** after expiry of the fixed-term.[75] If, however, the employment relationship is not being renewed because of the worker's pregnancy, this constitutes direct discrimination on grounds of sex which is prohibited by Articles 2(1) and 14(1) SDD (§9 para. 46 above and para. 30 above).[76] Following Article 2 MPD, protection against dismissal presupposes that the worker has informed the employer of her situation. The protection is not compromised by the fact that the worker did not reveal her pregnancy or the fact that she would be unable to work during a substantial part of her fixed-term employment when she was hired (see also §9 para. 63).[77] Member States may provide for a period of time within which the worker must invoke the unlawfulness of her termination or bring an action in court. Under the implementation obligations (§1 paras. 65 sq.), however, such procedural requirements must be equivalent to those provided for similar prohibitions of dismissal in national law and must not render the prohibition illusory.[78]

---

[70] Where the national law of a Member State provides for a longer period of maternity leave, Article 10(1) MPD, which specifically refers to Article 8(1) MPD, *does not* require prohibition against dismissal; to this effect also ECJ Case C-66/96 *Pedersen* [1998] ECR I-7327 paras. 56, 62. Differently S. Klein-Jahns, in *EAS*, B 5100 para. 33.

[71] On the *ratio legis* ECJ Case C-460/06 *Paquay* [2007] ECR I-8511 para. 30; Case C-191/03 *McKenna* [2005] ECR I-7631 para. 48; Case C-394/95 *Mary Brown* [1998] ECR I-4185 para. 18; Case C-32/93 *Webb* [1993] ECR I-3567 paras. 21 sq.

[72] ECJ Case C-506/06 *Mayr* [2008] ECR I-1017 para. 34.

[73] ECJ Case C-460/06 *Paquay* [2007] ECR I-8511 paras. 33–35; approving note by M. Schmidt, 'Kündigungsschutz während Mutterschutz – Vorbereitungsmaßnahmen des Arbeitgebers', *ZESAR* 2008, 193 sq.; case note by M. Benecke, *EuZA* 2008, 385–394 (critical on the compatibility of this interpretation with the wording of the Directive and with references to the German provision of §9 MuSchG).

[74] ECJ Case C-438/99 *Jiménez Melgar* [2001] ECR I-6915 para. 43; Case C-109/00 *Tele Danmark* [2001] ECR I-6993 paras. 31–34.

[75] ECJ Case C-438/99 *Jiménez Melgar* [2001] ECR I-6915 paras. 43–45.

[76] ECJ Case C-438/99 *Jiménez Melgar* [2001] ECR I-6915 para. 46.

[77] ECJ Case C-109/00 *Tele Danmark* [2001] ECR I-6993 paras. 25–34. Critically E. Herrmann, *SAE* 2003, 125–134 (arguing for a bad faith objection of the employer).

[78] ECJ Case C-63/08 *Pontin* [2009] ECR I-10467 paras. 43–49 (as to the principles) and 50–69 (as to their application to the questions put before the Court).

33. The *'beginning of pregnancy'* was unclear in a case of **in vitro fertilisation** (i.e. the fertilisation of the ovum outside the woman's body). In *Mayr* the employer gave notice to the worker after the ova taken from her had already been fertilised with her partner's sperm, but before the fertilised ova had been transferred to her uterus. On the basis of the wording and the purpose of the provision, the Court considered that in a case of in vitro fertilisation pregnancy begins with the implantation of the ova into the woman's uterus.[79] This conforms both with the language which is used and with the worker's needs for protection.[80] The Court also took account of the interest of legal certainty (that argued in favour of the employer's position): As fertilised ova could be retained for up to ten years, a different interpretation would lead to unbearable legal uncertainty. The case at hand also illustrates the supplementary protection which is provided by the prohibition of sex discrimination (para. 30 above): If the employer had dismissed Ms Mayr because of the in-vitro fertilisation or the upcoming pregnancy, that would have constituted discrimination on grounds of sex as prohibited by Articles 14(1)(c) and 2 SDD.[81]

34. The protection against dismissal contained in Article 10 MPD is **not absolute**. Protected workers may be dismissed in exceptional cases, as permitted by national legislation, for reasons which are unconnected with their pregnancy, recent childbirth or breastfeeding.[82] With regard to the burden of proof, the workers may benefit from the reversal which is provided for by Article 19(4)(a) SDD.[83] The employer must cite duly substantiated grounds for the dismissal in writing, Article 10(2) MPD. Member States must protect the workers from the consequences of an unlawful dismissal under Article 10(1) MPD. Such protection may be afforded by requiring the prior consent of a supervisory authority (see also Article 10(1) MPD), but the Directive does not require Member States to introduce such administrative control.[84] The protection against discrimination on maternity-related grounds which the Court has established under the prohibition of discrimination,[85] (§9 paras. 46 sq. above) is no longer important within the scope of Article 10 MPD, but may afford supplementary protection in other cases, e.g. during a period of breastfeeding.[86]

---

[79] ECJ Case C-506/06 *Mayr* [2008] ECR I-1017 paras. 29–42.

[80] Critically M. Reiner, *EuZA* 2009, 79–87.

[81] ECJ Case C-506/06 *Mayr* [2008] ECR I-1017 paras. 45–52.

[82] Cf. ECJ Case C-460/06 *Paquay* [2007] ECR I-8511 paras. 31, 36. The Member States may afford employees more stringent protection (Article 1(3) MPD); they do not have to determine the acceptable grounds for termination by legislation; see Case C-438/99 *Jiménez Melgar* [2001] ECR I-6915 para. 37.

[83] ECJ Case C-460/06 *Paquay* [2007] ECR I-8511 para. 37.

[84] ECJ Case C-438/99 *Jiménez Melgar* [2001] ECR I-6915 para. 51.

[85] ECJ Case C-32/93 *Webb* [1994] ECR I-3567.

[86] Cf. ECJ Case C-66/96 *Pedersen* [1998] ECR I-7327 paras. 33–37 (concerning continued pay in case of pregnancy related illness).

2. A General Prohibition of Less Favourable Treatment or Victimisation

35. The Maternity Protection Directive affords (only) partial protection through its prohibition of dismissal. The Directive protects women only from the beginning of pregnancy until the end of maternity leave, and only protects against termination, but not, e.g., for breastfeeding women beyond their maternity leave and not against any other less favourable treatment outside dismissal.[87] As, however, any less favourable treatment on grounds of pregnancy, childbirth or breastfeeding, constitutes sex discrimination following the Court of Justice's case law, Articles 14, 2 and 15 Sex Discrimination Directive provide for comprehensive protection against less favourable treatment, even beyond the scope of the Maternity Protection Directive (see in more detail §9 para. 63 above and para. 2 above).[88]

VI. IMPLEMENTATION

36. In **Germany**,[89] the Directive was implemented – with delay – by the Act to Amend the Maternity Protection Law (*Gesetz zur Änderung des Mutterschutzrechts*) of 20 December 1996,[90] amending the Maternity Protection Act (*Mutterschutzgesetz,* MuSchG).[91] With regard to health and safety (Article 4–6 MPD), the Directive was implemented by the Regulation on Maternity Protection (*Verordnung zum Schutze der Mütter am Arbeitsplatz*) of 15 April 1997.[92,93] In substance, the Directive necessitated only minor changes to existing German law (14 weeks maternity leave in every case; restriction of exceptions to the prohibition of dismissal).[94] In the **United Kingdom**, the Maternity and Parental Leave etc. Regulations 1999[95] implement the Directive.[96]

---

[87] Article 11(1) MPD further provides for a – limited – guarantee of rights with regard to risk avoidance and prohibitions of work.

[88] ECJ Case C-232/09 *Danosa* 11 November 2010 paras. 59 sqq., 65 sqq.; Case C-294/04 *Herrero* [2006] ECR I-1513 paras. 38 sq., 41; Case C-284/02 *Sass* [2004] ECR I-11143 paras. 32–37; Case C-207/98 *Mahlburg* [2000] ECR I-549 para. 27; Case C-394/95 *Mary Brown* [1998] ECR I-4185 para. 27 (giving up the more restrictive decision in Case C-400/95 *Larsson* [1997] ECR I-2757 para. 23). For pension rights (Article 9(1)(g) GDRL) Case C-356/03 *Mayer* [2005] ECR I-295.

[89] See in more detail S. Klein-Jahns, in *EAS*, B 5100 paras. 58 sq.; R. Wank, in P. Hanau/H.-D. Steinmeyer/R. Wank (eds.), *Handbuch des Europäischen Arbeits- und Sozialrechts*, §18 paras. 368, 925.

[90] BGBl. 1996 I, 2110.

[91] BGBl. 2000 I, 2318; also available at www.gesetze-im-internet.de/muschg/index.html; bilingual German-English version in S. Lingemann/R. v. Steinau-Steinrück/A. Mengel (eds.), *Employment and Labour Law in Germany*, Part II, XV.

[92] BGBl. 1997 I 782.

[93] See e.g. H. Marburger, *BB* 1997, 521–524; H.-H. Sowka, *NZA* 1997, 296–298; id., *NZA* 1997, 927–928; J. T. Thau, *AuA* 1997, 213–215; J. Zmarzlik, *DB* 1994, 96–97. On the implementation in the UK, see V. Cromack, *J. Soc. Wel. & Fam. L.* 15 (1993), 261–272.

[94] M. Lenz, *NJW* 1997, 1491.

[95] Available at www.legislation.gov.uk/uksi/1999/3312/contents/made.

[96] For a discussion, see S. Deakin/G. Morris, *Labour Law*, paras. 6.105–6.111.

VII. THE EXAMPLE OF THE *LEWEN* CASE[97]

37. Suanne Lewen had been employed by Mr Denda in his firm, Denda Zahntechnik since 1 September 1990. Her monthly salary was DM 5 500 gross for a working week of 39.25 hours. Mrs Lewen, who became pregnant at the beginning of 1996, worked from 1 January to 8 April 1996 and 15 to 18 April 1996. She was on leave from 9 to 12 April 1996 and 19 April to 15 May 1996. *16 May* 1996 marked the start of the six-week period for the protection of mothers provided for by §3(2) Maternity Protection Act (*Mutterschutzgesetz*, MuSchG), the expected due date for delivery being 27 June 1996. Mrs Lewen's daughter was born on 12 July 1996. Under §6(1) MuSchG, Mrs Lewen's period of protection came to an end on 6 September 1996. From 7 September 1996 Mrs Lewen, at her own request, took parental leave, as provided for by §§15 sqq. Federal Parental Benefit and Parental Leave Act (*Bundeserziehungsgeldgesetz*, BErzGG)[98], for a period ending on 12 July 1999.

38. In her action, which she commenced against Mr Denda before the *Arbeitsgericht* (Labour Court, ArbG) Gelsenkirchen on 10 January 1997, Mrs Lewen sought an order requiring the defendant to pay her a 1996 Christmas bonus of DM 5 500. Mr Denda had previously paid her and other workers such bonuses.

39. The Labour Court referred various questions concerning the compatibility of Mrs Lewen's exclusion from the Christmas bonus with the Maternity Protection Directive to the Court of Justice. An initial question was whether the Christmas bonus, paid as an incentive for future services or loyalty to the undertaking, constituted 'payment' within the meaning of Article 11(2)(b) MPD and as such had to be maintained during maternity leave. The Court of Justice answered the question in the negative, considering that the bonus was not intended to grant the workers 'adequate' remuneration within the meaning of Article 11(3) MPD. The bonus also did not constitute a 'right connected with the employment contract' under Article 11(2)(a) MPD as, following the clear systematic order of the provisions, lit. b) exhaustively regulates issues of remuneration.

40. The Labour Court further asked whether it was compatible with Article 11(2) MPD to exclude workers *entirely* from the benefit of a bonus for the preceding year, without taking account of the work done during the year in which the bonus is paid or of the periods for the protection of mothers (in which

---

97 ECJ Case 333/97 *Lewen* [1999] ECR I-7243.
98 Bilingual German-English version in S. Lingemann/R. v. Steinau-Steinrück/A. Mengel (eds.), *Employment and Labour Law in Germany*, Part II, XVI.

they were prohibited from working). Again, the Court of Justice did not find an incompatibility with the Maternity Protection Directive, even irrespective of whether the bonus was paid as retroactive remuneration for preceding services or whether it was paid as an encouragement to those who are in 'active' employment when it was awarded. A bonus is neither a 'right' under Article 11(2)(a) MPD nor 'payment' under Article 11(2)(b) MPD (see para. 39). However, if under different circumstances, the bonus is awarded retroactively as pay for work performed in the course of that year, Article 157 TFEU precludes the employer from excluding female workers entirely from the benefit of a bonus paid voluntarily, without taking account of the work done in the year in which the bonus is paid or of the periods for the protection of mothers (in which they were prohibited from working) (differentiation on grounds of pregnancy constitutes direct sex discrimination, see §9 para. 45 above).

§21. THE PARENTAL LEAVE DIRECTIVE

CONTENT

Bibliography:

E. Caracciolo Di Torella, 'Childcare, Employment and Equality in the European Community: First (False) Steps of the Court', *E.L. Rev.* 25 (2000), 310–316; D. Coester-Waltjen, *Mutterschutz in Europa – Der Schutz der erwerbstätigen Frau während der Schwangerschaft und Mutterschaft in den Mitgliedstaaten der Europäischen Gemeinschaft* (Munich: Schweitzer, 1986) (also Euro.Dok. V/1829/84-EN, Brussels 1984/85); K. Dahm, Die neue Richtlinie zum Elternurlaub, EuZA 2011, 30–52; F. P. Davidson, 'Parental Leave – Time for Action?', *J. Soc. Wel. & Fam. L.* 8 (1986), 281–289; E. Ellis, 'Parents and Employment: An Opportunity for Progress', *ILJ* 15 (1986), 97–109; S. Hardy/N. Adnett, 'The Parental Leave Directive, Towards a 'Family Friendly' Social Europe?', *EJIR* 8 (2002), 157–170; K. Hiller, 'Fallstudie: Elternurlaubsrichtlinie', in G. Falkner/W. Müller (eds.), *Österreich im europäischen Mehrebenensystem, Schriftenreihe des Zentrums für angewandte Politikforschung* (Vienna: Signum-Verlag, 1998), 111–138; R. Hornung-Draus, 'Abkommen zum Elternurlaub verabschiedet', *Arbeitgeber* 1996, 62–63; J. P. Jacobsen, 'Accomodating Families', in: K. G. Dau-Schmidt/S. D. Harris/O. Lobel (eds.), Labor and Employment Law and Economics – Encyclopedia of Law and Economics (2nd edn. Cheltenham, UK/Northampton, MA, 2009), 320–341; J. Joussen, 'Die vorzeitige Beendigung des Elternurlaubs bei erneuter Schwangerschaft', *EuZA* 2008, 375–384; A. Junker, 'Arbeitsrecht zwischen Markt und gesellschaftspolitischen Herausforderungen –

Differenzierung nach Unternehmensgröße – Familiengerechte Strukturen – Gutachten B zum 65. Deutschen Juristentag', in Ständige Deputation des Deutschen Juristentages (ed.), *Verhandlungen des fünfundsechzigsten Deutschen Juristentages* (Munich: C.H. Beck, 2004); S. Klein-Jahns, 'Mutterschutz und Erziehungsurlaub', in H. Oetker/U. Preis (eds.), *Europäisches Arbeits- und Sozialrecht, EAS, part B – Systematische Darstellungen,* looseleaf (Heidelberg: Forkel, last update: January 1999), B 5100; G. Lester, 'A Defense of Paid Family Leave', *Harv. J. L. & Gender* 28 (2005), 1–83; C. A. McCaffrey/A. Graff, 'European Union Directive on Parental Leave: Will the European Union Face the same Problems as those Faced by the United States Under the 1993 Family and Medical Leave Act?', *Hofstra Lab. & Emp. J.* 17 (1999), 229–267; S. Peters-Lange/C. Rolfs, 'Reformbedarf und Reformgesetzgebung im Mutterschutz- und Erziehungsgeldrecht', *NZA* 2000, 682–687; S. Piffl-Pavelec, 'Richtlinie des Rates 96/34 v. 3.6.1996 zu der von UNICE, CEEP und EGB geschlossenen Rahmenvereinbarung über Elternurlaub', *DRdA* 1996, 531–534; Marlene Schmidt, 'Parental Leave: Contested Procedure, Creditable Results', *IJCLLIR* 13 (1997), 113–126, also published as: 'The EU Directive on Parental Leave', in R. Blanpain (ed.), *Labour Law and Industrial Relations in the European Union, Bulletin of Comparative Labour Relations* 32 (The Hague: Kluwer, 1998), 181–192; Marlene Schmidt, 'Family Friendly Policy and the Law', *Comp. Lab. L. & Pol'y J.* 27 (2006), 451–485.

Cases:

ECJ Case 184/83 *Hofmann* [1984] ECR 3047; ECJ Case C-333/97 *Lewen* [1999] ECR I-7243; ECJ Case C-519/03 *Commission* v. *Luxembourg* [2005] ECR I-3067; ECJ Case C-185/04 *Öberg* [2006] ECR I-1453 (on free movement of workers); ECJ Case C-116/06 *Kiiski* [2007] ECR I-7643; ECJ Case C-537/07 *Gómez-Limón* [2009] ECR I-6525; ECJ Case C-116/08 *Meerts* [2009] ECR I-10063; ECJ Case C-486/08 *Zentralbetriebsrat der Landeskrankenhäuser Tirols* [2010] ECR I-3527; ECJ Case C-149/10 *Chatzi* [2010] ECR I-8489; ECJ Case C-104/09 *Roca Álvarez* [2010] ECR I-8661; CFI Case T-135/96 *UEAPME* v. *Council* [1998] ECR II-2335.

I. ISSUES, OVERVIEW, COMPETENCES, REGULATORY CONTEXT

1. Professional and family life are often difficult to reconcile, especially where there are children.[1] Central issues are[2] care for the new-born child during its first years and care for older children in cases of sickness. Parents who have taken time off work in order to care for their children often face difficulties when trying to re-enter professional life. In practice, it is often women who feel confronted with the choice of either raising children or engaging in a professional career.

---

[1]   On the economic and social development, see e.g. S. Hardy/N. Adnett, *EJIR* 8 (2002), 157, 159–161 (with references to the economic evaluation pp. 163–165 and to comparative law pp. 169–169); C. A. McCaffrey/A. Graff, *Hofstra Lab. & Emp. J.* 17 (1999), 229–267 (comparative: USA); M. Schmidt, *Comp. Lab. L. & Pol'y J.* 27 (2006), 451–485; see also D. Coester-Waltjen, *Mutterschutz in Europa,* 32–35, 76–91, 95–100; H. Collins, *Employment Law,* 91 sqq.

[2]   For a comprehensive discussion, see G. Lester, *Harv. J. L. & Gender* 28 (2005), 1–83.

2. The Parental Leave Directive (PLD),[3] which implements the Parental Leave Framework Agreement (PLFA) of the social partners, is intended to contribute to the reconciliation of family and professional life.[4] It provides for a right for fathers and mothers to three months' parental leave on occasion of the birth or adoption of a child (Clauses 2–6 PLFA) as well as a right to time off from work in family emergencies (Clause 7 PLFA).

3. An initial proposal for a directive dating from 1983/84[5] failed due to opposition from the United Kingdom, whose government was concerned about the costs involved and the potentially negative impact upon the economy.[6] Subsequently, the 1989 Community Charter of Fundamental Social Rights (§2 paras. 65–77 above) renewed the demand to develop 'measures … enabling men and women to reconcile their occupational and family obligations' (No. 16(3) CFSR). The **original Parental Leave Framework Agreement** 1995 (PLFA 1995) was finally concluded on 14 December 1995 on the **basis** of the social dialogue procedure[7] under the Social Policy Protocol (§4 para. 4). It was implemented by the 1996 Parental Leave Directive (the Parental Leave Directive 1996, PLD 1996).[8] An action for annulment on the basis of alleged lack of Community competence, brought before the Court of First Instance by an association of small and medium-sized enterprises, was dismissed as inadmissible (see in more detail §4 para. 30 above).[9]

4. In September 2008, the European social partners began negotiating under Article 154 TFEU with the aim of concluding a new framework agreement on parental leave (on the procedural aspects, cf. §4 paras. 31–39). The Commission had already announced its intention to adopt a directive to implement the new framework agreement. The Commission had further announced that, if

---

3   Council Directive 2010/18/EU of 8 March 2010 implementing the revised Framework Agreement on parental leave concluded by BUSINESSEUROPE, UEAPME, CEEP and ETUC and repealing Directive 96/34/EC, OJ 2010 L 68/13.

4   S. Piffl-Pavelec, *DRdA* 1996, 531. On rationales and effects of family-accomodating policies (from a law and economics perspective) see J. P. Jacobsen, in: K. G. Dau-Schmidt/S. D. Harris/O. Lobel (eds.), *Labor and Employment Law and Economics*, 320–341.

5   Commission, Proposal for a Council Directive on parental leave and leave for family reasons of 24 November 1983, COM(83) 686 final, OJ 1983 C 333/6; Commission, Amended proposal for a Council Directive on parental leave and leave for family reasons of 15 November 1984, COM(84) 631 final, OJ 1984 C 316/7. Economic and Social Committee, Opinion on the proposal for a Council Directive on parental leave and leave for family reasons of 24 May 1984, OJ 1984 C 206/47. On the proposal see e.g. F. P. Davidson, *J. Soc. Wel. & Fam. L.* 8 (1986), 281–289; E. Ellis, *ILJ* 15 (1986), 97–109.

6   M. Schmidt, *IJCLLIR* 13 (1997), 113 sq.; see also F. P. Davidson, *J. Soc. Wel. & Fam. L.* 8 (1986), 281–289; S. Piffl-Pavelec, *DRdA* 1996, 531, 532.

7   On the negotiations, see M. Schmidt, *IJCLLIR* 13 (1997), 113, 114 sq.

8   Council Directive 96/34/EC of 3 June 1996 on the framework agreement on parental leave concluded by UNICE, CEEP and the ETUC, OJ 1996 L 145/4.

9   CFI Case T-135/96 *UEAPME* v. *Council* [1998] ECR II- 2335.

negotiations between the social partners should fail, it would make proposals to amend the existing provisions in order to further pursue its preliminary work to promote the balancing of professional and family life.[10] In its preliminary work, the Commission also considered new models of family-related leave: paternity leave (short period of leave for fathers at the time of birth or adoption of a child), adoption leave (leave at the time of adoption, comparable to maternity leave) and care leave (leave for purposes of caring for dependants who require care).[11]

5. The social partners concluded a **new Parental Leave Framework Agreement** (PLFA) on 18 June 2009 which was subsequently implemented by the 2010 Parental Leave Directive (PLD).[12] Apart from a number of editorial amendments, the new Framework Agreement also brought about some substantive changes. The minimum duration of parental leave increased from three to four months (Clause 2(2) sent. 1 PLFA); return to work is facilitated by additional (soft) mechanisms (Clause 6 PLFA); issues of pay are still not covered, but the social partners remind Member States to take the role of income into account in connection with parental leave (Clause 5(5)(2) PLFA).

6. The **regulatory context** of the Parental Leave Directive consists,[13] on the one hand, of the provisions on equal treatment of men and women (§9)[14] and, on the other, provisions of the Maternity Protection Directive (§20).[15] In practice, it is predominantly women who may be deterred from taking up (or further pursuing) work (or from having children) because of the task of child-rearing. From this perspective, the provisions of the Parental Leave Directive can be considered to promote equal treatment. As both men *and* women benefit from the rights under the Directive, it signals that professional activity and childcare are regarded as tasks for both the father and the mother, and thus workers of both gender may require assistance in balancing work and family commitments. The ensuing benefit for the children is a positive side-effect. The Parental Leave Directive supplements the Maternity Protection Directive.

---

[10]   Commission, Communication to the European Parliament, the Council, the European Economic and Social Committee and the Committee of the Regions of 3 October 2008 entitled 'A better work-life balance: stronger support for reconciling professional, private and family life', COM(2008) 635 final, 6–8.

[11]   Ibid. with further references.

[12]   See note 3 above.

[13]   Apart from the legal acts mentioned in the following, see also Council recommendation of 31 March 1992 on child care, OJ 1992 L 123/16.

[14]   ECJ Case 184/83 *Hofmann* [1984] ECR 3047 proved that the prohibitions of sex discrimination could only to a limited extent contribute the promoting compatibility of family and work life.

[15]   With regard to freedom of movement for workers, see also ECJ Case C-185/04 *Öberg* [2006] ECR I-1453.

II. SCOPE OF APPLICATION

7. The personal scope of application of the Framework Agreement is delineated by the parties to the employment contract, namely the worker (Clause 1(2) PLFA) and the employer. The term **'worker'** is **not determined autonomously**,[16] but rather with reference to the laws of the Member States.[17] The Framework Agreement also expressly applies to part-time workers, fixed-term workers and temporary agency workers (Clause 1(3) PLFA). As a rule, there is no minimum occupation requirement. However, Member States may make the right to parental leave (not that to time off from work on grounds of *force majeure*) subject to a minimum period of service of up to one year, Clause 3(1)(b) PLFA. The Framework Agreement applies to all **employers**, in the private and public sectors, irrespective of whether they are operating for profit or not. Member States may take the size of the undertaking into account (Clause 3(1)(d) PLFA), but only in respect of modifications, not for exceptions, from the Directive's scope of application.

III. RIGHT TO PARENTAL LEAVE

8. At the heart of the Framework Agreement is the individual right to four months' parental leave on grounds of birth or adoption.

1. Individual Right, Non-Transferability

9. Pursuant to Clause 2(1) PLFA, men and women have a right to parental leave.[18] The Framework Agreement refers to an *individual* right, i.e. a **claim** of the worker against the employer. For the express purpose of promoting equal opportunities and equal treatment of men and women, the right to parental leave should, in principle, be granted on a **non-transferable** basis. Its non-transferable nature should give an incentive for fathers to take parental leave as the right would otherwise be forfeited, cf. Clause 2(2) sent. 2 PLFA ('to encourage equal

---

[16] R. Wank, in P. Hanau/H.-D. Steinmeyer/R. Wank (eds.), *Handbuch des europäischen Arbeits- und Sozialrechts*, §18 para. 416; differently S. Klein-Jahns, in *EAS*, B 5100 para. 64.

[17] The Court's observations in Case C-149/10 *Chatzi* [2010] ECR I-8489 paras. 27 sqq. are imclear and ambiguous. At para. 27, the Court raises the question 'whether Directive 96/34 and the Framework Agreement which is annexed to it are intended to apply also to public officials', thus suggesting it intended to interpret the term 'worker' in the PLFA autonomously. At para. 28, though, the Court explains that the Directive does 'not contain anything permitting the inference that public officials are excluded from their scope'; this seems to suggest that it assumes that the term 'worker' refers to the national laws of the Member States but does not exclude the possibility that, still, public officials could be specifically excluded.

[18] ECJ Case C-149/10 *Chatzi* [2010] ECR I-8489 paras. 31 sqq. confirms that the right to parental leave is conferred on the parents but not on the child; this question was raised in the context of a birth of twins with the aim of arguing that the parents should have an individual right to parental leave for each child. What was in issue, in other words, was not the entitled person but the length of parental leave; see also para. 17.

take-up of leave by both parents'). However, this restriction only applies 'in principle' and only one month is strictly non-transferable. This leaves room for the Member States to take account of special circumstances, such as where one partner is prevented from availing himself of parental leave due to sickness. It also follows from this conception that the right to parental leave may not be made subject to proof of need of care,[19] and that both parents may claim their right to parental leave for the same period of time.[20]

10. The Framework Agreement only partially determines the prerequisites and legal consequences of the right to parental leave, Clause 2(1) PLFA. The details must be determined by Member States, to the extent necessary to implement the right. Other conditions and modalities are left to their discretion. Clause 3 PLFA enumerates a number of issues that the Member States may address.

2. Prerequisites for the Right to Parental Leave

a) General Prerequisites in Union Law

11. The Framework Agreement provides for two prerequisites: First – positively – the reason for parental leave: **birth or adoption** of a child; second – negatively – the temporal limitation: until a given age of up to **eight years**.[21] This upper age limit accommodates the countervailing interests of the parties to the employment contract and is thus well founded on the basis of teleological reasons. It may not be exceeded even under the minimum standard clause contained in Clause 8(1) PLFA.

b) Additional Requirements and Modalities

12. There are a number of additional requirements and modalities, some of which are optional for the Member States or the national social partners. Clause 3(1)(a)-(d) PLFA provides for a non-exhaustive ('in particular') list of potential subjects for national regulation. However, the supplementary prerequisites (and modalities), must satisfy the minimum standards of the Directive (Framework Agreement) and may not (while respecting the Directive's requirements) render parental leave so unattractive as to thwart it in practice.[22] Of the potential subjects of national regulation in lit. (a)-(d), lit. (a) concerns aspects of the legal

---

[19]   S. Klein-Jahns, in *EAS,* B 5100 para. 66.

[20]   S. Klein-Jahns, in *EAS,* B 5100 para. 66; S. Peters-Lange/C. Rolfs, *NZA* 2000, 682, 685; S. Piffl-Pavelec, *DRdA* 1996, 531; M. Schmidt, *IJCLLIR* 13 (1997), 113, 120.

[21]   The restriction in the Luxembourg implementation laws, restricting the right to parental leave to parents of children born after the end of the implementation period was considered incompatible with the PLFA; ECJ Case C-519/03 *Commission* v. *Luxembourg* [2005] ECR I-3067 paras. 40–45.

[22]   C. A. McCaffrey/A. Graff, *Hofstra Lab. & Emp. J.* 17 (1999), 229–267 (emphasising the great practical importance of formal requirements which are easily administered).

consequences, lit. (b) the option to use a period of work qualification and/or a length of service qualification and lit. c) and d) leave room to accommodate specific interests of the undertakings. Clause 3(2) concerns notice periods, Clause 4 specific aspects of adoption.

13. There are two **formal requirements**.

– The first is optional. The Member States or national social partners may make the entitlement to parental leave subject to a **period of work qualification** and/or a minimum length of service qualification of up to one year, Clause 3(1)(b). The terms 'period of work' and 'length of service' appear to refer to the national laws (collective agreements, practices)[23] as the Framework Agreement does not give any guiding principles for an autonomous definition.
– While the original 1995 Framework Agreement left it to the discretion of the Member States or national social partners to provide for **notice periods**, Clause 3(2) PFLA now requires them to provide for notice periods specifying the beginning and end of the period of leave. This takes account of the important employer interest in planning security. In determining the length of such notice periods, the interests of both workers and employers must be taken into account.

14. National laws or collective agreements may accommodate **entrepreneurial interests** in two respects.

– First, they may allow the employer to **postpone** granting parental leave for justifiable reasons relating to the operation of the undertaking, Clause 3(1)(c) PLFA. The original provision of Clause 2(3)(e) PLFA 1995 provided examples of potentially justifiable reasons: 'where work is of a seasonal nature, where a replacement cannot be found within the notice period, where a significant proportion of the workforce applies for parental leave at the same time, where a specific function is of strategic importance'. (All but the last of the examples are convincing on the basis of teleological considerations; with regard to a 'specific function of strategic importance', it is difficult to see how that could justify *temporarily* postponing parental leave.)
– Second, they may authorise 'special arrangements' to meet the operational and organisational **requirements of small** (not medium-sized)[24] **undertakings** (not establishments), Clause 3(1)(d) PLFA. This does not justify excluding parental leave for small undertakings altogether, especially since

---

[23] S. Klein-Jahns, in *EAS*, B 5100 para. 81.
[24] Clause 3(1)(c) PLFA takes the interests of medium-sized undertakings into account (see the text of the preceding indent); S. Klein-Jahns, in *EAS*, B 5100 paras. 84–86.

Clause 3(1)(c) already takes operational interests into account. One may think of procedural alleviations such as longer notice periods.

15. Clause 4 PLFA requires the Member States and/or social partners to assess the need for additional measures to address the **specific needs of adoptive parents**.[25]

16. The Directive does not expressly regulate whether and under which conditions parental leave, once granted, may **subsequently be changed**. The issue is thus left to the discretion of the Member States, subject to the limits that follow from the implementation duties (§1 paras. 65 sq.) and the prohibition of sex discrimination (§9).[26] The Court of Justice has emphasised two guidelines for legitimate considerations: On the one hand, the employer's organisational interest is an argument in favour of making any change subject to strict prerequisites. On the other hand, the purpose of parental leave as such may be an argument in favour of allowing changes if the objective of providing care for the child concerned would otherwise be spoiled.[27] In light of the specific purposes of *maternity leave* (Article 8 MPD, see §20 para. 4 above) of protecting the special relationship between a mother and her (unborn or newly born) child and avoiding double burdens for the mother for a period of 14 weeks around the date of birth, the Court considered that the purposes of parental leave could not be achieved effectively during the period of maternity leave.[28] The Court did not conclude, though, that parental leave had to necessarily be suspended during the time of maternity leave.[29] If, however, the national law of a Member State authorised changing the period of parental leave on grounds of similar weight such as divorce, serious sickness or death of the other parent or of the child, then it would constitute unlawful sex discrimination not to recognise pregnancy as a legitimate ground to allow a change to the period of parental leave (see §9 para. 46).[30]

---

[25] S. Klein-Jahns, in *EAS*, B 5100 para. 82 (considering, e.g., shorter notice periods pursuant to Clause 2(3)(3) PLFA 1995).

[26] Cf. ECJ Case C-104/09 *Roca Álvarez* [2010] ECR I-8661 (access of fathers to a so-called 'breastfeeding leave' – which did not, in fact, serve the purpose of allowing the mother to breastfeed the child but was granted also to mothers who were bottle-feeding – considered discrimination contrary to SDD).

[27] ECJ Case C-116/06 *Kiiski* [2007] ECR I-7643 paras. 37 sq.

[28] ECJ Case C-116/06 *Kiiski* [2007] ECR I-7643 para. 51.

[29] In ECJ Case C-116/06 *Kiiski* [2007] ECR I-7643 para. 56, the Court considers only 'moreover' that it had previously held that a period of parental leave guaranteed by EU law could not affect to take another period of leave guaranteed by EU law.

[30] ECJ Case C-116/06 *Kiiski* [2007] ECR I-7643 paras. 52–55; differently AG Kokott, Opinion in Case C-116/06 *Kiiski* [2007] ECR I-7643 pts. 29–48. See also J. Joussen, *EuZA* 2008, 375–384 (agreeing with the Court; with references on the conformity of the provision of the §16(3) of the German Parental Leave Act with the Directive at pp. 382–384).

3. Legal Consequences

a) Leave from Work

17. The central legal consequence is that the worker is to be granted **leave from work** for (at least) a period of **four months**.[31] The period of leave must actually be granted for the purpose of parental leave.[32] The Framework Agreement does not provide for any other obligations, in particular, it does not provide for a right to continued pay. It is for the Member States or national social partners to determine the details ('**modalities**', Clause 3 PLFA) such as the status of the employment contract or relationship (Clause 5(3) PLFA). However, with regard to the status of the employment contract, the Court has interpreted the scope for national regulation narrowly. The provision presupposes that the employment relationship is maintained during the period of parental leave, and consequently, national provisions may merely regulate the formal qualification.[33] They may determine, though, whether the worker acquires rights vis-à-vis the employer during the period of parental leave.[34] National law or collective agreements may also decide whether parental leave is granted on a full-time or part-time basis, in a piecemeal way or in the form of a time-credit system, Clause 3(1)(a) PLFA.

18. Taking care of children with special needs raises specific problems. The social partners left it for Member States and/or (national) social partners to 'assess the need to adjust the conditions for access and modalities of application of parental leave to the needs of parents of children with a disability or a long-term illness', Clause 3(3) PLFA.

---

[31] Where twins or multiples are born, Article 2(1) and (2) PLFA does not mean that the entitlement to four months parental leave is to be multiplied by the number of children born. In the light of the principle of equal treatment (as a general principle of EU primary law), the Court has interpreted the provision as requiring, that the Member States ensure 'that the parents of twins receive treatment that takes due account of their particular needs'. The Member States enjoy 'wide freedom of action when establishing the parental leave regime that is applicable to parents of twins and enables them to receive treatment that takes due account of their particular needs'. ECJ Case C-149/10 *Chatzi* [2010] ECR I-8489 paras. 41 sqq.

[32] The Court considered incompatible with the requirements of the PLFA a provision of Luxembourg law pursuant to which parental leave was terminated automatically without – a possibility of taking the remaining parental leave at a later date – if the worker took maternity leave. ECJ Case C-519/03 *Commission v. Luxembourg* [2005] ECR I-3067 paras. 31–39; see also Case C-124/05 *Federatie Nederlandse Vakbeweging* [2006] ECR I-3423 para. 24; Case C-116/06 *Kiiski* [2007] ECR I-7643 para. 56.

[33] ECJ Case C-116/06 *Kiiski* [2007] ECR I-7643 para. 32.

[34] ECJ Case C-116/08 *Meerts* [2009] ECR I-10063 para. 45.

b) Job Protection: The Right to Return to the Same Job

19. At the end of parental leave, the worker has a right to return to his or her job, i.e. the previous workplace and occupation, Clause 5(1) PLFA. If that is not possible, he or she has a right to be assigned to an equivalent or similar job consistent with the employment contract. It is **not possible** to return to the same job where it is not available (e.g. outsourced) or no longer vacant (permanent replacement has been found). Inquiry in this regard must start from the premise that the employer retains entrepreneurial freedom to eliminate jobs, and this decision may be based upon the employer's experience during a worker's parental leave which mean that the employer concludes that a particular worker's job can now be dispensed with. In light of the obligations of effective implementation of Union law (§1 paras. 65 sq. above), the employer may not, however, purposefully spoil the worker's right to return. That is, however, not the case where the employer can only fill the vacancy with a fixed-term replacement due to the current labour market. The Framework Agreement does not explicitly provide that the employer must bear the **burden of proof** with regard to the impossibility of return,[35] but that follows from the principles of effective implementation.

c) Acquired Rights

20. Rights acquired or in the process of being acquired by the worker on the date on which parental leave starts, are maintained as they stand until the end of parental leave, Clause 5(2) PLFA.[36] The concept of 'rights acquired or in the process of being acquired' should be interpreted **autonomously**; in light of the Framework Agreement's objective of the equal treatment of men and women, the Court held that the concept 'cannot be interpreted restrictively'.[37] It 'covers all the rights and benefits, whether in cash or in kind, derived directly or indirectly from the employment relationship, which the worker is entitled to claim from the employer at the date on which parental leave starts'.[38] However, the scope of protection offered by this provision is restricted in a number of respects. First, it only applies to **rights**, and the Court of Justice did not consider voluntary bonuses such as a Christmas bonus to constitute rights.[39] Furthermore, Clause 5(2) PLFA merely guarantees the **maintenance** of rights as they stand but **not**

---

[35]   Thus, however, S. Klein-Jahns, in *EAS*, B 5100 para. 72.

[36]   The provision can be relied on by individuals before a national court in proceedings against the Member State; ECJ Case C-537/07 *Gómez-Limón* [2009] ECR I-6525 paras. 32–37.

[37]   ECJ Case C-116/08 *Meerts* [2009] ECR I-10063 paras. 39–42.

[38]   ECJ Case C-116/08 *Meerts* [2009] ECR I-10063 para. 43; Case C-486/08 *Zentralbetriebsrat der Landeskrankenhäuser Tirols* [2010] ECR I-3527 paras. 53 sqq. (paid annual leave).

[39]   ECJ Case C-333/97 *Lewen* [1999] ECR I-7243 para. 31; consequently, also a prorated cutback of such benefits for the time of parental leave is compatible with Clause 5(2) PLFA; Case C-333/97 *Lewen* [1999] ECR I-7243 para. 46. Critically E. Caracciolo Di Torella, *E.L. Rev.* 25 (2000), 310–316 (but rather on policy considerations [*de lege ferenda*] than *de lege lata*).

their **continuation**. Thus, for example, the time of parental leave does not have to be taken into consideration for the calculation of length of service (although, of course, national provisions may provide so).[40] It 'does not ... govern the entitlements and obligations derived from an employment relationship during parental leave, which are defined, pursuant to [Clause 5(3)], by the Member States and/or by management and labour'.[41] Finally, rights acquired or in the process of being acquired are only maintained **until the end** of parental leave. At the end of the period of parental leave, these rights apply with any changes arising from national law, collective agreement or practice, Clause 5(2) sent. 2 PLFA.

21.   In *Meerts,* a full-time worker with an employment contract for an indefinite period was dismissed while she was on part-time parental leave. The termination was without urgent cause and without observing the statutory notice period. It had immediate effect subject to payment of compensation for dismissal equal to ten months' salary calculated on the part-time work salary. The Court considered this calculation to be incompatible with the acquired rights provision of Clause 5(2) PLFA and the status of employment provision of Clause 5(3) PLFA. While the Court does not say so explicitly, it appears from the facts of the case that the employer chose to terminate her contract of employment at that time so as to reduce the amount of compensation which would be payable. In light of this consideration, the case would fall under the prohibition of less favourable treatment contained in Clause 5(4) PLFA. The Court had to decide the case under the original 1995 Framework Agreement which contained a more narrowly defined prohibition of dismissal (see para. 22 below). Yet, a general prohibition of less favourable treatment could also have been inferred from the 1995 Framework Agreement, and the case could have been considered to be a 'dismissal on the grounds of ... the taking of parental leave'. Under yet another analysis, where national law places the worker on parental leave in a more vulnerable position, the Member States' duties of implementation, particularly the principle of effectiveness, could be considered to be violated. The Court's analysis may be based on considerations of burden of proof; it does not require the proof of causation necessary under Article 5(4) PLFA.

d)   Protection Against Less Favourable Treatment

22.   In order to ensure that workers may effectively avail themselves of the right to parental leave, the Member States or social partners must protect

---

[40]   Cf. ECJ Case C-116/08 *Meerts* [2009] ECR I-10063 para. 45. S. Klein-Jahns, in *EAS*, B 5100 para. 73.
[41]   ECJ Case C-537/07 *Gómez-Limón* [2009] ECR I-6525 paras. 38–40 (concerning continued acquisition of future entitlements under the statutory social security schemes during periods of parental leave).

workers against **less favourable treatment or dismissal** *on grounds of* an application for, or the taking of, parental leave, Clause 5(4) PLFA. The unusual wording, specifically highlighting dismissal, despite it certainly constituting a form of 'less favourable treatment', is due to the fact that Clause 2(4) PLFA 1995 had only provided for protection against dismissal. Yet, even then, without specific provisions, the general prohibition of victimisation could already be construed on teleological considerations even without specific provision in the Directive.[42] The general prohibition of less favourable treatment does not play an important role, though, as the most important aspects are already covered by the specific provisions on the right to return to the same job in Clause 5(1) PLFA (para. 19 above) and maintenance of rights in Clause 5(2) PLFA (para. 20 above). In light of its purpose, the provision merely prohibits less favourable treatment or dismissal *on grounds of* parental leave, not any dismissal on other grounds.

e)   Issues of Social Security

23.   Clause 5(5) PLFA leaves all matters of **social security** to the Member States. It is doubtful whether the social partners have competence in this area. The provision does, however, provide first, that Member States must deal with the issues involved and second, that they must take 'into account the importance of the continuity of the entitlements to social security cover under the different schemes'. The Court has rightly construed the provision to be a mere recommendation. Since the Framework Agreement was concluded by the social partners, it 'could not impose obligations on the national social security organisations, which were not party to that agreement' or establish entitlements for employees.[43]

24.   Continuity of entitlements is particularly relevant with regard to health insurance which should be continued during the time of parental leave even if the worker does not pay any contributions (Recital 18 PLFA). However, the Framework Agreement does not provide that times of parental leave must be treated as times of employment, e.g. with regard to pension schemes. It 'does not require the Member States to give workers a guarantee that, during the period of their part-time parental leave, they will continue to acquire entitlements to future social security benefits to the same extent as if they had continued to work on a full-time basis'.[44]

---

[42]   Cf. R. Wank, in P. Hanau/H.-D. Steinmeyer/R. Wank (eds.), *Handbuch des europäischen Arbeits- und Sozialrechts*, §18 para. 419.

[43]   ECJ Case C-537/07 *Gómez-Limón* [2009] ECR I-6525 paras. 47 sq., 50.

[44]   ECJ Case C-537/07 *Gómez-Limón* [2009] ECR I-6525 paras. 41–43. S. Klein-Jahns, in *EAS*, B 5100 para. 75.

IV. TIME OFF FROM WORK ON GROUNDS OF *FORCE MAJEURE*

25. The second main area where family and occupation conflict, is family-related emergencies which often occur due to sickness and accidents (primarily) of the children. If a worker's child is sick and cannot therefore go to school or childcare, one parent has to stay at home and yet cannot take sick leave of his or her own right. Worry about these sorts of conflict, between parental and occupational obligations, tend to particularly deter women from returning to work. In order to mitigate this concern, Clause 7 PLFA provides for a right to time off from work.

26. In line with the purpose of the Directive, Clause 7 provides for a right to time off from work only 'on grounds of **force majeure** for urgent family reasons', in other words not on grounds of force majeure in general.[45] The definition of **'family reasons'** is controversial: Does the term merely cover the sickness of children or also of parents? Certainly, the provision was not intended to provide for time off work on account of sickness of a partner of a childless couple. But even sickness of one *parent* can only justify time off under the provision where this is necessary to take care of the children. Again, in accordance with the purpose of the Framework Agreement, the provision does not cover emergencies of other close relatives (such as the worker's parents or siblings).[46] Furthermore, **'family reasons'** are specified so as to cover only 'sickness or accident',[47] in other words not family celebrations or deaths. This is convincing given that the purpose of the provision only relates to care for the (close) family.[48] Finally, the term **'force majeure'** is further limited by the requirement that **immediate presence of the worker** is indispensable.

27. The right to time off work is not made conditional upon a minimum period of service or the size of the undertaking, and the Framework Agreement does not leave any discretion to the Member States in this respect. National law or collective agreements may only specify the conditions of access and detailed rules of application and may limit entitlement to time off from work to a certain amount of time per year and/or per case.

---

[45] Thus, however, R. Wank, in P. Hanau/H.-D. Steinmeyer/R. Wank (eds.), *Handbuch des europäischen Arbeits- und Sozialrechts,* §18 para. 422.

[46] For a different perspective see S. Klein-Jahns, in *EAS,* B 5100 para. 90 (no restriction to children); with approval see M. Schmidt, *IJCLLIR* 13 (1997), 113, 122.

[47] The examples illustrate that the provision is not concerned with *force majeure* in the sense of an exogenous incident (illness!). Also a recklessly caused accident (hang-gliding, drug consumption) may constitute *force majeure* within the meaning of this provision.

[48] S. Klein-Jahns, in *EAS,* B 5100 para. 88.

28. The Framework Agreement thus gives rise to a right to time off from work, but leaves it for the worker to decide whether or not he or she avails him or herself of that right. The Framework Agreement does not require **continued pay** but national law or collective agreements may do so by way of providing more stringent protection (Clause 8(1) PLFA). With regard to the right to time off from work, the Framework Agreement does not expressly prohibit less favourable treatment; however, such a prohibition is required on teleological grounds and should be provided for in the course of implementation.

V.   IMPLEMENTATION

29. Implementation of the original Directive[49] into **German** law merely required selective amendments to pre-existing legislation, the Federal Parental Benefit and Parental Leave Act (*Bundeserziehungsgeldgesetz*, BErzGG),[50] which largely already conformed to the requirements of the Framework Agreement. Maintenance of rights follows from the concept of 'dormant employment' pursuant to which only the main obligations of the parties are suspended while the employment relationship as such continues to exist. Implementation is defective in that it does not (expressly) provide for a right to return to the same job as required by Clause 5(1) PLFA (para. 19 above). The right to time off from work is guaranteed by §616 Civil Code (*Bürgerliches Gesetzbuch*, BGB) and §45 Social Security Code V (*Sozialgesetzbuch V*, SGB V). The amended 2010 Directive does not require major changes to German law.[51] In the **United Kingdom**, the Parental Leave Directive is implemented by the Employment Relations Act 1999[52] in connection with the Employment Rights Act 1996[53] and the Maternity and Parental Leave etc. Regulations 1999.[54,55]

---

[49]   For an overview, see R. Wank, in P. Hanau/H.-D. Steinmeyer/R. Wank (eds.), *Handbuch des europäischen Arbeits- und Sozialrechts*, §18 paras. 423–429; S. Klein-Jahns, in *EAS*, B 5100 paras. 105 sq.

[50]   Bilingual German-English version in S. Lingemann/R. v. Steinau-Steinrück/A. Mengel (eds.), Employment and Labor Law in Germany, Part II, XVI.

[51]   K. Dahm, EuZA 2011, 30–52 (with comparative references).

[52]   Available at www.legislation.gov.uk/ukpga/1999/26/enacted.

[53]   Available at www.legislation.gov.uk/ukpga/1996/18.

[54]   Available at www.legislation.gov.uk/uksi/1999/3312/contents/made.

[55]   For an overview, see S. Deakin/G. Morris, *Labour Law*, para. 6.112.

§22. THE YOUNG PEOPLE AT WORK DIRECTIVE

CONTENT

Sources:

W. Balze, 'Jugendarbeitsschutz', in H. Oetker/U. Preis (eds.), *Europäisches Arbeits- und Sozialrecht, EAS, part B – Systematische Darstellungen,* loose-leaf (Heidelberg: Forkel, last update: August 1998), B 5200; A. Bond, 'The Young Persons Directive – Council Directive 94/33/EC on the Protection of Young People at Work', *ILJ* 24 (1995), 377–382; M. Grisenthwaite, 'Protecting the Young: Legislation to Prevent Exploitation', *I.C.C.L.R.* 8 (1997), 256–258; C. Hamilton/B. Watt, 'The Employment of Children', *C.F.L.Q* 16

(2004), 135–149; N. Kollmer, 'Grundzüge der neuen Kinderarbeitsschutz-Verordnung', *NZA* 1998, 1268–1272; K. Lörcher, 'Die Jugendarbeitsschutzrichtlinie der EU', *AuR* 1994, 360–364; S. Piffl-Pavelec/K. Peherstorfer, 'Jugendarbeitsschutzrichtlinie', *DRdA* 1994, 441–444; Marlene Schmidt, 'Defizite im Jugendarbeitsschutz – Erneut: Mangelhafte Umsetzung einer EG-Richtlinie durch den deutschen Gesetzgeber', *BB* 1998, 1362–1366; H.-H. Sowka, 'Änderungen im Mutterschutzrecht und im Jugendarbeitsschutzrecht', *NZA* 1997, 296–298; J. Zmarzlik, 'Änderung des Jugendarbeitsschutzgesetzes', *DB* 1997, 674–677.

Cases:

ECJ Case C-47/99 *Commission* v. *Luxembourg* [1999] ECR I-8999; ECJ Case C-45/99 *Commission* v. *France* [2000] ECR I-3615.

I.   ISSUES, OVERVIEW, COMPETENCES, REGULATORY CONTEXT

1.   Young people under the age of 18 are particularly exposed to risks when they pursue occupational activities. Lack of experience, insufficient awareness of risks and their incomplete physical and mental development may lead to a higher level of risk exposure in an environment that is adapted to the experience and needs of adults.[1] Furthermore, the requirements of professional life are in many respects not well adapted to the physical and psychological needs of young people who are growing up. Young people also lack business experience and are thus exposed to a higher risk of economic exploitation. The Young People at Work Directive[2] (YPWD) seeks to address these dangers.

2.   The Directive was preceded by a 1967 recommendation on the protection of young workers[3] and a 1987 resolution of the European Parliament on child labour[4] (see Recital 5 YPWD). Central aspects of the protection of young people at work have been further addressed by Nos. 20–23 of the 1989 Community Charter of Fundamental Social Rights (see §2 paras. 65–77 above) (cf. Recital 3 YPWD). The Commission announced its proposal for a directive in its action programme to implement the Community Charter. This directive was

---

[1]   Young people sustain twice as many work accidents as adults during their first year of employment; cf. Opinion of the Economic and Social Committee of 1 April 1992 on the proposal for a Council Decision on the Protection of Young People at Work, OJ 1992 C 313/70.

[2]   Council Directive 94/33/EC of 22 June 1994 on the protection of young people at work, OJ 1994 L 216/12.

[3]   Commission, Recommendation 67/125/EEC of 31 January 1967 to the Member States on the protection of young workers, OJ 1967 L 25/405.

[4]   European Parliament, Resolution of 16 June 1987 on Child Labour, OJ 1987 C 190/44. See W. Balze, in *EAS*, B 5200 para. 7.

adopted in 1992.[5] The United Kingdom's opposition to the Directive – which was based upon the view that its subject-matter was irrelevant for the proper functioning of the Internal Market and had no connection with the safety and health of workers – led to the Directive affording a lower standard of protection for young workers. The United Kingdom was also granted longer implementation periods (Article 17 YPWD). However, Article 32 of the 2000 Charter of Fundamental Rights now also provides for a prohibition of child labour (§2 paras. 58 sq. above).

3. Based upon Article 118a EEC (merged in Article 153 TFEU), the Young People at Work Directive, pursuant to Article 1(1)-(3) sent. 1, has three central provisions: *First,* it prohibits child labour, subject to narrowly restricted exceptions; 'child' is defined here as a young person who is less than 15 years old or subject to full-time compulsory school attendance. *Secondly,* the Directive requires that work by adolescents, i.e. persons less than 18 years old who are not children, be strictly regulated. The Directive concretises this general requirement by prohibiting occupation in a number of specifically dangerous activities, by requiring the employer to assess dangers for adolescent workers and adopt the necessary protective measures and through special provisions on working time (including a prohibition of night work), rest periods (including annual leave) and breaks. *Thirdly,* Article 1(3) sent. 1 YPWD imposes a general requirement that the working conditions of young people be adapted to their age. This general requirement overlaps with some of the individual protective rules of the Directive.

4. The Directive is closely related to the general provisions on industrial safety of EU employment law, particularly those found in the Safety and Health Framework Directive (§13) and the Working Time Directive (§14).

II. SCOPE OF APPLICATION

5. The Young People at Work Directive applies to people under 18 years of age (which Article 3(a) defines as '**young persons**') who have an employment contract or are in an employment relationship, Article 2(1) YPWD. The employment relationship must be defined and/or governed by the law in force in a Member State. The definition of worker and employment contract or relationship is thus determined by reference to the national laws of the Member States, subject to the qualification that the validity of the employment *contract*

---

[5]   Commission, Proposal for a Council Directive on the protection of young people at work, COM(91) 543 final, OJ 1992 C 84/7; Amended Proposal for a Council Directive on the protection of young people at work, COM(93) 35 final, OJ 1993 C 77/1.

under national law is not decisive. As the Directive does not contain any restrictions, it applies without distinction to all employment relationships and activities. In particular, there are no exceptions for small and medium-sized undertakings; the size of the undertaking is irrelevant. There is some uncertainty whether the Directive also applies to undertakings in the public sector[6] or non-profit sector.[7] While the purpose of the Directive argues in favour of their inclusion, it is in these areas in particular that the national definitions of worker differ. If the reference to the laws of the Member States in the Directive is not to be rendered meaningless, these questions must be left to national law.

6. There is only narrow scope for Member States to provide for **exceptions** with regard to the areas of home and family: (a) domestic service in a private household or (b) work (of a family-related young person)[8] in a family undertaking[9] which is regarded as not being harmful, damaging or dangerous to young people, Article 2(2) YPWD.

III. PROHIBITION OF CHILD LABOUR

7. The first and fundamental regulatory objective of the Directive is the prohibition of child labour. The general prohibition is followed by a differentiated catalogue of optional exceptions.

1. The General Prohibition

8. Child labour is prohibited, Article 4(1) YPWD. 'Child' means any young person (meaning under 18 years of age, see para. 5 above) of less than 15 years of age or who is still subject to compulsory full-time schooling under national law, Article 3(b) YPWD. The prohibition of child labour thus pursues the dual objective of protecting the physical and mental development of young children and giving preference to full-time schooling (under national law) over occupational activity.

2. Optional Exceptions

9. Articles 4 and 5 YPWD provide for a differentiated set of optional exceptions for the Member States. They concern different subject matters and may, to some

---

[6]   Thus e.g. M. Schmidt, *BB* 1998, 1362, 1365.

[7]   Denied with reference to the national concept of worker by A. Bond, *ILJ* 24 (1995), 377, 381.

[8]   This is what both the wording and the purpose of the provision seem to suggest; this is doubted however by M. Grisenthwaite, *I.C.C.L.R.* 8 (1997), 256 (any child working in a family undertaking).

[9]   On the development, see A. Bond, *ILJ* 24 (1995), 377, 380.

extent, be provided for as legal exceptions; others require authorisation by the supervisory authority. Next to a 'small general clause' for 'light work', there are further optional exceptions for cultural or similar activities and for work in the context of training. These optional exceptions in principle only apply to the prohibition of child labour, leaving the prohibition of night work for children of Article 9(1)(a) and the rest periods of Article 10(1)(a) unaffected. Only the exception for cultural activities (paras. 11 sq. below) also allows for deviations from the prohibition of night work and the provision of rest periods.

a)   Light Work

10.   The exception for 'light work', contained in Article 4(2)(c) YPWD, is addressed first in the Directive. Pursuant to Article 3(d) YPWD, light work is work which, on account of the inherent nature of the tasks involved and the particular conditions under which they are performed (e.g. time and place of work), does not have a negative effect upon children. Negative effects can be such as affect health or development, but also such as affect their school or vocational education. Member States may permit children of at least 14 years of age to engage in light work, and, for a limited number of working hours, may also permit children aged 13 years and above. The exception must be provided for by a legislative or regulatory provision which must also determine the working conditions (subject to the provisions of the Directive), Article 4(3) YPWD.

b)   Cultural, Artistic, Sports or Advertising Activities

11.   The employment of children for purposes of performing cultural, artistic, sports or advertising activities is of considerable practical importance and in many areas, is considered to be socially desirable. At the same time, such employment may raise specific needs for protection. In light of the multitude of scenarios and the specific needs for protection of children in this area, an exception cannot be granted in an abstract, general matter (by law) but rather can be granted only by **prior consent of the competent authority** in the individual case based upon a general legislative framework. The legislative framework of child labour in this case must ensure that the activities do not have a harmful effect upon the child: its safety, health, development, its school or vocational education or its capacity to benefit from the instructions received.

12.   In the case of children of at least 13 years of age, national law may derogate from the requirement of consent of the competent authority and instead determine the conditions of child labour by legislative or regulatory provision. This is in line with the exception for 'light work'.

c)   Combined Work-Training Schemes

13.   Internships and practical experience often play an important role in school education or vocational training. This is taken into account by Article 4(2)(b) YPWD. Children of at least 14 years of age may be allowed to work pursuant to a combined work/training scheme or an in-plant work-experience scheme. The national law of the Member States may provide for such exception in general terms, and the detailed conditions must then be determined by the competent authority in a general fashion; there is no need for consent in each individual case. The provision is based upon the assumption that the very purpose of the exception, as well as the conditions laid down by the competent authority, are sufficient to take account of the needs of children for protection.

IV.   ASSESSMENT AND PREVENTION OF RISKS

1.   Specific Needs of Protection

14.   Assessment and prevention of risks are the central instruments of EU industrial safety regulation (see §13 paras. 16–24 above). The Young People at Work Directive leaves the general provisions of the Safety and Health Framework Directive unaffected and supplements them with specific provisions to protect the particular needs of young people. Pursuant to Article 7(1), the Directive is concerned with the specific risks to young people's health, safety and development, which arise from their lack of experience, lower risk awareness and the fact that young people have not yet fully matured. With regard to these specific risks, the employer must adopt the measures necessary to protect the safety and health of young people, Article 6(1) YPWD.

2.   Assessment of Risks

15.   As under the Safety and Health Framework Directive (see §13 para. 21 above), the employer is initially obliged to assess the specific risks ('assessment of the hazards to young people in connection with their work'), Article 6(2)(1) YPWD. The assessment must be conducted before young people begin work and whenever there is a major change in working conditions. In a non-exhaustive ('in particular') list, the assessment must take into account:

(a)   the fitting-out and layout of the workplace and workstation;
(b)   the nature, degree and duration of exposure to physical, biological and chemical agents;
(c)   the form, range and use of work equipment, in particular agents, machines, apparatus and devices, and the way in which they are handled;

(d)   the arrangement of work processes and operations and the way in which these are combined (organisation of work); and

(e)   the level of training and instruction given to young people.

3.   Prevention of Risks

a)   General Clause

16.   The general clause of Article 6(1) with Article 7(1) YPWD obliges the employer to take the necessary risk prevention measures. The general clause is concretised by a number of specific rules. Only exceptionally, does the Directive provide for abstract, general prohibitions of work; as a rule, it merely requires assessment and monitoring of the health of young workers.

b)   Prohibitions of Work

17.   With regard to a number of **particularly severe risks**, Article 7(2) YPWD provides for general prohibitions of work. They concern

–   cases of exposure to specifically harmful substances, radiation, noise, cold or heat, lit. (b), (c), (e); and
–   cases where young people would be overwhelmed in regard to their physical or psychological capacity or their risk awareness, lit. (a), (d).

18.   Pursuant to Article 7(3) YPWD, Member States may provide for **derogations** from the general prohibition if they are *indispensable* for the young people's vocational training and if their safety and health is ensured by the fact that the work is performed under the supervision of the protective and preventive services (to be installed under Article 7 SHFD; see §13 paras. 30 sq. above). As a matter of course, the general requirements of the Safety and Health Framework Directive must be guaranteed.

c)   Assessment and Monitoring of Health

19.   Outside this area of prohibited work, where the employer's assessment (Article 6(2) YPWD) shows that there is a risk to the safety, physical or mental health or development of young people, the Directive does not provide for a prohibition of work but rather for a **monitoring of risks**. In addition to the general health examinations under the Safety and Health Framework Directive, the Young People at Work Directive requires 'an appropriate free assessment and monitoring of their health' at regular intervals. The Directive does not specify the employer's obligations in cases where their assessment reveals that risks outweigh the interests of activity or occupation. In this case, the general clause of Article 6(1) applies (see para. 16 above).

4. *Information*

20. As in the case of the Safety and Health Framework Directive, the Young People at Work Directive not only provides for paternalistic protection through prohibitions of work and a duty to assess and prevent risks, but also seeks to reinforce individual autonomy and responsibility. The provisions on assessment and prevention of risks are thus supplemented by a duty to inform young people and their legal representatives of possible risks and measures adopted for their prevention, Article 6(3) YPWD.[10] This can be understood as an expression of the benchmark of the responsible employee (see §13 para. 37).

21. In addition, the **protective and preventive services** – to be installed pursuant to Article 7 SHFD (see §13 para. 30 above) – should be involved in the planning, implementation and monitoring of the safety and health conditions which are applicable to young persons, Article 6(4) YPWD.

V. WORKING TIME AND REST PERIODS

22. Finally, the Young People at Work Directive regulates working time and rest periods, providing for differentiated rules for children and adolescents. With regard to children, these provisions largely (except for rest periods) only concern the optional exceptions of Article 4(2)(b) and (c) YPWD for a combined work/training scheme or an in-plant work-experience scheme and for 'light work' (paras. 10, 13 above). With regard to cultural and similar activities pursuant to Article 5 (paras. 11 sq. above), the Directive does not explicitly provide for restrictions. To the extent that it contains provisions for adolescents in this area, these should *a fortiori* apply to children (thus with regard to night-work, Article 9(2)(b) indent 4 YPWD).

1. *Daily and Weekly Working Time*

23. As **child** labour is in principle prohibited (paras. 7 sq. above), working time regulation is only required with regard to the few exceptions: for a combined work/training scheme or an in-plant work experience scheme and for light work, Article 4(2)(b) and (c) YPWD (paras. 10, 13 above). The provision draws a distinction which is based upon whether the children are still subject to compulsory full-time schooling, Article 8(1)(a)-(d) YPWD. The maximum working hours for work performed in a combined work/training scheme or in an in-plant work experience scheme is eight hours per day, 40 hours per week, lit. (a). During term-time, the maximum limits are two hours per school day

---

[10] A. Bond, *ILJ* 24 (1995), 377, 379.

(outside the time fixed for school attendance), twelve hours per week, lit. (b), during a period when school is not operating seven hours per day, 35 hours per week, lit. (c). Children who are not subject to compulsory full-time schooling may perform light work (Article 4(2)(c)) for a maximum of seven hours per day, 35 hours per week, lit. (d). For **adolescents** who, by definition, are not subject to compulsory full-time schooling (para. 8 above), the maximum working hours are eight hours per day, 40 hours per week, Article 8(2) YPWD.

24. As in the Working Time Directive (§14 para. 15), **working time** is defined broadly as any period during which the young person is at work, at the employer's disposal and carrying out his activity or duties, Article 3(e) YPWD. For young persons working under a theoretical and/or practical combined work/ training scheme or in an in-plant work-experience scheme, time spent on training counts as working time, Article 8(3) YPWD.

25. Member States may provide for **derogations** from the provisions on maximum working hours pursuant to the rather broadly worded provision of Article 8(5) YPWD, either by way of exception or where there are of objective grounds for doing so.

2.   Night Work

26. Night work is strictly prohibited for **children** (in the cases of Article 4(2)(b), (c)) during the time between 8 p.m. and 6 a.m. For **adolescents**, night work is in principle prohibited during an eight-hour period from 10 p.m. to 6 a.m. or from 11 p.m. to 7 a.m. Article 9(1) YPWD.

27. Member States may, first, provide for **exceptions** for adolescents in '*specific areas of activity*', i.e. such as require derogation due to their nature, Article 9(2)(a) YPWD. Work at a bakery may provide an example.[11] Even then, work in the core night-time from midnight to 4 a.m. must remain prohibited. Furthermore, Member States must ensure that the adolescent is supervised by an adult where that is necessary for his protection. Secondly, Member States may authorise night work of adolescents in *certain areas* enumerated by the Directive where there are objective grounds for doing so: in the shipping or fishing sectors; in the context of the armed forces or the police; in hospitals or similar establishments; in cultural, artistic, sports or advertising activities, Article 9(2)(b)(2) YPWD. This latter exception further presupposes that adolescents are allowed suitable compensatory rest time and that the objectives of the Directive – protection against economic exploitation and protection of the physical, mental, moral and social development of young workers – are not called into question.

---

[11]   See in German law §14(2)(4) JArbSchG.

28. Prior to an assignment to night work and at regular intervals thereafter, adolescents are entitled to a free assessment of their health and capacities unless they only exceptionally perform night work, Article 9(3) YPWD.

3. Daily and Weekly Rest Periods

29. Where children are allowed to work pursuant to an exception under Article 4(2)(b) and (c), they are entitled to a **daily** rest period – per 24-hour-period – of at least 14 consecutive hours, for adolescents the minimum daily rest period is twelve hours, Article 10(1) YPWD. The **weekly** rest period – per seven-day-period – for both groups is two days which should be consecutive days where possible, Article 10(2) YPWD.

30. Again, there are two groups of exceptions, Article 10(3) and (4) YPWD. First, Member States may provide for the minimum (daily or weekly) rest periods to be interrupted in the case of activities involving periods of work that are split up over the day or are of short duration. Secondly, national legislation may provide for exceptions in respect of adolescents in certain enumerated areas where this is justified on objective grounds, provided that the adolescents get compensatory rest periods and that the objectives of the Directive are still achieved: work performed in the shipping or fishing sectors, in the context of the armed forces or the police, in hospitals or similar establishments, in agriculture, in the tourism industry or in the hotel, restaurant and café sectors, and activities involving periods of work split up over the day.

4. Breaks

31. Young people (see para. 5 above) are entitled to a break of 30 – if possible consecutive – minutes where the daily working time exceeds four and a half hours.

5. Annual Rest

32. With regard to 'annual rest' – in other words, annual leave – the Young People at Work Directive supplements the Working Time Directive only in certain individual aspects. For *children* (who permissibly work under Article 4(2)(b) and (c)) who are subject to full-time schooling, a period free of any work should, as far as possible, be included in the school holidays. This provision takes account of the concern that children should be able to have holidays with their peers, which is particularly important for their social integration and development.

6.   Optional Exception for Force Majeure

33.   In cases of *force majeure* as defined in Article 4(5) SHFD, the national law of the Member States may authorise derogations from

- the maximum working hours for adolescents of Article 8(2) YPWD;
- the night-rest-period for adolescents of Article 9(1)(b) YPWD; and
- the minimum rest periods for adolescents of Article 10(1)(b) YPWD.

Such derogations presuppose that the work in question is of a temporary nature and must be performed immediately and that the adolescents are allowed equivalent compensatory rest time within the following three weeks.

7.   Sanctions

34.   The Directive does not specifically provide for sanctions for a violation of its obligations but rather leaves the issue to the Member States. Article 14 YPWD merely reiterates the general obligations of implementation (see §1 paras. 65 sq. above): Member States must determine the measures necessary to enforce the provisions; such measures must be effective and proportionate.

VI. IMPLEMENTATION

35.   The Young People at Work Directive has been implemented in **Germany** by the Second Act Amending the Young Persons in Employment Protection Act (*Zweites Änderungsgesetz zum Jugendarbeitsschutzgesetz*) (with some delay)[12].[13] To a large extent, the pre-existing legislation already satisfied the requirements of the Directive.[14]

---

[12]   The implementation period fort he Directive had expired already on 22 June 1996; see Article 17(a) YPWD. Some authors have expressed doubt as to the direct applicability of the Young People at Work Directive (in public employment), arguing that the Directive did not intend to give rise to direct claims; K. Lörcher, *AuR* 1994, 360, 362. On the belated implementation in Luxembourg and France, see ECJ Case C-47/99 Commission v. Luxembourg [1999] ECR I-8999; ECJ Case C-45/99 Commission v. France [2000] ECR I-3615. On the implementation in the UK see M. Grisenthwaite, *I.C.C.L.R.* 8 (1997), 256–258; C. Hamilton/B. Watt, *C.F.L.Q.* 16 (2004), 135–149; S. Deakin/G. Morris, *Labour Law*, para. 4.91.

[13]   For an overview, see R. Wank, in P. Hanau/H.-D. Steinmeyer/R. Wank (eds.), *Handbuch des europäischen Arbeits- und Sozialrechts*, §18 paras. 403–411; for a synopsis of the YPWD and the German JArbSchG, see W. Balze, in *EAS*, B 5200 para. 60; see also ibid. para. 12. See also N. Kollmer, *NZA* 1998, 1268–1272.

[14]   M. Schmidt, *BB* 1998, 1362–1364 (discussing implementation deficits in individual respects).

CHAPTER 6

EMPLOYEE PROTECTION IN BUSINESS RESTRUCTURING AND INSOLVENCY

§23. THE COLLECTIVE REDUNDANCIES DIRECTIVE

CONTENT

Bibliography:

S. Alber, 'Die Rechtsprechung des EuGH zur Richtlinie über Massenentlassungen', in W. Kothe/H. Dörner/R. Anzinger (eds.), *Arbeitsrecht im sozialen Dialog – Festschrift für Hellmut Wißmann zum 65. Geburtstag* (Munich: C.H. Beck, 2005), 507–522; F. Becker, 'Die EG-Richtlinie zur Angleichung des Massenkündigungsschutzes', *NJW* 1976, 2057 sqq.; B. Bercusson, Case Comment, CMLR 33 (1996), 589–610; B. Boemke, 'Die Massenentlassungsrichtlinie', in H. Oetker/U. Preis (eds.), *Europäisches Arbeits- und Sozialrecht, EAS, part B – Systematische Darstellungen,* loose-leaf (Heidelberg: Forkel, last update: November 2007), B 7100; C. Bourn, 'Amending the Collective Dismissals Directive: A Case of Re-arranging the Deckchairs?', *IJCLLIR* 9 (1993), 227–243; L. Dolding, 'Collective Redundancy and Community Law', *ILJ* 21 (1992), 310–315; G. Forst, 'Zum Begriff des abhängigen Unternehmens im europäischen Arbeitsrecht', *ZESAR* 2010, 154–163; M. Franzen, 'Europarecht und betriebliche Mitbestimmung – Überlegungen zur Umsetzung der Rahmen-Richtlinie 2002/14/EG über die Unterrichtung und Anhörung der Arbeitnehmer in Deutschland', in H. Konzen et al. (eds.), *Festschrift für Rolf Birk* (Tübingen: Mohr Siebeck, 2008), 97–114; M. Franzen, 'Massenentlassung und Betriebsänderung unter dem Einfluss des europäischen Gemeinschaftsrechts', *ZfA* 2006, 437–458; M. R. Freedland, 'Employment Protection: Redundancy Procedures and the EEC', *ILJ* 5 (1976), 24–34; R. Giesen, 'Massenentlassungsanzeige erst nach Abschluss von Sozialplanberatungen?', *SAE* 2006, 135–140; F. Gaudu, 'Collective Redundancies for economic motives: convergences and controversies', *ELLJ* 2 (2011), 5–26; B. A. Hepple, 'Community Measures for the Protection of Workers against Dismissal', *CMLR* 14 (1977), 489–500; O. Hinrichs, *Kündigungsschutz und Arbeitnehmerbeteiligung bei Massenentlassung – Europarechtliche Aspekte und Impulse* (Baden-Baden: Nomos, 2001); S. Klumpp, 'Der EuGH und die Massenentlassung – Zeit für "Junk II"?', *NZA* 2006, 703–709; A. M. Lofaso, 'Pretermination Job Rights of British Workers Affected by Collective Redundancies', *YEL* 16 (1996), 277–319; M. Löwisch, 'Änderungen des Kündigungsschutzgesetzes', *NJW* 1978, 1237–1238; A. Mauthner, *Die Massenentlassungsrichtlinie und ihre Bedeutung für das deutsche Massenentlassungsrecht* (Heidelberg: Recht und Wirtschaft, 2004); H. Oetker/C. Schubert, 'Europäisches Betriebsverfassungsrecht', in H. Oetker/U. Preis (eds.), *Europäisches Arbeits- und Sozialrecht, EAS, part B – Systematische Darstellungen,* loose-leaf (Heidelberg: Forkel, last update: January 2007), B 8300 paras. 398–443; B. Reinhard, 'Rechtsfolgen fehlerhafter Massenentlassungen', *RdA* 2007, 207–216; K. Riesenhuber/R. Domröse, 'Die "Entlassung" nach der Massenentlassungsrichtlinie – Bedeutung und Folgen des EuGH-Urteils v. 27.1.2005 – Rs. C-188/03, Junk', *EWS* 2005, 97–103; K. Riesenhuber/R. Domröse, 'Zur richtlinienkonformen Auslegung von §§17, 18 KSchG und den Rechtsfolgen fehlerhafter Massenentlassungen', *NZA* 2005, 568–570; M. Schlachter, *Casebook Europäisches Arbeitsrecht* (Baden-Baden: Nomos, 2005), Cases No. 15, 19; C. Weber, 'Schwellenwerte für die Beschäftigungszahlen bei Massenentlassungen – Urteil des Europäischen Gerichtshofs vom 18.1.2007 – Rechtssache CGT', *EuZA* 2008, 355–366; C. Weber, 'Information und Konsultation im europäischen und deutschen Mitbestimmungsrecht', in B. Dauner-Lieb et al. (eds.), *Festschrift für Horst Konzen* (Tübingen: Mohr Siebeck 2005), 921–956; C. Weber, 'Mitbestimmungsspirale im Recht der Massenentlassung? – Zum Vorlagebeschluss des Arbeitsgerichts Berlin vom 21.2.2006', in G. Annuß/E. Picker/H. Wißmann (eds.),

Festschrift für Reinhard Richardi (Munich: C.H. Beck, 2007), 461–473; C. Weber, 'Massenentlassung und Arbeitnehmerbeteiligung im deutschen und europäischen Mitbestimmungsrecht', *AuR* 2008, 365–380; Lord K. W. Wedderburn, 'Consultation and Collective Bargaining in Europe – Success or Ideology?', *ILJ* 26 (1997), 1–34; M. Weiss, 'Die europarechtliche Regelung der Massenentlassung', *RdA* 1992, 367–373; G. Wisskirchen/A. Bissels, 'Massenentlassungen in den Mitgliedstaaten der EU', *ZESAR* 2010, 164–171; H. Wißmann, 'Die Probleme bei der Umsetzung der EG-Richtlinie über Massenentlassungen in deutsches Recht', *RdA* 1998, 221–228; H. Wolter, 'Wende im Recht der Massenentlassung', *AuR* 2005, 135–141.

Cases:

ECJ Case 284/83 *Nielsen* [1985] ECR 553; ECJ Case 215/83 *Commission* v. *Belgium* [1985] ECR 1039; ECJ Case C-383/92 *Commission* v. *United Kingdom* [1994] ECR I-2479; ECJ Case C-449/93 *Rockfon* [1995] ECR I-4291; ECJ Case C-250/97 *Lauge* [1998] ECR I-8738; ECJ Case C-32/02 *Commission* v. *Italy* [2003] ECR I-12063; ECJ Case C-55/02 *Commission* v. *Portugal* [2004] ECR I-9387; ECJ Case C-188/03 *Junk* [2005] ECR I-885; ECJ Joined Cases C-187/05 to 190/05 *Agorastoudis* [2006] ECR I-7775; ECJ Case C-385/05 *Confédération générale du travail (CGT)* [2007] ECR I-611; ECJ Case C-270/05 *Athinaïki Chartopoiía* [2007] ECR I-1499; ECJ Case C-12/08 *Mono Car Styling* [2009] ECR I-6653; ECJ Case C-44/08 *AEK* v. *Fujitsu Siemens* [2009] ECR I-8163; ECJ Case C-323/08 *Rodríguez Mayor* [2009] ECR I-11621; ECJ Joined Cases C-235/10 to C-239/10 *Claes* 3 March 2011.

I. ISSUES, OVERVIEW, COMPETENCE, REGULATORY CONTEXT

1. In 1973, the German-Dutch **AKZO-Group** decided to make some 5,000 workers redundant as part of its business restructuring. As the group had subsidiaries in several Member States, it decided to lay off workers in those countries where the risks and costs involved would be lowest. This – economically sensible – approach met with considerable political criticism. Not least, because it demonstrated how a *high* standard of worker-protection could be a locational advantage – at least in the short run and with regard to disinvestment. On the whole, there was a concern that the standards of protection with regard to collective redundancies should not become a factor of competition. The AKZO case was thus one of the triggers for the enactment of the 1975 Collective Redundancies Directive.[1]

---

[1]   See B. A. Hepple, *CMLR* 14 (1977), 489 sq.; AG Mengozzi, Opinion in Case C-12/08 *Mono Car Styling* [2009] ECR I-6653 pt. 31. On the legislative history also B. Boemke, in *EAS*, B 7100 paras. 1–4; A. M. Lofaso, *YEL* 16 (1996), 277, 292–297. Commission, Proposal for a Directive on the harmonisation of the legislation of the Member States relating to redundancies, COM(72) 1400 final.

2. Collective redundancies are initially simply dismissals of workers. An employer's decision to terminate an employment contract cannot be called into question in so far as it is based upon an **entrepreneurial decision** (for restructuring).[2] Employee protection thus cannot be achieved by controlling the employer's underlying decision. Instead, the goal of protection in this field must be to structure the procedures so as to avoid dismissal to the greatest possible extent and otherwise alleviate the consequences of inevitable dismissals.

3. The **Collective Redundancies Directive**[3] (CRD) does not regulate the prerequisites for mass dismissals; in particular it does not prohibit them.[4] Instead, it aims to establish a minimum standard of protection (Article 5 CRD) through procedural safeguards. Before dismissing workers, the employer must inform the workers' representatives and conduct a consultation procedure, the aim of which is, *inter alia*, to avoid collective redundancies and alleviate their consequences. The employer must further notify the competent public authority of the projected redundancies so as to enable them 'to seek solutions to the problems raised'. After an employer's notification, a 30 day period begins, during which redundancies cannot take effect.

4. The original directive of 1975[5] was **amended in 1992**.[6] The 1992 amendment was intended to take account of the fact that in international groups of companies, structural decisions are often not made on the national level; this should not compromise information and consultation duties (see para. 29 below). In **1998**, the Directive was **codified** (i.e. systematically revised) 'for reasons of clarity and rationality' (Recital 1 CRD).[7] The original directive was based upon the Union's **competences** contained in Articles 100 and 117 EEC (see now Articles 115 and 153 TFEU). The Directive is thus on the one hand, intended to serve the establishment and functioning of the Common (Internal) Market, and on the other, is intended to 'promote improved working conditions and an

---

2   Thus also under the CRD, ECJ Joined Cases C-187/05 to C-190/05 *Agorastoudis* [2006] ECR I-7775 para. 35; Case 284/83 *Nielsen* [1985] ECR 553 para. 10; AG Mengozzi, Opinion in Case C-12/08 *Mono Car Styling* [2009] ECR I-6653 pt. 37. See also F. Gaudu, *ELLJ* 2 (2011), 5, 8 sq.

3   Council Directive 98/59/EC of 20 July 1998 on the approximation of the laws of the Member States relating to collective redundancies, OJ 1998 L 225/16.

4   M. Franzen, *ZfA* 2006, 437, 442.

5   Council Directive 75/129/EEC of 17 February 1975 on the approximation of the laws of the Member States relating to collective redundancies, OJ 1975 L 48/29. On the legislative history of the original directive, see M. R. Freedland, *ILJ* 5 (1976), 24–34; B. A. Hepple, *CMLR* 14 (1977), 489–500.

6   Council Directive 92/56/EEC of 24 June 1992 amending Directive 75/129/EEC on the approximation of the laws of the Member States relating to collective redundancies, OJ 1992 L 245/3. See C. Bourn, *IJCLLIR* 9 (1993), 227–243; L. Dolding, *ILJ* 21 (1992), 310–315.

7   See above note 3n.

improved standard of living for workers so as to make possible their harmonisation while the improvement is being maintained' (Article 117 EEC).[8]

5. In light of the objective of protecting workers in situations of restructuring or economic distress of the undertaking, the Transfer of Undertakings Directive (§24) and the Insolvency Protection Directive (§25) form part of the **regulatory context** of the Collective Redundancy Directive. As regards protection in cases of dismissal, the anti-discrimination directives are also applicable as they apply to 'employment and working conditions, including dismissal' (§§9–11).

II. SCOPE OF APPLICATION: 'COLLECTIVE REDUNDANCIES'

1. Alternatives for Implementation

6. The scope of application is defined by the term 'collective redundancies' as defined in Article 1 CRD. Collective redundancies are only redundancies for reasons **not related to the individual worker** concerned. In addition, there are qualitative requirements. Here, **Member States** have the option to chose between one of two models, No. i and No. ii.[9]

- Model No. i refers to the number or proportion of workers, in relation to the size of the establishment, who are made redundant within a period of 30 days.
- For model No. ii, the size of the establishment is irrelevant, a collective redundancy occurs where 20 or more workers have been made redundant within a period of 90 days.

Alternatives		Period of Time	Size of the Establishment	Number/Proportion of the Workers who are made Redundant
No. I	Indent 1	within a period of 30 days	20–100 workers	at least 10 workers
	Indent 2		100–299 workers	at least 10% of the number of workers
	Indent 3		300 workers or more	at least 30 workers
No. Ii		within a period of 90 days	Irrelevant	at least 20 workers

---

[8]   ECJ Cases C-187/05 to C-190/05 *Agorastoudis* [2006] ECR I-7775 para. 38.

[9]   For an overview of the implementation models see C. Barnard, *EC Employment Law*, 674–677.

2. The Individual Requirements

a) Establishment

7. The term 'establishment', which is central to the application of the Directive, is not expressly left for the Member States to determine, but is to be interpreted **autonomously**.[10] While some language versions would support its construction so as to refer to the 'undertaking', the Court of Justice has interpreted the term 'establishment' in light of the Directive's legislative history,[11] so as to refer to the unit to which the workers made redundant are assigned to carry out their duties. An 'establishment' 'may consist of a distinct entity, having a certain degree of permanence and stability, which is assigned to perform one or more given tasks and which has a workforce, technical means and a certain organisational structure allowing for the accomplishment of those tasks'.[12] It is not essential whether or not this unit is endowed with a management which can independently effect collective redundancies.[13] Such a requirement would be incompatible with the objectives of the Directive, as it would be liable to make its scope of application open to manipulation by undertakings.[14]

8. In the *Rockfon* case, this definition of establishment led to a *broadening* of the Directive's scope of application. The Rockfon A/S with 162 workers together with three other companies located in the same town in Denmark, Rockment A/S, Conrock A/S and Rockwool A/S, belonged to the Rockwool-Group. Altogether, the companies had some 1,435 workers. A central personnel department under the roof of the Rockwool A/S decided on recruitments and dismissals. Rockfon made 24 of its 162 workers redundant. Looking at all four companies, the threshold number of 30 workers had not been passed. If, however, the Rockfon A/S alone constituted an establishment, then the threshold of a minimum of 10% (= 16 workers) had been passed.

---

10   ECJ Case C-449/93 *Rockfon* [1995] ECR I-4291 para. 25; Case C-270/05 *Athinaïki Chartopoiía* [2007] ECR I-1499 para. 23. B. Boemke, in *EAS*, B 7100 paras. 15–18; S. Deakin/G. Morris, *Labour Law*, para. 9.32; generally on autonomous interpretation of EU law K. Riesenhuber, in id. (ed.), *Europäische Methodenlehre*, §11 paras. 4–8.

11   The proposal for the original directive still used the term *enterprise* but already defined it as the local employment unit. When the Council replaced this term with *établissement* it considered the definition to be unnecessary.

12   ECJ Case C-270/05 *Athinaïki Chartopoiía* [2007] ECR I-1499 para. 27.

13   This is now confirmed by the group of undertakings-clause of Article 2(4) CRD as inserted by the 1992 revision.

14   ECJ Case C-449/93 *Rockfon* [1995] ECR I-4291 paras. 26–33; Case C-270/05 *Athinaïki Chartopoiía* [2007] ECR I-1499 paras. 25–29. C. Weber, *AuR* 2008, 365, 367 sq.

b)   Employer and Worker

9. Notwithstanding their importance for the definition of collective redundancies, the Directive does not define the terms 'employer' and 'worker' but instead (implicitly) refers to the national laws of the Member States.[15] Yet, with respect to the employer, Article 2(4) CRD takes account of the issue of groups of companies (see para. 29 below). The Directive neither provides for exceptions with regard to employers[16] – e.g. undertakings that do not intend to make profits or small or medium sized undertakings – nor with regard to workers – e.g. executive staff. In light of the express exception of Article 1(2) (see para. 14 below), this lack of provision should be interpreted negatively so that the Member States may not provide for exceptions.[17] National law may not exempt specific groups of workers – such as workers under 26 years – from the scope of protection, be it fully or partly, permanently or temporarily; this may in particular not be justified by the Member States' right to choose one of the thresholds of Article 1(1)(a) CRD.[18]

c)   Redundancy

10. The ambiguous term 'redundancy' must be construed **autonomously**.[19] It can refer to (a) the expression by the employer of his intention to put an end to the contract of employment or (b) to the actual cessation of the employment relationship on the expiry of the period in the notices of redundancy. German courts and scholars had, for a long time, followed the latter interpretation. Based upon the wording, the system and the purpose of the Directive, the Court of Justice construes redundancy to refer to the employer's declaration of his intent to terminate the contract.[20] Redundancy refers to 'any termination of contract of employment not sought by the worker, and therefore without his consent'.[21]

---

[15]   B. Boemke, in *EAS*, B 7100 para. 57. Differently C. Weber, *AuR* 2008, 365, 367; id., *EuZA* 2008, 355, 363.

[16]   ECJ Case C-32/02 *Commission* v. *Italy* [2003] ECR I-12063 para. 26; the restriction of the scope to 'entrepreneur' in Italian law excluded non-profit organisations such as trade unions, foundations, political parties, partnerships, cooperatives and non-governmental organisations (see para. 18 of the decision).

[17]   §17(5) KSchG is thus incompatible with the CRD; G. Thüsing, *Europäisches Arbeitsrecht*, §6 para. 16; C. Weber, *AuR* 2008, 365, 367; with doubt also F. Marhold, in M. Fuchs/F. Marhold (eds.), *Europäisches Arbeitsrecht*, 176.

[18]   ECJ Case C-385/05 *Confédération générale du travail (CGT)* [2006] ECR I-611 paras. 43–48.

[19]   ECJ Case C-188/03 *Junk* [2005] ECR I-885 paras. 29 sq.; K. Riesenhuber/R. Domröse, *EWS* 2005, 97 (98).

[20]   ECJ Case C-188/03 *Junk* [2005] ECR I-885 paras. 31–39; K. Riesenhuber/R. Domröse, *EWS* 2005, 97, 98 sq.; C. Barnard, *EC Employment Law*, 679 sq.

[21]   ECJ Case C-55/02 *Commission* v. *Portugal* [2004] ECR I-9387 para. 49 sq.; Joined Cases C-187/05 to C-190/05 *Agorastoudis* [2006] ECR I-7775 para. 28.

11. Collective redundancies include dismissals on grounds **not related to the individual workers concerned**. This is in line with the purpose of the Directive to regulate mass dismissals as entrepreneurial measures in the course of restructuring but not general questions about the right of dismissal. Terminations on grounds 'related to the individual workers' are those related to their person (e.g. sickness) or their behaviour (e.g. harassment of co-workers). If, for example, the whole purchasing department is being terminated because of bribery, this is not a case covered by the concept of 'collective redundancy'. Reversing the (rather unconvincing) prior jurisprudence of the Court of Justice[22], Article 1(1)(2) CRD provides that terminations of an employment contract which occur on the employer's initiative for one or more reasons not related to the individual workers concerned shall be assimilated to redundancies. The prerequisite for this 'assimilation' is that there are at least five redundancies.[23]

12. What about the case where the employment relationship ends as a consequence of the employer's death (where the employer was a natural person)? On the basis of the wording ('dismissals') and purpose of the Directive (information and consultation; notification of the competent authority *prior* to the dismissal), as well as the consideration that the Directive only effected a partial harmonisation, the Court considered that such cases would not be covered by Article 1(1) CRD.[24] Arguably, this is a rather narrow view and it is well conceivable that the relevant procedures could be performed by a successor. It seems that the Directive is merely *partial* harmonisation could have been decisive, as this case is inherently linked to national inheritance laws.

13. Apart from the above requirements (paras. 10 sq.), the reasons behind the collective redundancy are irrelevant. The Directive also applies where collective redundancies result from the definitive **termination of the operation of an undertaking or establishment** which has been decided on by the employer of its own accord.[25] This was true even under the original 1975 directive which provided for an exception where the termination of the operation was the result of a judicial decision (see para. 15 below). Since the 1992 revision, the Directive also applies in cases where the employing establishment terminates its activities as a result of a judicial decision ordering its dissolution and winding up on grounds of insolvency (although Articles 3(1)(2) and 4(4) of the Directive allow for some

---

22 ECJ Case 284/83 *Nielsen* [1985] ECR 553 paras. 7–11.
23 M. Weiss, *RdA* 1992, 367, 371 sq.
24 ECJ Case C-323/08 *Rodríguez Mayor* [2009] ECR I-11621.
25 ECJ Joined Cases C-187/05 to C-190/05 *Agorastoudis* [2006] ECR I-7775. See also Case 215/83 *Commission* v. *Belgium* [1985] ECR 1039 paras. 13–19; Case C-55/02 *Commission* v. *Portugal* [2004] ECR I-9387 para. 66.

modifications).[26] If, in such case, the management of the undertaking has been completely taken over by liquidators, the liquidators must perform the employer's duties.[27]

3. Exceptions

14. In an exhaustive list, Article 1(2) CRD provides for three areas of exception from the Directive's scope of application:

- collective redundancies effected under contracts of employment concluded for limited periods of time or for specific tasks, except where such redundancies take place prior to the date of expiry or the completion of such contracts;[28]
- workers employed by public administrative bodies or by establishments governed by public law; and
- the crews of seagoing vessels.

The first exception is well founded on objective reasons. The procedural rules do not fit for the case that, e.g., the contracts of a large number of casual employees who have been hired for a trade fair expire after the end of the fair. The other exceptions for the public administration and seagoing vessels are rather unconvincing in light of the purpose of the Directive;[29] the latter has apparently been retained because of pressure exerted by Greece.[30]

15. Since the 1992-revision, redundancies of 'workers affected by the termination of an establishment's activities where that is the result of a **judicial decision**' are no longer excluded as such. The original exception was primarily related to insolvency proceedings.[31] However, not all provisions on the notification of the competent authorities in Articles 3 sq. CRD apply in such cases, see Articles 3(1)(2) and Article 4(4) CRD.[32]

---

26 ECJ Joined Cases C-235/10 to C-239/10 *Claes* 3 March 2011 paras. 29–49.

27 ECJ Joined Cases C-235/10 to C-239/10 *Claes* 3 March 2011 paras. 50–58.

28 The exception applies where the individual contract is for a limited period of time, not where contracts of that kind are typically or predominantly of a temporary nature; see ECJ Case 215/83 *Commission* v. *Belgium* [1985] ECR 1039 para. 24.

29 See ECJ Case 215/83 *Commission* v. *Belgium* [1985] ECR 1039 paras. 21–25 (ship repairers, port workers and manual workers in the building industry).

30 M. Weiss, *RdA* 1992, 367, 371.

31 See also M. Weiss, *RdA* 1992, 367, 371 sq.; ECJ Joined Cases C-187/05 to C-190/05 *Agorastoudis* [2006] ECR I-7775.

32 See ECJ Case C-270/05 *Athinaïki Chartopoiïa* [2007] ECR I-1499; Case C-250/97 *Lauge* [1998] ECR I-8738.

III.   THE CONSULTATION PROCEDURE

1.   Duty of Consultation

16.   Where an employer is contemplating collective redundancies, he[33] shall begin consultations with the workers' representatives in good time with a view to reaching an agreement, Article 2(1) CRD.

17.   The employer's **partners for the consultation** are the workers' representatives. The Directive leaves the designation of workers' representatives to the Member States, Article 1(1)(b) CRD. However, making worker representation subject to the voluntary recognition of trade unions by the employer (as had been the case in the UK), does not satisfy the requirements for effective implementation of Articles 2 and 3(2) CRD, as the employer could then frustrate the workers' rights at his whim.[34]

18.   **Topics** of the consultations pursuant to Article 2(2) CRD are ways and means[35]

- of avoiding collective redundancies or reducing the number of workers affected, and
- of mitigating the consequences by recourse to accompanying social measures. By way of example, the legislature considers 'measures aimed at aid for redeploying or retraining workers made redundant'. Such measures should be distinguished from measures aimed at alleviating the *economic* consequences, which the Directive does not require.[36]

19.   As the duty to conduct consultation is already triggered by the employer's *intention* ('contemplating') to make collective redundancies and as the consultation is aimed, among other matters, at avoiding or limiting collective redundancies (Article 2(2)(1) CRD), the concept of **redundancies** must be construed so as to refer to the employer's declaration of termination rather than

---

[33]   Note: the politically incorrect wording which could be misread as suggesting that the employer is a male person is in taken from the original text of the Directive which, apparently, has not been gender-mainstreamed.

[34]   ECJ Case C-383/92 *Commission* v. *United Kingdom* [1994] ECR I-2479 paras. 13–28; see also the parallel proceedings with regard to the TUD 1997 Case C-382/92 *Commission* v. *United Kingdom* [1994] ECR I-2435. On the initial situation under UK law and on the consequences of the decision B. Bercusson, *CMLR* 33 (1996), 589, 590–594; S. Deakin/G. Morris, *Labour Law*, paras. 9.30 sq.; M. Weiss, *RdA* 1992, 367, 369.

[35]   ECJ Case C-188/03 *Junk* [2005] ECR I-885 para. 38. On the implementation obligations in this regard Case C-383/92 *Commission* v. *United Kingdom* [1994] ECR I-2479 paras. 34–37; B. Bercusson *CMLR* 33 (1996), 589, 594–598.

[36]   M. Franzen, *ZfA* 2006, 437, 442.

to the actual cessation of the employment relationship (see already para. 10 above).[37] And, again, as consultation is aimed at avoiding or limiting collective redundancies, it must be conducted **before** the employer effects the redundancies, i.e. gives notices of termination (see again para. 10 above).[38] The employer may, in other words, only give notice of termination after the consultation has been completed.

20. The employer must **initiate consultation** as soon as he contemplates, or draws up a plan for, collective redundancies.[39] In the case of a group of undertakings (see Art. 4(2) CRD and para. 30 below) – but with potential relevance beyond that specific situation – the Court of Justice has ruled that 'the consultation procedure must be started by the employer once a strategic or commercial decision compelling him to contemplate or to plan for collective redundancies has been taken'.[40] In a group of undertakings, this responsibility exists irrespective of whether the employer has knowledge of the relevant decisions or facts. In particular, it cannot be inferred from Article 2(3) CRD on the employer's obligation to inform the workers' representatives, that the consultation must be commenced only once the employer has all relevant information (see also para. 30 below).

21. The *aim* of the consultation is 'reaching an agreement', Article 2(1) CRD. In other words, the Directive merely provides for a **duty to negotiate** but not for an obligation to reach an agreement.[41] The aim of reaching an agreement, however, implies the employer's obligation to **negotiate in good faith**.[42] Such duty implies that the employer must be open to negotiations. He may not, in particular, obstruct an agreement by creating a *fait accompli*, for example by giving notice before consultation is completed.[43] At the same time, there is no obligation to reach an agreement and the consultation may thus lead to an agreement, be terminated without agreement or fail;[44] the outcome of negotiations cannot support an inference as to whether or not the negotiations were conducted in good faith, particularly since the Directive is not intended to interfere with the

---

37   ECJ Case C-188/03 *Junk* [2005] ECR I-885 paras. 33–39, 41.
38   Ibid., paras. 42–54.
39   ECJ Case C-44/08 *AEK* v. *Fujitsu Siemens* [2009] ECR I-8163 para. 41. See also S. Deakin/G. Morris, *Labour Law*, para. 9.33; see also C. Barnard, *EC Employment Law*, 679 sq.
40   ECJ Case C-44/08 *AEK* v. *Fujitsu Siemens* [2009] ECR I-8163 para. 48.
41   M. Franzen, *ZfA* 2006, 437, 444 sq.; S. Klumpp, *NZA* 2007, 703, 705 sq.; B. Reinhard, *RdA* 2007, 207, 213; C. Weber, *AuR* 2008, 365, 370.
42   C. Weber, *AuR* 2008, 365, 370 ('Negotiations with a competent partner based on solid information in the context of a meeting of employer and the employees' representatives; it further includes the right of the employees' representatives to demand a reasoned statement of the employer' – my translation); S. Deakin/G. Morris, *Labour Law*, 9.37.
43   ECJ Case C-188/03 *Junk* [2005] ECR I-885 paras. 38, 43 sq.; C. Barnard, *EC Employment Law*, 682.
44   C. Weber, *Festschrift für Richardi*, 466.

employer's entrepreneurial decision (see para. 2 above). Between the duty to negotiate in good faith on the one hand, and the lack of a duty to reach an agreement and the autonomy of the entrepreneurial decision on the other, it is, however, not for the employer to decide unilaterally that consultation has failed,[45] as he could otherwise negotiate only *pro forma* and thus effectively frustrate the duty to negotiate.

22. As the details of consultation are not spelled out by the Directive, they may be fleshed out by the Member States in their implementing legislation.[46] Member States may choose to proceed in the same way as the Directive, and merely define the duration and termination of consultation by the duty to negotiate. Consultation is thus terminated when the parties reach agreement or fail to reach agreement in spite of their negotiating in good faith.[47] On the other hand, Member States may hammer out the details of the consultation procedure, e.g. by determining a reasonable period for negotiations after which negotiations are deemed to have failed.[48] There is no obligation to provide for **conciliation procedures or procedures to reach agreement**. Such mechanisms are not unknown to the EU legislator (cf. Article 7(3) TUD) and were considered during the legislative proceedings. However, ultimately the legislator decided against imposing them. An obligation to provide for such proceedings cannot be inferred from the duty to negotiate as it does not amount to a duty to reach an agreement (see para. 21 above).[49] Consequently, the principle of effectiveness cannot lead to a duty to provide for such conciliation procedures either.[50] Such obligation could only follow from the principle of equivalence for individual Member States where conciliation procedures are the instrument usually employed to enforce a duty to negotiate collectively.[51]

23. If the national law of a Member State provides for conciliation procedures as an instrument of implementing the Directive, then, as a rule, these procedures must be followed in order for the parties to complete the consultation stage. Matters are

---

[45] To this effect, however, M. Franzen, *ZfA* 2006, 437, 444 sq. (who does not overlook the duty to negotiate in good faith, though).

[46] See also C. Weber, *Festschrift für Richardi*, 466 sq.

[47] To the same effect H. Oetker/C. Schubert, in *EAS*, B 8300 paras. 413, 418.

[48] B. Reinhard, *RdA* 2007, 307, 213 sq.; C. Weber, *AuR* 2008, 365, 370.

[49] M. Franzen, *ZfA* 2006, 437, 445.

[50] See also C. Weber, *Festschrift für Richardi*, 468.

[51] Differently M. Franzen, *ZfA* 2006, 437, 445. The fact that this leads to an indirect obligation to provide for sanctions that the Directive does not expressly provide and that differences in the national laws may thus be perpetuated is an inevitably consequence of an only partial (!) approximation of the national laws (see Recitals 3 and 4 CRD) which only provides for duties and does not specifically prescribe sanctions. Also C. Weber, *Festschrift für Richardi*, 468–470 overlooks the equivalence principle when he interprets the reference for a preliminary ruling of the *Arbeitsgericht* (Labour Court, ArbG) Berlin as asking for an interpretation of Community law in the light of national law.

different where consultation and conciliation are separate. That is the case in the German implementing measures of §§17 sq. Protection Against Unfair Dismissal Act (*Kündigungsschutzgesetz*, KSchG) which are separate from the provisions on the 'reconciliation of interests' (*Interessenausgleich*) and on the 'social plan' (*Sozialplan*) and the 'conciliation board procedures' (*Einigungsstellenverfahren*) in §§111 sq. Works Constitution Act (*Betriebsverfassungsgesetz*, BetrVG). However, a problematic aspect of this implementation is that, in practice, consultation is usually conducted within the framework of a reconciliation of interests and of the social plan procedures (as collective redundancies will usually involve 'operational changes', thus triggering these procedures).[52] To the extent that the duty to (inform and) consult is being fulfilled within the framework of the reconciliation of interests, and this reconciliation of interests can be clearly separated from the social plan and conciliation board procedures, the requirements of Article 2(1) and (2) CRD are satisfied. If, however, the reconciliation of interests and the social plan (together with the reconciliation board procedure) are inextricably linked so that the consultation required by Article 2(1) and (2) CRD becomes part of negotiations over the social plan, then the latter are to be considered part of consultation within the meaning of the Directive, even though the Directive does not *per se* require a duty to reach agreement.[53]

2. Duty of Information

24. In preparation for consultation – namely 'to enable the workers' representatives to make constructive proposals' – the employer, pursuant to Article 2(3) CRD, must supply workers' representatives with **all relevant information** (lit. a) and **notify them in writing** about certain specified issues.[54] The list of topics about which the employer must notify the workers in writing 'in any event'[55] includes:[56]

i.   the reasons for the projected redundancies;

ii. the number of categories of workers to be made redundant;

---

52   Thus rightly M. Franzen, *ZfA* 2006, 437, 450 sq.; H. Oetker/C. Schubert, in *EAS*, B 8300 para. 417. With doubt, though, C. Weber, *Festschrift für Richardi*, 470.

53   To this effect rightly M. Franzen, *ZfA* 2006, 437, 451–455; differently C. Weber, *AuR* 2008, 365, 371 sq.; id., *Festschrift für Richardi*, 470–472; R. Giesen, *SAE* 2006, 135, 137 sq.; H. Oetker/C. Schubert, in *EAS*, B 8300 para. 417.

54   The 1992 revision inserted Nos. v. and vi and included the obligation in Nos. ii. and iii. to provide for the 'categories' of workers to be made redundant.

55   The listed topics of information only provide for a minimum. It may thus be doubted whether the legislature intended a restriction to such issues that the employer can control and over which he can consequently negotiate as M. Franzen, *ZfA* 2006, 437, 443 sq. suggests.

56   The group of undertakings-clause of Article 2(4) CRD as inserted 1992 cuts off the defence of the subsidiary that it had not received the necessary information from the controlling undertaking.

iii. the number and categories of workers normally employed;

iv. the period over which the projected redundancies are to be effected;

v. the criteria proposed for the selection of the workers to be made redundant in so far as national legislation and/or practice confers that power upon the employer; and

vi. the method for calculating any redundancy payments other than those arising out of national legislation and/or practice.

25. The different terms 'information' and 'notification' in Article 2(3) CRD and in the subheading of Section II do not refer to qualitatively different subjects but rather appear to have been chosen on grounds of linguistic convenience or elegance; this interpretation is also supported by other language versions (*Auskunft/Information; renseignements/communiquer par écrit*). In substance, the duty to inform in lit. a) provides for a general clause. The catalogue of lit. b) provides for minimum requirements and qualifies the general duty to inform in that the information must be given in writing. The general duty of lit. a) does not require information to be given in writing, yet, such requirement may follow from the purpose of the duty, e.g. with regard to the complexity of the subjects covered.

26. The information is to be provided **'in good time** during the course of the consultations'. While on the one hand, it seems to be desirable for the workers' representatives to be involved as early as possible during the proceedings, meaningful consultation requires a certain degree of concreteness and definiteness. The purpose of the consultation of avoiding redundancies where possible (see paras. 19 sq. above) and the purpose of the information of allowing the workers' representatives to make constructive proposals (see para. 24 above) indicate that the information should normally be given at the beginning of the consultation.[57] Yet it will sometimes not be practically possible for the employer to specify all information at the beginning; certain information may have to be updated during the course of the consultation process. In the words of the Court: 'the logic of [Article 2(3)] is that the employer is to supply to the workers' representatives the relevant information throughout the course of the consultations. Flexibility is essential, given, first, that that information may become available only at various stages in the consultation process, which implies that the employer both can and must add to the information supplied in the course of that process. Secondly, the purpose of the employer being under that obligation is to enable the workers' representatives to participate in the consultation process as fully and effectively as possible, and, to achieve that, any new relevant information must be supplied up to the end of the process'.[58] The employer's obligation to provide information is thus **dynamic**.

---

[57]   C. Bourn, *IJCLLIR* 9 (1993), 227, 235 sq.

[58]   ECJ Case C-44/08 *AEK* v. *Fujitsu Siemens* [2009] ECR I-8163 para. 53.

27. The employer is obliged to give a **copy** of the written communication which covers 'at least' the elements of nos. i. to v. to the competent public authority, Article 2(3)(2) CRD (see in detail paras. 33–37 below). The workers' representatives receive a copy of the notice given to the competent authority. This enables the workers' representatives to make use of their right to 'send any comments they may have' to the competent authority, Article 3(2) CRD.

3. Experts

28. Other than the Commission's proposal, the Directive does not provide for a right for workers' representatives to call upon the services of an expert, but rather leaves it to the Member States to provide for such a right, Article 2(2)(2) CRD. The provision does not amount to more than an explicit suggestion, as the same would already follow from the minimum standard clause of Article 5 CRD.

4. Groups of Undertakings

29. As described in the AKZO case at the beginning of this chapter (para. 1 above), decisions for restructuring an undertaking that is part of a group of undertakings are often made by 'an undertaking controlling the employer'.[59] The employer, who is obliged to provide information, may thus merely be the instrument implementing a decision which has been taken at another level of the company. Pursuant to the clause contained in Article 2(4) CRD, this does not relieve the employer from his information and consultation duties.[60] If workers or their representatives allege a breach of these duties, it will be no defence for the employer to argue that the necessary information had not been provided to him by the undertaking which took the decision leading to collective redundancies. However, Article 2(4) CRD does not also make the parent undertaking responsible. Addressee of the obligations under the Directive is only the *employer*.[61] This responsibility is irrespective of whether the collective redundancies were the employer's choice or whether the employer has been informed in due time.[62]

30. **Timing is of the essence** where groups of undertakings are concerned. The employer's obligation to commence consultation and inform the employee representatives 'in good time' (see para. 26 above) may prove particularly

---

[59]   On the definition of 'control', see G. Forst, *ZESAR* 2010, 154, 160 (an influence, based on legal relations, which allows the parent company to compel the other to effect the redundancies).

[60]   See also C. Bourn, *IJCLLIR* 9 (1993), 227, 236 sq.

[61]   R. Resch, *ZESAR* 2010, 35, 42 (suggesting as a rationale that the employees of different subsidiaries of a group have disparate interests).

[62]   ECJ Case C-44/08 *AEK* v. *Fujitsu Siemens* [2009] ECR I-8163 paras. 42 sqq., 57 sq.

difficult to perform, as the *AEK* v. *Fujitsu Siemens* case illustrates.[63] If, in a group of undertakings, the parent company adopts a strategic decision or a change of activity which compels the employer (i.e. the subsidiary) to contemplate or plan collective redundancies, this gives rise to the employer's duty to initiate consultations pursuant to Article 2(1) CRD. The obligation does not arise, though, until the subsidiary within which collective redundancies may be made, has been identified. This duty arises irrespective of whether the employer knows of the parent company's decision. Moreover, it is not dependent upon whether the employer is able to supply the information required by Article 2(3) CRD.

31. While the systematic location of paragraph (4) in Article 2 CRD indicates that the provision only applies with regard to the employer's duties to inform and consult, its wording ('notification', 'requirements laid down by this directive') implies that it also applies with regard to the duty to notify the competent authority pursuant to Article 3 CRD; this interpretation is also supported by teleological considerations.

5. Sanctions

32. The Directive does not specifically provide for sanctions for a breach of the information and consultation duties.[64] Yet, a framework for such sanctions follows from the duties of implementation: to enforce rights determined by Union law in a way equivalent to the enforcement of comparable rights under national law (principle of equivalence) and to provide for effective sanctions (principle of effectiveness) (see §1 paras. 65 sq. above).[65] In its decision in *Junk,* the Court did not expressly address the issue of sanctions but referred to it indirectly in holding that 'an employer is entitled to carry out collective redundancies after the conclusion of the consultation procedure provided for in Article 2 of the directive and after notification of the projected collective redundancies as provided for in Articles 3 and 4 of that directive'.[66] This does not prescribe specific sanctions but indicates that redundancies effected before consultation and notification may not be regarded as effective (be it that they are void or unenforceable under national law).[67] However, since the issue of

---

[63]   ECJ Case C-44/08 *AEK* v. *Fujitsu Siemens* [2009] ECR I-8163 with a note by R. Resch, *ZESAR* 2010, 35–43.

[64]   For a critical viewpoint see M. Weiss, *RdA* 1992, 367, 370 sq. See also C. Bourn, *IJCLLIR* 9 (1993), 227, 240 sq. discussing plans to concretise the sanctions of (today's) Article 6 CRD so as to provide for the ineffectiveness of the mass dismissal.

[65]   Specifically for the CRD ECJ Case C-383/92 *Commission* v. *United Kingdom* [1994] ECR I-2479 para. 40.

[66]   ECJ Case C-188/03 *Junk* [2005] ECR I-885 paras. 54, 41.

[67]   To the same effect already C. Bourn, *IJCLLIR* 9 (1993), 227, 240 sq.; further B. Reinhard, *RdA* 2007, 207, 211–214; K. Riesenhuber/R. Domröse, *NZA* 2005, 568, 569; M. Franzen, *Festschrift für Birk*, 110.

sanctions was not decided by the Court in that case, it is only an *obiter dictum*. Moreover, the Directive's legislative history argues compellingly against such a conclusion. The EU legislator had indeed considered imposing the sanction that collective redundancies carried out without prior consultation should be null and void. This proposal met with strong opposition and the legislator ultimately decided against it.[68]

IV. NOTIFICATION AND BLOCKING PERIOD FOR REDUNDANCIES

33. The employer must notify the competent authority – determined by the national law of the Member States – about the projected collective redundancies, Article 3(1) CRD. Redundancies cannot take effect before the expiry of a blocking period of at least 30 and at most 60 days after the notification, Article 4(1) CRD. The obligation to notify and the blocking period **aim** to give the competent authority an opportunity to 'seek solutions to the problems raised by the projected collective redundancies', Article 4(2) CRD.

1. Content of the Notification

34. Article 3(1)(3) CRD describes the **content** of the notification in the form of a general clause as 'all relevant information concerning the projected collective redundancies and the consultations with workers' representatives' and thus determines it with a view to the tasks assigned to the public authority under Article 4(2) CRD. Article 3(1)(3) CRD further concretises this obligation by a non-exhaustive ('particularly') list pursuant to which the notification must contain

- the reasons for the redundancies (conforms with Article 2(3)(b)(i) CRD),
- the number of workers to be made redundant (conforms with Article 2(3)(b)(ii) CRD),
- the number of workers normally employed (conforms with Article 2(3)(b)(iii) CRD), and
- the period over which the redundancies are to be effected (conforms with Article 2(3) lit b)(iv) CRD).

The notification must thus cover the facts which are essential for the application of the provisions on collective redundancies (under Article 1 CRD) and also the basic data needed by the authority for it to perform the tasks assigned to it by Article 4(2) CRD.

---

[68] C. Barnard, *EC Employment Law*, 684 sq. S. Deakin/G. Morris, *Labour Law*, para. 9.42 with note 490; C. Weber, *AuR* 2008, 365, 377 sq.

35. The employer must further forward to the competent authority in excerpts a copy of the written communication to the workers' representatives, Article 2(3)(2) CRD (see para. 27 above). As the systematic context reveals, this information is not, however, intended to enable the competent authority to perform its tasks under Article 4(2) CRD; if that had been intended, the legislator would presumably have included the issue in Article 3(1)(3) CRD. Requiring the employer to produce a copy of the written communication rather indicates that the legislator intended the competent authority to supervise compliance with the duty to inform under Article 2(3) CRD.[69]

2. Time for Notification

36. The relevant time for notification can only be indirectly inferred from the Directive.[70] As Article 3(1) CRD refers to *projected* collective redundancies and as 'redundancies' refers to the notice (rather than to the actual cessation of the employment relationship; see para. 19 above), it follows that the relevant supervisory body must be notified **before the redundancies are effected**, i.e. before the employer declares his intent to terminate the employment relationships. This interpretation is not only supported by the wording of the Directive, but also by the purpose of the blocking period of giving the competent authority (at least) 30 days to find solutions to the problems raised by the collective redundancies (Article 4(2) CRD). The Court has not expressed the decisive consideration very clearly though, which is that the legislator considered the blocking period of 30 days pursuant to Article 4(1)(1) CRD as a minimum period, leaving longer notice periods applicable to individual workers unaffected. This presupposes that the blocking period and any other applicable notice periods start running at the same time. As the Court correctly said, 'an employer is entitled to carry out collective redundancies ... after notification of the projected collective redundancies'[71] – but not before that.

37. It is a separate question whether notification must be given before or **after consultation**. There is no doubt that notification cannot precede consultation as, pursuant to Article 3(1)(3) CRD, it has to contain, *inter alia*, information concerning 'the consultation with workers' representatives'. Some authors consider that notification may be given *during* the consultation. They point out that the contents of information and notification correlate (Article 2(3), Article 3(1)(3)); that the workers' representatives receive a copy of the notification and may send comments to the competent authority (Article 3(3)); and that the blocking period of Article 4(1) has to be used by the competent authority to find

---

[69] Thus also H. Oetker/C. Schubert, in *EAS,* B 8300 para. 418.
[70] ECJ Case C-188/03 *Junk* [2005] ECR I-885.
[71] ECJ Case C-188/03 *Junk* [2005] ECR I-885 para. 54.

solution for the problems raised by the projected collective redundancies.[72] These considerations are, however, by no means compelling and they also lack teleological support. That the contents of information and notification are similar is due to the fact that they pursue *similar* objectives. The duty to give copies of written communication as well as the notification serve as a control of the consultation and notification processes, the implementation of which can thus be exerted by the competent authority and the workers' representatives (see paras. 27 and 35 above). And as the workers' representatives are not a body set up specifically for the consultation process, the fact that they receive a copy of the notification cannot support the conclusion that consultation does not have to be completed at that time. The decisive consideration is, though: The competent authority does not have to be involved in the consultation and the employer is under no obligation to negotiate with the competent authority with a view to avoiding redundancies. Instead, the employer, after informing and consulting with the workers' representatives, makes a decision about collective redundancies and the competent authority has to *deal with this decision* as a fact. It is thus not only unnecessary for consultation to be ongoing at the time of notification but, on the contrary, consultation should be completed and the employer should have come to a final decision about the collective redundancies at the point of notification.[73] On the basis of the same considerations, it cannot be considered that 'the sooner [the competent authority knows] the better'.[74] Indeed, an early notification about plans that ultimately do not come to fruition would only cause unnecessary work. The legislator considered that a period of 30 days should normally suffice for the competent authority to complete its tasks; while the national law of a Member State may reduce this period, an extension is permitted only under narrow conditions (see para. 39 below). Only this period of time is also covered by the blocking period.

3. The Blocking Period for Redundancies

38. Pursuant to Article 4(1) CRD, projected redundancies shall take effect not earlier than 30 days after notification of the competent authority. The purpose of this blocking period is to give the competent authority sufficient time to seek **solutions** to the problems raised by the collective redundancies, Article 4(2) CRD.[75] The provision also contains a **first sanction** for delay or omission of notification. As a rule, redundancies shall take effect not earlier than 30 days

---

72   M. Franzen, *ZfA* 2006, 437, 456 sq.; C. Weber, *AuR* 2008, 365, 371.
73   To the same effect S. Klumpp, *NZA* 2007, 703, 706 sq.; also *Arbeitsgericht* (Labour Court, ArbG) Berlin, *NZA* 2006, 739, 743; F. Temming, 'Offene Fragen im Verhältnis zwischen Konsultationsverfahren und Zeitpunkt der Massenentlassungsanzeige', *ZESAR* 2010, 277, 282 sq.; differently R. Giesen, *SAE* 2006, 135, 138.
74   Thus C. Weber, *AuR* 2008, 365, 371.
75   ECJ Case C-188/03 *Junk* [2005] ECR I-885 paras. 47 sq., 51.

after notification. Provisions regarding individual rights with regard to notice of dismissal remain unaffected. Apart from that, the Directive leaves Member States with considerable discretion for implementation, subject to a combination of time limits provided by the Directive and options for their extension or abbreviation.

39. The blocking period to be determined by the national law of the Member States runs for a **minimum of 30 days** and a maximum of 60 days, Articles 4(1)(1) and (3) CRD. National law may additionally authorise the competent authority **to reduce and to extend** the blocking period. It may authorise a reduction without any further requirements, Article 4(1)(2) CRD. As a protection of entrepreneurial freedom, the possibility of extending the blocking period is limited in two ways. First, the period may under no circumstances be extended beyond 60 days (in other words, it may not be extended at all where national law already provides for an initial period of 60 days). And secondly, the period of extension may only be granted where the problems raised by the projected collective redundancies are not likely to be solved within the initial period, Article 4(3)(1) CRD. The employer must then be informed about the extension and the grounds for it before the expiry of the initial period, Article 4(3)(3) CRD. This would be a convincing balancing of the conflicting interests, but for the provision of Article 4(3)(2) CRD which, without any qualification, allows Member States to grant the competent authority wider, unconditional powers of extension. If that is to make any sense in the context of the other provisions of Article 4, we must assume that the formal and substantive restrictions of Article 4(3) subparagraphs 1 and 3 CRD also apply. Furthermore, Article 4(3)(1) CRD expresses the legislator's evaluation that a period of 60 days will suffice even in complicated cases to find 'solutions to the problems raised'; an extension beyond 60 days may thus only be granted in truly exceptional cases. Finally, the decision to reduce or extend the blocking period taken by the competent authority under the applicable national law must be guided by the purpose of the Directive. The discretion of the competent authority is thus subject to control by the Court of Justice which – as in comparable cases – may scrutinise whether the national authority has manifestly exceeded its powers.[76]

40. The Directive provides for an initial sanction for non-compliance with the duty to notify the competent authority, by way of the rule that redundancies may not take effect before the expiry of the blocking period (see already para. 38 above). If we consider this provision in light of its purpose of guaranteeing the competent authority a period of 30 days for seeking solutions, this sanction could suffice as an effective implementation. Consequently, it could also suffice for the employer to

---

[76] See e.g. ECJ Case 174/82 *Sandoz* [1983] ECR 2445 paras. 15–20 ('wide discretion' and 'proportionality'); and, respectively, for the Union legislature: Case C-84/94 *United Kingdom v. Council* [1996] ECR I-5755 paras. 50–67.

notify the competent authority after he has already given notice to the workers: his failure to give prior notice would be sanctioned by the blocking period. That was indeed the way in which the German legislature chose to implement the Directive. The Court emphasised, though, that Member States must also follow the **temporal sequence of notification and redundancies** (see para. 36 above) as laid down by the Directive. It therefore held that 'an employer is entitled to carry out collective redundancies ... after notification of the projected collective redundancies as provided for in Articles 3 and 4'[77] (see already para. 19 above on the consultation procedure). More specifically, it has held that 'an employer cannot terminate contracts of employment before he has engaged in the two procedures in question'.[78] In order to effectively implement these requirements into national law, redundancies must be considered ineffective if the employer has given notice before making the required notification to the competent authority.[79] At the same time, the 30 day period merely prevents the redundancies from becoming *effective*. The employer may, in other words, give notice after having notified the competent authority but before the expiry of the blocking period.[80]

V.   SANCTIONS AND ENFORCEMENT OF RIGHTS

41. Apart from the specific exception of the blocking period (see para. 38 above), the Directive does not specifically provide for sanctions. Pursuant to Article 6 CRD, Member States must ensure 'that judicial and/or administrative procedures for the enforcement of obligations under this Directive are available to the workers' representatives and/or workers'. The Directive thus leaves a wide margin of discretion to Member States. In particular, it does not prescribe whether its duties be implemented in the form of individual or collective rights[81] – although the Court has emphasised the 'collective nature' of the right to information and consultation.[82] However, the general duties of implementation provide for a framework of obligations (principles of equivalence and effectiveness; see §1 paras. 65 sq.; see also para. 40).[83] The Court has accepted that a requirement of national law pursuant to which complaints may only be raised if (1) the workers' representatives have first raised objections and (2) the worker concerned has informed the employer in advance of his intention to

---

[77]   ECJ Case C-188/03 *Junk* [2005] ECR I-885 para. 54.

[78]   ECJ Case C-188/03 *Junk* [2005] ECR I-885 para. 41.

[79]   The details – such as the question whether the invalidity or ineffectiveness means that the employer cannot invoke the notice of dismissal – are to be determined by the national laws of the Member States. B. Reinhard, *RdA* 2007, 207, 210; critically C. Weber, *AuR* 2008, 365, 375.

[80]   ECJ Case C-188/03 *Junk* [2005] ECR I-885 para. 53; B. Boemke, in *EAS,* B 7100 para. 68; B. Reinhard, *RdA* 2007, 207, 209.

[81]   AG Mengozzi, Opinion in Case C-12/08 *Mono Car Styling* [2009] ECR I-6653 pts. 53–107.

[82]   ECJ Case C-12/08 *Mono Car Styling* [2009] ECR I-6653 paras. 38 sqq.

[83]   ECJ Case C-12/08 *Mono Car Styling* [2009] ECR I-6653 paras. 48 sq.

challenge compliance with the information and consultation procedure, is compatible with Articles 6 and 2 CRD and the implementation obligations.[84] Furthermore, such a requirement does not violate the general principle (and fundamental right) of effective judicial protection.[85]

VI. IMPLEMENTATION[86]

42. In **Germany**, the provisions of §§17 sq. Protection Against Unfair Dismissals Act (*Kündigungsschutzgesetz*, KSchG)[87] and, §§111–113 Works Constitution Act (*Betriebsverfassungsgesetz*, BetrVG) in respect of information and consultation[88] serve to implement the Directive.[89] With regard to 'terminations ... which occur on the employer's initiative', the provisions exceed the requirements of the Directive. In implementation, the temporal sequence of consultation, notification and termination proved to be problematic; it had initially been misconceived by the German implementing measures.[90]

43. Implementation in **other Member States**,[91] was also partly delayed or defective, and the Commission instituted several proceedings for infringement of the Treaty.[92]

VII. THE EXAMPLE OF THE *JUNK* CASE[93]

44. Mrs Junk was employed as a care assistant and domestic carer by the company AWO Gemeinnützige Pflegegesellschaft Südwest mbH (AWO). AWO,

---

[84] ECJ Case C-12/08 *Mono Car Styling* [2009] ECR I-6653 paras. 32–45.

[85] ECJ Case C-12/08 *Mono Car Styling* [2009] ECR I-6653 paras. 46–52.

[86] For a comparative discussion of (disparate) underlying values, (equivalent) results and methods of and frameworks for implementation, see F. Gaudu, *ELLJ* 2 (2011), 5–26.

[87] Bilingual German-English version in S. Lingemann/R. v. Steinau-Steinrück/A. Mengel (eds.), *Employment and Labour Law in Germany,* Part II, V.

[88] Bilingual German-English version in S. Lingemann/R. v. Steinau-Steinrück/A. Mengel (eds.), *Employment and Labor Law in Germany,* Part II, X.

[89] B. Boemke, in *EAS*, B 7100 paras. 23–58, 71–87 and 91–109; R. Wank, in P. Hanau/H.-D. Steinmeyer/R. Wank (eds.), *Handbuch des europäischen Arbeits- und Sozialrechts*, §18 paras. 205–212; G. Thüsing, *Europäisches Arbeitsrecht*, §6 paras. 5 sq. and 14–23 (discussing transformation deficits).

[90] See in more detail K. Riesenhuber/R. Domröse, *EWS* 2005, 97–103; iid., *NZA* 2005, 568–570.

[91] M. Weiss, *RdA* 1992, 367, 368; G. Wisskirchen/A. Bissels, *ZESAR* 2010, 164–171. For the implementation in the UK see S. Deakin/G. Morris, *Labour Law*, paras. 9.32 sqq.

[92] Infringement proceedings: ECJ Case 215/83 *Commission* v. *Belgium* [1985] ECR 1039; Case C-383/92 *Commission* v. *United Kingdom* [1994] ECR I-2479; Case 91/81 *Commission* v. *Italy* [1982] ECR 2133; Case 131/84 *Commission* v. *Italy* [1985] ECR 3531. On the deficient implementation in the UK, see A. M. Lofaso, *YEL* 16 (1996), 277, 295–301.

[93] ECJ Case C-188/03 *Junk* [2005] ECR I-885.

which had approximately 430 employees, was in the business of providing domestic care services. A works council had been established within the company. On 31 January 2002, AWO lodged a request to open insolvency proceedings on grounds of financial difficulties. Effective 1 February 2002, it released all of its employees from their obligation to work and did not pay them any remuneration for January 2002. Insolvency proceedings were initiated thereafter. By letter dated 19 June 2002, which was received the same day, the liquidator informed the chairman of the works council that, as a consequence of the closure of the company, he intended to terminate all remaining contracts of employment, including that of Mrs Junk, in compliance with the maximum three-month period of notice laid down in the insolvency proceedings, that is to say, effective 30 September 2002, and to carry out a collective redundancy. Attached to the letter was a list containing the names, addresses, dates of birth and other information of the workers who were to be made redundant. By letter dated 26 June 2002, the chairman of the works council informed the liquidator that it was also eager to see the matter resolved swiftly. By letter dated 27 June 2002, which Mrs Junk received on 29 June 2002, the liquidator terminated her contract of employment effective 30 September 2002 on grounds relating to the business. By letter dated 27 August 2002, which was received on the same date, the liquidator notified the labour office that 172 employees were to be made redundant effective 30 September 2002, in accordance with Paragraph 17(3) KSchG. He attached to that notification the opinion of the works council. Mrs Junk challenged her dismissal in the Labour Court and argued that it was ineffective.

45. The *Arbeitsgericht* (Labour Court, ArbG) Berlin[94] referred a question to the Court of Justice whether the term 'redundancies' should be construed as referring to the notice of dismissal as the first act in bringing the employment relationship to an end or to the termination of the employment relationship upon expiry of the notice period. If it referred to the notice of dismissal, the court further wanted to know whether both the consultation procedure (Article 2 CRD) and notification (Articles 3 and 4 CRD) had to be completed before the notices of dismissal were announced.

46. The Court of Justice construed the term 'redundancies' autonomously. The different language versions did not unambiguously say whether it was to be interpreted as giving notice or as termination of employment. However, the fact that Article 2(1) CRD referred to the employer 'contemplating collective redundancies' and that Article 3(1) CRD referred to 'projected redundancies'

---

[94]   The judge responsible for the reference for a preliminary ruling (at the time of the reference, though not at the time of the final decision in the national court) was Oda Hinrichs; see the bibliography before para. 1.

already indicated to the Court that the term 'redundancies' referred to the notice of dismissal rather than the point at which termination was effected. Teleological considerations confirm this interpretation, given that consultation, *inter alia,* serves the purpose of avoiding redundancies. This purpose could be compromised if the employer could give notice of dismissal before entering into consultation. 'Redundancies' thus refers to the notice of dismissal.

47.   This interpretation also paved the way for a reply to the second question. If the consultation procedure was to fulfil its purpose, then it had to be conducted before the employer gave notice of dismissal. The Court further inferred from the wording, system and purpose of the provisions that the competent authority must be notified before the employer gave notice of termination.

§24. THE TRANSFER OF UNDERTAKINGS DIRECTIVE – WITH AN APPENDIX ON THE TAKEOVER DIRECTIVE

CONTENT

Bibliography:

H. Alsbaek, *Der Betriebsübergang und seine individualarbeitsrechtlichen Folgen in Europa* (Berlin: Duncker & Humblot, 2001); C. v. Alvensleben, *Die Rechte der Arbeitnehmer bei Betriebsübergang im Europäischen Gemeinschaftsrecht – Eine Studie zu den gemeinschaftsrechtlichen Grundlagen des §613a BGB* (Baden-Baden: Nomos, 1992); G. Annuß, 'Der Betriebsübergang nach "Ayse Süzen"', *NZA* 1998, 70–77; J. Armour/S. Deakin, 'The Rover Case (2) – Bargaining in the Shadow of TUPE', *ILJ* 29 (2000), 395–402; J. Armour/S. Deakin, 'Insolvency and employment protection: the mixed effects of the Acquired Rights Directive', *Int'l Rev. L. & Econ.* 22 (2003), 1–23; R. Ascheid, 'Richtlinie 77/187/EWG: Harmonisierung europäischen und deutschen Richterrechts', in P. Hanau/R. Herzog/F. Heither (eds.), *Richterliches Arbeitsrecht – Festschrift für Thomas Dieterich zum 65. Geburtstag* (Munich: C.H. Beck, 1999), 9–27; G. Barrett, 'Light Acquired on Acquired Rights: Examining Developments in Employment Rights on Transfers of Undertaking', *CMLR* 42 (2005), 1053–1105; J. H. Bauer, 'Christel Schmidt lässt grüßen: Neue Hürden des EuGH für Auftragsvergabe', *NZA* 2004, 14–17; J. H. Bauer/R. Steinau-Steinrück, 'Neuregelung des Betriebsübergangs: Erhebliche Risiken und viel mehr Bürokratie!', *ZIP* 2002, 457–466; J. H. Bauer/R. v. Steinau-Steinrück v., 'Betriebsübergang: Haftungsrisiken und Handlungsvorschläge', *NZA* 2003, 72–76; D. W. Belling/M. Collas, 'Der Schutz der Arbeitnehmer vor den haftungsrechtlichen Folgen einer Betriebsaufspaltung', *NJW* 1991, 1919–1927; B. Bercusson, Case Comment, *CMLR* 33 (1996), 589–610; C. Bergwitz, 'Betriebsübergang und Insolvenz nach der neuen EG-Richtlinie zur Änderung der Betriebsübergangsrichtlinie', *DB* 1999, 2005–2010; H.

Buchner, 'Die Betriebsübertragung i.S. von §613a BGB im Spannungsfeld von Arbeitsplatzschutz und unternehmerischer Gestaltungsmöglichkeit – Übereinstimmung zwischen EuGH und BAG in der Abgrenzung des Betriebsbegriffs', *JZ* 1999, 593–597; N. Bruun, 'Employees' Participation Rights and Business Restructuring', *ELLJ* 2 (2011), 27–47; H. Collins, 'Dismissals on Transfer of a Business', *ILJ* 15 (1986) 244–255; H. Collins, 'Transfer of Undertakings and Insolvency', *ILJ* 18 (1989), 144–158; N. Colneric, 'Gemeinschaftsrechtliche Informations- und Konsultationspflichten beim Betriebsübergang', in J. F. Baur/K. J. Hopt/K. P. Mailänder (eds.), *Festschrift für Ernst Steindorff* (Berlin/New York: de Gruyter, 1990), 1129–1140; P. Davies, 'Acquired Rights, Creditor's Rights, Freedom of Contract, and Industrial Democracy', *YEL* 9 (1989), 21–53; P. Davies, 'Amendments to the Acquired Rights Directive', *ILJ* 27 (1998), 365–373; P. Davies, 'Taken to the Cleaners? Contracting out of Services yet again', *ILJ* 26 (1997), 193–197; C. De Groot, 'The Council Directive on the Safeguarding of Employees' rights in the event of transfers of undertakings: an Overview of Recent Case Law', *CMLR* 35 (1998), 707–729; B. Debong, *Die EG-Richtlinie über die Wahrung der Arbeitnehmeransprüche bei Betriebsübergang – ein Vergleich ihrer Umsetzung in der Bundesrepublik Deutschland und Frankreich* (Pfaffenweiler: Centaurus, 1988); D. Edward/J. Segan, 'Fragen und Probleme der Anwendung der Betriebsübergangsrichtlinie im Vereinigten Königreich', *RdA* 2006 Special Supplement to issue 6, 15–24; B. Eisele, *Die Richtlinie zum Betriebsübergang und ihre Umsetzung im englischen Recht – eine rechtsvergleichende Analyse* (Tübingen: Köhler, 2003); M. Felsner, *Arbeitsrechtliche Rahmenbedingungen von Unternehmensübernahmen in Europa – eine rechtsvergleichende Untersuchung zur Umsetzung der Richtlinie 77/187/ EWG in Italien sowie in Frankreich, Großbritannien und den Niederlanden, mit einigen Anmerkungen zum deutschen Recht* (Frankfurt a.M. et al.: Lang, 1997); B. W. Feudner, 'Grenzüberschreitende Anwendung von §613a BGB?', *NZA* 1999, 1184–1190; G. Forst, 'Leiharbeitnehmer im Betriebsübergang', *RdA* 2011, 228–236; M. Franzen, *Der Betriebsinhaberwechsel nach §613a BGB im internationalen Arbeitsrecht* (Heidelberg: Müller, 1994); M. Franzen, 'Die Richtlinie 98/50/EG zur Änderung der Betriebsübergangsrichtlinie 77/187/EWG und ihre Auswirkungen auf das deutsche Arbeitsrecht', *RdA* 1998, 361–374; M. Franzen, 'Informationspflichten und Widerspruchsrecht beim Betriebsübergang nach §613a Abs. 5 und 6 BGB', *RdA* 2002, 258–272; M. Franzen, 'Vorgaben des Europäischen Gemeinschaftsrechts für die arbeitsrechtliche Regulierung des Betriebsübergangs', *NZA* 2008 Supplement to issue 4, 139–145; M. Fuchs/M. Merkes, 'Der Begriff des Betriebsübergangs – Analyse und Bestandsaufnahme', *ZESAR* 2010, 257–267; B. Gaul/S. Jeffreys/A. Tinhofer/S. van Wassenhove, *Study on the Application of Directive 2001/23/EC to Cross Border Transfer of Undertakings*, http://ec.europa.eu/employment_social/labour_law/docs/crossborder_en. pdfn; S. Hardy/R. W. Painter, 'The New Acquired Rights Directive and its Implications for European Employee Relations in the Twenty-First Century', *MJ* 6 (1999), 366–379; F. Hartmann, 'Der Schutzzweck der Betriebsübergangsrichtlinie in historisch-rechtsvergleichender Perspektive', *EuZA* 2012, 35–53; B. Hepple, *The Legal Consequences of Cross Border Transfers of Undertakings within the European Union*, http://ec.europa.eu/ employment_social/labour_law/docs/transfer_crossborder_study_hepple_en.pdfn; B. Hepple, 'Workers' Rights in Mergers Rights and Takeovers: The EEC Proposals', *ILJ* 5 (1976), 197–210; J. Hunt, 'Success at last? The Amendment of the Acquired Rights Directive', *E.L. Rev.* 24 (1999) 215–230; J. Hunt, 'The Court of Justice as a Policy Actor:

the Case of the Acquired Rights Directive', *Leg.Stud.* 18 (1998) 336–359; M. Jacobs, 'Die arbeitsvertragliche Bezugnahme auf Tarifverträge bei Betriebsübergang', in H. Konzen et al. (eds.), *Festschrift für Rolf Birk* (Tübingen: Mohr Siebeck, 2008), 243–264; D. Joost, 'Betriebsübergang und Funktionsausgliederung', in R. Anzinger (eds.), *Entwicklungen im Arbeitsrecht und Arbeitsschutzrecht, Festschrift für Otfried Wlotzke zum 70. Geburtstag* (Munich: C.H. Beck, 1996), 683–700; J. Joussen, 'Betriebsübergangsrichtlinie', in H. Oetker/U. Preis (eds.), *Europäisches Arbeits- und Sozialrecht, EAS, part B – Systematische Darstellungen,* loose-leaf (Heidelberg: Forkel, last update: March 2007), B 7200; S. Klumpp, 'Betriebsübergang und Leiharbeit – Urteil des Europäischen Gerichtshofs vom 13.9.2007 – Rechtssache Jouini', *EuZA* 2009, 69–78; R. Krause, 'Das Übergangsmandat des Betriebsrats im Lichte der novellierten Betriebsübergangsrichtlinie', *NZA* 1998, 1201–1206; S. Krebber, 'Die volle Wirksamkeit von Richtlinien', *ZvglRWiss* 97 (1998), 124–160; F. Löw, *Die Betriebsveräußerung im Europäischen Arbeitsrecht – Die EG-Richtlinie 77/187 und ihre Umsetzung in Deutschland und Großbritannien* (Frankfurt a.M. et al.: Lang 1992); M. Löwisch, 'Unvereinbarkeit von Nachträglichkeit und Rückwirkung des Widerspruchs nach §613a Abs. 6 BGB mit der Richtlinie 01/23/EG', in H. Konzen et al. (eds.), *Festschrift für Rolf Birk,* (Tübingen: Mohr Siebeck, 2008), 541–545; J. McMullen, 'An Analysis of the Transfer of Undertakings (Protection of Employment) Regulations 2006', *ILJ* 35 (2006), 113–139; J. McMullen, 'Some Problems and Themes in the Application in Member States of Directive 2001/23/EC on Transfers of Undertakings', *IJCLLIR* 23 (2007), 335–374; J. McMullen, 'TUPE – Sidestepping Süzen', *ILJ* 28 (1999), 360–364; G. More, 'The Concept of 'Undertaking' in the Acquired Rights Directive: the Court of Justice under Pressure (again)', *YEL* 135 (1995), 135–155; M. Novella/M. L. Vallauri, 'Employee Rights on Transfer of Undertakings: Italian Legislation and EC Law', *ELJ* 14 (2008), 55–73; J. Novak, 'Der Betriebsübergang nach einem Systemwechsel in ein neues Arbeits- und Wirtschaftsrecht am Beispiel Sloweniens', *RdA* 2006 Special Supplement to issue 6, 25–30; H. Oetker, 'Die Vorgaben der Betriebsübergangsrichtlinie für die Beteiligungsrechte des Betriebsrats', *NZA* 1998, 1193–1201; H. Oetker/C. Schubert, 'Europäisches Betriebsverfassungsrecht', in H. Oetker/U. Preis (eds.), *Europäisches Arbeits- und Sozialrecht, EAS, part B – Systematische Darstellungen,* loose-leaf (Heidelberg: Forkel, last update: January 2007), B 8300 paras. 444–519; R. Rebhahn, 'Arbeitsrecht bei Betriebsübergang: Eintrittspflicht bei Insolvenz und Haftungsfragen', *JBl* 1999, 621–638 and 710–721; R. Rebhahn, 'Probleme der Ausführung der Betriebsübergangsrichtlinie in Kontinentaleuropa', *RdA* 2006 Special Supplement to issue 6, 4–15; H. Reichold, 'Neues zum grenzüberschreitenden Betriebsübergang', in H. Konzen et al. (eds.), *Festschrift für Rolf Birk* (Tübingen: Mohr Siebeck, 2008), 687–702; K. Riesenhuber, 'Arbeitnehmerschutz durch Information beim Betriebsübergang – Die Information von Arbeitnehmervertretern und Arbeitnehmern durch Veräußerer und Erwerber nach der Betriebsübergangsrichtlinie', in R. Krause/W. Veelken/K. Vieweg (eds.), *Recht der Wirtschaft und der Arbeit in Europa, Gedächtnisschrift für Wolfgang Blomeyer* (Berlin: Duncker & Humblot, 2004), 195–215; K. Riesenhuber, 'Informationspflichten beim Betriebsübergang: Fehler bei der Umsetzung der Richtlinie und Anlass für eine grundsätzliche Neuordnung', *RdA* 2004, 340–352; H. M. Schellhaaß, 'Das Europäische Arbeitsrecht aus ökonomischer Perspektive', in S. Grundmann (ed.), *Systembildung und Systemlücken in Kerngebieten des Europäischen Privatrechts* (Tübingen: Mohr Siebeck, 2000), 401–419; M. Schlachter,

Casebook Europäisches Arbeitsrecht (Baden-Baden: Nomos, 2005), cases No. 12–14; M. Schlachter, 'Betriebsübergang bei "eigenwirtschaftlicher Nutzung" von Betriebsmitteln des Auftraggebers', *NZA* 2006, 80–83; M. Schlachter, 'Die Rechtsstellung des widersprechenden Arbeitnehmers bei Betriebsübergang', *NZA* 1995, 705–711; R. Trümner, 'Mitbestimmungsvorgaben des Europäischen Arbeitsrechts bei Privatisierungen', *Der Personalrat* 1997, 197–205; B. Waas, 'Zur Konsolidierung des Betriebsbegriffs in der Rechtsprechung von EuGH und BAG zum Betriebsübergang', *ZfA* 2001, 377–395; B. Waas/A. Johanns, 'Die Änderung der Richtlinie zum Betriebsübergang', *EuZW* 1999, 458–463; R. Wank, 'Der Betriebsübergang in der Rechtsprechung des EuGH und des BAG – eine methodische Untersuchung', in H. Oetker/U. Preis/V. Rieble (eds.), *Festschrift 50 Jahre BAG* (Munich: C.H. Beck, 2004), 245–263; R. Wank/U. Börgmann, 'Der Übergang "durch Rechtsgeschäft" beim Betriebsübergang', *DB* 1997, 1229–1235; C. Weber, 'Information und Konsultation im europäischen und deutschen Mitbestimmungsrecht', in B. Dauner-Lieb et al. (eds.), *Festschrift für Horst Konzen* (Tübingen: Mohr Siebeck, 2005), 921–956; H. J. Willemsen, 'Europäisches und deutsches Arbeitsrecht im Widerstreit? – Aktuelle "Baustellen" im Recht des Betriebsübergangs', *NZA* 2008 Special Supplement to issue 4, 155–164; H. J. Willemsen/G. Annuß, 'Neue Betriebsübergangsrichtlinie – Anpassungsbedarf im deutschen Recht?', *NJW* 1999, 2073–2079; U. Zachert/E. Kocher, 'Die Richtlinie 98/50/EG zum Betriebsübergang – aus Brüssel, Luxemburg und Kassel etwas Neues?', in K. Schmidt (ed.), *Arbeitsrecht und Arbeitsgerichtsbarkeit – Festschrift zum 50jährigen Bestehen der Arbeitsgerichtsbarkeit in Rheinland-Pfalz* (Neuwied/Kriftel: Luchterhand, 1999), 51–65.

Cases:

ECJ Case 135/83 *Abels* [1985] ECR 469; ECJ Case 19/83 *Wendelboe* [1985] ECR 457; ECJ Case 186/83 *Botzen* [1985] ECR 519; ECJ Case 105/84 *Danmols Inventar* [1985] ECR 2639; ECJ Case 24/85 *Spijkers* [1986] ECR 1119; ECJ Case 237/84 *Commission v. Belgium* [1986] ECR 1247; ECJ Case 235/84 *Commission v. Italy* [1986] ECR 2291; ECJ Case 287/86 *Ny Mølle Kro* [1987] ECR 5465; ECJ Case 324/86 *Daddy's Dance Hall* [1988] ECR 739; ECJ Joined Cases 144/87 and 145/87 *Berg and Busschers* [1988] ECR 2559; ECJ Case 101/87 *Bork* [1988] ECR 3057; ECJ Case C-362/89 *d'Urso* [1991] ECR I-4105; ECJ Case C-209/91 *Rask* [1992] ECR I-5755; ECJ Joined Cases C-132/91, C-138/91 and C-139/91 *Katsikas and others,* [1992] ECR I-6577; ECJ Case C-29/91 *Redmond Stichting* [1992] ECR I-3189; ECJ Case C-392/92 *Christel Schmidt* [1994] ECR I-1311; ECJ Case C-382/92 *Commission v. Vereinigtes Königreich* [1994] ECR I-2435; ECJ Case C-48/94 *Rygaard* [1995] ECR I-2745; ECJ Case C-472/93 *Luigi Spano* [1995] ECR I-4321; ECJ Joined Cases C-171/94 and C-172/94 *Merckx and Neuhuys* [1997] ECR I-1253; ECJ Case C-298/94 *Henke* [1996] ECR I-4989; ECJ Case C-305/94 *Rotsart de Hertaing* [1996] ECR I-5927; ECJ Case C-13/95 *Süzen* [1997] ECR I-1259; ECJ Case C-336/95 *Pedro Burdalo Trevejo* [1997] ECR I-2115; ECJ Case C-319/94 *Dethier Equipement* [1998] ECR I-1061; ECJ Case C-399/96 *Europièces* [1998] ECR I-6965; ECJ Joined Cases C-127/96, C-229/96 and C-74/97 *Vidal and others* [1998] ECR I-8179; ECJ Joined Cases C-173/96 and C-247/96 *Hidalgo and Ziemann* [1998] ECR I-8237; ECJ Case C-234/98 *Allen* [1999] ECR I-8643; ECJ Case C-343/98 *Collino* [2000] ECR I-6659; ECJ Case C175/99 *Mayeur* [2000] ECR I-7755; ECJ Case C-172/99 *Oy Liikenne Ab* [2001] ECR I-745; ECJ Case C-51/00 *Temco Service Industries* [2002] ECR I-969; ECJ Case C-164/00 *Beckmann* [2002] ECR I-4893; ECJ Case C-32/02 *Commission v.*

Italy [2003] ECR I-12063; ECJ Case C-4/01 *Martin* [2003] ECR I-12859; ECJ Case C-340/01 *Abler* [2003] ECR I-14023; ECJ Case C-425/02 *Delahaye* [2004] ECR I-10823; ECJ Case C-297/03 *Sozialhilfeverband Rohrbach* [2005] ECR I-4305; ECJ Case C-478/03 *Celtec* [2005] ECR I-4389; ECJ Joined Cases C-232/04 and C-233/04 *Güney-Görres and Demir* [2005] ECR I-11237; ECJ Case C-499/04 *Werhof* [2006] ECR I-2397; ECJ Case C-458/05 *Jouini* [2007] ECR I-7301; ECJ Case C-313/07 *Kirtruna* [2008] ECR I-7907; ECJ Case C-396/07 *Juuri* [2008] ECR I-8883; ECJ Case C-466/07 *Klarenberg* [2009] ECR I-803; ECJ Case C-561/07 *Commission* v. *Italy* [2009] ECR I-4959; ECJ Case C-151/09 *UGT-FSP* [2010] ECR I-7591; ECJ Case C-386/09 *Briot* [2010] ECR I-8471; ECJ Case C-242/09 *Albron Catering* [2010] ECR I-10309; ECJ Case C-463/09 *CLECE* 20 January 2011; ECJ Case C-108/10 *Scattolon* 6 September 2011.

I. ISSUES, OVERVIEW, COMPETENCE, REGULATORY CONTEXT

1. *Issues and Interests*[1]

1. To transfer an undertaking or business or to merge it with another is, first of all, an **entrepreneurial decision** by its owner. In such cases, it may be in the interests of the parties to the transfer or merger agreement ('the transferor' and 'the transferee') to also transfer the employment relationships. Just as inventories or customer relations may be economically valuable for the transferee, so too, may workers ('human capital'). However, this is not always necessarily true. Where the transferee is already active in the relevant sector, it may intend to generate synergies by using its own employees – who may be specially trained and familiar with his business concept and management – in the new undertaking or business. Also, the transferred undertaking or business, on its own or in combination with the transferee's business, may have too many workers or workers who are not well-qualified. In other cases, it may be in the transferee's interest to keep only individual (selected) workers.[2]

2. The **workers'** interests may also be rather disparate.[3] For them, the employer will often not have any concrete personality or shape so that the owner

---

[1] We can only sketch the interests involved in an abstract and schematic fashion here. See also – with particular reference to the interests involved in case of insolvency – J. Armour/S. Deakin, *ILJ* 29 (2000), 395–402; iid., *Int'l Rev. L. & Econ.* 22 (2003), 1–23 (protection of firm-specific human capital; employee-voice in bargaining process); P. Davies, *YEL* 9 (1989), 21–25; R. Rebhahn, *JBl* 1999, 621, 624 sq., 629–633.

[2] H. M. Schellhaaß, in S. Grundmann (ed.), *Systembildung und Systemlücken in Kerngebieten des Europäischen Privatrechts*, 407 sq.; R. Wank, *Festschrift 50 Jahre BAG*, 245, 255 (on the reassignment of a contract). Cf. ECJ Case C-362/89 *d'Urso* [1991] ECR I-4105 para. 18; AG Geelhoed, Opinion in Case C-51/00 *Temco Service Industries* [2002] ECR I-969 pts. 40, 63 *et passim*.

[3] See e.g. B. Hepple, *ILJ* 5 (1976), 197–203.

of the undertaking or business may be of subordinate relevance. But even where they have chosen their employer specifically when entering into their employment contract, they will usually prefer having their employment relationship transferred together with the undertaking or business rather than being dismissed if their chances on the employment market are limited.

3. If we consider the chances of workers on the labour market, their interest in a transfer of the employment relationship will often be downright **opposite** to those of the transferee. A worker who is in high demand is not afraid of unemployment and would rather negotiate a transfer with the transferor and the transferee. Conversely, the transferee does not place great value on a 'weak' worker; he would more often than not rather choose new workers. As a **matter of economics and policy**, it is rather controversial whether and on the basis of which conditions, the law should provide for a transfer of the employment relationships (with all its rights and obligations) in the case of a transfer of the undertaking or business, particularly where undertakings or businesses are in a crisis.[4] Where an undertaking or business is in a crisis because of its workers or their conditions of employment, a transfer of the employment relationships is liable to exacerbate difficulties in reorganisation.[5] However, the issues involved certainly do not lie exclusively in the legal rules on the transfer of employment relationships. The general laws on unfair dismissal are also highly relevant which, as yet, remain largely unaffected by EU legislation.[6]

4. The European legislator opted for a transfer of the employment relationships together with the undertaking or business. As a matter of **social policy**, this general rule takes account of the workers' interest in continuity of their employment relationship.[7] The transfer should not affect the employees' rights, particularly their rights to unfair dismissal protection, where the business in its concrete structure – the 'substrate' of the employment relationship – continues to exist notwithstanding the transfer.[8] This aspect of continuity is also considered to be a justification *vis-à-vis* the transferee: The burden involved in a transfer of the employment relationship is considered to be the flip-side of the benefit he receives from taking over an entire organisational entity (which

---

4   See only H. M. Schellhaaß, in S. Grundmann (ed.), *Systembildung und Systemlücken in Kerngebieten des Europäischen Privatrechts*, 409–411.

5   D. W. Belling/M. Collas, *NJW* 1991 (1919); R. Rebhahn, *RdA* 2006 Special Supplement to issue 6, 4, 8. Cf. also ECJ Case C-362/89 *d'Urso* [1991] ECR I-4105 para. 18.

6   For a comparative survey on protection against unfair dismissal R. Rebhahn, *ZfA* 2003, 163–235.

7   ECJ Case 24/85 *Spijkers* [1986] ECR 1119 para. 11; R. Wank, *Festschrift 50 Jahre BAG*, 245, 248; R. Rebhahn, *RdA* 2006 Special Supplement to issue 6, 4, 5.

8   Thus F. Hartmann, *EuZA* 2012, 35–53 (based on a historical and comparative discussion of the rationale of the Directive and its predecessors in the national laws of the Member States).

transferee would otherwise have to build up himself).[9] As a matter of **internal market policy**, the effectiveness of the Directive can be doubted. Its effects largely depend upon the – disparate – national laws against unfair dismissal of the Member States which are being perpetuated by the transfer of the employment relationships. Consequently, the Directive does not lead to an approximation of the employment law costs of the transfer of an undertaking or business but rather effects a 'transposition' of those costs.[10]

5.   If a legislator, on a general assessment of the interests, opts for a transfer of the employment relationship with all its rights and obligations as the Union legislator did (see Recital 3 TUD), **further issues** arise and require regulation. Thus, the transfer of the employment relationship needs to be supplemented by a prohibition of dismissal. The position of the workers' representatives needs clarification: On the one hand, it seems consequential to also protect their position. On the other hand, their position may have to be brought in line with the (factual and legal) requirements of the transferee's undertaking. And finally, respect for the workers as subjects and contract partners demands that they should not be moved around like figures on a chess board, but rather be involved in the process through information and consultation.[11] Such rights of employee involvement must however be balanced with the owner's right to make an entrepreneurial decision.

2.   Legislative History and Development

6.   The **connection of the Directive to the internal market** – which had originally been enacted 1977 (as Directive 77/187/EEC; hereinafter TUD 1977)[12] and was based upon Article 100 EEC (Article 115 TFEU)[13] – is not easily understandable. The legislator argued that the new and increasingly

---

[9]   R. Wank, *Festschrift 50 Jahre BAG*, 245, 248 sq.

[10]   R. Rebhahn, *RdA* 2006 Special Supplement to issue 6, 4, 5 and 15 (suggesting that this may be considered the fundamental flaw of the directive's regime). G. Thüsing, *Europäisches Arbeitsrecht*, §5 para. 1 (who, from a German perspective, appears to consider protection against circumvention of the law against unfair dismissal the main purpose of the Directive).

[11]   Cf. No. 18 indent 2 CFSR; on the CFSR, see §2 para. 65 above. For other rationales of participation rights ('industrial democracy'; a discrete concept of protection of rights, arguably an alternative to the transfer of rights) P. Davies, *YEL* 9 (1989), 21–25.

[12]   Council Directive 77/187/EEC of 14 February 1977 on the approximation of the laws of the Member States relating to the safeguarding of employees' rights in the event of transfers of undertakings, businesses or parts of businesses, OJ 1977 L 61/26. On the development instructively B. Hepple, *ILJ* 5 (1976), 197–210. Proposal for a Directive on the harmonisation of the legislation of Member States on the retention of the rights and advantages of employees in the case of mergers, takeovers and amalgamations, COM(74) 351 final, OJ 1974 C 104/1, also reproduced in RdA 1975, 124 (corrected English version published as COM(74) 351 final/2; see also J. Joussen, in *EAS*, B 7200 paras. 1 sq.

[13]   There does not seem to be doubt as to the Union competence; see e.g. C. v. Alvensleben, *Die Rechte der Arbeitnehmer bei Betriebsübergang im Europäischen Gemeinschaftsrecht*, 124–129.

common phenomenon of restructuring of undertakings (Recital 1 TUD 1977) – through transfer and merger – required that workers were protected, particularly to ensure 'that their rights are safeguarded' (Recital 2 TUD 1977). Differences between the national laws of the Member States should be reduced (Recital 3 TUD 1977). The primary concern was thus to remove distortions of competition which could follow from disparate national standards of protection in the Member States (doubtful with a view to disparate general laws against unfair dismissal in the Member States; see para. 4 above).[14] At the same time, the plans for an approximation of national laws on mergers may also have contributed to the Directive's development. Here, disparate national concepts and standards of worker protection proved to be an obstacle.[15] While the Merger of Companies Directive[16] dealt with issues of company law, the Transfer of Undertakings Directive supplemented it in regard to issues of employment law.[17]

7. In **1998** the legislator revised and amended the original directive in many respects (hereinafter 'TUD 1998').[18] While the amendments may appear to be rather far-reaching in their wording, the amendments were largely only an **implementation of previous case law** of the Court of Justice. A **2001** '**codification**' (hereinafter the 'Transfer of Undertakings Directive' or 'TUD'),[19] adopted 'in the interests of clarity and rationality' (Recital 1 TUD) brought legislation to its current status quo. It did not significantly change the substance of the measure, but rather rearranged the numbering of the Directive.

---

14   ECJ Case C-382/92 *Commission* v. *United Kingdom* [1994] ECR I-2435 para. 15; on the development, see in detail C. v. *Alvensleben, Die Rechte der Arbeitnehmer bei Betriebsübergang im Europäischen Gemeinschaftsrecht*, 87–124; see also P. Davies, *YEL* 9 (1989), 21, 25–29.

15   C. v. Alvensleben, *Die Rechte der Arbeitnehmer bei Betriebsübergang im Europäischen Gemeinschaftsrecht*, 92–94.

16   Originally Third Council Directive 78/855/EEC of 9 October 1978 based on Article 54 (3)(g) of the Treaty concerning mergers of public limited liability companies, OJ 1978 L 295/36. On the Merger Directive see S. Grundmann, *European Company Law*, §28.

17   B. Hepple, *ILJ* 5 (1976), 197, 203–205.

18   Council Directive 98/50/EC of 29 June 1998 amending Directive 77/187/EEC on the approximation of the laws of the Member States relating to the safeguarding of employees' rights in the event of transfers of undertakings, businesses or parts of businesses, OJ 1998 L 201/88. On this directive P. Davies, *ILJ* 27 (1998), 365–373; M. Franzen, *RdA* 1998, 361–374; S. Hardy/R. W. Painter, *MJ* 6 (1999), 366–379; J. Hunt, *E.L. Rev.* 24 (1999), 215–230; B. Waas/A. Johanns, *EuZW* 1999, 458–463; H. J. Willemsen/G. Annuß, *NJW* 1999, 2073–2079.

19   Council Directive 2001/23/EC of 12 March 2001 on the approximation of the laws of the Member States relating to the safeguarding of employees' rights in the event of transfers of undertakings, businesses or parts of undertakings or businesses, OJ 2001 L 82/16. Proposal for a Council Directive on the approximation of the laws of the Member States relating to the safeguarding of employees' rights in the event of transfers of undertakings, businesses or parts of undertakings or businesses, COM(2000) 259 final.

8. Following a 2007 report on the impact of the Directive (cf. Article 10 TUD)[20], the Commission is currently considering further revising the Directive.[21] Central to its potential revision is ensuring that **cross-border transfers of undertakings** and businesses are covered by the Directive.[22] Strengthening the rights to information and consultation is also being discussed.[23]

3. Overview of the Directive

9. The Transfer of Undertakings Directive applies to private and public undertakings which pursue an economic activity. The central instrument of protection is the transfer of the rights and obligations from the existing employment relationships to the transferee. In addition, the Directive protects workers against dismissal. Existing bodies for worker representation are maintained, so long as the undertaking or business which is being transferred maintains its independence. Workers are involved in the process through information and consultation.

4. Regulatory Context

10. Other **legislative acts on measures of restructuring** and their effects in employment law are part of the regulatory context. For one thing, the Transfer of Undertakings Directive is the employment law counterpart of the company law directives on mergers[24] and divisions[25] of companies. The directives on employee involvement in the Societas Europaea (SE; §29) and on cross-border mergers (§30) provide for specific rules, and so does the preliminary draft for a directive on the cross-border transfer of the company seat (§31). The Collective Redundancies Directive (§23) also deals with the consequences in employment

---

[20] Commission Report on Council Directive 2001/23/EC of 12 March 2001 on the approximation of the laws of the Member States relating to the safeguarding of employees' rights in the event of transfers of undertakings, businesses or parts of undertakings or businesses, COM(2007) 334 final.

[21] The Commission has initiated the first phase consultation of the social partners in June under Article 138(2) EC (Article 154(2) TFEU) in June 2007; http://ec.europa.eu/social/BlobServlet?docId=2442&langId=en.

[22] See the Study by B. Gaul/S. Jeffreys/A. Tinhofer/S. van Wassenhove, 'Study on the Application of Directive 2001/23/EC to Cross Border Transfer of Undertakings', available at http://ec.europa.eu/social/BlobServlet?docId=2445&langId=en, and B. Hepple, 'The Legal Consequences of Cross Border Transfers of Undertakings within the European Union', available at http://ec.europa.eu/social/BlobServlet?docId=2446&langId=en; see H. Reichold, *Festschrift für Birk*, 687–702; on the current state of legislation, see the references para. 55 below.

[23] See e.g. J. McMullen, *IJCLLIR* 23 (2007), 335, 372 sq.; N. Bruun, *ELLJ* 2(2011), 27–47.

[24] See note 16 above.

[25] Sixth Council Directive 82/891/EEC of 17 December 1982 based on Article 54(3)(g) of the Treaty, concerning the division of public limited liability companies, OJ 1982 L 378/47.

law of the restructuring of an undertaking. While insolvency cannot properly be considered to be a structural measure, it may still have similar consequences for the workers; issues of employee protection are regulated in the Insolvency Protection Directive (§25). The Transfer of Undertakings Directive is also connected with dismissal protection, and here the various anti-discrimination directives (§§8–11) form part of the relevant regulatory context.

11. Alongside freedom of movement for workers and anti-discrimination, the Transfer of Undertakings Directive is probably the legislative measure that has lead to the largest number of **decisions of the Court of Justice** in the area of employment law. This is partly due to the economic relevance of the Directive. However, another reason for the volume of case law in this field is that the wording and systematic organisation of the Directive's rules (and probably also its purpose) was rather vague and unclear, even in the original 1977 Directive but also following later revisions. The Court's jurisprudence has also often raised more questions than it has answered, partly because of the Court's frequently unsound method of analysis.

II. SCOPE OF PROTECTION: TRANSFER OF AN UNDERTAKING

1. *Personal Scope of Protection*

a) Worker

12. The Directive addresses conceptual issues poorly. It defines the substantive scope of the Directive's application in Article 1 but not its personal scope. Instead, the personal scope can only be inferred from the substantive rules of protection (in particular Article 3 TUD), together with the definitions of Article 2 TUD. They reveal that the personal scope of protection is limited to **employees.**

13. As to the concept of employees, Article 2(1)(d) TUD in principle refers to the national laws of the Member States: 'employee' shall mean any person who, in the Member State concerned, is protected as an employee under national employment law.[26] Paragraph 2 subparagraph 1 of the provision expressly emphasises that the Directive is without prejudice to national law as regards the definition of contract of employment or employment relationship. Thus, in Germany, for example, civil servants are not covered as they do not qualify as

---

[26]   ECJ Case C-164/00 *Beckmann* [2002] ECR I-4893 para. 27.

employees under national law.[27] The provision, which was introduced in 1998, confirms previous case law of the Court of Justice:[28] Given that the Directive was merely aimed at partial harmonisation, the Court had **not interpreted** the term 'employee' **autonomously.**[29]

14. However, Article 2(2)(2) TUD at least sets a **framework** for national concepts. Member States may not exclude part-time, fixed-term or temporary agency[30] employment relationships from the scope of the Directive. Further limitations follow from the general duties of implementation (see §1 paras. 65 sq.).

b) Public and Private Undertakings

15. The Transfer of Undertakings Directive applies to 'public and private undertakings engaged in economic activities whether or not they are operating for gain', (Article 1(1)(c) sent. 1 TUD).[31] The Court defines an 'undertaking' as 'any economic entity organised on a stable basis, whatever its legal status and method of financing. Any grouping of persons and assets enabling the exercise of an economic activity pursuing a specific objective and which is sufficiently structured and independent will therefore constitute such an entity (...).The term 'economic activity' appearing in the definition given in the above paragraph covers any activity consisting in offering goods or services on a given market (...).'[32] If one accepts a need for protection of employees, then application of the Directive to public undertakings is naturally consequent. However, with regard to public undertakings, the rationale of avoiding distortions of competition (see

---

[27]   F. Marhold, in M. Fuchs/F. Marhold (eds.), *Europäisches Arbeitsrecht*, 182. See also ECJ Case C-343/98 *Collino* [2000] ECR I-6659 para. 40.

[28]   Recital 6 to Directive 98/50/EC.

[29]   ECJ Case C-343/98 *Collino* [2000] ECR I-6659 paras. 36–39; Joined Cases C-173/96 and C-247/96 *Hidalgo and Ziemann* [1998] ECR I-8237 para. 24; Case 105/84 *Danmols Inventar* [1985] ECR 2639 paras. 23–27. Critically G. Barrett, *CMLR* 42 (2005), 1053, 1084–1090; F. Marhold, in M. Fuchs/F. Marhold (eds.), *Europäisches Arbeitsrecht*, 182 sq. (wrongly considering a discrepancy with the applicability of the Directive also to 'public undertakings'; different from his considerations [at 183] the possibility of excluding whole groups of employees from the protective scope of the Directive is strictly limited by the transposition duties); R. Rebhahn, *RdA* 2006 Special Supplement to issue 6, 4, 9 sq. (leads to distortions of competition; narrow definition in national law as a competitive advantage).

[30]   For the definitions of temporary work and temporary agency work, the legislator refers to the Temporary Work Health and Safety Directive; see §19 above. See also ECJ Case C-458/05 *Jouini* [2007] ECR I-7301 para. 36.

[31]   The provision which was introduced in 1989 codifies the Court's jurisprudence; Recital 5 to Directive 98/50/EG; see e.g. ECJ Case C-343/98 *Collino* [2000] ECR I-6659 para. 30; Case C-382/92 *Commission* v. *United Kingdom* [1994] ECR I-2435 paras. 44–46. See B. Bercusson, *CMLR* 33 (1996), 589, 606–609. See also ECJ Case C-32/02 *Commission* v. *Italy* I-12063 para. 24 (deficient transposition).

[32]   ECJ Case C-108/10 *Scattolon* 6 September 2011 paras. 42 sq.

para. 6 above) does not apply with the same force, as public undertakings may often not be in competition to the same extent as private undertakings.

16.   An **exception** – first introduced in 1998 as codification of the Court of Justice's jurisprudence[33] – applies with regard to **administrative reorganisation of public administrative authorities** and the transfer of administrative functions between public administrative authorities, (Article 1(1)(c) sent. 2 TUD). However, this exception only applies if the activity in question involves the *exercise of public authority.*[34]

17.   The exercise of **public powers** does not cover advertising and information activities of a municipality,[35] or measures of care for persons in need,[36] or cleaning services.[37] Similarly, the transfer of telecommunication services which have hitherto been publicly administered to a private company by way of a concession is not outside the scope of application of the Directive, even if the transferee undertaking has been established by another public body.[38] Again, the Directive also applies where a public contract – e.g. for the provision of bus services – has been awarded in public procurement procedures – whether or not those procedures have been determined by the EU procurement directives – to another undertaking, as long as it does not involve the exercise of public authority.[39]

18.   Finally, the Directive provides for a specific exclusion – apparently introduced and maintained as a result of pressure from Denmark and Greece –[40] for **seagoing vessels.**

2.   *Substantive Scope of Application*

19.   The Transfer of Undertakings Directive applies where an undertaking or business is (a) being transferred (b) to another employer (c) as a result of a legal

---

[33]   ECJ Case C-425/02 *Delahaye* [2004] ECR I-10823 para. 30; Case C-175/99 *Mayeur* [2000] ECR I-7755 para. 28; Case C-343/98 *Collino* [2000] ECR I-6659 para. 31; Case C-298/94 *Henke* [1996] ECR I-4989 paras. 13–15. See also G. Barrett, *CMLR* 42 (2005), 1053, 1069–1072.

[34]   ECJ Case C-108/10 *Scattolon* 6 September 2011 paras. 53 sqq.; Case C-343/98 *Collino* [2000] ECR I-6659 para. 32; Joined Cases C-173/96 and C-247/96 *Hidalgo and Ziemann* [1998] ECR I-8237 para. 24.

[35]   ECJ Case C-175/99 *Mayeur* [2000] ECR I-7755 (taking over of the activities of information and advertising by a private association which had hitherto been performed by the municipality itself).

[36]   ECJ Joined Cases C-173/96 and C-247/96 *Hidalgo and Ziemann* [1998] ECR I-8237 para. 24.

[37]   ECJ Case C-108/10 *Scattolon* 6 September 2011 paras. 44 sqq.

[38]   ECJ Case C-343/98 *Collino* [2000] ECR I-6659 paras. 31–33.

[39]   ECJ Case C-172/99 *Oy Liikenne Ab* [2001] ECR I-745 paras. 19–21; Joined Cases C-173/96 and C-247/96 *Hidalgo and Ziemann* [1998] ECR I-8237 paras. 21 and 24.

[40]   M. Franzen, *RdA* 1999, 361, 365.

transfer or merger. There is an optional exception for transfers in the course of insolvency proceedings.

a)   Parties to the Transfer

aa)   Transfer *to another employer*

20.   The Directive only applies where the undertaking or business is being transferred *to another employer* (*Inhaber, employeur*). The legislator deliberately excluded transfer by way of a **share deal** from the scope of the Directive (even though it may be subject to the same rules under national law).[41] The Takeover Directive only partly covers this situation and its rules on employee protection are only rudimentary (see the survey paras. 117–121 below). This is criticised on the ground that the employees' interests in maintaining their jobs (prohibition against dismissal, Article 4 TUD; see paras. 80–82 below) and working conditions (see paras. 83–88) as well as their informational interests (Article 7 TUD, see paras. 89–94 below) may be similarly affected.[42] Indeed, a transfer of the shares of an undertaking may have similarly grave consequences, including asset stripping and breaking-up of the undertaking. Yet, the interests of protection are substantially different. Given that the contract partner (employer) remains unchanged, employees are initially protected both by the binding nature of their employment contracts, potentially limited by the employer's power of direction, and by unfair dismissal protection under national law. **Restructuring within the undertaking** (i.e. without a change of employer) is not covered by the Directive either.[43]

bb)   Determination of the Transferor in Case of 'Agency Work'

21.   The *Albron Catering case,* concerning the transfer of a unit that exclusively used '**(temporary) agency workers**', raised the question of who is the transferor.[44] Within the Heineken International group, all staff are employed by Heineken

---

[41]   See S. Deakin/G. Morris, *Labour Law,* para. 3.75; J. McMullen, *IJCLLIR* 23 (2007), 335, 338 sq. For a critical perspective N. Bruun, *ELLJ* 2(2011), 27, 45.

[42]   For a critical viewpoint see e.g. P. Davies, *YEL* 9 (1989), 21, 27 sq.; J. McMullen, *IJCLLIR* 23 (2007) 335, 337–342; R. Rebhahn, *RdA* 2006, 5, 6.

[43]   R. Rebhahn, *JBl* 1999, 621, 624.

[44]   ECJ Case C-242/09 *Albron Catering* [2010] ECR I-10309. Critical but, as to the case at hand, approving notes by J.-H. Bauer/A. v. Medem, '§613 a BGB: Übergang von Leiharbeitsverhältnissen bei Übertragung des Entleiherbetriebs?', *NZA* 2011, 20–23; T. Raab, 'Betriebsübergang und Leiharbeit – Rechtsfolgen der Übernahme des Entleiherbetriebs für die dort beschäftigten Leiharbeitnehmer', *EuZA* 2011, 357–353; R. Simon, 'Übergang einer Betriebsgesellschaft – Wahrung von Arbeitnehmeransprüchen', *E.L. Rep.* 2011, 98 sq.; H. J. Willemsen, 'Erosion des Arbeitgeberbegriffs nach der Albron-Entscheidung des EuGH? – Betriebsübergang bei gespaltener Arbeitgeberfunktion', *NJW* 2011, 1546–1551 (arguing that, instead of making the user undertaking 'non-contractual employer', the Court should have considered the work agency transferor). For a critical perspective see B. Gaul/D. Ludwig,

Nederlands Beheer BV ('HNB'). HNB performs the function of central employer and detaches the staff to the various operating companies of the Heineken group in the Netherlands. Mr Roest had been employed by HNB for some 20 years during which he had been assigned to Heineken Nederland, a catering department of the group.[45] When Heineken International transferred the catering department to Albron, Mr Roest claimed that there had been a transfer of an undertaking from Heineken Nederland to Albron. It appears that his interest was to maintain the working conditions he had enjoyed before the outsourcing. Technically, HNB was his employer. But, as is inherent in agency work, *de facto* Heineken Nederland performed some of the function of the employer (cf. §18 para. 1 above). The Court invented the concept of a '**non-contractual employer**' to deal with this issue, which was in this case Heineken Nederland. This concept finds some support from the fact that the Directive repeatedly refers to the 'employment contract or employment relationship' (see para. 13 above). The rationale of the concept is that, where there is a contractual as well as a non-contractual employer, the Directive does not give greater weight to either position and concludes that in the circumstances of the case, 'it is also possible' to regard the non-contractual employer as transferor. The decision is certainly understandable in the light of the facts of the case where Mr Roest had been working for Heineken Nederland for 20 years. Indeed, the Court has restricted its judgement accordingly: 'In the event of a transfer … of an undertaking belonging to a group to an undertaking outside that group, it is also possible to regard as a 'transferor', within the meaning of Article 2(1)(a) TUD, the group company to which the employees were assigned on a permanent basis without however being linked to the latter by a contract of employment, even though there exists within that group an undertaking with which the employees concerned were linked by such a contract of employment'. These considerations thus do not apply where the normal case of *temporary* agency work outside a group context is concerned.[46] Furthermore, the very limited wording should be noted: The Court does not say that the Directive *mandates* that national law consider the non-contractual employer transferor but merely states that this is 'also (!) possible (!)'. Finally, the judgement raises the question of *which rights and obligations are being transferred*; see paras. 56 sqq. below.

'Wird §613a BGB jetzt uferlos?', *DB* 2011, 298, 299 sq. (criticising the judgement as unprincipled and disproportionately protective of temporary agency workers).

[45] For the background of such 'long-term temporary work' in Dutch law, see F. B. J. Grapperhaus, *ELLJ* 1 (2010), 406 sq.

[46] Thus also J.-H. Bauer/A. v. Medem, *NZA* 2011, 20, 22 sq.; S. de Groof, *ELLJ* 1 (2010), 508, 511 (also arguing out that a different decision would have opened a loophole for groups of companies); H. J. Willemsen, *NJW* 2011, 1546–1551.

b)   Transfer of an Undertaking or Business

aa)   OVERVIEW AND GENERAL ISSUES

22.   The Transfer of Undertakings Directive applies to 'any transfer of an undertaking, business, or part of an undertaking or business', (Article 1(1)(a) TUD). The determination of which units are concerned – 'undertaking, business or part of an undertaking or business' – and whether there has been a transfer are thus central in establishing the Directive's scope. The legislator has not – as one could have expected – defined these concepts in Article 2 TUD (which contains other definitions) but rather in Article 1(1)(b) TUD, on the purpose of the Directive. Following the Court's jurisprudence,

> 'there is a transfer within the meaning of this Directive where there is a transfer of an economic entity which retains its identity, meaning an organised grouping of resources which has the objective of pursuing an economic activity, whether or not that activity is central or ancillary'.[47]

Furthermore,

> 'a structured group of workers may, despite the absence of significant material or immaterial assets, correspond to an economic entity for the purposes of [the TUD]'.[48]

23.   Taken together, the two provisions of lit. a) and lit. b) reveal that the Directive applies to the transfer of the smallest of the units mentioned, i.e. **part of a business**. The definition in lit. b) should thus be considered to be the definition of a part of a business.[49] A part of a business is, in other words, defined as 'an economic entity meaning an organised grouping of resources which has the objective of pursuing an economic activity, whether or not that activity is central or ancillary'. For convenience's sake, we will hereinafter only speak of 'transfer or an undertaking', keeping in mind that this is to be understood as a token for any unit covered by the Directive. The Directive does not define what constitutes a **transfer**. However, again, the definition of lit. b) indicates that *the retention of the unit's identity* is the decisive element of a transfer.[50]

---

[47]   See the seminal decisions in ECJ Case C-13/95 *Süzen* [1997] ECR I-1259 paras. 10, 13; and its progeny in Case C-340/01 *Abler* [2003] ECR I-14023 para. 30; Case C-51/00 *Temco Service Industries* [2002] ECR I-969 para. 23; Case C-234/98 *Allen* [1999] ECR I-8643 para. 24; Joined Cases C-173/96 and C-247/96 *Hidalgo and Ziemann* [1998] ECR I-8237 paras. 21, 25; Joined Cases C-127/96, C-229/96 and C-74/97 *Vidal* [1998] ECR I-8179 para. 26.

[48]   ECJ Case C-108/10 *Scattolon* 6 September 2011 para. 49.

[49]   F. Marhold, in M. Fuchs/F. Marhold (eds.), *Europäisches Arbeitsrecht*, 184.

[50]   Cf. ECJ Case C-108/10 *Scattolon* 6 September 2011 para. 60.

24. This definition was introduced into the Directive in 1998 and must be read in light of the Court's prior judgment on the 1977 directive which it was intended to codify.[51] The Court of Justice had also defined 'part of an undertaking',[52] yet it had considered the two criteria, business and transfer, as **two elements of a single criterion**. Following this analysis, which is now codified in the Directive, the two aspects 'business' and 'transfer' cannot be considered independently. Instead, the Court adopts a 'holistic' approach and analyses whether the 'economic unity' while transferred to a different employer in the course of a structural measure, is nonetheless maintained.[53] The Court's case law may be interpreted as an attempt to avoid as far as possible *any* circumvention of the Directive and to guarantee that its goals are effectively realised, especially those contained in Article 3(1) TUD (transfer of rights and obligations). In that sense, the Court's approach may be justified as a manifestation of a teleological interpretation. The Court has, though, in a somewhat single-edged approach rather emphasised the interests of the employees at the expense of those of the employer, and it is with respect to the Transfer of Undertakings Directive in particular that the reproach of 'one-dimensionality' of EU employment law (see §1 para. 63 above) appears to be quite apposite.

25. It is this 'holistic approach' in particular which has been criticised as **methodologically unsound**.[54] This criticism is obsolete, though, since the legislator codified the Court's analysis in 1998 (see Recital 4 TUD 1998).[55] Or, in other words: Criticism can no longer be directed against the Court, but against the legislator.

26. In the following sections, we will consider the Court's jurisprudence on the requirement of a 'transfer of an undertaking' in an analysis of the issues involved (bb)).[56] The issue of a 'succession in function' will be considered separately (cc) below.

---

[51] Recital 4 to Directive 98/50/EG; see the references to the Court's in note 47 above.

[52] For references see note 47 above.

[53] To this effect already ECJ Case 24/85 *Spijkers* [1986] ECR 1119; see C. v. Alvensleben, *Die Rechte der Arbeitnehmer bei Betriebsübergang im Europäischen Gemeinschaftsrecht*, 171–173; approvingly in princple G. Annuß, *NZA* 1998, 70, 73 ('not a term susceptible to subsumtion but a rather diffuse type-like term with fuzzy edges'; – my translation).

[54] See e.g. R. Wank, in P. Hanau/H.-D. Steinmeyer/R. Wank (eds.), *Handbuch des europäischen Arbeits- und Sozialrechts*, §18 para. 77 with further references; M. Franzen, *RdA* 1999, 361, 363.

[55] See also M. Schmidt, *Arbeitsrecht der EG*, III para. 246; F. Marhold, in M. Fuchs/F. Marhold (eds.), *Europäisches Arbeitsrecht*, 184.

[56] See also the analysis by G. Thüsing, *Europäisches Arbeitsrecht*, §5 paras. 7–25 ([1] business/ undertaking; [2] maintenance of identity; [3] transfer); and the stocktaking and analysis of M. Fuchs/M. Merkes, *ZESAR* 2010, 257–267.

bb)   TRANSFER OF AN UNDERTAKING IN THE COURT'S CASE LAW

27.   In the Court's view, whether or not there has been a **transfer of an undertaking** an evaluation of the facts of the individual case. Following its seminal judgement in *Spijkers*[57] the following elements should be considered:

- the type of undertaking or business,
- whether or not the business's tangible assets, such as buildings and movable property, are being transferred,
- the value of its intangible assets at the time of the transfer,
- whether or not the majority of its employees are being taken over by the new employer,
- whether or not its customers are being transferred,
- the degree of similarity between the activities carried on before and after the transfer, and
- the period, if any, for which those activities were suspended.

The Court considers these elements to be aspects of an **overall evaluation** which the national courts must make. The criteria must be assessed on an individual basis in light of their total number and relative weight.[58] In this evaluation, account should be taken of the specific circumstances of the undertaking or business concerned: individual criterion may have a different weight depending upon the activities pursued by the company and the methods of production or business.

28.   While the Court has, in general, interpreted the 'transfer of an undertaking' broadly, it has also imposed certain **limits**. Thus, a business presupposes 'a stable economic entity whose activity is not limited to performing one specific works contract'.[59] A construction site does not fulfil these criteria, and there is thus no transfer of an undertaking, where one undertaking transfers one of its building works to another undertaking with a view to the completion of that work.[60] The mere fact that the services offered by the old and the new

---

57   ECJ Case 24/85 *Spijkers* [1986] ECR 1119 paras. 11–14; the *Spijkers*-formula has been repeated since: Joined Cases C-232/04 and C-233/04 *Güney-Görres and Demir* [2005] ECR I-11237 paras. 33–35; Case C-340/01 *Abler* [2003] ECR I-14023 paras. 33–35; Case C-51/00 *Temco Service Industries* [2002] ECR I-969 paras. 24 sq.; Case C-234/98 *Allen* [1999] ECR I-8643 para. 26; Joined Cases C-127/96, C-229/96 and C-74/97 *Vidal* [1998] ECR I-8179 paras. 28 sq.; Case C-13/95 *Süzen* [1997] ECR I-1259 paras. 14, 18; Joined Cases C-171/94 and C-172/94 *Merckx and Neuhuys* [1997] ECR I-1253 para. 17; Case C-209/91 *Rask* [1992] ECR I-5755 para. 20; Case C-29/91 *Redmond Stichting* [1992] ECR I-3189 paras. 24 sq.

58   Similarly G. Thüsing, *Europäisches Arbeitsrecht*, §5 para. 13 ('type-like term'; – my translation).

59   ECJ Case C-48/94 *Rygaard* [1995] ECR I-2745 para. 20.

60   ECJ Case C-48/94 *Rygaard* [1995] ECR I-2745; it did not, therefore, matter that the second undertaking had taken over two apprentices, an employee and certain materials.

undertaking are similar cannot as such support the conclusion that the transfer of an economic unit has occurred.[61] Similarly, the mere transfer of assets does not as such constitute a transfer of an undertaking.[62] Again, the mere loss of a service contract to a competitor cannot by itself indicate the existence of a transfer within the meaning of the TUD (as to the 'succession in function', see paras. 34–41 below).[63]

29. In its evaluation, the Court attempts to take into account the **specificities of the sectors** covered by the Directive. This approach is, indeed, well-founded on the basis of teleological considerations, given that the organisational structures for the production and distribution of goods may differ considerably from those of the services sector. Organisational structures are very diverse even within the services sector. Consequently, taking over an essential part of the staff may in one case suffice to support the conclusion that an economic entity has been transferred, even if no assets have been taken over;[64] and at the same time, this is not a necessary requirement and it may be even irrelevant in another case (e.g. where a contract for the management of hospital catering services has been re-awarded; see also para. 45 below).[65]

30. In respect of sectors that require only few physical assets, the Court holds: 'Thus, in certain **labour-intensive sectors**, a group of workers engaged in a joint activity on a permanent basis may constitute an economic entity. Such an entity is, therefore, capable of maintaining its identity after it has been transferred where the new employer does not merely pursue the activity in question but also takes over a major part, in terms of their numbers and skills, of the employees specially assigned by his predecessor to that task. Thus, an organised grouping of wage earners who are specifically and permanently assigned to a common task may, in the absence of other factors of production, amount to an economic entity.'[66] In such instances, it may be of central importance whether or not the transferee takes over the employees with the relevant know how.[67]

---

61   ECJ Joined Cases C-173/96 and C-247/96 *Hidalgo and Ziemann* [1998] ECR I-8237 para. 30; Joined Cases C-127/96, C-229/96 and C-74/97 *Vidal* [1998] ECR I-8179 para. 30.
62   ECJ Case 24/85 *Spijkers* [1986] ECR 1119 para. 12.
63   ECJ Case C-13/95 *Süzen* [1997] ECR I-1259 para. 16.
64   ECJ Case C-51/00 *Temco Service Industries* [2002] ECR I-969 para. 25; Case C-13/95 *Süzen* [1997] ECR I-1259 para. 18.
65   ECJ Case C-340/01 *Abler* [2003] ECR I-14023 paras. 36 sq.
66   ECJ Case C-51/00 *Temco Service Industries* [2002] ECR I-969 para. 26; Case C-13/95 *Süzen* [1997] ECR I-1259 para. 21; Joined Cases C-173/96 and C-247/96 *Hidalgo and Ziemann* [1998] ECR I-8237 para. 32. Approvingly H. Collins, *ILJ* 18 (1989), 144, 153–157; critically ('an impossible distinction'?) G. Barrett, *CMLR* 42 (2005), 1053, 1059–1061, 1065 sq.
67   Critically B. Waas, *ZfA* 2001, 377, 389–392 (obstacle for the mobility of carriers of know how).

31.   So, for example, the Court has, with regard to *cleaning* or *surveillance work*, considered that an organised grouping of employees, who are specifically and permanently assigned to a common task, may constitute an economic entity.[68] The same considerations may apply with regard to the *driveage of a coal mine* where, as appears to be customary, the owner of the coal mine provides the essential parts of the machinery needed.[69] *Bus transport*, on the other hand, cannot be regarded as an activity based essentially on manpower, as it requires substantial plant and equipment.[70]

32.   The Court has also taken account of the special characteristics of *temporary work-agencies*. It considered such businesses to be characterised by the lack of a suitable business structure. 'The pursuit of such an activity requires, inter alia, expertise, an administrative structure capable of organising that assignment of employees and a grouping of temporary workers who are capable of integrating in the user undertakings and of carrying out the tasks required of them.'[71] Thus, a transfer of an undertaking may occur where (1) part of the administrative personnel and (2) part of the temporary workers are transferred to another temporary employment business (3) in order to carry out the same activities (4) in that business for the same clients and (5) the assets affected by the transfer are sufficient in themselves to allow the services characterising the economic activity in question to be provided without recourse to other significant assets or to other parts of the business.[72]

33.   Business transfer presupposes a certain **temporal connection** between the discontinuation of the transferor's business and the transferee taking up the business (see also paras. 44 sq. below). However, as the transfer of an undertaking is a 'complex legal and practical operation', a temporary suspension of work may be irrelevant.[73] On teleological considerations, the case where one employer definitely ceased trading and another later takes over the business may also be covered by the Directive.[74] The temporary closure of an undertaking and the resulting absence of staff at the time of the transfer do not of themselves preclude the possibility that there has been a transfer of an undertaking within the meaning of the Directive.[75]

---

[68]   ECJ Case C-392/92 *Christel Schmidt* [1994] ECR I-1311 para. 16; Joined Cases C-127/96, C-229/96 and C-74/97 *Vidal* [1998] ECR I-8179 30–32; Joined Cases C-173/96 and C-247/96 *Hidalgo and Ziemann* [1998] ECR I-8237 paras. 26, 32; ECJ Case C-151/09 *UGT-FSP* [2010] ECR I-7591 paras. 28 sq.

[69]   ECJ Case C-234/98 *Allen* [1999] ECR I-8643 para. 30.

[70]   ECJ Case C-172/99 *Oy Liikenne Ab* [2001] ECR I-745 para. 39.

[71]   ECJ Case C-458/05 *Jouini* [2007] ECR I-7301 paras. 33–36.

[72]   ECJ Case C-458/05 *Jouini* [2007] ECR I-7301. Critically S. Klumpp, *EuZA* 2009, 69, 73–76 (with a view to the difficulty of distinction with regard to the transfer of a part of the business).

[73]   ECJ Case C-234/98 *Allen* [1999] ECR I-8643 para. 32.

[74]   ECJ Joined Cases C-171/94 and C-172/94 *Merckx and Neuhuys* [1997] ECR I-1253 paras. 22 sq.

[75]   ECJ Case 101/87 *Bork* [1988] ECR 3057 para. 16; Case 287/86 *Ny Mølle Kro* [1987] ECR 5465 paras. 18–21.

cc) 'Functional Succession' as a particular type of business transfer

34. The Court's case law on the so-called succession in function as transfer of an undertaking has met with considerable attention and opposition.[76] The question is whether a transfer of an undertaking may be found where a certain **line of business** (such as cleaning services) has been contracted out or where a contract for such services has been terminated and re-awarded to a different partner, even where no tangible assets have been transferred. The Court tends to answer this question in the affirmative.[77] In a way, the Court's response sometimes appeared to be somewhat formalistic; it has relied upon the above principles (paras. 24, 27–30) and put them together like bricks. Indeed, the case law can be interpreted as saying that the individual elements must be evaluated 'holistically'. The transfer of tangible assets may not be necessary for finding that there has been a business transfer, depending upon the characteristics of the sector concerned.

35. The Court's judgement in *Christel Schmidt*[78] ('the most famous cleaning lady of Europe') is particularly far-reaching. The Court largely 'dematerialised' the concept of a transfer of an undertaking. The Sparkasse (savings bank) had terminated Mrs Schmidt's employment after it had contracted out the cleaning services it required to an independent contractor, a company named Spiegelblank (close to a textbook-example, the literal meaning of the contractor company's name is 'shiny as a mirror'). Spiegelblank offered to hire Mrs Schmidt to provide the same cleaning services, but at a reduced wage. Upon a reference of the *Landesarbeitsgericht* (Higher Labour Court, LAG) Schleswig-Holstein, the Court of Justice found that there had been a business transfer on these facts. The Court, in other words, accepted that a succession in function could constitute a business transfer.

36. The Court also followed this line of reasoning in *Merckx*.[79] Mr Merckx worked as a car salesman for Anfo Motors SA. When Anfo ceased trading, it informed customers and employees that Novarobel SA would from then on be the Ford dealer for the area which had hitherto been covered by Anfo. Novarobel took over 14 of Anfo's 64 employees. Again, the Court considered that there had been a business transfer. In the Court's view, a decisive element was that Novarobel had acquired the exclusive dealership for the region as well as that part of the staff and customers.[80]

---

76 See e.g. G. Annuß, *NZA* 1998, 70–77; H. Buchner, *JZ* 1999, 593–597; A. Junker, 'Europäisches individuelles Arbeitsrecht', in S. Grundmann (ed.), *Systembildung und Systemlücken in Kerngebieten des Europäischen Privatrechts*, 380–383; H. Alsbaek, *Der Betriebsübergang und seine individualrechtlichen Folgen in Europa*, 220–237 (with comparative reports).

77 R. Rebhahn, *RdA* 2006 Special Supplement to issue 6, 4, 6 sq.

78 ECJ Case C-392/92 *Christel Schmidt* [1994] ECR I-1311 para. 15. For a survey of the reactions in the different Member States G. More, *YEL* 135 (1995), 135–155.

79 ECJ Joined Cases C-171/94 and C-172/94 *Merckx and Neuhuys* [1997] ECR I-1253.

80 Ibid. paras. 20 sq.

37.   The Court subsequently drew a line in *Ayse Süzen*[81] which it later confirmed in *CLECE*.[82] The Aloisiuskolleg, a secondary school in Bonn-Bad Godesberg, had contracted with Zehnacker Gebäudereinigung GmbH for the provision of its cleaning services. Zehnacker *inter alia* employed Mrs Süzen to provide these services. After Aloisiuskolleg terminated the service contract and awarded it to Lefarth GmbH, Zehnacker gave Mrs Süzen and nine other employees notice of their dismissal. Lefarth did not take over any of the employees dismissed by Zehnacker. As there was no transfer of any assets or staff, the Court considered that no transfer of an undertaking had occurred. '[T]he mere fact that the service provided by the old and the new awardees of a contract is similar does not therefore support the conclusion that an economic entity has been transferred. An entity cannot be reduced to the activity entrusted to it. Its identity also emerges from other factors, such as its workforce, its management staff, the way in which its work is organized, its operating methods or indeed, where appropriate, the operational resources available to it.'[83]

38.   The Court's decision in *Abler* can also be considered in this line of cases.[84] The Orthopädisches Spital in Wien-Speising had initially contracted out its catering services to Sanrest Großküchen Betriebsgesellschaft mbH where Mr Abler was employed as a kitchen assistant. When, after a dispute, the contract with Sanrest came to an end, the Spital awarded it to Sodexho MM Catering Gesellschaft mbH. As Sodexho acquired the customers (employees of the hospital, patients and guests) as well as the equipment (i.e. the kitchen etc. which was supplied by the hospital), the Court found that a transfer of an undertaking had occurred.

39.   The Court continued and amended this line of cases in *Güney-Görres*. Ms Güney-Görres was assigned to carry out security checks on passengers at Düsseldorf airport. For this purpose, she used the equipment provided by the German government (*inter alia*, walk-through metal detectors, a baggage conveyor belt with automatic X-ray screening). When the servicing contract was awarded to a different undertaking, this new contractor used the same equipment. Again, the Court held that there had been a relevant transfer of an undertaking. It considered the fact that the contractor could not make

---

[81]   ECJ Case C-13/95 *Süzen* [1997] ECR I-1259. Barrett, *CMLR* 42 (2005), 1053, 1056 ('turning point'); critically P. Davies, *ILJ* 26 (1997), 193–197 (relation to *Christel Schmidt* unclear; 'perverse incentive' for employers).

[82]   ECJ Case C-463/09 *CLECE* 20 January 2011. Approving case note by F. Hartmann, '"Backsourcing" von Reinigungsaufgaben durch die öffentliche Hand – Betriebsübergang oder bloße Funktionsnachfolge?', *EuZA* 2011, 329–339.

[83]   ECJ Case C-13/95 *Süzen* [1997] ECR I-1259 para. 15; Joined Cases C-171/94 and C-172/94 *Merckx and Neuhuys* [1997] ECR I-1253 para. 15.

[84]   ECJ Case C-340/01 *Abler* [2003] ECR I-14023. Critically though F. Marhold, in M. Fuchs/F. Marhold (eds.), *Europäisches Arbeitsrecht*, 188 ('Currently, no clear line is discernible.' – my translation).

independent commercial use of the equipment to be immaterial.[85] The Court thus discarded a criterion established by German courts to delimit the transfer of an undertaking in the services sector.[86] The *Bundesarbeitsgericht* (Federal Labour Court) has since tried to distinguish cases by using a criterion of the 'core of the creation of value'.[87]

40. *Klarenberg* concerned another attempt to define the 'transfer of an undertaking'. The Court was asked to consider whether there had been a transfer of an undertaking where assets and staff had been taken over by the transferee and had been integrated into his organisation in a way so as to 'destroy their previous identity', i.e. where the transferee does not preserve the organisational autonomy of the business transferred.[88] Relying on considerations of the *effet utile*, the Court answered this question in the affirmative. 'In order not to frustrate in part the effectiveness' of the Transfer of Undertakings Directive, the condition of a preservation of the identity 'should be interpreted, not as requiring the retention of the specific organisation imposed by the undertaking on the various elements of production which are transferred, but … as requiring the retention of a functional link of interdependence, and complementarity, between those elements.'[89] While it has been criticised that in such cases the 'identity' was, in fact, not maintained,[90] others have pointed out that making the finding of a 'transfer of an undertaking' dependent upon the organisational measures of the transferee would have given the transferee room for circumventing the protection afforded by the Directive.[91]

dd) EVALUATION

41. The Court's case law on the transfer of an undertaking in general and its jurisprudence on the 'succession in function' remain unsatisfactory.[92] The case law has been criticised for a variety of different reasons. While the 1998 revision

---

[85] ECJ Joined Cases C-232/04 and C-233/04 *Güney-Görres and Demir* [2005] ECR I-11237 paras. 37–41.

[86] M. Franzen, *NZA* 2008 Special Supplement to issue 4, 139, 140; J. Joussen, in *EAS*, B 7200 para. 14; M. Schlachter, *NZA* 2006, 80–83. See also G. Thüsing, *Europäisches Arbeitsrecht*, §5 para. 15.

[87] See H. J. Willemsen, *NZA* 2008 Special Supplement to issue 4, 155–159 (with a discussion of the compatibility with EU law).

[88] Previous case law of the *Bundesarbeitsgericht* (Federal Labour Court, BAG) had answered the question in the negative; cf. BAG, *NZA* 2007, 1431, 1433 sq.; BAG, *NZA* 2006, 1039, 1042; BAG, *NZA* 2004, 316, 319. See also the reference for the preliminary ruling of the *Landesarbeitsgericht* (Higher Labour Court, LAG) Düsseldorf, *NZA-RR* 2008, 17.

[89] ECJ Case C-466/07 *Klarenberg* [2009] ECR I-803 paras. 37–52.

[90] R. Wank, *Festschrift 50 Jahre BAG*, 245, 250; H. J. Willemsen, *NZA* 2008 Special Supplement to issue 4, 155, 158 sq.

[91] R. Rebhahn, *RdA* 2006 Special Supplement to issue 6, 4, 8.

[92] Critically e.g. F. Marhold, in M. Fuchs/F. Marhold (eds.), *Europäisches Arbeitsrecht*, 186 sq.; B. Waas, *ZfA* 2001, 377–395; with a more positive assessment U. Zachert/E. Kocher, *Festschrift Arbeitsgerichtsbarkeit in Rheinland-Pfalz*, 51, 52–63.

brought the Directive into line with the Court's case law, it has done so at the price of creating a normative basis which is difficult to work with. Previously, the Court's case law has been described as methodologically unconvincing (see para. 25 above). Today, legislative technique is subject to similar criticism on methodological grounds.[93] As a consequence, the case law remains largely unpredictable, thus leading to high transaction cost and costs of enforcement;[94] indeed, the fact that more than fifteen years after *Christel Schmidt,* the Court still has to answer questions concerning cleaning services (with an uncertain outcome!; see *CLECE*) is ample proof of that unpredictability. The most important limitation in the area of 'succession in function', erected in the *Ayse Süzen* decision, is criticised on teleological considerations, as it partly opens the concept of 'transfer or business' up to manipulation by the transferor and the transferee; it also creates a counter-intentional incentive for the transferee not to hire any of the transferor's employees.[95] As the Directive provides for a minimum standard, Member States may only compensate these deficits by adopting an even wider concept of transfer of an undertaking; a path that the United Kingdom has taken.[96]

c)   Legal Transfer or Merger

42.   The Court has attached only little relevance to the further – restrictive – criterion that the transfer has to occur 'as a result of legal transfer or merger' (Article 1(1)(a) TUD). The fact that the provision refers to the special case of a merger is due to its genetic relationship to the Merger Directive (see para. 6 above). This latter directive also defines 'mergers'.[97] The definition of a 'legal transfer' is more difficult. This is, first, due to the vague wording of the Directive. The German language version speaks of *'vertragliche Übertragung',* i.e. a contractual transfer; similarly the French version (*'une cession conventionelle'*); the English wording is considerably broader and refers to a 'legal transfer'. Indeed, the fact that the German version uses words with a specific technical and legal meaning[98] ('contract') can be explained by reference to the Directive's legislative history (see para. 6 above). However, the restriction to *contractual* transfers is rather unconvincing on the basis of teleological considerations, since

---

[93]   Critically e.g. M. Franzen, *RdA* 1999, 361, 364; B. Waas/A. Johanns, *EuZW* 1999, 458.

[94]   R. Rebhahn, *RdA* 2006 Special Supplement to issue 6, 4, 5.

[95]   G. Barrett, *CMLR* 42 (2005), 1053, 165; G. Thüsing, *Europäisches Arbeitsrecht*, §5 para. 21. AG *Trstenjak,* Opinion in Case C-463/09 *CLECE* 26 October 2010 pt. 63 with note 47. See also J. McMullen, *ILJ* 28 (1999), 360–364 (on attempts of UK courts to side-step *Süzen*).

[96]   This appears to be the path taken by the UK which has, as a more favourable approach for employees, not adopted the *Süzen*-jurisprudence D. Edward/J. Segan, *RdA* 2006 Special Supplement to issue 6, 15, 23 sq.; J. McMullen, *IJCLLIR* 23 (2007) 335, 344 sq.

[97]   Article 3, 4 Cross Border Mergers Directive; see e.g. S. Grundmann, *European Company Law*, §28 paras. 12–16 and §29 para. 8.

[98]   See K. Riesenhuber, in id. (ed.), *Europäische Methodenlehre*, §11 para. 18.

this would attach critical relevance to rather technical national law structures, even though the different legal systems in effect reach the same result (transfer of an undertaking).

43. The Court thus rightly emphasised teleological rather than formal considerations.[99] The decisive element is not a transfer of ownership in the business but rather the consensual transition of **responsibility for the business or undertaking.**[100] Consequently, the Directive applies to a variety of instances that may not fall within the everyday understanding of the term 'transfer of an undertaking'.[101]

> 'The concept of legal transfer is thus capable of covering, as the case may be, a written or oral agreement between the transferor and the transferee relating to a change in the person responsible for the operation of the economic entity concerned and a tacit agreement between them resulting from aspects of practical co-operation which imply a common intention to make such a change.'[102]

The Court has, in one case, even relinquished the element of consensus: 'the circumstance that the transfer results from unilateral decisions of the public authority rather than from an agreement does not render the directive inapplicable'.[103]

44. The Directive, in particular, also applies to '**transfers in two steps**' where there is no direct link between the transferor and the transferee.[104] Thus, following

---

99   To the same effect R. Wank/U. Börgmann, *DB* 1997, 1229–1235; critically with regard to details and with regard to the lack of contours G. Barrett, *CMLR* 42 (2005), 1053, 1078–1085; R. Wank, *Festschrift 50 Jahre BAG*, 245, 253.

100   ECJ Case C-108/10 *Scattolon* 6 September 2011 para. 63 ('a sufficiently flexible interpretation in keeping with the objective of the directive, which is to safeguard employees in the event of a transfer of their undertaking'); Case C-340/01 *Abler* [2003] ECR I-14023 paras. 40 sq.; Case C-209/91 *Watson* [1992] I-5755 para. 15; Case C-209/91 *Rask* [1992] ECR I-5755 para. 15; Case C-29/91 *Redmond Stichting* [1992] ECR I-3189 para. 11; Joined Cases 144/87 and 145/87 *Berg and Busschers* [1988] ECR 2559 para. 17; Case 324/86 *Daddy's Dance Hall* [1988] ECR 739 para. 9; Case 287/86 *Ny Mølle Kro* [1987] ECR 5465 paras. 12 sq.

101   See also ECJ Case C-234/98 *Allen* [1999] ECR I-8643 paras. 15–20 (transfer between to undertakings of the same group of undertakings may constitute a 'transfer of undertaking' within the meaning of the Directive). In the preparation of the 1998 revision, the Commission had proposed to codify this jurisprudence but this supplementation was ultimately not adopted; see G. Barrett, *CMLR* 42 (2005), 1053, 1084. This cannot, though, be interpreted as a rejection of said jurisprudence which was based on the wording that now remained unchanged.

102   ECJ Case C-458/05 *Jouini* [2007] ECR I-7301 para. 25 ('cooperation' of two temporary work agencies who essentially shared the same directors which enabled the 'new' agency to start up an identical activity as the 'old' one, largely using the same employees who had previously worked for the latter).

103   ECJ Case C-343/98 *Collino* [2000] ECR I-6659 para. 34.

104   ECJ Case C-340/01 *Abler* [2003] ECR I-14023 paras. 38 sq.; Case C-51/00 *Temco Service Industries* [2002] ECR I-969 para. 31; Case C-172/99 *Oy Liikenne Ab* [2001] ECR I-745

---

the Court's jurisprudence, the Directive also applies where the owner of an undertaking, after giving notice to the lessee (= transferor) and bringing the lease to an end, retakes possession of the undertaking and thereafter leases or sells it to a third party (= transferee).[105] Similarly, where a contractor, who has entrusted the contract for cleaning its premises to a first undertaking which has the contract performed by a subcontractor (second undertaking), terminates that contract and enters into a new contract with the second undertaking, this may also constitute a transfer of an undertaking within the meaning of the Directive.[106]

45. Furthermore, **re-awarding a contract** may also constitute a transfer of an undertaking (see already paras. 34–41 above with regard to the 'succession in function'). For example, the Court found that there had been a business transfer where catering services for the hospital kitchen had been freshly assigned[107] (para. 38 above) and likewise in relation to airport security controls[108] (para. 39 above). It considered that it was irrelevant that, in the circumstances of the case at hand, the new contractor *had to* use the hospital's infrastructure (kitchen equipment, electricity, gas, water) and that it *had to* serve the same group of customers (staff, patients, guests). In the case of air security controls, the Court further stated that it was immaterial under the Directive that the contractor could not make *independent commercial use* of the supplied infra-structure (*inter alia*, walk-through metal detectors, a baggage conveyor belt with automatic X-ray screening).[109] The withdrawal of subsidies and their award to another legal entity pursuing a similar purpose can also fulfil the requirement of a 'legal transfer'.[110]

d) Limited Applicability to Insolvency and Serious Economic Crisis

46. The original 1977 directive did not expressly say whether it also applied in cases of insolvency. The wording was inconclusive, given that the German

---

paras. 28–30 (awarding of a contract purusant to EU public procurement rules); Joined Cases C-173/96 and C-247/96 *Hidalgo and Ziemann* [1998] ECR I-8237 paras. 22 sq.; Case C-29/91 *Redmond Stichting* [1992] ECR I-3189 paras. 11 sq. (lack of contractual relation is only an indication that there is no transfer of business but not conclusive); Case C-13/95 *Süzen* [1997] ECR I-1259 para. 12; Joined Cases C-171/94 and C-172/94 *Merckx and Neuhuys* [1997] ECR I-1253 paras. 28–30.

[105] ECJ Case 101/87 *Bork* [1988] ECR 3057 para. 14; Case 324/86 *Daddy's Dance Hall* [1988] ECR 739 para. 10; Case 287/86 *Ny Mølle Kro* [1987] ECR 5465 paras. 12–14. Similarly for a lease-purchase *and* its termination: ECJ Joined Cases 144/87 and 145/87 *Berg and Busschers* [1988] ECR 2559 paras. 17–19.

[106] ECJ Case C-51/00 *Temco Service Industries* [2002] ECR I-969.

[107] ECJ Case C-340/01 *Abler* [2003] ECR I-14023.

[108] ECJ Joined Cases C-232/04 and C-233/04 *Güney-Görres and Demir* [2005] ECR I-11237.

[109] ECJ Joined Cases C-232/04 and C-233/04 *Güney-Görres and Demir* [2005] ECR I-11237 paras. 37–41. See already para. 39 above.

[110] ECJ Case C-13/95 *Süzen* [1997] ECR I-1259 para. 8; Case C-29/91 *Redmond Stichting* [1992] ECR I-3189 para. 14.

version referred (and still refers) to *'vertragliche Übertragung'*, i.e. contractual transfer while the English version referred (and still refers) to a 'legal transfer', (see para. 42 above).[111] Neither phrasing is unambiguous, given that the technicalities of a transfer in insolvency proceedings may differ between Member States, involving a contractual transfer or a transfer, e.g., by an administrative act or by law. Yet, the national laws of the Member States, as well as Union law, agree that insolvency cases require special treatment; this indicates that the lack of express regulation in the (original) directive indicated that it was *not* intended to apply here.[112] The Court thus convincingly argued on teleological considerations that the original 1977 directive did **not apply** to the transfers of businesses that occurred in the case of insolvency.[113]

47.   In its reasoning, the Court also referred to the Directive's purpose of protecting employees. It did not follow the position advanced by some of the parties involved (including the Commission) that application of the Directive in cases of insolvency was contrary to the interests of employees as it would make the transfer of the undertaking more difficult and thus potentially lead to a loss of all jobs.[114] Rather more cautiously, the Court argued that the economic consequences were rather uncertain and that there was a serious risk of general deterioration of the working and living conditions of workers, which was contrary to the social objectives of the Treaty.[115] Rather than a judicial impact assessment, the Court uses these considerations as an indication of legislative intent. In light of the complex assessment of economic policy required, application of the Directive in cases of insolvency would have required an express provision.

48.   The legislator, in principle, **confirmed** this jurisprudence in the 1998 revision by its introduction of today's Article 5(1) TUD. Pursuant to this provision, the automatic transfer of employment relationships and the prohibition of dismissals of Article 3 and 4 do not apply to a transfer of an undertaking where the transferor is the subject of bankruptcy proceedings or any analogous insolvency proceedings which have been instituted with a view to the liquidation of the assets of the transferor and are under the supervision of a competent public authority, unless the Member States provide otherwise.[116]

---

111   From an English perspective on the interpretation of the wording P. Davies, *YEL* 9 (1989), 21, 45 ('To an English lawyer, this is a surprising question.').

112   ECJ Case 135/83 *Abels* [1985] ECR 469 paras. 11–24.

113   ECJ Case 135/83 *Abels* [1985] ECR 469 paras. 14–24; Case C-362/89 *D'Urso* [1991] ECR I-4105 paras. 22–33; Case 19/83 *Wendelboe* [1985] ECR 457 para. 10. Summarising the development M. Franzen, *RdA* 1999, 361, 365 sq.

114   Thus, however, R. Rebhahn, *JBl* 1999, 621, 627; for his own assessment with regard to economic policy, 629–633.

115   ECJ Case 135/83 *Abels* [1985] ECR 469 paras. 18–24.

116   See in more detail R. Rebhahn, *JBl* 1999, 621, 628 sq.

The remaining rules of employee protection in the Directive **remain applicable**, though, particularly provisions on information and consultation. Member States may apply the provisions on the transfer of obligations only with modifications (see in detail paras. 50–53 below).

49.   The scope of Article 5(1) TUD is recognisably drafted in light of the Court's previous jurisprudence which may thus be used for its interpretation. This is particularly relevant for the delimitation of **insolvency proceedings**. Following the Court's preceding case law – which is still good law under the revised Directive – the Directive 'does apply to the transfer of an undertaking subject to a procedure aimed at ensuring the **continuation of its business** ... where it has been decided that the undertaking is to continue trading for so long as that decision remains in effect'.[117] It also applies where court-ordered or voluntary liquidation proceedings have been initiated.[118] Similarly, the Directive applies to a transfer where the undertaking merely announced that it was suspending payment of its debts but before insolvency proceedings were opened.[119] As the legislator has now confirmed in Article 5(1) TUD, the decisive criterion is the *objective* of the proceeding: whether it is aimed at liquidation of the assets or at restructuring.[120]

50.   'Where Articles 3 and 4 apply to a transfer during insolvency proceedings which have been opened in relation to a transferor ... and provided that such proceedings are under the supervision of a competent public authority', the Member States, pursuant to Article 5(2)-(4) TUD, have **further options**, albeit within limits. These also apply in the case of insolvency proceedings which have been initiated with a view to liquidation. Under certain conditions, Member States may exclude the transferee's liability for the transferor's debts arising from contracts of employment and they may further enable the employers, in cooperation with the employees' representatives, to change the terms and conditions of employment.[121]

51.   The provision raises a number of questions. *First,* following its wording and systematic location, it seems to refer to paragraph 1 and could thus be interpreted

---

[117]   ECJ Case C-472/93 *Luigi Spano* [1995] ECR I-4321 para. 25; Case C-362/89 *D'Urso* [1991] ECR I-4105 paras. 22–33; Case 186/83 *Botzen* [1985] ECR 519; Case 135/83 *Abels* [1985] 469 paras. 25–31; see also Case C-561/07 *Commission* v. *Italy* [2009] ECR I-4959 paras. 37 sqq. Critically P. Davies, *YEL* 9 (1989) 21, 46 sq., and, with a view to the (confirming) revision 1998, id., *ILJ* 27 (1998), 365, 367 sq. On the rationale R. Rebhahn, *JBl* 1999, 621, 632 sq.

[118]   ECJ Case C-319/94 *Dethier Equipement* [1998] ECR I-1061 paras. 25–31; Case C-399/96 *Europièces* [1998] ECR I-6965 paras. 28–35.

[119]   ECJ Case 105/84 *Danmols Inventar* [1985] ECR 2639 paras. 9 sq.

[120]   ECJ Case 135/83 *Abels* [1985] ECR 469 paras. 28 sq.; Case C-362/89 *D'Urso* [1991] ECR I-4105 para. 26.

[121]   On this (critically) P. Davies, *ILJ* 27 (1998) 365, 368–370.

as meaning that these additional options only apply where a Member State applies Articles 3 and 4 TUD to all insolvency proceedings (irrespective of whether they are aimed at liquidating the undertaking); the provision of Article 5(2) TUD would, in other words, be read as '*only* where Articles 3 and 4 apply …'. However, the English and French language versions indicate that while the legislator refers to paragraph 1, the decisive prerequisite is that the proceedings are under the supervision of the competent public authority. The legislative history also indicates that the legislator intended to provide Member States with *additional* regulatory options in paragraph 2.[122] Consequently, a Member State may exclude the application of Articles 3 and 4 for insolvency proceedings which aim at liquidation and still make the provisions applicable to other insolvency proceedings. *Second,* paragraph 2 could be considered to be a restriction upon the Member States' discretion in their implementation of paragraph 1 as it leaves the Member States free *not to apply* Articles 3 and 4 to the insolvency proceedings aimed at liquidation *at all;* if, however, they decided to avail themselves of that option, its application must either be unconditional or with the restrictions of paragraphs 2–4. Paragraphs 2–4 would, in other words, restrict the Member States' discretion which appeared to be unfettered in paragraph 1 (for the insolvency proceedings mentioned therein). This interpretation does not seem to be supported by the systematic order of the provision, as it cannot be assumed that the legislator would take away with one hand what he has just given with the other. Such restriction of the Member States' discretion is not convincing on teleological considerations either as it is neither justified in the interests of employees nor in the interests of the internal market (which may, in certain cases, require that only certain types of structures be used). Paragraph 2 should thus be interpreted as opening up additional regulatory options, in addition to those of paragraph 1, applying to insolvency proceedings which are not aimed at liquidation. Paragraph 2 does not restrict the Member States' options under paragraph 1.[123]

52. If a Member State decides to apply Articles 3 and 4 TUD to a **transfer during insolvency proceedings** (whether aimed at liquidation or not) that is being conducted under the supervision of the competent public authority, then the employee protection provisions may be restricted in two ways:

– Pursuant to paragraph 2(a), Member States may provide that the **transferor's debts** arising from any employment relationship and payable before the opening of the insolvency proceedings shall not be transferred to the transferee; the assets are thus relieved in favour of other debtors. However, a condition for this option is that the proceedings in question give rise to

---

[122] Franzen, *RdA* 1999, 361, 367 sq.
[123] M. Franzen, *RdA* 1999, 561, 567 sq.; R. Rebhahn, *JBl* 1999, 621, 627.

protection at least equivalent to that provided for in the Insolvency Protection Directive (§25).

– Pursuant to paragraph 2(b), the transferor and the transferee and the employees' representatives may agree to a **change of the terms and conditions of employment** 'designed to safeguard employment opportunities by ensuring the survival of the undertaking, business or part of the undertaking or business'.[124]

Member States may also avail themselves of this latter option in the case where insolvency proceedings have not been initiated but the undertaking is in a **situation of serious economic crisis**, (Article 5(3) TUD).[125] This amendment refers to certain proceedings related to an inability to pay under Italian law.[126]

53. As the transfer of undertakings is thus (from an employer's perspective) alleviated in the case of insolvency, this may open up room for abuse. Article 5(4) TUD requires the Member States to take appropriate measures to prevent abuse.

3. Territorial Scope of Application

54. The Directive applies where and in so far as the business to be transferred is situated within the territorial scope of the Treaty, (Article 1(2) TUD). This also applies in cases of cross-border transfers which, as yet, have not been specifically regulated (see para. 8).[127]

4. Summary: Towards a Teleological Concept

55. The Court's jurisprudence is largely related to the circumstances of the individual case. So, too, are the *Spijkers*-criteria (para. 27 above) which only add little to the definition to the concept of 'transfer of an undertaking'. This is not least due to the fact that the Court chose to apply these criteria in a 'holistic' evaluation rather than in differentiated order of conceptual levels and with regard to the purpose of the Directive. Professor *Wank* has demonstrated that such approach is feasible, though, and has submitted a different analysis which distinguishes between different levels of concepts.[128] Pursuant to this approach, the concept of a transfer of an undertaking may be summarised as follows:

Elements of a 'transfer of an undertaking'

---

[124] On the negotiation solution under the TUD J. Armour/S. Deakin, *ILJ* 29 (2000), 395, 397–402.

[125] Cf. ECJ Case C-561/07 *Commission* v. *Italy* [2009] ECR I-4959 paras. 43 sqq.

[126] M. Franzen, *RdA* 1999, 561, 568; id., *NZA* 2008 Special Supplement to issue 4, 139, 143; Commission Report of 18 June 2007 on Council Directive 2001/23/EC, COM(2007) 334 final, 8.

[127] See B. W. Feudner, *NZA* 1999, 1184–1190; H. Reichold, *Festschrift für Birk*, 687–702.

[128] R. Wank, *Festschrift 50 Jahre BAG*, 245, 246–256 (though, of course, with criticisms in details).

(1) Economic Entity

    (a) Organised Grouping of Resources

        What this organised grouping of resources relates to depends upon the individual business (e.g. labour intensive businesses); depending on the sector concerned, the following elements must be considered in an evaluative assessment:

        (i)   assets

        (ii) (key) personnel

        (iii) customers

    (b) which has the objective of pursuing an economic activity, whether or not that activity is central or ancillary

    This element has little distinctive value, if any, as there is no organised grouping that does not pursue at least an ancillary objective.

(2) Transfer

    Whether a legally relevant transfer occurs should be ascertained by means of a comparison as to similarities with regard to two characteristics:

    (a)   similarity of activity

    (b)   length of an interruption of activity (if any)

    In most cases, the activity will be continued without any interruption; yet an interruption of not too long a duration is irrelevant.

(3) By a Private Legal Act

    A transfer by means of a private legal act is required. Such a legal act does not require a certain form and does not necessarily have to occur between transferor and transferee.

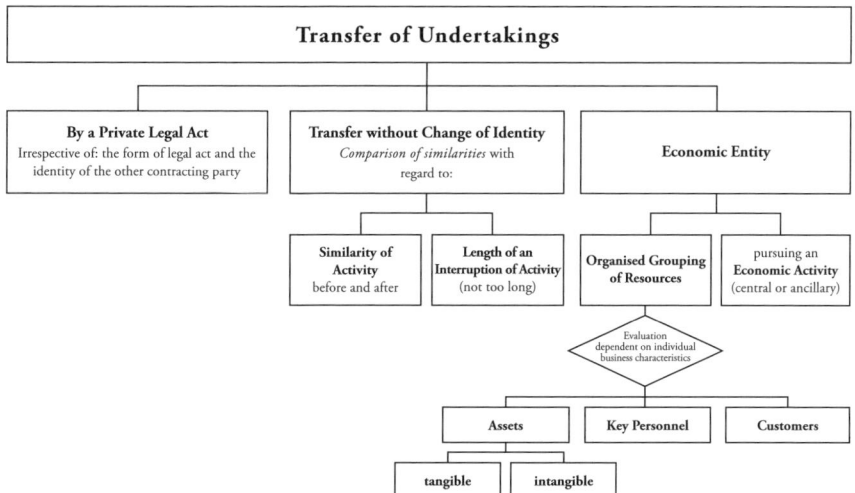

Table 1. Graphical exposition of the conceptual levels, following R. Wank, *Festschrift 50 Jahre Bundesarbeitsgericht*, 254.

III. LEGAL CONSEQUENCES

1. Transfer of the Rights and Obligations Arising from the Employment Relationship

56. The Directive's central instrument of protection is the transfer of rights and obligations provided for in Article 3 TUD: 'The transferor's rights and obligations arising from a contract of employment or from an employment relationship existing on the date of a transfer shall, by reason of such transfer, be transferred to the transferee.'

a) Transfer of the Rights and Obligations

aa) Principle

57. As a matter of Union law, an ***ipso iure* transfer** of employment rights and obligations is required. There is no need for a separate transfer of these rights and obligations from the transferor to the transferee; it rather instead occurs independently of the will of the parties.[129] Similarly, the date of the transfer (see para. 61 below) is not at the parties' discretion.[130]

58. The transferee acquires all rights and obligations arising from the employment relationship. The wording 'rights and obligations' should be broadly construed. It not only covers rights in a narrow sense but also contingent or temporary rights (such as rights contingent upon dismissal or the grant of early retirement).[131] Factual circumstances can also be of on-going relevance and may thus have to be taken into account by the transferee. For example, **length of service** with the transferor, while not in itself a right, must be taken into account by the transferee, e.g. for the purpose of calculating pay or compensation, in so far as the obligation to do so derives from the employment relationship with the transferor.[132] The expectation, though, that a dynamic reference to a collective agreement (in its respective version) will lead to corresponding adaptations of the wage in the future, is not part of the 'rights': On the basis of principled considerations (private autonomy of the transferee, his negative freedom of association) and a systematic interpretation of Article 3(2) TUD (temporal limitation to the continued application of collective

---

[129] ECJ Case C-478/03 *Celtec* [2005] ECR I-4389 paras. 39–43; Case C-51/00 *Temco Service Industries* [2002] ECR I-969 para. 35; Case C-305/94 *Rotsart de Hertaing* [1996] ECR I-5927 paras. 16–20: also where the transferee refuses to fulfill its obligations; Case C-362/89 *D'Urso* [1991] ECR I-4105 paras. 10–12; Joined Cases 144/87 and 145/87 *Berg and Busschers* [1988] ECR 2559 paras. 10–14.

[130] ECJ Case C-305/94 *Rotsart de Hertaing* [1996] ECR I-5927 paras. 23–25.

[131] ECJ Case C-4/01 *Martin* [2003] ECR I-12859 paras. 27–30.

[132] ECJ Case C-343/98 *Collino* [2000] ECR I-6659 paras. 49–51; confirmed by ECJ Case C-108/10 *Scattolon* 6 September 2011 para. 69. R. Rebhahn, *RdA* 2006 Special Supplement to issue 6, 4, 12.

agreements; see paras. 63–66 below), the Court held that the dynamic reference to a collective agreement will only be maintained as a *static* reference to the collective agreement in the version applicable at the time of the transfer.[133]

59.   Under special circumstances of a long-term intra-group assignment of 'agency workers', the Court considered that the user undertaking as a 'non-contractual employer' may also be considered to be the transferor; see para. 21 above. This raises the question, which rights and obligations will be transferred in such cases: those of the employment contract with the temporary work agency, those of the employment relationship with the user undertaking or a mixture of both? The purpose of the Directive (as interpreted by the Court) would suggest the latter: The employment contract and the employment relationship transfer to the transferee.[134]

60.   Article 3(1) TUD merely provides for the transfer of rights and obligations from the employment relationship but not rights and obligations from other relationships. Thus, a lease agreement for commercial premises entered into by the transferor with a third party is not automatically transferred to the transferee, even where this leads to its termination and the consequence that the business cannot be continued (in the same way).[135]

61.   The transfer concerns the employment relationships existing **at the time of the transfer**.[136] On the basis of the wording of the provision and considerations of legal certainty, the Court has held that the relevant point in time (not period of time!) is determined by the Directive. Following the concept of transfer of rights and obligations (see para. 57 above), this is the point of time to which responsibility for the business transfers to the transferee.[137] The rights transferred to the transferee also include those which came into being before the transfer but which have not yet been fulfilled.[138] Today, this jurisprudence is

---

[133]   ECJ Case C-499/04 *Werhof* [2006] ECR I-2397 paras. 23–37; approvingly J. McMullen, *IJCLLIR* 23 (2007), 335, 359–361. On this – and on the potential further-reaching effects of the judgement for German law (compatibility of the dynamic reference with EU law) – see M. Jacobs, *Festschrift für Birk*, 243–264; G. Thüsing, *Europäisches Arbeitsrecht*, §5 paras. 40–43.

[134]   Similarly J.-H. Bauer/A. v. Medem, *NZA* 2011, 20, 21 sq. Differently G. Forst, *RdA* 2011, 228, 232–236 (transfer of only the 'non-contractual' employment relationship while the contractual relationship to the work agency remains intact; with a detailed analysis of the various relationships).

[135]   ECJ Case C-313/07 *Kirtruna* [2008] ECR I-7907 paras. 40–46.

[136]   ECJ Case 19/83 *Wendelboe* [1985] ECR 457 paras. 12–17.

[137]   ECJ Case C-478/03 *Celtec* [2005] ECR I-4389 paras. 29–36. Transferor and transferee may neither determine the relevant point of time with the consent of the employee either; see para. 44 of the decision.

[138]   ECJ Case 135/83 *Abels* [1985] ECR 469 paras. 36 sq.; R. Rebhahn, *JBl* 1999, 710. This is not an *ex tunc*-effect, though; thus, however, J. Joussen, in *EAS,* B 7200 para. 38.

confirmed by a systematic interpretation of Article 5(2)(a) TUD. Matters are different where an employee has left the transferor's business before the transfer: His right, for example, to payment in lieu of annual leave is not transferred to the transferee under Article 3(1) TUD.[139]

62. Employment conditions cannot be altered for reasons which are connected with the transfer. Where the transfer is the reason for an unfavourable alteration, any consent given by the employee is in principle invalid.[140] Where the employer grants the employees less favourable employment conditions contrary to Article 3(1) TUD, he has to make good the consequences of his actions.[141] The transferor or transferee on the one hand and the employee on the other may, however, agree upon changes to the employment conditions in so far as such change is permitted by the applicable national law *independent of the transfer*.[142] It may be difficult in practice to draw the line between such admissible changes and those prohibited by the Directive.[143]

bb) ON-GOING EFFECTS OF CONDITIONS LAID DOWN IN COLLECTIVE
     AGREEMENTS

63. To a large extent, employment conditions are not only determined by individual contract but also by collective agreements on various levels.[144] Rights and obligations determined by collective agreements are, in principle, also transferred to the transferee (Article 3(3) TUD) (on the reference to a collective agreement in an individual employment contract, see para. 58 above).[145] The transferee must continue to abide by the terms and conditions agreed in any collective agreement **on the same terms** (*dans la même mesure, in dem gleichen Maße*) which were applicable to the transferor. This obligation ends when the collective agreement expires through termination or an expiry of its term,[146] or when another collective agreement enters into force or is being applied:[147] 'In other words, the directive permits the original collective agreement to be ousted by another collective agreement, even a less favourable one.'[148] As the Court

---

[139]   ECJ Case 19/83 *Wendelboe* [1985] ECR 457 paras. 12–17.
[140]   ECJ Case C-4/01 *Martin* [2003] ECR I-12859 paras. 44 sq.
[141]   ECJ Case C-4/01 *Martin* [2003] ECR I-12859 paras. 50–54.
[142]   ECJ Case C-4/01 *Martin* [2003] ECR I-12859 paras. 39–43; Case C-343/98 *Collino* [2000] ECR I-6659 para. 52; Case C-209/91 *Rask* [1992] ECR I-5755 paras. 26–28; Case 324/86 *Daddy's Dance Hall* [1988] ECR 739 paras. 16 sq.
[143]   See G. Barrett, *CMLR* 42 (2005), 1053, 1097–1100.
[144]   The Directive does not expressly define the term 'collective agreement'; for a comparative survey, see R. Rebhahn, *RdA* 2006 Special Supplement to issue 6, 4, 12 sq.
[145]   Cf. ECJ Case C-209/91 *Rask* [1992] ECR I-5755 para. 29.
[146]   This is also true where the termination coincides with the transfer of the undertaking; ECJ Case C-396/07 *Juuri* [2008] ECR I-8883 paras. 32–34.
[147]   ECJ Case C-4/01 *Martin* [2003] ECR I-12859 para. 46.
[148]   R. Rebhahn, *RdA* 2006 Special Supplement to issue 6, 4, 13.

recognises, this 'leaves a margin for manoeuvre allowing the transferee and the other contracting parties to arrange the salary integration of the transferred workers in such a way that the latter is duly adapted to the circumstances of the transfer in question'.[149] In addition, Member States may limit the period for observing such terms and conditions, but the transition period must be at least one year.

64. 'Terms and conditions of employment' is to be broadly construed here (as in para. 58 above). They do not only cover individual rights and conditions but, following the wording and purpose of the provision, all conditions. Terms and conditions thus do not only cover norms in collective agreements that give rise to individual rights, but also such as are related to the business as a whole or to the employees' representation.[150]

65. Consequently, that means that the collective agreement in effect is being transferred together with the business (within the temporal limits set out in para. 63 above). This is true, however, only to a limited extent. While a collective agreement is usually characterised by the fact that it applies to all employees (of the unit covered; perhaps subject to personal requirements such as union membership), a collective agreement carried over under Article 3(3) TUD only applies to the **transferred employees** and not to those whose employment relationship has been established only after the transfer or to any employees who had been previously employed by the transferee.[151]

66. It is a matter of controversy whether Article 3 TUD also determines the **legal effect** of terms and conditions resulting from collective agreements carried over to the transferee:[152] German law, for example, distinguishes between a

---

[149] ECJ Case C-108/10 *Scattolon* 6 September 2011 para. 75 (para. 74: 'it is lawful for the transferee to apply, from the date of the transfer, the working conditions laid down by the collective agreement in force with him, including those concerning remuneration'). With a view to the specific circumstances of the case, the Court emphasises, though, that the Member States are under an obligation effectively to implement the objective of the Directive of avoiding workers being placed, solely by reason of a transfer to another employer, in an unfavourable position compared with that which they previously enjoyed. This obligation may, in appropriate cases, require recognition of employment with the transferor with a view to length of services for the purposes of remuneration.

[150] Prevailing opinion; see C. v. Alvensleben, *Die Rechte der Arbeitnehmer bei Betriebsübergang im Europäischen Gemeinschaftsrecht*, 244–246; F. Marhold, in M. Fuchs/F. Marhold (eds.), *Europäisches Arbeitsrecht*, 200; R. Wank, in P. Hanau/H.-D. Steinmeyer/R. Wank (eds.), *Handbuch des europäischen Arbeits- und Sozialrechts*, §18 para. 98; J. Joussen, in *EAS*, B 7200 paras. 56 sq., 65; G. Thüsing, *Europäisches Arbeitsrecht*, §5 para. 56; differently e.g. B. Debong, *Die EG-Richtlinie über die Wahrung der Arbeitnehmeransprüche beim Betriebsübergang*, 68–73; U. Preis, in R. Müller-Glöge/U. Preis/I. Schmidt (eds.), *Erfurter Kommentar*, §613a BGB para. 114.

[151] ECJ Case 287/86 *Ny Mølle Kro* [1987] ECR 5465 para. 25.

[152] J. Joussen, in *EAS*, B 7200 para. 54 with further references.

---

collective effect and an *individual effect,* and the implementation norm of §613a(1) sent. 1 BGB only provides for the latter. Both effects differ considerably, for the collective effect is comparable to that of a legal norm and does not allow for derogations by individual contract. In substance, a merely individual effect thus constitutes a degradation of the protection which is incompatible with the wording ('on the same terms') and the purpose of Article 3(3) TUD. The predominant position among German scholars accepts it nonetheless.[153]

cc)   OPTIONAL JOINT AND SEVERAL LIABILITY OF TRANSFEROR AND TRANSFEREE

67.   Pursuant to Article 3(1)(2) TUD, the *ipso iure* transfer of rights and obligations (see para. 57 above) does not prevent Member States[154] from providing that the transferor and the transferee shall be jointly and severally liable in respect of obligations which arose from an employment relationship before the transfer.[155] While the transfer of the employment relationship satisfies the employee's interest in maintaining his job, joint and several liability may, to some extent, protect his interest in maintaining a **solvent debtor**. This takes account of the fact that the employee may have chosen his contract partner (= transferor) with a view to his financial standing (see also paras. 69–73 below). Providing for joint and several liability may also be an instrument to prevent abuse as may occur where the transferor wants to shed his obligations or liability by a transfer of the employment relations to another entity. To provide for joint and several liability thus takes account of fundamental employee interests, founded in the binding force of the contract, and it is surprising that such liability has not been made mandatory with regard to obligations which arose before the date of the transfer.[156]

68.   The provision does not interfere with the modalities of joint and several liability under national law.

dd)   RIGHT TO OBJECTION

69.   An issue not considered by the well-meaning legislator was whether the employee wanted to have his employment relationship transferred to the transferee in the first place. On the basis of a generalised evaluation of interests,

---

[153]   F. Marhold, in M. Fuchs/F. Marhold (eds.), *Europäisches Arbeitsrecht,* 200 (arguing that otherwise other employees than those who's employment relationship has been transferred, would be protected even though this was not justified; see para. 65 above); J. Joussen, in *EAS,* B 7200 para. 62; G. Thüsing, *Europäisches Arbeitsrecht,* §5 para. 56.

[154]   The UK hat opposed further reaching provisions of the Directive; S. Hardy/R. W. Painter, *MJ* 6 (1999), 366, 377.

[155]   ECJ Case C-305/94 *Rotsart de Hertaing* [1996] ECR I-5927 para. 19; Joined Cases 144/87 and 145/87 *Berg and Busschers* [1988] ECR 2559 paras. 11, 13.

[156]   Rightly critical R. Rebhahn, *RdA* 2006 Special Supplement to issue 6, 4, 12.

the legislator assumed that a transfer would normally be in the employee's best interest (see paras. 2 sq. above). This is, however, not always the case, and some Member States have taken the countervailing interest into account by granting employees a right to object.[157] The Court of Justice was initially opposed to such a right, considering that the Directive provided for a mandatory transfer and, conversely, a mandatory release of the transferor, subject only to the Member States' option to provide for joint and several liability (para. 67 above). 'Its purpose is not, however, to ensure that the contract of employment or the employment relationship with the transferor is continued where the undertaking's employees do not wish to remain in the transferee's employ.'[158]

70. Indeed, a mandatory transfer of the employment relationships may well be considered to be in the interests of all employees. However, such paternalistic provision of protection constitutes a particularly serious interference with the employee's freedom of contract: his right to hold the transferor to the contract and his right not to be obliged to work for the transferee with whom he has not concluded a contract.[159] As such, the mandatory transfer rule requires justification, particularly with regard to the principle of proportionality. The Court's interpretation of the Directive was certainly defensible. Yet, it had failed to recognise the fundamental rights aspect altogether. And it had wrongly assumed that the only option that the Directive provided for was either that the transferor was released from his obligations, or he was not, without considering a third possibility: that the legislator simply did not regulate the issue at all but left it for the Member States to decide.

71. The Court retreated from this position in later judgments. If an employee objects, his employment relationship will not be transferred to the transferee. Union law does not impose the protection by way of mandatory transfer upon the employee.[160] The details are left for Member States to expand upon. '[T]he

---

[157] For a comparative survey, see R. Rebhahn, *RdA* 2006 Special Supplement to issue 6, 4, 10 sq.

[158] ECJ Joined Cases 144/87 and 145/87 *Berg and Busschers* [1988] ECR 2559 para. 12.

[159] See the marked wording of Lord Atkins in *Nokes* v. *Doncaster Amalgamated Collieries Ltd.,* [1940] AC 1014, 1030, 1033: 'But why this beneficent procedure should be tainted with the oppression and confiscation which in some cases would certainly be caused, or why in the interests of companies big or small for the mere purposes of an amalgamation it should violate all the rules as to transferability depending on some occasions on principles of our law and on other occasions on contract I cannot imagine. ... My Lords, I should have thought that the principle that a man is not to be compelled to serve a master against his will is just as deep-seated in the common law of this country, as that which was under discussion in the case cited: and that here there is no clear, definite, or positive enactment overturning it.' See also B. Hepple, *ILJ* 5 (1976), 197, 202 sq., 206; P. Davies, *YEL* 9 (1989), 21, 22 sq.; R. Rebhahn, *RdA* 2006 Special Supplement to issue 6, 4, 10.

[160] ECJ Case C-399/96 *Europièces* [1998] ECR I-6965 para. 38; Joined Cases C-171/94 and C-172/94 *Merckx and Neuhuys* [1997] ECR I-1253 paras. 34 sq.; Joined Cases C-132/91, C-138/91 and C-139/91 *Katsikas* [1992] ECR I-6577 para. 30.

contract binding the employee to the transferring undertaking may be terminated either by the employee or by the employer or the contract may be maintained with that undertaking.'[161]

72. There is some uncertainty, though, about how far the Member States' discretion goes in this respect. This is due to the fact that it remains unclear whether the Court, in his above quotation (at the end of para. 69), wanted to *give examples* for possible national rules or *restrict* the Member States' discretion. The latter would be rather unconvincing, though, as the Court did not discuss existing national models or give any reasons for imposing such a restriction. It is further unclear whether the purpose of the Directive can justify restrictions upon national rights of objection. It has been considered, for example, that the retroactive effect of the right to object under German law (as construed by the *Bundesarbeitsgericht* [Federal Labour Court]) was incompatible with the Directive as it led to an unacceptable deterioration of the employee's position.[162] That, however, is what lies at the heart of the right to object: that the employee takes responsibility for his decision about whether or not to transfer his employment relationship. Consequently, the focus cannot be on the substantive effects of the right to object but rather has to be on ensuring that an employee has the information to make a rational decision (see also para. 74 below).

73. The Court relies upon two strands of arguments in accepting a right for employees to object to transfer under national law. For one thing, the Directive leaves the issue open. For another, the mandatory transfer of the employment contract to the transferee would violate the employee's freedom of contract and thus a fundamental right.[163] This latter justification does not refer to the fundamental rights in the national legal systems of the Member States (a violation of which the Court could not determine of his own right),[164] but rather to the fundamental right to **freedom of contract** as a general principle of Union law (see §2 para. 10 above), which is now also guaranteed by the Charter of Fundamental Rights (see §2 paras. 16 sq. above). Consequently, the Court does not consider Member States to be free to ignore the employee's objection to the

---

161 ECJ Case C-51/00 *Temco Service Industries* [2002] ECR I-969 para. 36; Case C-399/96 *Europièces* [1998] ECR I-6965 paras. 37–39; Joined Cases C-171/94 and C-172/94 *Merckx and Neuhuys* [1997] ECR I-1253 paras. 33–35; Joined Cases C-132/91, C-138/91 and C-139/91 *Katsikas* [1992] ECR I-6577 paras. 35 sq. Under German law, the effect of the objection is that the employment contract with the transferor continues; under English and French law, the objection leads to its termination with the effect that the employee loses his protection against unfair dismissal; C. Barnard, *EC Employment Law*, 662.

162 M. Löwisch, *Festschrift für Birk*, 541–545.

163 ECJ Joined Cases C-132/91, C-138/91 and C-139/91 *Katsikas* [1992] ECR I-6577 paras. 31 sq.; Joined Cases C-171/94 and C-172/94 *Merckx and Neuhuys* [1997] ECR I-1253 para. 34.

164 Thus, however, F. Marhold, in M. Fuchs/F. Marhold (eds.), *Europäisches Arbeitsrecht*, 197; apparently also G. Thüsing, *Europäisches Arbeitsrecht*, §5 paras. 48 sq.

transfer of his rights; instead, it only considers the alternatives that the employment relationship be terminated or continued with the transferor.[165]

74.   A right to object entails the problem, though, of ensuring that the employee objects of his own **free will**.[166] Where the employee is free to object to a transfer, he must also bear the responsibility for that decision. The Court tries to prevent an employee's decision being unlawfully influenced by Article 4(2) TUD, pursuant to which the employer is considered to be responsible for a termination of employment due to an unfavourable alteration of the terms and conditions of employment (see in detail paras. 83–88 below).

ee)   Termination by the Employee and Consensual Termination of the Employment Relationship

75.   Article 3(1) TUD does not prevent the termination of the employment relationship by the employee or a consensual termination agreement between the transferor or the transferee and the employee.[167] On teleological considerations, the Court emphasises, though, that such termination presupposes a decision by the employee 'of his own free will'. As the employee's free will is a necessary prerequisite of his (!) termination as well as a (consensual!) termination agreement, the Court's wording may be read as emphasising that Member States are required by their implementation duties (principle of effectiveness) to ensure the employee's self-determination in this particularly precarious situation.

b)   Exception for Benefits from Supplementary Company Schemes

76.   Statutory pensions or rights arising from statutory social security schemes will usually be independent of a transfer of an undertaking. However, rights to **old-age** or survivors' benefits under supplementary company or intercompany pension schemes require regulation. The Directive in principle leaves the issue to Member States.[168] It neither provides for a transfer of rights arising from individual employment relationships nor for those arising from collective agreement (Article 3(4) TUD: exception from paragraphs 1 and 3).

77.   Member States may also provide for a transfer of rights in this respect, (Article 3(4)(a) TUD). If they don't, they must at least protect the interests of employees and of persons no longer employed in the transferor's business at the time of the transfer in respect of rights which confer on them immediate or

---

[165]   Similarly F. Marhold, in M. Fuchs/F. Marhold (eds.), *Europäisches Arbeitsrecht*, 197 sq.; G. Thüsing, *Europäisches Arbeitsrecht*, §5 para. 49.
[166]   See the hints in ECJ Case C-399/96 *Europièces* [1998] ECR I-6965 paras. 39 sq.
[167]   ECJ Case 105/84 *Danmols Inventar* [1985] ECR 2639 paras. 13–17.
[168]   For a comparative survey, see R. Rebhahn, *RdA* 2006 Special Supplement to issue 6, 5, 12.

prospective entitlement to old age benefits, including survivors' benefits, under supplementary schemes, (Article 3(4)(b) TUD).[169]

78. As an exception to the general rule of Article 3(1) TUD, the Court has **interpreted** paragraph 4 **narrowly.**[170] It has thus classified old-age benefits as 'only benefits paid from the time when an employee reaches the end of his normal working life as laid down by the general structure of the pension scheme in question'.[171] Early retirement benefits and benefits intended to enhance the conditions of such retirement thus do not fall under the exception of paragraph 4,[172] but are instead transferred pursuant to the principles contained in paragraphs 1 and 3.[173]

c)   Optional Duty of the Transferor to Inform the Transferee

79. Regulating the transfer of rights and obligations, the Directive is almost exclusively concerned with the legal relationship between the employee and the transferor and transferee. It regulates the legal relationship between the transferor and transferee only with respect to specific issues, e.g. the (optional) joint and several liability (paras. 67 sq. above). Employee protection is also at stake with the optional duty to inform the transferor in Article 3(2) TUD.[174] Member States may provide that the transferor must inform the transferee of the rights and obligations that are being transferred under Article 3 TUD. More important than this option for implementation is the provision that the transfer of the rights and duties and the rights of the employee against either transferor or transferee are not affected by a failure of the transferor to fulfil such information duty.

2.   *Complementary Provisions on Dismissal*

a)   Prohibition of Dismissal due to Transfer

80. The provisions on the transfer of rights and obligations arising from the employment relationship are supplemented by a prohibition – addressed to both

---

169   Cf. ECJ Case C-561/07 *Commission* v. *Italy* [2009] ECR I-4959 paras. 31 sq.
170   ECJ Case C-164/00 *Beckmann* [2002] ECR I-4893 para. 29; ECJ Case C-561/07 *Commission* v. *Italy* [2009] ECR I-4959 para. 30. On the general principle of interpretation (critically) K. Riesenhuber, in id. (ed.), *Europäische Methodenlehre*, §11 paras. 61–66.
171   ECJ Case C-164/00 *Beckmann* [2002] ECR I-4893 para. 31.
172   ECJ Case C-164/00 *Beckmann* [2002] ECR I-4893 para. 31; confirmed by Case C-4/01 *Martin* [2003] ECR I-12859 paras. 29–32.
173   ECJ Case C-164/00 *Beckmann* [2002] ECR I-4893 paras. 36–40; Case C-4/01 *Martin* [2003] ECR I-12859 para. 35 (also where the obligations derive from statutory instruments or are implemented by such instruments).
174   See also P. Davies, *ILJ* 27 (1998), 365–370 sq. on potential other purposes (e.g. information for re-awarding the contract; critically B. Waas/A. Johanns, *EuZW* 1999, 458, 461.

transferor and transferee – to terminate[175] the employment relationship on grounds of the transfer, (Article. 4(1)(1) sent. 1 TUD).[176] In fact, such prohibition – as a general prohibition of unfavourable treatment – is teleologically necessary (and thus a matter of course) as transferor and transferee could otherwise escape from their obligations arising from the transfer.[177] Paragraph 1 subparagraph 1 sent. 1 already leaves unaffected the possibility to terminate the employment relationship for reasons unconnected to the transfer, e.g. on grounds of the employee's behaviour. The judicial assessment of causation takes into account the circumstances under which the dismissal occurred, e.g. whether it became effective close to the time of the transfer or whether the employee has been re-hired by the transferee.[178] As the prohibition of dismissal is addressed to the transferor as well, it also applies to dismissal *before the time of the transfer* -[179] which had long been considered lawful in the United Kingdom.[180]

81. However, **not every dismissal** that is in some way causally linked to the transfer can be considered unlawful. This would disproportionately restrict **entrepreneurial freedom**. Often the transferee will intend to generate synergies by integrating the new business within the structures of his undertaking or by merging it with other businesses which he operates. Where the transferred business is ailing, changes in the organisation will often be inevitable. This may lead to job losses and may, in other words, necessitate dismissals.[181] Consequently, the general prohibition of dismissal on grounds of transfer does not stand in the way of dismissals for **economic, technical or organisational**

---

[175] Termination is to be distinguished from the non-renewal of a fixed-term employment contract that ended, due to expiry of its term, on a date prior to the transfer; ECJ Case C-386/09 *Briot* [2010] ECR I-8481 paras. 29 sqq. To the same effect with regard to Article 10 MPD Case C-438/99 Jiménez Melgar [2001] ECR I-6915 para. 45; see §20 para. 32 above.

[176] Pursuant to subparagraph 2, the provision leaves unaffected exceptions for 'certain specific groups who are not covered by the laws or practice of the Member States in respect of protection against dismissal'. On this provision ECJ Case 237/84 *Commission v. Belgium* [1986] ECR 1247.

[177] Cf. also G. Barrett, *CMLR* 42 (2005), 1053, 1090.

[178] ECJ Case C-51/00 *Temco Service Industries* [2002] ECR I-969 para. 28; Case 101/87 *Bork* [1988] ECR 3057 para. 18.

[179] ECJ Case 101/87 *Bork* [1988] ECR 3057 para. 18; Case C-319/94 *Dethier Equipement* [1998] ECR I-1061 paras. 34–36.

[180] UK law accepted also a dismissal that occurred only a few hours before the transfer; see H. Collins, *ILJ* 18 (1989), 144, 148–152; also id., *ILJ* 15 (1986) 244–255; D. Edward/J. Segan, *RdA* 2006 Special Supplement to issue 6, 15, 17, 18; B. Eisele, *Die Richtlinie zum Betriebsübergang und ihre Umsetzung im englischen Recht*, 109–117; R. Rebhahn, *RdA* 2006 Special Supplement to issue 6, 4, 14.

[181] See already the reasoning on Article 4 of the Proposal of the Commission for a directive of the Council on harmonisation of the legislation of Member States on the retention of the rights and advantages of employees in the case of mergers, takeovers and amalgamations of 29 May 1974, COM(74) 351 final, OJ 1974 C 104/1 (corrected English version published as COM(74) 351 final/2).

reasons entailing changes in the workforce, (Article 4(1)(1) sent. 2 TUD).[182] This provision, of course, leaves national protection against unfair dismissal unaffected.

82. An unlawful dismissal in violation of Article 4(1) TUD is considered to be **ineffective.**[183] Consequently, an employee who was unlawfully dismissed by the transferor shortly before the transfer is still considered to be employed in the business or undertaking if he invokes the unlawfulness of the termination against the transferee.[184]

b) Responsibility of the Employer for a Termination Due to a Substantial Change in Working Conditions

83. Article 4(2) TUD contains a further supplementation, the scope of which is not easily understandable. 'If the contract of employment or the employment relationship is terminated because the transfer involves a substantial change in working conditions to the detriment of the employee, the employer shall be regarded as having been responsible for termination of the contract of employment or of the employment relationship.'[185]

84. Contrary to widespread opinion,[186] this provision is not concerned with changes of terms and conditions of employment which are transferred to the transferee under Article 3(1) and (3) TUD. A change of these conditions to the

---

[182]   ECJ Case C-313/07 *Kirtruna* [2008] ECR I-7907 paras. 40–46 (dismissal caused by the termination of the lease of the business premises); Case C-319/94 *Dethier Equipement* [1998] ECR I-1061 paras. 35 sq.; Case C-392/92 *Christel Schmidt* [1994] ECR I-1311 paras. 18 sq. See also Case C-209/91 *Rask* [1992] ECR I-5755 para. 29; ECJ Case C-561/07 *Commission* v. *Italy* [2009] ECR I-4959 paras. 35 sq. On the interpretation in English law, see C. Barnard, *EC Employment Law*, 664 sq.

[183]   To the same effect J. Joussen, in *EAS*, B 7200 para. 80. Apparently differently G. Barrett, *CMLR* 42 (2005), 1053, 1091–1093.

[184]   ECJ Case C-319/94 *Dethier Equipement* [1998] ECR I-1061 paras. 39–41. See alsready Joined Cases C-171/94 and C-172/94 *Merckx and Neuhuys* [1997] ECR I-1253 para. 26; Case 101/87 *Bork* [1988] ECR 3057 para. 18.

[185]   The Proposal of the Commission for a directive of the Council on harmonisation of the legislation of Member States on the retention of the rights and advantages of employees in the case of mergers, takeovers and amalgamations of 29 May 1974, COM(74) 351 final, OJ 1974 C 104/1 (corrected English version published as COM(74) 351 final/2) still provided that termination by the worker on grounds of a change of working conditions 'shall be deemed to be due to the action of the employer'. The explanatory memorandum states that this 'seems only fair'.

[186]   ECJ Joined Cases C-171/94 and C-172/94 *Merckx and Neuhuys* [1997] ECR I-1253 para. 38 (change of the amount of the remuneration is a substantial change in working conditions within the meaning of the provision); C. v. Alvensleben, *Die Rechte der Arbeitnehmer bei Betriebsübergang im Europäischen Gemeinschaftsrecht*, 254 sq., 257 sq.; F. Marhold, in M. Fuchs/F. Marhold (eds.), *Europäisches Arbeitsrecht*, 195; J. Joussen, in *EAS*, B 7200 para. 82. Rightly critical G. Barrett, *CMLR* 42 (2005), 1053, 1072, 1077.

---

detriment of the employee is prohibited by the Directive (see paras. 62 sq. above) and would thus be unlawful.[187] Therefore, as a matter of law, the transfer cannot 'involve' such a change in working conditions.[188] If, however, the change in working conditions is unlawful, then it already follows from a teleological interpretation of Article 3(1) and (3) TUD that a termination triggered by such a change should be equated with an (unlawful) termination by the employer. The provision of Article 4(2) TUD would then not only be unnecessary, it would also be misguided on teleological grounds: If Article 3(1) and (3) TUD, in principle,[189] prohibit *any* change in terms and conditions of employment, it would be inconsistent for Article 4(2) TUD to provide a sanction only for a *substantial* change in working conditions. And finally, the sanction would not be adequate either: A termination triggered by a substantial change in working conditions is not only to be attributed to the employer but must also be considered unlawful.

85. On these considerations, the **scope of application** may satisfactorily be explained in that it relates to

- any inevitable *factual changes* (in the framework of what is legally possible, e.g. under the direction of the transferee), as they may lie, for example, in a change of workplace; such changes will, however, normally be below the threshold of 'substantial' changes;[190]
- any *admissible* legal changes, as they are also addressed in the provision of Article 4(1)(1) sent. 2 TUD (see para. 81 above); and
- any admissible legal changes under Article 3(3) TUD, such as occur when the applicable collective agreement changes (see paras. 63–66 above).[191]

Thus construed, Article 4(2) TUD provides for an extension of protection in case where a *lawful* change in working conditions has considerable effects ('substantial')[192] which are to the detriment of the employee.[193]

---

[187] In this respect also C. v. Alvensleben, *Die Rechte der Arbeitnehmer bei Betriebsübergang im Europäischen Gemeinschaftsrecht*, 254; further F. Löw, *Die Betriebsveräußerung im Europäischen Arbeitsrecht*, 125 sq.

[188] Unclear J. Joussen, in *EAS*, B 7200 para. 82.

[189] On exceptions, see para. 85 below.

[190] B. Debong, *Die EG-Richtlinie über die Wahrung der Arbeitnehmeransprüche bei Betriebsübergang*, 69–72.

[191] J. Joussen, in *EAS*, B 7200 para. 82. Changes in collective agreements cannot normally be considered substantial given that collective agreements enjoy a presumption of reasonableness.

[192] Whether a change is to be considered substantial is a matter for the national courts to determine; ECJ Case C-399/96 *Europièces* [1998] ECR I-6965 para. 43.

[193] Apparently also M. Felsner, *Arbeitsrechtliche Rahmenbedingungen von Unternehmensübernahmen in Europa*, 275 sq. Article 30(2) of the Draft Convention on International Mergers (reproduced in C. v. Alvensleben, *Die Rechte der Arbeitnehmer bei Betriebsübergang im Europäischen Gemeinschaftsrecht*, 93) merely referred to dismissals that were effective under the applicable law.

86. The only **sanction** that the Directive specifically provides for is to hold the employer responsible for the termination. (The German language version is even more specific, requiring a fiction that the employer had dismissed the worker.) This sanction may make good sense in connection with the national law of the respective Member State. Thus, it may, under national law, enable a court to control the termination of employment, it may trigger a notice period or a right to compensation or it may be relevant for the right to (and/or amount of) social security benefits.[194] Under German law, this sanction is less important, given the employee's right to object.[195]

87. As the Directive only aims to achieve partial harmonisation of national laws, no further sanctions can be inferred from Article 4(2) TUD. In particular, the Directive does not oblige Member States to provide for compensation where the employer is held responsible for the dismissal.[196] However, the general duties of implementation (see §1 paras. 65 sq. above) may lead to Member States having further obligations in this respect.[197]

88. The Court of Justice occasionally refers to Article 4(2) TUD as an instrument to protect the **employee's self-determination**. Thus, when the Court is concerned that the employee should use the right to object in his 'own free will', i.e. without any undue influence from the employer (see para. 74 above), it invokes Article 4(2) TUD as an instrument of judicial control that the national courts may use.[198] This, however, only concerns cases where a lawful change of the terms and conditions of employment has triggered the employee's dismissal (see para. 85 above). If the employee's dismissal is prompted by a change of terms and conditions of employment that is unlawful under Article 3(1) and (3) TUD, it is subject to control and will already be considered to be unlawful under these provisions.

3. Information and Consultation

89. The Transfer of Undertakings Directive provides for extensive duties of information in Article 7.[199] It initially contains a 'basic model' in paragraphs 1 to 5 which provides for information and consultation of the employee's representatives (paras. 1, 2, 4) as well as exceptions to the basic model (paras. 3 and 5).[200] The final

---

[194] See also AG Léger, Opinion in ECJ Case C-425/02 *Delahaye* [2004] ECR I-10823 pt. 38 together with pt. 22. On the German law S. Krieger, 'Anmerkung zu EuGH, Urteil vom 27. 11. 2008 – C-396/07 (Mirja Juuri/Fazer Amica Oy)', *NJW* 2009, 47 sq.

[195] S. Krieger, previous note, 47 sq.

[196] ECJ Case C-396/07 *Juuri* [2008] ECR I-8883 paras. 22–25.

[197] ECJ Case C-396/07 *Juuri* [2008] ECR I-8883 paras. 26–29.

[198] See e.g. ECJ Case C-399/96 *Europièces* [1998] ECR I-6965 paras. 39–43.

[199] Information is in this case owed to all employees; ECJ Case 235/84 *Commission* v. *Italy* [1986] ECR 2291 paras. 20–23 (limited reach of information duties in a collective agreement).

[200] On the system also M. Franzen, *RdA* 2002, 258, 259–261.

paragraph 6 provides for a duty to inform the individual employee if no employee representation exists. Article 7 TUD is thus based upon a distinction between 'collective duties of information' and 'individual duties of information'.

a)   Collective Duties of Information and Consultation as the Rule

90.   Transferor and transferee have an obligation to **inform** their respective employee representatives about the details of the projected transfer, (Article 7(1)(1) TUD). National law determines the identity of the relevant employee representatives, (Article 2(1)(c) TUD). As under the Collective Redundancies Directive (see §23 para. 17 above), Member States are however bound to provide for *some* employee representation, which may be established independent of the employer's agreement.[201] Pursuant to Article 1(1)(1) TUD, the information must cover the following issues:[202]

–   the date or proposed date of the transfer,
–   the reasons for the transfer,
–   the legal, economic and social implications of the transfer for the employees, and
–   any measures envisaged in relation to the employees.

The relevant time for information to be shared is determined by subparagraphs 2 and 3, respectively, for the transferor and the transferee.[203]

91.   Where the transferor or the transferee envisages measures in relation to 'his' employees, he must also **consult** the employees' representatives on such measures with a view to reaching an agreement.[204] 'Measures' includes any legal, economic or social changes that have an effect upon the employees.[205] It covers, for example, moving workers to a different job, a redistribution of tasks or changes in the organisation of the business. A duty to consult is thus the rule rather than an exception. A duty to consult involves a **duty to negotiate** but not a duty to reach agreement. Other than in the Commission's proposal, the Directive does not contain provisions on reconciliation procedures.[206]

---

[201]   ECJ Case C-382/92 *Commission* v. *United Kingdom* [1994] ECR I-2435 paras. 8–30. F. Marhold, in M. Fuchs/F. Marhold (eds.), *Europäisches Arbeitsrecht*, 219 sq.; S. Deakin/G. Morris, *Labour Law*, paras. 9.30 sq.

[202]   Näher K. Riesenhuber, *Gedächtnisschrift für Blomeyer*, 195, 205–209.

[203]   H. Oetker, *NZA* 1998, 1193, 1194; K. Riesenhuber, *Gedächtnisschrift für Blomeyer*, 195, 209 sq.

[204]   On the development of the provision, see C. v. Alvensleben, *Die Rechte der Arbeitnehmer bei Betriebsübergang im Europäischen Gemeinschaftsrecht,* 121 sq.

[205]   With a tendency to a broader reading C. v. Alvensleben, *Die Rechte der Arbeitnehmer bei Betriebsübergang im Europäischen Gemeinschaftsrecht,* 121.

[206]   H. Oetker/C. Schubert, in *EAS*, B 8300 para. 479.

92. Pursuant to the **clause on groups of companies** contained in Article 7(4) TUD, the information and consultation duties also apply where the decision to transfer the business has been taken by an undertaking controlling the employer. A lack of information (from the controlling undertaking) does not relieve the transferor or the transferee of their duties to inform and consult (on the respective provision in the Article 2(4) CRD, see §23 para. 29 above).

93. Information and consultation duties may be limited under the national law of the Member States in two special cases:

–   Pursuant to paragraph 3, the Member States may limit obligations to inform and consult to cases where the transfer gives rise to a **change in the business** likely to entail serious disadvantages for a considerable number of employees.[207] This option is opened up for Member States whose law allows employees' representatives to have recourse to an **arbitration board** to obtain a decision on the measures to be taken in relation to employees.[208]
–   Pursuant to paragraph 5, Member States may limit obligations to inform and consult to undertakings or businesses which, in terms of the number of employees, meet the conditions for the election or nomination of a *collegiate body* representing the employees (**small businesses clause**).[209]

b)   Individual Duties of Information as an Exception

94. Only exceptionally,[210] Article 7(6) TUD imposes an obligation upon the employer to directly inform the employees concerned.[211] This occurs in cases where 'there **are no representatives of the employees** in an undertaking or business through no fault of their own'. This may, for example, be the case where the threshold for establishing an employee representative body has not been passed (where, in other words, the introduction of employee representation has failed for reasons which are not due to a lack of organisation). Pursuant to the systematic location of the provision, it appears that the legislator introduced the individual duty of information to complement the 'small businesses clause' of paragraph 5. This is, indeed, also convincing on teleological considerations, as the transfer of a small business may, in principle, be more readily comprehensible for the individual employee. The exception is however not very well conceived as

---

[207]   See in more detail K. Riesenhuber, *Gedächtnisschrift für Blomeyer*, 195, 210–215.
[208]   See in more detail N. Colneric, *Festschrift für Steindorff*, 1129, 1131–1133; H. Oetker, *NZA* 1998, 1193, 1195.
[209]   See in more detail N. Colneric, *Festschrift für Steindorff*, 1129, 1133; H. Oetker, *NZA* 1998, 1193, 1195 sq.
[210]   M. Franzen, *RdA* 2002, 258, 259.
[211]   The individual duty of information has first been introduced as a mandatory duty by Directive 98/50/EC. It previously existed only as an option for the national law.

complementary to paragraph 5, given that the latter provision already applies where the requirements for establishing a *collegiate body* of employee representatives have not been met, whereas paragraph 6 applies only where *no* employee representation exists.[212]

4. The Position of Employees' Representatives

95. Where employee representation is established in the transferred business, the question arises whether and how the transfer affects it and its members. On the one hand, the existence of employee representation must be safeguarded. The transfer of an undertaking cannot as such justify a change in its employee representation. Such protection may also be deemed necessary in order to prevent abuse ('demolition of the employee representation by way of transfer'). On the other hand, the structures of employee representation deserve recognition. The transfer of an undertaking cannot justify the creation of an employee representation that would not otherwise be required or lawful. Consequently, the transfer of an undertaking may require that employee representation is re-established in light of the new circumstances of the business. In such cases, provision must be made to safeguard employee interests in the interim period. The provisions of Article 6(1) TUD draw a distinction based upon whether or not the transferred unit (undertaking, business or part thereof) maintains its independence.

96. The provision applies to all '**representatives of employees**' under national law, (Article 2(1)(c) TUD). Unlike the original 1977 directive, 'members of administrative, governing or supervisory bodies of companies who represent employees on such bodies in certain Member States' (Article 2(c) TUD 1977) are no longer excluded from the Directive. This has been the case since the 1998 revision of the Directive.[213]

97. The status and function of the representatives or representative body (Article 2(1)(c) TUD; see para. 95 above) is preserved on the same terms and subject to the same conditions as existed prior to transfer, as long as the transferred unit **preserves its autonomy** (*seine Selbständigkeit behält, conserve son autonomie*) (Article 6(1)(1) TUD), and the conditions necessary for the body's constitution remain fulfilled.

98. The question whether the unit preserves its **autonomy** is to be distinguished from the question whether it maintains its 'identity' which determines whether

---

[212]   C. Weber, *Festschrift für Konzen*, 921, 935.
[213]   G. Thüsing, *Europäisches Arbeitsrecht*, §5 paras. 61 sq. Differently H. Oetker/C. Schubert, in *EAS*, B 8300 para. 447.

there is a transfer in the first place.[214] The concept of 'autonomy' must be interpreted autonomously.[215] According to the Court, 'autonomy is as a general rule preserved, … if, after the transfer, the organisational powers of those in charge of the entity transferred remain, within the organisational structures of the transferee, essentially unchanged as compared with the situation pertaining before the transfer'. The **organisational powers** refer to 'the powers, granted to those in charge of that entity, to organise, relatively freely and independently, the work within that entity in the pursuit of its specific economic activity and, more particularly, the powers to give orders and instructions, to allocate tasks to employees of the entity concerned and to determine the use of assets available to the entity, all without direct intervention from other organisational structures of the employer'.[216] However, not every change in a business' organisational structures affect its autonomy: 'The mere change of those ultimately in charge cannot in itself be detrimental to the autonomy of the entity transferred, except where those who have become ultimately in charge have available to them powers which enable them to organise directly the activities of the employees of that entity and therefore to substitute their decision-making within that entity for that of those immediately in charge of the employees.'[217]

99. Subparagraph 2 provides for an exception to the general rule of Article 6(1)(1) TUD where the conditions necessary for reappointment of the representatives or the **reconstitution** of the employee representative body are fulfilled under the applicable law or by agreement with the representatives. This may, in particular, be the case where the number of employees has increased as a consequence of the transfer.

100. The position of employee representation is not maintained in the case of **insolvency**. This is the premise underlying Article 6(1)(3) TUD for the insolvency proceedings defined therein,[218] even though Article 5 TUD merely provides for specific exceptions from Articles 3 and 4 rather than following the general exception that the Court had established under the original directive (see paras. 46 sq. above). Only the 'soft' provision of Article 6(1)(3) TUD suggests that the Member States 'may' take the necessary measures to ensure that the transferred employees are properly represented until new employee representatives are elected or designated.

---

[214] ECJ Case C-151/09 *UGT-FSP* [2010] ECR I-7591 paras. 33 sqq. Approving case note M. Fröhlich, 'Identität und Selbständigkeit der übertragenen wirtschaftlichen Einheit bei Betriebsübergang', *EuZA* 2011, 53–64.

[215] ECJ Case C-151/09 *UGT-FSP* [2010] ECR I-7591 paras. 37 sq.

[216] ECJ Case C-151/09 *UGT-FSP* [2010] ECR I-7591 paras. 42 sqq.

[217] ECJ Case C-151/09 *UGT-FSP* [2010] ECR I-7591 paras. 47 sqq.

[218] In this point as here H. Oetker/C. Schubert, in *EAS,* B 8300 para. 453.

101. The Directive assumes that the mandate of employee representation ends where the transferred unit does **not maintain its autonomy,** (Article 6(1)(4) TUD). Here, too, Member States are obliged to ensure adequate representation of employees in the interim period until new employee representation is established.[219] In this case, however, the obligation upon Member States is mandatory ('shall take the necessary measures').

102. As a supplementary measure, Article 6(2) provides for **continued protection** of the employee representatives whose term of office ends as a result of the transfer, i.e. where the transferred unit loses its autonomy and in the case of insolvency. The Directive does not provide for the protective instruments itself but rather requires that the representatives shall continue to enjoy the protection provided by national law.

IV. IMPLEMENTATION[220]

103. In **Germany**[221] **the Directive was implemented by** the pre-existing provision of §613a BGB,[222] which was amended by the Act on the Adaptation of Employment Law to EC Requirements (*Arbeitsrechtliches EG-Anpassungsgesetz*) of 13 August 1980.[223] In order to implement the continued effect of collective agreements provided for in Article 3(2) TUD, §613a(1) BGB was amended by sentences 2–4. They provide for a continued effect of the norms of collective agreements with the same force as if they were an individual agreement. Restriction of the continued effect of substantive norms, which gives rise to individual rights as opposed to those that affect the business as a whole, is incompatible with the Directive (see para. 62 above). As a consequence of the 1998 and 2001 revisions of the Directive, §613a BGB was amended by the new paragraphs 5 and 6[224] dealing with the modalities of information as well as the right to object.

---

[219] See in more detail M. Franzen, *RdA* 1999, 361, 369; R. Krause, *NZA* 1998, 1201, 1203 sq.

[220] For a comparative survey, see R. Rebhahn, *RdA* 2006 Special Supplement to issue 6, 4–15.

[221] See in detail R. Wank, in P. Hanau/H.-D. Steinmeyer/R. Wank (eds.), *Handbuch des europäischen Arbeits- und Sozialrechts*, §18 paras. 112–152 (on the TUD 1977); J. Joussen, in *EAS*, B 7200 *et passim* and H. Oetker/C. Schubert, in *EAS*, B 8300 *et passim*. Further M. Franzen, *RdA* 1999, 361–374.

[222] Bilingual German-English version in S. Lingemann/R. v. Steinau-Steinrück/A. Mengel (eds.), *Employment and Labor Law in Germany*, Part II, I.

[223] BGBl. 1980 I, 1308.

[224] Gesetz zur Änderung des Seemannsgesetzes und anderer Gesetze of 23 May 2002, BGBl. 2002 I, 1163.

104. Preservation of the mandate of works councils follows from general principles of the Works Constitution Act (*Betriebsverfassungsgesetz*, BetrVG)[225], the interim mandate of Article 6(1)(4) is provided for by §21 BetrVG. The on-going protection against dismissal follows from §15(1) sent. 2 Protection Against Unfair Dismissal Act (*Kündigungsschutzgesetz*, KSchG).[226]

105. There is some doubt whether the collective obligation to inform under Article 7(1) TUD, pursuant to which transferor and transferee inform their employee representatives, has been properly transposed into German law.[227] The German legislator did not implement the respective provisions specifically but rather considered §111 BetrVG to provide for sufficient implementation in the case of operational changes.[228] This is problematic as it largely restricts the term of a 'change in business' (which the Directive does not define) to the cases exhaustively defined by §111 BetrVG. A resulting discrepancy with the Directive's requirements can be cured by interpreting national law in conformity with the Directive.[229]

106. In the **United Kingdom**, the Directive was originally implemented by the Transfer of Undertakings (Protection of Employment) Regulations 1981 ('TUPE'),[230] now in force in a revised version of 2006.[231] The 2006 regulations go beyond the Directive's requirements and provide for more favourable rules for employees.[232]

107. Implementation in **other Member States**, or lack thereof, has resulted in a number of proceedings before the Court of Justice on account of delayed or defective transposition.[233]

---

[225] Bilingual German-English version in S. Lingemann/R. v. Steinau-Steinrück/A. Mengel (eds.), *Employment and Labor Law in Germany*, Part II, X.

[226] Bilingual German-English version in S. Lingemann/R. v. Steinau-Steinrück/A. Mengel (eds.), *Employment and Labor Law in Germany*, Part II, V.

[227] N. Colneric, *Festschrift für Steindorff*, 1129, 1133–1140; H. Oetker, *NZA* 1998, 1193, 1196–1201; K. Riesenhuber, *RdA* 2004, 340–352; C. Weber, *Festschrift für Konzen*, 921, 935–939.

[228] K. Riesenhuber, *RdA* 2004, 340, 342.

[229] K. Riesenhuber, *RdA* 2004, 340, 348 sq.; differently C. Weber, *Festschrift für Konzen*, 921, 935–938.

[230] S.I. 1981/1794.

[231] S.I. 2006/246; available at www.legislation.gov.uk/uksi/2006/246/contents/made.

[232] S. Deakin/G. Morris, *Labour Law*, para. 3.66; J. McMullen, *ILJ* 35 (2006), 113–139.

[233] ECJ Case 237/84 *Commission v. Belgium* [1986] ECR 1247 (undue limitation of the protection against dismissal); Case 235/84 *Commission v. Italy* [1986] ECR 2291; Case C-382/92 *Commission v. United Kingdom* [1994] ECR I-2435; Case C-32/02 *Commission v. Italy* ECR I-12063 (non-profit employers not covered); Case C-145/01 *Commission v. Italy* ECR I-5581 (inadmissible); Case C-333/03 *Commission v. Luxembourg* ECR I-6033 (implementation delayed). On the accession of Spain Case C-336/95 *Pedro Burdalo Trevejo* [1997] ECR I-2115. On the infringement procedures with regard to other Member States H. Alsbaek, *Der Betriebsübergang und seine individualarbeitsrechtlichen Folgen in Europa*, 48–165 (UK,

108. As **against Member States**, protected employees may directly invoke the Directive if it has not been properly or fully implemented. Member States, on the other hand, cannot rely upon the Directive against private individuals, i.e. **against the employee**, as the Directive, which is addressed to Member States, does not impose obligations upon private individuals.[234] On direct effect in general, see also §1 paras. 71 sq.

V.   THE EXAMPLE OF THE *DELAHAYE* CASE[235]

109. The – exceptional – *Delahaye* case raises a number of interesting methodological issues. Mrs Delahaye was an employee of Foprogest. There was no collective agreement governing her remuneration. An important purpose of Foprogest's business was to promote and implement training activities which were intended to improve the social and occupational position of persons seeking work and unemployed persons, in order to enable them to be integrated or reintegrated into the workforce. Its resources consisted essentially of grants, donations and legacies. Foprogest's activity was transferred to the Luxembourg State. The activity thus taken over is now carried on in the form of an administrative public service.

110. Effective 1 January 2000, Mrs Delahaye was taken on as an employee of the Luxembourg State. Other workers who had previously been employed by Foprogest were also taken over by the State. In connection with this transfer, the Luxembourg State and the employees entered into new employment contracts. In this context, Mrs Delahaye signed a contract for an indefinite period with the Minister concerned on 22 December 1999. By virtue of the Grand-Ducal regulation on the remuneration of employees of the Grand Duchy, Mrs Delahaye was then allocated lower remuneration than that she had received under the contract originally concluded with Foprogest. She had been classified by the Grand Duchy of Luxembourg in the first grade, last step, of the salary scale, with no allowance for length of service, which meant that she lost 37% of her monthly salary.

111. It appears from the facts of the case that Mrs Delahaye, in bringing her action, sought to maintain her previous remuneration; as a minimum she wanted to be classified at a higher grade on the salary scale. As the Court of

---

France, Denmark); P. Davies, *YEL* 9 (1989), 21, 29–37 (UK); D. Edward/J. Segan, *RdA* 2006 Special Supplement to issue 6, 15–24 (UK); B. Eisele, *Die Richtlinie zum Betriebsübergang und ihre Umsetzung im englischen Recht* (UK); J. Novak, *RdA* 2006 Special Supplement to issue 6, 25–30 (Slovenia); M. Novella/M. L. Vallauri, *ELJ* 14 (2008), 55–73 (Italy).

234   ECJ Case C-297/03 *Sozialhilfeverband Rohrbach* [2005] ECR I-4305.
235   ECJ Case C-425/02 *Delahaye* [2004] ECR I-10823.

Justice summarises, the parties 'disagree essentially on whether the is obliged, after the transfer in question, to maintain all the rights of the employees, including in particular the right to remuneration, deriving from the contract of employment concluded between them and the transferor association'.

112.   In substance, the case involved a normative collision. The Directive, which pursuant to its Article 1(1)(c) TUD is applicable to the present case, provides for the preservation of the previous terms and conditions of employment – including pay. Pursuant to the Grand-Ducal regulation on remuneration of employees of the Grand Duchy, Mrs Delahaye was to be paid at a lower level.

113.   The Court of Justice tries to solve the case by applying Article 4(2) TUD. It had already previously, in *Mayeur*,[236] held as follows: Where, in the course of the integration of a private legal entity into public administration, employment contracts under private law have to be terminated, this constitutes a substantial change in working conditions to the detriment of the employee, caused by the transfer. In those circumstances, pursuant to Article 4(2) TUD, the employer must be regarded as having been responsible for the termination.[237] In *Delahaye,* the Court goes beyond this previous judgement, declaring that under those circumstances the Directive did not prevent the termination of the employment contracts (wrongfully citing *Mayeur* as a precedent).[238] The termination was then to be regarded as resulting from an action of the employer. 'The same must apply', the Court considers, if, as in *Delahaye,* application of the national rules governing the position of public employees entails a reduction in the remuneration of the employees concerned by the transfer. If the reduction was substantial, it constituted a substantial change in working conditions to the detriment of the employee within the meaning of Article 4(2) TUD.[239] 'Moreover', the Court concludes, 'the competent authorities responsible for applying and interpreting the national law relating to public employees are obliged to do so as far as possible in the light of the purpose of Directive 77/187. It would be contrary to the spirit of that directive to treat an employee taken over from the transferor without taking length of service into account, in so far as the national rules governing the position of State employees take a State employee's length of service into consideration for calculating his remuneration.'[240]

114.   This reasoning is unconvincing. Article 4(2) TUD is not designed to regulate the case at hand and its legal consequences do not contribute to a satisfactory solution. If the Directive was applicable to the present case, then the

---

236   ECJ Case C-175/99 *Mayeur* [2000] ECR I-7755.
237   ECJ Case C-175/99 *Mayeur* [2000] ECR I-7755 para. 56.
238   ECJ Case C-425/02 *Delahaye* [2004] ECR I-10823 para. 32.
239   ECJ Case C-425/02 *Delahaye* [2004] ECR I-10823 para. 33.
240   ECJ Case C-425/02 *Delahaye* [2004] ECR I-10823 para. 34.

rights and obligations, including the right to pay, were transferred to the State of Luxemburg as transferee, pursuant to Article 3(1) TUD. An adaptation of the contract terms was not possible. A dismissal on grounds related to the transfer – which, of course, does not seem to have been considered at all – would not have to be evaluated under Article 4(2) TUD, but rather under Article 4(1)(1) sent. 1 TUD – and consequently would have to be considered unlawful. The Court's reference to the general implementation obligations (Article 288 TFEU and Article 4(3) TEU) is not as such incorrect, yet it appears rather helpless, given that it is utterly unspecific.

115. A methodologically sound solution would have been possible by creating an exception from the Directive's scope of application. This would not have necessitated the exclusion of all public undertakings. The integration of a private undertaking into public administration is a special case that requires special treatment, and here, indeed, the Court could have invoked the fact that the Directive merely provides for partial harmonisation.[241]

116. More to the point, the Court could have openly engaged in judicial development of the law by applying Article 3(3)(1) TUD (Article 3(2)(1) TUD 1977) by way of analogy.[242] If remuneration is regulated by a collective agreement, then another collective agreement terminates the effect of the original collective agreement. This is something that the employee must always expect. In addition, the new collective agreement, collectively negotiated as a whole, is presumed adequate in the same way as the original collective agreement was. Not least, uniform application of the new collective agreement serves the parties' interest in equal treatment. The Directive does not provide for specific regulation of the special case where remuneration is not regulated by collective agreement but by law. Yet, this case can be equated to that which is regulated by Article 3(3) TUD. While the level of remuneration is not legitimised by the bargaining process, it can rely on the legitimation of the legislative process.

VI. OVERVIEW: EMPLOYEE PROTECTION IN THE TAKEOVER DIRECTIVE

Bibliography:
C. Barnard/S. Deakin, 'Reinventing the European Corporation? Corporate Governance, Social Policy and the Single Market', *IRJ* 33 (2002), 484–499; H. Diekmann, 'Änderungen im Wertpapiererwerbs- und Übernahmegesetz anlässlich der Umsetzung der

---

[241] Such exception could have been justified all the more as the case was governed by the TUD 1977 (see ECJ Case C-425/02 *Delahaye* [2004] ECR I-10823 para. 28) where applicability to public undertakings was not expressly regulated.

[242] Pointing in this direction also R. Rebhahn, *RdA* 2006 Special Supplement to issue. 6, 5, 13.

EU-Übernahmerichtlinie in das deutsche Recht', *NJW* 2007, 17–21; S. Grundmann, *European Company Law*, 2nd edn. (Antwerpen: Intersentia, 2011), §30 paras. 16 sqq.; P. Kindler/H. Horstmann, 'Die EU-Übernahmerichtlinie – ein "europäischer" Kompromiss', *DStR* 2004, 868–873; P. O. Mülbert, 'Umsetzungsfragen der Übernahmerichtlinie – erheblicher Änderungsbedarf bei den heutigen Vorschriften des WpÜG', *NZG* 2004, 633–642.

117.   As we have seen above, the Transfer of Undertakings Directive only applies where the undertaking or business is being transferred to another employer and thus not to acquisitions of undertakings structured as stock purchases (para. 22 above). This latter case is only partially regulated by Union law, namely by the Takeover Directive (TOD).[243,244] The Takeover Directive is primarily aimed at the protection of shareholders ('holders of securities') and contains few provisions on employee protection. A transfer of the rights and obligations is not necessary in this case as the employer remains unchanged. Instead, a need for protection is indicated by the fact that a takeover will often lead to the restructuring of the undertaking and will often involve dismissals, both in the offeror and offeree companies.[245] The Directive takes account of the employees' interests by providing for their informational involvement in the bidding procedures (cf. Recital 13 TOD). But even with regard to their informational involvement, the legislator has largely relied upon the pre-existing provisions of the Information and Consultation Framework Directive and the EWC-Directive as well as the Collective Redundancies Directive and the Transfer of Undertakings Directive, Article 14 TOD (cf. Recital 23 TOD).

118.   In referring to Article 14 TOD, the Commission wanted to 'respond to concerns voiced by certain Members of the European Parliament regarding protection of the employees of the companies involved in a takeover bid (both the offeror and the offeree company).' In its explanatory memorandum, the Commission thus emphasises that 'the close and effective involvement of the companies' employees, via their representatives, is an important factor not only for the success of the operation but also for proper consideration of the different interests that may be affected by the takeover'.[246] However, as Article 14 TOD

---

[243]   Directive 2004/25/EC of the European Parliament and of the Council of 21 April 2004 on takeover bids, OJ 2004 L 142/12.

[244]   On the TOD e.g. S. Grundmann, *European Company Law*, §30 (on the scope of application see §30 para. 11); M. Habersack/D. A. Verse, *Europäisches Gesellschaftsrecht*, 4th edn. (Munich: C.H. Beck, 2011), §11. Pursuant to Article 1(1) TOD, the substantive scope of application covers only 'bids for the securities of companies governed by the laws of Member States, where all or some of those securities are admitted to trading on a regulated market'.

[245]   C. Barnard/S. Deakin, *IRJ* 33 (2002), 484, 490.

[246]   Commission, Proposal for a Directive of the European Parliament and of the Council on takeover bids, COM(2002) 534 final, OJ 2003 C 45 E/1, 7, comment to Article 13 of the proposed Directive.

merely refers to pre-existing provisions of Community law and does not have any substantive content of its own, it merely pays lip service to employee involvement and has rightly been characterised as an 'empty phrase'.[247]

119. Employee interests are taken into account in the **bidding process** by requiring both the offeror and offeree company to, *inter alia,* address the effects on jobs and locations of the companies' place of business and to give certain information to employee representatives or, where no employee representatives exist, to the employees.[248] As the same information, for the most part, must also be made public at the same time, the main concern is that employee representatives receive the information directly rather than being informed about the bid in other indirect ways.

120. As a first step, the **decision to make a bid** must be made public without delay, (Article 6(1) sent. 1 TOD). As soon as the bid has been made public, the boards of directors (or equivalent bodies) of the offeree and offeror must inform the representatives of their respective employees or, where there are no such representatives, the employees themselves, (Article 6(1) sent. 3 TOD). In addition, the **offer document** (which is primarily intended for the holders of the offeree company's securities) must be communicated to the employee representatives (the employees) when it is made public, (Article 6(2) sent. 3 TOD). This offer document should include information on 'the offeror's intentions with regard to the future business of the offeree company and, in so far as it is affected by the bid, the offeror company and with regard to the safeguarding of the jobs of their employees and management, including any material change in the conditions of employment, and in particular the offeror's strategic plans for the two companies and the likely repercussions on employment and the locations of the companies' places of business', (Article 6(3)(i) TOD). Such information and documents must be **disclosed** in a way that they are readily and promptly available to, *inter alia,* the employee representatives (employees) of the offeree company, (Article 8(2) TOD). The employee representatives then have an opportunity to give their **written opinion** (cf. Article 9(5) sent. 3 TOD): 'The offeree company's employees should be associated with the opinion and should be able, if they disagree, to communicate their own opinion at the same time. These opinions are addressed to the shareholders, who have the responsibility to decide on the bid.'[249]

---

[247]   P. Kindler/H. Horstmann, *DStR* 2004, 866, 870 (my translation).
[248]   The law of the offeree company applies, Article 4(2)(e) sent. 2 TOD.
[249]   Commission, Proposal for a Directive of the European Parliament and of the Council on takeover bids, COM(2002) 534 final, OJ 2003 C 45 E/1, 6, comment to Article 9 of the proposed Directive.

121.   The board of the offeree company is then under an obligation to draw up and make public a **reasoned opinion** on the bid which, among other matters, must include its views on the offerer's strategic plans for the offeree company and the likely repercussions on employment and the locations of the company's places of business as set out in the offer document; (Article 9(5) sent. 1 TOD). This opinion must be communicated to the employee representatives (employees) at the same time as it is made public.

§25. THE INSOLVENCY PROTECTION DIRECTIVE

CONTENT

Bibliography:

R. Abele, 'Staatshaftung wegen mangelhafter Richtlinientransformation', *ZEuP* 1995, 105–118; R. Birk, 'Das Konkursausfallgeld – Ein rechtsvergleichender Überblick über die Insolvenzsicherung für Arbeitnehmerforderungen', *RabelsZ* 39 (1975), 605–646; M. Franzen, 'Die Rechtsprechung des EuGH zum Schutz der Arbeitnehmer bei Zahlungsunfähigkeit des Arbeitgebers – Ausgewählte Beispielsfälle zur Insolvenzgeld-Richtlinie 80/987/EWG', *DZWIR* 2000, 441–449; M. Heinze, 'Europarechtliche Vorgaben für die Neuregelung des Insolvenzgeldes', in K. Schmidt (ed.), *Festschrift zum 50-jährigen Bestehen der Arbeitsgerichtsbarkeit in Rheinland-Pfalz* (Neuwied/Kriftel: Luchterhand, 1999) 67–83, also published in *KTS* 1998, 513–528; W. Holzer, 'Die Richtlinie zur Angleichung der Rechtsvorschriften der Mitgliedstaaten über den Schutz der Arbeitnehmer bei Zahlungsunfähigkeit des Arbeitgebers und das österreichische Recht', in U. Ruggaldier (eds.), *Österreichisches Arbeitsrecht und das Recht der EG* (Vienna: Orac-Verlag, 1990), 259–282; H. Kasten, 'Deutsche Insolvenzgeldsicherung und EG-Recht', *ZESAR* 2003, 318–326; H. Kasten, *Die deutsche Insolvenzsicherung und EG-Recht* (Frankfurt a.M. et al.: Peter Lang, 2003); A. Kraft/M. Thurner/T. Paintner, 'Gesetz über den Schutz der Arbeitnehmeransprüche im Falle der Insolvenz des Arbeitgebers – Die Sicherung von Arbeitnehmeransprüchen in der Insolvenz des

Arbeitgebers nach polnischem Recht. Mit einer Einführung zum gemeinschaftsrechtlichen Besitzstand im Bereich der Insolvenz-Entgeltsicherung', *WIRO* 2002, 370–375; R. Krauser, 'Europarechtliche Vorgaben für das Konkursausfallgeld', *ZIP* 1998, 56–62; R. Krause, 'Gemeinschaftsrechtlicher Insolvenzschutz für Betriebsrenten und Staatshaftung für fehlerhafte Richtlinienumsetzung', *EuZA* 1 (2008), 96–103; S. Peters-Lange, 'Konsequenzen der EuGH-Rechtsprechung für den Insolvenz-geldanspruch', *ZIP* 2003, 1877–1878; M. Sargeant, 'Protecting Employees with Insolvent Employers', *ILJ* 32 (2003), 53–59; C. Weber, 'Sicherung des Arbeitsentgelts bei Zahlungsunfähigkeit des Arbeitgebers', in H. Oetker/U. Preis (eds.), *Europäisches Arbeits- und Sozialrecht, EAS, part B – Systematische Darstellungen*, loose-leaf (Heidelberg: Forkel, last update: November 2008), B 3300.

Cases:
ECJ Case 22/87 *Commission* v. *Italy* [1989] ECR 143; ECJ Joined Cases C-6/90 and C-9/90 *Francovich I* [1991] ECR I-5357; ECJ Joined Cases C-140/91, C-141/91, C-278/91 and C-279/91 *Suffritti* [1992] ECR I-6337; ECJ Case C-334/92 *Wagner Miret* [1993] ECR I-6911; ECJ Case C-479/93 *Francovich II* [1995] ECR I-3843; ECJ Case C-373/95 *Maso* [1997] ECR I-4051; ECJ Joined Cases C-94/95 and C-95/95 *Bonifaci* [1997] ECR I-3969; ECJ Case C-117/96 *Mosbæk* [1997] ECR I-5017; ECJ Case C-125/97 *Regeling* [1998] ECR I-4493; ECJ Case C-235/95 *Dumon and Froment* [1998] ECR I-4531; ECJ Case C-321/97 *Andersson and Wåkerås-Andersson* [1999] ECR I-3551; ECJ Case C-198/98 *Everson* [1999] ECR I-8903; ECJ Case C-441/99 *Gharehveran* [2001] ECR I-7687; ECJ Case C-442/00 *Caballero* [2002] ECR I-11915; ECJ Case C-160/01 *Mau* [2003] ECR I-4791; ECJ Case C-201/01 *Walcher* [2003] ECR I-8827; ECJ Case C-125/01 *Pflücke* [2003] ECR I-9375; ECJ Joined Cases C-19/01, C-50/01 and C-84/01 *Barsotti* [2004] ECR I-2005; ECJ Case C-520/03 *Valero* [2004] ECR I-12065; ECJ Case C-177/05 *Guerrero Pecino* [2005] ECR I-10887; ECJ Case C-81/05 *Alonso* [2006] ECR I-7569; ECJ Case C-278/05 *Robins* [2007] ECR I-1053; ECJ Case C-9/07 *Commission* v. *France* [2007] ECR I-121; ECJ Case C-6/07 *Commission* v. *Spain* [2007] ECR I-174; ECJ Case C-246/06 *Velasco Navarro* [2008] ECR I-105; ECJ Case C-498/06 *Robledillo Núñez* [2008] ECR I-921; ECJ Case C-310/07 *Holmqvist* [2008] ECR I-7871; ECJ Case C-69/08 *Raffaelo Visciano* [2009] ECR I-6741; ECJ Case C-477/09 *Charles Defossez* 11 March 2011; ECJ Case C-30/10 *Lotta Andersson* 10 February 2011; ECJ Case C-435/10 *van Ardennen* 17 November 2011.

I. ISSUES, OVERVIEW, COMPETENCE, REGULATORY CONTEXT

1. If an employer becomes insolvent, he will in many cases cease to fully pay his employees or make social security (insurance) payments for a considerable time before the insolvency proceedings are initiated. In the insolvency proceedings, employees will usually be protected as any other (money) creditors. In addition, insolvency laws will often provide for special privileges for employees' payment claims. Still, the protection of employees is often considered to be insufficient.[1] The right to outstanding remuneration from the time before the initiation of the insolvency proceedings is not sufficiently protected. At the same time, the employee is not in a good position to take care of his own protection. If the employer company is in a crisis and (part of) the remuneration is not being paid, the employee may, depending on his chances on the labour market, be well-advised to hold still and neither terminate his employment nor try to judicially enforce his right to back pay. Indeed, he may often hope to contribute to the recovery of the undertaking by holding out. The employee is usually not in a position to demand any security (and more often than not, the employer would not be able to offer security either). Faced with the alternative of unemployment, the employee may consider continuing work at a (as he hopes: temporarily) reduced wage as the lesser evil.[2]

2. This is the central issue which the Insolvency Protection Directive (IPD)[3] is concerned with. Its objective is to establish a Union-wide standard of protection with a **guarantee institution** at the centre that secures outstanding payment claims. The Directive, however, largely (and even with regard to central aspects) refers to national law and further gives the Member States a wide margin of discretion. Consequently, the approximation of laws establishes no more than a broad framework.

3. Originally enacted in 1980,[4] the Directive[5] was subsequently amended on the occasion of the accession of new Member States and revised in 2002 by Directive 2002/74/EG[6] – also in light of the Court's case law.[7] The 2002 revision generalised the exceptions that had originally been included with a view to

---

[1]   See also M. Franzen, *DZWIR* 2000, 441, 442.

[2]   R. Birk, *RabelsZ* 39 (1975), 605, 636.

[3]   Directive 2008/94/EC of the European Parliament and the Council of 22 October 2008 on the Protection of Employees in the Event of the Insolvency of their Employer (Codified Version), OJ 2008 L 283/36–42.

[4]   The enactment followed comparatively soon after the Proposal for a Council Directive on the Approximation of the Laws of the Member States concerning the Protection of Employees in the Event of the Insolvency of their Employer of 13 April 1978, COM(79) C 131 final, OJ 1978 C 135/2. On the legislative history W. Holzer, in U. Ruggaldier (eds.), *Österreichisches Arbeitsrecht und das Recht der EG*, 260–262; C. Weber, in *EAS*, B 3300 paras. 1–7.

[5]   Council Directive 80/987/EEC of 20 October 1980 on the Approximation of the Laws of the Member States Relating to the Protection of Employees in the Event of the Insolvency of their Employer, OJ 1980 L 283/23.

[6]   Directive 2002/74/EC of the European Parliament and of the Council of 23 September 2002 Amending Council Directive 80/987/EEC on the Approximation of the Laws of the Member States Relating to the Protection of Employees in the Event of the Insolvency of their Employer, OJ 2002 L 270/10. This Directive, now based no longer on Article 94 EC (Article 115 TFEU, Article 100 ECT) but rather on Article 137 EC (Article 153 TFEU), also changed the title: Council Directive 80/987/EEC of 20 October 1980 on the Protection of Employees in the Event of the Insolvency of their Employer.

[7]   See M. Sargeant, *ILJ* 32 (2003), 53–59.

---

specific Member States listed in the Annex in that it now opened them to all Member States, but at the same time reduced their number and scope. In addition, the legislator also revised the provisions on guarantee institutions and maximum limits (Article 3 and 4 IPD). Further, building on the jurisprudence of the Court of Justice, it expressly defined the international scope of application of the Directive. A 2008 codification revised the text 'in the interests of clarity and rationality';[8] it is this latter version that will be considered exclusively in the analysis which follows.

4. The original 1980 directive had been based on the **competence** of Article 100 EEC (Article 115 TFEU). There is some doubt whether this provision can support the Directive[9] even though the legal situations in the Member States before its enactment were rather disparate.[10] As the Directive did not, in particular, ensure that the guarantee institution is financed by the employer (cf. Article 5 IPD; see para. 22 below), it cannot contribute to avoiding distortions of competition in respect of personnel costs. The Court of Justice, while ruling on the Directive in a considerable number of cases, has never expressed any concern about the competence on which it is based. The 2002 amendment, as well as the 2008 codification, were based upon Article 137 EC (Article 153 TFEU).

II. SCOPE OF APPLICATION

5. 'This Directive shall apply to employees' claims arising from contracts of employment or employment relationships and existing against employers who are in a state of insolvency within the meaning of Article 2(1)'; Article 1(1) IPD. The scope of the Directive is determined by Article 1 together with the definition norm of Article 2.

1. Employee

6. The personal scope of application of the Directive primarily extends to **employees** and employers. Neither concept is defined by the Directive, but Article 2(2) IPD expressly refers to the definitions in national laws of the Member States.[11] However, the Directive itself and the general implementation obligations (§1 paras. 65 sq.) do provide for a framework of limitations.

---

8   See note 3 above.
9   C. Weber, in *EAS*, B 3300 para. 10.
10   For a survey see R. Birk, *RabelsZ* 39 (1975), 605–646.
11   C. Weber, in *EAS*, B 3300 paras. 16 sq.; critically from a policy perspective M. Sargeant, *ILJ* 32 (2003), 53, 56 sq. Irrespective of Article 2(2) IPD, the Court has in ECJ Case C-160/01 *Mau* [2003] ECR I-4791 paras. 39–45 (based on an *argumentum e contrario* from Article 2(2) IPD, the *telos* and the principle of effectiveness) defined a framework for the term 'employment

7. First, Member States may **exclude** *certain categories* of employees from the scope of the Directive where those employees are covered by other forms of guarantees which provide an equivalent standard of protection, Article 1(2) IPD. Secondly, they may maintain existing exceptions for domestic servants employed by a natural person and share-fishermen, Article 1(3) IPD. And finally, Article 12(c) IPD allows for selective exceptions from the liability of Article 3(1) and the guarantee obligation of Article 7 for the case where the employee, on his own or together with close relatives, was the owner of an essential part of the employer's undertaking or business and had a considerable influence upon its activities (see also para. 23 below).[12] Conversely, employees in certain atypical employment relationships – part-time employees, fixed-term employees, temporary agency employees – may **not be excluded** from the scope of the Directive, Article 2(2)(2) IPD, and Member States may not set a **minimum duration** for the employment relationship in order for employees to qualify for claims under the Directive, Article 2(3) IPD.

8. It already follows from this specific and differentiated set of exceptions that, *e contrario,* Member States may not exclude further categories of workers from the scope of the Directive's protection. More generally, the **implementation obligations** require that Member States may not introduce a special concept of employee or exclude further categories of employees (!) in their implementation of the Directive.[13] A Spanish provision which implemented the Directive, pursuant to which executive employees were not regarded as employees, was thus incompatible with the Directive.[14] Finally, the Court of Justice has also employed the fundamental rights of the Union in respect of the Member States' implementation obligations, namely 'the general principle of equality and **non-discrimination**'.[15] From this, the Court inferred a prohibition of discrimination in regard to determining the personal scope of application of the Directive by the Member States (see paras. 11 sq. below).

---

relationship' autonomously so as to exclude the time of parental leave without pay; see also note 19 below.

[12] Narrowly construed by ECJ Case C-441/99 *Gharehveran* [2001] ECR I-7687 paras. 21–28 (concerning the original Directive). ECJ Case C-30/10 *Lotta Andersson* 10 February 2011 accepts that the Directive does not preclude the Member States from fixing a time period (in this case: six months before the insolvency) during which the criteria excluding the employee's entitlement must have been met; the implementation obligations (see §1 paras. 65 sq.), of course, limit this possibility.

[13] C. Weber, in *EAS,* B 3300 para. 18.

[14] ECJ Case C-334/92 *Wagner Miret* [1993] ECR I-6911 paras. 15–23. See also Case 22/87 *Commission* v. *Italy* [1989] ECR 143 paras. 15–19 (exception of executive staff, apprentices and homeworker).

[15] ECJ Case C-81/05 *Alonso* [2006] ECR I-7569 paras. 35–37; Case C-177/05 *Guerrero Pecino* [2005] ECR I-10887 paras. 26–30; Case C-520/03 *Valero* [2004] ECR I-12065 para. 34; Case C-442/00 *Caballero* [2002] ECR I-11915 para. 32.

2.   Insolvency

9.   The substantive scope of the Directive is determined by the definition of insolvency, as defined in Article 2(1) of the Directive. Notwithstanding its importance, the Directive largely refers to the **national laws of the Member States** with regard to defining insolvency. An employer is deemed to be in a state of insolvency within the meaning of Article 2(1) of the Directive where

(1) first, the applicable national law provides for certain collective proceedings (see in more detail para. 10 below),
(2) second, a request has been made for the opening of these proceedings and
(3) third, the competent authority has decided on the opening of these proceedings, be it that it decided to open the proceedings or that it established that the available assets are insufficient to warrant the opening of the proceedings.[16]

10.   **Collective proceedings** are proceedings which are based upon the insolvency of the employer and involve the partial or total divestment of the employer's assets and the appointment of a liquidator or a person performing a similar task. The definition entails, in particular, that the scope of application is restricted to proceedings as defined in national law. Owing to the lack of uniform rules on insolvency proceedings, national laws could not be approximated any further in this regard. Consequently, the protection of employees is also left to the Member States in this regard. In particular, employee protection is only ensured where national law *provides for collective proceedings*. Where national law, as has occasionally been the case, excludes certain (e.g. smaller) employers from such proceedings, then consequently their employees will not be afforded the protection intended by the Directive. This is a deliberate legislative decision which is also compatible with the principle of equality.[17] Member States are free, however, to also extend employee protection to other cases where no such formalised proceedings are being opened but the employer is *de facto* insolvent, Article 2(4) IPD.

3.   Payment of Outstanding Claims

11.   The Directive protects 'payment of outstanding claims resulting from contracts of employment or employment relationships', primarily pay,

---

[16]   On the – differently worded – original version of Article 2(1) IPD: ECJ Case C-160/01 *Mau* [2003] ECR I-4791 paras. 21–32; Case C-321/97 *Andersson und Wåkerås-Andersson* [1999] ECR I-3551 para. 42; Joined Cases C-94/95 and C-95/95 *Bonifaci* [1997] ECR I-3969 paras. 34 sq.; Case C-373/95 *Maso* [1997] ECR I-4051 para. 44; Case C-479/93 *Francovich II* [1995] ECR I-3843 para. 18.

[17]   ECJ Case C-479/93 *Francovich II* [1995] ECR I-3843.

Article 3(1) IPD.[18] Claims must result from the **employment relationship**,[19] and Article 3(1) IPD clarifies that this may, at the choice of the Member States, include severance pay. What constitutes **pay** is (unlike Article 157 TFEU; see §9 paras. 6–10 above) for the national laws of the Member States to determine, Article 2(2) IPD.[20] Here too, though, implementation obligations and Union fundamental rights (see para. 8 above) provide for a framework of limitations. The Court considered a Spanish provision to be incompatible with the principle of equality under Union law because only claims for compensation for unfair dismissal awarded by judgement were protected but not similar claims for compensation established in conciliation procedures.[21] Upon repeated reference for preliminary ruling, the Court has accepted that the different treatment of claims for compensation agreed upon outside judicial proceedings may be objectively justified to the extent that it is necessary for the prevention of abuse (cf. Article 12(a) IPD; para. 24 below).[22]

12. In respect of theory and methodology, such judicial control of national implementation laws with regard to the principle of equality under Union law deserves further discussion. Comparable to its approach in *Mangold* (see §8 para. 11, §11 paras. 3, 36, 39, 47–50), the Court seems to establish a prohibition of discrimination as a general principle of Union primary law. (Today, this could perhaps be inferred from the Charter of Fundamental Rights.) It then measures national implementation laws against this principle. However, the present analysis differs from that in *Mangold*. There, the Court invented and applied the prohibition of age discrimination, a principle that needs further elaboration as a matter of social policy (and the Court has, indeed, supplemented this principle of primary law with the grounds for justification established in the provision of Article 6 ETFD, i.e. in secondary legislation.) In the present cases, the Court's analysis instead involves a prohibition of arbitrary distinctions where the test is whether the (national) legislator used a distinction for which simply no objective justification can be found.

---

18   Cf. ECJ Case 22/87 *Commission* v. *Italy* [1989] ECR 143 para. 11.
19   In ECJ Case C-160/01 *Mau* [2003] ECR I-4791 paras. 39–45 the Court defined the employment relationship autonomously so as to not cover the time of parental leave without pay; see also note 11 above; approvingly H. Kasten, *ZESAR* 2003, 318, 321 sq.
20   ECJ Case C-69/08 *Raffaelo Visciano* [2009] ECR I-6741 paras. 25–30 and 32–35. See also M. Heinze, *Festschrift zum 50-jährigen Bestehen der Arbeitsgerichtsbarkeit in Rheinland-Pfalz*, 70 (proposing to exclude e.g. claims for damages as well as bonuses [this latter issue seems problematic; it may, however, be covered by ceilings; see para. 21 below]).
21   ECJ Case C-246/06 *Velasco Navarro* [2008] ECR I-105 paras. 31–39; Case C-81/05 *Alonso* [2006] ECR I-7569 paras. 35–42; Case C-177/05 *Guerrero Pecino* [2005] ECR I-10887 paras. 20–30; Case C-442/00 *Caballero* [2002] ECR I-11915 paras. 32–39.
22   ECJ Case C-498/06 *Robledillo Núñez* [2008] ECR I-921 paras. 28–43.

13. The Directive is primarily aimed at the protection of outstanding payment claims. Beyond that, it also protects **old-age benefits including survivors' benefits,** Article 8 IPD. Survivors of employees can thus also be protected.

4.   Cross-Border Cases

14. Articles 9 sq. IPD contain special provisions for cross-border cases.[23] Where an undertaking with activities in more than one Member State[24] becomes insolvent, the guarantee institution located in the Member State of the employee's **habitual place of work** is responsible.[25]

III.   THE GUARANTEE INSTITUTION

1.   Outstanding Claims Resulting from the Employment Relationship

15. The guarantee institutions, designed to ensure payment of outstanding claims of employees (where applicable others, para. 14 above) resulting from the employment relationship, is the central objective and instrument of the Directive. The 'insurance' covers claims resulting from the **employment contract or employment relationship**; the wording is intended to also cover cases where the contractual basis may be defective. The definitions of 'employment contract' and 'employment relationship' are for the national laws of the Member States to determine, as are the definitions of employee, employer and pay, Article 2(2) IPD.

16. The guarantee institution covers **outstanding claims.** Its aim is, in other words, not to provide for social benefits (which may be determined with a view to the needs of the employee) but rather to safeguard payment of the employees' earnings.[26] The Court has given the term *outstanding* claims an **autonomous**

---

[23]   See R. Birk, *RabelsZ* 39 (1975), 605, 642–646.

[24]   The term 'activities' has been construed broadly, ECJ Case C-310/07 *Holmqvist* [2008] ECR I-7871 paras. 19–35: It does not require a branch office or a place of business, but the undertaking 'must have a stable economic presence ..., featuring human resources which enable it to perform activities there'. Approving case note by O. Ricken, *EuZA* 2010, 109–118.

[25]   The issue was controversial before the insertion of this new provision by the 2002 reform. The Court had (based on a systematic interpretation) initially considered responsible the guarantee institution of the state where the request for opening the proceedings has been made; ECJ Case C-117/96 *Mosbæk* [1997] ECR I-5017; differently – guarantee institution of the place of work – Case C-198/98 *Everson* [1999] ECR I-8903 paras. 20–24 in a case where the employee of a foreign company which was subject to insolvency proceedings abroad had pursued his work in the domestic branch; see further ECJ Case C-477/09 *Charles Defossez* 11 March 2011 paras. 18–34 (also discussing the temporal scope of the different versions of the Directive).

[26]   This purpose is being compromised by the possibility of the Member States to provide for ceilings pursuant to Article 4(3) IPD; see para. 21 below.

definition in Union law.[27] From this, it has, *inter alia,* concluded that (legal or judicial) provisions addressing the question of which of several outstanding claims a payment must be offset against, must be interpreted in conformity with the Directive.[28]

17.   The employee had outstanding claims for pay against the employer in respect of periods of employment before and within the reference period for protected claims of Article 4 IPD. In accordance with national private law, the guarantee institution wanted to set off payments made by the employer during the reference period against the claims for pay for that period. As a consequence, the employee's claims against the guarantee institution would have been reduced by the respective amount. The Court considered this interpretation to be incompatible with the purpose of the Directive.

2.   Period of Protection

18.   The Directive contains two provisions on the **period** for which outstanding claims are protected.[29] Article 3(2) merely provides that the protected claims shall be outstanding payment claims *'relating to a period* prior to and/or, as applicable, after a given date determined by the Member States'.[30] The legislator had in mind that a period should be determined in relation to the insolvency proceedings. This conforms with the purpose of the Directive of protecting employees in the case of the employer's insolvency: Such protection is warranted only to the extent that the employer's non-performance has a certain temporal connection with the insolvency.

19.   Article 3(2) IPD already merely requires that 'a period' be set without determining its length. In other words, the Directive leaves it for Member States to determine the length of the reference period – within the limits that follow from the purpose of the Directive and the implementation obligations (see §1 paras. 65 sq. above). Article 4 IPD supplements the provision by giving Member States certain options for limiting the scope of protection in respect of the length of the reference period and the payments guaranteed.

---

27   ECJ Case C-201/01 *Walcher* [2003] ECR I-8827 para. 32.

28   ECJ Case C-125/97 *Regeling* [1998] ECR I-4493 paras. 18–22.

29   See also R. Birk, *RabelsZ* 39 (1975), 605, 636 sq. (discussing the possible starting points in a comparative analysis).

30   The original Directive still restricted the discretion for transposition in the Member States in Article 3(2) to three alternatives; the Court had interpreted that provision narrowly in the interest of the *effet utile;* ECJ Case C-373/95 *Maso* [1997] ECR I-4051 paras. 43–54; Joined Cases C-94/95 and C-95/95 *Bonifaci* [1997] ECR I-3969 paras. 30–44. The legislature corrected this with the 2002 Directive and broadened Member States' discretion; see S. Peters-Lange, *ZIP* 2003, 1877–1879 ('The legislature has completely undermined the harmonisation goal that the Court had expressed in its jurisprudence on the determination of the public minimum guarantees.' – my translation).

20. As regards temporal limitations, Article 4(1), (2) IPD provides an option for Member States to introduce a *minimum period* and a *reference period*. The **minimum period** covers at least the last three months[31] of the employment relationship and the outstanding payment claims connected with it; this minimum period may be prior to, or after, the reference date which is determined pursuant to Article 3(2) IPD (see para. 18 above). In addition, Member States may include this minimum period of three months in a **reference period** of at least six months. If the reference period is at least 18 months, the minimum period may be reduced to eight weeks.

3. Ceilings

21. Member States may also introduce ceilings on the payments made by the guarantee institutions, Article 4(3) IPD.[32,33] The Directive does not determine the level of these ceilings but requires that they 'must not fall below a level which is socially compatible with the social objective of this Directive'. As an indication for the concretisation of this provision, one may consider that the Directive is normally (i.e. without any limitations) intended to protect an employee's net income (Article 6 IPD; see para. 28 below) for the last three months (Article 4(2) IPD). However, the Court of Justice has accepted a ceiling that covered the basic needs of the employee, independent of the individual's earnings.[34] The Commission must be notified about such ceilings under Article 4(3)(2) IPD, although such notification is not, under Union law, a precondition for the ceiling taking effect.[35]

4. Organisation, Financing and Operation

22. The organisation, financing and operation of the guarantee institution are for Member States to determine. Article 5 IPD merely provides for a number of principles. First, the assets of the institution must be independent of the employers' operating capital and must be inaccessible to insolvency proceedings;

---

[31]   On the interpretation ECJ Case C-373/95 *Maso* [1997] ECR I-4051 paras. 60–64 ('three calendar months').

[32]   This corresponds with the situation in the national laws that the legislature found before the harmonisation; see R. Birk, *RabelsZ* 39 (1975), 605, 640 sq.

[33]   See ECJ Case C-373/95 *Maso* [1997] ECR I-4051 paras. 55–59 (Article 4(3), 10 IPD cannot justify the limitation of other claims not based on the employment contract or relationship).

[34]   Implicitly ECJ Joined Cases C-19/01, C-50/01 and C-84/01 *Barsotti* [2004] ECR I-2005 paras. 32–40, where the Court merely objects that payments made during the period covered by the guarantee are being deducted (which are already taken into account by the determination of the out standing claims). Critically C. Weber, in *EAS*, B 3300 para. 47 (arguing that what is at stake is not an insurance the subsistence level but the remuneration).

[35]   ECJ Case C-235/95 *Dumon and Froment* [1998] ECR I-4531 paras. 28–32.

this is a basic requirement which reflects the purpose of the Directive. Secondly, employers must, in principle, contribute to the financing of the guarantee institution. Funding may not, in other words, be left exclusively to the employees. National law may exempt the employer from contributions if the guarantee is fully covered by public authorities. Third, the institutions' liabilities must not depend upon whether or not the employer, employee and public authorities, as applicable, have fulfilled their obligations to contribute. Again, this is a basic requirement which follows from the purpose of the Directive.

5.   Optional Limitations or Reductions in National Law

23.   The option for Member States to exclude or reduce the liability of the guarantee institution is unaffected by the Directive in the three following areas: prevention of abuse, prevention of collusion and in cases where the employee had considerable influence upon the employer's undertaking, Article 12 IPD. The first two groups are concerned with the prevention of abuse. The third group concerns cases where an employee's claims may be excluded or restricted because he, on his own or together with close relatives, was the owner of an essential part of the employer's undertaking and had considerable influence over its activities and is thus concerned with the delimitation of entrepreneurial risks.[36] As such, the third group concerns the personal scope of protection of the Directive (see paras. 6 sq. above) rather than a restriction of claims on grounds of individual behaviour. As exceptions, the provisions have been narrowly interpreted by the Court of Justice.[37]

24.   First, the Directive does not affect the 'option' of the Member States 'to take measures necessary to avoid abuse', lit. a). 'The abuses referred to [in Article 12(a) IPD] are abusive practices that adversely affect the guarantee institutions by artificially giving rise to a claim for salary, thereby illegally triggering a payment obligation on the part of those institutions.'[38] Member States retain discretion as to their choice of measures for the prevention of abuse (e.g. an exclusion or reduction of the guarantee institution's liability, a criminal sanction…); but their choices must also satisfy the principle of proportionality ('necessary').[39]

---

[36]   It seems misguided, though, that the legislature also refers to the ownership of the *business*. This wording appears to result from an uncertainty and an excessive measure of caution.

[37]   ECJ Case C-201/01 *Walcher* [2003] ECR I-8827 paras. 37 sq.; Case C-441/99 *Gharehveran* [2001] ECR I-7687 para. 26 (on the original Directive). On the methodological issue (critically) K. Riesenhuber, in id. (ed.), *Europäische Methodenlehre,* §11 paras. 61–66.

[38]   ECJ Case C-201/01 *Walcher* [2003] ECR I-8827 para. 39.

[39]   ECJ Case C-201/01 *Walcher* [2003] ECR I-8827 para. 40. See also Case C-498/06 *Robledillo Núñez* [2008] ECR I-921 paras. 32 sq.

25. Collusion (lit. b) – consensual cooperation to harm a third person – is really a special case of abuse. The provision is rather clumsily worded. It presupposes the existence of a special link and shared interests between employee and employer, which result in collusion. The Member States' options are restricted in that they may merely refuse or reduce liability under Article 3(1) or the guarantee obligation under Article 7. However, these are, of course, an employee's central claims under the Directive.

6.   General Limitations of National Law

26. The Directive does not expressly leave **limitation periods** or other general limitations to claims unaffected, yet they are not restricted by the wording of the Directive either. Such general limitations may be provided for in national law within the limits set by the implementation obligations (see §1 paras. 65 sq. above).[40] However, the Court held that an **obligation** for employees **to register as job-seekers** in the event of their employer's insolvency which, if unfulfilled rendered their guarantee payment subject to a 20% deduction, was incompatible with Articles 3 and 4 IPD.[41]

IV.   SOCIAL SECURITY

27. Articles 6–8 of Chapter III IPD provide for three selective regulations on social security.

28. Member States may exclude **contributions** (of the employees; *Beiträge der Arbeitnehmer*) due under the national **social security schemes** or under supplementary occupational or inter-occupational schemes from the liability under Articles 3–5 of the Directive, Article 6 IPD. This makes sense in that these contributions do not directly support the employee's living expenses.[42] The social purpose of the Directive thus does not require them to be included as guaranteed claims. Consequently, the employee's social security protection may be put at risk.[43] This provision emphasises the social purpose of the Directive over the Directive's other purpose of safeguarding *contractual rights*.

---

[40]   ECJ Case C-125/01 *Pflücke* [2003] ECR I-9375 paras. 30–46; Case C-69/08 *Raffaelo Visciano* [2009] ECR I-6741 paras. 36–50. Still with doubt H. Kasten, *Die deutsche Insolvenzsicherung und EG-Recht*, 81–99; H. Kasten, *ZESAR* 2003, 318, 322 sq.

[41]   ECJ Case C-435/10 *van Ardennen* 17 November 2011 paras. 26–39 (arguing, *inter alia*, that such obligation 'is not by its nature comparable with a time limit for the submission of an application for an insolvency benefit' (para. 36).

[42]   If the Member States do not make use of this option, they decide whether the respective amounts should be payable to the directly to the social security institutions or to the employees.

[43]   C. Weber, in *EAS*, B 3300 paras. 49–51.

29. Article 7 IPD then provides for (what Article 12(b) and (c) refer to as) a **guarantee obligation**. If the employer does not pay compulsory contributions due before the onset of his insolvency to the insurance institution, even though he has deducted the employees' contributions at the source from the remuneration paid, this must not adversely affect employees' benefit entitlement in respect of these insurance institutions.[44] This provision addresses a problem that frequently occurs when an employer has reached a state of crisis (see para. 1 above). In that situation, the employer will often not pay social security contributions. The employees should not suffer from the employer's default.

30. Finally, Article 8 IPD is concerned with entitlements or prospective entitlements to **old-age benefits** and survivors' benefits under supplementary occupational or inter-occupational schemes.[45] The provision is, however, rather vaguely worded.[46] It aims to protect employees from the risk that non-statutory supplementary schemes in which they are members are defaulting in the course of the employer's insolvency. Article 8 merely requires Member States to 'ensure that the necessary measures are taken to protect the interests of employees' (as well as other claimants: former employees and survivors) 'in respect of rights conferring on them immediate or prospective entitlement to old-age benefits, including survivors' benefits under supplementary occupational or inter-occupational pension schemes outside the national statutory social security schemes'. The provision gives Member States a wide margin of discretion in their implementation. Their margin of discretion is, however, exceeded where a considerable number of protected employees receive less than half of the old-age benefits to which they are entitled.[47]

V. IMPLEMENTATION

31. **German law**[48] provided for the protection of outstanding employee claims even before the Directive had been enacted. Provisions regarding the so-called insolvency money (*Insolvenzgeld*) are today found in §§183 sqq. Social Security Code III (*Sozialgesetzbuch III*). In the **United Kingdom**, ss. 166–170 and 182–190

---

44   Cf. ECJ Case 22/87 *Commission* v. *Italy* [1989] ECR 143 paras. 25–33.
45   Critically on the systematic placement R. Krause, *EuZA* 2008, 96, 97; C. Weber, in *EAS*, B 3300 paras. 23 sq. (not an issue of social security but of safeguarding remuneration).
46   W. Holzer, in U. Ruggaldier (ed.), *Österreichisches Arbeitsrecht und das Recht der EG*, 272 ('The normative content of the Article is difficult to grasp.' – my translation).
47   ECJ Case C-278/05 *Robins* [2007] ECR I-1053 paras. 35–46 and 54–62; R. Krause, *EuZA* 2008, 96, 102 sq.
48   On the implementation in Germany in more detail C. Weber, in *EAS*, B 3300 paras. 74–90; R. Wank, in P. Hanau/H.-D. Steinmeyer/R. Wank (eds.), *Handbuch des europäischen Arbeits- und Sozialrechts*, §18 paras. 180–189.

Employment Rights Act 1996[49] implement the Directive.[50] An employee's claim to arrears of pay is limited to eight weeks and is subject to a ceiling of £ 380 per week.

32.   Implementation deficits in Italy have repeatedly given rise to a number of proceedings in the Court of Justice.[51] In particular, they provided an opportunity for the Court to develop its case law on **direct applicability**, the duty of interpretation in conformity with the Directive and **state liability** (see §1 paras. 69–77); the Court's seminal decision on state liability in *Francovich I*[52] concerned the Insolvency Protection Directive. The Court held that the Directive was not, in principle, directly applicable, because while the scope of persons protected was sufficiently clearly determined, as was the content of the guarantee – notwithstanding the Member States' implementation options –, the Directive did not identify the person liable to provide the guarantee.[53]

---

[49]   Available at www.legislation.gov.uk/ukpga/1996/18.

[50]   For a short survey, see S. Deakin/G. Morris, *Labour Law,* paras. 5.187 sqq.

[51]   Deficits in the implementation of the 2002 Directive: ECJ Case C-9/07 *Commission* v. *France* [2007] ECR I-121; Case C-6/07 *Commission* v. *Spain* [2007] ECR I-174. On the implementation in Poland: A. Kraft/M. Thurner/T. Paintner, *WIRO* 2002, 370–375.

[52]   ECJ Joined Cases C-6/90 and C-9/90 *Francovich I* [1991] ECR I-5357 paras. 38–46. Further Case C-373/95 *Maso* [1997] ECR I-4051 paras. 33–42 and Joined Cases C-94/95 and C-95/95 *Bonifaci* [1997] ECR I-3969 paras. 45–54 (compensation of damages by means of retroactive enactment of transposition norms). See also Case C-321/97 *Andersson and Wåkerås-Andersson* [1999] ECR I-3551 (on the accession of Sweden).

[53]   ECJ Joined Cases C-6/90 and C-9/90 *Francovich I* [1991] ECR I-5357 paras. 10–27; Case C-334/92 *Wagner Miret* [1993] ECR I-6911 paras. 16–19. In the cases underlying the decision in Joined Cases C-140/91, C-141/91, C-278/91 and C-279/91 *Suffritti* [1992] ECR I-6337 paras. 10–14 the implementation period had not yet expired. Differently (direct application possible) where the Member State has implemented the Directive in its central parts, making choices on the various options, and only individual provisions have not been properly implemented; Case C-441/99 *Gharehveran* [2001] ECR I-7687 paras. 33–46.

PART 4
COLLECTIVE EMPLOYMENT LAW

§26. EUROPEAN LAW ON EMPLOYEE INVOLVEMENT – INTRODUCTION AND OVERVIEW

CONTENTS

Sources:

J. Armour/S. Deakin/S. J. Konzelmann, 'Shareholder Primacy and the Trajectory of UK Corporate Governance', *BJIR* 41(2003), 531–555; T. Baums/P. Ulmer (eds.), *Unternehmens-Mitbestimmung der Arbeitnehmer im Recht der EU-Mitgliedstaaten* (Heidelberg: Recht und Wirtschaft, 2004) (with contributions by P. Krüger Andersen [DK], H. Toiviainen [FIN], I. Urbain-Parleani [F], V. Raynaud [L], L. Timmermann/S. Spanjaard [NL], S. Kalss [A], A. Victorin [S], M. Henssler [D] und P. Ulmer [general report]); R. Birk, 'Europäisches kollektives Arbeitsrecht – insbesondere der Europäische Betriebsrat', in S. Grundmann (ed.), *Systembildung und Systemlücken in Kerngebieten des Europäischen Privatrechts* (Tübingen: Mohr Siebeck, 2000), 387–399; S. Braun, *Die Sicherung der Unternehmensmitbestimmung im Lichte des europäischen Rechts* (Baden-Baden: Nomos, 2005); T. Brors, *Das System der Arbeitnehmer-Beteiligungs-Richtlinien* (Baden-Baden: Nomos, 2005); N. Bruun, 'Employees' Participation Rights and Business Restructuring', *EELJ* 2 (2011), 27–47; J. Dammann, 'The Future of Codetermination After Centros: Will German Corporate Law Move Closer to the US Model?', *Fordham JCFL* 8 (2003) 607–686; W. Däubler, 'The Employee Participation Directive – A Realistic Utopia?', *CMLR* 14 (1977), 457–487; C. Docksey, 'Employee Information and Consultation Rights in the Member States of the European Communities', *Comp. Lab. L.* 7 (1986), 32–48 (with a table in the Annex, 49–69); H. Eidenmüller/L. Hornuf/M. Reps, 'Contracting Employee Involvement: An Analysis of Bargaining over Employee Involvement Rules for a Societas Europaea', available at SSRN: http://ssrn.com/abstract=1979487 or doi:10.2139/ssrn.1979487; H. Eidenmüller, 'Forschungsperspektiven im Unternehmensrecht', *JZ* 2007, 487–494; J. Figge, *Mitbestimmung auf Unternehmensebene in Vorschlägen der Europäischen Gemeinschaften* (Baden-Baden: Nomos, 1992); W. Frenz/V. Götzkes, 'Ein europäisches Grundrecht der Arbeitnehmerinnen und Arbeitnehmer auf Unterrichtung und Anhörung im Unternehmen? – Zur rechtsdogmatischen Einordnung von Art. 27 EGRC', *RdA* 2007, 216–218; F. Gamillscheg, *Kollektives Arbeitsrecht Band II – Betriebsverfassung* (Munich: C.H. Beck, 2008); F. Gamillscheg, 'Wandlungen in der französischen Betriebsverfassung', in G. Annuß/E. Picker/H. Wißmann (eds.), *Festschrift für Richardi zum 70. Geburtstag* (Munich: C.H. Beck, 2007), 1025–1038; W. Goos, 'Ansätze zur Mitbestimmung der Arbeitnehmer in der Europäischen Rechtsetzung', in H. Oetker/U. Preis/V. Rieble (eds.), *50 Jahre Bundesarbeitsgericht* (Munich: C.H. Beck, 2004), 1179–1195; H. Hansmann, *The Ownership of Enterprise* (Cambridge, MA: Harvard University Press, 1996); H. Hansmann/R. Kraakman, 'The end of history for corporate law', *Geo. L. J.* 89 (2001) 439–468; M. Henssler, Mitbestimmung als Verhandlungsgegenstand grenzüberschreitender Strategien, in P.-C. Müller-Graff/C. Teichmann (eds.), *Europäisches Gesellschaftsrecht auf neuen Wegen* (Baden-Baden: Nomos, 2010), 143–168; M. Henssler, 'Erfahrungen und Reformbedarf bei der SE – Mitbestimmungsrechtliche Reformvorschläge', *ZHR* 173 (2009), 222–249; T. C. Hodge, 'The Treatment of Employees as Stakeholders in the European Union: Current and Future Trends', *Syracuse J. Int'l L. & Com.* 38 (2010), 91–171; P. Hommelhoff, 'Mitbestimmungsvereinbarungen zur

Modernisierung der deutschen Unternehmensmitbestimmung', *ZGR* 2010, 48–74; P. Hommelhoff/K. J. Hopt/A. v. Werder (eds.), *Handbuch Corporate Governance*, 2nd edn. (Stuttgart/Cologne: Schäffer-Poeschel and Otto Schmidt, 2009); K. J. Hopt, 'Grundprobleme der Mitbestimmung in Europa – Eine rechtsvergleichende Bestandsaufnahme und Einschätzung der Vorschläge zur Rechtsangleichung der Arbeitnehmermitbestimmung in den Europäischen Gemeinschaften', *ZfA* 1982, 207–235; K. J. Hopt, 'New Ways in Corporate Governance: European Experiments with Labour Representation on Corporate Boards', *Mich. L. Rev.* 82 (1984), 1338–1363; K. J. Hopt/E. Wymeersch (eds.), *Comparative Corporate Governance* (Berlin: de Gruyter, 1997); K. J. Hopt et al. (eds.), *Corporate Governance in Context* (Oxford: Oxford University Press, 2005); A. Junker, 'Betriebsverfassung im europäischen Vergleich', *ZfA* 2001, 225–243; A. Junker, 'Betriebsverfassung in Klein- und Mittelbetrieben', *NZA* 2001, 131–138; A. Junker, 'Der "Europäische Betriebsrat" in rechtsvergleichender Perspektive', *JZ* 1992, 1100–1106; A. Junker, 'Der Standort der deutschen Betriebsverfassung in Europa', *RIW* 2002, 81–87; A. Junker, 'Unternehmensmitbestimmung in Deutschland – Anpassungsbedarf durch internationale und europäische Entwicklungen', *ZfA* 2005, 1–44; C. Kirchner, 'Grundstrukturen eines neuen institutionellen Designs für die Arbeitnehmermitbestimmung auf der Unternehmensebene', *AG* 2004, 197–200; W. Kohte, 'Auf dem Weg zur betrieblichen Informationsverfassung', in H. Oetker/U. Preis/V. Rieble, *50 Jahre Bundesarbeitsgericht* (Munich: C.H. Beck, 2004), 1219–1252; D. Komo/C. Villiers, 'Are trends in European company law threatening industrial democracy?', *E.L. Rev.* 34 (2009), 175–204; M. Körner, 'Das andere Modell: Die französische Betriebsverfassung', *NZA* 2001, 429–435; M. Körner, *Formen der Arbeitnehmermitwirkung – Das französische Comité d'entreprise – Eine Länderstudie* (Baden-Baden: Nomos, 1999); R. R. Kraakman et al. (eds.), *The Anatomy of Corporate Law – A Comparative and Functional Approach* (Oxford: Oxford University Press, 2004); R. Krause, 'Gewerkschaften und Betriebsräte zwischen Kooperation und Konfrontation', *RdA* 2009, 129–143; I. Krolop, *Mitbestimmungsvereinbarungen im grenzüberschreitenden Konzern* (Berlin: Berliner Wissenschafts-Verlag, 2010); A. Lingscheid/K. Schmidt, 'Informations- und Anhörungsrechte für Arbeitnehmer in Großbritannien', *RIW* 2006, 424–429; U. R. Mayer, 'Betriebsverfassungs- und tarifvertragsrechtliche Fragen bei grenzüberschreitenden Personaleinsätzen', *BB* 1999, 842–847; F. Möslein/K. Riesenhuber, 'Contract Governance – A Draft Research Agenda', *ERCL* 2009, 248–289; H. Oetker/C. Schubert, 'Europäisches Betriebsverfassungsrecht', in H. Oetker/U. Preis (eds.), *Europäisches Arbeits- und Sozialrecht, EAS, part B – Systematische Darstellungen,* loose-leaf (Heidelberg: Forkel, last update: January 2007), B 8300; J. Pipkorn, 'Die Mitwirkung der Arbeitnehmer aufgrund der Kommissionsvorschläge der Strukturrichtlinie und die Unterrichtung und Anhörung der Arbeitnehmer', *ZGR* 1985, 567–593; J. Pipkorn, 'Arbeitnehmerbeteiligung in Unternehmen auf Europäischer Grundlage', *RdA* 1992, 120–127; J. Pipkorn, 'Europäische Aspekte der Informations- und Mitwirkungsrecht der Arbeitnehmer', in O. Due/M. Lutter/J. Schwarze (eds.), *Festschrift für Ulrich Everling* (Baden-Baden: Nomos, 1995), 1113–1131; T. Raiser, 'Unternehmensmitbestimmung vor dem Hintergrund europarechtlicher Entwicklungen – Gutachten B für den 66. Deutschen Juristentag', in Ständige Deputation des Deutschen Juristentages (ed.), *Verhandlungen des Sechsundsechzigsten Deutschen Juristentages* (Munich: C.H. Beck, 2006); R. Rebhahn, 'Collective Labour Law in Europe in a Comparative Perspective (Part I)', *IJCLLIR* 19 (2003), 271–295;

R. Rebhahn, 'Collective Labour Law in Europe in a Comparative Perspective (Part II)', *IJCCLIR* 20 (2004), 107–132 (English version of *NZA* 2001, 763–774 and *RdA* 2002, 214–218); R. Rebhahn, 'Das kollektive Arbeitsrecht im Rechtsvergleich', *NZA* 2001, 763–774; R. Rebhahn, 'Rechtsvergleichendes zur Tarifbindung ohne Verbandsmitgliedschaft', *RdA* 2002, 214–218; R. Rebhahn, 'Unternehmensmitbestimmung in Deutschland – ein Sonderweg im Rechtsvergleich', in V. Rieble (ed.), *Zukunft der Unternehmensmitbestimmung* (Munich: ZAAR, 2004), 42–85; M. Rehberg, 'Chancen und Risiken der Verhandlung über die Arbeitnehmerbeteiligung', in V. Rieble/A. Junker (eds.), *Vereinbarte Mitbestimmung in der SE* (Munich: ZAAR, 2008), 45–64; K. Riesenhuber, 'Die Verhandlungslösung der Mitbestimmung – Eigentumsgarantie, Verhältnismäßigkeit und "Contract Governance"', in F.-J. Peine/H. A. Wolff (eds.), *Nachdenken über Eigentum – Festschrift für Alexander v. Brünneck zur Vollendung seines siebzigsten Lebensjahres* (Baden-Baden: Nomos, 2011), 332–342; K. Riesenhuber, 'Schatten des Rechts – Contract Governance und Governance der Vertragsverhandlungen bei der SE-Mitbestimmung', in S. Grundmann et al. (eds.), *Festschrift für Klaus J. Hopt* (Berlin: de Gruyter, 2010), 1225–1243; K. Seitz, *Europäisches Rahmenrecht für eine Europäische Betriebsverfassung – Stand und Perspektiven* (Tübingen: no publisher, 2004); M. Stoffels, 'Die Betriebsverfassung unter dem Einfluss des Europarechts', in A. Söllner et al. (eds.), *Gedächtnisschrift für Meinhard Heinze* (Munich: C.H. Beck, 2005), 885–899; C. Weber, 'Arbeitnehmermitbestimmung im Europäischen Sozialraum', in H. Dreier/H. Forkel/K. Laubenthal (eds.), *Raum und Recht – Festschrift 600 Jahre Würzburger Juristenfakultät* (Berlin: Duncker & Humblot, 2002), 189–218; C. Weber, 'Information und Konsultation im europäischen und deutschen Mitbestimmungsrecht', in B. Dauner-Lieb et al. (eds.), *Festschrift für Horst Konzen zum siebzigsten Geburtstag* (Tübingen: Mohr Siebeck, 2005), 921–956; C. Weber, 'Massenentlassung und Arbeitnehmerbeteiligung im deutschen und europäischen Mitbestimmungsrecht', *AuR* 2008, 365–380; Lord K. W. Wedderburn, 'Consultation and Collective Bargaining in Europe: Success or Ideology?', *ILJ* 26 (1997), 1–34; P. C. Weiler, *Governing the Workplace – The Future of Labor and Employment Law* (Cambridge, MA/London: Harvard University Press, 1990); M. Weiss, 'Arbeitnehmermitwirkung in Europa', *NZA* 2003, 177–184; M. Weiss, 'Convergence and/or Divergence in Labor Law Systems?: A European Perspective', *Comp. Lab. L. & Pol'y J.* 28 (2007), 469–486; M. Weiss, 'Europäische Betriebsräte und Konzern – 20 Thesen', *ZIAS* 1995, 633–639; M. Weiss, 'Transnationale Kollektivvertragsstrukturen in der EG: Informalität oder Verrechtlichung?', in H. Konzen et al. (eds.), *Festschrift für Rolf Birk zum siebzigsten Geburtstag* (Tübingen: Mohr Siebeck, 2008), 957–975; M. Weiss, 'Workers' Participation in the European Union', in P. Davies et al. (eds.), *European Community Labour Law: Principles and Perspectives – Liber Amicorum Lord Wedderburn* (Oxford: Clarendon Press, 1996), 213–235; H. P. Westermann, 'Tendenzen der gegenwärtigen Mitbestimmungsdiskussion in der Europäischen Gemeinschaft', *RabelsZ* 48 (1984), 123–184; H. Wiedemann, *Gesellschaftsrecht Band I – Grundlagen* (Munich: C.H. Beck, 1980), §11; O. E. Williamson, 'Transaction-Cost Economics: The Governance of Contractual Relations', *J.L. & Econ.* 22 (1979) 233–261; C. Windbichler, 'Arbeitnehmerinteressen im Unternehmen und gegenüber Unternehmen – Eine Zwischenbilanz', *AG* 2004, 190–196; C. Windbichler, 'Cheers and Boos for Employee Involvement: Co-Determination as Corporate Governance Conundrum', *EBOR* 6 (2005) 507–537; C. Windbichler, 'Der gordische Mitbestimmungsknoten und das Vereinbarungsschwert – Regulierung durch Selbstregulierung?', in U. Jürgens et al. (eds.),

Perspektiven der Corporate Governance – Bestimmungsfaktoren unternehmerischer Ent-
scheidungsprozesse und Mitwirkung der Arbeitnehmer (Baden-Baden: Nomos, 2007), 282–
304; see also the bibliographies to §§27–29.

I. EMPLOYEE INVOLVEMENT: INFORMATION, CONSULTATION AND PARTICIPATION

1. Terminology

1. There are two forms of employee involvement under European employment
law, which vary according to the level at which employee involvement occurs:
employee involvement on the shop level and on the board level. With regard to
the central instruments of employee involvement, the former is sometimes
referred to as the law of **information and consultation** (cf. Article 4(2)(f) SED).[1]
Since the very beginning of European legislation in this field, rights to
information and consultation have been concerned not only with matters
involving the establishment but also with those matters involving the
undertaking: collective redundancies and the transfer of (not only businesses but
also) undertakings.[2] However, information and consultation rights do not give
employee representatives any influence upon entrepreneurial decisions.
Furthermore, the relevant directives largely leave question of who should be the
competent employees' representatives to the Member States, thus allowing them
also to employ the representatives at the shop level (as opposed to representatives
on the board level). Employee involvement at the board level can be termed the
European law of employee participation. It is characterised by enabling
employees' representatives to influence the company's supervisory or
administrative body.[3] Article 2(k) SE-Directive defines 'participation' as

> 'the influence of the body representative of the employees and/or the employees'
> representatives in the affairs of a company by way of:
> – the right to elect or appoint some of the members of the company's supervisory or
>   administrative organ, or
> – the right to recommend and/or oppose the appointment of some or all of the
>   members of the company's supervisory or administrative organ.'

2. Following the language used in the SE-Directive – the directive
supplementing the Statute for a European company with regard to the
involvement of employees – which is concerned with both shop and board levels,
'employee involvement' is the broader and generic term, covering both employee

---

[1] See also – with a focus on UK law – S. Deakin/G. Morris, *Labour Law*, paras. 9.29–9.58.

[2] C. Weber, *Festschrift 600 Jahre Würzburger Juristenfakultät,* 210.

[3] A. Junker, *ZfA* 2005, 1, 2; C. Windbichler, *AG* 2004, 190, 192.

participation and information and consultation. The term 'employee co-determination' is sometimes equated with 'employee participation' (as defined above), and sometimes used as the generic term. This latter term can be confusing as it may convey different national concepts, as information and consultation do not give a right to co-determination in the strict sense and as it is equivocal, referring to different conceptual levels.[4]

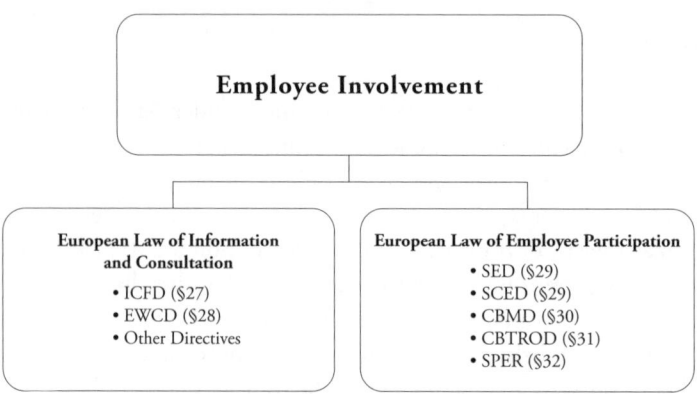

2. *Development*[5]

a) The Disparate National Solutions in the Member States as a Starting Point

3. The European law on employee involvement started from the premise that the models of interaction between employer and employees' representatives (cooperative or confrontational), the legal regulations and practical usages, had, on the basis of the principle of territoriality,[6] developed in disparate directions in the different Member States. With regard to *employee participation*,[7] national

---

4   Differently e.g. C. Weber, *Festschrift 600 Jahre Würzburger Juristenfakultät*, 211 sq. *et passim*.
5   For a summary see e.g. N. Bruun, *EELJ* 2 (2011), 27–47; W. Goos, *50 Jahre Bundesarbeitsgericht*, 1183–1192; J. Pipkorn, *RdA* 1992, 120–126; id., *Festschrift für Everling*, 1114–1131; in detail H. Oetker/C. Schubert, in *EAS*, B 8300 paras. 4–23 *et passim*; T. Raiser, *Unternehmensmitbestimmung vor dem Hintergrund europarechtlicher Entwicklungen*, B 33–41; C. Weber, *Festschrift 600 Jahre Würzburger Juristenfakultät*, 194–209.
6   U. R. Mayer, *BB* 1999, 842, 846.
7   T. Baums/P. Ulmer (eds.), *Unternehmens-Mitbestimmung der Arbeitnehmer im Recht der EU-Mitgliedstaaten*; K. J. Hopt, *ZfA* 1982, 207–235; id., *Mich. L. Rev.* 82 (1984), 1338, 1348–1352; T. Raiser, *Unternehmensmitbestimmung vor dem Hintergrund europarechtlicher Entwicklungen*, B 41–49; R. Rebhahn, *NZA* 2001, 763, 770–774; C. Weber, *Festschrift 600 Jahre Würzburger Juristenfakultät*, 191; D. Schiek, *Europäisches Arbeitsrecht*, 305–310; M. Weiss, *NZA* 2003, 177–184; M. Weiss, *Comp. Lab. L. & Pol'y J.* 28 (2007), 469–486; H. Wiedemann, *Gesellschaftsrecht I*, 584–607. See also Final Report of the Group of Experts 'European Systems of Workers Involvements' (Davignon-Report), ('National mechanisms for the information, consultation and participation of workers'); reproduced in English in A. C. Neal,

---

law starts with different organisational structures of the national company forms (two-tier-systems, one-tier-systems). Not all Member States provide for employee participation in the first place. And where the law provides for employee participation, the quora of employees' representatives in the supervisory or administrative organ (one-third participation, equal participation), procedures for appointment or election of representatives and their powers (from informational involvement to co-determination) vary considerably.[8] The German model of employee co-determination, in particular, is exceptional from a comparative perspective.[9]

4. Similarly, there are various different models of employee involvement at the shop floor level.[10] It is not always a given that an employee representative body should be established in the first place. The structures vary considerably: with regard to the composition of the representative body (employer as a member of the body or not); with regard the number or representative bodies and their constituencies (all employees or different groups of employees); with regard to the role of unions and their relation to representative bodies at the shop level;[11] with regard to the areas in which employees are involved, and the rights of the employees' representatives.

b) The Development of EU Primary Law and Secondary Legislation

5. Both the law of information and consultation and the law of employee participation have a common root in the legislative project of a **European Company**. Already the first draft regulation – which in many respects followed the German model – from 1970 provided for both, employee participation in the supervisory boards and a kind of European Works Council (see §29 para. 2 below). It took some 30 years, though, before this seed would blossom (see paras 37–39 below). The project suffered from the fact that the legislator – despite the disparate national laws and traditions of company organisation and employee involvement among the Member States – intended to install a uniform

---

European Labour Law and Social Policy – Cases and Materials, volume 1 (The Hague/London/ New York: Kluwer Law, 2002), 336–352; in German in *BR-Drs.* 572/97, Annex III.

[8]   R. Rebhahn, *NZA* 2001, 763, 770–774; Final Report of the Group of Experts 'European Systems of Workers Involvements' (Davignon-Report), reproduced in English in A. C. Neal, *European Labour Law and Social Policy – Cases and Materials, volume 1* (The Hague/London/ New York: Kluwer Law, 2002), 336–352; in German in *BR-Drs.* 572/97, Annex III sub I.

[9]   A. Junker, *ZfA* 2005, 1, 17–24; R. Rebhahn, in V. Rieble (ed.), *Zukunft der Unternehmensmitbestimmung*, 42–85.

[10]   F. Gamillscheg, *Festschrift für Richardi*, 1025–1038; A. Junker, *JZ* 1992, 1100–1106; id., *NZA* 2001, 131–138; id., *ZfA* 2001, 225–243; id., *RIW* 2002, 81–86; M. Körner, *Formen der Arbeitnehmermitwirkung*; ead., *NZA* 2001, 429–435; M. Weiss, *NZA* 2003, 177–184; id., *Festschrift für Birk*, 957–975; id., *Liber Amicorum Wedderburn*, 213–235.

[11]   See e.g. R. Krause, *RdA* 2009, 129–143 (discussing the origins and current structure of the 'interlaced dual model' under German law).

model. It was only over the course of many years that variation in implementation became possible. Proposals for a fifth company law directive on the structure of public limited companies[12] suffered the same defects:[13] They, too, were originally based upon the two-tier system of company structure and provided for employee involvement in the supervisory board.

6. The early beginnings of a European law of information and consultation were then developed following the 1974 **social action programme** (see §1 paras. 32 sq.) which voiced the demand for a 'progressive involvement of workers or their representatives in the life of undertakings in the Community'.[14] The 1975 Collective Redundancies Directive (see §23 above) and the 1977 Transfer of Undertakings Directive (see §24 above) were the first legislative measures to take account of this requirement; both included rights to information and consultation as a central protective instrument or to supplement other protective rules. The 1989 Safety and Health Framework Directive (§13 above) also provided for elements of employee involvement, if on a smaller scale.

7. The 1989 **Community Charter of Fundamental Social Rights** (1989; see §2 paras. 65–77) provided a new impulse for action in this field. In its Nos. 17 and 18 (and also, with regard to industrial safety, in No. 19(2)), it postulated that 'information, consultation and participation of workers' should be developed along appropriate lines, in particular with regard to structural measures in undertakings as well as collective redundancies.[15] The 1992 Social Policy Protocol (see §4 para. 4 above), introduced in the context of the Maastricht Treaty for eleven of the twelve Member States (without the UK), provided for a new social policy **competence**; the 1997 Amsterdam Treaty merged the provisions into the EC Treaty (see §4 para. 5 above). These new competences served as a basis initially for the enactment of the 1994 European Works Council Directive, or EWC Directive (see §28 below), and later also for the Information and Consultation Framework Directive (see §27 below) which is sometimes considered to provide the 'general part' of the EU law of information and consultation.[16]

---

[12] Proposal for a Fifth Directive on the Coordination of Safeguards Which for the Protection of the interests of Members and Outsiders, are Required by Member States of Companies within the Meaning of Article 59, Second Paragraph, with Respect to Company Structure and to the Power and Responsibilities of Company Boards, OJ 1972 C131/49; Amended Proposal for a Fifth Directive Founded on Article 54(3)(g) of the Treaty Concerning the Structure of Public Limited Companies and the Powers and Obligations of their Organs, OJ 1983 C 240/2.

[13] See e.g. S. Grundmann, *European Company Law*, paras. 401–404; M. Lutter, *Europäisches Unternehmensrecht*, 181; K. J. Hopt, *Mich. L. Rev.* 82 (1984), 1338, 1344–1348; J. Pipkorn, *ZGR* 1985, 567–593; T. Raiser, *Unternehmensmitbestimmung vor dem Hintergrund europarechtlicher Entwicklungen*, B 34.

[14] No. 8 of the Council Resolution of 21 January 1974 concerning a social action programme, OJ 1974 C 13/1.

[15] Nos. 17, 18, 19 CFSR; see §2 paras. 75 sq. above.

[16] W. Kohte, *Festschrift für Richardi*, 611, 615.

8. The **EWC Directive** marks a fundamental change in the Community's regulatory approach, away from substantive regulation and towards a **negotiation procedure**: employers and employees have the opportunity to agree on the installation of a European Works Council or, alternatively, special information and consultation procedures, and only if their negotiations fail, or if the parties so chose, subsidiary requirements laid down in the annex of the Directive apply. Subsequently, the so-called *Davignon*-Group also employed this approach in its final report.[17] Under the 2000 SE Directive (see §29 paras. 1–61 below) employer and employees, in a negotiation procedure, agree upon employee participation and a kind of European Works Council; the 2003 SCE Directive largely follows the same provisions (see §29 paras. 62–66 below). The 'before and after' principle, together with voting quota for the employee side, are intended to prevent a 'flight from employee participation'.

9. Finally, the legislator has also used these latter principles with regard to **cross-border restructuring** measures. The negotiation procedure and the 'before and after' principle are the central instruments of protection in the 2005 Cross-border Merger Directive (see §30 below), the Proposal for a Directive on the Cross-border Transfer of the Company Seat (§31 below) and the Proposal for a Regulation on the European Private Company (see §32 below).

10. The 2000 **Charter of Fundamental Rights** (see §2 paras. 16–64) does not provide for any substantial contribution to the development of the law in this field. As a general matter, the Charter is broadly enumerates a number of social rights, the content of which is, however, defined by reference to Union law and the laws of the Member States. This is also true with regard to the workers' right to information and consultation (not participation!) within the undertaking which, pursuant to Article 27 ChFR, is granted 'in the cases and under the conditions provided for by Union law and national laws and practices'. The provision constitutes a principle rather than a fundamental right.[18]

11. Parallel to this legislative development, the Court's case law (in particular) with regard to the **freedom of establishment** has also provided for impulses for the development of the law in this field. The obligation upon Member States, resulting from the freedom of establishment, to allow foreign companies (in their national form) into their territories has not only triggered a competition between national company laws, but also a competition between national laws of employee participation. And even though this is not, as of yet, of any practical

---

[17]   Final Report of the Group of Experts 'European Systems of Workers Involvements' (Davignon-Report), reproduced in English in A. C. Neal, *European Labour Law and Social Policy – Cases and Materials, volume 1* (The Hague/London/New York: Kluwer Law, 2002), 336–352; in German in *BR-Drs.* 572/97, Annex III.

[18]   W. Frenz/V. Götzkes, *RdA* 2007, 216–218.

relevance, this case law implies that the national laws of the Member States may be measured against the principle of proportionality under Union law (see in detail §3 para. 72 above). In this framework, the negotiation procedure may also exert pressure for reform of national laws on employee participation.

II. ELEMENTS OF THE EUROPEAN LAW OF INFORMATION AND CONSULTATION

12. The provisions on information and consultation which supplement the regulation on a number of specific issues have already been discussed in the respective context in earlier chapters. The horizontal provisions of the Information and Consultation Framework Directive and the EWC Directive, as well as the SE Directive and the SCE Directive, will be discussed in detail in the following chapters. At this point, we will first summarise the supplementary provisions on information and consultation (see 1. below)[19] and discuss some of the underlying principles (see 2. below) so as to open up the complete picture.

1. Overview of the Provisions on Information and Consultation in Individual Directives

a) Employee Involvement in the Collective Redundancies Directive

13. Where an employer foresees collective redundancies, he is bound to consult the employees' representatives with a view to reaching an agreement (duty to negotiate, no duty to reach an agreement), Article 2 CRD. These consultations cover ways and means of avoiding collective redundancies or reducing the number of workers affected, and mitigating the consequences of redundancies by recourse to accompanying social measures. In order to enable the employees' representatives to make constructive proposals, the employer must provide them with all relevant information and give them a list of detailed information in writing. See in detail §23 paras. 16–32 above.

b) Employee Involvement in the Transfer of Undertakings Directive

14. In the case of a transfer of undertaking, both transferor and transferee are under a duty to inform their employees' representatives about the basic terms of the transfer, the legal, economic and social consequences and any measures envisaged in relation to employees, Article 7 TUD. Where either of them

---

[19] For a survey, see P. Hanau, in id./H.-D. Steinmeyer/R. Wank (eds.), *Handbuch des europäischen Arbeits- und Sozialrechts*, §19 paras. 121–129; C. Weber, *Festschrift 600 Jahre Würzburger Juristenfakultät*, 195–209.

envisages measures in relation to the employees, he is further bound to consult with the employees' representatives with a view to reaching agreement (duty to negotiate, no duty to reach agreement). As an exception, where there is no employees' representative in the undertaking or business through no fault of the employees, the employees concerned must be informed about the details.

15. Since its 1998 revision, the Directive also regulates the position of the employees' representatives in the transferred business, namely the on-going or interim mandate and their protection, Article 6 TUD. In detail, see §24 paras. 89–94 above.

c)   Employee Involvement in the Area of Worker Safety and Health

16. The **Safety and Health Framework Directive** also contains supplementary provisions on information and consultation. 'Workers and/or their representatives' must receive 'all the necessary information' concerning risks to safety and health, protective measures as well as first aid, fire-fighting and evacuation of workers, Article 10 SHFD. In addition, the Directive provides for a 'right' of the workers and/or their representatives to consultation, which includes the right to be consulted and the right to make proposals but which ultimately (only) requires 'balanced participation in accordance with national laws and/or practices', Article 11 SHFD.[20] (The term 'participation' is used here in a non-technical sense and should be distinguished from the definition para. 1 above). See in detail §13 paras. 32–36 above.

17. The **Maternity Protection Directive**, as an individual directive to the Safety and Health Framework Directive, contains supplementary provisions. Female workers 'and/or their representatives'[21] should be informed of the results of the risk assessment, Article 4(2) MPD (§20 para. 17). In order to enable them to properly use this information, *Member States* must bring 'guidelines on the assessment of the chemical, physical and biological agents and industrial processes considered hazardous for the safety or health of workers' to the attention not only of employers but also to 'all female workers and/or their representatives', Article 3(2)(2) MPD.

18. There are two noteworthy particularities here. First, the employer is not only bound to forward information but must also collect information.[22] Secondly, it is only with qualification that these provisions can be considered to

---

20   C. Weber, *Festschrift 600 Jahre Würzburger Juristenfakultät*, 198 sq.
21   Irrespective of the linguistic confusion, the provision should not be construed to require a special representation for female workers.
22   See also W. Kohte, *50 Jahre Bundesarbeitsgericht*, 1226 sq., who, however, further generalises that '*Community law* [emphasis added] provides for an active duty of information; it binds

be part of our present subject. For while the Directives allow for their measures to be implemented by way of collective information provisions (of the workers' representatives), they do not require that this be the case. The Directives may also be implemented by way of a duty to inform each individual worker.[23]

d) Further Provisions

19. There are a number of directives that contain further provisions on information and consultation of employees' representatives, if only in a rather weak form.[24]

20. Closely connected with the Transfer of Undertakings Directive, the **Takeover Directive** provides for information duties. The boards of the offeror and offeree companies must inform their employees' representatives (where there are no employee representatives: the employees) of the decision to make a bid and communicate the offer document to them. The offer document should include information on the likely repercussions on employment and the locations of the company's places of business. The board of the offeree company must communicate its written opinion on the offer document to the employees' representatives or the employees, as applicable. See in detail §24 paras. 117–121.

21. The **Working Time Directive** provides for a specific duty to consult (with a view to reaching an agreement) with regard to exceptions from the weekly maximum working hours of doctors in training, Article 17(5)(6) WTD. See §14 para. 29 above.

22. Pursuant to Clause 5(3)(e) **Part-time Work Framework Agreement**, the employer should 'give consideration to the provision of appropriate information to existing bodies representing workers about part-time working in the enterprise'. See §16 paras. 44 sq. above.

23. Pursuant to Clause 7(3) **Fixed-term Work Framework Agreement** the employer should 'give consideration to' the provision of information on fixed term work to workers' representatives. See §17 para. 40.

---

the employer to compile information and documentations and gives employees access to inspection and information' (my translation).

23   C. Weber, *Festschrift für Konzen*, 924; id., *Festschrift 600 Jahre Würzburger Juristenfakultät*, 199.

24   C. Weber, *Festschrift für Konzen*, 924 (information duties in the directives on atypical employment relationships serve a 'function of a mere appeal' – my translation); id., *Festschrift 600 Jahre Würzburger Juristenfakultät*, 200.

24. Article 7 **Temporary Agency Work Directive** deals with the calculation of thresholds for the constitution of workers' representations. Article 8 TAWD provides that the user undertaking, in the context of information on the employment situation in the undertaking, should include suitable information on the use of temporary agency workers; §18 paras. 29 sqq.

2. Principles of the Law of Information and Consultation

25. There is no 'complete' set of rules on information and consultation in EU employment law. The beginnings of a European system of rules can be discerned in the European Works Council Directive and in the provisions on information and consultation for the supra-national forms of companies, the SE and the SCE. Whether or not the internal market or employment policy requires any further reaching approximation of law or the establishment of uniform structures is an open question. Existing legislation provides for a minimum platform of structures and concepts in Union law and a number of uniform principles can be discerned.[25]

a) Primacy of the Negotiation Solution

Provisions: Article 7, 13 EWCD, Article 5 ICFD, Article 7 SED, Article 7 SCED; cf. also Articles 16(3)(e) CBMD, 7 SED and Articles 34, 38 SPER

26. Where Union law itself provides for structures of employee representation, a preference of negotiation solutions over mandatory regimes can be discerned.[26] The legislator first developed the model for the EWC Directive (see in detail §28 paras. 47–85) which does not primarily require certain structures of employee involvement but rather installs a negotiation procedure which allows the employer side and the employee side to agree on a system of employee involvement that satisfies their own needs. Only in default, where negotiations fail, a legislative model of employee involvement applies. The transitional provision of Article 14 EWCD (Article 13 EWCD 1994) which has become considerably important in practice, can also be understood as an instance of the negotiation solution.[27]

---

[25]   T. Brors, *Das System der Arbeitnehmer-Beteiligungs-Richtlinien*; W. Kohte, *50 Jahre Bundesarbeitsgericht*, 1119–1252; K. Seitz, *Europäisches Rahmenrecht für eine Europäische Betriebsverfassung*; M. Stoffels, *Gedächtnisschrift für Heinze*, 885, 893 sq.; C. Weber, *Festschrift für Konzen*, 921–956 (who, beyond the issues covered in the following text, at pp. 941–950 also addresses the issue of protection of undertakings with ideological guidance as their purpose); C. Weber, *Festschrift 600 Jahre Würzburger Juristenfakultät*, 210–217. On the general issue of system-building in EU employment law, see already §1 paras. 42–48 above with further references.

[26]   W. Goos, *50 Jahre Bundesarbeitsgericht*, 1194; C. Weber, *Festschrift für Konzen*, 926; id., *FS 600 Jahre Würzburger Juristenfakultät*, 212–214.

[27]   C. Weber, *Festschrift für Konzen*, 926; id., *Festschrift 600 Jahre Würzburger Juristenfakultät*, 201, 213.

Here, the legislator exempted agreements which were already in force before the expiry of the implementation period of the original Directive from the Directive's requirements. The impending Directive as such thus functioned as a 'subsidiary structure'. The legislator has subsequently used similar procedural rules with regard to the SE and the SCE (see §29 para. 4 *et passim* below).

27. In the Information and Consultation Framework Directive, which itself does not install an employee representation but rather provides for information and consultation procedures and their modalities, a preference for negotiation solutions is expressed in Article 5. Pursuant to that provision, an agreement on the 'practical arrangements' takes precedence over the legal requirements of Article 4 ICFD. The provision places not only the execution of information and consultation in the hands of the employer and the employees' representatives, but also the rights to information and consultation as such, provided only that the principles of the Directive are respected (see in more detail §27 paras. 23 sq. below).

b)   Work in the Spirit of Cooperation – The Principle of Loyal Cooperation

Provisions: Article 9 EWCD, Article 9 SED, Article 11 SCED; cf. also Articles 1, 4 ICFD

28. The Information and Consultation Directive, the European Works Council Directive as well as the SE Directive and the SCE Directive emphasise the principle that management and employee representatives should work together 'in the spirit of cooperation'; one could also speak of a principle of *loyal cooperation*. The principle may be used for the interpretation of individual rights and obligations (e.g. information in good time, confidentiality) and may also serve as a basis for the judicial development of further obligations concerning the behaviour and cooperation of the parties.

c)   Forms of Employee Involvement: Information and Consultation

Provisions: Article 2(f), (g) EWCD, Article 2(f), (g) ICFD, Article 2(i), (j) SED, Article 2(i), (j) SCED, Article 2 CRD, Article 7(1)-(4) TUD

aa)   Rights of the Employees' Representatives

29. Existing legislation provides for the two basic forms of employee involvement: information and, building on information, consultation. So far, there are no further reaching instruments of employee involvement at this level.[28]

---

[28]   C. Weber, *Festschrift 600 Jahre Würzburger Juristenfakultät*, 211.

30. **Information** means the 'transmission of data'. More recent directives emphasise the purposes of information: to enable the employees' representatives to acquaint themselves with the subject matter and examine it (Article 2(f) ICFD; analogously Article 2(i) SED, Article 2(i) SCED). This purpose is also relevant for the modalities of the right to information (see also para. 34 below). For example, it may demand that dialogue is offered even at the point when information is first provided, giving the employees' representatives a right to ask questions and request further explanation.[29]

31. **Consultation** not only involves listening to the employees' representatives. It rather means 'the exchange of views and establishment of dialogue between the employees' representatives and the employer', Article 2(g) ICFD. Article 2(j) SED and Article 2(j) SCED even speak of 'the establishment of dialogue and exchange of views', thus hinting at a more institutional character. The – older – Collective Redundancies Directive emphasises the employees' representatives' right to make proposals, Article 2(3) CRD.[30] Normally, consultation builds upon prior information. This should be kept in mind with regard to the modalities of information.

32. A qualified form of consultation is consultation **with a view to reaching agreement**, Article 2(2) CRD, Article 7(2) TUD and Article 4(4)(c) ICFD. It includes a duty to negotiate but not a duty to reach agreement.

33. European employment law to date does not provide for any conciliation procedures. A proposal to this effect in the Transfer of Undertakings Directive[31] ultimately did not become law. The exception of Article 7(3) TUD, however, presupposes that the national law of Member States may provide for an arbitration board that has the power to make a decision. The provision does not, though, provide any guidance for the evaluation of conciliation procedures from a Union law perspective, given that – rather unconvincingly from a policy perspective – it sacrifices the protection of a larger group of employees for the

---

29   See already Final Report of the Group of Experts 'European Systems of Workers Involvements' (Davignon-Report), reproduced in English in A. C. Neal, *European Labour Law and Social Policy – Cases and Materials, volume 1* (The Hague/London/New York: Kluwer Law, 2002), 336–352; in German in *BR-Drs.* 572/97, Annex II.

30   Rather weaker Final Report of the Group of Experts 'European Systems of Workers Involvements' (Davignon-Report), reproduced in English in A. C. Neal, *European Labour Law and Social Policy – Cases and Materials, volume 1* (The Hague/London/New York: Kluwer Law, 2002), 336–352; in German in *BR-Drs.* 572/97, Annex II (only 'possibility … to express an opinion').

31   Article 8(2)(2) Proposal for a Directive on the harmonisation of the legislation of Member States on the retention of the rights and advantages of employees in the case of mergers, takeovers and amalgamations, COM(74) 351 final, OJ 1974 C 104/1 (corrected English version published as COM(74) 351 final/2).

benefit of more intensive protection of a smaller group. It cannot be inferred from Article 7(3), that the legislator considered both alternatives substantively equivalent. The fact that EU employment law to date does not provide for conciliation procedures cannot support any further reaching conclusions either.[32]

bb)   Purposive Performance of Participation Rights

Provisions: Article 2(f), (g) EWCD, Article 4(3) and (4) ICFD, Article 2(i), (j) SED, Article 2(i), (j) SCED, cf. also Article 2 CRD, Article 7(1)-(4) TUD

34.   The Information and Consultation Framework Directive further provides that the practical arrangements for information and consultation should be structured in a way so that their respective purposes will be fulfilled, Article 4(3) and (4) ICFD (see §27 paras. 19–21).[33] The SE Directive, the SCE Directive and, following their example, the new EWC Directive include such requirements in their definitions of information and consultation, Article 2(i), (j) SED, Article 2(i), (j) SCED and Article 2(f), (g) EWCD. Indeed, it can be inferred from the respective *purposes* that the information should be given 'in a manner and with a content which allows the employees' representatives to undertake an in-depth assessment of the possible impact' and that consultation should proceed 'in a manner and with a content which allows the employees' representatives, on the basis of information provided, to express an opinion on measures envisaged'. The Court had inferred the same from the information and consultation rights of the Collective Redundancies Directive notwithstanding the absence of an express provision in its judgement in *Junk*[34] (see §23 para. 19 above).

d)   Confidentiality[35]

Provisions: Article 8 EWCD, Article 6 ICFD, Article 8 SED, Article 10 SCED; cf. also Articles 16(3)(f) CBMD, 8 SED

35.   As a specific manifestation of the principle of loyal cooperation (see para. 28 above), the Directives provide for a minimum standard of uniform

---

[32]   Cautiously also C. Weber, *Festschrift für Richardi*, 467 sq. ('We can see that the rights on employee participation in European law have been drafted with a reluctance towards a compulsion to reach agreement for employers and employee representations and, beyond that, with reluctance towards formal guidelines for the consultation process as such.' – my translation).

[33]   W. Kohte, *50 Jahre Bundesarbeitsgericht*, 1241–1244.

[34]   ECJ Case C-188/03 *Junk* [2005] ECR I-885; see also C. Weber, *Festschrift für Konzen*, 940.

[35]   We leave out of consideration here the duties to confidentiality that result from Article 3(a) Directive Council Directive 89/592/EEC of 13 November 1989 coordinating regulations on insider dealing, OJ 1989 L 334/30, irrespective of their relevance for the law of employee participation. See e.g. ECJ Case C-384/02 *Grøngaard* [2005] ECR I-9939 (passing on of information by the employee representative to the union president).

confidentiality requirements. As a rule, the employer's confidentiality interest does not relieve him of the obligation to inform the employees' representatives but is instead reflected in confidentiality obligations. It is only on exceptional grounds that the employer may be allowed to hold back information.

e)   Protection of Employees' Representatives

Provisions: Article 10(3) EWCD, Article 7 ICFD, Article 10 SED, Article 12 SCED, Art. 6(2) TUD; cf. also Articles 16(3)(f) CBMD, 10 SED

36.   Finally, the employees' representatives enjoy specific protection against unfavourable treatment. Again, the same rule could already be inferred from the provisions establishing their rights; on teleological considerations, it is a necessary complement to the provision of employee rights.[36]

III.   ELEMENTS OF A EUROPEAN LAW OF EMPLOYEE PARTICIPATION[37]

1.   Overview

37.   The **scope** of European legislation on employee participation is comparatively smaller. Its provisions are to be found in:

- the SE-Directive (see §29 paras. 1–61 below);
- the SCE-Directive, which largely adopts the provisions of the SE-Directive with only few adaptations for the SCE (see §29 paras. 62–66 below);
- the Cross-border Merger Directive, which refers to selected provisions of the SE-Directive (see §30 below); as well as
- the Proposal for a Directive on the Cross-border Transfer of the Company Seat (see §31 below); and
- the Proposal for a Regulation on the Statute of the European Private Company (see §32 below).

2.   Safeguarding Pre-Existing Employee Participation

38.   None of the provisions are intended to establish a legislative system of employee participation at the EU level. Rather, the Directives and proposals contain provisions for the protection of pre-existing employee participation in

---

36   Cf. ECJ Case C-185/97 *Coote* [1998] ECR I-5199 paras. 20–27.
37   See also M. Henssler, in P.-C. Müller-Graff/C. Teichmann (eds.), *Europäisches Gesellschafts-recht auf neuen Wegen*, 143–168; id., *ZHR* 173 (2009), 222–249.

the affected companies. The legislator pursues three purposes. First, it intends to prevent undertakings from ridding themselves of a pre-existing employee participation regime and from reducing the participation level by adopting a new legal form. Consequently, in particular the formation of an SE through transformation (also 'conversion'; Articles 2(4), 37 SE-Regulation) strictly requires that the existing level of employee participation be maintained. Secondly, a structural measure (merger, transfer of the company seat) should not have the effect that the level of employee participation – measured as the proportion of employees' representatives in the organs of the company – is reduced for a substantial part of the employees. Thirdly, a structural measure should not lead to a new regime of employee participation that excludes a substantial part of the employees on the ground that they work in a different Member State.

3. Primacy of the Negotiation Solution

39. Here, too, the legislator opted for a negotiation solution, rather than requiring that the (highest level of) pre-existing participation regime be continued (although there are procedural and, in some instances, substantive safeguards; see 2. above). The negotiation approach serves several purposes.[38]

- As a matter of internal market policy, it proved to be the 'sword' that could cut the Gordian Knot of the longstanding controversy about employee participation in the SE.[39]
- As a matter of regulatory policy, the negotiation solution sets free potential for innovation[40] and opens up competition on models of employee participation (competition as a discovery procedure; v. Hayek).[41]

---

[38] As a matter of policy, the negotiation model is also being favoured for German law; see – with different emphasis – e.g. M. Henssler, in P.-C. Müller-Graff/C. Teichmann (eds.), *Europäisches Gesellschaftsrecht auf neuen Wegen*, 143–168; P. Hommelhoff, *ZGR* 2010, 48–74; C. Kirchner, *AG* 2005, 197–200; C. Windbichler, *AG* 2004, 190–196; T. Raiser, *Unternehmensmitbestimmung vor dem Hintergrund europarechtlicher Entwicklungen*, B 67 sq.; K. Riesenhuber, *Festschrift für v. Brünneck*, 332–342.

[39] C. Windbichler, in U. Jürgens et al. (eds.), *Perspektiven der Corporate Governance*, 282–304.

[40] M. Rehberg, in V. Rieble/A. Junker (eds.), *Vereinbarte Mitbestimmung in der SE*, 45–64.

[41] See already K. J. Hopt, *ZfA* 1982, 207, 232 sq.; id., *Festschrift für Everling*, 590 sq.; id., *IRLE* 14 (1994), 203, 212 sq.; more recently M. Rehberg, in V. Rieble/A. Junker, *Vereinbarte Mitbestimmung in der SE*, 51–53; see also H. Fleischer, *ZHR* 168 (2004), 673, 680 sq.; K. Riesenhuber, *Festschrift für Hopt*, 1225–1243. For an empirical analysis of employee involvement agreements of SEs incorporated in Germany and Austria see H. Eidenmüller/L. Hornuf/M. Reps, 'Contracting Employee Involvement: An Analysis of Bargaining over Employee Involvement Rules for a Societas Europaea', available at SSRN: http://papers.ssrn.com/sol3/papers.cfm?abstract_id=1979487.

- For the undertakings and employees concerned, determination by consent serves to legitimise the employee participation regime.[42]
- Within the limits of the parties' autonomy, it finally allows for flexible and custom-tailored solutions that can address the specific needs of the various sides.[43]

It is complemented with a set of subsidiary requirements (a fall-back solution) which the parties may also chose as the applicable regime. The fall-back solution is, however, primarily intended to apply if the parties do not reach agreement within the negotiation period.

IV. EMPLOYEE INVOLVEMENT AND GOVERNANCE – OVERVIEW

40. Employee involvement can be considered from various governance perspectives: as an element of corporate governance or as an instance of contract governance.

1. Corporate Governance[44]

41. Following the OECD definition, '**corporate governance** involves a set of relationships between a company's management, its board, its shareholders and other stakeholders. Corporate governance also provides the structure through which the objectives of the company are set, and the means of attaining those objectives and monitoring performance are determined.'[45] Whether corporate governance should focus on shareholders' rights exclusively or also accommodate the interests of other stakeholders, including **employees**, is a matter of debate.[46] Traditionally, Anglo-American law tends to favour the former position, continental-European systems the latter.[47] Following a stakeholder approach,

---

42   C. Kirchner, *AG* 2005, 197, 198.
43   T. Raiser, *Unternehmensmitbestimmung vor dem Hintergrund europarechtlicher Entwicklungen*, B 67 sq.; C. Windbichler, *AG* 2004, 190–196.
44   For a detailed discussion and with an extensive bibliography, see S. Grundmann, *European Company Law*, §14.
45   OECD Principles of Corporate Governance 2004, available at www.oecd.org/dataoecd/32/18/31557724.pdf. See also S. Grundmann, *European Company Law*, §14 para. 1; A. v. Werder, in P. Hommelhoff/K. J. Hopt/A. v. Werder (eds.), *Handbuch Corporate Governance*, 4 sqq.
46   For a survey from legal and economic perspectives, see the contributions of S. Grundmann, *European Company Law*, §14 paras. 20 sqq; R. H. Schmidt/Marco Weiß and H. Fleischer, in P. Hommelhoff/K. J. Hopt/A. v. Werder (eds.), *Handbuch Corporate Governance*, 161 sqq. and 185 sqq. See also H. Hansmann, *The Ownership of Enterprise*, 66 sqq. and 89 sqq.; R. Kraakman et al., *The Anatomy of Corporate Law*.
47   T. C. Hodge, *Syracuse J. Int'l L. & Com.* 38 (2010), 91–171 (comparative discussion of shareholder- and stakeholder approaches to corporate governance in the EU and in the USA).

employee involvement may be an element of corporate governance.[48] This is particularly obvious where employee participation in the company board is concerned. But other procedures of employee involvement, such as the information and consultation procedures, can also be considered to be part of the corporate governance structure.[49]

42. The EU Member States have different systems of corporate governance which are deeply rooted in the national legal systems and traditions.[50] The Union has, as yet, not attempted to replace these disparate systems,[51] though recent plans are more ambitious.[52] However, harmonisation of company laws and laws on employee involvement provides for a common framework in this area. Other elements of Union law, in particular the fundamental freedoms and EU employment legislation, have also left their mark on corporate governance. On the one hand, the Court's jurisprudence on freedom of establishment has paved the way for increased regulatory competition which, *inter alia,* exerts pressure on national systems of employee participation (see §3 paras. 92 sqq. above). Similarly, the *Societas Europaea* with its negotiation system (se §29 para. 31 below) and the negotiation mechanism of the Cross-Border Merger Directive (see §30 para. 14 below) result in competitive pressure for Member States like Germany with a particularly high level of employee participation (the co-determination model).[53] On the other hand, this legislation, together with the information and consultation directives (TUD, CRD, ICFD), installs a floor of employee involvement rights. The overall evaluation is controversial. While some are concerned that the development of EU law may negatively affect

---

[48] For a survey of the discussion, see K. Pistor, in P. Hommelhoff/K. J. Hopt/A. v. Werder (eds.), *Handbuch Corporate Governance,* 231 sqq.

[49] See e.g. J. Armour/S. Deakin/S. J. Konzelmann, *BJIR* 41(2003), 531, 541 sqq.

[50] S. Grundmann, *European Company Law,* §14 para. 21. For an (older) comparative survey, see e.g. K. J. Hopt/E. Wymeersch (eds.), *Comparative Corporate Governance.*

[51] Cf. Commission, Communication from the Commission to the Council and the European Parliament, 'Modernising Company Law and Enhancing Corporate Governance in the European Union – A Plan to Move Forward', COM(2003) 284 final, 10 sqq. For a discussion, see K. J. Hopt, in id. et al. (eds.), *Corporate Governance in Context,* 119 sqq.

[52] See Commission, Green Paper: The EU Corporate Governance Framework, COM(2001) 164 final. On the Green Paper, see S. Grundmann, *European Company Law,* §14 para. 6. The Green Paper mentions businesses' responsibility towards employees but emphasises that it 'has no bearing on ... board-level employee participation under national law' (p. 5 with note 18).

[53] See again H. Eidenmüller/L. Hornuf/M. Reps, 'Contracting Employee Involvement: An Analysis of Bargaining over Employee Involvement Rules for a Societas Europaea', available at SSRN: http://ssrn.com/abstract=1979487. On the resulting issues for trans-national groups of companies and on (voluntary) employee involvement agreements as a potential solution, see in detail I. Krolop, *Mitbestimmungsvereinbarungen im grenzüberschreitenden Konzern.*

employee involvement and promote a trend[54] towards the shareholder approach,[55] others are optimistic that the stakeholder approach will prevail.[56]

2. Contract Governance

43. Employee involvement may also be considered from a perspective of **contract governance**.[57] From a **regulatory perspective**, the negotiation model in EU law has been described as an instance of contract governance – as opposed to public governance by mandatory law.[58] The regulator (legislator) uses the contract mechanism, combined with a framework of procedural and substantive safeguards, to achieve its regulatory goal. Apart from the advantages discussed above, contract governance as a 'tool' may allow for regulation by less intrusive means.[59]

44. Employee involvement can also be regarded from the **perspective of the parties** to the employment contract. As a long-term relationship, the employment contract is typically and unavoidably of an open-ended nature; not all the details, indeed, many aspects cannot be spelled out at the time of the conclusion of the contract. The terms need to be concretised during the course of the relationship and must be adapted to the changing needs of the parties over time. As with other long-term relationships, the employment contract thus also requires a governance structure, and employee involvement can be considered one of its elements: 'Collective agreements and codetermination at the shop-floor level serve as tools for the necessary redefinition of rights and obligations over time, i.e., they are part of a sophisticated contract governance system.'[60]

---

54 For the general debate, see the seminal contribution by H. Hansmann/R. Kraakman, *Geo. L. J.* 89 (2001) 439–468 (submitting that a convergence of corporate governance in favour of the shareholder model took place).

55 D. Komo/C. Villiers, *E.L. Rev.* 34 (2009), 175–204.

56 T. C. Hodge, *Syracuse J. Int'l L. & Com.* 38 (2010), 91–171; J. Dammann, *Fordham JCFL* 8 (2003), 607–686. See also M. Weiss, *Comp. Lab. L. & Pol'y J.* 28 (2007), 469–486 (emphasising continuing national differences that oppose convergence); J. Armour/S. Deakin/S. J. Konzelmann, *BJIR* 41(2003), 531–555 (TUD and CRD as stakeholder-elements in the predominantly [enlightened] shareholder-oriented UK corporate governance system).

57 See the seminal article by O. E. Williamson, *J.L. & Econ.* 22 (1979) 233–261. For an analytical framework of contract governance, see F. Möslein/K. Riesenhuber, *ERCL* 2009, 248–289.

58 H. Eidenmüller, *JZ* 2007, 487, 493; K. Riesenhuber, *Festschrift für v. Brünneck*, 332–342.

59 On the general theme, see I. Ayres, 'Menus Matter', *Chicago L. Rev.* 73 (2006), 3, 4. In the context of employee involvement, see K. Riesenhuber, *Festschrift für v. Brünneck*, 332–342.

60 C. Windbichler, *EBOR* 6 (2005) 507–537; ead., *AG* 2004, 190, 195; ead., in U. Jürgens et al. (eds.), *Perspektiven der Corporate Governance*, 282–304.

§27. THE INFORMATION AND CONSULTATION FRAMEWORK DIRECTIVE

CONTENTS

Bibliography:

C. Barnard/S. Deakin, 'Reinventing the European Corporation? Corporate Governance, Social Policy and the Single Market', *IRJ* 33 (2002), 484–499; B. Bercusson, 'The European Social Model Comes to Britain', *ILJ* 31(2002), 209–244; O. Deinert, 'Vorschlag für eine europäische Mitbestimmungsrichtlinie und Umsetzungsbedarf im Betriebsverfassungsgesetz', *NZA* 1999, 800–805; F. J. Düwell, 'Auf dem Weg zu einem Europäischen Betriebsverfassungsrecht?', *FA* 2002, 172–175; K. D. Ewing/G. M. Truter, 'The Information and Consultation of Employees Regulations: Voluntarism's Bitter Legacy', *MLR* 68 (2005), 626–641; F. N. Fauser/M. Nacken, 'Die Sicherung des Unterrichtungs- und Beratungsanspruchs des Betriebsrats aus §§111, 112 BetrVG – Unter besonderer Berücksichtigung gemeinschaftsrechtlicher Vorgaben', *NZA* 2006, 1136–1143; M. Franzen, 'Europarecht und betriebliche Mitbestimmung – Überlegungen zur

Umsetzung der Rahmen-Richtlinie 2002/14/EG über die Unterrichtung und Anhörung der Arbeitnehmer in Deutschland', in H. Konzen et al. (eds.), *Festschrift für Rolf Birk zum siebzigsten Geburtstag* (Tübingen: Mohr Siebeck, 2008), 97–114; R. Giesen, 'EU-Richtlinienvorschlag zur Information und Anhörung der Arbeitnehmer', *RdA* 2000, 298–304; M. Hall, 'Assessing the Information and Consultation of Employees Regulations', *ILJ* 34 (2005), 103–126; A. Hassiotis, *Die Entwicklung des Rechts auf Arbeitnehmervertretung auf Information und Konsultation in der Europäischen Union: unter Berücksichtigung des deutschen, französischen, britischen und schweizerischen Rechts* (Zurich/Bern: Schulthess/Stämpfli, 2000); B. Karthaus, 'Betriebsübergang als interessenausgleichspflichtige Maßnahme nach der Richtlinie 2002/14/EG', *AuR* 2007, 114–120; W. Kohte, 'Auf dem Weg zur betrieblichen Informationsverfassung', in H. Oetker/U. Preis/V. Rieble (eds.), *50 Jahre Bundesarbeitsgericht* (Munich: C.H. Beck, 2004), 1219–1252; W. Kohte, 'Der Unterlassungsanspruch der betrieblichen Arbeitnehmervertretung', in G. Annuss/E. Picker/H. Wissmann (eds.), *Festschrift für Reinhard Richardi* (Munich, C.H. Beck, 2007), 601–615; W. Kolvenbach/D. W. Kolvenbach, 'Massenentlassungen bei Renault in Belgien', *NZA* 1997, 695–697; M. Körner, *Formen der Arbeitnehmermitwirkung – Das französische Comité d'entreprise – Eine Länderstudie* (Baden-Baden: Nomos, 1999); A. Lingscheid/K. Schmidt, 'Informations- und Anhörungsrechte für Arbeitnehmer in Großbritannien', *RIW* 2006, 424–429; T. Lobinger, 'Das individualrechtliche Fundament des Rechts der Betriebsänderung – Zur Dogmatik der §§111 ff. BetrVG im Lichte geschichtlicher und gemeinschaftsrechtlicher Betrachtung', *ZfA* 2006, 173–221; P. Lorber, 'Implementing the Information and Consultation Directive in Great Britain: A New Voice at Work', *IJCLLIR* 22 (2006), 231–258; P. Lorber, 'National Works Councils: "Opening the Door on a New Whole Era in United Kingdom Employment Relations"?', *IJCLLIR* 19 (2003), 297–319; F. Lorenz/M. Zumfelde, 'Der Europäische Betriebsrat und die Schließung des Renault-Werkes in Vilvoorde/Belgium', *RdA* 1998, 168–173; H. Oetker/C. Schubert, 'Europäisches Betriebsverfassungsrecht', in H. Oetker/U. Preis (eds.), *Europäisches Arbeits- und Sozialrecht, EAS, part B – Systematische Darstellungen*, loose-leaf (Heidelberg: Forkel, last update: January 2007), B 8300 paras. 386–395; H. Reichold, 'Durchbruch zu einer europäischen Betriebsverfassung – Die Rahmen-richtlinie 2002/14/EG zur Unterrichtung und Anhörung der Arbeitnehmer', *NZA* 2003, 289–299; T. Ritter, *Der Wirtschaftsausschuss nach dem Betriebsverfassungsgesetz und die Rahmenrichtlinie 2002/14/EG* (Baden-Baden: Nomos, 2006); D. Schäfer, *Der Europäische Rahmen für Arbeitnehmermitwirkung* (Frankfurt. a.M. et al.: Lang, 2005); B. Spreer, *Die Richtlinie 2002/14/EG zur Festlegung eines allgemeinen Rahmens für die Unterrichtung und Anhörung der Arbeitnehmer in der Europäischen Gemeinschaft* (Berlin: Logos, 2005); K. Vogelsang, 'Hat der Bundesgesetzgeber die Pflicht zur Umsetzung der Informationsrichtlinie 2002/14/EG zu Recht verstreichen lassen?', *PersV* 2006, 364–375; C. Weber, 'Information und Konsultation im europäischen und deutschen Mitbestimmungsrecht', in B. Dauner-Lieb et al. (eds.), *Festschrift für Horst Konzen* (Tübingen: Mohr Siebeck, 2005), 921–956; C. Weber, 'Massenentlassung und Arbeitnehmerbeteiligung im deutschen und europäischen Mitbestimmungsrecht', *AuR* 2008, 365–380; C. Weber, 'Schwellenwerte für die Beschäftigungszahlen bei Massenentlassungen – Urteil des Europäischen Gerichtshofs vom 18.1.2007 – Rechtssache CGT', *EuZA* 2008, 355–366; M. Weiss, 'Arbeitnehmermitwirkung in Europa', *NZA* 2003, 177–184; U. Wendeling-Schröder/H. Welkoborsky, 'Beschäftigungssicherung und

Transfersozialplan – Neue Handlungsfelder auf Grund BetrVG-Novelle und EG-Recht',
NZA 2002, 1370–1378; Lord K. W. Wedderburn, 'Consultation and Collective Bargaining
in Europe: Success or Ideology?', *ILJ* 26 (1997), 1–34; F. Wooldridge, 'The Framework
Directive on informing and consulting employees', *Co Lawyer* 24 (2003), 182–184; see also
the bibliography to §26 above.

Cases:
ECJ Case C-385/05 *Confédération générale du travail (CGT)* [2007] ECR I-611; ECJ Case
C-327/06 *Commission* v. *Italy* [2007] ECR I-22; ECJ Case C-320/06 *Commission* v. *Belgium*
[2007] ECR I-48; ECJ Case C-321/06 *Commission* v. *Luxembourg* [2007] ECR I-85; ECJ
Case C-317/06 *Commission* v. *Spain* [2007] ECR I-95; ECJ Case C-381/06 *Commission* v.
Greece [2007] ECR I-112; ECJ Case C-405/08 *Holst* [2010] ECR I-985.

I. ISSUES, OVERVIEW, COMPETENCE, REGULATORY CONTEXT

1. Issues

1. In 1997, **Renault** unexpectedly, and without prior information and
consultation of its employees' representatives, announced that it was going to
close its Brussels plant and dismiss all of its more than 3,000 employees. A court
in Brussels charged the chief executive officer of the undertaking with a small
fine for the violation of its duties to inform the employees' representatives. In
summary proceedings in Belgium and in France, the unions and the group's
works council, respectively, succeeded in having information and consultation
procedures ordered. Subsequently, two severance schemes were agreed upon.[1]
Despite these partial legal victories, the behaviour of the undertaking's
management outraged employees and unions as well as Member States and the
Commission. It also triggered the enactment of the Information and
Consultation Framework Directive[2] (ICFD).

2. The *Renault* case does not demonstrate that the European law of information
and consultation – as it then existed with the 1975 Collective Redundancies
Directive and the 1994 EWC Directive – was insufficient as such.[3] Rather, what

---

[1]   W. Kolvenbach/D. W. Kolvenbach, *NZA* 1997, 695–697; M. Körner, *Formen der
       Arbeitnehmermitwirkung*, 200–206; F. Lorenz/M. Zumfelde, *RdA* 1998, 168–173; H. Reichold,
       NZA 2003, 289 sq.; id., *Arbeitsrecht*, 3rd edn. (Munich: C.H. Beck, 2008), §14 para. 29.
[2]   Directive 2002/14/EC of the European Parliament and of the Council of 11 March 2002
       Establishing a General Framework for Informing and Consulting Employees in the European
       Community, OJ 2002 L 80/29.
[3]   But see C. Villiers, 'The Rover Case (1) The Sale of Rover Cars by BMW – the Role of the
       Works Council', *ILJ* 29 (2000), 386–394 on the reach of the EWC-Directive and the example
       of the sale of Rover by BWM.

was criticised rather was the **manner** in which Renault's management had proceeded – a French court characterized it as 'brutal'. In practice, the regime of employee involvement had failed to serve its purpose. A potential reason appeared to be that employer and employees' representatives did not meet on a regular basis to exchange views and they lacked a culture of trusting cooperation.[4] Moreover, breach of information and consultation rights proved to be insufficiently sanctioned. The Information and Consultation Framework Directive is designed to address these deficits.[5]

3. The Directive, which also serves to implement Nos. 17 and 18 of the Community Charter of Fundamental Social Rights (see §2 paras. 65–77), pursues the primary **purpose** of protecting employees by safeguarding their involvement in decisions concerning the undertaking or establishment through representation. However, individual provisions[6] and the Recitals of the Preamble (see in particular Recitals 7–14 ICFD) reveal that the legislator was not exclusively concerned with employee protection but also with issues of management and political economy. Information and consultation are conceived as components of a concept of 'anticipation' and 'prevention' that is intended to benefit both the employees and the undertaking.[7] This is best expressed by Recital 7 ICFD:

> 'There is a need to strengthen dialogue and promote mutual trust within undertakings in order to improve risk anticipation, make work organisation more flexible and facilitate employee access to training within the undertaking while maintaining security, make employees aware of adaptation needs, increase employees' availability to undertake measures and activities to increase their employability, promote employee involvement in the operation and future of the undertaking and increase its competitiveness.'

4. This has aptly been described as the legislator's 'dynamic motivation oriented at competition policy and internal market policy'.[8] The legislator starts from the premise of the inevitability of constant changes and adaptations in the undertaking and its establishments and the employer's **management prerogative**

---

4   Cf. M. Hall, *ILJ* 34 (2005), 103, 107.
5   Following T. Lobinger, *ZfA* 2006, 173, 218 sq., we may well categorise the Directive as a procedural instrument of protection, with a view to its collective instruments on the one hand and with its low degree of doctrinal determination, it may be doubted, though, whether it can – as Lobinger suggests – be considered proof for an individual conception of employee protection.
6   E.g. in Article 6 ICFRD on confidentiality, in Article 8 ICFD on the protection of rights or in Article 1(3) ICFD on cooperation and mutual respect.
7   H. Oetker/C. Schubert, in *EAS*, B 8300 para. 293.
8   H. Reichold, *NZA* 2003, 289, 291 (my translation).

and, at the same time, seeks to safeguard the interests of the employees, particularly their employability, namely by means of information rights.[9]

2. Legislative History and Development

5. While plans for the Information and Consultation Framework Directive date from further back,[10] the *Renault* case provided additional momentum for its enactment. In June 1997, the Commission instituted the consultation procedure pursuant to Article 2(2) and (3) Social Policy Protocol to the Maastricht Treaty (cf. Article 154(2) and (3) TFEU) on the projected directive and its contents. However, the social partners decided not to enter into social dialogue-proceedings (pursuant to Article 3(4) Social Policy Protocol; cf. Article 154(4) TFEU) on the matter.[11] On 17 November 1998, the Commission adopted a proposal for the Information and Consultation Framework Directive.[12] The proposal met with some initial resistance which blocked the project until 2001.[13] In 2001, the Commission presented an amended proposal to the European Parliament and Council which contained more stringent rules, based upon the new competence of Article 137 EC (Article 153 TFEU) which had entered into force in 1999.[14] The Common Position of 2001[15] basically reduced its rules back to the level of the original proposal.[16] The Directive was adopted on 11 March 2002. The Commission has recently **reviewed** the application of the

---

[9] W. Kohte, Festschrift *50 Jahre Bundesarbeitsgericht,* 1228–1230 ('concept of prevention and employability' – my translation).

[10] See in detail D. Schäfer, *Der Europäische Rahmen für Arbeitnehmermitwirkung,* 95–108 (and in detail on the draft versions 108–131). On the legislative history T. Ritter, *Der Wirtschaftsausschuss nach dem Betriebsverfassungsgesetz und die Rahmenrichtlinie 2002/14/ EG,* 67–82.

[11] It was namely the association of private employers UNICE that opposed the social dialogue proceedings; C. Barnard/S. Deakin, *IRJ* 33 (2002), 484, 488; M. Hall, *ILJ* 34 (2005), 103, 107; H. Reichold, *NZA* 2003, 289, 290.

[12] Commission, Proposal for a Council Directive establishing a general framework for informing and consulting employees in the European Community, COM(98) 612 final, OJ 1999 C 2/3. See O. Deinert, *NZA* 1999, 800–805; R. Giesen, *RdA* 2000, 298–304.

[13] On the backgrounds, see M. Hall, *ILJ* 34 (2005), 103, 107 sq.; S. Deakin/G. Morris, *Labour Law,* para. 9.30.

[14] Commission, Amended Proposal for a Directive of the European Parliament and of the Council Establishing a General Framework for Improving Information and Consultation Rights of Employees in the European Community, COM(2001) 296 final, OJ 2001 C 240E/133.

[15] Common Position (EC) No 33/2001 of 23 July 2001 adopted by the Council, acting in accordance with the procedure referred to in Article 251 of the Treaty establishing the European Community, with a view to adopting a Directive of the European Parliament and of the Council establishing a general framework for informing and consulting employees in the European Community OJ 2001 C 307/16.

[16] H. Reichold, *NZA* 2003, 289, 290.

Directive pursuant to Article 12 and has come to a positive conclusion, except for the delayed implementation in some Member States.[17]

3. Overview of the Directive

6. Similar to the EWC-Directive (see §28 below) and to the SE-Directive (see §29 below), the Information and Consultation Framework Directive is primarily characterised by procedural rules and an openness to autonomous regulation by the social partners.[18] The Directive applies to undertakings or establishments that exceed certain thresholds of numbers of employees, subject to further definition by Member States. Its core element is the determination of '[subjects and] practical arrangements for information and consultation' in Article 4 ICFD, with the option for Member States to leave the practical arrangements for information and consultation open to agreement between the social partners, Article 5 ICFD. These provisions are supplemented by the principle of loyal cooperation (Article 1(3) ICFD) and a number of other concretising provisions (Articles 6 and 7 ICFD).

II. SCOPE OF APPLICATION

7. Pursuant to Article 3(1) ICFD, the Directive, according to the choice of the Member States, applies to

- **undertakings** employing at least 50 employees in any one Member State; an undertaking is defined for the purposes of the directive as 'a public[19] or private undertaking carrying out an economic activity, whether or not operating for gain, which is located within the territory of the Member States', Article 2(a) ICFD;
  or
- **establishments** employing at least 20 employees in any one Member State; an establishment is defined as 'a unit of business defined in accordance with national law and practice, and located within the territory of a Member State, where an economic activity is carried out on an ongoing basis with human and material resources', Article 2(b) ICFD.

8. The *formula* for calculating the number of employees for the purposes of these thresholds is for the Member States to determine (e.g. how part-time

---

[17]   Communication from the Commission to the Council, the European Parliament, the European Economic and Social Committee and the Committee of the Regions on the review of the application of Directive 2002/14/EC in the EU, COM(2008) 146 final.

[18]   See also C. Barnard/S. Deakin, *IRJ* 33 (2002), 484, 490.

[19]   On the applicability in the public service, see K. Vogelsang, *PersV* 2006, 364, 365 sq.

employees are to be taken into account).[20] This determination, however, only includes rules to make the Directive manageable and not the delimitation of the scope of application as such.[21] With regard to the concept of **employee**, the Directive expressly refers to the national laws of the Member States.[22] Neither this reference to national law nor the competence to define the formula for calculating the number of employees allows Member States to exclude – fully or partly, permanently or temporarily – certain groups or categories of employees, e.g. on the basis of their age ('under 26').[23]

9. Pursuant to Article 3(2), Member States may *maintain* **particular provisions** applicable to undertakings or establishments which pursue directly and essentially

- political,
- professional organisational,
- religious,
- charitable,
- educational,
- scientific or
- artistic aims as well as
- aims involving information and the expression of opinions.

This option is, however, open only to Member States where provisions of that nature already existed in their national law on the effective date of the Directive (Article 13 ICFD: 23 March 2002). It is, in other words, merely respecting established legal traditions of individual Member States.[24] In addition, the optional exception is in substance limited in two ways: it does not allow for a complete exception but merely for 'particular provisions' and it binds Member States to respect the 'principles and objectives' of the Directive. In addition, Member States have the option to derogate from the Directive – again: 'through particular provisions' – with regard to crews of vessels plying the high seas, Article 3(3) ICFD.

10. The Directive does not define the **employees 'representatives** but rather refers to the employees' representatives established under national laws and/or

---

20 See also R. Waltermann, case note to ECJ Case C-385/05 *Confédération générale du travail (CGT)*, ZESAR 2007, 330.

21 C. Weber, *EuZA* 2008, 355, 361 sq.

22 As a consequence, civil servants are not covered under German law, K. Vogelsang, *PersV* 2006, 364, 366.

23 ECJ Case C-385/05 *Confédération générale du travail (CGT)* [2007] ECR I-611 paras. 31–39; approvingly R. Waltermann, *ZESAR* 2007, 330 sq.; C. Weber, *EuZA* 2008, 355, 359–362.

24 C. Weber, *Festschrift für Konzen*, 942.

practices, Article 2(e) ICFD. Apart from the European Works Council, the establishment and composition of employees' representations are thus not determined by Union law. Furthermore, there is no obligation under Union law to install an employee representation, either. Following the Court's jurisprudence with regard to the Collective Redundancies Directive (see §23 para. 17 above) and the Transfer of Undertakings Directive (see §24 para. 90 above), the Information and Consultation Framework Directive should be read as requiring Member States to provide that there is at least the *possibility* for employees in the undertakings and establishments covered by the Directive (see para. 7 above) to form a representative body (which is not conditional upon the employer's consent).[25]

III. RIGHTS OF THE EMPLOYEES' REPRESENTATIVES

1. Information and Consultation

11. Similar to the EWC-Directive which was originally adopted in 1994, the Information and Consultation Framework Directive provides for employee involvement through information and consultation. **Information** is (unlike in the EWCD) specifically defined as the transmission of data by the employer to the employees' representatives in order to enable the representatives to acquaint themselves with the subject matter and examine it, Article 2(f) ICFD. The definition designates information as an element of a *'constituted' workforce*, given that it is not the individual employees who are to be informed but rather their representatives. This is different from, for example, Article 7 TDU where Member States may resort to individual information (see §24 paras. 89–94). In addition, information is characterised by the purpose of giving the employees' representatives an opportunity to acquaint themselves with the subject matter and examine it.

12. **Consultation** is defined – in a similar way as in the EWC-Directive – as the exchange of views and the establishment of dialogue between the employees' representatives and the employer, Article 2(g) ICFD. This requires each party to listen to the opinion of the other side, consider and comment upon it. It thus goes beyond the mere acknowledgement of another opinion.[26]

---

[25] M. Franzen, *Festschrift für Birk*, 100 sq., 104; P. Hanau, in id./H.-D. Steinmeyer/R. Wank (eds.), *Handbuch des europäischen Arbeits- und Sozialrechts*, §19 para. 130; W. Kohte, *Festschrift 50 Jahre Bundesarbeitsgericht*, 1244–1247 (with further reaching inferences for the German Works Constitution Act); M. Stoffels, 'Die Betriebsverfassung unter dem Einfluss des Europarechts', in A. Söllner et al. (eds.), *Gedächtnisschrift für Meinhard Heinze* (Munich: C.H. Beck, 2005), 885, 897 sq.

[26] See also M. Franzen, *Festschrift für Birk*, 99 sq.

13. Information and consultation are designed as **two steps** of employee involvement. While there are instances that merely require information, information may be used in other instances as a first step, preparing for consultation.

2. *'Practical Arrangements for Information and Consultation': Subjects and Modalities*

14. The 'practical arrangements' (*modalités, Modalitäten*) of information and consultation are determined by the Directive. They take the form of minimum standards, Article 4 ICFD. The national law of Member States may entrust the social partners 'with defining [them] freely and at any time' through agreement, Article 5 ICFD. The term used to designate the subject matter of these provisions is rather misleading in the English language version as well as in the French and German language versions.[27] The provision initially regulates topics of information and consultation and then the 'modalities' or 'practical arrangements' in a narrow sense.

a) Topics of Information and Consultation

15. Article 4(2) ICFD provides for a list of topics of information (even though the heading of the provision merely speaks of 'modalities'). In the cases covered by lit. a), the provision requires information only; this is due to the fact that those topics are concerned with entrepreneurial decisions where no concrete measures (with relevance for the employees) are at stake. In the cases covered by lit. b) and c), the provision requires both information and consultation.

16. The Directive requires only **information** on 'the recent and probable development of the undertaking's or the establishment's activities and *economic situation*', Article 4(2)(a) ICFD.

17. **Information and consultation** is required on

– certain issues of *employment*, namely pursuant to lit. b):
  • employment situation,
  • employment structure and

---

27 Spanish 'las modalidades prácticas del ejercicio del derecho de información y de consulta' ('the practical modalities of information and consultation'); Polish 'praktyczne rozwiązania do celów wykonywania prawa do informacji i konsultacji' ('practical determinations in regard of information and consultation'). More aptly in the Dutch version: 'nadere regelingen inzake informatie en raadpleging' ('more detailed provisions on information and consultation').

- likely development of employment within the undertaking or establishment and
- any anticipatory measures envisaged, in particular where there is a threat to employment

and,

- pursuant to lit. c): decisions likely to lead to *substantial changes in work organisation or in contractual relations,* including those covered by the Collective Redundancies Directive, the Transfer of Undertakings Directive or the EWC-Directive.[28]

18. In particular the provision of lit. b) and the cases covered therein reflect the background of the rules in the *Renault* case (para. 1 above). The provision also expresses the specific purpose of the Directive: Employee involvement should be initiated at an early stage of planning in order to allow influence on the entrepreneurial planning (which, of course, as such remains free) (see Recital 10 ICFD: 'employment strategy based on the concepts of "anticipation", "prevention" and "employability"'). The rights to employee involvement provided here *supplement* specific rights as provided in the Collective Redundancies Directive, the Transfer of Undertakings Directive and the EWC-Directive but do not replace them.[29]

b) Modalities in the strict sense

19. The **information** is to be 'given at such time, in such fashion and with such content as are appropriate to enable, in particular, employees' representatives to conduct an adequate study and, where necessary, prepare for consultation'. As the Directive defines information so as to serve a specific purpose (see para. 11 above), this definition follows as a matter of course, and the same result would have been reached by means of teleological interpretation.

20. Similarly, **consultation** is to take place 'while ensuring that the timing, method and content thereof are appropriate', Article 4(4)(a) ICFD. This will usually imply that consultation must take place before the decision on the subject matter has been taken as the employer would otherwise not be in a position to consult with an open mind (cf. Recitals 6, 13 ICFD).[30] Consultation must take place at the relevant level of management and representation, depending upon the subject under discussion, lit. b).[31] Consultation proceeds on the basis of any information supplied by the employer and the opinions which the employees'

---

[28] M. Franzen, *RdA* 2002, 258, 262; B. Karthaus, *AuR* 2007, 114, 116 sq.; T. Lobinger, *ZfA* 2006, 173, 215 sq.

[29] B. Karthaus, *AuR* 2007, 114, 116.

[30] This is doubted by P. Lorber, *IJCLLIR* 19 (2003), 297, 302 sq.

[31] With further considerations B. Bercusson, *ILJ* 31 (2002), 209, 226 sq.

representatives are entitled to formulate, lit. c). The general requirement for dialogue and an exchange of opinions is then further concretised to the extent that the consultation should be conducted in a way so as to enable the employees' representatives to meet the employer and obtain a response, and the reasons for that response, to any opinion they might formulate, lit. d).

21. Where the consultation is concerned with decisions which are likely to lead to substantial changes in work organisation or contractual relations pursuant to Article 4(2)(c) ICFD,[32] consultation goes beyond dialogue and exchange and amounts to a duty to negotiate, Article 4(4)(e) ICFD.[33] Employer and employees' representatives then **consult with a view to reaching an agreement**. This is, in other words, a *qualified form of dialogue*. As in the Collective Redundancies Directive and the Transfer of Undertakings Directive, the duty to negotiate does not include a duty to reach an agreement. The employer may, if the negotiations do not lead to an agreement, decide unilaterally; indeed, Article 4(4)(e) ICFD specifically emphasises the employer's powers which remains unaffected by the provision.

c) The Autonomy of the Social Partners to Agree on Different 'Practical Arrangements'

22. Article 5 sent. 1 ICFD gives Member States the option to implement Article 4 ICFD as a default rule, subject to alterations by agreement between the social partners.[34] In addition and independent of national implementing measures, agreements that have been concluded before the implementation period as well as any subsequent renewals of such agreements may establish provisions that deviate from the requirements of Article 4, Article 5 sent. 2 ICFD. The legislator is, to some extent,[35] pursuing the same **procedural regulatory**

---

[32] Further reaching B. Bercusson, *ILJ* 31 (2002), 209, 224 sq., suggesting a duty to negotiate in all cases of Article 4(2) ICFD, if only they could have as a consequence that the employer, acting within the limits of his managerial authority, may take decisions within the scope of Article 4(2)(c) ICFD.

[33] With doubt B. Bercusson, *ILJ* 31 (2002), 209, 225, who seems to suggest a duty to negotiate in all cases.

[34] P. Lorber, *IJCLLIR* 19 (2003), 297, 302. Contrary to B. Spreer, *Die Richtlinie 2002/14/EG zur Festlegung eines allgemeinen Rahmens für die Unterrichtung und Anhörung der Arbeitnehmer*, 55 sq. and D. Schäfer, *Der Europäische Rahmen für Arbeitnehmermitwirkung*, 166–168, this is not a case of transposition of the directive by the social partners pursuant to Article 153(4) TFEU (on this provision, see §4 paras. 24 sq.), but rather an optional dispositivity by collective agreement.

[35] The approach is much weaker here, though. Unlike in the EWC-Directive, the legislative model applies not only as a default, subsidiary regime. The possibility of disposing of the legislative model by agreement and its limits are largely subject to the discretion of the Member States in the implementation process.

concept which is found in the EWC-Directive in these provisions,[36] and allows the social partners to regulate their own affairs in a way which meets their specific interests and needs.

23. Due to the misleading terminology (practical arrangements, *modalités, Modalitäten;* see para. 14 above) there could be doubt as to whether the social partners' autonomy also allows them to 'freely define' the topics of information and consultation. However, both the wording and the reference in Article 5 ICFD to the whole provision of Article 4 – including paragraph 2 – support the affirmative answer.[37]

24. The social partners may in their 'negotiated agreement' also agree upon a standard which **undercuts the Directive's minimum standards** (mandatory for Member States). They may, for example, restrict the topics for information and consultation. The national law of Member States may provide for conditions and limitations. And, in any case, the agreement must respect the principles set out in Article 1 ICFD. The modalities in a strict sense (see paras. 19–21 above) leave little room for lower standards, though, given that they are largely determined by the purpose of the Directive.

IV. SUPPLEMENTARY PROVISIONS

25. Finally, a number of provisions concern relationships between the social partners.

1. Work in the Spirit of Cooperation – The Principle of Loyal Cooperation

26. Article 9 EWC-Directive specifically emphasises the principle of loyal cooperation. Article 1(3) ICFD provides for the same principle. Its location at the start of the Directive can be seen as an expression of its fundamental importance rather than it being of merely declaratory purposive value. 'When defining or implementing practical arrangements[38] for information and consultation, the employer and the employees' representatives shall work in a *spirit of cooperation* and with due regard for their reciprocal rights and obligations, *taking into*

---

[36] M. Fuchs, in M. Fuchs/F. Marhold, *Europäisches Arbeitsrecht,* 226 sq.; D. Schiek, *Europäisches Arbeitsrecht,* 319.

[37] Differently C. Weber, 'Arbeitnehmermitbestimmung im Europäischen Sozialraum', in H. Dreier/H. Forkel/K. Laubenthal (eds.), *Raum und Recht – Festschrift 600 Jahre Würzburger Juristenfakultät* (Berlin: Duncker & Humblot, 2002), 189, 209.

[38] The interpretation, again, has to take account of the special terminology of the Directive pursuant to which the term 'modalities' covers both the topics of information as well as the manner in which it is to be provided; see Article 4 ICFD and on this the text at para. 14 above.

account the *interests* both of the undertaking or establishment and of the employees', Article 1(3) ICFD. This amounts to a **principle of good faith** for the European law of information and consultation, together with some concretisation in respect of individual duties.

27. The 'spirit of cooperation' is the basic principle of information and dialogue in the context of consultation (see in general §26 para. 28 above). Article 4(3) and (4) ICFD concretise the principle. The general clause of Article 1(3) ICFD may provide for a basis for the judicial development of individual duties of behaviour by the Court of Justice.[39] Respect for the respective rights of the parties and consideration of mutual *interests* (!) are central precepts of good faith, particularly in a long-term relationship such as that between the social partners.

2. Protection of Employees' Representatives

28. Protection against unfavourable treatment is a standard feature of EU employment law. Article 7 ICFD requires that provision is made for special protection. The employees' representatives are to enjoy 'adequate protection and *guarantees*' so as to enable them to properly perform the duties which have been assigned to them. This presupposes not only a prohibition of unfavourable treatment, but also effective enforcement mechanisms (see also paras. 33 sq. below). The Directive, which only provides for minimum standards and for a regulatory framework, leaves Member States broad discretion in transposing this provision into national law. Article 7 ICFD does *not* demand that employees' representatives enjoy *more extensive* protection than other employees. However, 'adequate' protection requires that employees' representatives are not treated less favourably because of either their status as employees' representatives or their performance of the concomitant functions. Effective protection implies that representatives are afforded an opportunity to ascertain whether unfavourable treatment (e.g. a dismissal) was based upon such prohibited grounds.[40]

3. Confidentiality

29. Finally, Article 6 ICFD provides detailed rules regarding the protection of confidential information. The provision can be characterised as a specific manifestation of the general principle of loyal cooperation, given that it is concerned with a **fundamental interest of the employer**. It contains a two-step

---

[39] See on this the determination of 'responsibility' in Article 4(1) EWCD by the ECJ in the context of information duties; §28 para. 54 above.
[40] ECJ Case C-405/08 *Holst* [2010] ECR I-985 paras. 46–66. With approving case note by M. Jacobs, *EuZA* 2010, 533–540.

instrument of protection (similar to the respective provision in the EWCD, see §28 paras. 77–79 below).

30. As a rule, the employers' interest in confidentiality is taken into account by prohibiting the employees' representatives (and any experts who assist them) from revealing confidential information. The employees' representatives (and the experts) may not reveal 'any information which, in the legitimate interest of the undertaking or establishment, has expressly been **provided to them in confidence**'. The prohibition continues to apply 'wherever said representatives or experts are, even after expiry of their term of office'. National law may, however, authorise the employees' representatives to pass on confidential information to third parties who are also bound by an obligation of confidentiality (e.g. lawyers, tax advisors, auditors). The duty of confidentiality is formally delimited by the criterion that the information has expressly been provided in confidence and further qualified by the substantive criterion that the confidentiality is in the **legitimate interest** of the undertaking or establishment. The mere (formal) characterisation of information as confidential is insufficient, as otherwise the work of the employees' representatives could be inhibited by the threat of a sanction (see also §28 para. 78 below on the EWCD). Conversely, it may constitute a violation of the principle of loyal cooperation of Article 1(3) ICFD if the employees' representatives reveal information which has not been expressly designated as confidential, but which has been or should have been recognised as confidential.

31. There are specific cases where the employer may **withhold information** or is **not obliged to undertake consultation**. This is the case where information or consultation would seriously harm the functioning of the undertaking or establishment or would be prejudicial to it. This is determined on the basis of objective criteria, Article 6(2) ICFD. In light of the purpose of the Directive and the system of Article 6 ICFD which, as a rule, considers the duty of confidentiality pursuant to paragraph 1 to satisfy the employer's interests, these prerequisites in paragraph 2 must be narrowly construed.

32. Where the disclosure of information is prohibited under paragraph 1 or the employer may withhold information under paragraph 2, these restrictions must be open to judicial or administrative **control**, Article 6(3) sent. 1 ICFD (correspondingly Article 11(4) EWCD). As an option, Member States may provide for procedures intended to safeguard the information in question, Article 6(3) sent. 2 ICFD. For example, one may consider a proviso that certain information may not be revealed to the employees' representatives but to a professional (e.g. an accountant) who is bound by an obligation of confidentiality and who then, in turn, may only reveal certain aspects of the information to the employees' representatives.

4. Sanctions and Protection of Rights

33. In light of the *Renault* case which triggered the enactment of the Directive, it is essential that information and consultation rights are protected; Article 8 ICFD is sometimes described as the *Renault* clause.[41] In this regard, the Directive lags behind the standard of the original proposal which provided that employer's decisions that have been taken without due information or consultation should be ineffective.[42] However, Article 8(2) ICFD is an expression of the general Member States' implementation obligations to ensure effective enforcement of rights and obligations flowing from the Directive and provide for adequate sanctions for a breach of obligations.[43] Mere symbolic sanctions such as in the *Renault* case (see para. 1 above) cannot satisfy this requirement (principle of effectiveness).

34. Beyond that, Article 8(1) ICFD emphasises the legislator's concern that rights and obligations flowing from the Directive should be *fulfilled*, thus going beyond mere sanctions for non-performance. This is in line with the concept of protection by means of anticipation and prevention (see para. 3 above). The national law of Member States must provide adequate administrative or judicial procedures to ensure effective enforcement of the obligations derived from the Directive.[44] Following general principles of the Member States' implementation obligations, an overall assessment of the enforcement mechanisms provided by the national law is required. Mere sanctions for breach, even if they are particularly severe, do not satisfy the requirement for national law procedures (!) that enable enforcement (!).[45] On the other hand, the Directive does not require Member States to provide for injunctive relief which employees' representatives could invoke against the employer;[46] such a proposal was insufficiently supported during the legislative proceedings prior to the Directive's enactment.[47] An obligation in Union law to provide for injunctive relief could only be derived from the implementation principles (see §1 paras. 65 sq.) if this

---

[41]   J. Kenner, 'Worker Involvement in the Societas Europaea: Integrating Company and Labour Law in the European Union?', *YEL* 24 (2005), 223, 241 sq.

[42]   See in more detail D. Schäfer, *Der Europäische Rahmen für Arbeitnehmermitwirkung*, 117–119. On the development C. Barnard/S. Deakin, *IRJ* 33 (2002), 484, 489 sq. Critically on the enacted version e.g. P. Lorber, *IJCLLIR* 19 (2003), 297, 303.

[43]   See M. Franzen, *Festschrift für Birk*, 105 sq. and 111–114.

[44]   W. Kohte, *Festschrift für Richardi*, 611 sq.: 'The right to information and consultation must be judicially enforceable' – my translation; in addition to that also injunctive relief.

[45]   B. Spreer, *Die Richtlinie 2002/14/EG zur Festlegung eines allgemeinen Rahmens für die Unterrichtung und Anhörung der Arbeitnehmer*, 61 sq. In this respect apparently differently C. Weber, *AuR* 2008, 365, 379.

[46]   More broadly W. Kohte, *Festschrift 50 Jahre Bundesarbeitsgericht*, 1248–1250 (injunctive relief as a safeguarding mechanism); id., *Festschrift für Richardi*, 611–613; F. N. Fauser/M. Nacken, *NZA* 2006, 1136, 1142 sq.; B. Karthaus, *AuR* 2007, 114,119.

[47]   H. Oetker/C. Schubert, in *EAS*, B 8300 para. 385; C. Weber, *AuR* 2008, 365, 379 sq.

was the mechanism that a given Member State used as a sanction for comparable rights derived from national law (principle of equivalence) or if it could be established that other remedies would in effect not lead to the required enforcement (principle of effectiveness).

V. IMPLEMENTATION

35. In **Germany**[48] implementing legislation was largely considered to be unnecessary, given the high level of employee involvement under the Works Constitution Act (*Betriebsverfassungsgesetz*, BetrVG).[49] As a consequence, there is no specific implementing measure in German law, and there is also no reference to the Directive as is required by Article 11(2) ICFD. The principle of loyal cooperation can be found in §74 BetrVG. The transposition of the rights of the employees' representatives under Article 4(2) ICFD is more problematic. Unlike the system of the BetrVG, the ICFD does not distinguish between employee participation in social, personal and economic matters; consequently, German implementation is difficult to assess.[50]

36. The requirements of Article 4(2)(a) (**economic development**) have not been sufficiently transposed into German law in more than one respect.[51] Participation of the economic committee pursuant to §106 BetrVG cannot satisfy the requirements of the Directive. (1) While §106 BetrVG largely covers the same subjects, it does not take the prospective element ('probable development') into account. (2) Secondly, the economic committee is not an employees' representation within the meaning of Article 2(e) ICFD;[52] instead, it is a special

---

[48] For a survey on the implementation, see Communication from the Commission to the Council, the European Parliament, the European Economic and Social Committee and the Committee of the Regions on the review of the application of Directive 2002/14/EC in the EU, COM(2008) 146 final.
Various Member States did not implement the Directive timely; see ECJ Case C-327/06 Commission v. Italy [2007] ECR I-22; Case C-320/06 Commission v. Belgium [2007] ECR I-48; Case C-321/06 Commission v. Luxembourg [2007] ECR I-85; Case C-317/06 Commission v. Spain [2007] ECR I-95; Case C-381/06 Commission v. Greece [2007] ECR I-112.

[49] Betriebsverfassungsgesetz of 15 January 1972, as amended on 25. September 2001, BGBl. 2001 I, 2518, also available at www.gesetze-im-internet.de/betrvg/index.html and English version at www.gesetze-im-internet.de/englisch_betrvg/index.html; bilingual German-English version in S. Lingemann/R. v. Steinau-Steinrück/A. Mengel (eds.), Employment and Labor Law in Germany, Part II, X. On implementation deficits in the public service K. Vogelsang, *PersV* 2006, 364–375.

[50] H. Reichold, *NZA* 2003, 289, 298; see also U. Wendeling-Schröder/H. Welkoborsky, *NZA* 2002, 1370, 1372. For a categorisation of the participation rights, see M. Franzen, *Festschrift für Birk*, 102–104.

[51] See in more detail M. Franzen, *Festschrift für Birk*, 102 sq.; T. Ritter, *Der Wirtschaftsausschuss nach dem Betriebsverfassungsgesetz und die Rahmenrichtlinie 2002/14/EG*, 168–292.

[52] See (with regard to the TUD) K. Riesenhuber, *RdA* 2004, 340, 342 sq.

body designed to advise the Works Council (*Betriebsrat*) which is the employees' representation proper ('auxiliary body for the works council'). Such 'split' definition of the employees' representation is incompatible with the principle of equivalence which is part of a Member State's implementation obligations.[53] (3) Finally, an economic committee must only be constituted in undertakings which permanently employ more than 100 employees. This threshold exceeds those in the Directive;[54] and this also leads to a change in the relevant level of employee involvement from the establishment to the undertaking, which is not allowed under Article 3(1) ICFD. The rights to information and consultation pursuant to Article 4(2)(b) ICFD (employment situation etc.) are implemented by §§92–95 and 96–98 BetrVG.[55] The rights pursuant to Article 4(2)(c) ICFD (work organisation) are covered by §87 BetrVG (here even providing for a right to co-determination) and §§90 sq. and 111 BetrVG. The procedural and substantive enforcement mechanisms required by Article 8 ICFD follow from §23(3) BetrVG.[56] Here, too, commentators have highlighted some specific implementation deficits.[57]

37. In the **United Kingdom**, the Directive was implemented by the Information and Consultation of Employees Regulations 2004 (ICER 2004).[58] The ICER 2004 emphasise flexibility and aim to preserve a culture of individual and custom-tailored information and consultation solutions.

38. **Denmark** has used the option contained in Article 11(1) ICFD which, in accordance with the Court's case law, allows Member States to leave implementation of the Directive to management and labour (see in more detail §4 paras. 24 sq. above). Such implementation by collective agreement is also possible where not all employees are members of the unions concluding the agreement, provided that, under the applicable national law, those employees are still guaranteed the same level of protection.[59]

---

[53]   Differently M. Franzen, *Festschrift für Birk,* 104 sq.; T. Ritter, *Der Wirtschaftsausschuss nach dem Betriebsverfassungsgesetz und die Rahmenrichtlinie 2002/14/EG, S. 225–228.*

[54]   M. Franzen, *Festschrift für Birk,* 105; H. Reichold, *NZA* 2003, 289, 299.

[55]   M. Franzen, *Festschrift für Birk,* 103.

[56]   With doubt in regard to injunctive relief P. Hanau, in id./H.-D. Steinmeyer/R. Wank (eds.), *Handbuch des europäischen Arbeits- und Sozialrechts,* §19 para. 134.

[57]   M. Franzen, *Festschrift für Birk,* 103 sq.

[58]   SI 2004/3426; also available at www.legislation.gov.uk/uksi/2004/3426/contents/made. On the implementation in the UK, S. Deakin/G. Morris, *Labour Law,* paras. 9.50–9.58 (discussing doubt as to the correct implementation at para. 9.58); K. D. Ewing/G. M. Truter, *MLR* 68 (2005), 626–641; M. Hall, *ILJ* 34 (2005), 103, 109–125; A. Lingscheid/K. Schmidt, *RIW* 2006, 424–429; P. Lorber, *IJCLLIR* 19 (2003), 297, 304–319; id., *IJCLLIR* 22 (2006), 231–258; see also the considerations of B. Bercusson, *ILJ* 31 (2002), 209, 231–243.

[59]   Cf. ECJ Case C-405/08 *Holst* [2010] ECR I-985 paras. 34–45.

§28. THE EUROPEAN WORKS COUNCIL DIRECTIVE

CONTENTS

Bibliography:

A. Alaimo, 'The New Directive on European Works Councils: Innovations and Omissions', *IJCLLIR* 26 (2010), 217–230; W. Altmeyer, 'Europäische Betriebsräte – Die aktuellsten Gerichtsurteile', *AiB* 2007, 503–506; F. Bauckhage, *Die Sanktionen des Europäische Betriebsräte-Gesetzes* (Berlin: wvb, 2006); J. R. Bellace, 'The European Works Council Directive: Transnational Information and Consultation in the European Union', *Comp. Lab. L. J.* 18 (1997), 325–361; T. Blanke, 'Die neue EBR-Richtlinie 2009/38/EG', *AuR* 2009, 242–250; T. Blanke/E. Rose, 'Die zeitliche Koordinierung der Informations- und Konsultationsansprüche Europäischer Betriebsräte und nationaler Interessenvertretungen bei grenzübergreifenden Umstrukturierungsmaßnahmen', *RdA* 2008, 65–81; T. Blanke, *Europäisches Betriebsräte-Gesetz – EBRG-Kommentar – Europäische Mitbestimmung SE,* 2nd edn. (Baden-Baden: Nomos, 2006); R. Birk, 'Europäisches kollektives Arbeitsrecht – insbesondere der Europäische Betriebsrat', in S.

Grundmann (ed.), *Systembildung und Systemlücken in Kerngebieten des Europäischen Privatrechts* (Tübingen: Mohr Siebeck, 2000), 387–399; M. Carley/M. Hall, 'The Implementation of the European Works Councils Directive', *ILJ* 29 (2000), 103–124; C. Docksey, 'Employee Information and Consultation Rights in the Member States of the European Communities', *Comp. Lab. L. 7* (1986), 32–48; C. Docksey, 'Information and Consultation of Employees: The United Kingdom and the Vredeling Directive', *MLR* 49 (1986), 281–313; F. Gamillscheg, *Kollektives Arbeitsrecht Band II – Betriebsverfassung* (Munich: C.H. Beck, 2008); G. Forst, 'Die Beteiligungsvereinbarung nach der neuen EBR-Richtlinie', *ZESAR* 2009, 469–476; G. Forst, 'Zum Begriff des abhängigen Unternehmens im europäischen Arbeitsrecht', *ZESAR* 2010, 154–163; M. Franzen, 'Die EU-Richtlinie 2009/38/EG über Europäische Betriebsräte', *EuZA* 2010, 180–197; B. Gaul, 'Die Einrichtung Europäischer Betriebsräte', *NJW* 1995, 228–232; R. Giesen, 'Merkwürdiges Übergangsrecht bei der Reform des Europäischen Betriebsrats', *NZA* 2009, 1174–1176; W. Goos, 'Ansätze zur Mitbestimmung der Arbeitnehmer in der europäischen Rechtsetzung', in H. Oetker/U. Preis/V. Rieble (eds.), *50 Jahre Bundesarbeitsgericht* (Munich: C.H. Beck, 2004), 1179–1195; W. Goos, 'Kommt der Europäische Betriebsrat?', *NZA* 1994, 776–781; M. Hall, 'Behind the European Works Councils Directive: The European Commission's Legislative Strategy', *BJIR* 30 (1992), 547–564; P. Hanau, in id./H. D. Steinmeyer/R. Wank (eds.), *Handbuch des Europäischen Arbeits- und Sozialrechts* (Munich: C.H. Beck, 2002), §19 paras. 22–100; P. Hanau, 'Nationale Regelungen für internationale (europäische) Betriebsräte', in J. F. Baur et al. (eds.), *Festschrift für Ralf Vieregge zum 70. Geburtstag am 6. November 1995* (Berlin/New York: de Gruyter, 1995), 319–334; M. Heinze, 'Der Europäische Betriebsrat, Die Richtlinie und ihre Alternativen', *AG* 1995, 385–402; M. Henssler, 'Konzernrechtliche Abhängigkeit im Mitbestimmungsrecht der Europäischen Aktiengesellschaft – Der Abhängigkeitsbegriff im Europäischen Mitbestimmungsrecht, EBRG, SEBG und nationalem Akt', in: G. Bitter et al. (eds.), *Festschrift für Karsten Schmidt* (Cologne: Otto Schmidt, 2009), 601–618; K. S. Hohenstatt, 'Der Europäische Betriebsrat und seine Alternativen', *EuZW* 1995, 169–172; W. Hromadka, 'Rechtsfragen zum Eurobetriebsrat', *DB* 1995, 1125–1131; D. Joost, 'Auskunftsansprüche bei Errichtung Europäischer Betriebsräte für Unternehmensgruppen mit zentraler Leitung in einem Drittstaat', *ZIP* 2004, 1034–1039; D. Joost, 'Auskunftsansprüche der Arbeitnehmervertreter zur Errichtung eines Europäischen Betriebsrats bei Unternehmensgruppen', *BB* 2001, 2214–2218; D. Joost, in R. Richardi et al. (eds.), *Münchener Handbuch zum Arbeitsrecht*, 3rd edn. (Munich: C.H. Beck, 2009) §§274, 275; A. Junker, 'Betriebsverfassung in Klein- und Mittelbetrieben – Ein europäischer Vergleich', *NZA* 2002, 131–138; A. Junker, 'Neues zum Europäischen Betriebsrat', *RdA* 2002, 32–35; A. Junker, 'Der "Europäische Betriebsrat" in rechtsvergleichender Perspektive', *JZ* 1992, 1100–1106; M. Kilian, 'Die Umsetzung der Richtlinie 94/45/EG ("Europäische Betriebsräte") im Vereinigten Königreich', *RdA* 2001, 166–171; W. Kolvenbach, 'Europäische Betriebsräte – Großbritannien', *NZA* 1998, 582–585; W. Kolvenbach, 'Europäische Betriebsräte – Neue Initiativen', *DB* 1991, 805–807; W. Kolvenbach, 'Europäische Betriebsräte, Umsetzung, Anwendung und Vorbildfunktion der Richtlinie 94/45/EG', *NZA* 2000, 518–527; S. Laulom, 'The Flawed Revision of the European Works Council Directive', *ILJ* 39 (2010), 202–208; P. Lorber, 'Reviewing the European Works Council Directive: European Progress and United Kingdom Perspective', *ILJ* 33 (2004), 191–199; F. Lorenz/M.

Zumfelde, 'Der Europäische Betriebsrat und die Schließung des Renault-Werkes in Vilvoorde/Belgien', *RdA* 1998, 168–173; C. McGlynn, 'European Works Councils: Towards Industrial Democracy?', *ILJ* 24 (1995), 78–84; R. H. Mnookin/L. Kornhauser, 'Bargaining in the Shadow of the Law: The Case of Divorce', *Yale L.J.* 88 (1979), 950–997; P. Mozet, 'Beteiligung der Arbeitnehmer auf europäischer Ebene, Anmerkungen zur EG-Richtlinie über den Europäischen Betriebsrat', *ZEuP* 1995, 552–563; H. Oetker, 'Europäischer Betriebsrat und Pressefreiheit – Zugleich ein Beitrag zu den Schranken der Mitbestimmung im Tendenzunternehmen', *DB* 1996, Supplement No. 10 to Issue 23, 1–16; H. Oetker/C. Schubert, 'Europäisches Betriebsverfassungsrecht', in H. Oetker/U. Preis (eds.), *Europäisches Arbeits- und Sozialrecht, EAS, part B – Systematische Darstellungen*, loose-leaf (Heidelberg: Forkel, last update: January 2007), B 8300 paras. 28–285; J. Pipkorn, 'The Draft Directive on Procedures for Informing and Consulting Employees', *CMLR* 20 (1983), 725–755; U. Rademacher, *Der Europäische Betriebsrat – Die Richtlinie des Rates vom 22.9.1994 und ihre Umsetzung in nationales Recht* (Baden-Baden: Nomos, 1996); M. E. Risak, 'Horizontale Auskunftspflicht bei der Errichtung europäischer Belegschaftsvertretung', *EuZA* 2008, 409–416; D. Sadowski/K. Kühne, 'Der europäische Betriebsrat – weder europäisch noch Betriebsrat', in H. Konzen et al. (eds.), *Festschrift für Rolf Birk zum siebzigsten Geburtstag* (Tübingen: Mohr Siebeck, 2008), 771–787; D. Schiek, 'Europäische Betriebsvereinbarung', *RdA* 2001, 218–236; I. Schmidt, 'Betriebliche Arbeitnehmervertretung insbesondere im Europäischen Recht', *RdA* 2001 Special Supplement to Issue 5, 12–22; Marlene Schmidt, 'Der Europäische Betriebsrat', *NZA* 1997, 180–183; G. Thüsing/G. Forst, 'Europäische Betriebsräte-Richtlinie: Neuerungen und Umsetzungserfordernisse', *NZA* 2009, 408–412; C. Villiers, 'The Rover Case (1) The Sale of Rover Cars by BMW – the Role of the Works Council', *ILJ* 29 (2000), 386–394; G. H. van Voss, 'The Directive on European Works Councils in Community-scale Undertakings – The Introduction of "Double Subsidiarity" in European Labour Law', *MJECL* 2 (1995), 339–356; B. Waas, 'Die neue EBR-Richtlinie 2009/38/EG', *KritV* 2009, 400–411; C. Weber, 'Information und Konsultation im europäischen und deutschen Mitbestimmungsrecht', in B. Dauner-Lieb et al. (eds.), *Festschrift für Horst Konzen zum siebzigsten Geburtstag* (Tübingen: Mohr Siebeck, 2005), 921–956; Lord K. W. Wedderburn, 'Consultation and Collective Bargaining in Europe: Success or Ideology?', *ILJ* 26 (1997), 1–34; Lord K. W. Wedderburn, 'Inderogability, Collective Agreements, and Community Law', *ILJ* 21 (1992), 245–264; M. Weiss, 'Arbeitnehmermitwirkung in Europa', *NZA* 2003, 177–184; M. Weiss, 'Die Umsetzung der Richtlinie über Europäische Betriebsräte', *AuR* 1995, 438–444; M. Weiss, 'Europäische Betriebsräte und Konzern – 20 Thesen', *ZIAS* 1995, 633–639; M. Weiss, 'Workers' Participation in the European Union', in P. Davies/ et al. (eds.), *European Community Labour Law: Principles and Perspectives – Liber Amicorum Lord Wedderburn* (Oxford: Clarendon Press, 1996), 213–235; C. Windbichler, 'Dependent Independence from a Labour Law Perspective', *JITE* 152 (1996), 250–261; C. Windbichler, 'Unternehmerisches Zusammenwirken von Arbeitgebern als arbeitsrechtliches Problem – Eine Skizze auch vor dem Hintergrund der EG-Richtlinie zum Europäischen Betriebsrat in Unternehmensgruppen', *ZfA* 1996, 1–18; C. Windbichler, 'Auskunftspflichten in der gemeinschaftsweit operierenden Unternehmensgruppe', in M. Lutter/M. Scholz/W. Sigle (eds.), *Festschrift für Martin Peltzer zum 70. Geburtstag* (Cologne: Otto Schmidt, 2001), 629–643; see also the bibliography to §26 above.

Cases:

ECJ Case C-430/98 *Commission* v. *Luxembourg* [1999] ECR I-7395; ECJ Case C-62/99 *bofrost* [2001] ECR I-2595; ECJ Case C-440/00 *Kühne & Nagel* [2004] ECR I-807; ECJ Case C-349/01 *ADS* [2004] ECR I-6819.

I. ISSUES, OVERVIEW, COMPETENCE, REGULATORY CONTEXT

1. Issues

1. The primary purpose of employee involvement on the shop level is to include employees, through the provision of information, in decisions concerning the workplace or the workforce and, as the case may be, let them participate in the decision-making process. This presupposes that the relevant decisions are being taken by the (national) employer-undertaking. Where undertakings in the internal market merge or cooperate across national borders, this premise may be called into question: Decisions that affect national establishments may be made outside the Member State concerned – and thus as a matter of fact be beyond the reach of the involvement of any employees' representatives.[1] In trans-national situations, national employees' representations may thus be rendered ineffective: 'The works council in Gunzenhausen will arguably have little influence on the group's central management in the United States or in Switzerland'.[2] The 'Directive on the establishment of a European Works Council or a procedure in Community-scale undertakings and Community-scale groups of undertakings for the purposes of informing and consulting employees' (European Works Council Directive, EWC-Directive, EWCD)[3] is an attempt to ensure information and consultation of employees in Union-scale undertakings or groups of undertakings (see Recitals 9–11 EWCD).[4]

---

[1]   Cf. B. Gaul, *NJW* 1995, 228, 231; I. Schmidt, *RdA* 2001 Special Supplement to Issue 5, 12, 13; M. Weiss, *ZIAS* 1995, 633. Cf. also Article 2(4) CRD, Article 7(4) TUD.

[2]   F. Gamillscheg, *Kollektives Arbeitsrecht II*, 1178 – my translation. See also A. Junker, *JZ* 1992, 1100, 1101 sq.; J. Pipkorn, *CMLR* 20 (1983), 725, 729 sq.

[3]   Directive 2009/38/EC of the European Parliament and of the Council of 6 May 2009 on the establishment of a European Works Council or a procedure in Community-scale undertakings and Community-scale groups of undertakings for the purposes of informing and consulting employees (Recast), OJ 2009 L 122/28. Occasionally, we will refer to the original Directive (cf. Article 17 EWCD): Council Directive 94/45/EC of 22 September 1994 on the establishment of a European Works Council or a procedure in Community-scale undertakings and Community-scale groups of undertakings for the purposes of informing and consulting employees, OJ 1994 L 254/64; we use the abbreviation 'EWCD 1994' to distinguish it from the current version.

[4]   D. Sadowski/K. Kühne, *Festschrift für Birk*, 771–787 (with an game theory-analysis of the effect of the EWC as a forum for communication for the employees' representatives in a international competition of various undertakings of a group.

2. Legislative History and Development of the Directive, Competence

2. The **preparatory work** for the Directive[5] dates back to the Council resolution on a social policy action programme of 21 January 1974 (see §1 paras. 32 sq. above) in which the progressive involvement of workers or their representatives was declared to be a goal of Community policy.[6] The original proposal for a directive of 1980,[7] often referred to as *Vredeling*, after the then responsible Commissioner, did not provide for the establishment of a specific representative organ but rather aimed to establish special rights of information and consultation for the national employees' representations which could, where appropriate, also bind decision-makers in the undertaking located in other Member States.[8] As the Council could not agree on the proposal, it was not further pursued after 1986.[9] The 1989 Community Charter with its emphasis upon information and consultation rights (Nos. 17 and 18 CSFR; see §2 para. 71 above) gave the project new momentum. In 1990, the Commission adopted a revised proposal.[10] Its acceptance was largely due to the fact that the Commission 'shifted gears from a substantive regulation, uniformly applicable to all cases, to the mere installation of a procedural structure'[11]: Employer and employees (representatives) are able to customise their system of employee involvement through the negotiation procedure.

3. The Commission had initially intended to base the Directive upon the internal market competence of Article 100 EC-Treaty (Article 115 TFEU) but could not secure the unanimity required by this provision. The Directive was

---

[5]   See in detail T. Blanke, *EBRG-Kommentar*, Einleitung paras. 18–82; U. Rademacher, *Der Europäische Betriebsrat*, 33–70 and 70–79; G. H. van Voss, *MJ* 2 (1995), 339–344.

[6]   On the legislative history R. Birk, in S. Grundmann (ed.), *Systembildung und Systemlücken in Kerngebieten des Europäischen Privatrechts*, 387, 391 sq.; see in detail U. Rademacher, *Der Europäische Betriebsrat*, 33 sqq.

[7]   Commission, Proposal for a Council Directive on Procedures for Informing and Consulting the Employees of Undertakings with Complex Structures, in Particular Transnational Undertakings, OJ 1980 C 297/3.

[8]   See also J. R. Bellace, *Comp. Lab. L. J.* 18 (1997), 325, 346–348; C. Docksey, *Comp. Lab. L.* 7 (1986), 32–48; id., *MLR* 49 (1986), 281–313; J. Pipkorn, *CMLR* 20 (1983), 725–755; M. Weiss, *Liber Amicorum Lord Wedderburn*, 213, 224–226; H. P. Westermann, 'Tendenzen der gegenwärtigen Mitbestimmungsdiskussion in der Europäischen Gemeinschaft', *RabelsZ* 48 (1984), 123, 169–179.

[9]   W. Kolvenbach, *DB* 1991, 805.

[10]   Commission, Proposal for a Council Directive on the Establishment of a European Works Council in Community-Scale Undertakings or Groups of Undertakings for the Purposes of Informing and Consulting Employees, COM(90) 581 final, OJ 1991 C 39/10; Amended proposal for a Council Directive on the establishment of a European Works Council in Community-Scale Undertakings or groups of undertakings for the purposes of informing and consulting employees, COM(91) 345 final, OJ 1991 C 336/11. On the proposals, see e.g. M. Hall, *BJIR* 30 (1992), 547–564; A. Junker, *JZ* 1992, 1100–1106.

[11]   M. Weiss, *NZA* 2003, 177, 179 – my translation; M. Weiss, *ZIAS* 1995, 633, 635 (paradigm change).

ultimately adopted on the basis of the 1992 Social Policy Protocol to the Amsterdam Treaty to which the United Kingdom was not a party (see §4 para. 4 above). Social dialogue, which was introduced as part of the Social Policy Protocol (cf. today Articles 154 sq. TFEU; see §4 paras. 26–41 above), did not however lead to an agreement as the employers' association UNICE felt unable to give its consent owing to the intervention of the British employers' association.[12] The original Directive 94/45/EC (hereinafter 'EWCD 1994') entered into force on 22 September 1994.

4.   Based upon Article 100 ECT (Article 115 TFEU), a 1997 amendment, Directive 97/45/EG,[13] extended the scope of the Directive so as to also cover the **United Kingdom** (to be implemented by 14 December 1999).[14] Apart from that, the Directive only provided for minor changes in connection with the extension of the territorial scope of application.[15]

5.   Following a first report on the application of the Directive (cf. Article 15 EWCD 1994) submitted in 2000,[16] the Commission initiated a revision in 2003. It primarily considered the Directive to be deficient with regard to information and enforcement; here too, the *Renault* case, which had triggered the Information and Consultation Framework Directive (see §27 para. 1), left its marks.[17] On 2 July 2008, the Commission submitted a **proposal for a revised directive**.[18] The European Parliament adopted the proposal on 16 December 2008 with amendments,[19] after the Council had consented to its adoption thus

---

12   R. Birk, in S. Grundmann (ed.), *Systembildung im Europäischen Privatrecht,* 391; M. Heinze, *AG* 1995, 385, 386. On the consultation procedure see also: C.-N. Lerche, *Der europäische Betriebsrat und der deutsche Wirtschaftsausschuss* (Frankfurt a. M. et al.: Lang, 1997), 139.

13   Council Directive 97/74/EC of 15 December 1997 extending, to the United Kingdom of Great Britain and Northern Ireland, Directive 94/45/EC on the establishment of a European Works Council or a procedure in Community-scale undertakings and Community-scale groups of undertakings for the purposes of informing and consulting employees, OJ 1997 L 10/22.

14   See W. Kolvenbach, *NZA* 1998, 582–585; M. Kilian, *RdA* 2001, 166–171.

15   W. Kolvenbach, *NZA* 1998, 582, 583.

16   Report from the Commission to the European Parliament and the Council on the application of the Directive on the establishment of a European works council or a procedure in Community-scale undertakings and Community-scale groups of undertakings for the purposes of informing and consulting employees (Council Directive 94/45/EC of 22 September 1994), COM(2000) 188 final.

17   See e.g. W. Altmeyer, *AiB* 2007, 503–506; P. Lorber, *ILJ* 33 (2004), 191–199; M. Schmidt, *EuZA* 2008, 196, 205–207.

18   Commission, Proposal for a European Parliament and Council Directive on the establishment of a European Works Council or a procedure in Community-scale undertakings and Community-scale groups of undertakings for the purposes of informing and consulting employees (Recast) of 2 July 2008, COM(2008) 419 final, See also the preceding Communication from the Commission on the Social Agenda of 9 February 2005, COM(2005) 33 final.

19   European Parliament legislative resolution 16 December 2008 on the proposal for a directive of the European Parliament and of the Council on the establishment of a European Works

amended pursuant to Article 251(2)(2) indent 1 EC (cf. Article 294(4) TFEU). Political agreement on the adoption was reached on 17 December 2008. On 6 May 2009, the Directive was formally **enacted**.[20] In this book, we will only refer to the 2009 revision as the 'EWC-Directive'. A central objective of the revision was to make the work of the EWC more effective (cf. Recitals 7, 14 sq. EWCD and the newly inserted provisions of Article 1(2) sent. 2, (3) EWCD). At the same time, burdens on undertakings and establishments should be limited to an unavoidable minimum (Recital 9 sent. 1, Article 1(2) sent. 2 EWCD). In substance, the Directive strengthened the rights of employees' representatives (e.g. already in the definitions of Article 2(2)(f) and (g)), expanded the assistance which was available to employees' representatives from experts and union representatives (Article 5(4) EWCD), and emphasised the 'role' of employees' representatives (Article 10(1), (2), (4) EWCD).

6. Some undertakings had established forms of cross-border cooperation of employees' representatives even before the enactment of the Directive on the basis of agreements (on their perpetuation, see Article 14 EWCD).[21] Since its adoption, a large number of undertakings have established European Works Councils.[22] A database on EWC agreements, which was set up by the European Trade Union Institute (ETUI), can be found at www.ewcdb.eu.

3.   *Overview of the Directive*

7. The Directive primarily provides for a *procedure* (Articles 4–6) pursuant to which the *central management* of a Community-scale undertaking or group of undertakings on the one side and a *special negotiating body* (SNB) which is constituted by the employee-side on the other side (scope of application; Articles 1–3 EWCD) autonomously agree on creation of

– either an EWC
– or special information and consultation procedures

Council or a procedure in Community-scale undertakings and Community-scale groups of undertakings for the purposes of informing and consulting employees (recast), OJ 2010 C 45 E/112.

[20]   See already note 3 above. For a discussion of the new Directive, see M. Franzen, *EuZA* 2010, 180–197. For a critical assessment of the reform (and also of the peculiar process of involvement of the social partners in this case) see A. Alaimo, *IJCLLIR* 26 (2010), 217–230; S. Laulom, *ILJ* 39 (2010), 202–208. For critical discussion of the intertemporal provisions of the Directive by R. Giesen, *NZA* 2009, 1174–1176.

[21]   See the references in C. Barnard, *EC Employment Law,* 526 sq.; B. Gaul, *NJW* 1995, 228 sq.; I. Schmidt, *RdA* 2001 Special Supplement to Issue 5, 12, 17.

[22]   On practical experience, see in detail M. Fuchs, in M. Fuchs/F. Marhold (eds.), *Europäisches Arbeitsrecht,* 315–322.

in addition to any procedures of employee involvement existing under national law. The practical arrangements and modalities are largely left for the parties to determine autonomously (cf. Article 6(2) introductory sentence EWCD); the Directive merely provides for principles of cooperation (Articles 8–10 EWCD). Mainly for cases of procrastination or negotiation failure, the Directive provides for subsidiary requirements for the installation of an EWC and its competences (which, of course, the parties can also agree to autonomously) in its Annex (Article 7 EWCD; 'fall-back solution').

4.   Note regarding the Presentation of the following Sections

8.   The subsidiary requirements in the Annex thus constitute a legislative model and a crucial guideline that is likely to shape the expectations of the parties during negotiations. Given that the rules in the Annex will apply if the negotiations fail, the parties thus 'bargain in the shadow of the law'.[23] On the basis of these considerations, it appears apt in the following to first consider the subsidiary requirements (III. below) before looking at the central provisions of the Directive concerning the negotiation procedures for the creation of an EWC or special information and consultation procedures by agreement (IV. below). Both parts are largely independent, so that readers who are primarily interested in the negotiation regime of the Directive may proceed directly to part IV.

II.   SCOPE OF APPLICATION AND DEFINITIONS

9.   'The purpose of [the EWC] Directive is to improve the right to information and to consultation of employees in Community-scale undertakings and Community-scale groups of undertakings.' Consequently, '[t]o that end, a European Works Council or a procedure for informing and consulting employees shall be established in every Community-scale undertaking and every Community-scale group of undertakings … with the purpose of informing and consulting employees', Article 1(1) and (2) sent. 1 EWCD. The Directive thus applies to Community-scale undertakings and groups of undertakings as defined in Article 2(1)(a)-(c), (2) EWCD with regard to (1) the number of employees and (2) the activity in different Member States.

---

[23]   Cf. M. Carley/M. Hall, *ILJ* 29 (2000), 103, 105, 107. The concept is based on the seminal contribution by R. H. Mnookin/L. Kornhauser, *Yale L.J.* 88 (1979), 950–997.

1.   Substantive Scope of Application

a)   Community-scale Undertaking

10.   Pursuant to Article 2(1)(a) EWCD, a '**Community-scale undertaking**' is an undertaking

- with at least 1,000 employees within the Member States and
- at least 150 employees in each of two Member States.

11.   The requirement of at least 1,000 employees exempts small and medium-size undertakings which the legislator did not want to expose to the (financial) burdens involved with the installation of an EWC or special information and consultation procedures.[24] The requirement of at least 150 employees in each of two Member States reflects the transnational ('Community-scale') element.[25]

12.   The term **undertaking** should be construed autonomously in Union law as disparate interpretations in the national laws of the Member States would call the uniform scope of application of the Directive into question.[26] For a definition, we can refer to the concept of undertaking in **competition law**:[27] 'the concept of an undertaking encompasses every entity engaged in an economic activity, regardless of the legal status of the entity and the way in which it is financed'.[28] Matters are different with regard to the concept of **employee**. As is clear from Article 2(2) EWCD, the Community legislator merely intended to set out a regulatory framework for Member States. The basic concept is thus for the Member States to define.[29] The Directive merely provides that for the calculation of thresholds, the average number of employees, including part-time employees, employed during the previous two years should be taken into account.[30]

13.   Where – as is the case in Germany – **executive staff members** are in principle regarded as employees, they cannot be exempted from the concept of employee for purposes of implementing the Directive. They must thus be taken

---

[24]   For a comparative survey of works constitution in small and medium-sized establishments, see A. Junker, *NZA* 2002, 131–138.

[25]   P. Mozet, *ZEuP* 1995, 552, 558.

[26]   P. Hanau, in id./H. D. Steinmeyer/R. Wank (eds.), *Handbuch des Europäischen Arbeits- und Sozialrechts*, §19 paras. 33 sq.; I. Schmidt, *RdA* 2001 Special Supplement to Issue 5, 12, 15.

[27]   P. Hanau, in id./H. D. Steinmeyer/R. Wank (eds.), *Handbuch des Europäischen Arbeits- und Sozialrechts*, §19 paras. 33 sq.; U. Rademacher, *Der Europäische Betriebsrat*, 84.

[28]   ECJ Case C-41/90 *Höfner & Elser* [1991] ECR I-2010 para. 21.

[29]   R. Birk, in S. Grundmann (ed.), *Systembildung und Systemlücken in Kerngebieten des Europäischen Privatrechts*, 387, 396 (critically); U. Rademacher, *Der Europäische Betriebsrat*, 93–96.

[30]   W. Hromadka, *DB* 1995, 1125, 1126.

into account when calculating the thresholds. To use a specific concept of employee in implementing the Directive would violate a Member State's implementation obligations.[31] Moreover, Article 2(2) EWCD does not authorise Member States to take national practices into account with regard to the *concept of employee*. Reference to national legislation or practices may only be made with regard to the *calculation* of the average number of employees. This is a specific issue, separate from that of the concept of employee.[32] The provision may, for example, be relevant for the method of taking part-time employees into account.

b)   Community-scale Groups of Undertakings

14.   Apart from Community-scale undertakings, the Directive also applies to **Community-scale groups of undertakings**.[33] Pursuant to Article 2(1)(b) EWCD, a group of undertakings is defined as (a group which consists of) 'a controlling undertaking and its controlled undertakings'. This definition is hybrid in the sense that it partly, with regard to the concept of undertaking, refers to an autonomous definition in Union law, although it is also partly inevitably dependent upon national company laws of which the Directive did not intend to harmonise with regard to the definition of 'control' (controlling, controlled).[34] While the concept of control should thus be defined autonomously, its application must be left to national laws of the Member States.

15.   The group consists of a **controlling undertaking** and at least one controlled undertaking.[35] Pursuant to Article 3(1) EWCD, an undertaking is 'controlling' if it can exercise a dominant influence over another undertaking by virtue, for example, of ownership, financial participation or the rules which govern it. The other undertaking then is the 'controlled undertaking'. There are three cases where a dominant influence will be presumed, although this presumption is rebuttable by proof of the contrary: where the undertaking (a) holds a majority

---

[31]   Cf. on the IPD ECJ Case C-334/92 *Wagner Miret* [1993] ECR I-6911 paras. 15–23; to the same effect as here M. Weiss, *AuR* 1995, 438, 442; differently F. Gamillscheg, *Kollektives Arbeitsrecht I*, 1185; P. Hanau, in id./H. D. Steinmeyer/R. Wank (eds.), *Handbuch des Europäischen Arbeits- und Sozialrechts*, §19 para. 55; id., *Festschrift für Vieregge*, 321 sq. (Member States discretion in the transposition); D. Joost, in R. Richardi et al. (eds.), *Münchener Handbuch zum Arbeitsrecht*, §274 paras. 24, 33; U. Rademacher, *Der Europäische Betriebsrat*, 96 sq.; I. Schmidt, *RdA* 2001 Special Supplement to Issue 5, 12, 15; M. Schmidt, *NZA* 1997, 180, 181.

[32]   See e.g. the comparative discussion – arranged pursuant to the issues involved – by A. Junker, *NZA* 2002, 131, 136.

[33]   With further considerations C. Windbichler, *JITE* 152 (1996), 250–261; ead., *ZfA* 1996, 1–18 (comparing the group of undertakings with the German concept of *Konzern* and with gradually different forms of entrepreneurial cooperation of different intensity); see also ead., *Festschrift für Peltzer*, 629–643 (criticising inconsistencies and an unrealistic picture of the group of undertakings in of the Directive).

[34]   M. Henssler, *Festschrift für Karsten Schmidt*, 601, 610; C. Windbichler, *ZfA* 1996, 1, 9 sq. For an entirely autonomous definition G. Forst, *ZESAR* 2010, 154, 155 sq.

[35]   See in more detail W. Hromadka, *DB* 1995, 1125 sq.

---

of that undertaking's subscribed capital; (b) controls a majority of the votes attached to that undertaking's issued share capital; or (c) can appoint more than half of the members of that undertaking's administrative, management or supervisory body, Article 3(2) EWCD.[36] These determinants in company law have not been approximated by the Directive. Whether an undertaking is 'controlling' consequently depends upon the application of national law of the Member State which governs that undertaking, Article 3(6)(1) EWCD (for undertakings in third countries, see subparagraph 2).[37]

16. Pursuant to Article 2(2)(c) EWCD, a group of undertakings is qualified as being of 'Community-scale' if it has the following (cumulative) characteristics:

- at least 1,000 employees within the Member States,
- at least two group undertakings in different Member States, *and*
- at least one group undertaking with at least 150 employees in one Member State and at least one other group undertaking with at least 150 employees in another Member State.

This definition transposes the criteria for a Community-scale undertaking (see para. 10 above) to a group of undertakings. Here too, a minimum size of at least 1,000 employees is required (see para. 11 above). Formulating the further requirements, the legislator has taken into account that the group may also comprise undertakings located outside the Community. The provisions first cover the standard case where two group undertakings located in two Member States each have at least 150 employees in each of two (say: their home) Member States. The elaborate wording takes into account the case where an undertaking does not have 150 employees in the (Member) State where it is located but in a(nother) Member State.

17. Some authors suggest that the definition should be construed so as to also cover cases where *one* group undertaking has 150 employees in one Member State and *several other* group undertakings, each of which has less than 150 employees, *together* have 150 employees in another Member State.[38] This may well be considered the case as a matter of policy and it may indeed be regarded as following from transposition of the requirements for (single) undertakings to groups of undertakings. Yet, the unequivocal wording of the provision leaves no room for such broad interpretation.

---

[36]   On the calculation of the voting rights, see paragraph (3); paragraph (7) resolves a potential collision of norms in the application of paragraph (2).

[37]   For reference points (also) in Union law, see C. Windbichler, *ZfA* 1996, 1, 9 sq.

[38]   G. Asshoff/M. Bachner/O. Kunz, *Europäisches Arbeitsrecht im Betrieb* (Cologne: Bund-Verlag GmbH, 1996), 192.

2. Territorial Scope of Application

18. The territorial scope of the powers and competences of European Works Councils or special procedures for information and consultation is primarily for the parties to the agreement to determine. Where they do not provide otherwise, the powers and competences pursuant to Article 1(6) extend to the Member States (in the course of Directive 97/74/EC: including the United Kingdom; see para. 4 above) and cover

- in the case of a Community-scale undertaking: all the establishments located within the Member States;
- in the case of a Community-scale group of undertakings: all group undertakings located within the Member States.

3. Exception for Pre-Existing Agreements

19. Pursuant to Article 13 EWCD 1994, the Directive did not apply to Community-scale undertakings or groups of undertakings in which an agreement, covering the whole workforce and providing for transnational information and consultation of employees was already in force upon expiry of the implementation period (22 September 1996). This provision, which received considerable attention by undertakings and scholars,[39] has been maintained in the 2009 revision and is now to be found in Article 14 EWCD. Such agreements may be maintained permanently if the parties so agree. Undertakings appear to have considered such prior agreements as advantageous; fearing that the 'corset of the directive' would be too narrow.[40] Article 13 EWCD 1994/14 EWCD may be considered to be another instance of bargaining in the shadow of the law, with the special characteristic that in this case, the shadow resulted from pending legislation. The provisions are remarkable for giving the parties a particularly broad margin of discretion, making application of the exception conditional upon only very few requirements. This is also the reason why there is little that can be said regarding the prior agreements as such, given that they were subject to the

---

[39] See in particular M. Heinze, *AG* 1995, 385, 393–400; P. Hanau, *Festschrift für Vieregge*, 319, 323–329, 330 sq.; P. Hanau, in id./H. D. Steinmeyer/R. Wank (eds.), *Handbuch des Europäischen Arbeits- und Sozialrechts*, §19 paras. 64–75; H. J. Willemsen/K.-S. Hohenstatt, 'Chancen und Risiken von Vereinbarungen gemäß Artikel 13 der "Euro-Betriebsrat"-Richtlinie', *NZA* 1995, 399–403; I. Schmidt, *RdA* 2001 Special Supplement to Issue 5, 12, 16–18; further J. R. Bellace, *Comp. Lab. L. J.* 18 (1997), 325, 351–354; M. Carley/M. Hall, *ILJ* 29 (2000), 103, 107 sq.; S. Deakin/G. Morris, *Labour Law*, para. 9.64; F. Gamillscheg, *Kollektives Arbeitsrecht II*, 1179 sq.

[40] P. Hanau, *Festschrift für Vieregge*, 323. See also I. Schmidt, *RdA* 2001 Special Supplement to Issue 5, 12, 16 sq. ('This privilege [sc. of Article 13 EWCD 1994] has in fact triggered a "boom" of EWCs.'; – my translation).

---

almost unfettered autonomy of the parties. However, they do raise specific private international law questions (questions of conflict of laws and of jurisdiction).[41]

III. THE SUBSIDIARY MODEL OF THE EUROPEAN WORKS COUNCIL

20. The Directive provides for a subsidiary European Works Council model which applies in three cases:

(1) where the parties so agree;
(2) where the employer refuses to begin negotiations within six months of the request by employees or their representatives to do so; and
(3) where the parties have not reached an agreement in their negotiations within three years after the request by the employees or their representatives to initiate negotiations.

The subsidiary rules in the Annex may thus serve as a model as well as constitute the fall-back solution if negotiations fail, whether the employer does not commence them in the first place or they do not lead to an agreement. The parties thus bargain 'in the shadow' of the subsidiary requirements (see para. 8 above).

1. Constitution of the European Works Council

21. The size and composition of the EWC depends upon the structure of the respective undertaking or group of undertakings. After determining the total number of employees employed by the undertaking or group of undertakings in all Member States, one seat is given to each 10% (or a fraction thereof) of such total number employed in one Member State, Annex No. 1(c) EWCD. It thus consists of a minimum of ten members. The 10% requirement, first introduced by the 2009 revision, follows the model of the SE-Directive. It is designed to ensure proportionate **representation** relative to the overall number of employees and their regional distribution.

22. EWC members must be recruited from the pool of employees of the undertaking or group. They are elected or appointed by the employees' representatives or, in the absence thereof, by the entire body of employees, Annex No. 1(b) EWCD. Their **election or appointment** is not regulated by the Directive but follows the laws and practices of the national laws of the Member States.

---

[41]   P. Hanau, *Festschrift für Vieregge*, 319–334.

23. The EWC elects a **select committee** comprising at most five Members, Annex No. 1(d) EWCD. The purpose of the select committee, the constitution of which was only optional prior to the 2009 revision of the Directive, is to coordinate the EWC's activities; at the same time, its activities may serve to limit costs. The select committee adopts its own rules of procedure.

24. Central management and any more appropriate level of management, for example a central human resources department, must be informed about the composition of the EWC, Annex 1(d) EWCD.

2. Competences

25. The competences of the EWC are defined in the Annex by the criterion of transnationality. The Annex provides for annual information and consultation and ad hoc-information in exceptional circumstances.

a) Subjects Covered: Transnational Issues

26. The competences of the EWC are generally limited to information and consultation on **transnational issues**, Annex No. 1a) with Article 1(3), (4) EWCD (see also Recital 16). These are matters which concern

– the Community-scale undertaking or group of undertakings[42] as a whole or
– at least two undertakings or establishments situated in two Member States.[43]

27. The original 1994 directive (Annex No. 1(a) EWCD 1994) specifically limited the competences of the EWC for groups of undertakings with their central management outside the Member States (cf. Article 4(2) EWCD) to matters where (a) all of the establishments or group undertakings in the Member States or (b) at least two of its establishments or group undertakings in the Member States were concerned. While the express provision was deleted in the 2009 revision, the substance of the rule still applies; it already follows from Annex No. 1(a) with Article 1(3) and (4) EWCD.

b) Regular (Annual) Information and Consultation

28. The EWC's rights comprise, first, the right to meet with central management once a year and be informed and consulted, Annex No. 2 EWCD.

---

[42] This should also include the sale of *Rover* by *BMW* in 2000; but see C. Villiers, *ILJ* 29 (2000), 386–394 (expressing doubt about the applicability of the EWCD).

[43] On the new definition M. Franzen, *EuZA* 2010, 180, 183 sq. (e.g. central management in Member State A decides to lay of workers in Member State B: covered).

29. The original 1994 Directive did not define the term **information**. The definition adopted in the 2009 revision follows that of the Information and Consultation Framework Directive (Recitals 21 sq. EWCD; see §27 para. 11 above). Information is defined as the transmission of data by the employer to the employees' representatives in order to enable them to acquaint themselves with the subject matter and examine it, Article 2(1)(f) EWCD. Going beyond a mere definition, the provision also determines the modalities of information. Information must be given 'at such time,[44] in such fashion and with such content as are appropriate to enable employees' representatives to undertake an in-depth assessment of the possible impact and, where appropriate, prepare for consultations with the competent organ of the Community-scale undertaking or Community-scale group of undertakings'. Limits to the employer's obligations follow from the rules on confidentiality, Article 8 EWCD, see paras. 77–79 below.

30. Consultation is defined as the establishment of dialogue and exchange of views between employees' representatives and central management or any more appropriate level of management, Article 2(1)(g) EWCD. *Dialogue* and *exchange of views* do not mean a duty to reach agreement but require more than just hearing the arguments of the other side.[45] A dialogue presupposes an exchange of arguments and the readiness to hear and consider the other party's opinion and to comment upon it.[46] Here too, the Directive now – following the Information and Consultation Framework Directive – provides for a number of consultation modalities (see Recitals 21, 23 EWCD), some of which can already be inferred from the Directive's purpose: Consultation has to take place 'at such time, in such fashion and with such content as enables employees' representatives to express an opinion on the basis of the information provided about the proposed measures to which the consultation is related, without prejudice to the responsibilities of the management, and within a reasonable time, which may be taken into account within the Community-scale undertaking or Community-scale group of undertakings'.

31. The aforementioned modalities are part of the definition of consultation and thus also apply to consultation procedures which are agreed upon during the negotiation procedure if the parties have not provided differently. In contrast, Annex No. 1(a) EWCD provides with regard to the subsidiary requirements that 'the consultation shall be conducted in such a way that the employees' representatives can meet with the central management and obtain a response, and the reasons for that response, to any opinion they might express' (cf.

---

[44] The relevant time for information and consultation was subject to doubt under the EWCD 1994; see T. Blanke/E. Rose, *RdA* 2008, 65–81.

[45] F. Bauckhage, *Die Sanktionen des Europäischen Betriebsräte-Gesetzes,* 104. Differently B. Gaul, *NJW* 1995, 228, 230.

[46] H. Oetker/C. Schubert, in *EAS,* B 8300 para. 124; H. Oetker, *DB* 1996, Supplement No. 10 to Issue 23, 7–9; apparently also I. Schmidt, *RdA* 2001 Special Supplement to Issue 5, 12, 20. Apparently narrower W. Goos, *NZA* 1994, 776, 777; W. Hromadka, *DB* 1995, 1125, 1130 sq.

Recital 44 EWCD). Pursuant to the general definitions, the requirements are: employer informs, EWC expresses an opinion, employer takes this into account; for the subsidiary model, requirements are the same plus *a response*. This dissonance does not seem to be supported by teleological considerations.

32. Timing is of the essence – for both the employee representatives and for the employer. There is a tension between the employees' interests in obtaining information at an early point in time and in deliberating extensively on the one hand and in the employer's interest in making quick decisions, in particular where decisions about the undertaking's structure are concerned. The Preamble recognises both sides' interests: 'informing and consulting the European Works Council should make it possible for it to give an opinion to the undertaking in a timely fashion, without calling into question the ability of undertakings to adapt' (Recital 14 EWCD; see also Recital 22: time, fashion and content of information 'as are appropriate without slowing down the decision-making process in undertakings'). Clearly, the legislator wanted to take both interests into account and not grant the employees unfettered rights. This fact should be taken into account when interpreting the definitions, particularly when it comes to concretising the general clauses of 'appropriateness' and 'reasonableness'.[47]

33. Information is initially provided by a **report** which is drawn up by central management (Article 2(1)(e) EWCD), Annex No. 2 EWCD. This report then serves as a basis for information and consultation with the EWC on the progress of the business of the undertaking or group and its prospects.

34. Topics of information of the EWC pursuant to Annex No. 1(a) EWCD are

(1)   the structure of the undertaking or group;
(2)   its economic and financial situation;
(3)   the probable development and production and sales;
(4)   the situation and probable trend of employment;
(5)   investments;
(6)   substantial changes concerning organisation;
(7)   introduction of new working methods or production processes;
(8)   transfers of production;
(9)   mergers, cut-backs or closures of undertakings, establishments or important parts thereof; and
(10) collective redundancies.

The subject matters of the above Nos. (4) to (10) are *also* topics for **consultations.**

---

[47]   Differently – and too one-dimensionally focused on employees' interests only – T. Blanke, *AuR* 2009, 242, 247 sq.

c) Ad hoc Information

35. In addition, Annex No. 3 EWCD requires employees' representatives to be given ad hoc information where there are **exceptional circumstances** which considerably affect the interests of employees. By way of example, the Annex mentions relocations, the closure of establishments or undertakings and collective redundancies.

36. The primary addressee of the ad hoc information duty is the **select committee** (see para. 23 above), and in the absence of such a committee, the EWC. The burdens and costs of an extraordinary meeting of the EWC should, where possible, be avoided. Annex No. 3 EWCD provides for a two-step procedure. As a first step, the select committee (or the EWC) must be informed. As a second step, it may request to meet central management (or any other appropriate level of management having its own powers of decision) so as to be informed and consulted. Information and consultation shall take place as soon as possible (but: leaving both sides sufficient time for preparation). In preparation for the meeting, central management must draw up a report and give it to the EWC; the EWC may then deliver an opinion on this report at the end of the meeting or within a reasonable time. Members of the EWC who have been appointed by the establishments or undertakings directly concerned may also participate in the meeting of central management and select committee.

37. The Annex explicitly confirms that 'this meeting shall not affect the **prerogatives of the central management**'. Information and consultation does not involve any co-determination or similar participation rights. The consultation does not, as a matter of law, have to have an effect upon the final decision taken by management.

3. Procedural Provisions

38. The Annex provides for only a few requirements as to the procedures of the EWC and largely leaves these issues for the Member States or the parties to determine, Annex No. 4 EWCD. Member States may provide for rules on the chairing of information and consultation meetings. Before meeting with central management, the EWC or select committee may meet and confer without management being present.

39. The EWC and select committee may be assisted by **experts** of its own choosing, e.g. lawyers, accountants or tax advisors, so far as this is necessary for it to carry out its task (Annex No. 5 EWCD).

40.   The **operating expenses** of the EWC are borne by central management (Annex No. 6 EWCD). These include in particular expenses incurred by meetings of the EWC and the select committees, especially travel and accommodation expenses and costs of interpreters (Annex No. 6(3) EWCD). Central management provides members of the EWC with such financial and material resources as will enable them to perform their duties in an appropriate manner. This includes an expenses allowance which must be paid in advance as appropriate (e.g. for travel expenses which the company does not provide as allowance in kind). The Directive further refers to putting in place adequate infrastructure provision, e.g. office space, phone, computer, internet, email, fax etc.

41.   These provisions only lay down principles (resources to enable the members of the EWC to perform their duties in an adequate manner), leaving it to Member States to hammer out the details (Annex No. 6(4) EWCD). The legislator specifically emphasised Member States' competence to 'limit funding to cover one expert only'. Other types of cost may also be restricted in accordance with the principle of proportionality.

4.   Revision Clause

42.   The subsidiary requirements will usually only apply if negotiations fail (Article 7(1) Indents 2 and 3 EWCD; see para. 20 above); this is different only in the – presumably rare – case where the parties agree on the subsidiary requirements (Indent 1). It can thus not be expected that they fully satisfy all the needs of the employer and the employee side. Again, the legislator assumes that a customised approach agreed upon by the parties would be preferable. It thus entrusts the EWC to examine whether to open negotiations for the conclusion of an agreement pursuant to Article 6 EWCD four years after it has been established, Annex No. 1(f) EWCD.

IV.   PROCEDURES FOR THE ESTABLISHMENT OF A EUROPEAN WORKS COUNCIL OR A PROCEDURE FOR INFORMATION AND CONSULTATION

1.   Autonomy and the Negotiation Procedure

43.   This model of a European Works Council (as introduced above, III.) only applies as a fall-back solution. Departing from earlier proposals, the enacted Directive primarily leaves the development of structures of information and consultation with regard to transnational matters to the parties. They make the fundamental decision whether to install an EWC or a special procedure for information and consultation (or not to have any special regime of employee

involvement at all), and they design the modalities of information and consultation autonomously. The Directive primarily determines the identity of the negotiation partners and the basic elements of the negotiation procedures: Within the scope of application of the Directive (II. above), central management (see 2. below) is responsible for creating the prerequisites for the establishment or a procedure for information and consultation (see 3. below). For these purposes central management – out of its own initiative or upon request of the employees – must set up a 'special negotiating body' (see 4. below) as the negotiation partner representing employees.

2. *Responsibility for Establishing a European Works Council or an Information and Consultation Procedure: Central Management*

44. 'The central management shall be responsible for creating the conditions and means necessary for the setting-up of a European Works Council or an information and consultation procedure, as provided for in Article 1(2), in a Community-scale undertaking and a Community-scale group of undertakings', Article 4(1) EWCD. Central management is also the negotiation partner for the employee-side (Article 6 EWCD). The Court of Justice has construed this 'responsibility' as a general clause which can provide the basis for the development of concrete duties of behaviour which are expected from central management; this proved to be of practical relevance with regard to the obligations to provide information (see paras. 47–53 below).

a) The Basic Case

45. Normally, central management will be identified in light of the factual aspects of the case as being 'the central management of the Community-scale undertaking' (Article 2(1)(e) EWCD), e.g. as the board of directors of a specific company. In the case of a Community-scale group of undertakings, it is the central management of the controlling undertaking.

b) Deemed Central Management

46. Special rules apply where the (factual) central management is not located in a Member State. In that case, pursuant to Article 4(2) EWCD, the responsibilities of central management are imposed upon:

– the designated central management's representative agent in a Member State; or
– if no such representative is designated: the management of the establishment or group undertaking employing the greatest number of employees in any one Member State (so-called 'hostage-principle'[48]).

---

[48]   W. Goos, *NZA* 1994, 776; C. Windbichler, *JITE* 152 (1996), 250, 253 sq.

The representative or management will then be deemed to be central management for the purposes of the Directive ('deemed central management').[49] It is, in other words, responsible for the establishment of an EWC or a procedure for information and consultation and functions as the negotiation partner for the employee side, Article 4(3) EWCD. These rules give rise to specific issues of information and information obligations which will be discussed below (paras. 47–53).

3.   Preparation and Initiation of the Negotiation Procedure

a)   The Initiative to Open the Procedure

47.   Both the employer and employee sides can initiate the negotiation procedure. The initiative on the employee side is presumably of greater practical importance. It requires the written request of

- at least 100 employees or
- their representatives

in at least two undertakings or establishments in at least two different Member States.

b)   Preparation of the Employee Initiative: Information Rights

aa)   THE BASIC CASE

48.   An initiative of the employee side will often require that the employees receive the information necessary to establish whether the prerequisites for the application of the Directive (see II. above) are fulfilled:

- the employee thresholds of Article 2(1)(a) and (c),
- but also the existence of a hierarchical group within the meaning of Article 2(1)(b)('controlling undertaking') and Article 3.

The Directive (now) provides for a corresponding right to information. In the original version of the directive, this right had been worded rather awkwardly, it had been systematically misplaced in the implementation provisions and finally, the provision soon proved to have substantial *lacunae*.[50] The 2009 revision introduced the right to information in the new provision of Article 4(4) EWCD. It not only provides for an obligation to **transmit** information but also to **obtain** the required information.

---

49   See also ECJ Case C-440/00 *Kühne & Nagel* [2004] ECR I-787 para. 54.
50   D. Joost, *BB* 2001, 2214 sq. Critically as to the purposive interpretation and the judicial development of the law by the ECJ C. Weber, *Festschrift für Konzen*, 952–955.

49. The right to information is granted to 'the parties concerned by the application of this Directive'. The non-technical term of 'parties' (*Parteien, des parties intéressées*) designates those who have a (legal) interest in the information. In the basic case of Article 5(1) EWCD, this refers to those who can initiate the procedure, i.e. the employees' representatives or a group of 100 employees.

50. The obligation is imposed upon **central management**, which will usually be in the best position to give the information required, but also on every **individual undertaking** of a group.[51] The obligation of the individual undertakings is necessary as the employees may often not be able to discern which of several undertakings of a group is controlling and which of the boards constitutes the central management. Furthermore, the initiative could be hampered if the employees (or their representatives) had to first contact the management of an undertaking in another Member State.[52] Article 4(4) EWCD allows the employees or their representatives to address their requests for information to every undertaking of the group, including for example 'their own' undertaking.

51. Since the 2009 revision, the right to **information includes** 'the information required for commencing the negotiations referred to in Article 5, and in particular the information concerning the structure of the undertaking or the group and its workforce', Article 4(4) and Recital 25 EWCD. Before that, the court had similarly broadly construed the right to information in the original directive, on the basis of teleological considerations.[53] The information which must be given includes the number of employees at the various locations (see Article 2(1)(a) and (c) EWCD) as well as the necessary details to establish whether a relationship of control within the meaning of Article 2(1)(b) EWCD, as specified by Article 3 EWCD, exists. The information right further includes information regarding whether a group of undertakings exists, even if the details of control have not yet been established.[54]

52. However, in the interest of the undertaking or the group of undertakings, the right to information is **restricted** in five respects:[55]

(1) In substance, the employees or their representatives may only request such information as is necessary for the establishment of an EWC or a procedure

---

[51]   Thus already on the basis of the original Directive ECJ Case C-62/99 *bofrost* [2001] ECR I-2595 para. 31; Case C-349/01 *ADS* [2004] ECR I-6819 para. 56. See also I. Schmidt, *RdA* 2001 Special Supplement to Issue 5, 12, 16.
[52]   ECJ Case C-349/01 *ADS* [2004] ECR I-6819 para. 56.
[53]   ECJ Case C-62/99 *bofrost* [2001] ECR I-2595 para. 38.
[54]   ECJ Case C-62/99 *bofrost* [2001] ECR I-2595 paras. 29–36.
[55]   ECJ Case C-440/00 *Kühne & Nagel* [2004] ECR I-787 paras. 59, 62 sq.

for information and consultation (principle of proportionality). Following the Court's jurisprudence, this includes (subject to a control of the necessity by the national courts in the individual case)[56]

- the average number of employees;
- their dispersion in the different Member States;
- the establishments of the undertaking and the undertakings of the group; as well as
- the structure of the undertaking and the undertakings of the group; and
- the designation and contact details of the employees' representatives, which would have to be involved in the establishment of a special negotiation body under Article 5 or in the creation of a European Works Council.[57]

(2) The information may only be used for the purposes set forth in the Directive.

(3) Member States must ensure that there is adequate protection of confidential information.

(4) The undertakings obliged to provide information must be afforded an opportunity to challenge the prerequisites and the limits of information in administrative or judicial procedures.

(5) Not least, the legal obligation is limited by the factual possibilities: the undertakings can only be obliged to give the information that is available to them.

53. In addition to information in a narrow sense, the employee-side may also request that they be given such **documents** as are necessary to specify and illustrate the information.[58]

bb) 'Horizontal' Information Obligations between Group Undertakings

54. Where a group of undertakings is concerned, the right to information may not only be directed at central management but also at individual undertakings (see para. 50 above). Local management of a controlled undertaking of a group may not have the required information at its disposal, though. On the basis of the general principle of responsibility pursuant to Article 4(1) EWCD (see para. 44 above), the Court has not only recognised a right of employees (or their representatives) to receive information from the (factual or deemed) central management but also a corresponding right of the individual undertakings that

---

[56] ECJ Case C-440/00 *Kühne & Nagel* [2004] ECR I-787 paras. 70 sq. (here with regard to an information right of the deemed central management against other undertakings of the group; see para. 54 below; the same considerations also apply here). On the necessity requirement, D. Joost, *ZIP* 2004, 1034, 1037.

[57] For a critical perspective see D. Joost, *ZIP* 2004, 1034, 1038 (not necessary).

[58] ECJ Case C-62/99 *bofrost* [2001] ECR I-2595 para. 40.

have received an information request to obtain information from their central management.[59] This is, indeed, an indispensable complement to the recognition of individual undertakings' duty to provide information, as otherwise the employees' (or their representatives') right to information would often fail on practical grounds. Central management, on the other hand, is not excessively burdened by such a right; from its perspective, the practical consequence is merely that instead of giving the required information directly to the employees (or their representatives) it is obliged to give the information indirectly via one of its group undertakings. The new provision of Article 4(4) EWCD, introduced by the 2009 revision, only indirectly expresses this 'horizontal' right to information when it speaks of a responsibility for '**obtaining** and transmitting' the information (see para. 48 above).

cc)   Special Information Obligations in Cases of Deemed Central Management

55.   In the basic case of a transnational undertaking, central management is obliged to provide the required information. It will usually be in the best position to perform this obligation, as is also the case where a group of undertakings is concerned. Matters are more complicated where central management is not located in a Member State. In this case, the Directive places the responsibilities which would otherwise lie with central management on the shoulders of the deemed central management. While the deemed central management is thus put in the place of the (actual) central management, it is in many ways not in the same position. In particular, the deemed central management will often not have access to the information required by the Directive (Article 4(4) EWCD). If in this situation the (actual) central management, *ex praemissione* located outside Union territory, refuses to transmit the necessary information, then the establishment of the EWC or information and consultation procedures are liable to fail.

56.   To overcome this deadlock, the Court has inferred from the principle of responsibility contained in Article 4(1) EWCD that the deemed central management has a **right to receive information** from the other group undertakings located in the Member States. The deemed central management 'must request the information essential to the opening of negotiations for the

---

[59]   ECJ Case C-349/01 *ADS* [2004] ECR I-6819 paras. 56, 60. See already D. Joost, *BB* 2001, 2214, 2218; I. Schmidt, *RdA* 2001 Special Supplement to Issue 5, 12, 15 sq.; on the fundamental principles (with comparative considerations); C. Windbichler, *Festschrift für Peltzer*, 629–643. On the implementation in Germany *Bundesarbeitsgericht* (Federal Labour Court, BAG). BAG, *BAGE* 111, 191; in Austria *Oberster Gerichtshof* (Supreme Court of Justice, OGH), *ZESAR* 2007, 331–336 with approving case note A. Ritzberger-Moser; for a critical case note see also M. E. Risak, *EuZA* 2008, 409–416.

establishment of [an EWC] from the other undertakings belonging to the group which are located in the Member States, and has a right to receive that information from them'.[60]

4. The Establishment of a 'Special Negotiating Body' for the Employee-Side

57. In order to commence the proceedings, the employee side must be organised for the purposes of the negotiations. While employees' representations may (or may not) exist in the establishments or undertakings in the different Member States, these do not represent the 'transnational' workforce of the undertaking or the group as such. On these grounds, a special negotiating body (hereinafter also referred to as 'SNB') must be established for the employee side, Article 5(2) introductory sentence EWCD. The SNB is entrusted with 'the task of determining, with the central management, by written agreement, the scope, composition, functions, and term of office of the European Works Council(s) or the arrangements for implementing a procedure for the information and consultation of employees', Article 5(3) EWCD.

58. The members of the special negotiating body are elected or appointed according to the rules and practices established by the Member States (cf. Article 5(2)(a) subparagraphs 1 and 2 EWCD). The Union legislator considered that the election or appointment should normally be made by the employees' representatives existing in the establishments or undertakings in the Member States. Where, through no fault of their own, the employees have not established a representative body for themselves, they have a right to elect or appoint the members for the special negotiating body, Article 5(2)(a)(2) EWCD.

59. The election or appointment procedures for the members of the special negotiating body must ensure **representation on two levels**: with regard to (1) the proportion of employees (2) in each Member State, Article 5(2)(b) EWCD. Every portion of employees employed in one Member State amounting to 10%, or a fraction thereof, of the number of employees employed in all the Member States taken together has one seat in the special negotiating body. Pursuant to Article 5(2)(c) EWCD, central and local management must be informed about both the composition of the special negotiating body and the start of the negotiations. In addition, the competent European workers' and employers' organisations must also be so informed.

---

[60] ECJ Case C-440/00 *Kühne & Nagel* [2004] I-787 para. 64 with approving case note R. Giesen, *RdA* 2004, 307–310.

5.   *The Negotiations*

a)   The Principle of Negotiating in Good Faith

60.   The negotiations are governed by the principle of good faith which is expressed in part, by Article 6(1) EWCD: 'The central management and the special negotiating body must negotiate in a spirit of cooperation with a view to reaching an agreement on the detailed arrangements for implementing the information and consultation of employees provided for in Article 1(1).' A number of individual rights and obligations further elaborate upon this principle (see in particular paras. 61, 63 below).

b)   Opening of the Negotiations and Refusal of Central Management

61.   Central management opens the negotiations by convening a meeting with the special negotiating body, Article 5(4) EWCD. Placed in the hands of the employer-side, the opening of negotiations is not only a right but also an obligation. If central management refuses to open the proceedings within six months of the employees' (representatives') request to initiate the proceedings, then the subsidiary requirements of the Annex apply, Article 7(1) indent 2 EWCD.

c)   The Special Negotiating Body's Decision not to Open or to Terminate the Negotiations

62.   Where central management refuses to negotiate in good faith, the primary concern is that the objectives of the Directive should not be defeated. Matters are different where the special negotiating body decides not to open or to terminate negotiations, e.g. on the basis that both an EWC and special information and consultation procedures were unnecessary. Based on the proposition that a higher level of employee involvement will normally be in the interest of the employee side, the central concern here is not that the objectives of the Directive would be defeated. Rather, the main concern here is a need to ensure that a decision to that effect is sufficiently legitimised and seriously intended. On the basis of these considerations, such a decision requires a **two-thirds majority**, Article 5(5)(1) EWCD. In that case, neither an EWC nor a special information and consultation procedure will be established; the provisions of the Annex do not apply, subparagraph 2 EWCD. The special negotiating body may not, in other words, cut short the negotiations and force an EWC pursuant to the Annex onto the employer by a decision not to open or to terminate negotiations. The interests of the employer also require protection: the employee-side should not be allowed to frivolously initiate and terminate the procedure. To take this interest into account, a new request to convene the special negotiating body may be made at the earliest two years after the special negotiating body's decision not to open or to terminate negotiations, subparagraph 3.

d)   Procrastination of Negotiations

63.   Procrastination is also a violation of the duty to negotiate in good faith. However, it is difficult to prove in practice. Article 7(1) indent 3 EWCD pursues a different path. The supplementary provisions of the Annex apply if the parties concluded an agreement (Article 6(1) EWCD) within **three years**[61] after the initial request to initiate proceedings (Article 5(1) EWCD) and the negotiations have not ended upon the special negotiating body's decision under Article 5(5) EWCD. Such failure of the negotiations may be due to the excessive demands of one side but it may also occur irrespective of the honest attempt of both sides. The provision is not concerned with issues of fault but rather intends to realise the objectives of the Directive where the employee side maintains an interest in the additional layer of transnational involvement (no decision pursuant to Article 5(5) EWCD).

e)   Experts and Costs

64.   The special negotiating body may seek assistance from an **expert** of its own choosing who may also be present at negotiation meetings in an advisory capacity, Article 5(4)(3) EWCD. In its original version, the Directive only allowed for assistance to be given by experts, for example lawyers, tax advisors or accountants. The 2009 revision expanded the scope of eligible advisors so as to also include 'representatives of competent recognised Community-level trade union organisations', Article 5(4)(3), Recital 27 EWCD.[62] The experts and trade union representatives may be present at negotiation meetings *in an advisory capacity* at the request of the special negotiating body.

65.   Any expenses relating to the negotiations should be borne by central management 'so as to enable the special negotiating body to carry out its task in an appropriate manner', Article 5(6)(1) EWCD. However, this statement of purpose also contains a limitation by reference to the principle of proportionality ('appropriate'). This merely provides for a principle (means appropriate to the performance of the tasks) which the Member States may flesh out in national law. The Directive specifically ('in particular'!) provides for a limitation upon the funding 'to cover one expert only' (*einen Sachverständigen, un seul expert*).

---

[61]   Critically M. Weiss, *ZIAS* 1995, 633, 637.
[62]   While sentence 1 of the provision seems to presuppose that the trade union representatives are experts, the following sentence distinguishes between experts and trade union representatives.

Other types of cost may be similarly proportionately limited in light of the tasks and purposes of the special negotiating body.

6. The Agreement

a) Legal Nature

66. The nature of the agreement between central management and the special negotiating body has been controversial (particularly in German literature). A number of ways in which agreements might be characterised have been suggested: collective agreement, works agreement, a contract (for the benefit of third parties), a company agreement or a collective agreement *sui generis*.[63] This issue, however, is not determined by the Directive but rather left for the national law to resolve.[64] National law must however still ensure that the agreement has the effects required by the Directive and is enforceable. National law must thus enable the establishment of a EWC and specify the rights and obligations of the undertaking or group of undertakings on the one hand and the EWC on the other. In addition, national law must provide for effective enforcement mechanisms. This raises specific difficulties as the assignment of the special negotiating body is completed with the conclusion of the agreement and there is consequently no person to ensure enforcement.

67. Union law neither provides for conflicts rules for collective agreements (see §5 para. 11 above) nor for a uniform contract law regime. It may thus be controversial which national law applies for such issues as the conclusion of the agreement, breach or termination to the extent that they are not covered by the Directive (or rather: its implementation provisions). In the absence of specific provision, it seems natural that the law of the state where the (deemed) central management is located would apply. In addition, the parties should be free to make a choice of law.[65]

b) Content

68. The content is, first of all, for the parties to determine. Article 6(2) EWCD emphasises the principle of private autonomy (freedom of contract, involving the freedom to determine the content of the contract).[66] The Directive limits the

---

[63] See e.g. D. Joost, in R. Richardi et al. (eds.), *Münchener Handbuch zum Arbeitsrecht*, §274 para. 98; M. Weiss, *NZA* 2003, 177, 180.

[64] To the same effect (but critically) M. Weiss, *AuR* 1995, 438, 439, 443.

[65] T. Blanke, *Europäische Betriebsräte-Gesetz, Europäische Mitbestimmung*, §17 EBRG paras. 13 sq; G. Forst, *ZESAR* 2009, 469, 471 sq.

[66] Critically G. Forst, *ZESAR* 2009, 469, 471 (arguing that the special negotiating body was no bearer of fundamental rights and could thus not invoke freedom of contract).

contents to two basic forms of transnational employee involvement: the establishment of an EWC (Article 6(2) EWCD) and special information and consultation procedures (Article 6(3) EWCD). Furthermore, certain *subjects* should be covered. Any *lacunae* are, however, not to be filled by the provisions of the Annex. The EWC provisions in the Annex are, in other words, subsidiary, but they do not constitute default rules.

aa)   ESTABLISHMENT OF AN EWC

69. Notwithstanding the autonomy (freedom of contract) of the parties, Article 6(2) EWCD defines the subjects that an EWC agreement should address. These include:

(a)   the undertakings or the establishments which are covered by the agreement;
(b)   the composition of the EWC, the number of members, the allocation of seats and the term of office;
(c)   the functions and the procedure for information and consultation of the EWC;
(d)   the venue, frequency and duration of meetings of the EWC;
(e)   where necessary, the composition, the appointment procedure, the functions and the procedural rules of the select committee set up within the EWC (cf. Recital 30 EWCD);
(f)   the financial and material resources to be allocated to the EWC;
(g)   the date of entry into force of the agreement and its duration, the arrangements for amending or terminating the agreement and the cases in which the agreement shall be renegotiated and the procedure[67] for its renegotiation.[68]

The provisions of the Annex may be used by the parties as an additional model for their agreement.

70. The 2009 revision has expanded the contents of Article 6(2) EWCD. Thus, with regard to the composition of the EWC and the allocation of seats, 'the need for balanced representation of employees with regard to their activities, category and gender' must be taken into account. The competences of the EWC (lit. c) and issues of re-negotiation (lit. g) and Recital 28) have also been further concretised.

---

[67]   See also G. Forst, *ZESAR* 2009, 469, 471: the parties may also determine the body responsible for the renegotiations, they may, in particular, charge the EWC with that task.
[68]   See G. Forst, *ZESAR* 2009, 469, 472, 475 (with a model renegotiation clause).

bb) ESTABLISHMENT OF INFORMATION AND CONSULTATION PROCEDURES

71. The parties may alternatively agree to establish one or more information and consultation procedures. Instead of installing another body of employee representation, existing institutions can be used and endowed with additional rights and competences.

72. The Directive imposes requirements for the design of the information and consultation procedures; they aim to achieve the objectives of the Directive if the parties choose this alternative. Thus the parties may decide to establish 'one or more' information and consultation procedures. They must further take the definitions of 'information' and 'consultation' in Article 2(1)(f) and (g) into account (see paras. 29 sq. above). This is also premised in Article 6(3)(2) EWCD pursuant to which the agreement 'must stipulate by what method the employees' representatives shall have the right to meet to discuss the information conveyed to them'. The information 'shall relate in particular to the transnational matters which significantly affect the workers' interests', Article 6(3)(3) EWCD.

c) Procedure and Form

73. The agreement requires a majority decision by the members of the special negotiating body, Article 6(5) EWCD. It is to be concluded in writing, Article 6(2) and (3) EWCD.

7. Renegotiation, Adaptation

74. The original 1994 Directive left the issues of renegotiation and adaptation to the autonomous determination of the parties of the agreement. Such renegotiation may be advisable after some time to take account of the experience gained with the procedures. It may become necessary to take account of a change in the structure of the undertaking. The 2009 revision also left the issue primarily in the hands of the parties. Article 6(2)(g) EWCD now includes in the list of contents *inter alia* the duration of the agreement, 'the arrangements for amending or terminating the agreement and the cases in which the agreement shall be renegotiated and the procedure for its renegotiation, including, where necessary, where the structure of the Community-scale undertaking or Community-scale group of undertakings changes'. In addition, Article 13 EWCD places the obligation to initiate negotiations pursuant to Article 5 EWCD (see para. 19 above) on central management if the structure of the undertaking or group significantly changes and (a) the agreements in force do not contain provisions for this case or (b) there is a conflict between the relevant provisions of two or more applicable agreements. Central management must commence negotiations on its own initiative or at the written request of at least 100 employees or their representatives in at least two undertakings or establishments in at least two different Member States. In this case, 'at least' three members of the existing European Works Council or, if there is more than one, of each of the existing European Works Councils should be members of the special negotiating body, *in addition to* the members elected or appointed pursuant to Article 5(2) EWCD, Article 13(2) EWCD. The existing EWC or EWCs remain in office during the period of negotiation, Article 13(3) EWCD.

8. Principles of Cooperation

75. Finally, the Directive provides for a handful of basic provisions on the cooperation between central management and the employee side (special negotiating body, EWC, employees' representatives in the special information and consultation procedures).

a) The Principle of Loyal Cooperation

76. The Directive provides for guidelines for the cooperation of central management on the one side and the EWC or the employees' representatives on the other in the form of a general clause.[69] The parties shall work 'in a spirit of cooperation with due regard to their reciprocal rights and obligations', Article 9(1) EWCD. Distinct from similar national concepts,[70] this may be termed the *principle of loyal cooperation*. The general clause is to be taken into account in the interpretation of the specified individual duties and it may also serve as a basis for the judicial development of other specific duties.

b) Confidentiality

77. During the course of the negotiation procedure, the employer must transmit a considerable amount of information to the special negotiating body. The transmission of information is therefore the essence of employee involvement in the EWC and in the special information and consultation procedures. The proper and effective functioning of employee involvement often requires central management to disclose **sensitive information**. The Directive takes the countervailing interests into account providing for a graded regulation in Article 8 EWCD.

78. In most cases, the **confidentiality** obligation of employees' representatives (and any experts involved) gives sufficient protection to the employers' interests.

---

[69]   See F. Gamillscheg, *Kollektives Arbeitsrecht II,* 1193 (with comparative considerations).
[70]   M. *Weiss, AuR* 1995, 438, 439.

The members of the EWC and, in information and consultation proceedings, the employees' representatives, are not authorised to reveal any information 'which has expressly been provided to them in confidence', Article 8(1)(1) EWCD. This obligation continues to apply 'wherever the persons referred ... are, even after the expiry of their terms of office', Article 8(1)(3) EWCD. This confidentiality duty is thus formally delimited by the criterion of information which has 'expressly been provided in confidence'. This requirement, however, it not sufficient and, in light of the **principle of loyal cooperation**, not necessary either. It is not sufficient as the mere (formal) characterisation of information as confidential would be open to abuse and could stifle the work of the employees' representatives. The information must also be characterised as confidential on objective grounds.[71] The criterion is not necessary either, for it could constitute a violation of the principle of loyal cooperation (Article 9 EWCD) if the employees' representatives revealed information that they recognised or should have recognised as confidential on the pretext that it had not expressly been labelled as such.

79. Only in exceptional cases may central management **withhold information**. This requires the nature of the information to be such that, according to objective criteria, its transmission would seriously harm the functioning of the undertaking or would be prejudicial to it, Article 8(2) EWCD. In light of the purpose of the Directive and the system of the provision which considers the duty to confidentiality contained in paragraph 1 to normally satisfy the employers' interests, the prerequisites of paragraphs 2 should be narrowly construed. The details must be fleshed out by the Member States which may also provide that withholding information requires prior administrative or judicial authorisation.

c)   The 'Role' of the Employees' Representatives

80. The 2009 revision introduced a number of new provisions on the 'role' of the employees' representatives. They address three issues.

81. The necessary **means**, Article 10(1) EWCD: Members of the EWC must be provided with the means necessary to apply the rights arising from the Directive and collectively represent the interests of the employees of the Community-scale undertaking or group of undertakings.

---

[71]   H. Oetker/C. Schubert, in *EAS,* B 8300 para. 256; M. Weiss, *ZIAS* 1995, 633, 638. Differently W. Hromadka, *DB* 1995, 1125, 1129 sq. (requiring only a 'certain relevance' of the confidentiality for the undertaking).

82.   Training for members of the special negotiating body and the EWC, Article 10(4) EWCD: To the extent necessary to perform their task in an international environment, the members of the special negotiating body and the EWC have a right to training without loss of wages.

83.   Sharing of information with the representatives of the establishments and group undertakings, Article 10(2) EWCD[72]: Members of the EWC inform these employees' representatives or, in the absence of such representatives, the employees about the content and results of the information and consultation conducted under the EWCD. This is in line with their function as information intermediaries;[73] Recital 33 even speaks of an obligation to 'report' (*render compte, Rechenschaft ablegen*).[74] This obligation does not, however, relieve the members of the EWC from their confidentiality obligations under Article 8 EWCD.

d)   Protection of Employees' Representatives

**84.   Pursuant to Article 10(3) EWCD, the members of the special negotiating body, the members of the EWC and the employees' representatives exercising their function in the special transnational information and consultation procedures enjoy the same protection and guarantees as the employees' representatives in the Member State where they are employed. This is merely an expression of the principle of equivalence (see §1 para. 66 above; for German law, cf. §§38, 78 BetrVG, §15 KSchG, §103 BetrVG). In substance, protection against unfavourable treatment is a teleologically necessary complement to the employees' rights. Pursuant to subparagraph 2, the prohibition of unfavourable treatment in particular applies with regard to the attendance of meetings of the special negotiating body, the EWC or other meetings within the framework of the agreement and to payment of wages for periods of absence of the employees' representatives necessary for the performance of their duties.

e)   Undertakings with Ideological Guidance as Business Purpose

**85.   The Directive only rudimentarily provides for an option for regulation of undertakings whose business purpose is 'ideological guidance'.[75] A Member

---

[72]   The provision had originally been located in Annex No. 5 EWCD 1994 and was thus (only) part of the fall-back solution. With the 2009 revision, it was 'promoted' to a general provision of the general operative part of the Directive.

[73]   W. Goos, *Festschrift 50 Jahre Bundesarbeitsgericht*, 1186 ('central function as a cross-border information intermediary and communicator between the central management and the employees' representatives' – my translation); C. Weber, *Festschrift für Konzen*, 927.

[74]   On possible conflicts in the temporal sequence with national rights of employee involvement T. Blanke/E. Rose, *RdA* 2008, 65–81.

[75]   For a critical perspective see e.g. C. Weber, *Festschrift für Konzen*, 948–950.

State may lay down particular provisions for the central management of undertakings in its territory 'which pursue directly and essentially the aim of **ideological guidance**'.[76] This regulatory option is, however, only available to Member States in which such particular provisions already existed at the time the (original)[77] directive was adopted (22 September 1994). Such particular provisions may apply with respect to **information and the expression of opinions**. The location of this regulatory option in Article 8(3) EWCD suggests that it is further limited to the preceding provisions of Article 8(1) and (2) EWCD on confidentiality (see para. 77 above).[78]

V. IMPLEMENTATION

86. In several countries, implementation of the original 1994 Directive was delayed.[79] In **Germany**, the original Directive was implemented by the Act on European Works Councils (*Gesetz über Europäische Betriebsräte,* EBRG) of 28 October 1996.[80] The 2009 Directive was implemented by the Act on European Works Councils (*Europäische Betriebsräte-Gesetz*) of 7 December 2011.[81] In the **United Kingdom**, the Directive was implemented by the Transnational Information and Consultation of Employees Regulations 1999 (TICER 1999).[82]

---

[76] On Article 8(3) EWCD see in detail M. Plum, *Tendenzschutz im europäischen Arbeitsrecht* (Berlin: Duncker & Humblot, 2011), 103–155.

[77] The wording is ambiguous and could also refer to the recast Directive of 2009. Yet, the purpose of the original provision rather suggests that its entry into force should be relevant, in particular since the 2009 Directive did not provide for substantive changes in this regard. To the same effect M. Plum, *Tendenzschutz im europäischen Arbeitsrecht* (Berlin: Duncker & Humblot, 2011), 146.

[78] For a different perspective see M. Plum, *Tendenzschutz im europäischen Arbeitsrecht*, 148.

[79] See e.g. ECJ Case C-430/98 *Commission* v. *Luxemburg* [1999] ECR I-7395; for further references see F. Gamillscheg, *Kollektives Arbeitsrecht II*, 1182; W. Kolvenbach, *NZA* 1998, 582; id., *NZA* 2000, 518–527; Report from the Commission to the European Parliament and the Council on the application of the Directive on the establishment of a European works council or a procedure in Community-scale undertakings and Community-scale groups of undertakings for the purposes of informing and consulting employees (Council Directive 94/45/EC of 22 September 1994), COM(2000) 188 final, 2–10.

[80] BGBl. 1996 I, 1548. On the implementation in **Germany** in detail D. Joost, in R. Richardi et al. (eds.), *Münchener Handbuch zum Arbeitsrecht*, §§274, 275; M. Fuchs, in id./F. Marhold (eds.), *Europäisches Arbeitsrecht*, 315 sq. (Germany and **Austria**); P. Hanau, in id./H. D. Steinmeyer/R. Wank (eds.), *Handbuch des Europäischen Arbeits- und Sozialrechts*, §19 para. 23; H. Oetker/C. Schubert, in *EAS*, B 8300 paras. 28–31. On the implementation in the **United Kingdom** M. Carley/M. Hall, *ILJ* 29 (2000), 103, 109–112 (general) und 112–122 (UK); M. Kilian, *RdA* 2001, 166–171; W. Kolvenbach, *NZA* 1998, 582–585.

[81] Europäische Betriebsräte-Gesetz of 7 December 2011, BGBl. 2011 I, 2650, also available at www.gesetze-im-internet.de/ebrg/index.html.

[82] SI 1999/3323; also available at www.legislation.gov.uk/uksi/1999/3323/contents/made. For a survey, see S. Deakin/G. Morris, *Labour Law*, paras. 9.60–9.64.

VI. THE EXAMPLE OF THE *KÜHNE & NAGEL* CASE[83]

87.   Kühne & Nagel, an undertaking with its seat in Germany, belongs to a Community-scale group of undertakings (the 'Kühne & Nagel Group'). The group's parent company and thus its central management, is located in Switzerland. Neither a European Works Council nor any procedure for informing and consulting employees has been established within the Kühne & Nagel Group. No information is available about the number of employees in the other undertakings of the Kühne & Nagel Group or about their distribution across the other Member States. However, according to the order for reference, Kühne & Nagel is the undertaking within the Kühne & Nagel Group with the greatest number of employees in any one Member State (cf. Article 4(2)(2) EWCD).

88.   In order to prepare for the establishment of a European Works Council the Kühne & Nagel Works Council asked management to provide it with the information about the average number of employees and their distribution across the Member States, the undertakings and the establishments and about the structure of the company and the group of companies, as well as the names and addresses of the Kühne & Nagel Group employees' representatives in the Member States.

89.   Kühne & Nagel did not dispute that it was under an obligation to provide the information but stated that it could not perform its obligation because central management, located in Switzerland, was not subject to Community law. The company therefore refused to supply the Works Council with the information. It stated that it did not itself have the information. It was therefore impossible to respond to the Works Council's request, which consequently had to be refused. Kühne & Nagel contended that there was no legal basis for the request that it provide information concerning the Group's employees' representative bodies in other Member States.

90.   The *Bundesarbeitsgericht* (Federal Labour Court, BAG) found that the EBRG does not expressly confer on Kühne & Nagel an information right which is enforceable against undertakings belonging to the Kühne & Nagel Group and established in Member States other than the Federal Republic of Germany. However, the management of an undertaking or group of undertakings which has its seat in Germany is legally bound to provide the information to the Works

---

[83]   ECJ Case C-440/00 *Kühne & Nagel* [2004] ECR I-787 with approving case note R. Giesen, *RdA* 2004, 307–310 (309 sq. on the practical implementation); D. Joost, *ZIP* 2004, 1034–1039; M. Kort, *JZ* 2004, 569–572.

Council. The EBRG thus appears to assume that the information necessary for that purpose will be obtained. In the view of the *Bundesarbeitsgericht*, the territorial scope of the EBRG is, however, such that it has no effect outside Germany and does not require foreign legal persons to provide information regarding undertakings established in Germany. The *Bundesarbeitsgericht* considers the defence thus relied on by Kühne & Nagel non-persuasive if the company has the ability to compel the undertakings of the group established in other Member States to supply the requisite information, on the basis of the national legislation enacted in those States to implement the Directive. In the referring court's view, that ability exists only if the Directive requires the creation of a horizontal entitlement to information in the case of groups of undertakings whose central management is not situated in a Member State.

91. At the heart of the case lies the issue of establishing an EWC (or specific information and consultation procedures) in a group of undertakings, the central management of which is located in a third country. Article 4(2) EWCD provides for the regulation for such cases: The function of central management is assumed in such case by the representative agent designated by central management, or in absence thereof, by the management of the group undertaking employing the greatest number of employees in any one Member State (the 'deemed central management'). In the case at hand, Kühne & Nagel was the deemed central management. The employees' (representatives') initiative to commence negotiation proceedings for the establishment of an EWC or information and consultation proceedings will normally start with a request for information, aimed at establishing whether the prerequisites of the Directive (in particular Article 2(1)(a) and c) EWCD) are fulfilled. The original directive provided for a right to request information in Article 11(2) EWCD 1994, and this right is now contained in Article 4(4) EWCD. But what if the deemed central management finds itself unable to (fully) provide the necessary information: Is it then under an obligation (and able) to request the necessary information from the other group undertakings located in the Member States?

92. The Court answers this question in the affirmative, based upon the principle of responsibility of the (here: deemed) central management under Article 4(1) EWCD. The deemed central management is under an obligation to require from the other group undertakings located in Union territory the information necessary for the initiation of proceedings for the establishment of an EWC or information and consultation procedures. Conversely, the other group undertakings located in the Member States are under an obligation to provide the information to the deemed central management. The Court bases this judicial development of obligations on the principle of *effet utile* in its negative form: To deny such horizontal right to information would effectively thwart the establishment of an EWC or information and consultation procedures where the central management is located in a third country – contrary to the legislator's intent as expressed in Article 4(2) EWCD. Methodologically, the Court bases the horizontal right to information to the principle of responsibility which Article 4(1) EWCD contains in the form of a general clause of the (also: deemed) central management. The 2009 revision has recognised such horizontal right to information in so far as it has established the central management's duty to obtain the necessary information in Article 4(4) sent. 1 EWCD (see para. 48 above).

§29. EMPLOYEE INVOLVEMENT IN THE EUROPEAN COMPANY AND IN THE EUROPEAN COOPERATIVE SOCIETY

CONTENTS

Bibliography[1]:

C. Barnard/S. Deakin, 'Reinventing the European Corporation? Corporate Governance, Social Policy and the Single Market', *IRJ* 33 (2002), 484–499; T. Blanke, *Europäisches Betriebsräte-Gesetz – Europäische Mitbestimmung SE*, 2nd edn. (Baden-Baden: Nomos, 2006); T. Blanke, 'Europäische Aktiengesellschaft ohne Arbeitnehmerbeteiligung?', *ZIP* 2006, 789–792; R. Blanpain, 'Representation of Employees at the Level of the Enterprise and the EEC', *RdA* 1992, 127–131; F. Blanquet, 'Das Statut der Europäischen Aktiengesellschaft (Societas Europaea "SE") – Ein Gemeinschaftsinstrument für die grenzüberschreitende Zusammenarbeit im Dienste der Unternehmen', *ZGR* 2000, 33–65; R. Birk, 'Europäische Aktiengesellschaft und nationales Betriebsverfassungsrecht – Bemerkungen zur Institution des Europäischen Betriebsrats (EBR) nach dem Vorschlag eines Statuts für Europäische Aktiengesellschaften', *ZfA* 1974, 47–81; S. Braun, *Die Sicherung der Unternehmensmitbestimmung im Lichte des europäischen Rechts* (Baden-Baden: Nomos, 2005); T. Brocker, *Unternehmensmitbestimmung und Corporate Governance* (Munich: ZAAR, 2006); I. Calle Lambach, 'Das Gesetz zur Beteiligung der Arbeitnehmer in der Europäischen Gesellschaft (SE-Beteiligungsgesetz – SEBG)', *RIW* 2005, 161–168; I. Calle Lambach, *Die Beteiligung der Arbeitnehmer in der Europäischen Gesellschaft (SE)* (Berlin: Logos, 2004); M. Casper, 'Numerus Clausus und Mehrstaatlichkeit bei der SE-Gründung', *AG* 2007, 97–105; M. Casper/C. Schäfer, 'Die Vorrats-SE – Zulässigkeit und wirtschaftliche Neugründung', *ZIP* 2007, 653–662; W. Däubler, 'The Employee Participation Directive – A Realistic Utopia?', *CMLR* 14 (1977),

---

[1] See also the vast amount of literature on company law, e.g. S. Grundmann, *European Company Law*, bibliography to §33; M. Habersack/D. A. Verse, *Europäisches Gesellschaftsrecht*, §13 before para. 1, both with further references.

457–487; P. L. Davies, 'Workers on the Board of the European Company?', *ILJ* 32 (2003), 75–96; M. Dreher, 'Sockellösung statt Optionsmodell für die Mitbestimmung in der Europäischen Aktiengesellschaft?', *EuZW* 1990, 476–478; H. Eidenmüller/L. Hornuf/M. Reps, 'Contracting Employee Involvement: An Analysis of Bargaining over Employee Involvement Rules for a Societas Europaea', available at SSRN: http://ssrn.com/abstract=1979487 or doi:10.2139/ssrn.1979487; H. Fleischer, 'Gesetz und Vertrag als alternative Problemlösungsmodelle im Gesellschaftsrecht – Prolegomena zu einer Theorie der gesellschaftsrechtlichen Regelsetzung', *ZHR* 268 (2004), 673–707; H. Fleischer, 'Der Einfluss der Societas Europaea auf die Dogmatik des deutschen Gesellschaftsrechts', *AcP* 204 (2004), 502–543; J. Figge, *Mitbestimmung auf Unternehmensebene in Vorschlägen der Europäischen Gemeinschaften* (Baden-Baden: Nomos, 1992); G. Forst, 'Beteiligung der Arbeitnehmer in der Vorrats-SE – Zugleich Besprechung des Beschlusses des OLG Düsseldorf v. 30. 3. 2009 – I-3 Wx 248/08', *RdA* 2010, 55–59; G. Forst, 'Die Beteiligung der Arbeitnehmer in der Vorrats-SE', *NZG* 2009, 687–692; G. Forst, *Die Beteiligungsvereinbarung nach §21 SEBG* (Cologne et al.: Carl Heymanns, 2010); G. Forst, 'Folgen der Beendigung einer SE-Beteiligungsvereinbarung', *EuZW* 2011, 333–336; M. Grobys, 'Das geplante Umsetzungsgesetz zur Beteiligung von Arbeitnehmern in der Europäischen Aktiengesellschaft', *NZA* 2004, 779–781; M. Grobys, 'SE-Betriebsrat und Mitbestimmung in der Europäischen Gesellschaft', *NZA* 2005, 84–91; J. Gruber/M.-P. Weller, 'Societas Europaea – Mitbestimmung ohne Aufsichtsrat? – Ideen für die Leitungsverfassung der monistischen Aktiengesellschaft in Deutschland', *NZG* 2003, 297–301; S. Grundmann, *European Company Law – Organization, Finance and Capital Markets,* 2nd edn. (Antwerpen: Intersentia, 2011); S. Grundmann, *Europäisches Gesellschaftsrecht,* 2nd edn. (Heidelberg: C.F. Müller, 2011); M. Habersack/D. A. Verse, *Europäisches Gesellschaftsrecht,* 4th edn. (Munich: C.H. Beck, 2011); M. Habersack, 'Grundsatzfragen der Mitbestimmung in SE und SCE sowie bei grenzüberschreitender Verschmelzung', *ZHR* 171 (2007), 613–643; M. Habersack, 'Schranken der Mitbestimmungsautonomie in der SE – Dargestellt am Beispiel der Größe und inneren Ordnung des Aufsichtsorgans', *AG* 2006, 345–355; H. Heckschen, 'Die SE als Option für den Mittelstand', in L. Aderhold/B. Grunewald/D. Klingberg/W. G. Paefgen (eds.), *Festschrift für Harm Peter Westermann* (Cologne: Otto Schmidt, 2008), 999–1018; M. Heinze, 'Die Europäische Aktiengesellschaft', *ZGR* 2002, 66–95; M. Heinze, 'Ein neuer Lösungsweg für die Europäische Aktiengesellschaft', *AG* 1997, 289–297; W. Heinze/A. Seifert/C. Teichmann, 'Verhandlungssache – Arbeitnehmerbeteiligung in der SE', *BB* 2005, 2524–2530; P. Hemeling, *Die Societas Europaea (SE) in der praktischen Anwendung* (Bonn: Zentrum für Europäisches Wirtschaftsrecht, 2007); M. Henssler, 'Bewegung in der deutschen Unternehmensmitbestimmung – Reformdruck durch Internationalisierung der Wirtschaft', *RdA* 2005, 330–337; M. Henssler, 'Erfahrungen und Reformbedarf bei der SE – Mitbestimmungsrechtliche Reformvorschläge', *ZHR* 173 (2009), 222–249; M. Henssler, 'Mitbestimmungsrechtliche Konsequenzen einer Sitzverlegung innerhalb der Europäischen Union – Inspirationen durch "Inspire Art"', in A. Söllner/W. Gitter/R. Waltermann/R. Giesen/O. Ricken (eds.), *Gedächtnisschrift für Meinhard Heinze* (Munich: C.H. Beck, 2005), 333–355; M. Henssler, 'Unternehmerische Mitbestimmung in der Societas Europaea – Neue Denkanstöße für die "Corporate Governance"-Diskussion', in M. Habersack/P. Hommelhoff/U. Hüffer/K. Schmidt (eds.), *Festschrift für Peter Ulmer*

(Berlin: de Gruyter, 2003), 193–210; E. Herfs-Röttgen, 'Arbeitnehmerbeteiligung in der Europäischen Aktiengesellschaft', NZA 2001, 424–429; E. Herfs-Röttgen, 'Probleme der Arbeitnehmerbeteiligung in der Europäischen Aktiengesellschaft', NZA 2002, 358–365; P. Hommelhoff, 'Einige Bemerkungen zur Organisationsverfassung der Europäischen Aktiengesellschaft', AG 2001, 279–288; P. Hommelhoff, 'Mitbestimmungsvereinbarungen zur Modernisierung der deutschen Unternehmensmitbestimmung', ZGR 2010, 48–74; P. Hommelhoff, 'Vereinbarte Mitbestimmung', ZHR 148 (1984), 118–148; K. J. Hopt, 'Arbeitnehmervertreter im Aufsichtsrat – Auswirkungen der Mitbestimmung auf corporate governance und wirtschaftliche Integration in Europa', in O. Due/M. Lutter/J. Schwarze (eds.), Festschrift für Ulrich Everling (Baden-Baden: Nomos, 1995), 475–509; K. J. Hopt, 'Labor Representation on Corporate Boards: Impacts and Problems for Corporate Governance and Economic Integration in Europe', Int'l Rev. L. & Econ. 14 (1994), 203–214; K. J. Hopt, 'Grundprobleme der Mitbestimmung in Europa – Eine rechtsvergleichende Bestandsaufnahme und Einschätzung der Vorschläge zur Rechtsangleichung der Arbeitnehmermitbestimmung in den Europäischen Gemeinschaften', ZfA 1982, 207–235; D. Joost, 'Mitbestimmung in der Europäischen Aktiengesellschaft', in H. Oetker/U. Preis (eds.), Europäisches Arbeits- und Sozialrecht, EAS, part B – Systematische Darstellungen, loose-leaf (Heidelberg: Forkel, last update: February 2006), B 8200; A. Junker, 'Sechsundsiebzig verweht – Die deutsche Mitbestimmung endet in Europa', NJW 2004, 728–730; A. Junker, 'Unternehmensmitbestimmung in Deutschland – Anpassungsbedarf durch internationale und europäische Entwicklungen', ZfA 2005, 1–44; A. Junker, 'Europäische Aktiengesellschaft und deutsche Mitbestimmung', ZfA 2005, 211–224; B. Keller, 'Die Europäische Aktiengesellschaft und Arbeitnehmerbeteiligung', WSI-Mitteilungen 2002, 203–212; J. Kenner, 'Worker Involvement in the Societas Europaea: Integrating Company and Labour Law in the European Union?', YEL 24 (2005), 223–259; R. Kiem, 'Vereinbarte Mitbestimmung und Verhandlungsmandat der Unternehmensleitung – Ein Beitrag zur mitbestimmungsrechtlichen Verhandlungslösung und guter Corporate Governance', ZHR 171 (2007), 713–730; C. Kirchner, 'Grundstrukturen eines neuen institutionellen Designs für die Arbeitnehmermitbestimmung auf der Unternehmensebene', AG 2004, 197–200; O. Kisker, 'Unternehmerische Mitbestimmung in der Europäischen Gesellschaft, der Europäischen Genossenschaft und bei grenzüberschreitender Verschmelzung im Vergleich', RdA 2006, 206–212; G. Kleinsorge, 'Europäische Gesellschaft und Beteiligungsrechte der Arbeitnehmer', RdA 2002, 343–352; W. Kolvenbach, 'Scheitert die Europa AG an der Mitbestimmung?', NZA 1998, 1323–1328; R. Köstler, 'Mitbestimmung', in M. R. Theisen/M. Wenz (eds.), Die Europäische Aktiengesellschaft – Recht, Steuern und Betriebswirtschaft der Societas Europaea (SE), 2nd edn. (Stuttgart: Schaeffer-Poeschel, 2005), 331–376; R. Köstler, 'Die Mitbestimmung in der SE', ZGR 2003, 800–809; R. Krause, 'Die Mitbestimmung der Arbeitnehmer in der Europäischen Gesellschaft (SE)', BB 2005, 1221–1229; M. Kraushaar, 'Europäische Aktiengesellschaft (SE) und Unternehmensmitbestimmung', BB 2003, 1614–1620; M. Kraushaar, 'Verhandelte Mitbestimmung und das Problem der Arbeitnehmerpluralität', AG 2008, 809–816; A. Krieger, 'Muss die Mitbestimmung der Arbeitnehmer das europäische Gesellschaftsrecht blockieren?', in M. Löwisch/C. Schmidt-Leithoff/B. Schmiedel (eds.), Beiträge zum Handels- und Wirtschaftsrecht – Festschrift für Fritz Rittner (Munich: C.H. Beck, 1991), 303–321; F. Kübler, 'Mitbestimmungsfeindlicher

Missbrauch der Societas Europaea?', in R. Damm/P. W. Heermann/R. Veil (eds.), *Festschrift für Thomas* Raiser (Berlin: de Gruyter, 2005), 247–258; F. Kübler, 'The Long Good-bye – Überlegungen zur Zukunft der Mitbestimmung der Arbeitnehmer im Europäischen Gesellschaftsrecht', in A. Höland et al. (eds.), *Arbeitnehmermitwirkung in einer sich globalisierenden Arbeitswelt – Liber Amicorum Manfred Weiss* (Berlin: BMV, 2005), 235–246; C. Leca, 'The Participation of Employees' Representatives in the Governance Structure of the Societas Europaea', *EBLR* 2007, 403–441; R. Lubitz, *Sicherung und Modernisierung der Unternehmensmitbestimmung* (Munich: ZAAR, 2005); M. Lutter (ed.), *Die Europäische Aktiengesellschaft,* 2nd edn. (Berlin: Heymanns, 1978); M. Lutter, *Europäisches Unternehmensrecht,* 4th edn. (Berlin/New York: de Gruyter, 1996) (in particular pp. 65–71 – overview; pp. 171–196 – on the 4th Directive; pp. 674 sq. on the SE-Directive; pp. 715–724 – on the SE Regulation); M. Lutter, 'Mitbestimmungsprobleme im internationalen Konzern', in H. Bernstein/U. Drobnig/H. Kötz (eds.), *Festschrift für Konrad Zweigert* (Tübingen: Mohr Siebeck, 1981), 251–274; H. Merkt, 'Die monistische Verfassung für die Europäische Aktiengesellschaft aus deutscher Sicht', *ZGR* 2003, 650–678; T. Müller-Bonanni/P. Melot de Beauregard, 'Mitbestimmung in der Societas Europaea', *GmbHR* 2005, 195–200; B. Nagel, 'Die Europäische Aktiengesellschaft (SE) und die Beteiligung der Arbeitnehmer', *AuR* 2004, 281–286; B. Nagel/A. Köklü, '"Societas Europaea" und Mitbestimmung', *ZESAR* 2004, 175–181; H.-W. Neye, 'Kein neuer Stolperstein für die Europäische Aktiengesellschaft', *ZGR* 2002, 377–382; J. Oechsler, 'Der praktische Weg zur Societas Europea (SE) – Gestaltungsspielraum und Typenzwang', *NZG* 2005, 697–702; H. Oetker, 'Beteiligung der Arbeitnehmer in der Europäischen Aktiengesellschaft (SE) im Überblick', *ZESAR* 2005, 3–12; H. Oetker, 'Die Beteiligung der Arbeitnehmer in der Europäischen Aktiengesellschaft (SE) unter besonderer Berücksichtigung der leitenden Angestellten', *BB* 2005 Beil. 11, 2–13; H. Oetker, 'Mitbestimmungssicherung bei der Errichtung einer Europäischen Gesellschaft (SE) durch formwechselnde Umwandlung einer Aktiengesellschaft mit Sitz in Deutschland', in H. Konzen et al. (eds.), *Festschrift für Rolf Birk* (Tübingen: Mohr Siebeck, 2008), 557–573; H. Oetker, 'Unternehmensmitbestimmung in der rechtspolitischen Diskussion – Ein Zwischenbericht', *RdA* 2005, 337–345; H. Oetker, 'Unternehmensmitbestimmung in der SE kraft Vereinbarung – Grenzen der Vereinbarungsautonomie im Hinblick auf die Größe des Aufsichtsrats', *ZIP* 2006, 1113–1121; K. Oplustil/C. Teichmann (eds.), *The European Company – all over Europe – A state-by-state account of the introduction of the European Company* (Berlin: de Gruyter, 2004); M. Pannier, 'The EU Cross Border Merger Directive – A New Dimension for Employee Participation and Company Restructuring', *EBLR* 2005, 1424–1442; J. Pipkorn, 'Arbeitnehmerbeteiligung in Unternehmen auf Europäischer Grundlage', *RdA* 1992, 120–127; S. Pluskat, 'Die Arbeitnehmerbeteiligung in der geplanten Europäischen AG', *DStR* 2001, 1483–1490; T. Raiser, 'Unternehmensmitbestimmung vor dem Hintergrund europarechtlicher Entwicklungen, Gutachten B für den 66. Deutschen Juristentag', in Ständige Deputation des Deutschen Juristentages (ed.), *Verhandlungen des Sechsundsechzigsten Deutschen Juristentages* (Munich: C.H. Beck, 2006); T. Raiser, 'Führungsstruktur und Mitbestimmung in der Europäischen Aktiengesellschaft nach dem Verordnungsvorschlag der Kommission vom 25. August 1989', in J. F. Baur/K. J. Hopt/ K.P. Mailänder (eds.), *Festschrift für Ernst Steindorff* (Munich: C.H. Beck, 1990), 201–214; R. Rebhahn, 'Unternehmensmitbestimmung in Deutschland – ein Sonderweg im

Rechtsvergleich', in V. Rieble (ed.), *Zukunft der Unternehmensmitbestimmung* (Munich: ZAAR, 2004), 42–85; M. Rehberg, 'Missbräuchliche Verkürzung der unternehmerischen Mitbestimmung durch die Societas Europaea – Zur Bedeutung, Reichweite und nationalen Umsetzung von Art. 11 sowie Erwägungsgrund 18 der SE-Richtlinie', *ZGR* 2005, 859–894; M. Rehberg, 'Chancen und Risiken der Verhandlung über die Arbeitnehmerbeteiligung', in V. Rieble/A. Junker (eds.), *Vereinbarte Mitbestimmung in der SE* (Munich: ZAAR, 2008), 45–64; T. Rehwinkel, 'Die gesetzliche Auffanglösung der Unternehmensmitbestimmung in der Europäischen Aktiengesellschaft', *ZESAR* 2008, 74–79; J. Reichert/S. Brandes, 'Mitbestimmung der Arbeitnehmer in der SE: Gestaltungsfreiheit und Bestandsschutz', *ZGR* 2003, 767–799; V. Rieble, 'Mitbestimmung zwischen Legitimationslast und Modernisierungsdruck', in V. Rieble (ed.), Zukunft der Unternehmensmitbestimmung (Munich: ZAAR, 2004), 9–32; V. Rieble, 'Schutz vor paritätischer Mitbestimmung', *BB* 2006, 2018–2023; V. Rieble, 'SE-Mitbestimmungsvereinbarung: Verfahren, Fehlerquellen und Rechtsschutz', in V. Rieble/A. Junker (eds.), *Vereinbarte Mitbestimmung in der SE* (Munich: ZAAR, 2008), 73–115; V. Rieble, 'Unternehmensmitbestimmung vor dem Hintergrund europarechtlicher Entwicklungen', *NJW* 2006, 2214–2217; V. Rieble (ed.), *Zukunft der Unternehmensmitbestimmung* (Munich: ZAAR, 2004); V. Rieble/A. Junker (eds.), *Vereinbarte Mitbestimmung in der SE* (Munich: ZAAR, 2008); W.-G. Ringe, 'Mitbestimmungsrechtliche Folgen einer SE-Sitzverlegung', *NZG* 2006, 931–935; M. Roth, 'Die unternehmerische Mitbestimmung in der monistischen SE', *ZfA* 2004, 431–461; P. Sanders, 'Auf dem Wege zu einer europäischen Aktiengesellschaft?', *AWD* 1960, 1–5; P. Sanders, 'Die Europäische Aktiengesellschaft – Probleme des Zugangs und der Mitbestimmung', *AG* 1967, 344–348; P. Sanders, 'Vorentwurf eines Statuts für Europäische Aktiengesellschaften', in Commission of the European Communities (ed.), *Kollektion Studien, Reihe Wettbewerb Nr. 6* (Brussels: Commission of the European Communities, 1967); C. Schäfer, 'SE und Gestaltung der Mitbestimmung aus gesellschaftsrechtlicher Sicht', in V. Rieble/A. Junker (eds.), *Vereinbarte Mitbestimmung in der SE* (Munich: ZAAR, 2008) 13–36; A. Scheibe, *Die Mitbestimmung der Arbeitnehmer in der SE unter besonderer Berücksichtigung des monistischen Systems* (Frankfurt a.M.: Peter Lang, 2007); C. Schubert, 'Die Arbeitnehmerbeteiligung bei der Europäischen Gesellschaft ohne Arbeitnehmer', *ZESAR* 2006, 340–348; C. H. Seibt, 'Arbeitnehmerlose Societas Europaea – Zugleich Besprechung von AG Hamburg v. 28-6-2005 – 66 AR 76/05 sowie LG Hamburg v 30-9-2005 – 417 T 15/05', *ZIP* 2005, 2248–2250; S. Simitis, 'Workers' Participation in the Enterprise – Transcending Company Law?', *MLR* 38 (1975), 1–22; C. Teichmann, *Binnenmarktkonformes Gesellschaftsrecht* (Berlin: de Gruyter, 2006); C. Teichmann, 'Gestaltungsfreiheit in Mitbestimmungsvereinbarungen', *AG* 2008, 797–800; C. Teichmann, 'Mitbestimmung und grenzüberschreitende Verschmelzung', *Konzern* 2007, 89–98; G. Thüsing, 'Europäische Perspektiven der deutschen Unternehmensmitbestimmung', in V. Rieble (ed.), *Zukunft der Unternehmensmitbestimmung* (Munich: ZAAR, 2004) 95–113; W. Veelken, 'Zur Mitbestimmung bei der Europäischen Aktiengesellschaft', in R. Kraus/W. Veelken/K. Vieweg (eds.), *Recht der Wirtschaft und der Arbeit in Europa – Gedächtnisschrift für Wolfgang Blomeyer* (Berlin: Duncker & Humblot, 2004), 491–523; C. Villiers, 'The Directive on Employee Involvement in the European Company: Its Role in European Corporate Governance and Industrial Relations', *IJCLLIR* 22 (2006), 183–211; J. Wagner,

'Praktische Erfahrungen mit der Europäischen Aktiengesellschaft', *EWS* 2005, 546–554;
K. M. Wagner, *Die wirtschaftliche Arbeitnehmermitbestimmung in einer Europäischen
Aktiengesellschaft* (Frankfurt a.m.: Alfred Metzner Verlag, 1977); H. P. Westermann,
'Tendenzen der gegenwärtigen Mitbestimmungsdiskussion in der Europäischen
Gemeinschaft', *RabelsZ* 48 (1984), 123–184; S. Weiss/H.-T. Wöhlert, 'Der Siegeszug des
deutschen Mitbestimmungsrechts in Europa?', *NZG* 2006, 121–126; C. Windbichler,
'Arbeitnehmerinteressen im Unternehmen und gegenüber Unternehmen – Eine
Zwischenbilanz', *AG* 2004, 190–196; C. Windbichler, 'Betriebliche Mitbestimmung als
institutionalisierte Vertragshilfe', in M. Lieb/U. Noack/H.P. Westermann (eds.),
Festschrift für Wolfgang Zöllner (Cologne/Berlin/Bonn/Munich: Carl Heymanns, 2007),
999–1009; C. Windbichler, 'Cheers and Boos for Employee-Involvement:
Co-Determination as Corporate Governance Conundrum', *EBOR* 6 (2006), 507–537; C.
Windbichler, 'Der gordische Mitbestimmungsknoten und das Vereinbarungsschwert –
Regulierung durch Selbstregulierung?', in U. Jürgens et al. (eds.), *Perspektiven der
Corporate Governance – Bestimmungsfaktoren unternehmerischer Entscheidungsprozesse
und Mitwirkung der Arbeitnehmer* (Baden-Baden: Nomos. 2007), 282–304; C.
Windbichler, 'Methodenfragen in einer gestuften Rechtsordnung – Mitbestimmung und
körperschaftliche Organisationsautonomie in der Europäischen Gesellschaft', in A.
Heldrich et al. (eds.), *Festschrift für Claus-Wilhelm Canaris* (Munich: C.H. Beck, 2007),
1423–1434; G. Wisskirchen/T. Prinz, 'Das Gesetz über die Beteiligung der Arbeitnehmer
in der Europäischen Gesellschaft (SE)', *BB* 2004, 2638–2643; H. Wißmann, '"Deutsche"
Europäische Aktiengesellschaft und Mitbestimmung', in R. Wank et al., *Festschrift für
Herbert Wiedemann zum 70. Geburtstag* (Munich: C.H. Beck, 2002), 685–700; H.
Wißmann, 'Die Mitbestimmung der Arbeitnehmer in der Europäischen Aktiengesell-
schaft (SE)', *RdA* 1992, 320–330; R. Wollburg/N. R. Banerjea, 'Die Reichweite der
Mitbestimmung in der Europäischen Gesellschaft – Die SE als attraktive neue
Rechtsform für grenzüberschreitende Zusammenschlüsse und für grenzüberschreitend
tätige Konzerne', *ZIP* 2005, 277–283; see also the bibliography in §26 above.

I. ISSUES, OVERVIEW, COMPETENCE, REGULATORY CONTEXT

1. Overview of the Legislative History

1. The idea underpinning the European Company (*Societas Europaea,* SE) to
create a supra-national company form dates back to the early days of the
European Community.[2] Similar to Community-scale undertakings which are

---

[2]   For a summary, see S. Grundmann, *European Company Law*, §33 paras. 1 sqq., 50–52;
further F. Blanquet, *ZGR* 2000, 33–65; M. Heinze, *ZGR* 2002, 66–77; E. Herfs-Röttgen, *NZA*
2001, 424 sq.; D. Joost, in *EAS*, B 8200 paras. 1–4; A. Junker, *ZfA* 2005, 1, 24–27; J. Kenner,
YEL 24 (2005), 223, 225–244; G. Kleinsorge, *RdA* 2002, 343, 343–345; C. Leca, *EBLR* 2007,
403, 406–411; H. Oetker, in M. Lutter/P. Hommelhoff (eds.), *SE-Kommentar,* Vor §1 SEBG
paras. 1–12; S. Pluskat, *DStR* 2001, 1483 sq.; W. Veelken, *Gedächtnisschrift für Blomeyer,* 493–
510.

covered by the EWC-Directive (see §28 above), issues of employee involvement
also arise here. Even beyond that, as a **supra-national legal form**, the SE requires
its own regime of employee involvement. In light of the disparate legal traditions
of the Member States,[3] in particular given the exceptionally high level of
employee involvement provided by German law,[4] employee involvement proved
to be a critical issue and, for a long time, an obstacle in the legislative proceedings.
In fact, the unusually long legislative proceedings have been described as a 'thirty
years' war',[5] and much of the debate centred on issues of employee involvement.
Ultimately, agreement was reached by switching from a uniform substantive
regime of employee involvement to a procedural regime, in principle leaving it to
the employer and the employees to agree upon a regime of employee involvement.[6]

2. Three different phases can be discerned in the **legislative proceedings**, each
moving towards greater autonomy and flexibility. Based on a proposal by *Pieter
Sanders*,[7] the SE was originally designed as a company form completely
regulated on the European level. The first draft of 1970[8] with its 284 Articles
provided for a full-fledged law of public limited companies.[9] In substance, it
largely adopted the German model. The company structure followed the two-tier
system, distinguishing between a management organ and a supervisory board,
with a one-third employee-participation in the supervisory board as well as a
kind of European Works Council.

3. A second proposal, adopted in 1975, was similarly ambitious.[10] The legislator
then gradually backed away from the core elements of the initial
proposal: Uniform regulation was gradually opened up for alternative
configurations, taking into account the different national traditions of the
Member States and the different forms of employee involvement. A simplified

---

3   For a comparative survey, see T. Baums/P. Ulmer (eds.), *Unternehmens-Mitbestimmung der
     Arbeitnehmer im Recht der EU-Mitgliedstaaten* (Heidelberg: Recht und Wirtschaft, 2004);
     R. Rebhahn, in V. Rieble (ed.), *Zukunft der Unternehmensmitbestimmung*, 42–85; also
     M. Pannier, *EBRL* 2005, 1424, 1425–1434; see also §26 paras. 3 sq.
4   R. Rebhahn, in V. Rieble (ed.), *Zukunft der Unternehmensmitbestimmung*, 42–85; A. Junker,
     NJW 2004, 728, 730.
5   Schwarz, *ZIP* 2001, 1847 sq.
6   It may thus be useful first to read §28.
7   P. Sanders, in Commission of the European Communities (ed.), *Kollektion Studien, Reihe
     Wettbewerb Nr. 6* (1967); id., *AG* 1967, 344–348; id., *AWD* 1960, 1–5.
8   Commission, Proposal for a Council Regulation Embodying a Statute fort he European
     Company of 30 June 1970, COM(70) 600, OJ 1970 C 124/1; Opinion of the European
     Parliament, OJ 1974 C 93/22 and of the Economic and Social Committee, OJ 1972 C 131/32.
     On the EWC in this proposal, see R. Birk, *ZfA* 1974, 47–81.
9   See in more detail S. Grundmann, *European Company Law*, §33 para. 2.
10   Amended Proposal for a Council Regulation on the Statute for European Companies of
     30 April 1975, COM(75) 150 final, reproduced in Bulletin of the European Communities
     Supplement 4/75 (1975).

1989 proposal,[11] amended in 1991,[12] separated the two issues of the company organisation on the one hand and employee involvement on the other, providing the former in a regulation regarding the statute of the European Company and the latter in a directive regarding employee involvement. The statute now allowed for a choice of either the two-tier system (of management and supervisory board) or the single-tier system. With regard to employee involvement, the proposal for a directive contained a choice of no less than four systems which the legislator considered to be equivalent.[13]

4. Ultimately, the *Davignon* report paved the way for the enactment of both the Regulation and the Directive. It employed the model of the 1994 EWC-Directive with its change from a substantive to a procedural approach ('paradigm change')[14].[15] As with the EWC, employee involvement is left for employer and employees' representatives to decide by way of agreement (**negotiation or agreement model**).[16] This allows undertakings and employees to develop a

---

[11] Proposal for a Council Regulation on the Statute for a European Company of 25 August 1989, COM(89) 268 final, OJ 1989 C 263/41; Opinion of the European Parliament, OJ 1991 C 48/99; Opinion of the Economic and Social Committee, OJ 1990 C 124/34; Proposal for a Council Directive Complementing the Statute for a European Company with Regard to the Involvement of Employees in the European Company, COM(1989) 268 final, OJ 1989 C 263/69. See the (critical) discussion by M. Dreher, *EuZW* 1990, 476–478; J. Figge, *Mitbestimmung auf Unternehmensebene in Vorschlägen der Europäischen Gemeinschaften*, 204–243; further A. Krieger, *Festschrift für Rittner*, 310–318; J. Pipkorn, *RdA* 1992, 120–127; T. Raiser, *Festschrift für Steindorff*, 201–214; H. Wißmann, *RdA* 1992, 320–330.

[12] Amended Proposal for a Council Directive Complementing the Statute for a European COmpany with Regard to the Involvement of Employees in the European Company of 6 May 1991, COM(1991) 174 final, OJ 1991 C 138/8; Amended Proposal for a Council Regulation on the Statute for a European Company of 16 May 1991, COM(1991) 174 final, OJ 1991 C 176/1 (also available at http://aei.pitt.edu/10895/1/10895.pdf); reproduced with annotations in M. Lutter, *Europäisches Unternehmensrecht*, 674 sq., 715–724.

[13] For a critical perspective see M. Dreher, *EuZW* 1990, 476, 477; J. Figge, *Mitbestimmung auf Unternehmensebene in Vorschlägen der Europäischen Gemeinschaften*, 230–234.

[14] H. Wißmann, *Festschrift für Wiedemann*, 693–697.

[15] Final Report of the Group of Experts 'European Systems of Workers Involvements' (Davignon-Report), reproduced in English in A. C. Neal, *European Labour Law and Social Policy – Cases and Materials, volume 1* (The Hague/London/New York: Kluwer Law, 2002), 336–352; in German in *BR-Drs.* 572/97. On the Davignon-report and the ensuing development see M. Heinze, *AG* 1997, 289–297; id., *ZGR* 2002, 66, 70–75; W. Kolvenbach, *NZA* 1998, 1323–1328.

[16] See K. J. Hopt, *ZfA* 1982, 207, 234 sq. (already considering a negotiation solution for international cases); M. Lutter, *Festschrift für Zweigert*, 267–270. On the (limited) possibilities of an 'agreed employee participation' under German law, see P. Hommelhoff, *ZHR* 148 (1984), 118–148. On basics of employee participation (and the necessity of its alignment with corporate governance) T. Brocker, *Unternehmensmitbestimmung und Corporate Governance*; C. Kirchner, *AG* 2005, 197–200 (at 198 on the legitimising effect of the agreement); C. Windbichler, *EBOR* 6 (2005), 507–537 (favouring a negotiation solution in principle but criticising the model of the SED as being overly concerned with safeguarding national employee participation and providing for overly complicated and costly procedures); ead., in U. Jürgens et al. (eds.), *Perspektiven der Corporate Governance*, 282–304.

---

customised employee involvement regime. At the same time, the agreement
model leads to a competition between different systems of employee involvement,
thus activating competition as a discovery procedure (*v. Hayek*).[17] Two
mechanisms in particular are designed to prevent a 'flight from employee
participation'[18] and a race to the bottom: the so-called 'before and after' principle
pursuant to which the level of employee involvement in the participating
companies will, in principle, be maintained; and procedural safeguards,
including quora for decisions of the employee-side, preventing rash decisions on
a decrease of the level of employee involvement.[19]

2. Competence

5. After agreement was reached at the 2000 Nice summit on the SE in
principle, including the issue of employee involvement (the 'Miracle of Nice),
the Regulation on the Statute for a European Company (SE-Regulation, SER)[20]
and the Directive Supplementing the SE-Statute with regard to the Involvement
of Employees (SE-Directive, SED)[21] were adopted on the basis of Article 308 EC
(today's Article 352 TFEU) in 2001.[22] The competence remained controversial.
The European Parliament argued that Article 95 EC (Article 114 TFEU) should
be used for the Regulation and Article 137 EC (Article 153 TFEU) for the
Directive: While Article 308 EC (the selected competence basis) merely
required the European Parliament to be heard, these provisions would have
given Parliament further participation rights.[23] After enactment of the
Regulation and Directive, the European Parliament considered an action for
annulment pursuant to Article 308 EC, but ultimately did not institute
proceedings.[24]

---

[17]   See already K. J. Hopt, *ZfA* 1982, 207, 232 sq.; id., *Festschrift für Everling*, 590 sq.; id., *Int'l Rev.
L. & Econ.* 14 (1994), 203, 212 sq.; more recently M. Rehberg, in V. Rieble/Junker (eds.),
Vereinbarte Mitbestimmung in der SE, 51–53; see also H. Fleischer, *ZHR* 168 (2004), 673, 680
sq., and §26 para. 39 above.

[18]   In substance already P. Sanders, *AG* 1967, 344, 347 sq. Critically against the topos and the
risks associated with it M. Heinze, *ZGR* 2002, 66, 69 sq.; M. Henssler, *Festschrift für Ulmer,*
199 sq. (with a view to freedom of establishment); A. Krieger, *Festschrift für Rittner,* 316–318;
C. Windbichler, *AG* 2004, 190, 192.

[19]   See also H. Wißmann, *Festschrift für Wiedemann,* 694.

[20]   Council Regulation (EC) No 2157/2001 of 8 October 2001 on the Statute for a European
company (SE), OJ 2001 L 294/1.

[21]   Council Directive 2001/86/EC of 8 October 2001 supplementing the Statute for a European
company with regard to the involvement of employees, OJ 2001 L 294/22.

[22]   See in more detail F. Blanquet, *ZGR* 2002, 20, 62 sq.

[23]   E. Herfs-Röttgen, *NZA* 2002, 358 sq.; G. Kleinsorge, *RdA* 2002, 343, 345 sq. On the EP's
proposals – that the Council rejected – see M. Heinze, *ZGR* 2002, 66, 92 sq.

[24]   H.-W. Neye, *ZGR* 2002, 377–382; see also P. Hommelhoff, *AG* 2001, 279 sq.

3. Overview of the Directive

6. After a provision on the Directive's purpose and on definitions (Articles 1
and 2 SED), the Directive provides for a negotiation procedure for the
determination of employee involvement (Articles 3–7 SED): The companies
participating in the establishment of an SE ('participating companies') on the one
hand and a 'special negotiating body' to be set up for the purposes of representing
the employees on the other have a chance to regulate issues of employee
involvement – information and consultation as well as participation –
autonomously. The subsidiary rules ('**standard rules**') of the Annex apply only
subordinately (Recital 8 SED). This model takes the disparate laws and traditions
of employee involvement in the Member States into account (Recital 5 SED). The
negotiation procedures and the standard subordinate rules of the Annex are
designed to preserve existing rights (Recital 7 SED); the 'before and after'
principle, which preserves an existing level of employee involvement in Member
States, aims to prevent a 'flight from employee participation'. In particular, the
formation of an SE by way of transformation should not give undertakings an
opportunity to shake off existing employee involvement standards. **Principles on
the cooperation** between employer/participating companies and employees and
their representatives supplement these provisions (Articles 8–10 SED). Within
the scope of the SE-Directive, the provisions of the EWC-Directive (see §28
above) do not apply; the SE-Directive contains equivalent provisions on
information and consultation for Community-scale undertakings (Article 13(1)
SED). National laws on information and consultation (such as the German Works
Constitution Act) remain applicable, but national laws on employee participation
do not (Article 13(2) SED; on the distinction, see §26 para. 1 above).

7. The SE is thus not as such a company form subject to employee participation.
The 'before and after' principle **merely safeguards** the pre-existing level of
employee participation. The SE may, in other words, not fall behind the employee
participation as it existed in a specific participating company; it 'freezes'
employee participation at that level. Conversely, the establishment of an SE
opens up the possibility of **avoiding a *higher level*** of employee participation in
the future. This is of particular interest for German companies which are subject
to a one-third co-determination requirement (under the One-Third Participation
Act, *Drittelbeteiligungsgesetz*, DrittelbG,[25] which applies to certain company
forms with more than 500 employees) but have a prospect to soon grow above
the employee threshold of 2,000 employees laid down in the Co-Determination

---

[25] Bilingual German-English version in S. Lingemann/R. v. Steinau-Steinrück/A. Mengel (eds.),
Employment and Labor Law in Germany, Part II, XIII.

Act (*Mitbestimmungsgesetz*, MitbestG)[26] which requires provision for equal
participation on the company board. If the company transforms or merges into
an SE before passing the 2,000- employees-threshold, the one-third participation
on the board will be preserved. As the SE is not subject to the national (e.g.
German) law of employee participation, it will not trigger the parity
co-determination of the Co-Determination Act if the SE subsequently surpasses
the threshold of 2,000 employees.[27] The Directive does not provide for a
mandatory **re-negotiation** duty but rather leaves the issue to the parties'
agreement (see para. 46 below). Furthermore, the Directive does not provide for
any 'safeguarding of employee participation' in the case of a subsequent
structural change in the SE; the general aim expressed in Recital 18 SED that
the 'before and after' principle should also apply to structural changes in an SE
does not find concrete expression in the operative part of the Directive.[28] As a
matter of Union law, this case is only covered by the prohibition of abuse (see
also paras. 59 sq. below).

4. Overview of the Formation Process

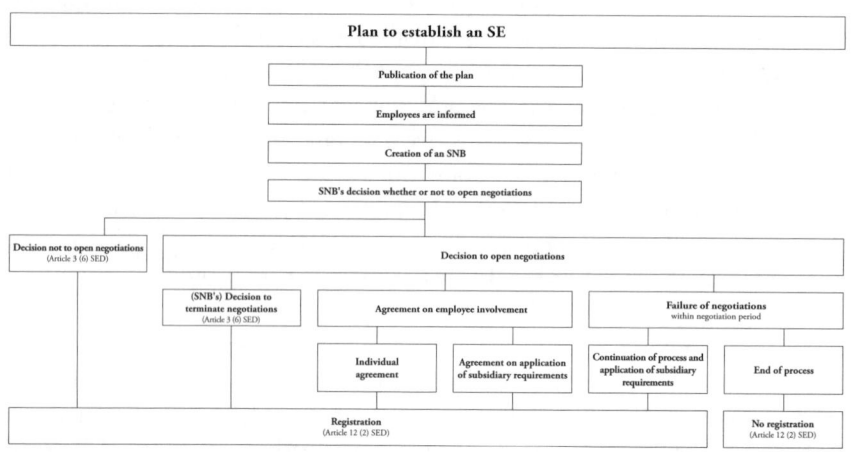

---

[26] Bilingual German-English version in S. Lingemann/R. v. Steinau-Steinrück/A. Mengel (eds.),
Employment and Labor Law in Germany, Part II, XII.

[27] See in detail V. Rieble, *BB* 2006, 2018–2023 ('protection against parity co-determination' –
my translation); further H. Heckschen, *Festschrift für H. P. Westermann*, 1013 sq.;
M. Henssler, *RdA* 2005, 330, 333 sq.; C. Schäfer, in V. Rieble/Junker (eds.), *Vereinbarte
Mitbestimmung in der SE*, 14–16.

[28] On the solution in German law see e.g. M. Rehberg, *ZGR* 2005, 859, 882–885; V. Rieble; *BB*
2006, 2018, 2022; id., in id./A. Junker (eds.), *Vereinbarte Mitbestimmung in der SE*, 87 sq.; R.
Wollburg/N. R. Banerjea, *ZIP* 2005, 277–283.

II. ESSENTIAL ASPECTS OF COMPANY LAW: FORMATION AND STRUCTURE OF THE SE

8. Employee involvement in the SE is linked to two variables, namely the different ways of forming an SE and its different company structures. These must be briefly sketched out,[29] before we can address issues of employee involvement.

1. Formation

9. Article 2 SER provides for an exhaustive list of four ways in which an SE may be formed, the details of which are found in Articles 15–37:[30]

- formation by means of **merger** pursuant to Articles 17–31 SER; here, the legislator could in many respects use the mechanisms first established by the Merger Directive;[31]
- formation by means of forming a **holding SE** pursuant to Articles 32–34 SER;
- formation by means of forming a **subsidiary SE** pursuant to Articles 35–36 SER; and
- formation by **transformation**[32] of an existing public limited liability company into an SE pursuant to Article 37 SER.

10. The Regulation does not provide for the formation of an SE by natural persons – the regular way of forming a company under national law. Furthermore, only specific national forms of companies are eligible to form an SE. All methods of SE formation also require there to be a cross-border element (**element of internationality**).[33]

11. Formation of an SE by way of **transformation** of an existing company was particularly controversial during the legislative proceedings. For a long time during the legislative negotiations, this mode of formation was not to be allowed, so as to prevent existing companies (with a high level of employee participation) from evading employee participation by transforming into an SE ('flight from employee participation'). This issue is now addressed by the 'before and after'

---

[29] See in detail S. Grundmann, *European Company Law*, §50 paras. 16–28; for a survey, see also D. Joost, in *EAS*, B 8200 paras. 24–41; A. Junker, *ZfA* 2005, 1, 27–30; id., *ZfA* 2005, 211, 218–221.

[30] See in more detail S. Grundmann, *European Company Law*, §50 paras. 16–28;. See also J. Oechsler, *NZG* 2005, 697–702 (discussing creative leeway that is opened up by combinations of the different modes of formation).

[31] Directive 2005/56/EC of the European Parliament and of the Council of 26 October 2005 on cross-border mergers of limited liability companies, OJ 2005 L 310/1.

[32] Articles 2(4), 37 SED define the term 'transformation' in a narrow sense.

[33] P. Hommelhoff, *AG* 2001, 279, 281. Critically e.g. M. Casper, *AG* 2007, 97 sqq. (pure formality with no protective effect for creditors or minorities); J. Oechsler, *NZG* 2005, 697, 698.

principle which preserves the pre-existing level of employee participation (in
particular) in case of transformation (see para. 48 below).[34]

2. Structure of the SE

12. In light of the different legal traditions of the Member States, the
SE-Regulation offers an option of different structures.[35] The SE comprises

(a) a **general meeting** of shareholders and
(b) – either a **supervisory organ** and a **management organ** (two-tier system)
     or
     – an **administrative organ** (single-tier system).

The founders of an SE must choose between the two-tier system and the single-
tier system in the company's statutes.

13. In the **two-tier system** (Articles 39–42 SER), the management organ is
responsible for managing the SE, Article 39(1) sent. 1 SER. Members of the
management organ are appointed by the supervisory organ, Article 39(2)(1) SER.
The supervisory organ, the members of which are appointed by the general
meeting of shareholders, supervises the work of the management organ. For this
purpose, the management organ reports regularly to the supervisory organ on
the progress and foreseeable development of the SE's business, Article 41(1) SER.
Furthermore, the supervisory organ has additional information and control
rights, Article 41(2)-(5) SER. Certain categories of transactions as listed in the
SE's statutes require authorisation by the supervisory organ, Article 48(1)(1) SER
(see also subparagraph 2).

14. The **single-tier system** (Articles 43–45 SER) does not have two separate
organs for management and supervision.[36] Instead, an administrative organ,
the members of which are appointed by the general meeting of shareholders,
manages the SE, Article 43(1) sent. 1, (3) SER. The number of members of the
administrative organ is specified in the SE's statutes; for an SE subject to
employee participation, the administrative organ must have at least three
members, Article 43(2) SER. The national law of Member States may provide

---

[34] On the transposition of these precautions in German law, see H. Oetker, *Festschrift für Birk*, 557–573.

[35] See in more detail S. Grundmann, *European Company Law*, §33 paras. 35–49.

[36] See in detail H. Merkt, *ZGR* 2003, 650–678; on the resulting issues of employee participation, see M. Henssler, *Festschrift für Ulmer*, 193–210; M. Roth, *ZfA* 2004, 431–461; J. Gruber/M.-P. Weller, *NZG* 2003, 297, 298 (with references to the transposition in Germany); A. Scheibe, *Die Mitbestimmung der Arbeitnehmer in der SE unter besonderer Berücksichtigung des monistischen Systems*.

that one or more managing directors shall be responsible for the day-to-day management of the SE, Article 43(1) sent. 2 SER. Supervision and control are achieved through regular meetings of the administrative organ, at least every three months, in which the progress and future development of the SE's business is discussed, Article 44(1) SER. Each member of the administrative organ is entitled to examine all information submitted to the organ, Article 44(2) SER.

III. THE SUBSIDIARY REQUIREMENTS OF THE ANNEX

15. Similar to the EWC-Directive, the SE-Directive does not primarily provide for substantive requirements for employee involvement but rather establishes a negotiation structure, thus enabling the parties (employer- and employee-side) to autonomously design a regime that satisfies their own preferences and needs. Here as well, the negotiation model is supplemented by a set of subsidiary rules. The parties may also agree on the application of the subsidiary rules. Their primary purpose, though, is to apply if the negotiations of the parties fail (Article 7 SED; see paras. 41 sq. below). Unlike the 2005 Directive on Cross-border Mergers (see §30 para. 16 below), the SE-Directive does not allow the participating companies to avoid negotiations and directly and unilaterally opt for the subsidiary requirements.[37] Negotiations between the parties thus take place 'in the shadow' of the supplementary rules (see already §28 paras. 8, 20 above with references) and will usually shape the expectations of the parties.[38] We therefore discuss them first.

16. The supplementary provisions are criticised as offering only few incentives for negotiation for the employee-side, given the 'before and after' principle.[39] Some authors consider the supplementary provisions to constitute a penalty default rule, i.e. a default rule that penalises one side if the parties do not agree on a different regime.[40] There is, of course, some pressure on the employee side

---

[37]   Often criticised as overly cumbersome and costly; see e.g. M. Henssler, *RdA* 2005, 330, 333.

[38]   See e.g. H. Fleischer, *AcP* 204 (2004), 502, 534 sq.; E. Herfs-Röttgen, *NZA* 2002, 358, 362; R. Krause, *BB* 2005, 1221, 1222; R. Köstler, in M. R. Theisen/R. Wenz (eds.), *Die Europäische Aktiengesellschaft*, 345 sq.

[39]   H. Fleischer, *AcP* 204 (2004), 502, 534 sq. ('cardinal construction fault' – my translation) and 541 sq.; id., *ZHR*, 268 (2004), 673, 694 sq.; A. Junker, *ZfA* 2005, 1, 34–36; id., *ZfA* 2005, 211, 222 sq.; F. Kübler, *Liber Amicorum Weiss*, S. 242; id., *Festschrift für Raiser*, 253; T. Raiser, *Unternehmensmitbestimmung vor dem Hintergrund europarechtlicher Entwicklungen*, B 27 sq.; V. Rieble, *NJW* 2006, 2214, 2216; G. Thüsing, in V. Rieble (ed.), *Zukunft der Unternehmensmitbestimmung*, 110; C. Windbichler, in U. Jürgens et al. (eds.), *Perspektiven der Corporate Governance*, 290; T. Brocker, *Unternehmensmitbestimmung und Corporate Governance*, 276 sq.

[40]   C. Barnard/S. Deakin, *IRJ* 33 (2002), 484, 486; C. Windbichler, in U. Jürgens et al. (eds.), *Perspektiven der Corporate Governance*, 294. For an introduction to penalty default rules, see

to reach agreement if they don't want to be blamed for the negotiations failing.[41] Additional incentives for negotiation may result from the employers' concessions in other areas than employee involvement ('increasing the pie') or from his threat to avail himself of other instruments for reaching his commercial goals.[42] As a matter of policy, a one-third employee participation, as suggested by the *Davignon*-report,[43] is considered to be preferable and to offer a more balanced negotiation situation. Theoretical and empirical analysis suggests that while there are certain impediments, negotiations actually do take place and lead to new and innovative solutions, often deviating from the standards of national participation laws.[44]

17. The supplementary provisions of the Annex are divided into three parts. The first two concern the representative body (cf. Article 2(f) SED) – sometimes called the 'SE works council', (1) its composition and (2) the information and consultation procedures. This part of the Annex largely follows the model of the EWC-Directive. Part 3 is concerned with employee participation at the level of the SE board: the supervisory board or the administrative board.

1. The Representative Body ('SE-Works Council')

a) Composition of the Representative Body

18. The representative body is composed of employees of the SE and its subsidiaries (as defined in Article 2(c) SED), Annex Part 1(a) SED. They are, in principle, elected or appointed **by the employees 'representatives from their ranks,** and in the absence of employees' representatives, are elected or appointed directly by the employees. The details of the election or appointment are for the Member States to determine; national law must also ensure that the number of members of, and the allocation of seats on, the representative body is to be adapted to changes occurring within the SE, its subsidiaries and establishments, Annex Part 1(b) SED. The Annex merely provides for a framework for the

---

R. Craswell, *'Contract Law: General Theories'*, in B. Bouckaert/G. De Geest (eds.), *Encyclopedia of Law and Economics* (Cheltenham: Edward Elgar, 2000), also available at http://encyclo.findlaw.com/4000book.pdf.

[41] W. Heinze/A. Seifert/C. Teichmann, *BB* 2005, 2524, 2525; C. Teichmann, *Konzern* 2007, 89, 94.

[42] M. Rehberg, in V. Rieble/A. Junker (eds.), *Vereinbarte Mitbestimmung in der SE*, 50 sq.

[43] Final Report of the Group of Experts 'European Systems of Workers Involvements' (Davignon-Report), reproduced in English in A. C. Neal, *European Labour Law and Social Policy – Cases and Materials, volume 1* (The Hague/London/New York: Kluwer Law, 2002), 336–352; in German in *BR-Drs.* 572/97, para. 83.

[44] H. Eidenmüller/L. Hornuf/M. Reps, 'Contracting Employee Involvement: An Analysis of Bargaining over Employee Involvement Rules for a Societas Europaea', available at SSRN: http://ssrn.com/abstract=1979487 or doi:10.2139/ssrn.1979487.

determination of the number of members of the representative body, namely by giving a representation ratio in Annex Part 1(e) SED. In respect of a Member State, one seat is to be allocated for every portion of employees employed in that Member State which equals 10%, or a fraction thereof, of the total number of employees employed by the participating companies (including subsidiaries and establishments) in all the Member States taken together. The rather technical wording means that one seat is allocated for every complete or commenced 10% tranche.[45] If an SE employs 55% of its employees in France and 45% in Germany, then six and five representatives respectively will be dispatched to the representative body.

19. The appropriate organ of the SE is to be informed about the composition of the representative body, Annex Part 1(f) SED. Where the size of the representation organ so justifies, it may elect a '**select committee**' from among its members, comprising not more than three members, Annex Part 1(c) SED. The representative body adopts its own rules of procedure, Annex Part 1(d) SED.

20. As in the EWC-Directive, here too, the subsidiary provisions are designed to provide a solution that is workable on a permanent basis. In pursuit of its general commitment to autonomous negotiation solutions, the Directive requires the representative organ to regularly examine whether to open negotiations for the conclusion of an agreement, Annex Part 1(g) SED.

b)   Information and Consultation

21. The first aspect of employee involvement provided for in the Annex is information and consultation. The provisions are comparable to those of the EWC-Directive: **Information** means 'the informing of the body of representatives of the employees', Article 2(i) SED. This definition emphasises that the modalities of giving information must be such as to serve the purpose of information, giving the representatives sufficient opportunity for examination and, where applicable, preparing the ensuing consultation. **Consultation** goes beyond hearing the opinion of the other side and requires a dialogue and the exchange of opinions, Article 2(j) SED. It thus presupposes the willingness to hear the opinion of the partner, to consider it and to comment upon it.

aa)   SUBJECTS COVERED

22. Information and consultation of the representative body cover issues that have a **transnational aspect**: 'questions which concern the SE itself and any of its

---

[45]   D. Joost, in *EAS*, B 8200 para. 140; H. Oetker, in M. Lutter/P. Hommelhoff (eds.). *SE-Kommentar,* §5 SEBG para. 8.

subsidiaries or establishments situated in another Member State or which exceed
the powers of the decision-making organs in a single Member State', Annex
Part 2(a) SED.

bb)   REGULAR (ANNUAL) INFORMATION AND CONSULTATION

23.   The representative body has the right to be informed and consulted on the
basis of regular reports drawn up by the competent organ on the progress of the
business of the SE and its prospects. For this purpose, it meets with the
competent organ **at least once a year**. Information and consultation in particular
relate to

(1)   the structure of the SE;
(2)   its economic and financial situation;
(3)   the probable development of the business, production and sales;
(4)   the situation and probable trend of employment;
(5)   the investments;
(6)   substantial changes concerning organisation;
(7)   the introduction of new working methods or production processes;
(8)   transfers of production;
(9)   mergers, cut-backs or closures of undertakings, establishments or
      important parts thereof; and
(10) collective redundancies.

These are the same subjects which are covered by the information and
consultation rights of the EWC; see §28 para. 34 above.

24.   In addition, the competent organ provides the representative organ with
the agenda for meetings of the administrative, or, where appropriate, the
management and supervisory organ, and with copies of all documents submitted
to the general meeting of its shareholders.

cc)   AD HOC INFORMATION AND CONSULTATION

25.   Regular information and consultation is supplemented by ad hoc
involvement in **exceptional circumstances** that significantly affect the interests
of employees, Annex Part 2(c) SED. These include, in a non-exhaustive list
('particularly')

–   relocations;
–   transfers;
–   the closure of establishments or undertakings; or
–   collective redundancies.

26. The competent organ of the SE must inform the representative organ about such incidents. The representative organ (or, where it so decides, in particular for reasons of urgency, the select committee) then has a right to meet at its request with the competent organ of the SE (or any more appropriate level of management within the SE with its own powers of decision) so as to be informed and consulted on measures significantly affecting employees' interests, Annex Part 2(c) SED. This right comes with a particularly severe sanction: Where the competent organ decides not to act in accordance with the opinion expressed by the representative body, the representative body has the right to a further meeting with the competent organ of the SE with a view to seeking agreement. In order to preserve the possibility of reaching an agreement, management may not begin to implement any measures before the meeting has been held.[46] At the same time, the Directive expressly emphasises that the representative body's rights do not affect the prerogatives of the competent organ, Annex Part 2(c)(4) SED.

c)   Procedural Norms

27. The Directive provides for only a few procedural requirements and leaves the details for Member States to determine. Again, the provisions largely follow those of the EWC-Directive (see also §28 paras. 8, 20 above):

–   Member States may provide for rules on the **chairing of** information and consultation **meetings**, Annex Part 2(d) SED.
–   Members of the representative body have a right and the duty to **inform the representatives** of the employees of the SE and its subsidiaries of the content and outcome of the information and consultation procedures, Annex Part 2(e) SED. This does not, of course, relieve them of their duties to confidentiality under Article 8 SED.
–   The representative body (or the select committee) may be assisted by **experts** of its own choosing, Annex Part 2(f) SED.
–   Members of the representative organ have a right to time off for **training** without loss of wages in so far as this is necessary for the fulfilment of their tasks, Annex Part 2(g) SED.
–   The **costs** of the representative organ are to be borne by the SE; the SE must provide the body's members with the financial (reimbursement of expenses, adequate advance) and material (office, computer, phone, etc.) resources needed (proportionality) to enable them to perform their duties in an appropriate manner, Annex Part 2(h) SED. Necessary costs include, in particular, the costs for meetings, namely accommodation and travelling expenses and interpretation facilities. The details should be determined by the Member States which may, in particular, limit the costs for experts to one expert only.

---

[46]   Thus also M. Grobys, *NZA* 2005, 84, 89 sq.

2.   Participation

28.   Secondly, the subsidiary rules of the Annex relate to employee participation
in the management organs of the SE. The rules are different, depending on
whether the SE has been formed by way of transformation or another way.

–   Where the SE is formed by way of **transformation**, the **'before and after'
    principle** strictly applies. If the company was subject to employee
    participation in the supervisory or administrative organ before registration
    of the SE,[47] 'all aspects' of employee participation continue to apply to the SE,
    Annex Part 3(a) SED.
–   In all **other cases of SE formation**, employees of the SE (including
    subsidiaries and establishments) and/or the representative organ (see 1.
    above) have the right to delegate (elect, appoint, recommend or oppose the
    appointment)[48] employees' representatives to the supervisory or
    administrative organ. The number of employees' representatives is equal to
    the **highest proportion** in place in the participating companies concerned
    before registration of the SE ('race to the top')[49], Annex Part 3(b)(1) SED.
–   As a rule for all modes of SE formation, (only) where none of the participating
    companies was governed by participation rules prior to registration of the SE,
    the SE is not required to establish a form of employee participation, Annex
    Part 3(b)(2) SED. This also follows from the 'before and after' principle.

29.   The **allocation of seats** on the supervisory or administrative body among
the members representing the employees from the various Member States is
determined by the representative body according to the proportion of the SE's
employees in each Member State. The employees of the Member States are, in
other words, represented in proportion to their relative number.

30.   The employees' representatives are 'full members' of the supervisory or
administrative organ with the same **rights and obligations** as the members
representing the shareholders, including the right to vote, Annex Part 3(b)(4)
SED. The reference to the rights and obligations includes the whole body of
applicable procedural rules with regard to such issues as confidentiality.

---

[47]   The same must apply where such employee participation has wrongfully not been established
    in the original undertaking; V. Rieble, in id./A. Junker (eds.), *Vereinbarte Mitbestimmung in
    der SE,* 111; S. Weiss/H.-T. Wöhlert, *NZG* 2006, 121, 122 sq.
[48]   The cumbersome wording used here and elsewhere in the Directive takes account of the
    different forms of appointing employees' representatives in different Member States.
    'recommend or oppose the appointment' refers in particular to the Dutch model of
    co-optation upon a proposal of the works council or the shareholders' meeting; on this model
    see e.g. R. Rebhahn, in V. Rieble (ed.), *Zukunft der Unternehmensmitbestimmung,* 51; L.
    Timmermann/S. Spanjaard, in T. Baums/P. Ulmer (eds.), *Unternehmens-Mitbestimmung der
    Arbeitnehmer im Recht der EU-Mitgliedstaaten* (Heidelberg: Recht und Wirtschaft, 2004),
    85–88; H. P. Westermann, *RabelsZ* 48 (1984), 123, 151–159.
[49]   M. Roth, *ZfA* 2004, 431, 442.

IV. NEGOTIATION PROCEDURE TO DETERMINE EMPLOYEE INVOLVEMENT

1. Initiation of Negotiation Procedures – Obligation to Provide Information

31. If the management or administrative organs of the participating companies plan to establish an SE, they must **start negotiations** with the representatives of the companies' employees on arrangements for employee involvement in the SE 'as soon as possible'[50] after publication of the respective plan[51].[52] This requires the respective organs to provide adequate **information** about the identity of the participating companies and the subsidiaries or establishments concerned as well as the number of their employees.[53] This information must be given to the employees' representatives of the participating companies.[54] In undertakings or establishments in which there are no employees' representatives through no fault of the employees, the information should be given to the employees, *argumentum e* Article 3(2)(b)(3) SED. In substance, the organs have to transmit all information necessary for setting up the special negotiating body.[55]

32. Unlike the EWC-Directive, the SE-Directive exclusively entrusts the management or administrative organs of the participating companies – in other words: the employer-side – with initiating the negotiation procedure. This is sufficient in this case, as the participating companies have an interest of their own to initiate the proceedings. This is because the SE cannot, pursuant to Article 12(2) SER, be **registered** unless

- an agreement on arrangements for employee involvement pursuant to Article 4 SED (see paras. 45–50 below) has been concluded; or
- the special negotiating body (see para. 35 below) has, pursuant to Article 3(6) SED, decided not to commence or to terminate negotiations (see paras. 41 sq. below); or

---

[50]   Thus also E. Herfs-Röttgen, *NZA* 2001, 424, 426; see also the implementation in Germany in §4(2) sent. 2 SEBG.

[51]   The forms of plan vary according to the forms of formation:
- the terms of merger, Article 20 SER;
- the terms of creating a holding-SE, Art. 32, 33 SER;
- the plan to form a subsidiary-SE, cf. Article 35 SER;
- the plan to transform into an SE, Article 37 SER.

[52]   See also B. Keller, *WSI-Mitteilungen* 2002, 202, 205 (with a process chart).

[53]   Reference is to concept of employee of the Member States; H. Oetker, *BB* 2005 Supplement 11, 2, 6.

[54]   This is not expressly provided but can be inferred from Article 3(2) and (3) SED as a special negotiating body is not yet installed and as the SNB has to be informed separately. Thus also §4(2) SEBG.

[55]   To this effect also R. Krause, *BB* 2005, 1221, 1223.

- the period for negotiations pursuant to Article 5 SED has expired without an agreement having been concluded (thus opening up the way for the application of the subsidiary requirements of the Annex; provided, of course, that the participating companies continue to pursue the registration) (see para. 37 below).

Registration, in other words, presupposes the successful completion or failure of negotiations; in any case, they must have been initiated.[56]

33. It is a matter of controversy whether registration also requires prior negotiation procedures in the case of an **SE without employees** (e.g. a shelf company) or the formation of an SE by undertakings that are not subject to employee participation.[57] Some (national) courts have considered the negotiation procedures to also be a prerequisite for registration in this case: The declaration by the participating companies that the subsidiary-SE is intended not to have any employees on a permanent basis would only be binding for the time it was made, and the register court was not in a position to control the issue in the future. It was exclusively a matter for the representative organs to agree on the establishment of a representative body.[58] Others have restricted the requirements of Article 12(2) SER on teleological considerations, arguing that the protection of employee interests (which the provision was to safeguard) does not require prior negotiations in such cases. At the same time, the SE should be obliged to initiate and conduct negotiations later if it employed (a relevant number of) employees.[59]

34. The negotiation procedure pursuant to Articles 3–5 SED is **subject to the national law** of the Member State where the registered office of the SE is to be located, Article 5 SED.

2. The Creation of a Special Negotiating Body

35. As in the case of the EWC-negotiations, here, too, a special employee representative body must first be constituted. In the negotiations regarding employee involvement in the SE, the employees of the participating companies

---

[56] F. Blanquet, *ZGR* 2002, 20, 56 sq.

[57] See in detail – distinguishing different factual situations – G. Forst, *Die Beteiligungsvereinbarung nach §21 SEBG,* 110–124.

[58] *Amtsgericht* (Local Court, AG) Hamburg, *ZIP* 2005, 2017 sq.; upheld by *Landgericht* (Regional Court, LG) Hamburg, *ZIP* 2005, 2017 sq. Approvingly T. Blanke, *ZIP* 2006, 789–792; D. Joost, in *EAS,* B 8200 para. 43.

[59] *Oberlandesgericht* (Higher Regional Court, OLG) Düsseldorf, *ZIP* 2009, 918–921 (concerning a shelf company). In the same direction M. Casper, *AG* 2007, 97, 99; id./C. Schäfer, *ZIP* 2007, 653–662: G. Forst, *NZG* 2009, 687–692; id., *RdA* 2010, 55–59; M. Henssler, *RdA* 2005, 330, 334 sq.; C. H. Seibt, *ZIP* 2005, 2248–2250; C. Schubert, *ZESAR* 2006, 340–348.

and the subsidiaries and establishments concerned are represented by a 'special negotiating body'.[60] The initiative for the election or appointment of the members of the special negotiating body is not specifically regulated (different in Article 5(1) EWCD, see §28 para. 47 above) as, again, participating companies have their own interest in beginning prompt negotiations – which are a prerequisite for registration (see para. 32 above).

36.   Election or appointment of the members of the special negotiating body is governed by Article 3(2) SED. The provision aims to achieve the representation of employees in a way which is proportionate to their relative number in each Member State.[61] In principle, one seat should be allocated to every portion of the employees which equals 10%, or a fraction thereof, of the number of all employees employed by the participating companies and concerned subsidiaries and establishments in the Member States, Article 3(2)(a)(i) SED.[62] In the case of an SE formed through merger there may be – subject to certain upper limits – additional members in order to ensure that the special negotiating body includes at least one member for each participating company which will cease to exist as a separate legal entity following the registration of the SE, Article 3(2)(a)(ii) SED. Member States determine the procedure for the election or appointment of the members of the special negotiating body from their territory, Article 3(2)(b) SED. These procedures must ensure that, as far as possible, each participating company is represented by at least one member in the special negotiating body. The legislator assumed that the members of the special negotiating body will normally be elected or appointed by the existing employees' representatives. Where there are no employees' representatives through no fault of their own, employees have the right to directly elect or appoint the members of the special negotiating body, Article 3(2)(b)(3) SED. The national law of Member States may allow for union representatives to be elected or appointed to the special negotiating body even if they are not employees of any of the participating companies, Article 3(2)(b)(2) SED (thus e.g. in Germany pursuant to §6(2) sent. 1 of the Act on SE Employee Involvement, *SE-Beteiligungsgesetz*, SEBG).[63]

---

[60]   The evaluation of the regulation of the special negotiating body is controversial, e.g. with a view to legitimation and costs; see e.g. C. Windbichler, in U. Jürgens et al. (eds.), *Perspektiven der Corporate Governance*, 292, 295.

[61]   On critical constellations, see E. Herfs-Röttgen, *NZA* 2002, 358, 360.

[62]   D. Joost, in *EAS*, B 8200 para. 53; see already para. 18 with note 45 above.

[63]   Critically M. Heinze, *ZGR* 2002, 66, 81.

3. Negotiations and Decisions within the Special Negotiating Body

a) Start and Duration of Negotiations, Information Obligations

37. Negotiations **begin** with the creation of the special negotiating body. They normally continue for six months; this period may be extended to up to one year by agreement of the parties, Article 5 SED. The **parties** to the negotiations – the competent organs of the participating companies[64] and the special negotiating body – 'negotiate in the spirit of cooperation and with a view to reaching an agreement on arrangements for the involvement of the employees within the SE', Article 4(1) SED.

38. The participating companies (their respective competent organs) **inform** the special negotiating body on the plan and actual process of establishing the SE, Article 3(3)(3) SED. Here, too, the contents of the information are determined teleologically and with regard to the special negotiating body's task of negotiating the agreement on employee involvement.[65]

b) Negotiation Options and Quorum Requirements

aa) THE GENERAL GOAL: AGREEMENT ON EMPLOYEE INVOLVEMENT

39. The **goal** of the negotiations is to reach an agreement on the involvement of employees within the SE, Article 3(3), (1) and (2) SED. The special negotiation body makes its decisions by way of an absolute majority; each member has one vote, Article 3(4) sent. 1 and 2 SED. However, the Directive provides for specific quora for decisions in order to safeguard the pre-existing level of employee involvement.

bb) REDUCTION OF PARTICIPATION RIGHTS

40. Where the agreement would lead to a reduction of participation rights, the decision requires the votes of (1) at least two thirds of the members of the special negotiating body (2) representing at least two thirds of the employees, (3) including the votes of members representing employees from at least two

---

[64] The role of these organs as negotiation partners is being criticised as it may lead to conflicts of interests; see F. Kübler, *Liber Amicorum Weiss,* 241; id., *Festschrift für Raiser,* 252. On the involvement of the shareholdes in the decision on the employee involvement agreement, see R. Kiem, *ZHR* 171 (2007), 713–730.

[65] Cf. on the EWCD ECJ Case C-62/99 *bofrost* [2001] ECR I-2595 para. 38 and §28 para. 51 above. See also G. Forst, *Die Beteiligungsvereinbarung nach §21 SEBG,* 108–110 (discussing *inter alia* whether the employee has an individual right to information or whether this is merely an obligation of the management and administrative organs of the participating companies).

Member States[66]; Article 3(4)(1) sent. 2, Recital 10 SED. These requirements apply if the pre-existing regime of employee participation covers

(a) in the case of an SE to be established through merger: at least 25%
(b) in the case of an SE to be established by way of creating a holding company or forming a subsidiary: at least 50%

of the employees of the participating companies.[67] **Reduction** of participation rights means that the proportion of members of the organs of the SE is lower than the highest proportion existing within the participating companies, Article 3(4)(2) SED. This formal determination has the advantages of simplicity and clarity, but it may lead to unsatisfactory results in individual cases.[68]

cc)   Decision not to Open or to Terminate Negotiations

41.   The special negotiating body may decide not to open or to terminate negotiations, Article 3(6) SED. This ends the negotiation procedure. In that case, however, the subsidiary provisions of the Annex do *not* apply. However, with regard to information and consultation, the national provisions of the Member States in which the SE employs workers continue to apply.[69] Subject to other agreement, a re-opening of negotiations (reconvention of the special negotiating body) is possible at the earliest two years after such decision and it requires the written request of a minimum of 10% of the employees of the SE, its subsidiaries and establishments or their representatives. If these ensuing negotiations fail, then, again, the subsidiary requirements of the Annex do not apply.

42.   The consequences of a decision not to open or to terminate negotiations are thus very serious, and consequently, the decision requires **special quora**. Again, the special two-thirds quorum applies (see para. 40 above): two thirds of the votes, representing two thirds of the employees including the votes of Members from at least two Member States, Article 3(6)(2) SED. In the case of an SE which is to be established through transformation, the special negotiating body cannot

---

[66]   This second requirement of a representation of two thirds of the employees seems to be designed to take account of the case where there is a deviation due to the relevance of the 10%-tranche (see para. 36 above); W. Veelken, *Gedächtnisschrift für Blomeyer*, 513, further refers to the case where union officials act as employee representatives (see para. 36 above).

[67]   This is intended to take account of the 'before and after' principle and of the protection of acquired rights; E. Herfs-Röttgen, *NZA* 2001, 424, 426 sq.; S. Pluskat, *DStR* 2001, 1483, 1487. The different percentages take account of the fact that, in the case of a formation by merger, the merging companies cease to exist (higher need of protection), different from the formation of a holding or subsidiary SE; G. Kleinsorge, *RdA* 2002, 343, 349.

[68]   Critically therefore P. L. Davies, *ILJ* 32 (2003), 75, 85–87; E. Herfs-Röttgen, *NZA* 2002, 358, 361; J. Reichert/S. Brandes, *ZGR* 2003, 767, 784–787; C. Windbichler, *AG* 2004, 190, 192; H. Wißmann, *Festschrift für Wiedemann*, 691 sq. (pointing out the difficulty of a comparison of systems using the example Germany-Netherlands).

[69]   In this case, of course, the EWCD remains applicable, Article 13(1) SED; see para. 6 above.

decide not to open or to terminate the negotiations if the original company is
governed by participation, Article 3(6)(3) with Recital 10 sent. 2 SED. Here, the
legislator considered the risk of an 'evasion' of employee participation to be
particularly likely.[70]

c) Experts and Costs

43. The special negotiation body may request **experts** of its own choosing to
provide assistance during the negotiations, Article 3(5) SED. In this context,
representatives of appropriate Community level trade union organisations are
deemed to be experts of whom the SNB can avail itself (see also §28 para. 64).[71]
The experts may, if the SNB so requests, also participate in the negotiations in an
advisory function, however, only where this is appropriate to further the
somewhat unusual purpose of 'promoting coherence and consistency at
Community level'.

44. The **costs** of the special negotiating body are to be borne by the
participating companies so as to enable it to fulfil its tasks in an appropriate
(proportionality!) manner, Article 3(7) SED. The details should be determined
by the Member States which may limit the costs to only one expert.[72]

4. The Agreement

a) Autonomy and Regular Contents

45. The contents of the agreement[73] – which should be concluded in writing,
Article 3(3)(1) SED – are to be autonomously agreed upon by the parties,
Article 4(2) SED.[74] They may, in particular, agree to apply the subsidiary
requirements of the Annex, Article 7(1)(2)(a) SED. The subsidiary requirements
are not intended to be default norms which apply where the agreement proves to
have gaps. More generally, given the primacy of the agreement under the

---

[70]   E. Herfs-Röttgen, *NZA* 2001, 424, 427; S. Pluskat, *DStR* 2001, 1483, 1487.

[71]   This may perhaps be justified with a view to the novelty of this subject of negotiations where
       the unions have built up respective expertise.

[72]   Only Germany, Ireland, Latvia and Sweden have not included any such limitation; see
       Commission, Communication on the review of Council Directive 2001/86/EC of 8 October
       2001 supplementing the Statute for a European company with regard to the involvement of
       employees, COM(2008) 591 final, 4 (note 8).

[73]   The legal nature of the agreement is controversial (as in the case of the agreement under the
       EWCD); see e.g. E. Herfs-Röttgen, *NZA* 2002, 358, 364; see further the references in §28
       para. 66 above.

[74]   F. Blanquet, *ZGR* 2002, 20, 58 ('freedom of contract' – my translation); W. Heinze/A.
       Seifert/C. Teichmann, *BB* 2005, 2525–2530 (emphasising the advantages of a legislative
       solution and proposing a model agreement). The SE-Regulation and, as we discuss below, the
       SE-Directive provide for a number of restrictions though.

negotiation model, the provisions of the Annex cannot, without further justification, be used to fill gaps in the agreement; such justification must be based upon the parties' intentions.[75]

46. The Directive does however provide for a number of regular contents[76] of the agreement. Pursuant to Article 4(2) SED, these include:

(a) **with regard to the agreement** as such:
- – its scope, lit. a);
- – its entry into force and its duration as well as grounds and procedures for renegotiation, lit. h);[77]
(b) **with regard to information and consultation**, which may, alternatively, provide for a representative body ('Works Council') or (one or more) procedure(s) for information and consultation:
- – the composition of the representative body, the number of its members and the allocation of seats, lit. b);
- – the competences and procedures for information and consultation of the representative organ, lit. c);
- – the frequency of the meetings of the representative body, lit. d);
- – the financial and material resources to be allocated to the representative body, lit. e),

or

- – the arrangements for implementing the procedure(s) for information and consultation (which the parties may agree upon as an alternative to the establishment of a representative body), lit. f);
(c) **with regard to participation**
- – if the parties want to provide for employee participation: the contents of an agreement regarding employee participation; lit. g); these include
  - • the number of employee representatives in the supervisory or administrative organ of the SE;[78]

---

[75] V. Rieble, in id./A. Junker (eds.), *Vereinbarte Mitbestimmung in der SE*, 98 ('supplementary interpretation of the contract' – my translation). See also G. Forst, *Die Beteiligungsvereinbarung nach §21 SEBG*, 190 sq.

[76] These are not 'minimum contents' as the parties (1) have a choice between the representative body and the information and consultation procedures and (2) they do not have to provide for employee participation at all.

[77] On the consequences of a cessation of the agreement, see G. Forst, *EuZW* 2011, 333–336 (primarily the consequences the parties have agreed; subsidiarily [for lack of agreement] distinguish: [a] in case of expiration of the agreed term: continuing effect of the original agreement and renegotiations; [b] in case of a termination by notice application of the subsidiary requirements).

[78] On the controversial issue whether this determines the size of the supervisory organ or merely the proportion of the employees' representatives, see e.g. M. Habersack, *ZHR* 171 (2007), 613, 632–634; C. Windbichler, *Festschrift für Canaris*, 1428–1430, both with further references; see also para. 50 below.

- the procedures as to how these members may be elected, appointed, recommended or opposed by the employees; and
- the rights of the members.

The subsidiary requirements of the Annex do not apply in this case, except if the parties have so agreed.

47. The parties thus **mandatorily** must agree upon (a) the basic data of the agreement and (b) – alternatively – the establishment of a representative body or one or more information and consultation procedures (see also Recital 6 SED).[79] The agreement on (c) employee participation is however **left to the parties**.[80] Special rules only apply where the SE is formed through transformation:

b)   'Before and After Principle' in Case of Transformation

48. The parties' freedom to agree upon the content of the agreement is primarily restricted in respect of SEs which have been formed by way of **transformation**. Here, the 'before and after' principle applies in a particularly strong form, Article 4(4) SED, as the legislator considered the danger of evasion from employee participation to be particularly likely (see Recital 10 sent. 2 SED): The agreement must provide for *at least the same level of all elements* of employee involvement as that which existed within the company before it was transformed into an SE.[81]

c)   Relationship to SE Statutes

49. The agreement may also contain provisions on employee participation in the supervisory or administrative board and thus refer to the structure of the SE. As a consequence, it may conflict with the statutes of the SE (defined in Article 6 SED), e.g. its provisions on the number of members of the supervisory organ.[82] Such conflict should be resolved by an amendment[83] of the statutes, Article 12(4)(1) SED (**primacy of the agreement**).[84] National law may provide

---

[79]   Thus also G. Kleinsorge, *RdA* 2002, 343, 347 sq.; E. Herfs-Röttgen, *NZA* 2001, 424, 427. Differently with respect to (b) however E. Herfs-Röttgen, *NZA* 2002, 358, 361 sq. (arg. e recital 4 and *a maiore* Article 3(6) SED).

[80]   E. Herfs-Röttgen, *NZA* 2002, 358, 363 (suggesting to apply the *quora* of Article 3(6) SED by analogy in this case; this would, however, presuppose a *lacuna*).

[81]   On the extent of which a safeguarding of participation rights is thus achieved, see G. Forst, *Die Beteiligungsvereinbarung nach §21 SEBG*, 201–209.

[82]   R. Krause, *BB* 2005, 1221, 1226; H. Oetker, *ZIP* 2006, 1113–1121.

[83]   This requires an amendment of the statutes; the agreement on employee involvement does not derogate the statutes; M. Habersack, *ZHR* 171 (2007), 613, 628; C. Schäfer, in V. Rieble/A. Junker (eds.), *Vereinbarte Mitbestimmung in der SE*, 27 sq.

[84]   See W. Heinze/A. Seifert/C. Teichmann, *BB* 2005, 2524, 2525 (considering this as additional potential for negotiations. For a critical view on the primacy of the agreement e.g.

that the management organ or the administrative organ of the SE is entitled to amend the statutes without any further decision from the general shareholder meeting, subparagraph 2.

50. Whether and how **limitations under national** law regarding the statutes of a company can **restrict autonomy of the parties** in respect of the participation agreement of an SE is considered controversial in German literature. Pursuant to a predominant opinion, the participation agreement should be restricted by mandatory law in the same way as the statutes of the SE.[85] Autonomy with regard to the participation agreement was based upon the autonomy of the statutes and should consequently be limited in the same way.[86] What the shareholders cannot provide for in the statutes of the SE cannot be provided for in the participation agreement either. An agreement, for example, following the Austrian model, pursuant to which the employee representatives had the right to appoint a member to every committee of the supervisory organ, would be excluded under German law, as the composition of the committees is subject to the organisational autonomy of the supervisory board.[87] Other authors argue, that pursuant to Article 12(4)(1) SED the agreement takes precedence over the statutes; they refer to the hierarchy of norms under Article 9 SED which is the basis for the autonomy of Article 4(2) SED; and, not least, to the purpose of the Directive to allow the parties to agree on all issues concerning the employees' influence on the decisions of the board.[88] The purpose of the Directive does, indeed, argue for an autonomous determination of the limits to the parties' autonomy in Union law. The wording and the purpose of Article 4(2) SED indicate that the legislator wanted to give the parties far-reaching autonomy to find customised solutions, in particular to agree on innovative solutions drawing inspiration from models under foreign laws.

5. Application of the Subsidiary Requirements

51. The subsidiary requirements of the Annex[89] may, for one thing, apply if the parties so agree (see para. 45 above). Apart from that, they only apply

---

C. Windbichler, in U. Jürgens et al. (eds.), *Perspektiven der Corporate Governance*, 293.

[85] M. Habersack, *AG* 2006, 345–355; id., *ZHR* 171 (2007), 613, 629–635; C. Schäfer, in V. Rieble/A, Junker (eds.), *Vereinbarte Mitbestimmung in der SE*, 27–35; C. Windbichler, *Festschrift für Canaris*, 1423–1434. Differentiating V. Rieble, in id./A. Junker (eds.), *Vereinbarte Mitbestimmung in der SE*, 100 sq. (size of the supervisory board but not authorisation rights). Further G. Forst, *Die Beteiligungsvereinbarung nach §21 SEBG*, 91 sqq.

[86] M. Habersack, *AG* 2006, 345, 348; id., *ZHR* 171 (2007), 613, 629.

[87] Example from C. Teichmann, *AG* 2008, 797, 801.

[88] See in detail C. Teichmann, *AG* 2008, 797, 800–805; id., *Konzern* 2007, 89, 94 sq.; further R. Krause, *BB* 2005, 1221, 1226; H. Oetker, *ZIP* 2006, 1113–1121; M. Rehberg, in V. Rieble/A. Junker (eds.), *Vereinbarte Mitbestimmung in der SE*, 57–63.

[89] Strictly speaking, of course, national rules implementing the requirements of the Annex.

subordinately and (depending upon the mode of SE formation) pursuant to the 'before and after' principle. Differentiation according to the various forms of establishing an SE (see b) below) is intended to address the different risks of evading employee participation requirements.[90]

a)   General Requirements

52.   There are three general requirements for the application of the subsidiary requirements, Article 7(1)(2)(b) SED. First, the parties have not reached agreement within the negotiation period of six months (which may consensually be extended to twelve months; Article 5 SED; see para. 37 above). Second, the competent organs of the participating companies have decided to accept the application of the subsidiary requirements and so also the continuation of the SE registration process. And third, the special negotiating body has not made a decision pursuant to Article 3(6)(1) SED not to commence or to terminate the negotiations (thus excluding the application of the subsidiary requirements; see para. 41 above).

b)   Specific Requirements Related to Different Modes of Formation and to the 'Before and After' Principle

53.   Further requirements for the application of the subsidiary requirements of the Annex are specifically related to the different ways in which an SE may be established.[91]

–   In the case of an SE established by **transformation**, the subsidiary requirements apply if, prior to transformation, the company was subject, under national law, to employee participation in the supervisory or administrative organ, Article 7(2)(a) SED.
–   In the case of an SE established by **merger**, one of two alternative requirements must be fulfilled, Article 7(2)(b) SED: (a) one or more of the merged companies was subject to one or more forms of employee participation which extended to at least 25% of the employees of all merged companies; or (b) as before, one or more of the merged companies was subject to employee participation which covered less than 25% and the special negotiating body decides that the subsidiary requirements should apply.[92]

---

[90]   E. Herfs-Röttgen, *NZA* 2001, 424, 427 sq.
[91]   For a critical perspective on differentiated threshold values see M. Heinze, *ZGR* 2002, 66, 76.
[92]   This latter variant may be excluded by the national law of the Member States; concession to Spain which was concerned with national demands for employee participation; E. Herfs-Röttgen, *NZA* 2001, 424, 428; M. Heinze, *ZGR* 2002, 66, 77; G. Kleinsorge, *RdA* 2002, 343, 350; W. Veelken, *Gedächtnisschrift für Blomeyer,* 516 sq.

–   In the case of the establishment of a **holding or subsidiary SE**, again, one of
    two alternative requirements must be fulfilled, Article 7(2)(d) SED: (a) one or
    more of the participating companies was subject to one or more forms of
    employee participation which covered at least 50% of the employees of all
    participating companies; or (b) as before, but the minimum coverage of 50%
    was not reached and the special negotiating body decided that the subsidiary
    requirements should apply.

At first sight, the differences in percentages appear to be arbitrarily determined.
They are intended to take the different intensities of an interest in participation
into account. This interest is particularly high in the case of transformation,
given the risk of an 'evasion of employee participation'. Where the establishment
of an SE by merger is concerned, the legislator considered the participation
interest to be higher than in the case of transformation of a holding SE or
subsidiary SE because, in the former case, the participating companies cease to
exist as separate entities.

6. Principles of Cooperation

a) The Principle of Loyal Cooperation

54. The principle of loyal cooperation, similar to that provided for by the
EWC-Directive (see §28 para. 76 above) applies with regard to cooperation with
the representative body ('SE Works Council') and with the employees'
representatives in information and consultation procedures: The parties work
together in a spirit of cooperation and with due regard to their mutual rights and
obligations, Article 9 SED.

55. This principle is, in other words, provided for only with regard to the
different forms of information and consultation and not with regard to employee
participation in the supervisory or administrative organ. In this latter case,
pursuant to Annex Part 3(b)(4) SED, the employees' representatives become 'full
members' of that body, with the same rights and obligations. Their legal position
is thus determined by the SE-Regulation and any supplementary national
legislation; these also determine the information rights of the members of the
supervisory or administrative organ (see already para. 31 above) as well as the
duties of loyalty, fiduciary duties and the duty of constructive cooperation.

b) Confidentiality

56. The rules on confidential information in Article 8 SED are also analogous
to the provisions of the EWC-Directive (see already §26 para. 25 and §28 para. 77

above).[93] The employer's interest in confidentiality is primarily protected by a duty of the members of the special negotiating body and the representative body not to reveal information which has been given to them in confidence, Article 8(1) SED. (Only) exceptionally, may the employer withhold information, Article 8(2) SED. The national law of Member States may provide for special requirements for SEs in its territory which pursue directly and essentially the aim of ideological guidance, Article 8(3) SED.[94] The application of paragraphs 1–3 must be subject to administrative or judicial review upon the request of the employees' representatives, Article 8(4) SED.

57. Again, these provisions do not relate to the employees' representatives in the supervisory or administrative organ. Their confidentiality duties are governed by Article 49 SED.[95] Additional requirements may follow from the Insider Trading Directive[96].[97]

c) Protection of Employee Representatives

58. Comprehensive protection of the employees' representatives is provided in respect of all of their functions, namely

- as members of the special negotiating body;
- as members of the representative body ('SE Works Council');
- the employees' representatives involved in the special procedures on information and consultation; and
- the employees' representatives in the supervisory or administrative organ of the SE.

They all enjoy the same level of protection in the fulfilment of their tasks as the employees' representatives under the national laws and practices of the Member States in which they are employed, Article 10(1) SED.[98]

---

[93] See M. Heinze, *ZGR* 2002, 66, 85 sq. (with a sober assessment of effectiveness of confidentiality duties).

[94] On the protection of ideological establishments in European Employment Law see in detail M. Plum, *Tendenzschutz im europäischen Arbeitsrecht* (Berlin: Duncker & Humblot, 2011) and esp. 155–171 on Article 8(3) SED.

[95] See in detail C. Teichmann, in M. Lutter/P. Hommelhoff (eds.), *SE-Kommentar*, Art. 49 SE-VO paras. 1 sqq.; J. Reichert/S. Brandes, in W. Goette/M. Habersack/S. Kalss (eds.), *Münchener Kommentar zum Aktiengesetz*, Art. 49 SE-VO paras. 1 sqq.

[96] Article 3(a) Council Directive 89/592/EEC of 13 November 1989 coordinating regulations on insider dealing, OJ 1989 L 334/30.

[97] See e.g. ECJ Case C-384/02 *Grøngaard* [2005] ECR I-9939 (communication of information by an employee representative to the union president).

[98] Critically with regard to the resulting differences in levels of protection and the consequences for cooperation of employee representatives from different countries M. Kiehn, *Die*

V. PREVENTION OF ABUSE

59. A large number of the provisions of the SE-Directive are designed to prevent 'flight from employee participation' (see paras. 4, 6 above). What is at stake, more precisely, is an accommodation of the interests of (some) Member States to maintain their national level of employee participation. This interest is to be balanced with the internal market interest to provide, with the SE, a company form suitable for the purposes of undertakings and open to adaptation with a view to their needs. The fear of a 'flight from employee participation', which had been a determining factor throughout the legislative proceedings, is also expressed in the prohibition of misuse of Article 11 SED, located at the beginning of the transposition provisions. It requires Member States to take appropriate measures 'with a view to preventing the misuse of an SE for the purpose of depriving employees of rights to employee involvement or withholding such rights'. The same objective is, if in more general terms, also expressed in Recital 18 SED.[99]

60. However, precisely what the prohibition of misuse entails is rather controversial. Some consider it to be a sharp sword;[100] others see its scope as limited to exceptional cases.[101] Interpretation of the provision should take into account the fact that the legislator has already balanced and accommodated the countervailing (employee) interests for a large number of cases in specific provisions. In this light, the remaining room for autonomous agreement or regulation should be left to the participating companies or the SE, respectively, and for the agreement on employee involvement. Article 11 SED should thus rather be considered to provide a pressure valve for exceptional cases. Where the parties make use of the leeway that the SE-Regulation and Directive provide for, this cannot as such be considered to be a 'misuse'.

---

betriebliche Beteiligung der Arbeitnehmer in der Societas Europea (SE) (Hamburg: Kovac, 2011), 150.

[99] Some authors appear to interpret Recital 18 SED as a rule leading to specific legal consequences; see e.g. G. Kleinsorge, *RdA* 2002, 343, 351; id., *ZGR* 2003, 800, 808; also M. Rehberg, *ZGR* 2005, 859, 882 sqq. (ultimately denying this though at p. 885); differently e.g. C. Schäfer, in V. Rieble/A. Junker (eds.), *Vereinbarte Mitbestimmung in der SE,* 20. Legal consequences may, however, only be inferred from rules of the operative part of the Directive; consequently, Recital 18 may only be used as an element of interpretation; on the methodological issue, see K. Riesenhuber, in id. (ed.), *Europäische Methodenlehre,* §11 paras. 36 sq.

[100] Thus, however M. Rehberg, *ZGR* 2005, 859–893, who considers Article 11 SED as a special emphasis of the purposive interpretation and the *effet utile.* In the Court's jurisprudence, these are the general principles of interpretation.

[101] To this effect D. Joost, in *EAS,* B 8200 para. 250; F. Kübler, *Festschrift für Raiser,* 254–257; M. Henssler, *Gedächtnisschrift für Heinze,* 340 sq.; V. Rieble, *BB* 2006, 2018, 2022; W.-G. Ringe, *NZG* 2006, 932, 934.

VI. IMPLEMENTATION

61. The **German** legislator[102] has enacted supplementary provisions to the
SE-Regulation and provisions for the implementation of the SE-Directive in the
SE-Introductory Act (*SE-Einführungsgesetz*, SEEG) of 22 December 2004.[103] The
Act contains the SE-Implementation Act in Article 1 (*SE-Ausführungsgesetz*,
SEAG) and the SE-Participation Act in Article 2 (*SE-Beteiligungsgesetz*, SEBG).[104]
Introduction of the SE with its procedural model of employee involvement has
contributed to, if not triggered, a broad discussion about employee participation
in Germany.[105] There are signs that it has also opened up a regulatory
competition in the field of employee involvement. In the **United Kingdom**, the
SE-Directive was implemented by the European Public Limited Liability
Company Regulations 2004.[106]

VII. REFERENCES REGARDING THE EUROPEAN COOPERATIVE COMPANY

Bibliography:[107]
M. Habersack, 'Grundsatzfragen der Mitbestimmung in SE und SCE sowie bei
grenzüberschreitender Verschmelzung', *ZHR* 171 (2007), 613–643; O. Kisker,
'Unternehmerische Mitbestimmung in der Europäischen Gesellschaft, der Europäischen

---

[102] For a discussion of implementation from a comparative perspective see C. Leca, *EBLR* 2007, 403, 424–432.

[103] BGBl. 2004 I, 3675.

[104] See e.g. I. Calle Lambach, *RIW* 2005, 161–168; M. Grobys, *NZA* 2004, 779–781; id., *NZA* 2005, 84–91; M. Jacobs, in W. Goette/M. Habersack/S. Kalss (eds.), *Münchener Kommentar zum Aktiengesetz*, vol. 9/2, Europäisches Aktienrecht A. III. SEBG; D. Joost, in *EAS*, B 8200 (discussing controversial issues of the implementation at para 15); R. Krause, *BB* 2005, 1221–1229; T. Müller-Bonanni/P. Melot de Beauregard, *GmbHR* 2005, 195–200; H. Oetker, *BB* 2005 Supplement 11, 2–13; id., *ZESAR* 2005, 3–12; id., in M. Lutter/P. Hommelhoff (eds.), *SE-Kommentar*, Vor §1 SEBR paras. 13–15 (on the SEBG) and paras. 16–23 (on the implementation in other Member States); G. Kleinsorge, 'MgVG', in B. Nagel/G. Freis/G. Kleinsorge (eds.), *Beteiligung der Arbeitnehmer im Unternehmen auf der Grundlage des europäischen Rechts*, 2nd edn. (Berlin: de Gruyter, 2009), Einf SE paras. 40–56 (on the legislative procedure) and paras. 68–86 (on the content of SEBG). On practical experiences J. Wagner, *EWS* 2005, 546–554. The evaluation of the German implementation is controversial, F. Kübler, *Liber Amicorum Weiss*, 235 sqq. (a tendency towards over-regulation); B. Nagel, *AuR* 2004, 281 sqq. (competitive implementation).

[105] See e.g. C. Kirchner, *AG* 2005, 197–200; T. Raiser, *Unternehmensmitbestimmung vor dem Hintergrund europarechtlicher Entwicklungen*; V. Rieble, *NJW* 2006, 2214–2217; id. (ed.), *Zukunft der Unternehmensmitbestimmung*; id./A. Junker (eds.), *Vereinbarte Mitbestimmung in der SE*; C. Windbichler, *AG* 2004, 190–196.

[106] SI 2004/2326; also available at www.legislation.gov.uk/uksi/2004/2326/contents/made. For a brief overview, see S. Deakin & G. Morris, *Labour Law*, para. 9.65.

[107] For the company law literature, see the references in M. Habersack/D. A. Verse, *Europäisches Gesellschaftsrecht*, §14 before para. 1.

Genossenschaft und bei grenzüberschreitender Verschmelzung im Vergleich', *RdA* 2006, 206–212; R. Schulze, 'Die Europäische Genossenschaft (SCE)', *NZG* 2004, 792–796; R. Schulze (ed.), Europäische Genossenschaft SCE (Baden-Baden: Nomos, 2004); I. Snaith, 'Employee Involvement in the European Cooperative Society: A Range of Stakeholders?', *IJCLLIR* 22 (2006), 213–230.

62. Following the success of the European Company and on the basis of the model there employed, the Community adopted the regulatory framework for another supra-national company form as early as 2003, the European Cooperative Society, *Societas Cooperativa Europaea* (SCE).[108] Issues of employee participation, which were again regulated in an accompanying directive (SCE-Directive, SCED),[109] were also addressed by way of the negotiation model which was first utilised in the EWC-Directive. The rules largely follow the model of the SE-Directive.[110]

63. As a **cooperative society**, the SCE's principal objective is to satisfy its members' needs and/or the development of their economic and social activities, in particular through the conclusion of agreements with them to supply goods or services or to execute work of the kind that the SCE carries out or commissions, Article 1(3) SCER. Its formation presupposes a transnational element. Unlike the European Company, the SCE may also be formed by natural persons, Article 2(1) SCER.

64. With regard to employee involvement, the Directive provides for a **negotiation model** (Articles 3–6 SCED), supplemented by **subsidiary requirements** (Article 7 SCED with the Annex). They primarily aim for the autonomous regulation of issues of employee involvement by the relevant parties, Article 4(2) SCED. At the same time, the provisions also safeguard the pre-existing level of employee participation, again using the mechanisms of the 'before and after' principle and of decision quora for (a) any reduction of the participation level (Article 3(4) SCED) and (b) the decision not to take up or to terminate negotiation (Article 3(6) SCED; pursuant to subparagraph 3 excluded in case of establishment of the SCE by way of transformation). The subsidiary requirements safeguard pre-existing participation with a view to the proportion of all employees that was previously governed by participation rules, Article 7(2) SCED.

---

[108] Council Regulation (EC) No 1435/2003 of 22 July 2003 on the Statute for a European Cooperative Society (SCE), OJ 2003 L 207/1.

[109] Council Directive 2003/72/EC of 22 July 2003 supplementing the Statute for a European Cooperative Society with regard to the involvement of employees, OJ 2003 L 207/25.

[110] For a comparison, see in particular O. Kisker, *RdA* 2006, 206–212 (overview at pp. 208 sq.); H. Oetker, in M. Lutter/P. Hommelhoff (eds.), *SE-Kommentar,* Vor §1 SEBG paras. 24 sq. and with a synopsis after para. 31.

65. Some peculiarities – in comparison to the SE – require specific rules. First, account must be taken of the fact that natural persons may be involved in the formation of an SCE and that consequently the **number of employees** may be **small**: In such cases, the legislator did not consider it to be justified to require negotiation procedures (Recital 12 SCE). Where the SCE is formed exclusively by natural persons or by natural person and only a single legal entity, the negotiation procedure only applies if the founders employ at least 50 employees in at least two different Member States, Article 8 SCED. In such cases, employee involvement is governed by the provisions of the Member State of the SCE's registered office which apply to other entities of the same type. However, upon a request by at least one third of the employees, the negotiation procedure must be commenced.

66. A second specific aspect is the **employees' right to participate in the general meeting** (where applicable, the section or sectorial meeting) with the right to vote if certain prerequisites are met. Some Member States provide for such right (not Germany), and pursuant to Article 9 SCED, this right is maintained under certain circumstances, particularly in the case of transformation.

§30. CROSS-BORDER MERGER AND EMPLOYEE PARTICIPATION

CONTENTS

Bibliography[1]:

W. Bayer/J. Schmidt, 'Die neue Richtlinie über die grenzüberschreitende Verschmelzung von Kapitalgesellschaften – Inhalt und Anregungen zur Umsetzung in

---

[1]   For a company law bibliography, see S. Grundmann, *European Company Law*, bibliography to §29; M. Habersack/D. A. Verse, *Europäisches Gesellschaftsrecht*, 4th edn. (Munich: C.H. Beck,

Deutschland', *NJW* 2006, 401–406; S. Brandes, 'Mitbestimmungsvermeidung mittels grenzüberschreitender Verschmelzung', *ZIP* 2008, 2193–2199; W. Däubler, 'Grenzüberschreitende Fusion und Arbeitsrecht – Zum Entwurf der Zehnten gesellschaftsrechtlichen Richtlinie', *DB* 1988, 1850–1854; M. Habersack, 'Grundsatzfragen der Mitbestimmung in SE und SCE sowie bei grenzüberschreitender Verschmelzung', *ZHR* 171 (2007), 613–643; M. Henssler, 'Mitbestimmung als Verhandlungsgegenstand grenzüberschreitender Strategien', in P.-C. Müller-Graff/C. Teichmann (eds.), *Europäisches Gesellschaftsrecht auf neuen Wegen* (Baden-Baden: Nomos, 2010), 143–168; S. Herrler, 'Ermöglichung grenzüberschreitender Verschmelzungen von Kapitalgesellschaften durch Änderung des Umwandlungsgesetzes – Umsetzung der Verschmelzungsrichtlinie unter Vernachlässigung der primärrechtlichen Rahmenbedingungen', *EuZW* 2007, 295–300; J. Heuschmid, 'Unternehmensmitbestimmung nach der Richtlinie zur grenzüberschreitenden Verschmelzung von Kapitalgesellschaften', *AuR* 2006, 184–192; O. Kisker, 'Unternehmerische Mitbestimmung in der Europäischen Gesellschaft, der Europäischen Genossenschaft und bei grenzüberschreitender Verschmelzung im Vergleich', *RdA* 2006, 206–212; W. Koberski, 'Fusionsrichtlinie und Arbeitnehmerbeteiligung', in W. Kohte/ H.-J. Dörner/R. Anzinger (eds.), *Arbeitsrecht im sozialen Dialog, Festschrift für Hellmut Wißmann* (Munich: C.H. Beck, 2005), 474–488; N. Krause/M. Janko, 'Grenzüberschreitende Verschmelzungen und Arbeitnehmermitbestimmung', *BB* 2007, 2194–2197; S. Lunk/L. Hinrichs, 'Die Mitbestimmung der Arbeitnehmer bei grenzüberschreitenden Verschmelzungen nach dem MgVG', *NZA* 2007, 773–780; M. Lutter, *Europäisches Unternehmensrecht*, 4th edn. (Berlin: de Gruyter, 1996); S. Maul/C. Teichmann/M. Wenz, 'Der Richtlinienvorschlag zur grenzüberschreitenden Verschmelzung von Kapitalgesellschaften', *BB* 2003, 2633–2641; T. Müller-Bonnani/M. Müntefering, 'AN-Beteiliugng bei SE-Gründung und grenzüberschreitender Verschmelzung im Vergleich', *BB* 2010, 1699–1703; B. Nagel, 'Das Gesetz über die Mitbestimmung der Arbeitnehmer bei grenzüberschreitenden Verschmelzungen (MgVG)', *NZG* 2007, 57–59; H.-W. Neye, 'Die neue Richtlinie zur grenzüberschreitenden Verschmelzung von Kapitalgesellschaften', *ZIP* 2005, 1893–1898; J. Oechsler, 'Die Richtlinie 2005/56/EG über die Verschmelzung von Kapitalgesellschaften aus verschiedenen Mitgliedstaaten', *NZG* 2006, 161–166; M. Pannier, 'The EU Cross Border Merger Directive – A New Dimension for Employee Participation and Company Restructuring', *EBLR* 2005, 1424–1442; T. Raiser, 'Unternehmensmitbestimmung vor dem Hintergrund europarechtlicher Entwicklungen, Gutachten B für den 66. Deutschen Juristentag', in Ständige Deputation des Deutschen Juristentages (ed.), *Verhandlungen des Sechsundsechzigsten Deutschen Juristentages* (Munich: C.H. Beck, 2006); K. Riesenhuber, 'Die Verschmelzungsrichtlinie: "Basisrechtsakt für ein Europäisches Recht der Strukturmaßnahmen" – Zum Schutz durch Information im Europäischen Gesellschaftsrecht', *NZG* 2004, 15–22; C. Schubert, 'Die Mitbestimmung der Arbeitnehmer bei grenzüberschreitender Verschmelzung', *RdA* 2007, 9–17; M. Siems, 'SEVIC: Der letzte Mosaikstein im Internationalen Gesellschaftsrecht der EU?', *EuZW* 2006, 135–140; S. Simon/L. Hinrichs, 'Unterrichtung der Arbeitnehmer und ihrer Vertretungen bei grenzüberschreitenden Verschmelzungen', *NZA* 2008, 391–397; C.

2011), §8 before para. 52.

Teichmann, 'Mitbestimmung und grenzüberschreitende Verschmelzung', *Konzern* 2007, 89–98; G. Thüsing, 'Europäische Perspektiven der deutschen Unternehmensmitbestimmung', in V. Rieble (ed.), *Zukunft der Unternehmensmitbestimmung* (Munich: ZAAR, 2004), 95–113; P. M. Wiesner, 'Die grenzüberschreitende Verschmelzung und der neue Mitbestimmungskompromiss', *DB* 2005, 91–94; F. Wooldridge, 'The Employee Participation Provisions of the Cross-Border Mergers Directive', *Comp.Law.* 28 (2007), 118–119.

Cases:
ECJ Case C-411/03 *SEVIC* [2005] ECR I-10805.

I. ISSUES, OVERVIEW, COMPETENCE, REGULATORY CONTEXT

1. One of the Communities' oldest projects for approximation of laws was – together with the Statute for a European Company – the Directive on Cross-Border Mergers. It is of obvious relevance for the internal market. The cross-border merger of undertakings raises similar issues of employee participation as the European Company (SE), even though the practical goal differs in that a cross-border merger results in a new national company rather than a new supranational company. Not surprisingly, it was again the issue of employee participation that stalled the legislative proceedings. The provisions on employee participation of the 2005 Directive on Cross-Border Mergers of Limited Liability Companies (Cross-Border Merger Directive, CBMD)[2] employ the model of the SE-Directive with appropriate adaptations.[3] For a better understanding of this, read §29 on employee involvement in the SE first.

2. The **legislative history**[4] of the Directive dates back to the origins of EU company law. A first draft in 1972[5] still contemplated regulation through an international treaty, based upon Article 220 EEC (Article 293 EC). Employee participation was to be governed by the law of the Member State where the emerging company would have its seat. The proposal failed, as did a subsequent

---

[2]   Directive 2005/56/EC of the European Parliament and of the Council of 26 October 2005 on cross-border mergers of limited liability companies, OJ 2005 L 310/1.

[3]   For a comparison of the rules on employee involvement, see T. Müller-Bonnani/M. Müntefering, *BB* 2010, 1699–1703.

[4]   See e.g. S. Grundmann, *European Company Law*, §29 paras. 2 sq.; M. Habersack/D. A. Verse, *Europäisches Gesellschaftsrecht*, §8 paras. 52 sq.; M. Lutter, *Europäisches Unternehmensrecht*, 257 sq.

[5]   Draft Convention on International Merger of Société Anonymes of 27 September 1972, Bulletin EC Supplement 13/73; reproduced e.g. in RabelsZ 39 (1975) 539–560; also available at http://aei.pitt.edu/5613.pdf; M. Lutter, *Europäisches Unternehmensrecht*, 2nd edn. (Berlin: de Gruyter, 1984), 351 sqq.

1985 draft of a directive based upon Article 54(3)(g) EEC (Article 50(2) TFEU).[6] It was not until after the breakthrough of the SE in 2000 (see §29 para. 5 above) that a new proposal from 2003 which employed the models developed for the SE,[7] finally succeeded and resulted in the adoption of the Directive. The Directive, adopted in October 2005, was not rendered obsolete by the Court's decision in *Sevic*[8] in December of the same year. Pursuant to that decision, it is held to be incompatible with the freedom of establishment as protected by Article 49 TFEU for a Member State, while allowing national mergers, to completely exclude trans-border mergers. Within the limits of proportionality, regulation for the protection of mandatory requirements of public interest, e.g. in the interest of employees or creditors, remain admissible, as long as such rules do not entirely prohibit trans-border mergers (see in more detail §3 paras. 86–91 above).

3. **The Directive** primarily addresses the company law aspects of cross-border mergers.[9] The provisions on employee involvement build upon the model of the **SE-Directive** to which Article 16 CBMD refers with some modifications. As a (theoretical) rule, employee participation is governed by the law of the state where the company resulting from the merger has its registered office. There are, however, three (practically important and far-reaching) categories of cases in which this would lead to a reduction in the level of employee participation compared to the standard of the original companies; in these groups of cases, the 'before and after' principle, taken from the SE-Directive, applies.[10] The managements of the merging companies and a special negotiating body, which must be created for this purpose, negotiate about employee participation. These negotiations are structured by procedural safeguards (majority requirements for certain decisions of the special negotiating body) and subsidiary requirements which apply if the parties so agree or if negotiations fail. However, more narrowly than under the SE-Directive, the subsidiary requirements, only apply if at least one third of the employees of the merging companies (in the SE: only one quarter) have been covered by employee participation regimes.

---

6   Proposal for a Tenth Directive of the Council based on Article 54(3)(g) of the Treaty Concerning Cross-Border Mergers of Public Limited Companies, COM(1984) 727 final, OJ 1985 C 23/11, reproduced and annotated in M. Lutter, *Europäisches Unternehmensrecht*, 257 sqq.; see also W. Däubler, *DB* 1988, 1850–1854.

7   Proposal for a Directive of the European Parliament and of the Council on cross border mergers of companies with share capital of 18 November 2003, COM(2003) 703 final; reference in OJ 2004 C 96/28. See in detail S. Grundmann, *European Company Law*, §29 paras. 1 sqq.; W. Koberski, *Festschrift für Wißmann*, 482 sqq.; S. Maul/C. Teichmann/M. Wenz, *BB* 2003, 2633–2641.

8   ECJ Case C-411/03 *SEVIC* [2005] ECR I-10805.

9   On company law issues see e.g. W. Bayer/J. Schmidt, *NJW* 2006, 401–406; S. Grundmann, *European Company Law*, §29; M. Habersack/D. A. Verse, *Europäisches Gesellschaftsrecht*, §8 paras. 62–66 and (on employee participation) paras. 67–71; J. Oechsler, *NZG* 2006, 161–166.

10   C. Schubert, *RdA* 2007, 9.

---

4.   The Directive on Cross-Border Mergers thus also proves to be a mere safeguarding mechanism, preserving a pre-existing level of employee participation but not providing for a substantive standard of its own. Given that the national law applicable to the (national) company resulting from the merger provides for an employee participation regime, the situation is different from that of the SE or SCE; there is no need to create a specific supra-national regime, either.[11]

5.   As the Directive merely provides for a mechanism for safeguarding the pre-existing level of participation, a cross-border merger opens up the possibility of avoiding a higher level of participation in a similar way to the formation of an SE (see §29 para. 7 above). This may, for example, be relevant for an undertaking that is subject to the German One-Third Participation Act (*Drittel-beteiligungsgesetz*, DrittelbG) and wishes to avoid equal participation under the Co-Determination Act (*Mitbestimmungsgesetz*, MitbestG) that would apply if it surpassed the threshold of 2,000 employees.[12]

II.   SCOPE OF APPLICATION: CROSS-BORDER MERGER

6.   Article 16 CBMD regulates issues of employee participation for the company resulting from the merger. A **cross-border merger** within the meaning of the Directive is a merger of limited liability companies (i.e. not only public limited companies)[13] incorporated under the national law of a Member State and having their registered office, central administration or principal place of business within the Community, provided that at least two of the companies are governed by laws of different Member States, Article 1 CBMD. The **merger** is an operation that can come in one of three different forms:

– as a merger by acquisition, Article 2(2)(a) CBMD;
– as a merger by formation of a new company, Article 2(2)(b) CBMD; or
– as a merger into the parent company, Article 2(2)(c) CBMD.

---

[11]   M. Habersack, *ZHR* 171 (2007), 613, 619 sq.

[12]   S. Brandes, *ZIP* 2008, 2193–2199.

[13]   Article 2(1) CBMD refers to the definitions of Article 1 Disclosure Directive (First Council Directive 68/151/EEC of 9 March 1968 on co-ordination of safeguards which, for the protection of interests of members and others, are required by Member States of companies within the meaning of the second paragraph of Article 58 of the Treaty, with a view to making such safeguards equivalent throughout the Community, OJ 1968 L 65/8 = OJ English Special Edition First Series I, p. 41); in Germany: Aktiengesellschaft (AG), Kommanditgesellschaft auf (KGaA), Gesellschaft mit beschränkter Haftung (GmbH); in the UK: public limited company (PLC), private limited company (Ltd.). On merger with participation of partnerships in the light of freedom of establishment, see S. Herrler, *EuZW* 2007, 295–300.

III. PROCEDURAL PROVISOS AND CONSIDERATION OF EMPLOYEE INTERESTS IN THE MERGER PROCEDURES – OVERVIEW

7.   The merger procedure provides for rules of employee protection in its various stages: procedural provisos with regard to employee participation and supplementary protective rules.

- Thus, pursuant to Article 4(1)(b) and (2) CBMD, it is a **prerequisite** for a merger that the merging companies comply with national provisions and formalities – in particular – with regard to the protection of employees.
- Secondly, already the **common draft terms of a cross-border merger** must contain information on the procedures by which the employee participation rights in the new or surviving company will be determined pursuant to Article 16 CBMD Article 5(j) CBMD.
- Subsequently, the **report** of the management or administrative organ, which primarily explains and justifies the legal and economic aspects of the merger, must also explain the implications of the cross-border merger for employees, Article 7 CBMD. The report should be made available to the employees' representatives or, where there are no such representatives, the employees, not less than one month before the date of the general meeting regarding the merger approval; the employee representatives may state their opinion on the report and such a statement must be appended to the report.[14]
- The general meetings of the merging companies decide on whether to approve the common draft terms of the proposed cross-border merger on the basis of the report (Article 7 CBMD) and an independent expert report (Article (8 CBMD), Article 9(1) CBMD. As issues of employee participation may be of central importance for this decision, Article 9(2) CBMD provides for the possibility that the general meeting of each of the merging companies may make implementation of the cross-border merger conditional upon express ratification by it of the arrangements regarding employee participation in the new or surviving company, Article 9(2) CBMD. This is not a decision on employee participation but a decision on the cross-border merger with a special view to employee participation as a central data.
- Within the framework of a (judicial, notarial or administrative) control of the legality of the merger to be instituted by the national law of the Member States, the respective authority in particular must ensure that the arrangements for employee participation have been determined in accordance with Article 16 CBMD, Article 11(1) sent. 2 CBMD.

---

14   On implementation in Germany (critically) S. Simon/L. Hinrichs, *NZA* 2008, 391–397.

IV. INFORMATION AND CONSULTATION

8. The Directive does **not regulate** issues of information and consultation (or other forms of shop-floor level employee involvement). Recital 12 CBMD merely explains that in this respect, the national law of Member States remains applicable, in particular as determined by the provisions of the Collective Redundancies Directive, the Transfer of Undertakings Directive, the Information and Consultation Framework Directive and the EWC-Directive. In these regards, existing Community (Union) legislation already provided for a Community-wide standard of information and consultations (see §26 paras. 12–36), so that no further regulation was required. Consequently, unlike for the SE, there is no need to reach an agreement on a European Works Council in advance.[15]

V. EMPLOYEE PARTICIPATION

1. Participation pursuant to the Law of the Member State of the Registered Office of the Company Resulting from the Merger

9. The (formal) rule on employee participation is as follows: The national provisions of the Member State, in which the company resulting from the cross-border merger has its registered[16] office, apply, Article 16(1) CBMD (**principle of the state of the registered office**). This (formal) general rule is, however, subject to the exceptions contained in paragraph 2: Where the applicable regime of employee participation thus determined involves a reduction in the level of participation compared to the level in the merging companies – as defined in more detail – then the negotiation model applies ('before and after' principle). As a practical matter, the majority of cases will probably fall under the categories of exceptions of paragraph 2.

2. Agreement on Participation – The Negotiation Model

10. The principle of the Member State of the registered seat pursuant to paragraph 1 does not apply if the level of employee participation in the company resulting from the merger lags behind the level of any of the merging companies in either of three ways, Article 16(2) CBMD (see a) below).[17] In that case, a negotiation procedure applies which follows the structure of the SE negotiation model with some adaptations, Article 16(3) and (4)(see b) below).

---

[15] C. Teichmann, *Konzern* 2007, 89, 91 ('gratifyingly pragmatic' – my translation).

[16] See C. Schubert, *RdA* 2007, 9 sq.

[17] The groups of cases overlap partly – taking account of the disparate prerequisites of employee participation in the different Member States; see C. Teichmann, *Konzern* 2007, 89, 91.

a)   Requirement of Negotiations on Employee Participation

aa)   Employee Participation in one of the Merging Companies

11.   The employee participation regime of the Member State where the registered office of the company resulting from the merger is located does not apply if

–   one of the merging companies had,
–   in the six months before the publication of the common draft terms of the cross-border merger (Article 6 CBMD),
–   an average number of more than 500 employees[18] and
–   was operating under a system of employee participation pursuant to which the employees' representatives had a right to select some or all of the members of the supervisory or administrative organ, Article 16(2) CBMD with Article 2(k) SED.

As is clear from the wording and system of the provision, the threshold number of 500 employees only applies with regard to this category of cases (but not with regard to the following ones).[19,20]

bb)   A Higher Level of Employee Participation in one of the Merging Companies

12.   Secondly, paragraph 1 does not apply where the law of the registered office of the company resulting from the merger does not provide for at least **the same level of participation** as existed in the merging companies, Article 16(2)(a) CBMD. On grounds of practicability and legal certainty, the *level of participation* is formally determined as the proportion of the employees' representatives in the supervisory or administrative organ.[21]

---

[18]   On teleological considerations (safeguarding the national employee participation), the term employee refers to the national laws of the Member States; C. Schubert, *RdA* 2007, 9, 12.

[19]   Thus also S. Brandes, *ZIP* 2008, 2193, 2195; J. Heuschmid, *AuA* 2006, 184, 187; O. Kisker, *RdA* 2006, 206, 210; B. Nagel, *NZG* 2007, 57 und 58; differently C. Schubert, *RdA* 2007, 9, 11 sq. (with teleological considerations).

[20]   As the cases covered by this group are, as regards the safeguarding of employee protection, also covered by the following group of Article 16(2)(a) CBMD (see para. 12), M. Pannier, *EBLR* 2005, 1424, 1437 sq., suggests that the provision is intended to open up the option of negotiations for the resulting company also in the case where it chooses as its seat the Member State with the highest level of employee participation.

[21]   C. Schubert, *RdA* 2007, 9, 10 sq. Following the example of Finland, also emploees' representatives in committees are taken into account; Article 16(2)(b) CBMD; see O. Kisker, *RdA* 2006, 206, 210 sq.; C. Schubert ibid.

cc)   No Unconditional Right to Participation for Employees of
       Establishments in other Member States

13.   Thirdly, the participation regime of the Member State where the registered
office of the company resulting from the merger is located does not apply if it
does not give employees employed in establishments in other Member States an
equal right to exercise rights of participation (active and passive voting rights),
Article 16(2)(b) CBMD;[22] that is, for example, the case in German employee-
participation law.[23] If the Member States extend participation rights to
employees employed in other Member States in light of this provision, this does
not entail an obligation to take those employees into account when calculating
the size of the workforce thresholds giving rise to participation rights under
national law, Article 16(5) CBMD.

b)   Negotiation Procedure

14.   In these categories of cases, a negotiation procedure applies. It is largely
modelled upon the negotiation procedure of the **SE-Directive** to which Article 16
CBMD refers in detail. **Modifications** of the rules of the SE-Directive are mainly
due to three reasons.[24]

–   Some of the provisions of the SE-Directive do not fit as they refer to modes of
    formation other than the merger which is the exclusive focus here.
–   Other provisions are specifically designed for the formation of a supra-
    national company form and thus cannot apply where the company resulting
    from the merger takes a national company form.
–   Finally, Article 16 CBMD only applies with regard to employee participation
    and not to information and consultation which is also covered by the
    SE-Directive.

aa)   The Subsidiary Requirements

15.   Reference to the SE-Directive is initially made with regard to the subsidiary
rules of the Annex. Pursuant to Article 16(3)(h) CBMD, the provisions of Annex
Part 3 (b) SED (see §29 paras. 28–30, 55) apply; it contains the rules on employee
participation (as opposed to those on information and consultation). Pursuant to
Article 16(3)(e) CBMD with Article 7 SED, the subsidiary rules apply if (a) the
parties so agree or (b) do not reach agreement within the negotiation period (§29

---

22   O. Kisker, *RdA* 2006, 206, 211.
23   Territoriality principle; see e.g. S. Brandes, *BB* 2008, 2193, 2196 (S. 2195: 'Discrimination of
      employees abroad in regard of employee participation is the rule in Europe.' – my translation);
      M. Henssler, *RdA* 2005, 330, 331 sq.; T. Raiser, *Unternehmensmitbestimmung vor dem
      Hintergrund europarechtlicher Entwicklungen*, B 62.
24   O. Kisker, *RdA* 2006, 206, 209 sq.

para. 15). The additional requirement of Article 7(2) SED on the level of employee participation in the participating (merging) companies only fit the purposes of the Cross-Border Merger Directive to the extent that they concern formation by way of merger (subparagraph 1(b)); the provisions on transformation (subparagraph 2(a)) and formation of a holding or subsidiary SE (subparagraph 2(c)) are consequently not referred to. The provision of Article 7(2)(1)(b) SED is further modified (and restricted) in that it only applies where one third (33 1/3%) of the employees of the merging companies had been subject to participation (as opposed to the participation threshold of one quarter [25%] that applies with regard to the SE; §29 para. 53).[25]

bb) Dispensability of Negotiations

16. As a peculiarity in comparison to the provisions in the SE-Directive, the Cross-Border Merger Directive gives the organs of the merging companies an option to avoid negotiations and decide to directly apply the subsidiary requirements, Article 16(4)(a) CBMD. Already under the SE-Directive, negotiations are being conducted 'in the shadow of the subsidiary requirements'. Given that the subsidiary requirements apply if the parties do not reach agreement, they form a minimum standard of employee participation (see §29 para. 15). It may thus appear only consequential to give the employer-side the possibility not to spend any time and money and to opt directly for the subsidiary requirements.[26] It should not be overlooked, though, that this entails a different model of cooperation. If negotiations are dispensable, this means that the other party (the employee-side as represented by the special negotiating body) and the chances of negotiated participation are not being taken as seriously.

cc) Procedures for the Negotiation of Employee Participation

17. With regard to the negotiation procedures, Article 16(3) CBMD largely refers to the provisions of the SE-Directive, namely in lit. a) with regard to:

– **initiation** of procedures with the employer-side (Article 3(1) SED; see §29 paras. 31 sq.);[27]
– the creation of a **special negotiating body** for the purposes of the negotiations and the election or appointment of its members pursuant to the rules of the national law (Article 3(2) SED; see §29 paras. 35 sq.);

---

25   C. Teichmann, *Konzern* 2007, 89, 92. Critically W. Koberski, *Festschrift für Wißmann,* 488. O. Kisker, *RdA* 2006, 206, 209, finds a certain inconsistency in the fact that, pursuant to Article 16(3)(a) CBMD, the 25% requirement of Article 3(4)(1) indent 1 SED applies unmodified (and has not been raised to one third).

26   S. Brandes, *ZIP* 2008, 2193, 2194, 2196 sq.; B. Nagel, *NZG* 2007, 57, 58; C. Teichmann, *Konzern* 2007, 89, 92.

27   See S. Lunk/L. Hinrichs, *NZA* 2007, 773, 775 sq.

- the **objective of negotiations** of concluding a written agreement on employee participation (Article 3(3) SED; see §29 para. 39);
- the **majority requirements** for decisions in the special negotiating body (Article 3(4) SED; except for the provision of subparagraph 1 indent 2 which is concerned with the formation of a holding or subsidiary SE and thus does not fit; see §29 paras. 39 sq.); in particular, the special negotiating body may decide on a reduction of the level of participation only with two thirds of the votes;
- the right to request the assistance of **experts** (Article 3(5) SED; see §29 para. 43); and
- the **costs** of the representative body (Article 3(7) SED; see §29 para. 44).

18. The Cross-Border Merger Directive does not refer to Article 3(5) SED pursuant to which the subsidiary requirements of the Annex do not apply if the special negotiating body decides **not to commence or to terminate negotiations**. Instead, Article 16(4)(b) CBMD requires quora for these decisions, analogous to those of the SE-Directive, and provides that as a consequence of such a decision, the employee participation regime of the law of the Member State where the company resulting from the merger has its registered office applies.

19. Furthermore, the provisions of the SE-Directive on the following subjects also apply to negotiations under the CBMD:

- **duty to negotiate**, Article 16(3)(b) CBMD with Article 4(1) SED (see §29 para. 37);
- **duration of negotiations**, Article 16(3)(c) CBMD with Article 5 SED (see §29 para. 37); and
- **applicable law**, Article 16(3)(d) CBMD with Article 6 SED (see §29 para. 34).

dd) CONTENT OF THE AGREEMENT

20. With regard to the content of the agreement, Article 16(3)(b) CBMD refers to the provisions of the SE-Directive concerned with employee participation (as opposed to information and consultation): Article 4(2)(a), g) and (h) SED (see §29 para. 46 above). Here, too, the principle of the **autonomy of the parties** applies.[28]

21. Article 16(4)(c) CBMD provides for the additional implementation option to **limit the proportion of employee representatives** in the *administrative organ* (i.e. in the single-tier system; cf. §29 para. 14 above) of the company resulting

---

[28] Its limits are as controversial here as in the case of the SED; see for the CBMD C. Teichmann, *Konzern* 2007, 89, 95 sq.; in more detail also §29 paras. 45–47 with further references.

from the cross-border merger. This may not, where one of the merging companies was governed by a one-third participation in the supervisory or administrative board, lead to a lower level of participation. As a bottom line, this means that the equal participation of employees in one of the merging companies, as it may apply under the two-tier system, does not have to be continued if the company resulting from the merger adopts a single-tier structure. The provision takes account of the fact that employee participation in the administrative board is of a qualitatively higher intensity than in the supervisory board.[29]

22. As employee participation takes place at the board level, it must be compatible with the company's organisation. As regards the SE, any discrepancy is to be resolved by a '**primacy of the participation agreement**' (Article 12(4) SER; see §29 paras. 49 sq. above). Where, under the negotiation procedure in the cases of Article 16(2) CBMD, one of the merging companies was governed by a regime of employee participation which, pursuant to the agreement or the subsidiary requirements, is to be transposed to the company resulting from the merger, Article 16(2) CBMD provides that the company resulting from the merger is obliged to take a legal form allowing for the exercise of the ensuing participation rights.

23. The principles of cooperation, again, follow the provisions of the SE-Directive, namely with regard to **confidentiality** (Article 16(3)(f) CBMD with Article 8 SED; see §29 paras 56 sq. above) and with regard to **protection of the employees' representatives** (Article 16(3)(f) CBMD with Article 10 SED; see §29 para. 58 above).

ee)   ENFORCEMENT THROUGH REGISTRATION PROCESS

24. As for the SE, in order to enforce these procedural requirements for a cross-border merger, the legislator has provided for a sanction in connection with registration: The company resulting from the merger may not be registered unless an agreement on participation has been concluded or the special negotiating body has decided not to commence or to terminate negotiations or the negotiation period has expired without the parties' reaching agreement, Article 16(3) CBMD with Article 12(2)-(4) SER (see §29 para. 32).

ff)   SAFEGUARDING EXISTING STANDARDS FOR THREE YEARS

25. Finally, the Directive provides for a minimum safeguarding of the participation regime thus determined in light of subsequent structural changes

---

[29]   J. Heuschmid, AuA 2006, 184, 188; W. Koberski, *Festschrift für Wißmann,* 488 ('acceptable'; 'just tenable' – my translation); O. Kisker, *RdA* 2006, 206, 210; C. Teichmann, *Konzern* 2007, 89, 92 sq.

in the company resulting from the merger. When the company resulting from the cross-border merger is governed by an employee participation system, it is obliged to ensure that the employees' participation rights will be preserved in the event of **subsequent domestic mergers** for a period of three years by applying mutatis mutandis the rules of Article 16 CBMD (negotiation procedure where the level of participation is being reduced; supplementary provisions; quora for decisions), Article 16(7) CBMD.[30] The provision imposes certain safeguards of existing rights but also prevents a special risk of misuse of the procedure.

26. However, Article 16(3) CBMD does not refer to the general provision against misuse in Article 11 SED (see §29 paras. 59 sq. above).[31] Given that the legislator was fully aware of the SE-Directive and referred to it specifically and in detail, this omission should be considered to constitute a deliberate decision. Instead of a general and unspecific prohibition of misuse, the legislator preferred a concrete and formal provision for safeguarding the rights of employees (for a limited period of time).[32]

VI. IMPLEMENTATION

27. In **Germany** the company law rules of the Directive were implemented by the amendment of the Transformation Act (*Umwandlungsgesetz*, UmwG).[33] The rules on employee participation were implemented by the Act on Employee Participation in the case of Cross-Border Mergers (*Gesetz über die Mitbestimmung der Arbeitnehmer bei einer grenzüberschreitenden Verschmelzung*, MgVG)[34].[35] In the **United Kingdom**, the Companies (Cross-Border Mergers) Regulations 2007 implement the Directive.[36] The employee participation rules can be found in Part 4 (ss. 22–64).

---

[30] See e.g. M. Habersack, *ZHR* 171 (2007), 613, 637–639; C. Teichmann, *Konzern* 2007, 89, 93, 96 sq.

[31] Critically e.g. O. Kisker, *RdA* 2006, 206, 210.

[32] C. Teichmann, *Konzern* 2007, 89, 97.

[33] Zweites Gesetz zur Änderung des Umwandlungsgesetzes of 19 April 2007, BGBl. 2007 I, 542. The German Transformation Act is available at www.gesetze-im-internet.de/bundesrecht/umwg_1995/gesamt.pdf.

[34] Gesetz über die Mitbestimmung der Arbeitnehmer bei einer grenzüberschreitenden Verschmelzung of 21 December 2006, BGBl. 2006 I, 3332; available at www.gesetze-im-internet.de/bundesrecht/mgvg/gesamt.pdf.

[35] C. Schubert, *RdA* 2007, 9–17 (pointing out some implementation deficits); S. Lunk/L. Hinrichs, *NZA* 2007, 773–780; N. Krause/M. Janko, *BB* 2007, 2194–2197; G. Kleinsorge, in B. Nagel/G. Freis/G. Kleinsorge (eds.), *Beteiligung der Arbeitnehmer im Unternehmen auf der Grundlage des europäischen Rechts*, 2nd edn. (Berlin: de Gruyter, 2009), Einf MgVG paras. 24–42.

[36] SI 2007/2974; also available at www.legislation.gov.uk/uksi/2007/2974/contents/made.

§31. CROSS-BORDER TRANSFER OF THE REGISTERED OFFICE AND EMPLOYEE PARTICIPATION

CONTENT

Bibliography[1]:

W. Bayer/J. Schmidt, 'Aktuelle Entwicklungen im Europäischen Gesellschaftsrecht', *BB* 2008, 454–460; R. R. Drury, 'Migrating Companies', *E.L. Rev.* 24 (1999), 354–372; H. Eidenmüller, 'Mobilität und Restrukturierung von Unternehmen im Binnenmarkt – Entwicklungsperspektiven des europäischen Gesellschaftsrechts im Schnittfeld von Gemeinschaftsgesetzgeber und EuGH', *JZ* 2004, 24–33; B. Großfeld/D. Jasper, 'Identitätswahrende Sitzverlegung und Fusion von Kapitalgesellschaften in die Bundesrepublik Deutschland', *RabelsZ* 53 (1989), 52–71; M. Heinze, 'Arbeitsrechtliche Probleme bei der grenzüberschreitenden Sitzverlegung in der Europäischen Gemeinschaft', *ZGR* 1999, 54–70; J. Hoffmann, 'Neue Möglichkeiten zur identitätswahrenden Sitzverlegung in Europa – Der Richtlinienvorentwurf zur Verlegung des Gesellschaftssitzes innerhalb der EU', *ZHR* 164 (2000) 43–66; O. Kisker, 'Unternehmerische Mitbestimmung in der Europäischen Gesellschaft, der Europäischen Genossenschaft und bei grenzüberschreitender Verschmelzung im Vergleich', *RdA* 2006, 206–212; S. Leible, 'Niederlassungsfreiheit und Sitzverlegungsrichtlinie', *ZGR* 2004, 531–558; S. Leible, 'Warten auf die Sitzverlegungsrichtlinie', in H. Altmeppen/H. Fitz/H. Honsell (eds.), *Festschrift für Günter H. Roth* (Munich: C.H. Beck, 2011), 447–460; H.-W. Neye, 'Die Vorstellungen der Bundesregierung zum Vorschlag einer 14. Richtlinie', *ZGR* 1999, 13–19; S. Rammeloo, 'Cross-border company mobility and the Proposal for a 14th EC Company Law Directive: "Daily Mail" surmounted', *MJ* 2 (1999), 105–110; S. Rammeloo, *Corporations in Private International Law – A European Perspective* (Oxford/New York: Oxford University Press, 2001); E. Vaccaro, 'Transfer of Seat and Freedom of Establishment in European Company Law', *EBLR* 2005, 1348–1365; H. Wicke, 'Mobilität europäischer Kapitalgesellschaften am Vorabend der 14. gesellschaftsrechtlichen Richtlinie', *GPR* 2010, 238–243; see also the bibliography in §3 before para. 4.; Commission website: http://ec.europa.eu/internal_market/company/seat-transfer/index_en.htm.

---

[1]   For the company law bibliography, see e.g. S. Grundmann, *European Company Law*, bibliography to §27; M. Habersack/D. A. Verse, *Europäisches Gesellschaftsrecht*, 4th edn. (Munich: C.H. Beck, 2011), §4 paras. 30 sq. (notes 119 sqq.); and the contributions by G. Di Marco, H.-W. Neye, K. Schmidt, H.-J. Priester, H.F. Hügel, H. Rajak, E. Wymeersch und L. Timmermann, *ZGR* 1999, 3–156.

Cases: (see also the references in §3 before para. 78)

ECJ Case C-79/85 *Segers* [1986] ECR 2375; ECJ Case C-81/87 *Daily Mail* [1988] ECR 5483; ECJ Case C-212/97 *Centros* [1999] ECR I-1459; ECJ Case C-208/00 *Überseering* [2002] ECR I-9919; ECJ Case C-167/01 *Inspire Art* [2003] ECR I-10155; ECJ Case C-411/03 *SEVIC* [2005] ECR I-10805; ECJ Case C-210/06 *Cartesio* [2008] ECR I-9641.

I. BACKGROUND IN COMPANY LAW

1. A cross-border transfer of the registered office first raises issues of **international private company law and substantive company law.** This may – depending upon the detail of the applicable national law – result in restrictions for companies intending to move into or move out of a Member State.[2] In the light of the freedom of establishment (Article 49 TFEU), such restrictions must meet different requirements, depending upon whether they apply to the transfer of the (factual) central administration or place of business of the company or its registered office.[3]

- *Transfer of the de facto head office* means that the company retains its registered office in the state of incorporation but establishes its central administration in another Member State. For example, a limited company incorporated under the law of the UK transfers its central administration to Düsseldorf. Under the freedom of establishment, national law may, in principle, not restrict this possibility. Restrictions with regard to the *procedure* of transfer are admissible only to the extent that they are necessary for the fulfilment of mandatory requirements of public interest (see in detail §3 paras. 88–90 above).
- This should be distinguished from the *transfer of a company's registered office* to another Member State, either subjecting itself to the law of the other Member State or continuing to rely upon the law of the Member State of incorporation. For example, an English limited company intends to transfer its registered office without dissolution, either choosing a German company form or maintaining the limited company form. Again, the national law of Member States may provide for restrictions. The – rather disparate – national legal systems either do not allow for a transfer of the registered office in the first place or require dissolution of the foreign company in the Member State

---

2   Cf. e.g. Commission, Pre-Draft of proposal for a 14th Company Law Directive on the cross-border transfer of the registered office or the de facto head office of a company from one member states to another of 20 April 1997 (internal Doc XV/6002/97), also reproduced in English (though without the explanatory memorandum) in S. Rammeloo, *Corporations in Private International Law*, 296–300, and in German in *ZIP* 1997, 1721–1724; *ZGR* 1999, 157–164, explanation sub A) I.

3   S. Leible, *ZGR* 2004, 531, 532–537.

of departure and re-incorporation in the Member State of destination. To enable companies to transfer their registered office requires more than removing restrictions, it necessitates legal approximation and coordination.[4]

2. The adoption of a 14th company law **Directive on the Cross-border Transfer of the Registered Seat** has thus long been an urgent *desideratum* in company law.[5] The harmonisation project has, however, not gone beyond a 1997 **draft proposal**[6] and consultation which was undertaken in 2002 and 2004.[7] While the adoption of the Directive had still been on the Commission's 2003 Action Plan[8] and had also been called for by the European Parliament[9], Commissioner *McCreevy* receded from the project after a 2007 impact assessment.[10,11] The Commissioner considered that the fundamental freedoms together with the Branches Directive[12] provided a sufficient legal framework for mobility of companies in the EU. The European Parliament maintains that there is a need for European legislation and has, in a resolution of March 2009, requested the Commission to submit a legislative proposal for a directive,[13]

---

4   S. Leible, *ZGR* 2004, 531, 534–537. See also Commission, Pre-Draft of proposal for a 14th Company Law Directive on the cross-border transfer of the registered office or the de facto head office of a company from one member states to another of 20 April 1997 (internal Doc. XV/6002/97), also reproduced (though without the explanatory memorandum) in S. Rameloo (ed.), *Corporations in Private International Law,* 296 sqq, explanation sub A) I.: 'This heterogeneity is one of the reasons why, for the companies, the national legal orders represent a closed and self-contained universe, at least in the case where they intend to transfer their seat to another Member State.' – my translation.

5   On the development, see e.g. S. Grundmann, *European Company Law,* §27 paras. 1 sq.; S. Leible, *ZGR* 2004, 531, 537–539. See also the Commission website http://ec.europa.eu/ internal_market/company/seat-transfer/index_en.htm.

6   Commission, Pre-Draft of proposal for a 14th Company Law Directive on the cross-border transfer of the registered office or the de facto head office of a company from one member states to another of 20 April 1997 (internal Doc XV/6002/97), also reproduced in English in S. Rammeloo, *Corporations in Private International Law* (Oxford/New York: Oxford University Press, 2001), 297–300, and in German in *ZIP* 1997, 1721–1724; *ZGR* 1999, 157–164.

7   http://ec.europa.eu/internal_market/company/seat-transfer/index_en.htm.

8   Communication from the Commission to the Council and the European Parliament 'Modernising Company Law and Enhancing Corporate Governance in the European Union – A Plan to Move Forward', COM(2003) 284 final, 23 (sub 3.4).

9   European Parliament resolution on recent developments and prospects in relation to company law (2006/2051(INI)), OJ 2006 C 303E/114.

10   Impact assessment on the Directive on the cross-border transfer of registered office, SEC(2007) 1707.

11   Speech by Commissioner McCreevy at the European Parliament's Legal Affairs Committee of 3 October 2007, SPEECH/07/592, http://europa.eu/rapid/pressReleasesAction. do?reference=SPEECH/07/592. See also W. Bayer/J. Schmidt, *BB* 2008, 454, 458.

12   Eleventh Council Directive 89/666/EEC of 21 December 1989 concerning disclosure requirements in respect of branches opened in a Member State by certain types of company governed by the law of another state, OJ 1989 L 395/36.

13   European Parliament resolution of 10 March 2009 with recommendations to the Commission on the cross-border transfer of the registered office of a company (2008/2196(INI)), P6_

though to no avail. Scholars urge that, notwithstanding the Court's jurisprudence on freedom of establishment, there is still a need for harmonisation for practical (legal certainty) and legal reasons.[14]

3. The Commission's most recent plans dating from 2004 distinguished between the two forms of transfer or the *de facto* head office on the one hand and of the registered office on the other for purposes of approximation of laws. In light of the Court's jurisprudence on freedom of establishment, they raise different questions (see para. 1 above).

– Transfer of the *de facto* head office in principle continues to be possible even without any approximation of national laws. The right to move into another Member State is guaranteed by the freedom of establishment. Here too, though, an approximation of laws would be desirable on grounds of legal certainty, given that the Member States may maintain national restrictions to the extent that they are justified as necessary for the protection of mandatory requirements of public interest.[15] Furthermore, the Court of Justice has considered that freedom of establishment does not 'as [Union] law now stands' fully comprise the freedom to leave the home Member State (see §3 para. 80 above).
– Cross-border transfer of the registered office, however, requires regulation in Union law; it would only be made possible by an approximation of national laws. The Commission had most recently focussed its endeavours on regulating the cross-border transfer of the registered office.

4. As a matter of company law, the central objective is to allow for a **transfer of the registered seat while maintaining the company's legal identity**, that is, without requiring liquidation and reincorporation, even though the destination Member State may require certain amendments to the company statutes so as to ensure compatibility with certain national requirements of company law. The Member State of departure may not remove the company from the company register or withdraw its legal capacity before the company is registered in the Member State of destination. In substance, the transfer of the company seat constitutes a type of structural change or transformation of the company[16] from a company type of the Member State of departure to a company type of the Member State of destination. The proceedings are designed accordingly.

TA(2009)0086, also available at www.europarl.europa.eu/sides/getDoc.do?pubRef=-//EP//TEXT+TA+20090310+ITEMS+DOC+XML+V0//EN&language=EN#BKMD-5.
[14]   See recently S. Leible, *Festschrift für G. H. Roth*, 447–460.
[15]   To the same effect O. Kisker, *RdA* 2006, 206, 212; S. Leible, *ZGR* 2004, 531, 546 sq.; see also the references §3 para. 84 above.
[16]   S. Grundmann, *European Company Law*, §27 para. 11.

II. EMPLOYEE PARTICIPATION

5. If the cross-border transfer of the company seat is comparable to a transformation, then it raises similar questions of employee participation as the formation of an SE by way of transformation.[17] There is a risk of a 'flight from employee participation'; a company could shake off the higher level of employee participation by transferring its registered office to another Member State.[18]

6. It is not by chance, then, that the Commission has once again followed the **negotiation model of the SE** (see §29 above) and the Cross-border Merger Directive (see §30 above).[19] As in the Cross-border Merger Directive, the **principle of the Member State of the registered office** is the starting point: The employee participation regime of the Member State where the registered office is located following the transfer, i.e. the Member State of destination, applies. If, however, the level of employee participation required in the Member State of destination lags behind that of the Member State of departure, then the negotiation model applies. Again, negotiations take place 'in the shadow of the subsidiary requirements'. The subsidiary requirements apply if the parties so agree (or possibly also where the employer-side so chooses unilaterally, so as to avoid lengthy and costly negotiations), they are primarily intended to apply, though, if the parties do not reach agreement within the negotiation period. Taking the SE-Directive as a model, it would be consequential to regard the cross-border transfer of the company seat equivalent to a transformation of the company type and thus strictly apply the 'before and after' principle.

7. The case of a cross-border transfer of the company is different from the establishment of an SE, though, in that, like in the cross-border merger, it seeks to form a *national company type* rather than a supra-national company type. If this national company type is subjected to the higher level of employee participation of the Member State of departure, it is effectively placed at a

---

17 M. Fuchs, in M. Fuchs/F. Marhold (eds.), *Europäisches Arbeitsrecht*, 353. See also the position of ETUC www.etuc.org/a/249 and the information provided by ETUI www.worker-participation.eu/Company-Law-and-CG/Company-Law/Transfer-of-seat-14th.

18 Here – as in the case of the *Societas Europaea* – the issue of employee involvement proved to be an obstacle to the introduction of the new company form; see e.g. B. Großfeld/D. Jasper, *RabelsZ* 53 (1989), 52, 64; J. Hoffmann, *ZHR* 164 (2000), 43, 61 sq.; H.-W. Neye, *ZGR* 1999, 13, 17.

19 Approving in principle (but critical to the perpetuation of the highest level of employee involvement) M. Heinze, *ZGR* 1999, 54, 61 sqq.; also J. Hoffmann, *ZHR* 164 (2000), 43, 61 sq.; H.-W. Neye, *ZGR* 1999, 13, 17 sq. Critically H. Eidenmüller, *JZ* 2004, 24, 32, criticising the proposal (including its employee involvement model) as anti-competitive and an intrusion into the sovereignty of the Member States.

disadvantage in comparison to other companies of the same type (a 'second-class Ltd').[20] From a practical perspective, implementation of the 'before and after' principle is, however, easier than in the case of the cross-border merger of *two or more* companies.[21]

---

[20]   M. Fuchs, in M. Fuchs/F. Marhold (eds.), *Europäisches Arbeitsrecht,* 353.
[21]   S. Grundmann, *European Company Law,* §27 para. 28.

§32. EMPLOYEE INVOLVEMENT IN THE EUROPEAN PRIVATE COMPANY

CONTENT

Bibliography:

J. Bormann/L. Böttcher, 'Vermeidungsstrategien bei der unternehmerischen Mitbestimmung in der SPE auf der Grundlage des ungarischen Kompromissvorschlags', *NZG* 2011, 411–416; J. Boucourechliev (ed.), *Propositions pour une société fermée européenne* (Luxembourg: Office des Publications Officielles des Communautés Européennes, 1997); J. Boucourechliev, *Pour une s.a.r.l. européenne: étude du C.R.E.D.A.* (Paris: Presses Universitaires de France, 1973); J. Boucourechliev/P. Hommelhoff (eds.), *Vorschläge für eine Europäische Privatgesellschaft – Strukturelemente einer kapitalmarktfernen europäischen Gesellschaftsform* (Cologne: Otto Schmidt, 1999); N. Bruun, 'Employees' Participation Rights and Business Restructuring', *EELJ* 1 (2011), 27–47; A. F. M. Dorresteijn/O. Uziahu-Santcroos, 'The Societas Privata Europaea under the

Magnifying Glass (Part 2)', *ECL* 6 (2009), 152–159; R. Drury/A. Hicks, 'The Proposal for a European Private Company', *J.B.L.* 1999, 429–451; S. Fischer, 'Brücken zur Europäischen Privatgesellschaft', *ZEuP* 2004, 737–761; G. Forst, 'Arbeitnehmerbeteiligung im Verordnungsvorschlag für eine Europäische Privatgesellschaft (SPE)', *ZESAR* 2009, 261–266; D. Helms, *Die Europäische Privatgesellschaft – Rechtliche Strukturen und Regelungsprobleme einer supranationalen Gesellschaft des Gemeinschaftsrechts* (Cologne: Otto Schmidt, 1998); W. Hadding/E. Kießling, 'Die Europäische Privatgesellschaft (Societas Europaea Privata – SPE)', *WM* 2009, 145–158; High-Level Group of Company Law Experts (Winter-Group), *A Modern Regulatory Framework for Company Law in Europe* (2002), available at: http://ec.europa.eu/internal_market/company/docs/modern/report_en.pdf.; P. Hommelhoff, *Die "Europäische Privatgesellschaft" am Beginn ihrer Normierung* (Bonn: Zentrum für Europäisches Wirtschaftsrecht, 2008); P. Hommelhoff, 'Die Gesetzgebungsinitiative des Europäischen Parlaments zur Europäischen Privatgesellschaft', in id./P. Rawert/K. Schmidt (eds.), *Festschrift für Hans-Joachim Priester* (Cologne: Otto Schmidt, 2007) 245–257; P. Hommelhoff, 'SPE-Mitbestimmung', *ZEuP* 2011, 7–40; P. Hommelhoff/D. Helms (eds.), *Neue Wege in die Europäischen Privatgesellschaft* (Cologne: Otto Schmidt, 2001); P. Hommelhoff/C. Teichmann, 'Auf dem Weg zur Europäischen Privatgesellschaft (SPE)', *DStR* 2008, 925–933; P. Hommelhoff/C. Teichmann, 'Die SPE vor dem Gipfelsturm – Zum Kompromissvorschlag der schwedischen EU-Ratspräsidentschaft', *GmbHR* 2010, 337–349; W. Koberski/J. Heuschmid, 'Die Beteiligung der Arbeitnehmer in der Europäischen Privatgesellschaft – Eine kritische Zwischenbilanz', *RdA* 2010, 207–216; R. Krause, 'Die Stellung von KMU im europäischen Gesellschaftsrecht', *EuZW* 2003, 747–751; R. Krause, 'Zum Vorhaben einer Europäischen Privatgesellschaft', in R. Krause/W. Veelken/K. Vieweg (eds.), *Recht der Wirtschaft und der Arbeit in Europa – Gedächtnisschrift für Wolfgang Blomeyer* (Berlin: Duncker & Humblot, 2004), 387–414; S. Maul/V. Röhricht, 'Die Europäische Privatgesellschaft – Überblick über eine neue supranationale Rechtsform', *BB* 2008, 1574–1579; K. Noussia, 'European Private Company ("Societas Privata Europaea")', *B.L.I.* 11 (2010) 277–296; O. Vossius, 'Die Europäische Privatgesellschaft – Societas Europaea Privata', *EWS* 2007, 438–444; see also the collection of materials at www.europeanprivatecompany.eu.

I. ISSUES AND OVERVIEW

1. A Supra-National Company-Structure for Small and Medium-Sized Undertakings

1. In creating the European Company (see §29 above), the Union has generated a supra-national company form designed, and of interest, primarily for large enterprises. For some time now, practitioners and scholars have felt that there is a need for a European company type for small and medium sized enterprises, a European limited liability company with uniform structures throughout the Union: a **European Private Company** (*Socieatas Europaea Privata,* SPE).[1]

---

[1]   See in detail R. Drury/A. Hicks, *J.B.L.* 1999, 429, 433 sqq.; W. Hadding, *WM* 2009, 145–158; P. Hommelhoff/C. Teichmann, *DStR* 2008, 925–928; S. Grundmann, *European Company Law,*

Its proponents argue that such company type would receive greater acceptance in the internal market and that it could lead to savings for its owners.[2] A 'European Limited' seems all the more desirable as most of the approximation of laws in the area of company law is primarily aimed at public limited companies and does not apply to small company forms to the same extent.[3]

2. Competence

2. Following the Union's experiences with the *Societas Europaea* and the *Societas Cooperativa Europaea* (see §29 para. 5 above), an SPE-Regulation can only be based upon the flexibility clause of Article 352 TFEU.[4] Consequently, it can only be adopted if the Member States reach unanimous support in the Council.

3. Development

3. The first suggestions to create such a type of company were made by the Paris Chamber of Industry and Commerce in the 1970s.[5] The project was taken up again by scholars and practitioners in the 1990s, which led to a 1998 draft proposal which had been prepared on the basis of a private initiative.[6] The Commission adopted the idea in its 2003 Action Plan;[7] the European Parliament embraced the project as well.[8]

4. In the summer of **2008**, the Commission presented an initial **Proposal** for a Council Regulation on the Statute for a European Private Company (SPE-Regulation Proposal 2008, SPER-P2008).[9] The Commission's proposal met with much sympathy and support, but also with considerable opposition. As was the

---

§34 paras. 25–34. On the development, see e.g. D. Helms, *Die Europäische Privatgesellschaft* (1998); R. Krause, *Gedächtnisschrift für Blomeyer,* 387–391; S. Grundmann, *European Company Law,* §34 para. 25. High-Level Group of Company Law Experts (Winter-Group), *A Modern Regulatory Framework for Company Law in Europe* (2002), 123 sq., available at: http://ec.europa.eu/internal_market/company/docs/modern/report_en.pdf.

2   W. Hadding, *WM* 2009, 145 sq.; O. Vossius, *EWS* 2007, 438–444.

3   R. Krause, *EuZW* 2003, 747 sq., 749.

4   G. Forst, *ZESAR* 2009, 261.

5   See J. Boucourechliev, *Pour une s.a.r.l. européenne.*

6   J. Boucourechliev/P. Hommelhoff (eds.), *Vorschläge für eine europäische Privatgesellschaft;* available at www.etudes.ccip.fr/dossiers/spe/de/index.html.

7   Communication from the Commission to the Council and the European Parliament 'Modernising Company Law and Enhancing Corporate Governance in the European Union – A Plan to Move Forward' of 21 May 2003, COM(2003) 284 final, 25 sq. (sub 3.5); on this R. Krause, *EuZW* 2003, 747, 750 sq.

8   European Parliament Resolution with Recommendations to the Commission on the European Private Company Statute of 1 February 2007, OJ 2007 C 250E/111; see P. Hommelhoff, *Festschrift für Priester,* 245–257.

9   Proposal for a Council Regulation on the statute for a European private company of 25 June 2008, COM(2008) 396 final.

---

case with the European Company, much of the opposition stemmed from a concern that the new company form could provide a vehicle for circumvention of employee participation.[10]

5. The European Parliament and Council have made an effort to overcome the ensuing halt in proceedings and have proposed various **compromises**.[11]

– On 10 March **2009**, the **European Parliament** adopted a resolution suggesting numerous amendments concerning, in particular, the company seat and employee involvement.[12]
– On 27 November **2009**, the **Swedish Council presidency** proposed a compromise for the Competitiveness Council (3/4 December 2009).[13] This proposal (SPE-Regulation Proposal 2009, SPER-P2009) also identified the issues of company seat and employee rights as the main matters which were outstanding and proposed changes accordingly.
– A new compromise was proposed under the **Hungarian presidency** on 23 May **2011** (SPE-Regulation Proposal 2011, SPER-P2011).[14] The controversial issues remained the same – seat and employee participation; and the new proposal provides further fine-tuning.

However, none of these proposals could secure the necessary support of all Member States in the Council.

II. OVERVIEW OF COMPANY LAW ISSUES

6. The Commission proposes to adopt a statute for a European Private Company in the form of a regulation containing a comprehensive company statute. The company type is a 'private company'. In line with the *Societas Europaea,* it is called *Societas Europaea Privata,* Article 1 SPER-P2008. The designation as 'European' highlights that it is another supra-national company

---

[10] See e.g. N. Bruun, *EELJ* 2 (2011), 27, 36.

[11] For an excellent survey and a thorough discussion of the regulatory and policy issues involved, comparing the original Commission proposal, the legislative resolution of the European Parliament and the Council proposal of 2009, see P. Hommelhoff, *ZEuP* 2011, 7–40.

[12] European Parliament legislative resolution of 10 March 2009 on the proposal for a Council regulation on the Statute for a European private company (COM(2008) 396), P6_TA(2009)0094, available at www.europarl.europa.eu/sides/getDoc.do?pubRef=-//EP//TEXT+TA+P6-TA-2009-0094+0+DOC+XML+V0//EN. On this, see A. F. M. Dorresteijn/O. Uziahu-Santcroos, *ECL* 6 (2009), 152–159.

[13] Revised Presidency compromise for a Council Regulation on a European Private Company, 16115/09, ADD1, DRS 71, SOC 711; also available at http://register.consilium.europa.eu/pdf/en/09/st16/st16115-ad01.en09.pdf.

[14] Revised Presidency compromise text – Proposal for a Council Regulation on a European Private Company, 10611/11, DRS 84, SOC 432; also available at http://register.consilium.europa.eu/pdf/en/11/st10/st10611.en11.pdf.

type. The designation as 'private' follows the English and French language usage[15] and indicates that the company is designed for a 'closed circle of members' (*société fermée européenne*)[16]: The SPE is designed as a company type outside the capital market, the shares of which are tradable only with restrictions, controlled by the shareholders. This concept makes it possible to give the shareholders far-reaching autonomy in respect of the company's statutes (as opposed to the mandatory rules which apply to the public limited company).

7. The **company seat** is of considerable importance for employee participation. Pursuant to Article 7(1) SPER-P2008, an SPE must have its registered office and its central administration or principal place of business in the Community. Yet, paragraph 2 of the provision provides that there is no obligation to have both, central administration or principal place of business *in the same Member State* as the registered office. The proposals of 2009 and 2011 have not maintained this flexibility. Article 7(2) SPER-P2009 provides that the registered office and the central administration may not be dislocated for a period of two years; thereafter, the admissibility of a separation is a matter of the applicable national law. And the 2011 compromise proposal leaves the issue to be determined entirely by reference to the applicable national law.

III. OVERVIEW OF EMPLOYEE PARTICIPATION

1. Issues of Employee Participation

8. The Commission considered these issues to be less pressing in the case of the SPE as only few Member States provide for employee participation in small undertakings, e.g. Sweden and Denmark.[17] At the same time, the fact that employee participation in limited company structures varies considerably with regard to (1) the applicable thresholds (e.g. Sweden: from 25 employees, Denmark: from 35 employees, Finland from 150 employees, Hungary from 200, Austria from 300 employees, Germany from 500 employees)[18] and (2) the 'level' of participation (e.g. in Denmark and Germany one third, in Finland one quarter, in Sweden, irrespective of the size of the supervisory organ two employee representatives in undertakings of up to 1,000 employees).[19]

---

[15]   P. Hommelhoff/C. Teichmann, *DStR* 2008, 925, 929.

[16]   See the designation by Boucourechliev (ed.), *Propositions pour une société fermée européenne*.

[17]   COM(2008) 396 final, 10.

[18]   Cf. P. Hommelhoff, *ZEuP* 2011, 7, 24.

[19]   See T. Baums/P. Ulmer (eds.), *Unternehmens-Mitbestimmung der Arbeitnehmer im Recht der EU-Mitgliedstaaten* (Heidelberg: Recht und Wirtschaft, 2004); P. Hommelhoff, *ZEuP* 2011, 7, 20 with note 44.

The disparate regulatory levels may be an incentive for legal arbitrage.[20] Issues of employee participation may occur at various stages:

- formation of an SPE raises particular issues of circumvention of national employee participation rules where (as in the original Commission proposal) the principal place of business and the registered company seat may be located in different Member States (see para. 7 above);
- formation of an SPE with employees in different Member States which provide for different levels of employee participation;
- a cross-border transfer of the company seat;
- a subsequent change of circumstances which are relevant for the determination of employee participation.

9. Several **models** for the determination of employee participation have been discussed in the course of the preparation of the (private and official) proposals:[21]

(1) Employee participation could be governed exclusively by the applicable law of the Member States.
(2) The SPE as a company type could be limited to undertakings with less than 500 employees.
(3) Employee participation could be regulated by collective agreements.
(4) Employer and employee side could negotiate employee participation, following the model of the SE-Directive, on the basis of the 'before and after' principle.

2.   Survey of the Legislative Proposals on Employee Participation

10. The **Commission proposal** pursues a middle path.[22] As a rule, it follows the home Member State principle. In other words, following model (1) above, employee participation is left for the national law of Member States to determine. In certain cases where there is a need to safeguard pre-existing employee participation, the proposal provides for precautions, namely

- in the case of formation of the SPE by way of transformation or merger;
- in the case of a transfer of the registered office of the SPE; and

---

[20] Cf. H. Eidenmüller/A. Engert/L. Hornuf, 'How Does the Market React to the Societas Europaea?', *EBOR* 10 (2009), 1–33.
[21] For an overview, see D. Helms, *Die Europäische Privatgesellschaft*, 91–96 sqq.; P. Hommelhoff, *Die "Europäische Privatgesellschaft" am Beginn ihrer Normierung*, 17–19; R. Krause, *Gedächtnisschrift für Blomeyer*, 410–412. See also High-Level Group of Company Law Experts (Winter-Group), *A Modern Regulatory Framework for Company Law in Europe*, 126 sq., available at: http://ec.europa.eu/internal_market/company/docs/modern/report_en.pdf.
[22] For a discussion, see G. Forst, *ZESAR* 2009, 261–266.

- in the case of a cross-border merger of the SPE with one or more companies in other Member States.

In these cases, a negotiation procedure applies. We will discuss the details of the Commission's proposal below.

11. The **European Parliament** resolution of 10 March 2009 proposed numerous amendments to the Commission proposal, concerning, *inter alia*, the employee participation regime. The proposal also starts from the home Member State principle as a general rule. Where the SPE has a multi-national workforce, a number of cumulative factors trigger the negotiation procedure; the proposal draws distinctions with regard to (a) the number of employees, (b) the mode of formation and (c) the proportion of the workforce which habitually works in a Member State with a greater level of employee participation than the Member State in which the SPE has its registered office:

Total number of employees	Way of formation	Proportion of the workforce that habitually works in a Member State which provides for a greater level of employee participation than the Member State in which the SPE has its registered office
More than 1.000	Irrelevant	More than one quarter (25%)
Between 500 and 1.000	Irrelevant	More than one third (33%)
Fewer than 500	– transformation of an existing company – merger of existing companies – division of an existing company	More than one third (33%)
Fewer than 500	Formation *ex nihilo* (pursuant to the provisions of the SPE Regulation)	More than half (50%)

In these cases, the negotiation procedure of the SE Employee Participation Directive (§29) (and, where appropriate, that of the Cross-Border Merger Directive) applies *mutatis mutandis*. This proposal has been criticised as being overly complicated, particularly for small and medium-sized undertakings; the SE employee participation rules are considered to be too complicated for them. Furthermore, it is doubtful whether the middle category of companies with 500–1.000 employees warrants specific rules.[23]

---

23   See P. Hommelhoff, *ZEuP* 2011, 7, 17 sqq.

12. The **Swedish Council presidency compromise** of 27 November 2009[24] also used the home Member State principle as its starting point. A specific negotiation procedure applies, however, in **two instances**:

(a) the company has at least 500 employees, at least half of which[25] habitually work in a Member State that provides for a higher level of employee participation rights for employees than those provided for in the Member State where the company has its registered office; or

(b) where the registered office of the SPE is being transferred [from 'the home Member State' to a 'host Member State'] and (1) at least 1/3 of its employees, at the time of registration in the host Member State, habitually work in the home Member State;[26] and (2) the employees in the home Member State were provided a higher level of participation rights than is provided for those employees in the host Member State.

In these cases, a **negotiation procedure** applies that is outlined specifically for the SPE in Articles 35a-35d of the proposal. As a '**standard rule**' that (basically) applies when negotiations fail, the employees of the SPE have the right to elect, appoint, recommend or oppose the appointment of a number of members of the administrative or supervisory board of the SPE equal to the proportion applicable in the Member State concerned providing for the highest level of participation rights. Furthermore, the proposal imposes an **obligation** upon the management body of the SPE **to review** at least every three years whether the conditions for establishing employee participation pursuant to the above case (a) are fulfilled.[27] Again, however, the Council could not reach agreement, given the disparate employee participation traditions of the Member States.

13. The proposal of 23 May 2011 builds upon the compromise proposal of the Swedish presidency.[28] Starting from the home Member State principle, the proposal suggests that a specific procedure negotiation (Article 35a-35d of the

---

[24] See P. Hommelhoff/C. Teichmann, *GmbHR* 2010, 337–349; W. Koberski/J. Heuschmid, *RdA* 2010, 207–216.

[25] On the 50% criterion, see on the one Hand P. Hommelhoff, *ZEuP* 2011, 7, 15 (approvingly, arguing that only coverage of a certain proportion of all employees justifies the extension of this regime to the workforce as a whole); and on the other W. Koberski/J. Heuschmid, *RdA* 2010, 207, 212 (criticising the 50%-criterion, arguing that (a) it could bring many cases out of the employee participation regime [e.g. an SPE with 5,000 employees, 2,400 in Germany, 2,600 in the UK]; and that (b) it was ambiguous [e.g. an SPE with 5,000 employees, 2,000 in Germany, 1,000 in Slovenia, 1,000 in Hungary and 500 in Spain, therefore not half of the employees in a single Member State]).

[26] For a critical evaluation, see. W. Koberski/J. Heuschmid, *RdA* 2010, 207, 213.

[27] Note that such review can go both ways and also lead to a reduction of the level of participation; P. Hommelhoff, *ZEuP* 2011, 7, 28 sq.

[28] For a discussion, see J. Bormann/L. Böttcher, *NZG* 2011, 411–416 (arguing that the proposal opens up various opportunities for avoiding the high level of German employee involvement).

proposal) should apply where the **single threshold** of at least 500 employees habitually working in a Member State that provides for a higher level of participation rights for employees than is provided for those employees in the Member State where the SPE has its registered office is passed. In the case of a transfer of the registered office, the provision is supplemented by the criterion of an absolute number: the special rules on employee participation apply if at least 1/3 – but not less than 500 – of the company's employees habitually work in the home Member State and this Member State provides for a higher level of participation rights than the host Member State. In addition, the compromise contains a provision pursuant to which existing information and consultation rights should also apply where the SPE has employees in different Member States.

IV. SAFEGUARDING EMPLOYEE PARTICIPATION IN THE SPE – THE COMMISSION PROPOSAL OF 2008

14. The Commission proposal takes safeguarding of employee participation into account in several ways. It applies the home Member State principle (see 1. below). With regard to formation, the Cross-border Mergers Directive (see §30 above) affords supplementary protection (see 2. below). It also applies to the cross-border merger of the SPE with other companies (see 3. below). Finally, the proposal provides for specific rules with regard to the transfer of the registered office (see 4. below).

1. General Rule: The Home Member State Principle

15. First and foremost, the home Member State principle contributes to safeguarding employee participation. The SPE is governed by the rules on employee participation applicable in the country where it has its registered office, Article 34(1) SPER-P2008. Here, the Commission adopts the approach of the Cross-border Merger Directive.[29] As a consequence, it is for the Member States to decide whether and to what extent the SPE should be subject to employee participation. Where the Member States subject undertakings, which take the form of national limited liability companies, to employee participation (if they exceed certain thresholds) – as is, e.g., the case in Germany -[30] it would appear consequential to also extend these rules to undertakings in the form of a European Private Company. The Regulation does not require that, though.[31]

---

[29] COM(2008) 396 final, 10.

[30] See §1(1) Participation Act (Mitbestimmungsgesetz, MitbestG), §1(1) One Third Participation Act (Drittelbeteiligungsgesetz, DrittelbG).

[31] For a different view see P. Hommelhoff, *ZEuP* 2011, 7, 10. Such obligation does not follow from the principle of equivalence in Union law either (see §1 para. 66). This principle also applies outside the context of implementation of directives; it requires that laws in Union law

16. As a matter of legislative technique, the provision seems to be worded rather laboriously. It would already follow from a systematic interpretation that paragraph 1 only applies 'subject to the [more precisely: other] provisions of this Article'. Similarly, it seems self-evident that national provisions on employee participation can only apply if they exist; the express note ('if any') is perhaps intended to clarify that the regulation does not require such rules and that it does not impose a duty on the Member States to introduce such rules. Finally, the reference in Article 34(2) SPER-P2008 to the subsequent provision of Article 38 SPER-P2008 also appears to be superfluous in light of the generally accepted method of systematic interpretation.

17. The home Member State principle is problematic where the central business administration and the registered office of the SPE are, as the original Commission proposal provided, located in different Member States (Article 7(2) SPER-P2008). This construction makes it possible to (or even provides an invitation to) avoid employee participation. An SPE could be registered in England while its central administration and principal place of business is located in Germany or Denmark.[32] While the 2009 and 2011 compromise proposals (see paras. 11 sqq. above) also start from the home Member State principle as a rule (see Article 35(1) SPER-P2009; Article 35(1) SPER-P2011), they have curtailed the possibility of a separation of registered office and central administration (see Article 7(2) SPER-P2009; Article 7 SPER-P2011: deferring the issue to national law).

2. Employee Participation and Formation of the SPE

a)   'National' Formation of an SPE

18. The SPE may, first, be established nationally. Unlike the European Company (see §29 para. 10), the formation of an SPE does not require a cross-border element ('internationality') (cf. Article 5 SPER-P2008).[33] Where a (national or international) original establishment of an SPE (see Article 5(1) lit. a) SPER-P2008) is concerned, no specific issues of employee participation arise; the home Member State principle applies.

---

be enforced equivalent to comparable rights in the national laws of the Member States. This does not exclude the possibility of treating the SPE – from the viewpoint of the undertaking – more favourably, not subjecting it to employee involvement.

[32]   G. Forst, *ZESAR* 2009, 261, 262; K. Noussia, *B.L.I.* 11 (2010) 277, 292; P. Hommelhoff/C. Teichmann, *GmbHR* 2010, 337, 341.

[33]   P. Hommelhoff/C. Teichmann, *DStR* 2008, 925, 928 sq. From the preceding discussion e.g. S. Fischer, *ZEuP* 2004, 737, 742 sq.; R. Krause, *Gedächtnisschrift für Blomeyer,* 397 sq.

19.   But where the SPE is formed by a 'national' transformation, merger or division (Article 5(1) lit. b)-d) SPER-P2008), there is also no danger of a 'flight from employee participation' as both the original company (companies) and the company resulting from the structural measure are subject to the national rules on employee participation. It thus remains a matter for the national legislators of the Member States to decide whether and to what extent the SPE – and the other types of companies under national law – should be subject to employee participation.

20.   The 2009 and 2011 proposals (see paras. 11 sqq. above) have taken a different approach. Rather than looking at the national character of company formation, they focus upon the SPE's workforce: If a substantial part (number and/or proportion) of the workforce (as defined by the proposals, see paras. 11 sqq. above) habitually works in a Member State with a higher level of employee participation than that applicable in the Member State of the registered office, then the negotiation procedure applies (see Article 35(2) SPER-P2009; Article 35(2) SPER-P2011).

b)   Formation by Cross-Border Merger

21.   Issues of safeguarding employee participation may arise, though, if the SPE is formed by way of cross-border merger. Whether that is possible in the first place is a question that the Proposal for a regulation does not explicitly answer. Article 5(1) lit. b) and Recital 7 SPER-P2008 refer to merger in general terms. However, Article 5(2) sent. 1 SPER-P2008 seems to be based upon the premise that *several* national merger-regimes could apply. The supra-national character of the company type would also suggest that a formation by cross-border merger should be possible.

22.   The Proposal does not contain any rules or references to other legal instruments with regard to employee participation in the case of a formation by way of cross-border merger. That is rather surprising, given that, with regard to the cross-border merger of *an (existing) SPE* with another company, the proposal makes explicit reference to the Cross-Border Merger Directive (CBMD) (see paras. 14 sq. below). This could be interpreted as a 'negative rule', implying by silence that the Commission assumed that the Cross-Border Mergers Directive would not apply to the formation of an SPE by way of merger of national companies from different Member States. It seems more likely, though, that, to the contrary, the Commission considered that the Cross-Border Merger Directive applies as a matter of course.

23.   The applicability of the Cross-Border Merger Directive is not self-evident, though. The SPE company type did not exist when the Cross-Border

Merger Directive was enacted. While the Directive's scope of application is restricted to 'limited liability companies' within the meaning of Article 2(1) CBMD as *merging companies*, it does not provide for any 'hard' limitations with regard to the company type of the *company resulting from the merger* for the case of merger by formation of a new company (Article 2(2) lit. b) CBMD).[34] The legislator of the Cross-border Merger Directive has premised the Directive on the company resulting from the merger being a company type which would be accepted in the national laws of the Member States (cf. Article 11(1) sent. 1 CBMD. It has further assumed that it would be a limited liability company (cf. Article 2(2) lit. b) CBMD). The SPE satisfies these two criteria. Pursuant to Article 3(1) lit. a), b) SPER-P2008, the SPE is a limited liability company, and it already follows from the nature of the regulation (Article 288(2) TFEU) that the SPE is a company form recognised by the Member States.

24. If then the Cross-Border Merger Directive applies to the formation of an SPE by way of cross-border merger, Article 16 CBMD provides sufficient safeguards for employee participation; see in detail §30 above.

3. Employee Participation in the Case of a Cross-border Merger of an SPE with other Companies

25. Employee participation could also be 'at risk' if an SPE that, pursuant to the applicable national law of the Member State of its registered office is subject to employee participation (Article 34(1) SPER-P2008), merges with one or more other companies and the company resulting from the merger is governed by the law of another Member State which does not provide for employee participation. Pursuant to Article 34(3) SPER-P2008, the Cross-border Merger Directive also applies to this case.

26. This reference appears to be declaratory only. The Cross-border Merger Directive only applies to limited liability companies within the meaning of Article 2(1) CMBD as merging companies. These include the company types listed in the Disclosure Directive[35] (Article 2(1) lit. a) CMBD), that is the various instances of national public limited companies and limited liability companies. The SPE is not among these company types. Article 2(1) lit. b) CBMD, however, extends the definition so as to also cover companies with

---

34   Article 2(2)(b) CBMD is based on the assumption that the resulting company is also a public company.

35   First Council Directive of 9 March 1968 on co-ordination of safeguards which, for the protection of the interests of members and others, are required by Member States of companies within the meaning of the second paragraph of Article 58 of the Treaty, with a view to making such safeguards equivalent throughout the Community, OJ 1968 L 65/8.

share capital and having legal personality, possessing separate assets which alone serve to cover its debts (cf. Articles 3(1) lit. a), b), 9(2), 19–25 SPER-P2008) and 'subject under the national law governing it to conditions concerning guarantees such as are provided for by [the Disclosure Directive] for the protection of the interests of members and others'. The Proposal for an SPE-Regulation repeatedly refers to the Disclosure Directive (in particular Article 11 SPER-P2008), and, in any case, the national implementation provisions apply via Article 4(2) SPER-P2008.

27. The 2009 and 2011 proposals (see paras. 11 sqq. above) have maintained this provision (see Article 35(3) SPER-P2009; Article 35(3) SPER-P2011).

4.   Employee Participation in the Case of Transfer of the Registered Office

28. The Proposal contains an autonomous regulation for safeguarding employee participation only in the case of transfer of the registered office, Article 38 SPER-P2008. The SPE should not be allowed to escape from employee participation under the applicable national law (Article 34(1) SPER-P2008) by transferring its registered office to another Member State where no (equivalent) employee participation exists. Again, the legislator has employed the model of the SE-Directive and the Cross-border Merger Directive: a negotiation model supplemented by the 'before and after' principle (see §29 paras. 7, 28–58, §30 paras. 9–26 above).

29. The starting point is, once again, the home Member State principle. With regard to employee participation, as of its registration, the SPE is governed by the rules on employee participation of the Member State of destination.

30. Article 38 SPER-P2008 applies to the 'arrangements for the participation of employees' (*modalités de participation des travailleurs*). This includes arrangements provided for by law or by agreement of the parties. The German language version refers more narrowly to *Vereinbarungen über die Mitbestimmungen,* thus only referring to *agreements,* but this appears to be a translation error.

31. Similar to the provisions of the Cross-Border Merger Directive, the home Member State principle does not apply if (somewhat simplified)

(1)   at least **one third of all employees** of the SPE are employed in the home Member State and
(2)   either
    (a)   the provisions of the host Member State provide for a **lower level of employee participation** than those of the home Member State; the

level of participation is again (as in the SE-Directive and in the Cross-border Mergers Directive) measured by reference to the proportion of employee representatives amongst the members of the supervisory or administrative body;

or

(b) the provisions of the host Member State do not give employees employed in other Member States the same rights to exercise rights of employee participation (active and passive voting rights) as they enjoyed before the transfer of the registered office.

32. The 2009 and 2011 proposals (see paras. 11 sqq. above) have, in principle, maintained the same approach. The criteria which trigger the negotiation model vary, though see Article 35(1a)(b) SPER-P2009; Article 35(1a)(b) SPER-P2011.

33. In these cases, the **negotiation model** applies, Article 38(3)-(6) SPER-P2008. The management organ is then obliged to take the necessary steps, as soon as possible, after disclosure of the transfer proposal, to start negotiations with the representatives of the SPE's employees with a view to reaching agreement on arrangements for employee participation (paragraph 3). Apart from providing for its substantive and temporal scope of application, the agreement must determine whether employee participation should be introduced or maintained in the SPE and, if so, how it should be structured (paragraph 4). The negotiation period normally lasts six months and can be extended by another six months by the agreement of the parties (paragraph 5). If the parties do not reach agreement, the rules on employee participation of the home Member State remain applicable (paragraph 6).

5.   The Negotiation Model

34. With regard to the negotiation procedures, the 2008 Commission proposal refers to the provisions of the Cross-Border Merger Directive, Article 34(3) SPER-P2008, with regard to the cross-border merger of the SPE with another company. It provides specific rules for the case of a cross-border transfer of the registered seat, Article 38(3)-(6) SPER-P2008.

35. The 2009 and 2011 proposals (see paras. 11 sqq. above) contain specific provisions for the negotiation procedure, see Articles 35a-35d SPER-P2009, Articles 35a-35d SPER-P2011.

6.   Change of Circumstances, Review

36. An issue that had raised considerable discussion with regard to the SE is that of review of a change of the circumstances relevant to the issue of employee participation: What happens if the relevant thresholds are subsequently exceeded or fallen beneath? The 2008 Commission proposal does not take account of this issue.[36] The subsequent proposals do so in two ways. First, they require the SPE's management body to carry out a review every three years to decide whether the conditions for the negotiation procedure are fulfilled, Article 35(1b) SPER-P2009 and Article 35(1b) SPER-P2011. It appears that this can go both ways: the review may lead to an increase in the level of employee participation as well as a decrease.[37] In addition, the provisions on the agreements provides that it 'shall include' *inter alia* 'the procedure for its renegotiation and the consequence of a failure to reach a new agreement', Article 35c(2)(c) SPER-P2009 and Article 35c(2)(c) SPER-P2011.

---

[36]   For a critical perspective see G. Forst, *ZESAR* 2009, 261, 264.
[37]   P. Hommelhoff, *ZEuP* 2011, 7, 27 sqq.

INDEX*

---

*   Numbers in **bold font style** refer to chapters, numbers in regular font style refer to paragraphs
    within the chapters.

IUS COMMUNITATIS SERIES

Published titles within the series:

1. STEFAN GRUNDMANN, *European Company Law. Organization, Finance and Capital Markets*, 2nd edn., Cambridge-Antwerp-Portland, Intersentia, 2012
    ISBN 978-1-78068-019-4
2. ANDRÉ KLIP, *European Criminal Law. An Integrative Approach*, 2nd edn., Cambridge-Antwerp-Portland, Intersentia, 2012
    ISBN 978-1-78068-001-9
3. PIETER BOELES, MAARTEN DEN HEIJER, GERRIE LODDER and KEES WOUTERS, *European Migration Law*, Antwerp-Oxford, Intersentia, 2009
    ISBN 978-90-5095-953-7